CRIMINAL PROCEDURE

Aspen Casebook Series

CRIMINAL PROCEDURE

Doctrine, Application, and Practice

JENS DAVID OHLIN
Vice Dean and Professor of Law
Cornell Law School

Published by Wolters Kluwer in New York.

Wolters Kluwer Legal & Regulatory U.S. serves customers worldwide with CCH, Aspen Publishers, and Kluwer Law International products. (www.WKLegaledu.com)

To contact Customer Service, e-mail customer.service@wolterskluwer.com, call 1-800-234-1660, fax 1-800-901-9075, or mail correspondence to:

Wolters Kluwer
Attn: Order Department
PO Box 990
Frederick, MD 21705

Printed in the United States of America.

2 3 4 5 6 7 8 9 0

ISBN 978-1-4548-9385-1

Library of Congress Cataloging-in-Publication Data

Names: Ohlin, Jens David, author.
Title: Criminal procedure: doctrine, application, and practice / Jens David Ohlin, Vice Dean and Professor of Law, Cornell Law School.
Description: New York: Wolters Kluwer, [2019] | Series: Aspen casebook series | Includes bibliographical references and index.
Identifiers: LCCN 2019021427 | ISBN 9781454893851
Subjects: LCSH: Criminal procedure–United States. | LCGFT: Casebooks (Law)
Classification: LCC KF9619.O325 2019 | DDC 345.73/05–dc23 LC record available at https://lccn.loc.gov/2019021427

About Wolters Kluwer Legal & Regulatory U.S.

Wolters Kluwer Legal & Regulatory U.S. delivers expert content and solutions in the areas of law, corporate compliance, health compliance, reimbursement, and legal education. Its practical solutions help customers successfully navigate the demands of a changing environment to drive their daily activities, enhance decision quality and inspire confident outcomes.

Serving customers worldwide, its legal and regulatory portfolio includes products under the Aspen Publishers, CCH Incorporated, Kluwer Law International, ftwilliam.com and MediRegs names. They are regarded as exceptional and trusted resources for general legal and practice-specific knowledge, compliance and risk management, dynamic workflow solutions, and expert commentary.

For my colleagues at Cornell Law School

Summary of Contents

Contents

CHAPTER 4
Exceptions to the Warrant Requirement 183

CHAPTER 5

Seizing Persons 315

CHAPTER 20

Appeals and Habeas Corpus 1351

Preface

I wrote this casebook because I wanted to achieve a middle ground between two well-known approaches to the teaching of criminal procedure.

One approach focuses on federal constitutional rules and the Supreme Court cases that articulate them. These rules provide the minimum floor below which states—and Congress—cannot go. This approach turns criminal procedure into a sub-discipline of constitutional law with the Fourth, Fifth, and Sixth Amendments as the primary object of study.

Another approach focuses on state constitutional rules in order to achieve a more "on the ground" perspective that will be especially helpful for the law school graduates who will enter the legal profession as criminal lawyers. In that case, what the lawyer needs to understand is not just the constitutional prohibitions but, more importantly, the particular rules in that jurisdiction, which might be articulated in state constitutions, state statutes, and state rules of criminal procedure.

Both approaches have merit, so I asked myself: *Why not do both?*

Criminal Procedure: Doctrine, Application, and Practice presents the constitutional cases decided by the Supreme Court, but legal requirements imposed by statute or by state law are highlighted in shaded call-out boxes in each chapter. These call-out boxes help the reader understand that local jurisdictions sometimes impose more demanding rules of criminal procedure. If you're in that jurisdiction, that's really all that matters. However, these call-out boxes are modular and do not disrupt the flow of the main text, thus allowing students and professors alike the flexibility to emphasize and discuss those aspects of the law of criminal procedure that they consider most important.

Another distinctive aspect of this casebook is highlighted in the volume's subtitle: *Doctrine, Application, and Practice.* It's not just enough to understand the principles and rules contained in caselaw and statute; it's also crucial to *apply* those rules to new fact patterns. So, each chapter includes Problem Cases—again, set as modular call-out boxes—that ask the reader to engage with a set of facts. Acquiring the skill of "law application to fact" can be difficult for the law school student, but it is the hallmark of an accomplished lawyer or jurist.

Finally, each chapter concludes with a brief Practice & Policy section. The goal of the section is to discuss higher-order questions that require a critical reflection on where the law is going and where it ought to be going. The materials are presented at the end of each chapter because the reader requires a firm grounding in the doctrine before tackling these advanced topics. In order to achieve this critical reflection on the law, students working through the Practice & Policy sections will gain important exposure to empirical, normative, and philosophical methodologies.

For professors who teach single-semester courses on either criminal investigations or criminal adjudication, please note that I have published versions of this casebook specifically designed for those classes. The titles of those volumes are *Investigative Criminal Procedure: Doctrine, Application, and Practice* and *Adjudicative Criminal Procedure: Doctrine, Application, and Practice*. Both of these "split" volumes start with the same introductory chapter from this volume, which provides an overview of the criminal process, highlights the constitutional debate over "incorporation," and discusses competing frameworks for understanding and analyzing criminal procedure.

Please note that I have followed several conventions while selecting and editing the cases in the book. First, internal citations within the cases are omitted without indication, in order to make the cases more readable. Second, deletions within cases are marked by ellipses (. . .) rather than asterisks (* * *). Third, the ellipses at the beginning or end of a paragraph may indicate that sentences were deleted from the paragraph or that entire paragraphs were deleted. In other words, the reader should not assume that ellipses at the end of a paragraph indicate that the deleted material was solely contained within that original paragraph. Fourth, ellipses were not used when numbered sections within a case make abundantly clear that entire sections of the opinion have been removed. Finally, parallel citations were removed without indication.

I hope that you enjoy the casebook. Please send suggestions for what you would like to see included in the next edition. I can be reached at jdo43@cornell.edu and would be happy to hear from you.

Jens David Ohlin
Ithaca, NY
June 2019

ACKNOWLEDGMENTS

Many people were instrumental in bringing this casebook to fruition.

I would first like to thank the entire team at Wolters Kluwer for helping with the acquisition, production, and marketing of this casebook. That includes senior acquisitions editor Richard Mixter, managing editor Anton Yakovlev, publisher Joe Terry, as well as Nicole Pinard and John Devins. I would also like to thank the entire sales and marketing team for their dedication and travel, as well as Maureen Kenealy and the Connected Casebook team for producing the digital version of this casebook.

I would like to thank the entire team at The Froebe Group for handling the production of the volume. This includes Kathy Langone, Sarah Hains, the copy editors, and the compositors. Geoffrey Lokke secured the necessary copyright permissions.

Several colleagues at Cornell Law School have provided advice to me about legal pedagogy in general and casebook structure in particular. I gained much wisdom from these conversations, and I am honored to be a member of a law faculty where teaching obligations are taken seriously.

Wolters Kluwer assembled an excellent team of criminal procedure professors across the country to review the draft chapters and provide suggestions for revisions. I am grateful for their feedback and hope that the resulting casebook will meet their needs in the classroom.

I am especially grateful for the assistance of Professor Geoff Corn, who provided me with extensive feedback on draft chapters of this casebook and also helped to edit some of the language. Professor Corn also worked on the charts that are included in the casebook, which are the product of his many years of teaching criminal procedure. I owe a huge debt to Professor Corn.

As always, Nancy Ohlin supported my work on this project, especially during the dark moments in the middle when the end appeared as far away—and as unreachable—as the horizon.

I would also like to thank the following copyright holders for granting permission to reproduce these materials in the text:

Booking photos of Ernesto Miranda at the Phoenix Police Museum. Copyright © by Matt York/AP/Shutterstock. Reprinted by permission. All rights reserved.

Bottles of the sedative midazolam at a hospital pharmacy. Copyright © by Sue Ogrocki/AP Images. Reprinted by permission. All rights reserved.

Buffalo herd in Yellowstone National Park. Courtesy of Shadowmeld Photography/Wikimedia Commons.

Computer screen with GPS locations of vehicles near Lexington, NE. Copyright © by Mikael Karlsson/Alamy. Reprinted by permission. All rights reserved.

Dallas police officer with victim in an alternative lineup. Copyright © by LM Otero/AP/Shutterstock. Reprinted by permission. All rights reserved.

Danny Lee Kyllo in Florence, OR. Copyright © by Don Ryan/AP/Shutterstock. Reprinted by permission. All rights reserved.

Datsun 710 in which reporter Don Bolles was fatally injured by a car bomb, on display at the Newseum, Washington, D.C. Courtesy of Steve Terrell/Flickr.

George W. Bush signs bill restructuring the Foreign Intelligence Surveillance Act. Copyright © by Matthew Cavanaugh/ EPA/Shutterstock. Reprinted by permission. All rights reserved.

Janet DiFiore, Westchester County district attorney, and United States Attorney for the Southern District of New York Michael Garcia. Copyright © by Chip East/Reuters. Reprinted by permission. All rights reserved.

Khalid al-Mihdhar at Dulles International Airport. Copyright © by AP Photo/ APTN. Reprinted by permission. All rights reserved.

Larry "Dudley" Hiibel outside U.S. Supreme Court. Copyright © by Manuel Balce Ceneta/AP/Shutterstock. Reprinted by permission. All rights reserved.

Las Vegas police at sobriety checkpoint. Copyright © by Jim West/Alamy. Reprinted by permission. All rights reserved.

Louis Capone and Emanuel "Mendy" Weiss at trial. Courtesy of New York World-Telegram and the Sun Newspaper Photograph Collection/Library of Congress.

Louis "Lepke" Buchalter stands in court during sentencing. Courtesy of New York World-Telegram and the Sun Newspaper Photograph Collection/ Library of Congress.

Marvin Anderson with unconditional pardon. Copyright © by Steve Helber/AP/ Shutterstock. Reprinted by permission. All rights reserved.

Max, the Los Angeles International Airport police dog. Copyright © by Kevork Djansezian/AP/Shutterstock. Reprinted by permission. All rights reserved.

NYPD officer with body camera during a news conference on the "Big Brother" pilot program. Copyright © by Shannon Stapleton/Reuters. Reprinted by permission. All rights reserved.

NYPD stop and frisk near Canal Street. Copyright © by Stacy Walsh Rosenstock/ Alamy. Reprinted by permission. All rights reserved.

Prisoner arraigned at a "Tenderloin" police station in New York. Courtesy of George Grantham Bain Collection/Library of Congress.

Protesters across from City Hall in Los Angeles in support of the Ferguson riots and Michael Brown. Copyright © by Chester Brown/Alamy. Reprinted by permission. All rights reserved.

Protestors at march to end New York's stop and frisk program. Copyright © by Seth Wenig/AP/Shutterstock. Reprinted by permission. All rights reserved.

Raymond Santana, Yusef Salaam, and Kevin Richardson at New York City Hall. Copyright © by Bebeto Matthews/AP/Shutterstock. Reprinted by permission. All rights reserved.

Ruhal Ahmed and Shafiq Rasul. Copyright © by Kim Kyung-Hoon/Reuters. Reprinted by permission. All rights reserved.

Sol Goldstein with Lt. Dan Costigan and Supt. Howard C. Barber. Courtesy of Greeley Photo Service/Library of Congress.

Tashfeen Malik and Syed Farook at O'Hare International Airport. Copyright © by U.S. Customs and Border Protection/AP. Reprinted by permission. All rights reserved.

Ted Kaczynski's cabin in the woods of Lincoln, Montana. Copyright © by Elaine Thompson/AP Images. Reprinted by permission. All rights reserved.

Thermal image of house. Copyright © by Dario Sabljak/Alamy. Reprinted by permission. All rights reserved.

Traveler removes shoes at LaGuardia Airport. Copyright © by Bebeto Matthews/AP/Shutterstock. Reprinted by permission. All rights reserved.

Unabomber sketch, drawn by forensic artist Jeanne Boylan. Courtesy of Wikimedia Commons.

U.S. Attorney General John Ashcroft. Copyright © by Scott J. Ferrell/Congressional Quarterly/Alamy. Reprinted by permission. All rights reserved.

Vials containing buccal swabs at the Avera Institute for Human Genetics in Sioux Falls, S.D. Copyright © by Regina Garcia Cano/AP/Shutterstock. Reprinted by permission. All rights reserved.

Yaser Esam Hamdi during a prayer service performed by detainees in Camp X-Ray. Courtesy of Photographer's Mate 1st Class Shawn P. Eklund, United States Navy.

PART I

FRAMEWORK FOR CRIMINAL PROCEDURE

CHAPTER 1

Introduction

INTRODUCTION

In the popular imagination, the essence of the criminal law is often understood in procedural terms: the execution of a search warrant, the use of a lineup at the police station, the adversarial trial process among attorneys, the cross-examination of witnesses at trial, or the influence of lawyers as advocates in this system. It can therefore come as a surprise to the first-year law student taking a basic course in criminal law to be taught no procedure at all, since first-year courses are usually, though not universally, focused on the substance of the criminal law doctrine to the exclusion of procedure. There is much to be said about whether the bifurcation between substance and procedure is a useful one, but it is a distraction in the present context. The undeniable reality is that most students of criminal procedure come to the subject with a firm prior grasp of the doctrine of substantive criminal law and are now faced with studying the procedural system as the second phase of their studies of criminal justice.

Students often falsely assume that a course in criminal procedure will be the criminal law analogue to their first-year course in civil procedure. While in some ways that analogy is accurate, in other ways it fails. A basic course in criminal procedure is more properly conceived of as a criminal law version of constitutional law, insofar as it articulates a set of constitutional constraints on the construction and application of criminal procedural rules in federal and state jurisdictions alike. While civil proceduralists certainly deal with some constitutional constraints, their field of study focuses more on the procedural rules—and the policy decisions that justify them—whereas criminal procedure is dominated by constitutional provisions that have set a minimum floor below which individual jurisdictions cannot go. The goal of a course in criminal procedure is to understand that floor and also appreciate the pluralism among jurisdictions above that constitutional floor.

What is the relationship between substance and procedure? There are, potentially, two fundamental views to consider. Under the first view, the reason to have "fair" procedures is to promote certain outcomes. For this view, then, procedure has *instrumental* value, i.e., a particular procedure has value because it is the necessary instrument to achieve a desired outcome. So, for example, one might say that the rule prohibiting inherently unreliable identifications that result from unnecessary suggestion has instrumental value because it limits the number of erroneous identifications. Or, consider the exclusionary rule, which generally prohibits the introduction of evidence obtained from police or state misconduct that violates the Constitution. Evidence is kept from the jury to deter future state misbehavior, though there are exceptions to the exclusionary rule that apply in situations where the Supreme Court has prioritized the interests of accuracy or where deterrence is unnecessary or unworkable. In either case, the instrumental methodology requires consideration of multiple objectives.

On the other hand, though, one might conceive of procedure as having an *inherent* value. Under this view, a particular procedure is valuable because the procedure accords with our sense of fair play, of justice, or equality of arms (between state authorities and the defense), or simply the rule of law abstractly construed. The idea here is that "fair" or "just" procedures are valuable simply because the procedural mechanism is inherently or intuitively just, where the justness of the procedure can be understood without an empirical investigation into whether that procedure tends to produce more accurate results or not. So, for example, one might coherently believe that the right of the defense to receive the evidence that the prosecutor intends to introduce at trial, through the "discovery" process prior to the commencement at trial, is justified simply by the inherent value of justice and fair play, and what it means to live under the rule of law, and not because discovery yields more accurate results in terms of convictions and acquittals.

Of course, it is not the case that procedures are 100 percent instrumentally valuable or inherently valuable. In reality, there will be a mixture of both types of arguments in each doctrinal controversy. These arguments are themes or patterns of thought that will reoccur frequently during the casebook.

As you read the rest of the materials in the casebook, you should be constantly re-evaluating one fundamental question: What does "justice" mean in our system? One conception of justice is *accuracy*, i.e., the factually guilty are convicted and the factually innocent are acquitted. Or, perhaps "justice" means something less epistemic; otherwise, we would not tolerate a Fourth Amendment exclusionary rule, which eschews accuracy and induces the state to treat the subjects of criminal investigations *fairly*. On the other hand, fairness cannot be the sole goal of the system either. If fairness were the sole goal, we would not have a harmless error doctrine, which prioritizes accuracy over fairness when it insists that defendants shall not get new trials when errors would not have made a difference to the outcome of their trial. The truth is that there is no settled answer to this question; the push and pull of these competing conceptions can be seen in each doctrine and its exceptions, in each case opinion and its dissents. Consider the following observation from Justice Scalia in *Crawford v. Washington*, 541 U.S. 36, 62 (2004): "Dispensing with confrontation because testimony is obviously reliable is akin to dispensing with jury trial because a defendant is obviously guilty." What exactly does this mean? How does he conceptualize the relationship between accuracy and fairness? Perhaps he was saying that truth is our horizon, but that the goal of our criminal process is fairness.

Because of its introductory nature, the present chapter departs from the structure of the rest of the casebook. Typical chapters will be divided into sections based on each major doctrine or doctrinal controversy—the materials interspersed with Problem Cases, hypotheticals, and call-out boxes focusing on statutory requirements imposed by local state codes.

This chapter, instead, will start in Section A with a narrative overview of the criminal process from the initiation of a criminal complaint all the way to appeal and sentencing. Then, Section B will outline the major constitutional provisions relevant for criminal procedure: The Fourth, Fifth, Sixth, and Fourteenth Amendments, followed by a selection of typical state constitutional provisions to demonstrate the relevance of state law for criminal procedure. Section C will then focus on the "incorporation" debate—the process by which the Fourteenth Amendment either selectively or totally incorporated the Bill of Rights, which by its terms applies to the federal government, and made its provisions applicable in state prosecutions as well. Finally, Section D will consider the inherent tension between two models of criminal justice: crime control versus due process.

A. THE CRIMINAL PROCESS

Before learning the doctrine and the constitutional foundation of criminal procedure, it is helpful to have an overview of the criminal process from the commencement of an investigation through appeal and punishment. It is important to remember, of course, that each jurisdiction retains unique procedures that vary from state to state. However, in most important respects, the procedure followed in the federal criminal justice system is mirrored in each state jurisdiction. There are two reasons for this. The first is that the U.S. Constitution, as interpreted by state and federal courts, mandates certain procedural protections that state jurisdictions are not permitted to deviate from. Second, all U.S. jurisdictions (with some variations) share a common legal heritage with Britain, and therefore some aspects of our criminal justice system have been inherited from the "common law" system, broadly construed, which influence the basic structure of the adversarial process. That being said, these commonalities do leave some room for local deviation or experimentation, as long as that local deviation respects the constitutional minimum. The following materials provide a basic overview of that common criminal process, though the materials in the casebook as a whole will go a long way toward exploring local deviation and evaluating when it is—or is not—constitutionally acceptable.

1. Criminal Complaint and Investigation

The criminal process usually begins with a criminal complaint sworn by a victim in a case. There are exceptions to this general practice: If the police encounter evidence of law breaking they will investigate and pursue the case in anticipation that a victim will be found who will complain about the conduct. Also, if the police encounter evidence of criminal conduct directed at the public at large—or if they personally witness the crime—they will issue a citation on their own volition. But for major crimes, a case usually begins with a complaining victim for mostly pragmatic reasons: It is difficult to successfully prosecute an offender unless there is a witness to testify about the offending conduct.

The investigation will be conducted by the relevant police agency with jurisdiction over the crime. This is not limited to the municipal police and the FBI. There are a host of other agencies with criminal jurisdiction apart from your local city police and the federal government. This includes county sheriffs, state police, and numerous federal and state agencies with statutory grants of jurisdiction over particular crimes or territory: state agencies that patrol state parks; agencies that prosecute environmental or safety offenses; federal agencies like the Bureau of Alcohol, Tobacco, and Firearms; and hundreds of obscure agencies that rarely get public attention (e.g., the Library of Congress used to have its own police force until Congress merged it with the U.S. Capitol Police). Also, the U.S. military conducts police investigations of its own servicemembers (and prosecutes them under the Uniform Code of Military Justice). Universities and colleges in most states have their own public safety officers entitled to exercise the same duties as police officers. Occasionally, police officers from multiple jurisdictions will collaborate together on a joint "task force" to investigate criminal activity, for example, a multi-jurisdictional drug task force. Regardless of which jurisdiction or agency conducts it, an "investigation" can be as swift or as protracted as the circumstances require.

During the investigation, the police will often discover evidence without ever engaging in conduct that even implicates the Fourth Amendment. But when police conduct a search or seizure, they may need to obtain judicial authorization in the form of a warrant, though there are many exceptions to the warrant requirement that allow the police to search for evidence without any prior judicial authorization (such as searching a car), as long as the police have probable cause to believe that they might find evidence of a crime or contraband at that location. In the case of exigent circumstances, the police might even be justified in conducting a search without a warrant. And other exceptions to the warrant requirement, such as consent, might also apply.

Investigators might also seek to interview either the target of the investigation or a witness to the crime. A suspect being interviewed might request the presence of counsel during the interview or might agree to speak to the authorities without the benefit of counsel. The suspect is not usually required to speak with the authorities and can decline to assist the police detectives in their investigative efforts. However, a suspect might be ordered by a judge to divulge, against his or her wishes, physical evidence, such as a blood or DNA sample.

2. Arrest

If the police have probable cause to believe that a particular individual committed a crime, they can arrest the suspect. If the suspect is apprehended in public, police normally do not require a warrant. However, if police need to enter the suspect's home to find him in order to conduct the arrest, or if the jurisdiction

Sol Goldstein being led out of building by detectives Lt. Dan Costigan and Supt. Howard C. Barber after a raid in Brooklyn, ca. 1915. (Greeley Photo Service/Library of Congress)

requires it, police will normally ask a judge to issue an arrest warrant unless a warrantless entry is justified by exigency or consent. Furthermore, most jurisdictions impose limitations on when and how a warrant will be executed, although again there are some exceptions that allow police officers to suspend those rules. Outside the home, a police officer might perform an arrest on his or her own authority if he or she personally witnesses the crime or if the officer has "good cause," based on an investigation, that the suspect committed the crime. As for the arresting officer's evidentiary burden, the standard is that the officer has "probable cause" to believe that the suspect committed the crime—a standard that is much less demanding than the level of certainty required to convict someone at trial (proof beyond a reasonable doubt) or to find liability in a civil case (a preponderance of the evidence).

In addition to the questioning that might occur before arrest, the police might also question the suspect after he or she is taken into custody, at or outside the police station. Once the suspect is in police custody, the police must issue *Miranda* warnings and obtain a "*Miranda* waiver" as a precondition to using those statements against the suspect at trial. These rights include the right, during an interrogation, to counsel at public expense and the right to remain silent. See *Miranda v. Arizona*, 384 U.S. 436 (1966). Failure to advise a detained suspect of his rights and obtain a valid waiver will normally trigger the exclusionary rule at trial.

In some larger jurisdictions, such as New York City, professional investigators working directly for the district attorney will continue to work on the case pending the trial. In other jurisdictions, the police detectives might continue the investigation. Regardless of who continues it, the investigatory work might include questioning of the suspect after he or she has been formally charged with a crime, or some kind of identification procedure that allows a witness—possibly the victim of the crime—to identify the suspect as the perpetrator of the crime. These additional investigatory steps will also trigger constitutional criminal procedure protections.

3. Arraignment and Bail

Before appearing in a courtroom, the arrested individual will go through a routinized "booking process" that involves the taking of fingerprints and photographs, the collection of biographical information, and creating a personal inventory of the arrestee's belongings on his or her person. Following this process, after a wait of a few hours in a jail cell, possibly with other detainees in a large cell, the arrested suspect will be brought before a judge for bail and arraignment hearings.

In a busy urban jurisdiction, the bail hearing might occur in the evening hours with judges working a night court; in a smaller town, the bail hearing might occur the following day. Bail will either be granted or denied depending on various

A prisoner being arraigned at a "Tenderloin" (midtown) police station in New York, ca. 1908. (George Grantham Bain Collection/Library of Congress)

factors, including the severity of the offense and the risk that the defendant might flee the jurisdiction. In making this determination, the judge will hear from both the prosecuting attorney and the defendant's attorney and will consider highly particularized information about the defendant's situation, including financial resources, connections overseas, family connections in the local jurisdiction (e.g., children), all of which should help predict whether the defendant might attempt to flee the jurisdiction prior to the commencement of trial.

If bail is granted, the suspect may either post cash (if they have enough) or apply for a bail bond. The defendant secures the bail bond by giving a percentage of the money to a bail bondsman, a private actor who then posts the required amount for bail with the court. If the defendant flees the jurisdiction or otherwise refuses to appear for trial, the bail is forfeited. To recoup the loss, the bail bondsman will then attempt to locate and forcibly bring the suspect to the court. In many cases, the lightly regulated bail bondsman industry has provoked substantial concern because these private actors work essentially as bounty hunters.

The defendant will also be "arraigned," either at the same time as the bail hearing or at a separate hearing. At this appearance, the defendant will be informed of his or her constitutional rights, including the right (if applicable) to an appointed counsel, and asked how he or she pleads to each charge—guilty, not guilty, or no contest. Normally, the answer to this question will be deferred, but once asked the defendant is considered arraigned.

4. Indictment and Preliminary Hearings

After arrest, the local district attorney is usually not permitted to proceed directly to a trial. In the case of felonies, many jurisdictions require the successful completion of either a preliminary hearing or a grand jury indictment before a judge will schedule a trial. These two pre-trial mechanisms are radically different. In jurisdictions that do not use a grand jury, the defendant is normally charged by "information," which is sworn out by a prosecutor under oath. Preliminary hearings are usually public, adversarial proceedings between the state represented by a prosecutor, and a defendant represented by a defense attorney; the prosecutor has the burden to demonstrate to the judge that there is a sufficient evidentiary basis (normally probable cause) to justify the charge and proceed to trial; if successful (which is normally the case), the defendant is "bound over" for trial. In contrast, grand jury proceedings are non-adversarial and involve only a prosecutor presenting his or her side of the case to a grand jury in a closed-door and confidential proceeding. The prosecutor has the burden to present evidence that provides probable cause to believe that the defendant committed the crime.

The target of the investigation typically does not appear in the grand jury proceeding, though in some rare instances the target might petition the court for permission to testify before the grand jury in an attempt to convince the grand jurors not to indict. A grand jury must indict the individual on a specific charge. If the grand jury chooses to indict, it issues a "true bill" of indictment, which includes the section of the penal code violated and a statement of the factual accusation. The state will then normally move forward to trial on the indictment (although there is no obligation to do so), where the state must then prove every material element of the alleged offense beyond a reasonable doubt. In both mechanisms, the grand jury and the preliminary hearing, if the prosecutor loses, the defendant is released and the case is concluded. On the other hand, if the prosecutor wins and a trial is ordered, both sides then begin work to prepare for trial.

5. Pre-Trial

Before trial, prosecutors are required to comply with both statutory and/or constitutional discovery obligations: provide defense with all favorable and material evidence. This process eliminates the danger of unfair surprise and gives the defendant the opportunity to prepare for trial and select an appropriate defense strategy. Also, the defense attorney and prosecutor may make informal predictions about their chance of success at trial and then negotiate a plea bargain in order to reduce the risk of losing. Usually a plea bargain involves the defendant pleading guilty to a lesser charge and coming to some agreement about the length (or range) of the penalty. For example, a murder suspect might plead guilty in exchange for a sentence of 20 years to life rather than 25 years to life. Or, an assault suspect might plead guilty to a lesser offense in exchange for a sentence of probation and therefore escape the prospect of imprisonment entirely. Prosecutors agree to these deals primarily to avoid the risk of a judgment of acquittal but also for other motivations, including the need to lower their caseload, mitigate the burden on victims and witnesses who may be spared the need to testify, and also their sense that the negotiated resolution is a just outcome for all involved. The prosecutor might consult (in some jurisdictions *must* consult) with the victim in the case before the plea deal is finalized, though the victim does not have a right to prevent the deal from being finalized, since the victim is not a formal party to the legal proceedings.

The deal is then presented to the judge for ratification and endorsement. Usually the judge will accept the deal after the defendant admits under oath that they committed the crime, although strictly speaking this is not a constitutional requirement and the judge might accept prosecution evidence in lieu of a formal admission under oath from the defendant. Although judges are entitled to reject plea offers if they wish, in most cases they welcome them as a way to reduce their caseloads. In the absence of plea bargaining, the criminal justice system in its current form (without additional resources) would collapse. More than 90 percent of all criminal cases are adjudicated through some form of plea bargaining, rather than a full trial followed by a verdict, so the sheer weight of the additional trials would require a massive and unprecedented reallocation of government resources to the judicial system.

If a plea deal is not reached, the parties will begin their preparations for trial. This process will often begin with motions "for appropriate relief," which could range from issues regarding inadmissible evidence, discovery disputes, dismissal of charges, requests for a new grand jury or preliminary hearing, severance of charges, change of venue, speedy trial issues, and many others. These legal questions will have to be resolved by the trial judge prior to the commencement of the case (although sometimes the judge will defer ruling until the trial begins). Importantly, a defendant may testify in these motion hearings without waiving the privilege against self-incrimination, although any such testimony may be used later at trial to impeach the defendant if he or she testifies under oath. The prosecution is required to satisfy its discovery obligations, i.e., to respond to requests by the defense to turn over evidence in the prosecution's possession, especially exculpatory evidence that might help the defendant prove his or her innocence. In some jurisdictions, the defense has a statutory obligation to turn over evidence to the prosecution if the defense has elected to receive discovery. If the defense believes that the police obtained evidence in violation of the defendant's constitutional rights, the defense might move for suppression of the evidence under the exclusionary rule, though the exclusionary rule is not always applicable.

Once all pre-trial matters are resolved, the trial process begins with *voir dire*, the selection of the jury, unless the defendant has voluntarily elected a bench trial with a judge acting as the fact finder. The defendant has no constitutional right to a bench trial, though in most jurisdictions the bench trial is allowed at the defendant's election. On the other hand, some jurisdictions dispense with juries in the case of minor infractions, though the Constitution requires a jury trial for all crimes yielding serious punishment. After lawyers from both sides ask questions to potential jurors about their attitudes about the police, about crime, and other matters related to their qualification as potential jurors, each side may strike potential jurors with a limited number of peremptory challenges (no cause required) and an unlimited number of challenges for cause based on indications that a juror cannot be impartial. The trial judge rules on all such challenges.

6. Trial

After opening statements from both attorneys, the trial commences with the prosecutor's presentation of evidence and witnesses, who can be cross-examined

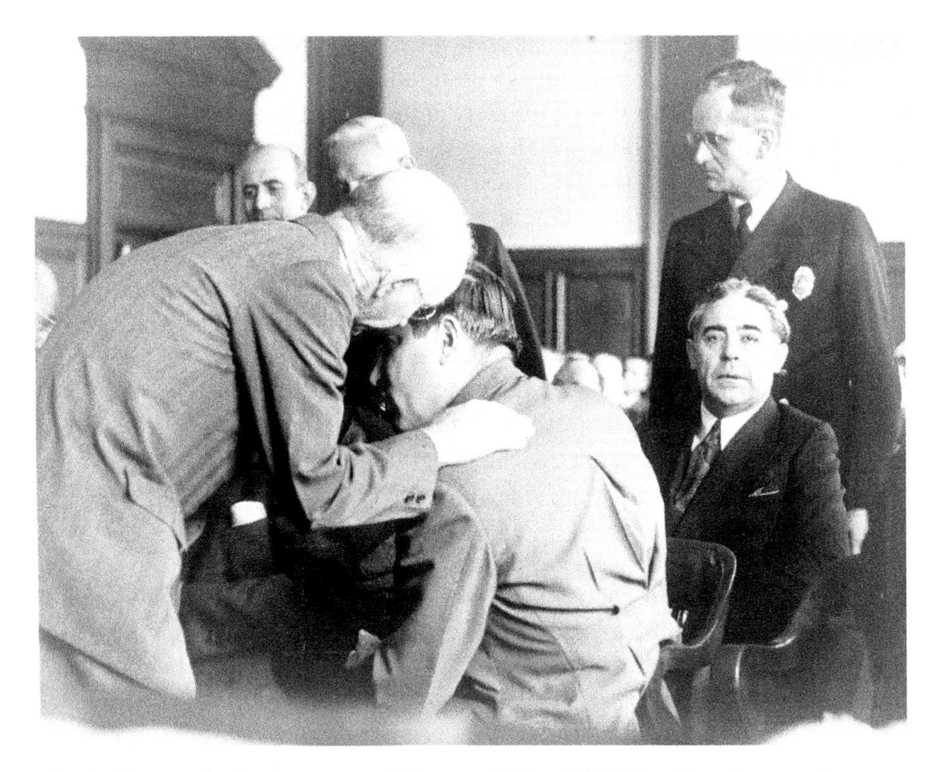

Louis Capone, facing camera, and Emanuel "Mendy" Weiss, listening to a lawyer, during a 1941 trial. (New York World-Telegram and the Sun Newspaper Photograph Collection/Library of Congress)

by the defense attorney. The prosecutor bears the initial burden to establish a prima facie case, i.e., evidence that is sufficient to support a reasonable conclusion that every material element of the alleged offense has been established. A defendant could be acquitted without his lawyer presenting a shred of evidence, if the prosecutor fails to meet his prima facie burden (for example, in a murder case, where the prosecution failed to offer any evidence that establishes the defendant caused the victim's death). Or, counsel for the defendant might decide to attack the evidence presented by the prosecution (for example, through cross-examination) but not introduce any independent evidence or defense witnesses. At the conclusion of the prosecution's case-in-chief, the judge can grant a motion for acquittal (sometimes called a motion for a finding of not guilty) if he or she determines that it would be unreasonable for any jury to convict (because of the prosecution's failure to satisfy this prima facie burden of production).

Otherwise, the defense presents its case and argues for an acquittal, followed by closing arguments. If the defendant has selected a bench trial, the judge deliberates and then hands down a decision. In the case of a jury trial, the judge must "charge" the jury with a set of instructions that explain the law to lay individuals who do not have prior legal training. Jurors then retire to deliberate in secret. With the exception of capital cases, the Constitution does not require the states to comply with the 12-person jury size or the unanimous jury verdict rule. Ultimately, the jury must decide whether the prosecution submitted enough admissible evidence to establish beyond a reasonable doubt that the defendant committed the crime. It is possible that the prosecution might submit enough evidence to meet its prima facie burden but not enough evidence to satisfy its ultimate burden of persuasion, especially in light of countervailing evidence presented by the defense: To convict the jury must find that the only reasonable conclusion supported by the totality of the evidence is guilt. If the jury is not so convinced, it means that the prosecution has not excluded reasonable doubt, and this should result in acquittal by the jury. After an acquittal, the prosecution cannot retry the case because the principle of double jeopardy precludes giving the government a second "bite at the apple." Otherwise, the government could simply retry cases indefinitely until it found a jury to convict the defendant. The one notable exception to the double jeopardy rule is the "dual sovereign" or "separate sovereign" doctrine that allows the federal government to prosecute after a state acquittal under the theory that the federal and state governments represent distinct sovereigns conducting independent prosecutions.

Sometimes juries engage in "nullification" by acquitting defendants even though the jury assesses that the prosecution established guilt beyond a reasonable doubt. The prosecution has no recourse if the jury engages in nullification because as just noted, defendants who are acquitted cannot be retried. Also, while the defendant can appeal a conviction, the prosecution cannot appeal an acquittal. Although the jury has the power to nullify, judges will not permit defense attorneys to *request* nullification during their closing statement.

7. Sentencing

If found guilty, a defendant will be subject to the criminal penalties defined by statute. In most cases, the sentencing determination is bifurcated into a separate proceeding that allows the judge or jury to consider aggravating, mitigating, and extenuating circumstances that may not have been relevant during the guilt phase of the trial. So, for example, defense counsel might call witnesses who could testify regarding the defendant's positive character or the factors beyond his control—such as early childhood abuse—that influenced his life trajectory. For some crimes, the statute will fix mandatory minimum and maximum penalties so as to constrain the discretion of the court in imposing its sentence. In some jurisdictions, a non-binding set of sentencing guidelines will provide a framework for the court to use in calculating an appropriate prison sentence or fine. If a factor triggers an automatic or *binding* statutory increase in the sentence, that factor must be found by the jury during the trial

Louis "Lepke" Buchalter stands in court during sentencing in 1941. (New York World-Telegram and the Sun Newspaper Photograph Collection/Library of Con-gress)

itself under the standard of proof beyond a reasonable doubt, rather than by the judge during sentencing.

8. Appeal

After sentencing, defendants are permitted to appeal their conviction unless they have knowingly waived their right to appeal (usually as part of a plea bargain). Generally speaking, the prosecutor cannot appeal an acquittal because the constitutional protection of double jeopardy attaches to the acquittal; if the prosecution believes a legal ruling before or during the trial will be "case dispositive," it must file an interlocutory appeal (if they are allowed in that jurisdiction) or risk the consequence of the judge's ruling.

Appeals are limited to questions of law. Usually, the disputed question of law will have been raised during the pre-trial process (such as a dispute over evidence that should have been excluded) or a procedural irregularity during the trial itself (such as a dispute over the judge's charge to the jury before deliberation). Indeed, the defense may have procedurally defaulted an appeal issue if they failed to raise it initially. In some cases, even if an appeals court concludes that the judge committed legal error, the conviction might not be overturned if it was a "harmless" error that would not have impacted the jury's decision, i.e., the result of the trial. On the other hand, if the appeals court finds that the legal error impacted the final outcome, the conviction will be tossed but the prosecution will have the option to retry the defendant in a new trial.

Matters of fact become reviewable as a question of law if an appellate court determines that no reasonable jury could find the defendant guilty under the evidence admitted in the case. This allows a small window for an appeals court to scrutinize the weight of evidence in a case to determine whether it was legally sufficient to support a conviction. In that case, the appeals court is effectively concluding that the prosecution failed to satisfy its prima facie burden and the case should never have been submitted to the jury for consideration because of evidentiary insufficiency. The result is that the appeals court will dismiss the case "with prejudice" so that the defendant cannot be retried on the same charges.

B. THE CONSTITUTIONAL PROTECTION OF INDIVIDUAL RIGHTS

In the immediate period after the negotiation and drafting of the U.S. Constitution, critics who had just finished fighting a war of independence against imperial Britain worried that the Constitution might have replaced one monarchical authority with another potential form of despotism, the federal government. In addition to the structural protections of federalism embedded in the Constitution, which limited the power of the federal government, critics sought to protect individual rights that might be compromised at the altar of federal authority. The result was the Bill of Rights, the first ten amendments to the Constitution.

1. The Bill of Rights

The Fourth, Fifth, and Sixth Amendments are of particular relevance to the criminal defendant and the conduct of the police and prosecutors and are reprinted in this section. They are the most important primary texts in this course and will inevitably, over the course of studying the doctrine, become committed to memory even in the absence of practice. However, they are not the sole constitutional provisions that are relevant for criminal procedure. Equally important is the Fourteenth Amendment, which, following the Civil War, required all states to respect "due process of law."

Fourth Amendment

The right of the people to be secure in their persons, houses, papers, and effects, against unreasonable searches and seizures, shall not be violated, and no warrants shall issue, but upon probable cause, supported by oath or affirmation, and particularly describing the place to be searched, and the persons or things to be seized.

Fifth Amendment

No person shall be held to answer for a capital, or otherwise infamous crime, unless on a presentment or indictment of a grand jury, except in cases arising in the land or naval forces, or in the militia, when in actual service in time of war or public danger; nor shall any person be subject for the same offense to be twice put in jeopardy of life or limb; nor shall be compelled in any criminal case to be a witness against himself, nor be deprived of life, liberty, or property, without due process of law; nor shall private property be taken for public use, without just compensation.

Sixth Amendment

In all criminal prosecutions, the accused shall enjoy the right to a speedy and public trial, by an impartial jury of the state and district wherein the crime shall have been committed, which district shall have been previously ascertained by law, and to be informed of the nature and cause of the accusation; to be confronted with the witnesses against him; to have compulsory process for obtaining witnesses in his favor, and to have the assistance of counsel for his defense.

Fourteenth Amendment

Section 1. All persons born or naturalized in the United States, and subject to the jurisdiction thereof, are citizens of the United States and of the State wherein they reside. No State shall make or enforce any law which shall abridge the privileges or immunities of citizens of the United States; nor shall any State deprive any person of life, liberty, or property, without due process of law; nor deny to any person within its jurisdiction the equal protection of the laws.

2. State Constitutional Provisions

It is sometimes tempting to view criminal procedure as simply a function of federal constitutional law, but the reality of the field is that state statutes and state constitutions play an indispensable role in articulating the rules that police and prosecutors must follow. Although the federal constitution, and the court decisions applying its provisions, set an absolute floor below which state law cannot descend, there is no prohibition on a state conferring extra protections on suspects and defendants, either through statutes or state constitutional law. Criminal procedure is just as much a function of state law as it is a function of federal law.

Below are three state law constitutional provisions, reprinted to demonstrate both their variety and their significance. Notice the difference among them. Specifically, state constitutional law provisions can be categorized in the following way: (1) provisions that establish *additional* protections over and above the federal baseline; (2) provisions that by their express terms are co-extensive with their federal counterparts; and (3) provisions that by case law precedent have been held to be co-extensive with their federal counterparts. In other words, some states have constitutional provisions that go beyond the federal constitution, while others simply have provisions that mirror the federal protections. Peruse the following provisions and pay particular attention to the diversity.

New York State Constitution Section 12

The right of the people to be secure in their persons, houses, papers and effects, against unreasonable searches and seizures, shall not be violated, and no warrants shall issue, but upon probable cause, supported by oath or affirmation, and particularly describing the place to be searched, and the persons or things to be seized.

The right of the people to be secure against unreasonable interception of telephone and telegraph communications shall not be violated, and ex parte orders or warrants shall issue only upon oath or affirmation that there is reasonable ground to believe that evidence of crime may be thus obtained, and identifying the particular means of communication, and particularly describing the person or persons whose communications are to be intercepted and the purpose thereof.

Massachusetts State Constitution Article XIV

Every subject has a right to be secure from all unreasonable searches, and seizures, of his person, his houses, his papers, and all his possessions. All warrants, therefore, are contrary to this right, if the cause or foundation of them be not previously supported by oath or affirmation; and if the order in the warrant to a civil officer, to make search in suspected places, or to arrest one or more suspected persons, or to seize their property, be not accompanied with a special designation of the persons or objects of search, arrest, or seizure: and no warrant ought to be issued but in cases, and with the formalities prescribed by the laws.

Florida State Constitution Article 12

The right of the people to be secure in their persons, houses, papers and effects against unreasonable searches and seizures, and against the unreasonable interception of private communications by any means, shall not be violated. No warrant shall be issued except upon probable cause, supported by affidavit, particularly describing the place or places to be searched, the person or persons, thing or things to be seized, the communication to be intercepted, and the nature of evidence to be obtained. This right shall be construed in conformity with the 4th Amendment to the United States Constitution, as interpreted by the United States Supreme Court. Articles or information obtained in violation of this right shall not be admissible in evidence if such articles or information would be inadmissible under decisions of the United States Supreme Court construing the 4th Amendment to the United States Constitution.

The materials in this casebook will mostly focus on the federal baseline, though where applicable call-out boxes will identify when state law statutes or state constitutional law provisions have established a higher standard for the local jurisdiction. From the perspective of national policy, the federal constitutional law standard is most important. From the perspective of the practice of a criminal lawyer, whether a prosecutor or a defense attorney, a local rule that establishes a stricter standard is equally important.

C. INCORPORATION

As noted above, the Fourteenth Amendment enacted after the Civil War required each state to respect due process of law. Although this much was certain, for many years the Supreme Court was engulfed in a highly intellectual debate over the meaning of this phrase. In short, there were three positions. The first position, originally articulated by the Supreme Court in *Twining v. New York*, was that the Fourteenth Amendment did *not* "incorporate" the Bill of Rights to make it applicable to the states. The second position was the exact opposite, i.e., that the Fourteenth Amendment performed a "total incorporation" of the Bill of Rights, thereby making all of its provisions applicable against the states. The third position was an intermediate between these polar extremes: The Fourteenth Amendment performed a "selective incorporation" of some but not all the provisions of the Bill of Rights. The debate between these theories was intellectually vicious and occupied the Supreme Court for years, filling scores of pages of the *United States Reports* with jurisprudential theories on the meaning of the Fourteenth Amendment. Behind the abstraction though was a legal fight of profound significance for the future of criminal procedure because it would determine whether the key protections of the Bill of Rights, including the right to counsel and the right against self-incrimination, applied in state prosecutions. Since the vast majority of criminal prosecutions are conducted at the state level, the debate would therefore determine whether local law enforcement was constrained by the federal constitution.

1. Selective Incorporation

In the following case, a majority of the Supreme Court supported the strategy of selective incorporation. In the foreground, the case deals with the right of the prosecution to appeal an acquittal in a crime case, and whether an appeal under these circumstances would violate the constitutional prohibition against double jeopardy. There is no question that the principle applies in federal cases, but does it also constrain state courts? Although this is the issue to be decided in the case, the significance of the holding swept far broader in that it articulated a standard for selective incorporation across the entire Bill of Rights. Which rights were incorporated by the Fourteenth Amendment? As you read the case, look for the phrase "scheme of ordered liberty" and assess its significance in this context. Does it provide a meaningful standard for the process of selective incorporation?

Palko v. Connecticut

Supreme Court of the United States
302 U.S. 319 (1937)

Mr. Justice CARDOZO delivered the opinion of the Court.

A statute of Connecticut permitting appeals in criminal cases to be taken by the state is challenged by appellant as an infringement of the Fourteenth Amendment of the Constitution of the United States. Whether the challenge should be upheld is now to be determined.

Appellant was indicted in Fairfield County, Conn., for the crime of murder in the first degree. A jury found him guilty of murder in the second degree, and he was sentenced to confinement in the state prison for life. Thereafter the State of Connecticut, with the permission of the judge presiding at the trial, gave notice of appeal to the Supreme Court of Errors. This it did pursuant to an act adopted in 1886 which is printed in the margin. Upon such appeal, the Supreme Court of Errors reversed the judgment and ordered a new trial. It found that there had been error of law to the prejudice of the state (1) in excluding testimony as to a confession by defendant; (2) in excluding testimony upon cross-examination of defendant to impeach his credibility; and (3) in the instructions to the jury as to the difference between first and second degree murder.

Pursuant to the mandate of the Supreme Court of Errors, defendant was brought to trial again. Before a jury was impaneled, and also at later stages of the case, he made the objection that the effect of the new trial was to place him twice in jeopardy for the same offense, and in so doing to violate the Fourteenth Amendment of the Constitution of the United States. Upon the overruling of the objection the trial proceeded. The jury returned a verdict of murder in the first degree, and the court sentenced the defendant to the punishment of death. The Supreme Court of Errors affirmed the judgment of conviction, adhering to a decision announced in 1894 which upheld the challenged statute. The case is here upon appeal. . . .

The argument for appellant is that whatever is forbidden by the Fifth Amendment is forbidden by the Fourteenth also. The Fifth Amendment, which is not directed to the States, but solely to the federal government, creates immunity from double jeopardy. No person shall be "subject for the same offense to be twice put in jeopardy of life or limb." The Fourteenth Amendment ordains, "nor shall any State deprive any person of life, liberty, or property, without due process of law." To retry a defendant, though under one indictment and only one, subjects him, it is said, to double jeopardy in violation of the Fifth Amendment, if the prosecution is one on behalf of the United States. From this the consequence is said to follow that there is a denial of life or liberty without due process of law, if the prosecution is one on behalf of the people of a state. . . .

We do not find it profitable to mark the precise limits of the prohibition of double jeopardy in federal prosecutions. The subject was much considered in *Kepner v. United States,* 195 U.S. 100, decided in 1904 by a closely divided court. The view was there expressed for a majority of the court that the prohibition was not confined to jeopardy in a new and independent case. It forbade jeopardy in the same case if the new trial was at the instance of the government and not upon defendant's motion. All this may be assumed for the purpose of the case at hand, though the dissenting opinions show how much was to be said in favor of a different ruling. Right-minded men, as we learn from those opinions, could reasonably, even if mistakenly, believe that a second trial was lawful in prosecutions subject to the Fifth Amendment, if it was all in the same case. Even more plainly, right-minded men could reasonably believe that in espousing that conclusion they were not favoring a practice repugnant to the conscience of mankind. Is double jeopardy in such circumstances, if double jeopardy it must be called, a denial of due process forbidden to the States? The tyranny of labels must not lead us to leap to a conclusion that a word which in one set of facts may stand for oppression or enormity is of like effect in every other.

We have said that in appellant's view the Fourteenth Amendment is to be taken as embodying the prohibitions of the Fifth. His thesis is even broader. Whatever would be a violation of the original bill of rights (Amendments 1 to 8) if done by the federal government is now equally unlawful by force of the Fourteenth Amendment if done by a state. There is no such general rule.

The Fifth Amendment provides, among other things, that no person shall be held to answer for a capital or otherwise infamous crime unless on presentment or indictment of a grand jury. This court has held that, in prosecutions by a state, presentment or indictment by a grand jury may give way to informations at the instance of a public officer. The Fifth Amendment provides also that no person shall be compelled in any criminal case to be a witness against himself. This court has said that, in prosecutions by a state, the exemption will fail if the state elects to end it. The Sixth Amendment calls for a jury trial in criminal cases and the Seventh for a jury trial in civil cases at common law where the value in controversy shall exceed $20. This court has ruled that consistently with those amendments trial by jury may be modified by a state or abolished altogether. . . .

On the other hand, the due process clause of the Fourteenth Amendment may make it unlawful for a state to abridge by its statutes the freedom of speech which the First Amendment safeguards against encroachment by the Congress or the like freedom of the press, or the free exercise of religion, or the right of peaceable assembly, without which speech would be unduly trammeled, or the right of one accused of crime to the benefit of counsel. In these and other situations immunities that are valid as against the federal government by force of the specific pledges of particular amendments have been found to be implicit in the concept of ordered liberty, and thus, through the Fourteenth Amendment, become valid as against the states.

The line of division may seem to be wavering and broken if there is a hasty catalogue of the cases on the one side and the other. Reflection and analysis will induce a different view. There emerges the perception of a rationalizing principle which gives to discrete instances a proper order and coherence. The right to trial by jury and the immunity from prosecution except as the result of an indictment may have value and importance. Even so, they are not of the very essence of a scheme of ordered liberty. To abolish them is not to violate a "principle of justice so rooted in the traditions and conscience of our people as to be ranked as fundamental." Few would be so narrow or provincial as to maintain that a fair and enlightened system of justice would be impossible without them. What is true of jury trials and indictments is true also, as the cases show, of the immunity from compulsory self-incrimination. This too might be lost, and justice still be done. Indeed, today as in the past there are students of our penal system who look upon the immunity as a mischief rather than a benefit, and who would limit its scope, or destroy it altogether. No doubt there would remain the need to give protection against torture, physical or mental. Justice, however, would not perish if the accused were subject to a duty to respond to orderly inquiry. The exclusion of these immunities and privileges from the privileges and immunities protected against the action of the States has not been arbitrary or casual. It has been dictated by a study and appreciation of the meaning, the essential implications, of liberty itself.

We reach a different plane of social and moral values when we pass to the privileges and immunities that have been taken over from the earlier articles of the Federal Bill of Rights and brought within the Fourteenth Amendment by a process of absorption. These in their origin were effective against the federal government alone. If the Fourteenth Amendment has absorbed them, the process of absorption has had its source in the belief that neither liberty nor justice would exist if they were sacrificed. This is true, for illustration, of freedom of thought and speech. Of that freedom one may say that it is the matrix, the indispensable condition, of nearly every other form of freedom. With rare aberrations a pervasive recognition of that truth can be traced in our history, political and legal. So it has come about that the domain of liberty, withdrawn by the Fourteenth Amendment from encroachment by the states, has been enlarged by latter-day judgments to include liberty of the mind as well as liberty of action. The extension became, indeed, a logical imperative when once it was recognized, as long ago it was, that liberty is something more than exemption from physical restraint, and that even in the field of substantive rights and duties the legislative judgment, if oppressive and arbitrary, may be overridden by the courts. Fundamental too in the concept of due process, and so in that of liberty, is the thought that condemnation shall be rendered only after trial. The hearing, moreover, must be a real one, not a sham or a pretense. For that reason, ignorant defendants in a capital case were held to have been condemned unlawfully when in truth, though not in form, they were refused the aid of counsel. The decision did not turn upon the fact that the benefit of counsel would have been guaranteed to the defendants by the provisions of the Sixth Amendment if they had been prosecuted in a federal court. The decision turned upon the fact that in the particular situation laid before us in the evidence the benefit of counsel was essential to the substance of a hearing.

Our survey of the cases serves, we think, to justify the statement that the dividing line between them, if not unfaltering throughout its course, has been true for the most part to a unifying principle. On which side of the line the case made out by the appellant has appropriate location must be the next inquiry and the final one. Is that kind of double jeopardy to which the statute has subjected him a hardship so acute and shocking that our policy will not endure it? Does it violate those "fundamental principles of liberty and justice which lie at the base of all our civil and political institutions"? The answer surely must be "no." What the answer would have to be if the state were permitted after a trial free from error to try the accused over again or to bring another case against him, we have no occasion to consider. We deal with the statute before us and no other. The state is not attempting to wear the accused out by a multitude of cases with accumulated trials. It asks no more than this, that the case against him shall go on until there shall be a trial free from the corrosion of substantial legal error. This is not cruelty at all, nor even vexation in any immoderate degree. If the trial had been infected with error adverse to the accused, there might have been review at his instance, and as often as necessary to purge the vicious taint. A reciprocal privilege, subject at all times to the discretion of the presiding judge, has now been granted to the state. There is here no seismic innovation. The edifice of justice stands, its symmetry, to many, greater than before. . . .

NOTES & QUESTIONS ON SELECTIVE INCORPORATION

1. *Scheme of ordered liberty.* The outcome of *Palko* throws into sharp relief the stinginess of the "scheme of ordered liberty" standard articulated by the Court. The Court fails to extend the protection of double jeopardy to state criminal prosecutions because double jeopardy is not a "principle of justice so rooted in the traditions and conscience of our people as to be ranked as fundamental." It is a bit unclear how double jeopardy could be so considered, but in any event it is clear that the standard offered the Supreme Court an opportunity to resist incorporation of a procedural right that is now regarded as both fundamental and deeply rooted in the common law tradition.

2. *The principle of double jeopardy.* Although the selective incorporation methodology from *Palko* was highly influential, its specific holding regarding retrials after acquittals was eventually overruled. In *Benton v. Maryland,* 395 U.S. 784 (1969), the Supreme Court concluded that the *Palko* reasoning was fundamentally flawed, and that federal double jeopardy standards applied against the states as well:

> The fundamental nature of the guarantee against double jeopardy can hardly be doubted. Its origins can be traced to Greek and Roman times, and it became established in the common law of England long before this Nation's independence. As with many other elements of the common law, it was carried into the jurisprudence of this Country through the medium of Blackstone, who codified the doctrine in his Commentaries. Today, every State incorporates some form of the prohibition in its constitution or common law. As this Court put it in *Green v. United States,* "(t)he underlying idea, one that is deeply ingrained in at least the Anglo-American system of jurisprudence, is that the State with all its resources and power should not be allowed to make repeated attempts to convict an individual for an alleged offense, thereby subjecting him to embarrassment, expense and ordeal and compelling him to live in a continuing state of anxiety and insecurity, as well as enhancing the possibility that even though innocent he may be found guilty." This underlying notion has from the very beginning been part of our constitutional tradition. Like the right to trial by jury, it is clearly "fundamental to the American scheme of justice." The validity of petitioner's larceny conviction must be judged, not by the watered-down standard enunciated in *Palko,* but under this Court's interpretations of the Fifth Amendment double jeopardy provision.

Benton v. Maryland, 395 U.S. 784, 795-96 (1969).

2. Total Incorporation

The most iconic expression of the argument for total incorporation came in Justice Black's dissenting opinion in *Adamson v. California.* In this opinion, reprinted here, Black explains why selective incorporation is both historically unjustified and also theoretically unsatisfying. As you read Black's dissenting opinion, think back on the rationale for a "scheme of ordered liberty" outlined in *Palko* and decide for yourself whether Black's criticisms are justified.

Adamson v. California

Supreme Court of the United States
332 U.S. 46 (1947)

Mr. Justice BLACK, dissenting.

The appellant was tried for murder in a California state court. He did not take the stand as a witness in his own behalf. The prosecuting attorney, under purported authority of a California statute, argued to the jury that an inference of guilt could be drawn because of appellant's failure to deny evidence offered against him. The appellant's contention in the state court and here has been that the statute denies him a right guaranteed by the Federal Constitution. The argument is that (1) permitting comment upon his failure to testify has the effect of compelling him to testify so as to violate that provision of the Bill of Rights contained in the Fifth Amendment that "No person . . . shall be compelled in any criminal case to be a witness against himself"; and (2) although this provision of the Fifth Amendment originally applied only as a restraint upon federal courts, the Fourteenth Amendment was intended to, and did make the prohibition against compelled testimony applicable to trials in state courts.

The Court refuses to meet and decide the appellant's first contention. But while the Court's opinion, as I read it, strongly implies that the Fifth Amendment does not, of itself, bar comment upon failure to testify in federal courts, the Court nevertheless assumes that it does in order to reach the second constitutional question involved in appellant's case. I must consider the case on the same assumption that the Court does. For the discussion of the second contention turns out to be a decision which reaches far beyond the relatively narrow issues on which this case might have turned.

This decision reasserts a constitutional theory spelled out in *Twining v. New Jersey*, 211 U.S. 78, that this Court is endowed by the Constitution with boundless power under "natural law" periodically to expand and contract constitutional standards to conform to the Court's conception of what at a particular time constitutes "civilized decency" and "fundamental principles of liberty and justice." Invoking this *Twining* rule, the Court concludes that although comment upon testimony in a federal court would violate the Fifth Amendment, identical comment in a state court does not violate today's fashion in civilized decency and fundamentals and is therefore not prohibited by the Federal Constitution as amended.

The *Twining* case was the first, as it is the only decision of this Court, which has squarely held that states were free, notwithstanding to Fifth and Fourteenth Amendments, to extort evidence from one accused of crime. I agree that if *Twining* be reaffirmed, the result reached might appropriately follow. But I would not reaffirm the *Twining* decision. I think that decision and the "natural law" theory of the Constitution upon which it relies, degrade the constitutional safeguards of the Bill of Rights and simultaneously appropriate for this Court a broad power which we are not authorized by the Constitution to exercise. Furthermore, the *Twining* decision rested on previous cases and broad hypotheses which have been undercut by intervening decisions of this Court. My reasons for believing that the *Twining* decision should not be revitalized can best be understood by reference to the constitutional, judicial, and general history that preceded and followed the case. That reference must be abbreviated far more than is justified but for the necessary limitations of opinion-writing.

The first 10 amendments were proposed and adopted largely because of fear that Government might unduly interfere with prized individual liberties. The people wanted and demanded a Bill of Rights written into their Constitution. The amendments embodying the Bill of Rights were intended to curb all branches of the Federal Government in the fields touched by the amendments—Legislative, Executive, and Judicial. The Fifth, Sixth, and Eighth Amendments were pointedly aimed at confining exercise of power by courts and judges within precise boundaries, particularly in the procedure used for the trial of criminal cases. Past history provided strong reasons for the apprehensions which brought these procedural amendments into being and attest the wisdom of their adoption. For the fears of arbitrary court action sprang largely from the past use of courts in the imposition of criminal punishments to suppress speech, press, and religion. Hence the constitutional limitations of courts' powers were, in the view of the Founders, essential supplements to the First Amendment, which was itself designed to protect the widest scope for all people to believe and to express the most divergent political, religious, and other views.

But these limitations were not expressly imposed upon state court action. In 1833, *Barron v. Baltimore*, was decided by this Court. It specifically held inapplicable to the states that provision of the Fifth Amendment which declares: "nor shall private property be taken for public use, without just compensation." In deciding the particular point raised, the Court there said that it could not hold that the first eight amendments applied to the states. This was the controlling constitutional rule when the Fourteenth Amendment was proposed in 1866.

My study of the historical events that culminated in the Fourteenth Amendment, and the expressions of those who sponsored and favored, as well as those who opposed its submission and passage, persuades me that one of the chief objects that the provisions of the Amendment's first section, separately, and as a whole, were intended to accomplish was to make the Bill of Rights, applicable to the states. With full knowledge of the import of the *Barron* decision, the framers and backers of the Fourteenth Amendment proclaimed its purpose to be to overturn the constitutional rule that case had announced. This historical purpose has never received full consideration or exposition in any opinion of this Court interpreting the Amendment.

In construing other constitutional provisions, this Court has almost uniformly followed the precept of *Ex parte Bain*, 121 U.S. 1, 12, that "It is never to be forgotten that in the construction of the language of the Constitution . . . , as indeed in all other instances where construction becomes necessary, we are to place ourselves as nearly as possible in the condition of the men who framed that instrument."

Investigation of the cases relied upon in *Twining v. New Jersey* to support the conclusion there reached that neither the Fifth Amendment's prohibition of compelled testimony, nor any of the Bill of Rights, applies to the States, reveals an unexplained departure from this salutary practice. Neither the briefs nor opinions in any of these cases . . . make reference to the legislative and contemporary history for the purpose of demonstrating that those who conceived, shaped, and brought about the adoption of the Fourteenth Amendment intended it to nullify this Court's decision in *Barron v. Baltimore*, and thereby to make the Bill of Rights applicable to the States. In *Maxwell v. Dow*, the issue turned on whether the Bill of Rights guarantee of a jury trial was, by the Fourteenth Amendment, extended to trials in state courts. In that case counsel for appellant did cite from the speech of Senator Howard, which so emphatically stated the understanding of the framers of the Amendment—the Committee on Reconstruction for which he spoke—that the Bill of Rights was to be made applicable to the states by the Amendment's first section. The Court's opinion in *Maxwell v. Dow*, acknowledged that counsel had "cited from the speech of one of the Senators," but indicated that it was not advised what other speeches were made in the Senate or in the House. The Court considered, moreover, that "What individual Senators or Representatives may have urged in debate, in regard to the meaning to be given to a proposed constitutional amendment, or bill, or resolution, does not furnish a firm ground for its proper construction, nor is it important as explanatory of the grounds upon which the members voted in adopting it."

In the *Twining* case itself, the Court was cited to a then recent book, Guthrie, *Fourteenth Amendment to the Constitution* (1898). A few pages of that work recited some of the legislative background of the Amendment, emphasizing the speech of Senator Howard. But Guthrie did not emphasize the speeches of Congressman Bingham, nor the part he played in the framing and adoption of the first section of the Fourteenth Amendment. Yet Congressman Bingham may, without extravagance, be called the Madison of the first section of the Fourteenth Amendment. In the *Twining* opinion the Court explicitly declined to give weight to the historical demonstration that the first section of the Amendment was intended to apply to the states the several protections of the Bill of Rights. It held that that question was "no longer open" because of previous decisions of this Court which, however, had not appraised the historical evidence on that subject. The Court admitted that its action had resulted in giving "much less effect to the 14th Amendment than some of the public men active in framing it" had intended it to have. With particular reference to the guarantee against compelled testimony, the Court stated that "Much might be said in favor of the view that the privilege was guaranteed against state impairment as a privilege and immunity of national citizenship, but, as has been shown, the decisions of this court have foreclosed that view." Thus the Court declined and again today declines, to appraise the relevant historical evidence of the intended scope of the first section of the Amendment. Instead it relied upon previous cases, none of which had analyzed the evidence showing that one purpose of those who framed, advocated, and adopted the Amendment had been to make the Bill of Rights applicable to the States. None of the cases relied upon by the Court today made such an analysis. . . .

In my judgment . . . history conclusively demonstrates that the language of the first section of the Fourteenth Amendment, taken as a whole, was thought by those responsible for its submission to the people, and by those who opposed its submission, sufficiently explicit to guarantee that thereafter no state could deprive its citizens of the privileges and protections of the Bill of Rights. Whether this Court ever will, or whether it now should, in the light of past decisions, give full effect to what the Amendment was intended to accomplish is not necessarily essential to a decision here. However that may be, our prior decisions, including *Twining*, do not prevent our carrying out that purpose, at least to the extent of making applicable to the states, not a mere part, as the Court has, but the full protection of the Fifth Amendment's provision against compelling evidence from an accused to convict him of crime. And I further contend that the "natural law" formula which the Court uses to reach its conclusion in this case should be abandoned as an incongruous excrescence on our Constitution. I believe that formula to be itself a violation of our Constitution, in that it subtly conveys to courts, at the expense of legislatures, ultimate power over public policies in fields where no specific provision of the Constitution limits legislative power. And my belief seems to be in accord with the views expressed by this Court, at least for the first two decades after the Fourteenth Amendment was adopted. . . .

Later decisions of this Court have completely undermined the phase of the *Twining* doctrine which broadly precluded reliance on the Bill of Rights to determine what is and what is not a "fundamental" right. . . . [T]his Court has now held that the Fourteenth Amendment protects from state invasion the following "fundamental" rights safeguarded by the Bill of Rights: right to counsel in criminal cases, *Powell v. Alabama*, 287 U.S. 45, 67; freedom of assembly, *De Jonge v. Oregon*, 299 U.S. 353, 364; at the very least, certain types of cruel and unusual punishment and former jeopardy, *State of Louisiana ex rel. Francis v. Resweber*, 329 U.S. 459; the right of an accused in a criminal case to be informed of the charge against him, see *Snyder v. Massachusetts*, 291 U.S. 97, 105; the right to receive just compensation on account of taking private property for public use. And the Court has now through the Fourteenth Amendment literally and emphatically applied the First Amendment to the States in its very terms.

In *Palko v. Connecticut*, a case which involved former jeopardy only, this Court re-examined the path it had traveled in interpreting the Fourteenth Amendment since the *Twining* opinion was written. In *Twining* the Court had declared that none of the rights enumerated in the first eight amendments were protected against state invasion because they were incorporated in the Bill of Rights. But the Court in *Palko*, answered a contention that all eight applied with the more guarded statement . . . that "there is no such general rule." Implicit in this statement, and in the cases decided in the interim between *Twining* and *Palko* and since, is the understanding that some of the eight amendments do apply by their very terms. . . . The Court went on to describe the Amendments made applicable to the States as "the privileges and immunities that have been taken over from the earlier articles of the Federal Bill of Rights and brought within the Fourteenth Amendment by a process of absorption." In the *Twining* case fundamental liberties were things apart from the Bill of Rights. Now it appears that at least some of the provisions of the Bill of Rights in their very terms satisfy the Court as sound and meaningful expressions of fundamental liberty. If the Fifth Amendment's protection against self-incrimination be such an expression of fundamental liberty, I ask, and have not found a satisfactory answer, why the Court today should consider that it should be "absorbed" in part but not in full? Nothing in the *Palko* opinion requires that when the Court decides that a Bill of Rights' provision is to be applied to the States, it is to be applied piecemeal. Nothing in the *Palko* opinion recommends that the Court apply part of an amendment's established meaning and discard that part which does not suit the current style of fundamentals. . . .

I cannot consider the Bill of Rights to be an outworn 18th Century "strait jacket" as the *Twining* opinion did. Its provisions may be thought outdated abstractions by some. And it is true that they were designed to meet ancient evils. But they are the same kind of human evils that have emerged from century to century wherever excessive power is sought by the few at the expense of the many. In my judgment the people of no nation can lose their liberty so long as a Bill of Rights like ours survives and its basic purposes are conscientiously interpreted, enforced and respected so as to afford continuous protection against old, as well as new, devices and practices which might thwart those purposes. I fear to see the consequences of the Court's practice of substituting its own concepts of decency and fundamental justice for the language of the Bill of Rights as its point of departure in interpreting and enforcing that Bill of Rights. If the choice must be between the selective process of the *Palko* decision applying some of the Bill of Rights to the States, or the *Twining* rule applying none of them, I would choose the *Palko* selective process. But rather than accept either of these choices. I would follow what I believe was the original purpose of the Fourteenth Amendment—to extend to all the people of the nation the complete protection of the Bill of Rights. To hold that this Court can determine what, if any, provisions of the Bill of Rights will be enforced, and if so to what degree, is to frustrate the great design of a written Constitution. . . .

Black's defense of total incorporation in *Adamson* did not win the day, but nor did it go gently into the good night; the fight over incorporation would linger for years on the Supreme Court. In the following case, *Duncan v. Louisiana*, one sees the slow accumulation of selective incorporation to the point where a large number of crucial rights were eventually incorporated—almost the same result as total incorporation would have produced. Indeed, pay particular attention to Justice Black's concurrence where he notes that he is happy to support selective incorporation since, in the final analysis, it ended up incorporating almost everything—a perfectly fine result from the perspective of a total incorporationist.

Duncan v. Louisiana

Supreme Court of the United States
391 U.S. 145 (1968)

Mr. Justice White delivered the opinion of the Court.

Appellant, Gary Duncan, was convicted of simple battery in the Twenty-fifth Judicial District Court of Louisiana. Under Louisiana law simple battery is a misdemeanor, punishable by a maximum of two years' imprisonment and a $300 fine. Appellant sought trial by jury, but because the Louisiana Constitution grants jury trials only in cases in which capital punishment or imprisonment at hard labor may be imposed, the trial judge denied the request. Appellant was convicted and sentenced to serve 60 days in the parish prison and pay a fine of $150. . . .

I

The Fourteenth Amendment denies the States the power to "deprive any person of life, liberty, or property, without due process of law." In resolving conflicting claims concerning the meaning of this spacious language, the Court has looked increasingly to the Bill of Rights for guidance; many of the rights guaranteed by the first eight Amendments to the Constitution have been held to be protected against state action by the Due Process Clause of the Fourteenth Amendment. That clause now protects the right to compensation for property taken by the State; the rights of speech, press, and religion covered by the First Amendment; the Fourth Amendment rights to be free from unreasonable searches and seizures and to have excluded from criminal trials any evidence illegally seized; the right guaranteed by the Fifth Amendment to be free of compelled self-incrimination; and the Sixth Amendment rights to counsel, to a speedy and public trial, to confrontation of opposing witnesses, and to compulsory process for obtaining witnesses.

The test for determining whether a right extended by the Fifth and Sixth Amendments with respect to federal criminal proceedings is also protected against state action by the Fourteenth Amendment has been phrased in a variety of ways in the opinions of this Court. The question has been asked whether a right is among those "fundamental principles of liberty and justice which lie at the base of all our civil and political institutions," whether it is "basic in our system of jurisprudence," and whether it is "a fundamental right, essential to a fair trial." The claim before us is that the right to trial by jury guaranteed by the Sixth Amendment meets these tests. The position of Louisiana, on the other hand, is that the Constitution imposes upon the States no duty to give a jury trial in any criminal case, regardless of the seriousness of the crime or the size of the punishment which may be imposed. Because we believe that trial by jury in criminal cases is fundamental to the American scheme of justice, we hold that the Fourteenth Amendment guarantees a right of jury trial in all criminal cases which—were they to be tried in a federal court—would come within the Sixth Amendment's guarantee. Since we consider the appeal before us to be such a case, we hold that the Constitution was violated when appellant's demand for jury trial was refused. . . .

We are aware of prior cases in this Court in which the prevailing opinion contains statements contrary to our holding today that the right to jury trial in serious criminal cases is a fundamental right and hence must be recognized by the States as part of their obligation to extend due process of law to all persons within their jurisdiction. Louisiana relies especially on *Maxwell v. Dow,* 176 U.S. 581 (1900); *Palko v. Connecticut,* 302 U.S. 319 (1937); and *Snyder v. Massachusetts,* 291 U.S. 97 (1934). None of these cases, however, dealt with a State which had purported to dispense entirely with a jury trial in serious criminal cases. Maxwell held that no provision of the Bill of Rights applied to the States—a position long since repudiated—and that the Due Process Clause of the Fourteenth Amendment did not prevent a State from trying a defendant for a noncapital offense with fewer than 12 men on the jury. It did not deal with a case in which no jury at all had been provided. In neither *Palko* nor *Snyder* was jury trial actually at issue, although both cases contain important dicta asserting that the right to jury trial is not essential to ordered liberty and may be dispensed with by the States regardless of the Sixth and Fourteenth Amendments. These observations, though weighty and respectable, are nevertheless dicta, unsupported by holdings in this Court that a State may refuse a defendant's demand for a jury trial when he is charged with a serious crime. Perhaps because the right to jury trial was not directly at stake, the Court's remarks about the jury in *Palko* and *Snyder* took no note of past or current developments regarding jury trials, did not consider its purposes and functions, attempted no inquiry into how well it was performing its job, and did not discuss possible distinctions between civil and criminal cases. In *Malloy v. Hogan*, the Court rejected *Palko*'s discussion of the self-incrimination clause. Respectfully, we reject the prior dicta regarding jury trial in criminal cases.

The guarantees of jury trial in the Federal and State Constitutions reflect a profound judgment about the way in which law should be enforced and justice administered. A right to jury trial is granted to criminal defendants in order to prevent oppression by the Government. Those who wrote our constitutions knew from history and experience that it was necessary to protect against unfounded criminal charges brought to eliminate enemies and against judges too responsive to the voice of higher authority. The framers of the constitutions strove to create an independent judiciary but insisted upon further protection against arbitrary action. Providing an accused with the right to be tried by a jury of his peers gave him an inestimable safeguard against the corrupt or overzealous prosecutor and against the compliant, biased, or eccentric judge. If the defendant preferred the common-sense judgment of a jury to the more tutored but perhaps less sympathetic reaction of the single judge, he was to have it. Beyond this, the jury trial provisions in the Federal and State Constitutions reflect a fundamental decision about the exercise of official power—a reluctance to entrust plenary powers over the life and liberty of the citizen to one judge or to a group of judges. Fear of unchecked power, so typical of our State and Federal Governments in other respects, found expression in the criminal law in this insistence upon community participation in the determination of guilt or innocence. The deep commitment of the Nation to the right of jury trial in serious criminal cases as a defense against arbitrary law enforcement qualifies for protection under the Due Process Clause of the Fourteenth Amendment, and must therefore be respected by the States. . . .

Mr. Justice Black, with whom Mr. Justice Douglas joins, concurring.

The Court today holds that the right to trial by jury guaranteed defendants in criminal cases in federal courts by Art. III of the United States Constitution and by the Sixth Amendment is also guaranteed by the Fourteenth Amendment to defendants tried in state courts. With this holding I agree for reasons given by the Court. I also agree because of reasons given in my dissent in *Adamson v. California*, 332 U.S. 47. In that dissent, I took the position . . . that the Fourteenth Amendment made all of the provisions of the Bill of Rights applicable to the States. . . .

In this situation I said in *Adamson v. California* that, while "I would . . . extend to all the people of the nation the complete protection of the Bill of Rights," that "(i)f the choice must be between the selective process of the *Palko* decision applying some of the Bill of Rights to the States, or the *Twining* rule applying none of them, I would choose the *Palko* selective process." And I am very happy to support this selective process through which our Court has since the *Adamson* case held most of the specific Bill of Rights' protections applicable to the States to the same extent they are applicable to the Federal Government. Among these are the right to trial by jury decided today, the right against compelled self-incrimination, the right to counsel, the right to compulsory process for witnesses, the right to confront witnesses, the right to a speedy and public trial, and the right to be free from unreasonable searches and seizures. . . .

Mr. Justice FORTAS, concurring.

. . . [A]lthough I agree with the decision of the Court, I cannot agree with the implication, that the tail must go with the hide: that when we hold, influenced by the Sixth Amendment, that "due process" requires that the States accord the right of jury trial for all but petty offenses, we automatically import all of the ancillary rules which have been or may hereafter be developed incidental to the right to jury trial in the federal courts. I see no reason whatever, for example, to assume that our decision today should require us to impose federal requirements such as unanimous verdicts or a jury of 12 upon the States. We may well conclude that these and other features of federal jury practice are by no means fundamental—that they are not essential to due process of law—and that they are not obligatory on the States.

I would make these points clear today. Neither logic nor history nor the intent of the draftsmen of the Fourteenth Amendment can possibly be said to require that the Sixth Amendment or its jury trial provision be applied to the States together with the total gloss that this Court's decisions have supplied. The draftsmen of the Fourteenth Amendment intended what they said, not more or less: that no State shall deprive any person of life, liberty, or property without due process of law. It is ultimately the duty of this Court to interpret, to ascribe specific meaning to this phrase. There is no reason whatever for us to conclude that, in so doing, we are bound slavishly to follow not only the Sixth Amendment but all of its bag and baggage, however securely or insecurely affixed they may be by law and precedent to federal proceedings. To take this course, in my judgment, would be not only unnecessary but mischievous because it would inflict a serious blow upon the principle of federalism. The Due Process Clause commands us to apply its great standard to state court proceedings to assure basis fairness. It does not command us rigidly and arbitrarily to impose the exact pattern of federal proceedings upon the 50 States. On the contrary, the Constitution's command, in my view, is that in our insistence upon state observance of due process, we should, so far as possible, allow the greatest latitude for state differences. It requires, within the limits of the lofty basic standards that it prescribes for the States as well as the Federal Government, maximum opportunity for diversity and minimal imposition of uniformity of method and detail upon the States. Our Constitution sets up a federal union, not a monolith.

This Court has heretofore held that various provisions of the Bill of Rights such as the freedom of speech and religion guarantees of the First Amendment, the prohibition of unreasonable searches and seizures in the Fourth Amendment, the privilege against self-incrimination of the Fifth Amendment, and the right to counsel and to confrontation under the Sixth Amendment "are all to be enforced against the States under the Fourteenth Amendment according to the same standards that protect those personal rights against federal encroachment." I need not quarrel with the specific conclusion in those specific instances. But unless one adheres slavishly to the incorporation theory, body and substance, the same conclusion need not be superimposed upon the jury trial right. I respectfully but urgently suggest that it should not be. Jury trial is more than a principle of justice applicable to individual cases. It is a system of administration of the business of the State. While we may believe (and I do believe) that the right of jury trial is fundamental, it does not follow that the particulars of according that right must be uniform. We should be ready to welcome state variations which do not impair—indeed, which may advance—the theory and purpose of trial by jury.

Mr. Justice HARLAN, whom Mr. Justice STEWART joins, dissenting.

Every American jurisdiction provides for trial by jury in criminal cases. The question before us is not whether jury trial is an ancient institution, which it is; nor whether it plays a significant role in the administration of criminal justice, which it does; nor whether it will endure, which it shall. The question in this case is whether the State of Louisiana, which provides trial by jury for all felonies, is prohibited by the Constitution from trying charges of simple battery to the court alone. In my view, the answer to that question, mandated alike by our constitutional history and by the longer history of trial by jury, is clearly "no."

The States have always borne primary responsibility for operating the machinery of criminal justice within their borders, and adapting it to their particular circumstances. In exercising this responsibility, each State is compelled to conform its procedures to the requirements of the Federal Constitution. The Due Process Clause of the Fourteenth Amendment requires that those procedures be fundamentally fair in all respects. It does not, in my view, impose or encourage nationwide uniformity for its own sake; it does not command adherence to forms that happen to be old; and it does not impose on the States the rules that may be in force in the federal courts except where such rules are also found to be essential to basic fairness.

The Court's approach to this case is an uneasy and illogical compromise among the views of various Justices on how the Due Process Clause should be interpreted. The Court does not say that those who framed the Fourteenth Amendment intended to make the Sixth Amendment applicable to the States. And the Court concedes that it finds nothing unfair about the procedure by which the present appellant was tried. Nevertheless, the Court reverses his conviction: it holds, for some reason not apparent to me, that the Due Process Clause incorporates the particular clause of the Sixth Amendment that requires trial by jury in federal criminal cases—including, as I read its opinion, the sometimes trivial accompanying baggage of judicial interpretation in federal contexts. I have raised my voice many times before against the Court's continuing undiscriminating insistence upon fastening on the States federal notions of criminal justice, and I must do so again in this instance. With all respect, the Court's approach and its reading of history are altogether topsy-turvy.

I believe I am correct in saying that every member of the Court for at least the last 135 years has agreed that our Founders did not consider the requirements of the Bill of Rights so fundamental that they should operate directly against the States. They were wont to believe rather that the security of liberty in America rested primarily upon the dispersion of governmental power across a federal system. The Bill of Rights was considered unnecessary by some but insisted upon by others in order to curb the possibility of abuse of power by the strong central government they were creating. . . .

A few members of the Court have taken the position that the intention of those who drafted the first section of the Fourteenth Amendment was simply, and exclusively, to make the provisions of the first eight Amendments applicable to state action. This view has never been accepted by this Court. In my view, often expressed elsewhere, the first section of the Fourteenth Amendment was meant neither to incorporate, nor to be limited to, the specific guarantees of the first eight Amendments. The overwhelming historical evidence . . . demonstrates, to me conclusively, that the Congressmen and state legislators who wrote, debated, and ratified the Fourteenth Amendment did not think they were "incorporating" the Bill of Rights and the very breadth and generality of the Amendment's provisions suggest that its authors did not suppose that the Nation would always be limited to mid-19th century conceptions of "liberty" and "due process of law" but that the increasing experience and evolving conscience of the American people would add new "intermediate premises." In short, neither history, nor sense, supports using the Fourteenth Amendment to put the States in a constitutional straitjacket with respect to their own development in the administration of criminal or civil law.

Although I therefore fundamentally disagree with the total incorporation view of the Fourteenth Amendment, it seems to me that such a position does at least have the virtue, lacking in the Court's selective incorporation approach, of internal consistency. . . .

Apart from the approach taken by the absolute incorporationists, I can see only one method of analysis that has any internal logic. That is to start with the words "liberty" and "due process of law" and attempt to define them in a way that accords with American traditions and our system of government. This approach, involving a much more discriminating process of adjudication than does "incorporation," is, albeit difficult, the one that was followed throughout the 19th and most of the present century. It entails a "gradual process of judicial inclusion and exclusion," seeking, with due recognition of constitutional tolerance for state experimentation and disparity, to ascertain those "immutable principles . . . of justice which inhere in the very idea of free government which no member of the Union may disregard." Due process was not restricted to rules fixed in the past, for that "would be to deny every quality of the law but its age, and to render it incapable of progress or improvement." Nor did it impose nationwide uniformity in details. . . .

Through this gradual process, this Court sought to define "liberty" by isolating freedoms that Americans of the past and of the present considered more important than any suggested countervailing public objective. The Court also, by interpretation of the phrase "due process of law," enforced the Constitution's guarantee that no State may imprison an individual except by fair and impartial procedures.

The relationship of the Bill of Rights to this "gradual process" seems to me to be twofold. In the first place it has long been clear that the Due Process Clause imposes some restrictions on state action that parallel Bill of Rights restrictions on federal action. Second, and more important than this accidental overlap, is the fact that the Bill of Rights is evidence, at various points, of the content Americans find in the term "liberty" and of American standards of fundamental fairness. . . .

NOTES & QUESTIONS ON TOTAL INCORPORATION

1. *The results of the incorporation debate.* Most of the individual rights relevant to criminal procedure were eventually incorporated through the Fourteenth Amendment and made applicable against the states. Among

these are the First Amendment freedoms of speech and religion; the Fourth Amendment prohibitions against unreasonable searches; the Fifth Amendment privilege against self-incrimination and its associated right to counsel; and the Sixth Amendment right to counsel and to "confront" witnesses at trial. In the end, how much does it really matter whether the result was achieved through selective or total incorporation?

2. *Justice Harlan's solution.* There are more than two options in the incorporation debate. In his dissent, Justice Harlan argues for an alternative methodology, one that eschews "incorporation" of any flavor and instead focuses on an *a priori* analysis of "liberty" and "due process of law," with reference to "American traditions and our system of government." What exactly does this mean and does the methodology differ significantly from selective incorporation? What is Harlan's view of Louisiana's authority to experiment with alternative arrangements to the jury? Does this give a clue to the real difference between selective incorporation and Harlan's "American tradition" methodology? For more discussion, see Stephen M. Dane, *"Ordered Liberty" and Self-Restraint: The Judicial Philosophy of the Second Justice Harlan,* 51 U. Cin. L. Rev. 545, 553 (1982).

3. *Incorporation and habeas jurisdiction.* In addition to direct appellate review in state court, defendants may also attack their convictions by filing petitions in federal court. Federal courts have the authority to entertain habeas corpus petitions alleging that a state criminal law proceeding violated the defendant's federal constitutional rights. With the incorporation of most federal rights into the Fourteenth Amendment, making those rights applicable against the individual states, the scope of federal habeas review has expanded greatly. Federal district judges entertaining habeas petitions now routinely evaluate state criminal procedure and may overturn convictions that were originally upheld by state appellate courts. Is this additional layer of habeas review to be celebrated as a key method for vindicating federal rights, or should it be viewed with suspicion as an unfortunate double layer of post-conviction review?

D. THE GOAL OF CRIMINAL PROCEDURE

What is the goal of criminal procedure and how does it relate to the field of criminal justice more broadly? How should we think of the procedural protections? Are they inherent rights that are deontologically justified regardless of how inconvenient they are for state authorities to abide by? Or are they justified by utilitarian principles since unfair procedures might cause the innocent to be falsely convicted, thus frustrating the state's legitimate desire to capture and punish the right people for their wrongdoing?

In the following excerpt, the scholar Herbert Packer suggested that criminal procedure inevitably involves a tension—or even a conflict—between two fundamental "models" of criminal justice. The first model, crime control, focuses on the state's desire to control crime by arresting and punishing suspects so that law and order is maintained in the polity. The second model, due process, focuses on the individual's need to resist state authority in order to ensure that procedural protections are respected for each individual, so that criminal justice outcomes are determined according to the rule of law. In a sense, every topic to be explored in this casebook will inevitably involve a tension between crime control and due process. The entire field of criminal procedure involves the navigation of this tension in a way that respects the legitimate needs of the state, acting on behalf of the community, and the legitimate needs of the individual as protected by the rules laid out in the Constitution and other legal instruments.

Two Models of the Criminal Process

Herbert Packer

113 U. Pa. L. Rev. 1 (1964)

In this section we shall develop two competing systems of values, the tension between which accounts for the intense activity now observable in the development of the criminal process. The models we are about to examine attempt to give operational content to these conflicting schemes of values. Like the values underlying them, the models are polarities. Just as the models are not to be taken as describing real-world situations, so the values that underlie them are not to be regarded as expressing the values held by any one person. The values are presented here as an aid to analysis, not as a program for action.

CRIME CONTROL VALUES

The value system that underlies the Crime Control Model is based on the proposition that the repression of criminal conduct is by far the most important function to be performed by the criminal process. The failure of law enforcement to bring criminal conduct under tight control is viewed as leading to the breakdown of public order and thence to the disappearance of an important condition of human freedom. If the laws go unenforced, which is to say, if it is perceived that there is a high percentage of failure to apprehend and convict in the criminal process, a general disregard for legal controls tends to develop. The law-abiding citizen then becomes the victim of all sorts of unjustifiable invasions of his interests. His security of person and property is sharply diminished and, therefore, so is his liberty to function as a member of society. The claim ultimately is that the criminal process is a positive guarantor of social freedom. In order to achieve this high purpose, the Crime Control Model requires that primary attention be paid to the efficiency with which the criminal process operates to screen suspects, determine guilt, and secure appropriate dispositions of persons convicted of crime.

Efficiency of operation is not, of course, a criterion that can be applied in a vacuum. By "efficiency" we mean the system's capacity to apprehend, try, convict, and dispose of a high proportion of criminal offenders whose offenses become known. In a society in which only the grossest forms of antisocial behavior were made criminal and in which the crime rate was exceedingly low, the criminal process might require many more man-hours of police, prosecutorial, and judicial time per case than ours does, and still operate with tolerable efficiency. On the other hand, a society that was prepared to increase substantially the resources devoted to the suppression of crime might cope with a rising crime rate without sacrifice of efficiency while continuing to maintain an elaborate and time-consuming set of criminal processes. However, neither of these hypotheses corresponds with social reality in this country. We use the criminal sanction to cover an increasingly wide spectrum of behavior thought to be antisocial, and the amount of crime is very large indeed. At the same time, while precise measures are not available, it does not appear that we are disposed in the public sector of the economy to increase very drastically the quantity, much less the quality, of the resources devoted to the suppression of criminal activity through the operation of the criminal process. These factors have an important bearing on the criteria of efficiency and, therefore, on the nature of the Crime Control Model.

The model, in order to operate successfully, must produce a high rate of apprehension and conviction and must do so in a context where the magnitudes being dealt with are very large, and the resources for dealing with them are very limited. There must then be a premium on speed and finality. Speed, in turn, depends on informality and on uniformity; finality depends on minimizing the occasions for challenge. The process must not be cluttered with ceremonious rituals that do not advance the progress of a case. Facts can be established more quickly through interrogation in a police station than through the formal process of examination and cross-examination in a court; it follows that extrajudicial processes should be preferred to judicial processes, informal to formal operations. Informality is not enough; there must also be uniformity. Routine stereotyped procedures are essential if large numbers are being handled. The model that will operate successfully on these presuppositions must be an administrative, almost a managerial, model. The image that comes to mind is an assembly line or a conveyor belt down which moves an endless stream of cases, never stopping, carrying the cases to workers who stand at fixed stations and who perform on each case as it comes by the same small but essential operation that brings it one step closer to being a finished product, or, to exchange the metaphor for the reality, a closed file.

The criminal process, on this model, is seen as a screening process in which each successive stage—prearrest investigation, arrest, post-arrest investigation, preparation for trial, trial or entry of plea, conviction, and disposition—involves a series of routinized operations whose success is gauged primarily by their tendency to pass the case along to a successful conclusion.

What is a successful conclusion? One that throws off at an early stage those cases in which it appears unlikely that the person apprehended is an offender and then secures, as expeditiously as possible, the conviction of the rest with a minimum of occasions for challenge, let alone postaudit. By the application of administrative expertness, primarily that of the police and prosecutors, an early determination of probable innocence or guilt emerges. The probably innocent are screened out. The probably guilty are passed quickly through the remaining stages of the process. The key to the operation of the model as to those who are not screened out is what I shall call a presumption of guilt. The concept requires some explanation, since it may appear startling to assert that what appears to be the precise converse of our generally accepted ideology of a presumption of innocence can be an essential element of a model that does correspond in some regards to the real-life operation of the criminal process.

The presumption of guilt allows the Crime Control Model to deal efficiently with large numbers. The supposition is that the screening processes operated by police and prosecutors are reliable indicators of probable guilt. Once a man has been investigated without being found to be probably innocent, or, to put it differently, once a determination has been made that there is enough evidence of guilt so that he should be held for further action rather than released from the process, then all subsequent activity directed toward him is based on the view that he is probably guilty. The precise point at which this occurs will vary from case to case; in many cases it will occur as soon as the suspect is arrested or even before, if the evidence of probable guilt that has come to the attention of the authorities is sufficiently strong. But in any case, the presumption of guilt will begin to operate well before the "suspect" becomes a "defendant."

The presumption of guilt is not, of course, a thing. Nor is it even a rule of law in the usual sense. It simply exemplifies a complex of attitudes, a mood. If there is confidence in the reliability of informal administrative factfinding activities that take place in the early stages of the criminal process, the remaining stages of the process can be relatively perfunctory without any loss in operating efficiency. The presumption of guilt, as it operates in the Crime Control Model, is the expression of that confidence.

It would be a mistake to think of the presumption of guilt as the opposite of the presumption of innocence that we are so used to thinking of as the polestar of the criminal process and which, as we shall see, occupies an important position in the Due Process Model. The presumption of innocence is not its opposite; it is irrelevant to the presumption of guilt; the two concepts embody different rather than opposite ideas. The difference can perhaps be epitomized by an example. A murderer, for reasons best known to himself, chooses to shoot his victim in plain view of a large number of people. When the police arrive, he hands them his gun and says: "I did it, and I'm glad." His account of what happened is corroborated by several eyewitnesses. He is placed under arrest and led off to jail. Under these circumstances, which may seem extreme but which in fact characterize with rough accuracy the factfinding situation in a large proportion of criminal cases, it would be plainly absurd to maintain that more probably than not the suspect did not commit the killing. But that is not what the presumption of innocence means. It means that until there has been an adjudication of guilt by an authority legally competent to make such an adjudication, the suspect is to be treated, for reasons that have nothing whatever to do with the probable outcome of the case, as if his guilt is an open question.

The presumption of innocence is a direction to officials how they are to proceed, not a prediction of outcome. The presumption of guilt, however, is basically a prediction of outcome. The presumption of innocence is really a direction to the authorities to ignore the presumption of guilt in their treatment of the suspect. It tells them, in effect, to close their eyes to what will frequently seem to be factual probabilities. The reasons why it tells them that are among the animating presuppositions of the Due Process Model, and we will come to them shortly. It is enough to note at this point that the presumption of guilt is descriptive and factual; the presumption of innocence is normative and legal. The pure Crime Control Model finds unacceptable the presumption of innocence although, as we shall see, its real-life emanations are brought into uneasy compromise with the dictates of this dominant ideological position. For this model the presumption of guilt assures the dominant goal of repressing crime through highly summary processes without any great loss of efficiency (as previously defined), for in the run of cases, the preliminary screening processes operated by the police and the prosecuting officials contain adequate guarantees of reliable factfinding. Indeed, the position is a stronger one. It is that subsequent processes, particularly of a formal adjudicatory nature, are unlikely to produce as reliable factfinding as the expert administrative process that precedes them. The criminal process thus must put special weight on the quality of administrative factfinding. It becomes important, then, to place as few restrictions as possible on the character of the administrative factfinding processes and to limit restrictions to those that enhance reliability, excluding those designed for other purposes. As we shall see, the desire to avoid restrictions on administrative factfinding is a consistent theme in the development of the Crime Control Model.

For this model the early administrative factfinding stages are centrally vital. The complementary proposition is that the subsequent stages are relatively unimportant and should be truncated as much as possible. This, too, produces tensions with presently dominant ideology. The pure Crime Control Model has very little use for many conspicuous features of the adjudicative process and in real life works a number of ingenious compromises with it. Even in the pure model, however, there have to be devices for dealing with the suspect after the preliminary screening process has resulted in a determination of probable guilt. The focal device, as we shall see, is the plea of guilty; through its use adjudicative factfinding is reduced to a minimum. It might be said of the Crime Control Model that, reduced to its barest essentials and when operating at its most successful pitch, it consists of two elements: (a) an administrative factfinding process leading to exoneration of the suspect, or to (b) the entry of a plea of guilty.

DUE PROCESS VALUES

If the Crime Control Model resembles an assembly line, the Due Process Model looks very much like an obstacle course. Each of its successive stages is designed to present formidable impediments to carrying the accused any further along in the process. Its ideology is not the converse of that underlying the Crime Control Model. It does not deny the social desirability of repressing crime, although its critics have been known to claim so. Its ideology is composed of a complex of ideas, some of them based on judgments about the efficacy of crime control devices. The ideology of due process is far more deeply impressed on the formal structure of the law than is the ideology of crime control; yet, an accurate tracing of the strands of which it is made is strangely difficult. What follows is only an attempt at an approximation.

The Due Process Model encounters its rival on the Crime Control Model's own ground in respect to the reliability of factfinding processes. The Crime Control Model, as we have suggested in a preliminary way, places heavy reliance on the ability of investigative and prosecutorial officers, acting in an informal setting in which their distinctive skills are given full sway, to elicit and reconstruct a tolerably accurate account of what actually took place in an alleged criminal event. The Due Process Model rejects this premise and substitutes for it a view of informal, nonadjudicative factfinding that stresses the possibility of error: people are notoriously poor observers of disturbing events—the more emotion-arousing the context, the greater the possibility that recollection will be incorrect; confessions and admissions by persons in police custody may be induced by physical or psychological coercion, so that the police end up hearing what the suspect thinks they want to hear rather than the truth; witnesses may be animated by a bias or interest that no one would trouble to discover except one specially charged with protecting the interests of the accused—which the police are not. Considerations of this kind all lead to the rejection of informal factfinding processes as definitive of factual guilt and to the insistence on formal, adjudicative, adversary factfinding processes in which the factual case against the accused is publicly heard by an impartial tribunal and is evaluated only after the accused has had a full opportunity to discredit the case against him. Even then the distrust of factfinding processes that animates the Due Process Model is not dissipated. The possibilities of human error being what they are, further scrutiny is necessary, or at least must be available, lest in the heat of battle facts have been overlooked or suppressed. How far this subsequent scrutiny must be available is hotly controverted today; in the pure Due Process Model the answer would be: at least as long as there is an allegation of factual error that has not received an adjudicative hearing in a factfinding context. The demand for finality is thus very low in the Due Process Model.

This strand of due process ideology is not enough to sustain the model. If all that were at issue between the two models was a series of questions about the reliability of factfinding processes, we would have but one model of the criminal process, the nature of whose constituent elements would pose questions of fact, not of value. Even if the discussion is confined for the moment to the question of reliability, it is apparent that more is at stake than simply an evaluation of what kinds of factfinding processes, alone or in combination, are likely to produce the most nearly reliable results. The stumbling-block is this: how much reliability is compatible with efficiency? Granted that informal factfinding will make some mistakes that will be remedied if backed up by adjudicative factfinding, the desirability of providing this backup is not affirmed or negated by factual demonstrations or predictions that the increase in reliability will be x percent or x plus n percent. It still remains to ask how much weight is to be given to the competing demands of reliability (a high degree of probability in each case that factual guilt has been accurately determined) and efficiency (a process that deals expeditiously with the large numbers of cases that it ingests). Just as the Crime Control Model is more optimistic about the unlikelihood of error in a significant number of cases, it is also more lenient in establishing a tolerable level of error. The Due Process Model insists on the prevention and elimination of mistakes to the extent possible; the Crime Control Model accepts the probability of mistakes up to the level at which they interfere with the goal of repressing crime, either because too many guilty people are escaping or, more subtly, because general awareness of the unreliability of the process leads to a decrease in the deterrent efficacy of the criminal law. On this view reliability and efficiency are not polar opposites but rather complementary characteristics. The system is reliable because efficient; reliability becomes a matter of independent concern only when it becomes so attenuated as to impair efficiency. All of this the Due Process Model rejects. If efficiency suggests shortcuts around reliability, those demands must be rejected. The aim of the process is at least as much to protect the factually innocent as it is to convict the factually guilty. It somewhat resembles quality control in industrial technology: tolerable deviation from standard varies with the importance of conformity to standard in the destined use of the product. The Due Process Model resembles a factory that has to devote a substantial part of its input to quality control. This necessarily reduces quantitative output.

This is only the beginning of the ideological difference between the two models. The Due Process Model could disclaim any attempt to provide enhanced reliability for the factfinding process and still produce a set of institutions and processes that would differ sharply from those posited by the demands of the Crime Control Model. Indeed, it may not be too great an oversimplification to assert that in point of historical development the doctrinal pressures that have emanated from the demands of the Due Process Model have tended to evolve from an original matrix of concern with the maximization of reliability into something quite different and more far-reaching. This complex of values can be symbolized although not adequately described by the concept of the primacy of the individual and the complementary concept of limitation on official power.

The combination of stigma and loss of liberty that is embodied in the end result of the criminal process is viewed as being the heaviest deprivation that government can inflict on the individual. Furthermore, the processes that culminate in these highly afflictive sanctions are in themselves coercive, restricting, and demeaning. Power is always subject to abuse, sometimes subtle, other times, as in the criminal process, open and ugly. Precisely because of its potency in subjecting the individual to the coercive power of the state, the criminal process must, on this model, be subjected to controls and safeguards that prevent it from operating with maximal efficiency. According to this ideology, maximal efficiency means maximal tyranny. And, while no one would assert that minimal efficiency means minimal tyranny, the proponents of the Due Process Model would accept with considerable equanimity a substantial diminution in the efficiency with which the criminal process operates in the interest of preventing official oppression of the individual.

The most modest-seeming but potentially far-reaching mechanism by which the Due Process Model implements these antiauthoritarian values is the doctrine of legal guilt. According to this doctrine, an individual is not to be held guilty of crime merely on a showing that in all probability, based upon reliable evidence, he did factually what he is said to have done. Instead, he is to be held guilty if and only if these factual determinations are made in procedurally regular fashion and by authorities acting within competences duly allocated to them. Furthermore, he is not to be held guilty, even though the factual determination is or might be adverse to him, if various rules designed to safeguard the integrity of the process are not given effect: the tribunal that convicts him must have the power to deal with his kind of case ("jurisdiction") and must be geographically appropriate ("venue"); too long a time must not have elapsed since the offense was committed ("statute of limitations"); he must not have been previously convicted or acquitted of the same or a substantially similar offense ("double jeopardy"); he must not fall within a category of persons, such as children or the insane, who are legally immune to conviction ("criminal responsibility"); and so on. None of these requirements has anything to do with the factual question of whether he did or did not engage in the conduct that is charged as the offense against him; yet favorable answers to any of them will mean that he is legally innocent. Wherever the competence to make adequate factual determinations lies, it is apparent that only a tribunal that is aware of these guilt-defeating doctrines and is willing to apply them can be viewed as competent to make determinations of legal guilt. The police and the prosecutors are ruled out by lack of capacity in the first instance and by lack of assurance of willingness in the second. Only an impartial tribunal can be trusted to make determinations of legal as opposed to factual guilt.

In this concept of legal guilt lies part of the explanation for the apparently quixotic presumption of innocence of which we spoke earlier. A man who after police investigation is charged with having committed a crime can hardly be said to be presumptively innocent, if what we mean is factual innocence. But if any of a myriad of legal doctrines may be appropriately invoked to exculpate this particular accused, it is apparent that as a matter of prediction it cannot be said with any confidence that more probably than not he will be found guilty.

Beyond the question of predictability this model posits a functional reason for observing the presumption of innocence: by forcing the state to prove its case against the accused in an adjudicative context, the presumption of innocence serves to force into play all the qualifying and disabling doctrines that limit the use of the criminal sanction against the individual, thereby enhancing his opportunity to secure a favorable outcome. In this sense the presumption of innocence may be seen to operate as a kind of self-fulfilling prophecy. By opening up a procedural situation that permits the successful assertion of defenses that have nothing to do with factual guilt, it vindicates the proposition that the factually guilty may nonetheless be legally innocent and should therefore be given a chance to qualify for that kind of treatment.

The possibility of legal innocence is expanded enormously when the criminal process is viewed as the appropriate forum for correcting its own abuses. This notion may well account for a greater amount of the distance between the two models than any other. In theory the Crime Control Model can tolerate rules that forbid illegal arrests, unreasonable searches, coercive interrogations, and the like if their enforcement is left primarily to managerial sanctions internally imposed. What it cannot tolerate is the vindication of those rules in the criminal process itself through the exclusion of evidence illegally obtained or through the reversal of convictions in cases where the criminal process has breached the rules laid down for its observance. The availability of these corrective devices fatally impairs the efficiency of the process. The Due Process Model, while it may in the first instance be addressed to the maintenance of reliable factfinding techniques, comes eventually to incorporate prophylactic and deterrent rules that result in the release of the factually guilty even in cases in which blotting out the illegality would still leave an adjudicative factfinder convinced of the accused's guilt.

Another strand in the complex of attitudes that underlies the Due Process Model is the idea—itself a shorthand statement for a complex of attitudes—of equality. This notion has only recently emerged as an explicit basis for pressing the demands of the Due Process Model, but it appears to represent, at least in its potential, a most powerful norm for influencing official conduct. Stated most starkly, the ideal of equality holds that "there can be no equal justice where the kind of trial a man gets depends on the amount of money he has."

The factual predicate underlying this assertion is that there are gross inequalities in the financial means of criminal defendants as a class, that in an adversary system of criminal justice, an effective defense is largely a function of the resources that can be mustered on behalf of the accused, and that a very large proportion of criminal defendants are, operationally speaking, "indigent" in terms of their ability to finance an effective defense. This factual premise has been strongly reinforced by recent studies that in turn have been both a cause and an effect of an increasing emphasis upon norms for the criminal process based on the premise.

The norms derived from the premise do not take the form of an insistence upon governmental responsibility to provide literally equal opportunities for all criminal defendants to challenge the process. Rather, they take as their point of departure the notion that the criminal process, initiated as it is by government and containing as it does the likelihood of severe deprivations at the hands of government, imposes some kind of public obligation to ensure that financial inability does not destroy the capacity of an accused to assert what may be meritorious challenges to the processes being invoked against him.

The demands made by a norm of this kind are likely by its very nature to be quite sweeping. Although its imperatives may be initially limited to determining whether in a particular case the accused was injured or prejudiced by his relative inability to make an appropriate challenge, the norm of equality very quickly moves to another level on which the demand is that the process in general be adapted to minimize discriminations rather than that a mere series of post hoc determinations of discrimination be made or makeable.

It should be observed that the impact of the equality norm will vary greatly depending upon the point in time at which it is introduced into a model of the criminal process. If one were starting from scratch to decide how the process ought to work, the norm of equality would have nothing very important to say on such questions as, for example, whether an accused should have the effective assistance of counsel in deciding whether to enter a plea of guilty. One could decide, on quite independent considerations, that it is or is not a good thing to afford that facility to the generality of persons accused of crime. But the impact of the equality norm becomes far greater when it is brought to bear on a process whose contours have already been shaped. If our model of the criminal process affords defendants who are in a financial position to consult a lawyer before entering a plea the right to do so, then the equality norm exerts powerful pressure to provide such an opportunity to all defendants and to regard the failure to do so as a malfunctioning of the process from whose consequences the accused is entitled to be relieved. In a sense that has been the role of the equality norm in affecting the real-world criminal process. It has made its appearance on the scene comparatively late and has therefore encountered a situation in which, in terms of the system as it operates, the relative financial inability of most persons accused of crime sharply distinguishes their treatment from the small minority of the financially capable. For that reason its impact has already been substantial and may be expected to be even more so in the future. . . .

NOTES & QUESTIONS ON PACKER'S TWO MODELS

1. ***Blackstone's calculation.*** Think of the various ways that Packer's two models will intersect internally to the doctrine. Take, for example, the requirement that a jury decide guilt beyond a reasonable doubt. The crime control model would suggest that the burden of proof should be lowered or that the government should be allowed to punish wrongdoers even in the absence of a jury determination—say, for example, after a determination by an administrative law judge housed within the executive branch. However, the due process model suggests that an individual has a right to demand that this determination be made by a jury, according to the highest possible standard, even if doing so frustrates the government's goal of maintaining law and order. Is this evidence

of Blackstone's formulation that it is better that ten guilty men go free than one innocent man be sent to prison? Consider the following assessment:

> Wholly apart from any effect on crime control, victims genuinely suffer in a variety of ways when crimes are not successfully solved and punished. But the experience is not uniform or always as clear and dramatic as when an innocent person is sent to prison or death row. Victimization studies show that most victims do not report crimes, and thus, most crimes are never prosecuted. And with the rise of the victims' rights movement, criticism has been leveled against the single-minded focus on criminal prosecution and incarceration "for taking disputes out of the hands of offenders, victims and the larger community." By focusing solely on criminal sanctions, we neglect the need of some victims for other methods to redress wrongs, including "family conferencing, restorative justice, and victim-offender reconciliation" and other forms of "re-integrative shaming through informal, non-punitive and non-adversarial interventions which shame offenders for their crimes, but offer support and re-integration through families and communities."

Keith A. Findley, *Toward a New Paradigm of Criminal Justice: How the Innocence Movement Merges Crime Control and Due Process*, 41 Tex. Tech L. Rev. 133, 137-38 (2008). Do you agree with Professor Findley's assessment? Is it true that sending an innocent person to prison is worse than the harm to a crime victim when his or her perpetrator is not caught or not punished? In some sense, the question of where to place the line between crime control and due process is one that is constantly debated throughout the doctrines in this casebook. The models themselves do not provide an answer but simply a framework for working out the inherent tensions of competing desiderata in the criminal justice system.

2. *The value of procedural fairness.* Consider the benefits associated with running a criminal justice system according to robust standards of due process. People will often ask defense attorneys how they can represent a defendant that they suspect is guilty, but people will rarely ask the same question of prosecutors: How can you seek a conviction against someone that you have evidence against but who you worry might be innocent? In that case, the emotional toll on the prosecutor is high. The prosecutor, though, plays a certain role in the entire process, which is to present evidence of guilt to the jury. Moreover, that evidence is presented within a framework of robust procedural fairness, giving the prosecutor some comfort that they can play their role with the security that the system is fair. But if those procedural protections vanish, or are loosened beyond reason, then that comfort disappears. The only way to get good people to play that prosecutorial role is to ensure them that the role is embedded in a larger system with procedural checks to ensure fairness. Perhaps the prosecutor—not just the defendant—is a beneficiary of that system.

PROBLEM CASE

Consider the case of the Ozie Powell, Willie Roberson, Andy Wright, Olen Montgomery, and Eugene Williams—each of whom were convicted of raping two white girls on a freight train in Alabama in 1931. The case was the subject of intense local scrutiny and was tinged with racism. News of the alleged assault spread quickly and when the freight train arrived in Scottsboro, Alabama, a large mob had gathered to harass the defendants. The local sheriff called soldiers to safeguard the prisoners from mob violence and retribution and they were successfully held for trial.

Unfortunately, the defendants were not given the opportunity to select their own counsel or speak to their families to arrange for the hiring of counsel to represent them prior to trial. The trial occurred just six days after the arraignment and no defense counsel was appointed to represent them until the morning of the trial, thus eliminating the possibility of adequate preparation.

In overturning the conviction, the Supreme Court concluded that the process of securing counsel was so bungled that the defendants were denied their right to counsel: "However guilty defendants, upon due inquiry, might prove to have been, they were, until convicted, presumed to be innocent. It was the duty of the court having their cases in charge to see that they were denied no necessary incident of a fair trial." *Powell v. Alabama*, 287 U.S. 45, 52 (1932). What role does guilt or innocence play in this statement? Is fairness a subsidiary norm to accuracy or is it an additional constraint that ought to be considered separate and apart from accuracy? What is the goal of fairness in a system designed to produce accuracy? One interpretation of the Court's statement in *Powell* is that fairness is a necessary prerequisite for accuracy, but another interpretation is that accuracy by itself does not exhaust the principle of justice—fairness is an important element too.

PART II

THE FOURTH AMENDMENT: REQUIREMENTS AND REMEDIES

CHAPTER 2

WHAT IS A SEARCH?

INTRODUCTION

The Fourth Amendment protects individuals from, among other things, unreasonable searches. Or, as the Supreme Court once said, the Fourth Amendment protects "people, not places." It is one of the most profound constitutional protections against government tyranny. The Fourth Amendment constrains and regulates—but of course does not eliminate—the government's power to transcend that most fundamental boundary between the public and private sphere. While intrusions are necessary to maintain public order and safety (to investigate wrongdoing, for example), they also contain the potential for widespread abuse.

The first step in the analysis is to determine whether the police activity constituted a "search" as that term is used in the Constitution. Over time, Justices on the Supreme Court have articulated two approaches for finding a search. The first approach asks whether there was a physical intrusion by the state, i.e., a trespass against private property. The second approach asks whether the individual had a reasonable expectation of privacy that was infringed by the state action. The following materials examine these two frameworks for defining searches. Then, after that, the chapter examines specific applications of the test in concrete and controversial circumstances: communications, either in person or by telephone; surveillance of property by airplane, thermal imaging, and contraband-sniffing canines; privacy in discarded garbage; and the tracking of public movements by GPS or cell phone location data.

In reading these materials, you should bear in mind that the question of what constitutes a search is a threshold inquiry. It merely determines whether the

Fourth Amendment will apply, although it does not wholly determine whether the search will be legal or not. The merits of that question will be the concern of Chapter 3, which will focus on the warrant requirement and the exceptions to it. Consequently, a search might be perfectly legal under the Fourth Amendment if the police requested or received a proper warrant authorized by a magistrate or if one of the many exceptions to the warrant requirement are applicable. But the question of the warrant is inapplicable if the state action did not constitute a search in the first place. There is, in other words, a natural order to the analysis. First determine whether the action constituted a search and only then ask whether the search complied with the Fourth Amendment's warrant requirement.

A. REASONABLE EXPECTATION OF PRIVACY

For much of the Supreme Court's history, the court defined searches essentially as a trespass—a physical invasion of a suspect's personal dominion. So, for example, the police entering a house would be considered an obvious search. But if searches could be conducted by not crossing onto private property, it was not a search in the sense of the Fourth Amendment. For example, in *United States v. Olmstead,* 277 U.S. 438 (1928), the police tapped the defendant's phone lines emerging from the telephone pole located on a public street, thus negating the need to enter the dwelling and tap the phone or its lines within the residence. The Court concluded that this was not a search because the authorities never performed an "actual physical invasion of his house or curtilage." This physical trespass-inspired framework for defining Fourth Amendment searches dominated for decades until the 1960s, when the Court decided *Katz v. United States*, 389 U.S. 347 (1967), which highlighted the notion of reasonableness. Under the *Katz* framework, the Court asks whether the police conduct violated the individual's reasonable expectation of privacy. This is a two-part test. First, the Court asks whether the individual acted under an expectation of privacy, i.e., whether the behavior in question was undertaken with the assumption that it would remain private. Second, the Court asks whether that expectation of privacy is objectively reasonable, in the sense that society is prepared to recognize that expectation as reasonable and deserving of constitutional protection.

As you read *Katz*, ask yourself what the Court means when it says that the Fourth Amendment protects "people, not places." In what situations does an individual have an "expectation of privacy" that triggers Fourth Amendment scrutiny? And more appropriately, how are lower courts (and the police) to determine that this expectation of privacy is a "reasonable" one under the circumstances?

Katz v. United States

Supreme Court of the United States
389 U.S. 347 (1967)

Mr. Justice STEWART delivered the opinion of the Court.

The petitioner was convicted in the District Court for the Southern District of California under an eight-count indictment charging him with transmitting wagering information by telephone from Los Angeles to Miami and Boston in violation of a federal statute. At trial the Government was permitted, over the petitioner's objection, to introduce evidence of the petitioner's end of telephone conversation, overheard by FBI agents who had attached an electronic listening and recording device to the outside of the public telephone booth from which he had placed his calls. In affirming his conviction, the Court of Appeals rejected the contention that the recordings had been obtained in violation of the Fourth Amendment, because "(t)here was no physical entrance into the area occupied by, (the petitioner)." . . .

We decline to adopt this formulation of the issues. In the first place the correct solution of Fourth Amendment problems is not necessarily promoted by incantation of the phrase "constitutionally protected area." Secondly, the Fourth Amendment cannot be translated into a general constitutional "right to privacy." That Amendment protects individual privacy against certain kinds of governmental intrusion, but its protections go further, and often have nothing to do with privacy at all. Other provisions of the Constitution protect personal privacy from other forms of governmental invasion. But the protection of a person's general right to privacy—his right to be let alone by other people—is, like the protection of his property and of his very life, left largely to the law of the individual States.

Because of the misleading way the issues have been formulated, the parties have attached great significance to the characterization of the telephone booth from which the petitioner placed his calls. The petitioner has strenuously argued that the booth was a "constitutionally protected area." The Government has maintained with equal vigor that it was not. But this effort to decide whether or not a given "area," viewed in the abstract, is "constitutionally protected" deflects attention from the problem presented by this case. For the Fourth Amendment protects people, not places. What a person knowingly exposes to the public, even in his own home or office, is not a subject of Fourth Amendment protection. But what he seeks to preserve as private, even in an area accessible to the public, may be constitutionally protected.

The Government stresses the fact that the telephone booth from which the petitioner made his calls was constructed partly of glass, so that he was as visible after he entered it as he would have been if he had remained outside. But what he sought to exclude when he entered the booth was not the intruding eye—it was the uninvited ear. He did not shed his right to do so simply because he made his calls from a place where he might be seen. No less than an individual in a business office, in a friend's apartment, or in a taxicab, a person in a telephone booth may rely upon the protection of the Fourth Amendment. One who occupies it, shuts the door behind him, and pays the toll that permits him to place a call is surely entitled to assume that the words he utters into the mouthpiece will not be broadcast to the world. To read the Constitution more narrowly is to ignore the vital role that the public telephone has come to play in private communication.

The Government contends, however, that the activities of its agents in this case should not be tested by Fourth Amendment requirements, for the surveillance technique they employed involved no physical penetration of the telephone booth from which the petitioner placed his calls. It is true that the absence of such penetration was at one time thought to foreclose further Fourth Amendment inquiry, for that Amendment was thought to limit only searches and seizures of tangible property. But "(t)he premise that property interests control the right of the Government to search and seize has been discredited." Thus, although a closely divided Court supposed in *Olmstead* that surveillance without any trespass and without the seizure of any material object fell outside the ambit of the Constitution, we have since departed from the narrow view on which that decision rested. Indeed, we have expressly held that the Fourth Amendment governs not only the seizure of tangible items, but extends as well to the recording of oral statements overheard without any "technical trespass under . . . local property law." Once this much is acknowledged, and once it is recognized that the Fourth Amendment protects people—and not simply "areas"—against unreasonable searches and seizures it becomes clear that the reach of that Amendment cannot turn upon the presence or absence of a physical intrusion into any given enclosure.

We conclude that the underpinnings of *Olmstead* and *Goldman* have been so eroded by our subsequent decisions that the "trespass" doctrine there enunciated can no longer be regarded as controlling. The Government's activities in electronically listening to and recording the petitioner's words violated the privacy upon which he justifiably relied while using the telephone booth and thus constituted a "search and seizure" within the meaning of the Fourth Amendment. The fact that the electronic device employed to achieve that end did not happen to penetrate the wall of the booth can have no constitutional significance. . . .

Mr. Justice Harlan, concurring.

I join the opinion of the Court, which I read to hold only (a) that an enclosed telephone booth is an area where, like a home, and unlike a field, a person has a constitutionally protected reasonable expectation of privacy; (b) that electronic as well as physical intrusion into a place that is in this sense private may constitute a violation of the Fourth Amendment; and (c) that the invasion of a constitutionally protected area by federal authorities is, as the Court has long held, presumptively unreasonable in the absence of a search warrant.

As the Court's opinion states, "the Fourth Amendment protects people, not places." The question, however, is what protection it affords to those people. Generally, as here, the answer to that question requires reference to a "place." My understanding of the rule that has emerged from prior decisions is that there is a twofold requirement, first that a person have exhibited an actual (subjective) expectation of privacy and, second, that the expectation be one that society is prepared to recognize as "reasonable." Thus a man's home is, for most purposes, a place where he expects privacy, but objects, activities, or statements that he exposes to the "plain view" of outsiders are not "protected" because no intention to keep them to himself has been exhibited. On the other hand, conversations in the open would not be protected against being overheard, for the expectation of privacy under the circumstances would be unreasonable.

The critical fact in this case is that "(o)ne who occupies it, (a telephone booth) shuts the door behind him, and pays the toll that permits him to place a call is surely entitled to assume" that his conversation is not being intercepted. The point is not that the booth is "accessible to the public" at other times, but that it is a temporarily private place whose momentary occupants' expectations of freedom from intrusion are recognized as reasonable. . . .

Finally, I do not read the Court's opinion to declare that no interception of a conversation one-half of which occurs in a public telephone booth can be reasonable in the absence of a warrant. As elsewhere under the Fourth Amendment, warrants are the general rule, to which the legitimate needs of law enforcement may demand specific exceptions. It will be time enough to consider any such exceptions when an appropriate occasion presents itself, and I agree with the Court that this is not one.

Mr. Justice Black, dissenting.

If I could agree with the Court that eavesdropping carried on by electronic means (equivalent to wiretapping) constitutes a "search" or "seizure," I would be happy to join the Court's opinion. . . .

My basic objection is twofold: (1) I do not believe that the words of the Amendment will bear the meaning given them by today's decision, and (2) I do not believe that it is the proper role of this Court to rewrite the Amendment in order "to bring it into harmony with the times" and thus reach a result that many people believe to be desirable.

While I realize that an argument based on the meaning of words lacks the scope, and no doubt the appeal, of broad policy discussions and philosophical discourses on such nebulous subjects as privacy, for me the language of the Amendment is the crucial place to look in construing a written document such as our Constitution. . . .

The first clause protects "persons, houses, papers, and effects, against unreasonable searches and seizures. . . ." These words connote the idea of tangible things with size, form, and weight, things capable of being searched, seized, or both. The second clause of the Amendment still further establishes its Framers' purpose to limit its protection to tangible things by providing that no warrants shall issue but those "particularly describing the place to be searched, and the persons or things to be seized." A conversation overheard by eavesdropping, whether by plain snooping or wiretapping, is not tangible and, under the normally accepted meanings of the words, can neither be searched nor seized. In addition the language of the second clause indicates that the Amendment refers not only to something tangible so it can be seized but to something already in existence so it can be described. Yet the Court's interpretation would have the Amendment apply to overhearing future conversations which by their very nature are nonexistent until they take place. How can one "describe" a future conversation, and, if one cannot, how can a magistrate issue a warrant to eavesdrop one in the future? It is argued that information showing what is expected to be said is sufficient to limit the boundaries of what later can be admitted into evidence; but does such general information really meet the specific language of the Amendment which says "particularly describing"? Rather than using language in a completely artificial way, I must conclude that the Fourth Amendment simply does not apply to eavesdropping.

Tapping telephone wires, of course, was an unknown possibility at the time the Fourth Amendment was adopted. But eavesdropping (and wiretapping is nothing more than eavesdropping by telephone) was . . . "an ancient practice which at common law was condemned as a nuisance". . . . There can be no doubt that the Framers were aware of this practice, and if they had desired to outlaw or restrict the use of evidence obtained by eavesdropping, I believe that they would have used the appropriate language to do so in the Fourth Amendment. They certainly would not have left such a task to the ingenuity of language-stretching judges. No one, it seems to me, can read the debates on the Bill of Rights without reaching the conclusion that its Framers and critics well knew the meaning of the words they used, what they would be understood to mean by others, their scope and their limitations. Under these circumstances it strikes me as a charge against their scholarship, their common sense and their candor to give to the Fourth Amendment's language the eavesdropping meaning the Court imputes to it today. . . .

The Fourth Amendment protects privacy only to the extent that it prohibits unreasonable searches and seizures of "persons, houses, papers, and effects." No general right is created by the Amendment so as to give this Court the unlimited power to hold unconstitutional everything which affects privacy. Certainly the Framers, well acquainted as they were with the excesses of governmental power, did not intend to grant this Court such omnipotent lawmaking authority as that. The history of governments proves that it is dangerous to freedom to repose such powers in courts.

NOTES & QUESTIONS ON EXPECTATIONS OF PRIVACY

1. *Justifiable reliance.* In *Katz,* Justice Stewart remarks that the defendant "justifiably relied" on the expected privacy when he entered the telephone booth and placed a call. What did the Court mean by this? Presumably, that if Katz had known that his conversation was not private, he would never had entered the booth and placed the call. This one phrase–justifiable reliance–could be considered an overarching theoretical framework for the Fourth Amendment doctrine on searches. In short, it would require a court to ask whether the defendant relied on a promise of privacy and whether that reliance was then justified. Is this different from the notion of a reasonable expectation of privacy? Or are the two standards identical? Certainly, both approaches would require a two-step analysis. For an argument that justifiable reliance promotes a more objective analysis, see Richard Sobel, Barry Horwitz & Gerald Jenkins, *The Fourth Amendment Beyond* Katz, Kyllo *and* Jones*: Reinstating Justifiable Reliance as a More Secure Constitutional Standard for Privacy,* 22 B.U. Pub. Int. L.J. 1 (2013) ("Justifiable reliance takes us out of the fickle realm of what the public expects today (and may no longer expect next month), and back to the actual words and intent of the Fourth Amendment.").

B. PRIVACY IN COMMUNICATIONS

Communications between individuals are often premised on an assumption of privacy. A person will tell his interlocutor things that he would not broadcast publicly. If there were no privacy in communication, the structure of relations would be fundamentally altered–not just intimate relations but also business and economic relationships as well. Government intrusions into putatively "private" communications should not be condoned lightly. They represent a serious form of state action. Although these intrusions raise many legal issues, the one discussed here is limited to whether these intrusions constitute a search for the purposes of the Fourth Amendment. The following materials focus on three distinct scenarios: (1) government undercover agents who wear a wire to record conversations with the target of a criminal investigation; (2) the installation of

PROBLEM CASE

A search is only a "search" under the Constitution if it is performed by the government; the conduct of private individuals is not circumscribed by the Fourth Amendment. With that limit in mind, consider the case of Walter Ackerman.

According to the police, Ackerman was charged with child pornography offenses after one of his emails was flagged by an AOL computer algorithm—using a technology called hash value matching that scans all email traffic to detect suspected examples of child pornography images. After the images were flagged, an AOL employee opened the email attachments and forwarded them to the National Center for Missing and Exploited Children (NCMEC), using one of its services called the CyberTipline. After receiving the tip, NCMEC viewed the email and attachments and contacted local police, which resulted in Ackerman's prosecution.

On appeal, Ackerman claimed that NCMEC was either a government entity or was acting as an "agent" of the government. The Tenth Circuit agreed with Ackerman because the government "knew of and acquiesced in" NCMEC's search. Specifically, "Congress statutorily required AOL to forward Mr. Ackerman's email to NCMEC; Congress statutorily required NCMEC to maintain the CyberTipline to receive emails like Mr. Ackerman's; Congress statutorily permitted NCMEC to review Mr. Ackerman's email and attachments; and Congress statutorily required NCMEC to pass along a report about Mr. Ackerman's activities to law enforcement authorities." *United States v. Ackerman*, 831 F.3d 1292, 1301-02 (10th Cir. 2016). If the *Ackerman* logic is accepted by other Circuits, NCMEC will need to start getting judicial warrants before opening and reading emails sent to it through the CyberTipline. Do you agree with this result, or would it represent an unnecessary restriction on law enforcement activities?

For a recent case where a court denied a similar argument, see *United States v. Stratton*, 2017 WL 169041, at *3 (D. Kan. Jan. 17, 2017) (concluding that Sony's search of an online PlayStation account did not make Sony an agent of the government for Fourth Amendment purposes).

devices ("pen registers") to record all numbers dialed from and received on a particular phone line; and (3) the bulk collection of telephony metadata. The last category is particularly important in the national security context, which is dominated by intelligence gathering techniques designed to scoop up vast sums of information that can be mined by intelligence analysts at a later date. But all three categories call to mind common themes and concerns: the degree to which the government can intrude upon interpersonal communication without triggering the protections of the Fourth Amendment.

1. Government Agents Wearing Wires

In *United States v. White*, the Supreme Court considered whether individuals have a reasonable expectation of privacy in conversations surreptitiously recorded, through a secret "wire," by a police informant. If the authorities can outfit a police informant with a secret wire, should this qualify as a search? In daily life, we all run the risk that conversational partners might be police informants and might run to the police with information gleamed from our conversations. Given this inherent risk in all conversations, should a secret recording by a government agent constitute a search within the meaning of the Fourth Amendment?

United States v. White

Supreme Court of the United States
401 U.S. 745 (1971)

Mr. Justice WHITE announced the judgment of the Court and an opinion in which THE CHIEF JUSTICE, Mr. Justice STEWART, and Mr. Justice BLACKMUN join.

In 1966, respondent James A. White was tried and convicted under two consolidated indictments charging various illegal transactions in narcotics.... The issue before us is whether the Fourth Amendment bars from evidence the testimony of governmental agents who related certain conversations which had occurred between defendant White and a government informant, Harvey Jackson, and which the agents overheard by monitoring the frequency of a radio transmitter carried by Jackson and concealed on his person. . . .

I

Until *Katz v. United States*, neither wiretapping nor electronic eavesdropping violated a defendant's Fourth Amendment rights "unless there has been an official search and seizure of his person, or such a seizure of his papers or his tangible material effects, or an actual physical invasion of his house 'or curtilage' for the purpose of making a seizure." But where "eavesdropping was accomplished by means of an unauthorized physical penetration into the premises occupied" by the defendant, although falling short of a "technical trespass under the local property law," the Fourth Amendment was violated and any evidence of what was seen and heard, as well as tangible objects seized, was considered the inadmissible fruit of an unlawful invasion.

Katz v. United States, however, finally swept away doctrines that electronic eavesdropping is permissible under the Fourth Amendment unless physical invasion of a constitutionally protected area produced the challenged evidence. In that case government agents, without petitioner's consent or knowledge, attached a listening device to the outside of a public telephone booth and recorded the defendant's end of his telephone conversations. In declaring the recordings inadmissible in evidence in the absence of a warrant authorizing the surveillance, the Court overruled *Olmstead* and *Goldman* and held that the absence of physical intrusion into the telephone booth did not justify using electronic devices in listening to and recording Katz' words, thereby violating the privacy on which he justifiably relied while using the telephone in those circumstances.

The Court of Appeals understood *Katz* to render inadmissible against White the agents' testimony concerning conversations that Jackson broadcast to them. We cannot agree. *Katz* involved no revelation to the Government by a party to conversations with the defendant nor did the Court indicate in any way that a defendant has a justifiable and constitutionally protected expectation that a person with whom he is conversing will not then or later reveal the conversation to the police. . . .

Concededly a police agent who conceals his police connections may write down for official use his conversations with a defendant and testify concerning them, without a warrant authorizing his encounters with the defendant and without otherwise violating the latter's Fourth Amendment rights. For constitutional purposes, no different result is required if the agent instead of immediately reporting and transcribing his conversations with defendant, either (1) simultaneously records them with electronic equipment which he is carrying on his person; (2) or carries radio equipment which simultaneously transmits the conversations either to recording equipment located elsewhere or to other agents monitoring the transmitting frequency. If the conduct and revelations of an agent operating without electronic equipment do not invade the defendant's constitutionally justifiable expectations of privacy, neither does a simultaneous recording of the same conversations made by the agent or by others from transmissions received from the agent to whom the defendant is talking and whose trustworthiness the defendant necessarily risks. . . .

Our problem is not what the privacy expectations of particular defendants in particular situations may be or the extent to which they may in fact have relied on the discretion of their companions. Very probably, individual defendants neither know nor suspect that their colleagues have gone or will go to the police or are carrying recorders or transmitters. Otherwise, conversation would cease and our problem with these encounters would be nonexistent or far different from those now before us. Our problem, in terms of the principles announced in *Katz*, is what expectations of privacy are constitutionally "justifiable"—what expectations the Fourth Amendment will protect in the absence of a warrant. So far, the law permits the frustration of actual expectations of privacy by permitting authorities to use the testimony of those associates who for one reason or another have determined to turn to the police, as well as by authorizing the use of informants in the manner exemplified by *Hoffa* and *Lewis*. If the law gives no protection to the wrongdoer whose trusted accomplice is or becomes a police agent, neither should it protect him when that same agent has recorded or transmitted the conversations which are later offered in evidence to prove the State's case.

Inescapably, one contemplating illegal activities must realize and risk that his companions may be reporting to the police. If he sufficiently doubts their trustworthiness, the association will very probably end or never materialize. But if he has no doubts, or allays them, or risks what doubt he has, the risk is his. In terms of what his course will be, what he will or will not do or say, we are unpersuaded that he would distinguish between probably informers on the one hand and probable informers with transmitters on the other. Given the possibility or probability that one of his colleagues is cooperating with the police, it is only speculation to assert that the defendant's utterances would be substantially different or his sense of security any less if he also thought it possible that the suspected colleague is wired for sound. At least there is no persuasive evidence that the difference in this respect between the electronically equipped and the unequipped agent is substantial enough to require discrete constitutional recognition, particularly under the Fourth Amendment which is ruled by fluid concepts of "reasonableness."

Nor should we be too ready to erect constitutional barriers to relevant and probative evidence which is also accurate and reliable. An electronic recording will many times produce a more reliable rendition of what a defendant has said than will the unaided memory of a police agent. It may also be that with the recording in existence it is less likely that the informant will change his mind, less chance that threat or injury will suppress unfavorable evidence and less chance that cross-examination will confound the testimony. Considerations like these obviously do not favor the defendant, but we are not prepared to hold that a defendant who has no constitutional right to exclude the informer's unaided testimony nevertheless has a Fourth Amendment privilege against a more accurate version of the events in question.

It is thus untenable to consider the activities and reports of the police agent himself, though acting without a warrant, to be a "reasonable" investigative effort and lawful under the Fourth Amendment but to view the same agent with a recorder or transmitter as conducting an "unreasonable" and unconstitutional search and seizure. . . .

Mr. Justice DOUGLAS, dissenting.

The issue in this case is clouded and concealed by the very discussion of it in legalistic terms. What the ancients knew as "eavesdropping," we now call "electronic surveillance"; but to equate the two is to treat man's first gunpowder on the same level as the nuclear bomb. Electronic surveillance is the greatest leveler of human privacy ever known. How most forms of it can be held "reasonable" within the meaning of the Fourth Amendment is a mystery. To be sure, the Constitution and Bill of Rights are not to be read as covering only the technology known in the 18th century. Otherwise its concept of "commerce" would be hopeless when it comes to the management of modern affairs. At the same time the concepts of privacy which the Founders enshrined in the Fourth Amendment vanish completely when we slavishly allow an all-powerful government, proclaiming law and order, efficiency, and other benign purposes, to penetrate all the walls and doors which men need to shield them from the pressures of a turbulent life around them and give them the health and strength to carry on.

That is why a "strict construction" of the Fourth Amendment is necessary if every man's liberty and privacy are to be constitutionally honored. . . . Today no one perhaps notices because only a small, obscure criminal is the victim. But every person is the victim, for the technology we exalt today is everyman's master. . . .

NOTES & QUESTIONS ON AGENTS WEARING WIRES

1. *The nature of conversation.* The Court in *White* viewed the conversation with the undercover police agent against a general assumption about conversations in general. It assumed that such conversations always—by definition—involve disclosure of information to a second party, the other conversant. By disclosing information to someone else, the Court said, you always run the risk that that person will provide the information to others, including state authorities. For that reason, there is no reasonable expectation of privacy in these conversations. Missing from this calculus is the *collective* privacy interest that is shared by the participants in a conversation and on which, in a sense, all private communication depends. If the *White* rationale were taken to its logical extreme, it would appear that no one ever has a reasonable expectation of privacy when they engage in a conversation with another individual. Do you agree with this conclusion?

2. Phone Records of Numbers Dialed and Received

In *Smith v. Maryland,* the Court must determine whether telephone users have a reasonable expectation of privacy in the phone numbers they dial. Specifically, the question is whether authorities can attach "pen registers" to telephone lines at the telephone company, which identify and record the numbers dialed and received on a particular customer's phone line. As you read this case, ask yourself whether callers have a reasonable expectation of privacy in the phone numbers that they dial, since this information is inevitably disclosed to a third party—the phone company. Is it reasonable for the customer of the phone company to assume, or hope, that these records will remain private?

Smith v. Maryland

Supreme Court of the United States
442 U.S. 735 (1979)

Mr. Justice Blackmun delivered the opinion of the Curt.

This case presents the question whether the installation and use of a pen register constitutes a "search" within the meaning of the Fourth Amendment, made applicable to the States through the Fourteenth Amendment.

I

On March 5, 1976, in Baltimore, Md., Patricia McDonough was robbed. She gave the police a description of the robber and of a 1975 Monte Carlo automobile she had observed near the scene of the crime. After the robbery, McDonough began receiving threatening and obscene phone calls from a man identifying himself as the robber. On one occasion, the caller asked that she step out on her front porch; she did so, and saw the 1975 Monte Carlo she had earlier described to police moving slowly past her home. On March 16, police spotted a man who met McDonough's description driving a 1975 Monte Carlo in her neighborhood. By tracing the license plate number, police learned that the car was registered in the name of petitioner, Michael Lee Smith.

The next day, the telephone company, at police request, installed a pen register at its central offices to record the numbers dialed from the telephone at petitioner's home. The police did not get a warrant or court order before having the pen register installed. The register revealed that on March 17 a call was placed from petitioner's home to McDonough's phone. On the basis of this and other evidence, the police obtained a warrant to search petitioner's residence. The search revealed that a page in petitioner's phone book was turned down to the name and number of Patricia McDonough; the phone book was seized. Petitioner was arrested, and a six-man lineup was held on March 19. McDonough identified petitioner as the man who had robbed her.

Petitioner was indicted in the Criminal Court of Baltimore for robbery. By pretrial motion, he sought to suppress "all fruits derived from the pen register" on the ground that the police had failed to secure a warrant prior to its installation. . . .

II

The Fourth Amendment guarantees "[t]he right of the people to be secure in their persons, houses, papers, and effects, against unreasonable searches and seizures." In determining whether a particular form of government-initiated electronic surveillance is a "search" within the meaning of the Fourth Amendment, our lodestar is *Katz v. United States,* 389

U.S. 347 (1967). In *Katz,* Government agents had intercepted the contents of a telephone conversation by attaching an electronic listening device to the outside of a public phone booth. The Court rejected the argument that a "search" can occur only when there has been a "physical intrusion" into a "constitutionally protected area," noting that the Fourth Amendment "protects people, not places." Because the Government's monitoring of Katz's conversation "violated the privacy upon which he justifiably relied while using the telephone booth," the Court held that it "constituted a 'search and seizure' within the meaning of the Fourth Amendment."

Consistently with *Katz,* this Court uniformly has held that the application of the Fourth Amendment depends on whether the person invoking its protection can claim a "justifiable," a "reasonable," or a "legitimate expectation of privacy" that has been invaded by government action. This inquiry, as Mr. Justice Harlan aptly noted in his *Katz* concurrence, normally embraces two discrete questions. The first is whether the individual, by his conduct, has "exhibited an actual (subjective) expectation of privacy"—whether, in the words of the *Katz* majority, the individual has shown that "he seeks to preserve [something] as private." The second question is whether the individual's subjective expectation of privacy is "one that society is prepared to recognize as 'reasonable'"—whether, in the words of the *Katz* majority, the individual's expectation, viewed objectively, is "justifiable" under the circumstances.

In applying the *Katz* analysis to this case, it is important to begin by specifying precisely the nature of the state activity that is challenged. The activity here took the form of installing and using a pen register. Since the pen register was installed on telephone company property at the telephone company's central offices, petitioner obviously cannot claim that his "property" was invaded or that police intruded into a "constitutionally protected area." Petitioner's claim, rather, is that, notwithstanding the absence of a trespass, the State, as did the Government in *Katz,* infringed a "legitimate expectation of privacy" that petitioner held. Yet a pen register differs significantly from the listening device employed in *Katz,* for pen registers do not acquire the *contents* of communications. This Court recently noted: "Indeed, a law enforcement official could not even determine from the use of a pen register whether a communication existed. These devices do not hear sound. They disclose only the telephone numbers that have been dialed—a means of establishing communication. Neither the purport of any communication between the caller and the recipient of the call, their identities, nor whether the call was even completed is disclosed by pen registers." Given a pen register's limited capabilities, therefore, petitioner's argument that its installation and use constituted a "search" necessarily rests upon a claim that he had a "legitimate expectation of privacy" regarding the numbers he dialed on his phone.

This claim must be rejected. First, we doubt that people in general entertain any actual expectation of privacy in the numbers they dial. All telephone users realize that they must "convey" phone numbers to the telephone company, since it is through telephone company switching equipment that their calls are completed. All subscribers realize, moreover, that the phone company has facilities for making permanent records of the numbers they dial, for they see a list of their long-distance (toll) calls on their monthly bills. In fact, pen registers and similar devices are routinely used by telephone companies "for the purposes of checking billing operations, detecting fraud and preventing violations of law." Electronic equipment is used not only to keep billing records of toll calls, but also "to keep a record of all calls dialed from a telephone which is subject to a special rate structure." Pen registers are regularly employed "to determine whether a home phone is being used to conduct a business, to check for a defective dial, or to check for overbilling." Although most people may be oblivious to a pen register's esoteric functions, they presumably have some awareness of one common use: to aid in the identification of persons making annoying or obscene calls. Most phone books tell subscribers, on a page entitled "Consumer Information," that the company "can frequently help in identifying to the authorities the origin of unwelcome and troublesome calls." Telephone users, in sum, typically know that they must convey numerical information to the phone company; that the phone company has facilities for recording this information; and that the phone company does in fact record this information for a variety of legitimate business purposes. Although subjective expectations cannot be scientifically gauged, it is too much to believe that telephone subscribers, under these circumstances, harbor any general expectation that the numbers they dial will remain secret.

Petitioner argues, however, that, whatever the expectations of telephone users in general, he demonstrated an expectation of privacy by his own conduct here, since he "us[ed] the telephone *in his house* to the exclusion of all others." But the site of the call is immaterial for purposes of analysis in this case. Although petitioner's conduct may have been calculated to keep the *contents* of his conversation private, his conduct was not and could not have been calculated to preserve the privacy of the number he dialed. Regardless of his location, petitioner had to convey that number to the telephone company in precisely the same way if he wished to complete his call. The fact that he dialed the number on his home phone rather than on some other phone could make no conceivable difference, nor could any subscriber rationally think that it would.

Second, even if petitioner did harbor some subjective expectation that the phone numbers he dialed would remain private, this expectation is not "one that society is prepared to recognize as 'reasonable.'" This Court consistently has held that a person has no legitimate expectation of privacy in information he voluntarily turns over to third parties. In *Miller,* for example, the Court held that a bank depositor has no "legitimate 'expectation of privacy'" in financial information "voluntarily conveyed to . . . banks and exposed to their employees in the ordinary course of business." . . . Because the depositor "assumed the risk" of disclosure, the Court held that it would be unreasonable for him to expect his financial records to remain private.

This analysis dictates that petitioner can claim no legitimate expectation of privacy here. When he used his phone, petitioner voluntarily conveyed numerical information to the telephone company and "exposed" that information to its equipment in the ordinary course of business. In so doing, petitioner assumed the risk that the company would reveal to police the numbers he dialed. The switching equipment that processed those numbers is merely the modern counterpart of the operator who, in an earlier day, personally completed calls for the subscriber. Petitioner concedes that if he had placed his calls through an operator, he could claim no legitimate expectation of privacy. We are not inclined to hold that a different constitutional result is required because the telephone company has decided to automate.

Petitioner argues, however, that automatic switching equipment differs from a live operator in one pertinent respect. An operator, in theory at least, is capable of remembering every number that is conveyed to him by callers. Electronic equipment, by contrast can "remember" only those numbers it is programmed to record, and telephone companies, in view of their present billing practices, usually do not record local calls. Since petitioner, in calling McDonough, was making a local call, his expectation of privacy as to her number, on this theory, would be "legitimate."

This argument does not withstand scrutiny. The fortuity of whether or not the phone company in fact elects to make a quasi-permanent record of a particular number dialed does not in our view, make any constitutional difference. Regardless of the phone company's election, petitioner voluntarily conveyed to it information that it had facilities for recording and that it was free to record. In these circumstances, petitioner assumed the risk that the information would be divulged to police. Under petitioner's theory, Fourth Amendment protection would exist, or not, depending on how the telephone company chose to define local-dialing zones, and depending on how it chose to bill its customers for local calls. Calls placed across town, or dialed directly, would be protected; calls placed across the river, or dialed with operator assistance, might not be. We are not inclined to make a crazy quilt of the Fourth Amendment, especially in circumstances where (as here) the pattern of protection would be dictated by billing practices of a private corporation.

We therefore conclude that petitioner in all probability entertained no actual expectation of privacy in the phone numbers he dialed, and that, even if he did, his expectation was not "legitimate." The installation and use of a pen register, consequently, was not a "search," and no warrant was required. . . .

Mr. Justice STEWART, with whom Mr. Justice BRENNAN joins, dissenting.

I am not persuaded that the numbers dialed from a private telephone fall outside the constitutional protection of the Fourth and Fourteenth Amendments.

In *Katz v. United States,* the Court acknowledged the "vital role that the public telephone has come to play in private communication[s]." The role played by a private telephone is even more vital, and since *Katz* it has been abundantly clear that telephone conversations carried on by people in their homes or offices are fully protected by the Fourth and Fourteenth Amendments. As the Court said in *United States v. United States District Court,* 407 U.S. 297, "the broad and unsuspected governmental incursions into conversational privacy which electronic surveillance entails necessitate the application of Fourth Amendment safeguards."

Nevertheless, the Court today says that those safeguards do not extend to the numbers dialed from a private telephone, apparently because when a caller dials a number the digits may be recorded by the telephone company for billing purposes. But that observation no more than describes the basic nature of telephone calls. A telephone call simply cannot be made without the use of telephone company property and without payment to the company for the service. The telephone conversation itself must be electronically transmitted by telephone company equipment, and may be recorded or overheard by the use of other company equipment. Yet we have squarely held that the user of even a public telephone is entitled "to assume that the words he utters into the mouthpiece will not be broadcast to the world."

The central question in this case is whether a person who makes telephone calls from his home is entitled to make a similar assumption about the numbers he dials. What the telephone company does or might do with those numbers is no more relevant to this inquiry than it would be in a case involving the conversation itself. It is simply not enough to say, after *Katz,* that there is no legitimate expectation of privacy in the numbers dialed because the caller assumes the risk that the telephone company will disclose them to the police.

I think that the numbers dialed from a private telephone—like the conversations that occur during a call—are within the constitutional protection recognized in *Katz.* It seems clear to me that information obtained by pen register surveillance of a private telephone is information in which the telephone subscriber has a legitimate expectation of privacy. The information captured by such surveillance emanates from private conduct within a person's home or office—locations that without question are entitled to Fourth and Fourteenth Amendment protection. Further, that information is an integral part of the telephonic communication that under *Katz* is entitled to constitutional protection, whether or not it is captured by a trespass into such an area.

The numbers dialed from a private telephone—although certainly more prosaic than the conversation itself—are not without "content." Most private telephone subscribers may have their own numbers listed in a publicly distributed directory, but I doubt there are any who would be happy to have broadcast to the world a list of the local or long distance numbers they have called. This is not because such a list might in some sense be incriminating, but because it easily could reveal the identities of the persons and the places called, and thus reveal the most intimate details of a person's life. . . .

AFTERMATH Although the Supreme Court decided that the use of a pen register did not constitute a search triggering the requirements of the Fourth Amendment, Congress passed a statute that specifically requires a warrant for its use. 18 U.S.C. § 3121. According to the statute, "the court shall enter an ex parte order authorizing the installation and use of a pen register or trap and trace device anywhere within the United States, if the court finds that the attorney for the Government has certified to the court that the information likely to be obtained by such installation and use is relevant to an ongoing criminal investigation." 18 U.S.C. § 3123.

There is a separate procedure for the issuance of warrants in foreign intelligence investigations, which are issued by the Foreign Intelligence Surveillance Court, a secret court that can issue "an order or an extension of an order authorizing or approving the installation and use of a pen register or trap and trace device for any investigation to obtain foreign intelligence information not concerning a United States person or to protect against international terrorism or clandestine intelligence activities, provided that such investigation of a United States person is not conducted solely upon the basis of activities protected by the first amendment to the Constitution. . . ." 50 U.S.C. § 1842. No warrant is required if the surveillance is "exclusively between or among foreign powers." 50 U.S.C. § 1802.

NOTES & QUESTIONS ON TELEPHONE PEN REGISTERS

1. *Third-party doctrine.* A central element of the *Smith* case and its progeny is the third-party doctrine, or the idea that people have no reasonable expectation of privacy in information or items that they disclose or transfer to third parties. Do you agree? What is the nature of privacy? Is it possible that a particular relationship and its conditions—such as an expectation of *confidentiality*—governs the transfer of information in some situations? If that is the case, might it be possible that individuals retain a reasonable

expectation of privacy even in situations where information is disclosed to third parties? For example, in *United States v. Miller,* 425 U.S. 435 (1976), the Court concluded that a depositor had no expectation of privacy in bank records since they were not "confidential communications" but rather negotiable instruments, located at the bank, which were required for a commercial transaction—which necessarily required third parties to have access to them. Does this adequately correspond with the expectation of confidentiality that bank customers expect in their commercial relationship with their bank? Consider Justice Sotomayor's statement in *Jones* that the third-party doctrine is "ill-suited to the digital age, in which people reveal a great deal of information about themselves to third parties in the course of carrying out mundane tasks." 132 S. Ct. at 957. For a discussion of the third-party doctrine, see Lucas Issacharoff & Kyle Wirshba, *Restoring Reason to the Third Party Doctrine*, 100 Minn. L. Rev. 985, 985-86 (2016) ("Unfortunately, the third party doctrine turned heavily on the limited forms of interaction in a prior technological era. As society has changed, the presumption of limited means of dissemination of information has all but collapsed, and the scope of what is covered by the third party doctrine has thus expanded."). Do you agree with Issacharoff's and Wirshba's statement?

2. *Alternatives to the phone company.* Assume that a customer is unhappy with the lack of privacy inherent in being a customer of the local phone company. What options are available to them? Is it reasonable to expect that the customer will find another mode of communication? The problem is that the other mode, assuming that it is provided by a commercial carrier, might create records too—thus creating the same problem. Or perhaps the customer should simply limit all confidential conversations to in-person interactions. Is this a reasonable expectation?

3. Bulk Collection of Telephony Metadata

Recent advances in technology have rendered the "pen register" device used in *Smith* utterly quaint in comparison to the modern surveillance technology used by the intelligence community to collect data on a national level. The final two cases in this section, *ACLU v. Clapper* and *Klayman v. Obama*, take opposite positions on a novel question: whether the National Security Agency's bulk collection of all communication metadata in the country constitutes a search that violates the Fourth Amendment. Essentially, the question here involves an application of the *Smith* precedent to a novel situation. Assuming that the government's collection of one piece of electronic metadata does not constitute a search for purposes of the Fourth Amendment, does the "collection of breathtaking amounts of" metadata transform the sweep into a search?

Khalid al-Mihdhar passing through security at Washington's Dulles International Airport, September 11, 2001. (AP Photo/APTN)

ACLU v. Clapper

Southern District of New York
959 F. Supp. 2d 724 (2013)

WILLIAM H. PAULEY III, District Judge:

The September 11th terrorist attacks revealed, in the starkest terms, just how dangerous and interconnected the world is. While Americans depended on technology for the conveniences of modernity, al-Qaeda plotted in a seventh-century milieu to use that technology against us. It was a bold jujitsu. And it succeeded because conventional intelligence gathering could not detect diffuse filaments connecting al-Qaeda.

Prior to the September 11th attacks, the National Security Agency ("NSA") intercepted seven calls made by hijacker Khalid al-Mihdhar, who was living in San Diego, California, to an al-Qaeda safe house in Yemen. The NSA intercepted those calls using overseas signals intelligence capabilities that could not capture al-Mihdhar's telephone number identifier. Without that identifier, NSA analysts concluded mistakenly that al-Mihdhar was overseas and not in the United States. Telephony metadata would have furnished the missing information and might have permitted the NSA to notify the Federal Bureau of Investigation ("FBI") of the fact that al-Mihdhar was calling the Yemeni safe house from inside the United States.

The Government learned from its mistake and adapted to confront a new enemy: a terror network capable of orchestrating attacks across the world. It launched a number of counter-measures, including a bulk telephony metadata collection program—a wide net that could find and isolate gossamer contacts among suspected terrorists in an ocean of seemingly disconnected data.

This blunt tool only works because it collects everything. Such a program, if unchecked, imperils the civil liberties of every citizen. Each time someone in the United States makes or receives a telephone call, the telecommunications provider makes a record of when, and to what telephone number the call was placed, and how long it lasted. The NSA collects that telephony metadata. If plumbed, such data can reveal a rich profile of every individual as well as a comprehensive record of people's associations with one another.

The natural tension between protecting the nation and preserving civil liberty is squarely presented by the Government's bulk telephony metadata collection program. Edward Snowden's unauthorized disclosure of Foreign Intelligence Surveillance Court ("FISC") orders has provoked a public debate and this litigation. While robust discussions are underway across the nation, in Congress, and at the White House, the question for this Court is whether the Government's bulk telephony metadata program is lawful. This Court finds it is. But the question of whether that program should be conducted is for the other two coordinate branches of Government to decide. . . .

FOREIGN INTELLIGENCE SURVEILLANCE ACT

In 1972, the Supreme Court recognized that "criminal surveillances and those involving domestic security" are distinct, and that "Congress may wish to consider protective standards for the latter which differ from those already prescribed for [criminal surveillances]." "Although the *Keith* opinion expressly disclaimed any ruling 'on the scope of the President's surveillance power with respect to the activities of foreign powers,' it implicitly suggested that a special framework for foreign intelligence surveillance might be constitutionally permissible."

In 1975, Congress organized the Senate Select Committee to Study Governmental Operations With Respect to Intelligence Activities, known as the "Church Committee," to investigate and report on the Government's intelligence-gathering operations. The Church Committee concluded that the Executive Branch had engaged in widespread surveillance of U.S. citizens and that Congress needed to provide clear boundaries for foreign intelligence gathering.

In 1978, Congress did just that. Legislating against the backdrop of *Keith* and the Church Committee findings, Congress enacted the Foreign

Intelligence Surveillance Act of 1978 (FISA). FISA requires the Government to obtain warrants or court orders for certain foreign intelligence surveillance activities and created the FISC to review those applications and grant them if appropriate.

While the FISC is composed of Article III judges, it operates unlike any other Article III court. Proceedings in Article III courts are public. . . . But FISC proceedings are secret. Congress created a secret court that operates in a secret environment to provide judicial oversight of secret Government activities. While the notion of secret proceedings may seem antithetical to democracy, the Founding Fathers recognized the need for the Government to keep secrets.

Congress has long appreciated the Executive's paramount need to keep matters of national security secret. FISC is an exception to the presumption of openness and transparency—in matters of national security, the Government must be able to keep its means and methods secret from its enemies.

In 1998, Congress amended FISA to allow for orders directing common carriers, public accommodation facilities, storage facilities, and vehicle rental facilities to provide business records to the Government. These amendments required the Government to make a showing of "specific and articulable facts giving reason to believe that the person to whom the records pertain is a foreign power or an agent of a foreign power."

After the September 11th attacks, Congress expanded the Government's authority to obtain additional records. See USA Patriot Act of 2001 (codified as amended at 50 U.S.C. § 1861) ("section 215"); Section 215 allows the Government to obtain an order "requiring the production of any tangible things (including books, records, papers, documents, and other items)," eliminating the restrictions on the types of businesses that can be served with such orders and the requirement that the target be a foreign power or their agent. The Government invoked this authority to collect virtually all call detail records or "telephony metadata." . . .

NSA BULK TELEPHONY METADATA COLLECTION

On June 5, 2013, *The Guardian* published a then-classified FISC "Secondary Order" directing Verizon Business Network Services to provide the NSA "on an ongoing daily basis ... all call detail records or 'telephony metadata'" for all telephone calls on its network from April 25, 2013 to July 19, 2013. "Telephony metadata" includes, as to each call, the telephone numbers that placed and received the call, the date, time, and duration of the call, other session-identifying information (for example, International Mobile Subscriber Identity number, International Mobile station Equipment Identity number, et cetera), trunk identifier, and any telephone calling card number. It does not include the content of any call, the name, address, or financial information of parties to the call, or any cell site location information. In response to the unauthorized disclosure of the Secondary Order, the Government acknowledged that since May 2006, it has collected this information for substantially every telephone call in the United States, including calls between the United States and a foreign country and calls entirely within the United States.

The Secondary Order was issued pursuant to a "*Primary Order*" setting out certain "minimization" requirements for the use of telephony metadata. The NSA stores the metadata in secure networks and access is limited to authorized personnel. Though metadata for all telephone calls is collected, there are restrictions on how and when it may be accessed and reviewed. The NSA may access the metadata to further a terrorism investigation only by "querying" the database with a telephone number, or "identifier," that is associated with a foreign terrorist organization. Before the database may be queried, a high-ranking NSA official or one of twenty specially-authorized officials must determine there is "reasonable articulable suspicion" that the identifier is associated with an international terrorist organization that is the subject of an FBI investigation. The "reasonable articulable suspicion" requirement ensures an "ordered and controlled" query and prevents general data browsing. An identifier reasonably believed to be used by a U.S. person may not be regarded as associated with a terrorist organization solely on the basis of activities protected by the First Amendment. An identifier used to query telephony metadata is referred to as a "seed."

The results of a query include telephone numbers that have been in contact with the seed, as well as the dates, times, and durations of those calls, but not the identities of the individuals or organizations associated with responsive telephone numbers. The query results also include second and third-tier contacts of the seed, referred to as "hops." The first "hop" captures telephony metadata for the set of telephone numbers in direct contact with the seed. The second "hop" reaches telephony metadata for the set of telephone numbers in direct contact with any first "hop" telephone number. The third "hop" corrals telephony metadata for the set of telephone numbers in direct contact with any second "hop" telephone number. The NSA takes this information and determines "which of the results are likely to contain foreign intelligence information, related to counterterrorism, that would be of investigative value to FBI (or other intelligence agencies)." They provide only this digest to the FBI. Moreover, metadata containing information concerning a U.S. person may only be shared outside the NSA if an official determines "that the information was related to counterterrorism information and necessary to understand counterterrorism information or to assess its importance."

Through this sifting, "only a very small percentage of the total data collected is ever reviewed by intelligence analysts." In 2012, fewer than 300 identifiers were queried. Because each query obtains information for contact numbers up to three hops out from the seed, the total number of responsive records was "substantially larger than 300, but . . . still a very small percentage of the total volume of metadata records." Between May 2006 and May 2009, the NSA provided the FBI and other agencies with 277 reports containing approximately 2,900 telephone numbers. . . .

CONSTITUTIONAL CLAIMS

. . . In *Smith v. Maryland,* 442 U.S. 735, the Supreme Court held individuals have no "legitimate expectation of privacy" regarding the telephone numbers they dial because they knowingly give that information to telephone companies when they dial a number. *Smith*'s bedrock holding is that an individual has no legitimate expectation of privacy in information provided to third parties. . . .

The privacy concerns at stake in *Smith* were far more individualized than those raised by the ACLU. *Smith* involved the investigation of a single crime and the collection of telephone call detail records collected by the telephone company at its central office, examined by the police, and related to the target of their investigation, a person identified previously by law enforcement. Nevertheless, the Supreme Court found there was no legitimate privacy expectation because "[t]elephone users . . . typically know that they must convey numerical information to the telephone company; that the telephone company has facilities for recording this information; and that the telephone company does in fact record this information for a variety of legitimate business purposes."

The ACLU argues that analysis of bulk telephony metadata allows the creation of a rich mosaic: it can "reveal a person's religion, political associations, use of a telephone-sex hotline, contemplation of suicide, addiction to gambling or drugs, experience with rape, grappling with sexuality, or support for particular political causes." But that is at least three inflections from the Government's bulk telephony metadata collection. First, without additional legal justification—subject to rigorous minimization procedures—the NSA cannot even query the telephony metadata database. Second, when it makes a query, it only learns the telephony metadata of the telephone numbers within three "hops" of the "seed." Third, without resort to additional techniques, the Government does not know who any of the telephone numbers belong to. In other words, all the Government sees is that telephone number A called telephone number B. It does not know who subscribes to telephone numbers A or B. Further, the Government repudiates any notion that it conducts the type of data mining the ACLU warns about in its parade of horribles.

The ACLU also argues that "[t]here are a number of ways in which the Government could perform three-hop analysis without first building its own database of every American's call records." That has no traction. At bottom, it is little more than an assertion that less intrusive means to collect and analyze telephony metadata could be employed. But, the Supreme Court has "repeatedly refused to declare that only the 'least intrusive' search practicable can be reasonable under the Fourth Amendment." That judicial-Monday-morning-quarterbacking "could raise insuperable barriers to the exercise of virtually all search-and-seizure powers" because judges engaging in after-the-fact evaluations of government conduct "can almost always imagine some alternative means by which the objectives might have been accomplished."

The ACLU's pleading reveals a fundamental misapprehension about ownership of telephony metadata. In its motion for a preliminary injunction, the ACLU seeks to: (1) bar the Government from collecting "Plaintiffs' call records" under the bulk telephony metadata collection program; (2) quarantine "all of Plaintiffs' call records" already collected under the bulk telephony metadata collection program; and (3) prohibit the Government from querying metadata obtained through the bulk telephony metadata collection program using any phone number or other identifier associated with Plaintiffs.

First, the business records created by Verizon are not "Plaintiffs' call records." Those records are created and maintained by the telecommunications provider, not the ACLU. Under the Constitution, that distinction is critical because when a person voluntarily conveys information to a third party, he forfeits his right to privacy in the information. Second, the Government's subsequent querying of the telephony metadata does not implicate the Fourth Amendment—anymore than a law enforcement officer's query of the FBI's fingerprint or DNA databases to identify someone. In the context of DNA querying, any match is of the DNA profile—and like telephony metadata additional investigative steps are required to link that DNA profile to an individual.

The collection of breathtaking amounts of information unprotected by the Fourth Amendment does not transform that sweep into a Fourth Amendment search. . . .

Some ponder the ubiquity of cellular telephones and how subscribers' relationships with their telephones have evolved since *Smith*. While people may "have an entirely different relationship with telephones than they did thirty-four years ago," this Court observes that their relationship with their telecommunications providers has not changed and is just as frustrating. Telephones have far more versatility now than when *Smith* was decided, but this case only concerns their use as telephones. The fact that there are more calls placed does not undermine the Supreme Court's finding that a person has no subjective expectation of privacy in telephony metadata. . . .

Klayman v. Obama

U.S. District Court for the District of Columbia
957 F. Supp. 2d 1 (2013)

RICHARD J. LEON, United States District Judge.

. . . The question before me is *not* the same question that the Supreme Court confronted in *Smith.* To say the least, "whether the installation and use of a pen register constitutes a 'search' within the meaning of the Fourth Amendment"—under the circumstances addressed and contemplated in that case—is a far cry from the issue in this case.

Indeed, the question in this case can more properly be styled as follows: When do present-day circumstances—the evolutions in the Government's surveillance capabilities, citizens' phone habits, and the relationship between the NSA and telecom companies—become so thoroughly unlike those considered by the Supreme Court thirty-four years ago that a precedent like *Smith* simply does not apply? The answer, unfortunately for the Government, is now. . . .

[T]he Court in *Smith* was not confronted with the NSA's Bulk Telephony Metadata Program. Nor could the Court in 1979 have ever imagined how the citizens of 2013 would interact with their phones. For the many reasons discussed below, I am convinced that the surveillance program now before me is so different from a simple pen register that *Smith* is of little value in assessing whether the Bulk Telephony Metadata Program constitutes a Fourth Amendment search. To the contrary, for the following reasons, I believe that bulk telephony metadata collection and analysis almost certainly does violate a reasonable expectation of privacy.

First, the pen register in *Smith* was operational for only a matter of days between March 6, 1976 and March 19, 1976, and there is no indication from the Court's opinion that it expected the Government to retain those limited phone records once the case was over. In his affidavit, Acting Assistant Director of the FBI Robert J. Holley himself noted that "[p]en-register and trap-and-trace (PR/TT) devices provide no historical contact information, only a record of contacts with the target occurring after the devices have been installed." This short-term, forward-looking (as opposed to historical), and highly-limited data collection is what the Supreme Court was assessing in *Smith.* The NSA telephony metadata program, on the other hand, involves the creation and maintenance of a historical database containing *five years'* worth of data. And I might add, there is the very real prospect that the program will go on for as long as America is combatting terrorism, which realistically could be forever!

Second, the relationship between the police and the phone company in *Smith* is *nothing* compared to the relationship that has apparently evolved over the last seven years between the Government and telecom companies. The Supreme Court itself has long-recognized a meaningful difference between cases in which a third party collects information and then turns it over to law enforcement, and cases in which the government and the third party create a formalized policy under which the service provider collects information for law enforcement purposes, with the latter raising Fourth Amendment concerns. In *Smith,* the Court considered a one-time, targeted request for data regarding an individual suspect in a criminal investigation, which in no way resembles the daily, all-encompassing, indiscriminate dump of phone metadata that the NSA now receives as part of its Bulk Telephony Metadata Program. It's one thing to say that people expect phone companies to occasionally provide information to law enforcement; it is quite another to suggest that our citizens expect all phone companies to operate what is effectively a joint intelligence-gathering operation with the Government.

Third, the almost-Orwellian technology that enables the Government to store and analyze the phone metadata of every telephone user in the United States is unlike anything that could have been conceived in 1979. In *Smith,* the Supreme Court was actually considering whether local police could collect one person's phone records for calls made after the pen register was installed and for the limited purpose of a small-scale investigation of harassing phone calls. The notion that the Government could collect similar data on hundreds of millions of people and retain that data for a five-year period, updating it with new data every day in perpetuity, was at best, in 1979, the stuff of science fiction. By comparison, the Government has at its disposal today the most advanced twenty-first century tools, allowing it to "store such records and efficiently mine them for information years into the future." And these technologies are "cheap in comparison to conventional surveillance techniques and, by design, proceed[ ] surreptitiously," thereby "evad[ing] the ordinary checks that constrain abusive law enforcement practices: limited police . . . resources and community hostility."

Finally, *and most importantly,* not only is the Government's ability to collect, store, and analyze phone data greater now than it was in 1979, but the nature and quantity of the information contained in people's telephony metadata is much greater, as well. According to the 1979 U.S. Census, in that year, 71,958,000 homes had telephones available, while 6,614,000 did not. In December 2012, there were a whopping 326,475,248 mobile subscriber connections in the United States, of which approximately 304 million were for phones and twenty-two million were for computers, tablets, and modems. The number of mobile subscribers in 2013 is more than *3,000 times* greater than the 91,600 subscriber connections in 1984, and more than *triple* the 97,035,925 subscribers in June 2000. It is now safe to assume that the vast majority of people reading this opinion have *at least* one cell phone within arm's reach (in addition to other mobile devices). In fact, some undoubtedly will be reading this opinion *on their cellphones.* Cell phones have also morphed into multipurpose devices. They are now maps and music players. They are cameras. They are even lighters that people hold up at rock concerts. They are ubiquitous as well. Count the phones at the bus stop, in a restaurant, or around the table at a work meeting or any given occasion. Thirty-four years ago, *none* of those phones would have been there. Thirty-four years ago, city streets were lined with pay phones. Thirty-four years ago, when people wanted to send "text messages," they wrote letters and attached postage stamps.

Admittedly, what metadata *is* has not changed over time. As in *Smith,* the *types* of information at issue in this case are relatively limited: phone numbers dialed, date, time, and the like. But the ubiquity of phones has dramatically altered the *quantity* of information that is now available and, *more importantly,* what that information can tell the Government about people's lives. Put simply, people in 2013 have an entirely different relationship with phones than they did thirty-four years ago. As a result, people make calls and send text messages now that they would not (really, *could not*) have made or sent back when *Smith* was decided—for example, every phone call today between two people trying to locate one another in a public place. This rapid and monumental shift towards a cell phone-centric culture means that the metadata from each person's phone "reflects a wealth of detail about her familial, political, professional, religious, and sexual associations," that could not have been gleaned from a data collection in 1979. Records that once would have revealed a few scattered tiles of information about a person now reveal an entire mosaic—a vibrant and constantly updating picture of the person's life. Whereas some may assume that these cultural changes will force people to "reconcile themselves" to an "inevitable" "diminution of privacy that new technology entails," I think it is more likely that these trends have resulted in a *greater* expectation of privacy and a recognition that society views that expectation as reasonable.

In sum, the *Smith* pen register and the ongoing NSA Bulk Telephony Metadata Program have so many significant distinctions between them that I cannot possibly navigate these uncharted Fourth Amendment waters using as my North Star a case that predates the rise of cell phones. . . .

AFTERMATH The conflict between *Clapper* and *Klayman* was never resolved. The Second Circuit heard an appeal to *Clapper* but decided the case on grounds of statutory interpretation, ultimately holding that the federal statute did not authorize the NSA to conduct bulk metadata collection. *ACLU v. Clapper*, 785 F.3d 787, 826 (2d Cir. 2015) ("the telephone metadata program exceeds the scope of what Congress has authorized and therefore violates § 215"). This statutory holding rendered the constitutional controversy unnecessary to resolve. The result is that much of the Fourth Amendment jurisprudence as it relates to telecommunications privacy remains unresolved.

NOTES & QUESTIONS ON BULK METADATA

1. *The USA Freedom Act.* Section 215 discussed in the above cases expired on June 1, 2015, and Congress subsequently passed the USA Freedom Act, which installed a new framework. The NSA no longer collects metadata, which is now maintained by the telecommunications provider. A court can issue an order for the government to access the information based on "a reasonable, articulable suspicion that such specific selection term is associated with a foreign power engaged in international terrorism or activities in preparation therefor, or an agent of a foreign power engaged in international terrorism or activities in preparation therefor. . . ." 50 U.S.C. § 1861. Also, the court can order that the telephone company turn over the records of phone numbers that are connected to the original number:

> If the government can demonstrate a reasonable, articulable suspicion that a specific selection term is associated with a foreign power or an agent of a foreign power engaged in international terrorism, the FISC may issue an order for the ongoing, daily production of call detail records held by telephone companies. The FISC may order the production of up to two "hops"–i.e., the call detail records associated with the initial telephone number and the records associated with the records returned in the initial hop.

Bart Forsyth, *Banning Bulk: Passage of the USA Freedom Act and Ending Bulk Collection*, 72 Wash. & Lee L. Rev. 1307, 1338-39 (2015). Does this new statutory scheme do enough to resolve the constitutional concerns raised in the prior cases?

2. *The mosaic theory.* Under traditional Fourth Amendment analysis, courts look to each individual intrusion to determine whether it is a search. Some jurists have suggested that this process is wrong and should be replaced by a mosaic theory, whereby courts should look to the collective effort rather than the individual components. If the collective effort is enough to constitute a search, then it should be so declared, rather than segmented into separate components, none of which is by itself significant enough to be considered a

search. The mosaic theory is particularly apt in the telecommunications context, where the state might engage in several individual steps, each one rather insignificant but which when taken together allow the state to create a "mosaic" of the individual concerned. For example, the D.C. Circuit offered the following compelling description of the mosaic theory:

> Prolonged surveillance reveals types of information not revealed by short-term surveillance, such as what a person does repeatedly, what he does not do, and what he does ensemble. These types of information can each reveal more about a person than does any individual trip viewed in isolation. Repeated visits to a church, a gym, a bar, or a bookie tell a story not told by any single visit, as does one's not visiting any of these places over the course of a month. The sequence of a person's movements can reveal still more; a single trip to a gynecologist's office tells little about a woman, but that trip followed a few weeks later by a visit to a baby supply store tells a different story. A person who knows all of another's travels can deduce whether he is a weekly church goer, a heavy drinker, a regular at the gym, an unfaithful husband, an outpatient receiving medical treatment, an associate of particular individuals or political groups—and not just one such fact about a person, but all such facts.

United States v. Maynard, 615 F.3d 544, 562 (D.C. Cir. 2010). Do you agree with the mosaic theory or do you think that courts should restrict themselves to a traditional Fourth Amendment methodology that looks at each component step? At least one commentator has spoken out against the theory:

> The approach is well intentioned. It aims to restore the balance of Fourth Amendment protection by disabling the new powers created by computerization of surveillance tools. But despite these good intentions, the mosaic theory represents a Pandora's Box that courts should leave closed. The theory raises so many novel and difficult questions that courts would struggle to provide reasonably coherent answers. By the time courts worked through answers for any one technology, the technology would likely be long obsolete.

Orin S. Kerr, *The Mosaic Theory of the Fourth Amendment*, 111 Mich. L. Rev. 311, 353 (2012). Do you agree that the mosaic theory would open a Pandora's Box?

C. SURVEILLANCE OF PROPERTY

In lieu of going inside a residence, which clearly constitutes a search (and by extension requires a warrant supported by probable cause unless one of the exceptions to the warrant requirement applies), the police might try to conduct surveillance of a suspect's property in order to collect information without physically going inside the residence. The question is when such surveillance might constitute a search within the meaning of the Fourth Amendment. In these cases, the police seek to collect, from a public vantage point and without performing a physical trespass, information about what is happening inside a property. Applying the *Katz* framework, the relevant questions are what expectations of privacy do residents have about their activities in their homes or property, and are these expectations reasonable or not?

As you read the following materials, ask yourself whether the police are engaging in an intrusion on privacy or whether the police are simply collecting the same kind of information that any member of the public might collect as they pass by a private property. Answering this question will help determine whether the state action outstrips the normal access to information that all members of the public have or whether the state action is an intrusive investigative technique. Recall that parcels of private property are by definition *private* but also not blackholes of information completely unseen to the rest of the world. Information escapes from every parcel of land, so the question is what technologies and techniques the police might use to collect it without it constituting a search under the Fourth Amendment. The following materials focus on (1) aerial fly-overs, (2) thermal imaging, and (3) contraband-sniffing canines.

1. Aerial Fly-Overs

Police sometimes use airplanes and helicopters to fly over a property in order to see into the yard or fields around a house. In multiple cases, the court has considered this police behavior and have asked whether the police are merely doing what any private citizen could do: launch an aircraft and look out the window, as many bored air passengers do. If a private citizen can do this, why not the police? In the following case, *Ciraolo,* the Court debates this very question. Specifically, does the police use of an airplane to view a property owner's yard constitute a search under the Fourth Amendment? Expressed in the terms of the *Katz* framework, what reasonable expectation of privacy does a resident have to areas of their property freely visible from the sky?

California v. Ciraolo

Supreme Court of the United States
476 U.S. 207 (1986)

Chief Justice Burger delivered the opinion of the Court.

We granted certiorari to determine whether the Fourth Amendment is violated by aerial observation without a warrant from an altitude of 1,000 feet of a fenced-in backyard within the curtilage of a home.

On September 2, 1982, Santa Clara Police received an anonymous telephone tip that marijuana was growing in respondent's backyard. Police were unable to observe the contents of respondent's yard from ground level because of a 6-foot outer fence and a 10-foot inner fence completely enclosing the yard. Later that day, Officer Shutz, who was assigned to investigate, secured a private plane and flew over respondent's house at an altitude of 1,000 feet, within navigable airspace; he was accompanied by Officer Rodriguez. Both officers were trained in marijuana identification. From the overflight, the officers readily identified marijuana plants 8 feet to 10 feet in height growing in a 15- by 25-foot plot in respondent's yard; they photographed the area with a standard 35mm camera.

On September 8, 1982, Officer Shutz obtained a search warrant on the basis of an affidavit describing the anonymous tip and their observations; a photograph depicting respondent's house, the backyard, and neighboring homes was attached to the affidavit as an exhibit. The warrant was executed the next day and 73 plants were seized; it is not disputed that these were marijuana.

The touchstone of Fourth Amendment analysis is whether a person has a "constitutionally protected reasonable expectation of privacy." *Katz* posits a two-part inquiry: first, has the individual manifested a subjective expectation of privacy in the object of the challenged search? Second, is society willing to recognize that expectation as reasonable?

Clearly–and understandably–respondent has met the test of manifesting his own subjective intent and desire to maintain privacy as to his unlawful agricultural pursuits. However, we need not address that issue, for the State has not challenged the finding of the California Court of Appeal that respondent had such an expectation. It can reasonably be assumed that the 10-foot fence was placed to conceal the marijuana crop from at least street-level views. So far as the normal sidewalk traffic was concerned, this fence served that purpose, because respondent "took normal precautions to maintain his privacy."

Yet a 10-foot fence might not shield these plants from the eyes of a citizen or a policeman perched on the top of a truck or a two-level bus. Whether respondent therefore manifested a subjective expectation of privacy from *all* observations of his backyard, or whether instead he manifested merely a hope that no one would observe his unlawful gardening pursuits, is not entirely clear in these circumstances. Respondent appears to challenge the authority of government to observe his activity from any vantage point or place if the viewing is motivated by a law enforcement purpose, and not the result of a casual, accidental observation.

We turn, therefore, to the second inquiry under *Katz, i.e.,* whether that expectation is reasonable. In pursuing this inquiry, we must keep in mind that "[t]he test of legitimacy is not whether the individual chooses to conceal assertedly 'private' activity," but instead "whether the government's intrusion infringes upon the personal and societal values protected by the Fourth Amendment."

Respondent argues that because his yard was in the curtilage of his home, no governmental aerial observation is permissible under the Fourth Amendment without a warrant. The history and genesis of the curtilage doctrine are instructive. "At common law, the curtilage is the area to which extends the intimate activity associated with the 'sanctity of a man's home and the privacies of life.'" The protection afforded the curtilage is essentially a protection of families and personal privacy in an area intimately linked to the home, both physically and psychologically, where privacy expectations are most heightened. The claimed area here was immediately adjacent to a suburban home, surrounded by high double fences. This close nexus to the home would appear to encompass this small area within the curtilage. Accepting, as the State does, that this yard and its crop fall within the curtilage, the question remains whether naked-eye observation of the curtilage by police from an aircraft lawfully operating at an altitude of 1,000 feet violates an expectation of privacy that is reasonable.

That the area is within the curtilage does not itself bar all police observation. The Fourth Amendment protection of the home has never been extended to require law enforcement officers to shield their eyes when passing by a home on public thoroughfares. Nor does the mere fact that an individual has taken measures to restrict some views of his activities preclude an officer's observations from a public vantage point where he has a right to be and which renders the activities clearly visible. "What a person knowingly exposes to the public, even in his own home or office, is not a subject of Fourth Amendment protection."

The observations by Officers Shutz and Rodriguez in this case took place within public navigable airspace, in a physically nonintrusive manner; from this point they were able to observe plants readily discernible to the naked eye as marijuana. That the observation from aircraft was directed at identifying the plants and the officers were trained to recognize marijuana is irrelevant. Such observation is precisely what a judicial officer needs to provide a basis for a warrant. Any member of the public flying in this airspace who glanced down could have seen everything that these officers observed. On this record, we readily conclude that respondent's expectation that his garden was protected from such observation is unreasonable and is not an expectation that society is prepared to honor.

The dissent contends that the Court ignores Justice Harlan's warning in his concurrence in *Katz v. United States,* the Fourth Amendment should not be limited to proscribing only physical intrusions onto private property. But Justice Harlan's observations about future electronic developments and the potential for electronic interference with private communications, were plainly not aimed at simple visual observations from a public place. Indeed, since *Katz* the Court has required warrants for electronic surveillance aimed at intercepting private conversations.

Justice Harlan made it crystal clear that he was resting on the reality that one who enters a telephone booth is entitled to assume that his conversation is not being intercepted. This does not translate readily into a rule of constitutional dimensions that one who grows illicit drugs in his backyard is "entitled to assume" his unlawful conduct will not be observed by a passing aircraft—or by a power company repair mechanic on a pole overlooking the yard. As Justice Harlan emphasized, "a man's home is, for most purposes, a place where he expects privacy, but objects, activities, or statements that he exposes to the 'plain view' of outsiders are not 'protected' because no intention to keep them to himself has been exhibited. On the other hand, conversations in the open would not be protected against being overheard, for the expectation of privacy under the circumstances would be unreasonable."

One can reasonably doubt that in 1967 Justice Harlan considered an aircraft within the category of future "electronic" developments that could stealthily intrude upon an individual's privacy. In an age where private and commercial flight in the public airways is routine, it is unreasonable for respondent to expect that his marijuana plants were constitutionally protected from being observed with the naked eye from an altitude of 1,000 feet. The Fourth Amendment simply does not require the police traveling in the public airways at this altitude to obtain a warrant in order to observe what is visible to the naked eye.

Justice POWELL, with whom Justice BRENNAN, Justice MARSHALL, and Justice BLACKMUN join, dissenting.

. . . Respondent contends that the police intruded on his constitutionally protected expectation of privacy when they conducted aerial surveillance of his home and photographed his backyard without first obtaining a warrant. The Court rejects that contention, holding that respondent's expectation of privacy in the curtilage of his home, although reasonable as to intrusions on the ground, was unreasonable as to surveillance from the navigable airspace. In my view, the Court's holding rests on only one obvious fact, namely, that the airspace generally is open to all persons for travel in airplanes. The Court does not explain why this single fact deprives citizens of their privacy interest in outdoor activities in an enclosed curtilage. . . .

As the decision in *Katz* held, and dissenting opinions written by Justices of this Court prior to *Katz* recognized, a standard that defines a Fourth Amendment "search" by reference to whether police have physically invaded a "constitutionally protected area" provides no real protection against surveillance techniques made possible through technology. Technological advances have enabled police to see people's activities and associations, and to hear their conversations, without being in physical proximity. Moreover, the capability now exists for police to conduct intrusive surveillance without any physical penetration of the walls of homes or other structures that citizens may believe shelters their privacy. Looking to the Fourth Amendment for protection against such "broad and unsuspected governmental incursions" into the "cherished privacy of law-abiding citizens," the Court in *Katz* abandoned its inquiry into whether police had committed a physical trespass. *Katz* announced a standard under which the occurrence of a search turned not on the physical position of the police conducting the surveillance, but on whether the surveillance in question had invaded a constitutionally protected reasonable expectation of privacy. . . .

The Court begins its analysis of the Fourth Amendment issue posed here by deciding that respondent had an expectation of privacy in his backyard. I agree with that conclusion because of the close proximity of the yard to the house, the nature of some of the activities respondent conducted there, and because he had taken steps to shield those activities from the view of passersby. The Court then implicitly acknowledges that society is prepared to recognize his expectation as reasonable with respect to ground-level surveillance, holding that the yard was within the curtilage, an area in which privacy interests have been afforded the "most heightened" protection. As the foregoing discussion of the curtilage doctrine demonstrates, respondent's yard unquestionably was within the curtilage. Since Officer Shutz could not see into this private family area from the street, the Court certainly would agree that he would have conducted an unreasonable search had he climbed over the fence, or used a ladder to peer into the yard without first securing a warrant.

The Court concludes, nevertheless, that Shutz could use an airplane—a product of modern technology—to intrude visually into respondent's yard. The Court argues that respondent had no reasonable expectation of privacy from aerial observation. It notes that Shutz was "within public navigable airspace," when he looked into and photographed respondent's yard. It then relies on the fact that the surveillance was not accompanied by a physical invasion of the curtilage. Reliance on the *manner* of surveillance is directly contrary to the standard of *Katz,* which identifies a constitutionally protected privacy right by focusing on the interests of the individual and of a free society. Since *Katz,* we have consistently held that the presence or absence of physical trespass by police is constitutionally irrelevant to the question whether society is prepared to recognize an asserted privacy interest as reasonable.

The Court's holding, therefore, must rest solely on the fact that members of the public fly in planes and may look down at homes as they fly over them. The Court does not explain why it finds this fact to be significant. One may assume that the Court believes that citizens bear the risk that air travelers will observe activities occurring within backyards that are open to the sun and air. This risk, the Court appears to hold, nullifies expectations

> of privacy in those yards even as to purposeful police surveillance from the air. . . .
>
> This line of reasoning is flawed. First, the actual risk to privacy from commercial or pleasure aircraft is virtually nonexistent. Travelers on commercial flights, as well as private planes used for business or personal reasons, normally obtain at most a fleeting, anonymous, and nondiscriminating glimpse of the landscape and buildings over which they pass. The risk that a passenger on such a plane might observe private activities, and might connect those activities with particular people, is simply too trivial to protect against. It is no accident that, as a matter of common experience, many people build fences around their residential areas, but few build roofs over their backyards. Therefore, contrary to the Court's suggestion, people do not "'knowingly expos[e]'" their residential yards "'to the public'" merely by failing to build barriers that prevent aerial surveillance. . . .

NOTES & QUESTIONS ON AERIAL SURVEILLANCE

1. *The significance of curtilage.* The Court in *Ciraolo* conceded that the yard fell within the curtilage of the home and was therefore possibly subject to Fourth Amendment protection, which includes "persons, houses, papers, and effects" but makes no explicit mention of yards. However, common law judges have long granted the same protections to the curtilage of a residence—the property adjacent to the home—that they do to the home itself. What effect did this conclusion have on the outcome of the case? What result if the Court had concluded that the police surveillance involved a piece of property *beyond* the curtilage of the house? For more discussion, see Catherine Hancock, *Justice Powell's Garden: The* Ciraolo *Dissent and Fourth Amendment Protection for Curtilage-Home Privacy*, 44 San Diego L. Rev. 551, 553 (2007) ("the *Ciraolo* Court implicitly discarded the 'personal and societal values' embodied in the curtilage barrier on the ground, by making the judgment that the same values did not justify the protection of the same home and garden privacy interest from a different point of police access").

2. *Drones and aerial surveillance.* The widespread adoption of drone technology will no doubt change the frequency of aerial surveillance. In the past, if the police wanted to conduct aerial surveillance of a suspect's privacy, they would need to rent an airplane and fly over a property. Few local police departments have the resources to maintain a fleet of aircraft for investigatory use, although some larger federal law enforcement agencies might have aircraft at their disposal. However, drone technology has become so widespread in the last decade that its cost has fallen dramatically, meaning that any local police

department could conceivably fly a drone with a camera over any property. Does the potential ubiquity of aerial surveillance change the constitutional calculus? The Supreme Court was particularly moved by the fact aerial surveillance by the police produces a vantage point that is no different from what a private citizen could achieve by flying an aircraft over someone else's private property. The same thing could be said regarding drone technology. Although the police can fly a drone over a property, so too could a private party. Does this fact make the situation less or more worrisome? For a discussion, see Robert Molko, *The Drones Are Coming! Will the Fourth Amendment Stop Their Threat to Our Privacy?*, 78 Brook. L. Rev. 1279, 1283 (2013) (concluding that "there must be some meaningful limit on how far overhead surveillance of our neighborhoods can stretch before the invasion of privacy reaches constitutional proportions" and the Supreme Court should "draw such a limit, whether under its current 'reasonable expectation' jurisprudence or perhaps under a different framework altogether").

STATUTORY REQUIREMENTS

Although the Fourth Amendment arguably does not require the police to secure a warrant before using a drone to conduct aerial surveillance, various state laws might specifically require a warrant under this circumstance. For example, consider the following Florida statute:

> (a) A law enforcement agency may not use a drone to gather evidence or other information.
> (b) A person, a state agency, or a political subdivision . . . may not use a drone equipped with an imaging device to record an image of privately owned real property or of the owner, tenant, occupant, invitee, or licensee of such property with the intent to conduct surveillance on the individual or property captured in the image in violation of such person's reasonable expectation of privacy without his or her written consent. For purposes of this section, a person is presumed to have a reasonable expectation of privacy on his or her privately owned real property if he or she is not observable by persons located at ground level in a place where they have a legal right to be, regardless of whether he or she is observable from the air with the use of a drone.

Fla. Stat. § 934.50. The statute then goes on to include exceptions for when the Department of Homeland Security believes that there is a high risk of a terrorist attack, when a judge issues a search warrant authorizing the use of a drone, or when "swift action is needed to prevent imminent danger to life or serious damage to property, to forestall the imminent escape of a suspect or the destruction of evidence, or to achieve purposes including, but not limited to, facilitating the search for a missing person." (The statute also includes exceptions for conducting real estate assessments and other non–law enforcement regulatory activities.)

A few other states have passed similar statutes, and legislation is pending in other jurisdictions. However, some law enforcement agencies (or their supporters) oppose the legislation because they believe that it needlessly hampers law enforcement. If you were a state legislator, how would you vote on a bill modeled after the Florida statute?

2. Thermal Imaging

The police have also used thermal imaging, from a public vantage point, to gain information about the activities inside a home that are shielded from visual inspection. In *Kyllo,* the Court considered a putative "search" by the police using one of these thermal imaging devices. At least at first glance, the investigative technique appears intrusive in that it reveals some information—though somewhat murky information—about what the residents of the dwelling might be doing inside. As you read the case, ask yourself how the Court should evaluate this investigatory technique. Should the Court follow the lead of *Ciraolo* and simply ask whether the police are doing what any private citizen could do as they drive by the house? And if this is the right inquiry, what is the answer to that question? Do private citizens have access to thermal imagers in the same way that any citizen could rent a plane and fly over a house or yard? Or is this wrong question to ask?

Danny Lee Kyllo in 2001, standing in front of the house in Florence, OR. (Don Ryan/AP/Shutterstock)

Kyllo v. United States

Supreme Court of the United States
533 U.S. 27 (2001)

Justice Scalia delivered the opinion of the Court.

This case presents the question whether the use of a thermal-imaging device aimed at a private home from a public street to detect relative amounts of heat within the home constitutes a "search" within the meaning of the Fourth Amendment.

I

In 1991 Agent William Elliott of the United States Department of the Interior came to suspect that marijuana was being grown in the home belonging to petitioner Danny Kyllo, part of a triplex on Rhododendron Drive in Florence, Oregon. Indoor marijuana growth typically requires high-intensity lamps. In order to determine whether an amount of heat was emanating from petitioner's home consistent with the use of such lamps, at 3:20 A.M. on January 16, 1992, Agent Elliott and Dan Haas used an Agema Thermovision 210 thermal imager to scan the triplex. Thermal imagers detect infrared radiation, which virtually all objects emit but which is not visible to the naked eye. The imager converts radiation into images based on relative warmth—black is cool, white is hot, shades of gray connote relative differences; in that respect, it operates somewhat like a video camera showing heat images. The scan of Kyllo's home took only a few minutes and was performed from the passenger seat of Agent Elliott's vehicle across the street from the front of the house and also from the street in back of the house. The scan showed that the roof over the garage and a side wall of petitioner's home were relatively hot compared to the rest of the home and substantially warmer than neighboring homes in the triplex. Agent Elliott concluded that petitioner was using halide lights to grow marijuana in his house, which indeed he was. Based on tips from informants, utility bills, and the thermal imaging, a Federal Magistrate Judge issued a warrant authorizing a search of petitioner's home, and the agents found an indoor growing operation involving more than 100 plants. Petitioner was indicted on one count of manufacturing marijuana. He unsuccessfully moved to suppress the evidence seized from his home and then entered a conditional guilty plea. . . .

II

The Fourth Amendment provides that "[t]he right of the people to be secure in their persons, houses, papers, and effects, against unreasonable searches and seizures, shall not be violated." "At the very core" of the Fourth Amendment "stands the right of a man to retreat into his own home and there be free from unreasonable governmental intrusion." With few exceptions, the question whether a warrantless search of a home is reasonable and hence constitutional must be answered no.

On the other hand, the antecedent question whether or not a Fourth Amendment "search" has occurred is not so simple under our precedent. The permissibility of ordinary visual surveillance of a home used to be clear because, well into the 20th century, our Fourth Amendment jurisprudence was tied to common-law trespass. Visual surveillance was unquestionably lawful because "'the eye cannot by the laws of England be guilty of a trespass.'" We have since decoupled violation of a person's Fourth Amendment

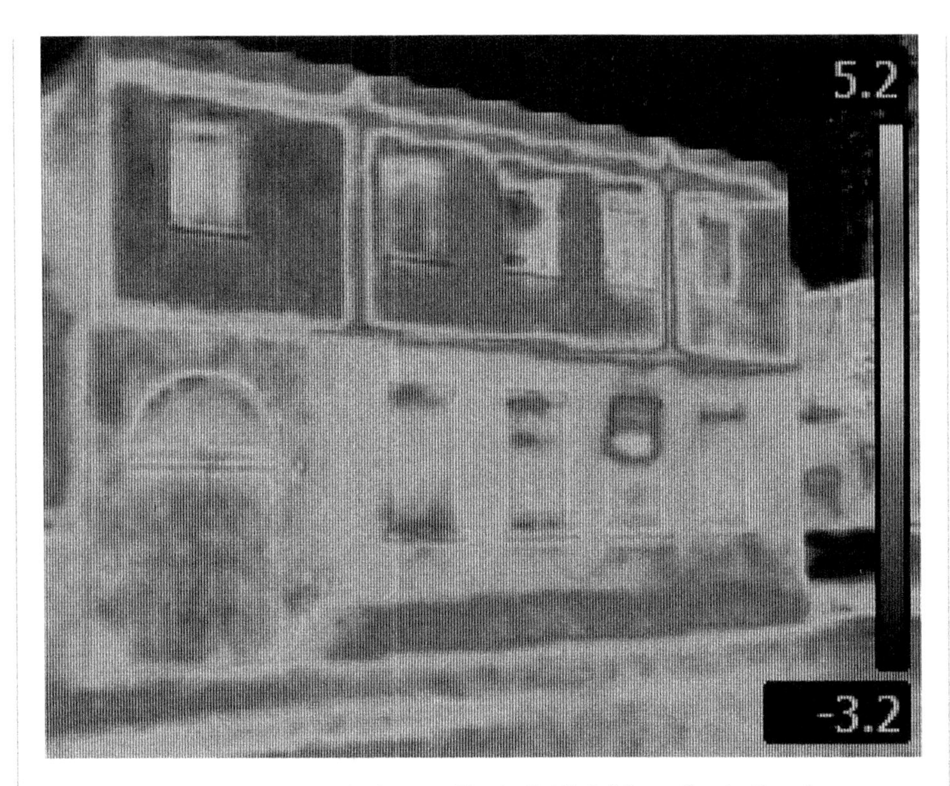

A thermal image of a house. (Dario Sabljak/Alamy Stock Photo)

rights from trespassory violation of his property, but the lawfulness of warrantless visual surveillance of a home has still been preserved. As we observed in *California v. Ciraolo,* 476 U.S. 207, 213 (1986) "[t]he Fourth Amendment protection of the home has never been extended to require law enforcement officers to shield their eyes when passing by a home on public thoroughfares."

One might think that the new validating rationale would be that examining the portion of a house that is in plain public view, while it is a "search" despite the absence of trespass, is not an "unreasonable" one under the Fourth Amendment. But in fact we have held that visual observation is no "search" at all—perhaps in order to preserve somewhat more intact our doctrine that warrantless searches are presumptively unconstitutional. In assessing when a search is not a search, we have applied somewhat in reverse the principle first enunciated in *Katz v. United States,* 389 U.S. 347 (1967). *Katz* involved eavesdropping by means of an electronic listening device placed on the outside of a telephone booth—a location not within the catalog ("persons, houses, papers, and effects") that the Fourth Amendment protects against unreasonable searches. We held that the Fourth Amendment nonetheless protected Katz from the warrantless eavesdropping because he "justifiably relied" upon the privacy of the telephone booth. As Justice Harlan's oft-quoted concurrence described it, a Fourth Amendment search occurs when the government violates a subjective expectation of privacy that society recognizes as reasonable. We have subsequently applied this principle to hold that a Fourth Amendment search does *not* occur—even when the explicitly protected location of a *house* is concerned—unless "the individual manifested a subjective expectation of privacy in the object of the challenged search," and "society [is] willing to recognize that expectation as reasonable." We have applied this test in holding that it is not a search for the police to use a pen register at the phone company to determine what numbers were dialed in a private home, and we have applied the test on two different occasions in holding that aerial surveillance of private homes and surrounding areas does not constitute a search.

The present case involves officers on a public street engaged in more than naked-eye surveillance of a home. We have previously reserved judgment as to how much technological enhancement of ordinary perception from such a vantage point, if any, is too much. While we upheld enhanced aerial photography of an industrial complex in *Dow Chemical*, we noted that we found "it important that this is *not* an area immediately adjacent to a private home, where privacy expectations are most heightened."

III

It would be foolish to contend that the degree of privacy secured to citizens by the Fourth Amendment has been entirely unaffected by the advance of technology. For example, as the cases discussed above make clear, the technology enabling human flight has exposed to public view (and hence, we have said, to official observation) uncovered portions of the house and its curtilage that once were private. The question we confront today is what limits there are upon this power of technology to shrink the realm of guaranteed privacy.

The *Katz* test—whether the individual has an expectation of privacy that society is prepared to recognize as reasonable—has often been criticized as circular, and hence subjective and unpredictable. While it may be difficult to refine *Katz* when the search of areas such as telephone booths, automobiles, or even the curtilage and uncovered portions of residences is at issue, in the case of the search of the interior of homes—the prototypical and hence most commonly litigated area of protected privacy—there is a ready criterion, with roots deep in the common law, of the minimal expectation of privacy that *exists*, and that is acknowledged to be *reasonable*. To withdraw protection of this minimum expectation would be to permit police technology to erode the privacy guaranteed by the Fourth Amendment. We think that obtaining by sense-enhancing technology any information regarding the interior of the home that could not otherwise have been obtained without physical "intrusion into a constitutionally protected area," constitutes a search—at least where (as here) the technology in question is not in general public use. This assures preservation of that degree of privacy against government that existed when the Fourth Amendment was adopted. On the basis of this criterion, the information obtained by the thermal imager in this case was the product of a search.

The Government maintains, however, that the thermal imaging must be upheld because it detected "only heat radiating from the external surface of the house." The dissent makes this its leading point, contending that there is a fundamental difference between what it calls "off-the-wall" observations and "through-the-wall surveillance." But just as a thermal imager captures only heat emanating from a house, so also a powerful directional microphone picks up only sound emanating from a house-and a satellite capable of scanning from many miles away would pick up only visible light emanating from a house. We rejected such a mechanical interpretation of the Fourth Amendment in *Katz,* where the eavesdropping device picked up only sound waves that reached the exterior of the phone booth. Reversing that approach would leave the homeowner at the mercy of advancing technology—including imaging technology that could discern all human activity in the home. While the technology used in the present case was relatively crude, the rule we adopt must take account of more sophisticated systems that are already in use or in development. The dissent's reliance on the distinction between "off-the-wall" and "through-the-wall" observation is entirely incompatible with the dissent's belief, which we discuss below, that thermal-imaging observations of the intimate details of a home are impermissible. The most sophisticated thermal-imaging devices continue to measure heat "off-the-wall" rather than "through-the-wall"; the dissent's disapproval of those more sophisticated thermal-imaging devices, is an acknowledgement that there is no substance to this distinction. As for the dissent's extraordinary assertion that anything learned through "an inference" cannot be a search, that would validate even the "through-the-wall" technologies that the dissent purports to disapprove. Surely the dissent does not believe that the through-the-wall radar or ultrasound technology produces an 8-by-10 Kodak glossy that needs no analysis (*i.e.,* the making of inferences). And, of course, the novel proposition that inference insulates a search is blatantly contrary to *United States v. Karo,* 468 U.S. 705 (1984), where the police "inferred" from the activation of a beeper that a certain can of ether was in the home. The police activity was held to be a search, and the search was held unlawful.

The Government also contends that the thermal imaging was constitutional because it did not "detect private activities occurring in private areas." It points out that in *Dow Chemical* we observed that the enhanced aerial photography did not reveal any "intimate details." *Dow Chemical,* however, involved enhanced aerial photography of an industrial complex, which does not share the Fourth Amendment sanctity of the home. The Fourth

Amendment's protection of the home has never been tied to measurement of the quality or quantity of information obtained. . . .

Limiting the prohibition of thermal imaging to "intimate details" would not only be wrong in principle; it would be impractical in application, failing to provide "a workable accommodation between the needs of law enforcement and the interests protected by the Fourth Amendment." To begin with, there is no necessary connection between the sophistication of the surveillance equipment and the "intimacy" of the details that it observes—which means that one cannot say (and the police cannot be assured) that use of the relatively crude equipment at issue here will always be lawful. The Agema Thermovision 210 might disclose, for example, at what hour each night the lady of the house takes her daily sauna and bath—a detail that many would consider "intimate"; and a much more sophisticated system might detect nothing more intimate than the fact that someone left a closet light on. We could not, in other words, develop a rule approving only that through-the-wall surveillance which identifies objects no smaller than 36 by 36 inches, but would have to develop a jurisprudence specifying which home activities are "intimate" and which are not. And even when (if ever) that jurisprudence were fully developed, no police officer would be able to know *in advance* whether his through-the-wall surveillance picks up "intimate" details—and thus would be unable to know in advance whether it is constitutional.

The dissent's proposed standard—whether the technology offers the "functional equivalent of actual presence in the area being searched"—would seem quite similar to our own at first blush. The dissent concludes that *Katz* was such a case, but then inexplicably asserts that if the same listening device only revealed the volume of the conversation, the surveillance would be permissible. Yet if, without technology, the police could not discern volume without being actually present in the phone booth, Justice Stevens should conclude a search has occurred. The same should hold for the interior heat of the home if only a person present in the home could discern the heat. Thus the driving force of the dissent, despite its recitation of the above standard, appears to be a distinction among different types of information—whether the "homeowner would even care if anybody noticed." The dissent offers no practical guidance for the application of this standard, and for reasons already discussed, we believe there can be none. The people in their houses, as well as the police, deserve more precision.

We have said that the Fourth Amendment draws "a firm line at the entrance to the house." That line, we think, must be not only firm but also bright—which requires clear specification of those methods of surveillance that require a warrant. While it is certainly possible to conclude from the videotape of the thermal imaging that occurred in this case that no "significant" compromise of the homeowner's privacy has occurred, we must take the long view, from the original meaning of the Fourth Amendment forward. . . . Where, as here, the Government uses a device that is not in general public use, to explore details of the home that would previously have been unknowable without physical intrusion, the surveillance is a "search" and is presumptively unreasonable without a warrant. . . .

Justice STEVENS, with whom THE CHIEF JUSTICE, Justice O'CONNOR, and Justice KENNEDY join, dissenting.

There is, in my judgment, a distinction of constitutional magnitude between "through-the-wall surveillance" that gives the observer or listener direct access to information in a private area, on the one hand, and the thought processes used to draw inferences from information in the public domain, on the other hand. The Court has crafted a rule that purports to deal with direct observations of the inside of the home, but the case before us merely involves indirect deductions from "off-the-wall" surveillance, that is, observations of the exterior of the home. Those observations were made with a fairly primitive thermal imager that gathered data exposed on the outside of petitioner's home but did not invade any constitutionally protected interest in privacy. Moreover, I believe that the supposedly "bright-line" rule the Court has created in response to its concerns about future technological developments is unnecessary, unwise, and inconsistent with the Fourth Amendment.

There is no need for the Court to craft a new rule to decide this case, as it is controlled by established principles from our Fourth Amendment jurisprudence. One of those core principles, of course, is that "searches and seizures *inside a home* without a warrant are presumptively unreasonable." But it is equally well settled that searches and seizures of property in plain view are presumptively reasonable. Whether that property is residential or commercial, the basic principle is the same: "What a person knowingly exposes to the public, even in his own home or office, is not a subject of Fourth Amendment protection." That is the principle implicated here.

While the Court "take[s] the long view" and decides this case based largely on the potential of yet-to-be-developed technology that might allow "through-the-wall surveillance," this case involves nothing more than off-the-wall surveillance by law enforcement officers to gather information exposed to the general public from the outside of petitioner's home. All that the infrared camera did in this case was passively measure heat emitted from the exterior surfaces of petitioner's home; all that those measurements showed were relative differences in emission levels, vaguely indicating that some areas of the roof and outside walls were warmer than others. As still images from the infrared scans show, no details regarding the interior of petitioner's home were revealed. Unlike an x-ray scan, or other possible "through-the-wall" techniques, the detection of infrared radiation emanating from the home did not accomplish "an unauthorized physical penetration into the premises," nor did it "obtain information that it could not have obtained by observation from outside the curtilage of the house."

Indeed, the ordinary use of the senses might enable a neighbor or passerby to notice the heat emanating from a building, particularly if it is vented, as was the case here. Additionally, any member of the public might notice that one part of a house is warmer than another part or a nearby building if, for example, rainwater evaporates or snow melts at different rates across its surfaces. Such use of the senses would not convert into an unreasonable search if, instead, an adjoining neighbor allowed an officer onto her property to verify her perceptions with a sensitive thermometer. Nor, in my view, does such observation become an unreasonable search if made from a distance with the aid of a device that merely discloses that the exterior of one house, or one area of the house, is much warmer than another. Nothing more occurred in this case.

Thus, the notion that heat emissions from the outside of a dwelling are a private matter implicating the protections of the Fourth Amendment (the text of which guarantees the right of people "to be secure *in* their . . . houses" against unreasonable searches and seizures (emphasis added)) is not only unprecedented but also quite difficult to take seriously. Heat waves, like aromas that are generated in a kitchen, or in a laboratory or opium den, enter the public domain if and when they leave a building. A subjective expectation that they would remain private is not only implausible but also surely not "one that society is prepared to recognize as 'reasonable.'"

To be sure, the homeowner has a reasonable expectation of privacy concerning what takes place within the home, and the Fourth Amendment's protection against physical invasions of the home should apply to their functional equivalent. But the equipment in this case did not penetrate the walls of petitioner's home, and while it did pick up "details of the home" that were exposed to the public, it did not obtain "any information regarding the *interior* of the home." In the Court's own words, based on what the thermal imager "showed" regarding the outside of petitioner's home, the officers "concluded" that petitioner was engaging in illegal activity inside the home. It would be quite absurd to characterize their thought processes as "searches," regardless of whether they inferred (rightly) that petitioner was growing marijuana in his house, or (wrongly) that "the lady of the house [was taking] her daily sauna and bath." In either case, the only conclusions the officers reached concerning the interior of the home were at least as indirect as those that might have been inferred from the contents of discarded garbage, or pen register data, or, as in this case, subpoenaed utility records. For the first time in its history, the Court assumes that an inference can amount to a Fourth Amendment violation. . . .

NOTES & QUESTIONS ON THERMAL IMAGING

1. *General public use.* The animating distinction in *Kyllo* is between devices and technology that are in "general public use" and those that are not. The thermal imaging in *Kyllo* constituted a search because it involved the state's use of technology that was not in general public use. Do you agree that this should be the dividing line? Furthermore, what does this portend for the future of Fourth Amendment jurisprudence? As technology becomes cheaper, smaller, and more accessible to the general public, the number of devices that the police can point at a house will only increase. It is, in other words, a one-way ratchet that will inure to the benefit of state power. Will homeowners have the technological capacity to resist these intrusions with *defensive* technologies?

2. *The open fields exception.* At common law, the police were allowed to search open fields, even on private property, without a warrant. The one requirement was that the field must not be within the "curtilage" of the house–i.e., the area adjacent to or surrounding the house. In *Oliver v. United States,* 466 U.S. 170 (1984), the defendant was growing marijuana on his property. The police conducted a warrantless search of the open field by easily walking around a locked gate with a no-trespassing sign (the gate was not connected to a fence that surrounded the field). Although it was clear that this constituted a trespass, the Court reasoned that an open field fell beyond the protection of the Fourth Amendment, which protects "persons, houses, papers, and effects." Since an open field, even on private property, is none of those things, the Fourth Amendment does not protect it. Also, "open fields do not provide the setting for those intimate activities that the Amendment is intended to shelter from government interference or surveillance. There is no societal interest in protecting the privacy of those activities, such as the cultivation of crops, that occur in open fields. Moreover, as a practical matter these lands usually are accessible to the public and the police in ways that a home, an office, or commercial structure would not be." 466 U.S. at 179. For a critical discussion, see Elizabeth Kingston, *Keeping Up with* Jones*: The Need to Abandon the Open Fields Doctrine,* 52 Crim. L. Bull. (2016) ("The open fields doctrine allows the government to enter land and acquire information even when its agents are criminally trespassing upon the land in question. It permits the government's warrantless unauthorized entrance onto property, crossing of several fences, ignoring of 'No Trespassing' signs, and scrutinizing of an outbuilding as constitutional."); *Commonwealth v. Lutz,* 512 Pa. 192, 206 (1986) ("The basic premise of the open fields doctrine, that there can be no reasonable expectation of privacy in an open field, is at times incompatible with the idea that a business owner has a reasonable expectation of privacy in his property.").

STATE LAW REQUIREMENTS

A few state courts had considered the issue of thermal imagers before the Supreme Court decided *Kyllo*. For example, in *State v. Young* (1994), the Supreme Court of Washington considered a marijuana investigation conducted in the City of Edmunds. A police officer used a thermal imaging device to record heat signatures coming from the house of someone the police suspected of growing marijuana. The heat imaging displayed patterns that could not be explained by regular house heating, either in the fireplace or through conventional heating systems. The police compared the heat signatures with similar houses in the neighborhood and again considered them unusual. Based on this information, a search warrant was obtained and marijuana was found. The defendant, Robert Young, contested the validity of the warrant because it was based on information initially procured from an illegal search. Applying Article I of the Washington State Constitution, the Washington Supreme Court concluded:

> The police used an infrared thermal detection device to detect heat distribution patterns undetectable by the naked eye or other senses. With this device the officer was able to, in effect, "see through the walls" of the home. The device goes well beyond an enhancement of natural senses. In addition, the night-time infrared surveillance enabled the officers to conduct their surveillance without Mr. Young's knowledge. The infrared device thus represents a particularly intrusive means of observation that exceeds our established surveillance limits.

123 Wash. 2d 173, 183, 867 P.2d 593, 598 (1994). Seven years later, the U.S. Supreme Court adopted a similar view, effectively adopting the state rule as the federal rule as well.

3. Contraband-Sniffing Dogs

In *United States v. Place*, 462 U.S. 696 (1983), the Supreme Court upheld the use of a drug-sniffing dog to examine an unopened piece of luggage for possible contraband. And in *Illinois v. Caballes*, 543 U.S. 405 (2005), the Court concluded that the use of a contraband-sniffing dog during a traffic stop was permissible. But *Florida v. Jardines* involved a different set of facts and offered the Court an opportunity to continue its revival of the trespass theory. The police will often cross private property to knock on the front door of a house or ring its doorbell. The Supreme Court has held that such requests to "knock and talk" are constitutional. But what if the police bring a dog that sniffs for drugs or other contraband? As you read the following case, ask yourself what role the law of trespass plays in the outcome of the case, and whether you agree that trespass is the correct framework for resolving such disputes.

Florida v. Jardines

Supreme Court of the United States
133 S. Ct. 1409 (2013)

Justice SCALIA delivered the opinion of the Court.

. . . In 2006, Detective William Pedraja of the Miami-Dade Police Department received an unverified tip that marijuana was being grown in the home of respondent Joelis Jardines. One month later, the Department and the Drug Enforcement Administration sent a joint surveillance team to Jardines' home. Detective Pedraja was part of that team. He watched the home for fifteen minutes and saw no vehicles in the driveway or activity around the home, and could not see inside because the blinds were drawn. Detective Pedraja then approached Jardines' home accompanied by Detective Douglas Bartelt, a trained canine handler who had just arrived at the scene with his drug-sniffing dog. The dog was trained to detect the scent of marijuana, cocaine, heroin, and several other drugs, indicating the presence of any of these substances through particular behavioral changes recognizable by his handler.

Detective Bartelt had the dog on a six-foot leash, owing in part to the dog's "wild" nature, and tendency to dart around erratically while searching. As the dog approached Jardines' front porch, he apparently sensed one of the odors he had been trained to detect, and began energetically exploring the area for the strongest point source of that odor. . . .

On the basis of what he had learned at the home, Detective Pedraja applied for and received a warrant to search the residence. When the warrant was executed later that day, Jardines attempted to flee and was arrested; the search revealed marijuana plants, and he was charged with trafficking in cannabis. . . .

The Fourth Amendment provides in relevant part that the "right of the people to be secure in their persons, houses, papers, and effects, against unreasonable searches and seizures, shall not be violated." The Amendment establishes a simple baseline, one that for much of our history formed the exclusive basis for its protections: When "the Government obtains information by physically intruding" on persons, houses, papers, or effects, "a 'search' within the original meaning of the Fourth Amendment" has "undoubtedly occurred." By reason of our decision in *Katz v. United States,* 389 U.S. 347 (1967), property rights "are not the sole measure of Fourth Amendment violations"—but though *Katz* may add to the baseline, it does not subtract anything from the Amendment's protections "when the Government *does* engage in [a] physical intrusion of a constitutionally protected area."

That principle renders this case a straightforward one. The officers were gathering information in an area belonging to Jardines and immediately surrounding his house—in the curtilage of the house, which we have held enjoys protection as part of the home itself. And they gathered that information by physically entering and occupying the area to engage in conduct not explicitly or implicitly permitted by the homeowner.

The Fourth Amendment "indicates with some precision the places and things encompassed by its protections": persons, houses, papers, and effects. The Fourth Amendment does not, therefore, prevent all investigations conducted on private property; for example, an officer may (subject to *Katz*) gather information in what we have called "open fields"—even if those fields are privately owned—because such fields are not enumerated in the Amendment's text.

But when it comes to the Fourth Amendment, the home is first among equals. At the Amendment's "very core" stands "the right of a man to retreat into his own home and there be free from unreasonable governmental intrusion." This right would be of little practical value if the State's agents could stand in a home's porch or side garden and trawl for evidence with impunity; the right to retreat would be significantly diminished if the police could enter a man's property to observe his repose from just outside the front window.

We therefore regard the area "immediately surrounding and associated with the home"—what our cases call the curtilage—as "part of the home itself for Fourth Amendment purposes." That principle has ancient and durable roots. Just as the distinction between the home and the open fields is "as old as the common law," so too is the identity of home and what Blackstone called the "curtilage or homestall," for the "house protects and privileges all its branches and appurtenants." This area around the home is "intimately linked to the home, both physically and psychologically," and is where "privacy expectations are most heightened."

While the boundaries of the curtilage are generally "clearly marked," the "conception defining the curtilage" is at any rate familiar enough that it is "easily understood from our daily experience." Here there is no doubt that the officers entered it: The front porch is the classic exemplar of an area adjacent to the home and "to which the activity of home life extends."

Since the officers' investigation took place in a constitutionally protected area, we turn to the question of whether it was accomplished through an unlicensed physical intrusion. While law enforcement officers need not "shield their eyes" when passing by the home "on public thoroughfares," an officer's leave to gather information is sharply circumscribed when he steps off those thoroughfares and enters the Fourth Amendment's protected areas. In permitting, for example, visual observation of the home from "public navigable airspace," we were careful to note that it was done "in a physically nonintrusive manner." *Entick v. Carrington,* 95 Eng. Rep. 807 (K.B. 1765), a case "undoubtedly familiar" to "every American statesman" at the time of the Founding, states the general rule clearly: "[O]ur law holds the property of every man so sacred, that no man can set his foot upon his neighbour's close without his leave." As it is undisputed that the detectives had all four of their feet and all four of their companion's firmly planted on the constitutionally protected extension of Jardines' home, the only question is whether he had given his leave (even implicitly) for them to do so. He had not.

"A license may be implied from the habits of the country," notwithstanding the "strict rule of the English common law as to entry upon a close." We have accordingly recognized that "the knocker on the front door is treated as an invitation or license to attempt an entry, justifying ingress to the home by solicitors, hawkers and peddlers of all kinds." This implicit license typically permits the visitor to approach the home by the front path, knock promptly, wait briefly to be received, and then (absent invitation to linger longer) leave. Complying with the terms of that traditional invitation does not require fine-grained legal knowledge; it is generally managed without incident by the Nation's Girl Scouts and trick-or-treaters. Thus, a police officer not armed with a warrant may approach a home and knock, precisely because that is "no more than any private citizen might do."

But introducing a trained police dog to explore the area around the home in hopes of discovering incriminating evidence is something else. There is no customary invitation to do *that*. An invitation to engage in canine forensic investigation assuredly does not inhere in the very act of hanging a knocker. To find a visitor knocking on the door is routine (even if sometimes unwelcome); to spot that same visitor exploring the front path with a metal detector, or marching his bloodhound into the garden before saying hello and asking permission, would inspire most of us to—well, call the police. The scope of a license—express or implied—is limited not only to a particular area but also to a specific purpose. Consent at a traffic stop to an officer's checking out an anonymous tip that there is a body in the trunk does not permit the officer to rummage through the trunk for narcotics. Here, the background social norms that invite a visitor to the front door do not invite him there to conduct a search.

The State points to our decisions holding that the subjective intent of the officer is irrelevant. But those cases merely hold that a stop or search *that is objectively reasonable* is not vitiated by the fact that the officer's real reason for making the stop or search has nothing to do with the validating reason. Thus, the defendant will not be heard to complain that although he was speeding the officer's real reason for the stop was racial harassment. Here, however, the question before the court is precisely *whether* the officer's conduct was an objectively reasonable search. As we have described, that depends upon whether the officers had an implied license to enter the porch, which in turn depends upon the purpose for which they entered. Here, their behavior objectively reveals a purpose to conduct a search, which is not what anyone would think he had license to do.

The State argues that investigation by a forensic narcotics dog by definition cannot implicate any legitimate privacy interest. The State cites for authority our decisions in *United States v. Place,* 462 U.S. 696 (1983), *United States v. Jacobsen,* 466 U.S. 109 (1984), and *Illinois v. Caballes,*

543 U.S. 405 (2005), which held, respectively, that canine inspection of luggage in an airport, chemical testing of a substance that had fallen from a parcel in transit, and canine inspection of an automobile during a lawful traffic stop, do not violate the "reasonable expectation of privacy" described in *Katz*.

Just last Term, we considered an argument much like this. *Jones* held that tracking an automobile's whereabouts using a physically-mounted GPS receiver is a Fourth Amendment search. The Government argued that the *Katz* standard "show[ed] that no search occurred," as the defendant had "no 'reasonable expectation of privacy'" in his whereabouts on the public roads—a proposition with at least as much support in our case law as the one the State marshals here. But because the GPS receiver had been physically mounted on the defendant's automobile (thus intruding on his "effects"), we held that tracking the vehicle's movements was a search: a person's "Fourth Amendment rights do not rise or fall with the *Katz* formulation." The *Katz* reasonable-expectations test "has been *added to,* not *substituted for,*" the traditional property-based understanding of the Fourth Amendment, and so is unnecessary to consider when the government gains evidence by physically intruding on constitutionally protected areas.

Thus, we need not decide whether the officers' investigation of Jardines' home violated his expectation of privacy under *Katz*. One virtue of the Fourth Amendment's property-rights baseline is that it keeps easy cases easy. That the officers learned what they learned only by physically intruding on Jardines' property to gather evidence is enough to establish that a search occurred. . . .

Justice ALITO, with whom THE CHIEF JUSTICE, Justice KENNEDY, and Justice BREYER join, dissenting.

The Court's decision in this important Fourth Amendment case is based on a putative rule of trespass law that is nowhere to be found in the annals of Anglo-American jurisprudence.

The law of trespass generally gives members of the public a license to use a walkway to approach the front door of a house and to remain there for a brief time. This license is not limited to persons who intend to speak to an occupant or who actually do so. (Mail carriers and persons delivering packages and flyers are examples of individuals who may lawfully approach a front door without intending to converse.) Nor is the license restricted to categories of visitors whom an occupant of the dwelling is likely to welcome; as the Court acknowledges, this license applies even to "solicitors, hawkers and peddlers of all kinds." And the license even extends to police officers who wish to gather evidence against an occupant (by asking potentially incriminating questions).

According to the Court, however, the police officer in this case, Detective Bartelt, committed a trespass because he was accompanied during his otherwise lawful visit to the front door of respondent's house by his dog, Franky. Where is the authority evidencing such a rule? Dogs have been domesticated for about 12,000 years; they were ubiquitous in both this country and Britain at the time of the adoption of the Fourth Amendment; and their acute sense of smell has been used in law enforcement for centuries. Yet the Court has been unable to find a single case—from the United States or any other common-law nation—that supports the rule on which its decision is based. Thus, trespass law provides no support for the Court's holding today.

The Court's decision is also inconsistent with the reasonable-expectations-of-privacy test that the Court adopted in *Katz v. United States.* A reasonable person understands that odors emanating from a house may be detected from locations that are open to the public, and a reasonable person will not count on the strength of those odors remaining within the range that, while detectible by a dog, cannot be smelled by a human. . . .

The opinion of the Court may leave a reader with the mistaken impression that Detective Bartelt and Franky remained on respondent's property for a prolonged period of time and conducted a far-flung exploration of the front yard. But that is not what happened. . . . A critical fact that the Court omits is that, as respondent's counsel explained at oral argument, this entire process—walking down the driveway and front path to the front door, waiting for Franky to find the strongest source of the odor, and walking back to the car—took approximately a minute or two. Thus, the amount of time that Franky and the detective remained at the front porch was even less. The Court also fails to mention that, while Detective Bartelt apparently did not personally smell the odor of marijuana coming from the house, another officer who subsequently stood on the front porch, Detective Pedraja, did notice that smell and was able to identify it.

The Court concludes that the conduct in this case was a search because Detective Bartelt exceeded the boundaries of the license to approach the house that is recognized by the law of trespass, but the Court's interpretation of the scope of that license is unfounded.

It is said that members of the public may lawfully proceed along a walkway leading to the front door of a house because custom grants them a license to do so. This rule encompasses categories of visitors whom most homeowners almost certainly wish to allow to approach their front doors—friends, relatives, mail carriers, persons making deliveries. But it also reaches categories of visitors who are less universally welcome—"solicitors," "hawkers," "peddlers," and the like. The law might attempt to draw fine lines between categories of welcome and unwelcome visitors, distinguishing, for example, between tolerable and intolerable door-to-door peddlers (Girl Scouts selling cookies versus adults selling aluminum siding) or between police officers on agreeable and disagreeable missions (gathering information about a bothersome neighbor versus asking potentially incriminating questions). But the law of trespass has not attempted such a difficult taxonomy.

Of course, this license has certain spatial and temporal limits. A visitor must stick to the path that is typically used to approach a front door, such as a paved walkway. A visitor cannot traipse through the garden, meander into the backyard, or take other circuitous detours that veer from the pathway that a visitor would customarily use. . . . Nor, as a general matter, may a visitor come to the front door in the middle of the night without an express invitation. . . . Similarly, a visitor may not linger at the front door for an extended period. The license is limited to the amount of time it would customarily take to approach the door, pause long enough to see if someone is home, and (if not expressly invited to stay longer), leave.

As I understand the law of trespass and the scope of the implied license, a visitor who adheres to these limitations is not necessarily required to ring the doorbell, knock on the door, or attempt to speak with an occupant. For example, mail carriers, persons making deliveries, and individuals distributing flyers may leave the items they are carrying and depart without making any attempt to converse. A pedestrian or motorist looking for a particular address may walk up to a front door in order to check a house number that is hard to see from the sidewalk or road. A neighbor who knows that the residents are away may approach the door to retrieve an accumulation of newspapers that might signal to a potential burglar that the house is unoccupied.

As the majority acknowledges, this implied license to approach the front door extends to the police. As we recognized in *Kentucky v. King*, 131 S. Ct. 1849 (2011), police officers do not engage in a search when they approach the front door of a residence and seek to engage in what is termed a "knock and talk," *i.e.*, knocking on the door and seeking to speak to an occupant for the purpose of gathering evidence. Even when the objective of a "knock and talk" is to obtain evidence that will lead to the homeowner's arrest and prosecution, the license to approach still applies. In other words, gathering evidence—even damning evidence—is a lawful activity that falls within the scope of the license to approach. And when officers walk up to the front door of a house, they are permitted to see, hear, and smell whatever can be detected from a lawful vantage point. . . .

The Court concludes that Detective Bartelt went too far because he had the "*objectiv[e] ... purpose* to conduct a search." What this means, I take it, is that anyone aware of what Detective Bartelt did would infer that his subjective purpose was to gather evidence. But if this is the Court's point, then a standard "knock and talk" and most other police visits would likewise constitute searches. With the exception of visits to serve warrants or civil process, police almost always approach homes with a purpose of discovering information. That is certainly the objective of a "knock and talk." The Court offers no meaningful way of distinguishing the "objective purpose" of a "knock and talk" from the "objective purpose" of Detective Bartelt's conduct here.

The Court contends that a "knock and talk" is different because it involves talking, and "all are invited" to do that. But a police officer who approaches the front door of a house in accordance with the limitations already discussed may gather evidence by means other than talking. The officer may observe items in plain view and smell odors coming from the house. So the Court's "objective purpose" argument cannot stand.

What the Court must fall back on, then, is the particular instrument that Detective Bartelt used to detect the odor of marijuana, namely, his dog. But in the entire body of common-law decisions, the Court has not found a single case holding that a visitor to the front door of a home commits a trespass if the visitor is accompanied by a dog on a leash. On the contrary, the common law allowed even unleashed dogs to wander on private property without committing a trespass.

The Court responds that "[i]t is not the dog that is the problem, but the behavior that here involved use of the dog." But where is the support in the law of trespass for *this* proposition? Dogs' keen sense of smell has been used in law enforcement for centuries. The antiquity of this practice is evidenced by a Scottish law from 1318 that made it a crime to "disturb a tracking dog or the men coming with it for pursuing thieves or seizing malefactors." If bringing a tracking dog to the front door of a home constituted a trespass, one would expect at least one case to have arisen during the past 800 years. But the Court has found none.

For these reasons, the real law of trespass provides no support for the Court's holding today. While the Court claims that its reasoning has "ancient and durable roots," its trespass rule is really a newly struck counterfeit. . . .

NOTES & QUESTIONS ON CONTRABAND-SNIFFING DOGS

1. *Reconsidering trespass.* In *Jardines*, the police crossed private property and used a drug-sniffing dog on the front porch of a house. Yet again, the Court invoked a trespass theory to explain why the dog's use in *Jardines* was impermissible, but the dog's use in *Caballes* was not. According to the Court, the police trespassed on the property to get to the porch. Although there exists an implied permission for all visitors to cross personal property to knock on the front door of a house, the Court concluded that this limited license for the purpose of knocking on the front door did not extend to the use of a canine unit to smell odors emanating from the house. Once again, the *Katz* "reasonable expectations" framework played little or no role in the

analysis. The majority speaks of a "physical intrusion" on the property but does not use the actual term "trespass." Does the avoidance of this legal term of art carry any significance? Certainly the dissent believed not and argued that the Court applied the trespass theory once again. Which concept—reasonable expectation of privacy or physical trespass—best resolves this case?

2. *Original meaning of the Fourth Amendment.* Did the framers of the Fourth Amendment understand its meaning in terms of trespass? Or was the concept of reasonableness (à la *Katz*) in the forefront of their minds? On this issue, see Laura Donahue, *The Original Fourth Amendment*, 83 U. Chi. L. Rev. 1181 (2016) (arguing that the Fourth Amendment originally had nothing to do with reasonableness but simply meant that the state could not enter a home without a specific warrant or to effectuate a felony arrest). Donahue argues that although the Fourth Amendment refers to *unreasonable* searches, the framers believed that "reasonable" searches of the home required a specific warrant, and that the absence of a specific warrant rendered such searches patently "unreasonable."

3. *Implied license.* In *Jardines*, much of the dispute between the majority and the dissent involves the scope of the implied license that homeowners typically give to the public to approach their property and knock on the front door or otherwise attempt to make contact (absent a gate or no-trespassing sign). The majority viewed the license as not extending to a police officer approaching the home with the goal of securing evidence against the resident, while Justice Alito in dissent concluded that the implied license applies as much to the police as it does to other members of the public. Which side do you agree with? For more discussion, see *Fourth Amendment—Trespass Test—Florida v. Jardines*, 127 Harv. L. Rev. 228, 232 (2013).

4. *Canine technology.* Is the sniffing of a police dog any different from the smelling that a member of the public could engage in as they approach the door of a house? In other words, should courts consider a dog as a type of advanced "technology"—like a machine-like sensor—or should they view the dog's ability as a biological "sense," analogous to the sights and smells that police officers could certainly receive, without a warrant, as they approach a house? Certainly, police officers are not required to turn off their eyes or ears or noses when they approach a house. Can the same thing be said of a police dog specifically trained to engage in contraband detection? For a discussion, see Irus Braverman, *Passing the Sniff Test: Police Dogs as Surveillance Technology*, 61 Buff. L. Rev. 81, 108 (2013). Or perhaps dogs are in neither category because "the canine sniff is sui generis." *United States v. Place*, 462 U.S. 696, 707 (1983). If the latter is true, does this suggest that dog-sniffing is not analogous to other investigatory conduct and therefore should be elevated independently?

D. PRIVACY IN DISCARDED GARBAGE

Generally speaking, the police are permitted to rummage through refuse deposited curbside that is intended for garbage collection by the local sanitation department. What expectations does a resident have with regard to garbage destined for the dump? Certainly, the resident expects others to handle and view the garbage, though probably with the assumption that the garbage will only be identified after it is commingled with the refuse of others, making it impossible to identify which garbage came from which house once it is rotting in the collective mass of the landfill or even in the back of the sanitation truck. However, under the *Katz* framework, a mere expectation of privacy (or in this case, anonymity) is insufficient. The expectation must also be *reasonable*, which in the case of garbage it is not.

In the following case, the Supreme Court must determine whether the police may, without a warrant, rummage through refuse left at the curb for garbage collection. As you read the case, think about what expectations of privacy residents might have with regard to items that they no longer wish to own and have designated for transfer to a third party. The take-away from *Greenwood* may be simple: Be careful what you throw away.

California v. Greenwood

Supreme Court of the United States
486 U.S. 35 (1988)

Justice WHITE delivered the opinion of the Court.

The issue here is whether the Fourth Amendment prohibits the warrantless search and seizure of garbage left for collection outside the curtilage of a home. We conclude, in accordance with the vast majority of lower courts that have addressed the issue, that it does not.

I

In early 1984, Investigator Jenny Stracner of the Laguna Beach Police Department received information indicating that respondent Greenwood might be engaged in narcotics trafficking. Stracner learned that a criminal suspect had informed a federal drug enforcement agent in February 1984 that a truck filled with illegal drugs was en route to the Laguna Beach address at which Greenwood resided. In addition, a neighbor complained of heavy vehicular traffic late at night in front of Greenwood's single-family home. The neighbor reported that the vehicles remained at Greenwood's house for only a few minutes.

Stracner sought to investigate this information by conducting a surveillance of Greenwood's home. She observed several vehicles make brief stops at the house during the late-night and early morning hours, and she followed a truck from the house to a residence that had previously been under investigation as a narcotics-trafficking location.

On April 6, 1984, Stracner asked the neighborhood's regular trash collector to pick up the plastic garbage bags that Greenwood had left on the curb in front of his house and to turn the bags over to her without mixing their contents with garbage from other houses. The trash collector cleaned his truck bin of other refuse, collected the garbage bags from the street in front of Greenwood's house, and turned the bags over to Stracner. The officer searched through the rubbish and found items indicative of narcotics use. She recited the information that she had gleaned from the trash search in an affidavit in support of a warrant to search Greenwood's home.

Police officers encountered both respondents at the house later that day when they arrived to execute the warrant. The police discovered quantities of cocaine and hashish during their search of the house. Respondents were arrested on felony narcotics charges. They subsequently posted bail.

The police continued to receive reports of many late-night visitors to the Greenwood house. On May 4, Investigator Robert Rahaeuser obtained Greenwood's garbage from the regular trash collector in the same manner as had Stracner. The garbage again contained evidence of narcotics use.

Rahaeuser secured another search warrant for Greenwood's home based on the information from the second trash search. The police found more narcotics and evidence of narcotics trafficking when they executed the warrant. Greenwood was again arrested. . . .

II

The warrantless search and seizure of the garbage bags left at the curb outside the Greenwood house would violate the Fourth Amendment only if respondents manifested a subjective expectation of privacy in their garbage that society accepts as objectively reasonable. Respondents do not disagree with this standard.

They assert, however, that they had, and exhibited, an expectation of privacy with respect to the trash that was searched by the police: The trash, which was placed on the street for collection at a fixed time, was contained in opaque plastic bags, which the garbage collector was expected to pick up, mingle with the trash of others, and deposit at the garbage dump. The trash was only temporarily on the street, and there was little likelihood that it would be inspected by anyone.

It may well be that respondents did not expect that the contents of their garbage bags would become known to the police or other members of the public. An expectation of privacy does not give rise to Fourth Amendment protection, however, unless society is prepared to accept that expectation as objectively reasonable.

Here, we conclude that respondents exposed their garbage to the public sufficiently to defeat their claim to Fourth Amendment protection. It is common knowledge that plastic garbage bags left on or at the side of a public street are readily accessible to animals, children, scavengers, snoops, and other members of the public. Moreover, respondents placed their refuse at the curb for the express purpose of conveying it to a third party, the trash collector, who might himself have sorted through respondents' trash or permitted others, such as the police, to do so. Accordingly, having deposited their garbage "in an area particularly suited for public inspection and, in a manner of speaking, public consumption, for the express purpose of having strangers take it," respondents could have had no reasonable expectation of privacy in the inculpatory items that they discarded.

Furthermore, as we have held, the police cannot reasonably be expected to avert their eyes from evidence of criminal activity that could have been observed by any member of the public. Hence, "[w]hat a person knowingly exposes to the public, even in his own home or office, is not a subject of Fourth Amendment protection." We held in *Smith v. Maryland,* 442 U.S. 735 (1979), for example, that the police did not violate the Fourth Amendment by causing a pen register to be installed at the telephone company's offices to record the telephone numbers dialed by a criminal suspect. An individual has no legitimate expectation of privacy in the numbers dialed on his telephone, we reasoned, because he voluntarily conveys those numbers to the telephone company when he uses the telephone. Again, we observed that "a person has no legitimate expectation of privacy in information he voluntarily turns over to third parties."

Similarly, we held in *California v. Ciraolo,* that the police were not required by the Fourth Amendment to obtain a warrant before conducting surveillance of the respondent's fenced backyard from a private plane flying at an altitude of 1,000 feet. We concluded that the respondent's expectation that his yard was protected from such surveillance was unreasonable because "[a]ny member of the public flying in this airspace who glanced down could have seen everything that these officers observed."

Our conclusion that society would not accept as reasonable respondents' claim to an expectation of privacy in trash left for collection in an area accessible to the public is reinforced by the unanimous rejection of similar claims by the Federal Courts of Appeals. . . .

Justice BRENNAN, with whom Justice MARSHALL joins, dissenting.

Every week for two months, and at least once more a month later, the Laguna Beach police clawed through the trash that respondent Greenwood left in opaque, sealed bags on the curb outside his home. Complete strangers minutely scrutinized their bounty, undoubtedly dredging up intimate details of Greenwood's private life and habits. The intrusions proceeded without a warrant, and no court before or since has concluded that the police acted on probable cause to believe Greenwood was engaged in any criminal activity.

Scrutiny of another's trash is contrary to commonly accepted notions of civilized behavior. I suspect, therefore, that members of our society will be shocked to learn that the Court, the ultimate guarantor of liberty, deems unreasonable our expectation that the aspects of our private lives that are concealed safely in a trash bag will not become public.

I

. . . The Framers of the Fourth Amendment understood that "unreasonable searches" of "paper[s] and effects"—no less than "unreasonable searches" of "person[s] and houses"—infringe privacy. As early as 1878, this Court acknowledged that the contents of "[l]etters and sealed packages . . . in the mail are as fully guarded from examination and inspection . . . as if they were retained by the parties forwarding them in their own domiciles." In short, so long as a package is "closed against inspection," the Fourth Amendment protects its contents, "wherever they may be," and the police must obtain a warrant to search it just "as is required when papers are subjected to search in one's own household."

With the emergence of the reasonable-expectation-of-privacy analysis, we have reaffirmed this fundamental principle. In *Robbins v. California,* 453 U.S. 420 (1981), for example, Justice Stewart, writing for a plurality of four, pronounced that "unless the container is such that its contents may be said to be in plain view, those contents are fully protected by the Fourth Amendment," and soundly rejected any distinction for Fourth Amendment purposes among various opaque, sealed containers. . . . Accordingly, we have found a reasonable expectation of privacy in the contents of a 200-pound "double-locked footlocker," a "comparatively small, unlocked suitcase," a "totebag," and "packages wrapped in green opaque plastic."

Our precedent, therefore, leaves no room to doubt that had respondents been carrying their personal effects in opaque, sealed plastic bags—identical to the ones they placed on the curb—their privacy would have been protected from warrantless police intrusion. So far as Fourth Amendment protection is concerned, opaque plastic bags are every bit as worthy as "packages wrapped in green opaque plastic" and "double-locked footlocker[s]."

II

Respondents deserve no less protection just because Greenwood used the bags to discard rather than to transport his personal effects. Their contents are not inherently any less private, and Greenwood's decision to discard them, at least in the manner in which he did, does not diminish his expectation of privacy.

A trash bag, like any of the above-mentioned containers, "is a common repository for one's personal effects" and, even more than many of them, is "therefore . . . inevitably associated with the expectation of privacy." A single bag of trash testifies eloquently to the eating, reading, and recreational habits of the person who produced it. A search of trash, like a search of the bedroom, can relate intimate details about sexual practices, health, and personal hygiene. Like rifling through desk drawers or intercepting phone calls, rummaging through trash can divulge the target's financial and professional status, political affiliations and inclinations, private thoughts, personal relationships, and romantic interests. It cannot be doubted that a sealed trash bag harbors telling evidence of the "intimate activity associated with the 'sanctity of a man's home and the privacies of life,'" which the Fourth Amendment is designed to protect. . . .

Beyond a generalized expectation of privacy, many municipalities, whether for reasons of privacy, sanitation, or both, reinforce confidence in the integrity of sealed trash containers by "prohibit[ing] anyone, except authorized employees of the Town . . . , to rummage into, pick up, collect, move or otherwise interfere with articles or materials placed on . . . any public street for collection." In fact, the California Constitution, as interpreted by the State's highest court, guarantees a right of privacy in trash vis-à-vis government officials.

That is not to deny that isolated intrusions into opaque, sealed trash containers occur. When, acting on their own, "animals, children, scavengers, snoops, [or] other members of the public," *actually* rummage through a bag of trash and expose its contents to plain view, "police cannot reasonably be expected to avert their eyes from evidence of criminal activity that could have been observed by any member of the public." . . .

Had Greenwood flaunted his intimate activity by strewing his trash all over the curb for all to see, or had some nongovernmental intruder invaded his privacy and done the same, I could accept the Court's conclusion that an expectation of privacy would have been unreasonable. Similarly, had police searching the city dump run across incriminating evidence that, despite commingling with the trash of others, still retained its identity as Greenwood's, we would have a different case. But all that Greenwood "exposed . . . to the public," were the exteriors of several opaque, sealed containers. Until the bags were opened by police, they hid their contents from the public's view every bit as much as did Chadwick's double-locked footlocker and Robbins' green, plastic wrapping. Faithful application of the warrant requirement does not require police to "avert their eyes from evidence of criminal activity that could have been observed by any member of the public." Rather, it only requires them to adhere to norms of privacy that members of the public plainly acknowledge. . . .

PROBLEM CASE

Joseph R. Redmon was indicted in 1996 for possession of cocaine. A multi-jurisdictional task force was tracking a shipment of cocaine from California to Illinois. An investigation by the task force led agents to Redmon, who lived in a townhouse in Urbana, Illinois. The police approached the townhouse and noticed a garbage can located against the wall of his garage on a shared driveway that connected eight townhouses together. The police removed the contents of the garbage can without a warrant and found evidence that led them to charge Redmon with cocaine possession.

Did this constitute a search? Redmon argued that it did and was far different from the police activity in *Greenwood,* which involved trash left at the curbside by a public road. In contrast, Redmon's garbage was still within the "curtilage" of his home, i.e., the property just adjacent to the structure. How would you resolve Redmon's claim? Was this a search? Did Redmon have a reasonable expectation of privacy for garbage that could be accessed by a shared driveway? Does it matter if the municipality had an ordinance prohibiting garbage left at the curb for collection? What result if Redmon lived in a single-family home and left his garbage against the garage at the end of a *private* driveway?

For more on this case, see *United States v. Redmon,* 138 F.3d 1109, 1110 (7th Cir. 1998) ("While most people have a good idea what 'garbage' is, many people do not realize that garbage can cause some serious constitutional issues. This is such a case.").

NOTES & QUESTIONS ON GARBAGE

1. *The color of the trash bag.* Does it matter what color of trash bag the resident uses to discard his or her garbage? Justices Brennan and Marshall seem to think so. When a resident places garbage in a sealed and opaque bag, the resident has a reasonable expectation of privacy, as opposed to the resident who uses a transparent bag whose contents are visible to all who walk by. For a discussion, see Mary Elizabeth Minor, *Was the Right of Privacy Trashed in* California v. Greenwood*?,* 24 Tulsa L.J. 401 (1989) ("Greenwood's garbage bags were sealed at the top, and nothing was visible to onlookers."); *People v. Edwards,* 71 Cal. 2d 1096, 1104 (1969) ("We can readily ascribe many reasons why residents would not want their castaway clothing, letters, medicine bottles or other telltale refuse and trash to be examined by neighbors or others, at least not until the trash has lost its identity and meaning by becoming part of a large conglomeration of trash elsewhere. Half truths leading to rumor and gossip may readily flow from an attempt to 'read' the contents of another's trash."). However, courts have held that residents do not have a reasonable expectation of privacy in trash left out for garbage collection in opaque containers at the curb. See *United States v. Wilkinson,* 926 F.2d 22, 27 (1st Cir. 1991).

STATE LAW REQUIREMENTS

Several states have adopted more protective notions of garbage privacy under state constitutional provisions, which need not dovetail with the Supreme Court's interpretation of the Fourth Amendment. See, e.g., *State v. Boland*, 115 Wash. 2d 571, 581 (1990) ("While a person must reasonably expect a licensed trash collector will remove the contents of his trash can, this expectation does not also infer an expectation of governmental intrusion."); *State v. Evans*, 159 Wash. 2d 402, 412 (2007) ("garbage in a curbside garbage container is not abandoned and police, therefore, needed a warrant to search it"); *State v. Hempele*, 120 N.J. 182, 202 (1990) ("Given the secrets that refuse can disclose, it is reasonable for a person to prefer that his or her garbage remain private.").

In *Hempele*, the court applied Article 1(7) of the New Jersey Constitution, which states that "[t]he right of the people to be secure in their persons, houses, papers, and effects, against unreasonable searches and seizures, shall not be violated; and no warrant shall issue except upon probable cause, supported by oath or affirmation, and particularly describing the place to be searched and the papers and things to be seized." N.J. Const. art. I, ¶7. Similarly, as noted by the dissent in *Greenwood*, the California Supreme Court concluded that the privacy of discarded garbage was protected by the California Constitution: "The placement of one's trash barrels onto the sidewalk for collection is not, however, necessarily an abandonment of one's trash to the police or general public." *People v. Krivda*, 5 Cal. 3d 357, 366, 486 P.2d 1262, 1268 (1971).

E. PRIVACY IN PUBLIC MOVEMENTS

When we move around in public, usually nobody notices. Or nobody cares. People *could* track our movements if they really cared to. Think of celebrities and the paparazzi who chase them—in that situation, the intense public interest causes the celebrity to lose the typical anonymity of urban life. But that is very much the exception that proves the rule. Those who are not celebrities move around in public with relative freedom to blend into the crowd.

What happens when the police seek to collect data regarding public movements? It is not private data, strictly speaking, because it involves movement in public. On the other hand, it has the potential to tell so much about our lives, especially when aggregated in bulk form. Knowing where someone went at one hour of one day is not significant, but knowing where someone went every moment of every day for months at a time will allow state authorities to construct a surprisingly rich portrait of an individual's existence. The following two cases involve precisely this form of aggregation. The first involves a GPS tracker attached to a car; the second involves the collection of cell phone location data.

1. GPS Tracking of Automobiles

The use of GPS tracking technology has long been in common use. In the following case, police authorities attached a GPS tracker to a suspect's car and by doing so

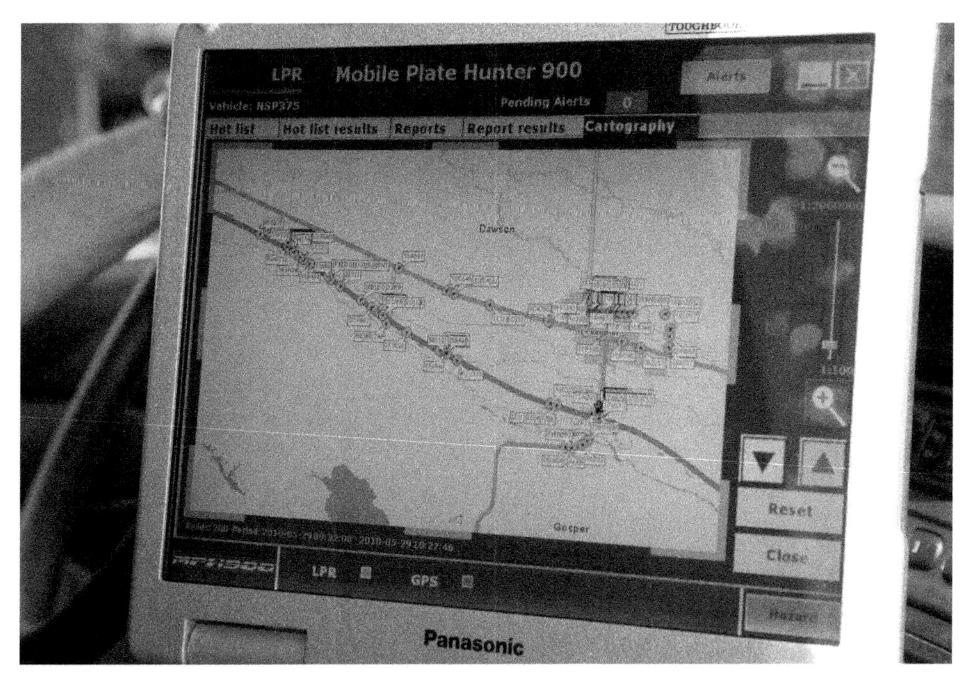

A computer screen displaying GPS locations of vehicles near Lexington, NE. Automated License Plate Readers scan and compare plates against a national database of stolen plates and vehicles, missing persons, and vehicle owners with outstanding felony warrants. (Mikael Karlsson/Alamy Stock Photo)

were able to catalog his movements—to the extent that he used his car—over an extended period of time (almost a month). On the one hand, the GPS tracker was clearly intrusive because the police officers attached it to his private property—his car—and did so without a warrant. On the other hand, the information collected by the GPS was information that the "public"—broadly construed—could collect simply by observing his vehicle on public roadways. The question this case asks is whether this investigative technique constitutes a search for purposes of the Fourth Amendment and if so, why? Is it because the driver has a reasonable expectation of privacy in his car's movements on public roadways or is it because the police performed a trespass when they placed the tracker on his vehicle?

United States v. Jones

Supreme Court of the United States
565 U.S. 400 (2012)

Justice Scalia delivered the opinion of the Court.

In 2004 respondent Antoine Jones, owner and operator of a nightclub in the District of Columbia, came under suspicion of trafficking in narcotics and was made the target of an investigation by a joint FBI and Metropolitan Police Department task force. Officers employed various investigative techniques, including visual surveillance of the nightclub, installation of a camera focused on the front door of the club, and a pen register and wiretap covering Jones's cellular phone.

Based in part on information gathered from these sources, in 2005 the Government applied to the United States District Court for the District of Columbia for a warrant authorizing the use of an electronic tracking device on the Jeep Grand Cherokee registered to Jones's wife. A warrant issued, authorizing installation of the device in the District of Columbia and within 10 days.

On the 11th day, and not in the District of Columbia but in Maryland, agents installed a GPS tracking device on the undercarriage of the Jeep while it was parked in a public parking lot. Over the next 28 days, the Government used the device to track the vehicle's movements, and once had to replace the device's battery when the vehicle was parked in a different public lot in Maryland. By means of signals from multiple satellites, the device established the vehicle's location within 50 to 100 feet, and communicated that location by cellular phone to a Government computer. It relayed more than 2,000 pages of data over the 4-week period.

The Government ultimately obtained a multiple-count indictment charging Jones and several alleged co-conspirators with, as relevant here, conspiracy to distribute and possess with intent to distribute five kilograms or more of cocaine and 50 grams or more of cocaine base. . . .

II

The Fourth Amendment provides in relevant part that "[t]he right of the people to be secure in their persons, houses, papers, and effects, against unreasonable searches and seizures, shall not be violated." It is beyond dispute that a vehicle is an "effect" as that term is used in the Amendment. We hold that the Government's installation of a GPS device on a target's vehicle, and its use of that device to monitor the vehicle's movements, constitutes a "search."

It is important to be clear about what occurred in this case: The Government physically occupied private property for the purpose of obtaining information. We have no doubt that such a physical intrusion would have been considered a "search" within the meaning of the Fourth Amendment when it was adopted. [In] *Entick v. Carrington,* 95 Eng. Rep. 807 (C.P. 1765) . . . Lord Camden expressed in plain terms the significance of property rights in search-and-seizure analysis: "[O]ur law holds the property of every man so sacred, that no man can set his foot upon his neighbour's close without his leave; if he does he is a trespasser, though he does no damage at all; if he will tread upon his neighbour's ground, he must justify it by law."

The text of the Fourth Amendment reflects its close connection to property, since otherwise it would have referred simply to "the right of the people to be secure against unreasonable searches and seizures"; the phrase "in their persons, houses, papers, and effects" would have been superfluous.

Consistent with this understanding, our Fourth Amendment jurisprudence was tied to common law trespass, at least until the latter half of the 20th century. Thus, in *Olmstead v. United States,* 277 U.S. 438 (1928), we held that wiretaps attached to telephone wires on the public streets did not constitute a Fourth Amendment search because "[t]here was no entry of the houses or offices of the defendants."

Our later cases, of course, have deviated from that exclusively property-based approach. In *Katz v. United States,* 389 U.S. 347, 351 (1967), we said that "the Fourth Amendment protects people, not places," and found a violation in attachment of an eavesdropping device to a public telephone booth. Our later cases have applied the analysis of Justice Harlan's concurrence in that case, which said that a violation occurs when government officers violate a person's "reasonable expectation of privacy."

The Government contends that the Harlan standard shows that no search occurred here, since Jones had no "reasonable expectation of privacy" in the area of the Jeep accessed by Government agents (its underbody) and in the locations of the Jeep on the public roads, which were visible to all. But we need not address the Government's contentions, because Jones's Fourth Amendment rights do not rise or fall with the *Katz* formulation. At bottom, we must "assur[e] preservation of that degree of privacy against government that existed when the Fourth Amendment was adopted." As explained, for most of our history the Fourth Amendment was understood to embody a particular concern for government trespass upon the areas ("persons, houses, papers, and effects") it enumerates. *Katz* did not repudiate that understanding. Less than two years later the Court upheld defendants' contention that the Government could not introduce against them conversations between *other* people obtained by warrantless placement of electronic surveillance devices in their homes. The opinion rejected the dissent's contention that there was no Fourth Amendment violation "unless the conversational privacy of the homeowner himself is invaded." . . .

More recently, in *Soldal v. Cook County,* 506 U.S. 56 (1992), the Court unanimously rejected the argument that although a "seizure" had occurred "in a 'technical' sense" when a trailer home was forcibly removed, no Fourth Amendment violation occurred because law enforcement had not "invade[d] the [individuals'] privacy." *Katz,* the Court explained, established that "property rights are not the sole measure of Fourth Amendment violations," but did not "snuf[f] out the previously recognized protection for property." As Justice Brennan explained in his concurrence in *Knotts, Katz* did not erode the principle "that, when the Government *does* engage in physical intrusion of a constitutionally protected area in order to obtain information, that intrusion may constitute a violation of the Fourth Amendment." We have embodied that preservation of past rights in our very definition of "reasonable expectation of privacy" which we have said to be an expectation "that has a source outside of the Fourth Amendment, either by reference to concepts of real or personal property law or to understandings that are recognized and permitted by society." *Katz* did not narrow the Fourth Amendment's scope.

The Government contends that several of our post-*Katz* cases foreclose the conclusion that what occurred here constituted a search. It relies principally on two cases in which we rejected Fourth Amendment challenges to "beepers," electronic tracking devices that represent another form of electronic monitoring. The first case, *Knotts,* upheld against Fourth Amendment challenge the use of a "beeper" that had been placed in a container of chloroform, allowing law enforcement to monitor the location of the container. We said that there had been no infringement of Knotts' reasonable expectation of privacy since the information obtained—the location of the automobile carrying the container on public roads, and the location of the off-loaded container in open fields near Knotts' cabin—had been voluntarily conveyed to the public. But as we have discussed, the *Katz* reasonable-expectation-of-privacy test has been *added to,* not *substituted for,* the common-law trespassory test. The holding in *Knotts* addressed only the former, since the latter was not at issue. The beeper had been placed in the container before it came into Knotts' possession, with the consent of the then-owner. Knotts did not challenge that installation, and we specifically declined to consider its effect on the Fourth Amendment analysis. *Knotts* would be relevant, perhaps, if the Government were making the argument that what would otherwise be an unconstitutional search is not such where it produces only public information. The Government does not make that argument, and we know of no case that would support it. . . .

Finally, the Government's position gains little support from our conclusion in *Oliver v. United States,* 466 U.S. 170 (1984), that officers' information-gathering intrusion on an "open field" did not constitute a Fourth Amendment search even though it was a trespass at common law. Quite simply, an open field, unlike the curtilage of a home, is not one of those protected areas enumerated in the Fourth Amendment. The Government's physical intrusion on such an area—unlike its intrusion on the "effect" at issue here—is of no Fourth Amendment significance.

Justice ALITO, with whom Justice GINSBURG, Justice BREYER, and Justice KAGAN join, concurring in the judgment.

This case requires us to apply the Fourth Amendment's prohibition of unreasonable searches and seizures to a 21st-century surveillance technique, the use of a Global Positioning System (GPS) device to monitor a vehicle's movements for an extended period of time. Ironically, the Court has chosen to decide this case based on 18th-century tort law. By attaching a small GPS device to the underside of the vehicle that respondent drove, the law enforcement officers in this case engaged in conduct that might have provided grounds in 1791 for a suit for trespass to chattels. And for this reason, the Court concludes, the installation and use of the GPS device constituted a search. . . .

The Fourth Amendment prohibits "unreasonable searches and seizures," and the Court makes very little effort to explain how the attachment or use of the GPS device fits within these terms. The Court does not contend that there was a seizure. A seizure of property occurs when there is "some meaningful interference with an individual's possessory interests in that property," and here there was none. Indeed, the success of the surveillance technique that the officers employed was dependent on the fact that the GPS did not interfere in any way with the operation of the vehicle, for if any such interference had been detected, the device might have been discovered.

The Court does claim that the installation and use of the GPS constituted a search, but this conclusion is dependent on the questionable proposition that these two procedures cannot be separated for purposes of Fourth Amendment analysis. If these two procedures are analyzed separately, it is not at all clear from the Court's opinion why either should be regarded as a search. It is clear that the attachment of the GPS device was not itself a search; if the device had not functioned or if the officers had not used it, no information would have been obtained. And the Court does not contend that the use of the device constituted a search either. On the contrary, the Court accepts the holding in *United States v. Knotts*, 460 U.S. 276 (1983), that the use of a surreptitiously planted electronic device to monitor a vehicle's movements on public roads did not amount to a search.

The Court argues—and I agree—that "we must 'assur[e] preservation of that degree of privacy against government that existed when the Fourth Amendment was adopted.'" But it is almost impossible to think of late-18th-century situations that are analogous to what took place in this case. (Is it possible to imagine a case in which a constable secreted himself somewhere in a coach and remained there for a period of time in order to monitor the movements of the coach's owner?) The Court's theory seems to be that the concept of a search, as originally understood, comprehended any technical trespass that led to the gathering of evidence, but we know that this is incorrect. At common law, any unauthorized intrusion on private property was actionable, but a trespass on open fields, as opposed to the "curtilage" of a home, does not fall within the scope of the Fourth Amendment because private property outside the curtilage is not part of a "hous[e]" within the meaning of the Fourth Amendment.

The Court's reasoning in this case is very similar to that in the Court's early decisions involving wiretapping and electronic eavesdropping, namely, that a technical trespass followed by the gathering of evidence constitutes a search. In the early electronic surveillance cases, the Court concluded that a Fourth Amendment search occurred when private conversations were monitored as a result of an "unauthorized physical penetration into the premises occupied" by the defendant. In *Silverman,* 365 U.S. 505, 509 (1961), police officers listened to conversations in an attached home by inserting a "spike mike" through the wall that this house shared with the vacant house next door. This procedure was held to be a search because the mike made contact with a heating duct on the other side of the wall and thus "usurp[ed] . . . an integral part of the premises."

By contrast, in cases in which there was no trespass, it was held that there was no search. Thus, in *Olmstead v. United States,* 277 U.S. 438 (1928), the Court found that the Fourth Amendment did not apply because "[t]he taps from house lines were made in the streets near the houses." Similarly, the Court concluded that no search occurred in *Goldman v. United States,* 316 U.S. 129 (1942), where a "detectaphone" was placed on the outer wall of defendant's office for the purpose of overhearing conversations held within the room. . . .

Katz v. United States, 389 U.S. 347 (1967), finally did away with the old approach, holding that a trespass was not required for a Fourth Amendment violation. *Katz* involved the use of a listening device that was attached to the outside of a public telephone booth and that allowed police officers to eavesdrop on one end of the target's phone conversation. This procedure did not physically intrude on the area occupied by the target, but the *Katz* Court "repudiate[ed]" the old doctrine, and held that "[t]he fact that the electronic device employed . . . did not happen to penetrate the wall of the booth can have no constitutional significance." What mattered, the Court now held, was whether the conduct at issue "violated the privacy upon which [the defendant] justifiably relied while using the telephone booth."

Under this approach, as the Court later put it when addressing the relevance of a technical trespass, "an actual trespass is neither necessary *nor sufficient* to establish a constitutional violation." . . .

Disharmony with a substantial body of existing case law is only one of the problems with the Court's approach in this case. . . . First, the Court's reasoning largely disregards what is really important (the *use* of a GPS for the purpose of long-term tracking) and instead attaches great significance to something that most would view as relatively minor (attaching to the bottom of a car a small, light object that does not interfere in any way with the car's operation). . . . Second, the Court's approach leads to incongruous results. If the police attach a GPS device to a car and use the device to follow the car for even a brief time, under the Court's theory, the Fourth Amendment applies. But if the police follow the same car for a much longer period using unmarked cars and aerial assistance, this tracking is not subject to any Fourth Amendment constraints. . . . Third, under the Court's theory, the coverage of the Fourth Amendment may vary from State to State. If the events at issue here had occurred in a community property State or a State that has adopted the Uniform Marital Property Act, respondent would likely be an owner of the vehicle, and it would not matter whether the GPS was installed before or after his wife turned over the keys. . . . Fourth, the Court's reliance on the law of trespass will present particularly vexing problems in cases involving surveillance that is carried out by making electronic, as opposed to physical, contact with the item to be tracked. For example, suppose that the officers in the present case had followed respondent by surreptitiously activating a stolen vehicle detection system that came with the car when it was purchased. . . .

Justice SOTOMAYOR, concurring.

I join the Court's opinion because I agree that a search within the meaning of the Fourth Amendment occurs, at a minimum, "[w]here, as here, the Government obtains information by physically intruding on a constitutionally protected area." . . . Of course, the Fourth Amendment is not concerned only with trespassory intrusions on property. Rather, even in the absence of a trespass, "a Fourth Amendment search occurs when the government violates a subjective expectation of privacy that society recognizes as reasonable." . . . As the majority's opinion makes clear, however, *Katz*'s reasonable-expectation-of-privacy test augmented, but did not displace or diminish, the common-law trespassory test that preceded it. . . . Justice Alito's approach, which discounts altogether the constitutional relevance of the Government's physical intrusion on Jones' Jeep, erodes that longstanding protection for privacy expectations inherent in items of property that people possess or control. By contrast, the trespassory test applied in the majority's opinion reflects an irreducible constitutional minimum: When the Government physically invades personal property to gather information, a search occurs. The reaffirmation of that principle suffices to decide this case.

Nonetheless . . . physical intrusion is now unnecessary to many forms of surveillance. With increasing regularity, the Government will be capable of duplicating the monitoring undertaken in this case by enlisting factory- or owner-installed vehicle tracking devices or GPS-enabled smartphones. In cases of electronic or other novel modes of surveillance that do not depend upon a physical invasion on property, the majority opinion's trespassory test may provide little guidance. . . .

In cases involving even short-term monitoring, some unique attributes of GPS surveillance relevant to the *Katz* analysis will require particular attention. GPS monitoring generates a precise, comprehensive record of a person's public movements that reflects a wealth of detail about her familial, political, professional, religious, and sexual associations. The Government can store such records and efficiently mine them for information years into the future. And because GPS monitoring is cheap in comparison to conventional surveillance techniques and, by design, proceeds surreptitiously, it evades the ordinary checks that constrain abusive law enforcement practices: "limited police resources and community hostility."

Awareness that the Government may be watching chills associational and expressive freedoms. And the Government's unrestrained power to assemble data that reveal private aspects of identity is susceptible to abuse. The net result is that GPS monitoring—by making available at a relatively low cost such a substantial quantum of intimate information about any person whom the Government, in its unfettered discretion, chooses to track—may "alter the relationship between citizen and government in a way that is inimical to democratic society."

I would take these attributes of GPS monitoring into account when considering the existence of a reasonable societal expectation of privacy in the sum of one's public movements. I would ask whether people reasonably expect that their movements will be recorded and aggregated in a manner that enables the Government to ascertain, more or less at will, their political and religious beliefs, sexual habits, and so on. I do not regard as dispositive the fact that the Government might obtain the fruits of GPS monitoring through lawful conventional surveillance techniques. I would also consider the appropriateness of entrusting to the Executive, in the absence of any oversight from a coordinate branch, a tool so amenable to misuse, especially in light of the Fourth Amendment's goal to curb arbitrary exercises of police power to and prevent "a too permeating police surveillance."

More fundamentally, it may be necessary to reconsider the premise that an individual has no reasonable expectation of privacy in information voluntarily disclosed to third parties. This approach is ill suited to the digital age, in which people reveal a great deal of information about themselves to third parties in the course of carrying out mundane tasks. People disclose the phone numbers that they dial or text to their cellular providers; the URLs that they visit and the e-mail addresses with which they correspond to their Internet service providers; and the books,

> groceries, and medications they purchase to online retailers. Perhaps . . . some people may find the "tradeoff" of privacy for convenience "worthwhile," or come to accept this "diminution of privacy" as "inevitable," and perhaps not. I for one doubt that people would accept without complaint the warrantless disclosure to the Government of a list of every Web site they had visited in the last week, or month, or year. But whatever the societal expectations, they can attain constitutionally protected status only if our Fourth Amendment jurisprudence ceases to treat secrecy as a prerequisite for privacy. I would not assume that all information voluntarily disclosed to some member of the public for a limited purpose is, for that reason alone, disentitled to Fourth Amendment protection. . . . Resolution of these difficult questions in this case is unnecessary, however, because the Government's physical intrusion on Jones' Jeep supplies a narrower basis for decision. I therefore join the majority's opinion.

NOTES & QUESTIONS ON GPS TRACKING

1. *The inherent publicity of automobiles.* Justice Scalia concluded that placing a GPS tracker on a car constituted a search. In one sense, it is odd to think that a driver should have a reasonable expectation of privacy with regard to the public movements of their car. In reality, members of the public can see where a car is driven—the cities you visit, the streets the car takes, and so on. None of this is secret. What the GPS tracker does is record and maximize the type of information that a traditional police "tail" (an undercover police officer following a suspect) would collect. Nonetheless, the Court in *Jones* concluded that the *Katz* "reasonable expectation of privacy" framework was irrelevant because the police performed a physical trespass of the car, making it a search for Fourth Amendment purposes.

2. *Evaluating the trespass theory.* In *Jones*, the Justices largely agreed that the use of the GPS device constituted a search. However, they disagreed sharply about the application of the trespass theory, which several Justices found implausible and an unfortunate throwback to the pre-*Katz* jurisprudence on searches. Did *Jones* signal the end to the *Katz* framework? The majority insisted no. How can the two be consistent with each other? The two frameworks are supposedly additive. Either a physical trespass *or* a violation of a reasonable expectation of privacy will constitute a search. As you read this case, ask yourself what expectations of privacy an individual has with regard to movements in the public sphere, especially on public roadways. Also, does it matter that the police accomplished the tracking by touching (and attaching an object to) the private property of the suspect?

3. *Trespass theory and property law.* Do you agree with Justice Scalia's historical argument for the common law trespass test? Which law of trespass should be applied? The law of trespass at the time the Fourth Amendment was drafted or the law of trespass today? For a discussion of the test, see Laurent Sacharoff, *Constitutional Trespass*, 81 Tenn. L. Rev. 877, 882 (2014) (arguing that courts should apply "the majority trespass rule from the states—modified to conform to Fourth Amendment purposes").

2. Cell Phone Location Data

In the following case, the Supreme Court considers whether government access to cell phone location records constitutes a search. By using this information, government investigators can, in theory, produce a complete picture of an individual's location and movements over days, weeks, months, and even years. Given that people often travel without their cars (by using other modes of transport, including someone else's car), but almost always keep their cellphones at their side, cell phone location data will produce a far more intrusive picture of a person's life than a GPS tracker on an automobile. If police can look at cell phone location data without it being considered a search, does this produce the kind of intrusion that Justice Sotomayor predicted—and lamented—in her *Jones* concurrence?

Carpenter v. United States

Supreme Court of the United States
138 S. Ct. 2206 (2018)

Chief Justice Roberts delivered the opinion of the Court.

This case presents the question whether the Government conducts a search under the Fourth Amendment when it accesses historical cell phone records that provide a comprehensive chronicle of the user's past movements.

I

There are 396 million cell phone service accounts in the United States—for a Nation of 326 million people. Cell phones perform their wide and growing variety of functions by connecting to a set of radio antennas called "cell sites." Although cell sites are usually mounted on a tower, they can also be found on light posts, flagpoles, church steeples, or the sides of buildings. Cell sites typically have several directional antennas that divide the covered area into sectors.

Cell phones continuously scan their environment looking for the best signal, which generally comes from the closest cell site. Most modern devices, such as smartphones, tap into the wireless network several times a minute whenever their signal is on, even if the owner is not using one of the phone's features. Each time the phone connects to a cell site, it generates a time-stamped record known as cell-site location information (CSLI). The precision of this information depends on the size of the geographic area covered by the cell site. The greater the concentration of cell sites, the smaller the coverage area. As data usage from cell phones has increased, wireless carriers have installed more cell sites to handle the traffic. That has led to increasingly compact coverage areas, especially in urban areas.

Wireless carriers collect and store CSLI for their own business purposes, including finding weak spots in their network and applying "roaming" charges when another carrier routes data through their cell sites. In addition, wireless carriers often sell aggregated location records to data brokers, without individual identifying information of the sort at issue here. While carriers have long retained CSLI for the start and end of incoming calls, in recent years phone companies have also collected location information from the transmission of text messages and routine data connections. Accordingly, modern cell phones generate increasingly vast amounts of increasingly precise CSLI.

In 2011, police officers arrested four men suspected of robbing a series of Radio Shack and (ironically enough) T-Mobile stores in Detroit. One of the men confessed that, over the previous four months, the group (along with a rotating cast of getaway drivers and lookouts) had robbed nine different stores in Michigan and Ohio. The suspect identified 15 accomplices who had participated in the heists and gave the FBI some of their cell phone numbers; the FBI then reviewed his call records to identify additional numbers that he had called around the time of the robberies.

Based on that information, the prosecutors applied for court orders under the Stored Communications Act to obtain cell phone records for petitioner Timothy Carpenter and several other suspects. That statute, as amended in 1994, permits the Government to compel the disclosure of certain telecommunications records when it "offers specific and articulable facts showing that there are reasonable grounds to believe" that the records sought "are relevant and material to an ongoing criminal investigation." . . . Carpenter was charged with six counts of robbery and an additional six counts of carrying a firearm during a federal crime of violence. Prior to trial, Carpenter moved to suppress the cell-site data provided by the wireless carriers. He argued that the Government's seizure of the records violated the Fourth Amendment because they had been obtained without a warrant supported by probable cause. . . .

II

. . . For much of our history, Fourth Amendment search doctrine was "tied to common-law trespass" and focused on whether the Government "obtains information by physically intruding on a constitutionally protected area." More recently, the Court has recognized that "property rights are not the sole measure of Fourth Amendment violations." . . . Although no single rubric definitively resolves which expectations of privacy are entitled to protection, the analysis is informed by historical understandings "of what was deemed an unreasonable search and seizure when [the Fourth Amendment] was adopted." On this score, our cases have recognized some basic guideposts. First, that the Amendment seeks to secure "the privacies of life" against "arbitrary power." Second, and relatedly, that a central aim of the Framers was "to place obstacles in the way of a too permeating police surveillance." . . .

The case before us involves the Government's acquisition of wireless carrier cell-site records revealing the location of Carpenter's cell phone whenever it made or received calls. This sort of digital data—personal location information maintained by a third party—does not fit neatly under existing precedents. Instead, requests for cell-site records lie at the intersection of two lines of cases, both of which inform our understanding of the privacy interests at stake.

The first set of cases addresses a person's expectation of privacy in his physical location and movements. In *United States v. Knotts,* 460 U.S. 276 (1983), we considered the Government's use of a "beeper" to aid in tracking a vehicle through traffic. Police officers in that case planted a beeper in a container of chloroform before it was purchased by one of Knotts's co-conspirators. The officers (with intermittent aerial assistance) then followed the automobile carrying the container from Minneapolis to Knotts's cabin in Wisconsin, relying on the beeper's signal to help keep the vehicle in view. The Court concluded that the "augment[ed]" visual surveillance did not constitute a search because "[a] person traveling in an automobile on public thoroughfares has no reasonable expectation of privacy in his movements from one place to another." Since the movements of the vehicle and its final destination had been "voluntarily conveyed to anyone who wanted to look," Knotts could not assert a privacy interest in the information obtained.

This Court in *Knotts,* however, was careful to distinguish between the rudimentary tracking facilitated by the beeper and more sweeping modes of surveillance. The Court emphasized the "limited use which the government made of the signals from this particular beeper" during a discrete "automotive journey." Significantly, the Court reserved the question whether "different constitutional principles may be applicable" if "twenty-four hour surveillance of any citizen of this country [were] possible."

Three decades later, the Court considered more sophisticated surveillance of the sort envisioned in *Knotts* and found that different principles did indeed apply. In *United States v. Jones,* FBI agents installed a GPS tracking device on Jones's vehicle and remotely monitored the vehicle's movements for 28 days. The Court decided the case based on the Government's physical trespass of the vehicle. At the same time, five Justices agreed that related privacy concerns would be raised by, for example, "surreptitiously activating a stolen vehicle detection system" in Jones's car to track Jones himself, or conducting GPS tracking of his cell phone. Since GPS monitoring of a vehicle tracks "every movement" a person makes in that vehicle, the concurring Justices concluded that "longer term GPS monitoring in investigations of most offenses impinges on expectations of privacy"—regardless whether those movements were disclosed to the public at large.

In a second set of decisions, the Court has drawn a line between what a person keeps to himself and what he shares with others. We have previously held that "a person has no legitimate expectation of privacy in information he voluntarily turns over to third parties." That remains true "even if the information is revealed on the assumption that it will be used only for a limited purpose." *United States v. Miller,* 425 U.S. 435, 443 (1976). As a result, the Government is typically free to obtain such information from the recipient without triggering Fourth Amendment protections.

This third-party doctrine largely traces its roots to *Miller*. While investigating Miller for tax evasion, the Government subpoenaed his banks, seeking several months of canceled checks, deposit slips, and monthly statements. The Court rejected a Fourth Amendment challenge to the records collection. For one, Miller could "assert neither ownership nor possession" of the documents; they were "business records of the banks." For another, the nature of those records confirmed Miller's limited expectation of privacy, because the checks were "not confidential communications but negotiable instruments to be used in commercial transactions," and the bank statements contained information "exposed to [bank] employees in the ordinary course of business." The Court thus concluded that Miller had "take[n] the risk, in revealing his affairs to another, that the information [would] be conveyed by that person to the Government."

Three years later, *Smith* applied the same principles in the context of information conveyed to a telephone company. The Court ruled that the Government's use of a pen register—a device that recorded the outgoing phone numbers dialed on a landline telephone—was not a search. Noting the pen register's "limited capabilities," the Court "doubt[ed] that people in general entertain any actual expectation of privacy in the numbers they dial." Telephone subscribers know, after all, that the numbers are used by the telephone company "for a variety of legitimate business purposes," including routing calls. And at any rate, the Court explained, such an expectation "is not one that society is prepared to recognize as reasonable." When Smith placed a call, he "voluntarily conveyed" the dialed numbers to the phone company by "expos[ing] that information to its equipment in the ordinary course of business." Once again, we held that the defendant "assumed the risk" that the company's records "would be divulged to police."

III

The question we confront today is how to apply the Fourth Amendment to a new phenomenon: the ability to chronicle a person's past movements through the record of his cell phone signals. Such tracking partakes of many of the qualities of the GPS monitoring we considered in *Jones*. Much like GPS tracking of a vehicle, cell phone location information is detailed, encyclopedic, and effortlessly compiled.

At the same time, the fact that the individual continuously reveals his location to his wireless carrier implicates the third-party principle of *Smith* and *Miller*. But while the third-party doctrine applies to telephone numbers and bank records, it is not clear whether its logic extends to the qualitatively different category of cell-site records. After all, when *Smith* was decided in 1979, few could have imagined a society in which a phone goes wherever its owner goes, conveying to the wireless carrier not just dialed digits, but a detailed and comprehensive record of the person's movements.

We decline to extend *Smith* and *Miller* to cover these novel circumstances. Given the unique nature of cell phone location records, the fact that the information is held by a third party does not by itself overcome the user's claim to Fourth Amendment protection. Whether the Government employs its own surveillance technology as in *Jones* or leverages the technology of a wireless carrier, we hold that an individual maintains a legitimate expectation of privacy in the record of his physical movements as captured through CSLI. The location information obtained from Carpenter's wireless carriers was the product of a search.

A person does not surrender all Fourth Amendment protection by venturing into the public sphere. To the contrary, "what [one] seeks to preserve as private, even in an area accessible to the public, may be constitutionally protected." . . . Prior to the digital age, law enforcement might have pursued a suspect for a brief stretch, but doing so "for any extended period of time was difficult and costly and therefore rarely undertaken." For that reason, "society's expectation has been that law enforcement agents and others would not—and indeed, in the main, simply could not—secretly monitor and catalogue every single movement of an individual's car for a very long period."

Allowing government access to cell-site records contravenes that expectation. Although such records are generated for commercial purposes, that distinction does not negate Carpenter's anticipation of privacy in his physical location. Mapping a cell phone's location over the course of 127 days provides an all-encompassing record of the holder's whereabouts. As with

GPS information, the time-stamped data provides an intimate window into a person's life, revealing not only his particular movements, but through them his "familial, political, professional, religious, and sexual associations." These location records "hold for many Americans the privacies of life." And like GPS monitoring, cell phone tracking is remarkably easy, cheap, and efficient compared to traditional investigative tools. With just the click of a button, the Government can access each carrier's deep repository of historical location information at practically no expense.

In fact, historical cell-site records present even greater privacy concerns than the GPS monitoring of a vehicle we considered in *Jones*. Unlike the bugged container in *Knotts* or the car in *Jones*, a cell phone—almost a "feature of human anatomy"—tracks nearly exactly the movements of its owner. While individuals regularly leave their vehicles, they compulsively carry cell phones with them all the time. A cell phone faithfully follows its owner beyond public thoroughfares and into private residences, doctor's offices, political headquarters, and other potentially revealing locales. Accordingly, when the Government tracks the location of a cell phone it achieves near perfect surveillance, as if it had attached an ankle monitor to the phone's user.

Moreover, the retrospective quality of the data here gives police access to a category of information otherwise unknowable. In the past, attempts to reconstruct a person's movements were limited by a dearth of records and the frailties of recollection. With access to CSLI, the Government can now travel back in time to retrace a person's whereabouts, subject only to the retention polices of the wireless carriers, which currently maintain records for up to five years. Critically, because location information is continually logged for all of the 400 million devices in the United States—not just those belonging to persons who might happen to come under investigation—this newfound tracking capacity runs against everyone. Unlike with the GPS device in *Jones*, police need not even know in advance whether they want to follow a particular individual, or when. . . .

NOTES & QUESTIONS ON CELL PHONE LOCATION DATA

1. *Reasonable expectation of privacy.* Does it matter that in *Carpenter* the intrusion on privacy involved no physical trespass? As a matter of current doctrine, it would appear that a physical trespass is a sufficient but not a necessary condition for concluding that a search occurred. In cases like *Jones*, physical trespass provides an easy way to resolve the question, but cases like *Carpenter* that involve no physical trespass require consideration of the more vexing question of a reasonable expectation of privacy. Do you agree that cell

phone users have a reasonable expectation of privacy in the data collected about their whereabouts over a long period of time?

2. *The mosaic theory and public movements.* Reconsider the mosaic theory discussed earlier in this chapter. Recall that the mosaic theory suggests that courts should aggregate individual actions into a combined effort in order to determine whether they qualify as a constitutional "search," especially when the combined efforts create a mosaic of a person's life. Apply the mosaic framework to public movements. The fact that an individual leaves a residence to go to the store, or to go to work, might not seem significant enough to count as a search. However, if the government were to track a person's public movements, every minute of every day, over a long period of time, might this construct a "mosaic" of a person's life that would far surpass the information that the rest of the public could reasonably acquire about another individual? Indeed, the D.C. Circuit applied the theory in the *Jones* case before the case reached the Supreme Court:

> The whole of one's movements over the course of a month is not constructively exposed to the public because, like a rap sheet, that whole reveals far more than the individual movements it comprises. The difference is not one of degree but of kind, for no single journey reveals the habits and patterns that mark the distinction between a day in the life and a way of life, nor the departure from a routine that, like the dog that did not bark in the Sherlock Holmes story, may reveal even more.

United States v. Maynard, 615 F.3d 544, 561-62 (D.C. Cir. 2010). For more discussion, see David Gray, *A Collective Right to Be Secure from Unreasonable Tracking,* 48 Tex. Tech L. Rev. 189, 193 (2015) (noting that "we quite reasonably assume a basic level of anonymity in the aggregate of our public movements" and that we "lead our lives on the assumption that nobody is cataloguing our comings and goings, or assembling informational 'mosaics' based on where we go over the course of a week or a month").

3. *Third-party doctrine.* Reconsider the third-party doctrine first discussed in *Smith.* Why did the Court reject the application of that doctrine in *Carpenter*? Should we consider *Carpenter* as the demise of the third-party doctrine or is it best viewed as a limited exception? Do the factors that led the Court to reject the application of the third-party doctrine to cell phone location data apply to other situations as well? Consider the following statement from the majority in *Carpenter* that when *Smith* was decided, "few could have imagined a society in which a phone goes wherever its owner goes, conveying to the wireless carrier not just dialed digits, but a detailed and comprehensive record of the person's movements." Do you agree?

F. PRACTICE & POLICY

The following section takes a step back and asks about the future of privacy in the advent of technological changes that have radically changed how people communicate. Smart phones are technically phones but function as mobile computers; the world has come a long way from pen registers and simple wiretaps. In some ways, this technology risks undermining and protecting privacy at the same time. As noted in several of the key cases excerpted in this chapter, technology is becoming so embedded in our daily lives that government access to that technology might abrogate the private sphere entirely. On the other hand, technology brings the possibility of high-level encryption that might protect our private data in the absence of constitutional or statutory protections. In that vein, consider the following developments:

July 27, 2014 photo provided by U.S. Customs and Border Protection showing Tashfeen Malik, left, and Syed Farook, as they passed through O'Hare International Airport in Chicago. (U.S. Customs and Border Protection via AP)

Data encryption on smart phones. On December 2, 2015, Syed Rizwan Farook and his wife Tashfeen Malik burst into a room at a San Bernardino County office building and started spraying the occupants with automatic gunfire. In just a few moments, Farook managed to murder 14 individuals and seriously wound many others—all of whom were his coworkers at the county health department, who had gathered for an office holiday party. Farook and Malik fled the scene of the murders without detection, but were soon located driving a black SUV nearby. After a violent confrontation with the police, both were killed on the street. In the weeks that followed, authorities were desperate to determine what had motivated their attack. Police authorities indicated that the couple were radicalized over the Internet and had adopted violent and extreme beliefs that eventually sparked the deadly attack.

As part of this investigation, the FBI wanted to search Farook's iPhone and read his electronic communications. Unfortunately for the FBI, the iPhone was locked with a password and the phone's data was encrypted—meaning that the data was unusable unless the police had the password to unlock the phone or could otherwise "de-encrypt" the data. The iPhone could not be connected to a random password generator because the phone was built with a security feature that freezes the phone for an extended period of time after a few unsuccessful attempts to unlock the phone. As such, it would take the FBI decades to unlock the phone by randomly guessing the passcode.

Apple refused to assist the FBI in unlocking the phone or providing a back door into the device. Company officials argued that strong encryption—indeed *unbreakable* encryption—was an essential attribute of the iPhone as a product. Moreover, they defended that attribute on moral and political grounds. According to Apple, consumers have a right to secure and private communications that cannot be deciphered by the government, even when the government has secured a warrant and even when a national security emergency arises.

The FBI filed suit in federal court, asking a judge to order Apple to assist the government in cracking the encryption on Farook's phone. On February 16, 2016, a federal magistrate judge ordered Apple to assist the FBI in revising the phone's operating system so that the government could use a random password generator to gain access to the phone. *Matter of Search of an Apple Iphone Seized During Execution of a Search Warrant on a Black Lexus IS300 California License Plate 35KGD203*, 2016 WL 618401, at *1 (C.D. Cal. Feb. 16, 2016). On February 25, Apple filed a motion to vacate the order, arguing:

> The order demanded by the government compels Apple to create a new operating system—effectively a "back door" to the iPhone—that Apple

> believes is too dangerous to build. Specifically, the government would force Apple to create new software with functions to remove security features and add a new capability to the operating system to attack iPhone encryption, allowing a passcode to be input electronically. This would make it easier to unlock the iPhone by "brute force," trying thousands or millions of passcode combinations with the speed of a modern computer. In short, the government wants to compel Apple to create a crippled and insecure product. Once the process is created, it provides an avenue for criminals and foreign agents to access millions of iPhones. And once developed for our government, it is only a matter of time before foreign governments demand the same tool.

Ultimately, the FBI was able to crack Farook's phone without Apple's assistance, and the government dropped its request for a judicial order forcing the company to assist in its efforts. Although the FBI was able to gain access to Farook's communications in this one instance, security experts believe that phones in the very near future will feature encryption and password protection that is literally impossible for the government to defeat.

This raises a larger issue about communication privacy. Should consumers have access to communication technology that remains shielded from the prying eyes of the government?

One framework for understanding the dispute between Apple and the FBI is to view it against the background of *Smith v. Maryland*. In that case, the Supreme Court held that telecommunications customers do not have a reasonable expectation of privacy in communication records that are revealed to third parties (such as phone or Internet companies). Since it is impossible to engage in communications without using third-party telecommunication providers, it is almost always the case that customers will have commercial relationships with third parties, which according to existing Supreme Court jurisprudence renders the Fourth Amendment inapplicable to the records in question. Consequently, the Constitution does not prohibit the police from requesting those records, although federal and state statutes might impose limitations. In this vein, consider Justice Marshall's sharp dissent in *Smith v. Maryland* and his conclusion that "whether privacy expectations are legitimate within the meaning of *Katz* depends not on the risks an individual can be presumed to accept when imparting information to third parties, but on the risks he should be forced to assume in a free and open society."

In the absence of constitutional protection, technology companies have filled the gap by offering technological solutions to the privacy problem. If the Constitution does not protect communications privacy, strong encryption can do it instead. If the Supreme Court had decided *Smith v. Maryland* differently, and imposed substantial protections for the privacy of telecommunications records, would the need for strong encryption be reduced? Should the Fourth Amendment be interpreted so that it protects communication records more robustly? Or should Congress be more involved? For an argument that Congress should require technology firms to create "front-door" entry for encryption systems, see Geoffrey S. Corn, *Averting the Inherent Dangers of Going Dark: Why Congress Must Require a Locked Front Door to Encrypted Data*, 72 Wash. & Lee L. Rev. 1433 (2015) ("legislation should require manufacturers and developers to create encryption keys that would be bifurcated and placed under the control of the manufacturer and some non-government entity devoted to privacy protection").

CHAPTER 3

THE WARRANT REQUIREMENT

INTRODUCTION

The Fourth Amendment explicitly prohibits unreasonable searches and also regulates the content of warrants, requiring that they describe with particularity the person or things to be seized by the police. Over the years, the Supreme Court has inferred from this that there is a general requirement that police have a search warrant to authorize their intrusion on personal liberty, unless one of the recognized exceptions to the warrant requirement apply. In other words, the Fourth Amendment expresses a strong *preference* for warrants, unless an exception to the warrant requirement applies. (These exceptions are the focus of Chapter 4.) Although this view has certainly carried the day, it is not universally held. In other cases, the Supreme Court has concluded that the Fourth Amendment simply requires that police searches be reasonable and that the reasonableness of the search does not require that it be judicially authorized in advance with a warrant. *Groh v. Ramirez*, 540 U.S. 551, 571 (2004) ("The precise relationship between the Amendment's Warrant Clause and Unreasonableness Clause is unclear. But neither Clause explicitly requires a warrant."). Under this view, the Warrant Clause regulates the content of warrants but does not express a general preference or requirement for the use of warrants. Over the years, Supreme Court opinions have vacillated between these two competing visions of the Fourth Amendment's Warrant Clause.

If warrants are central and indispensable to searches, the next question is what requirements apply to them. First, a search warrant must be issued by a "neutral and detached magistrate," i.e., a judicial officer rather than a police officer or other executive official tasked with solving or stopping crime. So, for example, a state attorney general would not be a neutral and detached magistrate because that official is charged with investigating and prosecuting crime as the state government's chief enforcement agent. See *Coolidge v. New Hampshire*, 403 U.S. 443, 450 (1971). The magistrate should only issue warrants that are supported by the standard of probable cause to believe that contraband or evidence is present at the location to be searched. The warrant must describe with "particularity" the items or things to be seized, and the police must knock and announce their presence before using physical force to enter the location. If the police make a "good faith" mistake while executing the search warrant, the mistake will not be judged to violate the Fourth Amendment, thus giving the police officers a margin of appreciation for well-intentioned errors.

One structural weakness of the warrant framework is that police officers are generally allowed to select which judge to approach for authorization of the warrant. In a small jurisdiction, the police officer might not have many choices, but in any medium or large city, the number of judges who might authorize a warrant is quite substantial. Consequently, the police officer can select from a number of judges and could, in theory, "forum shop" for the most sympathetic audience—the judge who would be most likely to sign the warrant. The purpose of the Fourth Amendment's Warrant Clause is to require judicial pre-authorization for searches to ensure that they satisfy the probable cause standard, but one should never forget that in practice judges are exercising their discretion when applying that standard. As is the case with any other legal actor, two judges applying the same standard might disagree as to whether probable cause is satisfied by the information brought forth by the officer.

The following sections work through the doctrinal requirements in order: Section A on probable cause; Section B on the particularity requirement; Section C on the knock-and-announce requirement; Section D on detentions incident to a search; and Section E on good faith mistakes. The practice and policy section concludes with a consideration of the warrant application process for securing warrants from the United States Foreign Intelligence Surveillance Court (FISC), whose procedures are shrouded in secrecy.

A. PROBABLE CAUSE

It is well-settled law that the standard for issuing a search warrant is probable cause to believe that there is contraband or evidence located at the place to be searched. The difficulty comes in applying that standard to particular factual scenarios that police and courts face on an ongoing basis when they apply for, authorize, and execute such warrants. The case law on the probable cause standard for issuing a search warrant clusters around a variety of factual paradigms,

STATUTORY REQUIREMENTS

In addition to the constitutional requirements discussed below for the issuance and execution of search warrants, state and federal statutes impose specific requirements that structure the search warrant process for law enforcement officials. Although the details of these statutory schemes vary across jurisdictions, common themes emerge in these regulations. The minimum floor set by the Constitution, and enforced by state and federal courts, should not obscure the fact that state statutes impose requirements as well. Some of these requirements simply replicate the constitutional requirement, but in other cases the statutory requirement might impose even greater requirements that go well beyond the requirements of the Fourth Amendment. Consequently, the practice of both prosecutors and criminal defense attorneys are guided by the statutory requirements in their jurisdiction. Consider carefully the following requirements:

First, state statutes typically require that the warrant application be made by a police officer or other public servant, and the application usually can be presented in writing or in person with sworn testimony.

Second, the warrant document usually must be signed by a "magistrate" or judge; the warrant cannot be signed by an executive official. Also, statutes usually require that the warrant be issued in the jurisdiction or locality of the residence or vehicle to be searched.

Third, state statutes usually set temporal parameters for the execution of search warrants. These parameters often require that the search warrant must be executed within a certain number of days after it is signed by the magistrate, so that it does not become an eternal warrant that authorizes searches in perpetuity. Also, most state statutes say that the search warrant must be executed during the day, or during normal business hours, unless otherwise indicated in the warrant. Once the search is complete, the police officer is supposed to "return" the warrant to the magistrate with a list of items that were taken from the property, and this return process is often confined to a specific time limit expressly provided by the statute. However, at least some courts have considered a violation of the "return" time period, or a failure to list one item on the inventory, as "merely a technical violation" that does not require suppression of the evidence at trial. *State v. Roy*, 167 N.H. 276, 283 (2015).

Finally, many states regulate the *content* of search warrants, requiring that they list the things or items that are the target of the search—essentially codifying the constitutionally protected "particularity" requirement that will be discussed below in Section B.

including (1) information from informants and tipsters; (2) information from witnesses and victims; and (3) first-hand information from the police.

1. Information from Informants

Frequently, police officers use information from confidential informants or anonymous tips as evidence in warrant applications. In *Aguilar v. Texas*, 378 U.S. 108 (1964), the Supreme Court concluded that "an affidavit may be based on hearsay information" but "the magistrate must be informed of . . . some of the underlying circumstances from which the officer concluded that the informant, whose identity need not be disclosed, was 'credible' or his information 'reliable.'" The Court's rationale for this conclusion was that the magistrate needs this information—otherwise the warrant will not be issued by a "neutral and detached magistrate," as the Fourth Amendment requires, but rather by a police officer "engaged in the often competitive enterprise of ferreting out crime." In *Spinelli v. United States,* 393 U.S. 410 (1969), the Supreme Court nullified a warrant that was based on an informant's conclusion that two phones were being used in a gambling operation, because the magistrate was not given the underlying reasons that formed the basis for the informant's conclusion. Specifically, the Court noted that though the affiant "swore that his confidant was 'reliable,' he offered the magistrate no reason in support of this conclusion" and the tip did not "contain a sufficient statement of the underlying circumstances from which the informant concluded that Spinelli was running a bookmaking operation." 393 U.S. at 410.

In the following case, though, the Supreme Court upheld a warrant, finding that there was probable cause to support the warrant even though it was based solely on allegations of criminal activity made in an unsolicited letter mailed to the police. As you read the case, ask yourself why the warrant was upheld when the warrants in *Aguilar* and *Spinelli* were deemed unsupported by probable cause.

Illinois v. Gates

Supreme Court of the United States
462 U.S. 213 (1983)

Justice Rehnquist delivered the opinion of the Court.

Respondents Lance and Susan Gates were indicted for violation of state drug laws after police officers, executing a search warrant, discovered marijuana and other contraband in their automobile and home. Prior to trial the Gates' moved to suppress evidence seized during this search. The Illinois Supreme Court affirmed the decisions of lower state courts granting the motion. It held that the affidavit submitted in support of the State's application for a warrant to search the Gates' property was inadequate under this Court's decisions in *Aguilar v. Texas,* 378 U.S. 108 (1964) and *Spinelli v. United States,* 393 U.S. 410 (1969). We granted certiorari to consider the application of the Fourth Amendment to a magistrate's issuance of a search warrant on the basis of a partially corroborated anonymous informant's tip. . . .

II

. . . On May 3, 1978, the Bloomingdale Police Department received by mail an anonymous handwritten letter which read as follows:

> This letter is to inform you that you have a couple in your town who strictly make their living on selling drugs. They are Sue and Lance Gates, they live on Greenway, off Bloomingdale Rd. in the condominiums. Most of their

buys are done in Florida. Sue his wife drives their car to Florida, where she leaves it to be loaded up with drugs, then Lance flys down and drives it back. Sue flys back after she drops the car off in Florida. May 3 she is driving down there again and Lance will be flying down in a few days to drive it back. At the time Lance drives the car back he has the trunk loaded with over $100,000.00 in drugs. Presently they have over $100,000.00 worth of drugs in their basement.

They brag about the fact they never have to work, and make their entire living on pushers.

I guarantee if you watch them carefully you will make a big catch. They are friends with some big drugs dealers, who visit their house often.

Lance & Susan Gates
Greenway
in Condominiums

The letter was referred by the Chief of Police of the Bloomingdale Police Department to Detective Mader, who decided to pursue the tip. Mader learned, from the office of the Illinois Secretary of State, that an Illinois driver's license had been issued to one Lance Gates, residing at a stated address in Bloomingdale. He contacted a confidential informant, whose examination of certain financial records revealed a more recent address for the Gates, and he also learned from a police officer assigned to O'Hare Airport that "L. Gates" had made a reservation on Eastern Airlines flight 245 to West Palm Beach, Fla., scheduled to depart from Chicago on May 5 at 4:15 P.M.

Mader then made arrangements with an agent of the Drug Enforcement Administration for surveillance of the May 5 Eastern Airlines flight. The agent later reported to Mader that Gates had boarded the flight, and that federal agents in Florida had observed him arrive in West Palm Beach and take a taxi to the nearby Holiday Inn. They also reported that Gates went to a room registered to one Susan Gates and that, at 7:00 A.M. the next morning, Gates and an unidentified woman left the motel in a Mercury bearing Illinois license plates and drove northbound on an interstate frequently used by travelers to the Chicago area. In addition, the DEA agent informed Mader that the license plate number on the Mercury registered to a Hornet station wagon owned by Gates. The agent also advised Mader that the driving time between West Palm Beach and Bloomingdale was approximately 22 to 24 hours.

Mader signed an affidavit setting forth the foregoing facts, and submitted it to a judge of the Circuit Court of DuPage County, together with a copy of the anonymous letter. The judge of that court thereupon issued a search warrant for the Gates' residence and for their automobile. The judge, in deciding to issue the warrant, could have determined that the *modus operandi* of the Gates had been substantially corroborated. As the anonymous letter predicted, Lance Gates had flown from Chicago to West Palm Beach late in the afternoon of May 5th, had checked into a hotel room registered in the name of his wife, and, at 7:00 A.M. the following morning, had headed north, accompanied by an unidentified woman, out of West Palm Beach on an interstate highway used by travelers from South Florida to Chicago in an automobile bearing a license plate issued to him.

At 5:15 A.M. on March 7th, only 36 hours after he had flown out of Chicago, Lance Gates, and his wife, returned to their home in Bloomingdale, driving the car in which they had left West Palm Beach some 22 hours earlier. The Bloomingdale police were awaiting them, searched the trunk of the Mercury, and uncovered approximately 350 pounds of marijuana. A search of the Gates' home revealed marijuana, weapons, and other contraband. The Illinois Circuit Court ordered suppression of all these items, on the ground that the affidavit submitted to the Circuit Judge failed to support the necessary determination of probable cause to believe that the Gates' automobile and home contained the contraband in question. This decision was affirmed in turn by the Illinois Appellate Court and by a divided vote of the Supreme Court of Illinois.

The Illinois Supreme Court concluded—and we are inclined to agree—that, standing alone, the anonymous letter sent to the Bloomingdale Police Department would not provide the basis for a magistrate's determination that there was probable cause to believe contraband would be found in the Gates' car and home. The letter provides virtually nothing from which one might conclude that its author is either honest or his information reliable; likewise, the letter gives absolutely no indication of the basis for the writer's predictions regarding the Gates' criminal activities. Something more was required, then, before a magistrate could conclude that there was probable cause to believe that contraband would be found in the Gates' home and car.

The Illinois Supreme Court also properly recognized that Detective Mader's affidavit might be capable of supplementing the anonymous letter with information sufficient to permit a determination of probable cause. In holding that the affidavit in fact did not contain sufficient additional information to sustain a determination of probable cause, the Illinois court applied a "two-pronged test," derived from our decision in *Spinelli v. United States,* 393 U.S. 410 (1969). The Illinois Supreme Court, like some others, apparently understood *Spinelli* as requiring that the anonymous letter satisfy each of two independent requirements before it could be relied on. According to this view, the letter, as supplemented by Mader's affidavit, first had to adequately reveal the "basis of knowledge" of the letter writer—the particular means by which he came by the information given in his report. Second, it had to provide facts sufficiently establishing either the "veracity" of the affiant's informant, or, alternatively, the "reliability" of the informant's report in this particular case. . . .

We agree with the Illinois Supreme Court that an informant's "veracity," "reliability" and "basis of knowledge" are all highly relevant in determining the value of his report. We do not agree, however, that these elements should be understood as entirely separate and independent requirements to be rigidly exacted in every case, which the opinion of the Supreme Court of Illinois would imply. Rather, as detailed below, they should be understood simply as closely intertwined issues that may usefully illuminate the commonsense, practical question whether there is "probable cause" to believe that contraband or evidence is located in a particular place.

III

This totality-of-the-circumstances approach is far more consistent with our prior treatment of probable cause than is any rigid demand that specific "tests" be satisfied by every informant's tip. Perhaps the central teaching of our decisions bearing on the probable cause standard is that it is a "practical, nontechnical conception." . . . [P]robable cause is a fluid concept—turning on the assessment of probabilities in particular factual contexts—not readily, or even usefully, reduced to a neat set of legal rules. Informants' tips doubtless come in many shapes and sizes from many different types of persons. . . . Rigid legal rules are ill-suited to an area of such diversity. "One simple rule will not cover every situation."

Moreover, the "two-pronged test" directs analysis into two largely independent channels—the informant's "veracity" or "reliability" and his "basis of knowledge." There are persuasive arguments against according these two elements such independent status. Instead, they are better understood as relevant considerations in the totality-of-the-circumstances analysis that traditionally has guided probable cause determinations: a deficiency in one may be compensated for, in determining the overall reliability of a tip, by a strong showing as to the other, or by some other indicia of reliability.

If, for example, a particular informant is known for the unusual reliability of his predictions of certain types of criminal activities in a locality, his failure, in a particular case, to thoroughly set forth the basis of his knowledge surely should not serve as an absolute bar to a finding of probable cause based on his tip. Likewise, if an unquestionably honest citizen comes forward with a report of criminal activity—which if fabricated would subject him to criminal liability—we have found rigorous scrutiny of the basis of his knowledge unnecessary. Conversely, even if we entertain some doubt as to an informant's motives, his explicit and detailed description of alleged wrongdoing, along with a statement that the event was observed first-hand, entitles his tip to greater weight than might otherwise be the case. Unlike a totality-of-the-circumstances analysis, which permits a balanced assessment of the relative weights of all the various indicia of reliability (and unreliability) attending an informant's tip, the "two-pronged test" has encouraged an excessively technical dissection of informants' tips, with undue attention being focused on isolated issues that cannot sensibly be divorced from the other facts presented to the magistrate.

. . . Finely-tuned standards such as proof beyond a reasonable doubt or by a preponderance of the evidence, useful in formal trials, have no place in the magistrate's decision. While an effort to fix some general, numerically precise degree of certainty corresponding to "probable cause" may not be helpful, it is clear that "only the probability, and not a prima facie showing, of criminal activity is the standard of probable cause."

We also have recognized that affidavits "are normally drafted by nonlawyers in the midst and haste of a criminal investigation. Technical requirements of elaborate specificity once exacted under common law pleading have no proper place in this area." Likewise, search and arrest warrants long have been issued by persons who are neither lawyers nor judges, and who certainly do not remain abreast of each judicial refinement of the nature of "probable cause." The rigorous inquiry into the *Spinelli* prongs and the complex superstructure of evidentiary and analytical rules that some have seen implicit in our *Spinelli* decision, cannot be reconciled with the fact that many warrants are—quite properly—issued on the basis of nontechnical, common-sense judgments of laymen applying a standard less demanding than those used in more formal legal proceedings. Likewise, given the informal, often hurried context in which it must be applied, the "built-in subtleties" of the "two-pronged test" are particularly unlikely to assist magistrates in determining probable cause.

Similarly, we have repeatedly said that after-the-fact scrutiny by courts of the sufficiency of an affidavit should not take the form of *de novo* review. A magistrate's "determination of probable cause should be paid great deference by reviewing courts." *Spinelli,* 393 U.S. at 419. "A grudging or negative attitude by reviewing courts toward warrants," *Ventresca,* 380 U.S. at 108, is inconsistent with the Fourth Amendment's strong preference for searches conducted pursuant to a warrant "courts should not invalidate . . . warrant[s] by interpreting affidavit [s] in a hypertechnical, rather than a commonsense, manner." . . .

For all these reasons, we conclude that it is wiser to abandon the "two-pronged test" established by our decisions in *Aguilar* and *Spinelli.* In its place we reaffirm the totality-of-the-circumstances analysis that traditionally has informed probable cause determinations. The task of the issuing magistrate is simply to make a practical, common-sense decision whether, given all the circumstances set forth in the affidavit before him, including the "veracity" and "basis of knowledge" of persons supplying hearsay information, there is a fair probability that contraband or evidence of a crime will be found in a particular place. And the duty of a reviewing court is simply to ensure that the magistrate had a "substantial basis for . . . conclud[ing]" that probable cause existed. We are convinced that this flexible, easily applied standard will better achieve the accommodation of public and private interests that the Fourth Amendment requires than does the approach that has developed from *Aguilar* and *Spinelli*. . . .

IV

. . . Even standing alone, the facts obtained through the independent investigation of Mader and the DEA at least suggested that the Gates were involved in drug trafficking. In addition to being a popular vacation site, Florida is well-known as a source of narcotics and other illegal drugs. Lance Gates' flight to Palm Beach, his brief, overnight stay in a motel, and apparent immediate return north to Chicago in the family car, conveniently awaiting him in West Palm Beach, is as suggestive of a pre-arranged drug run, as it is of an ordinary vacation trip.

In addition, the magistrate could rely on the anonymous letter, which had been corroborated in major part by Mader's efforts. . . . [T]he anonymous letter contained a range of details relating not just to easily obtained facts and conditions existing at the time of the tip, but to future actions of third parties ordinarily not easily predicted. The letter writer's accurate information as to the travel plans of each of the Gates was of a character likely obtained only from the Gates themselves, or from someone familiar with their not entirely ordinary travel plans. If the informant had access to accurate information of this type a magistrate could properly conclude that it was not unlikely that he also had access to reliable information of the Gates' alleged illegal activities. Of course, the Gates' travel plans might have been learned from a talkative neighbor or travel agent; under the "two-pronged test" developed from *Spinelli*, the character of the details in the anonymous letter might well not permit a sufficiently clear inference regarding the letter writer's "basis of knowledge." But, as discussed previously, probable cause does not demand the certainty we associate with formal trials. It is enough that there was a fair probability that the writer of the anonymous letter had obtained his entire story either from the Gates or someone they trusted. And corroboration of major portions of the letter's predictions provides just this probability. It is apparent, therefore, that the judge issuing the warrant had a "substantial basis for . . . conclud[ing]" that probable cause to search the Gates' home and car existed. . . .

NOTES & QUESTIONS ON INFORMANTS

1. *Totality of the circumstances.* The Supreme Court concluded in *Gates* that probable cause should be assessed by a flexible totality-of-the-circumstances test. Applying this newer, more flexible, approach to the facts of the

case, the Court conceded that the anonymous letter was, by itself, insufficient to meet the probable cause standard, but that other information developed by the police corroborated aspects of the allegations in the anonymous letter. Do you agree that this approach is sufficient to satisfy probable cause, or should a magistrate always have specific information that explains how the informant came to have this information *and* specific information about the informant's veracity? In reality, this standard would appear to doom warrants based on anonymous tips, since establishing the veracity of the informant usually requires linking their statement with past statements that turned out to be true, a process that is difficult if one does not know the identity of the informant.

2. *Anonymous tips.* The Supreme Court concluded that anonymous tips are an essential and legitimate ingredient of modern policing. Do you agree with this assumption? Are there inherent dangers involved in relying on this form of citizen participation in policing? For example, one study of narcotic search warrants in San Diego found that it "is noteworthy that only a handful (8%) of warrants targeting White suspects involved an anonymous tip as a source of probable cause. In marked contrast, anonymous tips played a much more frequent role in establishing probable cause for warrants targeting Blacks (35%) and Hispanics (19%)." Laurence A. Benner, *Racial Disparity in Narcotics Search Warrants*, 6 J. Gender Race & Just. 183, 221 (2002). Is this finding cause for alarm given the holding of *Illinois v. Gates*?

2. Information from Victims and Eyewitnesses

Courts have held that the specific concerns about the reliability of information provided by informants does not apply to information provided by victims or eyewitnesses to a crime. Although the issue has not been directly considered by the Supreme Court, both lower federal courts and state appellate courts have concluded that the totality of the circumstances test is less contentious to apply when the police receive information from victims or eyewitnesses. Why would this be so? Consider the following explanation:

> [T]here has been a growing recognition that the language in *Aguilar* and *Spinelli* was addressed to the particular problem of professional informers and should not be applied in a wooden fashion to cases where the information comes from an alleged victim of or witness to a crime. Indeed any other view would mean that, despite the 1972 amendment to F.R.Crim.P. 41(c) to the effect that "(t)he finding of probable cause may be based upon hearsay evidence in whole or in part," it would generally be impossible to use hearsay statements of victims or witnesses since ordinarily they would not be previously known to the police.

United States v. Burke, 517 F.2d 377, 380 (2d Cir. 1975). Also, courts are entitled to assume that victims and eyewitnesses are motivated by a desire to help law enforcement solve crimes, whereas something about the informant-police relationship naturally raises the possibility of ulterior motives.

It is important to remember that mere anonymity is not enough to transform an eyewitness into an informant. For example, if an eyewitness calls police and speaks with a detective but does so anonymously, courts might consider this individual an eyewitness rather than an informant. Nor will the payment of a reward necessarily transform an eyewitness into an informant with a credibility concern. See *People v. Stevens*, 98 Ill. App. 3d 158, 423 N.E.2d 1340 (1981).

3. Information from the Police

Probable cause might be established with information that comes from the police, rather than an informant, eyewitness, or victim. Should information flowing from the police be treated with the same assumption of credibility that is given to citizen-witnesses? In most cases, courts do not treat police officers with the same level of scrutiny, or skepticism, as informants or tipsters. Consider the following statement from the Supreme Court:

> We disagree with the conclusion of the Court of Appeals. Its determination that the affidavit might have been based wholly upon hearsay cannot be supported in light of the fact that Mazaka, a Government Investigator, swore under oath that the relevant information was in part based "upon observations made by me" and "upon personal knowledge" as well as upon "information which has been obtained from Investigators of the Alcohol and Tobacco Tax Division, Internal Revenue Service, who have been assigned to this investigation." It also seems to us that the assumption of the Court of Appeals that all of the information in Mazaka's affidavit may in fact have come from unreliable anonymous informers passed on to Government Investigators, who in turn related this information to Mazaka is without foundation. Mazaka swore that, insofar as the affidavit was not based upon his own observations, it was "based upon information received officially from other Investigators attached to the Alcohol and Tobacco Tax Division assigned to this investigation, and reports orally made to me describing the results of their observations and investigation." The Court of Appeals itself recognized that the affidavit stated that "Investigators' (employees of the Service) smelled the odor of fermenting mash in the vicinity of the suspected dwelling." A qualified officer's detection of the smell of mash has often been held a very strong factor in determining that probable cause exists so as to allow issuance of a warrant. Moreover, upon reading the affidavit as a whole, it becomes clear that the detailed observations recounted in the affidavit cannot fairly be regarded as having been made in any significant part by persons other than full-time Investigators of the Alcohol and Tobacco Tax Division of the Internal Revenue Service. Observations of fellow officers of the Government engaged in a common

investigation are plainly a reliable basis for a warrant applied for by one of their number.

United States v. Ventresca, 380 U.S. 102, 110-11 (1965).

B. THE PARTICULARITY REQUIREMENT

The Fourth Amendment's particularity requirement flows from the text of the amendment itself, which requires that warrants include statements "particularly describing the place to be searched, and the persons or things to be seized." The historical basis for this particularity requirement was the framer's rejection of the British practice of using "general warrants." These warrants granted broad discretion to the police to arrest any individual suspected of wrongdoing or search any property that the police believed would contain evidence of wrongdoing; the general warrants never listed the particular person to be arrested or the particular dwelling to be searched. In other words, it was a directive to the police to fight crime with little to no judicial oversight of the police power. The use of general warrants generated immense distrust of British power in the colonies, thus resulting in a constitutionally protected right to be free from unreasonable searches. To pass constitutional muster, the judicially authorized warrant must state with particularity "the things to be seized," rather than a general statement to look for any and all evidence of criminal behavior.

Although the text of the Fourth Amendment is clear on this point, the notion of "particularity" is not self-applying. What does it mean for something to be described particularly? How specific must the description be? An object or objects can be described with greater or lesser degrees of specificity. For example, if the police are looking for evidence of a financial fraud, can they seek a warrant for any and all business records? Or all bank records? Or must they seek a warrant for bank records during particular time periods or detailing particular types of transactions? In the following case, the Supreme Court tackles this question of specificity.

Groh v. Ramirez

Supreme Court of the United States
540 U.S. 551 (2004)

Justice STEVENS delivered the opinion of the Court.

Petitioner conducted a search of respondents' home pursuant to a warrant that failed to describe the "persons or things to be seized." The questions presented [include] whether the search violated the Fourth Amendment. . . .

I

Respondents, Joseph Ramirez and members of his family, live on a large ranch in Butte–Silver Bow County, Montana. Petitioner, Jeff Groh, has been a Special Agent for the Bureau of Alcohol, Tobacco and Firearms (ATF) since 1989. In February 1997, a concerned citizen informed petitioner that on a number of visits to respondents' ranch the visitor had seen a large stock of weaponry, including an automatic rifle, grenades, a grenade launcher, and a rocket launcher. Based on that information, petitioner prepared and signed an application for a warrant to search the ranch. The application stated that the search was for "any automatic firearms or parts to automatic weapons, destructive devices to include but not limited to grenades, grenade launchers, rocket launchers, and any and all receipts pertaining to the purchase or manufacture of automatic weapons or explosive devices or launchers." Petitioner supported the application with a detailed affidavit, which he also prepared and executed, that set forth the basis for his belief that the listed items were concealed on the ranch. Petitioner then presented these documents to a Magistrate, along with a warrant form that petitioner also had completed. The Magistrate signed the warrant form.

Although the application particularly described the place to be searched and the contraband petitioner expected to find, the warrant itself was less specific; it failed to identify any of the items that petitioner intended to seize. In the portion of the form that called for a description of the "person or property" to be seized, petitioner typed a description of respondents' two-story blue house rather than the alleged stockpile of firearms. The warrant did not incorporate by reference the itemized list contained in the application. It did, however, recite that the Magistrate was satisfied the affidavit established probable cause to believe that contraband was concealed on the premises, and that sufficient grounds existed for the warrant's issuance.

The day after the Magistrate issued the warrant, petitioner led a team of law enforcement officers, including both federal agents and members of the local sheriff's department, in the search of respondents' premises. Although respondent Joseph Ramirez was not home, his wife and children were. Petitioner states that he orally described the objects of the search to Mrs. Ramirez in person and to Mr. Ramirez by telephone. According to Mrs. Ramirez, however, petitioner explained only that he was searching for "an explosive device in a box." At any rate, the officers' search uncovered no illegal weapons or explosives. When the officers left, petitioner gave Mrs. Ramirez a copy of the search warrant, but not a copy of the application, which had been sealed. The following day, in response to a request from respondents' attorney, petitioner faxed the attorney a copy of the page of the application that listed the items to be seized. No charges were filed against the Ramirezes.

Respondents sued petitioner and the other officers . . . raising eight claims, including violation of the Fourth Amendment. The District Court entered summary judgment for all defendants. The court found no Fourth Amendment violation, because it considered the case comparable to one in which the warrant contained an inaccurate address, and in such a case, the court reasoned, the warrant is sufficiently detailed if the executing officers can locate the correct house. . . .

The Court of Appeals affirmed the judgment with respect to all defendants and all claims, with the exception of respondents' Fourth Amendment claim against petitioner. On that claim, the court held that the warrant was invalid because it did not "describe with particularity the place to be searched and the items to be seized," and that oral statements by petitioner during or after the search could not cure the omission. The court observed that the warrant's facial defect "increased the likelihood and degree of confrontation between the Ramirezes and the police" and deprived respondents of the means "to challenge officers who might have exceeded the limits imposed by the magistrate." . . .

II

The warrant was plainly invalid. The Fourth Amendment states unambiguously that "no Warrants shall issue, but upon probable cause, supported by Oath or affirmation, and *particularly describing* the place to be searched, and *the persons or things to be seized.*" The warrant in this case complied with the first three of these requirements: It was based on probable cause and supported by a sworn affidavit, and it described particularly the place of the search. On the fourth requirement, however, the warrant failed altogether. Indeed, petitioner concedes that "the warrant . . . was deficient in particularity because it provided no description of the type of evidence sought."

The fact that the *application* adequately described the "things to be seized" does not save the *warrant* from its facial invalidity. The Fourth Amendment by its terms requires particularity in the warrant, not in the supporting documents. And for good reason: "The presence of a search warrant serves a high function," *McDonald v. United States,* 335 U.S. 451, 455 (1948), and that high function is not necessarily vindicated when some other document, somewhere, says something about the objects of the search, but the contents of that document are neither known to the person whose home is being searched nor available for her inspection. We do not say that the Fourth Amendment prohibits a warrant from cross-referencing other documents. Indeed, most Courts of Appeals have held that a court may construe a warrant with reference to a supporting application or affidavit if the warrant uses appropriate words of incorporation, and if the supporting document accompanies the warrant. But in this case the warrant did not incorporate other documents by reference, nor did either the affidavit or the application (which had been placed under seal) accompany the warrant. Hence, we need not further explore the matter of incorporation.

Petitioner argues that even though the warrant was invalid, the search nevertheless was "reasonable" within the meaning of the Fourth Amendment. He notes that a Magistrate authorized the search on the basis of adequate evidence of probable cause, that petitioner orally described to respondents the items to be seized, and that the search did not exceed the limits intended by the Magistrate and described by petitioner. Thus, petitioner maintains, his search of respondents' ranch was functionally equivalent to a search authorized by a valid warrant.

We disagree. This warrant did not simply omit a few items from a list of many to be seized, or misdescribe a few of several items. Nor did it make what fairly could be characterized as a mere technical mistake or typographical error. Rather, in the space set aside for a description of the items to be seized, the warrant stated that the items consisted of a "single dwelling residence . . . blue in color." In other words, the warrant did not describe the items to be seized *at all.* In this respect the warrant was so obviously deficient that we must regard the search as "warrantless" within the meaning of our case law. . . .

We have clearly stated that the presumptive rule against warrantless searches applies with equal force to searches whose only defect is a lack of particularity in the warrant. . . . Petitioner asks us to hold that a search conducted pursuant to a warrant lacking particularity should be exempt from the presumption of unreasonableness if the goals served by the particularity requirement are otherwise satisfied. He maintains that the search in this case satisfied those goals—which he says are "to prevent general searches, to prevent the seizure of one thing under a warrant describing another, and to prevent warrants from being issued on vague or dubious information"—because the scope of the search did not exceed the limits set forth in the application. But unless the particular items described in the affidavit are also set forth in the warrant itself (or at least incorporated by reference, and the affidavit present at the search), there can be no written assurance that the Magistrate actually found probable cause to search for, and to seize, every item mentioned in the affidavit. In this case, for example, it is at least theoretically possible that the Magistrate was satisfied that the search for weapons and explosives was justified by the showing in the affidavit, but not convinced that any evidentiary basis existed for rummaging through respondents' files and papers for receipts pertaining to the purchase or manufacture of such items. Or, conceivably, the Magistrate might have believed that some of the weapons mentioned in the affidavit could have been lawfully possessed and therefore should not be seized. The mere fact that the Magistrate issued a warrant does not necessarily establish that he agreed that the scope of the search should be as broad as the affiant's request. Even though petitioner acted with restraint in conducting the search, "the inescapable fact is that this restraint was imposed by the agents themselves, not by a judicial officer." *Katz v. United States,* 389 U.S. 347, 356 (1967).

We have long held, moreover, that the purpose of the particularity requirement is not limited to the prevention of general searches. A particular warrant also "assures the individual whose property is searched or seized of the lawful authority of the executing officer, his need to search, and the limits of his power to search."

Petitioner argues that even if the goals of the particularity requirement are broader than he acknowledges, those goals nevertheless were served because he orally described to respondents the items for which he was searching. Thus, he submits, respondents had all of the notice that a proper warrant would have accorded. But this case presents no occasion even to reach this argument, since respondents, as noted above, dispute petitioner's account. According to Mrs. Ramirez, petitioner stated only that he was looking for an "explosive device in a box." Because this dispute is before us on petitioner's motion for summary judgment, "[t]he evidence of the nonmovant is to be believed, and all justifiable inferences are to be drawn in [her] favor." The posture of the case therefore obliges us to credit Mrs. Ramirez's account, and we find that petitioner's description of "an explosive device in a box" was little better than no guidance at all.

It is incumbent on the officer executing a search warrant to ensure the search is lawfully authorized and lawfully conducted. Because petitioner did not have in his possession a warrant particularly describing the things he intended to seize, proceeding with the search was clearly "unreasonable" under the Fourth Amendment. The Court of Appeals correctly held that the search was unconstitutional. . . .

PROBLEM CASE

Federal authorities charged 36 defendants with conspiracy to commit racketeering, health care fraud, mail fraud, and money laundering arising from an illegal no-fault automobile insurance scam. Three of the defendants moved for dismissal, arguing that evidence seized from a search of the Tri-State Billing Corp. was inadmissible because the underlying warrant failed to satisfy the particularity requirement.

The warrant did not include a list of items to be searched but it did include an attachment that listed the following items as the target of the search: "1. Bank account information; 2. Ledgers documenting patient medical treatment, tests provided, and other records related to patient care; 3. Signature stamps; 4. Calendars and patient appointment records; 5. Cellphones of target subjects found at subject premises; 6. Checks, cash, and other financial instruments; 7. Computers; 8. Thumb drives." The attachment also included a further list of eight categories of computer hardware where the documents might be located. However, the attachment was not incorporated by reference into the warrant itself. Also, the warrant did not list the crimes to which the documents allegedly related nor did it include a temporal restriction.

If you were the judge hearing the case, would this warrant satisfy the particularity requirement? If yes, why? If not, why not? See *United States v. Zemlyansky*, 945 F. Supp. 2d 438 (S.D.N.Y. 2013).

NOTES & QUESTIONS ON THE PARTICULARITY REQUIREMENT

1. *Application versus warrant.* The search in *Groh* was deemed invalid because the list of particular items that the police were searching for was included in the application for the warrant but not in the warrant itself. What difference does this make? Is this an exercise in formalism? Is the difference significant for the occupant of the dwelling? If the police show the warrant itself to the occupant, he or she may not have access to the warrant *application*; without the latter, the occupant will not know the nature of the search and thus be capable of objecting to an overbroad search. In *Groh*, the warrant did not incorporate "by reference" the list from the application. If it had, would the outcome of the case have differed?

2. *Reasonableness versus bright-line rules.* Another way of understanding *Groh* is to see it as a rejection of, or at the very least a limit on, the role of reasonableness in Fourth Amendment jurisprudence. Instead of upholding the search because the warrant was reasonable, the Court interpreted the particularity requirement in the strictest way possible. As one commentator noted:

> The majority's strict application of the Warrant Clause's particularity requirement reflected a bright-line approach that is not flexible enough to accommodate the competing demands of effective law enforcement and robust civil liberties. Historically, when determining the Fourth Amendment's scope, the Supreme Court has treated the amendment as extremely opentextured. Not only has the Court reshaped the words "search" and "seizure" to accommodate the needs of law enforcement, but it also has expanded the concept of security in "persons, houses, papers, and effects" to include autonomy rights not obvious in the amendment's text. This approach is fitting because an inquiry into "reasonableness," which the Fourth Amendment plainly invites, is the quintessential equitable balancing test. Although the Court has been stricter in its interpretation of the Warrant Clause, it nevertheless has tempered this strictness with the reasonableness inquiries involved in considerations of qualified immunity and exceptions to the exclusionary rule. In *Groh*, however, the Court effectively confined the reasonableness inquiry to the Reasonableness Clause and ossified the Warrant Clause with the unmitigated strictness of the particularity requirement, thus trading the flexibility of the reasonableness inquiry for a rigid bright-line rule.

Constitutional Law, 118 Harv. L. Rev. 276, 281 (2004). Do you agree?

3. *The all-records exception.* Some courts have recognized an exception to the particularity requirement in situations where an "entire" business

enterprise is "permeated" with fraud. In that situation, there is reason to believe that all records found at the location potentially relate to the crime, thus alleviating the requirement that a search warrant state with particularity the items to be seized. Instead, the search warrant could simply list "all records" of the business. To uphold a search warrant in this situation, however, a court would have to be satisfied that the business is indeed "permeated by fraud"—in other words, that the entire enterprise, rather than simply a portion of it, is illegal. As one court noted regarding the doctrine: "The principle is not so much an 'exception' to the particularity requirement of the Fourth Amendment as a recognition that a warrant—no matter how broad—is, nonetheless, legitimate if its scope does not exceed the probable cause upon which it is based. The more extensive the probable wrongdoing, the greater the permissible breadth of the warrant." *United States v. Hickey*, 16 F. Supp. 2d 223, 240 (E.D.N.Y. 1998).

C. THE KNOCK-AND-ANNOUNCE REQUIREMENT

At the time of the framing, the common law permitted the police to forcibly enter a dwelling for the purpose of executing a search warrant, but only after first announcing their presence and identifying themselves as police officers. In, *Wilson v. Arkansas*, 514 U.S. 927 (1995), the Supreme Court concluded that this requirement was permanently enshrined in the Fourth Amendment. Of course, the Fourth Amendment simply protects the right of the people to be free from "unreasonable searches and seizures" and says nothing per se about the police announcing their presence before entering a residence. Nonetheless, the Supreme Court concluded in *Wilson* that the knock-and-announce requirement

WHAT DOES A WARRANT LOOK LIKE?

To better understand the warrant application process, first take a look at the following blank warrant application used in federal courts. Pay particular attention to each blank section and the information that must be provided to the court. These include: (i) the name of the person; (ii) the location of the property; (iii) the exact items to be searched or seized; and (iv) what the search will reveal in terms of evidence of a crime. However, do not be fooled by the small size of the box where the police must list, with particularity, the items to be searched or seized. If the box is too small, the warrant will typically include a lengthy list attached as a typewritten appendix that may run several pages in length. Second, notice that the warrant includes a place for a date and a requirement that the warrant be executed within 14 days of issuance, and within specific hours of the day. Finally, scrutinize the "return" portion of the warrant on the second page, which must include an inventory of all items seized during the search, and must then be promptly filed with the judge who signed the warrant.

AO 442 (Rev. 11/11) Arrest Warrant

UNITED STATES DISTRICT COURT

for the

United States of America
v.
) Case No.

Defendant

ARREST WARRANT

To: Any authorized law enforcement officer

YOU ARE COMMANDED to arrest and bring before a United States magistrate judge without unnecessary delay *(name of person to be arrested)* ____________________,
who is accused of an offense or violation based on the following document filed with the court:

❒ Indictment ❒ Superseding Indictment ❒ Information ❒ Superseding Information ❒ Complaint
❒ Probation Violation Petition ❒ Supervised Release Violation Petition ❒ Violation Notice ❒ Order of the Court

This offense is briefly described as follows:

Date: ____________________ *Issuing officer's signature*

City and state: ____________________ *Printed name and title*

Return

This warrant was received on *(date)* ________, and the person was arrested on *(date)* ________
at *(city and state)* ____________________.

Date: ____________________ *Arresting officer's signature*

Printed name and title

AO 442 (Rev. 11/11) Arrest Warrant (Page 2)

This second page contains personal identifiers provided for law-enforcement use only and therefore should not be filed in court with the executed warrant unless under seal.

(Not for Public Disclosure)

Name of defendant/offender: ______

Known aliases: ______

Last known residence: ______

Prior addresses to which defendant/offender may still have ties: ______

Last known employment: ______

Last known telephone numbers: ______

Place of birth: ______

Date of birth: ______

Social Security number: ______

Height: ______ Weight: ______

Sex: ______ Race: ______

Hair: ______ Eyes: ______

Scars, tattoos, other distinguishing marks: ______

History of violence, weapons, drug use: ______

Known family, friends, and other associates *(name, relation, address, phone number)*: ______

FBI number: ______

Complete description of auto: ______

Investigative agency and address: ______

Name and telephone numbers (office and cell) of pretrial services or probation officer *(if applicable)*: ______

Date of last contact with pretrial services or probation officer *(if applicable)*: ______

was implicit within the Fourth Amendment's notion of *reasonableness* and was "woven quickly into the fabric of early American law." *Id.* at 933.

Because the knock-and-announce requirement was subsumed under the Fourth Amendment's notion of reasonableness, it is not a categorical rule. The reasonableness inquiry is designed to balance the privacy interest of the individual with the legitimate needs of law enforcement to pursue investigations and maintain safety while doing so. Consequently, the rule expresses a general background norm that can be dispensed with in exigent circumstances. Examples of exigent circumstances would include situations where the police have specific reason to believe that knocking first during the search will either result in the evidence's destruction or in a violent encounter. So, for example, if the police are aware that the inhabitants of the house have several grenade launchers and are prepared to use them to foil a police incursion, the police might reasonably conclude that announcing their presence prior to forcible entry might give the occupants of the dwelling the chance to kill the police officers before they even manage to get through the door. Similarly, if the police reasonably believe that the occupants might flush a bag of cocaine down the toilet before the police get inside the house, their refusal to knock and announce first might be judicially sanctioned.

In the following case, the Wisconsin courts crafted a blanket rule declaring that exigent circumstances existed in *all* felony drug searches, thus obviating the knock-and-announce requirement in all cases falling under that category. The Supreme Court was asked to rule on whether this scheme was consistent with the requirements of the Fourth Amendment as expressed in *Wilson v. Arkansas*.

Richards v. Wisconsin

Supreme Court of the United States
520 U.S. 385 (1997)

Justice STEVENS delivered the opinion of the Court.

In *Wilson v. Arkansas*, 514 U.S. 927 (1995), we held that the Fourth Amendment incorporates the common law requirement that police officers entering a dwelling must knock on the door and announce their identity and purpose before attempting forcible entry. At the same time, we recognized that the "flexible requirement of reasonableness should not be read to mandate a rigid rule of announcement that ignores countervailing law enforcement interests," and left "to the lower courts the task of determining the circumstances under which an unannounced entry is reasonable under the Fourth Amendment."

In this case, the Wisconsin Supreme Court concluded that police officers are *never* required to knock and announce their presence when executing a search warrant in a felony drug investigation. In so doing, it reaffirmed a pre-*Wilson* holding and concluded that *Wilson* did not preclude this *per se* rule. We disagree with the court's conclusion that the Fourth Amendment permits a blanket exception to the knock-and-announce requirement for this entire category of criminal activity. But because the evidence presented to support the officers' actions in this case establishes that the decision not to knock and announce was a reasonable one under the circumstances, we affirm the judgment of the Wisconsin court.

I

On December 31, 1991, police officers in Madison, Wisconsin, obtained a warrant to search Steiney Richards' motel room for drugs and related paraphernalia. The search warrant was the culmination of an investigation that had uncovered substantial evidence that Richards was one of several individuals dealing drugs out of motel rooms in Madison. The police requested a warrant that would have given advance authorization for a "no-knock" entry into the motel room, but the Magistrate explicitly deleted those portions of the warrant.

The officers arrived at the motel room at 3:40 A.M. Officer Pharo, dressed as a maintenance man, led the team. With him were several plainclothes officers and at least one man in uniform. Officer Pharo knocked on Richards' door and, responding to the query from inside the room, stated that he was a maintenance man. With the chain still on the door, Richards cracked it open. Although there is some dispute as to what occurred next, Richards acknowledges that when he opened the door he saw the man in uniform standing behind Officer Pharo. He quickly slammed the door closed and, after waiting two or three seconds, the officers began kicking and ramming the door to gain entry to the locked room. At trial, the officers testified that they identified themselves as police while they were kicking the door in. When they finally did break into the room, the officers caught Richards trying to escape through the window. They also found cash and cocaine hidden in plastic bags above the bathroom ceiling tiles.

Richards sought to have the evidence from his motel room suppressed on the ground that the officers had failed to knock and announce their presence prior to forcing entry into the room. The trial court denied the motion, concluding that the officers could gather from Richards' strange behavior when they first sought entry that he knew they were police officers and that he might try to destroy evidence or to escape. The judge emphasized that the easily disposable nature of the drugs the police were searching for further justified their decision to identify themselves as they crossed the threshold instead of announcing their presence before seeking entry. . . .

II

We recognized in *Wilson* that the knock-and-announce requirement could give way "under circumstances presenting a threat of physical violence," or "where police officers have reason to believe that evidence would likely be destroyed if advance notice were given." It is indisputable that felony drug investigations may frequently involve both of these circumstances. The question we must resolve is whether this fact justifies dispensing with case-by-case evaluation of the manner in which a search was executed.

The Wisconsin court explained its blanket exception as necessitated by the special circumstances of today's drug culture and the State asserted at oral argument that the blanket exception was reasonable in "felony drug cases because of the convergence in a violent and dangerous form of commerce of weapons and the destruction of drugs." But creating exceptions to the knock-and-announce rule based on the "culture" surrounding a general category of criminal behavior presents at least two serious concerns.

First, the exception contains considerable overgeneralization. For example, while drug investigation frequently does pose special risks to officer safety and the preservation of evidence, not every drug investigation will pose these risks to a substantial degree. For example, a search could be conducted at a time when the only individuals present in a residence have no connection with the drug activity and thus will be unlikely to threaten officers or destroy evidence. Or the police could know that the drugs being searched for were of a type or in a location that made them impossible to destroy quickly. In those situations, the asserted governmental interests in preserving evidence and maintaining safety may not outweigh the individual privacy interests intruded upon by a no-knock entry. Wisconsin's blanket rule impermissibly insulates these cases from judicial review.

A second difficulty with permitting a criminal-category exception to the knock-and-announce requirement is that the reasons for creating an exception in one category can, relatively easily, be applied to others. Armed bank robbers, for example, are, by definition, likely to have weapons, and the fruits of their crime may be destroyed without too much difficulty. If a *per se* exception were allowed for each category of criminal investigation that included a considerable—albeit hypothetical—risk of danger to officers or destruction of evidence, the knock-and-announce element of the Fourth Amendment's reasonableness requirement would be meaningless.

Thus, the fact that felony drug investigations may frequently present circumstances warranting a no-knock entry cannot remove from the neutral scrutiny of a reviewing court the reasonableness of the police decision not to knock and announce in a particular case. Instead, in each case, it is the duty of a court confronted with the question to determine whether the facts and circumstances of the particular entry justified dispensing with the knock-and-announce requirement.

In order to justify a "no-knock" entry, the police must have a reasonable suspicion that knocking and announcing their presence, under the particular circumstances, would be dangerous or futile, or that it would inhibit the effective investigation of the crime by, for example, allowing the destruction of evidence. This standard—as opposed to a probable-cause requirement—strikes the appropriate balance between the legitimate law enforcement concerns at issue in the execution of search warrants and the individual privacy interests affected by no-knock entries. This showing is not high, but the police should be required to make it whenever the reasonableness of a no-knock entry is challenged.

III

Although we reject the Wisconsin court's blanket exception to the knock-and-announce requirement, we conclude that the officers' no-knock entry into Richards' motel room did not violate the Fourth Amendment. We agree with the trial court . . . that the circumstances in this case show that the officers had a reasonable suspicion that Richards might destroy evidence if given further opportunity to do so.

The judge who heard testimony at Richards' suppression hearing concluded that it was reasonable for the officers executing the warrant to believe that Richards knew, after opening the door to his motel room the first time, that the men seeking entry to his room were the police. Once the officers reasonably believed that Richards knew who they were, the court concluded, it was reasonable for them to force entry immediately given the disposable nature of the drugs.

In arguing that the officers' entry was unreasonable, Richards places great emphasis on the fact that the Magistrate who signed the search warrant for his motel room deleted the portions of the proposed warrant that would have given the officers permission to execute a no-knock entry. But this fact does not alter the reasonableness of the officers' decision, which must be evaluated as of the time they entered the motel room. At the time the officers obtained the warrant, they did not have evidence sufficient, in the judgment of the Magistrate, to justify a no-knock warrant. Of course, the Magistrate could not have anticipated in every particular the circumstances that would confront the officers when they arrived at Richards' motel room. These actual circumstances—petitioner's apparent recognition of the officers combined with the easily disposable nature of the drugs—justified the officers' ultimate decision to enter without first announcing their presence and authority.

Accordingly, although we reject the blanket exception to the knock-and-announce requirement for felony drug investigations, the judgment of the Wisconsin Supreme Court is affirmed.

STATUTORY REQUIREMENTS

Many states *codify* a knock-and-announce requirement in statutes that mirror the constitutional standard discussed in this section. For example, 18 U.S.C. § 3109 states that an "officer may break open any outer or inner door or window of a house, or any part of a house, or anything therein, to execute a search warrant, if, *after notice of his authority and purpose*, he is refused admittance or when necessary to liberate himself or a person aiding him in the execution of the warrant." Similarly, Florida's statute states that if "a peace officer fails to gain admittance after she or he has announced her or his authority and purpose in order to make an arrest either by a warrant or when authorized to make an arrest for a felony without a warrant, the officer may use all necessary and reasonable force to enter any building or property where the person to be arrested is or is reasonably believed to be." Fla. Stat. Ann. § 901.19.

Almost all states have similar statutory requirements, though Illinois is a notable exception, and its knock-and-announce requirement is solely a creature of judicial application of constitutional law. See *People v. Condon*, 148 Ill. 2d 96, 108-09, 592 N.E.2d 951, 957 (1992) (applying knock-and-announce rule as a requirement of constitutional law as part of Fourth Amendment reasonableness inquiry). Most of the statutory knock-and-announce requirements also include an exception, either explicitly or implicitly, for exigent circumstances.

NOTES & QUESTIONS ON ANNOUNCEMENT

1. *Exigent circumstances.* Generally speaking, there are two types of situations that might qualify as exigent circumstances: danger to a person or risk of destruction of evidence. For example, courts have held that the destruction of evidence exception would apply in a situation where the police know that a "a small amount of narcotics is always kept near a toilet" or the police "announce and then hear indications that evidence is being destroyed," thus requiring immediate forcible entry. *State v. Gassner*, 6 Or. App. 452, 461, 488 P.2d 822, 826 (1971). Similarly, police would be entitled to forcibly enter without knocking to "to rescue a victim in peril." *Wong Sun v. United States*, 371 U.S. 471, 484 (1963). Prior to *Richards*, some in law enforcement supported categorical rules that allow entire categories of cases to be excepted from the knock-and-announce requirement, because these cases usually present fact patterns that involve exigency. On the other hand, civil libertarians wanted the exigency evaluated at the level of the individual case. For more discussion of this dilemma, see Charles Patrick Garcia, *The Knock and Announce Rule: A New Approach to the Destruction-of-Evidence Exception*, 93 Colum. L. Rev. 685, 713 (1993). *Richards* clearly resolved that dispute in favor of case-by-case particularity.

Have these exceptions impermissibly watered down the knock-and-announce requirement beyond its common law origin? Some commentators have argued that the destruction of evidence exception was not originally available to the police at common law when the Constitution was adopted. See Robert J. Driscoll, *Unannounced Police Entries and Destruction of Evidence After* Wilson v. Arkansas, 29 Colum. J.L. & Soc. Probs. 1, 27 (1995) ("the destruction-of-evidence exception appears to be a relatively recent judicial invention"). Here is Justice Brennan's assessment:

> I have found no English decision which clearly recognizes any exception to the requirement that the police first give notice of their authority and purpose before forcibly entering a home: Exceptions were early sanctioned in American cases, but these were rigidly and narrowly confined to situations not within the reason and spirit of the general requirement. Specifically, exceptional circumstances have been thought to exist only when, as one element, the facts surrounding the particular entry support a finding that those within actually knew or must have known of the officer's presence and purpose to seek admission. . . . The rationale of such an exception is clear, and serves to underscore the consistency and the purpose of the general requirement of notice: Where such circumstances as an escape and hot pursuit by the arresting officer leave no doubt that the fleeing felon is aware of the officer's presence and purpose, pausing at the threshold to make the ordinarily requisite announcement and demand would be a superfluous act which the law does not require. But no exceptions have heretofore permitted unannounced entries in the absence of such awareness on the part of the occupants—unless possibly where the officers are justified in the belief that someone within is in immediate danger of bodily harm.

Ker v. California, 374 U.S. 23, 54-55 (1963) (Brennan, J.). Has the current doctrine strayed from the historical understanding of the requirement?

2. *No-knock warrants.* In *United States v. Banks*, 540 U.S. 31, 36 (2003), the Supreme Court noted that when a "warrant applicant gives reasonable grounds to expect futility or to suspect that one or another such exigency already exists or will arise instantly upon knocking, a magistrate judge is acting within the Constitution to authorize a 'no-knock' entry." Some state statutes specifically contemplate the issuance of these warrants that pre-authorize the police to search a premise without first announcing their presence. For example, New York's statute on warrants includes the following provision:

> (b) A request that the search warrant authorize the executing police officer to enter premises to be searched without giving notice of his authority and purpose, upon the ground that there is reasonable cause to believe that (i) the property sought may be easily and quickly destroyed or disposed of, or (ii) the giving of such notice may endanger the life or safety of the executing officer or another person, or (iii) in the case of an application for a

> search warrant . . . for the purpose of searching for and arresting a person who is the subject of a warrant for a felony, the person sought is likely to commit another felony, or may endanger the life or safety of the executing officer or another person.

N.Y. Crim. Proc. Law § 690.35. Such warrants might be issued when, for example, "the information provided supported a reasonable belief that defendant might have weapons in his apartment subjecting the police to a substantial risk of physical injury." *People v. Walker*, 257 A.D.2d 769, 770, 684 N.Y.S.2d 26, 28 (1999). The point of these warrants is to provide a pre-authorization that necessarily evaluates the existence of exigent circumstances based on information provided in advance to the magistrate. However, the *absence* of a no-knock warrant does not preclude the police from claiming exigent circumstances if they arise at the moment in time when the warrant is executed. See *United States v. Scroggins*, 361 F.3d 1075, 1082 (8th Cir. 2004) ("Although the standards are the same regardless of whether the police visit a judge before or after they search, if they do so beforehand, and the judge is wrong, the police can rely upon [a] good-faith exception."); *United States v. Tisdale*, 195 F.3d 70, 72 (2d Cir. 1999) ("[T]he issuance of a warrant with a no-knock provision potentially insulates the police against a subsequent finding that exigent circumstances . . . did not exist.").

3. *How much announcement is required?* Although the concept of "knocking" is relatively straightforward, the notion of "announcing" one's presence is self-defining. In practice, what precisely must the police do? For example, after shouting "police," must the police wait for the occupant to respond before barging in forcibly? If yes, how long must they wait? What if the police announce themselves but then barge through the door a split second later? In *United States v. Banks*, 540 U.S. 31 (2003), the police

> officers posted in front called out "police search warrant" and rapped hard enough on the door to be heard by officers at the back door. There was no indication whether anyone was home, and after waiting for 15 to 20 seconds with no answer, the officers broke open the front door with a battering ram. Banks was in the shower and testified that he heard nothing until the crash of the door, which brought him out dripping to confront the police. The search produced weapons, crack cocaine, and other evidence of drug dealing.

The Supreme Court concluded that the search complied with the knock-and-announce requirement because "after 15 or 20 seconds without a response, police could fairly suspect that cocaine would be gone if they were reticent any longer." In other words, 20 seconds was a "reasonable wait time."

However, in *People v. Asher,* 203 Mich. App. 621, 623, 513 N.W.2d 144, 144 (1994), the police entered a residence after waiting only five seconds after knocking. After noting that five seconds was insufficient under the knock-and-announce requirement, the Michigan appellate court concluded that "nothing in this case indicates that there was any evidence that drugs were kept in a manner that would facilitate their immediate destruction or that these particular defendants possessed weapons." The Supreme Court of Nebraska held that a ten-second delay satisfies the requirement. *State v. Lammers,* 267 Neb. 679, 676 N.W.2d 716 (2004). Although there is no magic number of seconds sufficient to satisfy the knock-and-announce requirement, the basic idea is that the occupant should have the "reasonable opportunity" to respond before the authorities enter with force. See *Spradley v. State,* 933 So. 2d 51, 53 (Fla. Dist. Ct. App. 2006).

4. *Excluding evidence from no-knock searches.* What happens if the police enter a residence with force and a court concludes that the officers violated the knock-and-announce requirement? In the past, courts were split on whether the Constitution required suppressing evidence of the illegal search. Although the exclusionary rule will be studied in greater depth in Chapter 6, it should be noted here because the question speaks to the underlying rationale for the knock-and-announce requirement. In *Hudson v. Michigan,* 547 U.S. 586 (2006), the Supreme Court concluded that the exclusionary rule did not require the suppression of all evidence found in these illegal searches. The Court based this conclusion on the fact that announcement is designed to protect an individual's privacy—by giving them time to collect themselves before answering the door—and to protect human life and limb, but was not designed to protect the occupant's "interest in preventing the government from seeing or taking evidence described in a warrant."

D. DETENTION INCIDENT TO A SEARCH

During a search, how are police officers to treat the occupants of the premises? Assuming that the police are there simply to search the premise and do not, for example, have an arrest warrant for the occupant, their primary goal is to locate and secure the evidence described in the search warrant. Nonetheless, police will sometimes detain—perhaps even handcuff—the occupants during the course of the search, even though they do not meet the typical probable cause standard for an arrest. Is this practice consistent with the Fourth Amendment? In *Michigan v. Summers,* 452 U.S. 692 (1981), the Supreme Court ratified the practice on the assumption that some limited

PROBLEM CASE

On May 28, 2014, a SWAT team burst into a home in the small town of Cornelia, Georgia. It was 2:15 A.M., and the team was heavily armed with automatic rifles, stun grenades, and a battering ram. The officers approached the side of the house and burst through the door, shouting that they were police officers. One of the officers lobbed a stun grenade into the darkened room. The grenade landed directly in the crib of 19-month-old Bounkham Phonesavanh, affectionately referred to by family members as "Baby Bou Bou." Although the charge was a mere "stun" grenade, it was powerful enough to rip through his abdomen, exposing his ribs and causing serious burns to his face and body. The baby was placed in a coma but survived with lasting injuries.

The story of how the raid was approved did not inspire confidence. The drug task force of the local police force had previously caught a local methamphetamine user and turned him into an informant. The informant had provided an address of a house that might be connected to drug activity. A police officer woke up the local magistrate and provided sworn testimony to support the warrant application, stating that the informant had indicated that he had bought drugs at that house and that police surveillance confirmed an unusually high rate of visitors to the location. The magistrate signed a no-knock warrant authorizing the raid.

Subsequent investigations cast doubt on these assertions. The informant had not personally bought drugs at that location, and the police had not performed the surveillance that would be required to assert that the house was subject to a suspicious amount of traffic or activity. Federal authorities eventually charged the officer who sought the warrant with lying to a judge, though at trial she was acquitted of the charge. The family received a multi-million-dollar settlement to settle a civil claim against the city.

Critics of no-knock warrants, including the ACLU, see the injury of Baby Bou Bou as symptomatic of a larger problem: the militarization of local police forces combined with liberal legal standards that make it too easy for police officers to receive judicial authorization for no-knock entry. Do you agree? Do these raids comport with the spirit behind the Fourth Amendment? As a state legislator, would you vote in favor of repealing no-knock warrant statutes? See Alecia Phonesavanh, *A SWAT Team Blew a Hole in My 2-Year-Old Son*, Salon, June 24, 2014 ("Now my kids don't want to go to sleep at night because they're afraid the cops will kill them or their family. It's time to remind the cops that they should be serving and protecting our neighborhoods, not waging war on the people in them."); Kevin Sack, *Door-Busting Drug Raids Leave a Trail of Blood*, N.Y. Times, Mar. 18, 2017.

detention might be necessary to prevent the destruction of evidence and to protect the safety of the police officers conducting the search. In *Summers*, the occupants were detained in the immediate vicinity of the search and the Court concluded that this represented only "an incremental intrusion on personal liberty." In the following case, the Supreme Court asks whether the *Summers* holding can be extended to individuals detained some distance from the premise to be searched. As you read the case, ask yourself whether the detention in *Bailey* constituted an "incremental intrusion on personal liberty" or was more severe.

Bailey v. United States

Supreme Court of the United States
568 U.S. 186 (2013)

Justice KENNEDY delivered the opinion of the Court.

The Fourth Amendment guarantees the right to be free from unreasonable searches and seizures. A search may be of a person, a thing, or a place. So too a seizure may be of a person, a thing, or even a place. A search or a seizure may occur singly or in combination, and in differing sequence. In some cases the validity of one determines the validity of the other. The instant case involves the search of a place (an apartment dwelling) and the seizure of a person. But here, though it is acknowledged that the search was lawful, it does not follow that the seizure was lawful as well. The seizure of the person is quite in question. The issue to be resolved is whether the seizure of the person was reasonable when he was stopped and detained at some distance away from the premises to be searched when the only justification for the detention was to ensure the safety and efficacy of the search.

I

At 8:45 P.M. on July 28, 2005, local police obtained a warrant to search a residence for a .380-caliber handgun. The residence was a basement apartment at 103 Lake Drive, in Wyandanch, New York. A confidential informant had told police he observed the gun when he was at the apartment to purchase drugs from "a heavy set black male with short hair" known as "Polo." As the search unit began preparations for executing the warrant, two officers, Detectives Richard Sneider and Richard Gorbecki, were conducting surveillance in an unmarked car outside the residence. About 9:56 P.M., Sneider and Gorbecki observed two men—later identified as petitioner Chunon Bailey and Bryant Middleton—leave the gated area above the basement apartment and enter a car parked in the driveway. Both matched the general physical description of "Polo" provided by the informant. There was no indication that the men were aware of the officers' presence or had any knowledge of the impending search. The detectives watched the car leave the driveway. They waited for it to go a few hundred yards down the street and followed. The detectives informed the search team of their intent to follow and detain the departing occupants. The search team then executed the search warrant at the apartment.

Detectives Sneider and Gorbecki tailed Bailey's car for about a mile—and for about five minutes—before pulling the vehicle over in a parking lot by a fire station. They ordered Bailey and Middleton out of the car and did a patdown search of both men. The officers found no weapons but discovered a ring of keys in Bailey's pocket. Bailey identified himself and said he was coming from his home at 103 Lake Drive. His driver's license, however, showed his address as Bayshore, New York, the town where the confidential informant told the police the suspect, "Polo," used to live.

Bailey's passenger, Middleton, said Bailey was giving him a ride home and confirmed they were coming from Bailey's residence at 103 Lake Drive. The officers put both men in handcuffs. When Bailey asked why, Gorbecki stated that they were being detained incident to the execution of a search warrant at 103 Lake Drive. Bailey responded: "I don't live there. Anything you find there ain't mine, and I'm not cooperating with your investigation."

The detectives called for a patrol car to take Bailey and Middleton back to the Lake Drive apartment. Detective Sneider drove the unmarked car back, while Detective Gorbecki used Bailey's set of keys to drive Bailey's car back to the search scene. By the time the group returned to 103 Lake Drive, the search team had discovered a gun and drugs in plain view inside the apartment. Bailey and Middleton were placed under arrest, and Bailey's keys were seized incident to the arrest. Officers later discovered that one of Bailey's keys opened the door of the basement apartment. . . .

II

. . . In *Michigan v. Summers,* 452 U.S. 692, 697-698 (1981), the Court defined an important category of cases in which detention is allowed without probable cause to arrest for a crime. It permitted officers executing a search warrant "to detain the occupants of the premises while a proper search is conducted." The rule in *Summers* extends farther than some earlier exceptions because it does not require law enforcement to have particular suspicion that an individual is involved in criminal activity or poses a specific danger to the officers. *Muehler v. Mena,* 544 U.S. 93 (2005). In *Muehler,* applying the rule in *Summers,* the Court stated: "An officer's authority to detain incident to a search is categorical; it does not depend on the 'quantum of proof justifying detention or the extent of the intrusion to be imposed by the seizure.'" The rule announced in *Summers* allows detention incident to the execution of a search warrant "because the character of the additional intrusion caused by detention is slight and because the justifications for detention are substantial." . . .

In *Summers,* the Court recognized three important law enforcement interests that, taken together, justify the detention of an occupant who is on the premises during the execution of a search warrant: officer safety, facilitating the completion of the search, and preventing flight.

The first interest identified in *Summers* was "the interest in minimizing the risk of harm to the officers." There the Court held that "the execution of a warrant to search for narcotics is the kind of transaction that may give rise to sudden violence or frantic efforts to conceal or destroy evidence," and "[t]he risk of harm to both the police and the occupants is minimized if the officers routinely exercise unquestioned command of the situation."

When law enforcement officers execute a search warrant, safety considerations require that they secure the premises, which may include detaining current occupants. By taking "unquestioned command of the situation," the officers can search without fear that occupants, who are on the premises and able to observe the course of the search, will become disruptive, dangerous, or otherwise frustrate the search. . . .

It is likely, indeed almost inevitable in the case of a resident, that an occupant will return to the premises at some point; and this might occur when the officers are still conducting the search. Officers can and do mitigate that risk, however, by taking routine precautions, for instance by erecting barricades or posting someone on the perimeter or at the door. In the instant case Bailey had left the premises, apparently without knowledge of the search. He posed little risk to the officers at the scene. If Bailey had rushed back to his apartment, the police could have apprehended and detained him under *Summers*. There is no established principle, however, that allows the arrest of anyone away from the premises who is likely to return.

The risk, furthermore, that someone could return home during the execution of a search warrant is not limited to occupants who depart shortly before the start of a search. The risk that a resident might return home, either for reasons unrelated to the search or after being alerted by someone at the scene, exists whether he left five minutes or five hours earlier. Unexpected arrivals by occupants or other persons accustomed to visiting the premises might occur in many instances. Were police to have the authority to detain those persons away from the premises, the authority to detain incident to the execution of a search warrant would reach beyond the rationale of ensuring the integrity of the search by detaining those who are in fact on the scene. . . .

The risk that a departing occupant might notice the police surveillance and alert others still inside the residence is also an insufficient safety rationale to justify expanding the existing categorical authority to detain so that it extends beyond the immediate vicinity of the premises to be searched. If extended in this way the rationale would justify detaining anyone in the neighborhood who could alert occupants that the police are outside, all without individualized suspicion of criminal activity or connection to the residence to be searched. This possibility demonstrates why it is necessary to confine the *Summers* rule to those who are present when and where the search is being conducted.

The second law enforcement interest relied on in *Summers* was that "the orderly completion of the search may be facilitated if the occupants of the premises are present." This interest in efficiency derives from distinct, but related, concerns.

If occupants are permitted to wander around the premises, there is the potential for interference with the execution of the search warrant. They can hide or destroy evidence, seek to distract the officers, or simply get in the way. Those risks are not presented by an occupant who departs beforehand. So, in this case, after Bailey drove away from the Lake Drive apartment, he was not a threat to the proper execution of the search. Had he returned, officers would have been free to detain him at that point. A general interest in avoiding obstruction of a search, however, cannot justify detention beyond the vicinity of the premises to be searched.

Summers also noted that occupants can assist the officers. Under the reasoning in *Summers,* the occupants' "self-interest may induce them to open locked doors or locked containers to avoid the use of force that is not only damaging to property but may also delay the completion of the task at hand." This justification must be confined to those persons who are on site and so in a position, when detained, to at once observe the progression of the search; and it would have no limiting principle were it to be applied to persons beyond the premises of the search. Here, it appears the police officers decided to wait until Bailey had left the vicinity of the search before detaining him. In any event it later became clear to the officers that Bailey did not wish to cooperate. And, by the time the officers brought Bailey back to the apartment, the search team had discovered contraband. Bailey's detention thus served no purpose in ensuring the efficient completion of the search.

The third law enforcement interest addressed in *Summers* was the "the legitimate law enforcement interest in preventing flight in the event that incriminating evidence is found." The proper interpretation of this language, in the context of *Summers* and in the broader context of the reasonableness standard that must govern and inform the detention incident to a search, is that the police can prohibit an occupant from leaving the scene of the search. As with the other interests identified in *Summers,* this justification serves to preserve the integrity of the search by controlling those persons who are on the scene. If police officers are concerned about flight, and have to keep close supervision of occupants who are not restrained, they might rush the search, causing unnecessary damage to property or compromising its careful execution. Allowing officers to secure the scene by detaining those present also prevents the search from being impeded by occupants leaving with the evidence being sought or the means to find it.

The concern over flight is not because of the danger of flight itself but because of the damage that potential flight can cause to the integrity of the search. This interest does not independently justify detention of an occupant beyond the immediate vicinity of the premises to be searched. The need to prevent flight, if unbounded, might be used to argue for detention, while a search is underway, of any regular occupant regardless of his or her location at the time of the search. If not circumscribed, the rationale of preventing flight would justify, for instance, detaining a suspect who is 10 miles away, ready to board a plane. The interest in preventing escape from police cannot extend this far without undermining the usual rules for arrest based on probable cause or a brief stop for questioning. . . .

In sum, of the three law enforcement interests identified to justify the detention in *Summers,* none applies with the same or similar force to the detention of recent occupants beyond the immediate vicinity of the premises to be searched. Any of the individual interests is also insufficient, on its own, to justify an expansion of the rule in *Summers* to permit the detention of a former occupant, wherever he may be found away from the scene of the search. This would give officers too much discretion. The categorical authority to detain incident to the execution of a search warrant must be limited to the immediate vicinity of the premises to be searched.

In *Summers,* the Court recognized the authority to detain occupants incident to the execution of a search warrant not only in light of the law enforcement interests at stake but also because the intrusion on personal liberty was limited. The Court held detention of a current occupant "represents only an incremental intrusion on personal liberty when the search of a home has been authorized by a valid warrant." Because the detention occurs in the individual's own home, "it could add only minimally to the public stigma associated with the search itself and would involve neither the inconvenience nor the indignity associated with a compelled visit to the police station."

Where officers arrest an individual away from his home, however, there is an additional level of intrusiveness. A public detention, even if merely incident to a search, will resemble a full-fledged arrest. As demonstrated here, detention beyond the immediate vicinity can involve an initial detention away from the scene and a second detention at the residence. In between, the individual will suffer the additional indignity of a compelled transfer back to the premises, giving all the appearances of an arrest. The detention here was more intrusive than a usual detention at the search scene. Bailey's car was stopped; he was ordered to step out and was detained in full public view; he was handcuffed, transported in a marked patrol car, and detained further outside the apartment. These facts illustrate that detention away from a premises where police are already present often will be more intrusive than detentions at the scene. . . .

A spatial constraint defined by the immediate vicinity of the premises to be searched is therefore required for detentions incident to the execution of a search warrant. The police action permitted here—the search of a residence—has a spatial dimension, and so a spatial or geographical boundary can be used to determine the area within which both the search and detention incident to that search may occur. Limiting the rule in *Summers* to the area in which an occupant poses a real threat to the safe and efficient execution of a search warrant ensures that the scope of the detention incident to a search is confined to its underlying justification. Once an occupant is beyond the immediate vicinity of the premises to be searched, the search-related law enforcement interests are diminished and the intrusiveness of the detention is more severe. Here, petitioner was detained at a point beyond any reasonable understanding of the immediate vicinity of the premises in question; and so this case presents neither the necessity nor the occasion to further define the meaning of immediate vicinity. In closer cases courts can consider a number of factors to determine whether an occupant was detained within the immediate vicinity of the premises to be searched, including the lawful limits of the premises, whether the occupant was within the line of sight of his dwelling, the ease of reentry from the occupant's location, and other relevant factors. . . .

NOTES & QUESTIONS ON DETENTIONS DURING SEARCHES

1. *Three government interests.* The Supreme Court has justified detention incidental to arrest because it serves three important governmental interests: preventing flight if incriminating evidence is found; the safety of the officers; and the "orderly completion" of the search. Consider these government interests in light of the facts in *Bailey*. Were any of the interests advanced by the detention of the defendants in this case?

2. *What is the boundary?.* *Summers* permits detention on the premises while *Bailey* prohibits detention far removed from the location of the search. But what is the dividing line between the two results? What result if, say, the occupant is outside of the house on the street? Would that constitute the "immediate vicinity" and would detention be appropriate in that context? More importantly, do *Summers* and *Bailey* provide a workable standard for lower courts to make this determination? The Court suggested in *Bailey* that courts should consider whether the individual was in the "line of sight" of the dwelling or could easily reenter the dwelling from his or her position. As one commentator noted:

> [I]f a suspect whose home is about to be searched steps off of his property and reaches the street before being seized, will the detention be valid? The answer would seem to be yes, even though the occupant left his property, because he likely still has a line of sight to the property and could easily

> reenter it. On the other hand, what about a suspect who lives in an apartment building and enters the stairwell next to his room before police seize him? Even though he would probably be closer to the premises than the other suspect and would therefore pose a greater danger to police, his seizure would likely be found impermissible; he was off of his property and did not have a line of sight to it.

David Torreblanca, *Applying* Michigan v. Summers *to Off-Premises Seizures: The "As Early As Practicable" Standard,* 87 St. John's L. Rev. 763, 788-89 (2013). Can you craft a better set of guidelines?

3. *Search versus seizure.* The preceding cases, including *Bailey* and *Summers*, deal with the detention of individuals at the scene, which for purposes of the Fourth Amendment is a seizure of those individuals. *Summers* and *Bailey* both stand for the proposition that those individuals may be briefly seized by police in order to ensure the proper conclusion of the search. However, a further question is whether those individuals may be searched. In *Ybarra v. Illinois*, 444 U.S. 85 (1979), the Supreme Court concluded that police were not authorized to search an individual's pocket simply because he was located at the scene when a search warrant was executed. The Court noted that "Ybarra, whose hands were empty, gave no indication of possessing a weapon, made no gestures or other actions indicative of an intent to commit an assault, and acted generally in a manner that was not threatening." In other words, searching his pockets was not necessary to ensure the protection and safety of the officers conducting the search of the premises and therefore fell outside of the rationale for a seizure incident to a search.

E. MISTAKES

What happens when police make a mistake during a search and exceed the parameters of a lawful search warrant? In some situations, the police might deliberately go beyond the four corners of the search warrant, which is clearly impermissible. But what if the police encounter a confusing situation and, in good faith, make a simple and understandable mistake? Should the search be declared unconstitutional, perhaps even triggering the exclusionary rule? In the following case, the police were confronted with a confusing configuration of doors on the third floor of a building and entered Garrison's apartment thinking that it was part of the apartment that they were authorized to search. As you read the case, ask yourself whether this mistake strikes you as objectively reasonable.

Maryland v. Garrison

Supreme Court of the United States
480 U.S. 79 (1987)

Justice STEVENS delivered the opinion of the Court.

Baltimore police officers obtained and executed a warrant to search the person of Lawrence McWebb and "the premises known as 2036 Park Avenue third floor apartment." When the police applied for the warrant and when they conducted the search pursuant to the warrant, they reasonably believed that there was only one apartment on the premises described in the warrant. In fact, the third floor was divided into two apartments, one occupied by McWebb and one by respondent Garrison. Before the officers executing the warrant became aware that they were in a separate apartment occupied by respondent, they had discovered the contraband that provided the basis for respondent's conviction for violating Maryland's Controlled Substances Act. The question presented is whether the seizure of that contraband was prohibited by the Fourth Amendment.

The trial court denied respondent's motion to suppress the evidence seized from his apartment and the Maryland Court of Special Appeals affirmed. The Court of Appeals of Maryland reversed and remanded with instructions to remand the case for a new trial.

There is no question that the warrant was valid and was supported by probable cause. The trial court found, and the two appellate courts did not dispute, that after making a reasonable investigation, including a verification of information obtained from a reliable informant, an exterior examination of the three-story building at 2036 Park Avenue, and an inquiry of the utility company, the officer who obtained the warrant reasonably concluded that there was only one apartment on the third floor and that it was occupied by McWebb. When six Baltimore police officers executed the warrant, they fortuitously encountered McWebb in front of the building and used his key to gain admittance to the first-floor hallway and to the locked door at the top of the stairs to the third floor. As they entered the vestibule on the third floor, they encountered respondent, who was standing in the hallway area. The police could see into the interior of both McWebb's apartment to the left and respondent's to the right, for the doors to both were open. Only after respondent's apartment had been entered and heroin, cash, and drug paraphernalia had been found did any of the officers realize that the third floor contained two apartments. As soon as they became aware of that fact, the search was discontinued. All of the officers reasonably believed that they were searching McWebb's apartment. No further search of respondent's apartment was made.

The matter on which there is a difference of opinion concerns the proper interpretation of the warrant. A literal reading of its plain language, as well as the language used in the application for the warrant, indicates that it was intended to authorize a search of the entire third floor. This is the construction adopted by the intermediate appellate court, and it also appears to be the construction adopted by the trial judge. One sentence in the trial judge's oral opinion, however, lends support to the construction adopted by the Court of Appeals, namely, that the warrant authorized a search of McWebb's apartment only. Under that interpretation, the Court of Appeals concluded that the warrant did not authorize the search of respondent's apartment and the police had no justification for making a warrantless entry into his premises.

The opinion of the Maryland Court of Appeals relies on Article 26 of the Maryland Declaration of Rights and Maryland cases as well as the Fourth Amendment to the Federal Constitution and federal cases. Rather than containing any "plain statement" that the decision rests upon adequate and independent state grounds, the opinion indicates that the Maryland constitutional provision is construed *in pari materia* with the Fourth Amendment. We therefore have jurisdiction. . . .

II

The question whether the execution of the warrant violated respondent's constitutional right to be secure in his home is somewhat less clear. We have no difficulty concluding that the officers' entry into the third-floor common area was legal; they carried a warrant for those premises, and they were accompanied by McWebb, who provided the key that they used to open the door giving access to the third-floor common area. If the officers had known, or should have known, that the third floor contained two apartments before they entered the living quarters on the third floor, and thus had been aware of the error in the warrant, they would have been obligated to limit their search to McWebb's apartment. Moreover, as the officers recognized, they were required to discontinue the search of respondent's apartment as soon as they discovered that there were two separate units on the third floor and therefore were put on notice of the risk that they might be in a unit erroneously included within the terms of the warrant. The officers' conduct and the limits of the search were based on the information available as the search proceeded. While the purposes justifying a police search strictly limit the permissible extent of the search, the Court has also recognized the need to allow some latitude for honest mistakes that are made by officers in the dangerous and difficult process of making arrests and executing search warrants.

In *Hill v. California,* 401 U.S. 797 (1971), we considered the validity of the arrest of a man named Miller based on the mistaken belief that he was Hill. The police had probable cause to arrest Hill and they in good faith believed that Miller was Hill when they found him in Hill's apartment. As we explained:

> The upshot was that the officers in good faith believed Miller was Hill and arrested him. They were quite wrong as it turned out, and subjective good-faith belief would not in itself justify either the arrest or the subsequent search. But sufficient probability, not certainty, is the touchstone of reasonableness under the Fourth Amendment and on the record before us the officers' mistake was understandable and the arrest a reasonable response to the situation facing them at the time.

While *Hill* involved an arrest without a warrant, its underlying rationale that an officer's reasonable misidentification of a person does not invalidate a valid arrest is equally applicable to an officer's reasonable failure to appreciate that a valid warrant describes too broadly the premises to be searched. Under the reasoning in *Hill,* the validity of the search of respondent's apartment pursuant to a warrant authorizing the search of the entire third floor depends on whether the officers' failure to realize the overbreadth of the warrant was objectively understandable and reasonable. Here it unquestionably was. The objective facts available to the officers at the time suggested no distinction between McWebb's apartment and the third-floor premises.

For that reason, the officers properly responded to the command contained in a valid warrant even if the warrant is interpreted as authorizing a search limited to McWebb's apartment rather than the entire third floor. Prior to the officers' discovery of the factual mistake, they perceived McWebb's apartment and the third-floor premises as one and the same; therefore their execution of the warrant reasonably included the entire third floor. Under either interpretation of the warrant, the officers' conduct was consistent with a reasonable effort to ascertain and identify the place intended to be searched within the meaning of the Fourth Amendment.

The judgment of the Court of Appeals is reversed, and the case is remanded for further proceedings not inconsistent with this opinion.

Justice Blackmun, with whom Justice Brennan and Justice Marshall join, dissenting.

Under this Court's precedents, the search of respondent Garrison's apartment violated the Fourth Amendment. While executing a warrant specifically limited to McWebb's residence, the officers expanded their search to include respondent's adjacent apartment, an expansion made without a warrant and in the absence of exigent circumstances. In my view, Maryland's highest court correctly concluded that the trial judge should have granted respondent's motion to suppress the evidence seized as a result of this warrantless search of his apartment. Moreover, even if I were to accept the majority's analysis of this case as one involving a mistake on the part of the police officers, I would find that the officers' error, either in obtaining or in executing the warrant, was not reasonable under the circumstances. . . .

Because the Court cannot justify the officers' search under the "exceptional circumstances" rubric, it analyzes the police conduct here in terms of "mistake." According to the Court, hindsight makes it clear that the officers were mistaken, first, in not describing McWebb's apartment with greater specificity in the warrant, and, second, in including respondent's apartment within the scope of the execution of the warrant. The Court's inquiry focuses on what the officers knew or should have known at these particular junctures. The Court reasons that if, in light of the officers' actual or imputed knowledge, their behavior was reasonable, then their mistakes did not constitute an infringement on respondent's Fourth Amendment rights. In this case, the Court finds no Fourth Amendment violation because the officers could not reasonably have drawn the warrant with any greater particularity and because, until the moment when the officers realized that they were in fact searching two different apartments, they had no reason to believe that McWebb's residence did not cover the entire third floor. . . .

Even if one accepts the majority's view that there is no Fourth Amendment violation where the officers' mistake is reasonable, it is questionable whether that standard was met in this case. To repeat Justice Harlan's observation, although the proper question in Fourth Amendment analysis is "what protection it affords to ... people, ... that question requires reference to a 'place.'" *Katz v. United States,* 389 U.S., at 361 (concurring opinion). The "place" at issue here is a small multiple-occupancy building. Such forms of habitation are now common in this country, particularly in neighborhoods with changing populations and of declining affluence. Accordingly, any analysis of the "reasonableness" of the officers' behavior here must be done with this context in mind. . . .

The efforts of Detective Marcus, the officer who procured the search warrant, do not meet a standard of reasonableness, particularly considering that the detective knew the search concerned a unit in a multiple-occupancy building. Upon learning from his informant that McWebb was selling marijuana in his third-floor apartment, Marcus inspected the outside of the building. He did not approach it, however, to gather information about the configuration of the apartments. Had he done so, he would have discovered, as did another officer on the day of executing the warrant, that there were seven separate mailboxes and bells on the porch outside the main entrance to the house. Although there is some dispute over whether names were affixed near these boxes and bells, their existence alone puts a reasonable observer on notice that the three-story structure (with, possibly, a basement) had seven individual units. The detective, therefore, should

> have been aware that further investigation was necessary to eliminate the possibility of more than one unit's being located on the third floor. . . . Moreover, a reasonable officer would have realized the mistake in the warrant during the moments following the officers' entrance to the third floor. . . .
>
> Accordingly, even if a reasonable error on the part of police officers prevents a Fourth Amendment violation, the mistakes here, both with respect to obtaining and executing the warrant, are not reasonable and could easily have been avoided. I respectfully dissent.

NOTES & QUESTIONS ON GOOD FAITH MISTAKES

1. *Objectively understandable and reasonable.* In *Garrison*, the Supreme Court articulated the following standard for excusing good faith mistakes in the execution of a warrant: The mistake was objectively understandable and reasonable. Review the facts of the search. Do you consider the police mistake to be objectively reasonable, or do you endorse Justice Blackmun's conclusion that a reasonable police officer would not have made such a mistake? Does the rule emerging from *Garrison* give police officers enough incentive to comply with the requirements of their search warrants or does it incentivize loose and sloppy search practices?

2. *Can mistakes of law be objectively reasonable?* In *Garrison*, the police officers made a factual mistake—they misunderstood the configuration of rooms on the third floor. But what if the mistake is a legal one, such as a mistake regarding the content of a statute? In *Heien v. North Carolina*, 135 S. Ct. 530 (2014), the police stopped a motorist with a broken brake light and after a search of the car discovered cocaine. However, state law required only *one* functional brake light—not two—though the police officer falsely believed that state law required two functioning brake lights. In finding no Fourth Amendment violation, the Supreme Court noted that "reasonable men make mistakes of law, too. . . ." Does the holding discourage police officers from educating themselves about the content of the law?

3. *Mistakes in the warrant application.* What result if the warrant application includes mistakes, such as falsehoods contained in the sworn affidavit that was used to support the warrant application? The general rule is that innocent mistakes will not vitiate the warrant, but that "where the defendant makes a substantial preliminary showing that a false statement knowingly and intentionally, or with reckless disregard for the truth, was included by the affiant in the warrant affidavit, and if the allegedly false statement is necessary to the finding of probable cause, the Fourth Amendment requires that a hearing be held at the defendant's request." *Franks v. Delaware*, 438 U.S. 154, 155-56 (1978).

At the hearing, the court must evaluate the claim of perjury or reckless disregard based on a standard of "preponderance of the evidence." If the allegations of perjury or reckless disregard are established by that standard, the court will set aside the false material and ask whether the uncompromised information in the affidavit is sufficient to meet the Fourth Amendment's probable cause standard. If the probable cause standard is satisfied with the remaining information, then the warrant and the search are vindicated; if the probable cause standard is not met, then the warrant is vitiated and the results of the search are set aside.

F. PRACTICE & POLICY

The materials in this chapter have outlined how the warrant process traditionally works. However, there are warrant procedures in isolated contexts that are *sui generis*. For example, federal intelligence agencies can apply for, and receive, a warrant to conduct surveillance in sensitive national security cases. The following section looks at these unique procedures. As you read materials, and in particular the statutory scheme laid out by Congress, ask yourself whether the procedures in place are adequate to meet the demands of the Fourth Amendment and in particular the requirements of the Warrant Clause.

The creation of the FISA court. The Foreign Intelligence Surveillance Court was created by an act of Congress in 1978. Although the court is abbreviated FISC, it is often referred to as the "FISA Court" after its authorizing statute, the Foreign Intelligence Surveillance Act (FISA), 50 U.S.C. §§ 1801-1885c. Although originally enacted decades ago, the Act has been amended and revised several times in the ensuing years.

The court's central responsibility is to approve applications for search warrants in highly sensitive national security cases. The court is composed of eleven federal court judges, who are assigned to the court for a maximum of seven years each. The assignments are made by the Chief Justice of the U.S. Supreme Court. While most of the court's work involves the consideration of warrants for electronic surveillance, the court also considers warrant applications for physical searches, pen registers, and access to business records—all in the intelligence context. The judges usually sit at the court in overlapping one-week stints so there are always several judges at the FISC on any given week. The names of the judges assigned to the court are not released to the public.

Pursuant to FISA, the President has authority to order surveillance without a warrant for the electronic surveillance of "communications used exclusively between or among foreign powers," and "there is no substantial likelihood that the surveillance will acquire the contents of any communication to which a United States person is a party. . . ." 50 U.S.C. § 1802.

President George W. Bush signs a bill that restructured the Foreign Intelligence Surveillance Act (FISA) on July 10, 2008. The changes provided authorities broader latitude to surveil individuals at home and abroad believed to have ties to terrorist groups. (Matthew Cavanaugh/EPA/Shutterstock)

However, if the government wishes to conduct surveillance of foreign individuals that involve conversations with or among United States citizens, the government is required to seek a warrant approved by the FISA court. The standard for issuing a warrant is probable cause, specifically "probable cause to believe that . . . the target of the electronic surveillance is a foreign power or an agent of a foreign power" and "each of the facilities or places at which the electronic surveillance is directed is being used, or is about to be used, by a foreign power or an agent of a foreign power. . . ." 50 U.S.C. § 1805. If the court grants the request, a warrant is signed and the government agency engages in the surveillance or collects the information identified in the warrant. If the court denies the request, the government has the right to appeal the denial to a three-judge appellate panel called the Foreign Intelligence Surveillance Court of Review. Again, like the FISC, the judges of the court of review are selected by the Chief Justice. 50 U.S.C. § 1803.

Minimization procedures. The statute also requires that the government engage in the necessary "minimization procedures," which are

> specific procedures, which shall be adopted by the Attorney General, that are reasonably designed in light of the purpose and technique of

> the particular surveillance, to minimize the acquisition and retention, and prohibit the dissemination, of nonpublicly available information concerning unconsenting United States persons consistent with the need of the United States to obtain, produce, and disseminate foreign intelligence information. . . .

50 U.S.C. § 1801(h). In practice, typical minimization procedures include rules that analysts and agents at federal intelligence agencies must follow to maintain the privacy of U.S. citizens whose communications are captured in FISA intelligence gathering operations. In other words, FISA contemplates that foreign surveillance might involve "incidental collection" of communications from U.S. citizens who are not the subject of a valid FISA warrant.

For example, imagine that the federal government is wiretapping a foreign individual that the government has probable cause to believe is an agent of a foreign power. If that individual then has a conversation with a U.S. citizen, that communication might be collected by the intelligence agency, even though the federal government has neither sought nor received a FISA warrant against that U.S. person. Pursuant to the requirement to engage in minimization procedures, the intelligence agency will redact the name and other identifiable information of the U.S. citizen from intelligence reports in order to maintain the individual's privacy. There are, however, exceptions to this practice, and intelligence analysts can request that the identity of the U.S. person be "unmasked" for various reasons, including if such unmasking is essential to understand the nature of an immediate threat against the United States. These minimization procedures were submitted by the government to the FISA court and ultimately approved by that court in an April 2017 decision. The heavily redacted opinion and order concluded that minimization procedures are consistent with both the statutory scheme and the Fourth Amendment. However, the court also noted that the analysts with the National Security Agency (NSA) had, on occasion, "used U.S.-person identifiers . . . even though NSA's . . . minimization procedures prohibited" these actions. In a previous 2011 opinion, the court had found the NSA's minimization procedures constitutionally deficient "with respect to their protection of U.S. person information" and required the NSA to revise its procedures to cure the defect. However, the 2017 order concluded that "NSA analysts had been conducting such queries in violation of that prohibition, with much greater frequency than had previously been disclosed to the Court."

Does this finding suggest that the FISA warrant system fails to protect the Fourth Amendment rights of American citizens? Or does this finding suggest the exact opposite, i.e., that the FISC is providing meaningful oversight of the intelligence community and is prohibiting activities when they cross constitutional boundaries?

As with any warrant application, the FISA proceedings are ex parte, meaning the government submits the application and the judicial officer signs the warrant without hearing from the target of the search. What adds to the severity of the ex parte process is its secrecy—the target may never know that they were subjected to surveillance or that this surveillance was performed subject to a lawfully issued warrant, unless the federal government commences a prosecution, in which case the prosecutor is required to provide notice that evidence collected through the FISA process will be used at trial. Furthermore, the operation of the FISA court is largely shielded from the prying eyes of the public, which might scrutinize whether search warrants were issued too frequently, not frequently enough, or somewhere in between. Although the proceedings are ex parte, the FISA statute specifically contemplates the possibility of filings by amicus curiae—such as civil liberties advocacy organizations—selected to argue issues before the court, though such amicus curiae must have adequate security clearances and are selected by court officials.

What recourse does an individual have if they believe that a FISA warrant was authorized inappropriately? In some circumstances, if the individual is eventually indicted by the federal government in connection with information received from the wiretap, the individual could file a suppression motion that would require the trial court to determine whether the warrant was valid.

Access to information. Some jurists are particularly concerned that criminal defendants are given inadequate information with which to challenge FISA warrants and vindicate their constitutional rights. As noted above, prosecutors must disclose to the defense that they intend to introduce evidence at trial that was procured through FISA. For the evidence to be introduced, it must first be declassified. However, the affidavits that the government submitted to FISA to secure the warrant are not disclosed to the defense. Consequently, if the defendant intends to attack the constitutionality of the search, he or she must do so without knowing the basis for the government's request for the warrant or the reasons why the court granted the request.

For example, in *United States v. Daoud*, 755 F.3d 479 (7th Cir. 2014), the defendant was charged with attempting to use a weapon of mass destruction, attempting to damage and destroy a building by means of an explosive, soliciting a crime of violence, murder for hire, and witness tampering. The government notified Daoud's lawyers that it intended to introduce evidence procured through FISA surveillance. Daoud's lawyers filed a motion requesting access to the "classified materials submitted in support of the government's FISA warrant applications" in order to show that the evidence was "unlawfully acquired." The government gave the district court a *classified* response and gave the defense counsel a "heavily redacted" and unclassified version of the same response. At the same time, the Attorney General filed an affidavit stating that disclosure of the classified information in the unredacted classified version would be harmful to the national interests of the United States. The district judge ordered the information turned over to the defense counsel, who had the necessary security clearances, noting that "the supposed national security interest at stake is not implicated where defense counsel has the necessary security clearances."

On appeal, the Seventh Circuit disagreed:

> The judge appears to have believed that adversary procedure is always essential to resolve contested issues of fact. That is an incomplete description of the American judicial system in general and the federal judicial system in particular. There are *ex parte* or *in camera* hearings in the federal courts as well as hearings that are neither or both. And there are federal judicial proceedings that though entirely public are nonadversarial, either partly or entirely. For example, a federal district judge presiding over a class action is required to determine the fairness of a settlement agreed to by the parties even if no member of the class objects to it. And when in a criminal case the prosecutor and the defendant agree on the sentence to recommend, the judge must make an independent determination whether the sentence is appropriate. If, though it is within the range fixed by Congress, he thinks the agreed-upon sentence too harsh or too lenient, he is empowered (indeed required) to reject the agreed-upon sentence and impose a different one within the statutory range. . . .
>
> Not only is federal judicial procedure not always adversarial; it is not always fully public. Child witnesses, especially in sexual abuse cases, are often allowed to testify behind a screen. Criminal defendants typically are allowed to conceal from the jury most or even all of their criminal history. . . . Documents placed in evidence may be redacted to conceal embarrassing material. Trade secrets—and classified materials are a form of "trade secret"—are routinely concealed in judicial proceedings. And of course judicial deliberations, though critical to the outcome of a case, are secret. . . .
>
> Everyone recognizes that privacy is a legally protectable interest, and it is not an interest of private individuals alone. The Foreign Intelligence Surveillance Act is an attempt to strike a balance between the interest in full openness of legal proceedings and the interest in national security, which requires a degree of secrecy concerning the government's efforts to protect the nation. . . . Conventional adversary procedure thus has to be compromised in recognition of valid social interests that compete with the social interest in openness. . . .

> [The district judge] seems to have thought that any concerns about disclosure were dissolved by defense counsel's security clearances. She said that "the government had no meaningful response to the argument by defense counsel that the supposed national security interest at stake is not implicated where defense counsel has the necessary security clearances"—as if disclosing state secrets to cleared lawyers could not harm national security. Not true. Though it is certainly highly unlikely that Daoud's lawyers would, Snowden-like, publicize classified information in violation of federal law, they might in their zeal to defend their client, to whom they owe a duty of candid communication, or misremembering what is classified and what not, inadvertently say things that would provide clues to classified material. . . .
>
> Our own study of the classified materials has convinced us that there are indeed compelling reasons of national security for their being classified—that the government was being truthful in advising the district judge that their being made public "would harm the national security of the United States"—and that their disclosure to the defendant's lawyers is (in the language of section 1806(f)) not "necessary" for "an accurate determination of the legality of the surveillance." . . . [O]ur study of the materials convinces us that the investigation did not violate FISA. We shall issue a classified opinion explaining (as we are forbidden to do in a public document) these conclusions. . . .

United States v. Daoud, 755 F.3d 479, 482-85 (7th Cir.), *supplemented*, 761 F.3d 678 (7th Cir. 2014). Do you agree with the Seventh Circuit that defense counsel should, in some cases, be prohibited from seeing FISA-related evidence even if the lawyer has the appropriate clearances? As one commentator pointed out, there are significant costs associated with denying defendants access to this information:

> The defendant, who is attempting to challenge the validity of orders and affidavits that he cannot review, is at a significant disadvantage as compared to the defendant challenging traditional warrants. Defendants cannot review the FISA orders to determine whether they are overbroad, whether there are significant typographical errors, or whether they permit searches beyond that for which there is a justification in the affidavits. Defendants cannot review the FISA affidavits to determine if there are false statements, material omissions, a lack of probable cause, or other information that may be useful to a defendant in challenging the admissibility of the evidence. This is a significant disadvantage to defendants against whom FISA-derived evidence is being introduced.

Patrick Walsh, *Foreign Intelligence, Criminal Prosecutions, and Special Advocates*, 47 U. Mem. L. Rev. 1011, 1039 (2017).

CHAPTER 4

Exceptions to the Warrant Requirement

INTRODUCTION

Although judges are fond of referring to the Fourth Amendment's preference for, or presumption of, warrants, courts have articulated a lengthy list of exceptions to the warrant requirement. The exceptions fall under the following broad category, each one with distinct sub-categories: exigent circumstances (including hot pursuit and preservation of evidence), plain view, automobiles, searches incident to arrest, inventory searches (during arrest), protective sweeps, consent, special needs situations, and individuals on conditional release (i.e., probation or parole). Indeed, the category of "special needs situations" includes no fewer than a half-dozen contexts where warrants would be impractical and are therefore not required by the Fourth Amendment. Stepping back and viewing the exceptions from a wide angle, one might question where it is still the case that the Supreme Court interprets the Fourth Amendment as including a presumption in favor of warrants. A more nuanced reading of the current jurisprudence might conclude that the preference for warrants is highly context dependent. In some situations, warrants are required, in other situations not, and the goal of this chapter is to clarify which is which.

One might expect or hope that the exceptions would demonstrate an overall level of coherence in terms of a unified standard that applied in all contexts and that would help predict which situations would qualify for an exception to the warrant requirement. But this is not necessarily the case. The Supreme Court has taken the liberty to articulate different standards for different exceptions. Of course, the Court does sometimes fall back on a general Fourth Amendment totality-of-the-circumstances test, which in this case would balance the state's interest in conducting warrantless searches with the individual's reasonable expectation of privacy, if any. But in many cases, the Court has fashioned more specific standards that apply to a specific exception and that are designed to guide lower courts who are tasked with overseeing the exception in particular cases. The goal of this chapter is not only to identify these specific standards but also to gain fluency in making arguments in their application.

Overall, there is a special burden on individual liberty when the constitutional requirement of a warrant is dispatched. By definition, the warrantless search is not authorized in advance by a neutral and detached magistrate. The scope of the search is not identified in writing for the target of the search to scrutinize at the moment of the search. All judicial scrutiny of the parameters of the search comes after, not before, the infringement of liberty involved in the search. Consequently, the existence of the warrantless search is a moment for pause and reflection. The result of this scrutiny is the recognized exceptions detailed below.

One should not assume that just because the law sanctions a warrantless search in a particular context that the police are entitled to conduct the search in the absence of all suspicion. Sometimes this is the case but sometimes not. For some of the categories listed below, the Supreme Court has sanctioned a particular search practice that is warrantless but nonetheless requires that the state officials ordering the search have a degree of "reasonable suspicion" that the search will yield evidence of contraband, evidence of crime, or evidence of a regulatory or safety violation. In a few cases, the search procedure might go further and only be conducted if the state officials have "probable cause"—a standard that surpasses reasonable suspicion. On the other hand, some of the search protocols are both warrantless and suspicionless, either because they are random searches (such as random drug tests of high school athletes), or because they involve a dragnet that ensnares everyone in a given area (such as a DWI checkpoint or a border inspection search)—all examples of suspicionless searches that the Supreme Court has endorsed. Consequently, in each context, it is imperative to clarify the precise situation that the court is evaluating. Is it: (i) a warrantless search conducted with probable cause; (ii) a warrantless search conducted with reasonable suspicion; or (iii) a warrantless and suspicionless search?

Finally, do not fall into the trap of evaluating the fact pattern as a single unified search. To be sure, in some situations the court will address the entirety of the search in one fell swoop. But it is far more common for courts to segment the "search," as one might colloquially refer to it, into a sequence of component searches, each one inviting judicial scrutiny and each one requiring some constitutional justification. To take a simple example, a "search" of a residence might include the search of each individual room, the search of closets, and the protective sweep from room to room to ensure that the officers are not endangered by other occupants with weapons. Each of these actions are separate, and the fact that one is justified does not entail that the rest of these actions are also justified. Similarly, when the Supreme Court asks whether school officials were justified in searching a student and her possessions for drugs, it is another question whether the officials were also justified in conducting a strip search to find the drugs. To take one more example, the police stopping of motorists at a DWI checkpoint is one question; the taking of a motorist to a secondary area for a field sobriety test, another question. In these situations, there is the question of whether the initial search was justified at its inception, and the further question of whether the search then exceeded its legitimate scope.

A. EXIGENT CIRCUMSTANCES

The Supreme Court has consistently said that warrants are not required during situations of "exigency." However, what counts as "exigent circumstances" has been narrowly defined by courts and generally falls into three categories: (1) hot pursuit, (2) emergency aid, and (3) evidence protection. Whether there is any conceptual unity to these three categories is unclear. What unites them is a shared context of *temporal* exigency: The nature of the situation makes it uniquely impractical for the police to go through the time-consuming process of seeking and obtaining a warrant from a magistrate to either search for, or seize, evidence. The one opportunity for the police to act is *at that moment in time*, and a delayed search or seizure with a warrant will be too late. In each case, the nature of the temporal exigency outweighs the intrusion on personal liberty due to forgoing the warrant requirement. However, it should be remembered that exigent circumstances is an exception to the warrant requirement, but not the deeper requirement of probable cause. In other words, a police officer conducting a search or seizure of evidence during a situation of exigent circumstances must act pursuant to probable cause.

There are several situations where the Supreme Court has declined to find exigent circumstances justifying the abrogation of the warrant requirement. For example, in *Payton v. New York*, 445 U.S. 573 (1980), the Court concluded that the Fourth Amendment requires the police to have a warrant to enter a private residence to make a routine arrest, because "[i]t is a 'basic principle of Fourth Amendment law' that searches and seizures inside a home without a warrant are presumptively unreasonable." Although the Court noted that many state courts had authorized the practice, the Court nonetheless concluded that a "longstanding, widespread practice is not immune from constitutional scrutiny." Also, in *Mincey v. Arizona*, 437 U.S. 385 (1978), the Court refused to carve out a specific exception to the warrant requirement for the collection of evidence at all murder scenes, ultimately declining to hold that "the seriousness of the offense under investigation itself creates exigent circumstances of the kind that under the Fourth Amendment justify a warrantless search." Consequently, exigent circumstances must flow from the nature of the situation itself, not the crime that the police are investigating.

1. Hot Pursuit

The Supreme Court has, though, consistently held that the hot pursuit of a felon will justify a warrantless search and seizure. In the following case, the police were responding to a report of an armed robbery. In the course of that response, the police entered a residence after acquiring information that the suspect had entered the residence only five minutes prior. As you read the following case, ask yourself whether that time lag is sufficiently minor to qualify as "hot pursuit." More importantly, ask yourself why "hot pursuit" is an exception to the warrant requirement at all. Would it be reasonable to insist that the police receive a warrant to enter a residence under a such a situation? Which principles underlying the Fourth Amendment are implicated by this question?

Warden, Maryland Penitentiary v. Hayden

Supreme Court of the United States
387 U.S. 294 (1967)

Mr. Justice BRENNAN delivered the opinion of the Court.

About 8 A.M. on March 17, 1962, an armed robber entered the business premises of the Diamond Cab Company in Baltimore, Maryland. He took some $363 and ran. Two cab drivers in the vicinity, attracted by shouts of "Holdup," followed the man to 2111 Cocoa Lane. One driver notified the company dispatcher by radio that the man was a Negro about 5'8" tall, wearing a light cap and dark jacket, and that he had entered the house on Cocoa Lane. The dispatcher relayed the information to police who were proceeding to the scene of the robbery. Within minutes, police arrived at the house in a number of patrol cars. An officer knocked and announced their presence. Mrs. Hayden answered, and the officers told her they believed that a robber had entered the house, and asked to search the house. She offered no objection.

The officers spread out through the first and second floors and the cellar in search of the robber. Hayden was found in an upstairs bedroom feigning sleep. He was arrested when the officers on the first floor and in the cellar reported that no other man was in the house. Meanwhile an officer was attracted to an adjoining bathroom by the noise of running water, and discovered a shotgun and a pistol in a flush tank; another officer who, according to the District Court, 'was searching the cellar for a man or the money' found in a washing machine a jacket and trousers of the type the fleeing man was said to have worn. A clip of ammunition for the pistol and a cap were found under the mattress of Hayden's bed, and ammunition for the shotgun was found in a bureau drawer in Hayden's room. All these items of evidence were introduced against respondent at his trial.

We agree with the Court of Appeals that neither the entry without warrant to search for the robber, nor the search for him without warrant was invalid. Under the circumstances of this case, "the exigencies of the situation made that course imperative." The police were informed that an armed robbery had taken place, and that the suspect had entered 2111 Cocoa Lane less than five minutes before they reached it. They acted reasonably when they entered the house and began to search for a man of the description they had been given and for weapons which he had used in the robbery or might use against them. The Fourth Amendment does not require police officers to delay in the course of an investigation if to do so would gravely endanger their lives or the lives of others. Speed here was essential, and only a thorough search of the house for persons and weapons could have insured that Hayden was the only man present and that the police had control of all weapons which could be used against them or to effect an escape. . . .

It is argued that, while the weapons, ammunition, and cap may have been seized in the course of a search for weapons, the officer who seized the clothing was searching neither for the suspect nor for weapons when he looked into the washing machine in which he found the clothing. But even if we assume, although we do not decide, that the exigent circumstances in this case made lawful a search without warrant only for the suspect or his weapons, it cannot be said on this record that the officer who found the clothes in the washing machine was not searching for weapons. He testified that he was searching for the man or the money, but his failure to state explicitly that he was searching for weapons, in the absence of a specific question to that effect, can hardly be accorded controlling weight. He knew that the robber was armed and he did not know that some weapons had been found at the time he opened the machine. In these circumstances the inference that he was in fact also looking for weapons is fully justified. . . .

NOTES & QUESTIONS ON HOT PURSUIT

1. *Hot pursuit for misdemeanors.* In *Warden v. Hayden,* the police were responding to reports of an armed robbery, which is a violent felony. What if the police are responding to a report of a non-violent felony? More dramatically, what if the police are responding to a misdemeanor? Does the Fourth Amendment require a warrant in that situation, or is the felonious nature of the alleged conduct an essential aspect of the "hot pursuit" exception? In *Middletown v. Flinchum,* 95 Ohio St. 3d 43, 765 N.E.2d 330 (2002), the Ohio

Supreme Court considered a Fourth Amendment challenge to the warrantless entry into a house after chasing a man suspected of engaging in DWI and other vehicular offenses. According to the court, "the officers observed appellant engage in the reckless operation of his vehicle on more than one occasion. Once the officers attempted to approach appellant to arrest him, he not only ignored their commands to stop after they had identified themselves as police officers, but he also fled to his home in order to avoid arrest." Consequently, the Ohio Supreme Court concluded that the Fourth Amendment "hot pursuit" exception is not limited to fleeing felons, but would include fleeing misdemeanants as well.

Do you agree with this extension of the *Warden v. Hayden* framework? Jurisdictions are split on this point, with several courts ruling that the Fourth Amendment prohibits warrantless entry during hot pursuit of a minor offense. See, e.g., *Mascorro v. Billings*, 656 F.3d 1198, 1207 (10th Cir. 2011) (warrantless entry to home inappropriate after police pursued minor suspected of a traffic misdemeanor); *Butler v. State*, 309 Ark. 211, 217, 829 S.W.2d 412, 415 (1992) (hot pursuit rationale not available for pursuit of suspect for minor offense that constituted a "petty disturbance").

Although the Supreme Court has so far declined to create a bright-line rule regarding misdemeanors, it has nonetheless concluded that the classification of the suspected crime is relevant to the Fourth Amendment question. The Supreme Court has stated that the gravity of the offense is an important factor to consider in the analysis, at least where a minor crime is concerned:

> We therefore conclude that the common-sense approach utilized by most lower courts is required by the Fourth Amendment prohibition on "unreasonable searches and seizures," and hold that an important factor to be considered when determining whether any exigency exists is the gravity of the underlying offense for which the arrest is being made. Moreover, although no exigency is created simply because there is probable cause to believe that a serious crime has been committed, see *Payton*, application of the exigent-circumstances exception in the context of a home entry should rarely be sanctioned when there is probable cause to believe that only a minor offense, such as the kind at issue in this case, has been committed.

Welsh v. Wisconsin, 466 U.S. 740, 753 (1984).

2. *From public to private.* For the hot pursuit doctrine to apply, the police chase must involve a constitutionally acceptable search or seizure at the beginning of the chase. In other words, if the police seek to arrest an individual in a public place, they may follow the suspect to a private residence, and seek warrantless entry, in order to complete the chase that originated in the public location. See, e.g., *United States v. Santana*, 427 U.S. 38, 43 (1976) ("We thus conclude that a suspect may not defeat an arrest which

PROBLEM CASE

To understand some of the collateral consequences with the hot pursuit exception, consider the following case. On March 19, 2018, police officers in Sacramento responded to reports of a man breaking car windows. When the police responded to the scene, they located a suspect and chased him by foot through the streets. In a backyard, they came upon a black male and shouted, "Show me your hands! Stop! Stop!" Instead of complying, the suspect ran again before the police caught up to him on the other side of the house. The police again yelled for him to show his hands. One of the officers believed that he saw the suspect holding a gun, and yelled "Gun!" to warn his fellow officers. In a few seconds, the police unleashed 20 shots and killed the suspect.

The name of the suspect was Stephon Clark, age 22. He was not holding a gun; it was a white iPhone in his hand. Moreover, he was in his own backyard in the house that he shared with his grandmother.

Why were the police entitled to enter the property without a warrant? As a matter of Fourth Amendment jurisprudence, the warrantless entry to the backyard was justified by the hot pursuit doctrine. Police had received a report of a possible burglary in progress and located a suspect near the scene of that report. Reevaluate the hot pursuit doctrine within this context. Does the doctrine make it more or less likely that the police will exercise excessive force, especially against African-American suspects? For more discussion of this case, see Alex Horton & Wesley Lowery, *'Our City Is Hurting': Protesters Swarm Downtown Sacramento Following Deadly Police Shooting,* Wash. Post, Mar. 23, 2018. To see video footage of this incident, see https://tinyurl.com/Clark-Shooting.

has been set in motion in a public place . . . by the expedient of escaping to a private place."). To understand the rationale for this limitation, imagine that the police make a warrantless entry to a *private* residence to effectuate an arrest, at which point the suspect flees into the street and the police give chase. If the police then arrest the suspect in a public area, the hot pursuit will do nothing to cure the original Fourth Amendment violation. In that situation, the hot pursuit came after, rather than before, the unconstitutional entry into the private area, and therefore cannot justify the original warrantless entry.

2. Emergency Aid

What if the police learn that someone inside a private area is in need of emergency medical attention? Or that a suspect is about to commit a violent crime against an innocent victim? Are the police required to wait for the issuance of a valid warrant before intervening? Certainly not—hence the conclusion that "emergency aid" situations qualify as exigent circumstances that are an exception to the Fourth Amendment's warrant requirement. Although the underlying rationale for the emergency aid exception is fairly obvious, the application of the doctrine to specific facts can be more difficult. As you read the following case, ask yourself whether the police were faced with a situation where sudden action, inconsistent with the time delay associated with a warrant, was necessary to render emergency aid.

Michigan v. Fisher

Supreme Court of the United States
558 U.S. 451 (2009)

PER CURIAM.

Police officers responded to a complaint of a disturbance near Allen Road in Brownstown, Michigan. Officer Christopher Goolsby later testified that, as he and his partner approached the area, a couple directed them to a residence where a man was "going crazy." Upon their arrival, the officers found a household in considerable chaos: a pickup truck in the driveway with its front smashed, damaged fenceposts along the side of the property, and three broken house windows, the glass still on the ground outside. The officers also noticed blood on the hood of the pickup and on clothes inside of it, as well as on one of the doors to the house. (It is disputed whether they noticed this immediately upon reaching the house, but undisputed that they noticed it before the allegedly unconstitutional entry.) Through a window, the officers could see respondent, Jeremy Fisher, inside the house, screaming and throwing things. The back door was locked, and a couch had been placed to block the front door.

The officers knocked, but Fisher refused to answer. They saw that Fisher had a cut on his hand, and they asked him whether he needed medical attention. Fisher ignored these questions and demanded, with accompanying profanity, that the officers go to get a search warrant. Officer Goolsby then pushed the front door partway open and ventured into the house. Through the window of the open door he saw Fisher pointing a long gun at him. Officer Goolsby withdrew.

Fisher was charged under Michigan law with assault with a dangerous weapon and possession of a firearm during the commission of a felony. The trial court concluded that Officer Goolsby violated the Fourth Amendment when he entered Fisher's house, and granted Fisher's motion to suppress the evidence obtained as a result—that is, Officer Goolsby's statement that Fisher pointed a rifle at him. . . .

"[T]he ultimate touchstone of the Fourth Amendment," we have often said, "is 'reasonableness.'" Therefore, although "searches and seizures inside a home without a warrant are presumptively unreasonable," *Groh v. Ramirez,* 540 U.S. 551, 559 (2004), that presumption can be overcome. For example, "the exigencies of the situation [may] make the needs of law enforcement so compelling that the warrantless search is objectively reasonable." *Mincey v. Arizona,* 437 U.S. 385, 393-394 (1978).

Brigham City identified one such exigency: "the need to assist persons who are seriously injured or threatened with such injury." 547 U.S., at 403. Thus, law enforcement officers "may enter a home without a warrant to render emergency assistance to an injured occupant or to protect an occupant from imminent injury." This "emergency aid exception" does not depend on the officers' subjective intent or the seriousness of any crime they are investigating when the emergency arises. It requires only "an objectively reasonable basis for believing," that "a person within [the house] is in need of immediate aid."

Brigham City illustrates the application of this standard. There, police officers responded to a noise complaint in the early hours of the morning. "As they approached the house, they could hear from within an altercation occurring, some kind of fight." Following the tumult to the back of the house whence it came, the officers saw juveniles drinking beer in the backyard and a fight unfolding in the kitchen. They watched through the window as a juvenile broke free from the adults restraining him and punched another adult in the face, who recoiled to the sink, spitting blood. Under these circumstances, we found it "plainly reasonable" for the officers to enter the house and quell the violence, for they had "an objectively reasonable basis for believing both that the injured adult might need help and that the violence in the kitchen was just beginning."

A straightforward application of the emergency aid exception, as in *Brigham City,* dictates that the officer's entry was reasonable. Just as in *Brigham City,* the police officers here were responding to a report of a disturbance. Just as in *Brigham City,* when they arrived on the scene they encountered a tumultuous situation in the house—and here they also found signs of a recent injury, perhaps from a car accident, outside. And just as in *Brigham City,* the officers could see violent behavior inside. Although Officer Goolsby and his partner did not see punches thrown, as did the officers in *Brigham City,* they did see Fisher screaming and throwing things. It would be objectively reasonable to believe that Fisher's projectiles might have a human target (perhaps a spouse or a child), or that Fisher would hurt himself in the course of his rage. In short, we find it as plain here as we did in *Brigham City* that the officer's entry was reasonable under the Fourth Amendment.

The Michigan Court of Appeals, however, thought the situation "did not rise to a level of emergency justifying the warrantless intrusion into a residence." Although the Court of Appeals conceded that "there was evidence an injured person was on the premises," it found it significant that "the mere drops of blood did not signal a likely serious, life-threatening injury." The court added that the cut Officer Goolsby observed on Fisher's hand "likely explained the trail of blood" and that Fisher "was very much on his feet and apparently able to see to his own needs."

Even a casual review of *Brigham City* reveals the flaw in this reasoning. Officers do not need ironclad proof of "a likely serious, life-threatening" injury to invoke the emergency aid exception. The only injury police could confirm in *Brigham City* was the bloody lip they saw the juvenile inflict upon the adult. Fisher argues that the officers here could not have been motivated by a perceived need to provide medical assistance, since they never summoned emergency medical personnel. This would have no bearing, of course, upon their need to ensure that Fisher was not endangering someone else in the house. Moreover, even if the failure to summon medical personnel conclusively established that Goolsby did not subjectively believe, when he entered the house, that Fisher or someone else was seriously injured (which is doubtful), the test, as we have said, is not what Goolsby believed, but whether there was "an objectively reasonable basis for believing" that medical assistance was needed, or persons were in danger. *Brigham City, supra,* at 406.

It was error for the Michigan Court of Appeals to replace that objective inquiry into appearances with its hindsight determination that there was in fact no emergency. It does not meet the needs of law enforcement or the demands of public safety to require officers to walk away from a situation like the one they encountered here. Only when an apparent threat has become an actual harm can officers rule out innocuous explanations for ominous circumstances. But "[t]he role of a peace officer includes preventing violence and restoring order, not simply rendering first aid to casualties." *Brigham City, supra,* at 406. It sufficed to invoke the emergency aid exception that it was reasonable to believe that Fisher had hurt himself (albeit nonfatally) and needed treatment that in his rage he was unable to provide, or that Fisher was about to hurt, or had already hurt, someone else. The Michigan Court of Appeals required more than what the Fourth Amendment demands.

Justice STEVENS, with whom Justice SOTOMAYOR joins, dissenting.

On October 31, 2003, Jeremy Fisher pointed a rifle at Officer Christopher Goolsby when Goolsby attempted to force his way into Fisher's home without a warrant. Fisher was charged with assault with a dangerous weapon and possession of a dangerous weapon during the commission of a felony. The charges were dismissed after the trial judge granted a motion to suppress evidence of the assault because it was the product of Goolsby's unlawful entry. In 2005 the Michigan Court of Appeals held that the trial court had erred because it had decided the suppression motion without conducting a full evidentiary hearing. On remand, the trial court conducted such a hearing and again granted the motion to suppress.

As a matter of Michigan law it is well settled that police officers may enter a home without a warrant "when they reasonably believe that a person within is in need of immediate aid." We have stated the rule in the same way under federal law, *Mincey v. Arizona,* 437 U.S. 385, 392 (1978), and have explained that a warrantless entry is justified by the "need to protect or preserve life or avoid serious injury." The State bears the burden of proof on that factual issue and relied entirely on the testimony of Officer Goolsby in its attempt to carry that burden. Since three years had passed, Goolsby was not sure about certain facts—such as whether Fisher had a cut on his hand—but he did remember that Fisher repeatedly swore at the officers and told them to get a warrant, and that Fisher was screaming and throwing things. Goolsby also testified that he saw "mere drops" of blood outside Fisher's home, and that he did not ask whether anyone else was inside. Goolsby did not testify that he had any reason to believe that anyone else was in the house. Thus, the factual question was whether Goolsby had "an objectively reasonable basis for believing that [Fisher was] seriously injured or imminently threatened with such injury." *Brigham City v. Stuart,* 547 U.S. 398, at 400.

After hearing the testimony, the trial judge was "even more convinced" that the entry was unlawful. He noted the issue was "whether or not there was a reasonable basis to [enter the house] or whether [Goolsby] was just acting on some possibilities," and evidently found the record supported the latter rather than the former. He found the police decision to leave the scene and not return for several hours—without resolving any potentially dangerous situation and without calling for medical assistance—inconsistent with a reasonable belief that Fisher was in need of immediate aid. In sum, the one judge who heard Officer Goolsby's testimony was not persuaded that Goolsby had an objectively reasonable basis for believing that entering Fisher's home was necessary to avoid *serious* injury. . . .

Today, without having heard Officer Goolsby's testimony, this Court decides that the trial judge got it wrong. I am not persuaded that he did, but even if we make that assumption, it is hard to see how the Court is justified in micromanaging the day-to-day business of state tribunals making fact-intensive decisions of this kind. We ought not usurp the role of the factfinder when faced with a close question of the reasonableness of an officer's actions, particularly in a case tried in a state court. I therefore respectfully dissent.

NOTES & QUESTIONS ON EMERGENCY AID

1. *Emergency aid without crime?* In some situations, the police will need to enter a home to render emergency aid because an individual has been victimized by a past or ongoing crime. In that situation, the police response would be governed by a probable cause standard—probable cause that a crime has occurred or is occurring and an emergency response is required. However, in other circumstances, the police might face an emergency situation caused by something other than criminal behavior, such as an accident. In that situation,

the police are still permitted to enter, but there is no requirement that the police have probable cause to believe that a crime has occurred; they must simply have a reasonable basis to believe that an individual requires help that cannot wait. As the Court has said, "law enforcement officers may enter a home without a warrant to render emergency assistance to an injured occupant or to protect an occupant from imminent injury." *Brigham City, Utah v. Stuart*, 547 U.S. 398, 403 (2006). The standard is judged from an objective point of view and the "officer's subjective motivation is irrelevant." *Id.* at 404. Consequently, if a defense attorney argues that the police entry was actually motivated by a desire to complete an arrest, rather than the need to render emergency aid, the entry will still be justified if the officer had reason to believe (objectively speaking) that the aid was required.

Some courts use different labels for the two scenarios. If the case involves criminal behavior, it counts as an exception under the label of "exigent circumstances," whereas if the case does not involve a crime, it might qualify for an exception under the broader "emergency aid" label. Either way, regardless of which label is used in the jurisdiction, the doctrine is clear that the Fourth Amendment does not require police to forgo warrantless entry when necessary to render immediate care to an individual in a private residence.

2. *Emergency aid for animals?* What if the emergency situation requires that the police render assistance to an animal rather than a human being? In *State v. Fessenden*, 355 Or. 759, 333 P.3d 278 (2014), the prosecutors contended that the police were justified in making a warrantless entry to seize an emaciated horse and transport it to a veterinarian for life-saving care. The Oregon court noted that the "parties' arguments thus call on this court to consider the past and current societal interests in protecting the lives of animals and the peoples' constitutional rights to possession and privacy and to decide in what instances and as to which animals, if any, society's interests are sufficiently compelling to justify a warrantless search or seizure." Ultimately, the court ratified the warrantless entry because the "exigent circumstances exception permits warrantless action when necessary to prevent serious damage to property. The parties acknowledge that, even if a horse is not a person, it is property." *Id.* at 771, 333 P.3d at 285.

3. Destruction of Evidence

The third major category of exigent circumstances deals with the destruction of evidence. If the police have reason to believe that waiting for a warrant will result in destruction of evidence, a warrantless entry is permitted. Again, like the emergency aid exception, this exception to the warrant requirement is relatively uncontroversial in theory, and the controversy arises when courts apply the exception to specific cases. Courts require more than a vague assumption

PROBLEM CASE

Consider the following two invocations of the emergency aid exception:

(1) In April 2007, the police received a 911 call from an anonymous individual who reported that there was a disturbance in her neighbor's house. The caller reported that she could hear an acquaintance of hers, Sherry Turnage, inside the house, having an argument. Also, the caller reported that she heard Turnage use a pre-arranged "code word" indicating that she was in trouble and needed police assistance. The dispatcher relayed this information to two members of the police department, Officers Venables and Wileman, who raced to the scene separately in their police cruisers. When Venables and Wileman approached the house, they saw two people sitting on the front porch who indicated that they had exited the house and were waiting on the porch because there was a disturbance inside. Venables walked to the back of the house and through a window saw two people inside of the house arguing but not hitting each other. One of the individuals saw Venables outside and yelled "Cops!"–prompting the other individual to attempt to dispose of marijuana. The police officers opened the back door and entered the dwelling. An investigation revealed that no assault had taken place, but the officers found several marijuana plants in the residence. Was the warrantless entry justified by the emergency aid exception? See *State v. Baker*, 350 Or. 641, 260 P.3d 476 (2011).

(2) The police received a report of a fight at a motel and dispatched nine officers to the location. When they arrived at the motel there was no fight, but a man comes forward to say that his girlfriend might be the victim of an ongoing rape in Room 9 by a man wielding a pistol. The police draw their weapons and knock on the door of Room 9; after a brief pause, a fully clothed woman exits the room. The woman does not act scared or victimized or traumatized and simply walks away. A man in the room hides behind the open door, and the police order him to come out with his hands up. The man faithfully complies with these commands and emerges with his hands in the air. The man does not have a weapon on him. The police enter the room. The man asks them to leave, but they refuse. Instead they look around the room and find a gun and illegal drugs. Was the warrantless entry of the room justified by the emergency aid exception? See *State v. Davis*, 295 Or. 227, 666 P.2d 802 (1983).

that a delay will cause a loss of evidence; what is required is a specific reason in that particular case that the suspect might destroy the evidence in question. As you read the following case, apply the standard to the particular facts of the case and ask yourself whether a delay to secure a warrant in this case would have doomed the police effort to secure the evidence.

Kentucky v. King

Supreme Court of the United States
563 U.S. 452 (2011)

Justice Alito delivered the opinion of the Court.

It is well established that "exigent circumstances," including the need to prevent the destruction of evidence, permit police officers to conduct an otherwise permissible search without first obtaining a warrant. In this case, we consider whether this rule applies when police, by knocking on the door of a residence and announcing their presence, cause the occupants to attempt to destroy evidence. The Kentucky Supreme Court held that the exigent circumstances rule does not apply in the case at hand because the police should have foreseen that their conduct would prompt the occupants to attempt to destroy evidence. We reject this interpretation of the exigent circumstances rule. The conduct of the police prior to their entry into the apartment was entirely lawful. They did not violate the Fourth Amendment or threaten to do so. In such a situation, the exigent circumstances rule applies.

This case concerns the search of an apartment in Lexington, Kentucky. Police officers set up a controlled buy of crack cocaine outside an apartment complex. Undercover Officer Gibbons watched the deal take place from an unmarked car in a nearby parking lot. After the deal occurred, Gibbons radioed uniformed officers to move in on the suspect. He told the officers that the suspect was moving quickly toward the breezeway of an apartment building, and he urged them to "hurry up and get there" before the suspect entered an apartment.

In response to the radio alert, the uniformed officers drove into the nearby parking lot, left their vehicles, and ran to the breezeway. Just as they entered the breezeway, they heard a door shut and detected a very strong odor of burnt marijuana. At the end of the breezeway, the officers saw two apartments, one on the left and one on the right, and they did not know which apartment the suspect had entered. Gibbons had radioed that the suspect was running into the apartment on the right, but the officers did not hear this statement because they had already left their vehicles. Because they smelled marijuana smoke emanating from the apartment on the left, they approached the door of that apartment.

Officer Steven Cobb, one of the uniformed officers who approached the door, testified that the officers banged on the left apartment door "as loud as [they] could" and announced, "This is the police" or "Police, police, police." Cobb said that "[a]s soon as [the officers] started banging on the door," they "could hear people inside moving," and "[i]t sounded as [though] things were being moved inside the apartment." These noises, Cobb testified, led the officers to believe that drug-related evidence was about to be destroyed.

At that point, the officers announced that they "were going to make entry inside the apartment." Cobb then kicked in the door, the officers entered the apartment, and they found three people in the front room: respondent Hollis King, respondent's girlfriend, and a guest who was smoking marijuana. The officers performed a protective sweep of the apartment during which they saw marijuana and powder cocaine in plain view. In a subsequent search, they also discovered crack cocaine, cash, and drug paraphernalia.

Police eventually entered the apartment on the right. Inside, they found the suspected drug dealer who was the initial target of their investigation. . . .

This Court has identified several exigencies that may justify a warrantless search of a home. . . . [T]he need "to prevent the imminent destruction of evidence" has long been recognized as a sufficient justification for a warrantless search. Over the years, lower courts have developed an exception to the exigent circumstances rule, the so-called "police-created exigency" doctrine. Under this doctrine, police may not rely on the need to prevent destruction of evidence when that exigency was "created" or "manufactured" by the conduct of the police.

In applying this exception for the "creation" or "manufacturing" of an exigency by the police, courts require something more than mere proof that fear of detection by the police caused the destruction of evidence. An additional showing is obviously needed because, as the Eighth Circuit has recognized, "in some sense the police always create the exigent circumstances." That is to say, in the vast majority of cases in which evidence is destroyed by persons who are engaged in illegal conduct, the reason for the destruction is fear that the evidence will fall into the hands of law enforcement. Destruction of evidence issues probably occur most frequently in drug cases because drugs may be easily destroyed by flushing them down a toilet or rinsing them down a drain. Persons in possession of valuable drugs are unlikely to destroy them unless they fear discovery by the police. Consequently, a rule that precludes the police from making a warrantless entry to prevent the destruction of evidence whenever their conduct causes the exigency would unreasonably shrink the reach of this well-established exception to the warrant requirement. . . .

Despite the welter of tests devised by the lower courts, the answer to the question presented in this case follows directly and clearly from the principle that permits warrantless searches in the first place. As previously noted, warrantless searches are allowed when the circumstances make it reasonable, within the meaning of the Fourth Amendment, to dispense with the warrant requirement. Therefore, the answer to the question before us is that the exigent circumstances rule justifies a warrantless search when the conduct of the police preceding the exigency is reasonable in the same sense. Where, as here, the police did not create the exigency by engaging or threatening to engage in conduct that violates the Fourth Amendment, warrantless entry to prevent the destruction of evidence is reasonable and thus allowed. . . .

For these reasons, we conclude that the exigent circumstances rule applies when the police do not gain entry to premises by means of an actual or threatened violation of the Fourth Amendment. This holding provides ample protection for the privacy rights that the Amendment protects.

When law enforcement officers who are not armed with a warrant knock on a door, they do no more than any private citizen might do. And whether the person who knocks on the door and requests the opportunity to speak is a police officer or a private citizen, the occupant has no obligation to open the door or to speak. . . . And even if an occupant chooses to open the door and speak with the officers, the occupant need not allow the officers to enter the premises and may refuse to answer any questions at any time. . . . Occupants who choose not to stand on their constitutional rights but instead elect to attempt to destroy evidence have only themselves to blame for the warrantless exigent-circumstances search that may ensue. . . .

We need not decide whether exigent circumstances existed in this case. . . . We decide only the question on which the Kentucky Supreme Court ruled and on which we granted certiorari: Under what circumstances do police impermissibly create an exigency? . . . In this case, we see no evidence that the officers either violated the Fourth Amendment or threatened to do so prior to the point when they entered the apartment. Officer Cobb testified without contradiction that the officers "banged on the door as loud as [they] could" and announced either "Police, police, police" or "This is the police." This conduct was entirely consistent with the Fourth Amendment, and we are aware of no other evidence that might show that the officers either violated the Fourth Amendment or threatened to do so (for example, by announcing that they would break down the door if the occupants did not open the door voluntarily). . . .

Justice Ginsburg, dissenting.

The Court today arms the police with a way routinely to dishonor the Fourth Amendment's warrant requirement in drug cases. In lieu of presenting their evidence to a neutral magistrate, police officers may now knock, listen, then break the door down, nevermind that they had ample time to obtain a warrant. I dissent from the Court's reduction of the Fourth Amendment's force. . . .

This case involves a principal exception to the warrant requirement, the exception applicable in "exigent circumstances." . . . Circumstances qualify as "exigent" when there is an imminent risk of death or serious injury, or danger that evidence will be immediately destroyed, or that a suspect will escape. The question presented: May police, who could pause to gain the approval of a neutral magistrate, dispense with the need to get a warrant by themselves creating exigent circumstances? I would answer no, as did the Kentucky Supreme Court. The urgency must exist, I would rule, when the police come on the scene, not subsequent to their arrival, prompted by their own conduct. . . .

There was little risk that drug-related evidence would have been destroyed had the police delayed the search pending a magistrate's authorization. As the Court recognizes, "[p]ersons in possession of valuable drugs are unlikely to destroy them unless they fear discovery by the police." Nothing in the record shows that, prior to the knock at the apartment door, the occupants were apprehensive about police proximity. . . .

The existence of a genuine emergency depends not only on the state of necessity at the time of the warrantless search; it depends, first and foremost, on "actions taken by the police preceding the warrantless search." . . . Under an appropriately reined-in "emergency" or "exigent circumstances" exception, the result in this case should not be in doubt. The target of the investigation's entry into the building, and the smell of marijuana seeping under the apartment door into the hallway, the Kentucky Supreme Court rightly determined, gave the police "probable cause . . . sufficient . . . to obtain a warrant to search the . . . apartment." As that court observed, nothing made it impracticable for the police to post officers on the premises while proceeding to obtain a warrant authorizing their entry. . . . There is every reason to conclude that securing a warrant was entirely feasible in this case, and no reason to contract the Fourth Amendment's dominion.

NOTES & QUESTIONS ON DESTRUCTION OF EVIDENCE

1. *The police-created exigency doctrine.* According to the police-created exigency doctrine, the police may not "bootstrap" their way into "exigent circumstances"—thus removing the need for a warrant—by creating the exigent circumstances through their own conduct. The question is how to apply this theory in concrete cases. Under one application, the police cannot claim that the destruction of evidence is an exigent circumstance if the destruction of evidence is triggered by their knocking on the door. It was this view that the majority in *Kentucky v. King* rejected, holding instead that the police-created exigency doctrine only applies if the triggering conduct by the police violates the Fourth Amendment. In this case, is knocking on the door of the residence a Fourth Amendment violation? The majority suggested that when police knock on the door they "do no more than any private citizen might do." Do you agree that this is the relevant question? Or do you agree with Justice Ginsburg that the relevant question is the state of affairs *before* the police arrived on the scene, not what happened once they knocked on the door? Prior to knocking on the door, there was no danger of evidence being destroyed, and therefore every opportunity to apply for, and secure, a warrant.

2. *Objective or subjective standard.* Should courts apply a subjective or objective standard for the destruction of evidence exception? In *Kentucky v. King*, the majority concluded that what mattered is whether there was an objective justification flowing from the potential destruction of evidence, and

PROBLEM CASE

Consider the following scenario. Two police officers in Asheville, North Carolina, received a tip from a repeat confidential informant that someone was dealing cocaine at a local motel, the Roadway Inn and Suites. The officers drove their squad car to the motel. The car was not discrete; it was a drug unit vehicle painted with the words "Drug Suppression Unit" on the side. The officers approached a vehicle in the motel parking lot that belonged to the suspect; inside the car was the suspect's girlfriend who had gone to fetch food for him but had returned empty-handed. The officers and the girlfriend went to the fifth floor of the motel and approached the suspect's room, at which point they heard a noise that sounded like a door opening and closing suddenly.

The officers asked the hotel manager to open the suspect's room, and the police proceeded to search the suspect's hotel room without a warrant. In court, the officers testified that they were worried that the suspect had seen or heard them coming and might flush the cocaine down the toilet. How would you resolve this case? Is the warrantless search of the room justified by exigency? If yes, which facts support this conclusion. If no, why not? See *State v. Wood*, 215 N.C. App. 393, 716 S.E.2d 86 (2011).

that the subjective motivation of the police was irrelevant. Even if the police entered the building in "bad faith," the Court concluded that this factor should be irrelevant. Do you agree? Applying an objective standard, is the mere fact that the police heard sounds of movement inside the apartment enough to justify a warrantless entry to prevent the destruction of evidence?

3. *No blanket exclusion for murder scenes.* The Supreme Court has made clear that there is no blanket warrant exception for murder scenes. In *Mincey v. Arizona*, 437 U.S. 385 (1978), the Arizona Supreme Court had articulated a blanket murder scene exception to the Fourth Amendment's warrant requirement. The State of Arizona argued that a "possible homicide presents an emergency situation demanding immediate action," thus bringing the putative doctrine within the umbrella of "exigent circumstances." The U.S. Supreme Court reversed, concluding that "the mere fact that law enforcement may be made more efficient can never by itself justify disregard of the Fourth Amendment" and the "investigation of crime would always be simplified if warrants were unnecessary." Do you agree with Arizona that the commission of a homicide in a community is a sufficiently dangerous event as to constitute—by itself—an exigent circumstance?

B. PLAIN VIEW

If the police are engaged in constitutional activity but come across an item in "plain view," the Constitution permits them to seize the item, the Fourth Amendment notwithstanding. So, for example, if the police lawfully enter a residence and while there see an illegal gun or some narcotics on the bed, they are permitted to seize the prohibited items because they were in "plain view" from the vantage point of the officers. However, it is important to remember that the police must be acting from a lawful "vantage point" when the item comes into plain view. This requirement is necessary because otherwise the plain view exception would sweep far too broadly, since all items are in plain view once a police officer is holding it in his or her hands. In making this point, Justice Stewart said in *Coolidge v. New Hampshire*, 403 U.S. 443, 466 (1971):

> What the "plain view" cases have in common is that the police officer in each of them had a prior justification for an intrusion in the course of which he came inadvertently across a piece of evidence incriminating the accused. The doctrine serves to supplement the prior justification—whether it be a warrant for another object, hot pursuit, search incident to lawful arrest, or some other legitimate reason for being present unconnected with a search directed against the accused—and permits the warrantless seizure.

In other words, plain view is never, by itself, enough to justify the entirety of the police conduct. The police still need a justification for the original behavior. In the same opinion, Justice Stewart also articulated another requirement: that it is immediately apparent that the item is incriminating.

The following case involves an application of the *Coolidge* framework. Specifically, Justice Stewart stated in his plurality opinion in *Coolidge* that for the exception to apply, "the discovery of evidence in plain view must be inadvertent," though that holding did not garner five votes. Here was his explanation:

> The rationale of the exception to the warrant requirement, as just stated, is that a plain-view seizure will not turn an initially valid (and therefore limited) search into a "general" one, while the inconvenience of procuring a warrant to cover an inadvertent discovery is great. But where the discovery is anticipated, where the police know in advance the location of the evidence and intend to seize it, the situation is altogether different. The requirement of a warrant to seize imposes no inconvenience whatever, or at least none which is constitutionally cognizable in a legal system that regards warrantless searches as "*per se* unreasonable" in the absence of "exigent circumstances." . . .

Id. at 469-71. In *Horton v. California*, 496 U.S. 128 (1990), however, the Supreme Court reconsidered the requirement of inadvertence and concluded that it was not a necessary condition of the plain view doctrine. The Court argued that the doctrine should not depend on the subjective intent of the officers, i.e., what they were looking for, but should focus on objective criteria. The Court also rejected Justice Stewart's rationale for the requirement:

> [T]he suggestion that the inadvertence requirement is necessary to prevent the police from conducting general searches, or from converting specific warrants into general warrants, is not persuasive because that interest is already served by the requirements that no warrant issue unless it "particularly desc rib[es] the place to be searched and the persons or things to be seized," and that a warrantless search be circumscribed by the exigencies which justify its initiation. Scrupulous adherence to these requirements serves the interests in limiting the area and duration of the search that the inadvertence requirement inadequately protects. . . .

Id. at 129.

The resolution of this doctrinal debate still leaves open the question of what *standard* the police must satisfy in order to seize an item that is in plain view during a lawful search. In the following case, the Justices debate the relative merits of "probable cause" and "reasonable suspicion" as appropriate standards.

Arizona v. Hicks

Supreme Court of the United States
480 U.S. 321 (1987)

Justice Scalia delivered the opinion of the Court.

In *Coolidge v. New Hampshire*, 403 U.S. 443 (1971), we said that in certain circumstances a warrantless seizure by police of an item that comes within plain view during their lawful search of a private area may be reasonable under the Fourth Amendment. We granted certiorari in the present case to decide whether this "plain view" doctrine may be invoked when the police have less than probable cause to believe that the item in question is evidence of a crime or is contraband.

I

On April 18, 1984, a bullet was fired through the floor of respondent's apartment, striking and injuring a man in the apartment below. Police officers arrived and entered respondent's apartment to search for the shooter, for other victims, and for weapons. They found and seized three weapons, including a sawed-off rifle, and in the course of their search also discovered a stocking-cap mask.

One of the policemen, Officer Nelson, noticed two sets of expensive stereo components, which seemed out of place in the squalid and otherwise ill-appointed four-room apartment. Suspecting that they were stolen, he read and recorded their serial numbers—moving some of the components, including a Bang and Olufsen turntable, in order to do so—which he then reported by phone to his headquarters. On being advised that the turntable had been taken in an armed robbery, he seized it immediately. It was later determined that some of the other serial numbers matched those on other stereo equipment taken in the same armed robbery, and a warrant was obtained and executed to seize that equipment as well. Respondent was subsequently indicted for the robbery.

III

The remaining question is whether the search was "reasonable" under the Fourth Amendment.

On this aspect of the case we reject, at the outset, the apparent position of the Arizona Court of Appeals that because the officers' action directed to the stereo equipment was unrelated to the justification for their entry into respondent's apartment, it was ipso facto unreasonable. That lack of relationship always exists with regard to action validated under the "plain view" doctrine; where action is taken for the purpose justifying the entry, invocation of the doctrine is superfluous. . . .

We turn, then, to application of the doctrine to the facts of this case. "It is well established that under certain circumstances the police may seize evidence in plain view without a warrant." Those circumstances include situations "[w]here the initial intrusion that brings the police within plain view of such [evidence] is supported . . . by one of the recognized exceptions to the warrant requirement," such as the exigent-circumstances intrusion here. It would be absurd to say that an object could lawfully be seized and taken from the premises, but could not be moved for closer examination. It is clear, therefore, that the search here was valid if the "plain view" doctrine would have sustained a seizure of the equipment.

There is no doubt it would have done so if Officer Nelson had probable cause to believe that the equipment was stolen. The State has conceded, however, that he had only a "reasonable suspicion," by which it means something less than probable cause. We have not ruled on the question whether probable cause is required in order to invoke the "plain view" doctrine. Dicta in *Payton v. New York*, 445 U.S. 573, 587 (1980), suggested that the standard of probable cause must be met, but our later opinions . . . explicitly regarded the issue as unresolved.

We now hold that probable cause is required. To say otherwise would be to cut the "plain view" doctrine loose from its theoretical and practical moorings. The theory of that doctrine consists of extending to nonpublic places such as the home, where searches and seizures without a warrant are presumptively unreasonable, the police's longstanding authority to make warrantless seizures in public places of such objects as weapons and contraband. And the practical justification for that extension is the desirability of sparing police, whose viewing of the object in the course of a lawful search is as legitimate as it would have been in a public place, the inconvenience and the risk—to themselves or to preservation of the evidence—of going to obtain a warrant. Dispensing with the need for a warrant is worlds apart from permitting a lesser standard of cause for the seizure than a warrant would require, i.e., the standard of probable cause. No reason is apparent why an object should routinely be seizable on lesser grounds, during an unrelated search and seizure, than would have been needed to obtain a warrant for that same object if it had been known to be on the premises.

We do not say, of course, that a seizure can never be justified on less than probable cause. We have held that it can—where, for example, the seizure is minimally intrusive and operational necessities render it the only practicable means of detecting certain types of crime. No special operational necessities are relied on here, however—but rather the mere fact that the items in question came lawfully within the officer's plain view. That alone cannot supplant the requirement of probable cause.

Justice O'Connor, with whom The Chief Justice and Justice Powell join, dissenting.

. . . In *Coolidge v. New Hampshire*, 403 U.S. 443 (1971), Justice Stewart summarized three requirements that the plurality thought must be satisfied for a plain-view search or seizure. First, the police must lawfully make an initial intrusion or otherwise be in a position from which they can view a particular area. Second, the officer must discover incriminating evidence "inadvertently." Third, it must be "immediately apparent" to the police that the items they observe may be evidence of a crime, contraband, or otherwise subject to seizure. . . . There is no dispute in this case that the first two requirements have been satisfied. . . . [T]he dispute in this case focuses on the application of the "immediately apparent" requirement; at issue is whether a police officer's reasonable suspicion is adequate to justify a cursory examination of an item in plain view. . . .

[I] agree with the Court that even under the plain-view doctrine, probable cause is required before the police seize an item, or conduct a full-blown search of evidence in plain view. Such a requirement of probable cause will prevent the plain-view doctrine from authorizing general searches. This is not to say, however, that even a mere inspection of a suspicious item must be supported by probable cause. When a police officer makes a cursory inspection of a suspicious item in plain view in order to determine whether it is indeed evidence of a crime, there is no "exploratory rummaging." Only those items that the police officer "reasonably suspects" as evidence of a crime may be inspected, and perhaps more importantly, the scope of such an inspection is quite limited. In short, if police officers have a reasonable, articulable suspicion that an object they come across during the course of a lawful search is evidence of crime, in my view they may make a cursory examination of the object to verify their suspicion. If the officers wish to go beyond such a cursory examination of the object, however, they must have probable cause. . . .

[T]he overwhelming majority of both state and federal courts have held that probable cause is not required for a minimal inspection of an item in plain view. . . . Thus, while courts require probable cause for more extensive examination, cursory inspections—including picking up or moving objects for a better view—require only a reasonable suspicion. This distinction between searches based on their relative intrusiveness—and its subsequent adoption by a consensus of American courts—is entirely consistent with our Fourth Amendment jurisprudence. We have long recognized that searches can vary in intrusiveness, and that some brief searches "may be so minimally intrusive of Fourth Amendment interests that strong countervailing governmental interests will justify a [search] based only on specific articulable facts" that the item in question is contraband or evidence of a crime. . . .

In my view, the balance of the governmental and privacy interests strongly supports a reasonable-suspicion standard for the cursory examination of items in plain view. The additional intrusion caused by an inspection of an item in plain view for its serial number is miniscule. . . . Weighed against this minimal additional invasion of privacy are rather major gains in law enforcement. . . . The balance of governmental and private interests strongly supports the view accepted by a majority of courts that a standard of reasonable suspicion meets the requirements of the Fourth Amendment. . . .

NOTES & QUESTIONS ON THE PLAIN VIEW EXCEPTION

1. *Inadvertence.* In *Horton v. California,* the Supreme Court declined to ratify Justice Stewart's view of the inadvertence requirement. Do you agree with the Court that "evenhanded law enforcement is best achieved by the application of objective standards of conduct, rather than standards that depend upon the subjective state of mind of the officer"? Or do you agree with Justice Stewart that bad faith on the part of the officer—intentionally looking for items that might be in plain view—should be prohibited by the Fourth Amendment?

2. *Immediately apparent.* What does it mean that an item's incriminating nature is "immediately apparent"? In *Coolidge,* the Supreme Court explained that the rationale for the requirement was to prevent "general, exploratory rummaging in a person's belongings." 403 U.S. at 467. However, the Court was vague about the exact standard to be applied in these situations. In *Arizona v. Hicks,* the Supreme Court clarified that appropriate standard is whether the officer has "probable cause to believe that the item in question is evidence of

a crime or is contraband." 480 U.S. 321, 323 (1987). For example, in *Hicks*, the police officer noticed that the stereo components were "out of place in the squalid" apartment. The Court concluded that the state could not rely on the plain view exception because the officer only had a "reasonable suspicion," rather than probable cause to believe, that the stereo components were stolen. Do you agree? How significant was the fact that the apartment was "squalid" and the stereo was expensive?

3. *Plain view in the digital world.* Should the plain view exception apply to computer searches? Imagine that the police are looking for a particular piece of information on a suspect's hard drive. But in the course of examining the hard drive, the examiner comes across a series of documents that, on their face, give the technician probable cause to believe that a crime has occurred. For example, perhaps image files clearly involve child pornography, or a spreadsheet file is labeled "narcotic transactions." By analogy to a physical search, can the state claim that the files were in "plain view" when the investigators were looking for the files targeted in the original search warrant? The worry, of course, is that it might be hard for courts to distinguish a claim that a file was truly in plain view from a case of impermissible "general rummaging." Furthermore, one commentator has asked: "Does the [plain view] doctrine ever apply to a second seizure—a seizure of property already seized? In a typical electronic search, all the contents of all the computers already have been seized from the target at the physical search stage. Assuming that using nonresponsive data is a seizure of that data, does the plain view doctrine determine whether the government can conduct a second seizure?" Orin S. Kerr, *Executing Warrants for Digital Evidence: The Case for Use Restrictions on Nonresponsive Data*, 48 Tex. Tech L. Rev. 1, 22 (2015).

C. AUTOMOBILES

The police do not need a warrant to search an automobile as long as they have probable cause to believe that there is evidence of a crime or contraband inside the car. To understand the rationale for the exception, first consider the bare language of the Fourth Amendment: "The right of the people to be secure in their persons, houses, papers, and effects, against unreasonable searches and seizures, shall not be violated. . . ." Notice the explicit reference to houses and persons but no mention of automobiles or other moving vehicles. The automobile exception was first discussed in *Carroll v. United States*, 267 U.S. 132 (1925), in which the Supreme Court noted that automobiles had the capacity to be "quickly moved," thus increasing the likelihood that a vehicle might disappear before the police can secure a warrant. In *California v. Carney*, 471 U.S. 386 (1985), the Supreme Court further explained the rationale for the automobile exception: Motorists have a "lesser expectation of privacy resulting from its use as a readily mobile vehicle" and the "public is fully aware that it is accorded less privacy in its automobiles because of this compelling governmental need for regulation." The Court has said that the lesser expectation to privacy applies in situations where the passenger seats are open to public viewing (due to windows), *Cardwell v. Lewis*, 417 U.S. 583, 590 (1974), but also in situations where enclosed areas, such as the glove compartment, within the car are shielded from public view. Indeed, the Court has emphasized that because automobiles are used for transportation on public roads, motorists do not operate them with the same expectation of privacy that they have in their private homes.

1. Containers Located in Automobiles

In the following case, the Court considers the more tricky application of the automobile exception: What if the motorist has a closed container in the trunk of his car? On the one hand, since the container is in the automobile, it would seem that the entire contents of the automobile should fall under the exception and therefore not require a warrant. On the other hand, it seems counterintuitive that a closed container located in the trunk of a car should receive less Fourth Amendment protection simply because the container is located inside the car, rather than elsewhere. As you read the following case, notice how the Court navigates the contradiction.

California v. Acevedo

Supreme Court of the United States
500 U.S. 565 (1991)

Justice BLACKMUN delivered the opinion of the Court.

This case requires us once again to consider the so-called "automobile exception" to the warrant requirement of the Fourth Amendment and its application to the search of a closed container in the trunk of a car.

I

On October 28, 1987, Officer Coleman of the Santa Ana, Cal., Police Department received a telephone call from a federal drug enforcement agent in Hawaii. The agent informed Coleman that he had seized a package containing marijuana which was to have been delivered to the Federal Express Office in Santa Ana and which was addressed to J.R. Daza at 805 West Stevens Avenue in that city. The agent arranged to send the package to Coleman instead. Coleman then was to take the package to the Federal Express office and arrest the person who arrived to claim it.

Coleman received the package on October 29, verified its contents, and took it to the Senior Operations Manager at the Federal Express office.

At about 10:30 A.M. on October 30, a man, who identified himself as Jamie Daza, arrived to claim the package. He accepted it and drove to his apartment on West Stevens. He carried the package into the apartment.

At 11:45 A.M., officers observed Daza leave the apartment and drop the box and paper that had contained the marijuana into a trash bin. Coleman at that point left the scene to get a search warrant. About 12:05 P.M., the officers saw Richard St. George leave the apartment carrying a blue knapsack which appeared to be half full. The officers stopped him as he was driving off, searched the knapsack, and found 1½ pounds of marijuana.

At 12:30 P.M., respondent Charles Steven Acevedo arrived. He entered Daza's apartment, stayed for about 10 minutes, and reappeared carrying a brown paper bag that looked full. The officers noticed that the bag was the size of one of the wrapped marijuana packages sent from Hawaii.

Acevedo walked to a silver Honda in the parking lot. He placed the bag in the trunk of the car and started to drive away. Fearing the loss of evidence, officers in a marked police car stopped him. They opened the trunk and the bag, and found marijuana.

Respondent was charged in state court with possession of marijuana for sale. . . . He moved to suppress the marijuana found in the car. The motion was denied. He then pleaded guilty but appealed the denial of the suppression motion. . . .

II

. . . Contemporaneously with the adoption of the Fourth Amendment, the First Congress, and, later, the Second and Fourth Congresses, distinguished between the need for a warrant to search for contraband concealed in "a dwelling house or similar place" and the need for a warrant to search for contraband concealed in a movable vessel. See *Carroll v. United States,* 267 U.S. 132, 151 (1925). In *Carroll,* this Court established an exception to the warrant requirement for moving vehicles. . . . It therefore held that a warrantless search of an automobile, based upon probable cause to believe that the vehicle contained evidence of crime in the light of an exigency arising out of the likely disappearance of the vehicle, did not contravene the Warrant Clause of the Fourth Amendment.

The Court refined the exigency requirement in *Chambers v. Maroney,* 399 U.S. 42 (1970), when it held that the existence of exigent circumstances was to be determined at the time the automobile is seized. The car search at issue in *Chambers* took place at the police station, where the vehicle was immobilized, some time after the driver had been arrested. Given probable cause and exigent circumstances at the time the vehicle was first stopped, the Court held that the later warrantless search at the station passed constitutional muster. The validity of the later search derived from the ruling in *Carroll* that an immediate search without a warrant at the moment of seizure would have been permissible. The Court reasoned in *Chambers* that the police could search later whenever they could have searched earlier, had they so chosen. Following *Chambers,* if the police have probable cause to justify a warrantless seizure of an automobile on a public roadway, they may conduct either an immediate or a delayed search of the vehicle.

In *United States v. Ross,* 456 U.S. 798, decided in 1982, we held that a warrantless search of an automobile under the *Carroll* doctrine could include a search of a container or package found inside the car when such a search was supported by probable cause. . . . [W]e clarified the scope of the *Carroll* doctrine as properly including a "probing search" of compartments and containers within the automobile so long as the search is supported by probable cause.

In addition to this clarification, *Ross* distinguished the *Carroll* doctrine from the separate rule that governed the search of closed containers. The Court had announced this separate rule, unique to luggage and other closed packages, bags, and containers, in *United States v. Chadwick,* 433 U.S. 1 (1977). In *Chadwick,* federal narcotics agents had probable cause to believe that a 200-pound double-locked footlocker contained marijuana. . . . The Court . . . reasoned [that] a person expects more privacy in his luggage and personal effects than he does in his automobile. . . . In *Arkansas v. Sanders,* 442 U.S. 753 (1979), the Court extended *Chadwick*'s rule to apply to a suitcase actually being transported in the trunk of a car. . . . [The] *Sanders* majority stressed the heightened privacy expectation in personal luggage and concluded that the presence of luggage in an automobile did not diminish the owner's expectation of privacy in his personal items.

In *Ross,* the Court endeavored to distinguish between *Carroll,* which governed the *Ross* automobile search, and *Chadwick,* which governed the *Sanders* automobile search. It held that the *Carroll* doctrine covered searches of automobiles when the police had probable cause to search an entire vehicle, but that the *Chadwick* doctrine governed searches of luggage when the officers had probable cause to search only a container within the vehicle. Thus, in a *Ross* situation, the police could conduct a reasonable search under the Fourth Amendment without obtaining a warrant, whereas in a *Sanders* situation, the police had to obtain a warrant before they searched. . . .

III

The facts in this case closely resemble the facts in *Ross.* In *Ross,* the police had probable cause to believe that drugs were stored in the trunk of a particular car. Here, the California Court of Appeal concluded that the police had probable cause to believe that respondent was carrying marijuana in a bag in his car's trunk. Furthermore, for what it is worth, in *Ross,* as here, the drugs in the trunk were contained in a brown paper bag.

This Court in *Ross* rejected *Chadwick*'s distinction between containers and cars. It concluded that the expectation of privacy in one's vehicle is equal to one's expectation of privacy in the container, and noted that "the privacy interests in a car's trunk or glove compartment may be no less than those in a movable container." It also recognized that it was arguable that the same exigent circumstances that permit a warrantless search of an automobile would justify the warrantless search of a movable container. In deference to the rule of *Chadwick* and *Sanders,* however, the Court put that question to one side. It concluded that the time and expense of the warrant process would be misdirected if the police could search every cubic inch of an automobile until they discovered a paper sack, at which point the Fourth Amendment required them to take the sack to a magistrate for permission to look inside. We now must decide the question deferred in *Ross*: whether the Fourth Amendment requires the police to obtain a warrant to open the sack in a movable vehicle simply because they lack probable cause to search the entire car. We conclude that it does not. . . .

IV

. . . We now agree that a container found after a general search of the automobile and a container found in a car after a limited search for the container are equally easy for the police to store and for the suspect to hide or destroy. In fact, we see no principled distinction in terms of either the privacy expectation or the exigent circumstances between the paper bag found by the police in *Ross* and the paper bag found by the police here. Furthermore, by attempting to distinguish between a container for which the police are specifically searching and a container which they come across in a car, we have provided only minimal protection for privacy and have impeded effective law enforcement.

The line between probable cause to search a vehicle and probable cause to search a package in that vehicle is not always clear, and separate rules that govern the two objects to be searched may enable the police to broaden their power to make warrantless searches and disserve privacy interests. We noted this in *Ross* in the context of a search of an entire vehicle. Recognizing that under *Carroll,* the "entire vehicle itself . . . could be searched without a warrant," we concluded that "prohibiting police from opening immediately a container in which the object of the search is most likely to be found and instead forcing them first to comb the entire vehicle would actually exacerbate the intrusion on privacy interests." At the moment when officers stop an automobile, it may be less than clear whether they suspect with a high degree of certainty that the vehicle contains drugs in a bag or simply contains drugs. If the police know that they may open a bag only if they are actually searching the entire car, they may search more extensively than they otherwise would in order to establish the general probable cause required by *Ross*. . . .

VI

. . . Until today, this Court has drawn a curious line between the search of an automobile that coincidentally turns up a container and the search of a container that coincidentally turns up in an automobile. The protections of the Fourth Amendment must not turn on such coincidences. We therefore interpret *Carroll* as providing one rule to govern all automobile searches. The police may search an automobile and the containers within it where they have probable cause to believe contraband or evidence is contained. . . .

2. Automobiles in the Curtilage

What if an automobile is parked in a private driveway next to a house? In traditional Fourth Amendment jurisprudence, the "curtilage" of the house—the area adjacent to the structure—is often given similar constitutional protection as the home itself. At the same time, though, automobiles have long been considered an exception to the warrant requirement and can be searched as long as the officer has probable cause. Automobiles located within the curtilage therefore pose a special problem. As automobiles they ought to be exempt from the warrant requirement but their special location next to a home gives one pause before reaching this hasty conclusion. In the following case, the Supreme Court answers the question.

Collins v. Virginia

Supreme Court of the United States
138 S.Ct. 1663 (2018)

Justice SOTOMAYOR delivered the opinion of the Court.

This case presents the question whether the automobile exception to the Fourth Amendment permits a police officer, uninvited and without a warrant, to enter the curtilage of a home in order to search a vehicle parked therein. It does not.

II

. . . The "ready mobility" of vehicles served as the core justification for the automobile exception for many years. Later cases then introduced an additional rationale based on "the pervasive regulation of vehicles capable of traveling on the public highways." . . . In announcing each of these two justifications, the Court took care to emphasize that the rationales applied only to automobiles and not to houses, and therefore supported "treating automobiles differently from houses" as a constitutional matter. . . .

. . . In physically intruding on the curtilage of Collins' home to search the motorcycle, Officer Rhodes not only invaded Collins' Fourth Amendment interest in the item searched, i.e., the motorcycle, but also invaded Collins' Fourth Amendment interest in the curtilage of his home. The question before the Court is whether the automobile exception justifies the invasion of the curtilage. The answer is no.

Applying the relevant legal principles to a slightly different factual scenario confirms that this is an easy case. Imagine a motorcycle parked inside the living room of a house, visible through a window to a passerby on the street. Imagine further that an officer has probable cause to believe that the motorcycle was involved in a traffic infraction. Can the officer, acting without a warrant, enter the house to search the motorcycle and confirm whether it is the right one? Surely not.

The reason is that the scope of the automobile exception extends no further than the automobile itself. Virginia asks the Court to expand the scope of the automobile exception to permit police to invade any space outside an automobile even if the Fourth Amendment protects that space. Nothing in our case law, however, suggests that the automobile exception gives an officer the right to enter a home or its curtilage to access a vehicle without a warrant. Expanding the scope of the automobile exception in this way would both undervalue the core Fourth Amendment protection afforded to the home and its curtilage and "untether" the automobile exception "from the justifications underlying" it. . . .

Just as an officer must have a lawful right of access to any contraband he discovers in plain view in order to seize it without a warrant, and just as an officer must have a lawful right of access in order to arrest a person in his home, so, too, an officer must have a lawful right of access to a vehicle in order to search it pursuant to the automobile exception. The automobile exception does not afford the necessary lawful right of access to search a vehicle parked within a home or its curtilage because it does not justify an intrusion on a person's separate and substantial Fourth Amendment interest in his home and curtilage.

As noted, the rationales underlying the automobile exception are specific to the nature of a vehicle and the ways in which it is distinct from a house. The rationales thus take account only of the balance between the intrusion on an individual's Fourth Amendment interest in his vehicle and the governmental interests in an expedient search of that vehicle; they do not account for the distinct privacy interest in one's home or curtilage. To allow an officer to rely on the automobile exception to gain entry into a house or its curtilage for the purpose of conducting a vehicle search would unmoor the exception from its justifications, render hollow the core Fourth

Amendment protection the Constitution extends to the house and its curtilage, and transform what was meant to be an exception into a tool with far broader application. Indeed, its name alone should make all this clear enough: It is, after all, an exception for automobiles. . . .

Justice ALITO, dissenting.

The Fourth Amendment prohibits "unreasonable" searches. What the police did in this case was entirely reasonable. The Court's decision is not.

. . . [W]hy does the Court come to the conclusion that Officer Rhodes needed a warrant in this case? Because, in order to reach the motorcycle, he had to walk 30 feet or so up the driveway of the house rented by petitioner's girlfriend, and by doing that, Rhodes invaded the home's "curtilage." The Court does not dispute that the motorcycle, when parked in the driveway, was just as mobile as it would have been had it been parked at the curb. Nor does the Court claim that Officer Rhodes's short walk up the driveway did petitioner or his girlfriend any harm. Rhodes did not damage any property or observe anything along the way that he could not have seen from the street. But, the Court insists, Rhodes could not enter the driveway without a warrant, and therefore his search of the motorcycle was unreasonable and the evidence obtained in that search must be suppressed.

An ordinary person of common sense would react to the Court's decision the way Mr. Bumble famously responded when told about a legal rule that did not comport with the reality of everyday life. If that is the law, he exclaimed, "the law is a ass—a idiot." C. Dickens, Oliver Twist 277 (1867). The Fourth Amendment is neither an "ass" nor an "idiot." Its hallmark is reasonableness, and the Court's strikingly unreasonable decision is based on a misunderstanding of Fourth Amendment basics. . . .

In considering that question, we should ask whether the reasons for the "automobile exception" are any less valid in this new situation. Is the vehicle parked in the driveway any less mobile? Are any greater privacy interests at stake? If the answer to those questions is "no," then the automobile exception should apply. And here, the answer to each question is emphatically "no." The tarp-covered motorcycle parked in the driveway could have been uncovered and ridden away in a matter of seconds. And Officer Rhodes's brief walk up the driveway impaired no real privacy interests. . . .

NOTES & QUESTIONS ON THE AUTOMOBILE EXCEPTION

1. *Closed containers.* Reconsider the dilemma described before this case excerpt. The Court ultimately resolved the issue by concluding that everything within the car is governed by the automobile exception and its probable cause standard, regardless of whether the item is located within a closed container

or not. Do you believe that motorists have a different expectation of privacy for items in closed containers, as opposed to items, say, strewn about in the back seat?

2. *Car or package.* Despite the decision in *Acevedo*, the distinction between probable cause regarding a package and probable case regarding a car is still relevant. That's because the probable cause will define the proper scope of the search. If the police have probable cause with regard to the package, then the search should be confined to the package. If, on the other hand, the police have probable cause with regard to the car, then the police can search the entire car. The holding in *Acevedo* makes clear that the exception to the *warrant* requirement applies equally to the automobile as it does to containers located therein.

3. *Passenger belongings.* The cases discussed above deal with the belongings of the motorist located within his or her car. But a slightly different calculus is implicated when the belongings in question belong to the passenger of the vehicle. Does the passenger have a greater expectation of privacy in his or her belongings located in someone else's car? In *Wyoming v. Houghton*, 526 U.S. 295 (1999), the Supreme Court considered this very question, and concluded that as long as the police have probable cause to believe that the car contains evidence of a crime or contraband, the police are entitled to inspect the belongings of both the motorist and the passenger. Writing for the majority, Justice Scalia noted that "[w]hereas the passenger's privacy expectations are . . . considerably diminished, the governmental interests at stake are substantial. Effective law enforcement would be appreciably impaired without the ability to search a passenger's personal belongings when there is reason to believe contraband or evidence of criminal wrongdoing is hidden in the car." *Id.* at 304. Do you agree? In dissent, Justice Stevens concluded that "the State's legitimate interest in effective law enforcement does not outweigh the privacy concerns at issue." In *Houghton*, the police searched the passenger's purse without a warrant, relying on the automobile exception. What expectation of privacy do passengers expect with regard to their purses or other personal items?

4. *Parked in the curtilage of the house.* What if the automobile is parked in the curtilage of the house on private property? Should the police be permitted to search the car without a warrant? In *Collins v. Virginia*, above, the Supreme Court concluded that a car parked in the curtilage of the house is entitled to the same constitutional protection that is usually afforded to the curtilage, which as a matter of Fourth Amendment law is given a similar level of protection as the house itself. Do you agree with this reasoning? Consider Justice Alito's claim, in dissent, that a car parked within the curtilage of a house is just as moveable as a car parked anywhere else, and therefore should fall under the

automobile exception to the warrant requirement. If the owner of the car could move it before a search warrant is issued, should this fact prevail regardless of where the car is located? On the other hand, a car parked on private property is not travelling on public roadways or parked in a public area, thus raising the question whether the owner of a car parked within the curtilage has a greater expectation of privacy than the typical automobile owner.

5. *Mobile homes—car or house?* Which rule should apply to mobile motor homes? For Fourth Amendment purposes, they could be classified as automobiles, exempt from the warrant requirement, or as residences, requiring a warrant. After all, if the owner is capable of *living* in the mobile motor home, then it would stand to reason that the occupant has a heightened expectation of privacy—the home is an owner's castle. However, in *California v. Carney*, 471 U.S. 386 (1985), the Supreme Court ruled otherwise: "To distinguish between respondent's motor home and an ordinary sedan for purposes of the vehicle exception would require that we apply the exception depending upon the size of the vehicle and the quality of its appointments. Moreover, to fail to apply the exception to vehicles such as a motor home ignores the fact that a motor home lends itself easily to use as an instrument of illicit drug traffic and other illegal activity." *Id.* at 393-94. Do you agree with the Court that it would be impossible or impractical to draw a coherent line between regular automobiles and motor *homes*?

SUMMARY

When may the police search a car?[1]

1. If located within the curtilage of private residence, only with a warrant.
2. If impounded, it may be searched in accordance with the jurisdiction's inventory policy, and any evidence discovered may be used.
3. Interior and any container in the interior: Can be searched with probable case if the probable cause "points" to that area. When applying the automobile exception, the scope is what it would have been had the officer obtained a warrant.
4. If the police have consent.
5. Pursuant to an arrest but only if:
   a. The officer is searching for evidence related to the crime of arrest with reason to believe it is in the car; or
   b. The person arrested has not been fully secured and still has genuine access to the interior of the car.
   c. Trunk search is permitted only with consent or with probable cause that the evidence the officer is looking for is in the trunk. An arrest will never alone allow for a search of the trunk.

1. The casebook author would like to thank Professor Geoffrey Corn for compiling this summary.

D. SEARCH INCIDENT TO ARREST

The search incident to arrest exception is highly important because it is an exception not just to the warrant requirement but also the probable cause requirement. During the course of a *lawful* arrest, the police are permitted to search a detainee without a warrant and without any prior showing of probable cause. See *Weeks v. United States*, 232 U.S. 383, 392 (1914) (referring to "the right on the part of the Government, always recognized under English and American law, to search the person of the accused when legally arrested to discover and seize the fruits or evidences of crime"). The limitation applies regardless of the crime for which the defendant is arrested. See *United States v. Robinson*, 414 U.S. 218 (1973).

In *Chimel v. California*, 395 U.S. 752 (1969), the Supreme Court concluded that the search incident to arrest exception allowed the police to search both the detainee and the area around him. In articulating a standard for the spatial scope of the "area" around the detainee, the Court focused on the possibility that the detainee might reach for a weapon in the course of his or her arrest:

> When an arrest is made, it is reasonable for the arresting officer to search the person arrested in order to remove any weapons that the latter might seek to use in order to resist arrest or effect his escape. Otherwise, the officer's safety might well be endangered, and the arrest itself frustrated. In addition, it is entirely reasonable for the arresting officer to search for and seize any evidence on the arrestee's person in order to prevent its concealment or destruction. And the area into which an arrestee might reach in order to grab a weapon or evidentiary items must, of course, be governed by a like rule. A gun on a table or in a drawer in front of one who is arrested can be as dangerous to the arresting officer as one concealed in the clothing of the person arrested. There is ample justification, therefore, for a search of the arrestee's person and the area "within his immediate control"—construing that phrase to mean the area from within which he might gain possession of a weapon or destructible evidence.

Id. at 762-63. The notion of the area within the arrestee's "immediate control" has come to define the limit of this exception. In *Chimel*, the police searched an entire three-bedroom house, which the Court rejected and declared an illegitimate application of the "search incident to arrest exception." Such a widespread search was not necessary for the safety of the arresting officers. Focusing on the safety of the officers helps explain the holding of *United States v. Robinson* that searches are permissible during arrests for even minor crimes. The "danger" comes not from the nature of the underlying crime but the possibility of violent encounters triggered by the process of arrest.

In the following case, the Court is confronted with the question of whether the exception allows the police to search an arrestee's vehicle *after* the arrestee has been handcuffed and placed in a patrol car. The Supreme Court had previously ruled in *New York v. Belton*, 453 U.S. 454 (1981), that the exception applied to automobiles as well, so that the police arresting an individual in the course of a vehicle stop could search the vehicle. However, in *Belton*, the defendant was not yet handcuffed during the search of the car. *Arizona v. Gant* tests the outer limit of the vehicle-search rule first articulated in *Belton*. As you read the case, ask yourself what level of danger remained for the arresting officers after the arrestee was handcuffed and secured.

Arizona v. Gant

Supreme Court of the United States
556 U.S. 332 (2009)

Justice STEVENS delivered the opinion of the Court.

After Rodney Gant was arrested for driving with a suspended license, handcuffed, and locked in the back of a patrol car, police officers searched his car and discovered cocaine in the pocket of a jacket on the backseat. Because Gant could not have accessed his car to retrieve weapons or evidence at the time of the search, the Arizona Supreme Court held that the search-incident-to-arrest exception to the Fourth Amendment's warrant requirement, as defined in *Chimel v. California*, 395 U.S. 752 (1969), and applied to vehicle searches in *New York v. Belton*, 453 U.S. 454 (1981), did not justify the search in this case. We agree with that conclusion.

Under *Chimel*, police may search incident to arrest only the space within an arrestee's "immediate control," meaning "the area from within which he might gain possession of a weapon or destructible evidence." The safety and evidentiary justifications underlying *Chimel*'s reaching-distance rule determine *Belton*'s scope. Accordingly, we hold that *Belton* does not authorize a vehicle search incident to a recent occupant's arrest after the arrestee has been secured and cannot access the interior of the vehicle. Consistent with the holding in *Thornton v. United States*, 541 U.S. 615 (2004), and following the suggestion in Justice Scalia's opinion concurring in the judgment in that case, we also conclude that circumstances unique to the automobile context justify a search incident to arrest when it is reasonable to believe that evidence of the offense of arrest might be found in the vehicle.

I

On August 25, 1999, acting on an anonymous tip that the residence at 2524 North Walnut Avenue was being used to sell drugs, Tucson police officers Griffith and Reed knocked on the front door and asked to speak to the owner. Gant answered the door and, after identifying himself, stated that he expected the owner to return later. The officers left the residence and conducted a records check, which revealed that Gant's driver's license had been suspended and there was an outstanding warrant for his arrest for driving with a suspended license.

When the officers returned to the house that evening, they found a man near the back of the house and a woman in a car parked in front of it. After a third officer arrived, they arrested the man for providing a false name and the woman for possessing drug paraphernalia. Both arrestees were handcuffed and secured in separate patrol cars when Gant arrived. The officers recognized his car as it entered the driveway, and Officer Griffith confirmed that Gant was the driver by shining a flashlight into the car as it drove by him. Gant parked at the end of the driveway, got out of his car, and shut the door. Griffith, who was about 30 feet away, called to Gant, and they approached each other, meeting 10-to-12 feet from Gant's car. Griffith immediately arrested Gant and handcuffed him.

Because the other arrestees were secured in the only patrol cars at the scene, Griffith called for backup. When two more officers arrived, they locked Gant in the backseat of their vehicle. After Gant had been handcuffed and placed in the back of a patrol car, two officers searched his car: One of them found a gun, and the other discovered a bag of cocaine in the pocket of a jacket on the backseat.

Gant was charged with two offenses—possession of a narcotic drug for sale and possession of drug paraphernalia (i.e., the plastic bag in which the cocaine was found). He moved to suppress the evidence seized from his car on the ground that the warrantless search violated the Fourth Amendment. Among other things, Gant argued that Belton did not authorize the search of his vehicle because he posed no threat to the officers after he was handcuffed in the patrol car and because he was arrested for a traffic offense for which no evidence could be found in his vehicle. When asked at the suppression hearing why the search was conducted, Officer Griffith responded: "Because the law says we can do it." . . .

II

. . . In *Chimel*, we held that a search incident to arrest may only include "the arrestee's person and the area 'within his immediate control'—construing that phrase to mean the area from within which he might gain possession of a weapon or destructible evidence." That limitation, which continues to define the boundaries of the exception, ensures that the scope of a search incident to arrest is commensurate with its purposes of protecting arresting officers and safeguarding any evidence of the offense of arrest that an arrestee might conceal or destroy. If there is no possibility that an arrestee could reach into the area that law enforcement officers seek to search, both justifications for the search-incident-to-arrest exception are absent and the rule does not apply.

In *Belton,* we considered *Chimel*'s application to the automobile context. . . . [W]e held that when an officer lawfully arrests "the occupant of an automobile, he may, as a contemporaneous incident of that arrest, search the passenger compartment of the automobile" and any containers therein. That holding was based in large part on our assumption "that articles inside the relatively narrow compass of the passenger compartment of an automobile are in fact generally, even if not inevitably, within 'the area into which an arrestee might reach.'"

The Arizona Supreme Court read our decision in *Belton* as merely delineating "the proper scope of a search of the interior of an automobile" incident to an arrest. That is, when the passenger compartment is within an arrestee's reaching distance, *Belton* supplies the generalization that the entire compartment and any containers therein may be reached. On that view of *Belton,* the state court concluded that the search of Gant's car was unreasonable because Gant clearly could not have accessed his car at the time of the search. It also found that no other exception to the warrant requirement applied in this case. Gant now urges us to adopt the reading of *Belton* followed by the Arizona Supreme Court.

III

Despite the textual and evidentiary support for the Arizona Supreme Court's reading of *Belton,* our opinion has been widely understood to allow a vehicle search incident to the arrest of a recent occupant even if there is no possibility the arrestee could gain access to the vehicle at the time of the search. . . . Under this broad reading of *Belton,* a vehicle search would be authorized incident to every arrest of a recent occupant notwithstanding that in most cases the vehicle's passenger compartment will not be within the arrestee's reach at the time of the search. To read *Belton* as authorizing a vehicle search incident to every recent occupant's arrest would thus untether the rule from the justifications underlying the *Chimel* exception—a result clearly incompatible with our statement in *Belton* that it "in no way alters the fundamental principles established in the *Chimel* case regarding the basic scope of searches incident to lawful custodial arrests." Accordingly, we reject this reading of *Belton* and hold that the *Chimel* rationale authorizes police to search a vehicle incident to a recent occupant's arrest only when the arrestee is unsecured and within reaching distance of the passenger compartment at the time of the search.

Although it does not follow from *Chimel,* we also conclude that circumstances unique to the vehicle context justify a search incident to a lawful arrest when it is "reasonable to believe evidence relevant to the crime of arrest might be found in the vehicle." In many cases, as when a recent occupant is arrested for a traffic violation, there will be no reasonable basis to believe the vehicle contains relevant evidence. But in others . . . the offense of arrest will supply a basis for searching the passenger compartment of an arrestee's vehicle and any containers therein.

Neither the possibility of access nor the likelihood of discovering offense-related evidence authorized the search in this case. Unlike in *Belton,* which involved a single officer confronted with four unsecured arrestees, the five officers in this case outnumbered the three arrestees, all of whom had been handcuffed and secured in separate patrol cars before the officers searched Gant's car. Under those circumstances, Gant clearly was not within reaching distance of his car at the time of the search. An evidentiary basis for the search was also lacking in this case. . . . Gant was arrested for driving with a suspended license—an offense for which police could not expect to find evidence in the passenger compartment of Gant's car. Because police could not reasonably have believed either that Gant could have accessed his car at the time of the search or that evidence of the offense for which he was arrested might have been found therein, the search in this case was unreasonable.

IV

The State does not seriously disagree with the Arizona Supreme Court's conclusion that Gant could not have accessed his vehicle at the time of the search, but it nevertheless asks us to uphold the search of his vehicle under the broad reading of *Belton* discussed above. . . .

For several reasons, we reject the State's argument. First, the State seriously undervalues the privacy interests at stake. Although we have recognized that a motorist's privacy interest in his vehicle is less substantial than in his home, the former interest is nevertheless important and deserving of constitutional protection. It is particularly significant that *Belton* searches authorize police officers to search not just the passenger compartment but every purse, briefcase, or other container within that space. A rule that gives police the power to conduct such a search whenever an individual is caught committing a traffic offense, when there is no basis for believing evidence of the offense might be found in the vehicle, creates a serious and recurring threat to the privacy of countless individuals. Indeed, the character of that threat implicates the central concern underlying the Fourth Amendment—the concern about giving police officers unbridled discretion to rummage at will among a person's private effects.

At the same time as it undervalues these privacy concerns, the State exaggerates the clarity that its reading of *Belton* provides. Courts that have read *Belton* expansively are at odds regarding how close in time to the arrest and how proximate to the arrestee's vehicle an officer's first contact with the arrestee must be to bring the encounter within *Belton*'s purview and whether a search is reasonable when it commences or continues after the arrestee has been removed from the scene. The rule has thus generated a great deal of uncertainty, particularly for a rule touted as providing a "bright line." . . .

VI

Police may search a vehicle incident to a recent occupant's arrest only if the arrestee is within reaching distance of the passenger compartment at the time of the search or it is reasonable to believe the vehicle contains evidence of the offense of arrest. When these justifications are absent, a search of an arrestee's vehicle will be unreasonable unless police obtain a warrant or show that another exception to the warrant requirement applies. The Arizona Supreme Court correctly held that this case involved an unreasonable search. . . .

Justice ALITO, with whom THE CHIEF JUSTICE and Justice KENNEDY join, and with whom Justice BREYER joins except as to Part II-E, dissenting.

. . . Although the Court refuses to acknowledge that it is overruling *Belton* and *Thornton*, there can be no doubt that it does so. . . . Viewing this disagreement about the application of the *Chimel* rule as illustrative of a persistent and important problem, the *Belton* Court concluded that "[a] single familiar standard" was "essential to guide police officers" who make roadside arrests. The Court acknowledged that articles in the passenger compartment of a car are not always within an arrestee's reach, but "[i]n order to establish the workable rule this category of cases requires," the Court adopted a rule that categorically permits the search of a car's passenger compartment incident to the lawful arrest of an occupant. . . .

Because the Court has substantially overruled *Belton* and *Thornton*, the Court must explain why its departure from the usual rule of stare decisis is justified. . . . Relevant factors identified in prior cases include whether the precedent has engendered reliance, whether there has been an important change in circumstances in the outside world, whether the precedent has proved to be unworkable, whether the precedent has been undermined by later decisions, and whether the decision was badly reasoned. These factors weigh in favor of retaining the rule established in *Belton*.

Reliance. While reliance is most important in "cases involving property and contract rights," the Court has recognized that reliance by law enforcement officers is also entitled to weight. . . . The *Belton* rule has been taught to police officers for more than a quarter century. Many searches—almost certainly including more than a few that figure in cases now on appeal—were conducted in scrupulous reliance on that precedent. It is likely that, on the very day when this opinion is announced, numerous vehicle searches will be conducted in good faith by police officers who were taught the *Belton* rule. . . .

Changed circumstances. Abandonment of the *Belton* rule cannot be justified on the ground that the dangers surrounding the arrest of a vehicle occupant are different today than they were 28 years ago. The Court claims that "[w]e now know that articles inside the passenger compartment are rarely 'within "the area into which an arrestee might reach,"'" but surely it was well known in 1981 that a person who is taken from a vehicle, handcuffed, and placed in the back of a patrol car is unlikely to make it back into his own car to retrieve a weapon or destroy evidence.

Workability. The *Belton* rule has not proved to be unworkable. On the contrary, the rule was adopted for the express purpose of providing a test that would be relatively easy for police officers and judges to apply. The Court correctly notes that even the *Belton* rule is not perfectly clear in all situations. Specifically, it is sometimes debatable whether a search is or is not contemporaneous with an arrest, but that problem is small in comparison with the problems that the Court's new two-part rule will produce.

Consistency with later cases. The *Belton* bright-line rule has not been undermined by subsequent cases. On the contrary, that rule was reaffirmed and extended just five years ago in *Thornton*.

Bad reasoning. The Court is harshly critical of *Belton*'s reasoning, but the problem that the Court perceives cannot be remedied simply by overruling *Belton*. *Belton* represented only a modest—and quite defensible—extension of *Chimel*, as I understand that decision. Prior to *Chimel*, the Court's precedents permitted an arresting officer to search the area within an arrestee's "possession" and "control" for the purpose of gathering evidence. Based on this "abstract doctrine," the Court had sustained searches that extended far beyond an arrestee's grabbing area. The *Chimel* Court, in an opinion written by Justice Stewart, overruled these cases. Concluding that there are only two justifications for a warrantless search incident to arrest—officer safety and the preservation of evidence—the Court stated that such a search must be confined to "the arrestee's person" and "the area from within which he might gain possession of a weapon or destructible evidence." Unfortunately, *Chimel* did not say whether "the area from within which [an arrestee] might gain possession of a weapon or destructible evidence" is to be measured at the time of the arrest or at the time of the search, but unless the *Chimel* rule was meant to be a specialty rule, applicable to only a few unusual cases, the Court must have intended for this area to be measured at the time of arrest. . . .

NOTES & QUESTIONS ON SEARCHES INCIDENT TO ARREST

1. *Search incident to arrest or vehicle exception?* Why did the police in *Gant* need to rely on the search incident to arrest exception to the warrant

requirement? As noted above, the police already have the ability to search automobiles without securing a warrant. Does the automobile exception sweep broader and render the question in *Gant* irrelevant? No. Recall that the automobile exception requires probable cause to believe that the car contains evidence of a crime or contraband. In contrast, the search incident to arrest is performed to locate weapons and ensure officer safety and does not require a prior determination of probable cause. In other words, an officer may invoke—and will need to invoke—the search incident to arrest exception to justify searching the vehicle in the absence of probable cause to believe that the car contains evidence of a crime or contraband. However, as noted above, although the search incident to arrest exception is triggered more easily, it is more limited in scope because it only applies to areas within the immediate control of the arrestee and does not apply at all once the arrestee has been secured in a police vehicle.

2. *Cell phone searches incident to arrest.* Can the police search a motorist's cell phone during an arrest, relying on the exception for searches incident to arrest? In *Riley v. California*, 134 S. Ct. 2473 (2014), the Supreme Court said no. The Court conceded that the "search incident to arrest exception rests not only on the heightened government interests at stake in a volatile arrest situation, but also on an arrestee's reduced privacy interests upon being taken into police custody." However, the Court went on to note that the "fact that an arrestee has diminished privacy interests does not mean that the Fourth Amendment falls out of the picture entirely." In *Riley*, the government had asserted that the *Chimel* line of reasoning applied just as much to electronic searches as it did to the physical searches conducted in *Chimel* and its progeny. The Court, apparently, was unconvinced: "[T]hat is like saying a ride on horseback is materially indistinguishable from a flight to the moon." Ultimately, the majority in *Riley* noted that modern cell phones operate as powerful mobile computing devices that contain the "sum of an individual's private life"; therefore, the privacy interests at stake are paramount. The primary rationale articulated in *Chimel* and *Gant* was officer safety. Is there some way to construct an argument for cell phone searches based on officer safety? Could the search of a cell phone help police determine whether co-felons or conspirators were en route to the scene? For its part, the Supreme Court found these hypotheticals unmoored from empirical evidence. Although the search incident to arrest exception does not apply to cell phones, this is not to say that *other* exceptions, such as exigent circumstances, might not justify a cell phone search under unique circumstances.

E. INVENTORY SEARCHES

Police are entitled to "inventory" the property in their possession, which out of logical necessity entails a certain amount of "searching" of the property. The underlying rationale of the exception is to protect the property interest of the owner in question. If the police are taking custody of large amounts of cash or expensive jewelry, the police need to know of the existence of the property and properly document it. Typically, contemporary police practice implicates two types of inventory searches: of the arrestee's person and the arrestee's vehicle. Although both types of searches fall under the same exception to the warrant requirement, they each involve unique application of the principles underlying the exception.

1. Impounded Cars

When the police impound a car, they will perform a full inventory of its contents. But how far can they go? Can they open closed containers within the car, force open locked glove compartments, perform forensic testing of the carpet on the floor of the automobile to look for trace evidence? The following case does not address all of these questions of application, but does address the central issue of the police power to inventory the contents of impounded vehicles without a warrant and even in the absence of probable cause. As you read the case, ask yourself why it was reasonable for the police to search the glove compartment of the arrestee's car.

South Dakota v. Opperman

Supreme Court of the United States
428 U.S. 364 (1976)

Mr. Chief Justice BURGER delivered the opinion of the Court.

We review the judgment of the Supreme Court of South Dakota, holding that local police violated the Fourth Amendment to the Federal Constitution, as applicable to the States under the Fourteenth Amendment, when they conducted a routine inventory search of an automobile lawfully impounded by police for violations of municipal parking ordinances.

I

Local ordinances prohibit parking in certain areas of downtown Vermillion, S. D., between the hours of 2 A.M. and 6 A.M. During the early morning hours of December 10, 1973, a Vermillion police officer observed respondent's unoccupied vehicle illegally parked in the restricted zone. At approximately 3 A.M., the officer issued an overtime parking ticket and placed it on the car's windshield. The citation warned: "Vehicles in violation of any parking ordinance may be towed from the area."

At approximately 10 o'clock on the same morning, another officer issued a second ticket for an overtime parking violation. These circumstances were routinely reported to police headquarters, and after the vehicle was inspected, the car was towed to the city impound lot.

From outside the car at the impound lot, a police officer observed a watch on the dashboard and other items of personal property located on the back seat and back floorboard. At the officer's direction, the car door was then unlocked and, using a standard inventory form pursuant to standard police procedures, the officer inventoried the contents of the car, including the contents of the glove compartment which was unlocked. There he found marihuana contained in a plastic bag. All items, including the contraband, were removed to the police department for safekeeping. During the late afternoon of December 10, respondent appeared at the police department to claim his property. The marihuana was retained by police.

Respondent was subsequently arrested on charges of possession of marihuana. His motion to suppress the evidence yielded by the inventory search was denied; he was convicted after a jury trial and sentenced to a fine of $100 and 14 days' incarceration in the county jail. On appeal, the Supreme Court of South Dakota reversed the conviction. The court concluded that the evidence had been obtained in violation of the Fourth Amendment prohibition against unreasonable searches and seizures. We granted certiorari and we reverse.

II

This Court has traditionally drawn a distinction between automobiles and homes or offices in relation to the Fourth Amendment. Although automobiles are "effects" and thus within the reach of the Fourth Amendment, warrantless examinations of automobiles have been upheld in circumstances in which a search of a home or office would not.

The reason for this well-settled distinction is twofold. First, the inherent mobility of automobiles creates circumstances of such exigency that, as a practical necessity, rigorous enforcement of the warrant requirement is impossible. But the Court has also upheld warrantless searches where no immediate danger was presented that the car would be removed from the jurisdiction. Besides the element of mobility, less rigorous warrant requirements govern because the expectation of privacy with respect to one's automobile is significantly less than that relating to one's home or office. In discharging their varied responsibilities for ensuring the public safety, law enforcement officials are necessarily brought into frequent contact with automobiles. Most of this contact is distinctly noncriminal in nature. Automobiles, unlike homes, are subjected to pervasive and continuing governmental regulation and controls, including periodic inspection and licensing requirements. As an everyday occurrence, police stop and examine vehicles when license plates or inspection stickers have expired, or if other violations, such as exhaust fumes or excessive noise, are noted, or if headlights or other safety equipment are not in proper working order.

The expectation of privacy as to automobiles is further diminished by the obviously public nature of automobile travel. Only two Terms ago, the Court noted: "One has a lesser expectation of privacy in a motor vehicle because its function is transportation and it seldom serves as one's residence or as the repository of personal effects. . . . A car has little capacity for escaping public scrutiny. It travels public thoroughfares where both its occupants and its contents are in plain view."

In the interests of public safety and as part of what the Court has called "community caretaking functions," automobiles are frequently taken into police custody. Vehicle accidents present one such occasion. To permit the uninterrupted flow of traffic and in some circumstances to preserve evidence, disabled or damaged vehicles will often be removed from the highways or streets at the behest of police engaged solely in caretaking and traffic-control activities. Police will also frequently remove and impound automobiles which violate parking ordinances and which thereby jeopardize both the public safety and the efficient movement of vehicular traffic. The authority of police to seize and remove from the streets vehicles impeding traffic or threatening public safety and convenience is beyond challenge.

When vehicles are impounded, local police departments generally follow a routine practice of securing and inventorying the automobiles' contents. These procedures developed in response to three distinct needs: the protection of the owner's property while it remains in police custody; the protection the police against claims or disputes over lost or stolen property; and the protection of the police from potential danger. The practice has been viewed as essential to respond to incidents of theft or vandalism. In addition, police frequently attempt to determine whether a vehicle has been stolen and thereafter abandoned.

These caretaking procedures have almost uniformly been upheld by the state courts, which by virtue of the localized nature of traffic regulation have had considerable occasion to deal with the issue. Applying the Fourth Amendment standard of "reasonableness," the state courts have overwhelmingly concluded that, even if an inventory is characterized as a "search," the intrusion is constitutionally permissible. Even the seminal state decision relied on by the South Dakota Supreme Court in reaching the contrary result, expressly approved police caretaking activities resulting in the securing of property within the officer's plain view. The majority of the Federal Courts of Appeals have likewise sustained inventory procedures as reasonable police intrusions. . . . These cases have recognized that standard inventories often include an examination of the glove compartment, since it is a customary place for documents of ownership and registration, as well as a place for the temporary storage of valuables.

III

The decisions of this Court point unmistakably to the conclusion reached by both federal and state courts that inventories pursuant to standard police procedures are reasonable. . . . In applying the reasonableness standard adopted by the Framers, this Court has consistently sustained police intrusions into automobiles impounded or otherwise in lawful police custody where the process is aimed at securing or protecting the car and its contents. In *Cooper v. California*, the Court upheld the inventory of a car impounded under the authority of a state forfeiture statute. Even though the inventory was conducted in a distinctly criminal setting and carried out a week after the car had been impounded, the Court nonetheless found that the car search, including examination of the glove compartment where contraband was found, was reasonable under the circumstances. This conclusion was reached despite the fact that no warrant had issued and probable cause to search for the contraband in the vehicle had not been established. . . .

The Vermillion police were indisputably engaged in a caretaking search of a lawfully impounded automobile. The inventory was conducted only after the car had been impounded for multiple parking violations. The owner, having left his car illegally parked for an extended period, and thus subject to impoundment, was not present to make other arrangements for the safekeeping of his belongings. The inventory itself was prompted by the presence in plain view of a number of valuables inside the car. As in *Cady*, there is no suggestion whatever that this standard procedure, essentially like that followed throughout the country, was a pretext concealing an investigatory police motive.

On this record we conclude that in following standard police procedures, prevailing throughout the country and approved by the overwhelming majority of courts, the conduct of the police was not "unreasonable" under the Fourth Amendment. . . .

Mr. Justice MARSHALL, with whom Mr. Justice BRENNAN and Mr. Justice STEWART join, dissenting.

. . . The Court's opinion appears to suggest that its result may in any event be justified because the inventory search procedure is a "reasonable" response to "three distinct needs: the protection of the owner's property while it remains in police custody . . .; the protection of the police against claims or disputes over lost or stolen property . . .; and the protection of the police from potential danger."

This suggestion is flagrantly misleading, however, because the record of this case explicitly belies any relevance of the last two concerns. In any event it is my view that none of these "needs," separately or together, can suffice to justify the inventory search procedure approved by the Court.

First, this search cannot be justified in any way as a safety measure, for—though the Court ignores it—the sole purpose given by the State for the Vermillion police's inventory procedure was to secure valuables. Nor is there any indication that the officer's search in this case was tailored in any way to safety concerns, or that ordinarily it is so circumscribed. Even aside from the actual basis for the police practice in this case, however, I do not believe that any blanket safety argument could justify a program of routine searches of the scope permitted here. . . . Thus, while the safety rationale may not be entirely discounted when it is actually relied upon, it surely cannot justify the search of every car upon the basis of undifferentiated possibility of harm; on the contrary, such an intrusion could ordinarily be justified only in those individual cases where the officer's inspection was prompted by specific circumstances indicating the possibility of a particular danger.

Second, the Court suggests that the search for valuables in the closed glove compartment might be justified as a measure to protect the police against lost property claims. Again, this suggestion is belied by the record, since—although the Court declines to discuss it—the South Dakota Supreme Court's interpretation of state law explicitly absolves the police, as "gratuitous depositors," from any obligation beyond inventorying objects in plain view and locking the car. . . .

Finally, the Court suggests that the public interest in protecting valuables that may be found inside a closed compartment of an impounded car may justify the inventory procedure. I recognize the genuineness of this governmental interest in protecting property from pilferage. But even if I assume that the posting of a guard would be fiscally impossible as an alternative means to the same protective end, I cannot agree with the Court's conclusion. The Court's result authorizes—indeed it appears to require—the routine search of nearly every car impounded. In my view, the Constitution does not permit such searches as a matter of routine; absent specific consent, such a search is permissible only in exceptional circumstances of particular necessity. . . .

Because the record in this case shows that the procedures followed by the Vermillion police in searching respondent's car fall far short of these standards, in my view the search was impermissible and its fruits must be suppressed. First, so far as the record shows, the police in this case had no reason to believe that the glove compartment of the impounded car contained particular property of any substantial value. Moreover, the owner had apparently thought it adequate to protect whatever he left in the car overnight on the street in a business area simply to lock the car, and there is nothing in the record to show that the impoundment lot would prove a less secure location against pilferage, particularly when it would seem likely that the owner would claim his car and its contents promptly, at least if it contained valuables worth protecting. Even if the police had cause to believe that the impounded car's glove compartment contained particular valuables, however, they made no effort to secure the owner's consent to the search. Although the Court relies, as it must, upon the fact that respondent was not present to make other arrangements for the care of his belongings, in my view that is not the end of the inquiry. Here the police readily ascertained the ownership of the vehicle, yet they searched it immediately without taking any steps to locate respondent and procure his consent to the inventory or advise him to make alternative arrangements to safeguard his property. Such a failure is inconsistent with the rationale that the inventory procedure is carried out for the benefit of the owner. . . .

NOTES & QUESTIONS ON AUTOMOBILE INVENTORY SEARCHES

1. *Community caretaking functions.* According to the Court, the inventory of a car is necessary to: (i) protect the owner's property interests; (ii) protect the police from claims regarding lost or stolen property; and (iii) protect the police from possible danger (such as a hidden incendiary or explosive device). Do you agree with the majority that these rationales justify the type of search that led to the marijuana in the glove compartment in this case? Justice Marshall, in dissent, noted that an "undifferentiated possibility of harm" was insufficient to justify a universal practice of performing an inventory of *every* car in police possession. If Marshall is correct, the police should have some reason to suspect danger because a search can be justified by the third caretaking function listed above (protection from danger). Do you agree with the majority or with Marshall?

2. *Limits on police discretion.* What if the police decide to impound and inventory some cars but not others? The Supreme Court has said that the standards in place for inventory searches must provide some limits on police discretion. Put another way, if police follow "standardized procedures" and act in good faith, the inventory search exception will apply "so long as that discretion is exercised according to standard criteria and on the basis of something other than suspicion of evidence of criminal activity." *Colorado v. Bertine*, 479 U.S. 367, 375 (1987). However, if the decision to impound and search is based on suspicion of evidence of criminal activity, rather than the standardized criteria designed to implement the caretaking function of inventory searches, then the warrantless search would be unconstitutional.

3. *Sufficiently regulated.* An inventory search must be conducted in accordance with departmental policies or procedures to be consistent with the Fourth Amendment. In the words of the Supreme Court, it must be "sufficiently regulated." *Florida v. Wells*, 495 U.S. 1, 5 (1990). This requirement prohibits

PROBLEM CASE

The Oak Lawn Police Department had a policy regarding inventory searches of automobiles. The policy called for police officers to conduct the inventory search at the scene of the arrest: "[The] arresting officer . . . will make an inspection of the arrestee's vehicle prior to leaving it parked or removed from the scene. . . ." On March 15, 1994, officers from the department and the DEA conducted surveillance of two cars that they suspected were involved in cocaine distribution. After observing what they thought might be a delivery, the officers moved to pull over both cars. One of the cars stopped immediately and was arrested. The second car only stopped after its driver reached into the back-passenger side of the car. During the arrest of the second driver, the arresting officer conducted a visual search of the car and did not see anything. The car was transported to the police station, at which point a confidential informant told the police that the car had secret compartments and told them how to access them. The police searched the compartments and found weapons and ammunition. At trial, the officer testified that he believed that the policy gave him discretion to conduct the search at the station rather than on a dimly lit street at night. Was this search constitutional? See *United States v. Lomeli,* 76 F.3d 146, 148 (7th Cir. 1996).

"uncanalized discretion" but at the same time does not prohibit all discretion whatsoever, because the policy might "allow the opening of closed containers whose contents officers determine they are unable to ascertain from examining the containers' exteriors. The allowance of the exercise of judgment based on concerns related to the purposes of an inventory search does not violate the Fourth Amendment."

2. Arrested Persons

Police typically perform an inventory search of individuals they place under arrest: pockets, wallets, purses, etc. In *Illinois v. Lafayette,* 462 U.S. 640 (1983), the Supreme Court asked whether an inventory search of an arrestee's shoulder bag, without a warrant and without probable cause, is consistent with the Fourth Amendment. The Court concluded that such a search was reasonable, echoing many of the same rationales that it used to justify inventory searches of automobiles discussed above:

> At the stationhouse, it is entirely proper for police to remove and list or inventory property found on the person or in the possession of an arrested person who is to be jailed. A range of governmental interests support an inventory process. It is not unheard of for persons employed in police activities to steal property taken from arrested persons; similarly, arrested persons have been known to make false claims regarding what was taken from

their possession at the stationhouse. A standardized procedure for making a list or inventory as soon as reasonable after reaching the stationhouse not only deters false claims but also inhibits theft or careless handling of articles taken from the arrested person. Arrested persons have also been known to injure themselves—or others—with belts, knives, drugs or other items on their person while being detained. Dangerous instrumentalities—such as razor blades, bombs, or weapons—can be concealed in innocent-looking articles taken from the arrestee's possession. The bare recital of these mundane realities justifies reasonable measures by police to limit these risks—either while the items are in police possession or at the time they are returned to the arrestee upon his release. Examining all the items removed from the arrestee's person or possession and listing or inventorying them is an entirely reasonable administrative procedure. It is immaterial whether the police actually fear any particular package or container; the need to protect against such risks arises independent of a particular officer's subjective concerns. Finally, inspection of an arrestee's personal property may assist the police in ascertaining or verifying his identity. In short, every consideration of orderly police administration benefiting both police and the public points toward the appropriateness of the examination of respondent's shoulder bag prior to his incarceration.

The following case presents a far more difficult application of the inventory search concept. In *Maryland v. King*, the defendant was charged with a felony and then a cotton swab was used to collect a DNA sample from his cheek. As the case below indicates, the results of this "inventory" search would have profound consequences for the arrestee's future criminal responsibility.

Maryland v. King

Supreme Court of the United States
569 U.S. 435 (2013)

Justice KENNEDY delivered the opinion of the Court.

In 2003 a man concealing his face and armed with a gun broke into a woman's home in Salisbury, Maryland. He raped her. The police were unable to identify or apprehend the assailant based on any detailed description or other evidence they then had, but they did obtain from the victim a sample of the perpetrator's DNA.

In 2009 Alonzo King was arrested in Wicomico County, Maryland, and charged with first- and second-degree assault for menacing a group of people with a shotgun. As part of a routine booking procedure for serious offenses, his DNA sample was taken by applying a cotton swab or filter paper—known as a buccal swab—to the inside of his cheeks. The DNA was found to match the DNA taken from the Salisbury rape victim. King was tried and convicted for the rape. Additional DNA samples were taken from him and used in the rape trial, but there seems to be no doubt that it was the DNA from the cheek sample taken at the time he was booked in 2009 that led to his first having been linked to the rape and charged with its commission.

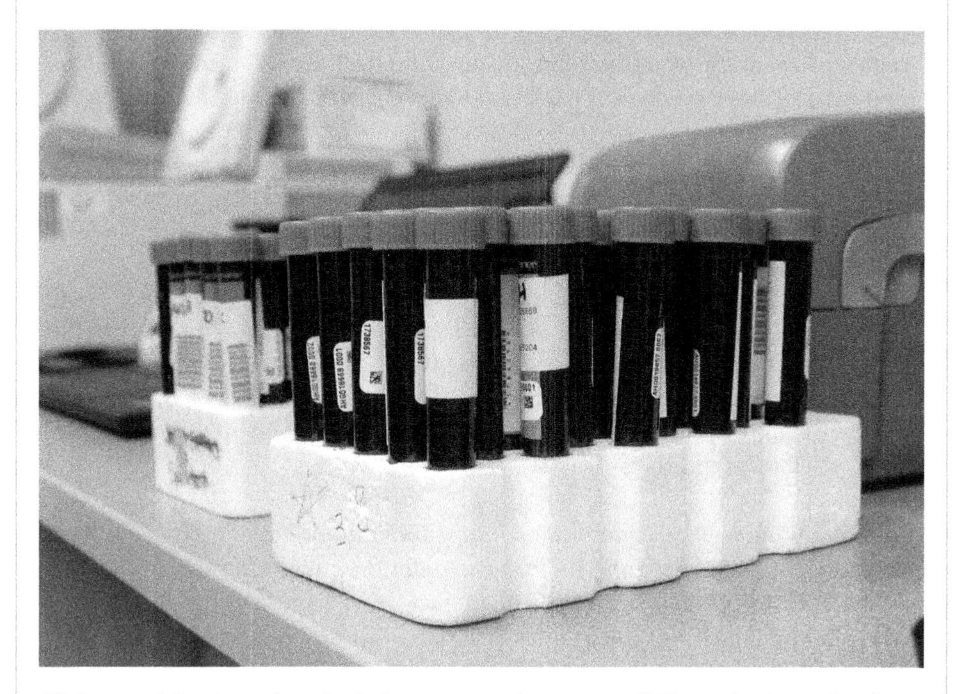

Vials containing buccal swabs being processed to extract DNA at the Avera Institute for Human Genetics in Sioux Falls, S.D. (Regina Garcia Cano/AP/Shutterstock)

The Court of Appeals of Maryland, on review of King's rape conviction, ruled that the DNA taken when King was booked for the 2009 charge was an unlawful seizure because obtaining and using the cheek swab was an unreasonable search of the person. It set the rape conviction aside. This Court granted certiorari and now reverses the judgment of the Maryland court.

I

When King was arrested on April 10, 2009, for menacing a group of people with a shotgun and charged in state court with both first- and second-degree assault, he was processed for detention in custody at the Wicomico County Central Booking facility. Booking personnel used a cheek swab to take the DNA sample from him pursuant to provisions of the Maryland DNA Collection Act (or Act).

On July 13, 2009, King's DNA record was uploaded to the Maryland DNA database, and three weeks later, on August 4, 2009, his DNA profile was matched to the DNA sample collected in the unsolved 2003 rape case. Once the DNA was matched to King, detectives presented the forensic evidence to a grand jury, which indicted him for the rape. Detectives obtained a search warrant and took a second sample of DNA from King, which again matched the evidence from the rape. . . .

II

. . . The Act authorizes Maryland law enforcement authorities to collect DNA samples from "an individual who is charged with . . . a crime of violence or an attempt to commit a crime of violence; or . . . burglary or an attempt to commit burglary." Md. Pub. Saf. Code § 2-504(a)(3)(i). Maryland law defines a crime of violence to include murder, rape, first-degree assault, kidnaping, arson, sexual assault, and a variety of other serious crimes. Once taken, a DNA sample may not be processed or placed in a database before the individual is arraigned (unless the individual consents). It is at this point that a judicial officer ensures that there is probable cause to detain the arrestee on a qualifying serious offense. If "all qualifying criminal charges are determined to be unsupported by probable cause . . . the DNA sample shall be immediately destroyed." § 2-504(d)(2)(i). DNA samples are also destroyed if "a criminal action begun against the individual . . . does not result in a conviction," "the conviction is finally reversed or vacated and no new trial is permitted," or "the individual is granted an unconditional pardon." . . .

All 50 States require the collection of DNA from felony convicts, and respondent does not dispute the validity of that practice. Twenty-eight States and the Federal Government have adopted laws similar to the Maryland Act authorizing the collection of DNA from some or all arrestees. Although those statutes vary in their particulars, such as what charges require a DNA sample, their similarity means that this case implicates more than the specific Maryland law. At issue is a standard, expanding technology already in widespread use throughout the Nation.

III

. . . A buccal swab is a far more gentle process than a venipuncture to draw blood. It involves but a light touch on the inside of the cheek; and although it can be deemed a search within the body of the arrestee, it requires no "surgical intrusions beneath the skin." The fact than an intrusion is negligible is of central relevance to determining reasonableness, although it is still a search as the law defines that term.

To say that the Fourth Amendment applies here is the beginning point, not the end of the analysis. . . . In giving content to the inquiry whether an intrusion is reasonable, the Court has preferred "some quantum of individualized suspicion . . . [as] a prerequisite to a constitutional search or seizure. But the Fourth Amendment imposes no irreducible requirement of such suspicion." . . .

Even if a warrant is not required, a search is not beyond Fourth Amendment scrutiny; for it must be reasonable in its scope and manner of execution. Urgent government interests are not a license for indiscriminate police behavior. To say that no warrant is required is merely to acknowledge that "rather than employing a per se rule of unreasonableness, we balance the privacy-related and law enforcement-related concerns to determine if the intrusion was reasonable." This application of "traditional standards of reasonableness" requires a court to weigh "the promotion of legitimate governmental interests" against "the degree to which [the search] intrudes upon an individual's privacy." An assessment of reasonableness to determine the lawfulness of requiring this class of arrestees to provide a DNA sample is central to the instant case.

IV

The legitimate government interest served by the Maryland DNA Collection Act is one that is well established: the need for law enforcement officers in a safe and accurate way to process and identify the persons and possessions they must take into custody. It is beyond dispute that "probable cause provides legal justification for arresting a person suspected of crime, and for a brief period of detention to take the administrative steps incident to arrest." Also uncontested is the "right on the part of the Government, always recognized under English and American law, to search the person of the accused when legally arrested." Even in that context, the Court has been clear that individual suspicion is not necessary, because "[t]he constitutionality of a search incident to an arrest does not depend on whether there is any indication that the person arrested possesses weapons or evidence. The fact of a lawful arrest, standing alone, authorizes a search."

The "routine administrative procedure[s] at a police station house incident to booking and jailing the suspect" derive from different origins and have different constitutional justifications than, say, the search of a place; for the search of a place not incident to an arrest depends on the "fair probability that contraband or evidence of a crime will be found in a particular place." The interests are further different when an individual is formally processed into police custody. Then "the law is in the act of subjecting the body of the accused to its physical dominion." When probable cause exists to remove an individual from the normal channels of society and hold him in legal custody, DNA identification plays a critical role in serving those interests.

First, "[i]n every criminal case, it is known and must be known who has been arrested and who is being tried." An individual's identity is more than just his name or Social Security number, and the government's interest in identification goes beyond ensuring that the proper name is typed on the indictment. Identity has never been considered limited to the name on the arrestee's birth certificate. In fact, a name is of little value compared to the real interest in identification at stake when an individual is brought into custody. . . .

A suspect's criminal history is a critical part of his identity that officers should know when processing him for detention. It is a common occurrence that "[p]eople detained for minor offenses can turn out to be the most devious and dangerous criminals. Hours after the Oklahoma City bombing, Timothy McVeigh was stopped by a state trooper who noticed he was driving without a license plate. Police stopped serial killer Joel Rifkin for the same reason. One of the terrorists involved in the September 11 attacks was stopped and ticketed for speeding just two days before hijacking Flight 93." Police already seek this crucial identifying information. They use routine and accepted means as varied as comparing the suspect's booking photograph to sketch artists' depictions of persons of interest, showing his mugshot to potential witnesses, and of course making a computerized comparison of the arrestee's fingerprints against electronic databases of known criminals and unsolved crimes. In this respect the only difference between DNA analysis and the accepted use of fingerprint databases is the unparalleled accuracy DNA provides. . . .

Second, law enforcement officers bear a responsibility for ensuring that the custody of an arrestee does not create inordinate "risks for facility staff, for the existing detainee population, and for a new detainee." DNA identification can provide untainted information to those charged with detaining suspects and detaining the property of any felon. For these purposes officers must know the type of person whom they are detaining, and DNA allows them to make critical choices about how to proceed. . . . Recognizing that a name alone cannot address this interest in identity, the Court has approved, for example, "a visual inspection for certain tattoos and other signs of gang affiliation as part of the intake process," because "[t]he identification and isolation of gang members before they are admitted protects everyone."

Third, looking forward to future stages of criminal prosecution, "the Government has a substantial interest in ensuring that persons accused of crimes are available for trials." A person who is arrested for one offense but knows that he has yet to answer for some past crime may be more inclined to flee the instant charges, lest continued contact with the criminal justice system expose one or more other serious offenses. For example, a defendant who had committed a prior sexual assault might be inclined to flee on a burglary charge, knowing that in every State a DNA sample would be taken from him after his conviction on the burglary charge that would tie him to the more serious charge of rape. In addition to subverting the administration of justice with respect to the crime of arrest, this ties back to the interest in safety; for a detainee who absconds from custody presents a risk to law enforcement officers, other detainees, victims of previous crimes, witnesses, and society at large.

Fourth, an arrestee's past conduct is essential to an assessment of the danger he poses to the public, and this will inform a court's determination whether the individual should be released on bail. DNA identification of a suspect in a violent crime provides critical information to the police and judicial officials in making a determination of the arrestee's future dangerousness. This inquiry always has entailed some scrutiny beyond the name on the defendant's driver's license. . . . Knowing that the defendant is wanted for a previous violent crime based on DNA identification is especially probative of the court's consideration of "the danger of the defendant to the alleged victim, another person, or the community." . . .

Finally, in the interests of justice, the identification of an arrestee as the perpetrator of some heinous crime may have the salutary effect of freeing a person wrongfully imprisoned for the same offense. . . . DNA identification represents an important advance in the techniques used by law enforcement to serve legitimate police concerns for as long as there have been arrests, concerns the courts have acknowledged and approved for more than a century. Law enforcement agencies routinely have used scientific advancements in their standard procedures for the identification of arrestees. "Police had been using photography to capture the faces of criminals almost since its invention." Courts did not dispute that practice. . . .

V

By comparison to this substantial government interest and the unique effectiveness of DNA identification, the intrusion of a cheek swab to obtain a DNA sample is a minimal one. True, a significant government interest does not alone suffice to justify a search. The government interest must outweigh the degree to which the search invades an individual's legitimate expectations of privacy. In considering those expectations in this case, however, the necessary predicate of a valid arrest for a serious offense is fundamental. . . .

The reasonableness of any search must be considered in the context of the person's legitimate expectations of privacy. . . . The expectations of privacy of an individual taken into police custody "necessarily [are] of a diminished scope." "[B]oth the person and the property in his immediate possession may be searched at the station house." A search of the detainee's person when he is booked into custody may "involve a relatively extensive exploration," including "requir[ing] at least some detainees to lift their genitals or cough in a squatting position." . . .

The reasonableness inquiry here considers two other circumstances in which the Court has held that particularized suspicion is not categorically required: "diminished expectations of privacy [and] minimal intrusions." This is not to suggest that any search is acceptable solely because a person is in custody. Some searches, such as invasive surgery, or a search of the arrestee's home, involve either greater intrusions or higher expectations of privacy than are present in this case. In those situations, when the Court must "balance the privacy-related and law enforcement-related concerns to determine if the intrusion was reasonable," the privacy-related concerns are weighty enough that the search may require a warrant, notwithstanding the diminished expectations of privacy of the arrestee.

Here, by contrast to the approved standard procedures incident to any arrest detailed above, a buccal swab involves an even more brief and still minimal intrusion. A gentle rub along the inside of the cheek does not break the skin, and it "involves virtually no risk, trauma, or pain." "A crucial factor in analyzing the magnitude of the intrusion . . . is the extent to which the procedure may threaten the safety or health of the individual," and nothing suggests that a buccal swab poses any physical danger whatsoever. A brief intrusion of an arrestee's person is subject to the Fourth Amendment, but a swab of this nature does not increase the indignity already attendant to normal incidents of arrest. . . .

Justice Scalia, with whom Justice Ginsburg, Justice Sotomayor, and Justice Kagan join, dissenting.

. . . [T]he Court elaborates at length the ways that the search here served the special purpose of "identifying" King. But that seems to me quite wrong—unless what one means by "identifying" someone is "searching for evidence that he has committed crimes unrelated to the crime of his arrest." At points the Court does appear to use "identifying" in that peculiar sense—claiming, for example, that knowing "an arrestee's past conduct is essential to an assessment of the danger he poses." If identifying someone means finding out what unsolved crimes he has committed, then identification is indistinguishable from the ordinary law-enforcement aims that have never been thought to justify a suspicionless search. Searching every lawfully stopped car, for example, might turn up information about unsolved crimes the driver had committed, but no one would say that such a search was aimed at "identifying" him, and no court would hold such a search lawful. I will therefore assume that the Court means that the DNA search at issue here was useful to "identify" King in the normal sense of that word. . . .

The portion of the Court's opinion that explains the identification rationale is strangely silent on the actual workings of the DNA search at issue here. To know those facts is to be instantly disabused of the notion that what happened had anything to do with identifying King. . . .

In fact, if anything was "identified" at the moment that the DNA database returned a match, it was not King–his identity was already known. (The docket for the original criminal charges lists his full name, his race, his sex, his height, his weight, his date of birth, and his address.) Rather, what the August 4 match "identified" was the previously-taken sample from the earlier crime. That sample was genuinely mysterious to Maryland; the State knew that it had probably been left by the victim's attacker, but nothing else. King was not identified by his association with the sample; rather, the sample was identified by its association with King. The Court effectively destroys its own "identification" theory when it acknowledges that the object of this search was "to see what [was] already known about [King]." King was who he was, and volumes of his biography could not make him any more or any less King. No minimally competent speaker of English would say, upon noticing a known arrestee's similarity "to a wanted poster of a previously unidentified suspect," that the arrestee had thereby been identified. It was the previously unidentified suspect who had been identified–just as, here, it was the previously unidentified rapist.

That taking DNA samples from arrestees has nothing to do with identifying them is confirmed not just by actual practice (which the Court ignores) but by the enabling statute itself (which the Court also ignores). The Maryland Act at issue has a section helpfully entitled "Purpose of collecting and testing DNA samples." That provision lists five purposes for which DNA samples may be tested. By this point, it will not surprise the reader to learn that the Court's imagined purpose is not among them.

Instead, the law provides that DNA samples are collected and tested, as a matter of Maryland law, "as part of an official investigation into a crime." That is certainly how everyone has always understood the Maryland Act until today. . . . More devastating still for the Court's "identification" theory, the statute does enumerate two instances in which a DNA sample may be tested for the purpose of identification: "to help identify human remains," and "to help identify missing individuals." No mention of identifying arrestees. . . . The Maryland regulations implementing the Act confirm what is now monotonously obvious: These DNA searches have nothing to do with identification. . . .

The Court also attempts to bolster its identification theory with a series of inapposite analogies. Is not taking DNA samples the same, asks the Court, as taking a person's photograph? No–because that is not a Fourth Amendment search at all. It does not involve a physical intrusion onto the person, and we have never held that merely taking a person's photograph invades any recognized "expectation of privacy." Thus, it is unsurprising that the cases the Court cites as authorizing photo-taking do not even mention the Fourth Amendment. . . .

It is on the fingerprinting of arrestees, however, that the Court relies most heavily. The Court does not actually say whether it believes that taking a person's fingerprints is a Fourth Amendment search, and our cases provide no ready answer to that question. Even assuming so, however, law enforcement's post-arrest use of fingerprints could not be more different from its post-arrest use of DNA. Fingerprints of arrestees are taken primarily to identify them (though that process sometimes solves crimes); the DNA of arrestees is taken to solve crimes (and nothing else). . . . The entire point of the DNA database is to check crime scene evidence against the profiles of arrestees and convicts as they come in. . . .

Today, it can fairly be said that fingerprints really are used to identify people—so well, in fact, that there would be no need for the expense of a separate, wholly redundant DNA confirmation of the same information. What DNA adds—what makes it a valuable weapon in the law-enforcement arsenal—is the ability to solve unsolved crimes, by matching old crime-scene evidence against the profiles of people whose identities are already known. That is what was going on when King's DNA was taken, and we should not disguise the fact. Solving unsolved crimes is a noble objective, but it occupies a lower place in the American pantheon of noble objectives than the protection of our people from suspicionless law-enforcement searches. The Fourth Amendment must prevail. . . .

NOTES & QUESTIONS ON PERSONAL INVENTORY SEARCHES

1. *Identification or crime-solving?* The majority and dissent in *Maryland v. King* disagree over the purpose of DNA testing. The majority calls it an identification procedure, like fingerprinting, while the dissent calls it an investigatory tool. Is it one, the other, or both? Which side of the debate has the better argument? In what does an individual's "identity" consist? For a discussion, see David H. Kaye, *Why So Contrived? Fourth Amendment Balancing, Per Se Rules, and DNA Databases After* Maryland v. King, 104 J. Crim. L. & Criminology 535, 544 (2014) (distinguishing between two types of identification: authentication-identification and association-identification).

2. *Limits to Maryland v. King?* Not every court has upheld its jurisdiction's policy of collecting DNA samples from arrestees. For example, in *People v. Buza*, 231 Cal. App. 4th 1446, 180 Cal. Rptr. 3d 753, 766 (2014), a California appeals court found a DNA search to be unreasonable because the California

PROBLEM CASE

The police arrested the defendant at his home during a domestic disturbance. The defendant was taken to the county detention center and ushered through the booking process by two officers. A court described what happened next:

> Officer Williams patted him down and took defendant's wallet and open pack of cigarettes, which he placed on a counter in the booking area. Officer Sellers processed the paperwork while Officer Williams completed the search of Defendant, supervised his change into prison clothes, and listed Defendant's possessions on a booking sheet. Shortly after the wallet and cigarettes were taken, Defendant asked for the return of his cigarettes. Although his request was denied, he continued to ask for the return of the cigarettes. He was told that detention facility rules precluded return of his cigarettes while he was in custody and that they would be stored with his other possessions. Defendant's repeated requests for his cigarettes aroused Officer Sellers' suspicion that the cigarette pack might contain contraband. Acting on his suspicion, as well as for other reasons, Officer Sellers searched the cigarette pack, taking each cigarette out. He found a packet of white powder in the bottom of the cigarette pack which was later stipulated to be cocaine.

State v. Shaw, 115 N.M. 174, 175-76, 848 P.2d 1101, 1102-03 (1993). At a suppression hearing, a training sergeant testified that "although there was no written procedure regarding searching personal items such as wallets or cigarette packs, the inventory procedure used at the facility required that all items in possession of an arrestee must be searched." Was the search constitutional?

statute authorized collection from individuals arrested for any felony, not just a violent felony:

> [W]e find it difficult to view *King* as controlling the outcome of the present case because of significant differences between the California DNA Act and the Maryland law. These include that the DNA Act applies to persons arrested for any felony, requires immediate collection and analysis of arrestees' DNA even before a judicial determination of probable cause, and does not provide for automatic expungement of DNA data if an arrestee is not in fact convicted of a qualifying crime.

Although the court's holding flowed from state constitutional law, the court strongly suggested in dicta that it believed that the California search was unreasonable under the Fourth Amendment as well. At this time, the more expansive policy of DNA testing has not yet been examined by the U.S. Supreme Court. How do you think the Supreme Court would react if the California statute were put before it? Is the intrusion on personal privacy more significant if it is applied to those arrested for non-violent felonies? What result if the DNA testing were applied to those arrested for misdemeanors?

F. PROTECTIVE SWEEPS

The arrest of an individual is an encounter fraught with danger. On the assumption that other dangers may lurk in the location of an arrest, police officers typically perform a "protective sweep" of the location. For example, if the arrest happens in a residence, the police might move from room to room conducting a quick search to determine if other individuals are in the house and determine if any of them are armed or dangerous. In the following case, the Supreme Court evaluates the constitutionality of this practice. As you read the case, ask yourself whether protective sweeps are exceptions from the warrant requirement or whether they are also exceptions from the probable cause requirement. Do police need probable cause to believe that the other rooms of a house conceal a hidden danger?

Maryland v. Buie

Supreme Court of the United States
494 U.S. 325 (1990)

Justice White delivered the opinion of the Court.

A "protective sweep" is a quick and limited search of premises, incident to an arrest and conducted to protect the safety of police officers or others. It is narrowly confined to a cursory visual inspection of those places in which a person might be hiding. In this case we must decide what level of justification is required by the Fourth and Fourteenth Amendments before police officers, while effecting the arrest of a suspect in his home pursuant to an arrest warrant, may conduct a warrantless protective sweep of all or part of the premises. The Court of Appeals of Maryland held that a running suit seized in plain view during such a protective sweep should have been suppressed at respondent's armed robbery trial because the officer who conducted the sweep did not have probable cause to believe that a serious and demonstrable potentiality for danger existed. We conclude that the Fourth Amendment would permit the protective sweep undertaken here if the searching officer "possesse[d] a reasonable belief based on 'specific and articulable facts which, taken together with the rational inferences from those facts, reasonably warrant[ed]' the officer in believing," *Michigan v. Long*, 463 U.S. 1032, 1049-1050 (1983), quoting *Terry v. Ohio*, 392 U.S. 1, 21 (1968), that the area swept harbored an individual posing a danger to the officer or others. We accordingly vacate the judgment below and remand for application of this standard.

I

On February 3, 1986, two men committed an armed robbery of a Godfather's Pizza restaurant in Prince George's County, Maryland. One of the robbers was wearing a red running suit. That same day, Prince George's County police obtained arrest warrants for respondent Jerome Edward Buie and his suspected accomplice in the robbery, Lloyd Allen. Buie's house was placed under police surveillance.

On February 5, the police executed the arrest warrant for Buie. They first had a police department secretary telephone Buie's house to verify that he was home. The secretary spoke to a female first, then to Buie himself. Six or seven officers proceeded to Buie's house. Once inside, the officers fanned out through the first and second floors. Corporal James Rozar announced that he would "freeze" the basement so that no one could come up and surprise the officers. With his service revolver drawn, Rozar twice shouted into the basement, ordering anyone down there to come out. When a voice asked who was calling, Rozar announced three times: "this is the police, show me your hands." Eventually, a pair of hands appeared around the bottom of the stairwell and Buie emerged from the basement. He was arrested, searched, and handcuffed by Rozar. Thereafter, Detective Joseph Frolich entered the basement "in case there was someone else" down there. He noticed a red running suit lying in plain view on a stack of clothing and seized it.

The trial court denied Buie's motion to suppress the running suit, stating in part: "The man comes out from a basement, the police don't know how many other people are down there. He is charged with a serious offense." The State introduced the running suit into evidence at Buie's trial. A jury convicted Buie of robbery with a deadly weapon and using a handgun in the commission of a felony. . . .

II

It is not disputed that until the point of Buie's arrest the police had the right, based on the authority of the arrest warrant, to search anywhere in the house that Buie might have been found, including the basement. "If there is sufficient evidence of a citizen's participation in a felony to persuade a judicial officer that his arrest is justified, it is constitutionally reasonable to require him to open his doors to the officers of the law." *Payton v. New York*, 445 U.S. 573, 602-603 (1980). There is also no dispute that if Detective Frolich's entry into the basement was lawful, the seizure of the red running suit, which was in plain view and which the officer had probable cause to believe was evidence of a crime, was also lawful under the Fourth Amendment. The issue in this case is what level of justification the Fourth Amendment required before Detective Frolich could legally enter the basement to see if someone else was there. . . .

III

It goes without saying that the Fourth Amendment bars only unreasonable searches and seizures. Our cases show that in determining reasonableness, we have balanced the intrusion on the individual's Fourth Amendment interests against its promotion of legitimate governmental interests. Under this test, a search of the house or office is generally not reasonable without a warrant issued on probable cause. There are other contexts, however, where the public interest is such that neither a warrant nor probable cause is required. . . .

That Buie had an expectation of privacy in those remaining areas of his house, however, does not mean such rooms were immune from entry. . . . In the instant case, there is an . . . interest of the officers in taking steps to assure themselves that the house in which a suspect is being, or has just been, arrested is not harboring other persons who are dangerous and who could unexpectedly launch an attack. The risk of danger in the context of an arrest in the home is as great as, if not greater than, it is in an on-the-street or roadside investigatory encounter. . . . A protective sweep . . . occurs as an adjunct to the serious step of taking a person into custody for the purpose of prosecuting him for a crime. Moreover, unlike an encounter on the street or along a highway, an in-home arrest puts the officer at the disadvantage of being on his adversary's "turf." An ambush in a confined setting of unknown configuration is more to be feared than it is in open, more familiar surroundings. . . .

We agree with the State, as did the court below, that a warrant was not required. We also hold that as an incident to the arrest the officers could, as a precautionary matter and without probable cause or reasonable suspicion, look in closets and other spaces immediately adjoining the place of arrest from which an attack could be immediately launched. Beyond that, however, we hold that there must be articulable facts which, taken together with the rational inferences from those facts, would warrant a reasonably prudent officer in believing that the area to be swept harbors an individual posing a danger to those on the arrest scene. . . .

We should emphasize that such a protective sweep, aimed at protecting the arresting officers, if justified by the circumstances, is nevertheless not a full search of the premises, but may extend only to a cursory inspection of those spaces where a person may be found. The sweep lasts no longer than is necessary to dispel the reasonable suspicion of danger and in any event no longer than it takes to complete the arrest and depart the premises. . . .

V

We conclude that by requiring a protective sweep to be justified by probable cause to believe that a serious and demonstrable potentiality for danger existed, the Court of Appeals of Maryland applied an unnecessarily strict Fourth Amendment standard. The Fourth Amendment permits a properly limited protective sweep in conjunction with an in-home arrest when the searching officer possesses a reasonable belief based on specific and articulable facts that the area to be swept harbors an individual posing a danger to those on the arrest scene. . . .

Justice STEVENS, concurring.

Today the Court holds that reasonable suspicion, rather than probable cause, is necessary to support a protective sweep while an arrest is in progress. I agree with that holding and with the Court's opinion, but I believe it is important to emphasize that the standard applies only to protective sweeps. Officers conducting such a sweep must have a reasonable basis for believing that their search will reduce the danger of harm to themselves or of violent interference with their mission; in short, the search must be protective.

In this case, to justify Officer Frolich's entry into the basement, it is the State's burden to demonstrate that the officers had a reasonable basis for believing not only that someone in the basement might attack them or otherwise try to interfere with the arrest, but also that it would be safer to go down the stairs instead of simply guarding them from above until respondent had been removed from the house. The fact that respondent offered no resistance when he emerged from the basement is somewhat inconsistent with the hypothesis that the danger of an attack by a hidden confederate persisted after the arrest. Moreover, Officer Rozar testified that he was not worried about any possible danger when he arrested Buie. Officer Frolich, who conducted the search, supplied no explanation for why he might have thought another person was in the basement. He said only that he "had no idea who lived there." This admission is made telling by Officer Frolich's participation in the 3-day prearrest surveillance of Buie's home. The Maryland Court of Appeals was under the impression that the search took place after "Buie was safely outside the house, handcuffed and unarmed." All of this suggests that no reasonable suspicion of danger justified the entry into the basement. . . .

Justice BRENNAN, with whom Justice Marshall joins, dissenting.

. . . While the Fourth Amendment protects a person's privacy interests in a variety of settings, "physical entry of the home is the chief evil against which the wording of the Fourth Amendment is directed." The Court discounts the nature of the intrusion because it believes that the scope of the intrusion is limited. The Court explains that a protective sweep's scope is "narrowly confined to a cursory visual inspection of those places in which a person might be hiding," and confined in duration to a period "no longer than is necessary to dispel the reasonable suspicion of danger and in any event no longer than it takes to complete the arrest and depart the premises." But these spatial and temporal restrictions are not particularly limiting. A protective sweep would bring within police purview virtually all personal possessions within the house not hidden from view in a small enclosed space. Police officers searching for potential ambushers might enter every room including basements and attics; open up closets, lockers, chests, wardrobes, and cars; and peer under beds and behind furniture. The officers will view letters, documents, and personal effects that are on tables or desks or are visible inside open drawers; books, records, tapes, and pictures on shelves; and clothing, medicines, toiletries and other paraphernalia not carefully stored in dresser drawers or bathroom cupboards. While perhaps not a "full-blown" or "top-to-bottom" search, a protective sweep is much closer to it than to a "limited patdown for weapons" or a "frisk of an automobile." . . .

In light of the special sanctity of a private residence and the highly intrusive nature of a protective sweep, I firmly believe that police officers must have probable cause to fear that their personal safety is threatened by a hidden confederate of an arrestee before they may sweep through the entire home. Given the state-court determination that the officers searching Buie's home lacked probable cause to perceive such a danger and therefore were not lawfully present in the basement, I would affirm the state court's decision to suppress the incriminating evidence. I respectfully dissent.

NOTES & QUESTIONS ON PROTECTIVE SWEEPS

1. *What is the* Buie *standard?* What standards are required for a protective sweep to be valid? In *Buie*, the Supreme Court explicitly said that neither probable cause nor reasonable suspicion are required, but "there must be articulable facts which, taken together with the rational inferences from those facts, would warrant a reasonably prudent officer in believing that the area to be swept harbors an individual posing a danger to those on the arrest scene. . . ." How is this "articulable facts" standard different from reasonable suspicion? One appeals court digested the requirements in the following way:

> A valid protective sweep must meet all of the following five requirements: (1) police must have entered or remained in the home legally; (2) police presence in the home must be for valid law enforcement purposes; (3) the sweep must be supported by a "reasonable, articulable suspicion" that the area harbors an individual who poses a danger to those on the scene; (4) the sweep may be no more than a "cursory inspection" of that area where such an individual may be found; and (5) the sweep may last only long enough to dispel the reasonable suspicion of danger and may not last longer than the police are justified in remaining on the premises.

Cooksey v. State, 350 S.W.3d 177, 185-86 (Tex. App. 2011). Is this a faithful distillation of the *Buie* standard?

PROBLEM CASE

As a matter of training, most police departments require that their officers have a reasonable belief or suspicion before conducting a sweep. For example, San Antonio's department mandates that "[o]fficers may conduct a quick and limited 'protective sweep' search for the safety of officers and persons in the area. . . . The protective sweep search may be made when an officer reasonably believes the area harbors an individual posing a danger to those at the scene." See San Antonio Police Department General Manual, Procedure 502–Warrantless Arrests, Searches, and Seizures. Similarly, Detroit's police department states:

> Officers may undertake a "protective sweep" of the premises where the arrest is for a violent crime and the arrest takes place without a warrant. The purpose of the "protective sweep" is to discover persons on the premises who might present a danger to officers. In order to extend a "protective sweep" beyond closets and adjoining spaces, officers must have reasonable suspicion for fearing that persons may be on the premises that pose a threat. In such cases the sweep is limited to places where a person may hide.

See Detroit Police Department Manual § 202.2-10 Executing Arrest Warrants. Tucson's department adds specificity and articulates two scenarios when police can engage in a protective sweep:

> (1) When an officer is lawfully within a residence to affect an arrest and there are circumstances that give the officer a reasonable belief that there might be others within the residence that pose an immediate danger to the officer.
> (2) When officers arrest someone near the door, but outside a residence and there is reason to believe that a confederate might be within the residence that poses a danger to the officers. This exception will apply only when there is reason for either the officers to fear violence based on the nature of the crime or other information related to the arrestee or the arrestee's confederates.

Tucson Police Department General Orders § 2235.7 (2016). Do the specific examples add different content to the general rules that the other police departments articulate? Is there a difference between a reasonable belief and a reasonable suspicion standard in this context?

G. CONSENT

In the absence of a warrant, or another exception to the warrant requirement, police officers will sometimes ask for permission to conduct a search. Since the individual has consented to the search, it stands to reason that no Fourth Amendment violation has occurred. Against this background of general agreement, however, several difficult questions arise. First, did the individual have the authorization to consent to the search in question, i.e., was the person who consented the same individual whose expectation of privacy was infringed by the search? Second, are there circumstances where police are prohibited from even asking for consent? Third, are the police required to inform the individual that they are free to withhold consent?

In *Schneckloth v. Bustamonte*, 412 U.S. 218 (1973), the Supreme Court addressed how to ascertain whether the consent to a search was granted "voluntarily," as opposed to coerced, and concluded that the answer can only come from a consideration of the "totality of the circumstances." The Court noted that "neither this Court's prior cases, nor the traditional definition of 'voluntariness' requires proof of knowledge of a right to refuse as the *sine qua non* of an effective consent to a search." In other words, police are not required to proactively inform the target of the search that they are free to withhold their consent, provided that a reasonable person, objectively construed, would understand that they are free to withhold their consent. *Id.* at 234. As the Court stated in *Florida v. Bostick*, 501 U.S. 429, 437 (1991), "the crucial test is whether, taking into account all of the circumstances surrounding the encounter, the police conduct would have communicated to a reasonable person that he was not at liberty to ignore the police presence and go about his business."

The following case involves a particularly tricky application of this principle. Police officers boarded a Greyhound bus and asked riders for permission to search their luggage. As you read the case, ask yourself if the riders understood that they were free to refuse. If you were on the bus, how would you have reacted to the presence of the police?

United States v. Drayton

Supreme Court of the United States
536 U.S. 194 (2002)

Justice Kennedy delivered the opinion of the Court.

The Fourth Amendment permits police officers to approach bus passengers at random to ask questions and to request their consent to searches, provided a reasonable person would understand that he or she is free to refuse. *Florida v. Bostick*, 501 U.S. 429 (1991). This case requires us to determine whether officers must advise bus passengers during these encounters of their right not to cooperate.

I

On February 4, 1999, respondents Christopher Drayton and Clifton Brown, Jr., were traveling on a Greyhound bus en route from Ft. Lauderdale, Florida, to Detroit, Michigan. The bus made a scheduled stop in Tallahassee, Florida. The passengers were required to disembark so the bus could be refueled and cleaned. As the passengers reboarded, the driver checked their tickets and then left to complete paperwork inside the terminal. As he left, the driver allowed three members of the Tallahassee Police Department to board the bus as part of a routine drug and weapons interdiction effort. The officers were dressed in plain clothes and carried concealed weapons and visible badges.

Once onboard Officer Hoover knelt on the driver's seat and faced the rear of the bus. He could observe the passengers and ensure the safety of the two other officers without blocking the aisle or otherwise obstructing the bus exit. Officers Lang and Blackburn went to the rear of the bus. Blackburn remained stationed there, facing forward. Lang worked his way toward the front of the bus, speaking with individual passengers as he went. He asked the passengers about their travel plans and sought to match passengers with luggage in the overhead racks. To avoid blocking the aisle, Lang stood next to or just behind each passenger with whom he spoke.

According to Lang's testimony, passengers who declined to cooperate with him or who chose to exit the bus at any time would have been allowed to do so without argument. In Lang's experience, however, most people are willing to cooperate. Some passengers go so far as to commend the police for their efforts to ensure the safety of their travel. Lang could recall five to six instances in the previous year in which passengers had declined to have their luggage searched. It also was common for passengers to leave the bus for a cigarette or a snack while the officers were on board. Lang sometimes informed passengers of their right to refuse to cooperate. On the day in question, however, he did not.

Respondents were seated next to each other on the bus. Drayton was in the aisle seat, Brown in the seat next to the window. Lang approached respondents from the rear and leaned over Drayton's shoulder. He held up his badge long enough for respondents to identify him as a police officer. With his face 12-to-18 inches away from Drayton's, Lang spoke in a voice just loud enough for respondents to hear: "I'm Investigator Lang with the Tallahassee Police Department. We're conducting bus interdiction [sic], attempting to deter drugs and illegal weapons being transported on the bus. Do you have any bags on the bus?"

Both respondents pointed to a single green bag in the overhead luggage rack. Lang asked, "Do you mind if I check it?," and Brown responded, "Go ahead." Lang handed the bag to Officer Blackburn to check. The bag contained no contraband.

Officer Lang noticed that both respondents were wearing heavy jackets and baggy pants despite the warm weather. In Lang's experience drug traffickers often use baggy clothing to conceal weapons or narcotics. The officer thus asked Brown if he had any weapons or drugs in his possession. And he asked Brown: "Do you mind if I check your person?" Brown answered, "Sure," and cooperated by leaning up in his seat, pulling a cell phone out of his pocket, and opening up his jacket. Lang reached across Drayton and patted down Brown's jacket and pockets, including his waist area, sides, and upper thighs. In both thigh areas, Lang detected hard objects similar to drug packages detected on other occasions. Lang arrested and handcuffed Brown. Officer Hoover escorted Brown from the bus.

Lang then asked Drayton, "Mind if I check you?" Drayton responded by lifting his hands about eight inches from his legs. Lang conducted a pat-down of Drayton's thighs and detected hard objects similar to those found on Brown. He arrested Drayton and escorted him from the bus. A further search revealed that respondents had duct-taped plastic bundles of powder cocaine between several pairs of their boxer shorts. Brown possessed three bundles containing 483 grams of cocaine. Drayton possessed two bundles containing 295 grams of cocaine.

Respondents were charged with conspiring to distribute cocaine and with possessing cocaine with intent to distribute it. . . . They moved to suppress the cocaine, arguing that the consent to the patdown search was invalid. . . .

II

Law enforcement officers do not violate the Fourth Amendment's prohibition of unreasonable seizures merely by approaching individuals on the street or in other public places and putting questions to them if they are willing to listen. Even when law enforcement officers have no basis for suspecting a particular individual, they may pose questions, ask for identification, and request consent to search luggage—provided they do not induce cooperation by coercive means. If a reasonable person would feel free to terminate the encounter, then he or she has not been seized.

The Court has addressed on a previous occasion the specific question of drug interdiction efforts on buses. In *Bostick*, two police officers requested a bus passenger's consent to a search of his luggage. The passenger agreed, and the resulting search revealed cocaine in his suitcase. The Florida Supreme Court suppressed the cocaine. In doing so it adopted a per se rule that due to the cramped confines onboard a bus the act of questioning would deprive a person of his or her freedom of movement and so constitute a seizure under the Fourth Amendment. This Court reversed. *Bostick* first made it clear that for the most part per se rules are inappropriate in the Fourth Amendment context. The proper inquiry necessitates a consideration of "all the circumstances surrounding the encounter." . . .

In light of the limited record, *Bostick* refrained from deciding whether a seizure occurred. The Court, however, identified two factors "particularly worth noting" on remand. First, although it was obvious that an officer was armed, he did not remove the gun from its pouch or use it in a threatening way. Second, the officer advised the passenger that he could refuse consent to the search. . . .

Applying the *Bostick* framework to the facts of this particular case, we conclude that the police did not seize respondents when they boarded the bus and began questioning passengers. The officers gave the passengers no reason to believe that they were required to answer the officers' questions.

When Officer Lang approached respondents, he did not brandish a weapon or make any intimidating movements. He left the aisle free so that respondents could exit. He spoke to passengers one by one and in a polite, quiet voice. Nothing he said would suggest to a reasonable person that he or she was barred from leaving the bus or otherwise terminating the encounter.

There were ample grounds for the District Court to conclude that "everything that took place between Officer Lang and [respondents] suggests that it was cooperative" and that there "was nothing coercive [or] confrontational" about the encounter. There was no application of force, no intimidating movement, no overwhelming show of force, no brandishing of weapons, no blocking of exits, no threat, no command, not even an authoritative tone of voice. It is beyond question that had this encounter occurred on the street, it would be constitutional. The fact that an encounter takes place on a bus does not on its own transform standard police questioning of citizens into an illegal seizure. Indeed, because many fellow passengers are present to witness officers' conduct, a reasonable person may feel even more secure in his or her decision not to cooperate with police on a bus than in other circumstances. . . . And while neither Lang nor his colleagues were in uniform or visibly armed, those factors should have little weight in the analysis. Officers are often required to wear uniforms and in many circumstances this is cause for assurance, not discomfort. Much the same can be said for wearing sidearms. That most law enforcement officers are armed is a fact well known to the public. The presence of a holstered firearm thus is unlikely to contribute to the coerciveness of the encounter absent active brandishing of the weapon. . . .

We turn now from the question whether respondents were seized to whether they were subjected to an unreasonable search, i.e., whether their consent to the suspicionless search was involuntary. In circumstances such as these, where the question of voluntariness pervades both the search and seizure inquiries, the respective analyses turn on very similar facts. And, as the facts above suggest, respondents' consent to the search of their luggage and their persons was voluntary. Nothing Officer Lang said indicated a command to consent to the search. Rather, when respondents informed Lang that they had a bag on the bus, he asked for their permission to check it. And when Lang requested to search Brown and Drayton's persons, he asked first if they objected, thus indicating to a reasonable person that he or she was free to refuse. Even after arresting Brown, Lang provided Drayton with no indication that he was required to consent to a search. To the contrary, Lang asked for Drayton's permission to search him ("Mind if I check you?"), and Drayton agreed.

The Court has rejected in specific terms the suggestion that police officers must always inform citizens of their right to refuse when seeking permission to conduct a warrantless consent search. Nor do this Court's decisions suggest that even though there are no per se rules, a presumption of invalidity attaches if a citizen consented without explicit notification that he or she was free to refuse to cooperate. Instead, the Court has repeated that the totality of the circumstances must control, without giving extra weight to the absence of this type of warning. Although Officer Lang did not inform respondents of their right to refuse the search, he did request permission to search, and the totality of the circumstances indicates that their consent was voluntary, so the searches were reasonable.

In a society based on law, the concept of agreement and consent should be given a weight and dignity of its own. Police officers act in full accord with the law when they ask citizens for consent. It reinforces the rule of law for the citizen to advise the police of his or her wishes and for the police to act in reliance on that understanding. When this exchange takes place, it dispels inferences of coercion. . . .

Justice SOUTER, with whom Justice STEVENS and Justice GINSBURG join, dissenting.

. . . *Florida v. Bostick*, 501 U.S. 429 (1991), established the framework for determining whether the bus passengers were seized in the constitutional sense. In that case, we rejected the position that police questioning of bus passengers was a per se seizure, and held instead that the issue of seizure was to be resolved under an objective test considering all circumstances: whether a reasonable passenger would have felt "free to decline the officers' requests or otherwise terminate the encounter." We thus applied to a bus passenger the more general criterion, whether the person questioned was free "to ignore the police presence and go about his business." . . .

When the bus in question made its scheduled stop in Tallahassee, the passengers were required to disembark while the vehicle was cleaned and refueled. When the passengers returned, they gave their tickets to the driver, who kept them and then left himself, after giving three police officers permission to board the bus in his absence. Although they were not in uniform, the officers displayed badges and identified themselves as police. One stationed himself in the driver's seat by the door at the front, facing back to observe the passengers. The two others went to the rear, from which they worked their way forward, with one of them speaking to passengers, the other backing him up. . . .

Thus, for reasons unexplained, the driver with the tickets entitling the passengers to travel had yielded his custody of the bus and its seated travelers to three police officers, whose authority apparently superseded the driver's own. The officers took control of the entire passenger compartment, one stationed at the door keeping surveillance of all the occupants, the others working forward from the back. With one officer right behind

> him and the other one forward, a third officer accosted each passenger at quarters extremely close and so cramped that as many as half the passengers could not even have stood to face the speaker. None was asked whether he was willing to converse with the police or to take part in the enquiry. Instead the officer said the police were "conducting bus interdiction," in the course of which they "would like . . . cooperation." The reasonable inference was that the "interdiction" was not a consensual exercise, but one the police would carry out whatever the circumstances; that they would prefer "cooperation" but would not let the lack of it stand in their way. There was no contrary indication that day, since no passenger had refused the cooperation requested, and there was no reason for any passenger to believe that the driver would return and the trip resume until the police were satisfied. The scene was set and an atmosphere of obligatory participation was established by this introduction. Later requests to search prefaced with "Do you mind . . ." would naturally have been understood in the terms with which the encounter began.
>
> It is very hard to imagine that either Brown or Drayton would have believed that he stood to lose nothing if he refused to cooperate with the police, or that he had any free choice to ignore the police altogether. No reasonable passenger could have believed that, only an uncomprehending one. . . .

NOTES & QUESTIONS ON CONSENT

1. *Voluntary searches and race.* The police in *Drayton* had guns, as one would expect. Does an encounter with a police officer carrying a gun in any way compromise the voluntariness of the situation? In this context, consider the added element of race. Young black males are sometimes counseled by their parents to *strictly* comply with instructions from police officers during these encounters in order to eliminate the potential for a misunderstanding that might lead a police officer to use physical force—or even lethal force—in response. Does this dynamic suggest that some individuals might "consent" to a search simply because they worry that an encounter with the police might turn violent? For more discussion of these issues, see Wesley MacNeil Oliver, *With an Evil Eye and an Unequal Hand: Pretextual Stops and Doctrinal Remedies to Racial Profiling*, 74 Tul. L. Rev. 1409 (2000); Adrian J. Barrio, *Rethinking* Schneckloth v. Bustamonte*: Incorporating Obedience Theory into the Supreme Court's Conception of Voluntary Consent*, 1997 U. Ill. L. Rev. 215.

2. *Who gets to consent?* In cases where multiple individuals share the same space, whether it is a shared dwelling or office space, the issue of consent can be tricky. Often, a court must decide which spaces are shared and which are private. For example, two individuals might share a common space but also

maintain separate rooms in which each has a legitimate expectation of privacy. But what of truly common areas, such as a residence shared by a husband and wife or other family members? In *United States v. Matlock*, 415 U.S. 164, 170 (1974), the Supreme Court concluded that "the consent of one who possesses common authority over premises or effects is valid as against the absent, non-consenting person with whom that authority is shared." However, in *Georgia v. Randolph*, 547 U.S. 103 (2006), the Supreme Court ruled a search unreasonable when the wife consented to a police search but her husband explicitly objected. The Court therefore concluded that the contents of the search could be used against the wife but not the husband. The court distinguished *Matlock* because in that earlier case, the non-consenting party was not present to object to the police search, whereas in *Randolph* the husband was present and specifically objected to the search, thus negating any presumption that the wife was consenting on his behalf. If this line appears thin, the Supreme Court apparently thought that it replicated the daily state of affairs when occupants share a residence. When one goes away, the nature of shared tenancy is that the non-present party runs the risk that the occupant who is present will let in whoever they want. However, when both occupants are present, either may object to a would-be visitor who comes to the door. To the Supreme Court, this is precisely what happened in *Matlock* and *Randolph*, except the visitor was the police:

> Since the co-tenant wishing to open the door to a third party has no recognized authority in law or social practice to prevail over a present and objecting co-tenant, his disputed invitation, without more, gives a police officer no better claim to reasonableness in entering than the officer would have in the absence of any consent at all. Accordingly, in the balancing of competing individual and governmental interests entailed by the bar to unreasonable searches, the cooperative occupant's invitation adds nothing to the government's side to counter the force of an objecting individual's claim to security against the government's intrusion into his dwelling place.

Randolph, 547 U.S. at 114-15.

In *Fernandez v. California*, the Supreme Court cut back on *Randolph*. In *Fernandez*, the police arrived at a shared dwelling after investigating a recent gang attack that was reported to the police. The police arrested a male occupant of the house and charged him with domestic abuse. After he was removed from the residence and despite his objections to a search of the residence, the police obtained consent to search the residence from his female partner, who remained behind. The Supreme Court concluded that because he was no longer physically present, his objection became legally irrelevant:

> Denying someone in [her] position the right to allow the police to enter her home would also show disrespect for her independence. Having beaten [her], petitioner would bar her from controlling access to her own home

> until such time as he chose to relent. The Fourth Amendment does not give him that power.

Fernandez v. California, 571 U.S. 292, 307 (2014).

3. *When consent is not an option.* A few courts have ruled that police should not even ask for consent to search in the absence of probable cause or reasonable suspicion of criminal activity. For example, consider the following interaction between the police and the occupants of a car during a vehicle stop:

> Abernathy asked for Servando's and Salvador's drivers' licenses, and he asked both men where they were going. Both of the brothers gave the trooper their licenses, and both answered that they were going to Chicago to visit a sick cousin. The license check came back clear, and both brothers answered the trooper's questions consistently. The Ramos brothers were cooperative, their licenses were clean, the truck was not stolen, their answers about their destination were consistent, and Servando had a reason for not wearing his seat belt—a colostomy bag.

United States v. Ramos, 42 F.3d 1160, 1163 (8th Cir. 1994). The court noted that "[a]ll of these facts were consistent with innocent behavior" and therefore concluded that the police officer, Abernathy, did not have probable cause to continue the vehicle stop any longer. However, *Ramos* is an outlier, and most courts that have considered the question concluded that neither reasonable suspicion nor probable cause is required to ask for consent to a search, as long as the *original* stop was lawful. See, e.g., *People v. Moore*, 341 Ill. App. 3d 804, 792 N.E.2d 836, 843-44 (2003); *State v. Harris*, 590 N.W.2d 90, 102 (Minn. 1999); *State v. Middleton*, 43 S.W.3d 881 (Mo. Ct. App. 2001); *State v. Everson*, 474 N.W.2d 695 (N.D. 1991). However, as noted immediately below, some states have imposed a probable cause standard by statute.

H. SPECIAL NEEDS

A large category of warrantless searches fall under the rubric of "special needs" searches. Generally, these searches do not require a warrant because the nature of the situation or the endeavor imposes a "special need" that does not arise in quotidian life, thus giving the state greater—but not unlimited—latitude to conduct warrantless searches. In this general category of special needs searches, courts have included: (1) administrative inspections in closely regulated industries; (2) border crossings; (3) checkpoints, such as DWI checkpoints to catch impaired drivers; (4) schools, particularly searches of students and their belongings, often looking for prohibited drugs; (5) government employment,

STATUTORY REQUIREMENTS

Some states impose specific statutory requirements regarding the search of vehicles during a motor vehicle stop by police officers. For example, Rhode Island law requires that

> [u]nless there exists reasonable suspicion or probable cause of criminal activity, no motor vehicle stopped for a traffic violation shall be detained beyond the time needed to address the violation. Nothing contained herein shall prohibit the detention of a motor vehicle for a reasonable period of time for the arrival of a canine unit or subsequent criminal investigation if there is reasonable suspicion or probable cause of criminal activity.

31 R.I. Gen. Laws Ann. § 31-21.2-5. The provision also requires that

> [n]o operator or owner-passenger of a motor vehicle shall be requested to consent to a search by a law enforcement officer of his or her motor vehicle, that is stopped solely for a traffic violation, unless there exists reasonable suspicion or probable cause of criminal activity. No pedestrian shall be requested to consent to a search by a law enforcement officer of his or her person, unless there exists reasonable suspicion or probable cause of criminal activity. No juvenile shall be requested to consent to a search by a law enforcement officer unless there exists reasonable suspicion or probable cause of criminal activity.

Notice that the probable cause requirement extends not only to vehicle searches but also to requests for *consent* to vehicle searches. This effectively eliminates consent as a method of getting around the probable cause requirement in the vehicle context—at least in Rhode Island. Why might the state legislature have imposed this requirement? For a clue, consider the title of the statute: The Racial Profiling Prevention Act of 2004. For more discussion of this issue, see Megan Annitto, *Consent Searches of Minors*, 38 N.Y.U. Rev. L. & Soc. Change 1, 50 (2014).

including drug testing and computer searches; and (6) jails and prisons, where guards search for weapons and contraband. In each of these contexts, something about the nature of the enterprise makes the use of a warrant, signed by a magistrate and supported by probable cause, particularly impractical. At the same time, each of these contexts also suggests a reduced expectation of privacy on the part of the individual searched, at least when compared to the baseline of an individual in the privacy of their own "castle," i.e., their home.

For these reasons, courts approach all of these special needs situations with a common methodology. As the Supreme Court said in *New Jersey v. T.L.O.*, 469 U.S. 325, 351 (1985), "[o]nly in those exceptional circumstances in which special needs, beyond the normal need for law enforcement, make the warrant and probable-cause requirement impracticable, is a court entitled to substitute its balancing of interests for that of the Framers." The key phrase to remember here is *beyond the normal need for law enforcement*. In other words, "special needs" situations do not include the need for the police to battle crime, prosecute offenders, or engage in other forms of traditional "crime control," since the Fourth Amendment clearly codifies a requirement for warrants in the law enforcement context. If the police were able to assert a "special need" to fight crime to justify a warrantless or suspicionless search, that would effectively unwind the entire Fourth Amendment Warrant Clause and render it meaningless. When courts refer to the "special needs *test*," they are referring to the requirement of an exceptional circumstance, outside of law enforcement, combined with a judicial balancing that weighs the government's need to conduct warrantless searches with the target's expectation of privacy.

Each section below explains the core rationale for warrantless searches in that particular category, and also presents a tricky application of the doctrine to a unique fact pattern. In each one, ask yourself whether the state has a special need for warrantless searches that is sufficiently urgent to outweigh whatever expectation of privacy the individual might have in that situation.

1. Administrative Inspections

Some industries are so closely regulated that periodic searches are part of the governmental regulatory regime. For example, health and safety regulations might require government officials to conduct inspections to ensure that narcotics are being properly handled in pharmacies, that restaurants are preparing food in a sanitary manner, or that toxic chemicals are being safeguarded in a factory. In each of these situations, the inspections should have a primary non–law enforcement goal, i.e., a regulatory goal. However, if regulatory violations are discovered, the target of the search might be subject to civil or even criminal penalties.

In the following case, the defendants were owners of an automobile junkyard. A routine, unannounced inspection, conducted without a warrant and without probable cause, unearthed violations that led to criminal charges. As you read the case, look for how the Court determined whether the searches had a rationale that fell outside of the law enforcement context, and therefore whether the searches were entitled to a "special needs" exception to the warrant requirement.

New York v. Burger

Supreme Court of the United States
482 U.S. 691 (1987)

Justice Blackmun delivered the opinion of the Court.

This case presents the question whether the warrantless search of an automobile junkyard, conducted pursuant to a statute authorizing such a search, falls within the exception to the warrant requirement for administrative inspections of pervasively regulated industries. The case also presents the question whether an otherwise proper administrative inspection is unconstitutional because the ultimate purpose of the regulatory statute pursuant to which the search is done—the deterrence of criminal behavior—is the same as that of penal laws, with the result that the inspection may disclose violations not only of the regulatory statute but also of the penal statutes.

I

Respondent Joseph Burger is the owner of a junkyard in Brooklyn, N.Y. His business consists, in part, of the dismantling of automobiles and the selling of their parts. His junkyard is an open lot with no buildings. A high metal fence surrounds it, wherein are located, among other things, vehicles and parts of vehicles. At approximately noon on November 17, 1982, Officer Joseph Vega and four other plainclothes officers, all members of the Auto Crimes Division of the New York City Police Department, entered respondent's junkyard to conduct an inspection pursuant to N.Y. Veh. & Traf. L. § 415-a5. On any given day, the Division conducts from 5 to 10 inspections of vehicle dismantlers, automobile junkyards, and related businesses.

Upon entering the junkyard, the officers asked to see Burger's license and his "police book"—the record of the automobiles and parts in his possession. Burger replied that he had neither a license nor a police book. The officers then announced their intention to conduct an . . . inspection. Burger did not object. In accordance with their practice, the officers copied down the Vehicle Identification Numbers (VINs) of several vehicles and parts of vehicles that were in the junkyard. After checking these numbers against a police computer, the officers determined that respondent was in possession of stolen vehicles and parts. Accordingly, Burger was arrested and charged with five counts of possession of stolen property and one count of unregistered operation as a vehicle dismantler. . . .

II

. . . An expectation of privacy in commercial premises, however, is different from, and indeed less than, a similar expectation in an individual's home. This expectation is particularly attenuated in commercial property employed in "closely regulated" industries. . . . The Court first examined the "unique" problem of inspections of "closely regulated" businesses in two enterprises that had "a long tradition of close government supervision." In *Colonnade Corp. v. United States*, 397 U.S. 72 (1970), it considered a warrantless search of a catering business pursuant to several federal revenue statutes authorizing the inspection of the premises of liquor dealers. Although the Court disapproved the search because the statute provided that a sanction be imposed when entry was refused, and because it did not authorize entry without a warrant as an alternative in this situation, it recognized that "the liquor industry [was] long subject to close supervision and inspection." We returned to this issue in *United States v. Biswell*, 406

U.S. 311 (1972), which involved a warrantless inspection of the premises of a pawnshop operator, who was federally licensed to sell sporting weapons. . . . We observed: "When a dealer chooses to engage in this pervasively regulated business and to accept a federal license, he does so with the knowledge that his business records, firearms, and ammunition will be subject to effective inspection." . . .

Because the owner or operator of commercial premises in a "closely regulated" industry has a reduced expectation of privacy, the warrant and probable-cause requirements, which fulfill the traditional Fourth Amendment standard of reasonableness for a government search, have lessened application in this context. Rather, we conclude that, as in other situations of "special need," where the privacy interests of the owner are weakened and the government interests in regulating particular businesses are concomitantly heightened, a warrantless inspection of commercial premises may well be reasonable within the meaning of the Fourth Amendment.

This warrantless inspection, however, even in the context of a pervasively regulated business, will be deemed to be reasonable only so long as three criteria are met. First, there must be a "substantial" government interest that informs the regulatory scheme pursuant to which the inspection is made. Second, the warrantless inspections must be "necessary to further [the] regulatory scheme." *Donovan v. Dewey*, 452 U.S., at 600. For example, in *Dewey* we recognized that forcing mine inspectors to obtain a warrant before every inspection might alert mine owners or operators to the impending inspection, thereby frustrating the purposes of the Mine Safety and Health Act—to detect and thus to deter safety and health violations.

Finally, "the statute's inspection program, in terms of the certainty and regularity of its application, [must] provid[e] a constitutionally adequate substitute for a warrant." In other words, the regulatory statute must perform the two basic functions of a warrant: it must advise the owner of the commercial premises that the search is being made pursuant to the law and has a properly defined scope, and it must limit the discretion of the inspecting officers. To perform this first function, the statute must be "sufficiently comprehensive and defined that the owner of commercial property cannot help but be aware that his property will be subject to periodic inspections undertaken for specific purposes." In addition, in defining how a statute limits the discretion of the inspectors, we have observed that it must be "carefully limited in time, place, and scope."

III

Searches made pursuant to § 415-a5, in our view, clearly fall within this established exception to the warrant requirement for administrative inspections in "closely regulated" businesses. First, the nature of the regulatory statute reveals that the operation of a junkyard, part of which is devoted to vehicle dismantling, is a "closely regulated" business in the State of New York. The provisions regulating the activity of vehicle dismantling are extensive. An operator cannot engage in this industry without first obtaining a license, which means that he must meet the registration requirements and must pay a fee. Under § 415-a5(a), the operator must maintain a police book recording the acquisition and disposition of motor vehicles and vehicle parts, and make such records and inventory available for inspection by the police or any agent of the Department of Motor Vehicles. The operator also must display his registration number prominently at his place of business, on business documentation, and on vehicles and parts that pass through his business. Moreover, the person engaged in this activity is subject to criminal penalties, as well as to loss of license or civil fines, for failure to comply with these provisions. That other States besides New York have imposed similarly extensive regulations on automobile junkyards further supports the "closely regulated" status of this industry. . . .

The automobile-junkyard business . . . is simply a new branch of an industry that has existed, and has been closely regulated, for many years. The automobile junkyard is closely akin to the secondhand shop or the general junkyard. Both share the purpose of recycling salvageable articles and components of items no longer usable in their original form. As such, vehicle dismantlers represent a modern, specialized version of a traditional activity. In New York, general junkyards and secondhand shops long have been subject to regulation. . . . The history of government regulation of junk-related activities argues strongly in favor of the "closely regulated" status of the automobile junkyard. Accordingly, in light of the regulatory framework governing his business and the history of regulation of related industries, an operator of a junkyard engaging in vehicle dismantling has a reduced expectation of privacy in this "closely regulated" business.

The New York regulatory scheme satisfies the three criteria necessary to make reasonable warrantless inspections pursuant to § 415-a5. First, the State has a substantial interest in regulating the vehicle-dismantling and automobile-junkyard industry because motor vehicle theft has increased in the State and because the problem of theft is associated with this industry. In this day, automobile theft has become a significant social problem, placing enormous economic and personal burdens upon the citizens of different States. . . . Because contemporary automobiles are made from standardized parts, the nationwide extent of vehicle theft and concern about it are understandable.

Second, regulation of the vehicle-dismantling industry reasonably serves the State's substantial interest in eradicating automobile theft. It is well established that the theft problem can be addressed effectively by controlling the receiver of, or market in, stolen property. Automobile junkyards and vehicle dismantlers provide the major market for stolen vehicles and vehicle parts. Thus, the State rationally may believe that it will reduce car theft by regulations that prevent automobile junkyards from becoming markets for stolen vehicles and that help trace the origin and destination of vehicle parts. Moreover, the warrantless administrative inspections pursuant to § 415-a5 "are necessary to further [the] regulatory scheme." [I]n the present case, a warrant requirement would interfere with the statute's purpose of deterring automobile theft accomplished by identifying vehicles and parts as stolen and shutting down the market in such items. Because stolen cars and parts often pass quickly through an automobile junkyard, "frequent" and "unannounced" inspections are necessary in order to detect them. In sum, surprise is crucial if the regulatory scheme aimed at remedying this major social problem is to function at all.

Third, § 415-a5 provides a "constitutionally adequate substitute for a warrant." The statute informs the operator of a vehicle dismantling business that inspections will be made on a regular basis. Thus, the vehicle dismantler knows that the inspections to which he is subject do not constitute discretionary acts by a government official but are conducted pursuant to statute. Section 415-a5 also sets forth the scope of the inspection and, accordingly, places the operator on notice as to how to comply with the statute. In addition, it notifies the operator as to who is authorized to conduct an inspection.

Finally, the "time, place, and scope" of the inspection is limited to place appropriate restraints upon the discretion of the inspecting officers. The officers are allowed to conduct an inspection only "during [the] regular and usual business hours." § 415-a5.[21] The inspections can be made only of vehicle-dismantling and related industries. And the permissible scope of these searches is narrowly defined: the inspectors may examine the records, as well as "any vehicles or parts of vehicles which are subject to the record keeping requirements of this section and which are on the premises."

IV

. . . Nor do we think that this administrative scheme is unconstitutional simply because, in the course of enforcing it, an inspecting officer may discover evidence of crimes, besides violations of the scheme itself. In *United States v. Biswell*, the pawnshop operator was charged not only with a violation of the recordkeeping provision, pursuant to which the inspection was made, but also with other violations detected during the inspection, and convicted of a failure to pay an occupational tax for dealing in specific firearms. The discovery of evidence of crimes in the course of an otherwise proper administrative inspection does not render that search illegal or the administrative scheme suspect. . . .

Justice BRENNAN, with whom Justice MARSHALL joins, and with whom Justice O'CONNOR joins as to all but Part III, dissenting.

Warrantless inspections of pervasively regulated businesses are valid if necessary to further an urgent state interest, and if authorized by a statute that carefully limits their time, place, and scope. I have no objection to this general rule. Today, however, the Court finds pervasive regulation in the barest of administrative schemes. Burger's vehicle-dismantling business is not closely regulated (unless most New York City businesses are), and an administrative warrant therefore was required to search it. The Court also perceives careful guidance and control of police discretion in a statute that is patently insufficient to eliminate the need for a warrant. Finally, the Court characterizes as administrative a search for evidence of only criminal wrongdoing. As a result, the Court renders virtually meaningless the general rule that a warrant is required for administrative searches of commercial property. . . .

The provisions governing vehicle dismantling in New York simply are not extensive. A vehicle dismantler must register and pay a fee, display the registration in various circumstances, maintain a police book, and allow inspections. Of course, the inspections themselves cannot be cited as proof of pervasive regulation justifying elimination of the warrant requirement; that would be obvious bootstrapping. Nor can registration and recordkeeping requirements be characterized as close regulation. New York City, like many States and municipalities, imposes similar, and often more stringent licensing, recordkeeping, and other regulatory requirements on a myriad of trades and businesses. Few substantive qualifications are required of an aspiring vehicle dismantler; no regulation governs the condition of the premises, the method of operation, the hours of operation, the equipment utilized, etc. This scheme stands in marked contrast to, e.g., the mine safety regulations relevant in *Donovan v. Dewey*. In sum, if New York City's administrative scheme renders the vehicle-dismantling business closely regulated, few businesses will escape such a finding. . . .

Even if vehicle dismantling were a closely regulated industry, I would nonetheless conclude that this search violated the Fourth Amendment. The warrant requirement protects the owner of a business from the "unbridled discretion [of] executive and administrative officers," by ensuring that "reasonable legislative or administrative standards for conducting an . . . inspection are satisfied with respect to a particular [business]." In order to serve as the equivalent of a warrant, an administrative statute must create "a predictable and guided [governmental] presence." Section 415-a5 does not approach the level of "certainty and regularity of . . . application" necessary to provide "a constitutionally adequate substitute for a warrant."

The statute does not inform the operator of a vehicle-dismantling business that inspections will be made on a regular basis; in fact, there is no assurance that any inspections at all will occur. There is neither an upper nor a lower limit on the number of searches that may be conducted at any given operator's establishment in any given time period. Neither the statute, nor any regulations, nor any regulatory body, provides limits or guidance on the selection of vehicle dismantlers for inspection. In fact, the State could not explain why Burger's operation was selected for inspection. This is precisely what was objectionable about the inspection scheme invalidated in *Marshall*: It failed to "provide any standards to guide inspectors either in their selection of establishments to be searched or in the exercise of their authority to search."

III

The fundamental defect in § 415-a5 is that it authorizes searches intended solely to uncover evidence of criminal acts. . . . In the law of administrative searches, one principle emerges with unusual clarity and unanimous acceptance: the government may not use an administrative inspection scheme to search for criminal violations.

Here the State has used an administrative scheme as a pretext to search without probable cause for evidence of criminal violations. It thus circumvented the requirements of the Fourth Amendment by altering the label placed on the search. This crucial point is most clearly illustrated by the fact that the police copied the serial numbers from a wheelchair and a handicapped person's walker that were found on the premises, and determined that these items had been stolen. Obviously, these objects are not vehicles or parts of vehicles, and were in no way relevant to the State's enforcement of its administrative scheme. The scope of the search alone reveals that it was undertaken solely to uncover evidence of criminal wrongdoing. . . .

NOTES & QUESTIONS ON ADMINISTRATIVE INSPECTIONS

1. *Who conducts the search?* Does it matter whether an administrative inspection is carried out by a police officer instead of a regular civil servant? In *Burger*, the junkyard inspections were carried out by regular police officers. Does this entail that the searches had a law enforcement purpose? Even if the answer to that question is no, does it create a *presumption* that the searches had a law enforcement purpose, albeit a presumption that can be rebutted by other circumstances?

2. *Is the exception too broad?* Does the administrative inspection exception allow the state to use so-called administrative inspections as a loophole to avoid the requirement of a warrant under the Fourth Amendment? Courts have upheld regulatory searches in many contexts, thus weakening the strength of the warrant requirement. See, e.g., *State v. Klager*, 797 N.W.2d 47, 51

(S.D. 2011) (upholding warrantless search of taxidermy business). As one commentator noted:

> The *Burger* decision is disturbing for two reasons. First, in the six years prior to *Burger*, lower court decisions had exhibited a strong need for refined standards concerning the administrative inspection doctrine. Judges were confused by the vagueness of previous Supreme Court decisions and, consequently, often misapplied the existent standards. The *Burger* Court failed to provide additional guidance concerning the doctrine, thereby missing a prime opportunity to both clarify the standards necessary for a warrantless administrative inspection and to prevent further expansion of the exception. Second, read broadly, the *Burger* decision provides positive sanction for warrantless administrative inspection of commercial operations in most industries. As the *Burger* dissent suggests, this expansion stretches the doctrine beyond its intended limits, and may virtually negate the fourth amendment warrant requirement as it applies to administrative inspections.

Jodi C. Remer, *The "Junking" of the Fourth Amendment: The Closely Regulated Industry Exception to the Warrant Requirement*, 25 Am. Crim. L. Rev. 791, 791 (1988). Do you agree with this assessment?

3. *Child abuse.* Perhaps the most compelling example of a regulatory regime that requires periodic and unannounced inspections is the child welfare context. State or city officials respond to reports of mistreatment and check in on families that they have previously identified as concerning, i.e., those households that are at a heightened risk for child mistreatment or neglect. The primary rationale for the inspections is to ensure the safety of children and to remove them from any unsafe conditions that might exist in their environment. However, charges for child neglect or child abuse are always possible if the inspectors uncover mistreatment that rises to a criminal level. Do these inspections satisfy the standards articulated in *Burger*? One difference between these child welfare inspections and the junkyard inspections at issue in *Burger* is that the junkyard inspections involved a place of business, whereas a child welfare inspection necessarily takes place in the home, where an individual's expectation of privacy is at its highest, and where arguably the protection of the Fourth Amendment is at its apex. Is child welfare a "highly regulated" industry? What result when one balances the state's interests in warrantless inspections versus the individual's expectations of privacy in the home? As one commentator put it, "most state statutory and administrative schemes governing child abuse investigations include provisions that either mandate or permit investigatory home visits, and many of these expressly give investigators authority to enter the home without obtaining a warrant or establishing reasonable cause. . . . The burden of meeting the [warrant] requirement, the courts

PROBLEM CASE

Consider the following description of an administrative search at an automobile repair body shop. The search was sparked by a complaint by a customer that they bought a used car from the shop whose Vehicle Identification Number (VIN) plate did not match the VIN sticker, suggesting the possibility of fraud. Florida Statute § 812.055 authorizes warrantless inspections "for the purpose of locating stolen vehicles[,] . . . investigating the titling and registration of vehicles[,] . . . inspecting vehicles[,] . . . or inspecting records. . . ."

> On January 15, 2001, at about 10:30 in the morning, Root, Glantz, and Edward Kelly led a group of approximately twenty officers to the Premises. The officers arrived in unmarked trucks and SUVs, and surrounded the entire Premises, blocking all exits. Some of the officers were dressed in SWAT uniforms—ballistic vests imprinted with SWAT in big letters, camouflage pants, and black boots. They entered the Premises with guns drawn—all were armed with Glock 21 sidearms; some carried Bennelli automatic shotguns. When the officers entered the Premises, they ordered the employees to line up along the fence. Vincent Lewis, who was working on a car, felt something touch his back and turned around to find an officer pointing a shotgun at him. The officers patted down and searched the employees. Pockets and purses were searched. The officers took at least Lewis's driver's license. . . .

Bruce v. Beary, 498 F.3d 1232, 1235-36 (11th Cir. 2007). Does this sound like a valid administrative search or was it a law enforcement search in disguise?

have reasoned, would seriously impair, if not wholly frustrate, the state's efforts to protect the child." Michael R. Beeman, *Investigating Child Abuse: The Fourth Amendment and Investigatory Home Visits*, 89 Colum. L. Rev. 1034, 1041-42 (1989).

2. Border Crossings

The Supreme Court has long held that the crossing of the border is a legitimate occasion for conducting a search of travelers and their belongings without a search warrant, and therefore clearly falls within the scope of the "special needs" exception to the Warrant Clause. As the Supreme Court stated in *United States v. Ramsey*, 431 U.S. 606, 616 (1977), "[t]hat searches made at the border, pursuant to the long-standing right of the sovereign to protect itself by stopping and examining persons and property crossing into this country, are reasonable simply by virtue of the fact that they occur at the border, should, by now, require no extended demonstration." Similarly, in *United States v. Thirty-seven Photographs*, 402 U.S. 363, 376 (1971), the Supreme Court explained that a traveler's expectation of privacy is far lower when crossing the border: "[A] port of entry is not a traveler's home. His right to be let alone neither prevents the search of his luggage nor the seizure of unprotected, but illegal, materials when his possession of them is discovered during such a search. Customs officials characteristically inspect luggage and their power to do so is not questioned in this case; it is an old practice and is intimately associated with excluding illegal articles from the country." Indeed, the *Ramsay* Court recognized in 1977 that in keeping with longstanding practice, routine border searches were not only exempt from the warrant requirement but also from the probable cause requirement as well, thus conferring broad discretion on custom officials to conduct these searches. However, the fact that routine border searches are generally permitted does not resolve the question of when or how border agents are entitled to conduct a search that goes beyond a "routine" search. Can border agents conduct a body cavity search to look for narcotics? Can border agents seize a cell phone and examine its digital contents?

In the following case, customs officials suspected that a traveler was a drug mule who had swallowed balloons filled with narcotics and detained her until she finally passed the balloons. As you read the case, ask yourself what standard customs officials must satisfy before they conduct this type of search. May customs officials conduct an invasive search in the absence of individualized suspicion?

United States v. Montoya de Hernandez

Supreme Court of the United States
473 U.S. 531 (1985)

Justice Rehnquist delivered the opinion of the Court.

Respondent Rosa Elvira Montoya de Hernandez was detained by customs officials upon her arrival at the Los Angeles Airport on a flight from Bogota, Colombia. . . . Respondent arrived at Los Angeles International Airport shortly after midnight, March 5, 1983, on Avianca Flight 080, a direct 10-hour flight from Bogota, Colombia. Her visa was in order so she was passed through Immigration and proceeded to the customs desk. At the customs desk she encountered Customs Inspector Talamantes, who reviewed her documents and noticed from her passport that she had made at least eight recent trips to either Miami or Los Angeles. Talamantes referred respondent to a secondary customs desk for further questioning. At this desk Talamantes and another inspector asked respondent general questions concerning herself and the purpose of her trip. Respondent revealed that she spoke no English and had no family or friends in the United States. She explained in Spanish that she had come to the United States to purchase goods for her husband's store in Bogota. The customs inspectors recognized Bogota as a "source city" for narcotics. Respondent possessed $5,000 in cash, mostly $50 bills, but had no billfold. She indicated to the inspectors that she had no appointments with merchandise vendors, but planned to ride around Los Angeles in taxicabs visiting retail stores such as J.C. Penney and K-Mart in order to buy goods for her husband's store with the $5,000.

Respondent admitted that she had no hotel reservations, but stated that she planned to stay at a Holiday Inn. Respondent could not recall how her airline ticket was purchased. When the inspectors opened respondent's one small valise they found about four changes of "cold weather" clothing. Respondent had no shoes other than the high-heeled pair she was wearing. Although respondent possessed no checks, waybills, credit cards, or letters of credit, she did produce a Colombian business card and a number of old receipts, waybills, and fabric swatches displayed in a photo album.

At this point Talamantes and the other inspector suspected that respondent was a "balloon swallower," one who attempts to smuggle narcotics into this country hidden in her alimentary canal. Over the years Inspector Talamantes had apprehended dozens of alimentary canal smugglers arriving on Avianca Flight 080.

The inspectors requested a female customs inspector to take respondent to a private area and conduct a patdown and strip search. During the search the female inspector felt respondent's abdomen area and noticed a firm fullness, as if respondent were wearing a girdle. The search revealed no contraband, but the inspector noticed that respondent was wearing two pairs of elastic underpants with a paper towel lining the crotch area.

When respondent returned to the customs area and the female inspector reported her discoveries, the inspector in charge told respondent that he suspected she was smuggling drugs in her alimentary canal. Respondent agreed to the inspector's request that she be x-rayed at a hospital but in answer to the inspector's query stated that she was pregnant. She agreed to a pregnancy test before the x-ray. Respondent withdrew the consent for an x-ray when she learned that she would have to be handcuffed en route to the hospital. The inspector then gave respondent the option of returning to Colombia on the next available flight, agreeing to an x-ray, or remaining in detention until she produced a monitored bowel movement that would confirm or rebut the inspectors' suspicions. Respondent chose the first option and was placed in a customs office under observation. She was told that if she went to the toilet she would have to use a wastebasket in the women's restroom, in order that female customs inspectors could inspect her stool for balloons or capsules carrying narcotics. The inspectors refused respondent's request to place a telephone call.

Respondent sat in the customs office, under observation, for the remainder of the night. During the night customs officials attempted to place respondent on a Mexican airline that was flying to Bogota via Mexico City in the morning. The airline refused to transport respondent because she lacked a Mexican visa necessary to land in Mexico City. Respondent was not permitted to leave, and was informed that she would be detained until she agreed to an x-ray or her bowels moved. She remained detained in the customs office under observation, for most of the time curled up in a chair leaning to one side. She refused all offers of food and drink, and refused to use the toilet facilities. The Court of Appeals noted that she exhibited symptoms of discomfort consistent with "heroic efforts to resist the usual calls of nature."

At the shift change at 4 o'clock the next afternoon, almost 16 hours after her flight had landed, respondent still had not defecated or urinated or partaken of food or drink. At that time customs officials sought a court order authorizing a pregnancy test, an x-ray, and a rectal examination. The Federal Magistrate issued an order just before midnight that evening, which authorized a rectal examination and involuntary x-ray, provided that the physician in charge considered respondent's claim of pregnancy. Respondent was taken to a hospital and given a pregnancy test, which later turned out to be negative. Before the results of the pregnancy test were known, a physician conducted a rectal examination and removed from respondent's rectum a balloon containing a foreign substance. Respondent was then placed formally under arrest. By 4:10 A.M. respondent had passed 6 similar balloons; over the next four days she passed 88 balloons containing a total of 528 grams of 80% pure cocaine hydrochloride.

After a suppression hearing the District Court admitted the cocaine in evidence against respondent. She was convicted of possession of cocaine with intent to distribute and unlawful importation of cocaine. . . .

The Fourth Amendment commands that searches and seizures be reasonable. What is reasonable depends upon all of the circumstances surrounding the search or seizure and the nature of the search or seizure itself. The permissibility of a particular law enforcement practice is judged by "balancing its intrusion on the individual's Fourth Amendment interests against its promotion of legitimate governmental interests."

Here the seizure of respondent took place at the international border. Since the founding of our Republic, Congress has granted the Executive plenary authority to conduct routine searches and seizures at the border, without probable cause or a warrant, in order to regulate the collection of duties and to prevent the introduction of contraband into this country. This Court has long recognized Congress' power to police entrants at the border. . . .

Consistently, therefore, with Congress' power to protect the Nation by stopping and examining persons entering this country, the Fourth Amendment's balance of reasonableness is qualitatively different at the international border than in the interior. Routine searches of the persons and effects of entrants are not subject to any requirement of reasonable suspicion, probable cause, or warrant, and first-class mail may be opened without a warrant on less than probable cause. Automotive travelers may be stopped at fixed checkpoints near the border without individualized suspicion even if the stop is based largely on ethnicity, and boats on inland waters with ready access to the sea may be hailed and boarded with no suspicion whatever. . . .

Balanced against the sovereign's interests at the border are the Fourth Amendment rights of respondent. Having presented herself at the border for admission, and having subjected herself to the criminal enforcement powers of the Federal Government, 19 U.S.C. § 482, respondent was entitled to be free from unreasonable search and seizure. But not only is the expectation of privacy less at the border than in the interior, the Fourth Amendment balance between the interests of the Government and the privacy right of the individual is also struck much more favorably to the Government at the border.

We have not previously decided what level of suspicion would justify a seizure of an incoming traveler for purposes other than a routine border search. . . . We hold that the detention of a traveler at the border, beyond the scope of a routine customs search and inspection, is justified at its inception if customs agents, considering all the facts surrounding the traveler and her trip, reasonably suspect that the traveler is smuggling contraband in her alimentary canal.

The "reasonable suspicion" standard has been applied in a number of contexts and effects a needed balance between private and public interests when law enforcement officials must make a limited intrusion on less than probable cause. It thus fits well into the situations involving alimentary canal smuggling at the border: this type of smuggling gives no external signs and inspectors will rarely possess probable cause to arrest or search, yet governmental interests in stopping smuggling at the border are high indeed. Under this standard officials at the border must have a "particularized and objective basis for suspecting the particular person" of alimentary canal smuggling.

The facts, and their rational inferences, known to customs inspectors in this case clearly supported a reasonable suspicion that respondent was an alimentary canal smuggler. We need not belabor the facts, including respondent's implausible story, that supported this suspicion. The trained customs inspectors had encountered many alimentary canal smugglers and certainly had more than an "inchoate and unparticularized suspicion or 'hunch,'" that respondent was smuggling narcotics in her alimentary canal. The inspectors' suspicion was a "common-sense conclusio[n] about human behavior upon which practical people, including government officials, are entitled to rely."

The final issue in this case is whether the detention of respondent was reasonably related in scope to the circumstances which justified it initially.

In this regard we have cautioned that courts should not indulge in "unrealistic second-guessing," and we have noted that "creative judge[s], engaged in post hoc evaluations of police conduct can almost always imagine some alternative means by which the objectives of the police might have been accomplished." But "[t]he fact that the protection of the public might, in the abstract, have been accomplished by 'less intrusive' means does not, in itself, render the search unreasonable." Authorities must be allowed "to graduate their response to the demands of any particular situation." Here, respondent was detained incommunicado for almost 16 hours before inspectors sought a warrant; the warrant then took a number of hours to procure, through no apparent fault of the inspectors. This length of time undoubtedly exceeds any other detention we have approved under reasonable suspicion. But we have also consistently rejected hard-and-fast time limits. Instead, "common sense and ordinary human experience must govern over rigid criteria."

. . . [T]he inspectors had available, as an alternative to simply awaiting her bowel movement, an x-ray. They offered her the alternative of submitting herself to that procedure. But when she refused that alternative, the customs inspectors were left with only two practical alternatives: detain her for such time as necessary to confirm their suspicions . . . or turn her loose into the interior carrying the reasonably suspected contraband drugs.

The inspectors in this case followed this former procedure. They no doubt expected that respondent, having recently disembarked from a 10-hour direct flight with a full and stiff abdomen, would produce a bowel movement without extended delay. But her visible efforts to resist the call of nature, which the court below labeled "heroic," disappointed this expectation and in turn caused her humiliation and discomfort. Our prior cases have refused to charge police with delays in investigatory detention attributable to the suspect's evasive actions, and that principle applies here as well. Respondent alone was responsible for much of the duration and discomfort of the seizure.

Under these circumstances, we conclude that the detention in this case was not unreasonably long. It occurred at the international border, where the Fourth Amendment balance of interests leans heavily to the Government. At the border, customs officials have more than merely an investigative law enforcement role. They are also charged, along with immigration officials, with protecting this Nation from entrants who may bring anything harmful into this country, whether that be communicable diseases, narcotics, or explosives. In this regard the detention of a suspected alimentary canal smuggler at the border is analogous to the detention of a suspected tuberculosis carrier at the border: both are detained until their bodily processes dispel the suspicion that they will introduce a harmful agent into this country.

Respondent's detention was long, uncomfortable, indeed, humiliating; but both its length and its discomfort resulted solely from the method by which she chose to smuggle illicit drugs into this country. . . . [I]n the presence of articulable suspicion of smuggling in her alimentary canal, the customs officers were not required by the Fourth Amendment to pass respondent and her 88 cocaine-filled balloons into the interior. Her detention for the period of time necessary to either verify or dispel the suspicion was not unreasonable. . . .

Justice BRENNAN, with whom Justice MARSHALL joins, dissenting.

We confront a "disgusting and saddening episode" at our Nation's border. Shortly after midnight on March 5, 1983, the respondent Rosa Elvira Montoya De Hernandez was detained by customs officers because she fit the profile of an "alimentary canal smuggler." This profile did not of course give the officers probable cause to believe that De Hernandez was smuggling drugs into the country, but at most a "reasonable suspicion" that she might be engaged in such an attempt. After a thorough strip search failed to uncover any contraband, De Hernandez agreed to go to a local hospital for an abdominal x-ray to resolve the matter. When the officers approached with handcuffs at the ready to lead her away, however, "she crossed her arms by her chest and began stepping backwards shaking her head negatively," protesting: "You are not going to put those on me. That is an insult to my character."

Stymied in their efforts, the officers decided on an alternative course: they would simply lock De Hernandez away in an adjacent manifest room "until her peristaltic functions produced a monitored bowel movement." The officers explained to De Hernandez that she could not leave until she had excreted by squatting over a wastebasket pursuant to the watchful eyes of two attending matrons. De Hernandez responded: "I will not submit to your degradation and I'd rather die." She was locked away with the matrons.

De Hernandez remained locked up in the room for almost 24 hours. Three shifts of matrons came and went during this time. The room had no bed or couch on which she could lie, but only hard chairs and a table. The matrons told her that if she wished to sleep she could lie down on the hard, uncarpeted floor. De Hernandez instead "sat in her chair clutching her purse," "occasionally putting her head down on the table to nap." Most of the time she simply wept and pleaded "to go home." She repeatedly begged for permission "to call my husband and tell him what you are doing to me."

Permission was denied. Sobbing, she insisted that she had to "make a phone call home so that she could talk to her children and to let them know that everything was all right." Permission again was denied. In fact, the matrons considered it highly "unusual" that "each time someone entered the search room, she would take out two small pictures of her children and show them to the person." De Hernandez also demanded that her attorney be contacted. Once again, permission was denied. As far as the outside world knew, Rosa de Hernandez had simply vanished. And although she already had been stripped and searched and probed, the customs officers decided about halfway through her ordeal to repeat that process—"to ensure the safety of the surveilling officers. The result was again negative."

After almost 24 hours had passed, someone finally had the presence of mind to consult a Magistrate and to obtain a court order for an x-ray and a body-cavity search. De Hernandez, "very agitated," was handcuffed and led away to the hospital. A rectal examination disclosed the presence of a cocaine-filled balloon. At approximately 3:15 on the morning of March 6, almost 27 hours after her initial detention, De Hernandez was formally placed under arrest and advised of her Miranda rights. Over the course of the next four days she excreted a total of 88 balloons. . . .

Travelers at the national border are routinely subjected to questioning, patdowns, and thorough searches of their belongings. These measures, which involve relatively limited invasions of privacy and which typically are conducted on all incoming travelers, do not violate the Fourth Amendment given the interests of "national self protection reasonably requiring one entering the country to identify himself as entitled to come in, and his belongings as effects which may be lawfully brought in." Individual travelers also may be singled out on "reasonable suspicion" and briefly held for further investigation. At some point, however, further investigation involves such severe intrusions on the values the Fourth Amendment protects that more stringent safeguards are required. For example, the length and nature of a detention may, at least when conducted for criminal-investigative purposes, ripen into something approximating a full-scale custodial arrest-indeed, the arrestee, unlike the detainee in cases such as this, is at least given such basic rights as a telephone call, Miranda warnings, a bed, a prompt hearing before the nearest federal magistrate, an appointed attorney, and consideration of bail. In addition, border detentions may involve the use of such highly intrusive investigative techniques as body-cavity searches, x-ray searches, and stomach-pumping.

I believe that detentions and searches falling into these more intrusive categories are presumptively "reasonable" within the meaning of the Fourth Amendment only if authorized by a judicial officer. . . . We have, to be sure, held that executive officials need not obtain prior judicial authorization where exigent circumstances would make such authorization impractical and counterproductive. In so holding, however, we have reaffirmed the general rule that "the police must, whenever practicable, obtain advance judicial approval of searches and seizures through the warrant procedure." *Terry v. Ohio*, 392 U.S., at 20. And even where a person has permissibly been taken into custody without a warrant, we have held that a prompt probable-cause determination by a detached magistrate is a constitutional "prerequisite to extended restraint of liberty following arrest."

There is no persuasive reason not to apply these principles to lengthy and intrusive criminal-investigative detentions occurring at the Nation's border. To be sure, the Court today invokes precedent stating that neither probable cause nor a warrant ever have been required for border searches. If this is the law as a general matter, I believe it is time that we reexamine its foundations. . . .

NOTES & QUESTIONS ON BORDER INSPECTIONS

1. *Reasonable suspicion.* Ultimately, the Court in *Montoya de Hernandez* concluded that customs officials need reasonable suspicion that an individual is carrying narcotics inside the body before conducting a search targeting the traveler's alimentary canal. This standard is less stringent than the probable cause requirement; it simply requires some level of *individualized* suspicion as opposed to generalities. Is the standard strict enough to protect the privacy interests of the traveler in question? What role in the analysis is played by the location of the search—the border? How would the case be resolved if the defendant were already located within the United States and was picked up by the local police department? Would probable cause be required by the Fourth Amendment? Would the warrant requirement apply?

2. *Gas tank search.* In *United States v. Flores-Montano,* 541 U.S. 149 (2004), the Supreme Court considered a case involving customs agents who took the extraordinary step of partially disassembling a traveler's car in order to inspect the vehicle's gas tank for hidden narcotics. Was this a reasonable search consistent with the Fourth Amendment? The Ninth Circuit Court of Appeals had ruled in earlier cases that a gas tank search was not a "routine" search as that term was used in *Montoya de Hernandez,* and that what determined whether a border search was routine or not was the "degree of intrusiveness." Consequently, the Ninth Circuit concluded that "reasonable suspicion" was required to justify a gas tank search, just as "reasonable suspicion" was the appropriate standard for the alimentary canal search in *Montoya de Hernandez.* However, on appeal, the U.S. Supreme Court rejected that approach and clarified that although reasonable suspicion is required for searches that involve a bodily intrusion, suspicionless searches of *vehicles* at the border are reasonable under the Fourth Amendment. The Court argued that "the reasons that might support a requirement of some level of suspicion in the case of highly intrusive searches of the person—dignity and privacy interests of the person being searched—simply do not carry over to vehicles" and then concluded that "[i]t is difficult to imagine how the search of a gas tank, which should be solely

a repository for fuel, could be more of an invasion of privacy than the search of the automobile's passenger compartment." *Flores-Montano*, 541 U.S. at 154. Do you agree with this analysis? Recall also that vehicles in the interior of the country receive far less protection than residences under the Fourth Amendment (under the automobile exception). Does this fact also support the Court's reasoning here?

3. *Fixed checkpoints near the border.* American border patrol agents occasionally set up fixed checkpoints on a highway or roadway in close proximity to the border, but not at the border per se. The goal of these checkpoints is to catch illegal immigrants who have crossed the border illegally. For example, an illegal immigrant might cross the border surreptitiously, away from the established border crossing area, but then return to a major roadway once on the U.S. side of the border. The roadway checkpoint allows border patrol agents to scrutinize travelers in the vicinity of the border. In *United States v. Martinez-Fuerte*, 428 U.S. 543 (1976), the Supreme Court sanctioned this procedure of warrantless and suspicionless vehicle stops at permanent checkpoints near the border. Moreover, the Supreme Court also concluded, with little analysis, that "it is constitutional to refer motorists selectively to the secondary inspection area . . . on the basis of criteria that would not sustain a roving-patrol stop" and "even if it be assumed that such referrals are made largely on the basis of apparent Mexican ancestry, we perceive no constitutional violation." *Id.* at 563. Is this form of racial profiling constitutionally acceptable? One commentator put the point sharply: "The United States border functions like a sort of constitutional black hole: the closer one gets to it, the more constitutional norms are bent and warped. On the border itself, these norms are almost entirely destabilized." Philip Mayor, *Borderline Constitutionalism: Reconstructing and Deconstructing Judicial Justifications for Constitutional Distortion in the Border Region*, 46 Harv. C.R.-C.L. L. Rev. 647 (2011). In light of *Martinez-Fuerte*, do you agree with this assessment?

4. *Cell phone searches at the border?* Can border officials or customs agents conduct a warrantless search of a cell phone or other digital device during a border crossing? The Supreme Court recognized in *Riley v. California* that police may not conduct a warrantless search of an arrestee's cell phone. However, the *Riley* decision involved the search incident to arrest exception and did not involve a border crossing, and the Supreme Court has not directly addressed the scope of the Fourth Amendment with regard to digital searches at the border. The Eleventh Circuit Court of Appeals has held that warrantless cell phone searches are permissible at the border, stating that "[b]order searches have long been excepted from warrant and probable cause requirements, and the holding of *Riley* does not change this rule." *United States v. Vergara*, No. 16-15059, 2018 WL 1324589, at *3 (11th Cir. Mar. 15, 2018). In *Vergara*, the customs agent conducted an initial search of the defendant's cell phone because

he had previously been convicted of child pornography offenses. Upon finding a few incriminating photos, the agent ordered a full forensic search of the device, which yielded several videos of child pornography. The Eleventh Circuit upheld the warrantless search but did not reach the issue of whether suspicionless searches were permitted, since the district court had concluded that the agent in this case had reasonable suspicion and the defendant did not contest this on appeal. Should courts impose a reasonable suspicion standard for warrantless digital searches at the border?

3. Checkpoints

Are police permitted to use checkpoints on public roadways to stop all motorists? Often, these checkpoints are used to look for drunk drivers. In the following case, the Michigan state police ran a checkpoint that involved stopping all drivers on a particular road and looking for signs of impairment. If signs of impairment were detected, the police would direct the motorist to a secondary area where sobriety tests would be conducted. In other words, the initial screening (the stopping of the car and the screening questions) were given to all motorists, without a finding of suspicion, but the secondary screening was only conducted if the police had some reason to suspect that the motorist was impaired. Was the Michigan checkpoint system consistent with the Fourth Amendment?

Michigan Department of State Police v. Sitz

Supreme Court of the United States
496 U.S. 444 (1990)

Chief Justice Rehnquist delivered the opinion of the Court.

This case poses the question whether a State's use of highway sobriety checkpoints violates the Fourth and Fourteenth Amendments to the United States Constitution. We hold that it does not and therefore reverse the contrary holding of the Court of Appeals of Michigan.

Petitioners, the Michigan Department of State Police and its director, established a sobriety checkpoint pilot program in early 1986. The director appointed a Sobriety Checkpoint Advisory Committee comprising representatives of the State Police force, local police forces, state prosecutors, and the University of Michigan Transportation Research Institute. Pursuant to its charge, the advisory committee created guidelines setting forth procedures governing checkpoint operations, site selection, and publicity.

Under the guidelines, checkpoints would be set up at selected sites along state roads. All vehicles passing through a checkpoint would be stopped and their drivers briefly examined for signs of intoxication. In cases where a checkpoint officer detected signs of intoxication, the motorist would be directed to a location out of the traffic flow where an officer would check the motorist's driver's license and car registration and, if warranted, conduct further sobriety tests. Should the field tests and the officer's observations suggest that the driver was intoxicated, an arrest would be made. All other drivers would be permitted to resume their journey immediately. . . .

To decide this case the trial court performed a balancing test derived from our opinion in *Brown v. Texas*, 443 U.S. 47 (1979). As described by the Court of Appeals, the test involved "balancing the state's interest in preventing accidents caused by drunk drivers, the effectiveness of sobriety checkpoints in achieving that goal, and the level of intrusion on an individual's privacy caused by the checkpoints." The Court of Appeals agreed that "the *Brown* three-prong balancing test was the correct test to be used to determine the constitutionality of the sobriety checkpoint plan."

As characterized by the Court of Appeals, the trial court's findings with respect to the balancing factors were that the State has "a grave and legitimate" interest in curbing drunken driving; that sobriety checkpoint programs are generally "ineffective" and, therefore, do not significantly further that interest; and that the checkpoints' "subjective intrusion" on individual liberties is substantial. According to the court, the record disclosed no basis for disturbing the trial court's findings, which were made within the context of an analytical framework prescribed by this Court for determining the constitutionality of seizures less intrusive than traditional arrests.

In this Court respondents seek to defend the judgment in their favor by insisting that the balancing test derived from *Brown v. Texas*, was not the proper method of analysis. Respondents maintain that the analysis must proceed from a basis of probable cause or reasonable suspicion. . . . Respondents argue that there must be a showing of some special governmental need "beyond the normal need" for criminal law enforcement before a balancing analysis is appropriate, and that petitioners have demonstrated no such special need. . . .

Petitioners concede, correctly in our view, that a Fourth Amendment "seizure" occurs when a vehicle is stopped at a checkpoint. The question thus becomes whether such seizures are "reasonable" under the Fourth Amendment. . . .

No one can seriously dispute the magnitude of the drunken driving problem or the States' interest in eradicating it. Media reports of alcohol-related death and mutilation on the Nation's roads are legion. The anecdotal is confirmed by the statistical. "Drunk drivers cause an annual death toll of over 25,000 and in the same time span cause nearly one million personal injuries and more than five billion dollars in property damage." For decades, this Court has "repeatedly lamented the tragedy."

Conversely, the weight bearing on the other scale—the measure of the intrusion on motorists stopped briefly at sobriety checkpoints—is slight. We reached a similar conclusion as to the intrusion on motorists subjected to a brief stop at a highway checkpoint for detecting illegal aliens. We see virtually no difference between the levels of intrusion on law-abiding motorists from the brief stops necessary to the effectuation of these two types of checkpoints, which to the average motorist would seem identical save for the nature of the questions the checkpoint officers might ask. The trial court and the Court of Appeals, thus, accurately gauged the "objective" intrusion, measured by the duration of the seizure and the intensity of the investigation, as minimal.

With respect to what it perceived to be the "subjective" intrusion on motorists, however, the Court of Appeals found such intrusion substantial. The court first affirmed the trial court's finding that the guidelines governing checkpoint operation minimize the discretion of the officers on the scene. But the court also agreed with the trial court's conclusion that the checkpoints have the potential to generate fear and surprise in motorists. This was so because the record failed to demonstrate that approaching motorists would be aware of their option to make U-turns or turnoffs to avoid the checkpoints. On that basis, the court deemed the subjective intrusion from the checkpoints unreasonable.

We believe the Michigan courts misread our cases concerning the degree of "subjective intrusion" and the potential for generating fear and surprise. The "fear and surprise" to be considered are not the natural fear of one who has been drinking over the prospect of being stopped at a sobriety checkpoint but, rather, the fear and surprise engendered in law-abiding motorists by the nature of the stop. This was made clear in *Martinez-Fuerte*. Comparing checkpoint stops to roving patrol stops considered in prior cases, we said: "[W]e view checkpoint stops in a different light because the subjective intrusion—the generating of concern or even fright on the part of lawful travelers—is appreciably less in the case of a checkpoint stop. . . ." Here, checkpoints are selected pursuant to the guidelines, and uniformed police officers stop every approaching vehicle. The intrusion resulting from the brief stop at the sobriety checkpoint is for constitutional purposes indistinguishable from the checkpoint stops we upheld in *Martinez-Fuerte*.

The Court of Appeals went on to consider as part of the balancing analysis the "effectiveness" of the proposed checkpoint program. Based on extensive testimony in the trial record, the court concluded that the checkpoint program failed the "effectiveness" part of the test, and that this failure materially discounted petitioners' strong interest in implementing the program. We think the Court of Appeals was wrong on this point as well. . . . During the operation of the Saginaw County checkpoint, the detention of the vehicles that entered the checkpoint resulted in the arrest of two drunken drivers. Stated as a percentage, approximately 1.6 percent of the drivers passing through the checkpoint were arrested for alcohol impairment. In addition, an expert witness testified at the trial that experience in other States demonstrated that, on the whole, sobriety checkpoints resulted in drunken driving arrests of around 1 percent of all motorists stopped. . . .

In sum, the balance of the State's interest in preventing drunken driving, the extent to which this system can reasonably be said to advance that interest, and the degree of intrusion upon individual motorists who are briefly stopped, weighs in favor of the state program. . . .

Justice BRENNAN, with whom Justice MARSHALL joins, dissenting.

. . . The majority opinion creates the impression that the Court generally engages in a balancing test in order to determine the constitutionality of all seizures, or at least those "dealing with police stops of motorists on public highways." This is not the case. In most cases, the police must possess probable cause for a seizure to be judged reasonable. See *Dunaway v. New York*, 442 U.S. 200, 209 (1979). Only when a seizure is "substantially less intrusive" than a typical arrest is the general rule replaced by a balancing test. I agree with the Court that the initial stop of a car at a roadblock under the Michigan State Police sobriety checkpoint policy is sufficiently less intrusive than an arrest so that the reasonableness of the seizure may be judged, not by the presence of probable cause, but by balancing "the gravity of the public concerns served by the seizure, the degree to which the seizure advances the public interest, and the severity of the interference with individual liberty." *Brown v. Texas*, 443 U.S. 47, 51 (1979). But one searches the majority opinion in vain for any acknowledgment that the reason for employing the balancing test is that the seizure is minimally intrusive.

Indeed, the opinion reads as if the minimal nature of the seizure ends rather than begins the inquiry into reasonableness. Once the Court establishes that the seizure is "slight," it asserts without explanation that the balance "weighs in favor of the state program." The Court ignores the fact that in this class of minimally intrusive searches, we have generally required the Government to prove that it had reasonable suspicion for a minimally intrusive seizure to be considered reasonable. Some level of individualized suspicion is a core component of the protection the Fourth Amendment provides against arbitrary government action. By holding that no level of suspicion is necessary before the police may stop a car for the purpose of preventing drunken driving, the Court potentially subjects the general public to arbitrary or harassing conduct by the police. I would have hoped that before taking such a step, the Court would carefully explain how such a plan fits within our constitutional framework. . . .

That stopping every car might make it easier to prevent drunken driving is an insufficient justification for abandoning the requirement of individualized suspicion. . . . Without proof that the police cannot develop individualized suspicion that a person is driving while impaired by alcohol, I believe the constitutional balance must be struck in favor of protecting the public against even the "minimally intrusive" seizures involved in this case. . . .

Justice STEVENS, with whom Justice BRENNAN and Justice MARSHALL join as to Parts I and II, dissenting.

A sobriety checkpoint is usually operated at night at an unannounced location. Surprise is crucial to its method. The test operation conducted by the Michigan State Police and the Saginaw County Sheriff's Department began shortly after midnight and lasted until about 1 A.M. During that period, the 19 officers participating in the operation made two arrests and stopped and questioned 124 other unsuspecting and innocent drivers. It is, of course, not known how many arrests would have been made during that period if those officers had been engaged in normal patrol activities. However, the findings of the trial court, based on an extensive record and affirmed by the Michigan Court of Appeals, indicate that the net effect of sobriety checkpoints on traffic safety is infinitesimal and possibly negative.

. . . Over a period of several years, Maryland operated 125 checkpoints; of the 41,000 motorists passing through those checkpoints, only 143 persons (0.3%) were arrested. The number of man-hours devoted to these operations is not in the record, but it seems inconceivable that a higher arrest rate could not have been achieved by more conventional means. . . .

In light of these considerations, it seems evident that the Court today misapplies the balancing test announced in *Brown v. Texas,* 443 U.S. 47, 50-51 (1979). The Court overvalues the law enforcement interest in using sobriety checkpoints, undervalues the citizen's interest in freedom from random, unannounced investigatory seizures, and mistakenly assumes that there is "virtually no difference" between a routine stop at a permanent, fixed checkpoint and a surprise stop at a sobriety checkpoint. I believe this case is controlled by our several precedents condemning suspicionless random stops of motorists for investigatory purposes.

I

There is a critical difference between a seizure that is preceded by fair notice and one that is effected by surprise. That is one reason why a border search, or indeed any search at a permanent and fixed checkpoint, is much less intrusive than a random stop. A motorist with advance notice of the location of a permanent checkpoint has an opportunity to avoid the search entirely, or at least to prepare for, and limit, the intrusion on her privacy.

No such opportunity is available in the case of a random stop or a temporary checkpoint, which both depend for their effectiveness on the element of surprise. A driver who discovers an unexpected checkpoint on a familiar local road will be startled and distressed. She may infer, correctly, that the checkpoint is not simply "business as usual," and may likewise infer, again correctly, that the police have made a discretionary decision to focus their law enforcement efforts upon her and others who pass the chosen point.

This element of surprise is the most obvious distinction between the sobriety checkpoints permitted by today's majority and the interior border checkpoints approved by this Court in *Martinez-Fuerte*. The distinction casts immediate doubt upon the majority's argument, for *Martinez-Fuerte* is the only case in which we have upheld suspicionless seizures of motorists. But the difference between notice and surprise is only one of the important reasons for distinguishing between permanent and mobile checkpoints. With respect to the former, there is no room for discretion in either the timing or the location of the stop—it is a permanent part of the landscape. In the latter case, however, although the checkpoint is most frequently employed during the hours of darkness on weekends (because that is when drivers with alcohol in their blood are most apt to be found on the road), the police have extremely broad discretion in determining the exact timing and placement of the roadblock.

There is also a significant difference between the kind of discretion that the officer exercises after the stop is made. A check for a driver's license, or for identification papers at an immigration checkpoint, is far more easily standardized than is a search for evidence of intoxication. A Michigan officer who questions a motorist at a sobriety checkpoint has virtually unlimited discretion to detain the driver on the basis of the slightest suspicion. A ruddy complexion, an unbuttoned shirt, bloodshot eyes, or a speech impediment may suffice to prolong the detention. Any driver who had just consumed a glass of beer, or even a sip of wine, would almost certainly have the burden of demonstrating to the officer that his or her driving ability was not impaired. . . .

These fears are not, as the Court would have it, solely the lot of the guilty. To be law abiding is not necessarily to be spotless, and even the most virtuous can be unlucky. Unwanted attention from the local police need not be less discomforting simply because one's secrets are not the stuff of criminal prosecutions. Moreover, those who have found—by reason of prejudice or misfortune—that encounters with the police may become adversarial or unpleasant without good cause will have grounds for worrying at any stop designed to elicit signs of suspicious behavior. Being stopped by the police is distressing even when it should not be terrifying, and what begins mildly may by happenstance turn severe. . . .

NOTES & QUESTIONS ON CHECKPOINTS

1. *Checkpoints for narcotics.* What if the police use a checkpoint to peer into stopped vehicles to look for illegal drugs? In *City of Indianapolis v. Edmond*, 531 U.S. 32 (2000), the Supreme Court considered such a checkpoint and concluded that it violated the Fourth Amendment. The Court distinguished the DWI checkpoints that were upheld in *Sitz*, noting that the "gravity of the drunk driving problem and the magnitude of the State's interest in getting drunk drivers off the road weighed heavily in our determination that the program was constitutional." On the other hand, the Court rejected the random stops at issue in *Delaware v. Prouse*, 440 U.S. 648, 661 (1979) because they involved "standardless and unconstrained discretion." The problem with the narcotics checkpoint was that its primary purpose was ordinary law enforcement, rather than the immediate public safety rationale at issue in *Sitz*. As the Court explained, "[w]e have never approved a checkpoint program whose primary purpose was to detect evidence of ordinary criminal wrongdoing. Rather, our checkpoint cases have recognized only limited exceptions to the general rule that a seizure must be accompanied by some measure of individualized suspicion." *Edmond*, 531 U.S. at 41. Under this framework, the narcotics checkpoints were clearly unconstitutional. Do you agree with this holding? Is the dividing line between "normal law enforcement" and an urgent public safety situation (as is the case with drunk drivers) so clean? As Justice Rehnquist noted in dissent, the narcotics checkpoint did not involve a bodily intrusion, and a motorist has a reduced expectation of privacy in their automobile as compared to their residence.

Las Vegas police at a sobriety checkpoint assessing for alcohol or drug impairment in June 2016. (Jim West/Alamy Stock Photo)

2. *Investigatory checkpoints.* In the midst of an ongoing investigation, police might set up a checkpoint to search for a suspect or even to look for potential witnesses who might have evidence regarding a recent crime. In *Illinois v. Lidster*, 540 U.S. 419 (2004), the Supreme Court considered a highway checkpoint designed to look for witnesses to a fatal hit-and-run accident that the police were investigating. One motorist swerved and almost hit one of the officers at the checkpoint. After an officer smelled alcohol on the motorist, he was given a sobriety test and failed, and was charged with DWI. The Supreme Court upheld the checkpoint, in part because the primary purpose was to elicit information from the motorists rather than to target the motorists for prosecution. Furthermore, the Court concluded that information-gathering checkpoints are far less intrusive than other checkpoints: "For another thing, information-seeking highway stops are less likely to provoke anxiety or to prove intrusive. The stops are likely brief. The police are not likely to ask questions designed to elicit self-incriminating information." *Id.* at 425. Do you agree with this assessment? How relevant is the goal or purpose of the checkpoint? From the perspective of Lidster, the defendant, he was still given a sobriety test, and failed. Should the constitutionality of the checkpoint be determined by the state's individual conduct toward the defendant or the general purpose in setting up the dragnet in the first place?

4. Schools

School officials search students and their belongings in order to enforce school regulations. But when does a school search go too far? The Supreme Court held in *New Jersey v. T.L.O.*, 469 U.S. 325 (1985), that warrantless school searches are appropriate if school officials have "reasonable suspicion" that in the search of the student they will discover contraband or evidence of a crime or violation of other school regulations. The Supreme Court described the sequence of events that led the school to conduct the search:

> On March 7, 1980, a teacher at Piscataway High School in Middlesex County, N.J., discovered two girls smoking in a lavatory. One of the two girls was the respondent T.L.O., who at that time was a 14-year-old high school freshman. Because smoking in the lavatory was a violation of a school rule, the teacher took the two girls to the Principal's office, where they met with Assistant Vice Principal Theodore Choplick. In response to questioning by Mr. Choplick, T.L.O.'s companion admitted that she had violated the rule. T.L.O., however, denied that she had been smoking in the lavatory and claimed that she did not smoke at all.
>
> Mr. Choplick asked T.L.O. to come into his private office and demanded to see her purse. Opening the purse, he found a pack of cigarettes, which he

> removed from the purse and held before T.L.O. as he accused her of having lied to him. As he reached into the purse for the cigarettes, Mr. Choplick also noticed a package of cigarette rolling papers. In his experience, possession of rolling papers by high school students was closely associated with the use of marihuana. Suspecting that a closer examination of the purse might yield further evidence of drug use, Mr. Choplick proceeded to search the purse thoroughly. The search revealed a small amount of marihuana, a pipe, a number of empty plastic bags, a substantial quantity of money in one-dollar bills, an index card that appeared to be a list of students who owed T.L.O. money, and two letters that implicated T.L.O. in marihuana dealing.

Id. at 328. The Supreme Court concluded that the search was reasonable because it was supported by reasonable suspicion, and that a school is a "special needs" situation that requires the state to conduct searches in order to maintain a proper educational environment for all students.

In the following case, school officials conducted a strip search to look for prohibited prescription drugs on the student, a 13-year-old girl. Did this action go too far and violate the Fourth Amendment? As you read the case, compare the facts to the suspicions that were at issue in *T.L.O.* Also, pay particular attention to the invasive nature of the search. Does the Court apply the same standard announced in *T.L.O.* or do strip searches require the application of a different legal standard entirely?

Safford Unified School Dist. No. 1 v. Redding

Supreme Court of the United States
557 U.S. 364 (2009)

Justice Souter delivered the opinion of the Court.

The issue here is whether a 13-year-old student's Fourth Amendment was violated when she was subjected to a search of her bra and underpants by school officials acting on reasonable suspicion that she had brought forbidden prescription and over-the-counter drugs to school. Because there were no reasons to suspect the drugs presented a danger or were concealed in her underwear, we hold that the search did violate the Constitution, but because there is reason to question the clarity with which the right was established, the official who ordered the unconstitutional search is entitled to qualified immunity from liability.

I

The events immediately prior to the search in question began in 13-year-old Savana Redding's math class at Safford Middle School one October day in 2003. The assistant principal of the school, Kerry Wilson, came into the room and asked Savana to go to his office. There, he showed her a day planner, unzipped and open flat on his desk, in which there were several knives, lighters, a permanent marker, and a cigarette. Wilson asked Savana whether the planner was hers; she said it was, but that a few days before she had lent it to her friend, Marissa Glines. Savana stated that none of the items in the planner belonged to her.

Wilson then showed Savana four white prescription-strength ibuprofen 400-mg pills, and one over-the-counter blue naproxen 200-mg pill, all used for pain and inflammation but banned under school rules without advance permission. He asked Savana if she knew anything about the pills. Savana answered that she did not. Wilson then told Savana that he had received a report that she was giving these pills to fellow students; Savana denied it and agreed to let Wilson search her belongings. Helen Romero, an administrative assistant, came into the office, and together with Wilson they searched Savana's backpack, finding nothing.

At that point, Wilson instructed Romero to take Savana to the school nurse's office to search her clothes for pills. Romero and the nurse, Peggy Schwallier, asked Savana to remove her jacket, socks, and shoes, leaving her in stretch pants and a T-shirt (both without pockets), which she was then asked to remove. Finally, Savana was told to pull her bra out and to the side and shake it, and to pull out the elastic on her underpants, thus exposing her breasts and pelvic area to some degree. No pills were found. . . .

II

The Fourth Amendment "right of the people to be secure in their persons . . . against unreasonable searches and seizures" generally requires a law enforcement officer to have probable cause for conducting a search. "Probable cause exists where 'the facts and circumstances within [an officer's] knowledge and of which [he] had reasonably trustworthy information [are] sufficient in themselves to warrant a man of reasonable caution in the belief that' an offense has been or is being committed," and that evidence bearing on that offense will be found in the place to be searched.

In *T.L.O.*, we recognized that the school setting "requires some modification of the level of suspicion of illicit activity needed to justify a search," 469 U.S., at 340, and held that for searches by school officials "a careful balancing of governmental and private interests suggests that the public interest is best served by a Fourth Amendment standard of reasonableness that stops short of probable cause." We have thus applied a standard of reasonable suspicion to determine the legality of a school administrator's search of a student, and have held that a school search "will be permissible in its scope when the measures adopted are reasonably related to the objectives of the search and not excessively intrusive in light of the age and sex of the student and the nature of the infraction."

A number of our cases on probable cause have an implicit bearing on the reliable knowledge element of reasonable suspicion, as we have attempted to flesh out the knowledge component by looking to the degree to which known facts imply prohibited conduct, the specificity of the information received, and the reliability of its source. . . . Perhaps the best that can be said generally about the required knowledge component of probable cause for a law enforcement officer's evidence search is that it raise a "fair probability," or a "substantial chance," of discovering evidence of criminal activity. The lesser standard for school searches could as readily be described as a moderate chance of finding evidence of wrongdoing.

III

In this case, the school's policies strictly prohibit the nonmedical use, possession, or sale of any drug on school grounds, including "[a]ny prescription or over-the-counter drug, except those for which permission to use in school has been granted pursuant to Board policy." A week before Savana was searched, another student, Jordan Romero (no relation of the school's administrative assistant), told the principal and Assistant Principal Wilson that "certain students were bringing drugs and weapons on campus," and that he had been sick after taking some pills that "he got from a classmate." On the morning of October 8, the same boy handed Wilson a white pill that he said Marissa Glines had given him. He told Wilson that students were planning to take the pills at lunch.

Wilson learned from Peggy Schwallier, the school nurse, that the pill was Ibuprofen 400 mg, available only by prescription. Wilson then called Marissa out of class. Outside the classroom, Marissa's teacher handed Wilson the day planner, found within Marissa's reach, containing various contraband items. Wilson escorted Marissa back to his office.

In the presence of Helen Romero, Wilson requested Marissa to turn out her pockets and open her wallet. Marissa produced a blue pill, several white ones, and a razor blade. Wilson asked where the blue pill came from, and Marissa answered, "I guess it slipped in when she gave me the IBU 400s." When Wilson asked whom she meant, Marissa replied, "Savana Redding." Wilson then enquired about the day planner and its contents; Marissa denied knowing anything about them. Wilson did not ask Marissa any followup questions to determine whether there was any likelihood that Savana presently had pills: neither asking when Marissa received the pills from Savana nor where Savana might be hiding them.

Schwallier did not immediately recognize the blue pill, but information provided through a poison control hotline indicated that the pill was a 200-mg dose of an anti-inflammatory drug, generically called naproxen, available over the counter. At Wilson's direction, Marissa was then subjected to a search of her bra and underpants by Romero and Schwallier, as Savana was later on. The search revealed no additional pills.

It was at this juncture that Wilson called Savana into his office and showed her the day planner. Their conversation established that Savana and Marissa were on friendly terms: while she denied knowledge of the contraband, Savana admitted that the day planner was hers and that she had lent it to Marissa. Wilson had other reports of their friendship from staff members, who had identified Savana and Marissa as part of an unusually rowdy group at the school's opening dance in August, during which alcohol and cigarettes were found in the girls' bathroom. Wilson had reason to connect the girls with this contraband, for Wilson knew that Jordan Romero had told the principal that before the dance, he had been at a party at Savana's house where alcohol was served. Marissa's statement that the pills came from Savana was thus sufficiently plausible to warrant suspicion that Savana was involved in pill distribution.

This suspicion of Wilson's was enough to justify a search of Savana's backpack and outer clothing. If a student is reasonably suspected of giving out contraband pills, she is reasonably suspected of carrying them on her person and in the carryall that has become an item of student uniform in most places today. If Wilson's reasonable suspicion of pill distribution were not understood to support searches of outer clothes and backpack, it would not justify any search worth making. And the look into Savana's bag, in her presence and in the relative privacy of Wilson's office, was not excessively intrusive, any more than Romero's subsequent search of her outer clothing.

Here it is that the parties part company, with Savana's claim that extending the search at Wilson's behest to the point of making her pull out her underwear was constitutionally unreasonable. The exact label for this final step in the intrusion is not important, though strip search is a fair way to speak of it. Romero and Schwallier directed Savana to remove her clothes down to her underwear, and then "pull out" her bra and the elastic band on her underpants. Although Romero and Schwallier stated that they did not see anything when Savana followed their instructions, we would not define strip search and its Fourth Amendment consequences in a way that would guarantee litigation about who was looking and how much was seen. The very fact of Savana's pulling her underwear away from her body in the presence of the two officials who were able to see her necessarily exposed her breasts and pelvic area to some degree, and both subjective and reasonable societal expectations of personal privacy support the treatment of such a search as categorically distinct, requiring distinct elements of justification on the part of school authorities for going beyond a search of outer clothing and belongings.

Savana's subjective expectation of privacy against such a search is inherent in her account of it as embarrassing, frightening, and humiliating. . . .

The indignity of the search does not, of course, outlaw it, but it does implicate the rule of reasonableness as stated in *T.L.O.*, that "the search as actually conducted [be] reasonably related in scope to the circumstances which justified the interference in the first place." 469 U.S., at 341. The scope will be permissible, that is, when it is "not excessively intrusive in light of the age and sex of the student and the nature of the infraction."

Here, the content of the suspicion failed to match the degree of intrusion. Wilson knew beforehand that the pills were prescription-strength ibuprofen and over-the-counter naproxen, common pain relievers equivalent to two Advil, or one Aleve. He must have been aware of the nature and limited threat of the specific drugs he was searching for, and while just about anything can be taken in quantities that will do real harm, Wilson had no reason to suspect that large amounts of the drugs were being passed around, or that individual students were receiving great numbers of pills.

Nor could Wilson have suspected that Savana was hiding common painkillers in her underwear. Petitioners suggest, as a truth universally acknowledged, that "students . . . hid[e] contraband in or under their clothing," and cite a smattering of cases of students with contraband in their underwear. But when the categorically extreme intrusiveness of a search down to the body of an adolescent requires some justification in suspected facts, general background possibilities fall short; a reasonable search that extensive calls for suspicion that it will pay off. But nondangerous school contraband does not raise the specter of stashes in intimate places, and there is no evidence in the record of any general practice among Safford Middle School students of hiding that sort of thing in underwear; neither Jordan nor Marissa suggested to Wilson that Savana was doing that, and the preceding search of Marissa that Wilson ordered yielded nothing. . . .

In sum, what was missing from the suspected facts that pointed to Savana was any indication of danger to the students from the power of the drugs or their quantity, and any reason to suppose that Savana was carrying pills in her underwear. We think that the combination of these deficiencies was fatal to finding the search reasonable. . . .

Justice STEVENS, with whom Justice GINSBURG joins, concurring in part and dissenting in part.

In *New Jersey v. T.L.O.*, 469 U.S. 325 (1985), the Court established a two-step inquiry for determining the reasonableness of a school official's decision to search a student. First, the Court explained, the search must be "justified at its inception" by the presence of "reasonable grounds for suspecting that the search will turn up evidence that the student has violated or is violating either the law or the rules of the school." Second, the search must be "permissible in its scope," which is achieved "when the measures adopted are reasonably related to the objectives of the search and not excessively intrusive in light of the age and sex of the student and the nature of the infraction."

Nothing the Court decides today alters this basic framework. It simply applies *T.L.O.* to declare unconstitutional a strip search of a 13-year-old honors student that was based on a groundless suspicion that she might be hiding medicine in her underwear. This is, in essence, a case in which clearly established law meets clearly outrageous conduct. I have long believed that "[i]t does not require a constitutional scholar to conclude that a nude search of a 13-year-old child is an invasion of constitutional rights of some magnitude." The strip search of Savana Redding in this case was both more intrusive and less justified than the search of the student's purse in *T.L.O.* . . .

Justice THOMAS, concurring in the judgment in part and dissenting in part.

. . . Unlike the majority . . . I would hold that the search of Savana Redding did not violate the Fourth Amendment. The majority imposes a vague and amorphous standard on school administrators. It also grants judges sweeping authority to second-guess the measures that these officials take to maintain discipline in their schools and ensure the health and safety of the students in their charge. This deep intrusion into the administration of public schools exemplifies why the Court should return to the common-law doctrine of in loco parentis. . . . But even under the prevailing Fourth Amendment test established by *T.L.O.*, 469 U.S. 325 (1985), all petitioners, including the school district, are entitled to judgment as a matter of law in their favor.

I

. . . Seeking to reconcile the Fourth Amendment with this unique public school setting, the Court in *T.L.O.* held that a school search is "reasonable" if it is "justified at its inception" and "reasonably related in scope to the circumstances which justified the interference in the first place." The search under review easily meets this standard.

A "search of a student by a teacher or other school official will be 'justified at its inception' when there are reasonable grounds for suspecting that the search will turn up evidence that the student has violated or is violating either the law or the rules of the school." *T.L.O.*, at 341-342. As the majority rightly concedes, this search was justified at its inception because there were reasonable grounds to suspect that Redding possessed medication that violated school rules. A finding of reasonable suspicion "does not deal with hard certainties, but with probabilities." To satisfy this standard, more than a mere "hunch" of wrongdoing is required, but "considerably" less suspicion is needed than would be required to "satisf[y] a preponderance of the evidence standard." . . .

Here, petitioners had reasonable grounds to suspect that Redding was in possession of prescription and nonprescription drugs in violation of the school's prohibition of the "non-medical use, possession, or sale of a drug" on school property or at school events. As an initial matter, school officials were aware that a few years earlier, a student had become "seriously ill" and "spent several days in intensive care" after ingesting prescription medication obtained from a classmate. Fourth Amendment searches do not occur in a vacuum; rather, context must inform the judicial inquiry. In this instance, the suspicion of drug possession arose at a middle school that had "a history of problems with students using and distributing prohibited and illegal substances on campus."

The school's substance-abuse problems had not abated by the 2003-2004 school year, which is when the challenged search of Redding took place. School officials had found alcohol and cigarettes in the girls' bathroom during the first school dance of the year and noticed that a group of students including Redding and Marissa Glines smelled of alcohol. Several weeks later, another student, Jordan Romero, reported that Redding had hosted a party before the dance where she served whiskey, vodka, and tequila. Romero had provided this report to school officials as a result of a meeting his mother scheduled with the officials after Romero "bec[a]me violent" and "sick to his stomach" one night and admitted that "he had taken some pills that he had got[ten] from a classmate." At that meeting, Romero admitted that "certain students were bringing drugs and weapons on campus." One week later, Romero handed the assistant principal a white pill that he said he had received from Glines. He reported "that a group of students [were] planning on taking the pills at lunch." School officials justifiably took quick action in light of the lunchtime deadline. . . .

The remaining question is whether the search was reasonable in scope. . . . Because the school officials searched in a location where the pills could have been hidden, the search was reasonable in scope under *T.L.O.* . . . Judges are not qualified to second-guess the best manner for maintaining quiet and order in the school environment. . . . It is a mistake for judges to assume the responsibility for deciding which school rules are important enough to allow for invasive searches and which rules are not. . . .

NOTES & QUESTIONS ON SCHOOL SEARCHES

1. *Standard for school searches.* In *Redding*, the Court applied the standard that it had previously articulated in prior school search cases, i.e., a search "will be permissible in its scope when the measures adopted are reasonably related to the objectives of the search and not excessively intrusive in light of the age and sex of the student and the nature of the infraction." Do you agree with the majority's application of this standard to the facts of the case?

Moreover, should the search in *Redding* be viewed as one single search or a series of progressively intrusive searches, culminating in the school's demand that the student partially remove her underwear? As one commentator noted:

> Given the uncertainties about whether the Court sees *Redding* as a single or multiple search situation and questions about the extent to which *T.L.O.* governs the strip search context, a single, coherent, analytical framework is not apparent from the *Redding* case and cannot be discerned until the Court answers the following questions: Is *Redding* a single search situation? If so, does satisfaction of the *Redding* factors necessarily satisfy the scope prong of *T.L.O.*? If not, how do *T.L.O.*'s concerns for the "age and sex of the student and the nature of the infraction" factor into the analysis?

Martin R. Gardner, *Strip Searching Students: The Supreme Court's Latest Failure to Articulate a "Sufficiently Clear" Statement of Fourth Amendment Law*, 80 Miss. L.J. 955, 968-69 (2011).

2. *School drug tests.* What result if the school officials in *Safford v. Redding* had required the student to take a urine drug test rather than demanding that the student submit to a strip search? In one sense, the strip search was uniquely embarrassing and intrusive; on the other hand, a procedure that requires a student to hand over bodily fluids such as urine to a state official is clearly invasive as well. In *Vernonia Sch. Dist. 47J v. Acton*, 515 U.S. 646 (1995), the Supreme Court upheld random drug tests of school athletes, finding that the searches were justified by the school's need to combat athletic drug abuse, and also noting that the manner in which the urine samples were collected was not unduly invasive: "These conditions are nearly identical to those typically encountered in public restrooms, which men, women, and especially schoolchildren use daily. Under such conditions, the privacy interests compromised by the process of obtaining the urine sample are in our view negligible." *Id.* at 658. In *Bd. of Educ. of Indep. Sch. Dist. No. 92 of Pottawatomie County v. Earls*, 536 U.S. 822 (2002), the Supreme Court went further, allowing a drug-testing program aimed at all students participating in school extra-curricular activities (not just athletics). In dissent, Justice Ginsburg noted that

> [i]t is a sad irony that the petitioning School District seeks to justify its edict here by trumpeting "the schools' custodial and tutelary responsibility for children." In regulating an athletic program or endeavoring to combat an exploding drug epidemic, a school's custodial obligations may permit searches that would otherwise unacceptably abridge students' rights. When custodial duties are not ascendant, however, schools' tutelary obligations to their students require them to "teach by example" by avoiding symbolic measures that diminish constitutional protections.

PROBLEM CASE

Consider the following description of an off-campus school search:

> Kissinger drove himself and another student to Ward [Public School] on August 26, 2015. He parked on Weibke Street, about one block away from Ward's campus. The administration questioned Kissinger as to why he had not turned in his application and whether he had driven another student to school that day. He provided untruthful responses. For example, Kissinger denied knowing where he was supposed to park, despite having previously been explicitly shown by Mr. Armstead. He also denied driving another student to school that morning, which was false. Based on Kissinger's evasiveness and several other factors, Mr. Pruitt suspected that Kissinger had contraband (specifically, drugs) in his car and ordered a search. Kissinger led a school administrator, Mr. Armstead, and the school resource officer, Officer Pruser, to his off campus vehicle. While Kissinger and Officer Pruser stood by, Mr. Armstead searched the vehicle and found a marijuana pipe containing burnt marijuana residue. Kissinger, Mr. Armstead, and Officer Pruser all returned to the school, where Officer Pruser handcuffed Kissinger and placed him under arrest.

Kissinger v. Fort Wayne Cmty. Sch., 293 F. Supp. 3d 796, 802 (N.D. Ind. 2018). The school's search policy permits the search of off-campus vehicles and vehicles "not involved in a school-sponsored activity." Is the search constitutional even though it occurred off campus?

Id. at 855. What result if the school district required *all* students to submit to random drug tests as a condition of attending public school?

5. Government Employees

When the state acts as an employer, does this give the state a special license to conduct searches of its own employees? After all, private employers frequently search the work areas of their employees, and these searches do not raise any constitutional concerns. First, there is no state action when a private employer acts in this way. Second, the work area of the employee, including, for example, the computer that the employee uses for work matters, usually belongs to the employer. Should the state be allowed to conduct similar work-related searches for public sector employees?

In the following case, the Supreme Court considers whether a government employment search falls under the "special needs" exception to the warrant requirement. As you read the case, ask yourself whether a government employment search is sufficiently distinct from the state's exercise of law enforcement powers that require a warrant. Also, what expectation of privacy did the employee have in the text messages that he sent using his government-issued pager?

City of Ontario v. Quon

Supreme Court of the United States
560 U.S. 746 (2010)

Justice KENNEDY delivered the opinion of the Court.

This case involves the assertion by a government employer of the right, in circumstances to be described, to read text messages sent and received on a pager the employer owned and issued to an employee. The employee contends that the privacy of the messages is protected by the ban on "unreasonable searches and seizures" found in the Fourth Amendment to the United States Constitution, made applicable to the States by the Due Process Clause of the Fourteenth Amendment. Though the case touches issues of farreaching significance, the Court concludes it can be resolved by settled principles determining when a search is reasonable.

I

. . . In October 2001, the City acquired 20 alphanumeric pagers capable of sending and receiving text messages. Arch Wireless Operating Company provided wireless service for the pagers. Under the City's service contract with Arch Wireless, each pager was allotted a limited number of characters sent or received each month. Usage in excess of that amount would result in an additional fee. The City issued pagers to Quon and other SWAT Team members in order to help the SWAT Team mobilize and respond to emergency situations. . . .

Within the first or second billing cycle after the pagers were distributed, Quon exceeded his monthly text message character allotment. . . . Over the next few months, Quon exceeded his character limit three or four times. Each time he reimbursed the City. . . . [A]n administrative assistant employed by the Ontario Police Department (OPD) contacted Arch Wireless. After verifying that the City was the subscriber on the accounts, Arch Wireless provided the desired transcripts. [A superior] reviewed the transcripts and discovered that many of the messages sent and received on Quon's pager were not work related, and some were sexually explicit. [The superior] . . . referred the matter to OPD's internal affairs division for an investigation into whether Quon was violating OPD rules by pursuing personal matters while on duty. . . .

II

. . . It is well settled that the Fourth Amendment's protection extends beyond the sphere of criminal investigations. The Fourth Amendment applies as well when the Government acts in its capacity as an employer.

The Court discussed this principle in *O'Connor*. There a physician employed by a state hospital alleged that hospital officials investigating workplace misconduct had violated his Fourth Amendment rights by searching his office and seizing personal items from his desk and filing cabinet. All Members of the Court agreed with the general principle that "[i]ndividuals do not lose Fourth Amendment rights merely because they work for the government instead of a private employer." 480 U.S., at 717. A majority of the Court further agreed that "special needs, beyond the normal need for law enforcement," make the warrant and probable-cause requirement impracticable for government employers.

The *O'Connor* Court did disagree on the proper analytical framework for Fourth Amendment claims against government employers. A four-Justice plurality concluded that the correct analysis has two steps. First, because "some government offices may be so open to fellow employees or the public that no expectation of privacy is reasonable," a court must consider "[t]he operational realities of the workplace" in order to determine whether an employee's Fourth Amendment rights are implicated. On this view, "the question whether an employee has a reasonable expectation of privacy must be addressed on a case-by-case basis." Next, where an employee has a legitimate privacy expectation, an employer's intrusion on that expectation "for noninvestigatory, work-related purposes, as well as for investigations of work-related misconduct, should be judged by the standard of reasonableness under all the circumstances."

Justice Scalia, concurring in the judgment, outlined a different approach. His opinion would have dispensed with an inquiry into "operational realities" and would conclude "that the offices of government employees . . . are covered by Fourth Amendment protections as a general matter." But he would also have held "that government searches to retrieve work-related materials or to investigate violations of workplace rules—searches of the sort that are regarded as reasonable and normal in the private-employer context—do not violate the Fourth Amendment." . . . Later, in the *Von Raab* decision, the Court explained that "operational realities" could diminish an employee's privacy expectations, and that this diminution could be taken into consideration when assessing the reasonableness of a workplace search. 489 U.S., at 671.

III

. . . At this point, were we to assume that inquiry into "operational realities" were called for, it would be necessary to ask whether Duke's statements could be taken as announcing a change in OPD policy, and if so, whether he had, in fact or appearance, the authority to make such a change and to guarantee the privacy of text messaging. It would also be necessary to consider whether a review of messages sent on police pagers, particularly those sent while officers are on duty, might be justified for other reasons, including performance evaluations, litigation concerning the lawfulness of police actions, and perhaps compliance with state open records laws. These matters would all bear on the legitimacy of an employee's privacy expectation.

The Court must proceed with care when considering the whole concept of privacy expectations in communications made on electronic equipment owned by a government employer. The judiciary risks error by elaborating too fully on the Fourth Amendment implications of emerging technology before its role in society has become clear. . . . Prudence counsels caution before the facts in the instant case are used to establish far-reaching premises that define the existence, and extent, of privacy expectations enjoyed by employees when using employer-provided communication devices. . . .

Even if the Court were certain that the *O'Connor* plurality's approach were the right one, the Court would have difficulty predicting how employees' privacy expectations will be shaped by those changes or the degree to which society will be prepared to recognize those expectations as reasonable. Cell phone and text message communications are so pervasive that some persons may consider them to be essential means or necessary instruments for self-expression, even self-identification. That might strengthen the case for an expectation of privacy. On the other hand, the ubiquity of those devices has made them generally affordable, so one could counter that employees who need cell phones or similar devices for personal matters can purchase and pay for their own. And employer policies concerning communications will of course shape the reasonable expectations of their employees, especially to the extent that such policies are clearly communicated.

A broad holding concerning employees' privacy expectations vis-à-vis employer-provided technological equipment might have implications for future cases that cannot be predicted. It is preferable to dispose of this case on narrower grounds. For present purposes we assume several propositions arguendo: First, Quon had a reasonable expectation of privacy in the text messages sent on the pager provided to him by the City; second, petitioners' review of the transcript constituted a search within the meaning of the Fourth Amendment; and third, the principles applicable to a government employer's search of an employee's physical office apply with at least the same force when the employer intrudes on the employee's privacy in the electronic sphere.

Even if Quon had a reasonable expectation of privacy in his text messages, petitioners did not necessarily violate the Fourth Amendment by obtaining and reviewing the transcripts. Although as a general matter, warrantless searches "are per se unreasonable under the Fourth Amendment," there are "a few specifically established and well-delineated exceptions" to that general rule. The Court has held that the "special needs" of the workplace justify one such exception.

Under the approach of the *O'Connor* plurality, when conducted for a "noninvestigatory, work-related purpos[e]" or for the "investigatio[n] of work-related misconduct," a government employer's warrantless search is reasonable if it is "justified at its inception" and if "the measures adopted are reasonably related to the objectives of the search and not excessively intrusive in light of" the circumstances giving rise to the search. The search here satisfied the standard of the *O'Connor* plurality and was reasonable under that approach.

The search was justified at its inception because there were "reasonable grounds for suspecting that the search [was] necessary for a non-investigatory work-related purpose." As a jury found, [the Ontario Police Chief] ordered the search in order to determine whether the character limit on the City's contract with Arch Wireless was sufficient to meet the City's needs. This was, as the Ninth Circuit noted, a "legitimate work-related rationale." The City and OPD had a legitimate interest in ensuring that employees were not being forced to pay out of their own pockets for work-related expenses, or on the other hand that the City was not paying for extensive personal communications.

As for the scope of the search, reviewing the transcripts was reasonable because it was an efficient and expedient way to determine whether Quon's overages were the result of work-related messaging or personal use. The review was also not "excessively intrusive." Although Quon had gone over his monthly allotment a number of times, OPD requested transcripts for only the months of August and September 2002. While it may have been reasonable as well for OPD to review transcripts of all the months in which Quon exceeded his allowance, it was certainly reasonable for OPD to review messages for just two months in order to obtain a large enough sample to decide whether the character limits were efficacious. . . .

Furthermore, and again on the assumption that Quon had a reasonable expectation of privacy in the contents of his messages, the extent of an expectation is relevant to assessing whether the search was too intrusive. Even if he could assume some level of privacy would inhere in his messages, it would not have been reasonable for Quon to conclude that his messages were in all circumstances immune from scrutiny. . . . Under the circumstances, a reasonable employee would be aware that sound management principles might require the audit of messages to determine whether the pager was being appropriately used. . . .

That the search did reveal intimate details of Quon's life does not make it unreasonable, for under the circumstances a reasonable employer would not expect that such a review would intrude on such matters. The search was permissible in its scope. . . .

NOTES & QUESTIONS ON GOVERNMENT EMPLOYMENT

1. *What is the standard?* In *Quon*, the Court resolved the case on "narrow" grounds by simply concluding that the search was reasonable under the Fourth Amendment, without resolving the lingering uncertainty produced by the lack of consensus in the prior *O'Connor* case. The Court in *Quon* decided that the result of the analysis would be the same under both of the *O'Connor* approaches. In so doing, the Court refused to explicitly address whether Quon had a reasonable expectation of privacy in the text messages that he sent during work hours. Under the first *O'Connor* approach, the search was reasonable because it had a legitimate work-related purpose at its inception and was not excessive in scope; under the second approach, the search was reasonable because it would be considered reasonable in the private sector context. Does it trouble you that the Supreme Court refused to adopt a particular standard for analyzing government employment searches? Or do the two approaches essentially converge in all cases, making the distinction utterly academic? Consider the following assessment:

> The Court's decision in *Quon* is a striking example of courts' recent difficulty in handling the intersection of the Fourth Amendment with technology. In declining to decide the expectation of privacy question in *Quon* on more principled grounds, the Court has provided no more guidance than did *O'Connor*—a case that did not involve technological issues—more than two decades ago. In fact, by declining to apply the *O'Connor* "operational realities" test where issues of technology are involved and opting instead to evaluate Fourth Amendment cases involving technology on a case-by-case basis, Justice Kennedy opened the door to *O'Connor*'s continued application in such circumstances and inevitably to inconsistent results on account of the flexibility of *O'Connor*'s fact-specific approach. Essentially, the Court has left the issue for future litigants and future Justices to solve. Instead, the Court should have ruled that government employees have no reasonable expectation of privacy in text messages sent from a government-issued device.

Fourth Amendment—Reasonable Expectation of Privacy, 124 Harv. L. Rev. 179, 184-85 (2010). Do you agree that the Supreme Court should adopt a clear rule that government employees have no expectation of privacy in messages sent from government-issued devices, including computers, pagers, and cell phones?

2. *Drug testing at work.* The Court has several times considered and upheld drug-testing programs in the public employment context. For example, in *Skinner v. Ry. Labor Executives' Ass'n*, 489 U.S. 602 (1989), the Supreme Court considered a Federal Railroad Administration (FRA) program that *required* blood and urine tests to detect alcohol and drug use among employees

involved in fatal accidents, and also *permitted* blood and urine tests for employees who violate some safety rules. The Court ruled that even if the tests were performed by private railroad companies, the federal regulations were enough state action to implicate the Fourth Amendment, and that "imposing a warrant requirement in the present context would add little to the assurances of certainty and regularity already afforded by the regulations, while significantly hindering, and in many cases frustrating, the objectives of the Government's testing program." *Id.* at 624. Similarly, in *National Treasury Employees Union v. Von Raab*, 489 U.S. 656 (1989), the Court approved a U.S. Customs Service drug-testing program for all employees applying for transfer or promotion to positions involving drug interdiction, use of firearms, or handling of classified material. The Court applied a balancing test that considered the diminished expectation of privacy for employees in these sensitive positions, which was weighed against the state's "compelling interest in ensuring that front-line interdiction personnel are physically fit, and have unimpeachable integrity and judgment." *Id.* at 670. The only major drug-testing program that the Supreme Court declined to endorse involved a mandatory drug test for all candidates for state political office in Georgia, which the Court considered unrelated to the public safety rationale at issue in *Von Raab* and *Skinner* and was mostly motivated by the state's desire to demonstrate its commitment to fighting the war on drugs. The Court concluded that the "candidate drug test Georgia has devised diminishes personal privacy for a symbol's sake." *Chandler v. Miller*, 520 U.S. 305, 322 (1997). Does the Georgia drug-testing program seem sufficiently distinct from the other programs to warrant a different treatment under the Fourth Amendment?

6. Jails and Prisons

The final category within the "special needs" exception incudes searches in jails and prisons. On the one hand, the state clearly has a legitimate interest in securing the safety and security of the prison population—both the inmates and the guards. On the other hand, the prisoners are "housed" within the jail or prison building, making it the only "home" that they have during their period of incarceration. Does this suggest that they might have some legitimate expectation of privacy in that context?

In *Bell v. Wolfish*, 441 U.S. 520 (1979), the Supreme Court upheld body cavity searches for both "convicted prisoners and pretrial detainees," even in situations where prison or jail officials lacked probable cause to conduct the cavity search.

In the following case, even the petitioner conceded that prison or jail officials could search incoming detainees as part of the regular screening process, consistent with the Fourth Amendment. The dispute centered over the scope of these searches, i.e., whether a strip search that exposed the most sensitive areas of the body was appropriate. Also at issue was which detainees could be subjected to these invasive body searches. Can the state conduct these searches on detainees arrested—and not yet convicted—for *minor* offenses? Recall that pre-trial detainees have not been convicted and are still entitled to the presumption of innocence.

Florence v. Board of Chosen Freeholders of County of Burlington

Supreme Court of the United States
566 U.S. 318 (2012)

Justice KENNEDY delivered the opinion of the Court, except as to Part IV.

Correctional officials have a legitimate interest, indeed a responsibility, to ensure that jails are not made less secure by reason of what new detainees may carry in on their bodies. Facility personnel, other inmates, and the new detainee himself or herself may be in danger if these threats are introduced into the jail population. This case presents the question of what rules, or limitations, the Constitution imposes on searches of arrested persons who are to be held in jail while their cases are being processed. . . . In addressing this type of constitutional claim courts must defer to the judgment of correctional officials unless the record contains substantial evidence showing their policies are an unnecessary or unjustified response to problems of jail security. That necessary showing has not been made in this case.

I

In 1998, seven years before the incidents at issue, petitioner Albert Florence was arrested after fleeing from police officers in Essex County, New Jersey. He was charged with obstruction of justice and use of a deadly weapon. Petitioner entered a plea of guilty to two lesser offenses and was sentenced to pay a fine in monthly installments. In 2003, after he fell behind on his payments and failed to appear at an enforcement hearing, a bench warrant was issued for his arrest. He paid the outstanding balance less than a week later; but, for some unexplained reason, the warrant remained in a statewide computer database.

Two years later, in Burlington County, New Jersey, petitioner and his wife were stopped in their automobile by a state trooper. Based on the outstanding warrant in the computer system, the officer arrested petitioner and took him to the Burlington County Detention Center. He was held there for six days and then was transferred to the Essex County Correctional Facility. It is not the arrest or confinement but the search process at each jail that gives rise to the claims before the Court.

Burlington County jail procedures required every arrestee to shower with a delousing agent. Officers would check arrestees for scars, marks, gang tattoos, and contraband as they disrobed. Petitioner claims he was also instructed to open his mouth, lift his tongue, hold out his arms, turn around, and lift his genitals. (It is not clear whether this last step was part of the normal practice.) Petitioner shared a cell with at least one other person and interacted with other inmates following his admission to the jail.

The Essex County Correctional Facility, where petitioner was taken after six days, is the largest county jail in New Jersey. It admits more than 25,000 inmates each year and houses about 1,000 gang members at any given time. When petitioner was transferred there, all arriving detainees passed through a metal detector and waited in a group holding cell for a more thorough search. When they left the holding cell, they were instructed to remove their clothing while an officer looked for body markings, wounds, and contraband. Apparently without touching the detainees, an officer looked at their ears, nose, mouth, hair, scalp, fingers, hands, arms, armpits, and other body openings. This policy applied regardless of the circumstances of the arrest, the suspected offense, or the detainee's behavior, demeanor, or criminal history. Petitioner alleges he was required to lift his genitals, turn around, and cough in a squatting position as part of the process. After a mandatory shower, during which his clothes were inspected, petitioner was admitted to the facility. He was released the next day, when the charges against him were dismissed. . . .

II

. . . The Court's opinion in *Bell v. Wolfish*, 441 U.S. 520 (1979), is the starting point for understanding how this framework applies to Fourth Amendment challenges. That case addressed a rule requiring pretrial detainees in any correctional facility run by the Federal Bureau of Prisons "to expose their body cavities for visual inspection as a part of a strip search conducted after every contact visit with a person from outside the institution." Inmates at the federal Metropolitan Correctional Center in New York City argued there was no security justification for these searches. Officers searched guests before they entered the visiting room, and the inmates were under constant surveillance during the visit. There had been but one instance in which an inmate attempted to sneak contraband back into the facility. The Court nonetheless upheld the search policy. It deferred to the judgment of correctional officials that the inspections served not only to discover but also to deter the smuggling of weapons, drugs, and other prohibited items inside. The Court explained that there is no mechanical way to determine whether intrusions on an inmate's privacy are reasonable. The need for a particular search must be balanced against the resulting invasion of personal rights. . . .

These cases establish that correctional officials must be permitted to devise reasonable search policies to detect and deter the possession of contraband in their facilities. The task of determining whether a policy is reasonably related to legitimate security interests is "peculiarly within the province and professional expertise of corrections officials." This Court has repeated the admonition that, "in the absence of substantial evidence in the record to indicate that the officials have exaggerated their response to these considerations courts should ordinarily defer to their expert judgment in such matters." . . .

III

The question here is whether undoubted security imperatives involved in jail supervision override the assertion that some detainees must be exempt from the more invasive search procedures at issue absent reasonable suspicion of a concealed weapon or other contraband. The Court has held that deference must be given to the officials in charge of the jail unless there is "substantial evidence" demonstrating their response to the situation is exaggerated. Petitioner has not met this standard, and the record provides full justifications for the procedures used.

Correctional officials have a significant interest in conducting a thorough search as a standard part of the intake process. The admission of inmates creates numerous risks for facility staff, for the existing detainee population, and for a new detainee himself or herself. The danger of introducing lice or contagious infections, for example, is well documented. . . . Persons just arrested may have wounds or other injuries requiring immediate medical attention. It may be difficult to identify and treat these problems until detainees remove their clothes for a visual inspection.

Jails and prisons also face grave threats posed by the increasing number of gang members who go through the intake process. The groups recruit new members by force, engage in assaults against staff, and give other inmates a reason to arm themselves. Fights among feuding gangs can be deadly, and the officers who must maintain order are put in harm's way. These considerations provide a reasonable basis to justify a visual inspection for certain tattoos and other signs of gang affiliation as part of the intake process. The identification and isolation of gang members before they are admitted protects everyone in the facility.

Detecting contraband concealed by new detainees, furthermore, is a most serious responsibility. . . . It is not surprising that correctional officials have sought to perform thorough searches at intake for disease, gang affiliation, and contraband. Jails are often crowded, unsanitary, and dangerous places. There is a substantial interest in preventing any new inmate, either of his own will or as a result of coercion, from putting all who live or work at these institutions at even greater risk when he is admitted to the general population.

Petitioner acknowledges that correctional officials must be allowed to conduct an effective search during the intake process and that this will require at least some detainees to lift their genitals or cough in a squatting position. These procedures, similar to the ones upheld in *Bell*, are designed to uncover contraband that can go undetected by a patdown, metal detector, and other less invasive searches. Petitioner maintains there is little benefit to conducting these more invasive steps on a new detainee who has not been arrested for a serious crime or for any offense involving a weapon or drugs. In his view these detainees should be exempt from this process unless they give officers a particular reason to suspect them of hiding contraband. It is reasonable, however, for correctional officials to conclude this standard would be unworkable. The record provides evidence that the seriousness of an offense is a poor predictor of who has contraband and that it would be difficult in practice to determine whether individual detainees fall within the proposed exemption.

People detained for minor offenses can turn out to be the most devious and dangerous criminals. Hours after the Oklahoma City bombing, Timothy McVeigh was stopped by a state trooper who noticed he was driving without a license plate. One of the terrorists involved in the September 11 attacks was stopped and ticketed for speeding just two days before hijacking Flight 93. Reasonable correctional officials could conclude these uncertainties mean they must conduct the same thorough search of everyone who will be admitted to their facilities.

Experience shows that people arrested for minor offenses have tried to smuggle prohibited items into jail, sometimes by using their rectal cavities or genitals for the concealment. They may have some of the same incentives as a serious criminal to hide contraband. . . . Even if people arrested for a minor offense do not themselves wish to introduce contraband into a jail, they may be coerced into doing so by others. . . . Exempting people arrested for minor offenses from a standard search protocol thus may put them at greater risk and result in more contraband being brought into the detention facility. This is a substantial reason not to mandate the exception petitioner seeks as a matter of constitutional law. . . .

The laborious administration of prisons would become less effective, and likely less fair and evenhanded, were the practical problems inevitable from the rules suggested by petitioner to be imposed as a constitutional mandate. Even if they had accurate information about a detainee's current and prior arrests, officers, under petitioner's proposed regime, would encounter serious implementation difficulties. They would be required, in a few minutes, to determine whether any of the underlying offenses were serious enough to authorize the more invasive search protocol. . . .

Justice BREYER, with whom Justice GINSBURG, Justice SOTOMAYOR, and Justice KAGAN join, dissenting.

The petition for certiorari asks us to decide "[w]hether the Fourth Amendment permits a . . . suspicionless strip search of every individual arrested for any minor offense. . . ." This question is phrased more broadly than what is at issue. The case is limited to strip searches of those arrestees entering a jail's general population. And the kind of strip search in question involves more than undressing and taking a shower (even if guards monitor the shower area for threatened disorder). Rather, the searches here involve close observation of the private areas of a person's body and for that reason constitute a far more serious invasion of that person's privacy. . . .

In my view, such a search of an individual arrested for a minor offense that does not involve drugs or violence—say a traffic offense, a regulatory offense, an essentially civil matter, or any other such misdemeanor—is an "unreasonable searc[h]" forbidden by the Fourth Amendment, unless prison authorities have reasonable suspicion to believe that the individual possesses drugs or other contraband. And I dissent from the Court's contrary determination. . . .

II

A strip search that involves a stranger peering without consent at a naked individual, and in particular at the most private portions of that person's body, is a serious invasion of privacy. We have recently said, in respect to a schoolchild (and a less intrusive search), that the "meaning of such a search, and the degradation its subject may reasonably feel, place a search that intrusive in a category of its own demanding its own specific suspicions." *Safford Unified School Dist. # 1 v. Redding*, 557 U.S. 364 (2009). . . . Even when carried out in a respectful manner, and even absent any physical touching, such searches are inherently harmful, humiliating, and degrading. And the harm to privacy interests would seem particularly acute where the person searched may well have no expectation of being subject to such a search, say, because she had simply received a traffic ticket for failing to buckle a seatbelt, because he had not previously paid a civil fine, or because she had been arrested for a minor trespass. . . .

I doubt that we seriously disagree about the nature of the strip search or about the serious affront to human dignity and to individual privacy that it presents. The basic question before us is whether such a search is nonetheless justified when an individual arrested for a minor offense is involuntarily placed in the general jail or prison population.

III

. . . I have found no convincing reason indicating that, in the absence of reasonable suspicion, involuntary strip searches of those arrested for minor offenses are necessary in order to further the penal interests mentioned. And there are strong reasons to believe they are not justified.

The lack of justification is fairly obvious with respect to the first two penological interests advanced. The searches already employed at Essex and Burlington include: (a) pat-frisking all inmates; (b) making inmates go through metal detectors (including the Body Orifice Screening

System (BOSS) chair used at Essex County Correctional Facility that identifies metal hidden within the body); (c) making inmates shower and use particular delousing agents or bathing supplies; and (d) searching inmates' clothing. In addition, petitioner concedes that detainees could be lawfully subject to being viewed in their undergarments by jail officers or during showering (for security purposes). No one here has offered any reason, example, or empirical evidence suggesting the inadequacy of such practices for detecting injuries, diseases, or tattoos. In particular, there is no connection between the genital lift and the "squat and cough" that Florence was allegedly subjected to and health or gang concerns. . . .

In my view, it is highly questionable that officials would be justified, for instance, in admitting to the dangerous world of the general jail population and subjecting to a strip search someone with no criminal background arrested for jaywalking or another similarly minor crime. Indeed, that consideration likely underlies why the Federal Government and many States segregate such individuals even when admitted to jail, and several jurisdictions provide that such individuals be released without detention in the ordinary case. . . . For the reasons set forth, I cannot find justification for the strip search policy at issue here—a policy that would subject those arrested for minor offenses to serious invasions of their personal privacy. I consequently dissent.

NOTES & QUESTIONS ON JAIL AND PRISON SEARCHES

1. *Searches in the carceral state.* Justice Kennedy and the majority showed great deference to the judgment of prison and jail officials regarding when body cavity searches are appropriate. One consequence of this deference is that the prison or jail population becomes the object of intrusive state action. This requires some consideration of which individuals are most likely to be targeted for incarceration. Consider the following description of the petitioner in the *Florence* case:

> Albert Florence was a black man who owned, and drove, one of the ultimate status symbols of the day—the coveted BMW X5 sport utility vehicle. The car was stopped by a state trooper patrolling outside the boundaries of urban New Jersey, in suburban Burlington County. Florence's past experiences with "Driving While Black" made him wary enough of traffic stops by police to store in his car a copy of the court document certifying that the unsatisfied judgment (fine) upon which the bench warrant was issued had been satisfied. The state trooper who stopped Florence's vehicle ignored his documentation and protestations that the outstanding warrant for his arrest

PROBLEM CASE

Consider the following description of a search at a local jail:

> Plaintiff alleges that he was an inmate at the Milwaukee County Jail in February 2017. Just prior to being booked into the jail, Defendant Emanuele and Defendant Zetting allegedly instructed Plaintiff to change into jail clothing, which he did. After changing, Plaintiff states he was handcuffed and escorted to the shower area by Defendants. One defendant allegedly asked Plaintiff if he had anything illegal on or in his body, to which he responded no. Plaintiff inquired as to why he was being searched and if he could speak to a sergeant. A defendant allegedly told Plaintiff that he could speak to a sergeant after the search. According to Plaintiff, he was ordered to lower his pants and underwear to his knees and squat while one defendant donned latex gloves and used a flashlight to spread open Plaintiff's buttocks. Plaintiff again requested to speak to a sergeant, and was denied.

Harris v. Schmidt, 2018 WL 4386101, at *1-2 (E.D. Wis. Sept. 14, 2018). If the plaintiff is correct that the local jail does not have a policy of strip searching every incoming detainee in this manner, is the search constitutional or unconstitutional?

> was erroneous. The trooper used his discretion in the field to apprehend and arrest Florence. Once taken into custody, Florence was subjected to a strip search at the Burlington County Jail in violation of both New Jersey law and the jail's own policy against strip searching persons arrested for minor offenses in the absence of reasonable suspicion. This procedural irregularity caused Florence to be visually inspected by a jail official at close range while standing naked and being directed to open his mouth and lift his tongue, lift his arms, rotate, and lift his genitals. Florence was then made to shower in the officer's sight.

Teresa A. Miller, *Bright Lines, Black Bodies: The* Florence *Strip Search Case and Its Dire Repercussions*, 46 Akron L. Rev. 433, 462-63 (2013). Does this assessment change your view of the case? Was it legitimate for the state to subject Florence to an intrusive body cavity search?

I. PROBATION AND PAROLE

Convicts on probation and parole are subject to post-incarceration scrutiny that may, on occasion, include a search of the individual's residence. In the following case, probation officials conducted a warrantless search of the probationer's apartment that was supported by reasonable suspicion and found evidence of a crime. One of the factors that makes probation and parole distinct from other exceptions to the warrant requirement is that the state's entitlement to search the probationer's residence is often an explicit condition of probation.

As you read the following case, ask yourself whether the probationer could have refused to confer blanket permission on the state to conduct these searches. In the event of this refusal, would Knights have received probation in the first place? As you read the case, ask yourself what role if any the concept of consent played in the Court's analysis. How would the case turn out if consent to search was not an explicit condition of probation?

United States v. Knights

Supreme Court of the United States
534 U.S. 112 (2001)

Chief Justice REHNQUIST delivered the opinion of the Court.

A California court sentenced respondent Mark James Knights to summary probation for a drug offense. The probation order included the following condition: that Knights would "[s]ubmit his . . . person, property, place of residence, vehicle, personal effects, to search at anytime, with or without a search warrant, warrant of arrest or reasonable cause by any probation officer or law enforcement officer." Knights signed the probation order, which stated immediately above his signature that "I HAVE RECEIVED A COPY, READ AND UNDERSTAND THE ABOVE TERMS AND CONDITIONS OF PROBATION AND AGREE TO ABIDE BY SAME." In this case, we decide whether a search pursuant to this probation condition, and supported by reasonable suspicion, satisfied the Fourth Amendment.

Three days after Knights was placed on probation, a Pacific Gas & Electric (PG&E) power transformer and adjacent Pacific Bell telecommunications vault near the Napa County Airport were pried open and set on fire, causing an estimated $1.5 million in damage. Brass padlocks had been removed and a gasoline accelerant had been used to ignite the fire. This incident was the latest in more than 30 recent acts of vandalism against PG&E facilities in Napa County. Suspicion for these acts had long focused on Knights and his friend, Steven Simoneau. The incidents began after PG&E had filed a theft-of-services complaint against Knights and discontinued his electrical service for failure to pay his bill. Detective Todd Hancock of the Napa County Sheriff's Department had noticed that the acts of vandalism coincided with Knights' court appearance dates concerning the theft of PG&E services. And just a week before the arson, a sheriff's deputy had stopped Knights and Simoneau near a PG&E gas line and observed pipes and gasoline in Simoneau's pickup truck.

After the PG&E arson, a sheriff's deputy drove by Knights' residence, where he saw Simoneau's truck parked in front. The deputy felt the hood of the truck. It was warm. Detective Hancock decided to set up surveillance of Knights' apartment. At about 3:10 the next morning, Simoneau exited the apartment carrying three cylindrical items. Detective Hancock believed the items were pipe bombs. Simoneau walked across the street to the bank of the Napa River, and Hancock heard three splashes. Simoneau returned without the cylinders and drove away in his truck. Simoneau then stopped in a driveway, parked, and left the area. Detective Hancock entered the driveway and observed a number of suspicious objects in the truck: a Molotov cocktail and explosive materials, a gasoline can, and two brass padlocks that fit the description of those removed from the PG&E transformer vault.

After viewing the objects in Simoneau's truck, Detective Hancock decided to conduct a search of Knights' apartment. Detective Hancock was aware of the search condition in Knights' probation order and thus believed that a warrant was not necessary. The search revealed a detonation cord, ammunition, liquid chemicals, instruction manuals on chemistry and electrical circuitry, bolt cutters, telephone pole-climbing spurs, drug paraphernalia, and a brass padlock stamped "PG&E."

Knights was arrested, and a federal grand jury subsequently indicted him for conspiracy to commit arson, for possession of an unregistered destructive device, and for being a felon in possession of ammunition. . . .

Certainly nothing in the condition of probation suggests that it was confined to searches bearing upon probationary status and nothing more. The search condition provides that Knights will submit to a search "by any probation officer or law enforcement officer" and does not mention anything about purpose. The question then is whether the Fourth Amendment limits searches pursuant to this probation condition to those with a "probationary" purpose.

Knights argues that this limitation follows from our decision in *Griffin v. Wisconsin*, 483 U.S. 868 (1987). In *Griffin*, we upheld a search of a probationer conducted pursuant to a Wisconsin regulation permitting "any probation officer to search a probationer's home without a warrant as long as his supervisor approves and as long as there are 'reasonable grounds' to believe the presence of contraband." The Wisconsin regulation that authorized the search was not an express condition of Griffin's probation; in fact, the regulation was not even promulgated at the time of Griffin's sentence. The regulation applied to all Wisconsin probationers, with no need for a judge to make an individualized determination that the probationer's conviction justified the need for warrantless searches. We held that a State's operation of its probation system presented a "special need" for the "exercise of supervision to assure that [probation] restrictions are in fact observed." That special need for supervision justified the Wisconsin regulation and the search pursuant to the regulation was thus reasonable.

In Knights' view, apparently shared by the Court of Appeals, a warrantless search of a probationer satisfies the Fourth Amendment only if it is just like the search at issue in *Griffin*—i.e., a "special needs" search conducted by a probation officer monitoring whether the probationer is complying with probation restrictions. This dubious logic—that an opinion upholding the constitutionality of a particular search implicitly holds unconstitutional any search that is not like it—runs contrary to *Griffin*'s express statement that its "special needs" holding made it "unnecessary to consider whether" warrantless searches of probationers were otherwise reasonable within the meaning of the Fourth Amendment.

We now consider that question in assessing the constitutionality of the search of Knights' apartment. . . . The touchstone of the Fourth Amendment is reasonableness, and the reasonableness of a search is determined "by assessing, on the one hand, the degree to which it intrudes upon an individual's privacy and, on the other, the degree to which it is needed for the promotion of legitimate governmental interests. Knights' status as a probationer subject to a search condition informs both sides of that balance. . . . Inherent in the very nature of probation is that probationers "do not enjoy the absolute liberty to which every citizen is entitled." Just as other punishments for criminal convictions curtail an offender's freedoms, a court granting probation may impose reasonable conditions that deprive the offender of some freedoms enjoyed by law-abiding citizens.

The judge who sentenced Knights to probation determined that it was necessary to condition the probation on Knights' acceptance of the search provision. It was reasonable to conclude that the search condition would further the two primary goals of probation—rehabilitation and protecting society from future criminal violations. The probation order clearly expressed the search condition and Knights was unambiguously informed of it. The probation condition thus significantly diminished Knights' reasonable expectation of privacy.

In assessing the governmental interest side of the balance, it must be remembered that "the very assumption of the institution of probation" is that the probationer "is more likely than the ordinary citizen to violate the law." *Griffin*, 483 U.S., at 880. The recidivism rate of probationers is significantly higher than the general crime rate. And probationers have even more of an incentive to conceal their criminal activities and quickly dispose of incriminating evidence than the ordinary criminal because probationers are aware that they may be subject to supervision and face revocation of probation, and possible incarceration, in proceedings in which the trial rights of a jury and proof beyond a reasonable doubt, among other things, do not apply.

The State has a dual concern with a probationer. On the one hand is the hope that he will successfully complete probation and be integrated back into the community. On the other is the concern, quite justified, that he will be more likely to engage in criminal conduct than an ordinary member of the community. The view of the Court of Appeals in this case would require the State to shut its eyes to the latter concern and concentrate only on the former. But we hold that the Fourth Amendment does not put the State to such a choice. Its interest in apprehending violators of the criminal law, thereby protecting potential victims of criminal enterprise, may therefore justifiably focus on probationers in a way that it does not on the ordinary citizen.

We hold that the balance of these considerations requires no more than reasonable suspicion to conduct a search of this probationer's house. The degree of individualized suspicion required of a search is a determination of when there is a sufficiently high probability that criminal conduct is occurring to make the intrusion on the individual's privacy interest reasonable. Although the Fourth Amendment ordinarily requires the degree of probability embodied in the term "probable cause," a lesser degree satisfies the Constitution when the balance of governmental and private interests makes such a standard reasonable. Those interests warrant a lesser than probable-cause standard here. When an officer has reasonable suspicion that a probationer subject to a search condition is engaged in criminal activity, there is enough likelihood that criminal conduct is occurring that an intrusion on the probationer's significantly diminished privacy interests is reasonable. . . .

NOTES & QUESTIONS ON PROBATION AND PAROLE

1. *Probation and DNA.* What if the search or seizure of the individual on probation or parole requires the production of a DNA sample? For example, consider the following federal statute: "The probation officer responsible for the supervision under Federal law of an individual on probation, parole, or supervised release shall collect a DNA sample from each such individual who is, or has been, convicted of a qualifying Federal offense (as determined under subsection (d)) or a qualifying military offense. . . ." 34 U.S.C. § 40702. Parallel statutes exist under state law. These DNA searches are far more intrusive than the searches conducted in *Knights* and are, by definition, suspicionless. The Supreme Court in *Knights* applied a totality-of-the-circumstances balancing test that weighs the state's need to conduct the warrantless search with the probationer's privacy interest. In *United States v. Kincade*, 379 F.3d 813 (9th Cir. 2004), the Ninth Circuit applied the same balancing

test in upholding the collection of DNA from an individual on conditional release from federal custody. In dissent, Judge Reinhardt made the following dire prediction:

> Were we to apply the totality of the circumstances analysis, I would hold that the balance of considerations makes the programmatic suspicionless searches unconstitutionally unreasonable. The invasions of privacy the Act authorizes are substantial; the probationers and parolees subjected to its provisions maintain reasonable expectations of privacy; and the government's interest, while significant, is no stronger than its ordinary interest in investigating and prosecuting crimes. On balance, the government's desire to create a comprehensive DNA databank must give way when weighed against the privacy interests at issue and the extent of the intrusion involved.
>
> When democratic values are lost, society often looks back, too late, and says when did this happen—why didn't we understand before it was too late? Today's decision marks one of those turning points—a fatally unwise and unconstitutional surrender to the government of our liberty for the sake of security, and, should the plurality's theory ever become law, the establishment of a doctrine that would leave us without the legal tools to halt further abolition of our privacy rights. The compulsory extraction of blood samples and the maintenance of permanent DNA profiles of American citizens is, unfortunately, the beginning not the end. 1984 arrives twenty years later than predicted.

Id. at 869-70. Do you agree with Reinhardt's invocation of George Orwell's dystopian classic *1984*?

J. PRACTICE & POLICY

Every day, more than a million individuals fly on a commercial airplane in the United States. Each one of them is subjected to an intrusive inspection of their body and baggage. If the individual has departed from a United States airport, the inspection is conducted by the Transportation Security Administration (TSA). If the individual departs from a foreign location, the inspections are performed by a foreign security service, or its contractors, which conform with TSA guidelines if the flight will land in the United States. These screenings are not covered by the border exception, since the TSA screens all airport travelers, including those traveling domestically. Therefore, the constitutional significance of the border plays no role in legitimizing the TSA screening process.

A traveler removes his shoes for screening at LaGuardia Airport in New York. (Bebeto Matthews/AP/Shutterstock)

Screening technologies at the airport. In the 1960s and 1970s, airports and airlines introduced the first wave of intensive security screenings at airports. This rudimentary screening (when viewed with hindsight and compared with today's technologically advanced screening) generated a wave of litigation over the procedures. In these cases, courts upheld special airport screening due to the heightened danger of terrorism or "skyjacking" that might kill other passengers. The fear of terrorism was very much a national concern, leading courts to conclude that security measures were justified by the special nature of air flight and the threat to national security posed by hijacking:

> The airport search is a direct reaction to the wave of airplane hijackings which began in 1968, at which time popular feelings of fear and anger, and ultimately rage, called out for some program to safeguard air flights, and understandably so. Airplane hijacking is a particularly frightening

> crime. Many hijackers have been psychotic or political fanatics, for whom death holds no fear and little consequence, willing to bargain with the lives of defenseless passengers for money, transportation to a safe haven, the release of "political" prisoners, or some other otherwise unattainable demand. Congress's penalty for hijacking reflects the public mood: death, if the jury so recommends. The present antihijacking system did not spring full blown into life. "Profiles" and selective investigation came first; plainclothes sky marshals became regular forward seat passengers; anathema as it was to some to do so, diplomatic overtures were made to Cuba to eliminate it as a refuge for hijackers. Finally, technology with magnetometers, metal detection devices and X-rays was brought to bear. Today, the general methodology of the airport search has become more or less routine.

United States v. Albarado, 495 F.2d 799, 803 (2d Cir. 1974). Courts invariably upheld against legal challenges both searches and seizures that occurred during the screening process. For more discussion, see Alexander A. Reinert, *Revisiting "Special Needs" Theory Via Airport Searches*, 106 Nw. U. L. Rev. 1513 (2012).

Consent or special needs. Courts disagreed over the conceptual ground for the basis of the warrantless and suspicionless searches and seizures that passengers were subjected to when they went through airport screening. Several courts concluded that the searches were inherently reasonable because they were based on consent. This view relied on the consent exception to the warrant requirement as outlined in *Schneckloth v. Bustamonte*, 412 U.S. 218, 222 (1973), discussed earlier in this chapter. Ticketed passengers seeking to board flights were voluntarily presenting themselves at security and agreeing to an inspection of their personal effects and baggage prior to admission to the secure area of the terminal and boarding on their flight. See, e.g., *United States v. Miner*, 484 F.2d 1075, 1076 (9th Cir. 1973) ("approaching the counter with the obvious intention of boarding a plane amounted to an implied 'consent'"); *United States v. Henry*, 615 F.2d 1223, 1229 (9th Cir. 1980) (defendant was "free to take the briefcase and leave the airport altogether or to board without taking or checking the briefcase, rather than submit it to the x-ray scan"); *United States v. Pulido-Baquerizo*, 800 F.2d 899, 901 (9th Cir. 1986) ("passengers placing luggage on an x-ray machine's conveyor belt for airplane travel at a secured boarding area impliedly consent to a visual inspection and limited hand search of their luggage if the x-ray scan is inconclusive in determining whether the luggage contains weapons or other dangerous objects").

The problem with this theory is that it failed to accord with the facts on the ground. If airport searches are inherently reasonable because they are based on the notion of consent, then passengers should be able to *withdraw* their consent and leave the screening area if they no longer wish to board an aircraft. This might happen if an individual seeks to board an airplane with illegal drugs on his body or in his bags. If the individual is selected for more intrusive secondary screening, the "consent" theory would suggest that the would-be passenger could declare that he was changing his mind—cancelling his vacation, for example—and going home. In practice, though, passengers are not given this option at screening. If screening agents discover something suspicious, they do not allow the individual the freedom to leave the screening area and return to the public side of the terminal. (The reason for this is simple: A terrorist might simply turn around and attack another target.) This uncomfortable reality caused a few courts to fashion the concept of "irrevocable implied consent," which once triggered by the passenger by presentment at the screening area was not reversible. *United States v. Doe*, 61 F.3d 107, 112 (1st Cir. 1995) (discussing but not applying the theory).

Over time, however, most courts have dropped the notion of implied consent and viewed airport screening as an "administrative search" justified by the special needs of air travel, and therefore covered by the special needs exception to the warrant requirement. *United States v. Aukai*, 497 F.3d 955, 962 (9th Cir. 2007) ("To the extent our cases have predicated the reasonableness of an airport screening search upon either ongoing consent or irrevocable implied consent, they are overruled."). Indeed, there is no question that air travel is a "closely regulated industry" with special administrative requirements.

But the notion of the screening as a special needs administrative search is only enough to satisfy the search aspect of the screening; the "seizure" aspect of the screening—the temporary detention of the passenger and his or her inability to leave the area during the search—is clearly a seizure. The only possible solution for justifying this seizure is to view it as a special kind of *Terry* stop—a specialized stop-and-frisk situation—which will be covered in greater detail in the next chapter of this casebook. See, e.g., *United States v. $90,000*, 2009 WL 6327469, at *13 (D. Minn. Sept. 23, 2009) ("the government's agents exceeded the scope of a reasonable *Terry* stop"); *United States v. Bell*, 464 F.2d 667, 672 (2d Cir. 1972) ("pat down did constitute a 'stop and frisk' but, in our view, did not offend any fourth amendment rights of the defendant in this case"). The other possibility is to craft a new exception to the warrant requirement just for airports. See Steven R. Minert, *Square Pegs, Round Hole: The Fourth Amendment and Preflight Searches of Airline Passengers in a Post-9/11 World*, 2006 BYU L. Rev. 1631, 1661 ("Consequently, the Supreme Court should grant certiorari to a preflight passenger search case and create a sui generis exception to the Warrant Clause in the Fourth Amendment, based upon the longstanding need to create greater rationality and unity in this area of Fourth Amendment jurisprudence.").

There is, however, a limit to what types of screening can be conducted consistent with the appropriate constitutional standard. The airport context does not automatically give the government carte blanche to throw the Fourth Amendment out the window. The searches must be reasonably related to finding explosives and weapons and materials that would subject other passengers and crew (or their property) to danger. Furthermore, the seizure should only last as long as necessary to assess the possible security threat posed by the passenger. See, e.g., *George v. Rehiel*, 738 F.3d 562, 579 (3d Cir. 2013) (federal agents' questioning of passenger for 30 minutes to determine if he was a security threat did not violate Fourth Amendment).

❧ **Post-9/11 screening enhancements.** After 9/11, the federal government overhauled airport security. The Transportation Security Administration (TSA) was created as part of the new Department of Homeland Security. The TSA also introduced more demanding screening protocols, which involved more invasive searches and lengthier seizures. This included the introduction of advanced imaging technology (AIT), which is far more accurate, but also far more invasive, than traditional metal detectors that were once the norm at airports. The new protocols generated significant pushback from both travelers and civil libertarians, who complained that some of the procedures were unreasonable. In addition to being concerned about invasive body scans performed by the AIT, some groups are also concerned about the process by which the government collects data on individual travelers to create a "profile" on each traveler to assess risk. See, e.g., Susan Stellin, *Airport Screening Concerns Civil Liberties Groups*, N.Y. Times, Mar. 11, 2013 ("As the focus turns more to identifying suspect travelers, not just suspect items, the government is also looking at data that airlines and travel agents have collected on their customers, ranging from birth dates and passport numbers to potentially confidential details apparent in travel itineraries (like a flight to Pakistan) and group discount codes (for a trip to a conference, for instance)."). The government tweaked which images were displayed on the scanners for the agents to view. By and large, federal courts have upheld the procedures as consistent with the Fourth Amendment. See, e.g., *Electronic Privacy Information Center v. U.S. Dep't of Homeland Security*, 653 F.3d 1, 10 (D.C. Cir. 2011):

> That balance clearly favors the Government here. The need to search airline passengers "to ensure public safety can be particularly acute," and, crucially, an AIT scanner, unlike a magnetometer, is capable of detecting, and therefore of deterring, attempts to carry aboard airplanes

> explosives in liquid or powder form. On the other side of the balance, we must acknowledge the steps the TSA has already taken to protect passenger privacy, in particular distorting the image created using AIT and deleting it as soon as the passenger has been cleared. More telling, any passenger may opt-out of AIT screening in favor of a patdown, which allows him to decide which of the two options for detecting a concealed, nonmetallic weapon or explosive is least invasive.

Does this assuage your concerns about privacy? The government interest is so strong in this context that it suggests that courts are inclined to give wide latitude to the TSA. By statute, the Department of Homeland Security must hire a senior privacy official who is tasked with "assuring that the use of technologies sustain, and do not erode, privacy protections relating to the use, collection, and disclosure of personal information." 6 U.S.C. § 142. Are there other mechanisms that the TSA or the Department of Homeland Security could use to limit the invasion of privacy caused by airport screening protocols?

CHAPTER 5

Seizing Persons

INTRODUCTION

Prior chapters focused on searches and seizures of evidence—as well as the warrants that are typically required for them. This chapter pivots to the seizure of *persons*, which implicates unique constitutional concerns given the intrusion on liberty that these seizures involve. While it is true that a person's home is their castle—and the law recognizes this special relationship—it is equally true, perhaps more so, that a person's body represents their own dominion and is, or ought to be, free from unwarranted governmental intrusion. For these and other reasons, the Fourth Amendment's promise that the people should be free from unreasonable searches and seizures has been taken to impose special doctrinal protections where the seizure of *persons* is concerned.

Indeed, legal restrictions on the power of the crown to "seize" its subjects date back at least as far as the Magna Carta, which included a provision that stated: "No free man shall be seized or imprisoned, or stripped of his rights or possessions, or outlawed, or deprived of his standing in any way, nor will we proceed with force against him, or send others to do so, except by the lawful judgment of his equals or by the law of the land." This provision combines a proto-due-process protection with a prohibition against unlawful seizures. Without going into a history lesson, it is clear that restrictions against governmental conduct against its own subjects have an ancient lineage and that the Fourth Amendment, and the doctrines articulated by the Supreme Court to bring it to practical life, are just the latest manifestations of this legal phenomenon.

As will be outlined below, the word "seizure" is a broad term, encompassing not just arrests but also lesser deprivations of physical liberty that are nonetheless significant enough to fall under the constitutional rubric of "seizures" and the protection of the Fourth Amendment. Consequently, Section A focuses on the general standard that the Supreme Court has articulated for what constitutes a "seizure" in the constitutional sense; Section B focuses on the constitutional requirements for arrests, in particular when warrantless arrests are permissible and whether the police can arrest someone for a minor infraction that does not carry the possibility of a jail sentence. Finally, Section C focuses on the "seizures" that have arguably generated the most controversy and litigation—the police procedure of stopping and frisking suspicious individuals. What unites the materials together is the judiciary's attempt to outline the outer scope of the government's legitimate authority to subject individuals to seizures during the investigatory process.

A. DEFINING PERSONAL SEIZURE

Individuals have many interactions with the police—some of them constitute seizures while others certainly do not. Consider these interactions on a spectrum from most confining to least confining. If the police handcuff a suspect, place them in a squad car and read them *Miranda* rights before hauling them off to the precinct for booking, this clearly constitutes a seizure as that term is used in the Fourth Amendment. On the other hand, if the police encounter someone on a public street and ask them for assistance, this innocent encounter may not be a seizure. In between these two extremes, there are countless daily transactions between police and residents, each one unique in its details. At what point do these encounters cross the line into a "seizure"?

In the following case, the Supreme Court articulated a standard to answer this question: whether "in view of all of the circumstances surrounding the incident, a reasonable person would have believed that he was not free to leave." This standard is easy to state but can be tricky to apply to particular facts. First of all, the standard calls for a counterfactual inquiry: What were to happen if the individual got up and started to leave or otherwise ignore the police requests? This is hard to know since it likely didn't happen. The individual did not leave but the standard invites us to imagine the result if he or she did. This question can be especially difficult to answer when the inquiry involves not just the question of leaving a precinct but the more subtle situation of refusing a police request that occurs outside the police station. As the Supreme Court states below, "a person is 'seized' only when, by means of physical force or *a show of authority*, his freedom of movement is restrained." As you read the following case, ask yourself whether Mendenhall was "seized" by the police by virtue of a show of authority.

United States v. Mendenhall

Supreme Court of the United States
446 U.S. 544 (1980)

Mr. Justice STEWART announced the judgment of the Court and delivered an opinion, in which Mr. Justice REHNQUIST joined.

The respondent was brought to trial in the United States District Court for the Eastern District of Michigan on a charge of possessing heroin with intent to distribute it. She moved to suppress the introduction at trial of the heroin as evidence against her on the ground that it had been acquired from her through an unconstitutional search and seizure by agents of the Drug Enforcement Administration (DEA). The District Court denied the respondent's motion, and she was convicted after a trial upon stipulated facts. . . .

I

At the hearing in the trial court on the respondent's motion to suppress, it was established how the heroin she was charged with possessing had been obtained from her. The respondent arrived at the Detroit Metropolitan Airport on a commercial airline flight from Los Angeles early in the morning on February 10, 1976. As she disembarked from the airplane, she was observed by two agents of the DEA, who were present at the airport for the purpose of detecting unlawful traffic in narcotics. After observing the respondent's conduct, which appeared to the agents to be characteristic of persons unlawfully carrying narcotics, the agents approached her as she was walking through the concourse, identified themselves as federal agents, and asked to see her identification and airline ticket. The respondent produced her driver's license, which was in the name of Sylvia Mendenhall, and, in answer to a question of one of the agents, stated that she resided at the address appearing on the license. The airline ticket was issued in the name of "Annette Ford." When asked why the ticket bore a name different from her own, the respondent stated that she "just felt like using that name." In response to a further question, the respondent indicated that she had been in California only two days. Agent Anderson then specifically identified himself as a federal narcotics agent and, according to his testimony, the respondent "became quite shaken, extremely nervous. She had a hard time speaking."

After returning the airline ticket and driver's license to her, Agent Anderson asked the respondent if she would accompany him to the airport DEA office for further questions. She did so, although the record does not indicate a verbal response to the request. The office, which was located up one flight of stairs about 50 feet from where the respondent had first been approached, consisted of a reception area adjoined by three other rooms.

At the office the agent asked the respondent if she would allow a search of her person and handbag and told her that she had the right to decline the search if she desired. She responded: "Go ahead." She then handed Agent Anderson her purse, which contained a receipt for an airline ticket that had been issued to "F. Bush" three days earlier for a flight from Pittsburgh through Chicago to Los Angeles. The agent asked whether this was the ticket that she had used for her flight to California, and the respondent stated that it was.

A female police officer then arrived to conduct the search of the respondent's person. She asked the agents if the respondent had consented to be searched. The agents said that she had, and the respondent followed the policewoman into a private room. There the policewoman again asked the respondent if she consented to the search, and the respondent replied that she did. The policewoman explained that the search would require that the respondent remove her clothing. The respondent stated that she had a plane to catch and was assured by the policewoman that if she were carrying no narcotics, there would be no problem. The respondent then began to disrobe without further comment. As the respondent removed her clothing, she took from her undergarments two small packages, one of which appeared to contain heroin, and handed both to the policewoman. The agents then arrested the respondent for possessing heroin.

II

. . . There is no question in this case that the respondent possessed this constitutional right of personal security as she walked through the Detroit Airport, for "the Fourth Amendment protects people, not places." Here the Government concedes that its agents had neither a warrant nor probable cause to believe that the respondent was carrying narcotics when the agents conducted a search of the respondent's person. It is the Government's position, however, that the search was conducted pursuant to the respondent's consent, and thus was excepted from the requirements of both a warrant and probable cause. Evidently, the Court of Appeals concluded that the respondent's apparent consent to the search was in fact not voluntarily given and was in any event the product of earlier official conduct violative of the Fourth Amendment. . . .

The Fourth Amendment's requirement that searches and seizures be founded upon an objective justification, governs all seizures of the person, "including seizures that involve only a brief detention short of traditional arrest." Accordingly, if the respondent was "seized" when the DEA agents approached her on the concourse and asked questions of her, the agents' conduct in doing so was constitutional only if they reasonably suspected the respondent of wrongdoing. But "[o]bviously, not all personal intercourse between policemen and citizens involves 'seizures' of persons. Only when the officer, by means of physical force or show of authority, has in some way restrained the liberty of a citizen may we conclude that a 'seizure' has occurred." . . .

We adhere to the view that a person is "seized" only when, by means of physical force or a show of authority, his freedom of movement is restrained. Only when such restraint is imposed is there any foundation whatever for invoking constitutional safeguards. The purpose of the Fourth Amendment is not to eliminate all contact between the police and the citizenry, but "to prevent arbitrary and oppressive interference by enforcement officials with the privacy and personal security of individuals." As long as the person to whom questions are put remains free to disregard the questions and walk away, there has been no intrusion upon that person's liberty or privacy as would under the Constitution require some particularized and objective justification.

Moreover, characterizing every street encounter between a citizen and the police as a "seizure," while not enhancing any interest secured by the Fourth Amendment, would impose wholly unrealistic restrictions upon a wide variety of legitimate law enforcement practices. The Court has on other occasions referred to the acknowledged need for police questioning as a tool in the effective enforcement of the criminal laws. "Without such investigation, those who were innocent might be falsely accused, those who were guilty might wholly escape prosecution, and many crimes would go unsolved. In short, the security of all would be diminished."

We conclude that a person has been "seized" within the meaning of the Fourth Amendment only if, in view of all of the circumstances surrounding the incident, a reasonable person would have believed that he was not free to leave. Examples of circumstances that might indicate a seizure, even where the person did not attempt to leave, would be the threatening presence of several officers, the display of a weapon by an officer, some physical touching of the person of the citizen, or the use of language or tone of voice indicating that compliance with the officer's request might be compelled. In the absence of some such evidence, otherwise inoffensive contact between a member of the public and the police cannot, as a matter of law, amount to a seizure of that person.

On the facts of this case, no "seizure" of the respondent occurred. The events took place in the public concourse. The agents wore no uniforms and displayed no weapons. They did not summon the respondent to their presence, but instead approached her and identified themselves as federal agents. They requested, but did not demand to see the respondent's identification and ticket. Such conduct without more, did not amount to an intrusion upon any constitutionally protected interest. The respondent was not seized simply by reason of the fact that the agents approached her, asked her if she would show them her ticket and identification, and posed to her a few questions. Nor was it enough to establish a seizure that the person asking the questions was a law enforcement official. In short, nothing in the record suggests that the respondent had any objective reason to believe that she was not free to end the conversation in the concourse and proceed on her way, and for that reason we conclude that the agents' initial approach to her was not a seizure.

Our conclusion that no seizure occurred is not affected by the fact that the respondent was not expressly told by the agents that she was free to decline to cooperate with their inquiry, for the voluntariness of her responses does not depend upon her having been so informed. We also reject the argument that the only inference to be drawn from the fact that the respondent acted in a manner so contrary to her self-interest is that she was compelled to answer the agents' questions. It may happen that a person makes statements to law enforcement officials that he later regrets, but the issue in such cases is not whether the statement was self-protective, but rather whether it was made voluntarily. . . .

Although we have concluded that the initial encounter between the DEA agents and the respondent on the concourse at the Detroit Airport did not constitute an unlawful seizure, it is still arguable that the respondent's Fourth Amendment protections were violated when she went from the concourse to the DEA office. Such a violation might in turn infect the subsequent search of the respondent's person.

The District Court specifically found that the respondent accompanied the agents to the office "voluntarily in a spirit of apparent cooperation." Notwithstanding this determination by the trial court, the Court of Appeals evidently concluded that the agents' request that the respondent accompany them converted the situation into an arrest requiring probable cause in order to be found lawful. But because the trial court's finding was sustained by the record, the Court of Appeals was mistaken in substituting for that finding its view of the evidence.

The question whether the respondent's consent to accompany the agents was in fact voluntary or was the product of duress or coercion, express or implied, is to be determined by the totality of all the circumstances and is a matter which the Government has the burden of proving. The respondent herself did not testify at the hearing. The Government's evidence showed that the respondent was not told that she had to go to the office, but was simply asked if she would accompany the officers. There were neither threats nor any show of force. The respondent had been questioned only briefly, and her ticket and identification were returned to her before she was asked to accompany the officers. . . .

Mr. Justice WHITE, with whom Mr. Justice BRENNAN, Mr. Justice MARSHALL, and Mr. Justice STEVENS join, dissenting.

. . . Throughout the lower court proceedings in this case, the Government never questioned that the initial stop of Ms. Mendenhall was a "seizure" that required reasonable suspicion. Rather, the Government sought to justify the stop by arguing that Ms. Mendenhall's behavior had given rise to reasonable suspicion because it was consistent with portions of the so-called "drug courier profile," an informal amalgam of characteristics thought to be associated with persons carrying illegal drugs. Having failed to convince the Court of Appeals that the DEA agents had reasonable suspicion for the stop, the Government seeks reversal here by arguing for the first time that no "seizure" occurred, an argument that Mr. Justice Stewart now accepts, thereby pretermitting the question whether there was reasonable suspicion to stop Ms. Mendenhall. Mr. Justice Stewart's opinion not only is inconsistent with our usual refusal to reverse judgments on grounds not raised below, but it also addresses a fact-bound question with a totality-of-circumstances assessment that is best left in the first instance to the trial court, particularly since the question was not litigated below and hence we cannot be sure is adequately addressed by the record before us.

Mr. Justice Stewart believes that a "seizure" within the meaning of the Fourth Amendment occurs when an individual's freedom of movement is restrained by means of physical force or a show of authority. Although it is undisputed that Ms. Mendenhall was not free to leave after the DEA agents stopped her and inspected her identification, Mr. Justice Stewart concludes that she was not "seized" because he finds that, under the totality of the circumstances, a reasonable person would have believed that she was free to leave. While basing this finding on an alleged absence from the record of objective evidence indicating that Ms. Mendenhall was not free to ignore the officer's inquiries and continue on her way, Mr. Justice Stewart's opinion brushes off the fact that this asserted evidentiary deficiency may be largely attributable to the fact that the "seizure" question was never raised below. In assessing what the record does reveal, the opinion discounts certain objective factors that would tend to support a "seizure" finding, while relying on contrary factors inconclusive even under its own illustrations of how a "seizure" may be established. Moreover, although Mr. Justice Stewart's opinion purports to make its "seizure" finding turn on objective factors known to the person accosted, in distinguishing prior decisions holding that investigatory stops constitute "seizures," it does not rely on differences in the extent to which persons accosted could reasonably believe that they were free to leave. Even if one believes the Government should be permitted to raise the "seizure" question in this Court, the proper course would be to direct a remand to the District Court for an evidentiary hearing on the question, rather than to decide it in the first instance in this Court. . . .

Whatever doubt there may be concerning whether Ms. Mendenhall's Fourth Amendment interests were implicated during the initial stages of her confrontation with the DEA agents, she undoubtedly was "seized" within the meaning of the Fourth Amendment when the agents escorted her from the public area of the terminal to the DEA office for questioning and a strip-search of her person. In *Dunaway v. New York*, 442 U.S. 200 (1979), we held that a person who accompanied police officers to a police station for purposes of interrogation undoubtedly "was 'seized' in the Fourth Amendment sense," even though "he was not told he was under arrest." We found it significant that the suspect was taken to a police station, "was never informed that he was 'free to go,'" and "would have been physically restrained if he had refused to accompany the officers or had tried to escape their custody." Like the "seizure" in *Dunaway*, the nature of the intrusion to which Ms. Mendenhall was subjected when she was escorted by DEA agents to their office and detained there for questioning and a strip-search was so great that it "was in important respects indistinguishable from a traditional arrest." Although Ms. Mendenhall was not told that she was under arrest, she in fact was not free to refuse to go to the DEA office and was not told that she was. Furthermore, once inside the office, Ms. Mendenhall would not have been permitted to leave without submitting to a strip-search. Because the intrusion to which Ms. Mendenhall was subjected when she was escorted to the DEA office is of the same character as that involved in *Dunaway*, probable cause, which concededly was absent, was required to support the intrusion. . . .

NOTES & QUESTIONS ON THE DEFINITION OF SEIZURE

1. *The reasonable person standard.* According to Justice Stewart, the standard for seizure requires asking whether an individual's freedom of movement is restrained by physical force or a show of authority by the police. In applying this standard, should courts view the situation from the perspective of the individual or the perspective of the police officer? In reality, the answer is: neither. The situation is analyzed from the objective perspective of the reasonable person. Consequently, it is possible that a particular individual might have sincerely believed that their freedom was restricted, but a court might conclude that no seizure existed because a reasonable person in the situation would not have come to the same conclusion. Regardless, the subjective intent of the officer is not determinative in the analysis. Even if a police officer testifies that he did not intend to restrict the individual's freedom of movement, a court could still find that seizure took place. The "reasonable person" standard, first articulated by Justice Stewart in *Mendenhall*, was later endorsed by the full Supreme Court in

Florida v. Royer, 460 U.S. 491, 502 (1983). Consider the following assessment of the reasonable person standard:

> Application of the test has created a broad "nonseizure" category of police-citizen encounters that permits officers substantial leeway in approaching and questioning citizens without being required to show objective justification for such conduct. This has been accomplished both by constructing a highly artificial "reasonable person," who is much more assertive in encounters with police officers than is the average citizen, and by ignoring the subjective intentions of the officer. The result is that fourth amendment rights of citizens are determined through a legal fiction. In many encounters with citizens, police conduct is not scrutinized under the fourth amendment because in the courts' view a reasonable person would feel free to end the encounter and walk away. However, given the reality that citizens virtually never feel free to walk away from an encounter initiated by a police officer, most of the citizens in these "nonseizure" encounters do not feel free to walk away. Moreover, in a significant number of these "nonseizure" cases, the police officers involved testified that the citizen in fact was not free to leave. The result is that citizens who do not feel free to end encounters with police and who, in fact, would not be permitted to do so, are left outside the scope of fourth amendment protections because the reasonable person constructed by the courts would have felt free to leave.

Edwin J. Butterfoss, *Bright Line Seizures: The Need for Clarity in Determining When Fourth Amendment Activity Begins*, 79 J. Crim. L. & Criminology 437, 439-40 (1988). Do you agree that the hypothetical "reasonable person" imagined by the judiciary is more assertive than the typical citizen?

2. *What constitutes a "show of authority"?* Consider the following fact pattern and ask yourself whether it constituted a seizure:

> Late one evening in April 1988, Officers Brian McColgin and Jerry Pertoso were on patrol in a high-crime area of Oakland, California. They were dressed in street clothes but wearing jackets with "Police" embossed on both front and back. Their unmarked car proceeded west on Foothill Boulevard, and turned south onto 63rd Avenue. As they rounded the corner, they saw four or five youths huddled around a small red car parked at the curb. When the youths saw the officers' car approaching they apparently panicked, and took flight. The respondent here, Hodari D., and one companion ran west through an alley; the others fled south. The red car also headed south, at a high rate of speed.
>
> The officers were suspicious and gave chase. McColgin remained in the car and continued south on 63rd Avenue; Pertoso left the car, ran back north along 63rd, then west on Foothill Boulevard, and turned south on

> 62nd Avenue. Hodari, meanwhile, emerged from the alley onto 62nd and ran north. Looking behind as he ran, he did not turn and see Pertoso until the officer was almost upon him, whereupon he tossed away what appeared to be a small rock. A moment later, Pertoso tackled Hodari, handcuffed him, and radioed for assistance. Hodari was found to be carrying $130 in cash and a pager; and the rock he had discarded was found to be crack cocaine.

California v. Hodari D., 499 U.S. 621, 622-23 (1991). There's no question that Hodari was seized when he was placed in handcuffs and formally arrested. But was Hodari "seized" during the chase, i.e., when he dropped the drugs? There was no physical force applied by the police against Hodari before the chase occurred. However, the police did yell out to Hodari to "halt" during the chase. Is that enough to constitute a "show of authority" under the *Mendenhall* test? The Court concluded no, because Hodari failed to comply when the police ordered him to stop, and instead took off running. Applying the *Mendenhall* test, why does this fact transform a putative seizure into a nonseizure?

B. REQUIREMENTS FOR ARREST

The arrest is the paradigmatic seizure. While not all seizures are arrests, it is certainly true that all arrests qualify as seizures. Consequently, the Supreme

PROBLEM CASE

Two police officers in Indiana tried to pull over an automobile that they believed was involved in a case of "road rage" that was reported to the police. The driver, Jadrion Griffin, slowed down but then took off, leading police on a brief, "slow-speed" car chase. Police say that Griffin slowly drove through a parking lot, threw a bag of cocaine out of his car window, and then eventually pulled over. Griffin moved to suppress as evidence the cocaine that was originally thrown out of his window because it occurred during an illegal seizure. To evaluate this claim that the seizure was improper, one must first determine if Griffin was "seized" at the moment in time when he allegedly tossed the cocaine out of the window. As noted in the case above, a person is seized for purposes of the Fourth Amendment when the police use physical force or a show of authority to restrain their freedom of movement. In pulling over Griffin's car by flashing their squad car lights, did the police officers restrain Griffin's freedom by physical force? If not, did the flashing of their squad car lights constitute a "show of authority"? If yes, when did the "res traint" on freedom begin? Did it begin when the police officers flashed their police sirens or only when Griffin's car came to a complete stop as he yielded to their authority? In other words, was Griffin "seized" during the period *between* the flashing of the police lights and his car coming to a complete stop? Was he "seized" during the slow-speed chase through the parking lot? See *United States v. Griffin*, 652 F.3d 793, 800-01 (7th Cir. 2011).

Court has articulated a series of specific requirements for arrests. Typically, warrants are required for misdemeanor arrests, unless the police officer personally witnessed the offense. For felonies, however, the police generally do not need a warrant as long as the police officer has probable cause to believe that the arrestee has committed a felony. If the felony arrestee is located in the home, however, a warrant is required beforehand because an arrest at an individual's home represents a far greater intrusion from the perspective of the Fourth Amendment. The cases that follow in the subsections below not only articulate these rules but also apply them to particular fact patterns.

1. The Warrant Requirement for Arrests

The Fourth Amendment specifically refers to warrants and provides that the probable cause standard shall be the required standard for the issuance of a warrant. But the Fourth Amendment says nothing about whether police are entitled to make an arrest *in the absence* of a warrant, for example, in a situation where a police officer has probable cause to believe that an individual has committed a crime but the police officer has not yet had a chance to apply for, or receive, an arrest warrant signed by a magistrate. The following case answers that question.

United States v. Watson

Supreme Court of the United States
423 U.S. 411 (1976)

Mr. Justice White delivered the opinion of the Court.

This case presents questions under the Fourth Amendment as to the legality of a warrantless arrest and of an ensuing search of the arrestee's automobile carried out with his purported consent.

I

The relevant events began on August 17, 1972, when an informant, one Khoury, telephoned a postal inspector informing him that respondent Watson was in possession of a stolen credit card and had asked Khoury to cooperate in using the card to their mutual advantage. On five to 10 previous occasions Khoury had provided the inspector with reliable information on postal inspection matters, some involving Watson. Later that day Khoury delivered the card to the inspector. On learning that Watson had agreed to furnish additional cards, the inspector asked Khoury to arrange to meet with Watson. Khoury did so, a meeting being scheduled for August 22. Watson canceled that engagement, but at noon on August 23, Khoury met with Watson at a restaurant designated by the latter. Khoury had been instructed that if Watson had additional stolen credit cards, Khoury was to give a designated signal. The signal was given, the officers closed in, and Watson was forthwith arrested. He was removed from the restaurant to the street where he was given the warnings required by *Miranda v. Arizona*. A search having revealed that Watson had no credit cards on his person, the inspector asked if he could look inside Watson's car, which was standing within view. Watson said, "Go ahead," and repeated these words when the inspector cautioned that "(i)f I find anything, it is going to go against you." Using keys furnished by Watson, the inspector entered the car and found under the floor mat an envelope containing two credit cards in the names of other persons. These cards were the basis for two counts of a four-count indictment charging Watson with possessing stolen mail. . . .

Prior to trial, Watson moved to suppress the cards, claiming that his arrest was illegal for want of probable cause and an arrest warrant and that his consent to search the car was involuntary and ineffective because he had not been told that he could withhold consent. The motion was denied, and Watson was convicted of illegally possessing the two cards seized from his car. . . .

II

. . . Watson's arrest was not invalid because executed without a warrant. Title 18 U.S.C. § 3061(a)(3) expressly empowers the Board of Governors of the Postal Service to authorize Postal Service officers and employees "performing duties related to the inspection of postal matters" to "make arrests without warrant for felonies cognizable under the laws of the United States if they have reasonable grounds to believe that the person to be arrested has committed or is committing such a felony."

By regulation, 39 CFR § 232.5(a)(3) (1975), and in identical language, the Board of Governors has exercised that power and authorized warrantless arrests. Because there was probable cause in this case to believe that Watson had violated section 1708, the inspector and his subordinates, in arresting Watson, were acting strictly in accordance with the governing statute and regulations. The effect of the judgment of the Court of Appeals was to invalidate the statute as applied in this case and as applied to all the situations where a court fails to find exigent circumstances justifying a warrantless arrest. We reverse that judgment.

. . . Section 3061 represents a judgment by Congress that it is not unreasonable under the Fourth Amendment for postal inspectors to arrest without a warrant provided they have probable cause to do so. This was not an isolated or quixotic judgment of the legislative branch. Other federal law enforcement officers have been expressly authorized by statute for many years to make felony arrests on probable cause but without a warrant. This is true of United States marshals and of agents of the Federal Bureau of

Investigation; the Drug Enforcement Administration; the Secret Service; and the Customs Service.

Because there is a "strong presumption of constitutionality due to an Act of Congress, especially when it turns on what is 'reasonable,'" "(o)bviously the Court should be reluctant to decide that a search thus authorized by Congress was unreasonable and that the Act was therefore unconstitutional." Moreover, there is nothing in the Court's prior cases indicating that under the Fourth Amendment a warrant is required to make a valid arrest for a felony. Indeed, the relevant prior decisions are uniformly to the contrary.

"The usual rule is that a police officer may arrest without warrant one believed by the officer upon reasonable cause to have been guilty of a felony. . . ." *Carroll v. United States,* 267 U.S. 132, 156 (1925). In *Henry v. United States,* 361 U.S. 98 (1959), the Court dealt with an FBI agent's warrantless arrest under 18 U.S.C. § 3052, which authorizes a warrantless arrest where there are reasonable grounds to believe that the person to be arrested has committed a felony. The Court declared that "(t)he statute states the constitutional standard. . . ." The necessary inquiry, therefore, was not whether there was a warrant or whether there was time to get one, but whether there was probable cause for the arrest. In *Abel v. United States,* 362 U.S. 217, 232 (1960), the Court sustained an administrative arrest made without "a judicial warrant within the scope of the Fourth Amendment." The crucial question in *Draper v. United States,* 358 U.S. 307 (1959), was whether there was probable cause for the warrantless arrest. If there was, the Court said, "the arrest, though without a warrant, was lawful. . . ." *Ker v. California,* 374 U.S. 23, 34-35 (1963), reiterated the rule that "(t)he lawfulness of the arrest without warrant, in turn, must be based upon probable cause . . ." and went on to sustain the warrantless arrest over other claims going to the mode of entry. Just last Term, while recognizing that maximum protection of individual rights could be assured by requiring a magistrate's review of the factual justification prior to any arrest, we stated that "such a requirement would constitute an intolerable handicap for legitimate law enforcement" and noted that the Court "has never invalidated an arrest supported by probable cause solely because the officers failed to secure a warrant." *Gerstein v. Pugh,* 420 U.S. 103, 113 (1975).

The cases construing the Fourth Amendment thus reflect the ancient common-law rule that a peace officer was permitted to arrest without a warrant for a misdemeanor or felony committed in his presence as well as for a felony not committed in his presence if there was reasonable ground for making the arrest. This has also been the prevailing rule under state constitutions and statutes. "The rule of the common law, that a peace officer or a private citizen may arrest a felon without a warrant, has been generally held by the courts of the several States to be in force in cases of felony punishable by the civil tribunals." . . .

The balance struck by the common law in generally authorizing felony arrests on probable cause, but without a warrant, has survived substantially intact. It appears in almost all of the States in the form of express statutory authorization. . . . This is the rule Congress has long directed its principal law enforcement officers to follow. Congress has plainly decided against conditioning warrantless arrest power on proof of exigent circumstances. Law enforcement officers may find it wise to seek arrest warrants where practicable to do so, and their judgments about probable cause may be more readily accepted where backed by a warrant issued by a magistrate. But we decline to transform this judicial preference into a constitutional rule when the judgment of the Nation and Congress has for so long been to authorize warrantless public arrests on probable cause rather than to encumber criminal prosecutions with endless litigation with respect to the existence of exigent circumstances, whether it was practicable to get a warrant, whether the suspect was about to flee, and the like.

Watson's arrest did not violate the Fourth Amendment, and the Court of Appeals erred in holding to the contrary. . . .

Mr. Justice MARSHALL, with whom Mr. Justice BRENNAN joins, dissenting.

. . . The Court has typically engaged in a two-part analysis in deciding whether the presumption favoring a warrant should be given effect in situations where a warrant has not previously been clearly required. Utilizing that approach we must now consider (1) whether the privacy of our citizens will be better protected by ordinarily required a warrant to be issued before they may be arrested; and (2) whether a warrant requirement would unduly burden legitimate governmental interests.

The first question is easily answered. Of course, the privacy of our citizens will be better protected by a warrant requirement. We have recognized that "the Fourth Amendment protects people, not places." Indeed, the privacy guaranteed by the Fourth Amendment is quintessentially personal. Thus a warrant is required in search situations not because of some high regard for property, but because of our regard for the individual, and his interest in his possessions and person. . . .

Not only is the Fourth Amendment directly addressed to the privacy of our citizens, but it speaks in indistinguishable terms about the freedom of both persons and property from unreasonable seizures. A warrant is required in the search situation to protect the privacy of the individual, but there can be no less invasion of privacy when the individual himself, rather than his property, is searched and seized. Indeed, an unjustified arrest that forces the individual temporarily to forfeit his right to control his person and movements and interrupts the course of his daily business may be more intrusive than an unjustified search. . . .

A warrant requirement for arrests would, of course, minimize the possibility that such an intrusion into the individual's sacred sphere of personal privacy would occur on less than probable cause. Primarily for this reason, a warrant is required for searches. Surely there is no reason to place greater trust in the partisan assessment of a police officer that there is probable cause for an arrest than in his determination that probable cause exists for a search. Last Term the Court unanimously recognized that detention of a person cannot be prolonged without judicial oversight of the probable-cause determination. *Gerstein v. Pugh*, 420 U.S. 103 (1975). But while Gerstein may provide the best protection possible against less-than-probable-cause warrantless arrests based on exigent circumstances, it does not fully protect the Fourth Amendment rights at stake here. A less-than-probable-cause arrest followed by a *Gerstein* release is as offensive to the Fourth Amendment as a less-than-probable-cause search that fails to uncover the evidence sought, and the requirement of a warrant is as instrumental in protecting against the one as the other. Indeed, the Court's opinion in *Gerstein* expressly recognizes that maximum protection of individual rights can only be realized "by requiring a magistrate's review of the factual justification prior to any arrest. . . ."

We come then to the second part of the warrant test: whether a warrant requirement would unduly burden legitimate law enforcement interests. Dicta in *Gerstein* answer this question in the affirmative. . . . I believe, however, that the suggested concerns are wholly illusory. Indeed, the argument that a warrant requirement for arrests would be an onerous chore for the police seems somewhat anomalous in light of the Government's concession that "it is the standard practice of the Federal Bureau of Investigation (FBI) to present its evidence to the United States Attorney, and to obtain a warrant, before making an arrest." In the past, the practice and experience of the FBI have been taken as a substantial indication that no intolerable burden would be presented by a proposed rule of procedure. There is no reason to accord less deference to the FBI practice here.

The Government's assertion that a warrant requirement would impose an intolerable burden stems, in large part, from the specious supposition that procurement of an arrest warrant would be necessary as soon as probable cause ripens. There is no requirement that a search warrant be obtained the moment police have probable cause to search. The rule is only that present probable cause be shown and a warrant obtained before a search is undertaken. The same rule should obtain for arrest warrants, where it may even make more sense. Certainly, there is less need for prompt procurement of a warrant in the arrest situation. Unlike probable cause to search, probable cause to arrest, once formed, will continue to exist for the indefinite future, at least if no intervening exculpatory facts come to light.

This sensible approach obviates most of the difficulties that have been suggested with an arrest warrant rule. Police would not have to cut their investigation short the moment they obtain probable cause to arrest, nor would undercover agents be forced suddenly to terminate their work and forfeit their covers. Moreover, if in the course of the continued police investigation exigent circumstances develop that demand an immediate arrest, the arrest may be made without fear of unconstitutionality, so long as the exigency was unanticipated and not used to avoid the arrest warrant requirement. Likewise, if in the course of the continued investigation police uncover evidence tying the suspect to another crime, they may immediately arrest him for that crime if exigency demands it, and still be in full conformity with the warrant rule. This is why the arrest in this case was not improper. Other than where police attempt to evade the warrant requirement, the rule would invalidate an arrest only in the obvious situation: where police, with probable cause but without exigent circumstances, set out to arrest a suspect. Such an arrest must be void, even if exigency develops in the course of the arrest that would ordinarily validate it; otherwise the warrant requirement would be reduced to a toothless prescription.

In sum, the requirement that officers about to arrest a suspect ordinarily obtain a warrant before they do so does not seem unduly burdensome, at least no more burdensome than any other requirement that law enforcement officials undertake a new procedure in order to comply with the dictates of the Constitution. . . .

NOTES & QUESTIONS ON ARREST WARRANTS

1. *Arrest warrants—what are they good for?* If *Watson* stands for the proposition that a police officer may conduct a felony arrest in the absence of a warrant, what value does an arrest warrant serve? The process of going to a magistrate ex ante and securing the warrant would appear to be a meaningless exercise. The answer, of course, is that the prior judicial determination involved in the issuance of the warrant makes it less likely that a court will later determine that a police officer acted improperly by arresting the suspect. In other words, the issuance of the warrant moves the judicial review of probable cause to before—rather than after—the arrest itself. This predetermination of probable cause is beneficial for police officers, who might otherwise worry that their assessment of probable cause will be overturned by the judiciary after the fact.

2. *Exigency.* Some states impose an exigency requirement on warrantless searches. In other words, a police officer is entitled to perform a warrantless

arrest as long as probable cause is satisfied *and* some exigent circumstance makes it impractical to secure an arrest warrant. For example, in *Campos v. State*, 117 N.M. 155, 159, 870 P.2d 117, 121 (1994), the New Mexico Supreme Court concluded that its state constitution prohibited warrantless arrests in the absence of exigency—in other words, when police officers could have secured a warrant. In *Campos*, the police received an anonymous tip that Campos would be conducting a drug transaction the following day, and the informant gave a description of Campos' car. The police set up surveillance and when they spotted Campos they arrested him without a warrant. After the arrest, the police conducted a search and found heroin. The court concluded that there were no exigent circumstances preventing the officers from securing a warrant. Exigent circumstances "means an emergency situation requiring swift action to prevent imminent danger to life or serious damage to property, or to forestall the imminent escape of a suspect or destruction of evidence." Do you think the Supreme Court should impose an exigency requirement under the Fourth Amendment?

3. *Misdemeanor arrests.* *Watson* deals with felony arrests. What is the rule for misdemeanor arrests? At common law, misdemeanor arrests were permissible without a warrant if the police officer witnessed the crime and the crime involved a breach of the peace. Over time, state jurisdictions have evolved a variety of different rules that now depart from the old common law scheme. For example, some states have eliminated the "breach of the peace" requirement, and a smaller number of states have repealed the requirement that the misdemeanor was committed in the presence of the officer, thus treating felonies and misdemeanors with the same standard. The overall trend involves great divergence at the state level, and the Supreme Court has not decided whether the Fourth Amendment requires a warrant for misdemeanor arrests and under what circumstances.

2. Home Arrests

But what if the police go directly to the home of an individual to conduct an arrest? Should the regular rule permitting warrantless arrests apply, as it does when the police officer has probable cause? Or is the home deserving of special Fourth Amendment protection on the theory that the home is a person's castle? State jurisdictions were split on this issue, with some prohibiting warrantless arrests in the home, and others, such as New York, specifically authorizing the practice by statute. As you read the following case, try to put yourself in the shoes of a homeowner facing the possibility of an arrest in their home. Would it provide extra comfort to you to know that the police could only arrest you in your home if a magistrate made a prior determination of probable cause?

Payton v. New York
Supreme Court of the United States
445 U.S. 573 (1980)

Mr. Justice STEVENS delivered the opinion of the Court.

These appeals challenge the constitutionality of New York statutes that authorize police officers to enter a private residence without a warrant and with force, if necessary, to make a routine felony arrest.

The important constitutional question presented by this challenge has been expressly left open in a number of our prior opinions. In *United States v. Watson*, 423 U.S. 411, we upheld a warrantless "midday public arrest," expressly noting that the case did not pose "the still unsettled question . . . whether and under what circumstances an officer may enter a suspect's home to make a warrantless arrest." The question has been answered in different ways by other appellate courts. The Supreme Court of Florida rejected the constitutional attack, as did the New York Court of Appeals in this case. The courts of last resort in 10 other States, however, have held that unless special circumstances are present, warrantless arrests in the home are unconstitutional. Of the seven United States Courts of Appeals that have considered the question, five have expressed the opinion that such arrests are unconstitutional. . . .

We now reverse the New York Court of Appeals and hold that the Fourth Amendment to the United States Constitution, made applicable to the States by the Fourteenth Amendment, prohibits the police from making a warrantless and nonconsensual entry into a suspect's home in order to make a routine felony arrest. . . .

I

On January 14, 1970, after two days of intensive investigation, New York detectives had assembled evidence sufficient to establish probable cause to believe that Theodore Payton had murdered the manager of a gas station two days earlier. At about 7:30 A.M. on January 15, six officers went to Payton's apartment in the Bronx, intending to arrest him. They had not obtained a warrant. Although light and music emanated from the apartment, there was no response to their knock on the metal door. They summoned emergency assistance and, about 30 minutes later, used crowbars to break open the door and enter the apartment. No one was there. In plain view, however, was a .30-caliber shell casing that was seized and later admitted into evidence at Payton's murder trial. . . .

On March 14, 1974, Obie Riddick was arrested for the commission of two armed robberies that had occurred in 1971. He had been identified by the victims in June 1973, and in January 1974 the police had learned his address. They did not obtain a warrant for his arrest. At about noon on March 14, a detective, accompanied by three other officers, knocked on the door of the Queens house where Riddick was living. When his young son opened the door, they could see Riddick sitting in bed covered by a sheet. They entered the house and placed him under arrest. Before permitting him to dress, they opened a chest of drawers two feet from the bed in search of weapons and found narcotics and related paraphernalia. Riddick was subsequently indicted on narcotics charges. . . .

II

It is familiar history that indiscriminate searches and seizures conducted under the authority of "general warrants" were the immediate evils that motivated the framing and adoption of the Fourth Amendment. Indeed, as originally proposed in the House of Representatives, the draft contained only one clause, which directly imposed limitations on the issuance of warrants, but imposed no express restrictions on warrantless searches or seizures. As it was ultimately adopted, however, the Amendment contained two separate clauses, the first protecting the basic right to be free from unreasonable searches and seizures and the second requiring that warrants be particular and supported by probable cause. . . .

It is thus perfectly clear that the evil the Amendment was designed to prevent was broader than the abuse of a general warrant. Unreasonable searches or seizures conducted without any warrant at all are condemned by the plain language of the first clause of the Amendment. Almost a century ago the Court stated in resounding terms that the principles reflected in the Amendment "reached farther than the concrete form" of the specific cases that gave it birth, and "apply to all invasions on the part of the government and its employees of the sanctity of a man's home and the privacies of life." Without pausing to consider whether that broad language may require some qualification, it is sufficient to note that the warrantless arrest of a person is a species of seizure required by the Amendment to be reasonable. . . .

The simple language of the Amendment applies equally to seizures of persons and to seizures of property. Our analysis in this case may therefore properly commence with rules that have been well established in Fourth Amendment litigation involving tangible items. As the Court reiterated just a few years ago, the "physical entry of the home is the chief evil against which the wording of the Fourth Amendment is directed." And we have long adhered to the view that the warrant procedure minimizes the danger of needless intrusions of that sort.

It is a "basic principle of Fourth Amendment law" that searches and seizures inside a home without a warrant are presumptively unreasonable. Yet it is also well settled that objects such as weapons or contraband found in a public place may be seized by the police without a warrant. The seizure of property in plain view involves no invasion of privacy and is presumptively reasonable, assuming that there is probable cause to associate the property with criminal activity. . . . The majority of the New York Court of Appeals, however, suggested that there is a substantial difference in the relative intrusiveness of an entry to search for property and an entry to search for a person. It is true that the area that may legally be searched is broader when executing a search warrant than when executing an arrest warrant in the home. This difference may be more theoretical than real, however, because the police may need to check the entire premises for safety reasons, and sometimes they ignore the restrictions on searches incident to arrest.

But the critical point is that any differences in the intrusiveness of entries to search and entries to arrest are merely ones of degree rather than kind. The two intrusions share this fundamental characteristic: the breach of the entrance to an individual's home. The Fourth Amendment protects the individual's privacy in a variety of settings. In none is the zone of privacy more clearly defined than when bounded by the unambiguous physical dimensions of an individual's home. . . . In terms that apply equally to seizures of property and to seizures of persons, the Fourth Amendment has drawn a firm line at the entrance to the house. Absent exigent circumstances, that threshold may not reasonably be crossed without a warrant.

III

. . . An examination of the common-law understanding of an officer's authority to arrest sheds light on the obviously relevant, if not entirely dispositive, consideration of what the Framers of the Amendment might have thought to be reasonable. Initially, it should be noted that the common-law rules of arrest developed in legal contexts that substantially differ from the cases now before us. In these cases, which involve application of the exclusionary rule, the issue is whether certain evidence is admissible at trial. At common law, the question whether an arrest was authorized typically arose in civil damages actions for trespass or false arrest, in which a constable's authority to make the arrest was a defense. Additionally, if an officer was killed while attempting to effect an arrest, the question whether the person resisting the arrest was guilty of murder or manslaughter turned on whether the officer was acting within the bounds of his authority.

A study of the common law on the question whether a constable had the authority to make warrantless arrests in the home on mere suspicion of a felony—as distinguished from an officer's right to arrest for a crime committed in his presence—reveals a surprising lack of judicial decisions and a deep divergence among scholars. . . . The common-law commentators disagreed sharply on the subject. . . . It is obvious that the common-law rule on warrantless home arrests was not as clear as the rule on arrests in public places. Indeed, particularly considering the prominence of Lord Coke, the weight of authority as it appeared to the Framers was to the effect that a warrant was required, or at the minimum that there were substantial risks in proceeding without one. The common-law sources display a sensitivity to privacy interests that could not have been lost on the Framers. The zealous and frequent repetition of the adage that a "man's house is his castle," made it abundantly clear that both in England and in the Colonies "the freedom of one's house" was one of the most vital elements of English liberty. . . .

A majority of the States that have taken a position on the question permit warrantless entry into the home to arrest even in the absence of exigent circumstances. At this time, 24 States permit such warrantless entries; 15 States clearly prohibit them, though 3 States do so on federal constitutional grounds alone; and 11 States have apparently taken no position on the question.

But these current figures reflect a significant decline during the last decade in the number of States permitting warrantless entries for arrest. . . . Virtually all of the state courts that have had to confront the constitutional issue directly have held warrantless entries into the home to arrest to be invalid in the absence of exigent circumstances. Three state courts have relied on Fourth Amendment grounds alone, while seven have squarely placed their decisions on both federal and state constitutional grounds. A number of other state courts, though not having had to confront the issue directly, have recognized the serious nature of the constitutional question. Apparently, only the Supreme Court of Florida and the New York Court of Appeals in this case have expressly upheld warrantless entries to arrest in the face of a constitutional challenge. . . .

IV

The parties have argued at some length about the practical consequences of a warrant requirement as a precondition to a felony arrest in the home. In the absence of any evidence that effective law enforcement has suffered in those States that already have such a requirement, we are inclined to view such arguments with skepticism. More fundamentally, however, such arguments of policy must give way to a constitutional command that we consider to be unequivocal. . . . Because no arrest warrant was obtained in either of these cases, the judgments must be reversed and the cases remanded to the New York Court of Appeals for further proceedings not inconsistent with this opinion.

Mr. Justice WHITE, with whom THE CHIEF JUSTICE and Mr. Justice REHNQUIST join, dissenting.

The Court today holds that absent exigent circumstances officers may never enter a home during the daytime to arrest for a dangerous felony unless they have first obtained a warrant. This hard-and-fast rule, founded on erroneous assumptions concerning the intrusiveness of home arrest entries, finds little or no support in the common law or in the text and history of the Fourth Amendment. I respectfully dissent. . . .

Today's decision rests, in large measure, on the premise that warrantless arrest entries constitute a particularly severe invasion of personal privacy. I do not dispute that the home is generally a very private area or that the common law displayed a special "reverence . . . for the individual's right of privacy in his house." However, the Fourth Amendment is concerned with protecting people, not places, and no talismanic significance is given to the fact that an arrest occurs in the home rather than elsewhere. It is necessary in each case to assess realistically the actual extent of invasion of constitutionally protected privacy. Further . . . all arrests involve serious intrusions into an individual's privacy and dignity. Yet we settled in *Watson* that the intrusiveness of a public arrest is not enough to mandate the obtaining of a warrant. The inquiry in the present case, therefore, is whether the incremental intrusiveness that results from an arrest's being made in the dwelling is enough to support an inflexible constitutional rule requiring warrants for such arrests whenever exigent circumstances are not present.

Today's decision ignores the carefully crafted restrictions on the common-law power of arrest entry and thereby overestimates the dangers inherent in that practice. At common law, absent exigent circumstances, entries to arrest could be made only for felony. Even in cases of felony, the officers were required to announce their presence, demand admission, and be refused entry before they were entitled to break doors. Further, it seems generally accepted that entries could be made only during daylight hours. And, in my view, the officer entering to arrest must have reasonable grounds to believe, not only that the arrestee has committed a crime, but also that the person suspected is present in the house at the time of the entry.

These four restrictions on home arrests—felony, knock and announce, daytime, and stringent probable cause—constitute powerful and complementary protections for the privacy interests associated with the home. The felony requirement guards against abusive or arbitrary enforcement and ensures that invasions of the home occur only in case of the most serious crimes. The knock-and-announce and daytime requirements protect individuals against the fear, humiliation, and embarrassment of being aroused from their beds in states of partial or complete undress. And these requirements allow the arrestee to surrender at his front door, thereby maintaining his dignity and preventing the officers from entering other rooms of the dwelling. The stringent probable-cause requirement would help ensure against the possibility that the police would enter when the suspect was not home, and, in searching for him, frighten members of the family or ransack parts of the house, seizing items in plain view. In short, these requirements, taken together, permit an individual suspected of a serious crime to surrender at the front door of his dwelling and thereby avoid most of the humiliation and indignity that the Court seems to believe necessarily accompany a house arrest entry. Such a front-door arrest, in my view, is no more intrusive on personal privacy than the public warrantless arrests which we found to pass constitutional muster in *Watson*. . . .

NOTES & QUESTIONS ON HOME ARRESTS

1. *Constructive entry. Payton* clearly stands for the proposition that the police need a warrant to arrest someone in their home. However, consider the following hypothetical: The police arrive at the front door of a suspect. They ring the bell and when he answers the door, they say: "Please step outside." The statement is ambiguous. Is it a command or is it request? Regardless, imagine that the resident feels compelled to step outside and then is immediately arrested—without a warrant. The police justify the search because the arrestee is no longer inside the home. Is this ruse consistent with the Fourth Amendment? Although some courts would sanction this behavior, others would disallow it under a theory that it constituted a "constructive entry" into the home. For example, consider the Sixth Circuit's conclusion in *United States v. Morgan*, 743 F.2d 1158 (6th Cir. 1984):

> Applying this rule here, it is undisputed that Morgan was peacefully residing in his mother's home until he was aroused by the police activities occurring outside. Morgan was then compelled to leave the house. Thus . . . "it cannot be said that [Morgan] voluntarily exposed himself to a warrantless arrest" by appearing at the door. On the contrary, Morgan appeared at the door only because of the coercive police behavior taking place outside of the house. Viewed in these terms, the arrest of Morgan occurred while he was present inside a private home. Although there was no direct police entry into the Morgan home prior to Morgan's arrest, the constructive entry accomplished the same thing, namely, the arrest of Morgan. Thus, the warrantless arrest of Morgan, as he stood within the door of a private home, after emerging in response to coercive police conduct, violated Morgan's Fourth Amendment rights. A contrary rule would undermine the constitutional precepts emphasized in *Payton*.

Id. at 1166. Do you think the Supreme Court should adopt the doctrine of "constructive entry" in this context? For a discussion, see Steven B. Dow, *"Step Outside, Please": Warrantless Doorway Arrests and the Problem of Constructive Entry*, 45 New Eng. L. Rev. 7 (2010).

2. *An open door policy.* Consider a different hypothetical situation. Imagine that the police arrive at a residence and find the front door wide open. Through the open door the police have an unobstructed view of the suspect that they want to arrest. Are they entitled to cross through the open door to

PROBLEM CASE

In 2015, police in Minnesota arrested and charged Leona Rose deLottinville with two drug felonies. A judge granted her pre-trial release on the condition that she refrain from using drugs and alcohol, which would be monitored by random drug tests. She failed a test and a judge issued an arrest warrant after finding probable cause that she had violated the conditions of her pre-trial release. Police went looking for deLottinville and after an investigation concluded that she might be staying at her boyfriend's apartment. A police officer entered the apartment, without knocking, through an open back door and arrested deLottinville. She filed a motion to suppress evidence of drugs found at the house, arguing that the arrest was illegal.

It is clear that the police required a warrant to arrest deLottinville in her home, but did that arrest warrant give the police authorization to enter her *boyfriend's* residence? This is really two questions: First, did the police violate the Fourth Amendment rights of the boyfriend when they entered the residence? Second, did the police violate the Fourth Amendment rights of deLottinville when they entered the apartment? Focus on the second question and ask yourself whether the police were required to act differently depending on whether they found deLottinville in her own or someone else's home. See *State v. deLottinville,* 890 N.W.2d 116, 120 (Minn. 2017).

perform a warrantless arrest of the suspect, provided that they have probable cause? Or consider a similar situation where the occupant opens the door for police but remains inside and carries on a conversation with police standing just outside the doorway. Courts are split on this issue. For example, compare *Hadley v. Williams,* 368 F.3d 747 (7th Cir. 2004) (open door arrest unconstitutional), with *United States v. Gori,* 230 F.3d 44 (2d Cir. 2000) (open door arrest permissible). In *Hadley,* the Seventh Circuit concluded: "Since few people will refuse to open the door to the police, the effect of the rule [permitting arrests] is to undermine, for no good reason that we can see, the principle that a warrant is required for entry into the home, in the absence of consent or compelling circumstances. Those cases equate knowledge (what the officer obtains from the plain view) with a right to enter, and by doing so permit the rule of *Payton* to be evaded." Do you agree that the underlying rationale of *Payton* does not permit these warrantless arrests?

3. Crimes Subject to Arrest

Can the police arrest an individual for a misdemeanor or other violation for which no jail time attaches? The answer to this question goes to the very heart of the underlying rationale for arrests as well as the burden that these arrests impose on the arrestee. Recall that the arrest triggers a number of collateral consequences, including the right of the police to conduct an inventory search of the arrested person and his automobile, and to subject the arrestee to booking procedures, which may include the taking of photographs and fingerprints. Furthermore, the arrest clearly involves a deprivation of liberty to the individual, who may be handcuffed, placed in a squad car, and held in detention at the police station while the arrest procedure is completed. In the case of an arrest for a crime that carries the possibility of prison or jail time, these deprivations have a certain logic. But in the case of misdemeanors or violations punishable only by fines, the deprivations of liberty associated with the process appear, to some, inherently disproportionate to the legitimate government need in the situation.

In the following case, the Supreme Court considers an arrest for a seatbelt violation. As you read the case, pay particular attention to the effect of the arrest on Gail Atwater (and her children). Did an arrest under these circumstances violate the Fourth Amendment?

Atwater v. City of Lago Vista

Supreme Court of the United States
532 U.S. 318 (2001)

Justice SOUTER delivered the opinion of the Court.

The question is whether the Fourth Amendment forbids a warrantless arrest for a minor criminal offense, such as a misdemeanor seatbelt violation punishable only by a fine. We hold that it does not.

I

In Texas, if a car is equipped with safety belts, a front-seat passenger must wear one and the driver must secure any small child riding in front. Violation of either provision is "a misdemeanor punishable by a fine not less than $25 or more than $50." Texas law expressly authorizes "[a]ny peace officer [to] arrest without warrant a person found committing a violation" of these seatbelt laws, although it permits police to issue citations in lieu of arrest.

In March 1997, petitioner Gail Atwater was driving her pickup truck in Lago Vista, Texas, with her 3-year-old son and 5-year-old daughter in the front seat. None of them was wearing a seatbelt. Respondent Bart Turek, a Lago Vista police officer at the time, observed the seatbelt violations and pulled Atwater over. According to Atwater's complaint (the allegations of which we assume to be true for present purposes), Turek approached the truck and "yell[ed]" something to the effect of "[w]e've met before" and "[y]ou're going to jail." He then called for backup and asked to see Atwater's driver's license and insurance documentation, which state law required her to carry. When Atwater told Turek that she did not have the papers because her purse had been stolen the day before, Turek said that he had "heard that story two-hundred times."

Atwater asked to take her "frightened, upset, and crying" children to a friend's house nearby, but Turek told her, "[y]ou're not going anywhere." As it turned out, Atwater's friend learned what was going on and soon arrived to take charge of the children. Turek then handcuffed Atwater, placed her in his squad car, and drove her to the local police station, where booking officers had her remove her shoes, jewelry, and eyeglasses, and empty her pockets. Officers took Atwater's "mug shot" and placed her, alone, in a jail cell for about one hour, after which she was taken before a magistrate and released on $310 bond.

Atwater was charged with driving without her seatbelt fastened, failing to secure her children in seatbelts, driving without a license, and failing to provide proof of insurance. She ultimately pleaded no contest to the misdemeanor seatbelt offenses and paid a $50 fine; the other charges were dismissed. Atwater and her husband, petitioner Michael Haas, filed suit in a Texas state court under 42 U.S.C. § 1983 against Turek and respondents City of Lago Vista and Chief of Police Frank Miller. . . .

II

. . . [T]he first step here is to assess Atwater's claim that peace officers' authority to make warrantless arrests for misdemeanors was restricted at common law. . . . Atwater's specific contention is that "founding-era common-law rules" forbade peace officers to make warrantless misdemeanor arrests except in cases of "breach of the peace," a category she claims was then understood narrowly as covering only those nonfelony offenses "involving or tending toward violence." Although her historical argument is by no means insubstantial, it ultimately fails.

We begin with the state of pre-founding English common law and find that, even after making some allowance for variations in the common-law usage of the term "breach of the peace," the "founding-era common-law rules" were not nearly as clear as Atwater claims; on the contrary, the common-law commentators (as well as the sparsely reported cases) reached divergent conclusions with respect to officers' warrantless misdemeanor arrest power. Moreover, in the years leading up to American independence, Parliament repeatedly extended express warrantless arrest authority to cover misdemeanor-level offenses not amounting to or involving any violent breach of the peace. . . .

We thus find disagreement, not unanimity, among both the common-law jurists and the text writers who sought to pull the cases together and summarize accepted practice. Having reviewed the relevant English decisions, as well as English and colonial American legal treatises, legal dictionaries, and procedure manuals, we simply are not convinced that Atwater's is the correct, or even necessarily the better, reading of the common-law history.

A second, and equally serious, problem for Atwater's historical argument is posed by the "divers Statutes" enacted by Parliament well before this Republic's founding that authorized warrantless misdemeanor arrests without reference to violence or turmoil. Quite apart from Hale and Blackstone, the legal background of any conception of reasonableness the Fourth Amendment's Framers might have entertained would have included English statutes, some centuries old, authorizing peace officers (and even private persons) to make warrantless arrests for all sorts of relatively minor offenses unaccompanied by violence. The so-called "nightwalker" statutes are perhaps the most notable examples. From the enactment of the Statute of Winchester in 1285, through its various readoptions and until its repeal in 1827, night watchmen were authorized and charged "as . . . in Times past" to "watch the Town continually all Night, from the Sun-setting unto the Sun-rising" and were directed that "if any Stranger do pass by them, he shall be arrested until Morning. . . ." . . .

The record thus supports Justice Powell's observation that "[t]here is no historical evidence that the Framers or proponents of the Fourth Amendment, outspokenly opposed to the infamous general warrants and writs of assistance, were at all concerned about warrantless arrests by local constables and other peace officers." We simply cannot conclude that the Fourth Amendment, as originally understood, forbade peace officers to arrest without a warrant for misdemeanors not amounting to or involving breach of the peace. . . .

Finally, both the legislative tradition of granting warrantless misdemeanor arrest authority and the judicial tradition of sustaining such statutes against constitutional attack are buttressed by legal commentary that, for more than a century now, has almost uniformly recognized the constitutionality of extending warrantless arrest power to misdemeanors without limitation to breaches of the peace.

Small wonder, then, that today statutes in all 50 States and the District of Columbia permit warrantless misdemeanor arrests by at least some (if not all) peace officers without requiring any breach of the peace, as do a host of congressional enactments. The American Law Institute has long endorsed the validity of such legislation and the consensus, as stated in the current literature, is that statutes "remov[ing] the breach of the peace limitation and thereby permit[ting] arrest without warrant for any misdemeanor committed in the arresting officer's presence" have "never been successfully challenged and stan[d] as the law of the land." . . .

III

. . . Atwater does not wager all on history. Instead, she asks us to mint a new rule of constitutional law on the understanding that when historical practice fails to speak conclusively to a claim grounded on the Fourth

Amendment, courts are left to strike a current balance between individual and societal interests by subjecting particular contemporary circumstances to traditional standards of reasonableness. Atwater accordingly argues for a modern arrest rule, one not necessarily requiring violent breach of the peace, but nonetheless forbidding custodial arrest, even upon probable cause, when conviction could not ultimately carry any jail time and when the government shows no compelling need for immediate detention.

If we were to derive a rule exclusively to address the uncontested facts of this case, Atwater might well prevail. She was a known and established resident of Lago Vista with no place to hide and no incentive to flee, and common sense says she would almost certainly have buckled up as a condition of driving off with a citation. In her case, the physical incidents of arrest were merely gratuitous humiliations imposed by a police officer who was (at best) exercising extremely poor judgment. Atwater's claim to live free of pointless indignity and confinement clearly outweighs anything the City can raise against it specific to her case.

But we have traditionally recognized that a responsible Fourth Amendment balance is not well served by standards requiring sensitive, case-by-case determinations of government need. . . . Courts attempting to strike a reasonable Fourth Amendment balance thus credit the government's side with an essential interest in readily administrable rules.

At first glance, Atwater's argument may seem to respect the values of clarity and simplicity, so far as she claims that the Fourth Amendment generally forbids warrantless arrests for minor crimes not accompanied by violence or some demonstrable threat of it (whether "minor crime" be defined as a fine-only traffic offense, a fine-only offense more generally, or a misdemeanor). But the claim is not ultimately so simple, nor could it be, for complications arise the moment we begin to think about the possible applications of the several criteria Atwater proposes for drawing a line between minor crimes with limited arrest authority and others not so restricted.

One line, she suggests, might be between "jailable" and "fine-only" offenses, between those for which conviction could result in commitment and those for which it could not. The trouble with this distinction, of course, is that an officer on the street might not be able to tell. It is not merely that we cannot expect every police officer to know the details of frequently complex penalty schemes, but that penalties for ostensibly identical conduct can vary on account of facts difficult (if not impossible) to know at the scene of an arrest. Is this the first offense or is the suspect a repeat offender? Is the weight of the marijuana a gram above or a gram below the fine-only line? Where conduct could implicate more than one criminal prohibition, which one will the district attorney ultimately decide to charge? And so on.

But Atwater's refinements would not end there. She represents that if the line were drawn at nonjailable traffic offenses, her proposed limitation should be qualified by a proviso authorizing warrantless arrests where "necessary for enforcement of the traffic laws or when [an] offense would otherwise continue and pose a danger to others on the road." The proviso only compounds the difficulties. Would, for instance, either exception apply to speeding? At oral argument, Atwater's counsel said that "it would not be reasonable to arrest a driver for speeding unless the speeding rose to the level of reckless driving." But is it not fair to expect that the chronic speeder will speed again despite a citation in his pocket, and should that not qualify as showing that the "offense would . . . continue" under Atwater's rule? And why, as a constitutional matter, should we assume that only reckless driving will "pose a danger to others on the road" while speeding will not? . . .

Accordingly, we confirm today what our prior cases have intimated: the standard of probable cause "applie[s] to all arrests, without the need to 'balance' the interests and circumstances involved in particular situations." If an officer has probable cause to believe that an individual has committed even a very minor criminal offense in his presence, he may, without violating the Fourth Amendment, arrest the offender. . . .

Justice O'CONNOR, with whom Justice STEVENS, Justice GINSBURG, and Justice BREYER join, dissenting.

. . . A custodial arrest exacts an obvious toll on an individual's liberty and privacy, even when the period of custody is relatively brief. The arrestee is subject to a full search of her person and confiscation of her possessions. If the arrestee is the occupant of a car, the entire passenger compartment of the car, including packages therein, is subject to search as well. The arrestee may be detained for up to 48 hours without having a magistrate determine whether there in fact was probable cause for the arrest. Because people arrested for all types of violent and nonviolent offenses may be housed together awaiting such review, this detention period is potentially dangerous. And once the period of custody is over, the fact of the arrest is a permanent part of the public record. . . .

Because a full custodial arrest is such a severe intrusion on an individual's liberty, its reasonableness hinges on "the degree to which it is needed for the promotion of legitimate governmental interests." In light of the availability of citations to promote a State's interests when a fine-only offense has been committed, I cannot concur in a rule which deems a full custodial arrest to be reasonable in every circumstance. Giving police officers constitutional carte blanche to effect an arrest whenever there is probable cause to believe a fine-only misdemeanor has been committed is irreconcilable with the Fourth Amendment's command that seizures be reasonable. Instead, I would require that when there is probable cause to believe that a fine-only offense has been committed, the police officer should issue a citation unless the officer is "able to point to specific and articulable facts which, taken together with rational inferences from those facts, reasonably warrant [the additional] intrusion" of a full custodial arrest. *Terry v. Ohio,* 392 U.S., at 21.

The majority insists that a bright-line rule focused on probable cause is necessary to vindicate the State's interest in easily administrable law enforcement rules. Probable cause itself, however, is not a model of precision. . . . The rule I propose—which merely requires a legitimate reason for the decision to escalate the seizure into a full custodial arrest—thus does not undermine an otherwise "clear and simple" rule. While clarity is certainly a value worthy of consideration in our Fourth Amendment jurisprudence, it by no means trumps the values of liberty and privacy at the heart of the Amendment's protections. . . .

. . . Ms. Atwater ultimately pleaded no contest to violating the seatbelt law and was fined $50. Even though that fine was the maximum penalty for her crime and even though Officer Turek has never articulated any justification for his actions, the city contends that arresting Atwater was constitutionally reasonable because it advanced two legitimate interests: "the enforcement of child safety laws and encouraging [Atwater] to appear for trial."

It is difficult to see how arresting Atwater served either of these goals any more effectively than the issuance of a citation. With respect to the goal of law enforcement generally, Atwater did not pose a great danger to the community. She had been driving very slowly—approximately 15 miles per hour—in broad daylight on a residential street that had no other traffic. Nor was she a repeat offender; until that day, she had received one traffic citation in her life—a ticket, more than 10 years earlier, for failure to signal a lane change. Although Officer Turek had stopped Atwater approximately three months earlier because he thought that Atwater's son was not wearing a seatbelt, Turek had been mistaken. Moreover, Atwater immediately accepted responsibility and apologized for her conduct. Thus, there was every indication that Atwater would have buckled herself and her children in had she been cited and allowed to leave.

With respect to the related goal of child welfare, the decision to arrest Atwater was nothing short of counterproductive. Atwater's children witnessed Officer Turek yell at their mother and threaten to take them all into custody. Ultimately, they were forced to leave her behind with Turek, knowing that she was being taken to jail. Understandably, the 3-year-old boy was "very, very, very traumatized." After the incident, he had to see a child psychologist regularly, who reported that the boy "felt very guilty that he couldn't stop this horrible thing . . . he was powerless to help his mother or sister." Both of Atwater's children are now terrified at the sight of any police car. According to Atwater, the arrest "just never leaves us. It's a conversation we have every other day, once a week, and it's—it raises its head constantly in our lives."

> Respondents also contend that the arrest was necessary to ensure Atwater's appearance in court. Atwater, however, was far from a flight risk. A 16-year resident of Lago Vista, population 2,486, Atwater was not likely to abscond. Although she was unable to produce her driver's license because it had been stolen, she gave Officer Turek her license number and address. In addition, Officer Turek knew from their previous encounter that Atwater was a local resident. . . . The city's justifications fall far short of rationalizing the extraordinary intrusion on Gail Atwater and her children. . . .

NOTES & QUESTIONS ON CRIMES SUBJECT TO ARREST

1. *Appearance in court.* One rationale for an arrest is to help increase the probability that the arrestee will appear in court to answer the charge. The booking process helps with identification procedures that can be used to track down the individual in the event of non-appearance. Does this rationale apply well for minor traffic infractions of the type that Gail Atwater was charged with? Why did the Supreme Court support an arrest in this case? As one commentator put it:

> The Supreme Court's decision in *Atwater* makes little sense based on the facts of the Petitioner's case, creates serious potential for abuse of the arrest power, and is not supported by the reasons stated in Justice Souter's majority opinion. The Court's apparent desire to limit further growth in the application of reasonableness balancing analysis may help to explain the result in *Atwater*, but does not justify it. The Court could easily have ruled in Ms. Atwater's favor without creating either unmanageably complex rules for the police and lower courts or a doctrinal slippery slope. A narrow ruling in her favor would have done justice in her case and prevented many similarly unjustified arrests in minor traffic cases.

Richard S. Frase, *What Were They Thinking? Fourth Amendment Unreasonableness in* Atwater v. City of Lago Vista, 71 Fordham L. Rev. 329, 415 (2002).

2. *State law.* If you were a state court justice deciding the same question under state law, would you follow the Supreme Court's Fourth Amendment rule or would you impose a more demanding standard for the police to follow? If you would conclude that the Atwater arrest was impermissible, what dividing line would you establish? What if a misdemeanor was punishable by up to a week in jail—would that be enough to trigger an arrest? Indeed, the majority in *Atwater* concluded that each of the petitioner's proposed standards were "readily administrable."

HYPOTHETICAL

A police officer notices a man walking down the street coming toward the officer. As the man and the officer get closer, the officer notices that the man is chewing tobacco. At that point, the officer witnesses the man spitting on the sidewalk. Three months earlier, the local city council passed a local ordinance banning spitting on public property. The ordinance was passed in order to respond to complaints from a number of local merchants who were unhappy about vagrants loitering in front of their business establishments. The ordinance calls for a $150 fine for the offense, which is classified as a violation. The police officer approaches the man and while writing the ticket gets into an argument with him. The officer decides to arrest the man instead, handcuffing him and placing him in the back of the cruiser. After being subjected to regular booking procedures at the police station, the man is eventually released with an appearance ticket and a $150 fine. Was the arrest consistent with the Fourth Amendment?

3. *State crimes.* In *Virginia v. Moore*, 553 U.S. 164 (2008), the Supreme Court considered the legality of an arrest for driving with a suspended license. The arrest clearly violated Virginia law, which required that the police officer believe that an arrest was necessary to ensure appearance or prevent injury. (Incidentally, state law required that the misdemeanor result in a summons, rather than an arrest.) But the Supreme Court concluded that the arrest was not unconstitutional as long as it was supported by probable cause. In *Moore*, the Court refused to "import" state limits into the constitutional analysis. So even when a police officer violates state law by arresting a misdemeanant, the officer has not violated the U.S. Constitution. According to the Court, the opposite "constitutional standard would be only as easy to apply as the underlying state law, and state law can be complicated indeed." *Id.* at 175. Do you agree that the restrictions embodied in the state law are too "complicated" to be a constitutional standard? See Va. Code § 19.2-74.

C. STOP AND FRISK

The spectrum of police encounters is not limited to innocent conversations on the one hand and full arrests on the other hand. What if the police stop suspicious individuals and ask them what they are doing, and then pat them down for weapons? These encounters fall into the netherworld of police encounters, and courts have invested enormous judicial resources to evaluate and oversee these encounters, which has proven difficult. As in the search context, it is important to segment the events into discrete components. Just because the police are justified in stopping an individual does not automatically entail that the police are justified in patting down or frisking that individual. Each event

STATUTORY REQUIREMENTS

State law may impose additional restrictions on misdemeanor arrests that go beyond the constitutional requirements. In other words, even though the Supreme Court is fine with police officers performing warrantless arrests for both felonies and misdemeanors, even minor infractions, state law might not be fine with it. State statutes vary considerably in whether they place restrictions on these warrantless arrests, but consider the following example from Nebraska:

> . . . [A] peace officer may arrest a person without a warrant if the officer has reasonable cause to believe that such person has committed:
>
> (a) A felony;
>
> (b) A misdemeanor, and the officer has reasonable cause to believe that such person either (i) will not be apprehended unless immediately arrested, (ii) may cause injury to himself or herself or others or damage to property unless immediately arrested, (iii) may destroy or conceal evidence of the commission of such misdemeanor, or (iv) has committed a misdemeanor in the presence of the officer; or
>
> (c) One or more of the following acts to one or more household members, whether or not committed in the presence of the peace officer:
>
> (i) Attempting to cause or intentionally and knowingly causing bodily injury with or without a dangerous instrument;
>
> (ii) Placing, by physical menace, another in fear of imminent bodily injury; or
>
> (iii) Engaging in sexual contact or sexual penetration without consent. . . .

Neb. Rev. Stat. § 29-404.02. Notice that there is no restriction on the severity of the misdemeanor, but the officer must believe that an arrest is necessary for apprehension, to prevent destruction of evidence or damage to property, or to prevent injury. Do you agree that these lines are "readily administrable," in the words of the *Atwater* majority?

is a unique Fourth Amendment event—requiring justification and some individualized suspicion.

In the following section, we analyze this distinctive police procedure and the enormous jurisprudence that has sprung up to regulate it. As you read these cases and materials, ask yourself whether the law has risen to the challenge or whether stop and frisk encounters fall into Herbert Packer's blind spot—somewhere in between due process and crime control. See James Stribopoulos, *Packer's Blind Spot: Low Visibility Encounters and the Limits of Due Process vs. Crime Control*, in *Rethinking Criminal Law Theory* (2012). Has the Supreme Court given the police enough authority to conduct these low visibility encounters or has the Court given state authorities too much power in this area?

1. The Authority to Stop and Frisk

The following case explains the concept of the "stop and frisk" procedure and establishes its legitimacy for the first time. Indeed, the case is so synonymous with "stop and frisk" that these encounters are often referred to simply as *Terry* stops in reference to this precedent. As you read *Terry v. Ohio,* look for the Court's articulation of the standard—reasonable suspicion—and more importantly evaluate the Court's application of that standard to the stop of Mr. Terry. Did the police have reasonable suspicion to believe that criminal behavior "may be afoot"?

Terry v. Ohio

Supreme Court of the United States
392 U.S. 1 (1968)

Mr. Chief Justice Warren delivered the opinion of the Court.

This case presents serious questions concerning the role of the Fourth Amendment in the confrontation on the street between the citizen and the policeman investigating suspicious circumstances.

Petitioner Terry was convicted of carrying a concealed weapon and sentenced to the statutorily prescribed term of one to three years in the penitentiary. Following the denial of a pretrial motion to suppress, the prosecution introduced in evidence two revolvers and a number of bullets seized from Terry and a codefendant, Richard Chilton, by Cleveland Police Detective Martin McFadden. At the hearing on the motion to suppress this evidence, Officer McFadden testified that while he was patrolling in plain clothes in downtown Cleveland at approximately 2:30 in the afternoon of October 31, 1963, his attention was attracted by two men, Chilton and Terry, standing on the corner of Huron Road and Euclid Avenue. He had never seen the two men before, and he was unable to say precisely what first drew his eye to them. However, he testified that he had been a policeman for 39 years and a detective for 35 and that he had been assigned to patrol this vicinity of downtown Cleveland for shoplifters and pickpockets for 30 years. He explained that he had developed routine habits of observation over the years and that he would "stand and watch people or walk and watch people at many intervals of the day." He added: "Now, in this case when I looked over they didn't look right to me at the time."

His interest aroused, Officer McFadden took up a post of observation in the entrance to a store 300 to 400 feet away from the two men. "I get more purpose to watch them when I seen their movements," he testified. He saw one of the men leave the other one and walk southwest on Huron Road, past some stores. The man paused for a moment and looked in a store window, then walked on a short distance, turned around and walked back toward the corner, pausing once again to look in the same store window. He rejoined his companion at the corner, and the two conferred briefly. Then the second man went through the same series of motions, strolling down Huron Road, looking in the same window, walking on a short distance, turning back, peering in the store window again, and returning to confer with the first man at the corner. The two men repeated this ritual alternately between five and six times apiece—in all, roughly a dozen trips. At one point, while the two were standing together on the corner, a third man approached them and engaged them briefly in conversation. This man then left the two others and walked west on Euclid Avenue. Chilton and Terry resumed their measured pacing, peering and conferring. After this had gone on for 10 to 12 minutes, the two men walked off together, heading west on Euclid Avenue, following the path taken earlier by the third man.

By this time Officer McFadden had become thoroughly suspicious. He testified that after observing their elaborately casual and oft-repeated reconnaissance of the store window on Huron Road, he suspected the two men of "casing a job, a stick-up," and that he considered it his duty as a police officer to investigate further. He added that he feared "they may have a gun." Thus, Officer McFadden followed Chilton and Terry and saw them stop in front of Zucker's store to talk to the same man who had conferred with them earlier on the street corner. Deciding that the situation was ripe for direct action, Officer McFadden approached the three men, identified himself as a police officer and asked for their names. At this point his knowledge was confined to what he had observed. He was not acquainted with any of the three men by name or by sight, and he had received no information concerning them from any other source. When the men "mumbled something" in response to his inquiries, Officer McFadden grabbed petitioner Terry, spun him around so that they were facing the other two, with Terry between McFadden and the others, and patted down the outside of his clothing. In the left breast pocket of Terry's overcoat Officer McFadden felt a pistol. He reached inside the overcoat pocket, but was unable to remove the gun. At this point, keeping Terry between himself and the others, the officer ordered all three men to enter Zucker's store. As they went in, he removed Terry's overcoat completely, removed a .38-caliber revolver from the pocket and ordered all three men to face the wall with their hands raised. Officer McFadden proceeded to pat down the outer clothing of Chilton and the third man, Katz. He discovered another revolver in the outer pocket of Chilton's overcoat, but no weapons were found on Katz. The officer testified that he only patted the men down to see whether they had weapons, and that he did not put his hands beneath the outer garments of either Terry or Chilton until he felt their guns. So far as appears from the record, he never placed his hands beneath Katz' outer garments. Officer McFadden seized Chilton's gun, asked the proprietor of the store to call a police wagon, and took all three men to the station, where Chilton and Terry were formally charged with carrying concealed weapons. . . .

I

. . . Unquestionably petitioner was entitled to the protection of the Fourth Amendment as he walked down the street in Cleveland. The question is whether in all the circumstances of this on-the-street encounter, his right to personal security was violated by an unreasonable search and seizure.

We would be less than candid if we did not acknowledge that this question thrusts to the fore difficult and troublesome issues regarding a sensitive area of police activity—issues which have never before been squarely presented to this Court. Reflective of the tensions involved are the practical and constitutional arguments pressed with great vigor on both sides of the public debate over the power of the police to "stop and frisk"—as it is sometimes euphemistically termed—suspicious persons.

New York police stop and frisk for illegal fireworks during crackdown near Canal Street in 1994. (Stacy Walsh Rosenstock/Alamy Stock Photo

On the one hand, it is frequently argued that in dealing with the rapidly unfolding and often dangerous situations on city streets the police are in need of an escalating set of flexible responses, graduated in relation to the amount of information they possess. For this purpose it is urged that distinctions should be made between a "stop" and an "arrest" (or a "seizure" of a person), and between a "frisk" and a "search." Thus, it is argued, the police should be allowed to "stop" a person and detain him briefly for questioning upon suspicion that he may be connected with criminal activity. Upon suspicion that the person may be armed, the police should have the power to "frisk" him for weapons. If the "stop" and the "frisk" give rise to probable cause to believe that the suspect has committed a crime, then the police should be empowered to make a formal "arrest," and a full incident "search" of the person. This scheme is justified in part upon the notion that a "stop" and a "frisk" amount to a mere "minor inconvenience and petty indignity," which can properly be imposed upon the citizen in the interest of effective law enforcement on the basis of a police officer's suspicion.

On the other side the argument is made that the authority of the police must be strictly circumscribed by the law of arrest and search as it has developed to date in the traditional jurisprudence of the Fourth Amendment. It is contended with some force that there is not—and cannot be—a variety of police activity which does not depend solely upon the voluntary cooperation of the citizen and yet which stops short of an arrest based upon probable cause to make such an arrest. The heart of the Fourth Amendment, the argument runs, is a severe requirement of specific justification for any intrusion upon protected personal security, coupled with a highly developed system of judicial controls to enforce upon the agents of the State the commands of the Constitution. Acquiescence by the courts in the compulsion inherent in the field interrogation practices at issue here, it is urged, would constitute an abdication of judicial control over, and indeed an encouragement of, substantial interference with liberty and personal security by police officers whose judgment is necessarily colored by their primary involvement in "the often competitive enterprise of ferreting out crime." This, it is argued, can only serve to exacerbate police-community tensions in the crowded centers of our Nation's cities. . . .

II

Our first task is to establish at what point in this encounter the Fourth Amendment becomes relevant. That is, we must decide whether and when Officer McFadden "seized" Terry and whether and when he conducted a "search." There is some suggestion in the use of such terms as "stop" and "frisk" that such police conduct is outside the purview of the Fourth Amendment because neither action rises to the level of a "search" or "seizure" within the meaning of the Constitution. We emphatically reject this notion. It is quite plain that the Fourth Amendment governs "seizures" of the person which do not eventuate in a trip to the station house and prosecution for crime—"arrests" in traditional terminology. It must be recognized that whenever a police officer accosts an individual and restrains his freedom to walk away, he has "seized" that person. And it is nothing less than sheer torture of the English language to suggest that a careful exploration of the outer surfaces of a person's clothing all over his or her body in an attempt to find weapons is not a "search." Moreover, it is simply fantastic to urge that such a procedure performed in public by a policeman while the citizen stands helpless, perhaps facing a wall with his hands raised, is a "petty indignity." It is a serious intrusion upon the sanctity of the person, which may inflict great indignity and arouse strong resentment, and it is not to be undertaken lightly.

The danger in the logic which proceeds upon distinctions between a "stop" and an "arrest," or "seizure" of the person, and between a "frisk" and a "search" is twofold. It seeks to isolate from constitutional scrutiny the initial stages of the contact between the policeman and the citizen. And by suggesting a rigid all-or-nothing model of justification and regulation under the Amendment, it obscures the utility of limitations upon the scope, as well as the initiation, of police action as a means of constitutional regulation. This Court has held in the past that a search which is reasonable at its inception may violate the Fourth Amendment by virtue of its intolerable intensity and scope. The scope of the search must be "strictly tied to and justified by" the circumstances which rendered its initiation permissible.

The distinctions of classical "stop-and-frisk" theory thus serve to divert attention from the central inquiry under the Fourth Amendment—the reasonableness in all the circumstances of the particular governmental invasion of a citizen's personal security. "Search" and "seizure" are not talismans. We therefore reject the notions that the Fourth Amendment does not come into play at all as a limitation upon police conduct if the officers stop short of something called a "technical arrest" or a "full-blown search."

In this case there can be no question, then, that Officer McFadden "seized" petitioner and subjected him to a "search" when he took hold of him and patted down the outer surfaces of his clothing. We must decide whether at that point it was reasonable for Officer McFadden to have interfered with petitioner's personal security as he did. And in determining whether the seizure and search were "unreasonable" our inquiry is a dual one—whether the officer's action was justified at its inception, and whether it was reasonably related in scope to the circumstances which justified the interference in the first place.

III

. . . [W]e deal here with an entire rubric of police conduct—necessarily swift action predicated upon the on-the-spot observations of the officer on the beat—which historically has not been, and as a practical matter could not be, subjected to the warrant procedure. Instead, the conduct involved in this case must be tested by the Fourth Amendment's general proscription against unreasonable searches and seizures.

Nonetheless, the notions which underlie both the warrant procedure and the requirement of probable cause remain fully relevant in this context. In order to assess the reasonableness of Officer McFadden's conduct as a general proposition, it is necessary "first to focus upon the governmental interest which allegedly justifies official intrusion upon the constitutionally protected interests of the private citizen," for there is "no ready test for determining reasonableness other than by balancing the need to search (or seize) against the invasion which the search (or seizure) entails." And in justifying the particular intrusion the police officer must be able to point to specific and articulable facts which, taken together with rational inferences from those facts, reasonably warrant that intrusion. The scheme of the Fourth Amendment becomes meaningful only when it is assured that at some point the conduct of those charged with enforcing the laws can be subjected to the more detached, neutral scrutiny of a judge who must evaluate the reasonableness of a particular search or seizure in light of the particular circumstances. And in making that assessment it is imperative that the facts be judged against an objective standard: would the facts available to the officer at the moment of the seizure or the search "warrant a man of reasonable caution in the belief" that the action taken was appropriate? Anything less would invite intrusions upon constitutionally guaranteed rights based on nothing more substantial than inarticulate hunches, a result this Court has consistently refused to sanction. And simple "good faith on the part of the arresting officer is not enough." . . .

Applying these principles to this case, we consider first the nature and extent of the governmental interests involved. One general interest is of course that of effective crime prevention and detection; it is this interest which underlies the recognition that a police officer may in appropriate circumstances and in an appropriate manner approach a person for purposes of investigating possibly criminal behavior even though there is no probable cause to make an arrest. It was this legitimate investigative function Officer McFadden was discharging when he decided to approach petitioner and his companions. He had observed Terry, Chilton, and Katz go through a series of acts, each of them perhaps innocent in itself, but which taken together warranted further investigation. There is nothing unusual in two men standing together on a street corner, perhaps waiting for someone. Nor is there anything suspicious about people in such circumstances strolling up and down the street, singly or in pairs. Store windows, moreover, are made to be looked in. But the story is quite different where, as here, two men hover about a street corner for an extended period of time, at the end of which it becomes apparent that they are not waiting for anyone or anything; where these men pace alternately along an identical route, pausing to stare in the same store window roughly times; where each completion of this route is followed immediately by a conference between the two men on the corner; where they are joined in one of these conferences by a third man who leaves swiftly; and where the two men finally follow the third and rejoin him a couple of blocks away. It would have been poor police work indeed for an officer of 30 years' experience in the detection of thievery from stores in this same neighborhood to have failed to investigate this behavior further.

The crux of this case, however, is not the propriety of Officer McFadden's taking steps to investigate petitioner's suspicious behavior, but rather, whether there was justification for McFadden's invasion of Terry's personal security by searching him for weapons in the course of that investigation. We are now concerned with more than the governmental interest in investigating crime; in addition, there is the more immediate interest of the police officer in taking steps to assure himself that the person with whom he is dealing is not armed with a weapon that could unexpectedly and fatally be used against him. Certainly it would be unreasonable to require that police officers take unnecessary risks in the performance of their duties. American criminals have a long tradition of armed violence, and every year in this country many law enforcement officers are killed in the line of duty, and thousands more are wounded. Virtually all of these deaths and a substantial portion of the injuries are inflicted with guns and knives.

In view of these facts, we cannot blind ourselves to the need for law enforcement officers to protect themselves and other prospective victims of violence in situations where they may lack probable cause for an arrest. When an officer is justified in believing that the individual whose suspicious behavior he is investigating at close range is armed and presently dangerous to the officer or to others, it would appear to be clearly unreasonable to deny the officer the power to take necessary measures to determine whether the person is in fact carrying a weapon and to neutralize the threat of physical harm.

We must still consider, however, the nature and quality of the intrusion on individual rights which must be accepted if police officers are to be conceded the right to search for weapons in situations where probable cause to arrest for crime is lacking. Even a limited search of the outer clothing for weapons constitutes a severe, though brief, intrusion upon cherished personal security, and it must surely be an annoying, frightening, and perhaps humiliating experience. . . .

Our evaluation of the proper balance that has to be struck in this type of case leads us to conclude that there must be a narrowly drawn authority to permit a reasonable search for weapons for the protection of the police officer, where he has reason to believe that he is dealing with an armed and dangerous individual, regardless of whether he has probable cause to arrest the individual for a crime. The officer need not be absolutely certain that the individual is armed; the issue is whether a reasonably prudent man in the circumstances would be warranted in the belief that his safety or that of others was in danger. And in determining whether the officer acted reasonably in such circumstances, due weight must be given, not to his inchoate and unparticularized suspicion or "hunch," but to the specific reasonable inferences which he is entitled to draw from the facts in light of his experience.

IV

We must now examine the conduct of Officer McFadden in this case to determine whether his search and seizure of petitioner were reasonable, both at their inception and as conducted. He had observed Terry, together with Chilton and another man, acting in a manner he took to be preface to a "stick-up." We think on the facts and circumstances Officer McFadden detailed before the trial judge a reasonably prudent man would have been warranted in believing petitioner was armed and thus presented a threat to the officer's safety while he was investigating his suspicious behavior. The actions of Terry and Chilton were consistent with McFadden's hypothesis that these men were contemplating a daylight robbery—which, it is reasonable to assume, would be likely to involve the use of weapons—and nothing in their conduct from the time he first noticed them until the time he confronted them and identified himself as a police officer gave him sufficient reason to negate that hypothesis. . . .

. . . Officer McFadden had reasonable grounds to believe that petitioner was armed and dangerous, and it was necessary for the protection of himself and others to take swift measures to discover the true facts and neutralize the threat of harm if it materialized. The policeman carefully restricted his search to what was appropriate to the discovery of the particular items which he sought. Each case of this sort will, of course, have to be decided on its own facts. We merely hold today that where a police officer observes unusual conduct which leads him reasonably to conclude in light of his experience that criminal activity may be afoot and that the persons with whom he is dealing may be armed and presently dangerous, where in the course of investigating this behavior he identifies himself as a policeman and makes reasonable inquiries, and where nothing in the initial stages of the encounter serves to dispel his reasonable fear for his own or others' safety, he is entitled for the protection of himself and others in the area to conduct a carefully limited search of the outer clothing of such persons in an attempt to discover weapons which might be used to assault him. Such a search is a reasonable search under the Fourth Amendment. . . .

Mr. Justice Douglas, dissenting.

. . . The infringement on personal liberty of any "seizure" of a person can only be "reasonable" under the Fourth Amendment if we require the police to possess "probable cause" before they seize him. Only that line draws a meaningful distinction between an officer's mere inkling and the presence of facts within the officer's personal knowledge which would convince a reasonable man that the person seized has committed, is committing, or is about to commit a particular crime. . . .

> To give the police greater power than a magistrate is to take a long step down the totalitarian path. Perhaps such a step is desirable to cope with modern forms of lawlessness. But if it is taken, it should be the deliberate choice of the people through a constitutional amendment. Until the Fourth Amendment, which is closely allied with the Fifth, is rewritten, the person and the effects of the individual are beyond the reach of all government agencies until there are reasonable grounds to believe (probable cause) that a criminal venture has been launched or is about to be launched.
>
> There have been powerful hydraulic pressures throughout our history that bear heavily on the Court to water down constitutional guarantees and give the police the upper hand. That hydraulic pressure has probably never been greater than it is today. Yet if the individual is no longer to be sovereign, if the police can pick him up whenever they do not like the cut of his jib, if they can "seize" and "search" him in their discretion, we enter a new regime. The decision to enter it should be made only after a full debate by the people of this country.

NOTES & QUESTIONS ON TERRY *STOPS*

1. *Specific and articulable facts versus hunches.* In *Terry*, the Court concluded that police officers need "specific and articulable facts which, taken together with rational inferences from those facts, reasonably warrant that intrusion." 392 U.S. at 21. Why do you think the Court required specific and articulable facts? The reasonable suspicion standard, based on the totality of the circumstances, is supposed to be based on something more definite than "inarticulable hunches." What is the problem with hunches? How would a court oversee the propriety of a *Terry* stop based on a mere hunch? However, remember that a police officer is entitled to rely on "specific reasonable inferences which he is entitled to draw from the facts in light of his experience." Are those inferences categorically distinct, and more reliable than, mere hunches? How should a court distinguish between "reasonable inferences" based on experience and hunches? In *United States v. Arvizu*, 534 U.S. 266 (2002), the Court explained that "[t]his process allows officers to draw on their own experiences and specialized training to make inferences from and deductions about the cumulative information available." Police officers have "specialized training" in police tactics, but they have no training in the social sciences, nor in statistics. Do courts defer to the judgments of police officers too much or is it appropriate to lend credence to common sense judgments made on the street by trained officers?

2. *Crime control.* Does *Terry v. Ohio* represent the final victory of the crime control model described by Herbert Packer? At least some commentators think so. Consider the following description from Professor Jeffrey Fagan, who was closely involved in *Terry* litigation on racial discrimination described later in this chapter:

> Beyond the costs of a wrong guess by police that leads to a temporary street detention, the *Terry* Court worried about a variety of "petty indignities." The indignities of this form of order maintenance in effect piled up from the accumulation of stops, not simply from publicly visible frisks. As *Terry*'s crime control agenda took root, the exposure of citizens, both innocents and those engaged in crime, to a new form street stops grew exponentially. The indignity problem arises not from the indignity of the frisk or the search, but from the context of the stop itself. And the dignity problem also arises not from the sheer prevalence of unproductive stops and the burden on innocents (although that itself is a concern), but from the ways those stops often are conducted. Even the most neutral of stops carries emotional freight and the threat of indignities. The concern here is what happens before, during, and after these stops, or how encounters with the police take place and *then unfold*, rather than on simply the regulatory questions of *whether, where*, and *how often* they occur.

Jeffrey Fagan, Terry*'s Original Sin*, 2016 U. Chi. Legal F. 43, 89-90. In other words, *Terry* has led to a persistent feeling in some communities that they are over-policed. Does this suggest that the Supreme Court should reconsider *Terry v. Ohio*, this time with greater attention to its psychological costs? This issue is explored in greater depth in the Practice & Policy section at the end of this chapter.

PROBLEM CASE

Terry states that police officers may stop an individual if they reasonably suspect that criminal activity is afoot and may then frisk an individual if they believe that the suspect is armed and dangerous. In applying that standard, consider the following case.

Police officers in Phoenix, Arizona, were patrolling at 10:00 p.m. a neighborhood they considered a "gang" area. The officers witnessed a man, Johnathon Serna, standing with a woman in the middle of the street. As the patrol car approached them, Serna and the woman walked in opposite directions away from each other. The officers stopped and got out of the car and approached Serna, who was cooperative and polite, and who agreed to speak with them. The officer noticed a bulge in Serna's waistband and therefore asked Serna if he was armed; Serna indicated that he had a gun. The officer asked Serna to put his hands over his head and the officer then removed the gun from Serna's waistband. As it turns out, Serna was a convicted felon who was not supposed to be carrying a gun, although in Arizona non-felons may carry a concealed firearm.

Did the police stop comply with *Terry*? When the police approached Serna, did they have evidence that criminal activity was afoot or, in the alternative, did they have Serna's consent to speak with him? When the police frisked Serna, did they have evidence that he was armed? Did they have evidence that Serna was dangerous? What role in the analysis is played by the fact that most citizens are permitted to carry weapons in public in Arizona? See *State v. Serna*, 235 Ariz. 270, 275, 331 P.3d 405, 410 (2014).

2. Failure to Disclose Identity

The previous subsection outlined the basic rationale or justification for the stop and frisk procedure. Now we turn to the *scope* of stop and frisk. What type of conduct is permissible during a stop and frisk encounter? Clearly the police are entitled to frisk the subject, but that still leaves many questions unanswered. What type of questions can the police ask and what consequences flow from a suspect's refusal to answer them? In the following case, the police stopped Larry Dudley Hiibel and then arrested him when he refused repeated requests to identify himself or provide identification documents in accordance with a state statute. Was Hiibel required to answer and did the Fourth Amendment permit his arrest when he failed to comply with this request during the *Terry* stop?

Hiibel v. Sixth Judicial District Court of Nevada, Humboldt County

Supreme Court of the United States
542 U.S. 177 (2004)

Justice KENNEDY delivered the opinion of the Court.

The petitioner was arrested and convicted for refusing to identify himself during a stop allowed by *Terry v. Ohio*, 392 U.S. 1 (1968). He challenges his conviction under the Fourth and Fifth Amendments to the United States Constitution, applicable to the States through the Fourteenth Amendment.

I

The sheriff's department in Humboldt County, Nevada, received an afternoon telephone call reporting an assault. The caller reported seeing a man assault a woman in a red and silver GMC truck on Grass Valley Road. Deputy Sheriff Lee Dove was dispatched to investigate. When the officer arrived at the scene, he found the truck parked on the side of the road. A man was standing by the truck, and a young woman was sitting inside it. The officer observed skid marks in the gravel behind the vehicle, leading him to believe it had come to a sudden stop.

The officer approached the man and explained that he was investigating a report of a fight. The man appeared to be intoxicated. The officer asked him if he had "any identification on [him]," which we understand as a request to produce a driver's license or some other form of written identification. The man refused and asked why the officer wanted to see identification. The officer responded that he was conducting an investigation and needed to see some identification. The unidentified man became agitated and insisted he had done nothing wrong. The officer explained that he wanted to find out who the man was and what he was doing there. After continued refusals to comply with the officer's request for identification, the man began to taunt the officer by placing his hands behind his back and telling the officer to arrest him and take him to jail. This routine kept up for several minutes: The officer asked for identification 11 times and was refused each time. After warning the man that he would be arrested if he continued to refuse to comply, the officer placed him under arrest.

We now know that the man arrested on Grass Valley Road is Larry Dudley Hiibel. Hiibel was charged with "willfully resist[ing], delay[ing] or obstruct [ing] a public officer in discharging or attempting to discharge any legal duty of his office" in violation of Nev. Rev. Stat. § 199.280 (2003). The government reasoned that Hiibel had obstructed the officer in carrying out his duties under § 171.123, a Nevada statute that defines the legal rights and duties of a police officer in the context of an investigative stop. Section 171.123 provides in relevant part:

> 1. Any peace officer may detain any person whom the officer encounters under circumstances which reasonably indicate that the person has committed, is committing or is about to commit a crime. . . .
> 3. The officer may detain the person pursuant to this section only to ascertain his identity and the suspicious circumstances surrounding his presence abroad. Any person so detained shall identify himself, but may not be compelled to answer any other inquiry of any peace officer.

Hiibel was tried in the Justice Court of Union Township. . . .

Larry "Dudley" Hiibel outside the U.S. Supreme Court in March 2004. (Manuel Balce Ceneta/AP/Shutterstock)

II

NRS § 171.123(3) is an enactment sometimes referred to as a "stop and identify" statute. Stop and identify statutes often combine elements of traditional vagrancy laws with provisions intended to regulate police behavior in the course of investigatory stops. The statutes vary from State to State, but all permit an officer to ask or require a suspect to disclose his identity. A few States model their statutes on the Uniform Arrest Act, a model code that permits an officer to stop a person reasonably suspected of committing a crime and "demand of him his name, address, business abroad and whither he is going." Other statutes are based on the text proposed by the American Law Institute as part of the Institute's Model Penal Code. . . . In some States, a suspect's refusal to identify himself is a misdemeanor offense or civil violation; in others, it is a factor to be considered in whether the suspect has violated loitering laws. In other States, a suspect may decline to identify himself without penalty.

Stop and identify statutes have their roots in early English vagrancy laws that required suspected vagrants to face arrest unless they gave "a good Account of themselves," a power that itself reflected common-law rights of private persons to "arrest any suspicious night-walker, and detain him till he give a good account of himself. . . ." In recent decades, the Court has found constitutional infirmity in traditional vagrancy laws. In *Papachristou v. Jacksonville*, 405 U.S. 156 (1972), the Court held that a traditional vagrancy law was void for vagueness. Its broad scope and imprecise terms denied proper notice to potential offenders and permitted police officers to exercise unfettered discretion in the enforcement of the law.

The Court has recognized similar constitutional limitations on the scope and operation of stop and identify statutes. In *Brown v. Texas*, 443 U.S. 47, 52 (1979), the Court invalidated a conviction for violating a Texas stop and identify statute on Fourth Amendment grounds. The Court ruled that the initial stop was not based on specific, objective facts establishing reasonable suspicion to believe the suspect was involved in criminal activity. Absent that factual basis for detaining the defendant, the Court held, the risk of "arbitrary and abusive police practices" was too great and the stop was impermissible. Four Terms later, the Court invalidated a modified stop and identify statute on vagueness grounds. See *Kolender v. Lawson*, 461 U.S. 352 (1983). The California law in *Kolender* required a suspect to give an officer "credible and reliable" identification when asked to identify himself. The Court held that the statute was void because it provided no standard for determining what a suspect must do to comply with it, resulting in "virtually unrestrained power to arrest and charge persons with a violation." The present case begins where our prior cases left off. . . .

III

Hiibel argues that his conviction cannot stand because the officer's conduct violated his Fourth Amendment rights. We disagree.

Asking questions is an essential part of police investigations. In the ordinary course a police officer is free to ask a person for identification without implicating the Fourth Amendment. "[I]nterrogation relating to one's identity or a request for identification by the police does not, by itself, constitute a Fourth Amendment seizure." Beginning with *Terry v. Ohio*, 392 U.S. 1 (1968), the Court has recognized that a law enforcement officer's reasonable suspicion that a person may be involved in criminal activity permits the officer to stop the person for a brief time and take additional steps to investigate further. To ensure that the resulting seizure is constitutionally reasonable, a *Terry* stop must be limited. The officer's action must be "justified at its inception, and . . . reasonably related in scope to the circumstances which justified the interference in the first place." For example, the seizure can not continue for an excessive period of time or resemble a traditional arrest.

Our decisions make clear that questions concerning a suspect's identity are a routine and accepted part of many *Terry* stops. Obtaining a suspect's name in the course of a *Terry* stop serves important government interests. Knowledge of identity may inform an officer that a suspect is wanted for another offense, or has a record of violence or mental disorder. On the other hand, knowing identity may help clear a suspect and allow the police to concentrate their efforts elsewhere. Identity may prove particularly important in cases such as this, where the police are investigating what appears to be a domestic assault. Officers called to investigate domestic disputes need to know whom they are dealing with in order to assess the situation, the threat to their own safety, and possible danger to the potential victim.

Although it is well established that an officer may ask a suspect to identify himself in the course of a *Terry* stop, it has been an open question whether the suspect can be arrested and prosecuted for refusal to answer. Petitioner draws our attention to statements in prior opinions that, according to him, answer the question in his favor. In *Terry*, Justice White stated in a concurring opinion that a person detained in an investigative stop can be questioned but is "not obliged to answer, answers may not be compelled, and refusal to answer furnishes no basis for an arrest." The Court cited this opinion in dicta in *Berkemer v. McCarty*, 468 U.S. 420, 439 (1984), a decision holding that a routine traffic stop is not a custodial stop requiring the protections of *Miranda v. Arizona*, 384 U.S. 436 (1966). In the course of explaining why *Terry* stops have not been subject to *Miranda*, the Court suggested reasons why *Terry* stops have a "nonthreatening character," among them the fact that a suspect detained during a *Terry* stop "is not obliged to respond" to questions. According to petitioner, these statements establish a right to refuse to answer questions during a *Terry* stop.

We do not read these statements as controlling. The passages recognize that the Fourth Amendment does not impose obligations on the citizen but instead provides rights against the government. As a result, the Fourth Amendment itself cannot require a suspect to answer questions. This case concerns a different issue, however. Here, the source of the legal obligation arises from Nevada state law, not the Fourth Amendment. Further, the statutory obligation does not go beyond answering an officer's request to disclose a name. As a result, we cannot view the dicta in *Berkemer* or Justice White's concurrence in *Terry* as answering the question whether a State can compel a suspect to disclose his name during a *Terry* stop.

The principles of *Terry* permit a State to require a suspect to disclose his name in the course of a *Terry* stop. The reasonableness of a seizure under the Fourth Amendment is determined "by balancing its intrusion on the individual's Fourth Amendment interests against its promotion of legitimate government interests." The Nevada statute satisfies that standard. The request for identity has an immediate relation to the purpose, rationale, and practical demands of a *Terry* stop. The threat of criminal sanction helps ensure that the request for identity does not become a legal nullity. On the other hand, the Nevada statute does not alter the nature of the stop itself: it does not change its duration or its location. A state law requiring a suspect to disclose his name in the course of a valid *Terry* stop is consistent with Fourth Amendment prohibitions against unreasonable searches and seizures.

Petitioner argues that the Nevada statute circumvents the probable-cause requirement, in effect allowing an officer to arrest a person for being suspicious. According to petitioner, this creates a risk of arbitrary police conduct that the Fourth Amendment does not permit. . . . Petitioner's concerns are met by the requirement that a *Terry* stop must be justified at its inception and "reasonably related in scope to the circumstances which justified" the initial stop. Under these principles, an officer may not arrest a suspect for failure to identify himself if the request for identification is not reasonably related to the circumstances justifying the stop. . . .

Justice BREYER, with whom Justice SOUTER and Justice GINSBURG join, dissenting.

Notwithstanding the vagrancy statutes to which the majority refers, this Court's Fourth Amendment precedents make clear that police may conduct a *Terry* stop only within circumscribed limits. And one of those limits invalidates laws that compel responses to police questioning.

In *Terry v. Ohio*, 392 U.S. 1 (1968), the Court considered whether police, in the absence of probable cause, can stop, question, or frisk an individual at all. The Court recognized that the Fourth Amendment protects the "right of every individual to the possession and control of his own person." At the same time, it recognized that in certain circumstances, public safety might require a limited "seizure," or stop, of an individual against his will. The Court consequently set forth conditions circumscribing when and how the police might conduct a *Terry* stop. They include what has become known as the "reasonable suspicion" standard. Justice White, in a separate concurring opinion, set forth further conditions. Justice White wrote: "Of course, the person stopped is not obliged to answer, answers may not be compelled, and refusal to answer furnishes no basis for an arrest, although it may alert the officer to the need for continued observation."

About 10 years later, the Court, in *Brown v. Texas*, 443 U.S. 47 (1979), held that police lacked "any reasonable suspicion" to detain the particular petitioner and require him to identify himself. The Court noted that the trial judge had asked the following: "I'm sure [officers conducting a *Terry* stop] should ask everything they possibly could find out. What I'm asking is what's the State's interest in putting a man in jail because he doesn't want to answer. . . ." The Court referred to Justice White's *Terry* concurrence. And it said that it "need not decide" the matter.

Then, five years later, the Court wrote that an "officer may ask the [*Terry*] detainee a moderate number of questions to determine his identity and to try to obtain information confirming or dispelling the officer's suspicions. But the detainee is not obliged to respond." *Berkemer v. McCarty*, 468 U.S. 420, 439 (1984). See also *Kolender v. Lawson*, 461 U.S. 352, 365 (1983) (Brennan, J., concurring) (*Terry* suspect "must be free to . . . decline to answer the questions put to him"); *Illinois v. Wardlow*, 528 U.S. 119, 125 (2000) (stating that allowing officers to stop and question a fleeing person "is quite consistent with the individual's right to go about his business or to stay put and remain silent in the face of police questioning").

This lengthy history—of concurring opinions, of references, and of clear explicit statements—means that the Court's statement in *Berkemer*, while technically dicta, is the kind of strong dicta that the legal community typically takes as a statement of the law. And that law has remained undisturbed for more than 20 years. . . .

NOTES & QUESTIONS ON FAILURE TO DISCLOSE IDENTITY

1. *What is identity?* The Court concluded that establishing an individual's identity, through questions, is a "routine and accepted part" of *Terry* stops. Do you agree? In any event, the question is really composed of two narrower

questions. First, may the police ask an individual questions about their identity during a *Terry* stop? Second, are the police permitted to arrest an individual who fails to comply with a request to identify themselves? The answer to the first question is undeniably yes, but the second question is more complicated and involves what consequences might flow from an individual's refusal to comply. How does the Court go about answering this question? The Court claimed that permitting this type of police conduct "does not alter the nature of the stop itself [and] does not change its duration or its location." Do you agree?

2. *What actually happened.* The following is the transcript of the full interaction between Hiibel and Deputy Dove. As you read the transcript, ask yourself whether this should be considered a "routine and accepted part" of all *Terry* stops.

Hiibel: How's it goin' Sheriff
Dove: How ya doin'?
Dove: Well, . . .
H: Looks like I'm parked ok
D: Well, I've got a report that there's been a fightin' going on between you two tonight.
H: I don't know nuttin' about that. — Of course, I've —
D: Why don't you come over here, ok?
H: I'm parked alright on the side of the road
D: You've got any identification on you?
H: No, — why should I have an ID? Why do you want me to . . .
D: The thing is this – we're doin' an investigation, ok and I wanna see some identification
H: Naw, I'm — gonna —
D: I need to see some identification
H: I don't, I don't think, I think I've —
D: Come over here. Sir . . .
H: Sir, don't grab onto me
D: I won't grab you if you'll come back over here
H: — sorry —
D: Come back over here, ok
H: Why in hell do I go over here? Why? Am I under arrest?
D: I just need to see some identification.
H: Why?
D: Because I'm investigating an investigation
H: Investigating what?
D: I'm investigating
H: I'm a legal
D:
H: I'm illegally parked, I mean, I mean I am illegally parked?
D: How'd you get home yesterday
H: That don't matter
D: —
H: —
D: It could be a searchable situation
H: Ok, take me to jail.
D: I didn't say that
H: Alright then I'm not illegally parked
D: Ok
H: I know what, I know what I'm talking to
D:
H: I know what you — type —
D: — registration —
H: Why?

D: Because I wanna find out who you are and I wanna find out what I've got going on here
H: ———
D: So, you're refusing to ——
H: ————
D: ————
H: ————
D: Show me your identification. . . .
H: Why?
D: and uh, uh fine. Show me your identification.
H: I'm uh, I'm uh, I'm being cooperative with you. I'm . . .
D: Show me your ID
H: I'm, I'm cooperating with you
D: Show me your ID
H: If you've got something take me to jail
D: Show me your ID
H: —————
D: ————
H:
D: . . . and then we'll talk, ok?
H: I don't want to talk. I've done nothin'. I've broken no laws. Take me to jail, I don't care.
D: Why would I, why would I take you to jail if you've broken no laws?
H: Because you wanna apparently. I'm not illegally parked, I'm not doin' nothin'. I've got a guy behind me who wants to take me to jail.
D: I want to see some ID, ok.
H: Why?
D: Because
H: Why
D: ————
H: ————
D: ————
H: I don't care
D: You're not going to cooperate?
H: Because I . . .
D: So then you're not gonna cooperate with me at all? Ok, turn around and put your hands on your back. Spread your feet.
M (Mimi): Nooo more!
D: Spread your feet, spread your feet,
M: No more!
D: Spread your feet wider, thank you sir.
M: Aaaahhhh
D: Ok, I'm going to tilt you back in a second. Do you got any —— or stick that will hurt me?
H: I . . .
D: I'm gonna take your knife and you'll get it back at a later time, now.
D: Ok, —— back here.
M: Aaahhhh.
Radio: ———
M: Aaahhhhhh
(Sirens)
M: Aaahhhhh! Get off of me! Get off of me!
H: Big man, big man, real big man!
Radio: ———
M: Aaahhh!
H: Big man, gee what a big man!
M: Stop!
H: I can't, I've never seen such a big man since you guys.
M: Get off of me! Get off of me!
M: Get off of me!
H: Oh, yes. Big men. Big men, I've never seen such big men since you guys.
M: Stop! Stop!
H: Big men!
M: Why are you doing this to me?
H: Big men, big men.
M: (expletive)
D: (to daughter) Can you explain to me what happened tonight?

M: I told you. We got in a fight (. . .) and I told ya what we we were arguing about because we were fightin'.
D: You feel like standin' up?
M: I feel like you getting this thing off of me
D: Can I help you stand up so then we can talk? Maybe we can take those off.
M: Come on . . .
D: Wanna stand up?
D: What's you're name?
H: Big man
D: What's your name?
M: Mimi.
D: Mimi what?
M: Hiibel

To see video of the encounter, go to youtube.com/watch?v=1dFRrFvuGsc. For more discussion of this case, see Arnold H. Loewy, *The Cowboy and the Cop: The Saga of Dudley Hiibel, 9/11, and the Vanishing Fourth Amendment*, 109 Penn St. L. Rev. 929, 937 (2005), who made the following observation:

> In this case, the reasonable suspicion was predicated upon an alleged assault on a female. Having found Hiibel by the side of the road and a young woman in the truck, one would have thought that the first step would be to ascertain the well-being of the female, not the name of the male. He could have observed the female to see if she had any injuries. He could have asked her if she had been attacked, and if either her affirmative response or the manner of her negative response led Deputy Dove to believe that she had been assau lted, he could have arrested her father. Had the officer done that, he would have learned that young Mimi Hiibel had not been assaulted and the whole matter would have been resolved.

See also Peter Koclanes, *Unreasonable Seizure: "Stop and Identify" Statutes Create an Illusion of Safety by Sacrificing Real Privacy*, 57 Fla. L. Rev. 431 (2005); William H. Weisman, *Where Everybody Knows Your Name: Compulsory Identification and the Fallacy of the* Hiibel *Majority*, 71 Brook. L. Rev. 1421, 1424 (2006).

3. *The right to refuse cooperation.* Is the *Hiibel* decision consistent with the general right to refuse to cooperate with the police? Wasn't Hiibel entitled by the Constitution to refuse to help the officer in his investigation? Consider the following statement from *Florida v. Bostick*, 501 U.S. 429, 430 (1991), that "a refusal, alone, does not furnish the minimal level of objective justification needed for detention or seizure."

3. The Reasonable Suspicion Standard

In practice, what does it mean that a police officer must have "reasonable suspicion" that criminal activity is afoot before commencing a *Terry* stop? The

Supreme Court decisions in this area have clustered around two general methodologies. First, the Court has articulated a general "reasonable person" standard and has explained how police officers and courts should apply it. These decisions have explained what type of inferences are—and are not—permissible, i.e., what should be considered an articulable fact and what should be considered an inarticulable "hunch." Second, the Court has articulated a series of bright-line rules, i.e., factual paradigms that it declares either can—or cannot—satisfy the reasonable suspicion standard.

This subsection includes excerpts from two cases that consider bright-line applications of the general standard. In the first case, *Florida v. J.L.*, the Supreme Court asks whether an anonymous tip that a suspect is carrying a gun might be enough to satisfy *Terry*'s reasonable suspicion standard. Previously, in *Adams v. Williams*, 407 U.S. 143 (1972), the Supreme Court upheld a stop and frisk that was based on a tip from an informant because the informant had provided information to the police officer in the past, and the information provided "was immediately verifiable at the scene." In *Florida v. J.L.*, the question is whether there is reasonable suspicion when the tip comes from an anonymous source unknown to the police.

Florida v. J.L.

Supreme Court of the United States
529 U.S. 266 (2000)

Justice Ginsburg delivered the opinion of the Court.

The question presented in this case is whether an anonymous tip that a person is carrying a gun is, without more, sufficient to justify a police officer's stop and frisk of that person. We hold that it is not.

I

On October 13, 1995, an anonymous caller reported to the Miami-Dade Police that a young black male standing at a particular bus stop and wearing a plaid shirt was carrying a gun. So far as the record reveals, there is no audio recording of the tip, and nothing is known about the informant. Sometime after the police received the tip—the record does not say how long—two officers were instructed to respond. They arrived at the bus stop about six minutes later and saw three black males "just hanging out [there]." One of the three, respondent J.L., was wearing a plaid shirt. Apart from the tip, the officers had no reason to suspect any of the three of illegal conduct. The officers did not see a firearm, and J.L. made no threatening or otherwise unusual movements. One of the officers approached J.L., told him to put his hands up on the bus stop, frisked him, and seized a gun from J.L.'s pocket. The second officer frisked the other two individuals, against whom no allegations had been made, and found nothing.

J.L., who was at the time of the frisk "10 days shy of his 16th birth[-day]," was charged under state law with carrying a concealed firearm without a license and possessing a firearm while under the age of 18. . . .

II

. . . In the instant case, the officers' suspicion that J.L. was carrying a weapon arose not from any observations of their own but solely from a call made from an unknown location by an unknown caller. Unlike a tip from a known informant whose reputation can be assessed and who can be held responsible if her allegations turn out to be fabricated, "an anonymous tip alone seldom demonstrates the informant's basis of knowledge or veracity," *Alabama v. White*, 496 U.S. 325, 329 (1990). As we have recognized, however, there are situations in which an anonymous tip, suitably corroborated, exhibits "sufficient indicia of reliability to provide reasonable suspicion to make the investigatory stop." The question we here confront is whether the tip pointing to J.L. had those indicia of reliability.

In *White*, the police received an anonymous tip asserting that a woman was carrying cocaine and predicting that she would leave an apartment building at a specified time, get into a car matching a particular description, and drive to a named motel. Standing alone, the tip would not have justified a *Terry* stop. Only after police observation showed that the informant had accurately predicted the woman's movements, we explained, did it become reasonable to think the tipster had inside knowledge about the suspect and therefore to credit his assertion about the cocaine. Although the Court held that the suspicion in *White* became reasonable after police surveillance, we regarded the case as borderline. Knowledge about a person's future movements indicates some familiarity with that person's affairs, but having such knowledge does not necessarily imply that the informant knows, in particular, whether that person is carrying hidden contraband. We accordingly classified *White* as a "close case."

The tip in the instant case lacked the moderate indicia of reliability present in *White* and essential to the Court's decision in that case. The anonymous call concerning J.L. provided no predictive information and therefore left the police without means to test the informant's knowledge or credibility. That the allegation about the gun turned out to be correct does not suggest that the officers, prior to the frisks, had a reasonable basis for suspecting J.L. of engaging in unlawful conduct: The reasonableness of official suspicion must be measured by what the officers knew before they conducted their search. All the police had to go on in this case was the bare report of an unknown, unaccountable informant who neither explained how he knew about the gun nor supplied any basis for believing he had inside information about J.L. If *White* was a close case on the reliability of anonymous tips, this one surely falls on the other side of the line.

Florida contends that the tip was reliable because its description of the suspect's visible attributes proved accurate: There really was a young black male wearing a plaid shirt at the bus stop. The United States as amicus curiae makes a similar argument, proposing that a stop and frisk should be permitted "when (1) an anonymous tip provides a description of a particular person at a particular location illegally carrying a concealed firearm, (2) police promptly verify the pertinent details of the tip except the existence of the firearm, and (3) there are no factors that cast doubt on the reliability of the tip. . . ." These contentions misapprehend the reliability needed for a tip to justify a *Terry* stop.

An accurate description of a subject's readily observable location and appearance is of course reliable in this limited sense: It will help the police correctly identify the person whom the tipster means to accuse. Such a tip, however, does not show that the tipster has knowledge of concealed criminal activity. The reasonable suspicion here at issue requires that a tip be reliable in its assertion of illegality, not just in its tendency to identify a determinate person.

A second major argument advanced by Florida and the United States as amicus is, in essence, that the standard *Terry* analysis should be modified to license a "firearm exception." Under such an exception, a tip alleging an illegal gun would justify a stop and frisk even if the accusation would fail standard pre-search reliability testing. We decline to adopt this position.

Firearms are dangerous, and extraordinary dangers sometimes justify unusual precautions. Our decisions recognize the serious threat that armed criminals pose to public safety; *Terry*'s rule, which permits protective police searches on the basis of reasonable suspicion rather than demanding that officers meet the higher standard of probable cause, responds to this very concern. But an automatic firearm exception to our established reliability analysis would rove too far. Such an exception would enable any person seeking to harass another to set in motion an intrusive, embarrassing police search of the targeted person simply by placing an anonymous call falsely reporting the target's unlawful carriage of a gun. Nor could one securely confine such an exception to allegations involving firearms. . . .

The facts of this case do not require us to speculate about the circumstances under which the danger alleged in an anonymous tip might be so great as to justify a search even without a showing of reliability. We do not say, for example, that a report of a person carrying a bomb need bear the indicia of reliability we demand for a report of a person carrying a firearm before the police can constitutionally conduct a frisk. Nor do we hold that public safety officials in quarters where the reasonable expectation of Fourth Amendment privacy is diminished, such as airports and schools, cannot conduct protective searches on the basis of information insufficient to justify searches elsewhere.

Finally, the requirement that an anonymous tip bear standard indicia of reliability in order to justify a stop in no way diminishes a police officer's prerogative, in accord with *Terry*, to conduct a protective search of a person who has already been legitimately stopped. We speak in today's decision only of cases in which the officer's authority to make the initial stop is at issue. In that context, we hold that an anonymous tip lacking indicia of reliability . . . does not justify a stop and frisk whenever and however it alleges the illegal possession of a firearm.

In the next case, the anonymous tip came from a 911 caller who reported witnessing a possible drunk driver. Does this type of report satisfy the reasonable suspicion standard—and justify a vehicle stop—given that the police had no prior contact with this 911 caller? As you read the case, pay particular attention to the Court's assessment of the caller's reliability.

Navarette v. California

Supreme Court of the United States
572 U.S. 393 (2014)

Justice THOMAS delivered the opinion of the Court.

After a 911 caller reported that a vehicle had run her off the road, a police officer located the vehicle she identified during the call and executed a traffic stop. We hold that the stop complied with the Fourth Amendment because, under the totality of the circumstances, the officer had reasonable suspicion that the driver was intoxicated.

I

On August 23, 2008, a Mendocino County 911 dispatch team for the California Highway Patrol (CHP) received a call from another CHP dispatcher in neighboring Humboldt County. The Humboldt County dispatcher relayed a tip from a 911 caller, which the Mendocino County team recorded as follows: "Showing southbound Highway 1 at mile marker 88, Silver Ford 150 pickup. Plate of 8-David-94925. Ran the reporting party off the roadway and was last seen approximately five [minutes] ago." . . .

A CHP officer heading northbound toward the reported vehicle responded to the broadcast. At 4:00 P.M., the officer passed the truck near mile marker 69. At about 4:05 P.M., after making a U-turn, he pulled the truck over. A second officer, who had separately responded to the broadcast, also arrived on the scene. As the two officers approached the truck, they smelled marijuana. A search of the truck bed revealed 30 pounds of marijuana. The officers arrested the driver, petitioner Lorenzo Prado Navarette, and the passenger, petitioner José Prado Navarette.

Petitioners moved to suppress the evidence, arguing that the traffic stop violated the Fourth Amendment because the officer lacked reasonable suspicion of criminal activity. . . .

II

. . . We have firmly rejected the argument "that reasonable cause for a[n investigative stop] can only be based on the officer's personal observation, rather than on information supplied by another person." Of course, "an anonymous tip alone seldom demonstrates the informant's basis of knowledge or veracity." That is because "ordinary citizens generally do not provide extensive recitations of the basis of their everyday observations," and an anonymous tipster's veracity is "by hypothesis largely unknown, and unknowable." But under appropriate circumstances, an anonymous tip can demonstrate "sufficient indicia of reliability to provide reasonable suspicion to make [an] investigatory stop." . . .

The initial question in this case is whether the 911 call was sufficiently reliable to credit the allegation that petitioners' truck "ran the [caller] off the roadway." Even assuming for present purposes that the 911 call was anonymous, we conclude that the call bore adequate indicia of reliability for the officer to credit the caller's account. The officer was therefore justified in proceeding from the premise that the truck had, in fact, caused the caller's car to be dangerously diverted from the highway.

By reporting that she had been run off the road by a specific vehicle—a silver Ford F-150 pickup, license plate 8D94925—the caller necessarily claimed eyewitness knowledge of the alleged dangerous driving. That basis of knowledge lends significant support to the tip's reliability. . . . A driver's claim that another vehicle ran her off the road . . . necessarily implies that the informant knows the other car was driven dangerously.

There is also reason to think that the 911 caller in this case was telling the truth. Police confirmed the truck's location near mile marker 69 (roughly 19 highway miles south of the location reported in the 911 call) at 4:00 P.M. (roughly 18 minutes after the 911 call). That timeline of events suggests that the caller reported the incident soon after she was run off the road. That sort of contemporaneous report has long been treated as especially reliable.

Another indicator of veracity is the caller's use of the 911 emergency system. A 911 call has some features that allow for identifying and tracing callers, and thus provide some safeguards against making false reports with immunity. As this case illustrates, 911 calls can be recorded, which provides victims with an opportunity to identify the false tipster's voice and subject him to prosecution. . . . None of this is to suggest that tips in 911 calls are per se reliable. Given the foregoing technological and regulatory developments, however, a reasonable officer could conclude that a false tipster would think twice before using such a system. The caller's use of the 911 system is therefore one of the relevant circumstances that, taken together, justified the officer's reliance on the information reported in the 911 call.

Even a reliable tip will justify an investigative stop only if it creates reasonable suspicion that "criminal activity may be afoot." We must therefore determine whether the 911 caller's report of being run off the roadway created reasonable suspicion of an ongoing crime such as drunk driving as opposed to an isolated episode of past recklessness. We conclude that the behavior alleged by the 911 caller, "viewed from the standpoint of an objectively reasonable police officer, amount[s] to reasonable suspicion" of drunk driving. The stop was therefore proper. . . .

The 911 caller in this case reported more than a minor traffic infraction and more than a conclusory allegation of drunk or reckless driving. Instead, she alleged a specific and dangerous result of the driver's conduct: running another car off the highway. That conduct bears too great a resemblance to paradigmatic manifestations of drunk driving to be dismissed as an isolated example of recklessness. Running another vehicle off the road suggests lane-positioning problems, decreased vigilance, impaired judgment, or some combination of those recognized drunk driving cues. And the experience of many officers suggests that a driver who almost strikes a vehicle or another object—the exact scenario that ordinarily causes "running [another vehicle] off the roadway"—is likely intoxicated. As a result, we cannot say that the officer acted unreasonably under these circumstances in stopping a driver whose alleged conduct was a significant indicator of drunk driving. . . .

PROBLEM CASE

In 2011, a police officer named Nathan Moore in Carthage, Missouri, was on patrol on New Year's Eve in his squad car when he noticed a car abort a turn into a driveway and then make two immediate turns while being followed by the police car. The car then parked at the side of the street. A passenger in the car got out and went to a nearby house. The police officer recognized the passenger, Larry Lee Smith, as a "known drug user and dealer." Smith had a brief conversation with the occupants of the house, which ended with the occupants shaking their heads as if to indicate "no." Smith then turned around to return to his car, but when Smith saw the police officer, Smith instead started walking briskly away through the yards of neighboring houses.

Moore exited his vehicle and asked Smith to put his hands on the patrol car. Moore started to search Smith for weapons, but as Moore touched Smith, Smith took his hands off the hood of the car and "reached for his right waistband and pocket area." A struggle ensued and resulted in Moore firing a Taser at Smith. Moore went to Smith's car, spoke with the driver, and performed a search that yielded marijuana.

Was Moore justified in performing a *Terry* stop on Smith? Did Moore have reasonable suspicion that criminal activity was afoot? Which "specific and articulable" facts might support such a finding? See *State v. Smith*, 448 S.W.3d 835, 840 (Mo. Ct. App. 2014).

In the following case, *Illinois v. Wardlow,* the Supreme Court asks whether a suspect's flight at the sight of the police can be enough to satisfy the reasonable suspicion standard. In the second case, ask yourself what role the nature of the "neighborhood" played in the analysis.

Illinois v. Wardlow

Supreme Court of the United States
528 U.S. 119 (2000)

Chief Justice REHNQUIST delivered the opinion of the Court.

Respondent Wardlow fled upon seeing police officers patrolling an area known for heavy narcotics trafficking. Two of the officers caught up with him, stopped him and conducted a protective patdown search for weapons. Discovering a .38-caliber handgun, the officers arrested Wardlow. We hold that the officers' stop did not violate the Fourth Amendment to the United States Constitution.

On September 9, 1995, Officers Nolan and Harvey were working as uniformed officers in the special operations section of the Chicago Police Department. The officers were driving the last car of a four car caravan converging on an area known for heavy narcotics trafficking in order to investigate drug transactions. The officers were traveling together because they expected to find a crowd of people in the area, including lookouts and customers.

As the caravan passed 4035 West Van Buren, Officer Nolan observed respondent Wardlow standing next to the building holding an opaque bag. Respondent looked in the direction of the officers and fled. Nolan and Harvey turned their car southbound, watched him as he ran through the gangway and an alley, and eventually cornered him on the street. Nolan then exited his car and stopped respondent. He immediately conducted a protective patdown search for weapons because in his experience it was common for there to be weapons in the near vicinity of narcotics transactions. During the frisk, Officer Nolan squeezed the bag respondent was carrying and felt a heavy, hard object similar to the shape of a gun. The officer then opened the bag and discovered a .38-caliber handgun with five live rounds of ammunition. The officers arrested Wardlow. . . .

This case, involving a brief encounter between a citizen and a police officer on a public street, is governed by the analysis we first applied in *Terry*. In *Terry,* we held that an officer may, consistent with the Fourth Amendment, conduct a brief, investigatory stop when the officer has a reasonable, articulable suspicion that criminal activity is afoot. While "reasonable suspicion" is a less demanding standard than probable cause and requires a showing considerably less than preponderance of the evidence, the Fourth Amendment requires at least a minimal level of objective justification for making the stop. *United States v. Sokolow*, 490 U.S. 1, 7 (1989). The officer must be able to articulate more than an "inchoate and unparticularized suspicion or hunch" of criminal activity.

Nolan and Harvey were among eight officers in a four-car caravan that was converging on an area known for heavy narcotics trafficking, and the officers anticipated encountering a large number of people in the area, including drug customers and individuals serving as lookouts. It was in this context that Officer Nolan decided to investigate Wardlow after observing him flee. An individual's presence in an area of expected criminal activity, standing alone, is not enough to support a reasonable, particularized suspicion that the person is committing a crime. *Brown v. Texas*, 443 U.S. 47 (1979). But officers are not required to ignore the relevant characteristics of a location in determining whether the circumstances are sufficiently suspicious to warrant further investigation. Accordingly, we have previously noted the fact that the stop occurred in a "high crime area" among the relevant contextual considerations in a *Terry* analysis. *Adams v. Williams*, 407 U.S. 143, 144, 147-148 (1972).

In this case, moreover, it was not merely respondent's presence in an area of heavy narcotics trafficking that aroused the officers' suspicion, but his unprovoked flight upon noticing the police. Our cases have also recognized that nervous, evasive behavior is a pertinent factor in determining reasonable suspicion. Headlong flight—wherever it occurs—is the consummate act of evasion: It is not necessarily indicative of wrongdoing, but it is certainly suggestive of such. In reviewing the propriety of an officer's conduct, courts do not have available empirical studies dealing with inferences drawn from suspicious behavior, and we cannot reasonably demand scientific certainty from judges or law enforcement officers where none exists. Thus, the determination of reasonable suspicion must be based on commonsense judgments and inferences about human behavior. We conclude Officer Nolan was justified in suspecting that Wardlow was involved in criminal activity, and, therefore, in investigating further.

Such a holding is entirely consistent with our decision in *Florida v. Royer*, 460 U.S. 491 (1983), where we held that when an officer, without reasonable suspicion or probable cause, approaches an individual, the individual has a right to ignore the police and go about his business. And any "refusal to cooperate, without more, does not furnish the minimal level of objective justification needed for a detention or seizure." *Florida v. Bostick*, 501 U.S. 429, 437 (1991). But unprovoked flight is simply not a mere refusal to cooperate. Flight, by its very nature, is not "going about one's business"; in fact, it is just the opposite. Allowing officers confronted with such flight to stop the fugitive and investigate further is quite consistent with the individual's right to go about his business or to stay put and remain silent in the face of police questioning.

Respondent and amici also argue that there are innocent reasons for flight from police and that, therefore, flight is not necessarily indicative of ongoing criminal activity. This fact is undoubtedly true, but does not establish a violation of the Fourth Amendment. Even in *Terry*, the conduct justifying the stop was ambiguous and susceptible of an innocent explanation. The officer observed two individuals pacing back and forth in front of a store, peering into the window and periodically conferring. All of this conduct was by itself lawful, but it also suggested that the individuals were casing the store for a planned robbery. *Terry* recognized that the officers could detain the individuals to resolve the ambiguity.

In allowing such detentions, *Terry* accepts the risk that officers may stop innocent people. Indeed, the Fourth Amendment accepts that risk in connection with more drastic police action; persons arrested and detained on probable cause to believe they have committed a crime may turn out to be innocent. The *Terry* stop is a far more minimal intrusion, simply allowing the officer to briefly investigate further. If the officer does not learn facts rising to the level of probable cause, the individual must be allowed to go on his way. But in this case the officers found respondent in possession of a handgun, and arrested him for violation of an Illinois firearms statute. No question of the propriety of the arrest itself is before us. . . .

Justice STEVENS, with whom Justice SOUTER, Justice GINSBURG, and Justice BREYER join, concurring in part and dissenting in part.

. . . Guided by that totality-of-the-circumstances test, the Court concludes that Officer Nolan had reasonable suspicion to stop respondent. In this respect, my view differs from the Court's. The entire justification for the stop is articulated in the brief testimony of Officer Nolan. Some facts are perfectly clear; others are not. This factual insufficiency leads me to conclude that the Court's judgment is mistaken.

Respondent Wardlow was arrested a few minutes after noon on September 9, 1995. Nolan was part of an eight-officer, four-car caravan patrol team. The officers were headed for "one of the areas in the 11th District [of Chicago] that's high [in] narcotics traffic." The reason why four cars were in the caravan was that "[n]ormally in these different areas there's an enormous amount of people, sometimes lookouts, customers." Officer Nolan testified that he was in uniform on that day, but he did not recall whether he was driving a marked or an unmarked car.

Officer Nolan and his partner were in the last of the four patrol cars that "were all caravaning eastbound down Van Buren." Nolan first observed respondent "in front of 4035 West Van Buren." Wardlow "looked in our direction and began fleeing." Nolan then "began driving southbound down the street observing [respondent] running through the gangway and the alley southbound," and observed that Wardlow was carrying a white, opaque bag under his arm. After the car turned south and intercepted respondent as he "ran right towards us," Officer Nolan stopped him and conducted a "protective search," which revealed that the bag under respondent's arm contained a loaded handgun.

This terse testimony is most noticeable for what it fails to reveal. Though asked whether he was in a marked or unmarked car, Officer Nolan could not recall the answer. He was not asked whether any of the other three cars in the caravan were marked, or whether any of the other seven officers were in uniform. Though he explained that the size of the caravan was because "[n]ormally in these different areas there's an enormous amount of people, sometimes lookouts, customers," Officer Nolan did not testify as to whether anyone besides Wardlow was nearby 4035 West Van Buren. Nor is it clear that that address was the intended destination of the caravan. As the Appellate Court of Illinois interpreted the record, "it appears that the officers were simply driving by, on their way to some unidentified location, when they noticed defendant standing at 4035 West Van Buren." Officer Nolan's testimony also does not reveal how fast the officers were driving. It does not indicate whether he saw respondent notice the other patrol cars. And it does not say whether the caravan, or any part of it, had already passed Wardlow by before he began to run.

Indeed, the Appellate Court thought the record was even "too vague to support the inference that . . . defendant's flight was related to his expectation of police focus on him." Presumably, respondent did not react to the first three cars, and we cannot even be sure that he recognized the occupants of the fourth as police officers. The adverse inference is based entirely on the officer's statement: "He looked in our direction and began fleeing."

No other factors sufficiently support a finding of reasonable suspicion. Though respondent was carrying a white, opaque bag under his arm, there is nothing at all suspicious about that. Certainly the time of day—shortly after noon—does not support Illinois' argument. Nor were the officers "responding to any call or report of suspicious activity in the area." Officer Nolan did testify that he expected to find "an enormous amount of people," including drug customers or lookouts, and the Court points out that "[i]t was in this context that Officer Nolan decided to investigate Wardlow after observing him flee." This observation, in my view, lends insufficient weight to the reasonable suspicion analysis; indeed, in light of the absence of testimony that anyone else was nearby when respondent began to run, this observation points in the opposite direction.

The State, along with the majority of the Court, relies as well on the assumption that this flight occurred in a high crime area. Even if that assumption is accurate, it is insufficient because even in a high crime neighborhood unprovoked flight does not invariably lead to reasonable suspicion.

> On the contrary, because many factors providing innocent motivations for unprovoked flight are concentrated in high crime areas, the character of the neighborhood arguably makes an inference of guilt less appropriate, rather than more so. Like unprovoked flight itself, presence in a high crime neighborhood is a fact too generic and susceptible to innocent explanation to satisfy the reasonable suspicion inquiry. . . .

NOTES & QUESTIONS ON REASONABLE SUSPICION

1. *Indicia of reliability.* In *J.L.*, the Supreme Court concluded that an anonymous tip lacks the "indicia of reliability" necessary to satisfy the reasonable suspicion standard. Why? An existing source has a track record with the police department that could be used to support a presumption of truthfulness on the part of the informant. However, no such presumption can be made for an anonymous source, since nobody knows who the source is. What happens, for example, if an anonymous source calls police to say that someone is driving drunk—should that be enough for the police to stop the car? Many of these questions were left open by *J.L.*, because the Court explicitly carved out the question of whether "a report of a person carrying a bomb need bear the indicia of reliability we demand for a report of a person carrying a firearm before the police can constitutionally conduct a frisk." 529 U.S. 266, 273-74. For more discussion, see James Michael Scears, *Anonymous Tips Alleging Drunk Driving: Why "One Free Swerve" Is One Too Many*, 64 Okla. L. Rev. 759, 771 (2012).

2. *High-crime neighborhoods.* In *Illinois v. Wardlow*, the Court made reference to the fact that the suspect was located in a high-crime area. How was this fact established by the police officer? Did the police officer have access to statistical data? Did the Court scrutinize the data? Moreover, should the fact that a neighborhood is "high crime" have any relevance to the analysis at all? In *United States v. Arvizu*, 232 F.3d 1241, 1250 (9th Cir. 2000), *rev'd*, 534 U.S. 266 (2002), the Ninth Circuit noted that "one's place of residence is simply not relevant to a determination of reasonable suspicion. Otherwise, persons forced to reside in high crime areas for economic reasons (who are frequently members of minority groups) would be compelled to assume a greater risk not only of becoming the victims of crimes but also of being victimized by the state's efforts to prevent those crimes—because their constitutional protections against unreasonable intrusions would be significantly reduced." Do you agree that the references to "high-crime areas" constitutes an articulable fact, or is it pseudo-science? For more critical discussion, see Paul Butler, *The White Fourth Amendment*, 43 Tex. Tech L. Rev. 245, 254 (2010); Reshaad Shirazi, *It's High Time to Dump the High-Crime Area Factor*, 21 Berkeley J. Crim.

L. 76, 88 (2016) ("The bottom line is that the single most significant variable in accounting for urban crime rates is the size of the African American population. Unsurprisingly, crime is a particularly severe problem in predominately poor neighborhoods of urban areas, where African Americans are more likely to reside. In other words, high-crime areas are usually high-black areas.").

3. *Criminal activity versus dangerousness*. Consider again the facts in *Illinois v. Wardlow*. The Court concluded that the officer had reasonable suspicion that criminal activity was afoot. However, did the officer have a reasonable suspicion that the suspect was armed? Remember, it is important to consider two questions: First, did the officer have reasonable suspicion to conduct the stop? Second, did the officer have a justification to frisk the suspect to search for weapons? Under *Terry*, a frisk for weapons is permitted in order to protect the officer's safety, but only if the officer possesses a reasonable fear for their safety. In *Wardlow*, the officer immediately frisked the suspect, based on the character of the neighborhood. The Supreme Court never reached the issue of whether this constituted a reasonable fear that justified the frisk. But if it had, what would the result be?

4. Profiling

Despite its call for basing determinations of "reasonable suspicion" on articulable facts, the Supreme Court has nonetheless allowed certain inferences to function as de facto profiles that make it more likely that criminal activity "may be afoot." These are heuristic devices used by law enforcement to make judgments based on patterns of activity. In *United States v. Sokolow*, the question is whether the suspect might be a drug courier simply because he flew roundtrip to Miami, Florida, with insufficient time for either vacation or business. As you read the case, construct alternative hypotheses that might yield non-criminal explanations for his behavior. Can you think of any? How plausible are they?

United States v. Sokolow

Supreme Court of the United States
490 U.S. 1 (1989)

Chief Justice REHNQUIST delivered the opinion of the Court.

Respondent Andrew Sokolow was stopped by Drug Enforcement Administration (DEA) agents upon his arrival at Honolulu International Airport. The agents found 1,063 grams of cocaine in his carry-on luggage. When respondent was stopped, the agents knew, inter alia, that (1) he paid $2,100 for two airplane tickets from a roll of $20 bills; (2) he traveled under a name that did not match the name under which his telephone number was listed; (3) his original destination was Miami, a source city for illicit drugs; (4) he stayed in Miami for only 48 hours, even though a round-trip flight from Honolulu to Miami takes 20 hours; (5) he appeared nervous during his trip; and (6) he checked none of his luggage. A divided panel of the United States Court of Appeals for the Ninth Circuit held that the DEA agents did not have a reasonable suspicion to stop respondent, as required by the Fourth Amendment. We take the contrary view.

This case involves a typical attempt to smuggle drugs through one of the Nation's airports. On a Sunday in July 1984, respondent went to the United Airlines ticket counter at Honolulu Airport, where he purchased two round-trip tickets for a flight to Miami leaving later that day. The tickets were purchased in the names of "Andrew Kray" and "Janet Norian" and had open return dates. Respondent paid $2,100 for the tickets from a large roll of $20 bills, which appeared to contain a total of $4,000. He also gave the ticket agent his home telephone number. The ticket agent noticed that respondent seemed nervous; he was about 25 years old; he was dressed in a black jumpsuit and wore gold jewelry; and he was accompanied by a woman, who turned out to be Janet Norian. Neither respondent nor his companion checked any of their four pieces of luggage.

After the couple left for their flight, the ticket agent informed Officer John McCarthy of the Honolulu Police Department of respondent's cash purchase of tickets to Miami. Officer McCarthy determined that the telephone number respondent gave to the ticket agent was subscribed to a "Karl Herman," who resided at 348-A Royal Hawaiian Avenue in Honolulu. Unbeknownst to McCarthy (and later to the DEA agents), respondent was Herman's roommate. The ticket agent identified respondent's voice on the answering machine at Herman's number. Officer McCarthy was unable to find any listing under the name "Andrew Kray" in Hawaii. McCarthy subsequently learned that return reservations from Miami to Honolulu had been made in the names of Kray and Norian, with their arrival scheduled for July 25, three days after respondent and his companion had left. He also learned that Kray and Norian were scheduled to make stopovers in Denver and Los Angeles.

On July 25, during the stopover in Los Angeles, DEA agents identified respondent. He "appeared to be very nervous and was looking all around the waiting area." Later that day, at 6:30 P.M., respondent and Norian arrived in Honolulu. As before, they had not checked their luggage. Respondent was still wearing a black jumpsuit and gold jewelry. The couple proceeded directly to the street and tried to hail a cab, where Agent Richard Kempshall and three other DEA agents approached them. Kempshall displayed his credentials, grabbed respondent by the arm, and moved him back onto the sidewalk. Kempshall asked respondent for his airline ticket and identification; respondent said that he had neither. He told the agents that his name was "Sokolow," but that he was traveling under his mother's maiden name, "Kray."

Respondent and Norian were escorted to the DEA office at the airport. There, the couple's luggage was examined by "Donker," a narcotics detector dog, which alerted on respondent's brown shoulder bag. The agents arrested respondent. He was advised of his constitutional rights and declined to make any statements. The agents obtained a warrant to search the shoulder bag. They found no illicit drugs, but the bag did contain several suspicious documents indicating respondent's involvement in drug trafficking. The agents had Donker reexamine the remaining luggage, and this time the dog alerted on a medium-sized Louis Vuitton bag. By now, it was 9:30 P.M., too late for the agents to obtain a second warrant. They allowed respondent to leave for the night, but kept his luggage. The next morning, after a second dog confirmed Donker's alert, the agents obtained a warrant and found 1,063 grams of cocaine inside the bag. Respondent was indicted for possession with the intent to distribute cocaine. . . .

. . . Our decision, then, turns on whether the agents had a reasonable suspicion that respondent was engaged in wrongdoing when they encountered him on the sidewalk. . . . The officer, of course, must be able to articulate something more than an "inchoate and unparticularized suspicion or hunch." The Fourth Amendment requires "some minimal level of objective justification" for making the stop. That level of suspicion is considerably less than proof of wrongdoing by a preponderance of the evidence. We have held that probable cause means "a fair probability that contraband or evidence of a crime will be found," and the level of suspicion required for a *Terry* stop is obviously less demanding than that for probable cause.

The concept of reasonable suspicion, like probable cause, is not "readily, or even usefully, reduced to a neat set of legal rules." We think the Court of Appeals' effort to refine and elaborate the requirements of "reasonable suspicion" in this case creates unnecessary difficulty in dealing with one of the relatively simple concepts embodied in the Fourth Amendment. In evaluating the validity of a stop such as this, we must consider "the totality of the circumstances–the whole picture." . . .

Paying $2,100 in cash for two airplane tickets is out of the ordinary, and it is even more out of the ordinary to pay that sum from a roll of $20 bills containing nearly twice that amount of cash. Most business travelers, we feel confident, purchase airline tickets by credit card or check so as to have a record for tax or business purposes, and few vacationers carry with them thousands of dollars in $20 bills. We also think the agents had a reasonable ground to believe that respondent was traveling under an alias; the evidence was by no means conclusive, but it was sufficient to warrant consideration. While a trip from Honolulu to Miami, standing alone, is not a cause for any sort of suspicion, here there was more: surely few residents of Honolulu travel from that city for 20 hours to spend 48 hours in Miami during the month of July.

Any one of these factors is not by itself proof of any illegal conduct and is quite consistent with innocent travel. But we think taken together they amount to reasonable suspicion. . . . *Terry* itself involved "a series of acts, each of them perhaps innocent" if viewed separately, "but which taken together warranted further investigation."

We do not agree with respondent that our analysis is somehow changed by the agents' belief that his behavior was consistent with one of the DEA's "drug courier profiles." A court sitting to determine the existence of reasonable suspicion must require the agent to articulate the factors leading to that conclusion, but the fact that these factors may be set forth in a "profile" does not somehow detract from their evidentiary significance as seen by a trained agent. . . . We hold that the agents had a reasonable basis to suspect that respondent was transporting illegal drugs on these facts. . . .

Justice Marshall, with whom Justice Brennan joins, dissenting.

. . . By requiring reasonable suspicion as a prerequisite to such seizures, the Fourth Amendment protects innocent persons from being subjected to "overbearing or harassing" police conduct carried out solely on the basis of imprecise stereotypes of what criminals look like, or on the basis of irrelevant personal characteristics such as race.

To deter such egregious police behavior, we have held that a suspicion is not reasonable unless officers have based it on "specific and articulable facts." It is not enough to suspect that an individual has committed crimes in the past, harbors unconsummated criminal designs, or has the propensity to commit crimes. On the contrary, before detaining an individual, law enforcement officers must reasonably suspect that he is engaged in, or poised to commit, a criminal act at that moment. The rationale for permitting brief, warrantless seizures is, after all, that it is impractical to demand strict compliance with the Fourth Amendment's ordinary probable-cause requirement in the face of ongoing or imminent criminal activity demanding "swift action predicated upon the on-the-spot observations of the officer on the beat." Observations raising suspicions of past criminality demand no such immediate action, but instead should appropriately trigger routine police investigation, which may ultimately generate sufficient information to blossom into probable cause.

Evaluated against this standard, the facts about Andrew Sokolow known to the DEA agents at the time they stopped him fall short of reasonably indicating that he was engaged at the time in criminal activity. It is highly significant that the DEA agents stopped Sokolow because he matched one of the DEA's "profiles" of a paradigmatic drug courier. In my view, a law enforcement officer's mechanistic application of a formula of personal and behavioral traits in deciding whom to detain can only dull the officer's ability and determination to make sensitive and fact-specific inferences "in light of his experience," particularly in ambiguous or borderline cases. Reflexive reliance on a profile of drug courier characteristics runs a far greater risk than does ordinary, case-by-case police work of subjecting innocent individuals to unwarranted police harassment and detention. . . .

NOTES & QUESTIONS ON PROFILING

1. *Stereotyping*. Do the assumptions in these cases amount to scientific profiling or are they merely rank stereotypes? Are there special dangers associated with making reasonable suspicion determinations based on statistical evidence? For a critical discussion, see Milton Heumann & Lance Cassak, *Profiles in Justice? Police Discretion, Symbolic Assailants, and Stereotyping*, 53 Rutgers L. Rev. 911, 948 (2001) ("what is most significant about the Supreme Court's treatment of profiling is the Court's refusal to give it any special attention or consideration as a unique or distinct law enforcement technique"). Do you agree with the final result in *Sokolow*?

5. Racial Disparities

After years of complaints that the *Terry* regime is applied in a racially discriminatory fashion, a federal district court finally considered this question directly

PROBLEM CASE

A patrolman observed Oswald Coleman driving a vehicle in Florida. Although Coleman had not broken any vehicle or traffic laws, the officer stopped the car because he believed it fit the profile of a drug courier. The Department of Highway Safety in Florida articulated the following elements of its drug courier profile:

1) a late model vehicle;
2) Florida rental tags;
3) two occupants observed initially in the vehicle;
4) the driver appeared to be male;
5) the driver appeared to be approximately 35 years of age;
6) the vehicle was traveling northbound on Interstate 95, a route frequently used by drug couriers;
7) the vehicle was traveling in the evening in an extremely cautious manner;
8) the driver did not look at the trooper as the Appellees' vehicle passed the patrol car.

Assuming that the officer was correct that Coleman satisfied these criteria, is this profile sufficient to justify a *Terry* stop? Did its application in this case produce a particularized and objective basis that would satisfy the reasonable suspicion standard, or was it merely the kind of "unparticularized suspicion or hunch" outlawed in *Terry*? Are there other reasons, besides drug trafficking, that an individual might drive on Interstate 95 in a late model vehicle? See *In re Forfeiture of $6,003.00 in U.S. Currency*, 505 So. 2d 668, 668 (Fla. Dist. Ct. App. 1987).

in class action litigation brought on behalf of African-American and Hispanic individuals stopped by New York City police pursuant to its stop and frisk policy. In the following case, Judge Shira Scheindlin concluded that the New York Police Department was conducting *Terry* stops in a racially discriminatory manner. As you read this case, ask yourself whether New York City's stop and frisk policy could be revised to satisfy Judge Scheindlin's concerns or whether the *Terry* regime is inherently problematic and should be scrapped entirely.

Floyd v. City of New York

U.S. District Court for the Southern District of New York
959 F. Supp. 2d 540 (2013)

SHIRA A. SCHEINDLIN, District Judge:[1]

New Yorkers are rightly proud of their city and seek to make it as safe as the largest city in America can be. New Yorkers also treasure their liberty. Countless individuals have come to New York in pursuit of that liberty. The goals of liberty and safety may be in tension, but they can coexist—indeed the Constitution mandates it.

This case is about the tension between liberty and public safety in the use of a proactive policing tool called "stop and frisk." The New York City Police Department ("NYPD") made 4.4 million stops between January 2004 and June 2012. Over 80% of these 4.4 million stops were of blacks or Hispanics. In each of these stops a person's life was interrupted. The person was detained and questioned, often on a public street. More than half of the time the police subjected the person to a frisk.

Plaintiffs—blacks and Hispanics who were stopped—argue that the NYPD's use of stop and frisk violated their constitutional rights in two ways: (1) they were stopped without a legal basis in violation of the Fourth Amendment, and (2) they were targeted for stops because of their race in violation of the Fourteenth Amendment. Plaintiffs do not seek to end the use of stop and frisk. Rather, they argue that it must be reformed to comply with constitutional limits. Two such limits are paramount here: first, that all stops be based on "reasonable suspicion" as defined by the Supreme Court of the United States; and second, that stops be conducted in a racially neutral manner.

I emphasize at the outset, as I have throughout the litigation, that this case is not about the effectiveness of stop and frisk in deterring or combating crime. This Court's mandate is solely to judge the constitutionality of police behavior, not its effectiveness as a law enforcement tool. Many police practices may be useful for fighting crime—preventive detention or coerced confessions, for example—but because they are unconstitutional

1. [Editor's Note: This excerpt is mostly drawn from the executive summary of Judge Scheindlin's opinion.]

they cannot be used, no matter how effective. "The enshrinement of constitutional rights necessarily takes certain policy choices off the table."

This case is also not primarily about the nineteen individual stops that were the subject of testimony at trial. Rather, this case is about whether the City has a policy or custom of violating the Constitution by making unlawful stops and conducting unlawful frisks.

The Supreme Court has recognized that "the degree of community resentment aroused by particular practices is clearly relevant to an assessment of the quality of the intrusion upon reasonable expectations of personal security." In light of the very active and public debate on the issues addressed in this Opinion—and the passionate positions taken by both sides—it is important to recognize the human toll of unconstitutional stops. While it is true that any one stop is a limited intrusion in duration and deprivation of liberty, each stop is also a demeaning and humiliating experience. No one should live in fear of being stopped whenever he leaves his home to go about the activities of daily life. Those who are routinely subjected to stops are overwhelmingly people of color, and they are justifiably troubled to be singled out when many of them have done nothing to attract the unwanted attention. Some plaintiffs testified that stops make them feel unwelcome in some parts of the City, and distrustful of the police. This alienation cannot be good for the police, the community, or its leaders. Fostering trust and confidence between the police and the community would be an improvement for everyone.

Plaintiffs requested that this case be tried to the Court without a jury. Because plaintiffs seek only injunctive relief, not damages, the City had no right to demand a jury. As a result, I must both find the facts and articulate the governing law. I have endeavored to exercise my judgment faithfully and impartially in making my findings of fact and conclusions of law based on the nine-week trial held from March through May of this year. . . .

Plaintiffs assert that the City, and its agent the NYPD, violated both the Fourth Amendment and the Equal Protection Clause of the Fourteenth Amendment of the United States Constitution. In order to hold a municipality liable for the violation of a constitutional right, plaintiffs "must prove that 'action pursuant to official municipal policy' caused the alleged constitutional injury." "Official municipal policy includes the decisions of a government's lawmakers, the acts of its policymaking officials, and practices so persistent and widespread as to practically have the force of law."

The Fourth Amendment protects all individuals against unreasonable searches or seizures. The Supreme Court has held that the Fourth Amendment permits the police to "stop and briefly detain a person for investigative purposes if the officer has a reasonable suspicion supported by articulable facts that criminal activity 'may be afoot,' even if the officer lacks probable cause." "Reasonable suspicion is an objective standard; hence, the subjective intentions or motives of the officer making the stop are irrelevant." The test for whether a stop has taken place in the context of a police encounter is whether a reasonable person would have felt free to terminate the encounter. "[T]o proceed from a stop to a frisk, the police officer must reasonably suspect that the person stopped is armed and dangerous."

The Equal Protection Clause of the Fourteenth Amendment guarantees to every person the equal protection of the laws. It prohibits intentional discrimination based on race. Intentional discrimination can be proved in several ways, two of which are relevant here. A plaintiff can show: (1) that a facially neutral law or policy has been applied in an intentionally discriminatory manner; or (2) that a law or policy expressly classifies persons on the basis of race, and that the classification does not survive strict scrutiny. Because there is rarely direct proof of discriminatory intent, circumstantial evidence of such intent is permitted. "The impact of the official action—whether it bears more heavily on one race than another—may provide an important starting point."

The following facts . . . are uncontested:

- Between January 2004 and June 2012, the NYPD conducted over 4.4 million *Terry* stops.
- The number of stops per year rose sharply from 314,000 in 2004 to a high of 686,000 in 2011.
- 52% of all stops were followed by a protective frisk for weapons. A weapon was found after 1.5% of these frisks. In other words, in 98.5% of the 2.3 million frisks, no weapon was found.
- 8% of all stops led to a search into the stopped person's clothing, ostensibly based on the officer feeling an object during the frisk that he suspected to be a weapon, or immediately perceived to be contraband other than a weapon. In 9% of these searches, the felt object was in fact a weapon. 91% of the time, it was not. In 14% of these searches, the felt object was in fact contraband. 86% of the time it was not.
- 6% of all stops resulted in an arrest, and 6% resulted in a summons. The remaining 88% of the 4.4 million stops resulted in no further law enforcement action.
- In 52% of the 4.4 million stops, the person stopped was black, in 31% the person was Hispanic, and in 10% the person was white.
- In 2010, New York City's resident population was roughly 23% black, 29% Hispanic, and 33% white.
- In 23% of the stops of blacks, and 24% of the stops of Hispanics, the officer recorded using force. The number for whites was 17%.
- Weapons were seized in 1.0% of the stops of blacks, 1.1% of the stops of Hispanics, and 1.4% of the stops of whites.

- Contraband other than weapons was seized in 1.8% of the stops of blacks, 1.7% of the stops of Hispanics, and 2.3% of the stops of whites.
- Between 2004 and 2009, the percentage of stops where the officer failed to state a specific suspected crime rose from 1% to 36%.

Both parties provided extensive expert submissions and testimony that is also discussed in detail below. Based on that testimony and the uncontested facts, I have made the following findings with respect to the expert testimony.

With respect to plaintiffs' Fourth Amendment claim, I begin by noting the inherent difficulty in making findings and conclusions regarding 4.4 million stops. Because it is impossible to individually analyze each of those stops, plaintiffs' case was based on the imperfect information contained in the NYPD's database of forms ("UF-250s") that officers are required to prepare after each stop. The central flaws in this database all skew toward underestimating the number of unconstitutional stops that occur: the database is incomplete, in that officers do not prepare a UF-250 for every stop they make; it is one-sided, in that the UF-250 only records the officer's version of the story; the UF-250 permits the officer to merely check a series of boxes, rather than requiring the officer to explain the basis for her suspicion; and many of the boxes on the form are inherently subjective and vague (such as "furtive movements"). Nonetheless, the analysis of the UF-250 database reveals that at least 200,000 stops were made without reasonable suspicion.

The actual number of stops lacking reasonable suspicion was likely far higher, based on the reasons stated above, and the following points: (1) Dr. Fagan was unnecessarily conservative in classifying stops as "apparently unjustified." For example, a UF-250 on which the officer checked only Furtive Movements (used on roughly 42% of forms) and High Crime Area (used on roughly 55% of forms) is not classified as "apparently unjustified." The same is true when only Furtive Movements and Suspicious Bulge (used on roughly 10% of forms) are checked. Finally, if an officer checked only the box marked "other" on either side of the form (used on roughly 26% of forms), Dr. Fagan categorized this as "ungeneralizable" rather than "apparently unjustified." (2) Many UF-250s did not identify any suspected crime (36% of all UF-250s in 2009). (3) The rate of arrests arising from stops is low (roughly 6%), and the yield of seizures of guns or other contraband is even lower (roughly 0.1% and 1.8% respectively). (4) "Furtive Movements," "High Crime Area," and "Suspicious Bulge" are vague and subjective terms. Without an accompanying narrative explanation for the stop, these checkmarks cannot reliably demonstrate individualized reasonable suspicion.

With respect to plaintiffs' Fourteenth Amendment claim, I reject the testimony of the City's experts that the race of crime suspects is the appropriate benchmark for measuring racial bias in stops. The City and its highest officials believe that blacks and Hispanics should be stopped at the same rate as their proportion of the local criminal suspect population. But this reasoning is flawed because the stopped population is overwhelmingly innocent—not criminal. There is no basis for assuming that an innocent population shares the same characteristics as the criminal suspect population in the same area. Instead, I conclude that the benchmark used by plaintiffs' expert—a combination of local population demographics and local crime rates (to account for police deployment) is the most sensible.

Based on the expert testimony I find the following: (1) The NYPD carries out more stops where there are more black and Hispanic residents, even when other relevant variables are held constant. The racial composition of a precinct or census tract predicts the stop rate above and beyond the crime rate. (2) Blacks and Hispanics are more likely than whites to be stopped within precincts and census tracts, even after controlling for other relevant variables. This is so even in areas with low crime rates, racially heterogenous populations, or predominately white populations. (3) For the period 2004 through 2009, when any law enforcement action was taken following a stop, blacks were 30% more likely to be arrested (as opposed to receiving a summons) than whites, for the same suspected crime. (4) For the period 2004 through 2009, after controlling for suspected crime and precinct characteristics, blacks who were stopped were about 14% more likely—and Hispanics 9% more likely—than whites to be subjected to the use of force. (5) For the period 2004 through 2009, all else being equal, the odds of a stop resulting in any further enforcement action were 8% lower if the person stopped was black than if the person stopped was white. In addition, the greater the black population in a precinct, the less likely that a stop would result in a sanction. Together, these results show that blacks are likely targeted for stops based on a lesser degree of objectively founded suspicion than whites.

With respect to both the Fourth and Fourteenth Amendment claims, one way to prove that the City has a custom of conducting unconstitutional stops and frisks is to show that it acted with deliberate indifference to constitutional deprivations caused by its employees—here, the NYPD. The evidence at trial revealed significant evidence that the NYPD acted with deliberate indifference.

Protestors gather before the start of a march to end New York's stop and frisk program in June 2012. (Seth Wenig/AP/Shutterstock)

As early as 1999, a report from New York's Attorney General placed the City on notice that stops and frisks were being conducted in a racially skewed manner. Nothing was done in response. In the years following this report, pressure was placed on supervisors to increase the number of stops. Evidence at trial revealed that officers have been pressured to make a certain number of stops and risk negative consequences if they fail to achieve the goal. Without a system to ensure that stops are justified, such pressure is a predictable formula for producing unconstitutional stops. As one high ranking police official noted in 2010, this pressure, without a comparable emphasis on ensuring that the activities are legally justified, "could result in an officer taking enforcement action for the purpose of meeting a quota rather than because a violation of the law has occurred."

In addition, the evidence at trial revealed that the NYPD has an unwritten policy of targeting "the right people" for stops. In practice, the policy encourages the targeting of young black and Hispanic men based on their prevalence in local crime complaints. This is a form of racial profiling. While a person's race may be important if it fits the description of a particular crime suspect, it is impermissible to subject all members of a racially defined group to heightened police enforcement because some members of that group are criminals. The Equal Protection Clause does not permit race-based suspicion.

Much evidence was introduced regarding inadequate monitoring and supervision of unconstitutional stops. Supervisors routinely review the productivity of officers, but do not review the facts of a stop to determine whether it was legally warranted. Nor do supervisors ensure that an officer has made a proper record of a stop so that it can be reviewed for constitutionality. Deficiencies were also shown in the training of officers with respect to stop and frisk and in the disciplining of officers when they were found to have made a bad stop or frisk. Despite the mounting evidence that many bad stops were made, that officers failed to make adequate records of stops, and that discipline was spotty or non-existent, little has been done to improve the situation.

One example of poor training is particularly telling. Two officers testified to their understanding of the term "furtive movements." One explained that "furtive movement is a very broad concept," and could include a person "changing direction," "walking in a certain way," "[a]cting a little suspicious," "making a movement that is not regular," being "very fidgety," "going in and out of his pocket," "going in and out of a location," "looking back and forth constantly," "looking over their shoulder," "adjusting their hip or their belt," "moving in and out of a car too quickly," "[t]urning a part of their body away from you," "[g]rabbing at a certain pocket or something at their waist," "getting a little nervous, maybe shaking," and "stutter[ing]." Another officer explained that "usually" a furtive movement is someone "hanging out in front of [a] building, sitting on the benches or something like that" and then making a "quick movement," such as "bending down and quickly standing back up," "going inside the lobby . . . and then quickly coming back out," or "all of a sudden becom[ing] very nervous, very aware." If officers believe that the behavior described above constitutes furtive movement that justifies a stop, then it is no surprise that stops so rarely produce evidence of criminal activity.

I now summarize my findings with respect to the individual stops that were the subject of testimony at trial. Twelve plaintiffs testified regarding nineteen stops. In twelve of those stops, both the plaintiffs and the officers testified. In seven stops no officer testified, either because the officers could not be identified or because the officers dispute that the stop ever occurred. I find that nine of the stops and frisks were unconstitutional—that is, they were not based on reasonable suspicion. I also find that while five other stops were constitutional, the frisks following those stops were unconstitutional. Finally, I find that plaintiffs have failed to prove an unconstitutional stop (or frisk) in five of the nineteen stops. The individual stop testimony corroborated much of the evidence about the NYPD's policies and practices with respect to carrying out and monitoring stops and frisks.

In making these decisions I note that evaluating a stop in hindsight is an imperfect procedure. Because there is no contemporaneous recording of the stop (such as could be achieved through the use of a body-worn camera), I am relegated to finding facts based on the often conflicting testimony of eyewitnesses. This task is not easy, as every witness has an interest in the outcome of the case, which may consciously or unconsciously affect the veracity of his or her testimony. Nonetheless, a judge is tasked with making decisions and I judged the evidence of each stop to the best of my ability. I am also aware that a judge deciding whether a stop is constitutional, with the time to reflect and consider all of the evidence, is in a far different position than officers on the street who must make split-second decisions in situations that may pose a danger to themselves or others. I respect that police officers have chosen a profession of public service involving dangers and challenges with few parallels in civilian life.

In conclusion, I find that the City is liable for violating plaintiffs' Fourth and Fourteenth Amendment rights. The City acted with deliberate indifference toward the NYPD's practice of making unconstitutional stops and conducting unconstitutional frisks. Even if the City had not been deliberately indifferent, the NYPD's unconstitutional practices were sufficiently widespread as to have the force of law. In addition, the City adopted a policy of indirect racial profiling by targeting racially defined groups for stops based on local crime suspect data. This has resulted in the disproportionate and discriminatory stopping of blacks and Hispanics in violation of the Equal Protection Clause. Both statistical and anecdotal evidence showed that minorities are indeed treated differently than whites. For example, once a stop is made, blacks and Hispanics are more likely to be subjected to the use of force than whites, despite the fact that whites are more likely to be found with weapons or contraband. I also conclude that the City's highest officials have turned a blind eye to the evidence that officers are conducting stops in a racially discriminatory manner. In their zeal to defend a policy that they believe to be effective, they have willfully ignored overwhelming proof that the policy of targeting "the right people" is racially discriminatory and therefore violates the United States Constitution. One NYPD official has even suggested that it is permissible to stop racially defined groups just to instill fear in them that they are subject to being stopped at any time for any reason—in the hope that this fear will deter them from carrying guns in the streets. The goal of deterring crime is laudable, but this method of doing so is unconstitutional.

I recognize that the police will deploy their limited resources to high crime areas. This benefits the communities where the need for policing is greatest. But the police are not permitted to target people for stops based on their race. Some may worry about the implications of this decision. They may wonder: if the police believe that a particular group of people is disproportionately responsible for crime in one area, why should the police not target that group with increased stops? Why should it matter if the group is defined in part by race? Indeed, there are contexts in which the Constitution permits considerations of race in law enforcement operations. What is clear, however, is that the Equal Protection Clause prohibits the practices described in this case. A police department may not target a racially defined group for stops in general—that is, for stops based on suspicions of general criminal wrongdoing—simply because members of that group appear frequently in the police department's suspect data. The Equal Protection Clause does not permit the police to target a racially defined group as a whole because of the misdeeds of some of its members.

To address the violations that I have found, I shall order various remedies including, but not limited to, an immediate change to certain policies and activities of the NYPD, a trial program requiring the use of body-worn cameras in one precinct per borough, a community-based joint remedial process to be conducted by a court-appointed facilitator, and the appointment of an independent monitor to ensure that the NYPD's conduct of stops and frisks is carried out in accordance with the Constitution and the principles enunciated in this Opinion, and to monitor the NYPD's compliance with the ordered remedies.

NOTES & QUESTIONS ON RACIAL DISPARITIES

1. *Flight from police—is it always suspicious?* Other courts have considered problems in the application of stop and frisk, particularly the assumption that suspects who flee from approaching police officers are probably involved in nefarious activity. For example, in *Commonwealth v. Warren,* the Massachusetts Supreme Judicial Court not only concluded that there were racial disparities in Boston's stop and frisk program but also explicitly linked this to the use of flight as one element of the reasonable suspicion analysis:

> [W]here the suspect is a black male stopped by the police on the streets of Boston, the analysis of flight as a factor in the reasonable suspicion calculus cannot be divorced from the findings in a recent Boston Police Department report documenting a pattern of racial profiling of black males in the city of Boston. According to the study . . . black men in the city of Boston were more likely to be targeted for police-civilian encounters such as stops, frisks, searches, observations, and interrogations. Black men were also disproportionally targeted for repeat police encounters. We do not eliminate flight as a factor in the reasonable suspicion analysis whenever a black male is the subject of an investigatory stop. However, in such circumstances, flight is not necessarily probative of a suspect's state of mind or consciousness of guilt. Rather, the finding that black males in Boston are disproportionately and repeatedly targeted for FIO encounters suggests a reason for flight totally unrelated to consciousness of guilt. Such an individual, when approached

> by the police, might just as easily be motivated by the desire to avoid the recurring indignity of being racially profiled as by the desire to hide criminal activity. Given this reality for black males in the city of Boston, a judge should, in appropriate cases, consider the report's findings in weighing flight as a factor in the reasonable suspicion calculus.

Commonwealth v. Warren, 475 Mass. 530, 539-40, 58 N.E.3d 333, 342 (2016). Do you agree that courts should discount flight as a reliable indicator if the defendant is a member of a minority group that is disproportionately targeted under a municipality's stop and frisk program? Finally, is this a sufficient judicial remedy to the problem? Or do you believe that flight is always a reliable indicator that criminal activity is afoot?

D. PRACTICE & POLICY

The following section focuses more deeply on New York City's stop and frisk program. The materials start with a detailed look at: (i) who is harmed by the racial profiling involved in New York's stop and frisk program; (ii) the evidence of discriminatory impact; (iii) the remedies imposed by the court in the New York City stop and frisk litigation; and (iv) the controversial Trespass Affidavit Program, which allowed city police officers to circumvent the requirements of individualized suspicion normally required by *Terry*. To critics of the New York City police department, the materials paint a disturbing portrait of a crime-control technique gone wrong. As you read these materials, ask yourself whether this on-the-ground practice is what the Supreme Court envisioned when it first decided *Terry v. Ohio* in 1968.

Who is Floyd? It is difficult to appreciate the human cost—the intrusion on liberty—imposed by stop and frisk unless one personalizes the experience. Although the *Floyd* litigation was a class action lawsuit on behalf of all African-American and Hispanic individuals stopped by the NYPD as part of the stop and frisk program, the named plaintiff and his experiences were explicitly discussed during the litigation. Here is the district court's description of Mr. Floyd's encounter with the police:

> On February 27, 2008, Floyd resided on Beach Avenue in a three-family home with a separate cottage. Floyd's Godmother owned the property and lived on the top floor, and tenants occupied the ground floor and the basement. Floyd lived in the cottage. Around 3:00 p.m., Floyd left the cottage carrying a backpack, with his wallet, cell phone, keys, and some change in his pocket. Before Floyd got to the street, the basement tenant, also a black male, told Floyd that he was locked out of his

apartment and asked for Floyd's assistance because Floyd had access to the spare keys.

Floyd retrieved seven to ten keys on separate key rings from his Godmother's apartment and went to the door of the basement apartment with the tenant. Because the keys were not marked, both Floyd and the tenant tried five or six different keys for a minute or two. At that point, three plainclothes officers, since identified as Officers Cormac Joyce and Eric Hernandez, and Sergeant James Kelly, approached and told Floyd and the tenant to stop what they were doing and put their hands up. Floyd obeyed. Officer Joyce patted Floyd down and searched Floyd's pockets without his consent. He did not remove anything from Floyd's pockets.

After frisking the men, the officers remained calm throughout the encounter. The officers asked the men for ID, and Floyd showed his Louisiana drivers' license. The tenant did not have ID on him. After additional inquiries, Floyd produced an electric bill with his name and address on it, and the tenant went inside his apartment and got ID. Floyd asked why he had been stopped and the officers informed him that there had been a pattern of burglaries in the area. Floyd asked for the officers' names and badge numbers and the officers provided them. The officers then left.

Earlier that day the officers had been patrolling Beach Avenue in response to reports of robberies and burglaries of private homes in the area—specifically the area of the 43rd Precinct near the Cross-Bronx Expressway. Proximity to the Cross-Bronx Expressway was significant because it provided easy access for a vehicle to get away from the area quickly. The majority of the burglaries in the pattern identified during trial occurred in January 2008, with the last occurring on February 2.

The officers observed Floyd and the tenant for about two minutes before approaching them. Sergeant Kelly observed them playing with the door knob, and also saw a bag on the ground next to Floyd. When he approached the men, he saw that they were trying numerous keys, which was consistent with his belief that they might be burglars, because burglars sometimes have master keys. The basis for the frisk was the belief that Floyd and the tenant were in the process of committing a violent felony.

Officer Joyce filled out a UF-250 in connection with this stop. He checked the box for Furtive Movements based on the jostling of the doorknob and the keys. He also checked time of day corresponding to criminal activity.

Floyd, 959 F. Supp. 2d 540, 651-52 (S.D.N.Y. 2013). What is your initial assessment of this stop? Was it justified under typical *Terry* standards?

Fagan's statistical analysis. In order to prove their contention that New York City's stop and frisk program had a discriminatory impact, plaintiffs retained the services of expert Jeffrey Fagan, a criminologist who works as a professor at Columbia Law School. Fagan conducted an empirical analysis of every UF-250 form filled out by a New York City police officer between 2004-2009, a total of 2.8 million forms. The UF-250 form is required after a police officer conducts a *Terry* stop and includes boxes that can be checked off so that the police officer can explain why they had a "reasonable suspicion" that the target of the stop and frisk was involved in criminal activity. For example, there are boxes for "furtive movements," "suspicious bulge," and "actions indicative of casing individual or location." There is also a write-in box where the police officer can indicate the type of location where the stop was made.

After performing a statistical analysis of his database of UF-250s, Fagan reached the following conclusions, quoted here:

> (1) The racial composition of a precinct, neighborhood, and census tract is a statistically significant, strong and robust predictor of NYPD stop-and-frisk patterns even after controlling for the simultaneous influences of crime, social conditions, and allocation of police resources.
>
> (2) NYPD stops-and-frisks are significantly more frequent for Black and Hispanic residents than they are for White residents, even after adjusting for local crime rates, racial composition of the local population, police patrol strength, and other social and economic factors predictive of police enforcement activity.
>
> (3) Blacks and Latinos are significantly more likely to be stopped by NYPD officers than are Whites even in areas where there are low crime rates and where residential populations are racially heterogenous or predominately White.
>
> (4) Black and Hispanic individuals are treated more harshly during stop-and-frisk encounters with NYPD officers than Whites who are stopped on suspicion of the same or similar crimes.

Fagan Decl. ¶ 23, cited in *Floyd,* 861 F. Supp. 2d, at 281. Do you agree that a statistical analysis alone is enough to prove that black and Hispanic individuals are treated more harshly during *Terry* stops?

The remedies ordered to reform New York's program. After deciding that New York City was responsible for conducting its stop and frisk program in a racially discriminatory fashion, Judge Scheindlin issued a second opinion, *Floyd,* 959 F. Supp. 2d 668 (S.D.N.Y. 2013), that outlined multiple remedies that she was ordering in the case. Although she

(COMPLETE ALL CAPTIONS)

STOP, QUESTION AND FRISK REPORT WORKSHEET
PD344-151A (Rev. 11-02)

Pct.Serial No.	
Date	Pct. Of Occ.

Time Of Stop	Period Of Observation Prior To Stop	Radio Run/Sprint #

Address/Intersection Or Cross Streets Of Stop

☐ Inside ☐ Outside	☐ Transit ☐ Housing	Type Of Location Describe:

Specify Which Felony/P.L. Misdemeanor Suspected	Duration Of Stop

What Were Circumstances Which Led To Stop?
(MUST CHECK AT LEAST ONE BOX)

- ☐ Carrying Objects In Plain View Used In Commission Of Crime e.g., Slim Jim/Pry Bar, etc.
- ☐ Fits Description.
- ☐ Actions Indicative Of "Casing" Victim Or Location.
- ☐ Actions Indicative of Acting As A Lookout.
- ☐ Suspicious Bulge/Object (Describe)
- ☐ Other Reasonable Suspicion Of Criminal Activity (Specify)
- ☐ Actions Indicative Of Engaging In Drug Transaction.
- ☐ Furtive Movements.
- ☐ Actions Indicative Of Engaging In Violent Crimes.
- ☐ Wearing Clothes/Disguises Commonly Used In Commission Of Crime.

Name Of Person Stopped	Nickname/ Street Name	Date Of Birth

Address	Apt. No.	Tel. No.

Identification: ☐ Verbal ☐ Photo I.D. ☐ Refused
☐ Other (Specify) ____________

Sex: ☐ Male ☐ Female	Race: ☐ White ☐ Black ☐ White Hispanic ☐ Black Hispanic ☐ Asian/Pacific Islander ☐ American Indian/Alaskan Native

Age	Height	Weight	Hair	Eyes	Build

Other (Scars, Tattoos, Etc.)

Did Officer Explain Reason For Stop ☐ Yes ☐ No	If No, Explain:

Were Other Persons Stopped/ Questioned/Frisked? ☐ Yes ☐ No	If Yes, List Pct. Serial Nos.

If Physical Force Was Used, Indicate Type:

- ☐ Hands On Suspect
- ☐ Suspect On Ground
- ☐ Pointing Firearm At Suspect
- ☐ Handcuffing Suspect
- ☐ Suspect Against Wall/Car
- ☐ Drawing Firearm
- ☐ Baton
- ☐ Pepper Spray
- ☐ Other (Describe)

Was Suspect Arrested? ☐ Yes ☐ No	Offense	Arrest No.
Was Summons Issued? ☐ Yes ☐ No	Offense	Summons No.

Officer In Uniform? ☐ Yes ☐ No	If No, How Identified? ☐ Shield ☐ I.D. Card ☐ Verbal

did not end the stop and frisk program entirely, she did order the following reforms:

- The appointment of an independent monitor—a law firm partner who previously worked as a law school professor—to oversee reforms.

- Revisions to policy and training documents to ensure that *Terry* stops meet the following constitutional standards: "In order to conduct a stop, an officer must have individualized, reasonable suspicion that the person stopped has committed, is committing, or is about to commit a crime. The officer must be able to articulate facts establishing a minimal level of objective justification for making the stop, which means more than an inchoate and unparticularized suspicion or hunch. 'Furtive movements' are an insufficient basis for a stop or frisk if the officer cannot articulate anything more specific about the suspicious nature of the movement. The same is true of merely being present in a 'high crime area.' Moreover, no person may be stopped solely because he matches a vague or generalized description—such as young black male 18 to 24—without further detail or indicia of reliability." *Id.* at 679.
- The training materials must also clarify that in order to move from a stop to a frisk, the officer must have reasonable suspicion, again based on articulable facts, that the individual is armed and dangerous.
- Training should be revised so that "[r]ace may only be considered where the stop is based on a specific and reliable suspect description."
- Revisions to the forms that police officers fill out after a *Terry* stop to explicitly require a separate justification for a pat-down, frisk, or search.
- Changes to monitoring, supervision, and discipline.
- Activity logs of *Terry* stops.
- Body cameras for all police officers.

The *Floyd* decision was appealed by New York City. However, before the case was heard by the Second Circuit, the City settled the case and reached an agreement with the plaintiffs to end the litigation. The settlement included New York City's agreement to a number of important reforms.

The Trespass Affidavit Program. Of particular importance in the settlement was an agreement to end the so-called Trespass Affidavit Program, whereby the owners of specific buildings in the city requested police assistance in monitoring their properties for trespassing and other illegal conduct. In practice, police interpreted the agreement as giving them the authority to search anyone for simply coming and going, since the police had the consent of the property owners. This activity often led the police to stop and frisk the lawful occupants or visitors of apartment units within these buildings as they were coming and going—most importantly without the individualized suspicion normally required by a *Terry* stop analysis. New York City agreed to end the program and agreed that police officers would conduct all stops only when they had individualized suspicion. For more discussion, see Carol S. Steiker, Terry *Unbound*, 82 Miss. L.J. 329, 330 (2013).

CHAPTER 6

The Exclusionary Rule

INTRODUCTION

The exclusionary rule is, first and foremost, a *remedy*. By definition, the exclusionary rule is only relevant if a court has determined that the authorities—either the police or some other state actor—violated a constitutional rule. If there is no violation of the Constitution, the exclusionary rule does not come into play. However, the rule is not a simple rule of evidence, as it was once considered by some courts. The Supreme Court eventually clarified that the exclusionary rule has constitutional significance, so it is neither optional nor a mere rule of evidence that could be created, and repealed, by statute. Although states are free to impose the exclusionary rule in additional circumstances, they cannot repeal the rule when it is constitutionally required. It is a constitutional necessity. For that reason, it applies not just to constitutional violations by the federal government but also constitutional violations by state and local police, by virtue of the Fourteenth Amendment.

The animating principle behind the exclusionary rule is deterrence. Police will have no incentive to comply with the constitutional requirements unless there are *consequences* for their misbehavior. In this case, the consequence is a severe one: The evidence discovered or seized during the offending event will be excluded from a criminal proceeding against the individual. Some have asked whether these consequences impose too high a price. While this is one way of asking the question, another way of putting the point is that the consequences are borne not just by the state authorities but also by the community itself, which is innocent of any wrongdoing. Hypothetically, if evidence must be excluded from a trial and thereby transform what would otherwise be a certain conviction into a certain acquittal—perhaps even a dismissal of the charges from the bench due to a lack of evidence—the community itself bears the burden of living with a potentially dangerous criminal who ought to be put in prison. The deterrence rationale points to the future, i.e., to future conduct by the police that will be ever more faithful to the constitutional standards. But that benefit is far in the future and somewhat diffuse. The cost of the exclusionary rule is borne in the here and now: the collapse of a criminal proceeding and the potential reintroduction of a criminal into a community that could be victimized by future wrongdoing of that individual. The police officer is the guilty party; the community pays the price. On the other hand, had the police not violated the Fourth Amendment in the first place, the prosecution probably would not have the evidence it needs to successfully prosecute the offender, who would remain free anyway.

There are alternate frameworks for understanding the exclusionary rule that do not depend on deterrence. For example, one might consider the exclusionary rule to be a requirement of judicial integrity. Under this rationale, the use of evidence obtained from unconstitutional police misconduct will infringe on the judicial integrity of the trial process—not just contaminating the result of the trial but also impairing the legitimacy of the *process* that yielded the result. Implicit in a system of due process, and indeed in the rule of law, is that the judicial system is conducted in a rule-bound way. To allow evidence at trial when it was seized in an illegal fashion undermines that rule-bound conception of the legal system.

Courts usually look to the deterrence rationale to define the outer boundaries of the exclusionary rule—when it applies and when it does not. Consequently, the law has evolved multiple categories of exceptions to the exclusionary rule, each of which will be outlined in greater detail below. If exclusion of the evidence will not function to deter future police misconduct, then the exclusionary rule loses its raison d'etre and should not be applied to the situation at hand. For example, the Supreme Court has carved out an exception for cases where the police officer acts in "good faith" but inadvertently crosses some constitutional line. In contrast with a case of intentional police misconduct, a future constable who crosses a constitutional line by mistake, while acting in good faith, is less likely to be influenced by the threat that the ill-gotten evidentiary gains will be thrown out and unavailable at trial. Of course, critics will argue that the negligent constable—or state authorities in general—could be more careful and that the risks associated with the exclusionary rule might incentivize them to build systems that are less likely to make mistakes that violate the Fourth Amendment. The other major exceptions, including the independent source doctrine, inevitable discovery, and knock-and-announce situations, will be discussed at the end of this chapter in Section E.

In a sense, the story of the exclusionary rule is paradoxically one of both expansion and contraction. On the one hand, the Supreme Court has consistently endorsed the basic premise behind the exclusionary rule and enlarged its application to Fourth Amendment violations, ultimately holding that it should also apply as a consequence for violations of the Fifth and Sixth Amendments as well. The basic structure of its deterrence rationale is so well regarded that the Supreme Court has gone back to the well time and time again to draw water to vindicate the Bill of Rights. At the same time, however, the Supreme Court has carved out the gaping exceptions for which the exclusionary rule will not apply, limiting its power in situations where it will do more damage than good according to a consequentialist calculation that balances the potential deterrence impact with the risk to the government's legitimate desire for crime control measures. This constant push and pull has produced a truly expansive doctrine with islands of exceptions. For both the student and the practitioner, the key is to understand which fact patterns land on the islands of exceptions and which do not.

The procedural mechanism for implementing the exclusionary rule is the suppression hearing. Typically, a defense attorney will make a pre-trial or trial motion to exclude evidence (sometimes called a motion *in limine*). The defense will assert that the authorities violated the Fourth, Fifth, or Sixth Amendment and that the situation does not fall under one of the previously articulated exceptions to the exclusionary rule. In order to establish the factual basis for the motion, the defense will bring witnesses to the stand—for example, the defendant and other witnesses might testify to the conduct of the police during the search of the defendant's residence. The prosecutor will have an opportunity to present its own case, perhaps calling police officers to the stand. Both sides have the opportunity to cross examine witnesses. The proceedings occur outside the presence of the jury since the issue is a legal one for a judge to decide. The judge decides the issue with a standard that is not as demanding as proof beyond a reasonable doubt; rather, the judge decides the issue using the standard of preponderance of the evidence. Generally speaking, courts allocate to the defendant the burden of establishing a constitutional violation that would trigger the exclusionary rule. However, if the government is relying on one of the established *exceptions* to the exclusionary rule, the burden shifts to the government to demonstrate the applicability of the exception, again by a preponderance of the evidence.

A. ORIGINS OF THE RULE

Why did the Supreme Court agree to recognize the exclusionary rule? There is no mention of it in the words of the Fourth or Fourteenth Amendments. But something about the nature of the constitutional protections necessarily entails a significant remedy. As you read the following case, which is often described as the canonical expression of the exclusionary rule, look for the Court's articulation of the underlying rationale for the rule. Is the remedy designed to protect the original victim of the police misconduct or is it designed to protect the rights of future, hypothetical victims? Or both? Finally, pay attention to the final result in the case. Why is some of the evidence excluded from consideration but other evidence is allowed to be introduced at trial?

Weeks v. United States

Supreme Court of the United States
232 U.S. 383 (1914)

Mr. Justice DAY delivered the opinion of the court:

An indictment was returned against the plaintiff in error, defendant below, and herein so designated, in the district court of the United States for the western district of Missouri, containing nine counts. The seventh count, upon which a conviction was had, charged the use of the mails for the purpose of transporting certain coupons or tickets representing chances or shares in a lottery or gift enterprise....

The defendant was arrested by a police officer, so far as the record shows, without warrant, at the Union Station in Kansas City, Missouri, where he was employed by an express company. Other police officers had gone to the house of the defendant, and being told by a neighbor where the key was kept, found it and entered the house. They searched the defendant's room and took possession of various papers and articles found there, which were afterwards turned over to the United States marshal. Later in the same day police officers returned with the marshal, who thought he might find additional evidence, and, being admitted by someone in the house, probably a boarder, in response to a rap, the marshal searched the defendant's room and carried away certain letters and envelops found in the drawer of a chiffonier. Neither the marshal nor the police officer had a search warrant....

The defendant assigns error, among other things, in the court's refusal to grant his petition for the return of his property, and in permitting the papers to be used at the trial.

It is thus apparent that the question presented involves the determination of the duty of the court with reference to the motion made by the defendant for the return of certain letters, as well as other papers, taken from his room by the United States marshal, who, without authority of process, if any such could have been legally issued, visited the room of the defendant for the declared purpose of obtaining additional testimony to support the charge against the accused, and, having gained admission to the house, took from the drawer of a chiffonier there found certain letters written to the defendant, tending to show his guilt. These letters were placed in the control of the district attorney, and were subsequently produced by him and offered in evidence against the accused at the trial. The defendant contends that such appropriation of his private correspondence was in violation of rights secured to him by the 4th and 5th Amendments to the Constitution of the United States. We shall deal with the 4th Amendment....

The history of this Amendment is given with particularity in the opinion of Mr. Justice Bradley, speaking for the court in *Boyd v. United States*, 116 U.S. 616. As was there shown, it took its origin in the determination of the framers of the Amendments to the Federal Constitution to provide for that instrument a Bill of Rights, securing to the American people, among other things, those safeguards which had grown up in England to protect the people from unreasonable searches and seizures, such as were permitted under the general warrants issued under authority of the government, by which there had been invasions of the home and privacy of the citizens, and the seizure of their private papers in support of charges, real or imaginary, make against them. Such practices had also received sanction under warrants and seizures under the so-called writs of assistance, issued in the American colonies. Resistance to these practices had established the principle which was enacted into the fundamental law in the 4th Amendment, that a man's house was his castle, and not to be invaded by any general authority to search and seize his goods and papers....

The effect of the 4th Amendment is to put the courts of the United States and Federal officials, in the exercise of their power and authority, under limitations and restraints as to the exercise of such power and authority, and to forever secure the people, their persons, houses, papers, and effects, against all unreasonable searches and seizures under the guise of law. This protection reaches all alike, whether accused of crime or not, and the duty of giving to it force and effect is obligatory upon all entrusted under our Federal system with the enforcement of the laws. The tendency of those who execute the criminal laws of the country to obtain conviction by means of unlawful seizures and enforced confessions, the latter often obtained after subjecting accused persons to unwarranted practices destructive of rights secured by the Federal Constitution, should find no sanction in the judgments of the courts, which are charged at all times with the support of the Constitution, and to which people of all conditions have a right to appeal for the maintenance of such fundamental rights.

What, then, is the present case? Before answering that inquiry specifically, it may be well by a process of exclusion to state what it is not. It is not an assertion of the right on the part of the government always recognized under English and American law, to search the person of the accused when legally arrested, to discover and seize the fruits or evidences of crime. This right has been uniformly maintained in many cases. Nor is it the case of testimony offered at a trial where the court is asked to stop and consider the illegal means by which proofs, otherwise competent, were obtained,—of which we shall have occasion to treat later in this opinion. Nor is it the case of burglar's tools or other proofs of guilt found upon his arrest within his control.

The case in the aspect in which we are dealing with it involves the right of the court in a criminal prosecution to retain for the purposes of evidence the letters and correspondence of the accused, seized in his house in his absence and without his authority, by a United States marshal holding no warrant for his arrest and none for the search of his premises. The accused, without awaiting his trial, made timely application to the court for an order for the return of these letters, as well or other property. This application was denied, the letters retained and put in evidence, after a further application at the beginning of the trial, both applications asserting the rights of the accused under the 4th and 5th Amendments to the Constitution. If letters and private documents can thus be seized and held and used in evidence against a citizen accused of an offense, the protection of the 4th Amendment, declaring his right to be secure against such searches and seizures, is of no value, and, so far as those thus placed are concerned, might as well be stricken from the Constitution. The efforts of the courts and their officials to bring the guilty to punishment, praiseworthy as they are, are not to be aided by the sacrifice of those great principles established by years of endeavor and suffering which have resulted in their embodiment in the fundamental law of the land. The United States marshal could only have invaded the house of the accused when armed with a warrant issued as required by the Constitution, upon sworn information, and describing with reasonable particularity the thing for which the search was to be made. Instead, he acted without sanction of law, doubtless prompted by the desire to bring further proof to the aid of the government, and under color of his office undertook to make a seizure of private papers in direct violation of the constitutional prohibition against such action. Under such circumstances, without sworn information and particular description, not even an order of court would have justified such procedure; much less was it within the authority of the United States marshal to thus invade the house and privacy of the accused. In *Adams v. New York*, 192 U.S. 585, this court said that the 4th Amendment was intended to secure the citizen in person and property against unlawful invasion of the sanctity of his home by officers of the law, acting under legislative or judicial sanction. This protection is equally extended to the action of the government and officers of the law acting under it. To sanction such proceedings would be to affirm by judicial decision a manifest neglect, if not an open defiance, of the prohibitions of the Constitution, intended for the protection of the people against such unauthorized action.

The court before which the application was made in this case recognized the illegal character of the seizure, and ordered the return of property not in its judgment competent to be offered at the trial, but refused the application of the accused to turn over the letters, which were afterwards put in evidence on behalf of the government....

We... reach the conclusion that the letters in question were taken from the house of the accused by an official of the United States, acting under color of his office, in direct violation of the constitutional rights of the defendant; that having made a seasonable application for their return, which was heard and passed upon by the court, there was involved in the order refusing the application a denial of the constitutional rights of the accused, and that the court should have restored these letters to the accused. In holding them and permitting their use upon the trial, we think prejudicial error was committed. As to the papers and property seized by the policemen, it does not appear that they acted under any claim of Federal authority such as would make the amendment applicable to such unauthorized seizures. The record shows that what they did by way of arrest and search and seizure was done before the finding of the indictment in the Federal court; under what supposed right or authority does not appear. What remedies the defendant may have against them we need not inquire, as the 4th Amendment is not directed to individual misconduct of such officials. Its limitations reach the Federal government and its agencies....

NOTES & QUESTIONS ON THE ORIGINS OF EXCLUSION

1. *Are there other remedies available?* It is important to remember that the exclusionary rule announced in *Weeks* was not inevitable. There are other ways—at least in theory—that constitutional rights might be vindicated in the face of a violation. For example, individuals could have a private right of action for money damages against state actors that violate their constitutional rights. Or state authorities might impose disciplinary measures—up to and including termination—against police officers that violate the Constitution. If the police cannot be trusted to oversee their own members, this process could be housed in an independent government agency created by statute. These are just theoretical examples, but they show that the exclusionary rule is not the only option available on the menu. The problem with the other options is that they require the cooperation of actors outside of the judiciary to implement. In contrast, the exclusionary rule as a remedy is articulated and implemented solely by judges. As James Madison said: "If they (the first ten Amendments) are incorporated into the Constitution, independent tribunals of justice will consider themselves in a peculiar manner the guardians of those rights; they will be an impenetrable bulwark against every assumption of power in the Legislative or Executive; they will be naturally led to resist every encroachment upon

rights expressly stipulated for in the Constitution by the declaration of rights." Annals of Congress 439 (1789), quoted in *Mapp v. Ohio*, 367 U.S. 643, 663 n.8 (1961).

Consider the following harsh assessment of the exclusionary rule:

> Considering the exclusionary rule's crumbling foundation, its structure riddled with exceptions, and its high costs in terms of both its effect on the justice system and on society's perception of this system, it is time to bid the rule farewell. This plea for the exclusionary rule's abandonment comes at a time when our cities are plagued with crime and where public sentiment encourages a "tough on crime" approach by the justice system. The exclusionary rule punishes society by allowing criminals back into our communities. The rule also punishes the justice system by acting to suppress truth in a trial that is intended to be a truthfinding process, thereby tarnishing the integrity of the judiciary in the public's eyes. Moreover, the exclusionary rule does not adequately punish or affect the officers who commit unlawful searches and seizures.

Christine M. D'Elia, *The Exclusionary Rule: Who Does It Punish?*, 5 Seton Hall Const. L.J. 563, 606 (1995). Do you agree with the author that the exclusionary rule is a blunt tool that fails to punish the appropriate actor?

2. *Judicial integrity*. Note that the Supreme Court in *Weeks* articulated a justification for the exclusionary rule that went beyond mere deterrence. For example, reconsider the following quote from the *Weeks* opinion: "To sanction such proceedings would be to affirm by judicial decision a manifest neglect, if not an open defiance, of the prohibitions of the Constitution, intended for the protection of the people against such unauthorized action." Also: "If letters and private documents can thus be seized and held and used in evidence against a citizen...the protection of the 4th Amendment...might as well be stricken from the Constitution." In reading these quotes, how would you describe the original justification for the exclusionary rule?

B. APPLICATION IN STATE COURTS

In *Weeks*, the Supreme Court refused to recognize the exclusionary rule as binding against the states—it was held to be a mandatory remedy for constitutional violations by *federal* officers acting under color of law. Although states were of course free to adopt an exclusionary rule as a matter of state law—either by state statute or judicial invention—the Supreme Court was not going to mandate it. This view was then reaffirmed in *Wolf v. Colorado*, 338 U.S. 25, 33 (1949), which held that "in a prosecution in a State court for a State crime the Fourteenth Amendment does not forbid the admission of evidence obtained by an unreasonable search and seizure." However, in the following case, the Supreme Court reverses course and finally recognizes that the exclusionary rule is binding on the states by virtue of the Fourteenth Amendment. As you read the case, ask yourself what had changed between 1914 when *Weeks* was decided and 1961 when the *Mapp* decision was handed down.

Mapp v. Ohio

Supreme Court of the United States
367 U.S. 643 (1961)

Mr. Justice CLARK delivered the opinion of the Court.

Appellant stands convicted of knowingly having had in her possession and under her control certain lewd and lascivious books, pictures, and photographs in violation of section 2905.34 of Ohio's Revised Code....

On May 23, 1957, three Cleveland police officers arrived at appellant's residence in that city pursuant to information that "a person (was) hiding out in the home, who was wanted for questioning in connection with a recent bombing, and that there was a large amount of policy paraphernalia being hidden in the home." Miss Mapp and her daughter by a former marriage lived on the top floor of the two-family dwelling. Upon their arrival at that house, the officers knocked on the door and demanded entrance but appellant, after telephoning her attorney, refused to admit them without a search warrant. They advised their headquarters of the situation and undertook a surveillance of the house.

The officers again sought entrance some three hours later when four or more additional officers arrived on the scene. When Miss Mapp did not come to the door immediately, at least one of the several doors to the house was forcibly opened and the policemen gained admittance. Meanwhile Miss Mapp's attorney arrived, but the officers, having secured their own entry, and continuing in their defiance of the law, would permit him neither to see Miss Mapp nor to enter the house. It appears that Miss Mapp was halfway down the stairs from the upper floor to the front door when the officers, in this highhanded manner, broke into the hall. She demanded to see the search warrant. A paper, claimed to be a warrant, was held up by one of the officers. She grabbed the "warrant" and placed it in her bosom. A struggle ensued in which the officers recovered the piece of paper and as a result of which they handcuffed appellant because she had been "belligerent" in resisting their official rescue of the "warrant" from her person. Running roughshod over appellant, a policeman "grabbed" her, "twisted (her) hand," and she "yelled (and) pleaded with him" because "it was hurting." Appellant, in handcuffs, was then forcibly taken upstairs to her bedroom where the officers searched a dresser, a chest of drawers, a closet and some suitcases. They also looked into a photo album and through personal papers belonging to the appellant. The search spread to the rest of the second floor including the child's bedroom, the living room, the kitchen and a dinette. The basement of the building and a trunk found therein were also searched. The obscene materials for possession of which she was ultimately convicted were discovered in the course of that widespread search.

At the trial no search warrant was produced by the prosecution, nor was the failure to produce one explained or accounted for.... The State says that even if the search were made without authority, or otherwise unreasonably, it is not prevented from using the unconstitutionally seized evidence at trial....

I

... [I]n the year 1914, in the *Weeks* case, this Court "for the first time" held that "in a federal prosecution the Fourth Amendment barred the use of evidence secured through an illegal search and seizure." *Wolf v. Colorado.* This Court has ever since required of federal law officers a strict adherence to that command which this Court has held to be a clear, specific, and constitutionally required—even if judicially implied—deterrent safeguard without insistence upon which the Fourth Amendment would have been reduced to "a form of words." It meant, quite simply, that "conviction by means of unlawful seizures and enforced confessions... should find no sanction in the judgments of the courts ..." *Weeks v. United States,* and that such evidence "shall not be used at all." *Silverthorne Lumber Co. v. United States,* 251 U.S. at 392.

There are in the cases of this Court some passing references to the *Weeks* rule as being one of evidence. But the plain and unequivocal language of *Weeks*—and its later paraphrase in *Wolf*—to the effect that the *Weeks* rule is of constitutional origin, remains entirely undisturbed. In *Byars v. United States,* 273 U.S. 28 (1927), a unanimous Court declared that "the doctrine (cannot)...be tolerated under our constitutional system, that evidences of crime discovered by a federal officer in making a search without lawful warrant may be used against the victim of the unlawful search where a timely challenge has been interposed." The Court, in *Olmstead v. United States,* 277 U.S. 438, 462 (1928), in unmistakable language restated the *Weeks* rule: "The striking outcome of the *Weeks* case and those which followed it was the sweeping declaration that the Fourth Amendment, although not referring to or limiting the use of evidence in court, really forbade its introduction if obtained by government officers through a violation of the amendment." ...

II

In 1949, 35 years after *Weeks* was announced, this Court, in *Wolf v. Colorado,* again for the first time, discussed the effect of the Fourth

Amendment upon the States through the operation of the Due Process Clause of the Fourteenth Amendment. It said: "(W)e have no hesitation in saying that were a State affirmatively to sanction such police incursion into privacy it would run counter to the guaranty of the Fourteenth Amendment."

Nevertheless, after declaring that the "security of one's privacy against arbitrary intrusion by the police" is "implicit in 'the concept of ordered liberty' and as such enforceable against the States through the Due Process Clause," and announcing that it "stoutly adhere(d)" to the *Weeks* decision, the Court decided that the *Weeks* exclusionary rule would not then be imposed upon the States as "an essential ingredient of the right." 338 U.S., at 27-29. The Court's reasons for not considering essential to the right to privacy, as a curb imposed upon the States by the Due Process Clause, that which decades before had been posited as part and parcel of the Fourth Amendment's limitations upon federal encroachment of individual privacy, were bottomed on factual considerations.

While they are not basically relevant to a decision that the exclusionary rule is an essential ingredient of the Fourth Amendment as the right it embodies is vouchsafed against the States by the Due Process Clause, we will consider the current validity of the factual grounds upon which *Wolf* was based.

The Court in *Wolf* first stated that "(t)he contrariety of views of the States" on the adoption of the exclusionary rule of *Weeks* was "particularly impressive"; and, in this connection that it could not "brush aside the experience of States which deem the incidence of such conduct by the police too slight to call for a deterrent remedy... by overriding the (States') relevant rules of evidence." While in 1949, prior to the *Wolf* case, almost two-thirds of the States were opposed to the use of the exclusionary rule, now, despite the *Wolf* case, more than half of those since passing upon it, by their own legislative or judicial decision, have wholly or partly adopted or adhered to the *Weeks* rule. Significantly, among those now following the rule is California, which, according to its highest court, was "compelled to reach that conclusion because other remedies have completely failed to secure compliance with the constitutional provisions...." In connection with this California case, we note that the second basis elaborated in *Wolf* in support of its failure to enforce the exclusionary doctrine against the States was that "other means of protection" have been afforded "the right to privacy." The experience of California that such other remedies have been worthless and futile is buttressed by the experience of other States. The obvious futility of relegating the Fourth Amendment of the protection of other remedies has, moreover, been recognized by this Court since *Wolf*....

It, therefore, plainly appears that the factual considerations supporting the failure of the *Wolf* Court to include the *Weeks* exclusionary rule when it recognized the enforceability of the right to privacy against the States in 1949, while not basically relevant to the constitutional consideration, could not, in any analysis, now be deemed controlling.

III

Some five years after *Wolf,* in answer to a plea made here Term after Term that we overturn its doctrine on applicability of the *Weeks* exclusionary rule, this Court indicated that such should not be done until the States had "adequate opportunity to adopt or reject the (*Weeks*) rule." There again it was said: "Never until June of 1949 did this Court hold the basic search-and-seizure prohibition in any way applicable to the states under the Fourteenth Amendment."

And only last Term, after again carefully re-examining the *Wolf* doctrine in *Elkins v. United States,* the Court pointed out that "the controlling principles" as to search and seizure and the problem of admissibility "seemed clear" until the announcement in *Wolf* "that the Due Process Clause of the Fourteenth Amendment does not itself require state courts to adopt the exclusionary rule" of the *Weeks* case. At the same time, the Court pointed out, "the underlying constitutional doctrine which *Wolf* established... that the Federal Constitution... prohibits unreasonable searches and seizures by state officers" had undermined the "foundation upon which the admissibility of state seized evidence in a federal trial originally rested...." The Court concluded that it was therefore obliged to hold, although it chose the narrower ground on which to do so, that all evidence obtained by an unconstitutional search and seizure was inadmissible in a federal court regardless of its source. Today we once again examine *Wolf's* constitutional documentation of the right to privacy free from unreasonable state intrusion, and, after its dozen years on our books, are led by it to close the only courtroom door remaining open to evidence secured by official lawlessness in flagrant abuse of that basic right, reserved to all persons as a specific guarantee against that very same unlawful conduct. We hold that all evidence obtained by searches and seizures in violation of the Constitution is, by that same authority, inadmissible in a state court.

IV

Since the Fourth Amendment's right of privacy has been declared enforceable against the States through the Due Process Clause of the Fourteenth, it is enforceable against them by the same sanction of exclusion as is used against the Federal Government. Were it otherwise, then just as without the *Weeks* rule the assurance against unreasonable federal searches and seizures would be "a form of words," valueless and undeserving of mention in a perpetual charter of inestimable human liberties, so too, without that rule the freedom from state invasions of privacy would be so ephemeral and so neatly severed from its conceptual nexus with the freedom from all brutish means of coercing evidence as not to merit this Court's high regard as a freedom implicit in "the concept of ordered liberty." At the time that the Court held in *Wolf* that the Amendment was applicable to the States through the Due Process Clause, the cases of this Court, as we have seen, had steadfastly held that as to federal officers the Fourth Amendment included the exclusion of the evidence seized in violation of its provisions. Even *Wolf* "stoutly adhered" to that proposition. The right to privacy, when conceded operatively enforceable against the States, was not susceptible of destruction by avulsion of the sanction upon which its protection and enjoyment had always been deemed dependent under the *Boyd, Weeks* and *Silverthorne* cases. Therefore, in extending the substantive protections of due process to all constitutionally unreasonable searches—state or federal—it was logically and constitutionally necessary that the exclusion doctrine—an essential part of the right to privacy—be also insisted upon as an essential ingredient of the right newly recognized by the *Wolf* case. In short, the admission of the new constitutional right by *Wolf* could not consistently tolerate denial of its most important constitutional privilege, namely, the exclusion of the evidence which an accused had been forced to give by reason of the unlawful seizure. To hold otherwise is to grant the right but in reality to withhold its privilege and enjoyment. Only last year the Court itself recognized that the purpose of the exclusionary rule "is to deter—to compel respect for the constitutional guaranty in the only effectively available way—by removing the incentive to disregard it."...

V

Moreover, our holding that the exclusionary rule is an essential part of both the Fourth and Fourteenth Amendments is not only the logical dictate of prior cases, but it also makes very good sense. There is no war between the Constitution and common sense. Presently, a federal prosecutor may make no use of evidence illegally seized, but a State's attorney across the street may, although he supposedly is operating under the enforceable prohibitions of the same Amendment. Thus the State, by admitting evidence unlawfully seized, serves to encourage disobedience to the Federal Constitution which it is bound to uphold.... In non-exclusionary States, federal officers, being human, were by it invited to and did, as our cases indicate, step across the street to the State's attorney with their unconstitutionally seized evidence. Prosecution on the basis of that evidence was then had in a state court in utter disregard of the enforceable Fourth Amendment. If the fruits of an unconstitutional search had been inadmissible in both state and federal courts, this inducement to evasion would have been sooner eliminated....

Federal-state cooperation in the solution of crime under constitutional standards will be promoted, if only by recognition of their now mutual obligation to respect the same fundamental criteria in their approaches.... Denying shortcuts to only one of two cooperating law enforcement agencies tends naturally to breed legitimate suspicion of "working arrangements" whose results are equally tainted.

There are those who say, as did Justice (then Judge) Cardozo, that under our constitutional exclusionary doctrine "(t)he criminal is to go free because the constable has blundered." *People v. Defore*, 242 N.Y. at 21. In some cases this will undoubtedly be the result. But, as was said in *Elkins*, "there is another consideration—the imperative of judicial integrity." 364 U.S. at 222. The criminal goes free, if he must, but it is the law that sets him free. Nothing can destroy a government more quickly than its failure to observe its own laws, or worse, its disregard of the charter of its own existence....

The ignoble shortcut to conviction left open to the State tends to destroy the entire system of constitutional restraints on which the liberties of the people rest. Having once recognized that the right to privacy embodied in the Fourth Amendment is enforceable against the States, and that the right to be secure against rude invasions of privacy by state officers is, therefore, constitutional in origin, we can no longer permit that right to remain an empty promise. Because it is enforceable in the same manner and to like effect as other basic rights secured by the Due Process Clause, we can no longer permit it to be revocable at the whim of any police officer who, in the name of law enforcement itself, chooses to suspend its enjoyment. Our decision, founded on reason and truth, gives to the individual no more than that which the Constitution guarantees him, to the police officer no less than that to which honest law enforcement is entitled, and, to the courts, that judicial integrity so necessary in the true administration of justice....

NOTES & QUESTIONS ON THE EXCLUSIONARY RULE IN STATE COURTS

1. *The silver platter problem.* Consider the following situation. Imagine that state police conduct an unconstitutional search and collect evidence at the scene. The local authorities decide to turn over the evidence to the local authorities; they deliver it on a "silver platter" so that federal prosecutors can launch a successful prosecution in federal court. Under the *Weeks* rule, only the federal government was constrained by the exclusionary rule. In this case, though, it is the local police who violated the Constitution, and according to *Weeks*, the exclusionary rule does not apply to misconduct by state officials. Should a federal prosecution be allowed in this context? In dicta, following *Weeks*, the Supreme Court suggested yes, as long as the federal authorities had

no role in the collection of evidence by the local authorities. See, e.g., *Gambino v. United States,* 275 U.S. 310, 317 (1927). Does the silver platter problem provide a reason for the holding in *Mapp*? The silver platter doctrine only emerges as a potential paradox when there is a split between federal and state courts over the exclusionary rule. If the rule applies in *both* courts, it is clear that the evidence cannot be used in either proceeding regardless of who collected the evidence in the first instance. The silver platter doctrine was repudiated by the Supreme Court when it concluded that "evidence obtained by state officers during a search which, if conducted by federal officers, would have violated the defendant's immunity from unreasonable searches and seizures under the Fourth Amendment is inadmissible." *Elkins v. United States,* 364 U.S. 206, 223 (1960). Does the *Elkins* decision foreshadow what was coming in *Mapp*?

2. *The reverse silver platter problem.* There also is a reverse silver platter situation. Imagine a situation where the federal authorities, such as the FBI, illegally obtain evidence. The federal exclusionary rule announced in *Weeks* prevents federal prosecutors from using the evidence. But the feds could turn the evidence over on a silver platter to local authorities in a state that does not have its own exclusionary rule. This looks like an end-run around the federal exclusionary rule. Once again, though, the *Mapp* ruling effectively solves the reverse silver platter problem by making the rule mandatory in all jurisdictions. For more discussion, see George C. Thomas III, Mapp v. Ohio*: Doomed from the Beginning?,* 12 Ohio St. J. Crim. L. 289, 290 (2014) (noting that "[a]pplying the exclusionary rule to the states allowed the Court to extricate itself from the complications of excluding reliable evidence in some criminal trials but not others"); Tracey Maclin, *The Supreme Court and the Fourth Amendment's Exclusionary Rule* (2013).

3. *The real story behind* Mapp. According to Justice Potter Stewart in his Harlan Fiske Stone lectures, the case was originally argued and briefed as a First Amendment case because the charges against Dollree Mapp involved obscenity, and civil libertarians argued that the charges should be thrown out on that basis. Justice Stewart describes what happened next when the Court's majority opinion was circulated among the Justices:

> What transpired in the month following our conference on the case is really a matter of speculation on my part, but I have always suspected that the members of the soon-to-be *Mapp* majority had met in what I affectionately call a "rump caucus" to discuss a different basis for their decision. But regardless of how they reached their decision, five Justices of the Court concluded that the fourth and fourteenth amendments required that evidence seized in an illegal search be excluded from state trials as well as federal ones.... I was shocked when Justice Clark's proposed Court opinion reached my desk. I immediately wrote him a note expressing my surprise and questioning the

> wisdom of overruling an important doctrine in a case in which the issue was not briefed, argued, or discussed by the state courts, by the parties' counsel, or at our conference following the oral argument. After my shock subsided, I wrote a brief memorandum concurring in the judgment on first and fourteenth amendment grounds, and agreeing with Justice Harlan's dissent that the issue which the majority decided was not properly before the Court. The *Mapp* majority stood its ground, however....

Potter Stewart, *The Road to* Mapp v. Ohio *and Beyond: The Origins, Development and Future of the Exclusionary Rule in Search-and-Seizure Cases,* 83 Colum. L. Rev. 1365, 1368 (1983).

4. *Stare decisis.* *Wolf* was decided in 1949 and the Supreme Court overruled it in *Mapp* just 12 years later, in 1961. What does it say about constitutional interpretation that such a major decision could be abandoned after only 12 years? Does this suggest concern that constitutional interpretation is not stable? Or, conversely, does it suggest confidence that mistakes will be quickly reversed?

C. DEFINING THE SCOPE OF POLICE MISCONDUCT

What type of police misconduct will trigger the exclusionary rule? Of course, state authorities must engage in conduct that is later judged to be unconstitutional for the rule to apply. But this basic statement leaves many specific situations to fall in between the cracks. In *Davis,* the Supreme Court considers the case of police officers who engage in a search that is consistent with legal precedent at the time of the search, but whose legality is subsequently undermined when an appellate court overturns that precedent. Should the exclusionary rule apply to this type of behavior? After all, the behavior is clearly unconstitutional—at least when judged with the benefit of hindsight. Should the exclusionary rule attach to misconduct that carries the imprimatur of legal precedent at the moment when the conduct occurs?

Davis v. United States

Supreme Court of the United States
564 U.S. 229 (2011)

Justice Alito delivered the opinion of the Court.

The Fourth Amendment protects the right to be free from "unreasonable searches and seizures," but it is silent about how this right is to be enforced. To supplement the bare text, this Court created the exclusionary rule, a deterrent sanction that bars the prosecution from introducing evidence obtained by way of a Fourth Amendment violation. The question here is whether to apply this sanction when the police conduct a search in compliance with binding precedent that is later overruled. Because suppression would do nothing to deter police misconduct in these circumstances, and because it would come at a high cost to both the truth and the public safety, we hold that searches conducted in objectively reasonable reliance on binding appellate precedent are not subject to the exclusionary rule.

I

The question presented arises in this case as a result of a shift in our Fourth Amendment jurisprudence on searches of automobiles incident to arrests of recent occupants. Under this Court's decision in *Chimel v. California,* 395 U.S. 752 (1969), a police officer who makes a lawful arrest may conduct a warrantless search of the arrestee's person and the area "within his immediate control." This rule "may be stated clearly enough," but in the early going after *Chimel* it proved difficult to apply, particularly in cases that involved searches "inside [of] automobile[s] after the arrestees [we]re no longer in [them]." A number of courts upheld the constitutionality of vehicle searches that were "substantially contemporaneous" with occupants' arrests. Other courts disapproved of automobile searches incident to arrests, at least absent some continuing threat that the arrestee might gain access to the vehicle and "destroy evidence or grab a weapon." In *New York v. Belton,* this Court granted certiorari to resolve the conflict.

In *Belton,* a police officer conducting a traffic stop lawfully arrested four occupants of a vehicle and ordered the arrestees to line up, un-handcuffed, along the side of the thruway. The officer then searched the vehicle's passenger compartment and found cocaine inside a jacket that lay on the backseat. This Court upheld the search as reasonable incident to the occupants' arrests. In an opinion that repeatedly stressed the need for a "straightforward," "workable rule" to guide police conduct, the Court announced "that when a policeman has made a lawful custodial arrest of the occupant of an automobile, he may, as a contemporaneous incident of that arrest, search the passenger compartment of that automobile."

For years, *Belton* was widely understood to have set down a simple, bright-line rule. Numerous courts read the decision to authorize automobile searches incident to arrests of recent occupants, regardless of whether the arrestee in any particular case was within reaching distance of the vehicle at the time of the search. Even after the arrestee had stepped out of the vehicle and had been subdued by police, the prevailing understanding was that *Belton* still authorized a substantially contemporaneous search of the automobile's passenger compartment.

Not every court, however, agreed with this reading of *Belton*. In *State v. Gant,* 216 Ariz. 1 (2007), the Arizona Supreme Court considered an automobile search conducted after the vehicle's occupant had been arrested, handcuffed, and locked in a patrol car. The court distinguished *Belton* as a case in which "four unsecured" arrestees "presented an immediate risk of loss of evidence and an obvious threat to [a] lone officer's safety." The court held that where no such "exigencies exis[t]"—where the arrestee has been subdued and the scene secured—the rule of *Belton* does not apply.

This Court granted certiorari in *Gant* and affirmed in a 5-to-4 decision. *Arizona v. Gant,* 556 U.S. 332 (2009). Four of the Justices in the majority agreed with the Arizona Supreme Court that *Belton*'s holding applies only where "the arrestee is unsecured and within reaching distance of the passenger compartment at the time of the search."... As a result, the Court adopted a new, two-part rule under which an automobile search incident to a recent occupant's arrest is constitutional (1) if the arrestee is within reaching distance of the vehicle during the search, or (2) if the police have reason to believe that the vehicle contains "evidence relevant to the crime of arrest."

The search at issue in this case took place a full two years before this Court announced its new rule in *Gant*. On an April evening in 2007, police officers in Greenville, Alabama, conducted a routine traffic stop that eventually resulted in the arrests of driver Stella Owens (for driving while intoxicated) and passenger Willie Davis (for giving a false name to police). The police handcuffed both Owens and Davis, and they placed the arrestees in the back of separate patrol cars. The police then searched the passenger compartment of Owens's vehicle and found a revolver inside Davis's jacket pocket.

Davis was indicted in the Middle District of Alabama on one count of possession of a firearm by a convicted felon. In his motion to suppress the revolver, Davis acknowledged that the officers' search fully complied with "existing Eleventh Circuit precedent." Like most courts, the Eleventh Circuit had long read *Belton* to establish a bright-line rule authorizing substantially contemporaneous vehicle searches incident to arrests of recent occupants. Davis recognized that the District Court was obligated to follow this precedent, but he raised a Fourth Amendment challenge to preserve "the issue for review" on appeal. The District Court denied the motion, and Davis was convicted on the firearms charge.

While Davis's appeal was pending, this Court decided *Gant*. The Eleventh Circuit, in the opinion below, applied *Gant*'s new rule and held that the vehicle search incident to Davis's arrest "violated [his] Fourth Amendment rights." As for whether this constitutional violation warranted suppression, the Eleventh Circuit viewed that as a separate issue that turned on "the potential of exclusion to deter wrongful police conduct." The court concluded that "penalizing the [arresting] officer" for following binding appellate precedent would do nothing to "dete[r]... Fourth

Amendment violations." It therefore declined to apply the exclusionary rule and affirmed Davis's conviction. We granted certiorari.

II

. . . Real deterrent value is a "necessary condition for exclusion," but it is not "a sufficient" one. The analysis must also account for the "substantial social costs" generated by the rule. Exclusion exacts a heavy toll on both the judicial system and society at large. It almost always requires courts to ignore reliable, trustworthy evidence bearing on guilt or innocence. And its bottom-line effect, in many cases, is to suppress the truth and set the criminal loose in the community without punishment. Our cases hold that society must swallow this bitter pill when necessary, but only as a "last resort." For exclusion to be appropriate, the deterrence benefits of suppression must outweigh its heavy costs.

Admittedly, there was a time when our exclusionary-rule cases were not nearly so discriminating in their approach to the doctrine. "Expansive dicta" in several decisions suggested that the rule was a self-executing mandate implicit in the Fourth Amendment itself. As late as our 1971 decision in *Whiteley v. Warden, Wyo. State Penitentiary*, 401 U.S. 560, 568-569, the Court "treated identification of a Fourth Amendment violation as synonymous with application of the exclusionary rule." *Arizona v. Evans*, 514 U.S. 1, 13 (1995). In time, however, we came to acknowledge the exclusionary rule for what it undoubtedly is—a "judicially created remedy" of this Court's own making. We abandoned the old, "reflexive" application of the doctrine, and imposed a more rigorous weighing of its costs and deterrence benefits. In a line of cases beginning with *United States v. Leon*, 468 U.S. 897, we also recalibrated our cost-benefit analysis in exclusion cases to focus the inquiry on the "flagrancy of the police misconduct" at issue.

The basic insight of the *Leon* line of cases is that the deterrence benefits of exclusion "var[y] with the culpability of the law enforcement conduct" at issue. When the police exhibit "deliberate," "reckless," or "grossly negligent" disregard for Fourth Amendment rights, the deterrent value of exclusion is strong and tends to outweigh the resulting costs. But when the police act with an objectively "reasonable good-faith belief" that their conduct is lawful, or when their conduct involves only simple, "isolated" negligence, the "deterrence rationale loses much of its force," and exclusion cannot "pay its way." The Court has over time applied this "good-faith" exception across a range of cases. . . .

III

The question in this case is whether to apply the exclusionary rule when the police conduct a search in objectively reasonable reliance on binding judicial precedent. At the time of the search at issue here, we had not yet decided *Arizona v. Gant* and the Eleventh Circuit had interpreted our decision in *New York v. Belton* to establish a bright-line rule authorizing the search of a vehicle's passenger compartment incident to a recent occupant's arrest. The search incident to Davis's arrest in this case followed the Eleventh Circuit's *Gonzalez* precedent to the letter. Although the search turned out to be unconstitutional under *Gant*, all agree that the officers' conduct was in strict compliance with then-binding Circuit law and was not culpable in any way.

Under our exclusionary-rule precedents, this acknowledged absence of police culpability dooms Davis's claim. Police practices trigger the harsh sanction of exclusion only when they are deliberate enough to yield "meaningfu[l]" deterrence, and culpable enough to be "worth the price paid by the justice system." The conduct of the officers here was neither of these things. The officers who conducted the search did not violate Davis's Fourth Amendment rights deliberately, recklessly, or with gross negligence. Nor does this case involve any "recurring or systemic negligence" on the part of law enforcement. The police acted in strict compliance with binding precedent and their behavior was not wrongful. Unless the exclusionary rule is to become a strict-liability regime, it can have no application in this case.

Indeed, in 27 years of practice under *Leon*'s good-faith exception, we have "never applied" the exclusionary rule to suppress evidence obtained as a result of nonculpable, innocent police conduct. If the police in this case had reasonably relied on a warrant in conducting their search or on an erroneous warrant record in a government database, the exclusionary rule would not apply.... About all that exclusion would deter in this case is conscientious police work. Responsible law-enforcement officers will take care to learn "what is required of them" under Fourth Amendment precedent and will conform their conduct to these rules. But by the same token, when binding appellate precedent specifically authorizes a particular police practice, well-trained officers will and should use that tool to fulfill their crime-detection and public-safety responsibilities. An officer who conducts a search in reliance on binding appellate precedent does no more than "ac[t] as a reasonable officer would and should act" under the circumstances. The deterrent effect of exclusion in such a case can only be to discourage the officer from "do[ing] his duty."

That is not the kind of deterrence the exclusionary rule seeks to foster. We have stated before, and we reaffirm today, that the harsh sanction of exclusion "should not be applied to deter objectively reasonable law enforcement activity." Evidence obtained during a search conducted in reasonable reliance on binding precedent is not subject to the exclusionary rule....

Justice BREYER, with whom Justice GINSBURG joins, dissenting.

... While conceding that, like the search *in* Gant, this search violated the Fourth Amendment, it holds that, unlike *Gant*, this defendant is not entitled to a remedy. That is because the Court finds a new "good faith" exception which prevents application of the normal remedy for a Fourth Amendment violation, namely, suppression of the illegally seized evidence....

At this point I can no longer agree with the Court. A new "good faith" exception and this Court's retroactivity decisions are incompatible. For one thing, the Court's distinction between (1) retroactive application of a new rule and (2) availability of a remedy is highly artificial and runs counter to precedent. To determine that a new rule is retroactive is to determine that, at least in the normal case, there is a remedy. As we have previously said, the "source of a 'new rule' is the Constitution itself, not any judicial power to create new rules of law"; hence, "[w]hat we are actually determining when we assess the 'retroactivity' of a new rule is not the temporal scope of a newly announced right, but whether a violation of the right that occurred prior to the announcement of the new rule will entitle a criminal defendant to the relief sought." The Court's "good faith" exception (unlike, say, inevitable discovery, a remedial doctrine that applies only upon occasion) creates "a categorical bar to obtaining redress" in every case pending when a precedent is overturned....

Perhaps more important, the Court's rationale for creating its new "good faith" exception threatens to undermine well-settled Fourth Amendment law. The Court correctly says that pre-*Gant* Eleventh Circuit precedent had held that a *Gant*-type search was constitutional; hence the police conduct in this case, consistent with that precedent, was "innocent." But the Court then finds this fact sufficient to create a new "good faith" exception to the exclusionary rule. It reasons that the "sole purpose" of the exclusionary rule "is to deter future Fourth Amendment violations." Those benefits are sufficient to justify exclusion where "police exhibit deliberate, reckless, or grossly negligent disregard for Fourth Amendment rights." But those benefits do not justify exclusion where, as here, the police act with "simple, isolated negligence" or an "objectively reasonable good-faith belief that their conduct is lawful."

If the Court means what it says, what will happen to the exclusionary rule, a rule that the Court adopted nearly a century ago for federal courts and made applicable to state courts a half century ago through the Fourteenth Amendment? The Court has thought of that rule not as punishment for the individual officer or as reparation for the individual defendant but more generally as an effective way to secure enforcement of the Fourth Amendment's commands. This Court has deviated from the "suppression" norm in the name of "good faith" only a handful of times and in limited, atypical circumstances: where a magistrate has erroneously issued a warrant; where a database has erroneously informed police that they have a warrant; and where an unconstitutional statute purported to authorize the search.

The fact that such exceptions are few and far between is understandable. Defendants frequently move to suppress evidence on Fourth Amendment grounds. In many, perhaps most, of these instances the police, uncertain of how the Fourth Amendment applied to the particular factual circumstances they faced, will have acted in objective good faith. Yet, in a significant percentage of these instances, courts will find that the police were wrong. And, unless the police conduct falls into one of the exceptions previously noted, courts have required the suppression of the evidence seized.

But an officer who conducts a search that he believes complies with the Constitution but which, it ultimately turns out, falls just outside the Fourth Amendment's bounds is no more culpable than an officer who follows erroneous "binding precedent." Nor is an officer more culpable where circuit precedent is simply suggestive rather than "binding," where it only describes how to treat roughly analogous instances, or where it just does not exist. Thus, if the Court means what it now says, if it would place determinative weight upon the culpability of an individual officer's conduct, and if it would apply the exclusionary rule only where a Fourth Amendment violation was "deliberate, reckless, or grossly negligent," then the "good faith" exception will swallow the exclusionary rule....

NOTES & QUESTIONS ON THE SCOPE OF MISCONDUCT

1. *Misconduct and deterrence.* What assumptions does the Court make about the possibility of deterrence in these cases? If the police were acting in accordance with legal precedent, it is hard to see how deterrence could be applicable. The only sliver of possibility is that police officers might be *extra* protective of Fourth Amendment concerns in situations where they suspect that a legal precedent is in danger of being overturned. Is it realistic to believe that a police officer would have the legal training to perform this subtle assessment?

2. *What is misconduct?* At issue in *Davis* is the very definition of police "misconduct." If misconduct means not following the Constitution, then the police engaged in misconduct. If, however, misconduct means not following the law at that moment in time, it is doubtful that the police engaged in misconduct. This necessarily implicates a jurisprudential question about the nature of

judging. When appellate courts reverse prior precedent and announce a new rule, have they *changed* the law? Or did they simply *recognize* the law that was always there, hiding underneath a layer of prior judicial mistakes? For legal realists, judges exercise their discretion and in so doing they make the law. Under this view, which is the best way of looking at the facts of *Davis*?

3. *Retroactivity.* One way of understanding *Davis* is as a retroactivity case. In situations where an appellate court articulates a Fourth Amendment rule triggering the exclusionary rule, they will not apply it retroactively to prior cases where police officers were acting according to legal direction that is subsequently overturned. However, is this result consistent with the Supreme Court's regular retroactivity doctrine? The rule stated in *Griffith v. Kentucky* is that "a new rule for the conduct of criminal prosecutions is to be applied retroactively to all cases, state or federal, pending on direct review or not yet final, with no exception for cases in which the new rule constitutes a 'clear break' with the past." 479 U.S. 314, 328 (1987). Does this rule suggest a different outcome for *Davis*? Or is the majority correct that the retroactivity rule applies only to the question of whether there is a constitutional violation, but does not apply to the question of whether there is a remedy for it (exclusion of evidence). According to Orin Kerr, "the Court's wish to limit the exclusionary rule for Fourth Amendment violations triggered what amounts in practice to a Fourth Amendment exception from traditional retroactivity rules." Orin S. Kerr, *Fourth Amendment Remedies and Development of the Law: A Comment on* Camreta v. Greene *and* Davis v. United States, Cato Sup. Ct. Rev., 2010-2011, at 237, 253.

D. STANDING

If the police violate the constitutional rights of person *x*, can person *y* raise this violation as a basis for excluding evidence in a prosecution against person *y*? This question might be understood under the general label of "standing," although there are other ways of conceptualizing the issue. In the following case, the Court must decide whether the exclusionary rule must apply when the prosecution seeks to introduce evidence against two defendants who were mere passengers in a car that was searched illegally. As you read the case, ask yourself whether the defendants were protected by the Fourth Amendment even though they did not own the car. Furthermore, what role, if any, should property law concepts play in the matter? Is it relevant that the defendants had no property interest—such as a rental agreement—with regard to the car that was searched?

Rakas v. Illinois

Supreme Court of the States
439 U.S. 128 (1978)

Mr. Justice Rehnquist delivered the opinion of the Court.

Petitioners were convicted of armed robbery in the Circuit Court of Kankakee County, Ill., and their convictions were affirmed on appeal. At their trial, the prosecution offered into evidence a sawed-off rifle and rifle shells that had been seized by police during a search of an automobile in which petitioners had been passengers. Neither petitioner is the owner of the automobile and neither has ever asserted that he owned the rifle or shells seized. The Illinois Appellate Court held that petitioners lacked standing to object to the allegedly unlawful search and seizure and denied their motion to suppress the evidence. We granted certiorari in light of the obvious importance of the issues raised to the administration of criminal justice and now affirm.

I

Because we are not here concerned with the issue of probable cause, a brief description of the events leading to the search of the automobile will suffice. A police officer on a routine patrol received a radio call notifying him of a robbery of a clothing store in Bourbonnais, Ill., and describing the getaway car. Shortly thereafter, the officer spotted an automobile which he thought might be the getaway car. After following the car for some time and after the arrival of assistance, he and several other officers stopped the vehicle. The occupants of the automobile, petitioners and two female companions, were ordered out of the car and, after the occupants had left the car, two officers searched the interior of the vehicle. They discovered a box of rifle shells in the glove compartment, which had been locked, and a sawed-off rifle under the front passenger seat. After discovering the rifle and the shells, the officers took petitioners to the station and placed them under arrest.

Before trial petitioners moved to suppress the rifle and shells seized from the car on the ground that the search violated the Fourth and Fourteenth Amendments. They conceded that they did not own the automobile and were simply passengers; the owner of the car had been the driver of the vehicle at the time of the search. Nor did they assert that they owned the rifle or the shells seized. The prosecutor challenged petitioners' standing to object to the lawfulness of the search of the car because neither the car, the shells nor the rifle belonged to them. The trial court agreed that petitioners lacked standing and denied the motion to suppress the evidence. In view of this holding, the court did not determine whether there was probable cause for the search and seizure. On appeal after petitioners' conviction, the Appellate Court of Illinois, Third Judicial District, affirmed the trial court's denial of petitioners' motion to suppress because it held that "without a proprietary or other similar interest in an automobile, a mere passenger therein lacks standing to challenge the legality of the search of the vehicle."...

II

Petitioners first urge us to relax or broaden the rule of standing enunciated in *Jones v. United States*, 362 U.S. 257 (1960), so that any criminal defendant at whom a search was "directed" would have standing to contest the legality of that search and object to the admission at trial of evidence obtained as a result of the search. Alternatively, petitioners argue that they have standing to object to the search under *Jones* because they were "legitimately on [the] premises" at the time of the search.

The concept of standing discussed in *Jones* focuses on whether the person seeking to challenge the legality of a search as a basis for suppressing evidence was himself the "victim" of the search or seizure. Adoption of the so-called "target" theory advanced by petitioners would in effect permit a defendant to assert that a violation of the Fourth Amendment rights of a third party entitled him to have evidence suppressed at his trial. If we reject petitioners' request for a broadened rule of standing such as this, and reaffirm the holding of *Jones* and other cases that Fourth Amendment rights are personal rights that may not be asserted vicariously, we will have occasion to re-examine the "standing" terminology emphasized in *Jones*. For we are not at all sure that the determination of a motion to suppress is materially aided by labeling the inquiry identified in *Jones* as one of standing, rather than simply recognizing it as one involving the substantive question of whether or not the proponent of the motion to suppress has had his own Fourth Amendment rights infringed by the search and seizure which he seeks to challenge. We shall therefore consider in turn petitioners' target theory, the necessity for continued adherence to the notion of standing discussed in *Jones* as a concept that is theoretically distinct from the merits of a defendant's Fourth Amendment claim, and, finally, the proper disposition of petitioners' ultimate claim in this case.

We decline to extend the rule of standing in Fourth Amendment cases in the manner suggested by petitioners. As we stated in *Alderman v. United States*, 394 U.S. 165, 174 (1969), "Fourth Amendment rights are personal rights which, like some other constitutional rights, may not be vicariously asserted." A person who is aggrieved by an illegal search and seizure only through the introduction of damaging evidence secured by a search of a third person's premises or property has not had any of his Fourth Amendment rights infringed. And since the exclusionary rule is an attempt to effectuate the guarantees of the Fourth Amendment, it is proper to permit only defendants whose Fourth Amendment rights have been violated to benefit from the rule's protections. There is no reason to think that a party whose rights have been infringed will not, if evidence is used against him, have ample motivation to move to suppress it. Even if such a person is not a defendant in the action, he may be able to recover damages for the violation of his Fourth Amendment rights or seek redress under state law for invasion of privacy or trespass....

Conferring standing to raise vicarious Fourth Amendment claims would necessarily mean a more widespread invocation of the exclusionary rule during criminal trials.... Each time the exclusionary rule is applied it exacts a substantial social cost for the vindication of Fourth Amendment rights. Relevant and reliable evidence is kept from the trier of fact and the search for truth at trial is deflected. Since our cases generally have held that one whose Fourth Amendment rights are violated may successfully suppress evidence obtained in the course of an illegal search and seizure, misgivings as to the benefit of enlarging the class of persons who may invoke that rule are properly considered when deciding whether to expand standing to assert Fourth Amendment violations.

Had we accepted petitioners' request to allow persons other than those whose own Fourth Amendment rights were violated by a challenged search and seizure to suppress evidence obtained in the course of such police activity, it would be appropriate to retain *Jones*' use of standing in Fourth Amendment analysis. Under petitioners' target theory, a court could determine that a defendant had standing to invoke the exclusionary rule without having to inquire into the substantive question of whether the challenged search or seizure violated the Fourth Amendment rights of that particular defendant. However, having rejected petitioners' target theory and reaffirmed the principle that the "rights assured by the Fourth Amendment are personal rights, [which]...may be enforced by exclusion of evidence only at the instance of one whose own protection was infringed by the search and seizure," *Simmons v. United States*, 390 U.S., at 389, the question necessarily arises whether it serves any useful analytical purpose to consider this principle a matter of standing, distinct from the merits of a defendant's Fourth Amendment claim. We can think of no decided cases of this Court that would have come out differently had we concluded, as we do now, that the type of standing requirement discussed in *Jones* and reaffirmed today is more properly subsumed under substantive Fourth Amendment doctrine. Rigorous application of the principle that the rights secured by this Amendment are personal, in place of a notion of "standing," will produce no additional situations in which evidence must be excluded. The inquiry under either approach is the same. But we think the better analysis forthrightly focuses on the extent of a particular defendant's rights under the Fourth Amendment, rather than on any theoretically separate, but invariably intertwined concept of standing. The Court in *Jones* also may have been aware that there was a certain artificiality in analyzing this question in terms of standing because in at least three separate places in its opinion the Court placed that term within quotation marks....

Analyzed in these terms, the question is whether the challenged search or seizure violated the Fourth Amendment rights of a criminal defendant who seeks to exclude the evidence obtained during it. That inquiry in turn requires a determination of whether the disputed search and seizure has infringed an interest of the defendant which the Fourth Amendment was designed to protect. We are under no illusion that by dispensing with the rubric of standing used in *Jones* we have rendered any simpler the determination of whether the proponent of a motion to suppress is entitled to contest the legality of a search and seizure. But by frankly recognizing that this aspect of the analysis belongs more properly under the heading of substantive Fourth Amendment doctrine than under the heading of standing, we think the decision of this issue will rest on sounder logical footing.

Here petitioners, who were passengers occupying a car which they neither owned nor leased, seek to analogize their position to that of the defendant in *Jones v. United States*. In *Jones*, petitioner was present at the time of the search of an apartment which was owned by a friend. The friend had given Jones permission to use the apartment and a key to it, with which Jones had admitted himself on the day of the search. He had a suit and shirt at the apartment and had slept there "maybe a night," but his home was elsewhere. At the time of the search, Jones was the only occupant of the apartment because the lessee was away for a period of several days. Under these circumstances, this Court stated that while one wrongfully on the premises could not move to suppress evidence obtained as a result of searching them, "anyone legitimately on premises where a search occurs may challenge its legality." Petitioners argue that their occupancy of the automobile in question was comparable to that of Jones in the apartment and that they therefore have standing to contest the legality of the search—or as we have rephrased the inquiry, that they, like Jones, had their Fourth Amendment rights violated by the search.

We do not question the conclusion in *Jones* that the defendant in that case suffered a violation of his personal Fourth Amendment rights if the search in question was unlawful. Nonetheless, we believe that the phrase "legitimately on premises" coined in *Jones* creates too broad a gauge for measurement of Fourth Amendment rights. For example, applied literally, this statement would permit a casual visitor who has never seen, or been permitted to visit, the basement of another's house to object to a search of the basement if the visitor happened to be in the kitchen of the house at the time of the search. Likewise, a casual visitor who walks into a house one minute before a search of the house commences and leaves one minute after the search ends would be able to contest the legality of the search. The first visitor would have absolutely no interest or legitimate expectation of privacy in the basement, the second would have none in the house, and it advances no purpose served by the Fourth Amendment to permit either of them to object to the lawfulness of the search.

We think that *Jones* on its facts merely stands for the unremarkable proposition that a person can have a legally sufficient interest in a place other than his own home so that the Fourth Amendment protects him from unreasonable governmental intrusion into that place. In defining the scope of that interest, we adhere to the view expressed in *Jones* and echoed in later cases that arcane distinctions developed in property and tort law between guests, licensees, invitees, and the like, ought not to control. But the *Jones* statement that a person need only be "legitimately on premises" in order to challenge the validity of the search of a dwelling place cannot be taken in its full sweep beyond the facts of that case....

Judged by the foregoing analysis, petitioners' claims must fail. They asserted neither a property nor a possessory interest in the automobile, nor an interest in the property seized. And as we have previously indicated, the fact that they were "legitimately on [the] premises" in the sense that they were in the car with the permission of its owner is not determinative of whether they had a legitimate expectation of privacy in the particular areas of the automobile searched. It is unnecessary for us to decide here whether the same expectations of privacy are warranted in a car as would be justified in a dwelling place in analogous circumstances. We have on numerous occasions pointed out that cars are not to be treated identically with houses or apartments for Fourth Amendment purposes. But here petitioners' claim is one which would fail even in an analogous situation in a dwelling place, since they made no showing that they had any legitimate expectation of privacy in the glove compartment or area under the seat of the car in which they were merely passengers. Like the trunk of an automobile, these are areas in which a passenger qua passenger simply would not normally have a legitimate expectation of privacy....

Mr. Justice WHITE, with whom Mr. Justice BRENNAN, Mr. Justice MARSHALL, and Mr. Justice STEVENS join, dissenting.

...Two intersecting doctrines long established in this Court's opinions control here. The first is the recognition of some cognizable level of privacy in the interior of an automobile. Though the reasonableness of the expectation of privacy in a vehicle may be somewhat weaker than that in a home, "[a] search even of an automobile, is a substantial invasion of privacy. To protect that privacy from official arbitrariness, the Court always has regarded probable cause as the minimum requirement for a lawful search." So far, the Court has not strayed from this application of the Fourth Amendment.

The second tenet is that when a person is legitimately present in a private place, his right to privacy is protected from unreasonable governmental interference even if he does not own the premises. Just a few years ago, the Chief Justice, for a unanimous Court, wrote that the "[p]resence of the defendant at the search and seizure was held, in *Jones*, to be a sufficient source of standing in itself." *Brown v. United States*, 411 U.S. 223, 227 n.2 (1973).... The Court in *Jones* itself was unanimous in this regard, and its holding is not the less binding because it was an alternative one.

These two fundamental aspects of Fourth Amendment law demand that petitioners be permitted to challenge the search and seizure of the automobile in this case. It is of no significance that a car is different for Fourth Amendment purposes from a house, for if there is some protection for the privacy of an automobile then the only relevant analogy is between a person legitimately in someone else's vehicle and a person legitimately in someone else's home. If both strands of the Fourth Amendment doctrine adumbrated above are valid, the Court must reach a different result. Instead, it chooses to eviscerate the *Jones* principle, an action in which I am unwilling to participate.

Though we had reserved the very issue over 50 years ago and never expressly dealt with it again until today, many of our opinions have assumed that a mere passenger in an automobile is entitled to protection against unreasonable searches occurring in his presence. In decisions upholding the validity of automobile searches, we have gone directly to the merits even though some of the petitioners did not own or possess the vehicles in question....

The logic of Fourth Amendment jurisprudence compels the result reached by the above decisions. Our starting point is "[t]he established principle... that suppression of the product of a Fourth Amendment violation can be successfully urged only by those whose rights were violated by the search itself...." Though the Amendment protects one's liberty and property interests against unreasonable seizures of self and effects, "the primary object of the Fourth Amendment [is]...the protection of privacy." And privacy is the interest asserted here, so the first step is to ascertain whether the premises searched "fall within a protected zone of privacy." My Brethren in the majority assertedly do not deny that automobiles warrant at least some protection from official interference with privacy. Thus, the next step is to decide who is entitled, vis-à-vis the State, to enjoy that privacy. The answer to that question must be found by determining "whether petitioner had an interest in connection with the searched premises that gave rise to a reasonable expectation [on his part] of freedom from governmental intrusion upon those premises."

...We have concluded on numerous occasions that the entitlement to an expectation of privacy does not hinge on ownership: "What a person knowingly exposes to the public, even in his own home or office, is not a subject of Fourth Amendment protection.... But what he seeks to preserve as private, even in an area accessible to the public, may be constitutionally protected." *Katz v. United States*, 389 U.S. 347, 351-352 (1967).

In *Alderman v. United States*, 394 U.S., at 196, Mr. Justice Harlan, concurring in part and dissenting in part, noted that "our own past decisions... have decisively rejected the notion that the accused must necessarily have a possessory interest in the premises before he may assert a Fourth Amendment claim." That rejection should not have been surprising in light of our conclusion as early as 1960 that "it is unnecessary and ill-advised to import into the law surrounding the constitutional right to be free from unreasonable searches and seizures subtle distinctions, developed and refined by the common law in evolving the body of private property law which, more than almost any other branch of law, has been shaped by distinctions whose validity is largely historical." *Jones*, 362 U.S., at 266....

The Court's holding is contrary not only to our past decisions and the logic of the Fourth Amendment but also to the everyday expectations of privacy that we all share. Because of that, it is unworkable in all the various situations that arise in real life. If the owner of the car had not only invited petitioners to join her but had said to them, "I give you a temporary possessory interest in my vehicle so that you will share the right to privacy that the Supreme Court says that I own," then apparently the majority would reverse. But people seldom say such things, though they may mean their invitation to encompass them if only they had thought of the problem. If the nonowner were the spouse or child of the owner, would the Court recognize a sufficient interest? If so, would distant relatives somehow have more of an expectation of privacy than close friends? What if the nonowner were driving with the owner's permission? Would nonowning drivers have more of an expectation of privacy than mere passengers? What about a passenger in a taxicab? *Katz* expressly recognized protection for such passengers. Why should Fourth Amendment rights be present when one pays a cabdriver for a ride but be absent when one is given a ride by a friend?

The distinctions the Court would draw are based on relationships between private parties, but the Fourth Amendment is concerned with the relationship of one of those parties to the government. Divorced as it is from the purpose of the Fourth Amendment, the Court's essentially property-based rationale can satisfactorily answer none of the questions posed above. That is reason enough to reject it. The *Jones* rule is relatively easily applied by police and courts; the rule announced today will not provide law enforcement officials with a bright line between the protected and the unprotected. Only rarely will police know whether one private party has or has not been granted a sufficient possessory or other interest by another private party. Surely in this case the officers had no such knowledge. The Court's rule will ensnare defendants and police in needless litigation over factors that should not be determinative of Fourth Amendment rights....

PROBLEM CASE

Gene Barry was a physician in Texas. In 2015, investigators from the Texas Medical Board authorized an administrative subpoena for records from the Red Bluff Medical Clinic, where Barry worked part-time. (Barry was neither a co-owner nor an equity partner in the medical practice.) Investigators from the medical board arrived at the clinic along with Drug Enforcement Agents and officers from the Texas Department of Public Safety and the Texas Board of Nursing. The investigators demanded access to the records listed in the subpoena, but Barry and his lawyer refused to provide access to the records. The agents threatened to detain the clinic's chief administrator unless she complied, so she did. She delivered the files to the agents; Barry alleged that the agents looked through files that were well beyond the scope of the administrative subpoena.

Barry alleged that the search violated his Fourth Amendment rights. Did he have standing to object? Barry was clearly a target of the drug investigation. However, did Barry have a protected property or privacy interest in the medical files? Clearly the patients had a privacy interest in their medical records, but could the same be said of the doctor who compiled the files? See *Barry v. Freshour*, No. 17-20726, 2018 WL 4793993, at *2 (5th Cir. Oct. 4, 2018).

In the following case, the Supreme Court confronts the tricky problem of what happens when the police make a traffic stop. Clearly the driver has been "seized," but what of the passenger? This issue is essential for determining whether the passenger can assert their Fourth Amendment rights. If the passenger is seized, the passenger might be able to argue a Fourth Amendment violation and ask a court to exclude the evidence that resulted from the seizure. On the other hand, if the passenger is *not* seized, then there is no violation of the passenger's Fourth Amendment rights and consequently the passenger has no basis to ask for exclusion of the evidence.

Brendlin v. California

Supreme Court of the United States
551 U.S. 249 (2007)

Justice Souter delivered the opinion of the Court.

When a police officer makes a traffic stop, the driver of the car is seized within the meaning of the Fourth Amendment. The question in this case is whether the same is true of a passenger. We hold that a passenger is seized as well and so may challenge the constitutionality of the stop.

I

Early in the morning of November 27, 2001, Deputy Sheriff Robert Brokenbrough and his partner saw a parked Buick with expired registration tags. In his ensuing conversation with the police dispatcher, Brokenbrough learned that an application for renewal of registration was being processed. The officers saw the car again on the road, and this time Brokenbrough noticed its display of a temporary operating permit with the number "11," indicating it was legal to drive the car through November. The officers decided to pull the Buick over to verify that the permit matched the vehicle, even though, as Brokenbrough admitted later, there was nothing unusual about the permit or the way it was affixed. Brokenbrough asked the driver, Karen Simeroth, for her license and saw a passenger in the front seat, petitioner Bruce Brendlin, whom he recognized as "one of the Brendlin brothers." He recalled that either Scott or Bruce Brendlin had dropped out of parole supervision and asked Brendlin to identify himself. Brokenbrough returned to his cruiser, called for backup, and verified that Brendlin was a parole violator with an outstanding no-bail warrant for his arrest. While he was in the patrol car, Brokenbrough saw Brendlin briefly open and then close the passenger door of the Buick. Once reinforcements arrived, Brokenbrough went to the passenger side of the Buick, ordered him out of the car at gunpoint, and declared him under arrest. When the police searched Brendlin incident to arrest, they found an orange syringe cap on his person. A patdown search of Simeroth revealed syringes and a plastic bag of a green leafy substance, and she was also formally arrested. Officers then searched the car and found tubing, a scale, and other things used to produce methamphetamine.

Brendlin was charged with possession and manufacture of methamphetamine, and he moved to suppress the evidence obtained in the searches of his person and the car as fruits of an unconstitutional seizure, arguing that the officers lacked probable cause or reasonable suspicion to make the traffic stop. He did not assert that his Fourth Amendment rights were violated by the search of Simeroth's vehicle, cf. *Rakas v. Illinois*, 439 U.S. 128 (1978), but claimed only that the traffic stop was an unlawful seizure of his person. The trial court denied the suppression motion after finding that the stop was lawful and Brendlin was not seized until Brokenbrough ordered him out of the car and formally arrested him. Brendlin pleaded guilty, subject to appeal on the suppression issue, and was sentenced to four years in prison. . . .

II

A person is seized by the police and thus entitled to challenge the government's action under the Fourth Amendment when the officer, "by means of physical force or show of authority," terminates or restrains his freedom of movement, "through means intentionally applied." Thus, an "unintended person . . . [may be] the object of the detention," so long as the detention is "willful" and not merely the consequence of "an unknowing act." A police officer may make a seizure by a show of authority and without the use of physical force, but there is no seizure without actual submission; otherwise, there is at most an attempted seizure, so far as the Fourth Amendment is concerned.

When the actions of the police do not show an unambiguous intent to restrain or when an individual's submission to a show of governmental authority takes the form of passive acquiescence, there needs to be some test for telling when a seizure occurs in response to authority, and when it does not. The test was devised by Justice Stewart in *United States v. Mendenhall*, 446 U.S. 544 (1980), who wrote that a seizure occurs if "in view of all of the circumstances surrounding the incident, a reasonable person would have believed that he was not free to leave." Later on, the Court adopted Justice Stewart's touchstone, but added that when a person "has no desire to leave" for reasons unrelated to the police presence, the "coercive effect of the encounter" can be measured better by asking whether "a reasonable person would feel free to decline the officers' requests or otherwise terminate the encounter." *Bostick* at 435-436.

The law is settled that in Fourth Amendment terms a traffic stop entails a seizure of the driver "even though the purpose of the stop is limited and the resulting detention quite brief." And although we have not, until today, squarely answered the question whether a passenger is also seized, we have said over and over in dicta that during a traffic stop an officer seizes everyone in the vehicle, not just the driver.

We have come closest to the question here in two cases dealing with unlawful seizure of a passenger, and neither time did we indicate any distinction between driver and passenger that would affect the Fourth Amendment analysis. *Delaware v. Prouse* considered grounds for stopping a car on the road and held that Prouse's suppression motion was properly granted. We spoke of the arresting officer's testimony that Prouse was in the back seat when the car was pulled over, 440 U.S., at 650, described Prouse as an occupant, not as the driver, and referred to the car's "occupants" as being seized. Justification for stopping a car was the issue again in *Whren v. United States,* where we passed upon a Fourth Amendment challenge by two petitioners who moved to suppress drug evidence found during the course of a traffic stop. 517 U.S., at 809. Both driver and passenger claimed to have been seized illegally when the police stopped the car; we agreed and held suppression unwarranted only because the stop rested on probable cause.

The State concedes that the police had no adequate justification to pull the car over but argues that the passenger was not seized and thus cannot claim that the evidence was tainted by an unconstitutional stop. We resolve this question by asking whether a reasonable person in Brendlin's position when the car stopped would have believed himself free to "terminate the encounter" between the police and himself. *Bostick*, 501 U.S., at 436. We

think that in these circumstances any reasonable passenger would have understood the police officers to be exercising control to the point that no one in the car was free to depart without police permission.

A traffic stop necessarily curtails the travel a passenger has chosen just as much as it halts the driver, diverting both from the stream of traffic to the side of the road, and the police activity that normally amounts to intrusion on "privacy and personal security" does not normally (and did not here) distinguish between passenger and driver. An officer who orders one particular car to pull over acts with an implicit claim of right based on fault of some sort, and a sensible person would not expect a police officer to allow people to come and go freely from the physical focal point of an investigation into faulty behavior or wrongdoing. If the likely wrongdoing is not the driving, the passenger will reasonably feel subject to suspicion owing to close association; but even when the wrongdoing is only bad driving, the passenger will expect to be subject to some scrutiny, and his attempt to leave the scene would be so obviously likely to prompt an objection from the officer that no passenger would feel free to leave in the first place.

It is also reasonable for passengers to expect that a police officer at the scene of a crime, arrest, or investigation will not let people move around in ways that could jeopardize his safety. In *Maryland v. Wilson*, 519 U.S. 408 (1997), we held that during a lawful traffic stop an officer may order a passenger out of the car as a precautionary measure, without reasonable suspicion that the passenger poses a safety risk. What we have said in these opinions probably reflects a societal expectation of "unquestioned [police] command" at odds with any notion that a passenger would feel free to leave, or to terminate the personal encounter any other way, without advance permission....

Brendlin was seized from the moment Simeroth's car came to a halt on the side of the road, and it was error to deny his suppression motion on the ground that seizure occurred only at the formal arrest....

NOTES & QUESTIONS ON STANDING

1. *Standing for searches.* The holdings of *Rakas* and *Brendlin* point in opposite directions. One allowed the passenger to raise the exclusionary rule, while the other does not. Under *Rakas*, the passengers were not entitled to seek exclusion of the evidence seized from the car because they could not assert either a property or privacy interest in the vehicle; they refused to assert that they owned the car and maintained that they were mere passengers. They also refused to assert that either of them owned the rifle or shells that were found during the search. Does this suggest a strategic error on the part of defense counsel? In other cases, a passenger might be able to assert a property interest in the contents of the car and therefore gain standing to object to a search. In

Brendlin, the passenger was permitted to challenge their seizure during the traffic stop because the court concluded that a traffic stop seizes the passenger just as much as the driver.

2. *Vehicle stops.* How important is it that under *Brendlin* passengers have standing to argue that a vehicle stop was illegal? The question can only be answered by referencing the standards for vehicle stops. As it turns out, under *Whren v. United States*, 517 U.S. 806 (1996), police officers are entitled to stop any vehicle engaged in a traffic infraction, even a minor one, regardless of the subjective motivation of the police officer. Consequently, a passenger complaint about being "seized" during a vehicle stop might be for naught; the seizure will be constitutional as long as the rather permissive *Whren* conditions are satisfied.

Max, a Los Angeles International Airport police dog, climbs out the trunk of a car after sniffing for explosives at a security checkpoint. (Kevork Djansezian/AP/Shutterstock)

3. *Dog sniff during a traffic stop.* Under *Brendlin*, both the driver and the passenger of the vehicle are seized during the traffic stop, thus implicating the conceptual machinery of the Fourth Amendment. What if the police use a trained contraband-sniffing dog during the vehicle stop to ascertain if drugs are located in the car? In *Illinois v. Caballes*, 543 U.S. 405 (2005), the Supreme Court upheld the practice, concluding that "conducting a dog sniff would not change the character of a traffic stop that is lawful at its inception and otherwise executed in a reasonable manner...." However, in *Rodriguez v. United States*, 135 S. Ct. 1609 (2015), the Supreme Court concluded that "[a]bsent reasonable suspicion, police extension of a traffic stop in order to conduct a dog sniff violates the Constitution's shield against unreasonable seizures." The issue, apparently, is one of timing. For example, if a police officer uses a dog to sniff around the outside of a car during a traffic stop while the officer's partner calls in the license plate number and driver's license number (to check

PROBLEM CASE

Consider the following fact pattern. A police officer on patrol in Idaho conducted a vehicle stop. A second police officer on patrol nearby heard on his radio about the traffic stop and decided on his own initiative to drive to the scene. The first officer briefly questioned the driver and the passenger and learned that the driver was on parole for a marijuana offense. The first officer then checked for outstanding warrants. He returned to the car and told the driver that he should exit the vehicle and that the officer's drug-sniffing dog would sniff the car while the officer wrote up a traffic citation. However, during this process, the second police officer offered to take over the task of writing the traffic citation so that the first officer could concentrate exclusively on the dog sniff. The dog sniff yielded evidence of marijuana, methamphetamine, and drug paraphernalia. Did this seizure violate the Fourth Amendment? See *State v. McGraw*, 163 Idaho 736, 418 P.3d 1245, 1247 (Ct. App. 2018).

for outstanding warrants) and writes a traffic ticket, that is not an unconstitutional seizure. On the other hand, if the police officer keeps the car detained for longer than is necessary to write the ticket, while he calls for a backup K-9 unit to arrive, for example, that would constitute an unlawful seizure of the driver and the passenger unless the extension of the traffic stop for this reason is supported by a reasonable suspicion.

E. EXCEPTIONS

Even if the police violate the Constitution during a search or seizure, application of the exclusionary rule is not a foregone conclusion. If the prosecutor can demonstrate that the evidence falls under one of the recognized exceptions, the exclusionary rule will not be applied. The exceptions include: (1) independent source, (2) inevitable discovery, (3) attenuation of the taint, (4) good faith, and (5) knock and announce. For each of these exceptions, something about the exception blunts the deterrent value of the exclusion. As you consider each of the exceptions, recall that the exclusionary rule involves a delicate balance: the need to deter the authorities from violating the Constitution with the need of the community to protect its members by prosecuting offenders. Generally, for most situations, the Supreme Court has concluded that the factors weigh in favor of deterrence, which is why the exclusionary rule applies in the first place. However, in isolated situations, the factors weigh in the opposite direction. The result is a general background of exclusion with specific exceptions. For each exception, there are two tasks required to master the doctrine. First, understand why the Court has identified the exception, i.e., why deterrence is unlikely to work in that instance. Second, understand the exception so that you can apply it in practice. Remember that a particular situation could involve multiple exceptions at the same time. In order to succeed in getting the evidence admitted at trial, the prosecution need only succeed on one of the exceptions. As a matter of advocacy, however, a careful prosecutor might assert multiple exceptions—as long as the facts support them—with the goal of prevailing on one of them. From the perspective of the defense counsel, they must succeed in defeating all of the asserting exceptions in order to keep the evidence from being admitted at trial.

1. Independent Source

If the police discovered the evidence through an "independent source," unrelated to the original constitutional violation, the evidence is admissible at trial. The Supreme Court first made reference to the exception when it referred to evidence "gained from an independent source" in *Silverthorne Lumber Co. v. United States*, 251 U.S. 385, 392 (1920). The most common fact pattern for the independent source exception involves unconstitutional entries into a residence, followed by a search or seizure on the basis of a warrant that was issued *without* relying on information obtained during the original entry. This is to be distinguished from a situation where the search warrant is obtained on the basis of the evidence noticed in plain view during the initial unconstitutional entry. In that situation, the exception does not apply because the warrant is connected to the illegal entry. However, in situations where the search warrant was based on an independent source, the exclusionary rule will not apply. *Segura v. United States*, 468 U.S. 796 (1984), involved preciously this fact pattern. Police officers entered a residence without a warrant but with probable cause and secured the occupants while their colleagues were obtaining a search warrant for the premises. Although the initial entry was unconstitutional, the Supreme Court held that the proceeds of the search need not be excluded because they flowed from an independent source—the valid search warrant—rather than the illegal entry.

In the following case, the Supreme Court advances a particular standard for the independent source doctrine. Is the *reason* for the magistrate's decision to issue the warrant relevant to the analysis? Does it matter whether the magistrate relied on information gleaned during the unlawful entry? What if the magistrate relied on multiple strands of evidence, i.e., independent evidence *and* evidence found at the scene of the illegal entry?

Murray v. United States

Supreme Court of the United States
487 U.S. 533 (1988)

Justice SCALIA delivered the opinion of the Court.

In *Segura v. United States*, 468 U.S. 796 (1984), we held that police officers' illegal entry upon private premises did not require suppression of evidence subsequently discovered at those premises when executing a search warrant obtained on the basis of information wholly unconnected with the initial entry. In these consolidated cases we are faced with the question whether, again assuming evidence obtained pursuant to an independently obtained search warrant, the portion of such evidence that had been observed in plain view at the time of a prior illegal entry must be suppressed.

I

Both cases arise out of the conviction of petitioner Michael F. Murray, petitioner James D. Carter, and others for conspiracy to possess and distribute illegal drugs. Insofar as relevant for our purposes, the facts are as follows: Based on information received from informants, federal law enforcement agents had been surveilling petitioner Murray and several of his co-conspirators. At about 1:45 P.M. on April 6, 1983, they observed Murray drive a truck and Carter drive a green camper, into a warehouse in South Boston. When the petitioners drove the vehicles out about 20 minutes later, the surveilling agents saw within the warehouse two individuals and a tractor-trailer rig bearing a long, dark container. Murray and Carter later turned over the truck and camper to other drivers, who were in turn followed and ultimately arrested, and the vehicles lawfully seized. Both vehicles were found to contain marijuana.

After receiving this information, several of the agents converged on the South Boston warehouse and forced entry. They found the warehouse unoccupied, but observed in plain view numerous burlap-wrapped bales that were later found to contain marijuana. They left without disturbing the bales, kept the warehouse under surveillance, and did not reenter it until they had a search warrant. In applying for the warrant, the agents did not mention the prior entry, and did not rely on any observations made during that entry. When the warrant was issued—at 10:40 P.M., approximately eight hours after the initial entry—the agents immediately reentered the warehouse and seized 270 bales of marijuana and notebooks listing customers for whom the bales were destined....

II

The exclusionary rule prohibits introduction into evidence of tangible materials seized during an unlawful search and of testimony concerning knowledge acquired during an unlawful search. Beyond that, the exclusionary rule also prohibits the introduction of derivative evidence, both tangible and testimonial, that is the product of the primary evidence, or that is otherwise acquired as an indirect result of the unlawful search, up to the point at which the connection with the unlawful search becomes "so attenuated as to dissipate the taint."

Almost simultaneously with our development of the exclusionary rule, in the first quarter of this century, we also announced what has come to be known as the "independent source" doctrine. *Silverthorne Lumber Co. v. United States*, 251 U.S. 385, 392 (1920). That doctrine, which has been applied to evidence acquired not only through Fourth Amendment violations but also through Fifth and Sixth Amendment violations, has recently been described as follows:

> [T]he interest of society in deterring unlawful police conduct and the public interest in having juries receive all probative evidence of a crime are properly balanced by putting the police in the same, not a worse, position that they would have been in if no police error or misconduct had occurred.... When the challenged evidence has an independent source, exclusion of such evidence would put the police in a worse position than they would have been in absent any error or violation.

Nix v. Williams, 467 U.S. 431, 443 (1984).

The dispute here is over the scope of this doctrine. Petitioners contend that it applies only to evidence obtained for the first time during an independent lawful search. The Government argues that it applies also to evidence initially discovered during, or as a consequence of, an unlawful search, but later obtained independently from activities untainted by the initial illegality. We think the Government's view has better support in both precedent and policy....

As the First Circuit has observed, "[i]n the classic independent source situation, information which is received through an illegal source is considered to be cleanly obtained when it arrives through an independent source." We recently assumed this application of the independent source doctrine (in the Sixth Amendment context) in *Nix v. Williams*. There incriminating statements obtained in violation of the defendant's right to counsel had led the police to the victim's body. The body had not in fact been found through an independent source as well, and so the independent source doctrine was not itself applicable. We held, however, that evidence concerning the body was nonetheless admissible because a search had been under way which would have discovered the body, had it not been called off because of the discovery produced by the unlawfully obtained statements. This "inevitable discovery" doctrine obviously assumes the validity of the independent source doctrine as applied to evidence initially acquired unlawfully. It would make no sense to admit the evidence because the independent search, had it not been aborted, would have found the body, but to exclude the evidence if the search had continued and had in fact found the body. The inevitable discovery doctrine, with its distinct requirements, is in reality an extrapolation from the independent source doctrine: Since the tainted evidence would be admissible if in fact discovered through an independent source, it should be admissible if it inevitably would have been discovered.

Petitioners' asserted policy basis for excluding evidence which is initially discovered during an illegal search, but is subsequently acquired through an independent and lawful source, is that a contrary rule will remove all deterrence to, and indeed positively encourage, unlawful police searches. As petitioners see the incentives, law enforcement officers will routinely enter without a warrant to make sure that what they expect to be on the premises is in fact there. If it is not, they will have spared themselves the time and trouble of getting a warrant; if it is, they can get the warrant and use the evidence despite the unlawful entry. We see the incentives differently. An officer with probable cause sufficient to obtain a search warrant would be foolish to enter the premises first in an unlawful manner. By doing so, he would risk suppression of all evidence on the premises, both seen and unseen, since his action would add to the normal burden of convincing a magistrate that there is probable cause the much more onerous burden of convincing a trial court that no information gained from the illegal entry affected either the law enforcement officers' decision to seek a warrant or the magistrate's decision to grant it. Nor would the officer without sufficient probable cause to obtain a search warrant have any added incentive to conduct an unlawful entry, since whatever he finds cannot be used to establish probable cause before a magistrate....

III

To apply what we have said to the present cases: Knowledge that the marijuana was in the warehouse was assuredly acquired at the time of the unlawful entry. But it was also acquired at the time of entry pursuant to the warrant, and if that later acquisition was not the result of the earlier entry there is no reason why the independent source doctrine should not apply. Invoking the exclusionary rule would put the police (and society) not in the same position they would have occupied if no violation occurred, but in a worse one.

We think this is also true with respect to the tangible evidence, the bales of marijuana.... The First Circuit has discerned a difference between tangible and intangible evidence that has been tainted, in that objects "once seized cannot be cleanly reseized without returning the objects to private control." It seems to us, however, that reseizure of tangible evidence already seized is no more impossible than rediscovery of intangible evidence already discovered. The independent source doctrine does not rest upon such metaphysical analysis, but upon the policy that, while the government should not profit from its illegal activity, neither should it be placed in a worse position than it would otherwise have occupied. So long as a later, lawful seizure is genuinely independent of an earlier, tainted one (which may well be difficult to establish where the seized goods are kept in the police's possession) there is no reason why the independent source doctrine should not apply.

The ultimate question, therefore, is whether the search pursuant to warrant was in fact a genuinely independent source of the information and tangible evidence at issue here. This would not have been the case if the agents' decision to seek the warrant was prompted by what they had seen during the initial entry, or if information obtained during that entry was presented to the Magistrate and affected his decision to issue the warrant.... Accordingly, we vacate the judgment and remand these cases to the Court of Appeals with instructions that it remand to the District Court for determination whether the warrant-authorized search of the warehouse was an independent source of the challenged evidence in the sense we have described.

Justice MARSHALL, with whom Justice STEVENS and Justice O'CONNOR join, dissenting.

The Court today holds that the "independent source" exception to the exclusionary rule may justify admitting evidence discovered during an illegal warrantless search that is later "rediscovered" by the same team of investigators during a search pursuant to a warrant obtained immediately after the illegal search. I believe the Court's decision, by failing to provide sufficient guarantees that the subsequent search was, in fact, independent of the illegal search, emasculates the Warrant Clause and undermines the deterrence function of the exclusionary rule. I therefore dissent.

This Court has stated frequently that the exclusionary rule is principally designed to deter violations of the Fourth Amendment. By excluding evidence discovered in violation of the Fourth Amendment, the rule "compel[s] respect for the constitutional guaranty in the only effectively available way, by removing the incentive to disregard it." The Court has crafted exceptions to the exclusionary rule when the purposes of the rule are not furthered by the exclusion. As the Court today recognizes, the independent source exception to the exclusionary rule "allows admission of evidence that has been discovered by means wholly independent of any constitutional violation." The independent source exception, like the inevitable discovery exception, is primarily based on a practical view that under certain circumstances the beneficial deterrent effect that exclusion will have on future constitutional violations is too slight to justify the social cost of excluding probative evidence from a criminal trial. When the seizure of the evidence at issue is "wholly independent of" the constitutional violation, then exclusion arguably will have no effect on a law enforcement officer's incentive to commit an unlawful search.

Given the underlying justification for the independent source exception, any inquiry into the exception's application must keep sight of the practical effect admission will have on the incentives facing law enforcement officers to engage in unlawful conduct. The proper scope of the independent source exception, and guidelines for its application, cannot be divined in a factual vacuum; instead, they must be informed by the nature of the constitutional violation and the deterrent effect of exclusion in particular circumstances. In holding that the independent source exception may apply to the facts of these cases, I believe the Court loses sight of the practical moorings of the independent source exception and creates an affirmative incentive for unconstitutional searches. This holding can find no justification in the purposes underlying both the exclusionary rule and the independent source exception....

It is undisputed that the agents made no effort to obtain a warrant prior to the initial entry. The agents had not begun to prepare a warrant affidavit, and according to FBI Agent Cleary, who supervised the FBI's involvement, they had not even engaged in any discussions of obtaining a warrant. The affidavit in support of the warrant obtained after the initial search was prepared by DEA Agent Keaney, who had tactical control over the DEA agents, and who had participated in the initial search of the warehouse. The affidavit did not mention the warrantless search of the warehouse, nor did it cite information obtained from that search. In determining that the challenged evidence was admissible, the Court of Appeals assumed that the initial warrantless entry was not justified by exigent circumstances and that the search therefore violated the Warrant Clause of the Fourth Amendment.

Under the circumstances of these cases, the admission of the evidence "reseized" during the second search severely undermines the deterrence function of the exclusionary rule. Indeed, admission in these cases affirmatively encourages illegal searches. The incentives for such illegal conduct are clear. Obtaining a warrant is inconvenient and time consuming. Even when officers have probable cause to support a warrant application, therefore, they have an incentive first to determine whether it is worthwhile to obtain a warrant. Probable cause is much less than certainty, and many "confirmatory" searches will result in the discovery that no evidence is present, thus saving the police the time and trouble of getting a warrant. If contraband is discovered, however, the officers may later seek a warrant to shield the evidence from the taint of the illegal search. The police thus know in advance that they have little to lose and much to gain by forgoing the bother of obtaining a warrant and undertaking an illegal search....

The strong Fourth Amendment interest in eliminating these incentives for illegal entry should cause this Court to scrutinize closely the application of the independent source exception to evidence obtained under the circumstances of the instant cases; respect for the constitutional guarantee requires a rule that does not undermine the deterrence function of the exclusionary rule. When, as here, the same team of investigators is involved in both the first and second search, there is a significant danger that the "independence" of the source will in fact be illusory, and that the initial search will have affected the decision to obtain a warrant notwithstanding the officers' subsequent assertions to the contrary. It is therefore crucial that the factual premise of the exception—complete independence—be clearly established before the exception can justify admission of the evidence. I believe the Court's reliance on the intent of the law enforcement officers who conducted the warrantless search provides insufficient guarantees that the subsequent legal search was unaffected by the prior illegal search.

To ensure that the source of the evidence is genuinely independent, the basis for a finding that a search was untainted by a prior illegal search must focus, as with the inevitable discovery doctrine, on "demonstrated historical facts capable of ready verification or impeachment." In the instant cases, there are no "demonstrated historical facts" capable of supporting a finding that the subsequent warrant search was wholly unaffected by the prior illegal search. The same team of investigators was involved in both searches. The warrant was obtained immediately after the illegal search, and no effort was made to obtain a warrant prior to the discovery of the marijuana during the illegal search. The only evidence available that the warrant search was wholly independent is the testimony of the agents who conducted the illegal search. Under these circumstances, the threat that the subsequent search was tainted by the illegal search is too great to allow for the application of the independent source exception. The Court's contrary holding lends itself to easy abuse, and offers an incentive to bypass the constitutional requirement that probable cause be assessed by a neutral and detached magistrate before the police invade an individual's privacy....

NOTES & QUESTIONS ON THE INDEPENDENT SOURCE EXCEPTION

1. *Is the exception really an exception?* Although doctrinally considered an "exception" to the exclusionary rule, is the independent source doctrine

really an *exception*? The exclusionary rule says that evidence seized illegally should be excluded from a criminal trial. But in *Segura* and *Murray*, the evidence was seized—at least in part—pursuant to a valid search warrant. In that sense, the independent source exception might be accused of restating the obvious. If the evidence comes from at least one valid source, it can be admitted at trial. For more discussion, see Robert M. Bloom, *Inevitable Discovery: An Exception Beyond the Fruits*, 20 Am. J. Crim. L. 79, 80 (1992) ("In the independent source situation, it can be said that the fruit not only grows from the poisonous tree, but also grows from another, non-poisonous tree").

2. *Scalia's two-part test.* In *Murray*, Justice Scalia established a two-part test for evaluating whether the issuance of a warrant will qualify as an independent source. First, did the officers decide to seek the warrant *after* they received information during the illegal entry? Second, was that information presented to the magistrate and did it impact the magistrate's decision? If the answer to all of these questions is yes, then the independent source exception cannot apply. Do you agree with this test? Apply the test to the facts of the *Murray* case. Is it clear that the search warrant was truly independent of the seizure during the unlawful entry? Finally, focus on the initial step of the two-part test, the subjective motivations of the police officer in seeking the search

PROBLEM CASE

On February 1, 2016, police investigated a report of a vehicle break-in. En route, an officer came across four young men, one of whom was Stephens, who the officer recognized from prior interactions. The officer talked with the men and then continued on to the scene of the vehicle break-in. Once there, the officer reviewed surveillance video of the break-in, which showed the four individuals that the officer had just interviewed. An armed robbery was also reported to the police, and the victim of the robbery identified Stephens from a lineup as the assailant who was carrying a pistol during the robbery. Police secured an arrest warrant for Stephens and found a pistol on him during the arrest.

At trial, Stephens argued that he had found the gun on the day of his arrest and therefore did not have the gun at the time of the armed robbery—thus suggesting a case of mistaken identity. Police impeached this testimony by showing a video of Stephens with the gun; the police found the video on Stephens' cell phone when they arrested him. The police used a bit of trickery to unlock the phone. Stephens asked for his phone at the police station so that he could retrieve a phone number stored on the phone. In doing so, Stephens had to unlock the phone with his passcode; when he unlocked the phone, an officer took the phone away and gave it to a computer forensics team for downloading. *After* downloading the data from the phone, the police requested and received a search warrant for the cell phone.

Stephens argued that the cell phone video should be excluded because at the time of his arrest, police had no authorization to search his cell phone. Should the video be excluded as evidence? *Stephens v. State*, 816 S.E.2d 748, 754 (Ga. Ct. App. 2018).

warrant from the magistrate. If the police officer testifies that the illegal entry played no role in their decision to seek the search warrant, is there any way that a defense counsel could counter this argument? For more discussion of this point, see *Exclusionary Rule-Independent Source Exception*, 102 Harv. L. Rev. 161, 167 (1988) (arguing that the "Court in *Murray* created a set of powerful incentives for police to conduct illegal 'confirmatory' searches before attempting to obtain a warrant"). Do you agree that the independent source exception gives police an incentive to conduct illegal confirmatory searches as long as they know that they have an independent basis for a search warrant? Is this reason enough to abandon the exception or should courts revise the first step of Scalia's two-part test?

2. Inevitable Discovery

If the police would have inevitably discovered the evidence, then the state may introduce the evidence at trial notwithstanding the fact that the evidence was procured during an unconstitutional search of seizure. In many cases, the inevitable discovery exception is hard to apply to a particular set of facts because it requires a counter-factual analysis: In the absence of finding the evidence, how would the investigation have proceeded? This question necessarily requires some conjecture: A judge is invited to speculate which steps the investigators would have taken and what evidence would have resulted from those efforts. If the tainted evidence would have been inevitably seized in the course of that hypothetical chain of events, then the evidence should be admitted at trial.

In reality, then, there is a close connection between the independent source and inevitable discovery exceptions. One might even describe the latter as merely a special example of the former. Because the evidence would have been obtained through another source anyway, the evidence can be logically separated from the unconstitutional search or seizure that tainted its collection. The major difference between the doctrines is that the independent source exception usually refers to an independent source—like a search warrant—that already happened. In contrast, inevitable discovery refers to a future, hypothetical source, i.e., a way that the investigation would have proceeded had the evidence not been collected through the unconstitutional event.

The following case involves the type of fact pattern where the inevitable discovery is easy to comprehend. The police were already engaged in a grid search when the police received additional information from an unconstitutional interrogation of the defendant. Although the interrogation yielded targeted information, the grid search had an air of inevitability to it—almost as a matter of geometry. As you read the case, apply its principles to more complex fact patterns where the next steps in the investigation are more difficult to envision.

Nix v. Williams

Supreme Court of the United States
467 U.S. 431 (1984)

Chief Justice BURGER delivered the opinion of the Court.

We granted certiorari to consider whether, at respondent Williams' second murder trial in state court, evidence pertaining to the discovery and condition of the victim's body was properly admitted on the ground that it would ultimately or inevitably have been discovered even if no violation of any constitutional or statutory provision had taken place.

I

On December 24, 1968, 10-year-old Pamela Powers disappeared from a YMCA building in Des Moines, Iowa, where she had accompanied her parents to watch an athletic contest. Shortly after she disappeared, Williams was seen leaving the YMCA carrying a large bundle wrapped in a blanket; a 14-year-old boy who had helped Williams open his car door reported that he had seen "two legs in it and they were skinny and white."

Williams' car was found the next day 160 miles east of Des Moines in Davenport, Iowa. Later several items of clothing belonging to the child, some of Williams' clothing, and an army blanket like the one used to wrap the bundle that Williams carried out of the YMCA were found at a rest stop on Interstate 80 near Grinnell, between Des Moines and Davenport. A warrant was issued for Williams' arrest.

Police surmised that Williams had left Pamela Powers or her body somewhere between Des Moines and the Grinnell rest stop where some of the young girl's clothing had been found. On December 26, the Iowa Bureau of Criminal Investigation initiated a large-scale search. Two hundred volunteers divided into teams began the search 21 miles east of Grinnell, covering an area several miles to the north and south of Interstate 80. They moved westward from Poweshiek County, in which Grinnell was located, into Jasper County. Searchers were instructed to check all roads, abandoned farm buildings, ditches, culverts, and any other place in which the body of a small child could be hidden.

Meanwhile, Williams surrendered to local police in Davenport, where he was promptly arraigned. Williams contacted a Des Moines attorney who arranged for an attorney in Davenport to meet Williams at the Davenport police station. Des Moines police informed counsel they would pick Williams up in Davenport and return him to Des Moines without questioning him. Two Des Moines detectives then drove to Davenport, took Williams into custody, and proceeded to drive him back to Des Moines.

During the return trip, one of the policemen, Detective Leaming, began a conversation with Williams, saying:

> I want to give you something to think about while we're traveling down the road.... They are predicting several inches of snow for tonight, and I feel that you yourself are the only person that knows where this little girl's body is...and if you get a snow on top of it you yourself may be unable to find it. And since we will be going right past the area [where the body is] on the way into Des Moines, I feel that we could stop and locate the body, that the parents of this little girl should be entitled to a Christian burial for the little girl who was snatched away from them on Christmas [E]ve and murdered.... A]fter a snow storm [we may not be] able to find it at all.

Leaming told Williams he knew the body was in the area of Mitchellville—a town they would be passing on the way to Des Moines. He concluded the conversation by saying "I do not want you to answer me.... Just think about it...."

Later, as the police car approached Grinnell, Williams asked Leaming whether the police had found the young girl's shoes. After Leaming replied that he was unsure, Williams directed the police to a point near a service station where he said he had left the shoes; they were not found. As they continued to drive to Des Moines, Williams asked whether the blanket had been found and then directed the officers to a rest area in Grinnell where he said he had disposed of the blanket; they did not find the blanket. At this point Leaming and his party were joined by the officers in charge of the search. As they approached Mitchellville, Williams, without any further conversation, agreed to direct the officers to the child's body.

The officers directing the search had called off the search at 3 P.M., when they left the Grinnell Police Department to join Leaming at the rest area. At that time, one search team near the Jasper County–Polk County line was only two and one-half miles from where Williams soon guided Leaming and his party to the body. The child's body was found next to a culvert in a ditch beside a gravel road in Polk County, about two miles south of Interstate 80, and essentially within the area to be searched.

In February 1969 Williams was indicted for first-degree murder. Before trial in the Iowa court, his counsel moved to suppress evidence of the body and all related evidence including the condition of the body as shown by the autopsy. The ground for the motion was that such evidence was the "fruit" or product of Williams' statements made during the automobile ride from Davenport to Des Moines and prompted by Leaming's statements....

II

The Iowa Supreme Court correctly stated that the "vast majority" of all courts, both state and federal, recognize an inevitable discovery exception to the exclusionary rule. We are now urged to adopt and apply the so-called ultimate or inevitable discovery exception to the exclusionary rule.

Williams contends that evidence of the body's location and condition is "fruit of the poisonous tree," i.e., the "fruit" or product of Detective Leaming's plea to help the child's parents give her "a Christian burial," which this Court had already held equated to interrogation. He contends that admitting the challenged evidence violated the Sixth Amendment whether it would have been inevitably discovered or not. Williams also contends that, if the inevitable discovery doctrine is constitutionally permissible, it must include a threshold showing of police good faith.

The doctrine requiring courts to suppress evidence as the tainted "fruit" of unlawful governmental conduct had its genesis in *Silverthorne Lumber Co. v. United States*, 251 U.S. 385 (1920); there, the Court held that the exclusionary rule applies not only to the illegally obtained evidence itself, but also to other incriminating evidence derived from the primary evidence. The holding of *Silverthorne* was carefully limited, however, for the Court emphasized that such information does not automatically become "sacred and inaccessible." "If knowledge of [such facts] is gained from an independent source, they may be proved like any others...." ...

The core rationale consistently advanced by this Court for extending the exclusionary rule to evidence that is the fruit of unlawful police conduct has been that this admittedly drastic and socially costly course is needed to deter police from violations of constitutional and statutory protections. This Court has accepted the argument that the way to ensure such protections is to exclude evidence seized as a result of such violations notwithstanding the high social cost of letting persons obviously guilty go unpunished for their crimes. On this rationale, the prosecution is not to be put in a better position than it would have been in if no illegality had transpired.

By contrast, the derivative evidence analysis ensures that the prosecution is not put in a worse position simply because of some earlier police error or misconduct. The independent source doctrine allows admission of evidence that has been discovered by means wholly independent of any constitutional violation. That doctrine, although closely related to the inevitable discovery doctrine, does not apply here; Williams' statements to Leaming indeed led police to the child's body, but that is not the whole story. The independent source doctrine teaches us that the interest of society in deterring unlawful police conduct and the public interest in having juries receive all probative evidence of a crime are properly balanced by putting the police in the same, not a worse, position that they would have been in if no police error or misconduct had occurred. When the challenged evidence has an independent source, exclusion of such evidence would put the police in a worse position than they would have been in absent any error or violation. There is a functional similarity between these two doctrines in that exclusion of evidence that would inevitably have been discovered would also put the government in a worse position, because the police would have obtained that evidence if no misconduct had taken place. Thus, while the independent source exception would not justify admission of evidence in this case, its rationale is wholly consistent with and justifies our adoption of the ultimate or inevitable discovery exception to the exclusionary rule.

It is clear that the cases implementing the exclusionary rule "begin with the premise that the challenged evidence is in some sense the product of illegal governmental activity." Of course, this does not end the inquiry. If the prosecution can establish by a preponderance of the evidence that the information ultimately or inevitably would have been discovered by lawful means—here the volunteers' search—then the deterrence rationale has so little basis that the evidence should be received. Anything less would reject logic, experience, and common sense.

The requirement that the prosecution must prove the absence of bad faith, imposed here by the Court of Appeals, would place courts in the position of withholding from juries relevant and undoubted truth that would have been available to police absent any unlawful police activity. Of course, that view would put the police in a worse position than they would have been in if no unlawful conduct had transpired. And, of equal importance, it wholly fails to take into account the enormous societal cost of excluding truth in the search for truth in the administration of justice. Nothing in this Court's prior holdings supports any such formalistic, pointless, and punitive approach.

The Court of Appeals concluded, without analysis, that if an absence-of-bad-faith requirement were not imposed, "the temptation to risk deliberate violations of the Sixth Amendment would be too great, and the deterrent effect of the Exclusionary Rule reduced too far." We reject that view. A police officer who is faced with the opportunity to obtain evidence illegally will rarely, if ever, be in a position to calculate whether the evidence sought would inevitably be discovered.

On the other hand, when an officer is aware that the evidence will inevitably be discovered, he will try to avoid engaging in any questionable practice. In that situation, there will be little to gain from taking any dubious "shortcuts" to obtain the evidence. Significant disincentives to obtaining evidence illegally—including the possibility of departmental discipline and civil liability—also lessen the likelihood that the ultimate or inevitable discovery exception will promote police misconduct. In these circumstances, the societal costs of the exclusionary rule far outweigh any possible benefits to deterrence that a good-faith requirement might produce....

Exclusion of physical evidence that would inevitably have been discovered adds nothing to either the integrity or fairness of a criminal trial. The Sixth Amendment right to counsel protects against unfairness by preserving the adversary process in which the reliability of proffered evidence may be tested in cross-examination. Here, however, Detective Leaming's conduct did nothing to impugn the reliability of the evidence in question—the body of the child and its condition as it was found, articles of clothing found on the body, and the autopsy. No one would seriously contend that the presence of counsel in the police car when Leaming appealed to Williams' decent human instincts would have had any bearing on the reliability of the body as evidence. Suppression, in these circumstances, would do nothing whatever to promote the integrity of the trial process, but would inflict a wholly unacceptable burden on the administration of criminal justice.

Nor would suppression ensure fairness on the theory that it tends to safeguard the adversary system of justice.... Fairness can be assured by placing the State and the accused in the same positions they would have been in had the impermissible conduct not taken place. However, if the government can prove that the evidence would have been obtained inevitably and, therefore, would have been admitted regardless of any overreaching by the police, there is no rational basis to keep that evidence from the jury in order to ensure the fairness of the trial proceedings. In that situation, the State has gained no advantage at trial and the defendant has suffered no prejudice....

The search had commenced at approximately 10 A.M. and moved westward through Poweshiek County into Jasper County. At approximately 3 P.M., after Williams had volunteered to cooperate with the police, Detective Leaming, who was in the police car with Williams, sent word to Ruxlow and the other Special Agent directing the search to meet him at the Grinnell truck stop and the search was suspended at that time. Ruxlow also stated that he was "under the impression that there was a possibility" that Williams would lead them to the child's body at that time. The search was not resumed once it was learned that Williams had led the police to the body, which was found two and one-half miles from where the search had stopped in what would have been the easternmost grid to be searched in Polk County. There was testimony that it would have taken an additional three to five hours to discover the body if the search had continued; the body was found near a culvert, one of the kinds of places the teams had been specifically directed to search.

On this record it is clear that the search parties were approaching the actual location of the body, and we are satisfied, along with three courts earlier, that the volunteer search teams would have resumed the search had Williams not earlier led the police to the body and the body inevitably would have been found....

Justice BRENNAN, with whom Justice MARSHALL joins, dissenting.

...In its zealous efforts to emasculate the exclusionary rule...the Court loses sight of the crucial difference between the "inevitable discovery" doctrine and the "independent source" exception from which it is derived. When properly applied, the "independent source" exception allows the prosecution to use evidence only if it was, in fact, obtained by fully lawful means. It therefore does no violence to the constitutional protections that the exclusionary rule is meant to enforce. The "inevitable discovery" exception is likewise compatible with the Constitution, though it differs in one key respect from its next of kin: specifically, the evidence sought to be introduced at trial has not actually been obtained from an independent source, but rather would have been discovered as a matter of course if independent investigations were allowed to proceed.

In my view, this distinction should require that the government satisfy a heightened burden of proof before it is allowed to use such evidence. The inevitable discovery exception necessarily implicates a hypothetical finding that differs in kind from the factual finding that precedes application of the independent source rule. To ensure that this hypothetical finding is narrowly confined to circumstances that are functionally equivalent to an independent source, and to protect fully the fundamental rights served by the exclusionary rule, I would require clear and convincing evidence before concluding that the government had met its burden of proof on this issue. Increasing the burden of proof serves to impress the factfinder with the importance of the decision and thereby reduces the risk that illegally obtained evidence will be admitted. Because the lower courts did not impose such a requirement, I would remand this case for application of this heightened burden of proof by the lower courts in the first instance....

NOTES & QUESTIONS ON INEVITABLE DISCOVERY

1. *Relationship to independent source doctrine.* Reconsider the point first raised at the start of this subsection: Are the inevitable discovery and independent source exceptions really separate doctrines?

2. *Is there an independence requirement?* If the inevitable discovery and independent source exceptions are closely intertwined, should courts impose an independence requirement for both doctrines? In 2006, the Supreme Court decided *Hudson v. Michigan* (reprinted below) and held that the exclusionary rule does not apply to knock-and-announce violations. In dissent, Justice Breyer considered the inevitable discovery doctrine, and noted that "'independent' or 'inevitable' discovery refers to discovery that did occur or that would have occurred (1) despite (not simply in the absence of) the unlawful behavior and (2) independently of that unlawful behavior." 547 U.S. 586, 616. Apply this

standard to the facts of the *Nix* case. Was the inevitable discovery of the body "independent" of the impermissible interrogation of the defendant?

3. *The "active pursuit" requirement.* Some lower courts have required that an alternative investigatory avenue must be under "active pursuit" in order for the inevitable discovery exception to apply. For example, in *United States v. Terzado-Madruga*, the Eleventh Circuit concluded that "[t]o qualify for admissibility, there must be a reasonable probability that the evidence in question would have been discovered by lawful means, and the prosecution must demonstrate that the lawful means which made discovery inevitable were possessed by the police and were being actively pursued prior to the occurrence of the illegal conduct." 897 F.2d 1099, 1114 (11th Cir. 1990). Obviously, this imposes a substantial doctrinal limitation that will exclude certain fact patterns from the application of the exception. However, other Circuits have rejected the requirement. For example, the Tenth Circuit concluded that "the inevitable discovery exception applies whenever an independent investigation inevitably would have led to discovery of the evidence, whether or not the investigation was ongoing at the time of the illegal police conduct." *United States v. Larsen*, 127 F.3d 984, 986 (10th Cir. 1997). Does a close reading of the *Nix* case support one view over the other? In *Nix*, the other investigatory avenue—the grid search—was already underway when the police engaged in the unlawful interrogation of the defendant. Was this a necessary or contingent element of the fact pattern? For more discussion, see Eugene L. Shapiro, *Active Pursuit, Inevitable Discovery, and the Federal Circuits: The Search for Manageable Limitations upon an Expansive Doctrine*, 39 Gonz. L. Rev. 295 (2004).

3. Attenuation of the Taint

The third exception, attenuation of the taint, expresses a causal relationship. Imagine that a defendant is arrested illegally by the police. Is all evidence—including a confession received while the defendant is in custody—automatically subject to the exclusionary rule? Or is there some way of cutting off the "taint" from the original constitutional violation? As the Supreme Court said in *Wong Sun v. United States*, 371 U.S. 471, 487-88 (1963): "We need not hold that all evidence is 'fruit of the poisonous tree' simply because it would not have come to light but for the illegal actions of the police. Rather, the more apt question in such a case is 'whether, granting establishment of the primary illegality, the evidence to which instant objection is made has been come at by exploitation of that illegality or instead by means sufficiently distinguishable to be purged of the primary taint,' Maguire, *Evidence of Guilt* 221 (1959)."

In the following case, the police issued *Miranda* warnings to the defendant, notifying him that, among other things, he had the right to counsel and the right to remain silent. The question then is whether the *Miranda* warnings interrupt the causal chain leading back to the original illegal detention. Was the statement "caused" by the original arrest or was it sufficiently voluntary so as to be considered a product of free will? In other words, did the *Miranda* warnings attenuate the taint from the illegal arrest?

Brown v. Illinois

Supreme Court of the United States
422 U.S. 590 (1975)

Mr. Justice BLACKMUN delivered the opinion of the Court.

This case lies at the crossroads of the Fourth and the Fifth Amendments. Petitioner was arrested without probable cause and without a warrant. He was given, in full, the warnings prescribed by *Miranda v. Arizona*, 384 U.S. 436 (1966). Thereafter, while in custody, he made two inculpatory statements. The issue is whether evidence of those statements was properly admitted, or should have been excluded, in petitioner's subsequent trial for murder in state court. Expressed another way, the issue is whether the statements were to be excluded as the fruit of the illegal arrest or were admissible because the giving of the *Miranda* warnings sufficiently attenuated the taint of the arrest.

I

As petitioner Richard Brown was climbing the last of the stairs leading to the rear entrance of his Chicago apartment in the early evening of May 13, 1968, he happened to glance at the window near the door. He saw, pointed at him through the window, a revolver held by a stranger who was inside the apartment. The man said: "Don't move, you are under arrest." Another man, also with a gun, came up behind Brown and repeated the statement that he was under arrest. It was about 7:45 P.M. The two men turned out to be Detectives William Nolan and William Lenz of the Chicago police force. It is not clear from the record exactly when they advised Brown of their identity, but it is not disputed that they broke into his apartment, searched it, and then arrested Brown, all without probable cause and without any warrant, when he arrived. They later testified that they made the arrest for the purpose of questioning Brown as part of their investigation of the murder of a man named Roger Corpus.

Corpus was murdered one week earlier, on May 6, with a .38-caliber revolver in his Chicago West Side second-floor apartment. Shortly thereafter, Detective Lenz obtained petitioners' name, among others, from Corpus' brother. Petitioner and the others were identified as acquaintances of the victim, not as suspects.

On the day of petitioner's arrest, Detectives Lenz and Nolan, armed with a photograph of Brown, and another officer arrived at petitioner's apartment about 5 P.M. While the third officer covered the front entrance downstairs, the two detectives broke into Brown's apartment and searched it. Lenz then positioned himself near the rear door and watched through the adjacent window which opened onto the back porch. Nolan sat near the front door. He described the situation at the later suppression hearing:

> After we were there for a while, Detective Lenz told me that somebody was coming up the back stairs. I walked out the front door through the hall and around the corner, and I stayed there behind a door leading on the back porch. At this time I heard Detective Lenz say, "Don't move, you are under arrest." I looked out. I saw Mr. Brown backing away from the window. I walked up behind him, I told him he is under arrest, come back inside the apartment with us.

As both officers held him at gunpoint, the three entered the apartment. Brown was ordered to stand against the wall and was searched. No weapon was found. He was asked his name. When he denied being Richard Brown, Detective Lenz showed him the photograph, informed him that he was under arrest for the murder of Roger Corpus, handcuffed him, and escorted him to the squad car.

The two detectives took petitioner to the Maxwell Street police station. During the 20-minute drive Nolan again asked Brown, who then was sitting with him in the back seat of the car, whether his name was Richard Brown and whether he owned a 1966 Oldsmobile. Brown alternately evaded these questions or answered them falsely. Upon arrival at the station house Brown was placed in the second-floor central interrogation room. The room was bare, except for a table and four chairs. He was left alone, apparently without handcuffs, for some minutes while the officers obtained the file on the Corpus homicide. They returned with the file, sat down at the table, one across from Brown and the other to his left, and spread the file on the table in front of him.

The officers warned Brown of his rights under *Miranda*. They then informed him that they knew of an incident that had occurred in a poolroom on May 5, when Brown, angry at having been cheated at dice, fired a shot from a revolver into the ceiling. Brown answered: "Oh, you know about that." Lenz informed him that a bullet had been obtained from the ceiling of the poolroom and had been taken to the crime laboratory to be compared with bullets taken from Corpus' body. Brown responded: "Oh, you know that, too." At this point—it was about 8:45 P.M.—Lenz asked Brown whether he wanted to talk about the Corpus homicide. Petitioner answered that he did. For the next 20 to 25 minutes Brown answered questions put to him by Nolan, as Lenz typed.

This questioning produced a two-page statement in which Brown acknowledged that he and a man named Jimmy Claggett visited Corpus on the evening of May 5; that the three for some time sat drinking and smoking marihuana; that Claggett ordered him at gunpoint to bind Corpus' hands and feet with cord from the headphone of a stereo set; and that Claggett, using a .38-caliber revolver sold to him by Brown, shot Corpus three times through a pillow. The statement was signed by Brown.

About 9:30 P.M. the two detectives and Brown left the station house to look for Claggett in an area of Chicago Brown knew him to frequent. They made a tour of that area but did not locate their quarry. They then went to police headquarters where they endeavored, without success, to obtain a photograph of Claggett. They resumed their search—it was now about 11 P.M.—and they finally observed Claggett crossing at an intersection. Lenz and Nolan arrested him. All four, the two detectives and the two arrested men, returned to the Maxwell Street station about 12:15 A.M.

Brown was again placed in the interrogation room. He was given coffee and was left alone, for the most part, until 2 A.M. when Assistant State's Attorney Crilly arrived. Crilly, too, informed Brown of his *Miranda* rights. After a half hour's conversation, a court reporter appeared. Once again, the Miranda warnings were given: "I read him the card." Crilly told him that he "was sure he would be charged with murder." Brown gave a second statement, providing a factual account of the murder substantially in accord with his first statement, but containing factual inaccuracies with respect to his personal background. When the statement was completed, at about 3 A.M., Brown refused to sign it. An hour later he made a phone call to his mother. At 9:30 that morning, about 14 hours after his arrest, he was taken before a magistrate....

III

The Illinois courts refrained from resolving the question...whether Brown's statements were obtained by exploitation of the illegality of his arrest. They assumed that the *Miranda* warnings, by themselves, assured that the statements (verbal acts, as contrasted with physical evidence) were of sufficient free will as to purge the primary taint of the unlawful arrest....

If *Miranda* warnings, by themselves, were held to attenuate the taint of an unconstitutional arrest, regardless of how wanton and purposeful the Fourth Amendment violation, the effect of the exclusionary rule would be substantially diluted. Arrests made without warrant or without probable cause, for questioning or "investigation," would be encouraged by the knowledge that evidence derived therefrom could well be made admissible at trial by the simple expedient of giving *Miranda* warnings. Any incentive to avoid Fourth Amendment violations would be eviscerated by making the warnings, in effect, a "cure-all," and the constitutional guarantee against unlawful searches and seizures could be said to be reduced to "a form of words."

It is entirely possible, of course, as the State here argues, that persons arrested illegally frequently may decide to confess, as an act of free will unaffected by the initial illegality. But the *Miranda* warnings, alone and per se, cannot always make the act sufficiently a product of free will to break, for Fourth Amendment purposes, the causal connection between the illegality and the confession. They cannot assure in every case that the Fourth Amendment violation has not been unduly exploited.

While we therefore reject the per se rule which the Illinois courts appear to have accepted, we also decline to adopt any alternative per se or "but for" rule. The petitioner himself professes not to demand so much. The question whether a confession is the product of a free will... must be answered on the facts of each case. No single fact is dispositive. The workings of the human mind are too complex, and the possibilities of misconduct too diverse, to permit protection of the Fourth Amendment to turn on such a talismanic test. The *Miranda* warnings are an important factor, to be sure, in determining whether the confession is obtained by exploitation of an illegal arrest. But they are not the only factor to be considered. The temporal proximity of the arrest and the confession, the presence of intervening circumstances, and, particularly, the purpose and flagrancy of the official misconduct are all relevant. The voluntariness of the statement is a threshold requirement. And the burden of showing admissibility rests, of course, on the prosecution.

IV

Although the Illinois courts failed to undertake the inquiry mandated by *Wong Sun* to evaluate the circumstances of this case in the light of the policy served by the exclusionary rule, the trial resulted in a record of amply sufficient detail and depth from which the determination may be made.... Brown's first statement was separated from his illegal arrest by less than two hours, and there was no intervening event of significance whatsoever....

The illegality here, moreover, had a quality of purposefulness. The impropriety of the arrest was obvious; awareness of that fact was virtually conceded by the two detectives when they repeatedly acknowledged, in their testimony, that the purpose of their action was "for investigation" or for "questioning." The arrest, both in design and in execution, was investigatory. The detectives embarked upon this expedition for evidence in the hope that something might turn up. The manner in which Brown's arrest was affected gives the appearance of having been calculated to cause surprise, fright, and confusion.

We emphasize that our holding is a limited one. We decide only that the Illinois courts were in error in assuming that the *Miranda* warnings, by themselves... always purge the taint of an illegal arrest....

Mr. Justice POWELL, with whom Mr. Justice REHNQUIST joins, concurring in part.

I join the Court insofar as it holds that the per se rule adopted by the Illinois Supreme Court for determining the admissibility of petitioner's two statements inadequately accommodates the diverse interests underlying the Fourth Amendment exclusionary rule. I would, however, remand the case for reconsideration under the general standards articulated in the Court's opinion and elaborated herein. . . .

I would require the clearest indication of attenuation in cases in which official conduct was flagrantly abusive of Fourth Amendment rights. If, for example, the factors relied on by the police in determining to make the arrest were so lacking in indicia of probable cause as to render official belief in its existence entirely unreasonable, or if the evidence clearly suggested that the arrest was effectuated as a pretext for collateral objectives or the physical circumstances of the arrest unnecessarily intrusive on personal privacy, I would consider the equalizing potential of *Miranda* warnings rarely sufficient to dissipate the taint. In such cases the deterrent value of the exclusionary rule is most likely to be effective, and the corresponding mandate to preserve judicial integrity most clearly demands that the fruits of official misconduct be denied. I thus would require some demonstrably effective break in the chain of events leading from the illegal arrest to the statement, such as actual consultation with counsel or the accused's presentation before a magistrate for a determination of probable cause before the taint can be deemed removed.

At the opposite end of the spectrum lie "technical" violations of Fourth Amendment rights where, for example, officers in good faith arrest an individual in reliance on a warrant later invalidated or pursuant to a statute that subsequently is declared unconstitutional. In cases in which this underlying premise is lacking, the deterrence rationale of the exclusionary rule does not obtain, and I can see no legitimate justification for depriving the prosecution of reliable and probative evidence. Thus, with the exception of statements given in the immediate circumstances of the illegal arrest—a constraint I think is imposed by existing exclusionary-rule law—I would not require more than proof that effective *Miranda* warnings were given and that the ensuing statement was voluntary in the Fifth Amendment sense. Absent aggravating circumstances, I would consider a statement given at the station house after one has been advised of *Miranda* rights to be sufficiently removed from the immediate circumstances of the illegal arrest to justify its admission at trial.

Between these extremes lies a wide range of situations that defy ready categorization, and I will not attempt to embellish on the factors set forth in the Court's opinion other than to emphasize that the *Wong Sun* inquiry always should be conducted with the deterrent purpose of the Fourth Amendment exclusionary rule sharply in focus. . . .

NOTES & QUESTIONS ON ATTENUATION OF THE TAINT

1. *Rejecting a per se rule.* In *Brown,* the Supreme Court rejected the idea that *Miranda* warnings by themselves necessarily attenuate the taint of an illegal seizure. The attenuation will come from the totality of the circumstances and in particular whether the confession was an act of free will that broke the chain of causation leading back to the original violation. Consequently, the issuance of the *Miranda* warnings may be one factor in the overall analysis, but not enough to establish attenuation by itself as a matter of legal necessity. Do you agree with the Court's decision to reject a per se rule that *Miranda* warnings always attenuate the taint?

2. *Other forms of attenuation.* *Brown* involved *Miranda* warnings as the relevant attenuation. But since the warnings by themselves are not outcome determinative, a court must look to other factors to determine if there is attenuation of the taint. For example, the defendant's *consent* to a search—outside of the *Miranda* context—could attenuate the taint of the original constitutional violation. Consider *State v. Zavala,* 134 Idaho 532, 5 P.3d 993 (Ct. App. 2000). Zavala was stopped for speeding. During the stop, the police officer radioed for backup, including a canine unit. After writing the ticket, the police officer did not give the ticket to Zavala. Instead, the officer asked Zavala and his passenger to step out of the car and began questioning them. Eventually, the other officers arrived with a canine unit. At that point, the officer gave the ticket to Zavala and told him he was free to go. However, the officer also requested permission to search the vehicle and Zavala consented. Drugs were found in the vehicle. On appeal, the Idaho court concluded that the original detention was illegal because it was unconnected to the vehicle stop and occurred after the officer finished writing the ticket. The court remanded to the trial court to determine attenuation:

> The state bears the burden of showing that the causal connection between an impermissible seizure and a statement made by a detainee, has been sufficiently broken to render those statements admissible at trial. When analyzing whether the state has met its burden, the district court should consider, the temporal proximity of the arrest and the statement, the presence of intervening circumstances, and the purpose and flagrancy of the official misconduct.

Id. at 537, 5 P.3d 993, 998.

3. *Can a warrant attenuate the taint from an illegal stop?* In *Utah v. Strieff,* 136 S.Ct. 2056 (2016), the Supreme Court considered whether an officer's discovery of the existence of a warrant, after an illegal stop, attenuates the taint from the original constitutional violation. After receiving an

anonymous tip, the police conducted surveillance of a house that the police believed was connected with the drug trade, based on the number of visitors that the house received over the course of a week. On the night in question, a police officer observed an individual leaving the house on foot. The police stopped him and asked him questions, and during that process learned that he had an outstanding warrant. The police arrested the man, searched him, and found illegal drugs on him. The man argued that the evidence should be suppressed because the original investigatory stop was unconstitutional because the officer lacked reasonable suspicion. A majority of the Supreme Court, applying the factors outlined in *Brown v. Illinois*, concluded that even if the original stop was suspicionless, the existence of the valid warrant attenuated the taint from the constitutional violation. Justice Thomas, writing for the majority, concluded that "there is no indication that this unlawful stop was part of any systemic or recurrent police misconduct" and "all the evidence suggests that the stop was an isolated instance of negligence that occurred in connection with a bona fide investigation of a suspected drug house." *Id.* at 2064. In dissent, Justice Sotomayor argued that the *Strieff* ruling would have a profound impact on all citizens, but especially racial minorities:

> This case involves a suspicionless stop, one in which the officer initiated this chain of events without justification. As the Justice Department notes, many innocent people are subjected to the humiliations of these unconstitutional searches. The white defendant in this case shows that anyone's dignity can be violated in this manner. But it is no secret that people of color are disproportionate victims of this type of scrutiny. For generations, black and brown parents have given their children "the talk"—instructing them never to run down the street; always keep your hands where they can be seen; do not even think of talking back to a stranger—all out of fear of how an officer with a gun will react to them. By legitimizing the conduct that produces this double consciousness, this case tells everyone, white and black, guilty and innocent, that an officer can verify your legal status at any time. It says that your body is subject to invasion while courts excuse the violation of your rights. It implies that you are not a citizen of a democracy but the subject of a carceral state, just waiting to be cataloged. We must not pretend that the countless people who are routinely targeted by police are "isolated." They are the canaries in the coal mine whose deaths, civil and literal, warn us that no one can breathe in this atmosphere. See L. Guinier & G. Torres, *The Miner's Canary* 274–283 (2002). They are the ones who recognize that unlawful police stops corrode all our civil liberties and threaten all our lives. Until their voices matter too, our justice system will continue to be anything but.

Id. at 2070-71.

PROBLEM CASE

Consider the following case:

> Four men (one armed with a handgun) entered and ransacked an apartment, bound and beat its occupants, and stole various items, including a mountain bike. Days later, one of the men confessed to Lowell police his involvement in the armed home invasion and robbery, implicated the defendant, Victor Marquez, and provided the police with the defendant's address. The police made a warrantless arrest of the defendant after one of the victims positively identified him from a photographic array. The arrest was made after the defendant opened the door of his apartment in response to a knock by a police officer, who recognized the defendant as the person being sought; saw, in plain view inside the defendant's apartment through its open doorway, what appeared to be the stolen mountain bike; and heard the defendant say, "The bike's not mine." After his arrest and booking, the defendant was interviewed by the police and made incriminatory statements [at the police station house].

Commonwealth v. Marquez, 434 Mass. 370, 371, 749 N.E.2d 673 (2001). Since the police did not have a warrant to arrest the defendant, their arrest of him at his home was clearly a violation of the Fourth Amendment. The defendant argued that the following evidence should be excluded: the stolen mountain bike recovered from his apartment, his statement at his arrest about the bike not being his, and his statement to police during the interview at the station house. Which of these pieces of evidence should be excluded at his trial?

4. Good Faith

The fourth major exception to the exclusionary rule involves situations in which the police act in good faith. In *United States v. Leon,* 468 U.S. 897 (1984), the Supreme Court considered the fate of evidence seized pursuant to a warrant that was duly issued by a judge. On appeal, the warrant was invalidated because the supporting affidavit was insufficient to establish probable cause; the appeals court concluded that the magistrate was wrong to issue the warrant in the first place. However, since the police officers relied on the facially valid warrant, the question was whether the evidence seized pursuant to it could be used at trial or whether the exclusionary rule applied. The Court concluded that "the marginal or nonexistent benefits produced by suppressing evidence obtained in objectively reasonable reliance on a subsequently invalidated search warrant cannot justify the substantial costs of exclusion." *Id.* at 922.

In *Arizona v. Evans,* 514 U.S. 1 (1995), the arresting police officer checked his computer database indicating that there was an outstanding misdemeanor warrant against the defendant. A search during the arrest yielded marijuana. Unbeknownst to the arresting officer, the prior misdemeanor warrant had been quashed 17 days prior but a court clerk had failed to remove the warrant from the police database. The Supreme Court ruled that the evidence resulting from the illegal result could still be admitted at trial and that exclusion would do nothing to further the goal of deterring police officers from violating the Fourth Amendment. After all, the mistake was committed by court personnel—not the police.

In the following case, *Herring v. United States*, the Supreme Court considers the behavior of a police officer who arrested the defendant believing that there was a valid warrant for the individual's arrest. In fact, the warrant had been withdrawn but a clerical error by police and court officials in a neighboring jurisdiction resulted in incorrect information being provided to the police officer. In that sense, the material facts are different from *Leon*, which involved a warrant whose illegitimacy was only determined after the arrest. In contrast, *Herring* involves a phantom warrant. The case therefore raises complex questions of agency and deterrence. Although the police officer acted without fault, other police officials were clearly negligent in how they handled the warrant withdrawal, resulting in the Fourth Amendment violation to the defendant. This raises a fundamental question: Is the exclusionary rule designed to deter individual police officers from violating the Fourth Amendment or is it designed to deter the *state*—writ large—from violating the Fourth Amendment? More importantly, as you read the case, ask yourself whether the exclusionary rule is a mere remedy or whether it confers a right on individual defendants.

Herring v. United States

Supreme Court of the United States
555 U.S. 135 (2009)

Chief Justice Roberts delivered the opinion of the Court.

The Fourth Amendment forbids "unreasonable searches and seizures," and this usually requires the police to have probable cause or a warrant before making an arrest. What if an officer reasonably believes there is an outstanding arrest warrant, but that belief turns out to be wrong because of a negligent bookkeeping error by another police employee? The parties here agree that the ensuing arrest is still a violation of the Fourth Amendment, but dispute whether contraband found during a search incident to that arrest must be excluded in a later prosecution.

Our cases establish that such suppression is not an automatic consequence of a Fourth Amendment violation. Instead, the question turns on the culpability of the police and the potential of exclusion to deter wrongful police conduct. Here the error was the result of isolated negligence attenuated from the arrest. We hold that in these circumstances the jury should not be barred from considering all the evidence.

I

On July 7, 2004, Investigator Mark Anderson learned that Bennie Dean Herring had driven to the Coffee County Sheriff's Department to retrieve something from his impounded truck. Herring was no stranger to law enforcement, and Anderson asked the county's warrant clerk, Sandy Pope, to check for any outstanding warrants for Herring's arrest. When she found none, Anderson asked Pope to check with Sharon Morgan, her counterpart in neighboring Dale County. After checking Dale County's computer database, Morgan replied that there was an active arrest warrant for Herring's failure to appear on a felony charge. Pope relayed the information to Anderson and asked Morgan to fax over a copy of the warrant as confirmation. Anderson and a deputy followed Herring as he left the impound lot, pulled him over, and arrested him. A search incident to the arrest revealed methamphetamine in Herring's pocket, and a pistol (which as a felon he could not possess) in his vehicle.

There had, however, been a mistake about the warrant. The Dale County sheriff's computer records are supposed to correspond to actual arrest warrants, which the office also maintains. But when Morgan went to the files to retrieve the actual warrant to fax to Pope, Morgan was unable to find it. She called a court clerk and learned that the warrant had been recalled five months earlier. Normally when a warrant is recalled the court clerk's office or a judge's chambers calls Morgan, who enters the information in the sheriff's computer database and disposes of the physical copy. For whatever reason, the information about the recall of the warrant for Herring did not appear in the database. Morgan immediately called Pope to alert her to the mixup, and Pope contacted Anderson over a secure radio. This all unfolded in 10 to 15 minutes, but Herring had already been arrested and found with the gun and drugs, just a few hundred yards from the sheriff's office....

II

When a probable-cause determination was based on reasonable but mistaken assumptions, the person subjected to a search or seizure has not necessarily been the victim of a constitutional violation. The very phrase "probable cause" confirms that the Fourth Amendment does not demand all possible precision. And whether the error can be traced to a mistake by a state actor or some other source may bear on the analysis. For purposes of deciding this case, however, we accept the parties' assumption that there was a Fourth Amendment violation. The issue is whether the exclusionary rule should be applied....

In analyzing the applicability of the rule, *Leon* admonished that we must consider the actions of all the police officers involved. 468 U.S., at 923,

n. 24 ("It is necessary to consider the objective reasonableness, not only of the officers who eventually executed a warrant, but also of the officers who originally obtained it or who provided information material to the probable-cause determination"). The Coffee County officers did nothing improper. Indeed, the error was noticed so quickly because Coffee County requested a faxed confirmation of the warrant.

The Eleventh Circuit concluded, however, that somebody in Dale County should have updated the computer database to reflect the recall of the arrest warrant. The court also concluded that this error was negligent, but did not find it to be reckless or deliberate. That fact is crucial to our holding that this error is not enough by itself to require "the extreme sanction of exclusion."

The fact that a Fourth Amendment violation occurred—i.e., that a search or arrest was unreasonable—does not necessarily mean that the exclusionary rule applies. Indeed, exclusion "has always been our last resort, not our first impulse," and our precedents establish important principles that constrain application of the exclusionary rule.

First, the exclusionary rule is not an individual right and applies only where it "result[s] in appreciable deterrence." We have repeatedly rejected the argument that exclusion is a necessary consequence of a Fourth Amendment violation. Instead we have focused on the efficacy of the rule in deterring Fourth Amendment violations in the future.

In addition, the benefits of deterrence must outweigh the costs. "We have never suggested that the exclusionary rule must apply in every circumstance in which it might provide marginal deterrence." "[T]o the extent that application of the exclusionary rule could provide some incremental deterrent, that possible benefit must be weighed against [its] substantial social costs." The principal cost of applying the rule is, of course, letting guilty and possibly dangerous defendants go free—something that "offends basic concepts of the criminal justice system." "[T]he rule's costly toll upon truth-seeking and law enforcement objectives presents a high obstacle for those urging [its] application."

These principles are reflected in the holding of *Leon*: When police act under a warrant that is invalid for lack of probable cause, the exclusionary rule does not apply if the police acted "in objectively reasonable reliance" on the subsequently invalidated search warrant. We (perhaps confusingly) called this objectively reasonable reliance "good faith." In a companion case, *Massachusetts v. Sheppard,* 468 U.S. 981 (1984), we held that the exclusionary rule did not apply when a warrant was invalid because a judge forgot to make "clerical corrections" to it.

Shortly thereafter we extended these holdings to warrantless administrative searches performed in good-faith reliance on a statute later declared unconstitutional. Finally, in *Evans,* 514 U.S. 1, we applied this good-faith rule to police who reasonably relied on mistaken information in a court's database that an arrest warrant was outstanding. We held that a mistake made by a judicial employee could not give rise to exclusion for three reasons: The exclusionary rule was crafted to curb police rather than judicial misconduct; court employees were unlikely to try to subvert the Fourth Amendment; and "most important, there [was] no basis for believing that application of the exclusionary rule in [those] circumstances" would have any significant effect in deterring the errors. *Evans* left unresolved "whether the evidence should be suppressed if police personnel were responsible for the error," an issue not argued by the State in that case, but one that we now confront.

The extent to which the exclusionary rule is justified by these deterrence principles varies with the culpability of the law enforcement conduct. As we said in *Leon*, "an assessment of the flagrancy of the police misconduct constitutes an important step in the calculus" of applying the exclusionary rule. Similarly, in *Krull* we elaborated that "evidence should be suppressed only if it can be said that the law enforcement officer had knowledge, or may properly be charged with knowledge, that the search was unconstitutional under the Fourth Amendment."...

...[F]lagrant conduct was at issue in *Mapp v. Ohio*, 367 U.S. 643 (1961), which overruled *Wolf v. Colorado*, 338 U.S. 25 (1949), and extended the exclusionary rule to the States. Officers forced open a door to Ms. Mapp's house, kept her lawyer from entering, brandished what the court concluded was a false warrant, then forced her into handcuffs and canvassed the house for obscenity. An error that arises from nonrecurring and attenuated negligence is thus far removed from the core concerns that led us to adopt the rule in the first place. And in fact since *Leon*, we have never applied the rule to exclude evidence obtained in violation of the Fourth Amendment, where the police conduct was no more intentional or culpable than this.

To trigger the exclusionary rule, police conduct must be sufficiently deliberate that exclusion can meaningfully deter it, and sufficiently culpable that such deterrence is worth the price paid by the justice system. As laid out in our cases, the exclusionary rule serves to deter deliberate, reckless, or grossly negligent conduct, or in some circumstances recurring or systemic negligence. The error in this case does not rise to that level....

We do not suggest that all recordkeeping errors by the police are immune from the exclusionary rule. In this case, however, the conduct at issue was not so objectively culpable as to require exclusion. In *Leon*, we held that "the marginal or nonexistent benefits produced by suppressing evidence obtained in objectively reasonable reliance on a subsequently invalidated search warrant cannot justify the substantial costs of exclusion." The same is true when evidence is obtained in objectively reasonable reliance on a subsequently recalled warrant.

If the police have been shown to be reckless in maintaining a warrant system, or to have knowingly made false entries to lay the groundwork for future false arrests, exclusion would certainly be justified under our cases should such misconduct cause a Fourth Amendment violation. We said as much in *Leon*, explaining that an officer could not "obtain a warrant on the basis of a 'bare bones' affidavit and then rely on colleagues who are ignorant of the circumstances under which the warrant was obtained to conduct the search." Petitioner's fears that our decision will cause police departments to deliberately keep their officers ignorant are thus unfounded....

Petitioner's claim that police negligence automatically triggers suppression cannot be squared with the principles underlying the exclusionary rule, as they have been explained in our cases. In light of our repeated holdings that the deterrent effect of suppression must be substantial and outweigh any harm to the justice system, we conclude that when police mistakes are the result of negligence such as that described here, rather than systemic error or reckless disregard of constitutional requirements, any marginal deterrence does not "pay its way." In such a case, the criminal should not "go free because the constable has blundered...."

Justice GINSBURG, with whom Justice STEVENS, Justice SOUTER, and Justice BREYER join, dissenting.

...The Court states that the exclusionary rule is not a defendant's right; rather, it is simply a remedy applicable only when suppression would result in appreciable deterrence that outweighs the cost to the justice system. The Court's discussion invokes a view of the exclusionary rule famously held by renowned jurist[] Henry J. Friendly.... "The sole reason for exclusion," Friendly wrote, "is that experience has demonstrated this to be the only effective method for deterring the police from violating the Constitution." He thought it excessive, in light of the rule's aim to deter police conduct, to require exclusion when the constable had merely "blundered"—when a police officer committed a technical error in an on-the-spot judgment or made a "slight and unintentional miscalculation." As the Court recounts, Judge Friendly suggested that deterrence of police improprieties could be "sufficiently accomplished" by confining the rule to "evidence obtained by flagrant or deliberate violation of rights."

Others have described "a more majestic conception" of the Fourth Amendment and its adjunct, the exclusionary rule. Protective of the fundamental "right of the people to be secure in their persons, houses, papers, and effects," the Amendment "is a constraint on the power of the sovereign, not merely on some of its agents." I share that vision of the Amendment.

The exclusionary rule is "a remedy necessary to ensure that" the Fourth Amendment's prohibitions "are observed in fact." The rule's service as an essential auxiliary to the Amendment earlier inclined the Court to hold the two inseparable.

Beyond doubt, a main objective of the rule "is to deter—to compel respect for the constitutional guaranty in the only effectively available way—by removing the incentive to disregard it." *Elkins v. United States*, 364 U.S. 206, 217 (1960). But the rule also serves other important purposes: It "enabl[es] the judiciary to avoid the taint of partnership in official lawlessness," and it "assur[es] the people—all potential victims of unlawful government conduct—that the government would not profit from its lawless behavior, thus minimizing the risk of seriously undermining popular trust in government."

The exclusionary rule, it bears emphasis, is often the only remedy effective to redress a Fourth Amendment violation. Civil liability will not lie for "the vast majority of [F]ourth [A]mendment violations—the frequent infringements motivated by commendable zeal, not condemnable malice." Criminal prosecutions or administrative sanctions against the offending officers and injunctive relief against widespread violations are an even farther cry.

The Court maintains that Herring's case is one in which the exclusionary rule could have scant deterrent effect and therefore would not "pay its way." I disagree.

The exclusionary rule, the Court suggests, is capable of only marginal deterrence when the misconduct at issue is merely careless, not intentional or reckless. The suggestion runs counter to a foundational premise of tort law—that liability for negligence, i.e., lack of due care, creates an incentive to act with greater care. The Government so acknowledges....

Is the potential deterrence here worth the costs it imposes? In light of the paramount importance of accurate recordkeeping in law enforcement, I would answer yes.... Electronic databases form the nervous system of contemporary criminal justice operations.... The risk of error stemming from these databases is not slim. Herring's amici warn that law enforcement databases are insufficiently monitored and often out of date. Government reports describe, for example, flaws in NCIC databases, terrorist watchlist databases, and databases associated with the Federal Government's employment eligibility verification system. Inaccuracies in expansive, interconnected collections of electronic information raise grave concerns for individual liberty....

The Court assures that "exclusion would certainly be justified" if "the police have been shown to be reckless in maintaining a warrant system, or to have knowingly made false entries to lay the groundwork for future false arrests." This concession provides little comfort.

> First, by restricting suppression to bookkeeping errors that are deliberate or reckless, the majority leaves Herring, and others like him, with no remedy for violations of their constitutional rights.... Second, I doubt that police forces already possess sufficient incentives to maintain up-to-date records.... Third, even when deliberate or reckless conduct is afoot, the Court's assurance will often be an empty promise: How is an impecunious defendant to make the required showing? If the answer is that a defendant is entitled to discovery (and if necessary, an audit of police databases), then the Court has imposed a considerable administrative burden on courts and law enforcement....

NOTES & QUESTIONS ON GOOD FAITH

1. *Reasonable reliance on case law.* What if the police officer conducts the arrest on the basis of case law that is subsequently overruled? In that situation, should the trial court exclude evidence flowing from the illegal arrest? Or does the good faith exception suggest that the evidence should be admitted at trial? Consider, first, the underlying rationale behind the exclusionary rule, which is deterrence. If the police officer is acting in good faith on precedent, this seems to suggest that deterrence (and the exclusionary rule) ought to have no role to play in the situation. In this vein, consider *United States v. McCane*, 573 F.3d 1037 (10th Cir. 2009). In *McCane*, a police officer in Oklahoma pulled over a vehicle suspected of drunken driving and other traffic violations. The officer arrested McCane, handcuffed him, then placed him in the back of his police cruiser. At this point, the police officer searched the vehicle and found an illegal firearm. McCane was charged with being a felon in possession of a firearm, a federal offense. Subsequently, the Supreme Court decided *Arizona v. Gant,* 556 U.S. 332, which held that the search incident to arrest exception to the warrant requirement did not apply when suspects are handcuffed and not capable of reaching back into the car. The question for McCane's case is whether the police officer acted in good faith, given that *Gant* had not yet been decided. On appeal, the Tenth Circuit concluded that the good faith exception should apply and the evidence could be admitted at trial, because "excluding evidence based on judicial error would serve no deterrent purpose." 573 F.3d at 1045. The Supreme Court adopted the same position in *Davis v. United States*, 564 U.S. 229 (2011).

2. *Totality of the circumstances.* What is the standard for determining whether a police officer acted in good faith? The majority adopts a standard that basically tracks a "totality of the circumstances" test. Do you agree that this is the correct standard?

STATE LAW REQUIREMENTS

Although the Constitution does not require state courts to exclude evidence collected during a police officer's good faith violation of the Fourth Amendment, states are certainly free to adopt a more restrictive approach. Some states have done precisely this and direct their state courts to exclude such evidence. For example, in *Commonwealth v. Johnson,* 624 Pa. 325, 327, 86 A.3d 182, 184 (2014), the Supreme Court of Pennsylvania ruled that the good faith exception did not apply under Article I, Section 8 of the Pennsylvania Constitution. *Johnson* involved a police officer who conducted an arrest based on an expired arrest warrant, though the police officer acted in good faith at the time of the arrest and reasonably believed that the warrant was valid. Nonetheless, the Pennsylvania Supreme Court ruled that the evidence should be suppressed by virtue of state law because doing so would vindicate the privacy interests of Pennsylvania citizens and also serve a general deterrence rationale.

Similarly, in *People v. Bigelow,* 488 N.E.2d 451 (N.Y. 1985), the New York Court of Appeals also rejected the good faith exception, ruling that excluding evidence in these cases *could* deter police misconduct. In *Bigelow,* the defendant was stopped in his vehicle. The police seized the vehicle and after a search warrant was issued by a magistrate, found contraband drugs, leading to a conviction for possession of a controlled substance. However, the search warrant, though facially valid, was invalidated after the arrest because it was not supported by probable cause; it was based on an informant's tip and "the informant's statement contained no allegations indicating that the information was based upon personal observation." The New York Court of Appeals insisted that the resulting evidence required exclusion and declined to follow the U.S. Supreme Court in recognizing a good faith exception to the exclusionary rule. Instead, the court ruled that under the New York State Constitution, the evidence must be excluded from trial because "if the People are permitted to use the seized evidence, the exclusionary rule's purpose is completely frustrated, a premium is placed on the illegal police action and a positive incentive is provided to others to engage in similar lawless acts in the future." 488 N.E.2d, at 458.

The result of these state law–based decisions is that the federal rule imposes a constitutional minimum that states are free to supplement with additional protections, either by statute or by state constitutional interpretation. While states are not under a Fourth Amendment obligation to exclude evidence when the police acted in good faith, states are *permitted* to exclude that evidence should they desire to do so. One practical impact of these conflicting state-court decisions is that evidence that is admissible in federal court might be inadmissible in a state court prosecution by a local district attorney—depending on which state is prosecuting the crime. For more discussion, see Megan McGlynn, *Competing Exclusionary Rules in Multistate Investigations: Resolving Conflicts of State Search-and-Seizure Law,* 127 Yale L.J. 246 (2017).

5. Knock and Announce

The last category is unique in the sense that it targets an entire category of Fourth Amendment violations. The other exceptions to the exclusionary rule cut across the various requirements imposed by the Fourth Amendment. In contrast, the knock-and-announce requirement, as explored in prior chapters, is generally required by the Fourth Amendment for all warrants unless officers have reasonable suspicion of exigent circumstances, including destruction of evidence or a threat to human safety.

In the following case, the Supreme Court tackles the consequences of a knock-and-announce violation, i.e., whether the exclusionary rule should apply or not. Instead of articulating and adopting a standard to judge trial courts in their exercise of discretion, the Court instead adopts a blanket rule. As you read the case, look for the Court's rationale for why a blanket rule is appropriate in this context.

Hudson v. Michigan

Supreme Court of the United States
547 U.S. 586 (2006)

Justice Scalia delivered the opinion of the Court.

We decide whether violation of the "knock-and-announce" rule requires the suppression of all evidence found in the search.

I

Police obtained a warrant authorizing a search for drugs and firearms at the home of petitioner Booker Hudson. They discovered both. Large quantities of drugs were found, including cocaine rocks in Hudson's pocket. A loaded gun was lodged between the cushion and armrest of the chair in which he was sitting. Hudson was charged under Michigan law with unlawful drug and firearm possession.

This case is before us only because of the method of entry into the house. When the police arrived to execute the warrant, they announced their presence, but waited only a short time—perhaps "three to five seconds"—before turning the knob of the unlocked front door and entering Hudson's home. Hudson moved to suppress all the inculpatory evidence, arguing that the premature entry violated his Fourth Amendment rights....

II

The common-law principle that law enforcement officers must announce their presence and provide residents an opportunity to open the door is an ancient one. Since 1917, when Congress passed the Espionage Act, this traditional protection has been part of federal statutory law and is currently codified at 18 U.S.C. § 3109.... [I]n *Wilson*, we were asked whether the rule was also a command of the Fourth Amendment. Tracing its origins in our English legal heritage, we concluded that it was. 514 U.S., at 931-936.

We recognized that the new constitutional rule we had announced is not easily applied. *Wilson* and cases following it have noted the many situations in which it is not necessary to knock and announce. It is not necessary when "circumstances presen[t] a threat of physical violence," or if there is "reason to believe that evidence would likely be destroyed if advance notice were given," or if knocking and announcing would be "futile." We require only that police "have a reasonable suspicion... under the particular circumstances" that one of these grounds for failing to knock and announce exists, and we have acknowledged that "[t]his showing is not high."

When the knock-and-announce rule does apply, it is not easy to determine precisely what officers must do. How many seconds' wait are too few? Our "reasonable wait time" standard is necessarily vague. *Banks* (a drug case, like this one) held that the proper measure was not how long it would take the resident to reach the door, but how long it would take to dispose of the suspected drugs—but that such a time (15 to 20 seconds in that case) would necessarily be extended when, for instance, the suspected contraband was not easily concealed. If our ex post evaluation is subject to such calculations, it is unsurprising that, ex ante, police officers about to encounter someone who may try to harm them will be uncertain how long to wait.

Happily, these issues do not confront us here. From the trial level onward, Michigan has conceded that the entry was a knock-and-announce violation. The issue here is remedy. *Wilson* specifically declined to decide whether the exclusionary rule is appropriate for violation of the knock-and-announce requirement. That question is squarely before us now.

III

... [E]xclusion may not be premised on the mere fact that a constitutional violation was a "but-for" cause of obtaining evidence. Our cases show that but-for causality is only a necessary, not a sufficient, condition for suppression. In this case, of course, the constitutional violation of an illegal manner of entry was not a but-for cause of obtaining the evidence. Whether that preliminary misstep had occurred or not, the police would have executed the warrant they had obtained, and would have discovered the gun and drugs inside the house. But even if the illegal entry here could be characterized as a but-for cause of discovering what was inside, we have "never held that evidence is fruit of the poisonous tree simply because it would not have come to light but for the illegal actions of the police." Rather, but-for cause, or "causation in the logical sense alone" can be too attenuated to justify exclusion....

Attenuation can occur, of course, when the causal connection is remote. Attenuation also occurs when, even given a direct causal connection, the interest protected by the constitutional guarantee that has been violated would not be served by suppression of the evidence obtained. "The penalties visited upon the Government, and in turn upon the public, because its officers have violated the law must bear some relation to the purposes which the law is to serve."... [C]ases excluding the fruits of unlawful warrantless searches say nothing about the appropriateness of exclusion to vindicate the interests protected by the knock-and-announce requirement. Until a valid warrant has issued, citizens are entitled to shield "their persons, houses, papers, and effects" from the government's scrutiny. Exclusion of the evidence obtained by a warrantless search vindicates that entitlement. The interests protected by the knock-and-announce requirement are quite different—and do not include the shielding of potential evidence from the government's eyes.

One of those interests is the protection of human life and limb, because an unannounced entry may provoke violence in supposed self-defense by the surprised resident. Another interest is the protection of property. Breaking a house (as the old cases typically put it) absent an announcement would penalize someone who "did not know of the process, of which, if he had notice, it is to be presumed that he would obey it. . . ." The knock-and-announce rule gives individuals "the opportunity to comply with the law and to avoid the destruction of property occasioned by a forcible entry." And thirdly, the knock-and-announce rule protects those elements of privacy and dignity that can be destroyed by a sudden entrance. It gives residents the "opportunity to prepare themselves for" the entry of the police. "The brief interlude between announcement and entry with a warrant may be the opportunity that an individual has to pull on clothes or get out of bed." In other words, it assures the opportunity to collect oneself before answering the door.

What the knock-and-announce rule has never protected, however, is one's interest in preventing the government from seeing or taking evidence described in a warrant. Since the interests that were violated in this case have nothing to do with the seizure of the evidence, the exclusionary rule is inapplicable.

Quite apart from the requirement of unattenuated causation, the exclusionary rule has never been applied except "where its deterrence benefits outweigh its substantial social costs." The costs here are considerable. In addition to the grave adverse consequence that exclusion of relevant incriminating evidence always entails (viz., the risk of releasing dangerous criminals into society), imposing that massive remedy for a knock-and-announce violation would generate a constant flood of alleged failures to observe the rule. . . . The cost of entering this lottery would be small, but the jackpot enormous. . . .

Another consequence of the incongruent remedy Hudson proposes would be police officers' refraining from timely entry after knocking and announcing. As we have observed, the amount of time they must wait is necessarily uncertain. If the consequences of running afoul of the rule were so massive, officers would be inclined to wait longer than the law requires—producing preventable violence against officers in some cases, and the destruction of evidence in many others. We deemed these consequences severe enough to produce our unanimous agreement that a mere "reasonable suspicion" that knocking and announcing "under the particular circumstances, would be dangerous or futile, or that it would inhibit the effective investigation of the crime," will cause the requirement to yield.

Next to these "substantial social costs" we must consider the deterrence benefits, existence of which is a necessary condition for exclusion.... To begin with, the value of deterrence depends upon the strength of the incentive to commit the forbidden act. Viewed from this perspective, deterrence of knock-and-announce violations is not worth a lot. Violation of the warrant requirement sometimes produces incriminating evidence that could not otherwise be obtained. But ignoring knock-and-announce can realistically be expected to achieve absolutely nothing except the prevention of destruction of evidence and the avoidance of life-threatening resistance by occupants of the premises—dangers which, if there is even "reasonable suspicion" of their existence, suspend the knock-and-announce requirement anyway. Massive deterrence is hardly required....

We cannot assume that exclusion in this context is necessary deterrence simply because we found that it was necessary deterrence in different contexts and long ago. That would be forcing the public today to pay for the sins and inadequacies of a legal regime that existed almost half a century ago. Dollree Mapp could not turn to 42 U.S.C. § 1983, for meaningful relief; *Monroe v. Pape*, 365 U.S. 167 (1961), which began the slow but steady expansion of that remedy, was decided the same Term as *Mapp*. It would be another 17 years before the § 1983 remedy was extended to reach the deep pocket of municipalities. Citizens whose Fourth Amendment rights were violated by federal officers could not bring suit until 10 years after *Mapp*, with this Court's decision in *Bivens v. Six Unknown Fed. Narcotics Agents*, 403 U.S. 388 (1971)....

Another development over the past half-century that deters civil-rights violations is the increasing professionalism of police forces, including a new emphasis on internal police discipline.... Failure to teach and enforce constitutional requirements exposes municipalities to financial liability. Moreover, modern police forces are staffed with professionals; it is not credible to assert that internal discipline, which can limit successful careers, will not have a deterrent effect. There is also evidence that the increasing use of various forms of citizen review can enhance police accountability.

In sum, the social costs of applying the exclusionary rule to knock-and-announce violations are considerable; the incentive to such violations is minimal to begin with, and the extant deterrences against them are substantial—incomparably greater than the factors deterring warrantless entries when *Mapp* was decided. Resort to the massive remedy of suppressing evidence of guilt is unjustified....

Justice BREYER, with whom Justice STEVENS, Justice SOUTER, and Justice GINSBURG join, dissenting.

II

...[T]he driving legal purpose underlying the exclusionary rule, namely, the deterrence of unlawful government behavior, argues strongly for suppression. In *Weeks*, *Silverthorne*, and *Mapp*, the Court based its holdings requiring suppression of unlawfully obtained evidence upon the recognition that admission of that evidence would seriously undermine the Fourth Amendment's promise. All three cases recognized that failure to apply the exclusionary rule would make that promise a hollow one, reducing it to "a form of words," "of no value" to those whom it seeks to protect. Indeed, this Court in *Mapp* held that the exclusionary rule applies to the States in large part due to its belief that alternative state mechanisms for enforcing the Fourth Amendment's guarantees had proved "worthless and futile."

Why is application of the exclusionary rule any the less necessary here? Without such a rule, as in *Mapp*, police know that they can ignore the Constitution's requirements without risking suppression of evidence discovered after an unreasonable entry. As in *Mapp*, some government officers will find it easier, or believe it less risky, to proceed with what they consider a necessary search immediately and without the requisite constitutional (say, warrant or knock-and-announce) compliance.

Of course, the State or the Federal Government may provide alternative remedies for knock-and-announce violations. But that circumstance was true of *Mapp* as well. What reason is there to believe that those remedies (such as private damages actions under 42 U.S.C. § 1983), which the Court found inadequate in *Mapp*, can adequately deter unconstitutional police behavior here?...

To argue, as the majority does, that new remedies, such as 42 U.S.C. § 1983 actions or better trained police, make suppression unnecessary is to argue that *Wolf*, not *Mapp*, is now the law. To argue that there may be few civil suits because violations may produce nothing "more than nominal injury" is to confirm, not to deny, the inability of civil suits to deter violations. And to argue without evidence (and despite myriad reported cases of violations, no reported case of civil damages, and Michigan's concession of their nonexistence) that civil suits may provide deterrence because claims may "have been settled" is, perhaps, to search in desperation for an argument. Rather, the majority, as it candidly admits, has simply "assumed" that, "[a]s far as [it] know[s], civil liability is an effective deterrent," a support-free assumption that *Mapp* and subsequent cases make clear does not embody the Court's normal approach to difficult questions of Fourth Amendment law.

It is not surprising, then, that after looking at virtually every pertinent Supreme Court case decided since *Weeks*, I can find no precedent that might offer the majority support for its contrary conclusion. The Court has, of course, recognized that not every Fourth Amendment violation necessarily triggers the exclusionary rule. But the class of Fourth Amendment violations that do not result in suppression of the evidence seized, however, is limited. The Court has declined to apply the exclusionary rule only: (1) where there is a specific reason to believe that application of the rule would "not result in appreciable deterrence," or (2) where admissibility in proceedings other than criminal trials was at issue.

Neither of these two exceptions applies here. The second does not apply because this case is an ordinary criminal trial. The first does not apply because (1) officers who violate the rule are not acting "as a reasonable officer would and should act in similar circumstances," (2) this case does not involve government employees other than police, and (3), most importantly, the key rationale for any exception, "lack of deterrence," is missing. That critical latter rationale, which underlies every exception, does not apply here, as there is no reason to think that, in the case of knock-and-announce violations by the police, "the exclusion of evidence at trial would not sufficiently deter future errors," or "further the ends of the exclusionary rule in any appreciable way."...

NOTES & QUESTIONS ON KNOCK AND ANNOUNCE

1. *Attenuation.* Among other things, Justice Scalia's majority opinion argues that there is insufficient causal connection between the illegally seized evidence and the original Fourth Amendment violation in knock-and-announce situations. Does this suggest that the knock-and-announce exception owes its birth to the attenuation of the taint exception? Scalia notes that but-for causation is a necessary but not sufficient condition for exclusion, and then goes on to note that "[w]hether that preliminary misstep had occurred or not, the police would have executed the warrant they had obtained, and would have discovered the gun and drugs inside the house." Does this bring to mind another exception to the exclusionary rule? Does it suggest a conceptual connection between the knock-and-announce exception and the inevitable discovery doctrine? If the evidence would have been located and seized by the police if the officers had knocked and announced their presence, then in some sense the evidence would have been inevitably discovered. This appeal to the abstract principle of inevitable discovery operates in the background to justify the creation of a new exclusionary rule exception.

2. *Alternative remedies.* What alternative remedies other than exclusion exist to ensure that police officers comply with the knock-and-announce

requirement? The majority notes in particular one important remedy: the victim's ability to file a private suit for money damages under 42 U.S.C. § 1983. Is this possibility enough to deter the behavior of rogue police officers who might ignore the knock-and-announce requirement? Do all residents have access to the legal resources to file a section 1983 action against the police? How many residents are even aware that a private right of action exists for police misconduct in such cases? For a discussion, see Brian S. Uholik, *Who Cares If It's Open?:* Hudson v. Michigan *and the United States Supreme Court's Evisceration of the Knock and Announce Rule,* 112 Penn St. L. Rev. 261, 287 (2007) (concluding that Scalia's argument about the success of 1983 actions "strikes an optimistic tone" but is "founded on little more than assumption").

STATE LAW REQUIREMENTS

Several states have declined to follow the Supreme Court's lead in crafting a knock-and-announce exception to the exclusionary rule. For example, in ***State v. Cable,*** 51 So. 3d 434, 435 (Fla. 2010), the Supreme Court of Florida ruled that violations of the knock-and-announce requirement would require exclusion from trials in state court. The Florida court took notice of the U.S. Supreme Court's holding in *Hudson* and was unpersuaded.

Florida has a knock-and-announce statute but it does not explicitly deal with the question of consequences: "(1) If a peace officer fails to gain admittance after she or he has announced her or his authority and purpose in order to make an arrest either by a warrant or when authorized to make an arrest for a felony without a warrant, the officer may use all necessary and reasonable force to enter any building or property where the person to be arrested is or is reasonably believed to be." Fla. Stat. § 901.19. Before the Supreme Court decided *Hudson,* Florida courts routinely excluded evidence gathered from knock-and-announce violations.

In ***Cable,*** Florida was confronted with the question of whether *Hudson* was binding on state courts and concluded that "[a]s a matter of state law, a state may provide a remedy for violations of state knock-and-announce statutes, and nothing in *Hudson* prohibits it from doing so." As for its reasoning, the Supreme Court of Florida noted that "without a basis in the statute for civil remedies, and because of the difficulties faced by a defendant seeking to recover money damages for a statutory violation against the police, we are concerned that the important values represented by the knock-and-announce statute, which is based on common law origins, would be undermined if the exclusionary rule did not apply to its violation." 51 So. 3d at 443.

For a contrary ruling, see ***State v. Bembry,*** 151 Ohio St. 3d 502, 509, 90 N.E.3d 891, 898 (2017) (concluding that the exclusionary rule is not an appropriate remedy under Ohio law for knock-and-announce violations because "[s]uppressing evidence found during a warranted search of a home will not heal a physical injury, fix a door, or undo the shock of embarrassment when police enter without notice of their presence and purpose"). The Supreme Court of Ohio also suggested that there was little possibility for effective deterrence because "[t]here is minimal incentive to violate the knock-and-announce principle in the first place, and the rule gives way in the name of safety, investigative necessity, or futility" and "[t]here is a danger that the risk of suppression would dissuade police from risking a knock-and-announce violation in exigent circumstances."

F. PRACTICE & POLICY

The following materials take a deeper dive into the conceptual underpinnings of the exclusionary rule. The cases discussed above raised questions about the ultimate goal that the rule was supposed to accomplish, but often with little hard data or sustained reflection about whether the exclusionary rule can really accomplish the tasks it is assigned. So, this last section explicitly considers: (i) the law and economics model underpinning suppression, (ii) the empirical evidence for deterrence, (iii) the risk of perjury, and (iv) alternative approaches for deterring Fourth Amendment violations.

A law and economics approach to the exclusionary rule. Which framework should courts adopt to analyze the scope of the exclusionary rule and determine which exceptions, if any, should be recognized? One possible approach is to use the tools from economics to model the incentives created by the rule in order to determine whether the legal system's goal is likely to be maximized by suppressing at trial illegally obtained evidence. This approach focuses on the incentives that the rule gives to police officers and when the possibility of suppression will alter their behavior. As one law and economics scholar noted, the deterrence value of the exclusionary rule is impacted by a selection bias that prevents the identification of costs and benefits of the rule, simply because "[t]he impact of the rule is felt when the police fail to arrest, or prosecutors fail to prosecute, in anticipation of future exercise of the rule. . . . Exclusionary rule precedent is thus developed without the courts ever seeing all of the instances that the Amendment was primarily designed to protect: preventing police harassment of innocent citizens." Tonja Jacobi, *The Law and Economics of the Exclusionary Rule*, 87 Notre Dame L. Rev. 585, 596-97, 599 (2011). See also Hugo M. Mialon & Sue H. Mialon, *The Effects of the Fourth Amendment: An Economic Analysis*, 24 J.L. Econ. & Org. 22 (2008). These results will not be counted in court or litigation records. Based on a model, Jacobi concluded that "[t]he intended effect of the exclusionary rule will only work under very strict assumptions about police incentives. When the odds of successful search and admissibility are 50:50, the rule will have no effect unless the police care three times as much about admission than they do about letting a criminal escape with contraband they believe he probably possesses."

There is also a substantial risk of overdeterrence. In addition to the risk that the exclusionary rule will under-deter police misconduct, there is also the risk that the exclusionary risk will inappropriately deter police searches that are justified by exigent circumstances. The theory here is that some police officers will envision that their search or seizure might be questioned by a court and the evidence suppressed, leading the officer to either forgo the investigatory opportunity entirely or require a warrant to conduct a search when the Fourth Amendment would permit a warrantless search. Consequently, the question of deterrence shows up as both a cost and a benefit in the model. The benefit is that police misconduct will be deterred. The cost is that some guilty individuals will be acquitted (or not even charged) when evidence is suppressed. In addition, however, some individuals will not be charged because an over-cautious police officer fails to conduct a search or seizure under the false belief that suppression would result from the action. The question is whether both of these costs, taken together, are outweighed by the benefits, which include greater police fidelity to the Fourth Amendment in future cases. See William J. Stuntz, *The Virtues and Vices of the Exclusionary Rule*, 20 Harv. J.L. & Pub. Pol'y 443, 445 (1997). However, at least some scholars have questioned whether overdeterrence is really a problem. See, e.g., Donald Dripps, *The Fourth Amendment, the Exclusionary Rule, and the Roberts Court: Normative and Empirical Dimensions of the Over-Deterrence Hypothesis*, 85 Chi.-Kent L. Rev. 209, 238 (2010) (concluding that "the available empirical evidence suggests that the current remedial mix is not over-deterring Fourth Amendment violations" and "when opportunity cost and the risk of tort damages are both low, the current mix is probably under-deterring, perhaps substantially"). Furthermore, some scholars reject the notion that freeing individuals should be considered a cost of the exclusionary rule rather than simply a cost of the Fourth Amendment. See Dallin H. Oaks, *Studying the Exclusionary Rule in Search and Seizure*, 37 U. Chi. L. Rev. 665, 754 (1970) ("Police officials and prosecutors should stop claiming that the exclusionary rule prevents effective law enforcement. In doing so they attribute far greater effect to the exclusionary rule than the evidence warrants, and they also are in the untenable position of urging that the sanctions be abolished so that they can continue to violate the rules with impunity.").

❧ **The empirical evidence of deterrence.** In addition to producing an abstract model using the tools of economics, psychologists and criminologists have conducted empirical studies to determine whether the exclusionary rule in fact deters the police from violating the Fourth Amendment. For example, one study examined Chicago police officers engaged in narcotics investigations and found that the experience of defending their conduct during suppression hearings had caused police officers to be more cautious in their approach, and to more often seek warrants, than in the past. Myron W. Orfield, Jr., *The Exclusionary Rule and Deterrence: An Empirical Study of Chicago Narcotics Officers*, 54 U. Chi. L. Rev. 1016 (1987). In particular, the study concluded that suppression hearings function as a form of "punishment" because the officer's conduct is effectively on trial, with the court passing judgment on the officer. Furthermore, multiple suppressions can result in an officer being transferred or demoted. Other studies using a survey method have found a deterrent effect at the level of police chiefs. See Christopher Totten, Sutham Cobkit (Cheurprakobkit), *The Knock-and-Announce Rule and Police Searches After* Hudson v. Michigan*: Can Alternative Deterrents Effectively Replace Exclusion for Rule Violations?*, 15 New Crim. L. Rev. 414, 456 (2012). However, Orfield's empirical results were based on surveys and interviews with police officers combined with an increase in the number of search warrants over time. Causality is inferred based on these data points, and it is always possible that police officers' self-assessment is not accurate. Other empirical studies have failed to find a meaningful deterrence effect or only a modest one.

Is it possible that the exclusionary rule could be empirically justified on grounds other than deterrence? In one study, researchers found support for the "integrity" justification for the rule that expresses the sentiment that using the fruits of an illegal search would threaten the integrity or legitimacy of the judicial proceedings. An experimental test "demonstrated that being induced to use evidence that was produced from a police officer's racially-motivated search caused participants not only to feel bad (upset, guilty, dissatisfied and less certain of the justness of their actions), but also to experience a literal sensation of dirtiness. These findings are consistent with the idea that people value the exclusionary rule for its ability to maintain the integrity of the courts." See Kenworthey Bilz, *Dirty Hands or Deterrence? An Experimental Examination of the Exclusionary Rule*, 9 J. Empirical Legal Stud. 149 (2012). This suggests that even if the exclusionary rule fails to deter future police misconduct, it could be justified because failure to suppress tainted evidence would cause the public to question the legitimacy of the legal system. This finding suggests that the entire focus on deterrence in the exclusionary rule jurisprudence—to the exclusion of other justifications—is misguided.

The risk of perjury. Strictly speaking, the looming possibility of a suppression hearing is supposed to prevent the police from violating the Fourth Amendment. But there is a third strategy, which is for the police to conceal the constitutional violation from the court, thus avoiding the constraints of the constitutional rule while at the same time allowing the use of evidence at trial. As noted above, some judges have worried that the exclusionary rule does more to encourage perjury than it does to deter police misconduct. In response, several researchers have tried to test this hypothesis. In one well-known study, a researcher concluded that the perjury problem was not just with police officers but that judges were also complicit in the problem. See Myron W. Orfield, Jr., *Deterrence, Perjury, and the Heater Factor: An Exclusionary Rule in the Chicago Criminal*

Courts, 63 U. Colo. L. Rev. 75, 76 (1992) ("This study demonstrates that judges in Chicago often knowingly credit police perjury and distort the meaning of the law to prevent the suppression of evidence and assure conviction."). Another study used embedded observers who rode with police units instead of relying on surveys or interviews with police officers. With this technique, the study could identify situations of perjury or lack of candor in police paperwork. Jerome H. Skolnick, *Justice Without Trial: Law Enforcement in a Democratic Society* 215 (3d ed. 1966). Skolnick's study found that up to a third of searches violated the Fourth Amendment and that the exclusionary rule failed to deter police; instead it encouraged perjury and other forms of deception. While it is unclear if the risk of perjury is significant enough to outweigh the benefits of deterrence, these findings certainly suggest that the risk of perjury is actual as opposed to hypothetical.

Alternative remedies to the exclusionary rule. Part of the justification for the exclusionary rule is that no other adequate remedy is available, thus making suppression the only game in town. Justice Murphy once famously stated that "there is but one alternative to the rule of exclusion. That is no sanction at all." *Wolf v. People of the State of Colo.*, 338 U.S. 25, 41 (1949). This suggests that there really is no alternative remedy for dealing with Fourth Amendment violations. This, of course, is an exaggeration, since victims of police misconduct can file civil suits against police officers who engage in misconduct; conversely, suppression of evidence is hardly a perfect solution either. As several jurists have noted, the "remedy" of suppression is not ideal, not only because it imposes a high toll on the community but also because it arguably does not make the victim of the police misconduct whole again. So, the question is whether alternative remedies might be more direct and successful in remediating the harm of police misconduct. The most obvious alternative is private suits for money damages against government officials under 42 U.S.C. § 1983, which states:

> Every person who, under color of any statute, ordinance, regulation, custom, or usage, of any State or Territory or the District of Columbia, subjects, or causes to be subjected, any citizen of the United States or other person within the jurisdiction thereof to the deprivation of any rights, privileges, or immunities secured by the Constitution and laws, shall be liable to the party injured in an action at law, suit in equity, or other proper proceeding for redress....

If the Fourth Amendment violation is conducted by federal agents (as opposed to state officers), a similar suit for money damages can be brought pursuant to *Bivens v. Six Unknown Named Agents of Fed. Bureau of Narcotics*, 403 U.S. 388, 389 (1971).

The problem with section 1983 or *Bivens* actions is that they are imperfect remedies for asserting Fourth Amendment claims and deterring police misconduct. However, it is important to correctly identify the nature of the deficiency. In an empirical study of all section 1983 actions filed in a two-year period in the Central District of California, Professor Ted Eisenberg concluded that section 1983 actions were not overwhelming federal courts, nor were the cases pursuing trivial constitutional claims—a frequent complaint about section 1983 actions. Theodore Eisenberg, *Section 1983: Doctrinal Foundations and an Empirical Study,* 67 Cornell L. Rev. 482, 484 (1982). The real problem is that section 1983 actions too often fail to yield liability and damages that will change state behavior. For multiple reasons, meritorious actions either are not filed in the first instance or do not individually punish the officers involved. For example, courts are often very generous in how they understand the qualified immunity that state actors are entitled to in these actions.

Consequently, one legal scholar proposed the following changes to section 1983 actions that would make them more effective than the current exclusionary rule:

> [A] regime that directly sanctions officers and their departments is preferable to the rule. Although there are many versions of such a regime, it should have several core components: (1) a liquidated damages/penalty for all unconstitutional actions, preferably based on the average officer's salary; (2) personal liability, at the liquidated damages sum, of officers who knowingly or recklessly violate the Fourth Amendment; (3) entity liability, at the liquidated damages sum, for all other violations; (4) state-paid legal assistance for those with Fourth Amendment claims; and (5) a judicial decisionmaker.

Christopher Slobogin, *Why Liberals Should Chuck the Exclusionary Rule*, 1999 U. Ill. L. Rev. 363, 442. Unfortunately, key elements of this plan, including state-paid legal assistance for plaintiffs filing civil suits asserting Fourth Amendment violations, are unlikely to materialize anytime soon. Although state-paid legal assistance is constitutionally required in criminal cases, there is no similar requirement for *civil* cases and state legislatures are notoriously unwilling to devote state financial resources to these efforts. This stands in marked contrast to some European countries where state-funded legal assistance is available not only in criminal cases but also in civil suits that are filed against the government. In the absence of this ideal civil litigation system, perhaps the exclusionary rule remains the best option in an imperfect world.

PART III

THE FIFTH AND SIXTH AMENDMENTS: DUE PROCESS AND COUNSEL

CHAPTER 7

SELF-INCRIMINATION AND THE FIFTH AMENDMENT

INTRODUCTION

The Fifth Amendment states, among other things, that no person "shall be compelled in any criminal case to be a witness against himself." For this reason, the state cannot force or "compel" a defendant to testify at his own trial; giving testimony is a right (recognized ever since *Ferguson v. Georgia*) but not a requirement. From this one simple example, several observations are in order.

First, the right not to give testimony against oneself is generally labeled as a privilege against self-incrimination. Though the text of the Fifth Amendment does not use the term self-incrimination, the phrase is useful because it brings to the forefront the interest protected by this clause of the Fifth Amendment: an individual's interest in not doing anything that will serve to incriminate himself or herself. Dwelling for a moment on the notion of *incrimination* will help scope out the various doctrinal issues that have faced courts in giving teeth to the Fifth Amendment. If, for example, the witness has received immunity from prosecution and therefore cannot incriminate himself in a way that will generate criminal responsibility, the Fifth Amendment will not prohibit a judge from forcing the witness to testify under the threat of contempt for failing to do so. Also, what are the ways that a witness might incriminate himself? By testifying, certainly. Along the way, however, litigants also have asserted a Fifth Amendment right to be free from various bodily intrusions (blood tests, DNA samples, etc.), or subpoenas for documents, in each case meeting with very limited success because the act must be *testimonial* in order to be protected by the Fifth Amendment right against self-incrimination.

Second, the privilege against self-incrimination applies not just at trial or in other judicial proceedings but also more importantly in less formal encounters with government authorities, to include other types of hearings or proceedings, and also interrogations by police. In fact, it is in the context of police interrogation where the rubber normally meets the road for the privilege against self-incrimination. Every day, thousands of suspects across the country are questioned by police, and many are taken into custody and brought to police stations by local police detectives investigating everything from narcotics violations to murder. As will become clear, sometimes just answering the police question is sufficient proof that the suspect waived his privilege not to; but in many situations, the prosecution must prove "something more" than just answering to establish a waiver of the privilege allowing introduction of the statement as evidence against the suspect brought to trial. And while forensic evidence may play a role in the most serious of violent felonies, the most important step in any police investigation is most likely to be an interview with the suspect(s). The following sections will begin to answer the key questions regarding the structure of this most consequential encounter with state authority: When must the prosecution establish that investigators obtained a valid *Miranda* waiver in order to be able to use the suspect's statement as evidence to prove guilt? If the right is triggered, when can questioning resume, if ever? Are there some situations when police may dispense with the notification requirement entirely?

Another key aspect of the investigative process is the right to counsel, which applies not only at trial but also during police interrogations. In addition to the right to counsel present during custodial interrogations that the *Miranda* Court held was part of the package of rights necessary to protect the Fifth Amendment privilege against compelled self-incrimination, there is also a Sixth Amendment right to counsel that applies during police interrogations of a suspect after he or she has been formally accused of a crime. For the sake of structure and clarity, the Sixth Amendment right to counsel during interrogations will be covered by Chapter 8. One of the challenges of confession admissibility analysis is distinguishing between the *Miranda* right to counsel and the Sixth Amendment right to counsel. Conceptually, it will help to distinguish between "suspects" and "defendants." A suspect is someone who the police are interested in but who has not yet been formally charged; a defendant is a suspect who has been formally charged. In this sense, all defendants are suspects, but not all suspects are defendants. The importance lies in the fact that the *Miranda* rule protects all suspects, but the Sixth Amendment right to counsel applies only to defendants, and only for questioning related to the charged offense.

The present chapter outlines the vast majority of the constitutional restrictions that restrain governmental conduct during police investigations. As you read the materials, think back to Herbert Packer's notion of the two models of the criminal process: due process and crime control. Notice the push and pull between the two interests and how the Supreme Court, and other legal actors, seek to accommodate these seemingly irreconcilable paradigms.

A. REQUIREMENTS FOR THE PRIVILEGE

The privilege of self-incrimination does not apply to every instance where evidence might be collected by the government. Nor does it apply to every statement that an individual might give to state officials. Over time, courts have limited the invocation of the privilege against self-incrimination to situations that: (i) involve the real possibility of incrimination; and (ii) involve a testimonial act. The following two sub-sections explain how courts understand these requirements and how they function to limit the Fifth Amendment privilege against self-incrimination.

1. Risk of Incrimination

The first requirement is somewhat obvious because it is implicit in the very notion of a privilege against self-*incrimination*. If the statement is not incriminating, the individual has no right to remain silent. Indeed, the only time when a statement will be incriminating is when it leads, either directly or indirectly, to evidence of criminal responsibility. Evidence of civil liability is not enough; the person asserting the privilege needs to have a reasonable fear of criminal liability. Nor will fear of foreign prosecution qualify. The invocation of the privilege might occur during interrogation, during the individual's criminal trial, appearing at the criminal trial of another, or even testifying during a civil trial or some other government hearing—as long as there is a reasonable fear of criminal liability.

The most common situation where the risk of incrimination is zero involves immunity from prosecution. If the witness has received immunity from prosecution, then their testimony would seem to be exempt from the risk of incrimination since the possibility of prosecution has been removed. However, two major questions remain. If state authorities confer immunity, can the witness invoke the privilege and refuse to testify based on a fear of federal prosecution if federal prosecutors have failed to confer immunity of their own? The answer to this question is an emphatic yes since the witness still faces a risk of incrimination and criminal exposure to another prosecutorial sovereign.

The second question is the one at issue in the following case. What type of immunity is sufficient to eliminate the risk of incrimination? In criminal practice, prosecutors typically confer one of two possible forms of immunity. So-called use immunity involves the promise not to use the defendant's testimony against him or her at a trial. In contrast, "transactional immunity" is far broader and represents a form of amnesty: The prosecutor promises not to charge the witness for any criminal transactions described by the witness during his or her testimony—a veritable get-out-of-jail-free card. Clearly, if the witness receives transactional immunity, there is no risk of incrimination and the privilege cannot be asserted. But what if the prosecutor simply offers use immunity? Can the witness still invoke the constitutional privilege and refuse to testify? In the following case, the Supreme Court answers this question.

Kastigar v. United States

Supreme Court of the United States
406 U.S. 441 (1972)

Mr. Justice POWELL delivered the opinion of the Court.

This case presents the question whether the United States Government may compel testimony from an unwilling witness, who invokes the Fifth Amendment privilege against compulsory self-incrimination, by conferring on the witness immunity from use of the compelled testimony in subsequent criminal proceedings, as well as immunity from use of evidence derived from the testimony.

Petitioners were subpoenaed to appear before a United States grand jury in the Central District of California on February 4, 1971. The Government believed that petitioners were likely to assert their Fifth Amendment privilege. Prior to the scheduled appearances, the Government applied to the District Court for an order directing petitioners to answer questions and produce evidence before the grand jury under a grant of immunity conferred pursuant to 18 U.S.C. §§ 6002, 6003. Petitioners opposed issuance of the order, contending primarily that the scope of the immunity provided by the statute was not coextensive with the scope of the privilege against self-incrimination, and therefore was not sufficient to supplant the privilege and compel their testimony. The District Court rejected this contention, and ordered petitioners to appear before the grand jury and answer its questions under the grant of immunity.

Petitioners appeared but refused to answer questions, asserting their privilege against compulsory self-incrimination. They were brought before the District Court, and each persisted in his refusal to answer the grand jury's questions, notwithstanding the grant of immunity. The court found both in contempt, and committed them to the custody of the Attorney General until either they answered the grand jury's questions or the term of the grand jury expired. The Court of Appeals for the Ninth Circuit affirmed. This Court granted certiorari to resolve the important question whether testimony may be compelled by granting immunity from the use of compelled testimony and evidence derived therefrom ("use and derivative use" immunity), or whether it is necessary to grant immunity from prosecution for offenses to which compelled testimony relates ("transactional" immunity).

I

The power of government to compel persons to testify in court or before grand juries and other governmental agencies is firmly established in Anglo-American jurisprudence. The power with respect to courts was established by statute in England as early as 1562, and Lord Bacon observed in 1612 that all subjects owed the King their "knowledge and discovery." While it is not clear when grand juries first resorted to compulsory process to secure the attendance and testimony of witnesses, the general common-law principle that "the public has a right to every man's evidence" was considered an "indubitable certainty" that "cannot be denied" by 1742. The power to compel testimony, and the corresponding duty to testify, are recognized in the Sixth Amendment requirements that an accused be confronted with the witnesses against him, and have compulsory process for obtaining witnesses in his favor. The first Congress recognized the testimonial duty in the Judiciary Act of 1789, which provided for compulsory attendance of witnesses in the federal courts. . . .

But the power to compel testimony is not absolute. There are a number of exemptions from the testimonial duty, the most important of which is the Fifth Amendment privilege against compulsory self-incrimination. The privilege reflects a complex of our fundamental values and aspirations, and marks an important advance in the development of our liberty. It can be asserted in any proceeding, civil or criminal, administrative or judicial, investigatory or adjudicatory; and it protects against any disclosures which the witness reasonably believes could be used in a criminal prosecution or could lead to other evidence that might be so used. This Court has been zealous to safeguard the values which underlie the privilege.

Immunity statutes, which have historical roots deep in Anglo-American jurisprudence, are not incompatible with these values. Rather, they seek a rational accommodation between the imperatives of the privilege and the legitimate demands of government to compel citizens to testify. The existence of these statutes reflects the importance of testimony, and the fact that many offenses are of such a character that the only persons capable of giving useful testimony are those implicated in the crime. Indeed, their origins were in the context of such offenses, and their primary use has been to investigate such offenses. Congress included immunity statutes in many of the regulatory measures adopted in the first half of this century. Indeed, prior to the enactment of the statute under consideration in this case, there were in force over 50 federal immunity statutes. In addition, every State in the Union, as well as the District of Columbia and Puerto Rico, has one or more such statutes. The commentators, and this Court on several occasions, have characterized immunity statutes as essential to the effective enforcement of various criminal statutes. . . .

III

Petitioners' second contention is that the scope of immunity provided by the federal witness immunity statute is not coextensive with the scope of the Fifth Amendment privilege against compulsory self-incrimination, and therefore is not sufficient to supplant the privilege and compel testimony over a claim of the privilege. The statute provides that when a witness is compelled by district court order to testify over a claim of the privilege:

> the witness may not refuse to comply with the order on the basis of his privilege against self-incrimination; but no testimony or other information compelled under the order (or any information directly or indirectly derived from such testimony or other information) may be used against the witness in any criminal case, except a prosecution for perjury, giving a false statement, or otherwise failing to comply with the order.

18 U.S.C. § 6002. The constitutional inquiry, rooted in logic and history, as well as in the decisions of this Court, is whether the immunity granted under this statute is coextensive with the scope of the privilege. If so, petitioners' refusals to answer based on the privilege were unjustified, and the judgments of contempt were proper, for the grant of immunity has removed the dangers against which the privilege protects. If, on the other hand, the immunity granted is not as comprehensive as the protection afforded by the privilege, petitioners were justified in refusing to answer, and the judgments of contempt must be vacated.

Petitioners draw a distinction between statutes that provide transactional immunity and those that provide, as does the statute before us, immunity from use and derivative use. They contend that a statute must at a minimum grant full transactional immunity in order to be coextensive with the scope of the privilege. In support of this contention, they rely on *Counselman v. Hitchcock*, 142 U.S. 547 (1892), the first case in which this Court considered a constitutional challenge to an immunity statute. The statute, a reenactment of the Immunity Act of 1868, provided that no "evidence obtained from a party or witness by means of a judicial proceeding . . . shall be given in evidence, or in any manner used against him . . . in any court of the United States. . . ." Notwithstanding a grant of immunity and order to testify under the revised 1868 Act, the witness, asserting his privilege against compulsory self-incrimination, refused to testify before a federal grand jury. He was consequently adjudged in contempt of court. On appeal, this Court construed the statute as affording a witness protection only against the use of the specific testimony compelled from him under the grant of immunity. This construction meant that the statute "could not, and would not, prevent the use of his testimony to search out other testimony to be used in evidence against him." Since the revised 1868 Act, as construed by the Court, would permit the use against the immunized witness of evidence derived from his compelled testimony, it did not protect the witness to the same extent that a claim of the privilege would protect him. Accordingly, under the principle that a grant of immunity cannot supplant the privilege, and is not sufficient to compel testimony over a claim of the privilege, unless the scope of the grant of immunity is coextensive with the scope of the privilege, the witness' refusal to testify was held proper. In the course of its opinion, the Court made the following statement, on which petitioners heavily rely:

> We are clearly of opinion that no statute which leaves the party or witness subject to prosecution after he answers the criminating question put to him, can have the effect of supplanting the privilege conferred by the Constitution of the United States. (The immunity statute under consideration) does not supply a complete protection from all the perils against which the constitutional prohibition was designed to guard, and is not a full substitute for that prohibition. In view of the constitutional provision, a statutory enactment, to be valid, must afford absolute immunity against future prosecution for the offence to which the question relates.

Sixteen days after the *Counselman* decision, a new immunity bill was introduced by Senator Cullom, who urged that enforcement of the Interstate Commerce Act would be impossible in the absence of an effective immunity statute. The bill, which became the Compulsory Testimony Act of 1893, was drafted specifically to meet the broad language in *Counselman* set forth above. The new Act removed the privilege against self-incrimination in hearings before the Interstate Commerce Commission and provided that: "no person shall be prosecuted or subjected to any penalty or forfeiture for or on account of any transaction, matter or thing, concerning which he may testify, or produce evidence, documentary or otherwise. . . ." Act of Feb. 11, 1893, 27 Stat. 444.

This transactional immunity statute became the basic form for the numerous federal immunity statutes until 1970, when, after re-examining applicable constitutional principles and the adequacy of existing law, Congress enacted the statute here under consideration. The new statute, which does not "afford (the) absolute immunity against future prosecution" referred to in *Counselman*, was drafted to meet what Congress judged to be the conceptual basis of *Counselman*, as elaborated in subsequent decisions of the Court, namely, that immunity from the use of compelled testimony and evidence derived therefrom is coextensive with the scope of the privilege.

The statute's explicit proscription of the use in any criminal case of "testimony or other information compelled under the order (or any information directly or indirectly derived from such testimony or other information)" is consonant with Fifth Amendment standards. We hold that such immunity from use and derivative use is coextensive with the scope of the privilege against self-incrimination, and therefore is sufficient to compel testimony over a claim of the privilege. While a grant of immunity must afford protection commensurate with that afforded by the privilege, it need not be broader. Transactional immunity, which accords full immunity from prosecution for the offense to which the compelled testimony relates, affords the witness considerably broader protection than does the Fifth Amendment privilege. The privilege has never been construed to mean that one who invokes it cannot subsequently be prosecuted. Its sole concern is to afford protection against being "forced to give testimony leading to the infliction of penalties affixed to . . . criminal acts." Immunity from the use of compelled testimony, as well as evidence derived directly and indirectly therefrom, affords this protection. It prohibits the prosecutorial authorities from using the compelled testimony in any respect, and it therefore insures that the testimony cannot lead to the infliction of criminal penalties on the witness.

Our holding is consistent with the conceptual basis of *Counselman*. The *Counselman* statute, as construed by the Court, was plainly deficient in its failure to prohibit the use against the immunized witness of evidence derived from his compelled testimony. . . . The basis of the Court's decision was recognized in *Ullmann v. United States*, 350 U.S. 422 (1956), in which the Court reiterated that the *Counselman* statute was insufficient: "because the immunity granted was incomplete, in that it merely forbade the use of the testimony given and failed to protect a witness from future prosecution based on knowledge and sources of information obtained from the compelled testimony." . . .

IV

Although an analysis of prior decisions and the purpose of the Fifth Amendment privilege indicates that use and derivative-use immunity is coextensive with the privilege, we must consider additional arguments advanced by petitioners against the sufficiency of such immunity. We start from the premise, repeatedly affirmed by this Court, that an appropriately broad immunity grant is compatible with the Constitution.

Petitioners argue that use and derivative-use immunity will not adequately protect a witness from various possible incriminating uses of the compelled testimony: for example, the prosecutor or other law enforcement officials may obtain leads, names of witnesses, or other information not otherwise available that might result in a prosecution. It will be difficult and perhaps impossible, the argument goes, to identify, by testimony or cross-examination, the subtle ways in which the compelled testimony may disadvantage a witness, especially in the jurisdiction granting the immunity.

This argument presupposes that the statute's prohibition will prove impossible to enforce. The statute provides a sweeping proscription of any use, direct or indirect, of the compelled testimony and any information derived therefrom: "(N)o testimony or other information compelled under the order (or any information directly or indirectly derived from such testimony or other information) may be used against the witness in any criminal case. . . ." 18 U.S.C. § 6002.

This total prohibition on use provides a comprehensive safeguard, barring the use of compelled testimony as an "investigatory lead," and also barring the use of any evidence obtained by focusing investigation on a witness as a result of his compelled disclosures. A person accorded this immunity under 18 U.S.C. § 6002, and subsequently prosecuted, is not dependent for the preservation of his rights upon the integrity and good faith of the prosecuting authorities. As stated in *Murphy*:

> Once a defendant demonstrates that he has testified, under a state grant of immunity, to matters related to the federal prosecution, the federal authorities have the burden of showing that their evidence is not tainted by establishing that they had an independent, legitimate source for the disputed evidence.

This burden of proof, which we reaffirm as appropriate, is not limited to a negation of taint; rather, it imposes on the prosecution the affirmative duty to prove that the evidence it proposes to use is derived from a legitimate source wholly independent of the compelled testimony.

This is very substantial protection, commensurate with that resulting from invoking the privilege itself. The privilege assures that a citizen is not compelled to incriminate himself by his own testimony. It usually operates to allow a citizen to remain silent when asked a question requiring an incriminatory answer. This statute, which operates after a witness has given incriminatory testimony, affords the same protection by assuring that the compelled testimony can in no way lead to the infliction of criminal penalties. The statute, like the Fifth Amendment, grants neither pardon nor amnesty. Both the statute and the Fifth Amendment allow the government to prosecute using evidence from legitimate independent sources.

The statutory proscription is analogous to the Fifth Amendment requirement in cases of coerced confessions. A coerced confession, as revealing of leads as testimony given in exchange for immunity, is inadmissible in a criminal trial, but it does not bar prosecution. Moreover, a defendant against whom incriminating evidence has been obtained through a grant of immunity may be in a stronger position at trial than a defendant who asserts a Fifth Amendment coerced-confession claim. One raising a claim under this statute need only show that he testified under a grant of immunity in order to shift to the government the heavy burden of proving that all of the evidence it proposes to use was derived from legitimate independent sources. On the other hand, a defendant raising a coerced-confession claim under the Fifth Amendment must first prevail in a voluntariness hearing before his confession and evidence derived from it become inadmissible.

There can be no justification in reason or policy for holding that the Constitution requires an amnesty grant where, acting pursuant to statute and accompanying safeguards, testimony is compelled in exchange for immunity from use and derivative use when no such amnesty is required where the government, acting without colorable right, coerces a defendant into incriminating himself.

We conclude that the immunity provided by 18 U.S.C. § 6002 leaves the witness and the prosecutorial authorities in substantially the same position as if the witness had claimed the Fifth Amendment privilege. The immunity therefore is coextensive with the privilege and suffices to supplant it.

Mr. Justice MARSHALL, dissenting.

Today the Court holds that the United States may compel a witness to give incriminating testimony, and subsequently prosecute him for crimes to which that testimony relates. I cannot believe the Fifth Amendment permits that result.

The Fifth Amendment gives a witness an absolute right to resist interrogation, if the testimony sought would tend to incriminate him. A grant of immunity may strip the witness of the right to refuse to testify, but only if it is broad enough to eliminate all possibility that the testimony will in fact operate to incriminate him. It must put him in precisely the same position, vis-a-vis the government that has compelled his testimony, as he would have been in had he remained silent in reliance on the privilege.

The Court recognizes that an immunity statute must be tested by that standard, that the relevant inquiry is whether it "leaves the witness and the prosecutorial authorities in substantially the same position as if the witness had claimed the Fifth Amendment privilege." I assume, moreover, that in theory that test would be met by a complete ban on the use of the compelled testimony, including all derivative, use, however remote and indirect. But I cannot agree that a ban on use will in practice be total, if it remains open for the government to convict the witness on the basis of evidence derived from a legitimate independent source. The Court asserts that the witness is adequately protected by a rule imposing on the government a heavy burden of proof if it would establish the independent character of evidence to be used against the witness. But in light of the inevitable uncertainties of the fact-finding process, a greater margin of protection is required in order to provide a reliable guarantee that the witness is in exactly the same position as if he had not testified. That margin can be provided only by immunity from prosecution for the offenses to which the testimony relates, i.e., transactional immunity.

I do not see how it can suffice merely to put the burden of proof on the government. First, contrary to the Court's assertion, the Court's rule does leave the witness "dependent for the preservation of his rights upon the integrity and good faith of the prosecuting authorities." For the information relevant to the question of taint is uniquely within the knowledge of the prosecuting authorities. They alone are in a position to trace the chains of information and investigation that lead to the evidence to be used in a criminal prosecution. A witness who suspects that his compelled testimony was used to develop a lead will be hard pressed indeed to ferret out the evidence necessary to prove it. And of course it is no answer to say he need not prove it, for though the Court puts the burden of proof on the government, the government will have no difficulty in meeting its burden by mere assertion if the witness produces no contrary evidence. The good faith of the prosecuting authorities is thus the sole safeguard of the witness' rights. Second, even their good faith is not a sufficient safeguard. For the paths of information through the investigative bureaucracy may well be long and winding, and even a prosecutor acting in the best of faith cannot be certain that somewhere in the depths of his investigative apparatus, often including hundreds of employees, there was not some prohibited use of the compelled testimony. The Court today sets out a loose net to trap tainted evidence and prevent its use against the witness, but it accepts an intolerably great risk that tainted evidence will in fact slip through that net. . . .

NOTES & QUESTIONS ON RISK OF INCRIMINATION

1. *Use versus transaction immunity.* In *Kastigar*, the Supreme Court concluded that a witness must testify if they have received the far narrower "use" immunity, as opposed to transactional immunity. Is this enough to protect the Fifth Amendment privilege? Do you agree with Justice Marshall that it is too hard to determine whether prosecutors have made secret "derivative use" of the testimony in constructing a case against the witness? How can lower courts effectively enforce the standard articulated by the majority when much of this happens behind closed doors?

2. *Consequences of non-compliance.* If a judge rules that an immune witness cannot claim the Fifth Amendment privilege, but the witness refuses to testify anyway, what consequences might follow? In practical terms, the judge might hold the witness in civil contempt and order the witness confined in jail until the witness agrees to testify. This contempt power is defined as "civil"

PROBLEM CASE

On January 11, 2005, the defendant pled guilty to one count of receipt and distribution of child pornography in violation of federal law. He was sentenced to 121 months, followed by a term of supervised release of three years. As a condition of his supervised release, defendant was required to live in a residential reentry center for treatment. As part of that process, the defendant was required to participate in a "non-deceptive sexual history polygraph process." In other words, the defendant was required to reveal everything about his sexual past during this polygraph examination. The defendant objected, arguing that doing so would violate his privilege against self-incrimination because disclosing that information might involve a "risk of incrimination." Is the polygraph requirement constitutional? Is it relevant that the required statement would take place only during supervised release rather than during some other judicial process? See *United States v. Behren*, 65 F. Supp. 3d 1140, 1145 (D. Colo. 2014).

because it is not backward-looking, i.e., imposed as criminal punishment for prior misdeeds, but rather forward-looking because it seeks to induce compliance with the judge's directives. For example, Susan McDougal was imprisoned by a judge for civil contempt after she refused to testify as part of an investigation commenced by Independent Counsel Kenneth Starr, who was investigating associates of President Bill Clinton in the Whitewater case. McDougal received immunity but still refused to testify before a grand jury. She ultimately spent 18 months in custody for civil contempt. McDougal challenged the contempt finding on constitutional grounds, arguing that she still faced a risk of incrimination based on a perjury charge for her testimony: "Because I believe that my truthful answers to the grand jury's inquiries would be inconsistent with the testimony and statements of others and/or inconsistent with the independent counsel's view of those facts . . . it is my belief that my answers would and could be used against me in future criminal prosecution." The Eighth Circuit rejected McDougal's argument, holding that a generalized fear of perjury could apply just as easily to anyone who receives immunity and would frustrate the investigative function of grand juries. *In re Grand Jury Subpoena*, 97 F.3d 1090, 1094 (8th Cir. 1996). McDougal was convicted of mail fraud and other charges but was later pardoned by Clinton before he left office.

2. What and Who Does the Privilege Protect?

The second requirement is that the privilege must be invoked to avoid a *testimonial* act. The Fifth Amendment says that no one shall be compelled to be a witness against himself, which implies a form of compelled *testimony*. But what if the individual is compelled to engage in some action? Or what if judicial officers perform an act *on the* individual? The following two cases deal with common situations. The first case involves the drawing of a motorist's blood for a blood-alcohol test, against the wishes of the motorist. Does this effectively force the defendant's body to give evidence against himself? The second case deals with a subpoena for documents—another situation where it might be said that turning over one's private papers to the authorities requires the individual to be a witness against himself. As you read both cases, pay attention to how the Supreme Court defines the outer contours of the concept of a "testimonial act."

Schmerber v. California

Supreme Court of the United States
384 U.S. 757 (1966)

Mr. Justice BRENNAN delivered the opinion of the Court.

Petitioner was convicted in Los Angeles Municipal Court of the criminal offense of driving an automobile while under the influence of intoxicating liquor. He had been arrested at a hospital while receiving treatment for injuries suffered in an accident involving the automobile that he had apparently been driving. At the direction of a police officer, a blood sample was then withdrawn from petitioner's body by a physician at the hospital. The chemical analysis of this sample revealed a percent by weight of alcohol in his blood at the time of the offense which indicated intoxication, and the report of this analysis was admitted in evidence at the trial. Petitioner objected to receipt of this evidence of the analysis on the ground that the blood had been withdrawn despite his refusal, on the advice of his counsel, to consent to the test. He contended that in that circumstance the withdrawal of the blood and the admission of the analysis in evidence denied him due process of law under the Fourteenth Amendment, as well as specific guarantees of the Bill of Rights secured against the States by that Amendment: [including] his privilege against self-incrimination under the Fifth Amendment. . . .

II

Breithaupt summarily rejected an argument that the withdrawal of blood and the admission of the analysis report involved in that state case violated the Fifth Amendment privilege of any person not to "be compelled in any criminal case to be a witness against himself." But that case, holding that the protections of the Fourteenth Amendment do not embrace this Fifth Amendment privilege, has been succeeded by *Malloy v. Hogan*, 378 U.S. 1, 8. We there held that "(t)he Fourteenth Amendment secures against state invasion the same privilege that the Fifth Amendment guarantees against federal infringement—the right of a person to remain silent unless he chooses to speak in the unfettered exercise of his own will, and to suffer no penalty . . . for such silence." We therefore must now decide whether the withdrawal of the blood and admission in evidence of the analysis involved in this case violated petitioner's privilege. We hold that the privilege protects an accused only from being compelled to testify against himself, or otherwise provide the State with evidence of a testimonial or communicative nature, and that the withdrawal of blood and use of the analysis in question in this case did not involve compulsion to these ends.

It could not be denied that in requiring petitioner to submit to the withdrawal and chemical analysis of his blood the State compelled him to submit to an attempt to discover evidence that might be used to prosecute him for a criminal offense. He submitted only after the police officer rejected his objection and directed the physician to proceed. The officer's direction to the physician to administer the test over petitioner's objection constituted compulsion for the purposes of the privilege. The critical question, then, is whether petitioner was thus compelled "to be a witness against himself." . . .

. . . History and a long line of authorities in lower courts have consistently limited [the privilege] to situations in which the State seeks to submerge those values by obtaining the evidence against an accused through "the cruel, simple expedient of compelling it from his own mouth. . . . In sum, the privilege is fulfilled only when the person is guaranteed the right to remain silent unless he chooses to speak in the unfettered exercise of his own will." The leading case in this Court is *Holt v. United States,* 218 U.S. 245. There the question was whether evidence was admissible that the accused, prior to trial and over his protest, put on a blouse that fitted him. It was contended that compelling the accused to submit to the demand that he model the blouse violated the privilege. Mr. Justice Holmes, speaking for the Court, rejected the argument as "based upon an extravagant extension of the 5th Amendment," and went on to say: "(T)he prohibition of compelling a man in a criminal court to be witness against himself is a prohibition of the use of physical or moral compulsion to extort communications from him, not an exclusion of his body as evidence when it may be material. The objection in principle would forbid a jury to look at a prisoner and compare his features with a photograph in proof."

It is clear that the protection of the privilege reaches an accused's communications, whatever form they might take, and the compulsion of responses which are also communications, for example, compliance with a subpoena to produce one's papers. On the other hand, both federal and state courts have usually held that it offers no protection against compulsion to submit to fingerprinting, photographing, or measurements, to write or speak for identification, to appear in court, to stand, to assume a stance, to walk, or to make a particular gesture. The distinction which has emerged, often expressed in different ways, is that the privilege is a bar against compelling "communications" or "testimony," but that compulsion which makes a suspect or accused the source of "real or physical evidence" does not violate it.

Although we agree that this distinction is a helpful framework for analysis, we are not to be understood to agree with past applications in all instances. There will be many cases in which such a distinction is not readily drawn. Some tests seemingly directed to obtain "physical evidence," for example, lie detector tests measuring changes in body function during interrogation, may actually be directed to eliciting responses which are essentially testimonial. To compel a person to submit to testing in which an effort will be made to determine his guilt or innocence on the basis of physiological responses, whether willed or not, is to evoke the spirit and history of the Fifth Amendment. Such situations call to mind the principle that the protection of the privilege "is as broad as the mischief against which it seeks to guard."

In the present case, however, no such problem of application is presented. Not even a shadow of testimonial compulsion upon or enforced communication by the accused was involved either in the extraction or in the chemical analysis. Petitioner's testimonial capacities were in no way implicated. . . .

Fisher v. United States

Supreme Court of the United States
425 U.S. 391 (1976)

Mr. Justice White delivered the opinion of the Court.

In these two cases we are called upon to decide whether a summons directing an attorney to produce documents delivered to him by his client in connection with the attorney-client relationship is enforceable over claims that the documents were constitutionally immune from summons in the hands of the client and retained that immunity in the hands of the attorney. . . . In each case, an Internal Revenue agent visited the taxpayer or taxpayers and interviewed them in connection with an investigation of possible civil or criminal liability under the federal income tax laws. . . .

II

All of the parties in these cases and the Court of Appeals for the Fifth Circuit have concurred in the proposition that if the Fifth Amendment would have excused a Taxpayer from turning over the accountant's papers had he possessed them, the Attorney to whom they are delivered for the purpose of obtaining legal advice should also be immune from subpoena. Although we agree with this proposition . . . we are convinced that, under our decision in *Couch v. United States*, 409 U.S. 322 (1973), it is not the taxpayer's Fifth

Amendment privilege that would excuse the Attorney from production. The relevant part of that Amendment provides: "No person . . . shall be Compelled in any criminal case to be a Witness against himself."

The taxpayer's privilege under this Amendment is not violated by enforcement of the summonses involved in these cases because enforcement against a taxpayer's lawyer would not "compel" the taxpayer to do anything and certainly would not compel him to be a "witness" against himself. The Court has held repeatedly that the Fifth Amendment is limited to prohibiting the use of "physical or moral compulsion" exerted on the person asserting the privilege. In *Couch*, we recently ruled that the Fifth Amendment rights of a taxpayer were not violated by the enforcement of a documentary summons directed to her accountant and requiring production of the taxpayer's own records in the possession of the accountant. We did so on the ground that in such a case "the ingredient of personal compulsion against an accused is lacking."

Here, the taxpayers are compelled to do no more than was the taxpayer in *Couch*. The taxpayers' Fifth Amendment privilege is therefore not violated by enforcement of the summonses directed toward their attorneys. This is true whether or not the Amendment would have barred a subpoena directing the taxpayer to produce the documents while they were in his hands.

The fact that the attorneys are agents of the taxpayers does not change this result. *Couch* held as much, since the accountant there was also the taxpayer's agent, and in this respect reflected a longstanding view. In *Hale v. Henkel*, 201 U.S. 43, 69-70 (1906), the Court said that the privilege "was never intended to permit (a person) to plead the fact that some third person might be incriminated by his testimony, even though he were the agent of such person. . . . (T)he Amendment is limited to a person who shall be compelled in any criminal case to be a witness against Himself." "It is extortion of information from the accused himself that offends our sense of justice." *Couch*, 409 U.S., at 328. Agent or no, the lawyer is not the taxpayer. The taxpayer is the "accused," and nothing is being extorted from him.

Nor is this one of those situations, which *Couch* suggested might exist, where constructive possession is so clear or relinquishment of possession so temporary and insignificant as to leave the personal compulsion upon the taxpayer substantially intact. In this respect we see no difference between the delivery to the attorneys in these cases and delivery to the accountant in the *Couch* case. As was true in *Couch*, the documents sought were obtainable without personal compulsion on the accused.

. . . The [Fifth] Amendment protects a person from being compelled to be a witness against himself. Here, the taxpayers retained any privilege they ever had not to be compelled to testify against themselves and not to be compelled themselves to produce private papers in their possession. This personal privilege was in no way decreased by the transfer. It is simply that by reason of the transfer of the documents to the attorneys, those papers may be subpoenaed without compulsion on the taxpayer. The protection of the Fifth Amendment is therefore not available. "A party is privileged from producing evidence but not from its production."

The Court of Appeals for the Fifth Circuit suggested that because legally and ethically the attorney was required to respect the confidences of his client, the latter had a reasonable expectation of privacy for the records in the hands of the attorney and therefore did not forfeit his Fifth Amendment privilege with respect to the records by transferring them in order to obtain legal advice. It is true that the Court has often stated that one of the several purposes served by the constitutional privilege against compelled testimonial self-incrimination is that of protecting personal privacy. But the Court has never suggested that every invasion of privacy violates the privilege. Within the limits imposed by the language of the Fifth Amendment, which we necessarily observe, the privilege truly serves privacy interests; but the Court has never on any ground, personal privacy included, applied the Fifth Amendment to prevent the otherwise proper acquisition or use of evidence which, in the Court's view, did not involve compelled testimonial self-incrimination of some sort.

The proposition that the Fifth Amendment protects private information obtained without compelling self-incriminating testimony is contrary to the clear statements of this Court that under appropriate safeguards private incriminating statements of an accused may be overheard and used in evidence, if they are not compelled at the time they were uttered, and that disclosure of private information may be compelled if immunity removes the risk of incrimination. If the Fifth Amendment protected generally against the obtaining of private information from a man's mouth or pen or house, its protections would presumably not be lifted by probable cause and a warrant or by immunity. The privacy invasion is not mitigated by immunity; and the Fifth Amendment's strictures, unlike the Fourth's, are not removed by showing reasonableness. The Framers addressed the subject of personal privacy directly in the Fourth Amendment. They struck a balance so that when the State's reason to believe incriminating evidence will be found becomes sufficiently great, the invasion of privacy becomes justified and a warrant to search and seize will issue. They did not seek in still another Amendment—the Fifth—to achieve a general protection of privacy but to deal with the more specific issue of compelled self-incrimination.

We cannot cut the Fifth Amendment completely loose from the moorings of its language, and make it serve as a general protector of privacy—a word not mentioned in its text and a concept directly addressed in the Fourth Amendment. We adhere to the view that the Fifth Amendment protects against "compelled self-incrimination, not (the disclosure of) private information."

> Insofar as private information not obtained through compelled self-incriminating testimony is legally protected, its protection stems from other sources: the Fourth Amendment's protection against seizures without warrant or probable cause and against subpoenas which suffer from "too much indefiniteness or breadth in the things required to be 'particularly described,'" or evidentiary privileges such as the attorney-client privilege. . . .

NOTES & QUESTIONS ON TESTIMONIAL ACTS

1. *Physical acts.* The holding in *Schmerber* is that a blood draw is not a testimonial act. Under what situations can a physical act qualify as "testimonial"? Recall that other constitutional protections, include the Fourth Amendment, limit the government's ability to conduct an unreasonable search and seizure. So, the government's power in this area is constrained by the "reasonableness" requirement of the Fourth Amendment, as drawing blood is unquestionably a search. But *Schmerber* stands for the proposition that the Fifth Amendment prohibition against compelled self-incrimination is not a significant constraint on the state's ability to collect physical evidence such as blood, hair, or DNA against a suspect in a criminal case. Other examples include handwriting samples (*Gilbert v. California*), voice samples (*United States v. Dionisio*), compelled lineups (*United States v. Wade*), and trying on clothing (*Holt v. United States*). Even voice exemplars, where the suspect must say some words not to convey evidentiary content, but for identification purposes, fall outside the scope of the privilege.

2. *Document production.* Under some circumstances, the turning over of incriminating documents could be a testimonial act—especially if the documents were created by the defendant. Or, consider a judicial order requiring a defendant to turn over the combination to her safe, a key to a locked safe, or the password for her cell phone. The underlying principle is that the privilege prevents the individual from being forced to reveal the "contents of their mind." But courts have struggled with drawing bright lines in this area. In *Doe v. United States*, 487 U.S. 201 (1988), the petitioner was held in civil contempt for refusing to sign a consent directive authorizing foreign banks to release his account records. The Supreme Court concluded that the order did not violate the Fifth Amendment privilege because it was not testimonial:

> The consent directive itself is not "testimonial." It is carefully drafted not to make reference to a specific account, but only to speak in the hypothetical. Thus, the form does not acknowledge that an account in a foreign financial institution is in existence or that it is controlled by petitioner. Nor does the form indicate whether documents or any other information relating to

> petitioner are present at the foreign bank, assuming that such an account does exist. The form does not even identify the relevant bank. Although the executed form allows the Government access to a potential source of evidence, the directive itself does not point the Government toward hidden accounts or otherwise provide information that will assist the prosecution in uncovering evidence.

However, Justice Stevens noted in dissent that

> [a] defendant can be compelled to produce material evidence that is incriminating. Fingerprints, blood samples, voice exemplars, handwriting specimens, or other items of physical evidence may be extracted from a defendant against his will. But can he be compelled to use his mind to assist the prosecution in convicting him of a crime? I think not. He may in some cases be forced to surrender a key to a strongbox containing incriminating documents, but I do not believe he can be compelled to reveal the combination to his wall safe—by word or deed.

Why does Stevens draw a distinction between a combination and a physical key? Is signing the bank consent direction akin to divulging the "combination" to his bank "vault"?

B. VOLUNTARINESS

The Due Process Clauses of the Fifth and Fourteenth Amendments prohibit government agents from using coercion to compel a confession, and bar for any use at trial (even impeachment) all actually coerced statements. At the most extreme end of the spectrum, this would prohibit the state from using torture against a detainee to extract a confession and then use that evidence at trial against the defendant. However, the Fifth Amendment does far more than protect against such egregious abuses—other forms of police misconduct have been deemed sufficiently coercive so as to be impermissible under the Fifth Amendment because they render the detainee's statements involuntary. These include: (1) threats of physical force; (2) deception; and (3) psychological coercion.

1. Threats of Physical Force

In addition to actual force, the *threat* of physical force will render a detainee's statements involuntary and therefore violates the Fifth Amendment. What type of threat is enough to qualify? More importantly, must the police threaten to harm the detainee themselves? The following case involves a situation where the detainee was induced by the police to cooperate based on a fear of an impending assault committed by third parties. As you read the case, ask yourself what values the Fifth Amendment prohibition is designed to promote. With this understanding in mind, what makes a threat of physical force constitutionally impermissible?

Arizona v. Fulminante

Supreme Court of the United States
499 U.S. 279 (1991)

Justice WHITE:

The Arizona Supreme Court ruled in this case that respondent Oreste Fulminante's confession, received in evidence at his trial for murder, had been coerced and that its use against him was barred by the Fifth and Fourteenth Amendments to the United States Constitution. The court also held that the harmless-error rule could not be used to save the conviction. We affirm the judgment of the Arizona court, although for different reasons than those upon which that court relied.

I

Early in the morning of September 14, 1982, Fulminante called the Mesa, Arizona, Police Department to report that his 11-year-old stepdaughter, Jeneane Michelle Hunt, was missing. He had been caring for Jeneane while his wife, Jeneane's mother, was in the hospital. Two days later, Jeneane's body was found in the desert east of Mesa. She had been shot twice in the head at close range with a large caliber weapon, and a ligature was around her neck. Because of the decomposed condition of the body, it was impossible to tell whether she had been sexually assaulted.

Fulminante's statements to police concerning Jeneane's disappearance and his relationship with her contained a number of inconsistencies, and he became a suspect in her killing. When no charges were filed against him, Fulminante left Arizona for New Jersey. Fulminante was later convicted in New Jersey on federal charges of possession of a firearm by a felon.

Fulminante was incarcerated in the Ray Brook Federal Correctional Institution in New York. There he became friends with another inmate, Anthony Sarivola, then serving a 60-day sentence for extortion. The two men came to spend several hours a day together. Sarivola, a former police officer, had been involved in loansharking for organized crime but then became a paid informant for the Federal Bureau of Investigation. While at Ray Brook, he masqueraded as an organized crime figure. After becoming friends with Fulminante, Sarivola heard a rumor that Fulminante was suspected of killing a child in Arizona. Sarivola then raised the subject with Fulminante in several conversations, but Fulminante repeatedly denied any involvement in Jeneane's death. During one conversation, he told Sarivola that Jeneane had been killed by bikers looking for drugs; on another occasion, he said he did not know what had happened. Sarivola passed this information on to an agent of the Federal Bureau of Investigation, who instructed Sarivola to find out more.

Sarivola learned more one evening in October 1983, as he and Fulminante walked together around the prison track. Sarivola said that he knew Fulminante was "starting to get some tough treatment and whatnot" from other inmates because of the rumor. Sarivola offered to protect Fulminante from his fellow inmates, but told him, "'You have to tell me about it,' you know. I mean, in other words, 'For me to give you any help.'" Fulminante then admitted to Sarivola that he had driven Jeneane to the desert on his motorcycle, where he choked her, sexually assaulted her, and made her beg for her life, before shooting her twice in the head. . . .

II

We deal first with the State's contention that the court below erred in holding Fulminante's confession to have been coerced. The State argues that it is the totality of the circumstances that determines whether Fulminante's confession was coerced, but contends that rather than apply this standard, the Arizona court applied a "but for" test, under which the court found that but for the promise given by Sarivola, Fulminante would not have confessed. . . . [However], the Arizona Supreme Court stated that a "determination regarding the voluntariness of a confession . . . must be viewed in a totality of the circumstances" and under that standard plainly found that Fulminante's statement to Sarivola had been coerced.

In applying the totality of the circumstances test to determine that the confession to Sarivola was coerced, the Arizona Supreme Court focused on a number of relevant facts. First, the court noted that "because [Fulminante] was an alleged child murderer, he was in danger of physical harm at the hands of other inmates." In addition, Sarivola was aware that Fulminante had been receiving "rough treatment from the guys." Using his knowledge of these threats, Sarivola offered to protect Fulminante in exchange for a confession to Jeneane's murder and "[i]n response to Sarivola's offer of protection, [Fulminante] confessed." Agreeing with Fulminante that "Sarivola's promise was extremely coercive," the Arizona court declared: "[T]he confession was obtained as a direct result of extreme coercion and was tendered in the belief that the defendant's life was in jeopardy if he did not confess. This is a true coerced confession in every sense of the word." . . .

Although the question is a close one, we agree with the Arizona Supreme Court's conclusion that Fulminante's confession was coerced. The Arizona Supreme Court found a credible threat of physical violence unless Fulminante confessed. Our cases have made clear that a finding of coercion need not depend upon actual violence by a government agent; a credible

> threat is sufficient. As we have said, "coercion can be mental as well as physical, and . . . the blood of the accused is not the only hallmark of an unconstitutional inquisition." As in *Payne*, where the Court found that a confession was coerced because the interrogating police officer had promised that if the accused confessed, the officer would protect the accused from an angry mob outside the jailhouse door, 356 U.S., at 564-565, 567, so too here, the Arizona Supreme Court found that it was fear of physical violence, absent protection from his friend (and Government agent) Sarivola, which motivated Fulminante to confess. Accepting the Arizona court's finding, permissible on this record, that there was a credible threat of physical violence, we agree with its conclusion that Fulminante's will was overborne in such a way as to render his confession the product of coercion. . . .

NOTES & QUESTIONS ON THREATS OF FORCE

1. *Totality-of-the-circumstances test.* In order to determine if a threat is sufficiently grave so as to vitiate the voluntariness of a confession, the Supreme Court looks to the totality of the circumstances, which is a free-ranging standard that requires consideration of all factors. In both *Payne* and *Fulminante,* the threat of force came from third parties, but the police threat to not protect the detainee was enough to make the detainee's statement involuntary under the totality-of-the-circumstances test. It does not matter whether the threat is a "but-for" cause of the statement and whether an appellate court finds that the detainee might have confessed anyway.

2. *Harmless error.* In a portion of the opinion not reprinted above, the Supreme Court analyzed the harmless error doctrine and concluded that it applies to coerced confessions. In other words, if the State can prove that the evidence would have established guilt beyond a reasonable doubt even without the coerced confession, the defendant's conviction need not be overturned. In that situation, the trial judge's error in admitting the confession is deemed harmless. But the Court then concluded that Arizona was unable to meet that burden, and concluded the error required reversal. This aspect of the *Fulminante* decision was immediately controversial because it substantially limited the impact of its other holding. Although many convictions based on coerced confessions would be overturned, the overturning of the conviction is not *automatic*. However, the rule is not binding on state courts, which are free to impose a rule requiring automatic reversal in these cases:

> Given the potency of confession evidence, state appellate courts should adopt an automatic reversal rule in most cases for coerced confessions because confession evidence is different from other forms of proof. Moreover, the courts should adopt the effect-on-the-verdict approach to harmless error

analysis and avoid applying the "guilty as hell rule" as a super jury determining the defendant's guilt.

Dennis J. Braithwaite, *Coerced Confessions, Harmless Error: The "Guilty as Hell" Rule in State Courts*, 36 Am. J. Trial Advoc. 233, 261 (2012).

PROBLEM CASE

Despite what the law says, police officials will sometimes engage in physical violence—or threats of physical violence—in order to extract confessions from a suspect. It goes without saying that physical violence used to extract a confession violates the Fifth Amendment and goes well beyond the threats of physical violence described in *Fulminante*.

In the immediate aftermath of 9/11, the administration of President George W. Bush authorized security services such as the Central Intelligence Agency to use torture techniques such as waterboarding against detainees suspected of involvement in terrorist networks. The use of these techniques violated both domestic statutes and international legal commitments prohibited torture.

Professor Alan Dershowitz of Harvard Law School argued that it was inevitable that state agents would resort to torture in some situations of national emergency. Rather than simply hew to the idea that torture is always unconstitutional, the better outcome in terms of the Fifth Amendment would be to allow state officials to seek a "torture warrant" from a federal court to ensure that the use of torture was truly limited to "ticking time bomb" situations. According to Dershowitz:

> If torture is in fact being used and/or would in fact be used in an actual ticking bomb mass terrorism case, would it be normatively better or worse to have such torture regulated by some kind of warrant, with accountability, record-keeping, standards, and limitations? This is an important debate, and a different one from the old, abstract Benthamite debate over whether torture can ever be justified. It is not so much about the substantive issue of torture, as it is over accountability, visibility, and candor in a democracy that is confronting a choice of evils.

Alan M. Dershowitz, *The Torture Warrant: A Response to Professor Strauss*, 48 N.Y.L. Sch. L. Rev. 275, 277-78 (2004). Dershowitz's proposal was widely, though not universally, condemned. One legal commentator suggested that the problem was that normalizing torture would put it in conflict with the rule of law:

> If the rule of law rests on the archetypal ban on torture, and that ban collapses, then one of two things happens: either the rule of law itself dissolves, or—perhaps even worse—the rule of law continues, but on a foundation that allows torture and other forms of state violence. Indeed, one might even say that under the second scenario the rule of law would become founded on violence (rather than merely employing force in a constrained way as a necessary tool of law enforcement). Such a result would be nonsensical and perhaps even paradoxical to many commentators.

John T. Parry, *Torture Warrants and the Rule of Law*, 71 Alb. L. Rev. 885, 902 (2008). Do you agree that normalizing torture in extreme situations is incompatible with the rule of law? Furthermore, can the "torture warrant" exception be generalized to other contexts? This section of the casebook details the other situations that can render an interrogation involuntary. Should courts issue "deception warrants" or "psychological pressure warrants"?

2. Deception

The Constitution permits the police to lie to a suspect under interrogation. Because the "totality of the circumstances" is the test for coercion, the mere fact that the police lied will rarely by itself render a confession involuntary. Some forms of deception, however, become so egregious that they render the resulting confession involuntary. As you read the following two cases, identify the standard that the Supreme Court uses to distinguish between permissible and impermissible deception. How do we know when the questioning has overcome the will of the interrogee?

Leyra v. Dennis

Supreme Court of the United States
347 U.S. 556 (1954)

Mr. Justice BLACK delivered the opinion of the Court.

Camilo Leyra, age 75, and his wife, age 80, were found dead in their Brooklyn apartment. Several days later petitioner, their son, age 50, was indicted in a state court charged with having murdered them with a hammer. He was convicted and sentenced to death, chiefly on several alleged confessions of guilt. The New York Court of Appeals reversed on the ground that one of the confessions, made to a state-employed psychiatrist, had been extorted from petitioner by coercion and promises of leniency in violation of the Due Process Clause of the Fourteenth Amendment. Petitioner was then tried again. This time the invalidated confession was not used to convict him but several other confessions that followed it the same day were used. . . .

The use in a state criminal trial of a defendant's confession obtained by coercion–whether physical or mental–is forbidden by the Fourteenth Amendment. The question for our decision is therefore whether the present confessions were so coerced. This question can only be answered by reviewing the circumstances surrounding the confessions. We therefore examine the circumstances as shown by the undisputed facts of this case.

When the father failed to appear at his place of business on Tuesday, January 10, 1950, petitioner, his business partner, and others went to the father's apartment about 3 P.M. and found the bodies of the aged parents. Police were called. Although they first suspected a prowling intruder, the presence on the couple's disarranged breakfast table of a third teacup led them to think that the killer was a welcome guest. This and other circumstances drew suspicion toward petitioner. He and others were questioned by the police until about 11 P.M. on the evening of the day the bodies were discovered. On Wednesday, police again questioned petitioner from about 10 in the morning to midnight. Once more, beginning about 9 Thursday morning petitioner was subjected to almost constant police questioning throughout the day and much of the night until about 8:30 Friday morning. At that time petitioner was taken by police to his parents' funeral. While petitioner was at the funeral and until he returned in the late afternoon, Captain Meenahan, his chief police questioner, went home to get some "rest." After the funeral petitioner himself was permitted to go to a hotel and sleep an hour and a half. He was returned to the police station about 5 P.M. on this Friday afternoon. During his absence a concealed microphone had been installed with wire connections to another room in which the state prosecutor, the police, and possibly some others were stationed to overhear what petitioner might say. Up to this time he had not confessed to the crime.

The petitioner had been suffering from an acutely painful attack of sinus and Captain Meenahan had promised to get a physician to help him. When petitioner returned to the questioning room after the funeral, Captain Meenahan introduced him to "Dr. Helfand," supposedly to give petitioner medical relief. Dr. Helfand, however, was not a general practitioner but a psychiatrist with considerable knowledge of hypnosis. Petitioner was left with Dr. Helfand while Captain Meenahan joined the state District Attorney in the nearby listening room. Instead of giving petitioner the medical advice and treatment he expected, the psychiatrist by subtle and suggestive questions simply continued the police effort of the past days and nights to induce petitioner to admit his guilt. For an hour and a half or more the techniques of a highly trained psychiatrist were used to break petitioner's will in order to get him to say he had murdered his parents. Time and time and time again the psychiatrist told petitioner how much he wanted to and could help him, how bad it would be for petitioner if he did not confess, and how much better he would feel, and how much lighter and easier it would be on him if he would just unbosom himself to the doctor. Yet the doctor was at that very time the paid representative of the state whose prosecuting officials were listening in on every threat made and every promise of leniency given.

A tape recording of the psychiatric examination was made and a transcription of the tape was read into the record of this case. To show exactly what transpired we attach rather lengthy excerpts from that transcription as an appendix. The petitioner's answers indicate a mind dazed and bewildered. Time after time the petitioner complains about how tired and how sleepy he is and how he cannot think. On occasion after occasion the doctor told petitioner either to open his eyes or to shut his eyes. Apparently many of petitioner's answers were barely audible. On occasions the doctor informed petitioner that his lips were moving but no sound could be heard. Many times petitioner was asked to speak louder. As time went on, the record indicates that petitioner began to accept suggestions of the psychiatrist. For instance, Dr. Helfand suggested that petitioner had hit his parents with a hammer and after some minutes petitioner agreed that must have been the weapon.

Finally, after an hour and a half or longer, petitioner, encouraged by the doctor's assurances that he had done no moral wrong and would be let off easily, called for Captain Meenahan. The captain immediately appeared. It was then that the confession was given to him which was admitted against petitioner in this trial. Immediately following this confession to Captain Meenahan, petitioner's business partner was called from an adjoining room. The police had apparently brought the business partner there to have him talk to petitioner at an opportune moment. Petitioner repeated to his partner in a very brief way some of the things he had told the psychiatrist and the captain. Following this, petitioner was questioned by the two assistant state prosecutors. What purports to be his formal confession was taken down by their stenographer, with a notation that it was given at 10 P.M., several hours after the psychiatrist took petitioner in charge.

. . . [T]he undisputed facts in this case are irreconcilable with petitioner's mental freedom "to confess to or deny a suspected participation in a crime," and the relation of the confessions made to the psychiatrist, the police captain and the state prosecutors, is "so close that one must say the facts of one control the character of the other. . . ." All were simply parts of one continuous process. All were extracted in the same place within a period of about five hours as the climax of days and nights of intermittent, intensive police questioning. First, an already physically and emotionally exhausted suspect's ability to resist interrogation was broken to almost trance-like submission by use of the arts of a highly skilled psychiatrist. Then the confession petitioner

PROBLEM CASE

In 1995, Christopher Jennett was accused of abusing his children during a visitation period. During his interrogation by the police at the station house, detectives told him that they had a warrant to search his apartment, which they did not. The detectives also implied that they would be able to find DNA evidence to substantiate the claims of abuse. They told him, "Have you ever—I am sure you have probably seen some of this testing with the O.J. trial—it's been all over the T.V. forever and they are doing a lot of blood samples and things like that." The police officer then went on to describe the methods that forensics examiners often use to extract DNA from clothing found at a crime scene or from the skin of a victim. However, the police had not collected any DNA evidence of the crimes. Jennett confessed to the abuse on videotape but later argued that the statement was involuntary because it was the product of a deceptive interrogation. Jennett was 35 years old and had a tenth-grade education. Was the interrogational strategy deceptive, and if so did it render Jennett's statement involuntary? Should Jennett have carefully parsed the detective's statement about DNA evidence and understood the difference between general discussions of forensics and a specific claim about the evidence collected in his case? See *State v. Jennett*, 574 N.W.2d 361, 364 (Iowa Ct. App. 1997).

began making to the psychiatrist was filled in and perfected by additional statements given in rapid succession to a police officer, a trusted friend, and two state prosecutors. We hold that use of confessions extracted in such a manner from a lone defendant unprotected by counsel is not consistent with due process of law as required by our Constitution. . . .

Lynumn v. Illinois

Supreme Court of the United States
372 U.S. 528 (1963)

Mr. Justice Stewart delivered the opinion of the Court.

The petitioner was tried in the Criminal Court of Cook County, Illinois, on an indictment charging her with the unlawful possession and sale of marijuana. . . . For the reasons stated in this opinion, we hold that the petitioner's trial did not meet the demands of due process of law, and we accordingly set aside the judgment. . . .

On January 17, 1959, three Chicago police officers arrested James Zeno for unlawful possession of narcotics. They took him to a district police station. There they told him that if he "would set somebody up for them, they would go light" on him. He agreed to "cooperate" and telephoned the petitioner, telling her that he was coming over to her apartment. The officers and Zeno then went to the petitioner's apartment house, and Zeno went upstairs to the third floor while the officers waited below. Some time later, variously estimated as from five to 20 minutes, Zeno emerged from the petitioner's third floor apartment with a package containing a substance later determined to be marijuana. The officers took the package and told Zeno to return to the petitioner's apartment on the pretext that he had left his glasses there. When the petitioner walked out into the hallway in response to Zeno's call, one of the officers seized her and placed her under arrest. The officers and Zeno then entered the petitioner's apartment. The petitioner at first denied she had sold the marijuana to Zeno, insisting that while he was in her apartment Zeno had merely repaid a loan. After further conversations with the officers, however, she told them that she had sold the marijuana to Zeno.

The officers testified to this oral confession at the petitioner's trial, and it is this testimony which, we now hold, fatally infected the petitioner's conviction. The petitioner testified at the trial that she had not in fact sold any marijuana to Zeno, that Zeno had merely repaid a long-standing loan. She also testified, however, that she had told the officers on the day of her arrest that she had sold Zeno marijuana, describing the circumstances under which this statement was made as follows:

> I told him (Officer Sims) I hadn't sold Zeno; I didn't know anything about narcotics and I had no source of supply. He kept insisting I had a source of supply and had been dealing in narcotics. I kept telling him I did not and that I knew nothing about it. Then he started telling me I could get 10 years and the children could be taken away, and after I got out they would be taken away and strangers would have them, and if I could cooperate he would see they weren't; and he would recommend leniency and I had better do what they told me if I wanted to see my kids again. The two children are three and four years old. Their father is dead; they live with me. I love my children very much. I have never been arrested for anything in my whole life before. I did not know how much power a policeman had in a recommendation to the State's Attorney or to the Court. I did not know that a Court and a State's Attorney are not bound by a police officer's recommendations. I did not know anything about it. All the officers talked to me about my children and the time I could get for not cooperating. All three officers did. After that conversation I believed that if I cooperated with them and answered the questions the way they wanted me to answer, I believed that I would not be prosecuted. They had said I had better say what they wanted me to, or I would lose the kids. I said I would say anything they wanted me to say. I asked what I was to say. I was told to say "You must admit you gave Zeno the package" so I said, "Yes, I gave it to him."
>
> . . . The only reason I had for admitting it to the police was the hope of saving myself from going to jail and being taken away from my children. The statement I made to the police after they promised that they would intercede for me, the statements admitting the crime, were false.
>
> . . . My statement to the police officers that I sold the marijuana to Zeno was false. I lied to the police at that time. I lied because the police told me they were going to send me to jail for 10 years and take my children, and I would never see them again; so I agreed to say whatever they wanted me to say.

The police officers did not deny that these were the circumstances under which the petitioner told them that she had sold marijuana to Zeno. To the contrary, their testimony largely corroborated the petitioner's testimony. Officer Sims testified:

> I told her then that Zeno had been trapped and we asked him to cooperate; that he had made a phone call to her and subsequently had purchased the evidence from her. I told her then if she wished to cooperate, we would be willing to recommend to the State leniency in her case. At that time, she said, "Yes, I did sell it to him."
>
> . . . While I was talking to her in the bedroom, she told me that she had children and she had taken the children over to her mother-in-law, to keep her children.

> **Q.** Did you or anybody in your presence indicate or suggest or say to her that her children would be taken away from her if she didn't do what you asked her to do?
> **Witness:** I believe there was some mention of her children being taken away from her if she was arrested.
> **The Court:** By whom? Who made mention of it?
> **The Witness:** I believe Officer Bryson made that statement and I think I made the statement at some time during the course of our discussion that her children could be taken from her. We did not say if she cooperated they wouldn't be taken. I don't know whether Kobar said that to her or not. I don't recall if Kobar said that to her or not.
>
> I asked her who the clothing belonged to. She said they were her children's. I asked how many she had and she said 2. I asked her where they were or who took care of them. She said the children were over at the mother's or mother-in-law. I asked her how did she take care of herself and she said she was on ADC. I told her that if we took her into the station and charged her with the offense, that the ADC would probably be cut off and also that she would probably lose custody of her children. That was not before I said if she cooperated, it would go light on her. It was during the same conversation.
>
> . . . I made the statement to her more than once; but I don't know how many times, that she had been set up and if she cooperated we would go light with her.

Officer Bryson testified:

> Miss Lynumn said she was thinking about her children and she didn't want to go to jail. I was present and heard something pertaining to her being promised leniency if she would cooperate. I don't know exactly who said it. I could have, myself, or Sims.

It is thus abundantly clear that the petitioner's oral confession was made only after the police had told her that state financial aid for her infant children would be cut off, and her children taken from her, if she did not "cooperate." These threats were made while she was encircled in her apartment by three police officers and a twice convicted felon who had purportedly "set her up." There was no friend or adviser to whom she might turn. She had had no previous experience with the criminal law, and had no reason not to believe that the police had ample power to carry out their threats.

We think it clear that a confession made under such circumstances must be deemed not voluntary, but coerced. That is the teaching of our cases. We have said that the question in each case is whether the defendant's will was overborne at the time he confessed. If so, the confession cannot be deemed "the product of a rational intellect and a free will." . . .

NOTES & QUESTIONS ON DECEPTION

1. *What type of deception?* In *Lynumn*, the police deceived the suspect into believing that she would lose her children unless she confessed to the crime—a lie that was so severe that her will was "overborne" at the time of confession. But does *Lynumn* offer much in the way of a standard to guide lower courts in determining whether a deception is so severe that it might overcome a suspect's free will? As noted in the prior subsection, voluntariness is governed by a fact-intensive inquiry into the totality of the circumstances. This includes consideration of the characteristics of the defendant, the nature of the interrogation, and the police behavior. For example, in *Leyra v. Dennis*, the Court considered everything from the suspect's sinus infection to the length of the interrogation to the number of officials involved in the interrogation before deciding that the police had deceived him—telling him he had done nothing morally wrong—into confessing,

2. *Necessary deception?* Certainly, police almost always "trick" defendants into thinking that a confession will help their legal situation because society or the legal system might view the defendant in a charitable light. For example, a police officer might trick a suspect into confessing to a murder by suggesting that he assert in his confession that the victim was "asking for it," and telling the suspect that no one could condemn him under these circumstances, all the while knowing full well that the situation does not meet the standard for the provocation or extreme emotional disturbance defense. Is this an unconstitutional deception? It certainly happens every day in precincts across the country. As one scholar noted:

PROBLEM CASE

Consider a case that involves an outright police falsehood. In 2005, the defendant was found guilty of petit larceny for stealing lottery tickets from her employer, a restaurant owner. During the police investigation, the defendant initially denied having stolen the lottery tickets, but a state trooper confronted her with the following evidence: He said that there was surveillance video of her taking the lottery tickets. The defendant then changed her story and admitted to taking some of the lottery tickets, an admission that was later used against her at trial. In reality, though, there was no video surveillance of the theft at all. The statement by the trooper was a ruse designed to elicit an incriminating statement. The trooper even went so far as to theatrically dump the "bogus videotape on the table in front of her." The ruse succeeded in getting the defendant to confess because she assumed that the state trooper was telling the truth. Did the deception render her confession involuntary? See *People v. Dishaw*, 30 A.D.3d 689, 690, 816 N.Y.S.2d 235, 236 (2006).

> The more relevant statistic for present purposes is the extent to which trickery is necessary to obtain confessions that are important to successful prosecutions. Unfortunately, studies of the interrogation process produce equivocal findings on this score. But the combined results of observational studies, simulation research, and the conduct of the police themselves suggest that a non-trivial number of guilty people would not confess in the absence of investigative techniques that go beyond non-deceptive questioning.

Christopher Slobogin, *Lying and Confessing*, 39 Tex. Tech L. Rev. 1275, 1280 (2007).

3. Psychological Pressure

The third category of cases involves psychological pressure. Under some situations, psychological pressure can be sufficiently grave so as to make the confession involuntary and a violation of due process. Like the other two categories, though, the lines are not clear and are always evaluated with reference to the totality of the circumstances.

Spano v. New York

Supreme Court of the United States
360 U.S. 315 (1959)

Mr. Chief Justice WARREN delivered the opinion of the Court.

This is another in the long line of cases presenting the question whether a confession was properly admitted into evidence under the Fourteenth Amendment. As in all such cases, we are forced to resolve a conflict between two fundamental interests of society; its interest in prompt and efficient law enforcement, and its interest in preventing the rights of its individual members from being abridged by unconstitutional methods of law enforcement. Because of the delicate nature of the constitutional determination which we must make, we cannot escape the responsibility of making our own examination of the record.

The State's evidence reveals the following: Petitioner Vincent Joseph Spano is a derivative citizen of this country, having been born in Messina, Italy. He was 25 years old at the time of the shooting in question and had graduated from junior high school. He had a record of regular employment. The shooting took place on January 22, 1957.

On that day, petitioner was drinking in a bar. The decedent, a former professional boxer weighing almost 200 pounds who had fought in Madison Square Garden, took some of petitioner's money from the bar. Petitioner followed him out of the bar to recover it. A fight ensued, with the decedent knocking petitioner down and then kicking him in the head three or four times. Shock from the force of these blow caused petitioner to vomit. After the bartender applied some ice to his head, petitioner left the bar, walked to his apartment, secured a gun, and walked eight or nine blocks to a candy store where the decedent was frequently to be found. He entered the store in which decedent, three friends of decedent, at least two of whom were ex-convicts, and a boy who was supervising the store were present. He fired five shots, two of which entered the decedent's body, causing his death. The boy was the only eyewitness; the three friends of decedent did not see the person who fired the shot. Petitioner then disappeared for the next week or so.

On February 1, 1957, the Bronx County Grand Jury returned an indictment for first-degree murder against petitioner. Accordingly, a bench warrant was issued for his arrest, commanding that he be forthwith brought before the court to answer the indictment, or, if the court had adjourned for the term, that he be delivered into the custody of the Sheriff of Bronx County.

On February 3, 1957, petitioner called one Gaspar Bruno, a close friend of 8 or 10 years' standing who had attended school with him. Bruno was a fledgling police officer, having at that time not yet finished attending police academy. According to Bruno's testimony, petitioner told him "that he took a terrific beating, that the deceased hurt him real bad and he dropped him a couple of times and he was dazed; he didn't know what he was doing and that he went and shot at him." Petitioner told Bruno that he intended to get a lawyer and give himself up. Bruno relayed this information to his superiors.

The following day, February 4, at 7:10 P.M., petitioner, accompanied by counsel, surrendered himself to the authorities in front of the Bronx County Building, where both the office of the Assistant District Attorney who ultimately prosecuted his case and the court-room in which he was ultimately tried were located. His attorney had cautioned him to answer no questions, and left him in the custody of the officers. He was promptly taken to the office of the Assistant District Attorney and at 7:15 P.M. the questioning began, being conducted by Assistant District Attorney Goldsmith, Lt. Gannon, Detectives Farrell, Lehrer and Motta, and Sgt. Clarke. The record reveals that the questioning was both persistent and continuous. Petitioner, in accordance with his attorney's instructions, steadfastly refused to answer. Detective Motta testified: "He refused to talk to me." "He just looked up to the ceiling and refused to talk to me." Detective Farrell testified:

Q. And you started to interrogate him? A. That is right.
Q. What did he say? A. He said "you would have to see my attorney. I tell you nothing but my name."
Q. Did you continue to examine him? A. Verbally, yes, sir.

He asked one officer, Detective Ciccone, if he could speak to his attorney, but that request was denied. Detective Ciccone testified that he could not find the attorney's name in the telephone book. He was given two sandwiches, coffee and cake at 11 P.M.

At 12:15 A.M. on the morning of February 5, after five hours of questioning in which it became evident that petitioner was following his attorney's instructions, on the Assistant District Attorney's orders petitioner was transferred to the 46th Squad, Ryer Avenue Police Station. The Assistant District Attorney also went to the police station and to some extent continued to participate in the interrogation. Petitioner arrived at 12:30 and questioning was resumed at 12:40. The character of the questioning is revealed by the testimony of Detective Farrell:

> **Q.** Who did you leave him in the room with? A. With Detective Lehrer and Sergeant Clarke came in and Mr. Goldsmith came in or Inspector Halk came in. It was back and forth. People just came in, spoke a few words to the defendant or they listened a few minutes and they left.

But petitioner persisted in his refusal to answer, and again requested permission to see his attorney, this time from Detective Lehrer. His request was again denied.

It was then that those in charge of the investigation decided that petitioner's close friend, Bruno, could be of use. He had been called out on the case around 10 or 11 P.M., although he was not connected with the 46th Squad or Precinct in any way. Although, in fact, his job was in no way threatened, Bruno was told to tell petitioner that petitioner's telephone call had gotten him "in a lot of trouble," and that he should seek to extract sympathy from petitioner for Bruno's pregnant wife and three children. Bruno developed this theme with petitioner without success, and petitioner, also without success, again sought to see his attorney, a request which Bruno relayed unavailingly to his superiors. After this first session with petitioner, Bruno was again directed by Lt. Gannon to play on petitioner's sympathies, but again no confession was forthcoming. But the Lieutenant a third time ordered Bruno falsely to importune his friend to confess but again petitioner clung to his attorney's advice. Inevitably, in the fourth such session directed by the Lieutenant, lasting a full hour, petitioner succumbed to his friend's prevarications and agreed to make a statement. Accordingly, at 3:25 A.M. the Assistant District Attorney, a stenographer, and several other law enforcement officials entered the room where petitioner was being questioned, and took his statement in question and answer form with the Assistant District Attorney asking the questions. The statement was completed at 4:05 A.M.

But this was not the end. At 4:30 A.M. three detectives took petitioner to Police Headquarters in Manhattan. On the way they attempted to find the bridge from which petitioner said he had thrown the murder weapon. They crossed the Triborough Bridge into Manhattan, arriving at Police Headquarters at 5 A.M., and left Manhattan for the Bronx at 5:40 A.M. via the Willis Avenue Bridge. When petitioner recognized neither bridge as the one from which he had thrown the weapon, they re-entered Manhattan via the Third Avenue Bridge, which petitioner stated was the right one, and then returned to the Bronx well after 6 A.M. During that trip the officers also elicited a statement from petitioner that the deceased was always "on (his) back," "always pushing" him and that he was "not sorry" he had shot the deceased. All three detectives testified to that statement at the trial. . . .

The abhorrence of society to the use of involuntary confessions does not turn alone on their inherent untrustworthiness. It also turns on the deep-rooted feeling that the police must obey the law while enforcing the law; that in the end life and liberty can be as much endangered from illegal methods used to convict those thought to be criminals as from the actual criminals themselves. Accordingly, the actions of police in obtaining confessions have come under scrutiny in a long series of cases. Those cases suggest that in recent years law enforcement officials have become increasingly aware of the burden which they share, along with our courts, in protecting fundamental rights of our citizenry, including that portion of our citizenry suspected of crime. The facts of no case recently in this Court have quite approached the brutal beatings in *Brown v. State of Mississippi*, 297 U.S. 278 (1936), or the 36 consecutive hours of questioning present in *Ashcraft v. State of Tennessee*, 322 U.S. 143 (1944). But as law enforcement officers become more responsible, and the methods used to extract confessions more sophisticated, our duty to enforce federal constitutional protections does not cease. It only becomes more difficult because of the more delicate judgments to be made. Our judgment here is that, on all the facts, this conviction cannot stand.

Petitioner was a foreign-born young man of 25 with no past history of law violation or of subjection to official interrogation, at least insofar as the record shows. He had progressed only one-half year into high school and the record indicates that he had a history of emotional instability. He did not make a narrative statement, but was subject to the leading questions of a skillful prosecutor in a question and answer confession. He was subjected to questioning not by a few men, but by many . . . and the effect of such massive official interrogation [by approximately 15 officials] must have been felt. Petitioner was questioned for virtually eight straight hours before he confessed, with his only respite being a transfer to an arena presumably considered more appropriate by the police for the task at hand. Nor was the questioning conducted during normal business hours, but began in early evening, continued into the night, and did not bear fruition until the not-too-early morning. The drama was not played out, with the final admissions obtained, until almost sunrise. In such circumstances slowly mounting fatigue does, and is calculated to, play its part. The questioners persisted in the face of his repeated refusals to answer on the advice of his attorney, and they ignored his reasonable requests to contact the local attorney whom he had already retained and who had personally delivered him into the custody of these officers in obedience to the bench warrant.

The use of Bruno, characterized in this Court by counsel for the State as a "childhood friend" of petitioner's, is another factor which deserves mention in the totality of the situation. Bruno's was the one face visible to petitioner in which he could put some trust. There was a bond of friendship between them going back a decade into adolescence. It was with this material that the officers felt that they could overcome petitioner's will. They instructed Bruno falsely to state that petitioner's telephone call had gotten him into trouble, that his job was in jeopardy, and that loss of his job would be disastrous to his three children, his wife and his unborn child. And Bruno played this part of a worried father, harried by his superiors, in not one, but four different acts, the final one lasting an hour. Petitioner was apparently unaware of John Gay's famous couplet: "An open foe may prove a curse, But a pretended friend is worse," and he yielded to his false friend's entreaties.

We conclude that petitioner's will was overborne by official pressure, fatigue and sympathy falsely aroused after considering all the facts in their post-indictment setting. . . .

NOTES & QUESTIONS ON PSYCHOLOGICAL PRESSURE

1. *Psychological pressure.* Why does psychological pressure during an interrogation violate the Fifth Amendment? One argument might be that involuntary confessions are unreliable—they are often false—and on that basis alone are intolerable in a system built on the rule of law. But in *Rogers v. Richmond*, 365 U.S. 534, 540-42 (1961), the Supreme Court specifically rejected that possible rationale:

> Our decisions under that Amendment have made clear that convictions following the admission into evidence of confessions which are involuntary, i.e., the product of coercion, either physical or psychological, cannot stand. This is so not because such confessions are unlikely to be true but because the methods used to extract them offend an underlying principle in the enforcement of our criminal law: that ours is an accusatorial and not an inquisitorial system—a system in which the State must establish guilt by

PROBLEM CASE

Katrina Ann Tingle was investigated by FBI agents regarding her suspected involvement in a robbery at the San Diego Navy Federal Credit Union. Tingle worked at the credit union and reported that a robbery had occurred there. FBI officials believed that the robbery report was a ruse and that Tingle and her boyfriend had staged the scene and had, in fact, taken the money for themselves. Here is the court's description of the interrogation:

> Sibley [the agent] explained that it would be in Tingle's best interest to cooperate. There was some discussion about Tingle's release on her own recognizance during court proceedings. Sibley stated that he would inform the prosecutor if Tingle were to cooperate, or would alternatively inform the prosecutor that she was "stubborn or hard-headed" if she refused. Sibley suggested that it was quite possible that he had been told by Tingle's boyfriend that she was the one responsible for the entire planning and execution of the staged robbery. At the beginning of the interrogation Sibley had determined that Tingle was the mother of a two-year-old child. In an effort to obtain a confession, Sibley told her either that she would not see the child for a while if she went to prison or that she might not see the child for a while if she went to prison. His purpose was to make it clear to her that she had "a lot at stake." During Sibley's interrogation Tingle began to sob. She was noticeably shaking. She continued to cry for at least ten minutes. She confessed. . . .

Does threatening to take a child away from a parent constitute psychological pressure? See *United States v. Tingle*, 658 F.2d 1332, 1334 (9th Cir. 1981).

> evidence independently and freely secured and may not by coercion prove its charge against an accused out of his own mouth. To be sure, confessions cruelly extorted may be and have been, to an unascertained extent, found to be untrustworthy. But the constitutional principle of excluding confessions that are not voluntary does not rest on this consideration. Indeed, in many of the cases in which the command of the Due Process Clause has compelled us to reverse state convictions involving the use of confessions obtained by impermissible methods, independent corroborating evidence left little doubt of the truth of what the defendant had confessed. Despite such verification, confessions were found to be the product of constitutionally impermissible methods in their inducement. Since a defendant had been subjected to pressures to which, under our accusatorial system, an accused should not be subjected, we were constrained to find that the procedures leading to his conviction had failed to afford him that due process of law which the Fourteenth Amendment guarantees.

What type of consideration is this? Clearly, the untrustworthy nature of the interrogation method is not the key consideration here. If it were, what remedy would be appropriate? Arguably, it would entail a court's inquiring into the veracity of the confession and excluding it if it is uncorroborated by other evidence. But the current rule is that involuntary confessions should be excluded even if the court is convinced that the statement was true. Why? The Court talks of the nature of an "accusatorial system," without fully explicating its essential elements. Can you articulate the key foundations of an accusatorial system that operates according to the rule of law? For a discussion, see Jeremy Waldron, *Torture and Positive Law: Jurisprudence for the White House*, 105 Colum. L. Rev. 1681, 1743 (2005) ("the prohibition on torture is archetypal of our particular legal heritage, as well as a certain sort of commitment to the rule of law").

2. *State action.* There must be some state action in order for there to be a due process violation based on psychological pressure. Consider the case of Francis Connelly, who flew all the way from Boston to Denver just to find a police officer to speak with to confess that he had murdered someone. The following excerpt explains what motivated his desire to confess:

> At a preliminary hearing, respondent moved to suppress all of his statements. Dr. Jeffrey Metzner, a psychiatrist employed by the state hospital, testified that respondent was suffering from chronic schizophrenia and was in a psychotic state at least as of August 17, 1983, the day before he confessed. Metzner's interviews with respondent revealed that respondent was following the "voice of God." This voice instructed respondent to withdraw money from the bank, to buy an airplane ticket, and to fly from Boston to Denver. When respondent arrived from Boston, God's voice became stronger and told respondent either to confess to the killing or to commit suicide. Reluctantly following the command of the voices, respondent approached Officer Anderson and confessed.

Colorado v. Connelly, 479 U.S. 157, 161 (1986). Arguably, the defendant's psychosis rendered his statement involuntary because it was the result of a psychological pressure. However, the Supreme Court rejected this argument and concluded that its involuntariness standard required state action, which was noticeably missing in this case.

C. WARNINGS DURING CUSTODIAL INTERROGATION

Police are required to do more than simply respect a suspect's Fifth Amendment rights during interrogation. The police are also required to issue affirmative warnings to the suspect. The following sections outline the basic parameters of this constitutional obligation: (1) the derivation of the rule in the original *Miranda* decision, which has effectively become the ur-text for interrogational warnings, and its status as a "constitutional rule"; (2) the definition of custody; (3) the definition of interrogation; (4) waiver of *Miranda* rights; and (5) exceptions to the *Miranda* rule. These sections highlight the degree to which the *Miranda* obligation is broad but not all-encompassing. In fact, certain factual predicates, dealing with the nature of the custodial moment and the nature of the police questioning, must apply before the rule is triggered. Also, though the *Miranda* warnings are relatively straightforward and easy for any layperson—or criminal suspect—to understand (which is their point), the *Miranda* rule

PROBLEM CASE

On the evening of April 19, 1989, a woman jogging in New York City's Central Park was raped and badly beaten. Her injuries were so severe that she fell into a coma and barely survived the attack. Though the New York City public was widely accustomed to reports of crime in their city, this particular crime—given its central location—was shocking. Also, other visitors to Central Park that night reported being harassed by a group of teenagers roaming the park. The New York Police Department immediately felt intense public pressure to solve the case.

Two days later, the NYPD solved the crime and arrested five teenagers and charged them with rape. The arrests were supported by confessions that the NYPD detectives had obtained from the five teenagers. Although DNA tests failed to link the suspects to the rape, all five were convicted and sent to prison.

In 2002, another individual, Matias Reyes, who was already incarcerated, confessed to the crime. DNA evidence corroborated the confession from Reyes and proved that he was the rapist. The convictions for the original five defendants were vacated, though their vindication in some sense came too late, given that four of them had finished their prison sentences for the crime.

Why would the original five have confessed to the crime? Each one admitted to being a mere accomplice to someone else and none of them admitted to being the principal perpetrator in the rape. It is unclear if the teenagers falsely believed that their admitted involvement was so minor that it fell beyond the scope of criminal responsibility; in other words, they might have misunderstood the rules regarding complicity. Also, one of the defendants later asserted that he confessed because he heard one of the other suspects being beaten in a neighboring interrogation room and confessed to avoid a similar fate. It is unclear whether this was a police ruse or whether detectives used inappropriate physical force during some of the interrogations. Although each of the suspects was given *Miranda* warnings, none of the suspects exercised their right to counsel during the police interviews.

Three of the five men exonerated in the Central Park jogger rape case. Raymond Santana, Yusef Salaam, and Kevin Richardson at a news conference at City Hall in 2014. (Bebeto Matthews/AP/Shutterstock)

Does this case suggest that the standards for what counts as unconstitutional psychological pressure are not restrictive enough? As one commentator noted:

> If the trial judge was right that the police and prosecutor violated no constitutional commands when securing the five confessions, it follows that it is possible for the police to obtain a confession that is false without constitutional error. This acknowledgment has potentially devastating implications for a system committed to taking all proper steps to bringing the guilty to justice while avoiding the conviction of the innocent. If the time-tested interrogation techniques used in the Central Park case could produce five false confessions within a forty-eight hour period, it is likely that the same techniques produced similar results in the past, and will produce them again. This alone should convince us of the necessity to explore where the fault lines of interrogation techniques lie and what can be done to minimize their most harmful consequences.

Sharon L. Davies, *The Reality of False Confessions–Lessons of the Central Park Jogger Case*, 30 N.Y.U. Rev. L. & Soc. Change 209, 223 (2006).

is not without its exceptions or nuances, suggesting a constitutional framework designed to balance the requirements of the Fifth Amendment with the community's need for the police to conduct interrogations consistent with the demands of crime control. This dynamic plays out in different ways in the doctrine as explored in the following subsections.

1. The *Miranda* Rule

There is always the possibility of an epistemic gap between a suspect's constitutional rights and their knowledge (or lack thereof) of those rights. What obligations do police have to inform suspects of their rights—especially their right to remain silent? Indeed, the right itself will have no impact on suspects' decision-making process if they are not aware of the right and do not factor it into their options. However, there are few areas in the law where state officials are required to affirmatively announce legal rights to those who are in the position of exercising them.

Normally, when the government (a judge, a court, a police officer) asks a question, the mere act of answering results in the inference that the individual voluntarily waived her right to refuse to answer based on the privilege against self-incrimination. However, is that inference valid when police create an atmosphere that seems intended to disable the individual's ability to make a rational choice? And if so, should the State be required to offer "something more" to prove the waiver was in fact valid as a prerequisite to using the statement as evidence against the individual? This is the question that the Court addressed in the seminal opinion below. As you read *Miranda*, identify the Supreme Court's rationale for this "prophylactic" rule that was created to protect the underlying privilege *not* to answer questions. Identifying the rationale for the eponymous rule is the first step in understanding the exceptions and waivers that will be articulated in the following subsections.

Miranda v. Arizona

Supreme Court of the United States
384 U.S. 436 (1966)

Mr. Chief Justice WARREN delivered the opinion of the Court.

The cases before us raise questions which go to the roots of our concepts of American criminal jurisprudence: the restraints society must observe consistent with the Federal Constitution in prosecuting individuals for crime. More specifically, we deal with the admissibility of statements obtained from an individual who is subjected to custodial police interrogation and the necessity for procedures which assure that the individual is accorded his privilege under the Fifth Amendment to the Constitution not to be compelled to incriminate himself.

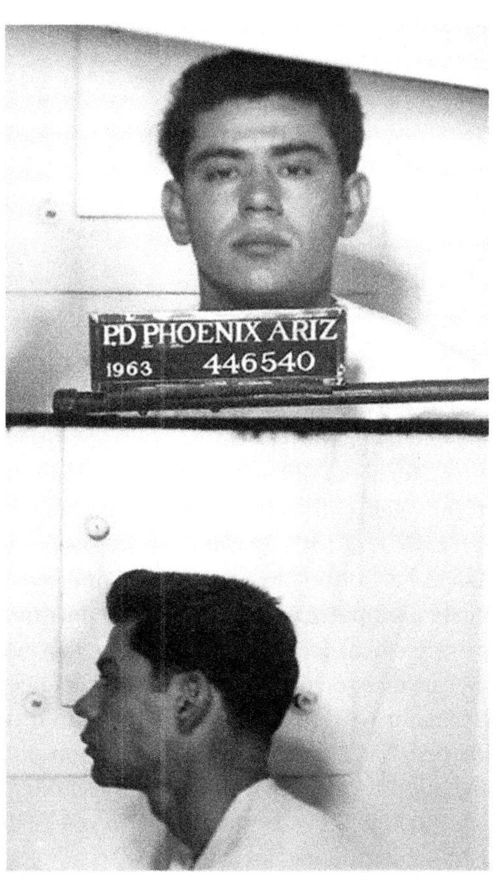

Booking photos of Ernesto Miranda on display at the Phoenix Police Museum in Phoenix, AZ. (Matt York/AP/Shutterstock)

We dealt with certain phases of this problem recently in *Escobedo v. Illinois*, 378 U.S. 478 (1964). There, as in the four cases before us, law enforcement officials took the defendant into custody and interrogated him in a police station for the purpose of obtaining a confession. The police did not effectively advise him of his right to remain silent or of his right to consult with his attorney. Rather, they confronted him with an alleged accomplice who accused him of having perpetrated a murder. When the defendant denied the accusation and said "I didn't shoot Manuel, you did it," they handcuffed him and took him to an interrogation room. There, while handcuffed and standing, he was questioned for four hours until he confessed. During this interrogation, the police denied his request to speak to his attorney, and they prevented his retained attorney, who had come to the police station, from consulting with him. At his trial, the State, over his objection, introduced the confession against him. We held that the statements thus made were constitutionally inadmissible. . . .

We start here, as we did in *Escobedo*, with the premise that our holding is not an innovation in our jurisprudence, but is an application of principles long recognized and applied in other settings. We have undertaken a thorough re-examination of the *Escobedo* decision and the principles it announced, and we reaffirm it. That case was but an explication of basic rights that are enshrined in our Constitution—that "No person . . . shall be compelled in any criminal case to be a witness against himself," and that "the accused shall . . . have the Assistance of Counsel"—rights which were put in jeopardy in that case through official overbearing. These precious rights were fixed in our Constitution only after centuries of persecution and struggle. And in the words of Chief Justice Marshall, they were secured "for ages to come, and . . . designed to approach immortality as nearly as human institutions can approach it." . . .

It was necessary in *Escobedo*, as here, to insure that what was proclaimed in the Constitution had not become but a "form of words," in the hands of government officials. And it is in this spirit, consistent with our role as judges, that we adhere to the principles of *Escobedo* today.

Our holding will be spelled out with some specificity in the pages which follow but briefly stated it is this: the prosecution may not use statements, whether exculpatory or inculpatory, stemming from custodial interrogation of the defendant unless it demonstrates the use of procedural safeguards effective to secure the privilege against self-incrimination. By custodial interrogation, we mean questioning initiated by law enforcement officers after a person has been taken into custody or otherwise deprived of his freedom of action in any significant way. As for the procedural safeguards to be employed, unless other fully effective means are devised to inform accused persons of their right of silence and to assure a continuous opportunity to exercise it, the following measures are required. Prior to any questioning, the person must be warned that he has a right to remain silent, that any statement he does make may be used as evidence against him, and that he has a right to the presence of an attorney, either retained or appointed. The defendant may waive effectuation of these rights, provided the waiver is made voluntarily, knowingly and intelligently. If, however, he indicates in any manner and at any stage of the process that he wishes to consult with an attorney before speaking there can be no questioning. Likewise, if the individual is alone and indicates in any manner that he does not wish to be interrogated, the police may not question him. The mere fact that he may have answered some questions or volunteered some statements on his own does not deprive him of the right to refrain from answering any further inquiries until he has consulted with an attorney and thereafter consents to be questioned.

I

The constitutional issue we decide in each of these cases is the admissibility of statements obtained from a defendant questioned while in custody or otherwise deprived of his freedom of action in any significant way. In each, the defendant was questioned by police officers, detectives, or a prosecuting attorney in a room in which he was cut off from the outside world. In none of these cases was the defendant given a full and effective warning of his rights at the outset of the interrogation process. In all the cases, the questioning elicited oral admissions, and in three of them, signed statements as well which were admitted at their trials. They all thus share salient features—incommunicado interrogation of individuals in a police-dominated atmosphere, resulting in self-incriminating statements without full warnings of constitutional rights.

An understanding of the nature and setting of this in-custody interrogation is essential to our decisions today. The difficulty in depicting what transpires at such interrogations stems from the fact that in this country they have largely taken place incommunicado. From extensive factual studies undertaken in the early 1930's, including the famous Wickersham Report to Congress by a Presidential Commission, it is clear that police violence and the "third degree" flourished at that time. In a series of cases decided by this Court long after these studies, the police resorted to physical brutality—beatings, hanging, whipping—and to sustained and protracted questioning incommunicado in order to extort confessions. The Commission on Civil Rights in 1961 found much evidence to indicate that "some policemen still resort to physical force to obtain confessions." The use of physical brutality and violence is not, unfortunately, relegated to the past or to any part of the country. Only recently in Kings County, New York, the police brutally beat, kicked and placed lighted cigarette butts on the back of a potential witness under interrogation for the purpose of securing a statement incriminating a third party.

The examples given above are undoubtedly the exception now, but they are sufficiently widespread to be the object of concern. Unless a proper limitation upon custodial interrogation is achieved—such as these decisions will advance—there can be no assurance that practices of this nature will be eradicated in the foreseeable future. . . .

Again we stress that the modern practice of in-custody interrogation is psychologically rather than physically oriented. As we have stated before, ". . . coercion can be mental as well as physical, and . . . the blood of the accused is not the only hallmark of an unconstitutional inquisition." Interrogation still takes place in privacy. Privacy results in secrecy and this in turn results in a gap in our knowledge as to what in fact goes on in the interrogation rooms. A valuable source of information about present police practices, however, may be found in various police manuals and texts which document procedures employed with success in the past, and which recommend various other effective tactics. These texts are used by law enforcement agencies themselves as guides. It should be noted that these texts professedly present the most enlightened and effective means presently used to obtain statements through custodial interrogation. By considering these texts and other data, it is possible to describe procedures observed and noted around the country.

The officers are told by the manuals that the "principal psychological factor contributing to a successful interrogation is privacy—being alone with the person under interrogation." . . . The manuals suggest that the suspect be offered legal excuses for his actions in order to obtain an initial admission of guilt. Where there is a suspected revenge-killing, for example, the interrogator may say:

> Joe, you probably didn't go out looking for this fellow with the purpose of shooting him. My guess is, however, that you expected something from him and that's why you carried a gun—for your own protection. You knew him for what he was, no good. Then when you met him he probably started using foul, abusive language and he gave some indication that he was about to pull a gun on you, and that's when you had to act to save your own life. That's about it, isn't it, Joe?

Having then obtained the admission of shooting, the interrogator is advised to refer to circumstantial evidence which negates the self-defense explanation. This should enable him to secure the entire story. One text notes that "Even if he fails to do so, the inconsistency between the subject's original denial of the shooting and his present admission of at least doing the shooting will serve to deprive him of a self-defense 'out' at the time of trial."

When the techniques described above prove unavailing, the texts recommend they be alternated with a show of some hostility. One ploy often used has been termed the "friendly-unfriendly" or the "Mutt and Jeff" act. . . .[1]

The interrogators sometimes are instructed to induce a confession out of trickery. The technique here is quite effective in crimes which require identification or which run in series. In the identification situation, the interrogator may take a break in his questioning to place the subject among a group of men in a line-up. "The witness or complainant (previously

1. [Editor's Note: In modern parlance, this technique is usually referred to as "good cop/bad cop."]

coached, if necessary) studies the line-up and confidently points out the subject as the guilty party." Then the questioning resumes "as though there were now no doubt about the guilt of the subject." A variation on this technique is called the "reverse line-up":

> The accused is placed in a line-up, but this time he is identified by several fictitious witnesses or victims who associated him with different offenses. It is expected that the subject will become desperate and confess to the offense under investigation in order to escape from the false accusations.

. . . From these representative samples of interrogation techniques, the setting prescribed by the manuals and observed in practice becomes clear. In essence, it is this: To be alone with the subject is essential to prevent distraction and to deprive him of any outside support. The aura of confidence in his guilt undermines his will to resist. He merely confirms the preconceived story the police seek to have him describe. Patience and persistence, at times relentless questioning, are employed. . . . When normal procedures fail to produce the needed result, the police may resort to deceptive stratagems such as giving false legal advice. . . . The police then persuade, trick, or cajole him out of exercising his constitutional rights. Even without employing brutality, the "third degree" or the specific stratagems described above, the very fact of custodial interrogation exacts a heavy toll on individual liberty and trades on the weakness of individuals. . . .

In these cases, we might not find the defendants' statements to have been involuntary in traditional terms. Our concern for adequate safeguards to protect precious Fifth Amendment rights is, of course, not lessened in the slightest. In each of the cases, the defendant was thrust into an unfamiliar atmosphere and run through menacing police interrogation procedures. . . . To be sure, the records do not evince overt physical coercion or patent psychological ploys. The fact remains that in none of these cases did the officers undertake to afford appropriate safeguards at the outset of the interrogation to insure that the statements were truly the product of free choice.

It is obvious that such an interrogation environment is created for no purpose other than to subjugate the individual to the will of his examiner. This atmosphere carries its own badge of intimidation. To be sure, this is not physical intimidation, but it is equally destructive of human dignity. The current practice of incommunicado interrogation is at odds with one of our Nation's most cherished principles—that the individual may not be compelled to incriminate himself. Unless adequate protective devices are employed to dispel the compulsion inherent in custodial surroundings, no statement obtained from the defendant can truly be the product of his free choice. . . .

III

Today, then, there can be no doubt that the Fifth Amendment privilege is available outside of criminal court proceedings and serves to protect persons in all settings in which their freedom of action is curtailed in any significant way from being compelled to incriminate themselves. We have concluded that without proper safeguards the process of in-custody interrogation of persons suspected or accused of crime contains inherently compelling pressures which work to undermine the individual's will to resist and to compel him to speak where he would not otherwise do so freely. In order to combat these pressures and to permit a full opportunity to exercise the privilege against self-incrimination, the accused must be adequately and effectively apprised of his rights and the exercise of those rights must be fully honored.

It is impossible for us to foresee the potential alternatives for protecting the privilege which might be devised by Congress or the States in the exercise of their creative rule-making capacities. Therefore we cannot say that the Constitution necessarily requires adherence to any particular solution for the inherent compulsions of the interrogation process as it is presently conducted. Our decision in no way creates a constitutional straitjacket which will handicap sound efforts at reform, nor is it intended to have this effect. We encourage Congress and the States to continue their laudable search for increasingly effective ways of protecting the rights of the individual while promoting efficient enforcement of our criminal laws. However, unless we are shown other procedures which are at least as effective in apprising accused persons of their right of silence and in assuring a continuous opportunity to exercise it, the following safeguards must be observed.

At the outset, if a person in custody is to be subjected to interrogation, he must first be informed in clear and unequivocal terms that he has the right to remain silent. For those unaware of the privilege, the warning is needed simply to make them aware of it—the threshold requirement for an intelligent decision as to its exercise. More important, such a warning is an absolute prerequisite in overcoming the inherent pressures of the interrogation atmosphere. It is not just the subnormal or woefully ignorant who succumb to an interrogator's imprecations, whether implied or expressly stated, that the interrogation will continue until a confession is obtained or that silence in the face of accusation is itself damning and will bode ill when presented to a jury. Further, the warning will show the individual that his interrogators are prepared to recognize his privilege should he choose to exercise it.

The Fifth Amendment privilege is so fundamental to our system of constitutional rule and the expedient of giving an adequate warning as to the availability of the privilege so simple, we will not pause to inquire in individual cases whether the defendant was aware of his rights without a warning being given. Assessments of the knowledge the defendant possessed, based on information as to his age, education, intelligence, or prior contact with authorities, can never be more than speculation; a warning is a clearcut fact. More important, whatever the background of the person interrogated, a warning at the time of the interrogation is indispensable to overcome its pressures and to insure that the individual knows he is free to exercise the privilege at that point in time.

The warning of the right to remain silent must be accompanied by the explanation that anything said can and will be used against the individual in court. This warning is needed in order to make him aware not only of the privilege, but also of the consequences of forgoing it. It is only through an awareness of these consequences that there can be any assurance of real understanding and intelligent exercise of the privilege. Moreover, this warning may serve to make the individual more acutely aware that he is faced with a phase of the adversary system—that he is not in the presence of persons acting solely in his interest.

The circumstances surrounding in-custody interrogation can operate very quickly to overbear the will of one merely made aware of his privilege by his interrogators. Therefore, the right to have counsel present at the interrogation is indispensable to the protection of the Fifth Amendment privilege under the system we delineate today. Our aim is to assure that the individual's right to choose between silence and speech remains unfettered throughout the interrogation process. A once-stated warning, delivered by those who will conduct the interrogation, cannot itself suffice to that end among those who most require knowledge of their rights. A mere warning given by the interrogators is not alone sufficient to accomplish that end. Prosecutors themselves claim that the admonishment of the right to remain silent without more "will benefit only the recidivist and the professional." Even preliminary advice given to the accused by his own attorney can be swiftly overcome by the secret interrogation process. Thus, the need for counsel to protect the Fifth Amendment privilege comprehends not merely a right to consult with counsel prior to questioning, but also to have counsel present during any questioning if the defendant so desires. . . .

The presence of counsel at the interrogation may serve several significant subsidiary functions as well. If the accused decides to talk to his interrogators, the assistance of counsel can mitigate the dangers of untrustworthiness. With a lawyer present the likelihood that the police will practice coercion is reduced, and if coercion is nevertheless exercised the lawyer can testify to it in court. The presence of a lawyer can also help to guarantee that the accused gives a fully accurate statement to the police and that the statement is rightly reported by the prosecution at trial.

An individual need not make a pre-interrogation request for a lawyer. While such request affirmatively secures his right to have one, his failure to ask for a lawyer does not constitute a waiver. No effective waiver of the right to counsel during interrogation can be recognized unless specifically made after the warnings we here delineate have been given. The accused who does not know his rights and therefore does not make a request may be the person who most needs counsel. . . .

Accordingly we hold that an individual held for interrogation must be clearly informed that he has the right to consult with a lawyer and to have the lawyer with him during interrogation under the system for protecting the privilege we delineate today. As with the warnings of the right to remain silent and that anything stated can be used in evidence against him, this warning is an absolute prerequisite to interrogation. No amount of circumstantial evidence that the person may have been aware of this right will suffice to stand in its stead. Only through such a warning is there ascertainable assurance that the accused was aware of this right.

If an individual indicates that he wishes the assistance of counsel before any interrogation occurs, the authorities cannot rationally ignore or deny his request on the basis that the individual does not have or cannot afford a retained attorney. The financial ability of the individual has no relationship to the scope of the rights involved here. The privilege against self-incrimination secured by the Constitution applies to all individuals. The need for counsel in order to protect the privilege exists for the indigent as well as the affluent. In fact, were we to limit these constitutional rights to those who can retain an attorney, our decisions today would be of little significance. The cases before us as well as the vast majority of confession cases with which we have dealt in the past involve those unable to retain counsel. While authorities are not required to relieve the accused of his poverty, they have the obligation not to take advantage of indigence in the administration of justice. Denial of counsel to the indigent at the time of interrogation while allowing an attorney to those who can afford one would be no more supportable by reason or logic than the similar situation at trial. . . .

In order fully to apprise a person interrogated of the extent of his rights under this system then, it is necessary to warn him not only that he has the right to consult with an attorney, but also that if he is indigent a lawyer will be appointed to represent him. Without this additional warning, the admonition of the right to consult with counsel would often be understood as meaning only that he can consult with a lawyer if he has one or has the funds to obtain one. The warning of a right to counsel would be hollow if not couched in terms that would convey to the indigent—the person most often subjected to interrogation—the knowledge that he too has a right to have counsel present. As with the warnings of the right to remain silent and of the general right to counsel, only by effective and express explanation to the indigent of this right can there be assurance that he was truly in a position to exercise it.

Once warnings have been given, the subsequent procedure is clear. If the individual indicates in any manner, at any time prior to or during questioning, that he wishes to remain silent, the interrogation must cease. At this point he has shown that he intends to exercise his Fifth Amendment privilege; any statement taken after the person invokes his privilege cannot be other than the product of compulsion, subtle or otherwise. Without the right to cut off questioning, the setting of in-custody interrogation operates on the individual to overcome free choice in producing a statement after the privilege has been once invoked. If the individual states that he wants an attorney, the interrogation must cease until an attorney is present. At that time, the individual must have an opportunity to confer with the attorney and to have him present during any subsequent questioning. If the individual cannot obtain an attorney and he indicates that he wants one before speaking to police, they must respect his decision to remain silent.

This does not mean, as some have suggested, that each police station must have a "station house lawyer" present at all times to advise prisoners. It does mean, however, that if police propose to interrogate a person they must make known to him that he is entitled to a lawyer and that if he cannot afford one, a lawyer will be provided for him prior to any interrogation. If authorities conclude that they will not provide counsel during a reasonable period of time in which investigation in the field is carried out, they may refrain from doing so without violating the person's Fifth Amendment privilege so long as they do not question him during that time.

If the interrogation continues without the presence of an attorney and a statement is taken, a heavy burden rests on the government to demonstrate that the defendant knowingly and intelligently waived his privilege against self-incrimination and his right to retained or appointed counsel. This Court has always set high standards of proof for the waiver of constitutional rights and we reassert these standards as applied to in-custody interrogation. Since the State is responsible for establishing the isolated circumstances under which the interrogation takes place and has the only means of making available corroborated evidence of warnings given during incommunicado interrogation, the burden is rightly on its shoulders.

An express statement that the individual is willing to make a statement and does not want an attorney followed closely by a statement could constitute a waiver. But a valid waiver will not be presumed simply from the silence of the accused after warnings are given or simply from the fact that a confession was in fact eventually obtained. . . . Moreover, where in-custody interrogation is involved, there is no room for the contention that the privilege is waived if the individual answers some questions or gives some information on his own prior to invoking his right to remain silent when interrogated.

Whatever the testimony of the authorities as to waiver of rights by an accused, the fact of lengthy interrogation or incommunicado incarceration before a statement is made is strong evidence that the accused did not validly waive his rights. In these circumstances the fact that the individual eventually made a statement is consistent with the conclusion that the compelling influence of the interrogation finally forced him to do so. It is inconsistent with any notion of a voluntary relinquishment of the privilege. Moreover, any evidence that the accused was threatened, tricked, or cajoled into a waiver will, of course, show that the defendant did not voluntarily waive his privilege. The requirement of warnings and waiver of rights is a fundamental with respect to the Fifth Amendment privilege and not simply a preliminary ritual to existing methods of interrogation.

The warnings required and the waiver necessary in accordance with our opinion today are, in the absence of a fully effective equivalent, prerequisites to the admissibility of any statement made by a defendant. No distinction can be drawn between statements which are direct confessions and statements which amount to "admissions" of part or all of an offense.

The privilege against self-incrimination protects the individual from being compelled to incriminate himself in any manner; it does not distinguish degrees of incrimination. Similarly, for precisely the same reason, no distinction may be drawn between inculpatory statements and statements alleged to be merely "exculpatory." If a statement made were in fact truly exculpatory it would, of course, never be used by the prosecution. In fact, statements merely intended to be exculpatory by the defendant are often used to impeach his testimony at trial or to demonstrate untruths in the statement given under interrogation and thus to prove guilt by implication. These statements are incriminating in any meaningful sense of the word and may not be used without the full warnings and effective waiver required for any other statement. In *Escobedo* itself, the defendant fully intended his accusation of another as the slayer to be exculpatory as to himself.

The principles announced today deal with the protection which must be given to the privilege against self-incrimination when the individual is first subjected to police interrogation while in custody at the station or otherwise deprived of his freedom of action in any significant way. It is at this point that our adversary system of criminal proceedings commences, distinguishing itself at the outset from the inquisitorial system recognized in some countries. Under the system of warnings we delineate today or under any other system which may be devised and found effective, the safeguards to be erected about the privilege must come into play at this point.

Our decision is not intended to hamper the traditional function of police officers in investigating crime. When an individual is in custody on probable cause, the police may, of course, seek out evidence in the field to be used at trial against him. Such investigation may include inquiry of persons not under restraint. General on-the-scene questioning as to facts surrounding a crime or other general questioning of citizens in the fact-finding process is not affected by our holding. It is an act of responsible citizenship for individuals to give whatever information they may have to aid in law enforcement. In such situations the compelling atmosphere inherent in the process of in-custody interrogation is not necessarily present.

In dealing with statements obtained through interrogation, we do not purport to find all confessions inadmissible. Confessions remain a proper element in law enforcement. Any statement given freely and voluntarily without any compelling influences is, of course, admissible in evidence. The fundamental import of the privilege while an individual is in custody is not whether he is allowed to talk to the police without the benefit of warnings and counsel, but whether he can be interrogated. There is no requirement that police stop a person who enters a police station and states that he wishes to confess to a crime, or a person who calls the police to offer a confession or any other statement he desires to make. Volunteered statements of any kind are not barred by the Fifth Amendment and their admissibility is not affected by our holding today.

To summarize, we hold that when an individual is taken into custody or otherwise deprived of his freedom by the authorities in any significant way and is subjected to questioning, the privilege against self-incrimination is jeopardized. Procedural safeguards must be employed to protect the privilege and unless other fully effective means are adopted to notify the person of his right of silence and to assure that the exercise of the right will be scrupulously honored, the following measures are required. He must be warned prior to any questioning that he has the right to remain silent, that anything he says can be used against him in a court of law, that he has the right to the presence of an attorney, and that if he cannot afford an attorney one will be appointed for him prior to any questioning if he so desires. Opportunity to exercise these rights must be afforded to him throughout the interrogation. After such warnings have been given, and such opportunity afforded him, the individual may knowingly and intelligently waive these rights and agree to answer questions or make a statement. But unless and until such warnings and waiver are demonstrated by the prosecution at trial, no evidence obtained as a result of interrogation can be used against him. . . .

Dickerson v. United States

Supreme Court of the United States
530 U.S. 428 (2000)

Chief Justice Rehnquist delivered the opinion of the Court.

In *Miranda v. Arizona*, 384 U.S. 436 (1966), we held that certain warnings must be given before a suspect's statement made during custodial interrogation could be admitted in evidence. In the wake of that decision, Congress enacted 18 U.S.C. § 3501, which in essence laid down a rule that the admissibility of such statements should turn only on whether or not they were voluntarily made. We hold that *Miranda*, being a constitutional decision of this Court, may not be in effect overruled by an Act of Congress, and we decline to overrule *Miranda* ourselves. We therefore hold that *Miranda* and its progeny in this Court govern the admissibility of statements made during custodial interrogation in both state and federal courts.

Petitioner Dickerson was indicted for bank robbery, conspiracy to commit bank robbery, and using a firearm in the course of committing a crime of violence, all in violation of the applicable provisions of Title 18 of the United States Code. Before trial, Dickerson moved to suppress a statement he had made at a Federal Bureau of Investigation field office, on the grounds that he had not received "*Miranda* warnings" before being interrogated. . . .

We begin with a brief historical account of the law governing the admission of confessions. Prior to *Miranda*, we evaluated the admissibility of a suspect's confession under a voluntariness test. The roots of this test developed in the common law, as the courts of England and then the United

States recognized that coerced confessions are inherently untrustworthy. Over time, our cases recognized two constitutional bases for the requirement that a confession be voluntary to be admitted into evidence: the Fifth Amendment right against self-incrimination and the Due Process Clause of the Fourteenth Amendment.

. . . For the middle third of the 20th century our cases based the rule against admitting coerced confessions primarily, if not exclusively, on notions of due process. We . . . refined the test into an inquiry that examines "whether a defendant's will was overborne" by the circumstances surrounding the giving of a confession. The due process test takes into consideration "the totality of all the surrounding circumstances—both the characteristics of the accused and the details of the interrogation." The determination "depend[s] upon a weighing of the circumstances of pressure against the power of resistance of the person confessing."

We have never abandoned this due process jurisprudence, and thus continue to exclude confessions that were obtained involuntarily. But our decisions in *Malloy v. Hogan*, 378 U.S. 1 (1964), and *Miranda* changed the focus of much of the inquiry in determining the admissibility of suspects' incriminating statements. In *Malloy*, we held that the Fifth Amendment's Self-Incrimination Clause is incorporated in the Due Process Clause of the Fourteenth Amendment and thus applies to the States. We decided *Miranda* on the heels of *Malloy*.

. . . Two years after *Miranda* was decided, Congress enacted § 3501. That section provides, in relevant part:

> (a) In any criminal prosecution brought by the United States or by the District of Columbia, a confession . . . shall be admissible in evidence if it is voluntarily given. Before such confession is received in evidence, the trial judge shall, out of the presence of the jury, determine any issue as to voluntariness. If the trial judge determines that the confession was voluntarily made it shall be admitted in evidence and the trial judge shall permit the jury to hear relevant evidence on the issue of voluntariness and shall instruct the jury to give such weight to the confession as the jury feels it deserves under all the circumstances.
>
> (b) The trial judge in determining the issue of voluntariness shall take into consideration all the circumstances surrounding the giving of the confession, including (1) the time elapsing between arrest and arraignment of the defendant making the confession, if it was made after arrest and before arraignment, (2) whether such defendant knew the nature of the offense with which he was charged or of which he was suspected at the time of making the confession, (3) whether or not such defendant was advised or knew that he was not required to make any statement and that any such statement could be used against him, (4) whether or not such defendant had been advised

> prior to questioning of his right to the assistance of counsel; and (5) whether or not such defendant was without the assistance of counsel when questioned and when giving such confession.
> The presence or absence of any of the above-mentioned factors to be taken into consideration by the judge need not be conclusive on the issue of voluntariness of the confession.

Given § 3501's express designation of voluntariness as the touchstone of admissibility, its omission of any warning requirement, and the instruction for trial courts to consider a nonexclusive list of factors relevant to the circumstances of a confession, we agree with the Court of Appeals that Congress intended by its enactment to overrule *Miranda*. Because of the obvious conflict between our decision in Miranda and § 3501, we must address whether Congress has constitutional authority to thus supersede *Miranda*. If Congress has such authority, § 3501's totality-of-the-circumstances approach must prevail over *Miranda*'s requirement of warnings; if not, that section must yield to *Miranda*'s more specific requirements.

The law in this area is clear. This Court has supervisory authority over the federal courts, and we may use that authority to prescribe rules of evidence and procedure that are binding in those tribunals. However, the power to judicially create and enforce nonconstitutional "rules of procedure and evidence for the federal courts exists only in the absence of a relevant Act of Congress." Congress retains the ultimate authority to modify or set aside any judicially created rules of evidence and procedure that are not required by the Constitution.

But Congress may not legislatively supersede our decisions interpreting and applying the Constitution. This case therefore turns on whether the *Miranda* Court announced a constitutional rule or merely exercised its supervisory authority to regulate evidence in the absence of congressional direction. Recognizing this point, the Court of Appeals surveyed *Miranda* and its progeny to determine the constitutional status of the *Miranda* decision. Relying on the fact that we have created several exceptions to *Miranda*'s warnings requirement and that we have repeatedly referred to the *Miranda* warnings as "prophylactic," and "not themselves rights protected by the Constitution," the Court of Appeals concluded that the protections announced in *Miranda* are not constitutionally required.

We disagree with the Court of Appeals' conclusion, although we concede that there is language in some of our opinions that supports the view taken by that court. But first and foremost of the factors on the other side—that *Miranda* is a constitutional decision—is that both *Miranda* and two of its companion cases applied the rule to proceedings in state courts—to wit, Arizona, California, and New York. Since that time, we have consistently applied *Miranda*'s rule to prosecutions arising in state courts. It is beyond dispute that we do not hold a supervisory power over the courts of the several States. With respect to proceedings in state courts, our "authority is limited to enforcing the commands of the United States Constitution." . . .

In sum, we conclude that *Miranda* announced a constitutional rule that Congress may not supersede legislatively. Following the rule of stare decisis, we decline to overrule *Miranda* ourselves. . . .

Justice Scalia, with whom Justice Thomas joins, dissenting.

. . . As the Court today acknowledges, since *Miranda* we have explicitly, and repeatedly, interpreted that decision as having announced, not the circumstances in which custodial interrogation runs afoul of the Fifth or Fourteenth Amendment, but rather only "prophylactic" rules that go beyond the right against compelled self-incrimination. Of course the seeds of this "prophylactic" interpretation of *Miranda* were present in the decision itself. In subsequent cases, the seeds have sprouted and borne fruit: The Court has squarely concluded that it is possible—indeed not uncommon—for the police to violate *Miranda* without also violating the Constitution.

Michigan v. Tucker, 417 U.S. 433 (1974), an opinion for the Court written by then-Justice Rehnquist, rejected the true-to-*Marbury*, failure-to-warn-as-constitutional-violation interpretation of *Miranda*. It held that exclusion of the "fruits" of a *Miranda* violation—the statement of a witness whose identity the defendant had revealed while in custody—was not required. The opinion explained that the question whether the "police conduct complained of directly infringed upon respondent's right against compulsory self-incrimination" was a "separate question" from "whether it instead violated only the prophylactic rules developed to protect that right." The "procedural safeguards" adopted in *Miranda*, the Court said, "were not themselves rights protected by the Constitution but were instead measures to insure that the right against compulsory self-incrimination was protected," and to "provide practical reinforcement for the right." Comparing the particular facts of the custodial interrogation with the "historical circumstances underlying the privilege," the Court concluded, unequivocally, that the defendant's statement could not be termed "involuntary as that term has been defined in the decisions of this Court," and thus that there had been no constitutional violation, notwithstanding the clear violation of the "procedural rules later established in *Miranda*." Lest there be any confusion on the point, the Court reiterated that the "police conduct at issue here did not abridge respondent's constitutional privilege against compulsory self-incrimination, but departed only from the prophylactic standards later laid down by this Court in *Miranda* to safeguard that privilege." It is clear from our cases, of course, that if the statement in *Tucker* had been obtained in violation of the Fifth Amendment, the statement and its fruits would have been excluded.

The next year, in *Oregon v. Hass*, 420 U.S. 714 (1975), the Court held that a defendant's statement taken in violation of *Miranda* that was nonetheless voluntary could be used at trial for impeachment purposes. This holding turned upon the recognition that violation of *Miranda* is not unconstitutional compulsion, since statements obtained in actual violation of the privilege against compelled self-incrimination, "as opposed to . . . taken in violation of *Miranda*," quite simply "may not be put to any testimonial use whatever against [the defendant] in a criminal trial," including as impeachment evidence.

Nearly a decade later, in *New York v. Quarles*, 467 U.S. 649 (1984), the Court relied upon the fact that "[t]he prophylactic *Miranda* warning . . . are not themselves rights protected by the Constitution," to create a "public safety" exception. In that case, police apprehended, after a chase in a grocery store, a rape suspect known to be carrying a gun. After handcuffing and searching him (and finding no gun)—but before reading him his *Miranda* warnings—the police demanded to know where the gun was. The defendant nodded in the direction of some empty cartons and responded that "the gun is over there." The Court held that both the unwarned statement—"the gun is over there"—and the recovered weapon were admissible in the prosecution's case in chief under a "public safety exception" to the "prophylactic rules enunciated in *Miranda*." It explicitly acknowledged that if the *Miranda* warnings were an imperative of the Fifth Amendment itself, such an exigency exception would be impossible, since the Fifth Amendment's bar on compelled self-incrimination is absolute, and its "strictures, unlike the Fourth's are not removed by showing reasonableness." . . .

In light of these cases, and our statements to the same effect in others, it is simply no longer possible for the Court to conclude, even if it wanted to, that a violation of *Miranda*'s rules is a violation of the Constitution. . . . By disregarding congressional action that concededly does not violate the Constitution, the Court flagrantly offends fundamental principles of separation of powers, and arrogates to itself prerogatives reserved to the representatives of the people. . . . Today's judgment converts *Miranda* from a milestone of judicial overreaching into the very Cheops' Pyramid (or perhaps the Sphinx would be a better analogue) of judicial arrogance. . . .

NOTES & QUESTIONS ON THE MIRANDA *RULE*

1. Miranda *and voluntariness.* What did the Court mean when it said, "we might not find the defendants' statements to have been involuntary in traditional terms"? If the Court was acknowledging the confessions were not in fact coerced, what "type" of coercion was it concerned with? And why the reference to "free choice" instead of "a voluntary" confession? Perhaps the Court was not so much concerned that the methods compromised the probative value

of the content of the statements—that was not the issue. The issue was whether the suspect made a voluntary decision to cooperate with the police and thereby gave up the right not to cooperate and force the police to solve the case without his help. Thus, the focus of *Miranda*, unlike due process, is the initial decision to submit to questioning, and the loss of confidence that this decision was truly voluntary because of the inherently coercive environment the police created.

2. *What is a constitutional holding?* The Supreme Court in *Dickerson* clearly disagreed over the status of the *Miranda* holding, concluding that it was a constitutional rule binding on the states but also conceding that its status, until then, had been ambiguous. Indeed, the very notion of a "prophylactic" rule suggests the possibility that the rule is merely prudential. The result is noteworthy because Justices Scalia and Thomas are not joined in their dissent by Chief Justice Rehnquist. How is this dispute resolved? What is the definition of a "constitutional" case? As one commentator noted:

> If it is possible to discern a rule of constitutional construction from a single case, *Dickerson* defines a constitutional case as one that creates rules or procedures to enforce a specific constitutional provision or principle not necessarily required by the Constitution. *Miranda* was determined to be a constitutional case, thus immune from congressional adjustment, because *Miranda* addressed a constitutional principle (the Fifth Amendment right against the use of compelled statements—and preventing the prosecution from profiting from a Fifth Amendment violation) and created rules to protect that principle (the *Miranda* warnings) and enforcement of those rules (the exclusion of statements in violation of those rules).

Arthur H. Garrison, *Rehnquist v. Scalia—The* Dickerson *and* Miranda *Cases: A Debate on What Makes a Decision Constitutional*, 25 Am. J. Trial Advoc. 91, 132 (2001).

2. Defining Custody

Police are not required to give *Miranda* warnings to every criminal suspect, but only those that are undergoing "custodial" interrogation. Prior to the commencement of the custodial interrogation, i.e., in that pre-custodial period—police are entitled to ask a suspect a question without advising them of their Fifth Amendment rights. But what does it mean for a suspect to be in "custody"? Clearly a formal arrest qualifies as custodial but the notion of a custodial interrogation, in fact, sweeps far broader than the one example of formal arrest. At the same time, perhaps *Miranda* did not intend to treat every situation of seizure as custody. The following cases explain and apply the concept of a "custodial" situation in greater detail. In reading these cases, ask yourself what it means for a suspect to have his or her "freedom of action in any significant way" limited or restricted. What factors should go into that analysis? And consider whether this statement might be accurate: "All custody is seizure, but not all seizure is custody."

Oregon v. Mathiason

Supreme Court of the United States
429 U.S. 492 (1977)

Per Curiam

Respondent Carl Mathiason was convicted of first-degree burglary after a bench trial in which his confession was critical to the State's case. At trial he moved to suppress the confession as the fruit of questioning by the police not preceded by the warnings required in *Miranda v. Arizona*, 384 U.S. 436 (1966). The trial court refused to exclude the confession because it found that Mathiason was not in custody at the time of the confession.

The Oregon Court of Appeals affirmed respondent's conviction, but on his petition for review in the Supreme Court of Oregon that court by a divided vote reversed the conviction. It found that although Mathiason had not been arrested or otherwise formally detained, "the interrogation took place in a 'coercive environment'" of the sort to which *Miranda* was intended to apply. The court conceded that its holding was contrary to decisions in other jurisdictions. . . . We think that court has read *Miranda* too broadly, and we therefore reverse its judgment.

The Supreme Court of Oregon described the factual situation surrounding the confession as follows:

> An officer of the State Police investigated a theft at a residence near Pendleton. He asked the lady of the house which had been burglarized if she suspected anyone. She replied that the defendant was the only one she could think of. The defendant was a parolee and a 'close associate' of her son. The officer tried to contact defendant on three or four occasions with no success. Finally, about 25 days after the burglary, the officer left his card at defendant's apartment with a note asking him to call because 'I'd like to discuss something with you.' The next afternoon the defendant did call. The officer asked where it would be convenient to meet. The defendant had no preference; so the officer asked if the defendant could meet him at the state patrol office in about an hour and a half, about 5:00 P.M. The patrol office was about two blocks from defendant's apartment. The building housed several state agencies.
>
> The officer met defendant in the hallway, shook hands and took him into an office. The defendant was told he was not under arrest. The door was closed. The two sat across a desk. The police radio in another room could be heard. The officer told defendant he wanted to talk to him about a burglary and that his truthfulness would possibly be

> considered by the district attorney or judge. The officer further advised that the police believed defendant was involved in the burglary and (falsely stated that) defendant's fingerprints were found at the scene. The defendant sat for a few minutes and then said he had taken the property. This occurred within five minutes after defendant had come to the office. The officer then advised defendant of his *Miranda* rights and took a taped confession.
>
> At the end of the taped conversation the officer told defendant he was not arresting him at this time; he was released to go about his job and return to his family. The officer said he was referring the case to the district attorney for him to determine whether criminal charges would be brought. It was 5:30 P.M. when the defendant left the office. . . .

Our decision in *Miranda* set forth rules of police procedure applicable to "custodial interrogation." "By custodial interrogation, we mean questioning initiated by law enforcement officers after a person has been taken into custody or otherwise deprived of his freedom of action in any significant way." Subsequently we have found the *Miranda* principle applicable to questioning which takes place in a prison setting during a suspect's term of imprisonment on a separate offense, *Mathis v. United States*, 391 U.S. 1 (1968), and to questioning taking place in a suspect's home, after he has been arrested and is no longer free to go where he pleases, *Orozco v. Texas*, 394 U.S. 324 (1969).

In the present case, however, there is no indication that the questioning took place in a context where respondent's freedom to depart was restricted in any way. He came voluntarily to the police station, where he was immediately informed that he was not under arrest. At the close of a 1/2-hour interview respondent did in fact leave the police station without hindrance. It is clear from these facts that Mathiason was not in custody "or otherwise deprived of his freedom of action in any significant way."

Such a noncustodial situation is not converted to one in which *Miranda* applies simply because a reviewing court concludes that, even in the absence of any formal arrest or restraint on freedom of movement, the questioning took place in a "coercive environment." Any interview of one suspected of a crime by a police officer will have coercive aspects to it, simply by virtue of the fact that the police officer is part of a law enforcement system which may ultimately cause the suspect to be charged with a crime. But police officers are not required to administer *Miranda* warnings to everyone whom they question. Nor is the requirement of warnings to be imposed simply because the questioning takes place in the station house, or because the questioned person is one whom the police suspect. *Miranda* warnings are required only where there has been such a restriction on a person's freedom as to render him "in custody." It was that sort of coercive environment to which *Miranda* by its terms was made applicable, and to which it is limited. . . .

Mr. Justice MARSHALL, dissenting.

The respondent in this case was interrogated behind closed doors at police headquarters in connection with a burglary investigation. He had been named by the victim of the burglary as a suspect, and was told by the police that they believed he was involved. He was falsely informed that his fingerprints had been found at the scene, and in effect was advised that by cooperating with the police he could help himself. Not until after he had confessed was he given the warnings set forth in *Miranda*.

The Court today holds that for constitutional purposes all this is irrelevant because respondent had not "been taken into custody or otherwise deprived of his freedom of action in any significant way." I do not believe that such a determination is possible on the record before us. It is true that respondent was not formally placed under arrest, but surely formalities alone cannot control. At the very least, if respondent entertained an objectively reasonable belief that he was not free to leave during the questioning, then he was "deprived of his freedom of action in a significant way." Plainly the respondent could have so believed, after being told by the police that they thought he was involved in a burglary and that his fingerprints had been found at the scene. Yet the majority is content to note that "there is no indication that . . . respondent's freedom to depart was restricted in any way," as if a silent record (and no state-court findings) means that the State has sustained its burden of demonstrating that respondent received his constitutional due.

More fundamentally, however, I cannot agree with the Court's conclusion that if respondent were not in custody no warnings were required. I recognize that *Miranda* is limited to custodial interrogations, but that is because, as we noted last Term, the facts in the *Miranda* cases raised only this "narrow issue." The rationale of *Miranda*, however, is not so easily cabined. . . . In my view, even if respondent were not in custody, the coercive elements in the instant case were so pervasive as to require *Miranda*-type warnings. . . .

Berkemer v. McCarty

Supreme Court of the United States
468 U.S. 420 (1984)

Justice MARSHALL delivered the opinion of the Court.

This case presents two related questions: First, does our decision in *Miranda v. Arizona*, 384 U.S. 436 (1966), govern the admissibility of statements made during custodial interrogation by a suspect accused of a misdemeanor traffic offense? Second, does the roadside questioning of a motorist detained pursuant to a traffic stop constitute custodial interrogation for the purposes of the doctrine enunciated in *Miranda*?

I

The parties have stipulated to the essential facts. On the evening of March 31, 1980, Trooper Williams of the Ohio State Highway Patrol observed respondent's car weaving in and out of a lane on Interstate Highway 270. After following the car for two miles, Williams forced respondent to stop and asked him to get out of the vehicle. When respondent complied, Williams noticed that he was having difficulty standing. At that point, "Williams concluded that [respondent] would be charged with a traffic offense and, therefore, his freedom to leave the scene was terminated." However, respondent was not told that he would be taken into custody. Williams then asked respondent to perform a field sobriety test, commonly known as a "balancing test." Respondent could not do so without falling.

While still at the scene of the traffic stop, Williams asked respondent whether he had been using intoxicants. Respondent replied that "he had consumed two beers and had smoked several joints of marijuana a short time before." Respondent's speech was slurred, and Williams had difficulty understanding him. Williams thereupon formally placed respondent under arrest and transported him in the patrol car to the Franklin County Jail.

At the jail, respondent was given an intoxilyzer test to determine the concentration of alcohol in his blood. The test did not detect any alcohol whatsoever in respondent's system. Williams then resumed questioning respondent in order to obtain information for inclusion in the State Highway Patrol Alcohol Influence Report. Respondent answered affirmatively a question whether he had been drinking. When then asked if he was under the influence of alcohol, he said, "I guess, barely." Williams next asked respondent to indicate on the form whether the marihuana he had smoked had been treated with any chemicals. In the section of the report headed "Remarks," respondent wrote, "No ang[el] dust or PCP in the pot. Rick McCarty."

At no point in this sequence of events did Williams or anyone else tell respondent that he had a right to remain silent, to consult with an attorney, and to have an attorney appointed for him if he could not afford one.

Respondent was charged with operating a motor vehicle while under the influence of alcohol and/or drugs. . . . Under Ohio law, that offense is a first-degree misdemeanor and is punishable by fine or imprisonment for up to six months. Incarceration for a minimum of three days is mandatory. . . .

III

To assess the admissibility of the self-incriminating statements made by respondent prior to his formal arrest, we are obliged to address a second issue concerning the scope of our decision in *Miranda*: whether the roadside questioning of a motorist detained pursuant to a routine traffic stop should be considered "custodial interrogation." Respondent urges that it should, on the ground that *Miranda* by its terms applies whenever "a person has been taken into custody or otherwise deprived of his freedom of action in any significant way." Petitioner contends that a holding that every detained motorist must be advised of his rights before being questioned would constitute an unwarranted extension of the *Miranda* doctrine.

It must be acknowledged at the outset that a traffic stop significantly curtails the "freedom of action" of the driver and the passengers, if any, of the detained vehicle. Under the law of most States, it is a crime either to ignore a policeman's signal to stop one's car or, once having stopped, to drive away without permission. Certainly few motorists would feel free either to disobey a directive to pull over or to leave the scene of a traffic stop without being told they might do so. Partly for these reasons, we have long acknowledged that "stopping an automobile and detaining its occupants constitute a 'seizure' within the meaning of [the Fourth] Amendmen[t], even though the purpose of the stop is limited and the resulting detention quite brief."

However, we decline to accord talismanic power to the phrase in the *Miranda* opinion emphasized by respondent. Fidelity to the doctrine announced in *Miranda* requires that it be enforced strictly, but only in those types of situations in which the concerns that powered the decision are implicated. Thus, we must decide whether a traffic stop exerts upon a detained person pressures that sufficiently impair his free exercise of his privilege against self-incrimination to require that he be warned of his constitutional rights.

Two features of an ordinary traffic stop mitigate the danger that a person questioned will be induced "to speak where he would not otherwise do so freely." First, detention of a motorist pursuant to a traffic stop is presumptively temporary and brief. The vast majority of roadside detentions last only a few minutes. A motorist's expectations, when he sees a policeman's light flashing behind him, are that he will be obliged to spend a short period of time answering questions and waiting while the officer checks his license and registration, that he may then be given a citation, but that in the end he most likely will be allowed to continue on his way. In this respect, questioning incident to an ordinary traffic stop is quite different from stationhouse interrogation, which frequently is prolonged, and in which the detainee often is aware that questioning will continue until he provides his interrogators the answers they seek.

Second, circumstances associated with the typical traffic stop are not such that the motorist feels completely at the mercy of the police. To be sure, the aura of authority surrounding an armed, uniformed officer and the knowledge that the officer has some discretion in deciding whether to issue a citation, in combination, exert some pressure on the detainee to respond to questions. But other aspects of the situation substantially offset these forces. Perhaps most importantly, the typical traffic stop is public, at least to some degree. Passersby, on foot or in other cars, witness the interaction of officer and motorist. This exposure to public view both reduces the ability of an unscrupulous policeman to use illegitimate means to elicit self-incriminating statements and diminishes the motorist's fear that, if he does not cooperate, he will be subjected to abuse. The fact that the detained motorist typically is confronted by only one or at most two policemen further mutes his sense of vulnerability. In short, the atmosphere surrounding an ordinary traffic stop is substantially less "police dominated" than that surrounding the kinds of interrogation at issue in *Miranda* itself, and in the subsequent cases in which we have applied *Miranda*.

In both of these respects, the usual traffic stop is more analogous to a so-called "*Terry* stop," see *Terry v. Ohio*, 392 U.S. 1 (1968), than to a formal arrest. Under the Fourth Amendment, we have held, a policeman who lacks probable cause but whose "observations lead him reasonably to suspect" that a particular person has committed, is committing, or is about to commit a crime, may detain that person briefly in order to "investigate the circumstances that provoke suspicion." Typically, this means that the officer may ask the detainee a moderate number of questions to determine his identity and to try to obtain information confirming or dispelling the officer's suspicions. But the detainee is not obliged to respond. And, unless the detainee's answers provide the officer with probable cause to arrest him, he must then be released. The comparatively nonthreatening character of detentions of this sort explains the absence of any suggestion in our opinions that *Terry* stops are subject to the dictates of *Miranda*. The similarly noncoercive aspect of ordinary traffic stops prompts us to hold that persons temporarily detained pursuant to such stops are not "in custody" for the purposes of *Miranda*.

Respondent contends that to "exempt" traffic stops from the coverage of *Miranda* will open the way to widespread abuse. Policemen will simply delay formally arresting detained motorists, and will subject them to sustained and intimidating interrogation at the scene of their initial detention. The net result, respondent contends, will be a serious threat to the rights that the *Miranda* doctrine is designed to protect.

We are confident that the state of affairs projected by respondent will not come to pass. It is settled that the safeguards prescribed by *Miranda* become applicable as soon as a suspect's freedom of action is curtailed to a "degree associated with formal arrest." If a motorist who has been detained pursuant to a traffic stop thereafter is subjected to treatment that renders him "in custody" for practical purposes, he will be entitled to the full panoply of protections prescribed by *Miranda*.

Admittedly, our adherence to the doctrine just recounted will mean that the police and lower courts will continue occasionally to have difficulty deciding exactly when a suspect has been taken into custody. Either a rule that *Miranda* applies to all traffic stops or a rule that a suspect need not be advised of his rights until he is formally placed under arrest would provide a clearer, more easily administered line. However, each of these two alternatives has drawbacks that make it unacceptable. The first would substantially impede the enforcement of the Nation's traffic laws—by compelling the police either to take the time to warn all detained motorists of their constitutional rights or to forgo use of self-incriminating statements made by those motorists—while doing little to protect citizens' Fifth Amendment rights. The second would enable the police to circumvent the constraints on custodial interrogations established by *Miranda*.

Turning to the case before us, we find nothing in the record that indicates that respondent should have been given *Miranda* warnings at any point prior to the time Trooper Williams placed him under arrest. For the reasons indicated above, we reject the contention that the initial stop of respondent's car, by itself, rendered him "in custody." And respondent has failed to demonstrate that, at any time between the initial stop and the arrest, he was subjected to restraints comparable to those associated with a formal arrest. Only a short period of time elapsed between the stop and the arrest. At no point during that interval was respondent informed that his detention would not be temporary. Although Trooper Williams apparently decided as soon as respondent stepped out of his car that respondent would be taken into custody and charged with a traffic offense, Williams never communicated his intention to respondent. A policeman's unarticulated plan has no bearing on the question whether a suspect was "in custody" at a particular time; the only relevant inquiry is how a reasonable man in the suspect's position would have understood his situation. Nor do other aspects of the interaction of Williams and respondent support the contention that respondent was exposed to "custodial interrogation" at the scene of the stop. From aught that appears in the stipulation of facts, a single police officer asked respondent a modest number of questions and requested him to perform a simple balancing test at a location visible to passing motorists. Treatment of this sort cannot fairly be characterized as the functional equivalent of formal arrest.

We conclude, in short, that respondent was not taken into custody for the purposes of *Miranda* until Williams arrested him. Consequently, the statements respondent made prior to that point were admissible against him. . . .

J.D.B. v. North Carolina

Supreme Court of the United States
564 U.S. 261 (2011)

Justice SOTOMAYOR delivered the opinion of the Court.

This case presents the question whether the age of a child subjected to police questioning is relevant to the custody analysis of *Miranda v. Arizona*, 384 U.S. 436 (1966). It is beyond dispute that children will often feel bound to submit to police questioning when an adult in the same circumstances would feel free to leave. Seeing no reason for police officers or courts to blind themselves to that commonsense reality, we hold that a child's age properly informs the *Miranda* custody analysis.

I

Petitioner J.D.B. was a 13-year-old, seventh-grade student attending class at Smith Middle School in Chapel Hill, North Carolina when he was removed from his classroom by a uniformed police officer, escorted to a closed-door conference room, and questioned by police for at least half an hour.

This was the second time that police questioned J.D.B. in the span of a week. Five days earlier, two home break-ins occurred, and various items were stolen. Police stopped and questioned J.D.B. after he was seen behind a residence in the neighborhood where the crimes occurred. That same day, police also spoke to J.D.B.'s grandmother—his legal guardian—as well as his aunt.

Police later learned that a digital camera matching the description of one of the stolen items had been found at J.D.B.'s middle school and seen in J.D.B.'s possession. Investigator DiCostanzo, the juvenile investigator with the local police force who had been assigned to the case, went to the school to question J.D.B. Upon arrival, DiCostanzo informed the uniformed police officer on detail to the school (a so-called school resource officer), the assistant principal, and an administrative intern that he was there to question J.D.B. about the break-ins. Although DiCostanzo asked the school administrators to verify J.D.B.'s date of birth, address, and parent contact information from school records, neither the police officers nor the school administrators contacted J.D.B.'s grandmother.

The uniformed officer interrupted J.D.B.'s afternoon social studies class, removed J.D.B. from the classroom, and escorted him to a school conference room. There, J.D.B. was met by DiCostanzo, the assistant principal, and the administrative intern. The door to the conference room was closed. With the two police officers and the two administrators present, J.D.B. was questioned for the next 30 to 45 minutes. Prior to the commencement of questioning, J.D.B. was given neither *Miranda* warnings nor the opportunity to speak to his grandmother. Nor was he informed that he was free to leave the room.

Questioning began with small talk—discussion of sports and J.D.B.'s family life. DiCostanzo asked, and J.D.B. agreed, to discuss the events of the prior weekend. Denying any wrongdoing, J.D.B. explained that he had been in the neighborhood where the crimes occurred because he was seeking work mowing lawns. DiCostanzo pressed J.D.B. for additional detail about his efforts to obtain work; asked J.D.B. to explain a prior incident, when one of the victims returned home to find J.D.B. behind her house; and confronted J.D.B. with the stolen camera. The assistant principal urged J.D.B. to "do the right thing," warning J.D.B. that "the truth always comes out in the end."

Eventually, J.D.B. asked whether he would "still be in trouble" if he returned the "stuff." In response, DiCostanzo explained that return of the stolen items would be helpful, but "this thing is going to court" regardless. DiCostanzo then warned that he may need to seek a secure custody order if he believed that J.D.B. would continue to break into other homes. When J.D.B. asked what a secure custody order was, DiCostanzo explained that "it's where you get sent to juvenile detention before court."

After learning of the prospect of juvenile detention, J.D.B. confessed that he and a friend were responsible for the break-ins. DiCostanzo only then informed J.D.B. that he could refuse to answer the investigator's questions and that he was free to leave. Asked whether he understood, J.D.B. nodded and provided further detail, including information about the location of the stolen items. Eventually J.D.B. wrote a statement, at DiCostanzo's request. When the bell rang indicating the end of the schoolday, J.D.B. was allowed to leave to catch the bus home. . . .

II

Any police interview of an individual suspected of a crime has "coercive aspects to it." Only those interrogations that occur while a suspect is in police custody, however, "heighte[n] the risk" that statements obtained are not the product of the suspect's free choice.

By its very nature, custodial police interrogation entails "inherently compelling pressures." Even for an adult, the physical and psychological isolation of custodial interrogation can "undermine the individual's will to resist and . . . compel him to speak where he would not otherwise do so freely." Indeed, the pressure of custodial interrogation is so immense that it "can induce a frighteningly high percentage of people to confess to crimes they never committed." That risk is all the more troubling—and recent studies suggest, all the more acute—when the subject of custodial interrogation is a juvenile.

Recognizing that the inherently coercive nature of custodial interrogation "blurs the line between voluntary and involuntary statements," this Court in *Miranda* adopted a set of prophylactic measures designed to safeguard the constitutional guarantee against self-incrimination. Prior to questioning, a suspect "must be warned that he has a right to remain silent, that any statement he does make may be used as evidence against him, and that he has a right to the presence of an attorney, either retained or appointed." And, if a suspect makes a statement during custodial interrogation, the burden is on the Government to show, as a "prerequisit[e]" to the statement's admissibility as evidence in the Government's case in chief, that the defendant "voluntarily, knowingly and intelligently" waived his rights.

Because these measures protect the individual against the coercive nature of custodial interrogation, they are required "only where there has been such a restriction on a person's freedom as to render him 'in custody.'" As we have repeatedly emphasized, whether a suspect is "in custody" is an objective inquiry. Rather than demarcate a limited set of relevant circumstances, we have required police officers and courts to "examine all of the circumstances surrounding the interrogation," including any circumstance that "would have affected how a reasonable person" in the suspect's position "would perceive his or her freedom to leave." On the other hand, the "subjective views harbored by either the interrogating officers or the person being questioned" are irrelevant. The test, in other words, involves no consideration of the "actual mindset" of the particular suspect subjected to police questioning.

The benefit of the objective custody analysis is that it is "designed to give clear guidance to the police." Police must make in-the-moment judgments as to when to administer *Miranda* warnings. By limiting analysis to the objective circumstances of the interrogation, and asking how a reasonable person in the suspect's position would understand his freedom to terminate questioning and leave, the objective test avoids burdening police with the task of anticipating the idiosyncrasies of every individual suspect and divining how those particular traits affect each person's subjective state of mind.

The State and its amici contend that a child's age has no place in the custody analysis, no matter how young the child subjected to police questioning. We cannot agree. In some circumstances, a child's age "would have affected how a reasonable person" in the suspect's position "would perceive his or her freedom to leave." That is, a reasonable child subjected to police questioning will sometimes feel pressured to submit when a reasonable adult would feel free to go. We think it clear that courts can account for that reality without doing any damage to the objective nature of the custody analysis.

A child's age is far "more than a chronological fact." It is a fact that "generates commonsense conclusions about behavior and perception."

Such conclusions apply broadly to children as a class. And, they are self-evident to anyone who was a child once himself, including any police officer or judge.

Time and again, this Court has drawn these commonsense conclusions for itself. We have observed that children "generally are less mature and responsible than adults," that they "often lack the experience, perspective, and judgment to recognize and avoid choices that could be detrimental to them," that they "are more vulnerable or susceptible to . . . outside pressures" than adults, and so on. Addressing the specific context of police interrogation, we have observed that events that "would leave a man cold and unimpressed can overawe and overwhelm a lad in his early teens." Describing no one child in particular, these observations restate what "any parent knows"—indeed, what any person knows—about children generally.

Our various statements to this effect are far from unique. The law has historically reflected the same assumption that children characteristically lack the capacity to exercise mature judgment and possess only an incomplete ability to understand the world around them. Like this Court's own generalizations, the legal disqualifications placed on children as a class—e.g., limitations on their ability to alienate property, enter a binding contract enforceable against them, and marry without parental consent—exhibit the settled understanding that the differentiating characteristics of youth are universal. . . .

As this discussion establishes, "[o]ur history is replete with laws and judicial recognition" that children cannot be viewed simply as miniature adults. We see no justification for taking a different course here. So long as the child's age was known to the officer at the time of the interview, or would have been objectively apparent to any reasonable officer, including age as part of the custody analysis requires officers neither to consider circumstances "unknowable" to them, nor to "anticipat[e] the frailties or idiosyncrasies" of the particular suspect whom they question. The same "wide basis of community experience" that makes it possible, as an objective matter, "to determine what is to be expected" of children in other contexts, likewise makes it possible to know what to expect of children subjected to police questioning. . . .

. . . [I[n many cases involving juvenile suspects, the custody analysis would be nonsensical absent some consideration of the suspect's age. This case is a prime example. Were the court precluded from taking J.D.B.'s youth into account, it would be forced to evaluate the circumstances present here through the eyes of a reasonable person of average years. In other words, how would a reasonable adult understand his situation, after being removed from a seventh-grade social studies class by a uniformed school resource officer; being encouraged by his assistant principal to "do the right thing"; and being warned by a police investigator of the prospect of juvenile detention and separation from his guardian and primary caretaker? To describe such an inquiry is to demonstrate its absurdity. Neither officers nor courts can reasonably evaluate the effect of objective circumstances that, by their nature, are specific to children without accounting for the age of the child subjected to those circumstances. . . .

Justice ALITO, with whom THE CHIEF JUSTICE, Justice SCALIA, and Justice THOMAS join, dissenting.

The Court's decision in this case may seem on first consideration to be modest and sensible, but in truth it is neither. It is fundamentally inconsistent with one of the main justifications for the *Miranda* rule: the perceived need for a clear rule that can be easily applied in all cases. And today's holding is not needed to protect the constitutional rights of minors who are questioned by the police.

Miranda's prophylactic regime places a high value on clarity and certainty. Dissatisfied with the highly fact-specific constitutional rule against the admission of involuntary confessions, the *Miranda* Court set down rigid standards that often require courts to ignore personal characteristics that may be highly relevant to a particular suspect's actual susceptibility to police pressure. This rigidity, however, has brought with it one of *Miranda*'s principal strengths—"the ease and clarity of its application" by law enforcement officials and courts. A key contributor to this clarity, at least up until now, has been *Miranda*'s objective reasonable-person test for determining custody. . . .

Today's decision shifts the *Miranda* custody determination from a one-size-fits-all reasonable-person test into an inquiry that must account for at least one individualized characteristic—age—that is thought to correlate with susceptibility to coercive pressures. Age, however, is in no way the only personal characteristic that may correlate with pliability, and in future cases the Court will be forced to choose between two unpalatable alternatives. It may choose to limit today's decision by arbitrarily distinguishing a suspect's age from other personal characteristics—such as intelligence, education, occupation, or prior experience with law enforcement—that may also correlate with susceptibility to coercive pressures. Or, if the Court is unwilling to draw these arbitrary lines, it will be forced to effect a fundamental transformation of the *Miranda* custody test—from a clear, easily applied prophylactic rule into a highly fact-intensive standard resembling the voluntariness test that the *Miranda* Court found to be unsatisfactory.

For at least three reasons, there is no need to go down this road. First, many minors subjected to police interrogation are near the age of majority, and for these suspects the one-size-fits-all *Miranda* custody rule may not be a bad fit. Second, many of the difficulties in applying the *Miranda* custody rule to minors arise because of the unique circumstances present when the police conduct interrogations at school. The *Miranda* custody rule has always taken into account the setting in which questioning occurs, and accounting for the school setting in such cases will address many of these problems. Third, in cases like the one now before us, where the suspect is especially young, courts applying the constitutional voluntariness standard can take special care to ensure that incriminating statements were not obtained through coercion.

Safeguarding the constitutional rights of minors does not require the extreme makeover of *Miranda* that today's decision may portend. . . .

. . . [T]here is no denying that, by incorporating age into its analysis, the Court is embarking on a new expansion of the established custody standard. . . . In its present form, *Miranda*'s prophylactic regime already imposes "high cost[s]" by requiring suppression of confessions that are often "highly probative" and "voluntary" by any traditional standard. Nonetheless, a "core virtue" of *Miranda* has been the clarity and precision of its guidance to "police and courts." This increased clarity "has been thought to outweigh the burdens" that *Miranda* imposes. The Court has, however, repeatedly cautioned against upsetting the careful "balance" that *Miranda* struck and it has "refused to sanction attempts to expand [the] *Miranda* holding" in ways that would reduce its "clarity." Given this practice, there should be a "strong presumption" against the Court's new departure from the established custody test. . . .

The Court's rationale for importing age into the custody standard is that minors tend to lack adults' "capacity to exercise mature judgment" and that failing to account for that "reality" will leave some minors unprotected under *Miranda* in situations where they perceive themselves to be confined. I do not dispute that many suspects who are under 18 will be more susceptible to police pressure than the average adult. As the Court notes, our pre-*Miranda* cases were particularly attuned to this "reality" in applying the constitutional requirement of voluntariness in fact. It is no less a "reality," however, that many persons over the age of 18 are also more susceptible to police pressure than the hypothetical reasonable person. Yet the *Miranda* custody standard has never accounted for the personal characteristics of these or any other individual defendants.

Indeed, it has always been the case under *Miranda* that the unusually meek or compliant are subject to the same fixed rules, including the same custody requirement, as those who are unusually resistant to police pressure. *Miranda*'s rigid standards are both overinclusive and underinclusive. They are overinclusive to the extent that they provide a windfall to the most hardened and savvy of suspects, who often have no need for *Miranda*'s protections. And *Miranda*'s requirements are underinclusive to the extent that they fail to account for "frailties," "idiosyncrasies," and other individualized considerations that might cause a person to bend more easily during a confrontation with the police. But if it is, then the weakness is an inescapable consequence of the *Miranda* Court's decision to supplement the more holistic voluntariness requirement with a one-size-fits-all prophylactic rule. . . .

The Court holds that age must be taken into account when it "was known to the officer at the time of the interview," or when it "would have been objectively apparent" to a reasonable officer. The first half of this test overturns the rule that the "initial determination of custody" does not depend on the "subjective views harbored by . . . interrogating officers." The second half will generate time-consuming satellite litigation over a reasonable officer's perceptions. When, as here, the interrogation takes place in school, the inquiry may be relatively simple. But not all police questioning of minors takes place in schools. In many cases, courts will presumably have to make findings as to whether a particular suspect had a sufficiently youthful look to alert a reasonable officer to the possibility that the suspect was under 18, or whether a reasonable officer would have recognized that a suspect's I.D. was a fake. The inquiry will be both "time-consuming and disruptive" for the police and the courts. . . .

NOTES & QUESTIONS ON THE CONCEPT OF CUSTODY

1. *Objective or subjective criteria.* The concept of custody could be defined in objective or subjective terms. In other words, the standard could depend on criteria objectively construed or criteria subjectively construed, i.e., as they are known to the police officers engaged in the interrogation. Prior cases such as *Mathiason* have construed "custody" in objective terms, i.e., whether there was a restriction on the individual's freedom to leave. See also *Stansbury v. California*, 511 U.S. 318, 323 (1994) ("Our decisions make clear that the initial determination of custody depends on the objective circumstances of the interrogation, not on the subjective views harbored by either the interrogating officers or the person being questioned.").

2. *Age and custody.* The legal issue in the *J.D.B.* case illustrates this dilemma with regard to the age of the suspect in especially stark terms. Minors will more readily consider a situation "custodial"—therefore suggesting that courts should consider the youthful age of the suspect in making the determination of whether the interrogation was custodial. But what if the police officers are generally unaware of the suspect's status as a minor? What if the suspect fails to volunteer their age or, more strikingly, lies to the police about their age? This possibility suggests that courts should view the criteria subjectively through the eyes of the police at the time of the interrogation. For this reason, the Supreme Court required that the age of the suspect must be "known to the officer at the time of police questioning, or would have been objectively apparent to a reasonable officer. . . ." *J.D.B. v. North Carolina*, 564 U.S. at 277.

Nonetheless, the Court embedded this requirement, somewhat uncomfortably, within an overall *objective* custody test:

> *Miranda* considered whether an individual was in custody on the premise that a custodial interrogation is "inherently compelling" and therefore likely to make an individual's confession coerced. Yet *J.D.B.* introduced into the custody analysis a question that has no bearing on the individual's sense of coercion: whether an officer knew or should reasonably have known a suspect's age. The Court insisted on this condition because it felt it was necessary to make the test administrable for officers. But in doing so it opened even greater distance between *Miranda* and the Fifth Amendment principle it is designed to protect, and thus violated the Court's own admonition "to maintain the closest possible fit between the Self-Incrimination Clause and any judge-made rule designed to protect it." Because *J.D.B.*'s test would ignore a suspect's age even when it makes him more likely to feel coerced simply because he reasonably looks like an adult, the Court's decision provides yet another rough, prophylactic rule that fails to tightly fit the constitutional protections in the Fifth Amendment. *J.D.B.*'s addition of the officer's knowledge to the custody inquiry is the most recent example "of prophylaxis built upon

PROBLEM CASE

Consider the following description of the interrogation of a teenager suspected of involvement in a shooting:

> Two seasoned detectives in the first team arrested defendant under the mistaken belief there was an outstanding warrant for his arrest. They took him in handcuffs to the station, seized his belongings including his cell phone, and left him shackled in an interrogation room for nearly an hour and a half. They did not tell the second team they had arrested and shackled him. They did not Mirandize him. When the first detective in the second team found defendant, he immediately unshackled him, told him he was not under arrest and was free to leave, and a ride would be arranged for him. Defendant answered some questions, but made no inculpatory statements. After defendant was left in that room again, a second detective from the second team came in and immediately demanded that defendant unlock his cell phone so its contents could be retrieved. Although this detective also initially told defendant he was not under arrest, when defendant asked how long he would be there, the detective indicated the answer hinged on completion of the data retrieval process. He then questioned defendant at length.

People v. Delgado, 2018 WL 4691176, at *2 (Cal. Ct. App. Oct. 1, 2018). The suspect then made a statement admitting that he shot the victims. Was the defendant in "custody" when he made the statement? Was he in "custody" the whole time or did he wax and wane in and out of custody as his circumstances changed? If he was in custody at the moment of interrogation, try to pin point the exact moment when the custody began.

> prophylaxis, producing a veritable fairyland castle of imagined constitutional restriction upon law enforcement" and upon the people.

Leading Cases, 125 Harv. L. Rev. 241, 248-49 (2011). Do you agree with the Court's inclusion of the subject requirement of the officer's knowledge of the suspect's age?

3. *Marshall.* Why would Justice Marshall, who dissented in the narrowing of the definition of custody in *Oregon v. Mathiason*, pen the majority opinion in *Berkemer* that concluded that "some" coercive effect of a seizure is not enough "coercive effect" to justify treating every seizure as custody? Perhaps the answer is that he recognized that the Court was not willing to subject every seizure to *Miranda*'s requirements, and that this compromise was an acceptable solution. Or is there some other explanation?

3. Defining Interrogation

The *Miranda* warning and waiver requirement is triggered by custodial interrogation. The concept of custody was explored in the prior subsection. Equally so, the concept of interrogation is not self-defining. In the following case, the Supreme Court attempts to provide a workable definition of what counts as an interrogation. Is it the asking of questions or does it also encompass, in some situations, the police officer listening to statements made by the suspect? As you read *Innis*, ask yourself what the Supreme Court means when it refers to "express questioning or its functional equivalent." What is encompassed by the phrase "functional equivalent"?

Rhode Island v. Innis

Supreme Court of the United States
446 U.S. 291 (1980)

Mr. Justice Stewart delivered the opinion of the Court.

In *Miranda v. Arizona*, 384 U.S. 436, 474, the Court held that, once a defendant in custody asks to speak with a lawyer, all interrogation must cease until a lawyer is present. The issue in this case is whether the respondent was "interrogated" in violation of the standards promulgated in the *Miranda* opinion.

I

On the night of January 12, 1975, John Mulvaney, a Providence, R.I., taxicab driver, disappeared after being dispatched to pick up a customer. His body was discovered four days later buried in a shallow grave in Coventry, R.I. He had died from a shotgun blast aimed at the back of his head.

On January 17, 1975, shortly after midnight, the Providence police received a telephone call from Gerald Aubin, also a taxicab driver, who reported that he had just been robbed by a man wielding a sawed-off shotgun. Aubin further reported that he had dropped off his assailant near Rhode Island College in a section of Providence known as Mount Pleasant. While at the Providence police station waiting to give a statement, Aubin noticed a picture of his assailant on a bulletin board. Aubin so informed one of the police officers present. The officer prepared a photo array, and again Aubin identified a picture of the same person. That person was the respondent. Shortly thereafter, the Providence police began a search of the Mount Pleasant area.

At approximately 4:30 A.M. on the same date, Patrolman Lovell, while cruising the streets of Mount Pleasant in a patrol car, spotted the respondent standing in the street facing him. When Patrolman Lovell stopped his car, the respondent walked towards it. Patrolman Lovell then arrested the respondent, who was unarmed, and advised him of his so-called *Miranda* rights. While the two men waited in the patrol car for other police officers to arrive, Patrolman Lovell did not converse with the respondent other than to respond to the latter's request for a cigarette.

Within minutes, Sergeant Sears arrived at the scene of the arrest, and he also gave the respondent the *Miranda* warnings. Immediately thereafter, Captain Leyden and other police officers arrived. Captain Leyden advised the respondent of his *Miranda* rights. The respondent stated that he understood those rights and wanted to speak with a lawyer. Captain Leyden then directed that the respondent be placed in a "caged wagon," a four-door police car with a wire screen mesh between the front and rear seats, and be driven to the central police station. Three officers, Patrolmen Gleckman, Williams, and McKenna, were assigned to accompany the respondent to the central station. They placed the respondent in the vehicle and shut the doors. Captain Leyden then instructed the officers not to question the respondent or intimidate or coerce him in any way. The three officers then entered the vehicle, and it departed.

While en route to the central station, Patrolman Gleckman initiated a conversation with Patrolman McKenna concerning the missing shotgun. As Patrolman Gleckman later testified:

> A. At this point, I was talking back and forth with Patrolman McKenna stating that I frequent this area while on patrol and [that because a school for handicapped children is located nearby,] there's a lot of handicapped children running around in this area, and God forbid one of them might find a weapon with shells and they might hurt themselves.

Patrolman McKenna apparently shared his fellow officer's concern: "A. I more or less concurred with him [Gleckman] that it was a safety factor and that we should, you know, continue to search for the weapon and try to find it."

While Patrolman Williams said nothing, he overheard the conversation between the two officers: "A. He [Gleckman] said it would be too bad if the little—I believe he said a girl—would pick up the gun, maybe kill herself."

The respondent then interrupted the conversation, stating that the officers should turn the car around so he could show them where the gun was located. At this point, Patrolman McKenna radioed back to Captain Leyden that they were returning to the scene of the arrest and that the respondent would inform them of the location of the gun. At the time the respondent indicated that the officers should turn back, they had traveled no more than a mile, a trip encompassing only a few minutes.

The police vehicle then returned to the scene of the arrest where a search for the shotgun was in progress. There, Captain Leyden again advised the respondent of his *Miranda* rights. The respondent replied that he understood those rights but that he "wanted to get the gun out of the way because of the kids in the area in the school." The respondent then led the police to a nearby field, where he pointed out the shotgun under some rocks by the side of the road. . . .

II

. . . In the present case, the parties are in agreement that the respondent was fully informed of his *Miranda* rights and that he invoked his *Miranda* right to counsel when he told Captain Leyden that he wished to consult with a lawyer. It is also uncontested that the respondent was "in custody" while being transported to the police station.

The issue, therefore, is whether the respondent was "interrogated" by the police officers in violation of the respondent's undisputed right under *Miranda* to remain silent until he had consulted with a lawyer. In resolving this issue, we first define the term "interrogation" under *Miranda* before turning to a consideration of the facts of this case.

The starting point for defining "interrogation" in this context is, of course, the Court's *Miranda* opinion. There the Court observed that "[b]y custodial interrogation, we mean questioning initiated by law enforcement officers after a person has been taken into custody or otherwise deprived of his freedom of action in any significant way." This passage and other references throughout the opinion to "questioning" might suggest that the *Miranda* rules were to apply only to those police interrogation practices that involve express questioning of a defendant while in custody.

We do not, however, construe the *Miranda* opinion so narrowly. The concern of the Court in *Miranda* was that the "interrogation environment" created by the interplay of interrogation and custody would "subjugate the individual to the will of his examiner" and thereby undermine the privilege against compulsory self-incrimination. The police practices that evoked this concern included several that did not involve express questioning. For example, one of the practices discussed in *Miranda* was the use of line-ups in which a coached witness would pick the defendant as the perpetrator. This was designed to establish that the defendant was in fact guilty as a predicate for further interrogation. A variation on this theme discussed in *Miranda* was the so-called "reverse line-up" in which a defendant would be identified by coached witnesses as the perpetrator of a fictitious crime, with the object of inducing him to confess to the actual crime of which he was suspected in order to escape the false prosecution. The Court in *Miranda* also included in its survey of interrogation practices the use of psychological ploys, such as to "posi[t]" "the guilt of the subject," to "minimize the moral seriousness of the offense," and "to cast blame on the victim or on society." It is clear that these techniques of persuasion, no less than express questioning, were thought, in a custodial setting, to amount to interrogation.

This is not to say, however, that all statements obtained by the police after a person has been taken into custody are to be considered the product of interrogation. . . . It is clear therefore that the special procedural safeguards outlined in *Miranda* are required not where a suspect is simply taken into custody, but rather where a suspect in custody is subjected to interrogation. "Interrogation," as conceptualized in the *Miranda* opinion, must reflect a measure of compulsion above and beyond that inherent in custody itself.

We conclude that the *Miranda* safeguards come into play whenever a person in custody is subjected to either express questioning or its functional equivalent. That is to say, the term "interrogation" under *Miranda* refers not only to express questioning, but also to any words or actions on the part of the police (other than those normally attendant to arrest and custody) that the police should know are reasonably likely to elicit an incriminating response from the suspect. The latter portion of this definition focuses primarily upon the perceptions of the suspect, rather than the intent of the police. This focus reflects the fact that the *Miranda* safeguards were designed to vest a suspect in custody with an added measure of protection against coercive police practices, without regard to objective proof of the underlying intent of the police. A practice that the police should know is reasonably likely to evoke an incriminating response from a suspect thus amounts to interrogation. But, since the police surely cannot be held accountable for the unforeseeable results of their words or actions, the definition of interrogation can extend only to words or actions on the part of police officers that they should have known were reasonably likely to elicit an incriminating response.

Turning to the facts of the present case, we conclude that the respondent was not "interrogated" within the meaning of *Miranda*. It is undisputed that the first prong of the definition of "interrogation" was not satisfied, for the conversation between Patrolmen Gleckman and McKenna included no express questioning of the respondent. Rather, that conversation was, at least in form, nothing more than a dialogue between the two officers to which no response from the respondent was invited.

Moreover, it cannot be fairly concluded that the respondent was subjected to the "functional equivalent" of questioning. It cannot be said, in short, that Patrolmen Gleckman and McKenna should have known that their conversation was reasonably likely to elicit an incriminating response from the respondent. There is nothing in the record to suggest that the officers were aware that the respondent was peculiarly susceptible to an appeal to his conscience concerning the safety of handicapped children. Nor is there anything in the record to suggest that the police knew that the respondent was unusually disoriented or upset at the time of his arrest.

The case thus boils down to whether, in the context of a brief conversation, the officers should have known that the respondent would suddenly be moved to make a self-incriminating response. Given the fact that the entire conversation appears to have consisted of no more than a few off hand remarks, we cannot say that the officers should have known that it was reasonably likely that Innis would so respond. This is not a case where the police carried on a lengthy harangue in the presence of the suspect. Nor does the record support the respondent's contention that, under the circumstances, the officers' comments were particularly "evocative." It is our view, therefore, that the respondent was not subjected by the police to words or actions that the police should have known were reasonably likely to elicit an incriminating response from him.

The Rhode Island Supreme Court erred, in short, in equating "subtle compulsion" with interrogation. That the officers' comments struck a responsive chord is readily apparent. Thus, it may be said . . . that the respondent was subjected to "subtle compulsion." But that is not the end of the inquiry. It must also be established that a suspect's incriminating response was the product of words or actions on the part of the police that they should have known were reasonably likely to elicit an incriminating response. This was not established in the present case. . . .

Mr. Justice STEVENS, dissenting.

. . . As the Court recognizes, *Miranda v. Arizona* makes it clear that, once respondent requested an attorney, he had an absolute right to have any type of interrogation cease until an attorney was present. As it also recognizes, *Miranda* requires that the term "interrogation" be broadly construed to include "either express questioning or its functional equivalent."

In my view any statement that would normally be understood by the average listener as calling for a response is the functional equivalent of a direct question, whether or not it is punctuated by a question mark. The Court, however, takes a much narrower view. It holds that police conduct is not the "functional equivalent" of direct questioning unless the police should have known that what they were saying or doing was likely to elicit an incriminating response from the suspect. This holding represents a plain departure from the principles set forth in *Miranda*. . . .

From the suspect's, point of view, the effectiveness of the warnings depends on whether it appears that the police are scrupulously honoring his rights. Apparent attempts to elicit information from a suspect after he has invoked his right to cut off questioning necessarily demean that right and tend to reinstate the imbalance between police and suspect that the *Miranda* warnings are designed to correct. Thus, if the rationale for requiring those warnings in the first place is to be respected, any police conduct or statements that would appear to a reasonable person in the suspect's position to call for a response must be considered "interrogation."

In short, in order to give full protection to a suspect's right to be free from any interrogation at all, the definition of "interrogation" must include any police statement or conduct that has the same purpose or effect as a direct question. Statements that appear to call for a response from the suspect, as well as those that are designed to do so, should be considered interrogation. By prohibiting only those relatively few statements or actions that a police officer should know are likely to elicit an incriminating response, the Court today accords a suspect considerably less protection. Indeed, since I suppose most suspects are unlikely to incriminate themselves even when questioned directly, this new definition will almost certainly exclude every statement that is not punctuated with a question mark from the concept of "interrogation."

The difference between the approach required by a faithful adherence to *Miranda* and the stinted test applied by the Court today can be illustrated by comparing three different ways in which Officer Gleckman could have communicated his fears about the possible dangers posed by the shotgun to handicapped children. He could have:

(1) directly asked Innis:
Will you please tell me where the shotgun is so we can protect handicapped school children from danger?
(2) announced to the other officers in the wagon:
If the man sitting in the back seat with me should decide to tell us where the gun is, we can protect handicapped children from danger.
or
(3) stated to the other officers:

It would be too bad if a little handicapped girl would pick up the gun that this man left in the area and maybe kill herself.

In my opinion, all three of these statements should be considered interrogation because all three appear to be designed to elicit a response from anyone who in fact knew where the gun was located. Under the Court's test, on the other hand, the form of the statements would be critical. The third statement would not be interrogation because in the Court's view there was no reason for Officer Gleckman to believe that Innis was susceptible to this type of an implied appeal; therefore, the statement would not be reasonably likely to elicit an incriminating response. Assuming that this is true, then it seems to me that the first two statements, which would be just as unlikely to elicit such a response, should also not be considered interrogation. But, because the first statement is clearly an express question, it would be considered interrogation under the Court's test. The second statement, although just as clearly a deliberate appeal to Innis to reveal the location of the gun, would presumably not be interrogation because (a) it was not in form a direct question and (b) it does not fit within the "reasonably likely to elicit an incriminating response" category that applies to indirect interrogation.

As this example illustrates, the Court's test creates an incentive for police to ignore a suspect's invocation of his rights in order to make continued attempts to extract information from him. If a suspect does not appear to be susceptible to a particular type of psychological pressure, the police are apparently free to exert that pressure on him despite his request for counsel, so long as they are careful not to punctuate their statements with question marks. And if, contrary to all reasonable expectations, the suspect makes an incriminating statement, that statement can be used against him at trial. The Court thus turns *Miranda*'s unequivocal rule against any interrogation at all into a trap in which unwary suspects may be caught by police deception. . . .

Illinois v. Perkins

Supreme Court of the United States
496 U.S. 292 (1990)

Justice KENNEDY delivered the opinion of the Court.

An undercover government agent was placed in the cell of respondent Perkins, who was incarcerated on charges unrelated to the subject of the agent's investigation. Respondent made statements that implicated him in the crime that the agent sought to solve. Respondent claims that the statements should be inadmissible because he had not been given *Miranda* warnings by the agent. We hold that the statements are admissible. *Miranda* warnings are not required when the suspect is unaware that he is speaking to a law enforcement officer and gives a voluntary statement.

I

In November 1984, Richard Stephenson was murdered in a suburb of East St. Louis, Illinois. The murder remained unsolved until March 1986, when one Donald Charlton told police that he had learned about a homicide from a fellow inmate at the Graham Correctional Facility, where Charlton had been serving a sentence for burglary. The fellow inmate was Lloyd Perkins, who is the respondent here. Charlton told police that, while at Graham, he had befriended respondent, who told him in detail about a murder that respondent had committed in East St. Louis. On hearing Charlton's account, the police recognized details of the Stephenson murder that were not well known, and so they treated Charlton's story as a credible one.

By the time the police heard Charlton's account, respondent had been released from Graham, but police traced him to a jail in Montgomery County, Illinois, where he was being held pending trial on a charge of aggravated battery, unrelated to the Stephenson murder. The police wanted to investigate further respondent's connection to the Stephenson murder, but feared that the use of an eavesdropping device would prove impracticable and unsafe. They decided instead to place an undercover agent in the cellblock with respondent and Charlton. The plan was for Charlton and undercover agent John Parisi to pose as escapees from a work release program who had been arrested in the course of a burglary. Parisi and Charlton were instructed to engage respondent in casual conversation and report anything he said about the Stephenson murder.

Parisi, using the alias "Vito Bianco," and Charlton, both clothed in jail garb, were placed in the cellblock with respondent at the Montgomery County jail. The cellblock consisted of 12 separate cells that opened onto a common room. Respondent greeted Charlton who, after a brief conversation with respondent, introduced Parisi by his alias. Parisi told respondent that he "wasn't going to do any more time" and suggested that the three of them escape. Respondent replied that the Montgomery County jail was "rinky-dink" and that they could "break out." The trio met in respondent's cell later that evening, after the other inmates were asleep, to refine their plan. Respondent said that his girlfriend could smuggle in a pistol. Charlton said: "Hey, I'm not a murderer, I'm a burglar. That's your guys' profession." After telling Charlton that he would be responsible for any murder that occurred, Parisi asked respondent if he had ever "done" anybody. Respondent said that he had and proceeded to describe at length the events of the Stephenson murder. Parisi and respondent then engaged in some casual conversation before respondent went to sleep. Parisi did not give respondent *Miranda* warnings before the conversations. . . .

II

. . . Conversations between suspects and undercover agents do not implicate the concerns underlying *Miranda*. The essential ingredients of a "police-dominated atmosphere" and compulsion are not present when an incarcerated person speaks freely to someone whom he believes to be a fellow inmate. Coercion is determined from the perspective of the suspect. When a suspect considers himself in the company of cellmates and not officers, the coercive atmosphere is lacking. There is no empirical basis for the assumption that a suspect speaking to those whom he assumes are not officers will feel compelled to speak by the fear of reprisal for remaining silent or in the hope of more lenient treatment should he confess.

It is the premise of *Miranda* that the danger of coercion results from the interaction of custody and official interrogation. We reject the argument that *Miranda* warnings are required whenever a suspect is in custody in a technical sense and converses with someone who happens to be a government agent. Questioning by captors, who appear to control the suspect's fate, may create mutually reinforcing pressures that the Court has assumed will weaken the suspect's will, but where a suspect does not know that he is conversing with a government agent, these pressures do not exist. The state court here mistakenly assumed that because the suspect was in custody, no undercover questioning could take place. When the suspect has no reason to think that the listeners have official power over him, it should not be assumed that his words are motivated by the reaction he expects from his listeners.

Miranda forbids coercion, not mere strategic deception by taking advantage of a suspect's misplaced trust in one he supposes to be a fellow prisoner. As we recognized in *Miranda*: "[C]onfessions remain a proper element in law enforcement. Any statement given freely and voluntarily without any compelling influences is, of course, admissible in evidence." Ploys to mislead a suspect or lull him into a false sense of security that do not rise to the level of compulsion or coercion to speak are not within *Miranda*'s concerns.

Miranda was not meant to protect suspects from boasting about their criminal activities in front of persons whom they believe to be their cellmates. This case is illustrative. Respondent had no reason to feel that undercover agent Parisi had any legal authority to force him to answer questions or that Parisi could affect respondent's future treatment. Respondent viewed the cellmate-agent as an equal and showed no hint of being intimidated by the atmosphere of the jail. In recounting the details of the Stephenson murder, respondent was motivated solely by the desire to impress his fellow inmates. He spoke at his own peril.

The tactic employed here to elicit a voluntary confession from a suspect does not violate the Self-Incrimination Clause. We held in *Hoffa v. United States*, 385 U.S. 293 (1966), that placing an undercover agent near a suspect in order to gather incriminating information was permissible under the Fifth Amendment. In *Hoffa*, while petitioner Hoffa was on trial, he met often with one Partin, who, unbeknownst to Hoffa, was cooperating with law enforcement officials. Partin reported to officials that Hoffa had divulged his attempts to bribe jury members. We approved using Hoffa's statements at his subsequent trial for jury tampering, on the rationale that "no claim ha[d] been or could [have been] made that [Hoffa's] incriminating statements were the product of any sort of coercion, legal or factual." In addition, we found that the fact that Partin had fooled Hoffa into thinking that Partin was a sympathetic colleague did not affect the voluntariness of the statements. The only difference between this case and *Hoffa* is that the suspect here was incarcerated, but detention, whether or not for the crime in question, does not warrant a presumption that the use of an undercover agent to speak with an incarcerated suspect makes any confession thus obtained involuntary. . . .

Respondent can seek no help from his argument that a bright-line rule for the application of *Miranda* is desirable. Law enforcement officers will have little difficulty putting into practice our holding that undercover agents need not give *Miranda* warnings to incarcerated suspects. The use of undercover agents is a recognized law enforcement technique, often employed in the prison context to detect violence against correctional officials or inmates, as well as for the purposes served here. The interests protected by *Miranda* are not implicated in these cases, and the warnings are not required to safeguard the constitutional rights of inmates who make voluntary statements to undercover agents. . . .

Justice MARSHALL, dissenting.

This Court clearly and simply stated its holding in *Miranda v. Arizona*: "[T]he prosecution may not use statements, whether exculpatory or inculpatory, stemming from custodial interrogation of the defendant unless it demonstrates the use of procedural safeguards effective to secure the privilege against self-incrimination." The conditions that require the police to apprise a defendant of his constitutional rights—custodial interrogation conducted by an agent of the police—were present in this case.

Because Lloyd Perkins received no *Miranda* warnings before he was subjected to custodial interrogation, his confession was not admissible.

The Court reaches the contrary conclusion by fashioning an exception to the *Miranda* rule that applies whenever "an undercover law enforcement officer posing as a fellow inmate . . . ask[s] questions that may elicit an incriminating response" from an incarcerated suspect. This exception is inconsistent with the rationale supporting *Miranda* and allows police officers intentionally to take advantage of suspects unaware of their constitutional rights. I therefore dissent.

The Court does not dispute that the police officer here conducted a custodial interrogation of a criminal suspect. Perkins was incarcerated in county jail during the questioning at issue here; under these circumstances, he was in custody as that term is defined in *Miranda.* The United States argues that Perkins was not in custody for purpose of *Miranda* because he was familiar with the custodial environment as a result of being in jail for two days and previously spending time in prison. Perkins' familiarity with confinement, however, does not transform his incarceration into some sort of noncustodial arrangement.

While Perkins was confined, an undercover police officer, with the help of a police informant, questioned him about a serious crime. Although the Court does not dispute that Perkins was interrogated, it downplays the nature of the 35-minute questioning by disingenuously referring to it as a "conversatio[n]." The officer's narration of the "conversation" at Perkins' suppression hearing however, reveals that it clearly was an interrogation:

> **[Agent:]** You ever do anyone?
> **[Perkins:]** Yeah, once in East St. Louis, in a rich white neighborhood.
> **Informant:** I didn't know they had any rich white neighborhoods in East St. Louis.
> **Perkins:** It wasn't in East St. Louis, it was by a race track in Fairview Heights. . . .
> **[Agent]:** You did a guy in Fairview Heights?
> **Perkins:** Yeah in a rich white section where most of the houses look the same.
> **[Informant]:** If all the houses look the same, how did you know you had the right house?
> **Perkins:** Me and two guys cased the house for about a week. I knew exactly which house, the second house on the left from the corner.
> **[Agent]:** How long ago did this happen?
> **Perkins:** Approximately about two years ago. I got paid $5,000 for that job.
> **[Agent]:** How did it go down?
> **Perkins:** I walked up [to] this guy['s] house with a sawed-off under my trench coat.
> **[Agent]:** What type gun[?]
> **Perkins:** A .12 gauge Remmington [sic] Automatic Model 1100 sawed-off.

The police officer continued the inquiry, asking a series of questions designed to elicit specific information about the victim, the crime scene, the weapon, Perkins' motive, and his actions during and after the shooting. This interaction was not a "conversation"; Perkins, the officer, and the informant were not equal participants in a free-ranging discussion, with each man offering his views on different topics. Rather, it was an interrogation: Perkins was subjected to express questioning likely to evoke an incriminating response.

Because Perkins was interrogated by police while he was in custody, *Miranda* required that the officer inform him of his rights. In rejecting that conclusion, the Court finds that "conversations" between undercover agents and suspects are devoid of the coercion inherent in station house interrogations conducted by law enforcement officials who openly represent the State. *Miranda* was not, however, concerned solely with police coercion. It dealt with any police tactics that may operate to compel a suspect in custody to make incriminating statements without full awareness of his constitutional rights. Thus, when a law enforcement agent structures a custodial interrogation so that a suspect feels compelled to reveal incriminating information, he must inform the suspect of his constitutional rights and give him an opportunity to decide whether or not to talk. . . .

The Court's adoption of an exception to the *Miranda* doctrine is incompatible with the principle, consistently applied by this Court, that the doctrine should remain simple and clear. . . . The Court's holding today complicates a previously clear and straightforward doctrine. The Court opines that "[l]aw enforcement officers will have little difficulty putting into practice our holding that undercover agents need not give *Miranda* warnings to incarcerated suspects." Perhaps this prediction is true with respect to fact patterns virtually identical to the one before the Court today. But the outer boundaries of the exception created by the Court are by no means clear. Would *Miranda* be violated, for instance, if an undercover police officer beat a confession out of a suspect, but the suspect thought the officer was another prisoner who wanted the information for his own purposes?

Even if *Miranda*, as interpreted by the Court, would not permit such obviously compelled confessions, the ramifications of today's opinion are still disturbing. The exception carved out of the *Miranda* doctrine today may well result in a proliferation of departmental policies to encourage police officers to conduct interrogations of confined suspects through undercover agents, thereby circumventing the need to administer *Miranda* warnings. Indeed, if *Miranda* now requires a police officer to issue warnings only in those situations in which the suspect might feel compelled "to speak by the fear of reprisal for remaining silent or in the hope of more lenient treatment should he confess," presumably it allows custodial interrogation by an undercover officer posing as a member of the clergy or a suspect's defense attorney. Although such abhorrent tricks would play on a suspect's need to confide in a trusted adviser, neither would cause the suspect to "think that the listeners have official power over him." The Court's adoption of the "undercover agent" exception to the *Miranda* rule thus is necessarily also the adoption of a substantial loophole in our jurisprudence protecting suspects' Fifth Amendment rights.

NOTES & QUESTIONS ON INTERROGATION

1. *Undercover "interrogation."* It can be hard to make sense of the conclusion that a police interrogation is not an "interrogation" for purposes of *Miranda* if the person doing the interrogation is an undercover police officer. After all, the police officer operating undercover might ask the very same questions as a police officer in uniform. Why then the difference? For one approach, consider the following explanation:

> Underlying *Perkins* is the core premise of *Miranda*—only the unique context of custodial interrogations inherently coerces a suspect and, thereby, necessitates the neutralizing effect of *Miranda* warnings to establish the voluntariness of a suspect's submission to police questioning. Thus, when a suspect is unaware that a police officer is questioning him, this special type of inherent coercion is lacking. Therefore, the neutralizing effect of a *Miranda* warning is unnecessary to establish that the suspect's answers were voluntary. In essence, the *Miranda* warning acts as a proverbial antacid, but one only prescribed by an especially corrosive acid produced when a suspect is in custody and aware that police are interrogating him. Although all questioning may produce some corrosive acid, unless and until the corrosion reaches the potency level of custodial interrogation, the special neutralizing antacid of *Miranda* is unnecessary.

Geoffrey S. Corn, Miranda, *Secret Questioning, and the Right to Counsel*, 66 Ark. L. Rev. 931, 933-34 (2013). What role is played by the suspect's *knowledge* that he or she is involved in a *police* interrogation?

2. *Drawing logical inferences.* In *Rhode Island v. Innis*, the police were investigating the murder of a taxi driver who was shot with a shotgun blast to the head. The police picked up Innis and read him *Miranda* warnings five different times, but when he offered to show the officers where the gun was, they did not immediately take him up on the offer but instead brought him back to their captain for more guidance, whereupon the suspect uttered a confession. Does this seem like officers who were using the conversation as a ploy to get him to confess? In such cases, evidence of police good faith can add important color to their "words and actions" when assessing whether they were reasonably expected to produce an incriminating response. Conversely, police bad faith can help establish that the police engaged in words and actions that were reasonably expected to elicit an incriminating statement.

PROBLEM CASE

Consider the following discussion, which occurred during the booking process. Martinez is the suspect and Navarro is the police officer.

Martinez: Alright. I'm willing to talk to you guys uh but just I would like to have an attorney present. That's it.
Navarro: Yeah, I don't know if we could get a hold of him right now.
Martinez: Yeah.
Navarro: All I wanted was your side of the story. That's it. OK. So, I'm pretty much done with you then. Um, I guess I don't know another option but to go ahead and book you. OK. Because
Martinez: What am I being booked under?
Navarro: You're going to be booked for murder because I only got one side of the story. OK.
Martinez: But how how's he going to go about that. If we talk, once you get a hold of my uh attorney.
Navarro: That's the thing, I don't know when we're going to get a hold of him. Maybe I don't know when he's going I don't know when you're going to call him.
Martinez: I have to get a hold of him.
Navarro: Huh?
Martinez: I have to get a hold of him?
Navarro: Yeah.
Martinez: You guys don't (unintelligible)
Navarro: No. No, you're going to have to call him and it's going to have to be from jail.

See *Martinez v. Cate*, 903 F.3d 982, 988-89 (9th Cir. 2018). Would you consider this conversation at the beginning of the booking process an interrogation? Did Navarro continue to engage in an "interrogation" after Martinez invoked his right to counsel? He later made incriminating statements after this colloquy. How would you evaluate Navarro's statement that "I don't know another option but to go ahead and book you"?

4. Waiver

Although every suspect has the right to remain silent, that right can be waived. Today, *Miranda* has so pervaded police practice that detectives typically ask suspects to acknowledge, in writing, that they have received their *Miranda* warnings and are waiving these rights. There is no question that *Miranda* rights can be waived in this fashion; a suspect is entitled, but not required, to remain silent and refuse to answer questions. But can *Miranda* rights also be waved implicitly, either through actions or words that indicate the suspect understands the rights that have been read and implies that the suspect is waiving his or her right to remain silent?

The following case deals with a suspect who refused to sign a *Miranda* waiver put before him but nonetheless made a very brief—but highly consequential—answer to one question put to him by the detective. Was his brief answer to the detective an implicit waiver of his right to remain silent during the interrogation? One way of getting a handle on the dispute is to ask whether the police need advance or separate permission from the suspect, or whether the suspect's answering a question is, by logical entailment, always a waiver of the right to remain silent.

According to *Davis v. United States*, 512 U.S. 452, 459 (1994), a suspect who wishes to invoke his *Miranda* right to counsel must "unambiguously request counsel." An invocation of the right that is equivocal or ambiguous is insufficient to trigger the *Miranda* prohibition that all interrogation was then to stop. Should the same rule—an unambiguous request—apply when a suspect wishes to invoke his or her *Miranda* right to silence? Does the logic of demanding an unambiguous request to invoke the right to a lawyer logically apply to silence? If police tell you that you have a right to remain silent, would it suggest to an average person that they then need to talk and say they want to remain silent?

Berghuis v. Thompkins

Supreme Court of the United States
560 U.S. 370 (2010)

Justice KENNEDY delivered the opinion of the Court.

The United States Court of Appeals for the Sixth Circuit, in a habeas corpus proceeding challenging a Michigan conviction for first-degree murder and certain other offenses, ruled . . . that a statement by the accused, relied on at trial by the prosecution, had been elicited in violation of *Miranda v. Arizona*. . . .

I

On January 10, 2000, a shooting occurred outside a mall in Southfield, Michigan. Among the victims was Samuel Morris, who died from multiple gunshot wounds. The other victim, Frederick France, recovered from his injuries and later testified. Thompkins, who was a suspect, fled. About one year later he was found in Ohio and arrested there.

Two Southfield police officers traveled to Ohio to interrogate Thompkins, then awaiting transfer to Michigan. The interrogation began around 1:30 P.M. and lasted about three hours. The interrogation was conducted in a room that was 8 by 10 feet, and Thompkins sat in a chair that resembled a school desk (it had an arm on it that swings around to provide a surface to write on). At the beginning of the interrogation, one of the officers, Detective Helgert, presented Thompkins with a form derived from the *Miranda* rule. It stated:

NOTIFICATION OF CONSTITUTIONAL RIGHTS AND STATEMENT

1. You have the right to remain silent.
2. Anything you say can and will be used against you in a court of law.
3. You have a right to talk to a lawyer before answering any questions and you have the right to have a lawyer present with you while you are answering any questions.
4. If you cannot afford to hire a lawyer, one will be appointed to represent you before any questioning, if you wish one.

5. You have the right to decide at any time before or during questioning to use your right to remain silent and your right to talk with a lawyer while you are being questioned.

Helgert asked Thompkins to read the fifth warning out loud. Thompkins complied. Helgert later said this was to ensure that Thompkins could read, and Helgert concluded that Thompkins understood English. Helgert then read the other four *Miranda* warnings out loud and asked Thompkins to sign the form to demonstrate that he understood his rights. Thompkins declined to sign the form. The record contains conflicting evidence about whether Thompkins then verbally confirmed that he understood the rights listed on the form.

Officers began an interrogation. At no point during the interrogation did Thompkins say that he wanted to remain silent, that he did not want to talk with the police, or that he wanted an attorney. Thompkins was "[l]argely" silent during the interrogation, which lasted about three hours. He did give a few limited verbal responses, however, such as "yeah," "no," or "I don't know." And on occasion he communicated by nodding his head. Thompkins also said that he "didn't want a peppermint" that was offered to him by the police and that the chair he was "sitting in was hard."

About 2 hours and 45 minutes into the interrogation, Helgert asked Thompkins, "Do you believe in God?" Thompkins made eye contact with Helgert and said "Yes," as his eyes "well[ed] up with tears." Helgert asked, "Do you pray to God?" Thompkins said "Yes." Helgert asked, "Do you pray to God to forgive you for shooting that boy down?" Thompkins answered "Yes" and looked away. Thompkins refused to make a written confession, and the interrogation ended about 15 minutes later. . . .

III

The *Miranda* Court formulated a warning that must be given to suspects before they can be subjected to custodial interrogation. . . . All concede that the warning given in this case was in full compliance with these requirements. The dispute centers on the response—or nonresponse—from the suspect.

Thompkins makes various arguments that his answers to questions from the detectives were inadmissible. He first contends that he "invoke[d] his privilege" to remain silent by not saying anything for a sufficient period of time, so the interrogation should have "cease[d]" before he made his inculpatory statements.

This argument is unpersuasive. In the context of invoking the *Miranda* right to counsel, the Court in *Davis v. United States*, 512 U.S. 452, 459 (1994), held that a suspect must do so "unambiguously." If an accused makes a statement concerning the right to counsel "that is ambiguous or equivocal" or makes no statement, the police are not required to end the interrogation or ask questions to clarify whether the accused wants to invoke his or her *Miranda* rights.

The Court has not yet stated whether an invocation of the right to remain silent can be ambiguous or equivocal, but there is no principled reason to adopt different standards for determining when an accused has invoked the *Miranda* right to remain silent and the *Miranda* right to counsel at issue in *Davis*. Both protect the privilege against compulsory self-incrimination by requiring an interrogation to cease when either right is invoked.

There is good reason to require an accused who wants to invoke his or her right to remain silent to do so unambiguously. A requirement of an unambiguous invocation of *Miranda* rights results in an objective inquiry that "avoid[s] difficulties of proof and . . . provide[s] guidance to officers" on how to proceed in the face of ambiguity. If an ambiguous act, omission, or statement could require police to end the interrogation, police would be required to make difficult decisions about an accused's unclear intent and face the consequence of suppression "if they guess wrong." Suppression of a voluntary confession in these circumstances would place a significant burden on society's interest in prosecuting criminal activity. Treating an ambiguous or equivocal act, omission, or statement as an invocation of *Miranda* rights "might add marginally to *Miranda*'s goal of dispelling the compulsion inherent in custodial interrogation." But "as *Miranda* holds, full comprehension of the rights to remain silent and request an attorney are sufficient to dispel whatever coercion is inherent in the interrogation process."

Thompkins did not say that he wanted to remain silent or that he did not want to talk with the police. Had he made either of these simple, unambiguous statements, he would have invoked his "right to cut off questioning." Here he did neither, so he did not invoke his right to remain silent.

We next consider whether Thompkins waived his right to remain silent. Even absent the accused's invocation of the right to remain silent, the accused's statement during a custodial interrogation is inadmissible at trial unless the prosecution can establish that the accused "in fact knowingly and voluntarily waived [*Miranda*] rights" when making the statement. The waiver inquiry "has two distinct dimensions": waiver must be "voluntary in the sense that it was the product of a free and deliberate choice rather than intimidation, coercion, or deception," and "made with a full awareness of both the nature of the right being abandoned and the consequences of the decision to abandon it."

Some language in *Miranda* could be read to indicate that waivers are difficult to establish absent an explicit written waiver or a formal, express oral statement. *Miranda* said "a valid waiver will not be presumed simply from the silence of the accused after warnings are given or simply from the fact that a confession was in fact eventually obtained." In addition, the *Miranda*

Court stated that "a heavy burden rests on the government to demonstrate that the defendant knowingly and intelligently waived his privilege against self-incrimination and his right to retained or appointed counsel."

The course of decisions since *Miranda*, informed by the application of *Miranda* warnings in the whole course of law enforcement, demonstrates that waivers can be established even absent formal or express statements of waiver that would be expected in, say, a judicial hearing to determine if a guilty plea has been properly entered. The main purpose of *Miranda* is to ensure that an accused is advised of and understands the right to remain silent and the right to counsel. Thus, "[i]f anything, our subsequent cases have reduced the impact of the *Miranda* rule on legitimate law enforcement while reaffirming the decision's core ruling that unwarned statements may not be used as evidence in the prosecution's case in chief."

One of the first cases to decide the meaning and import of *Miranda* with respect to the question of waiver was *North Carolina v. Butler*. The *Butler* Court, after discussing some of the problems created by the language in *Miranda*, established certain important propositions. *Butler* interpreted the *Miranda* language concerning the "heavy burden" to show waiver, 384 U.S., at 475, in accord with usual principles of determining waiver, which can include waiver implied from all the circumstances. And in a later case, the Court stated that this "heavy burden" is not more than the burden to establish waiver by a preponderance of the evidence.

The prosecution therefore does not need to show that a waiver of *Miranda* rights was express. An "implicit waiver" of the "right to remain silent" is sufficient to admit a suspect's statement into evidence. *Butler* made clear that a waiver of *Miranda* rights may be implied through "the defendant's silence, coupled with an understanding of his rights and a course of conduct indicating waiver." 441 U.S., at 373. The Court in *Butler* therefore "retreated" from the "language and tenor of the *Miranda* opinion," which "suggested that the Court would require that a waiver . . . be specifically made."

If the State establishes that a *Miranda* warning was given and the accused made an uncoerced statement, this showing, standing alone, is insufficient to demonstrate "a valid waiver" of *Miranda* rights. The prosecution must make the additional showing that the accused understood these rights. Where the prosecution shows that a *Miranda* warning was given and that it was understood by the accused, an accused's uncoerced statement establishes an implied waiver of the right to remain silent.

Although *Miranda* imposes on the police a rule that is both formalistic and practical when it prevents them from interrogating suspects without first providing them with a *Miranda* warning, it does not impose a formalistic waiver procedure that a suspect must follow to relinquish those rights. As a general proposition, the law can presume that an individual who, with a full understanding of his or her rights, acts in a manner inconsistent with their exercise has made a deliberate choice to relinquish the protection those rights afford. . . .

The record in this case shows that Thompkins waived his right to remain silent. There is no basis in this case to conclude that he did not understand his rights; and on these facts it follows that he chose not to invoke or rely on those rights when he did speak. First, there is no contention that Thompkins did not understand his rights; and from this it follows that he knew what he gave up when he spoke. There was more than enough evidence in the record to conclude that Thompkins understood his *Miranda* rights. Thompkins received a written copy of the *Miranda* warnings; Detective Helgert determined that Thompkins could read and understand English; and Thompkins was given time to read the warnings. Thompkins, furthermore, read aloud the fifth warning, which stated that "you have the right to decide at any time before or during questioning to use your right to remain silent and your right to talk with a lawyer while you are being questioned." He was thus aware that his right to remain silent would not dissipate after a certain amount of time and that police would have to honor his right to be silent and his right to counsel during the whole course of interrogation. Those rights, the warning made clear, could be asserted at any time. Helgert, moreover, read the warnings aloud.

Second, Thompkins's answer to Detective Helgert's question about whether Thompkins prayed to God for forgiveness for shooting the victim is a "course of conduct indicating waiver" of the right to remain silent. If Thompkins wanted to remain silent, he could have said nothing in response to Helgert's questions, or he could have unambiguously invoked his *Miranda* rights and ended the interrogation. The fact that Thompkins made a statement about three hours after receiving a *Miranda* warning does not overcome the fact that he engaged in a course of conduct indicating waiver. Police are not required to rewarn suspects from time to time. Thompkins's answer to Helgert's question about praying to God for forgiveness for shooting the victim was sufficient to show a course of conduct indicating waiver. This is confirmed by the fact that before then Thompkins had given sporadic answers to questions throughout the interrogation.

Third, there is no evidence that Thompkins's statement was coerced. Thompkins does not claim that police threatened or injured him during the interrogation or that he was in any way fearful. The interrogation was conducted in a standard-sized room in the middle of the afternoon. It is true that apparently he was in a straight-backed chair for three hours, but there is no authority for the proposition that an interrogation of this length is inherently coercive. Indeed, even where interrogations of greater duration were held to be improper, they were accompanied, as this one was not, by other facts indicating coercion, such as an incapacitated and sedated suspect, sleep and food deprivation, and threats. The fact that Helgert's question referred to Thompkins's religious beliefs also did not render Thompkins's statement involuntary. "[T]he Fifth Amendment privilege is not concerned with moral and psychological pressures to confess emanating from sources other than official coercion." In these circumstances, Thompkins knowingly and voluntarily made a statement to police, so he waived his right to remain silent.

Thompkins next argues that, even if his answer to Detective Helgert could constitute a waiver of his right to remain silent, the police were not allowed to question him until they obtained a waiver first. *Butler* forecloses this argument. The *Butler* Court held that courts can infer a waiver of Miranda rights "from the actions and words of the person interrogated." This principle would be inconsistent with a rule that requires a waiver at the outset. The *Butler* Court thus rejected the rule proposed by the *Butler* dissent, which would have "requir[ed] the police to obtain an express waiver of [*Miranda* rights] before proceeding with interrogation" (Brennan, J., dissenting). This holding also makes sense given that "the primary protection afforded suspects subject[ed] to custodial interrogation is the *Miranda* warnings themselves." The *Miranda* rule and its requirements are met if a suspect receives adequate *Miranda* warnings, understands them, and has an opportunity to invoke the rights before giving any answers or admissions. Any waiver, express or implied, may be contradicted by an invocation at any time. If the right to counsel or the right to remain silent is invoked at any point during questioning, further interrogation must cease.

Interrogation provides the suspect with additional information that can put his or her decision to waive, or not to invoke, into perspective. As questioning commences and then continues, the suspect has the opportunity to consider the choices he or she faces and to make a more informed decision, either to insist on silence or to cooperate. When the suspect knows that *Miranda* rights can be invoked at any time, he or she has the opportunity to reassess his or her immediate and long-term interests. Cooperation with the police may result in more favorable treatment for the suspect; the apprehension of accomplices; the prevention of continuing injury and fear; beginning steps towards relief or solace for the victims; and the beginning of the suspect's own return to the law and the social order it seeks to protect.

In order for an accused's statement to be admissible at trial, police must have given the accused a *Miranda* warning. If that condition is established, the court can proceed to consider whether there has been an express or implied waiver of *Miranda* rights. In making its ruling on the admissibility of a statement made during custodial questioning, the trial court, of course, considers whether there is evidence to support the conclusion that, from the whole course of questioning, an express or implied waiver has been established. Thus, after giving a *Miranda* warning, police may interrogate a suspect who has neither invoked nor waived his or her *Miranda* rights. On these premises, it follows the police were not required to obtain a waiver of Thompkins's *Miranda* rights before commencing the interrogation. . . .

Justice SOTOMAYOR, with whom Justice STEVENS, Justice GINSBURG, and Justice BREYER join, dissenting.

The Court concludes today that a criminal suspect waives his right to remain silent if, after sitting tacit and uncommunicative through nearly three hours of police interrogation, he utters a few one-word responses. The Court also concludes that a suspect who wishes to guard his right to remain silent against such a finding of "waiver" must, counterintuitively, speak—and must do so with sufficient precision to satisfy a clear-statement rule that construes ambiguity in favor of the police. Both propositions mark a substantial retreat from the protection against compelled self-incrimination that *Miranda v. Arizona* has long provided during custodial interrogation. . . .

. . . As to the *Miranda* claims, Thompkins argues first that through his conduct during the 3-hour custodial interrogation he effectively invoked his right to remain silent, requiring police to cut off questioning. . . . Thompkins also contends his statements were in any case inadmissible because the prosecution failed to meet its heavy burden under *Miranda* of proving that he knowingly and intelligently waived his right to remain silent. . . .

The strength of Thompkins' *Miranda* claims depends in large part on the circumstances of the 3-hour interrogation, at the end of which he made inculpatory statements later introduced at trial. The Court's opinion downplays record evidence that Thompkins remained almost completely silent and unresponsive throughout that session. One of the interrogating officers, Detective Helgert, testified that although Thompkins was administered *Miranda* warnings, the last of which he read aloud, Thompkins expressly declined to sign a written acknowledgment that he had been advised of and understood his rights. There is conflicting evidence in the record about whether Thompkins ever verbally confirmed understanding his rights. The record contains no indication that the officers sought or obtained an express waiver. . . .

Rarely do this Court's precedents provide clearly established law so closely on point with the facts of a particular case. Together, *Miranda* and *Butler* establish that a court "must presume that a defendant did not waive his right[s]"; the prosecution bears a "heavy burden" in attempting to demonstrate waiver; the fact of a "lengthy interrogation" prior to obtaining statements is "strong evidence" against a finding of valid waiver; "mere silence" in response to questioning is "not enough"; and waiver may not be presumed "simply from the fact that a confession was in fact eventually obtained."

It is undisputed here that Thompkins never expressly waived his right to remain silent. His refusal to sign even an acknowledgment that he understood his *Miranda* rights evinces, if anything, an intent not to waive those rights. That Thompkins did not make the inculpatory statements at issue until after approximately 2 hours and 45 minutes of interrogation serves as "strong evidence" against waiver. *Miranda* and *Butler* expressly preclude the possibility that the inculpatory statements themselves are sufficient to establish waiver.

In these circumstances, Thompkins' "actions and words" preceding the inculpatory statements simply do not evidence a "course of conduct indicating waiver" sufficient to carry the prosecution's burden. Although the Michigan court stated that Thompkins "sporadically" participated in the interview, that court's opinion and the record before us are silent as to the subject matter or context of even a single question to which Thompkins purportedly responded, other than the exchange about God and the statements respecting the peppermint and the chair. Unlike in *Butler*, Thompkins made no initial declaration akin to "I will talk to you." Indeed, Michigan and the United States concede that no waiver occurred in this case until Thompkins responded "yes" to the questions about God. I believe it is objectively unreasonable under our clearly established precedents to conclude the prosecution met its "heavy burden" of proof on a record consisting of three one-word answers, following 2 hours and 45 minutes of silence punctuated by a few largely nonverbal responses to unidentified questions. . . .

Once a suspect triggers his or her right to remain silent, the police must cease the interrogation. But for how long? Is the prohibition against further questioning permanent and ever-lasting? Or does it expire at some point? In the following case, the Supreme Court tackles this question. Does the Court offer clear guidance to local police officers about how long they must refrain from an interrogation after the right to remain silent has been triggered? What role in the analysis is played by the fact that the second interrogation was for a different crime?

Michigan v. Mosley

Supreme Court of the United States
423 U.S. 96 (1975)

Mr. Justice STEWART delivered the opinion of the Court.

The respondent, Richard Bert Mosley, was arrested in Detroit, Mich., in the early afternoon of April 8, 1971, in connection with robberies that had recently occurred at the Blue Goose Bar and the White Tower Restaurant on that city's lower east side. The arresting officer, Detective James Cowie of the Armed Robbery Section of the Detroit Police

Department, was acting on a tip implicating Mosley and three other men in the robberies. After effecting the arrest, Detective Cowie brought Mosley to the Robbery, Breaking and Entering Bureau of the Police Department, located on the fourth floor of the departmental headquarters building. The officer advised Mosley of his rights under this Court's decision in *Miranda v. Arizona* and had him read and sign the department's constitutional rights notification certificate. After filling out the necessary arrest papers, Cowie began questioning Mosley about the robbery of the White Tower Restaurant. When Mosley said he did not want to answer any questions about the robberies, Cowie promptly ceased the interrogation. The completion of the arrest papers and the questioning of Mosley together took approximately 20 minutes. At no time during the questioning did Mosley indicate a desire to consult with a lawyer, and there is no claim that the procedures followed to this point did not fully comply with the strictures of the *Miranda* opinion. Mosley was then taken to a ninth-floor cell block.

Shortly after 6 P.M., Detective Hill of the Detroit Police Department Homicide Bureau brought Mosley from the cell block to the fifth-floor office of the Homicide Bureau for questioning about the fatal shooting of a man named Leroy Williams. Williams had been killed on January 9, 1971, during a holdup attempt outside the 101 Ranch Bar in Detroit. Mosley had not been arrested on this charge or interrogated about it by Detective Cowie. Before questioning Mosley about this homicide, Detective Hill carefully advised him of his "*Miranda* rights." Mosley read the notification form both silently and aloud, and Detective Hill then read and explained the warnings to him and had him sign the form. Mosley at first denied any involvement in the Williams murder, but after the officer told him that Anthony Smith had confessed to participating in the slaying and had named him as the "shooter," Mosley made a statement implicating himself in the homicide. The interrogation by Detective Hill lasted approximately 15 minutes, and at no time during its course did Mosley ask to consult with a lawyer or indicate that he did not want to discuss the homicide. In short, there is no claim that the procedures followed during Detective Hill's interrogation of Mosley, standing alone, did not fully comply with the strictures of the *Miranda* opinion. . . .

In the *Miranda* case this Court promulgated a set of safeguards to protect the there-delineated constitutional rights of persons subjected to custodial police interrogation. In sum, the Court held in that case that unless law enforcement officers give certain specified warnings before questioning a person in custody, and follow certain specified procedures during the course of any subsequent interrogation, any statement made by the person in custody cannot over his objection be admitted in evidence against him as a defendant at trial, even though the statement may in fact be wholly voluntary.

Neither party in the present case challenges the continuing validity of the *Miranda* decision, or of any of the so-called guidelines it established to protect what the Court there said was a person's constitutional privilege against compulsory self-incrimination. The issue in this case, rather, is whether the conduct of the Detroit police that led to Mosley's incriminating statement did in fact violate the *Miranda* "guidelines," so as to render the statement inadmissible in evidence against Mosley at his trial. Resolution of the question turns almost entirely on the interpretation of a single passage in the *Miranda* opinion, upon which the Michigan appellate court relied in finding a per se violation of *Miranda*:

> Once warnings have been given, the subsequent procedure is clear. If the individual indicates in any manner, at any time prior to or during questioning, that he wishes to remain silent, the interrogation must cease. At this point he has shown that he intends to exercise his Fifth Amendment privilege; any statement taken after the person invokes his privilege cannot be other than the product of compulsion, subtle or otherwise. Without the right to cut off questioning, the setting of in-custody interrogation operates on the individual to overcome free choice in producing a statement after the privilege has been once invoked.

This passage states that "the interrogation must cease" when the person in custody indicates that "he wishes to remain silent." It does not state under what circumstances, if any, a resumption of questioning is permissible. The passage could be literally read to mean that a person who has invoked his "right to silence" can never again be subjected to custodial interrogation by any police officer at any time or place on any subject. Another possible construction of the passage would characterize "any statement taken after the person invokes his privilege" as "the product of compulsion" and would therefore mandate its exclusion from evidence, even if it were volunteered by the person in custody without any further interrogation whatever. Or the passage could be interpreted to require only the immediate cessation of questioning, and to permit a resumption of interrogation after a momentary respite.

It is evident that any of these possible literal interpretations would lead to absurd and unintended results. To permit the continuation of custodial interrogation after a momentary cessation would clearly frustrate the purposes of *Miranda* by allowing repeated rounds of questioning to undermine the will of the person being questioned. At the other extreme, a blanket prohibition against the taking of voluntary statements or a permanent immunity from further interrogation, regardless of the circumstances, would transform the *Miranda* safeguards into wholly irrational obstacles to legitimate police investigative activity, and deprive suspects of an opportunity to make informed and intelligent assessments of their interests. Clearly, therefore, neither this passage nor any other passage in the *Miranda* opinion can sensibly be read to create a per se proscription of indefinite duration upon any further questioning by any police officer on any subject, once the person in custody has indicated a desire to remain silent.

A reasonable and faithful interpretation of the *Miranda* opinion must rest on the intention of the Court in that case to adopt "fully effective means . . . to notify the person of his right of silence and to assure that the exercise of the right will be scrupulously honored. . . ." The critical safeguard identified in the passage at issue is a person's "right to cut off questioning." Through the exercise of his option to terminate questioning he can control the time at which questioning occurs, the subjects discussed, and the duration of the interrogation. The requirement that law enforcement authorities must respect a person's exercise of that option counteracts the coercive pressures of the custodial setting. We therefore conclude that the admissibility of statements obtained after the person in custody has decided to remain silent depends under *Miranda* on whether his "right to cut off questioning" was "scrupulously honored."

A review of the circumstances leading to Mosley's confession reveals that his "right to cut off questioning" was fully respected in this case. Before his initial interrogation, Mosley was carefully advised that he was under no obligation to answer any questions and could remain silent if he wished. He orally acknowledged that he understood the *Miranda* warnings and then signed a printed notification-of-rights form. When Mosley stated that he did not want to discuss the robberies, Detective Cowie immediately ceased the interrogation and did not try either to resume the questioning or in any way to persuade Mosley to reconsider his position. After an interval of more than two hours, Mosley was questioned by another police officer at another location about an unrelated holdup murder. He was given full and complete *Miranda* warnings at the outset of the second interrogation. He was thus reminded again that he could remain silent and could consult with a lawyer, and was carefully given a full and fair opportunity to exercise these options. The subsequent questioning did not undercut Mosley's previous decision not to answer Detective Cowie's inquiries. Detective Hill did not resume the interrogation about the White Tower Restaurant robbery or inquire about the Blue Goose Bar robbery, but instead focused exclusively on the Leroy Williams homicide, a crime different in nature and in time and place of occurrence from the robberies for which Mosley had been arrested and interrogated by Detective Cowie. Although it is not clear from the record how much Detective Hill knew about the earlier interrogation, his questioning of Mosley about an unrelated homicide was quite consistent with a reasonable interpretation of Mosley's earlier refusal to answer any questions about the robberies.

This is not a case, therefore, where the police failed to honor a decision of a person in custody to cut off questioning, either by refusing to discontinue the interrogation upon request or by persisting in repeated efforts to wear down his resistance and make him change his mind. In contrast to such practices, the police here immediately ceased the interrogation, resumed questioning only after the passage of a significant period of time and the provision of a fresh set of warnings, and restricted the second interrogation to a crime that had not been a subject of the earlier interrogation. . . .

Mr. Justice BRENNAN, with whom Mr. Justice MARSHALL joins, dissenting.

. . . [T]he process of eroding *Miranda* rights . . . continues with today's holding that police may renew the questioning of a suspect who has once exercised his right to remain silent, provided the suspect's right to cut off questioning has been "scrupulously honored." Today's distortion of *Miranda*'s constitutional principles can be viewed only as yet another stop in the erosion and, I suppose, ultimate overruling of *Miranda*'s enforcement of the privilege against self-incrimination. . . .

The task that confronts the Court in this case is to satisfy the *Miranda* approach by establishing "concrete constitutional guidelines" governing the resumption of questioning a suspect who, while in custody, has once clearly and unequivocally "indicate(d) . . . that he wishes to remain silent. . . ." As the Court today continues to recognize, under *Miranda*, the cost of assuring voluntariness by procedural tests, independent of any actual inquiry into voluntariness, is that some voluntary statements will be excluded. Thus the consideration in the task confronting the Court is not whether voluntary statements will be excluded, but whether the procedures approved will be sufficient to assure with reasonable certainty that a confession is not obtained under the influence of the compulsion inherent in interrogation and detention. The procedures approved by the Court today fail to provide that assurance. . . .

In formulating its procedural safeguard, the Court skirts the problem of compulsion and thereby fails to join issue with the dictates of *Miranda*. The language which the Court finds controlling in this case teaches that renewed questioning itself is part of the process which invariably operates to overcome the will of a suspect. That teaching is embodied in the form of a proscription on any further questioning once the suspect has exercised his right to remain silent. Today's decision uncritically abandons that teaching. The Court assumes, contrary to the controlling language, that "scrupulously honoring" an initial exercise of the right to remain silent preserves the efficaciousness of initial and future warnings despite the fact that the suspect has once been subjected to interrogation and then has been detained for a lengthy period of time.

Observing that the suspect can control the circumstances of interrogation "(t)hrough the exercise of his option to terminate questioning," the Court concludes "that the admissibility of statements obtained after the person in custody has decided to remain silent depends . . . on whether his 'right to cut off questioning' was 'scrupulously honored.'" But scrupulously honoring exercises of the right to cut off questioning is only meaningful insofar as the suspect's will to exercise that right remains wholly unfettered. The Court's formulation thus assumes the very matter at issue here: whether renewed questioning following a lengthy period of detention acts to overbear the suspect's will, irrespective of giving the *Miranda* warnings a second time (and scrupulously honoring them), thereby rendering inconsequential any failure to exercise the right to remain silent. . . .

I agree that *Miranda* is not to be read, on the one hand, to impose an absolute ban on resumption of questioning "at any time or place on any subject," or on the other hand, "to permit a resumption of interrogation after a momentary respite." But this surely cannot justify adoption of a vague and ineffective procedural standard that falls somewhere between those absurd extremes, for *Miranda* in flat and unambiguous terms requires that questioning "cease" when a suspect exercises the right to remain silent. *Miranda*'s terms, however, are not so uncompromising as to preclude the fashioning of guidelines to govern this case. . . .

The fashioning of guidelines for this case is an easy task. Adequate procedures are readily available. Michigan law requires that the suspect be arraigned before a judicial officer "without unnecessary delay," certainly not a burdensome requirement. Alternatively, a requirement that resumption of questioning should await appointment and arrival of counsel for the suspect would be an acceptable and readily satisfied precondition to resumption. *Miranda* expressly held that "(t)he presence of counsel . . . would be the adequate protective device necessary to make the process of police interrogation conform to the dictates of the privilege (against self-incrimination)." The Court expediently bypasses this alternative in its search for circumstances where renewed questioning would be permissible. . . .

NOTES & QUESTIONS ON WAIVER

1. *Appealing to God.* Do you consider the detective's invocation of religious themes in *Berghuis* to be underhanded, or was it simply a deft interrogational technique? Was the fact that Thompkins started crying an indication that the questioning was inappropriate, or was it simply evidence that the approach was devastatingly effective?

2. *Implied waiver.* The Court in *Berghuis* concluded that an individual can waive his or her right to remain silent implicitly, in this case by simply

PROBLEM CASE

A *Miranda* waiver must be knowing and intelligent. Consider the following situation. On May 21, 1994, the defendant Daoud stopped two Detroit police officers who were on patrol in their squad car. Daoud spontaneously told them that he had confessed to killing his mother (who was murdered in 1985). The police officers exited their squad car and advised Daoud of his *Miranda* rights. Daoud waived his rights and gave more statements to the officers, indicating exactly how he had killed his mother with blunt force and also strangled her—facts that were highly significant because they accorded with the condition of her body when it was found. Daoud was taken to the police station and Mirandized again, at which point he repeated the same information again. It later turned out that Doaud was delusional and was motivated to confess to the police officers because he believed that "God would set him free" if he confessed to killing his mother. Does this delusion suggest that his waiver was not knowing and intelligent? See *People v. Daoud*, 462 Mich. 621, 625-26, 614 N.W.2d 152, 154 (2000).

answering the detective's question. Is this enough to waive the right? Or should waiver involve something *more* than simply answering a question. As one commentator noted:

> [T]he most glaring contradiction is the majority's conclusion that Thompkins' incriminating statement—his "yes" response—amounted to a "course of conduct indicating waiver," despite *Miranda*'s warning that inculpatory statements alone are insufficient to establish waiver. . . . The *Berghuis* Court's novel application of the implied waiver doctrine leaves criminal suspects in a tough position: as long as they understand the substance of the *Miranda* warning, any uncoerced statement establishes an implied waiver, even if the only statement a suspect makes is an inculpatory one. In effect, the Court has endorsed a jurisprudence of confession-as-waiver.

Zachary Mueller, *Speaking to Remain Silent: Implied Waivers and the Right to Silence After* Berghuis, 73 U. Pitt. L. Rev. 587, 600 (2012). On the other hand, how else is one to interpret the answering of the question except as an implied waiver? Why else did Thompkins make the statement if not to communicate something to his interrogator?

5. Exceptions

The Supreme Court has crafted exceptions in limited categories where the demands of *Miranda* do not apply. In the first case, *Harris*, the Supreme Court must determine whether a statement made in violation of *Miranda* can nonetheless be introduced at trial, notwithstanding the typical *Miranda* framework, which requires suppression for a Fifth Amendment violation. In particular, *Harris* deals with the situation where prosecutors seek to introduce the suspect's statement into evidence to impeach the suspect's testimony, rather than seeking to introduce the statement during its case-in-chief to satisfy the prosecution's burden on the elements of the offense.

Harris v. New York

Supreme Court of the United States
401 U.S. 222 (1971)

Mr. Chief Justice Burger delivered the opinion of the Court.

We granted the writ in this case to consider petitioner's claim that a statement made by him to police under circumstances rendering it inadmissible to establish the prosecution's case in chief under *Miranda v. Arizona* may not be used to impeach his credibility.

The State of New York charged petitioner in a two-count indictment with twice selling heroin to an undercover police officer. At a subsequent jury trial the officer was the State's chief witness, and he testified as to details of the two sales. A second officer verified collateral details of the sales, and a third offered testimony about the chemical analysis of the heroin.

Petitioner took the stand in his own defense. He admitted knowing the undercover police officer but denied a sale on January 4, 1966. He admitted making a sale of contents of a glassine bag to the officer on January 6 but claimed it was baking powder and part of a scheme to defraud the purchaser.

On cross-examination petitioner was asked seriatim whether he had made specified statements to the police immediately following his arrest on January 7—statements that partially contradicted petitioner's direct testimony at trial. In response to the cross-examination, petitioner testified that he could not remember virtually any of the questions or answers recited by the prosecutor. At the request of petitioner's counsel the written statement from which the prosecutor had read questions and answers in his impeaching process was placed in the record for possible use on appeal; the statement was not shown to the jury.

The trial judge instructed the jury that the statements attributed to petitioner by the prosecution could be considered only in passing on petitioner's credibility and not as evidence of guilt. In closing summations both counsel argued the substance of the impeaching statements. The jury then found petitioner guilty on the second count of the indictment. . . .

At trial the prosecution made no effort in its case in chief to use the statements allegedly made by petitioner, conceding that they were inadmissible under *Miranda v. Arizona*. The transcript of the interrogation used in the impeachment, but not given to the jury, shows that no warning of a right to appointed counsel was given before questions were put to petitioner when he was taken into custody. Petitioner makes no claim that the statements made to the police were coerced or involuntary.

Some comments in the *Miranda* opinion can indeed be read as indicating a bar to use of an uncounseled statement for any purpose, but discussion of that issue was not at all necessary to the Court's holding and cannot be regarded as controlling. *Miranda* barred the prosecution from making its case with statements of an accused made while in custody prior to having or effectively waiving counsel. It does not follow from *Miranda* that evidence inadmissible against an accused in the prosecution's case in chief is barred for all purposes, provided of course that the trustworthiness of the evidence satisfies legal standards.

In *Walder v. United States,* 347 U.S. 62 (1954), the Court permitted physical evidence, inadmissible in the case in chief, to be used for impeachment purposes. . . .

It is true that Walder was impeached as to collateral matters included in his direct examination, whereas petitioner here was impeached as to testimony bearing more directly on the crimes charged. We are not persuaded that there is a difference in principle that warrants a result different from that reached by the Court in *Walder*. Petitioner's testimony in his own behalf concerning the events of January 7 contrasted sharply with what he told the police shortly after his arrest. The impeachment process here undoubtedly provided valuable aid to the jury in assessing petitioner's credibility, and the benefits of this process should not be lost, in our view, because of the speculative possibility that impermissible police conduct will be encouraged thereby. Assuming that the exclusionary rule has a deterrent effect on proscribed police conduct, sufficient deterrence flows when the evidence in question is made unavailable to the prosecution in its case in chief.

Every criminal defendant is privileged to testify in his own defense, or to refuse to do so. But that privilege cannot be construed to include the right to commit perjury. Having voluntarily taken the stand, petitioner was under an obligation to speak truthfully and accurately, and the prosecution here did no more than utilize the traditional truth-testing devices of the adversary process. Had inconsistent statements been made by the accused to some third person, it could hardly be contended that the conflict could not be laid before the jury by way of cross-examination and impeachment.

The shield provided by *Miranda* cannot be perverted into a license to use perjury by way of a defense, free from the risk of confrontation with prior inconsistent utterances. We hold, therefore, that petitioner's credibility was appropriately impeached by use of his earlier conflicting statements.

Mr. Justice BRENNAN, with whom Mr. Justice DOUGLAS and Mr. Justice MARSHALL, join, dissenting.

It is conceded that the question-and-answer statement used to impeach petitioner's direct testimony was, under *Miranda*, inadmissible as part of the State's direct case against petitioner. I think that the Constitution also denied the State the use of the statement on cross-examination to impeach the credibility of petitioner's testimony given in his own defense. The decision in *Walder v. United States* is not, as the Court today holds, dispositive to the contrary. Rather, that case supports my conclusion.

The State's case against Harris depended upon the jury's belief of the testimony of the undercover agent that petitioner "sold" the officer heroin on January 4 and again on January 6. Petitioner took the stand and flatly denied having sold anything to the officer on January 4. He countered the officer's testimony as to the January 6 sale with testimony that he had sold the officer two glassine bags containing what appeared to be heroin, but that actually the bags contained only baking powder intended to deceive the officer in order to obtain $12. The statement contradicted petitioner's direct testimony as to the events of both days. The statement's version of the events on January 4 was that the officer had used petitioner as a middleman to buy some heroin from a third person with money furnished by the officer. The version of the events on January 6 was that petitioner had again acted for the officer in buying two bags of heroin from a third person for which petitioner received $12 and a part of the heroin. Thus, it is clear that the statement was used to impeach petitioner's direct testimony not on collateral matters but on matters directly related to the crimes for which he was on trial.

Walder v. United States was not a case where tainted evidence was used to impeach an accused's direct testimony on matters directly related to the case against him. In *Walder* the evidence was used to impeach the accused's testimony on matters collateral to the crime charged. *Walder* had been indicted in 1950 for purchasing and possessing heroin. When his motion to suppress use of the narcotics as illegally seized was granted, the Government dismissed the prosecution. Two years later Walder was indicted for another narcotics violation completely unrelated to the 1950 one. Testifying in his own defense, he said on direct examination that he had never in his life possessed narcotics. On cross-examination he denied that law enforcement officers had seized narcotics from his home two years earlier. The Government was then permitted to introduce the testimony of one of the officers involved in the 1950 seizure, that when he had raided Walder's home at that time he had seized narcotics there. The Court held that on facts where "the defendant went beyond a mere denial of complicity in the crimes of which he was charged and made the sweeping claim that he had never dealt in or possessed any narcotics," the exclusionary rule . . . would not extend to bar the Government from rebutting this testimony with evidence, although tainted, that petitioner had in fact possessed narcotics two years before. The Court was careful, however, to distinguish the situation of an accused whose testimony, as in the instant case, was a "denial of complicity in the crimes of which he was charged," that is, where illegally obtained evidence was used to impeach the accused's direct testimony on matters directly related to the case against him. As to that situation, the Court said:

> Of course, the Constitution guarantees a defendant the fullest opportunity to meet the accusation against him. He must be free to deny all the elements of the case against him without thereby giving leave to the Government to introduce by way of rebuttal evidence illegally secured by it, and therefore not available for its case in chief.

From this recital of facts it is clear that the evidence used for impeachment in *Walder* was related to the earlier 1950 prosecution and had no direct bearing on "the elements of the case" being tried in 1952. The evidence tended solely to impeach the credibility of the defendant's direct testimony that he had never in his life possessed heroin. But that evidence was completely unrelated to the indictment on trial and did not in any way interfere with his freedom to deny all elements of that case against him. In contrast, here, the evidence used for impeachment, a statement concerning the details of the very sales alleged in the indictment, was directly related to the case against petitioner.

While *Walder* did not identify the constitutional specifics that guarantee "a defendant the fullest opportunity to meet the accusation against him . . . (and permit him to) be free to deny all the elements of the case against him," in my view *Miranda* identified the Fifth Amendment's privilege against self-incrimination as one of those specifics. . . . It is fulfilled only when an accused is guaranteed the right "to remain silent unless he chooses to speak in the unfettered exercise of his own will." The choice of whether to testify in one's own defense must therefore be "unfettered," since that choice is an exercise of the constitutional privilege. . . . [The] constitutional guarantee forbids the prosecution to use a tainted statement to impeach the accused who takes the stand: The prosecution's use of the tainted statement "cuts down on the privilege by making its assertion costly." Thus, the accused is denied an "unfettered" choice when the decision whether to take the stand is burdened by the risk that an illegally obtained prior statement may be introduced to impeach his direct testimony denying complicity in the crime charged against him. . . .

The next case, *Quarles*, asks whether there is an "emergency situation" exception to the *Miranda* framework, i.e., whether situations involving a risk to personal safety justify ignoring *Miranda* and interrogating a suspect without first issuing *Miranda* warnings. As you read *Quarles*, ask yourself what type of risk—if any—might be sufficiently grave to justify an exception to *Miranda* under the emergency situation doctrine.

New York v. Quarles

Supreme Court of the United States
467 U.S. 649 (1984)

Justice REHNQUIST delivered the opinion of the Court.

Respondent Benjamin Quarles was charged in the New York trial court with criminal possession of a weapon. The trial court suppressed the gun in question, and a statement made by respondent, because the statement was obtained by police before they read respondent his *Miranda* rights. . . . We conclude that under the circumstances involved in this case, overriding considerations of public safety justify the officer's failure to provide *Miranda* warnings before he asked questions devoted to locating the abandoned weapon.

On September 11, 1980, at approximately 12:30 A.M., Officer Frank Kraft and Officer Sal Scarring were on road patrol in Queens, N.Y., when a young woman approached their car. She told them that she had just been raped by a black male, approximately six feet tall, who was wearing a black jacket with the name "Big Ben" printed in yellow letters on the back. She told the officers that the man had just entered an A&P supermarket located nearby and that the man was carrying a gun.

The officers drove the woman to the supermarket, and Officer Kraft entered the store while Officer Scarring radioed for assistance. Officer Kraft quickly spotted respondent, who matched the description given by the woman, approaching a checkout counter. Apparently upon seeing the officer, respondent turned and ran toward the rear of the store, and Officer Kraft pursued him with a drawn gun. When respondent turned the corner at the end of an aisle, Officer Kraft lost sight of him for several seconds, and upon regaining sight of respondent, ordered him to stop and put his hands over his head.

Although more than three other officers had arrived on the scene by that time, Officer Kraft was the first to reach respondent. He frisked him and discovered that he was wearing a shoulder holster which was then empty. After handcuffing him, Officer Kraft asked him where the gun was. Respondent nodded in the direction of some empty cartons and responded, "the gun is over there." Officer Kraft thereafter retrieved a loaded .38-caliber revolver from one of the cartons, formally placed respondent under arrest, and read him his *Miranda* rights from a printed card. Respondent indicated that he would be willing to answer questions without an attorney present. Officer Kraft then asked respondent if he owned the gun and where he had purchased it. Respondent answered that he did own it and that he had purchased it in Miami, Fla.

In the subsequent prosecution of respondent for criminal possession of a weapon, the judge excluded the statement, "the gun is over there," and the gun because the officer had not given respondent the warnings required by our decision in *Miranda* before asking him where the gun was located. The judge excluded the other statements about respondent's ownership of the gun and the place of purchase, as evidence tainted by the prior *Miranda* violation. . . .

[I]n *Miranda* this Court for the first time extended the Fifth Amendment privilege against compulsory self-incrimination to individuals subjected to custodial interrogation by the police. The Fifth Amendment itself does not prohibit all incriminating admissions. . . . The *Miranda* Court, however, presumed that interrogation in certain custodial circumstances is inherently coercive and held that statements made under those circumstances are inadmissible unless the suspect is specifically informed of his *Miranda* rights and freely decides to forgo those rights. . . .

In this case we have before us no claim that respondent's statements were actually compelled by police conduct which overcame his will to resist. Thus the only issue before us is whether Officer Kraft was justified in failing to make available to respondent the procedural safeguards associated with the privilege against compulsory self-incrimination since *Miranda*.

. . . As the New York Court of Appeals observed, there was nothing to suggest that any of the officers were any longer concerned for their own physical safety. The New York Court of Appeals' majority declined to express an opinion as to whether there might be an exception to the *Miranda* rule if the police had been acting to protect the public, because the lower courts in New York had made no factual determination that the police had acted with that motive.

We hold that on these facts there is a "public safety" exception to the requirement that *Miranda* warnings be given before a suspect's answers may be admitted into evidence, and that the availability of that exception does not depend upon the motivation of the individual officers involved. In a kaleidoscopic situation such as the one confronting these officers, where spontaneity rather than adherence to a police manual is necessarily the order of the day, the application of the exception which we recognize today should not be made to depend on post hoc findings at a suppression hearing concerning the subjective motivation of the arresting officer. Undoubtedly most police officers, if placed in Officer Kraft's position, would act out of a host of different, instinctive, and largely unverifiable motives–their own safety, the safety of others, and perhaps as well the desire to obtain incriminating evidence from the suspect.

Whatever the motivation of individual officers in such a situation, we do not believe that the doctrinal underpinnings of *Miranda* require that it be applied in all its rigor to a situation in which police officers ask questions reasonably prompted by a concern for the public safety. The *Miranda* decision was based in large part on this Court's view that the warnings which it required police to give to suspects in custody would reduce the likelihood that the suspects would fall victim to constitutionally impermissible practices of police interrogation in the presumptively coercive environment of the station house. . . .

The police in this case, in the very act of apprehending a suspect, were confronted with the immediate necessity of ascertaining the whereabouts of a gun which they had every reason to believe the suspect had just removed from his empty holster and discarded in the supermarket. So long as the gun was concealed somewhere in the supermarket, with its actual whereabouts unknown, it obviously posed more than one danger to the public safety: an accomplice might make use of it, a customer or employee might later come upon it.

In such a situation, if the police are required to recite the familiar *Miranda* warnings before asking the whereabouts of the gun, suspects in Quarles' position might well be deterred from responding. Procedural safeguards which deter a suspect from responding were deemed acceptable in *Miranda* in order to protect the Fifth Amendment privilege; when the primary social cost of those added protections is the possibility of fewer convictions, the *Miranda* majority was willing to bear that cost. Here, had *Miranda* warnings deterred Quarles from responding to Officer Kraft's question about the whereabouts of the gun, the cost would have been something more than merely the failure to obtain evidence useful in convicting Quarles. Officer Kraft needed an answer to his question not simply to make his case against Quarles but to insure that further danger to the public did not result from the concealment of the gun in a public area.

We conclude that the need for answers to questions in a situation posing a threat to the public safety outweighs the need for the prophylactic rule protecting the Fifth Amendment's privilege against self-incrimination. We decline to place officers such as Officer Kraft in the untenable position of having to consider, often in a matter of seconds, whether it best serves society for them to ask the necessary questions without the *Miranda* warnings and render whatever probative evidence they uncover inadmissible, or for them to give the warnings in order to preserve the admissibility of evidence they might uncover but possibly damage or destroy their ability to obtain that evidence and neutralize the volatile situation confronting them.

In recognizing a narrow exception to the *Miranda* rule in this case, we acknowledge that to some degree we lessen the desirable clarity of that rule. At least in part in order to preserve its clarity, we have over the years refused to sanction attempts to expand our *Miranda* holding. As we have in other contexts, we recognize here the importance of a workable rule "to guide police officers, who have only limited time and expertise to reflect on and balance the social and individual interests involved in the specific circumstances they confront." But as we have pointed out, we believe that the exception which we recognize today lessens the necessity of that on-the-scene balancing process. The exception will not be difficult for police officers to apply because in each case it will be circumscribed by the exigency which justifies it. We think police officers can and will distinguish almost instinctively between questions necessary to secure their own safety or the safety of the public and questions designed solely to elicit testimonial evidence from a suspect.

The facts of this case clearly demonstrate that distinction and an officer's ability to recognize it. Officer Kraft asked only the question necessary to locate the missing gun before advising respondent of his rights. It was only after securing the loaded revolver and giving the warnings that he continued with investigatory questions about the ownership and place of purchase of the gun. The exception which we recognize today, far from complicating the thought processes and the on-the-scene judgments of police officers, will simply free them to follow their legitimate instincts when confronting situations presenting a danger to the public safety. . . .

Justice O'CONNOR, concurring in the judgment in part and dissenting in part.

In my view, a "public safety" exception unnecessarily blurs the edges of the clear line heretofore established and makes *Miranda*'s requirements more difficult to understand. In some cases, police will benefit because a reviewing court will find that an exigency excused their failure to administer the required warnings. But in other cases, police will suffer because, though they thought an exigency excused their noncompliance, a reviewing court will view the "objective" circumstances differently and require exclusion of admissions thereby obtained. The end result will be a finespun new doctrine on public safety exigencies incident to custodial interrogation, complete with the hair-splitting distinctions that currently plague our Fourth Amendment jurisprudence. . . .

The justification the Court provides for upsetting the equilibrium that has finally been achieved—that police cannot and should not balance considerations of public safety against the individual's interest in avoiding compulsory testimonial self-incrimination—really misses the critical question to be decided. *Miranda* has never been read to prohibit the police from asking questions to secure the public safety. Rather, the critical question *Miranda* addresses is who shall bear the cost of securing the public safety when such questions are asked and answered: the defendant or the State. *Miranda*, for better or worse, found the resolution of that question implicit in the prohibition against compulsory self-incrimination and placed the burden on the State. When police ask custodial questions without administering the required warnings, *Miranda* quite clearly requires that the answers received be presumed compelled and that they be excluded from evidence at trial.

The Court concedes, as it must, both that respondent was in "custody" and subject to "interrogation" and that his statement "the gun is over there" was compelled within the meaning of our precedent. In my view, since there is nothing about an exigency that makes custodial interrogation any less compelling, a principled application of *Miranda* requires that respondent's statement be suppressed. . . .

Justice MARSHALL, with whom Justice BRENNAN and Justice STEVENS join, dissenting.

The police in this case arrested a man suspected of possessing a firearm in violation of New York law. Once the suspect was in custody and found to be unarmed, the arresting officer initiated an interrogation. Without being advised of his right not to respond, the suspect incriminated himself by locating the gun. The majority concludes that the State may rely on this incriminating statement to convict the suspect of possessing a weapon. I disagree. The arresting officers had no legitimate reason to interrogate the suspect without advising him of his rights to remain silent and to obtain assistance of counsel. By finding on these facts justification for unconsented interrogation, the majority abandons the clear guidelines enunciated in *Miranda* and condemns the American judiciary to a new era of post hoc inquiry into the propriety of custodial interrogations. More significantly and in direct conflict with this Court's longstanding interpretation of the Fifth Amendment, the majority has endorsed the introduction of coerced self-incriminating statements in criminal prosecutions. I dissent. . . .

The majority's entire analysis rests on the factual assumption that the public was at risk during Quarles' interrogation. This assumption is completely in conflict with the facts. . . . Before the interrogation began, Quarles had been "reduced to a condition of physical powerlessness." Contrary to the majority's speculations, Quarles was not believed to have, nor did he in fact have, an accomplice to come to his rescue. When the questioning began, the arresting officers were sufficiently confident of their safety to put away their guns. As Officer Kraft acknowledged at the suppression hearing, "the situation was under control." . . . [T]here was no evidence that the interrogation was prompted by the arresting officers' concern for the public's safety.

. . . Again contrary to the majority's intimations, no customers or employees were wandering about the store in danger of coming across Quarles' discarded weapon. Although the supermarket was open to the public, Quarles' arrest took place during the middle of the night when the store was apparently deserted except for the clerks at the checkout counter. The police could easily have cordoned off the store and searched for the missing gun. Had they done so, they would have found the gun forthwith. . . .

This case is illustrative of the chaos the "public-safety" exception will unleash. . . . If after plenary review two appellate courts so fundamentally differ over the threat to public safety presented by the simple and uncontested facts of this case, one must seriously question how law enforcement officers will respond to the majority's new rule in the confusion and haste of the real world. . . . Not only will police officers have to decide whether the objective facts of an arrest justify an unconsented custodial interrogation; they will also have to remember to interrupt the interrogation and read the suspect his *Miranda* warnings once the focus of the inquiry shifts from protecting the public's safety to ascertaining the suspect's guilt. Disagreements of the scope of the "public-safety" exception and mistakes in its application are inevitable. . . .

NOTES & QUESTIONS ON MIRANDA *EXCEPTIONS*

1. *Imminence.* Does the emergency situations exception recognized in *Quarles* require a finding of imminence? In other words, in addition to the severity of the risk, there is a temporal question of the imminence or immediacy of the exigency. Other courts applying the doctrine have required imminence. See, e.g., *State v. Maloney*, 191 So. 3d 969, 975 (Fla. Dist. Ct. App. 2016) ("The imminence of the threat must be considered from the objective perspective of a reasonable person in the position of the officer at the time and without the benefit of hindsight."); *People v. Attebury*, 463 Mich. 662, 671-72, 624 N.W.2d 912, 917 (2001) (concluding that for the emergency situation exception "to apply, the police inquiry must have been an objectively reasonable question necessary to protect the police or the public from an immediate danger"). Do the facts in *Quarles*—the existence of the unsecured gun—satisfy this standard? Was it an immediate danger?

2. *Impeachment.* Why does the *Miranda* rule—or rather the exclusionary rule tied to it—not apply in situations of witness impeachment? Remember that the rule from *Harris* only applies to uncoerced testimony. If the police violate the Fifth Amendment by coercing a suspect into giving a statement, the prosecution cannot introduce the statement into evidence even for purposes of impeachment. Also, remember that the rule from *Harris* only applies if the suspect affirmatively testified on direct examination about the matter and therefore attempted to use the exclusionary rule as a sword with which to commit perjury. For example, in *People v. Taylor*, 8 Cal. 3d 174, 185, 501 P.2d 918, 925 (1972), the California Supreme Court considered the testimony of a defendant

who made a "general denial" that constituted, at most, "a technically inferable negation of one element of the crime." The California Court distinguished this from a more deliberate perjury attempt:

> Here the defendant on direct examination offered no elaborate justification for his conduct, and the prior illegally obtained evidence was therefore not "inconsistent" or "conflicting" with that testimony. Defendant did not rely on the illegality of the impeaching evidence as a sword to commit perjury, but simply as a shield against the consequences of concededly improper police practices.

For more discussion of the scope of the impeachment exception, see Mary Jo White, *The Impeachment Exception to the Constitutional Exclusionary Rules*, 73 Colum. L. Rev. 1476 (1973).

3. Miranda *as evidence rule*. Reconsider Justice O'Connor's concurring/dissenting opinion. O'Connor emphasizes that there is no abstract requirement to Mirandize a suspect—police always have the option of forgoing that measure in cases where the goal of the investigation is not prosecutorial but instead motivated by a public safety rationale. Consider the following example. The police might investigate a kidnapping because they want to prosecute the kidnapper, but they might also investigate a kidnapping to find and rescue the victim. In most investigations, these two rationales will dovetail together, because the police will be inclined to prosecute the perpetrator after they extinguish the threat to public safety. However, the two goals will not always dovetail. For example, the police might be in a situation where they need information to solve a public safety crisis, but the principal perpetrators will not survive to be prosecuted (such as a suicide bomber). Under this conception, *Miranda* is a rule of pure evidentiary consequence: It prohibits use of evidence. So, for O'Connor, police were permitted to do exactly what they did because they were engaged in a public safety investigation; they just should not have been allowed to use the statement at trial.

6. Evidentiary Consequences of *Miranda* Violations

What happens to evidence that is procured by the police from an interrogation conducted in violation of *Miranda*? Usually, the evidence in question is the statement itself. Can it be introduced at trial? Under standard Fourth Amendment doctrine, evidence procured through an illegal search or seizure would be subject to the exclusionary rule and suppressed at trial. Should a similar exclusionary rule apply by analogy to *Miranda* violations?

In the following two cases, the Supreme Court answers this question, with regard to statements that were initially given to the police *before* the police

PROBLEM CASE

Consider the following description of a vehicle traffic stop:

> At approximately 12:45 A.M., Police Officer Michael Adney stopped a car driven by Liddell for a loud music violation. Adney arrested Liddell when a check revealed that he was barred from driving in Iowa. After the arrest, a pat-down search uncovered a bag of marijuana, $183 in cash, and two cell phones. Adney handcuffed Liddell and placed him in the patrol car. Meanwhile, Police Officer Jon Melvin arrived to assist and began to search Liddell's car incident to the arrest. When Melvin discovered an unloaded .38 caliber revolver under the front seat, he showed the gun to Adney and asked whether Liddell's person had been thoroughly searched after the arrest. Adney removed Liddell from the patrol car and asked, referring to Liddell's car, "Is there anything else in there we need to know about?" Melvin added, "That's gonna hurt us?" Adney repeated, "That's gonna hurt us? Since we found the pistol already." Liddell laughed and said, "I knew it was there but . . . it's not mine," before telling the officers there were no other weapons in his car. Melvin completed the search of the car, finding .38 caliber ammunition and rolling papers used to make marijuana cigarettes.

United States v. Liddell, 517 F.3d 1007, 1008 (8th Cir. 2008). Is this pre-*Miranda* discussion admissible as evidence under the public safety exception? What was the officer's motivation for asking Liddell these questions? Is it possible that he had a dual motivation?

issued the *Miranda* warnings and were subsequently repeated again after the warnings were issued. Spoiler alert: The two case reach opposite conclusions about whether the statements can be introduced at trial. As you read the cases, pay particular attention to the relevant factual dissimilarities that might explain the divergent treatment they received from the Court.

Oregon v. Elstad

Supreme Court of the United States
470 U.S. 298 (1985)

Justice O'CONNOR delivered the opinion of the Court.

This case requires us to decide whether an initial failure of law enforcement officers to administer the warnings required by *Miranda v. Arizona*, 384 U.S. 436 (1966), without more, "taints" subsequent admissions made after a suspect has been fully advised of and has waived his *Miranda* rights. . . .

I

In December 1981, the home of Mr. and Mrs. Gilbert Gross, in the town of Salem, Polk County, Ore., was burglarized. Missing were art objects and furnishings valued at $150,000. A witness to the burglary contacted the Polk County Sheriff's office, implicating respondent Michael Elstad, an 18-year-old neighbor and friend of the Grosses' teenage son. Thereupon, Officers Burke and McAllister went to the home of respondent Elstad, with a warrant for his arrest. Elstad's mother answered the door. She led the officers to her son's room where he lay on his bed, clad in shorts and listening to his stereo. The officers asked him to get dressed and to accompany them into the living room. Officer McAllister asked respondent's mother to step into the kitchen, where he explained that they had a warrant for her son's arrest for the burglary of a neighbor's residence. Officer Burke remained with Elstad in the living room. He later testified:

> I sat down with Mr. Elstad and I asked him if he was aware of why Detective McAllister and myself were there to talk with him. He stated no, he had no idea why we were there. I then asked him if he knew a person by the name of Gross, and he said yes, he did, and also added that he heard that there was a robbery at the Gross house. And at that point I told Mr. Elstad that I felt he was involved in that, and he looked at me and stated, "Yes, I was there."

. . . Elstad was transported to the Sheriff's headquarters and approximately one hour later, Officers Burke and McAllister joined him in McAllister's office. McAllister then advised respondent for the first time of his *Miranda* rights, reading from a standard card. Respondent indicated he understood his rights, and, having these rights in mind, wished to speak with the officers. Elstad gave a full statement, explaining that he had known that the Gross family was out of town and had been paid to lead several acquaintances to the Gross residence and show them how to gain entry through a defective sliding glass door. The statement was typed, reviewed by respondent, read back to him for correction, initialed and signed by Elstad and both officers. . . .

II

The arguments advanced in favor of suppression of respondent's written confession rely heavily on metaphor. One metaphor, familiar from the Fourth Amendment context, would require that respondent's confession, regardless of its integrity, voluntariness, and probative value, be suppressed as the "tainted fruit of the poisonous tree" of the *Miranda* violation. A second metaphor questions whether a confession can be truly voluntary once the "cat is out of the bag." Taken out of context, each of these metaphors can be misleading. They should not be used to obscure fundamental differences between the role of the Fourth Amendment exclusionary rule and the function of *Miranda* in guarding against the prosecutorial use of compelled statements as prohibited by the Fifth Amendment. The Oregon court assumed and respondent here contends that a failure to administer *Miranda* warnings necessarily breeds the same consequences as police infringement of a constitutional right, so that evidence uncovered following an unwarned statement must be suppressed as "fruit of the poisonous tree." We believe this view misconstrues the nature of the protections afforded by *Miranda* warnings and therefore misreads the consequences of police failure to supply them. . . .

Respondent's contention that his confession was tainted by the earlier failure of the police to provide *Miranda* warnings and must be excluded as "fruit of the poisonous tree" assumes the existence of a constitutional violation. . . . But as we explained in *Quarles* and *Tucker*, a procedural *Miranda* violation differs in significant respects from violations of the Fourth Amendment, which have traditionally mandated a broad application of the "fruits" doctrine. The purpose of the Fourth Amendment exclusionary rule is to deter unreasonable searches, no matter how probative their fruits. Where a Fourth Amendment violation "taints" the confession, a finding of voluntariness for the purposes of the Fifth Amendment is merely a threshold requirement in determining whether the confession may be admitted in evidence. Beyond this, the prosecution must show a sufficient break in events to undermine the inference that the confession was caused by the Fourth Amendment violation.

The *Miranda* exclusionary rule, however, serves the Fifth Amendment and sweeps more broadly than the Fifth Amendment itself. It may be triggered even in the absence of a Fifth Amendment violation. The Fifth Amendment prohibits use by the prosecution in its case in chief only of compelled testimony. Failure to administer *Miranda* warnings creates a presumption of compulsion. Consequently, unwarned statements that are otherwise voluntary within the meaning of the Fifth Amendment must nevertheless be excluded from evidence under *Miranda*. Thus, in the individual case, *Miranda*'s preventive medicine provides a remedy even to the defendant who has suffered no identifiable constitutional harm.

But the *Miranda* presumption, though irrebuttable for purposes of the prosecution's case in chief, does not require that the statements and their fruits be discarded as inherently tainted. Despite the fact that patently voluntary statements taken in violation of *Miranda* must be excluded from the prosecution's case, the presumption of coercion does not bar their use for impeachment purposes on cross-examination. *Harris v. New York*, 401 U.S. 222 (1971). The Court in *Harris* rejected as an "extravagant extension of the Constitution," the theory that a defendant who had confessed under circumstances that made the confession inadmissible, could thereby enjoy the freedom to "deny every fact disclosed or discovered as a 'fruit' of his confession, free from confrontation with his prior statements" and that the voluntariness of his confession would be totally irrelevant. Where an unwarned statement is preserved for use in situations that fall outside the sweep of the *Miranda* presumption, "the primary criterion of admissibility [remains] the 'old' due process voluntariness test." . . .

Because *Miranda* warnings may inhibit persons from giving information, this Court has determined that they need be administered only after the person is taken into "custody" or his freedom has otherwise been significantly restrained. Unfortunately, the task of defining "custody" is a slippery one, and "policemen investigating serious crimes [cannot realistically be expected to] make no errors whatsoever." If errors are made by law enforcement officers in administering the prophylactic *Miranda* procedures, they should not breed the same irremediable consequences as police infringement of the Fifth Amendment itself. It is an unwarranted extension of *Miranda* to hold that a simple failure to administer the warnings, unaccompanied by any actual coercion or other circumstances calculated to undermine the suspect's ability to exercise his free will, so taints the investigatory process that a subsequent voluntary and informed waiver is ineffective for some indeterminate period. Though *Miranda* requires that the unwarned admission must be suppressed, the admissibility of any subsequent statement should turn in these circumstances solely on whether it is knowingly and voluntarily made. . . .

III

Though belated, the reading of respondent's rights was undeniably complete. McAllister testified that he read the *Miranda* warnings aloud from a printed card and recorded Elstad's responses. There is no question that respondent knowingly and voluntarily waived his right to remain silent before he described his participation in the burglary. It is also beyond dispute that respondent's earlier remark was voluntary, within the meaning of the Fifth Amendment. Neither the environment nor the manner of either "interrogation" was coercive. The initial conversation took place at midday, in the living room area of respondent's own home, with his mother in the kitchen area, a few steps away. Although in retrospect the officers testified that respondent was then in custody, at the time he made his statement he had not been informed that he was under arrest. The arresting officers' testimony indicates that the brief stop in the living room before proceeding to the station house was not to interrogate the suspect but to notify his mother of the reason for his arrest. . . .

IV

When police ask questions of a suspect in custody without administering the required warnings, *Miranda* dictates that the answers received be presumed compelled and that they be excluded from evidence at trial in the State's case in chief. The Court has carefully adhered to this principle, permitting a narrow exception only where pressing public safety concerns demanded. The Court today in no way retreats from the bright-line rule of *Miranda*. We do not imply that good faith excuses a failure to administer *Miranda* warnings; nor do we condone inherently coercive police tactics or methods offensive to due process that render the initial admission involuntary and undermine the suspect's will to invoke his rights once they are read to him. A handful of courts have, however, applied our precedents relating to confessions obtained under coercive circumstances to situations involving wholly voluntary admissions, requiring a passage of time or break in events before a second, fully warned statement can be deemed voluntary. Far from establishing a rigid rule, we direct courts to avoid one; there is no warrant for presuming coercive effect where the suspect's initial inculpatory statement, though technically in violation of *Miranda*, was voluntary. The relevant inquiry is whether, in fact, the second statement was also voluntarily made. As in any such inquiry, the finder of fact must examine the surrounding circumstances and the entire course of police conduct with respect to the suspect in evaluating the voluntariness of his statements. The fact that a suspect chooses to speak after being informed of his rights is, of course, highly probative. We find that the dictates of *Miranda* and the goals of the Fifth Amendment proscription against use of compelled testimony are fully satisfied in the circumstances of this case by barring use of the unwarned statement in the case in chief. No further purpose is served by imputing "taint" to subsequent statements obtained pursuant to a voluntary and knowing waiver. We hold today that a suspect who has once responded to unwarned yet uncoercive questioning is not thereby disabled from waiving his rights and confessing after he has been given the requisite *Miranda* warnings.

Missouri v. Seibert

Supreme Court of the United States
542 U.S. 600 (2004)

Justice Souter announced the judgment of the Court and delivered an opinion, in which Justice Stevens, Justice Ginsburg, and Justice Breyer join.

This case tests a police protocol for custodial interrogation that calls for giving no warnings of the rights to silence and counsel until interrogation has produced a confession. Although such a statement is generally inadmissible, since taken in violation of *Miranda v. Arizona*, the interrogating officer follows it with *Miranda* warnings and then leads the suspect to cover the same ground a second time. The question here is the admissibility of the repeated statement. Because this midstream recitation of warnings after interrogation and unwarned confession could not effectively comply with *Miranda*'s constitutional requirement, we hold that a statement repeated after a warning in such circumstances is inadmissible.

I

Respondent Patrice Seibert's 12-year-old son Jonathan had cerebral palsy, and when he died in his sleep she feared charges of neglect because of bedsores on his body. In her presence, two of her teenage sons and two of their friends devised a plan to conceal the facts surrounding Jonathan's death by incinerating his body in the course of burning the family's mobile home, in which they planned to leave Donald Rector, a mentally ill teenager living with the family, to avoid any appearance that Jonathan had been unattended. Seibert's son Darian and a friend set the fire, and Donald died.

Five days later, the police awakened Seibert at 3 A.M. at a hospital where Darian was being treated for burns. In arresting her, Officer Kevin Clinton followed instructions from Rolla, Missouri, Officer Richard Hanrahan that he refrain from giving *Miranda* warnings. After Seibert had been taken to the police station and left alone in an interview room for 15 to 20 minutes, Officer Hanrahan questioned her without *Miranda* warnings for 30 to 40 minutes, squeezing her arm and repeating "Donald was also to die in his sleep." After Seibert finally admitted she knew Donald was meant to die in the fire, she was given a 20-minute coffee and cigarette break. Officer Hanrahan then turned on a tape recorder, gave Seibert the *Miranda* warnings, and obtained a signed waiver of rights from her. He resumed the questioning with "Ok, 'trice, we've been talking for a little while about what happened on Wednesday the twelfth, haven't we?" and confronted her with her prewarning statements:

> **Hanrahan:** "Now, in discussion you told us, you told us that there was a[n] understanding about Donald."
> **Seibert:** "Yes."
> **Hanrahan:** "Did that take place earlier that morning?"
> **Seibert:** "Yes."
> **Hanrahan:** "And what was the understanding about Donald?"
> **Seibert:** "If they could get him out of the trailer, to take him out of the trailer."
> **Hanrahan:** "And if they couldn't?"
> **Seibert:** "I, I never even thought about it. I just figured they would."
> **Hanrahan:** "'Trice, didn't you tell me that he was supposed to die in his sleep?"
> **Seibert:** "If that would happen, 'cause he was on that new medicine, you know . . . ."
> **Hanrahan:** "The Prozac? And it makes him sleepy. So he was supposed to die in his sleep?"
> **Seibert:** "Yes."

Id., at 70.

After being charged with first-degree murder for her role in Donald's death, Seibert sought to exclude both her prewarning and postwarning statements. At the suppression hearing, Officer Hanrahan testified that he made a "conscious decision" to withhold *Miranda* warnings, thus resorting to an interrogation technique he had been taught: question first, then give the warnings, and then repeat the question "until I get the answer that she's already provided once." He acknowledged that Seibert's ultimate statement was "largely a repeat of information . . . obtained" prior to the warning.

III

. . . The technique of interrogating in successive, unwarned and warned phases raises a new challenge to *Miranda*. Although we have no statistics on the frequency of this practice, it is not confined to Rolla, Missouri. An officer of that police department testified that the strategy of withholding *Miranda* warnings until after interrogating and drawing out a confession was promoted not only by his own department, but by a national police training organization and other departments in which he had worked. Consistently with the officer's testimony, the Police Law Institute, for example, instructs that "officers may conduct a two-stage interrogation. . . . At any point during the pre-*Miranda* interrogation, usually after arrestees have confessed, officers may then *read* the *Miranda* warnings and ask for a waiver. If the arrestees waive their *Miranda* rights, officers will be able to repeat any subsequent incriminating statements later in court." The upshot of all this advice is a question-first practice of some popularity, as one can see from the reported cases describing its use, sometimes in obedience to departmental policy.

V

Missouri argues that a confession repeated at the end of an interrogation sequence envisioned in a question-first strategy is admissible on the authority of *Oregon v. Elstad,* 470 U.S. 298 (1985), but the argument disfigures that case. In *Elstad,* the police went to the young suspect's house to take him into custody on a charge of burglary. Before the arrest, one officer spoke with the suspect's mother, while the other one joined the suspect in a "brief stop in the living room," where the officer said he "felt" the young man was involved in a burglary. The suspect acknowledged he had been at the scene. This Court noted that the pause in the living room "was not to interrogate the suspect but to notify his mother of the reason for his arrest," and described the incident as having "none of the earmarks of coercion." The Court, indeed, took care to mention that the officer's initial failure to warn was an "oversight" that "may have been the result of confusion as to whether the brief exchange qualified as 'custodial interrogation' or . . . may simply have reflected . . . reluctance to initiate an alarming police procedure before [an officer] had spoken with respondent's mother." . . .

At the opposite extreme are the facts here, which by any objective measure reveal a police strategy adapted to undermine the *Miranda* warnings. The unwarned interrogation was conducted in the station house, and the questioning was systematic, exhaustive, and managed with psychological skill. When the police were finished there was little, if anything, of incriminating potential left unsaid. The warned phase of questioning proceeded after a pause of only 15 to 20 minutes, in the same place as the unwarned segment. When the same officer who had conducted the first phase recited the *Miranda* warnings, he said nothing to counter the probable misimpression that the advice that anything Seibert said could be used against her also applied to the details of the inculpatory statement previously elicited. In particular, the police did not advise that her prior statement could not be used. Nothing was said or done to dispel the oddity of warning about legal rights to silence and counsel right after the police had led her through a systematic interrogation. . . .

NOTES & QUESTIONS ON EVIDENTIARY CONSEQUENCES

1. ***Physical fruits of unwarned but voluntary statements.*** In *United States v. Patane*, 542 U.S. 630 (2004), the Supreme Court considered whether *Miranda* required suppression of physical evidence found because of a suspect's voluntary statements that nonetheless violated *Miranda* because police failed to give the required warnings. In standard Fourth Amendment doctrine, the exclusionary rule applies not just to the unconstitutional search or seizure but to any evidence that is fruit of the poisonous tree, unless one of the exceptions becomes applicable (such as independent source or inevitable discovery). The question is whether that "fruit of the poisonous tree" structure should apply to *Miranda* violations as well, especially ones where the violation is a technical violation of *Miranda* and not a violation of the Fifth Amendment requirement of voluntariness. The court said no—fruit of the poisonous tree did not apply. Do you agree with this conclusion? Recall that *Patane* was decided after *Dickerson*, which held in 2000 that *Miranda* was a constitutional rule. Is it surprising that the Court declined to apply "fruit of the poisonous tree" to a constitutional rule violation?

D. PRACTICE & POLICY

The materials in this chapter have highlighted the hazards of the interrogational encounter. Police use a variety of techniques to convince suspects to give statements notwithstanding their Fifth Amendment right against self-incrimination.

In some cases, those techniques are sufficiently coercive that a court will deem the statement involuntary. In other cases, the statement will be considered voluntary but will later turn out to be false; in other words, sometimes an innocent suspect will confess to a crime he did not commit. Why would an innocent individual confess to a crime? How often does this occur? More importantly, is there anything that the law can do to lower the rate of false confessions?

How common are false confessions? This is a difficult question to study empirically because only a limited number of confessions will be later investigated to determine their veracity. However, some studies are highly suggestive. For example, one interview study of inmates in Iceland found that 12 percent of those interviewed reported making false confessions for a variety of reasons. See Gisli H. Gudjonsson & Jon F. Sigurdsson, *How Frequently Do False Confessions Occur? An Empirical Study Among Prison Inmates*, 1 Psychology, Crime & Law 21-26 (1994). Some suspects are more vulnerable to false confession than others, depending on their age, intellectual ability, and of course the nature and tactics of the police investigation. A study by the Innocence Project of confessions that were later proven false based on DNA exoneration suggested that a large percentage of the confessions were linked to eyewitness misidentification and faulty forensic evidence. See Julie H. Kilborn, *Convicted But Innocent: Why Post-Conviction Lawyers Are Indispensable*, 57 La. B.J. 314, 315 (2010). Overall, false confessions were found in 25 percent of the cases of overturned convictions analyzed by the Innocence Project. See Innocence Project, Understand the Causes: False Confessions (2007). This raises a deeper question: Why do innocent people confess during police interrogations?

For more analysis of the phenomenon of false confessions, see Richard A. Leo, *False Confessions: Causes, Consequences, and Implications*, 37 J. Am. Acad. Psychiatry & L. 332-34 (2009); Gisli H. Gudjonsson, *The Psychology of Interrogations and Confessions: A Handbook* (2004); Saul M. Kassin & Katherine L. Kiechel, *The Social Psychology of False Confessions: Compliance, Internalization and Confabulation*, 7 Psychol. Sci. 125 (1996). For a dissenting opinion, see David A. Perez, *The (In) Admissibility of False Confession Expert Testimony*, 26 Touro L. Rev. 23, 25 (2010) (concluding that "a review of the empirical research demonstrates that false confessions are exceedingly rare and that the evidence upon which the leading false confession scholars rely on is very unreliable").

Why do innocent suspects confess? There are two major techniques for investigating and understanding the phenomenon of false confessions. The first is rational choice models and the second is empirical studies involving interviews or experiments. Rational choice models suggest that innocent suspects confess when it is believed that confessing confers some benefit. The assumption underlying this rational choice framework is that confession overlaps with rational self-interest. For example, Professors Ofshe and Leo built a rational choice model that predicts four types of false confession: stress-compliant, coerced-compliant, non–coerced-persuaded, and coerced-persuaded. However, Ofshe and Leo emphasized that the benefit must be substantial enough that it outweighs whatever negative impulse is associated with lying:

> The psychological benefits of reducing guilt, doing the right thing, showing empathy for the victim's family, straightening things out with God, and appearing honorable in the eyes of the investigator or the community are not likely to elicit a decision to confess from an innocent person for a variety of reasons. One reason is that telling a lie—confessing falsely—violates all of the cultural prescriptions activated by the investigator. Low-end incentives are actually negative incentives to confess for an innocent suspect.

Richard J. Ofshe & Richard A. Leo, *The Decision to Confess Falsely: Rational Choice and Irrational Action*, 74 Denv. U. L. Rev. 979, 997 (1997).

Although there are various reasons why an innocent individual might falsely confess, researchers generally point to the prevailing interrogational techniques and note that they are designed to produce confessions rather than the truth:

> First, investigators are advised to isolate the suspect in a small private room, which increases his or her anxiety and incentive to escape. A nine-step process then ensues in which an interrogator employs both negative and positive incentives. On one hand, the interrogator confronts the suspect with accusations of guilt, assertions that may be bolstered by evidence, real or manufactured, and refuses to accept alibis and denials. On the other hand, the interrogator offers sympathy and moral justification, introducing "themes" that minimize the crime and lead suspects to see confession as an expedient means of escape.

Saul M. Kassin et al., *Police-Induced Confessions: Risk Factors and Recommendations*, 34 Law & Hum. Behav. 3, 5 (2010). Consequently, the suspect may feel that conviction is inevitable and that mitigation of responsibility is the best outcome that they can hope for and that a false confession is the best avenue for achieving that mitigation. Or, the suspect may falsely believe that the confession will somehow exonerate them because they misunderstand the nature of justifications or excuses under the criminal law. For example, an interrogator might deceive a suspect into believing that if they confess to a crime under a particular set of facts, those facts will set up an affirmative defense. If, however, the suspect is ignorant of the affirmative defenses, they might not understand that they have just confessed to a crime and that the particular facts of the confession do not support a defense at all. Not only is this scenario not impossible; successful interrogation often depends on the questioner's ability to exploit these epistemic vulnerabilities.

Why do so many suspects waive *Miranda* rights? One would think that *Miranda* would encourage almost every suspect to invoke, rather than waive, key *Miranda* rights. In other words, one would expect the following result: Suspects would all keep quiet and demand to speak with an attorney right away, immediately after receiving the warnings. In practice this does not happen. Why? Consider the following hypothesis from Professor Corn:

> [P]erhaps the most important warning to facilitate a meaningful waiver choice has never been required: that silence in the face of police accusation produces no adverse evidentiary consequences and that it is not legally incriminating. This "missing" *Miranda* warning, although it is arguably just as, if not more, important than the existing warnings, is ironically the one warning that has never been required. Unless a suspect understands that his silence cannot be used against him, understanding that what he does say may be used against him seems far less significant. Without this additional warning, the suspect is left vulnerable to the instinctual lay expectation that the investigator will draw an inference of guilt from the decision to remain silent. Without being informed of the constitutional prohibition against this inferential guilt influence, the suspect is left to choose between standing on the right to silence and "looking guilty," or attempting to explain to the accuser why the accusation is erroneous.

Geoffrey S. Corn, *The Missing* Miranda *Warning: Why What You Don't Know Really Can Hurt You*, 2011 Utah L. Rev. 761, 770-71. Do you agree with the hypothesis? Should this "missing" *Miranda* warning be required?

Proposals for institutional change. Given the possibility for false convictions, what changes, either in law or policy, might be introduced to lower that risk? One possibility is to move from an adversarial model of criminal process to an inquisitorial model. Although an inquisitorial model *sounds* more harsh and more likely to result in false confessions, government actors, including investigating judges, are burdened with more robust obligations to find the truth and to investigate leads that might exonerate a suspect. However, even an inquisitorial model is subject to false confessions, as demonstrated by the Gudjonsson study cited above. (Iceland uses an inquisitorial model for its criminal procedure.) Furthermore, the wholesale change of the United States criminal justice model, which is rooted in the common law tradition, is unlikely to happen. Are there more modest changes that might help reduce the rate of false confessions?

First, several reformists have suggested the imposition of a rule, by local statute, requiring all interrogations to be recorded. While this is unlikely to be imposed by the Supreme Court as a matter of constitutional obligation, state legislatures could certainly pass regulations requiring video recording. In the absence of state legislation, local police agencies could enact discretionary policies requiring videotaping of all police interviews, as several agencies already require—at least in most situations. Existing practice does not necessary cover situations at the margins: i.e., spontaneous utterances that take place outside of formal interviews. But even if video recording is not universal, a general standard of videotaping police interviews might chasten the most egregious of police misconduct in the interview room.

Second, some reformists have suggested that judges should always hold evidentiary hearings to inquire into the validity of confessions before admitting them into evidence. This proposal is contingently related to the first proposal; it is easier for a judge to evaluate the legitimacy of the interrogation if there is video evidence of the interview. One proposal calls for judges to engage in the following analysis:

> Judges evaluating the reliability of confessions that are the product of a recorded interrogation should weigh three factors: (1) whether the confession contains nonpublic information that can be independently verified, would only be known by the true perpetrator or an accomplice, and cannot likely be guessed by chance; (2) whether the suspect's confession led the police to new evidence about the crime; and (3) whether the suspect's postadmission narrative "fits" (or fails to fit) with the crime facts and existing objective evidence.

Richard A. Leo et al., *Bringing Reliability Back In: False Confessions and Legal Safeguards in the Twenty-First Century*, 2006 Wis. L. Rev. 479, 531. However, in theory, the hearings could be conducted even in the absence of a video record of the interview.

The rationale for this proposal is to encourage judges to be gatekeepers to keep unreliable evidence from the jury. Judges already engage in this process when considering scientific evidence, i.e., so-called *Daubert* hearings in which judges assess whether a particular piece of scientific evidence, or its underlying process or method, is sufficiently reliable to be admitted into evidence. Judges could be encouraged to do the same for interrogations. Instead of simply examining whether the statement was voluntary, judges could, in addition, ask whether the statement is sufficiently *reliable* to be presented to the jury.

CHAPTER 8

RIGHT TO COUNSEL DURING INTERROGATIONS

INTRODUCTION

The right to have a lawyer present during police interrogation is obviously a valuable protection for any suspect in the government's cross-hairs. The source of that right, however, will depend on the timing of and circumstances surrounding the police questioning. Textually, the right to counsel is found in the Sixth Amendment, and is among the most central protections of the Constitution—without counsel, the individual's ability to stand against the awesome power of the state is effectively muted. The attorney both advocates for the individual's interests but more importantly provides valuable *counsel* to the individual, helping them decide how to respond to the threat posed by the government's criminal investigation. Should I cooperate? Should I stay silent? Should I provide information about other individuals? Although stories in the popular imagination focus on the role of the attorney during legal proceedings such as a trial, the attorney's role in the interrogational process is equally—if not more—consequential in the interrogation setting. Without an attorney, the interrogation is just one or more state officials speaking with a lone individual without any "medium" between them. That right comes into effect, however, only after a suspect has been formally accused of a crime—what the Supreme Court calls the initiation of formal adversarial proceedings—and applies only in relation to questioning related to that offense. However, as explained below, notice of a right to assistance of counsel was also included in the package of rights that the *Miranda* Court decided were needed to ensure a knowing and voluntary waiver of the *Fifth Amendment* privilege against self-incrimination. Hence, in addition to the textual Sixth Amendment right, it is also necessary to understand the function of the Court-created *Miranda* right to counsel.

To complicate matters, the right to counsel during interrogations also flows from the Sixth Amendment, which states: "In all criminal prosecutions, the accused shall enjoy the right to a speedy and public trial, by an impartial jury of the State and district wherein the crime shall have been committed; which district shall have been previously ascertained by law, and to be informed of the nature and cause of the accusation; to be confronted with the witnesses against him; to have compulsory process for obtaining witnesses in his favor, and to have the assistance of counsel for his defence." With this in mind, it is important to understand that police interrogations are not confined to the time period before charges are filed. In many instances, police may wish to speak with a criminal defendant after arraignment. Once the Sixth Amendment right to counsel has been triggered, subsequent police questioning of the defendant—even undercover questioning—takes place under the long shadow of the Sixth Amendment. And if this were not complicated enough, if the questioning of a defendant protected by the Sixth Amendment occurs while the defendant is in custody, *both* the Sixth Amendment *and* the *Miranda* rights to counsel will apply.

This chapter focuses on both the Fifth and Sixth Amendment right to counsel. Since the Fifth Amendment right to counsel flows from the privilege against self-incrimination, and is protected by the *Miranda* framework, it is a natural outgrowth of the jurisprudence explored in the prior chapter on self-incrimination. However, in practice, the right to counsel is a barrier to police interrogation, so both the Fifth and Sixth Amendment rights to counsel are analyzed below. However, it is important to remember that the requirements and consequences for each right are separate, even though both involve access to legal counsel. Consequently, Section A focuses on the Fifth Amendment right while Section B focuses on the Sixth Amendment right. Much of the debate in Section B involves how much of the "prophylactic" rationale for the Fifth Amendment *Miranda* right should be carried over to the Sixth Amendment context, which is not based on *Miranda*.

Conceptually, it is useful to distinguish a "suspect" from a "defendant": All defendants are suspects, but not all suspects are defendants. Only when formally charged does a suspect become a defendant, and only at that point does the Sixth Amendment right apply. And unlike the *Miranda* rule, which protects against a special type of inherent coercion, the Sixth Amendment is not intended to offset coercion, but instead ensures defense counsel can effectively protect the interests of the client. Thus, for example, there is no "custody" requirement to trigger the Sixth Amendment: Any police questioning once a suspect becomes a defendant implicates its protection. Other differences include the ability of police to approach a represented individual to request a waiver and the evidentiary consequence of violation: A Sixth Amendment violation is a "poison tree," while a *Miranda* violation is not.

A. THE FIFTH AMENDMENT RIGHT TO COUNSEL

As noted above, the Fifth Amendment right to counsel flows from *Miranda*. Recall that the Supreme Court stated in *Miranda* that "[t]he presence of counsel, in all the cases before us today, would be the adequate protective device necessary to make the process of police interrogation conform to the dictates of the privilege. His presence would insure that statements made in the government-established atmosphere are not the product of compulsion." *Miranda v. Arizona*, 384 U.S. 436, 466 (1966). The point of *Miranda* was that the presence of counsel to advise the suspect would surely offset the inherent coercion of custodial interrogation, and therefore advising a suspect of the right to that assistance, followed by a voluntary waiver of that assistance, indicates that the decision to submit to questioning was not the result of inherent coercive pressures.

The following cases outline the scope of the Fifth Amendment right to counsel and situate that right within the overall *Miranda* framework. Subsection 1 focuses on the requirement that police should cease the interrogation once a suspect invokes their right to counsel, while subsection 2 focuses on how police should respond to ambiguous statements that might or might not be interpreted as a demand for counsel. Subsection 3 focuses on the special problem of re-initiation: When, if at all, may police approach a suspect who has previously invoked the right to counsel to try again to obtain a *Miranda* waiver and question that suspect? Subsection 4 focuses on the effects of a break in the interrogation. What constraints operate when the police engage in a custodial interrogation, "release" the suspect, and then seek to interrogate the suspect a second time? What unites all of these questions is a central concern of the Supreme Court that once a suspect has invoked or "stood on" the Fifth Amendment right to counsel, procedures should be put in place to prevent the police from "badgering" the suspect into waiving the right to counsel.

1. Cessation of Interrogation

Assuming the *Miranda* right to counsel is triggered by custodial interrogation, the next question is what happens once a suspect invokes that right. In the following case, the suspect, Edwards, invoked his *Miranda* right to counsel and asked for a lawyer who could help negotiate a deal with prosecutors. In accordance with *Miranda*, police terminated the interrogation. However, the next day, the police approached Edwards, obtained a *Miranda* waiver, and interrogated him again. Did this "re-initiation"—without counsel present—violate his right to counsel? In other words, does invoking the Fifth Amendment right to counsel render the suspect "unapproachable" by police who want to try and get a new waiver unless counsel is present when police seek that waiver?

Edwards v. Arizona

Supreme Court of the United States
451 U.S. 477 (1981)

Justice WHITE delivered the opinion of the Court.

We granted certiorari in this case [to determine] "whether the Fifth, Sixth, and Fourteenth Amendments require suppression of a post-arrest confession, which was obtained after Edwards had invoked his right to consult counsel before further interrogation. . . ."

I

On January 19, 1976, a sworn complaint was filed against Edwards in Arizona state court charging him with robbery, burglary, and first-degree murder. An arrest warrant was issued pursuant to the complaint, and Edwards was arrested at his home later that same day. At the police station, he was informed of his rights as required by *Miranda v. Arizona*, 384 U.S. 436 (1966). Petitioner stated that he understood his rights, and was willing to submit to questioning. After being told that another suspect already in custody had implicated him in the crime, Edwards denied involvement and gave a taped statement presenting an alibi defense. He then sought to "make a deal." The interrogating officer told him that he wanted a statement, but that he did not have the authority to negotiate a deal. The officer provided Edwards with the telephone number of a county attorney. Petitioner made the call, but hung up after a few moments. Edwards then said: "I want an attorney before making a deal." At that point, questioning ceased and Edwards was taken to county jail.

At 9:15 the next morning, two detectives, colleagues of the officer who had interrogated Edwards the previous night, came to the jail and asked to see Edwards. When the detention officer informed Edwards that the detectives wished to speak with him, he replied that he did not want to talk to anyone. The guard told him that "he had" to talk and then took him to meet with the detectives. The officers identified themselves, stated they wanted to talk to him, and informed him of his *Miranda* rights. Edwards was willing to talk, but he first wanted to hear the taped statement of the alleged accomplice who had implicated him. After listening to the tape for several minutes, petitioner said that he would make a statement so long as it was not tape-recorded. The detectives informed him that the recording was irrelevant since they could testify in court concerning whatever he said.

Edwards replied: "I'll tell you anything you want to know, but I don't want it on tape." He thereupon implicated himself in the crime. . . .

II

In *Miranda v. Arizona*, the Court determined that the Fifth and Fourteenth Amendments' prohibition against compelled self-incrimination required that custodial interrogation be preceded by advice to the putative defendant that he has the right to remain silent and also the right to the presence of an attorney. The Court also indicated the procedures to be followed subsequent to the warnings. If the accused indicates that he wishes to remain silent, "the interrogation must cease." If he requests counsel, "the interrogation must cease until an attorney is present."

Miranda thus declared that an accused has a Fifth and Fourteenth Amendment right to have counsel present during custodial interrogation. Here, the critical facts as found by the Arizona Supreme Court are that Edwards asserted his right to counsel and his right to remain silent on January 19, but that the police, without furnishing him counsel, returned the next morning to confront him and as a result of the meeting secured incriminating oral admissions. Contrary to the holdings of the state courts, Edwards insists that having exercised his right on the 19th to have counsel present during interrogation, he did not validly waive that right on the 20th. For the following reasons, we agree.

First, the Arizona Supreme Court applied an erroneous standard for determining waiver where the accused has specifically invoked his right to counsel. It is reasonably clear under our cases that waivers of counsel must not only be voluntary, but must also constitute a knowing and intelligent relinquishment or abandonment of a known right or privilege, a matter which depends in each case "upon the particular facts and circumstances surrounding that case, including the background, experience, and conduct of the accused."

Considering the proceedings in the state courts in the light of this standard, we note that in denying petitioner's motion to suppress, the trial court found the admission to have been "voluntary" without separately focusing on whether Edwards had knowingly and intelligently relinquished his right to counsel. The Arizona Supreme Court, in a section of its opinion entitled "Voluntariness of Waiver," stated that in Arizona, confessions are prima facie involuntary and that the State had the burden of showing by a preponderance of the evidence that the confession was freely and voluntarily made. The court stated that the issue of voluntariness should be determined based on the totality of the circumstances as it related to whether an accused's action was "knowing and intelligent and whether his will [was] overborne." Once the trial court determines that "the confession is voluntary, the finding will not be upset on appeal absent clear and manifest error." The court then upheld the trial court's finding that the "waiver and confession were voluntarily and knowingly made."

In referring to the necessity to find Edwards' confession knowing and intelligent, the State Supreme Court cited *Schneckloth v. Bustamonte*, 412 U.S. 218, 226 (1973). Yet, it is clear that *Schneckloth* does not control the issue presented in this case. The issue in *Schneckloth* was under what conditions an individual could be found to have consented to a search and thereby waived his Fourth Amendment rights. The Court declined to impose the "intentional relinquishment or abandonment of a known right or privilege" standard and required only that the consent be voluntary under the totality of the circumstances. The Court specifically noted that the right to counsel was a prime example of those rights requiring the special protection of the knowing and intelligent waiver standard, but held that "[t]he considerations that informed the Court's holding in *Miranda* are simply inapplicable in the present case." *Schneckloth* itself thus emphasized that the voluntariness of a consent or an admission on the one hand, and a knowing and intelligent waiver on the other, are discrete inquiries. Here, however sound the conclusion of the state courts as to the voluntariness of Edwards' admission may be, neither the trial court nor the Arizona Supreme Court undertook to focus on whether Edwards understood his right to counsel and intelligently and knowingly relinquished it. It is thus apparent that the decision below misunderstood the requirement for finding a valid waiver of the right to counsel, once invoked.

Second, although we have held that after initially being advised of his *Miranda* rights, the accused may himself validly waive his rights and respond to interrogation, the Court has strongly indicated that additional safeguards are necessary when the accused asks for counsel; and we now hold that when an accused has invoked his right to have counsel present during custodial interrogation, a valid waiver of that right cannot be established by showing only that he responded to further police-initiated custodial interrogation even if he has been advised of his rights. We further hold that an accused, such as Edwards, having expressed his desire to deal with the police only through counsel, is not subject to further interrogation by the authorities until counsel has been made available to him, unless the accused himself initiates further communication, exchanges, or conversations with the police.

Miranda itself indicated that the assertion of the right to counsel was a significant event and that once exercised by the accused, "the interrogation must cease until an attorney is present." Our later cases have not abandoned that view. In *Michigan v. Mosley*, 423 U.S. 96 (1975), the Court noted that *Miranda* had distinguished between the procedural safeguards triggered by a request to remain silent and a request for an attorney and had required that interrogation cease until an attorney was present only if the individual stated that he wanted counsel. In *Fare v. Michael C.*, 442 U.S., at 719, the Court referred to *Miranda*'s "rigid rule that an accused's request for an attorney is per se an invocation of his Fifth Amendment rights, requiring that all interrogation cease." And just last Term, in a case where a suspect in custody had invoked his *Miranda* right to counsel, the Court again referred to the "undisputed right" under *Miranda* to remain silent and to be free of interrogation "until he had consulted with a lawyer." We reconfirm these views and, to lend them substance, emphasize that it is inconsistent with *Miranda* and its progeny for the authorities, at their instance, to reinterrogate an accused in custody if he has clearly asserted his right to counsel.

In concluding that the fruits of the interrogation initiated by the police on January 20 could not be used against Edwards, we do not hold or imply that Edwards was powerless to countermand his election or that the authorities could in no event use any incriminating statements made by Edwards prior to his having access to counsel. Had Edwards initiated the meeting on January 20, nothing in the Fifth and Fourteenth Amendments would prohibit the police from merely listening to his voluntary, volunteered statements and using them against him at the trial. The Fifth Amendment right identified in *Miranda* is the right to have counsel present at any custodial interrogation. Absent such interrogation, there would have been no infringement of the right that Edwards invoked and there would be no occasion to determine whether there had been a valid waiver.

But this is not what the facts of this case show. Here, the officers conducting the interrogation on the evening of January 19 ceased interrogation when Edwards requested counsel as he had been advised he had the right to do. The Arizona Supreme Court was of the opinion that this was a sufficient invocation of his *Miranda* rights, and we are in accord. It is also clear that without making counsel available to Edwards, the police returned to him the next day. This was not at his suggestion or request. Indeed, Edwards informed the detention officer that he did not want to talk to anyone. At the meeting, the detectives told Edwards that they wanted to talk to him and again advised him of his *Miranda* rights. Edwards stated that he would talk, but what prompted this action does not appear. He listened at his own request to part of the taped statement made by one of his alleged accomplices and then made an incriminating statement, which was used against him at his trial. We think it is clear that Edwards was subjected to custodial interrogation on January 20 . . . and that this occurred at the instance of the authorities. His statement made without having had access to counsel, did not amount to a valid waiver and hence was inadmissible. . . .

NOTES & QUESTIONS ON CESSATION OF INTERROGATION

1. *The* Edwards *"presumption."* The best way to think of the *Edwards* decision is to think of it as establishing a presumption of involuntariness. In other words, if the police continue to interrogate a suspect after he or she invokes the right to counsel, the law will conclude that the resulting statement is involuntary–i.e., compelled–and subject to suppression. This framework emerges from the fact that the *Edwards* right to counsel flows from the Fifth Amendment prohibition against compelled interrogation. The waiver is invalid because once the suspect says he needs help from a lawyer, there is no way a waiver without the lawyer's presence can be deemed valid. The suspect needs the lawyer to help him decide whether to waive. This also explains why the statement is admissible if the suspect *himself* reinitiates; the police are prohibited from exploiting the vulnerability the suspect signaled by procuring the waiver without a lawyer. Should this rule be so categorical? Should it be replaced with a presumption that might be rebutted depending on the particular facts of the case? For more discussion, see Eugene L. Shapiro, *Thinking the Unthinkable: Recasting the Presumption of* Edwards v. Arizona, 53 Okla. L. Rev. 11, 12 (2000).

2. Ambiguous Quasi-Invocations

On paper, the *Edwards* rule is simple: The suspect will say "Get me a lawyer," and then stops talking; the police are then required to stop questioning until the suspect has a lawyer present or reinitiates the conversation. However, in real life, statements are far more ambiguous and subject to interpretation. If a suspect makes a statement that could be construed as a request for counsel, how should–or must–the police respond? Can they treat it as a non-request? Or must they treat any ambiguous request as an invocation of the right to counsel? Or should they request clarification? In the following case, the rubber of the *Edwards* presumption hits the road. As you read the case, ask yourself whether the Supreme Court gives sufficiently clear guidance for how police officers should respond when faced with an ambiguous possible invocation of the right to counsel.

Davis v. United States

Supreme Court of the United States
512 U.S. 452 (1994)

Justice O'Connor delivered the opinion of the Court.

In *Edwards v. Arizona*, 451 U.S. 477 (1981), we held that law enforcement officers must immediately cease questioning a suspect who has clearly asserted his right to have counsel present during custodial interrogation.

In this case we decide how law enforcement officers should respond when a suspect makes a reference to counsel that is insufficiently clear to invoke the *Edwards* prohibition on further questioning.

I

Pool brought trouble—not to River City, but to the Charleston Naval Base. Petitioner, a member of the United States Navy, spent the evening of October 2, 1988, shooting pool at a club on the base. Another sailor, Keith Shackleton, lost a game and a $30 wager to petitioner, but Shackleton refused to pay. After the club closed, Shackleton was beaten to death with a pool cue on a loading dock behind the commissary. The body was found early the next morning.

The investigation by the Naval Investigative Service (NIS) gradually focused on petitioner. Investigative agents determined that petitioner was at the club that evening, and that he was absent without authorization from his duty station the next morning. The agents also learned that only privately owned pool cues could be removed from the club premises, and that petitioner owned two cues—one of which had a bloodstain on it. The agents were told by various people that petitioner either had admitted committing the crime or had recounted details that clearly indicated his involvement in the killing.

On November 4, 1988, petitioner was interviewed at the NIS office. As required by military law, the agents advised petitioner that he was a suspect in the killing, that he was not required to make a statement, that any statement could be used against him at a trial by court-martial, and that he was entitled to speak with an attorney and have an attorney present during questioning. Petitioner waived his rights to remain silent and to counsel, both orally and in writing.

About an hour and a half into the interview, petitioner said, "Maybe I should talk to a lawyer." According to the uncontradicted testimony of one of the interviewing agents, the interview then proceeded as follows:

> [We m]ade it very clear that we're not here to violate his rights, that if he wants a lawyer, then we will stop any kind of q uestioning with him, that we weren't going to pursue the matter unless we have it clarified is he asking for a lawyer or is he just making a comment about a lawyer, and he said, [']No, I'm not asking for a lawyer,' and then he continued on, and said, 'No, I don't want a lawyer.'

After a short break, the agents reminded petitioner of his rights to remain silent and to counsel. The interview then continued for another hour, until petitioner said, "I think I want a lawyer before I say anything else." At that point, questioning ceased. . . .

II

The Sixth Amendment right to counsel attaches only at the initiation of adversary criminal proceedings and before proceedings are initiated a suspect in a criminal investigation has no constitutional right to the assistance of counsel. Nevertheless, we held in *Miranda v. Arizona* that a suspect subject to custodial interrogation has the right to consult with an attorney and to have counsel present during questioning, and that the police must explain this right to him before questioning begins. The right to counsel established in *Miranda* was one of a "series of recommended 'procedural safeguards' ... [that] were not themselves rights protected by the Constitution but were instead measures to insure that the right against compulsory self-incrimination was protected."

The right to counsel recognized in *Miranda* is sufficiently important to suspects in criminal investigations, we have held, that it "requir[es] the special protection of the knowing and intelligent waiver standard." *Edwards v. Arizona,* 451 U.S., at 483. If the suspect effectively waives his right to counsel after receiving the warnings, law enforcement officers are free to question him. But if a suspect requests counsel at any time during the interview, he is not subject to further questioning until a lawyer has been made available or the suspect himself reinitiates conversation. This "second layer of prophylaxis for the *Miranda* right to counsel" is "designed to prevent police from badgering a defendant into waiving his previously asserted *Miranda* rights." To that end, we have held that a suspect who has invoked the right to counsel cannot be questioned regarding any offense unless an attorney is actually present. "It remains clear, however, that this prohibition on further questioning–like other aspects of *Miranda*–is not itself required by the Fifth Amendment's prohibition on coerced confessions, but is instead justified only by reference to its prophylactic purpose."

The applicability of the "'rigid' prophylactic rule" of *Edwards* requires courts to "determine whether the accused actually invoked his right to counsel." To avoid difficulties of proof and to provide guidance to officers conducting interrogations, this is an objective inquiry. Invocation of the *Miranda* right to counsel "requires, at a minimum, some statement that can reasonably be construed to be an expression of a desire for the assistance of an attorney." But if a suspect makes a reference to an attorney that is ambiguous or equivocal in that a reasonable officer in light of the circumstances would have understood only that the suspect might be invoking the right to counsel, our precedents do not require the cessation of questioning.

Rather, the suspect must unambiguously request counsel. As we have observed, "a statement either is such an assertion of the right to counsel or it is not." Although a suspect need not "speak with the discrimination of an Oxford don," he must articulate his desire to have counsel present sufficiently clearly that a reasonable police officer in the circumstances would understand the statement to be a request for an attorney. If the statement fails to meet the requisite level of clarity, *Edwards* does not require that the officers stop questioning the suspect.

We decline petitioner's invitation to extend *Edwards* and require law enforcement officers to cease questioning immediately upon the making of an ambiguous or equivocal reference to an attorney. The rationale underlying *Edwards* is that the police must respect a suspect's wishes regarding his right to have an attorney present during custodial interrogation. But when the officers conducting the questioning reasonably do not know whether or not the suspect wants a lawyer, a rule requiring the immediate cessation of questioning "would transform the *Miranda* safeguards into wholly irrational obstacles to legitimate police investigative activity," because it would needlessly prevent the police from questioning a suspect in the absence of counsel even if the suspect did not wish to have a lawyer present. Nothing in *Edwards* requires the provision of counsel to a suspect who consents to answer questions without the assistance of a lawyer. In *Miranda* itself, we expressly rejected the suggestion "that each police station must have a 'station house lawyer' present at all times to advise prisoners," and held instead that a suspect must be told of his right to have an attorney present and that he may not be questioned after invoking his right to counsel. We also noted that if a suspect is "indecisive in his request for counsel," the officers need not always cease questioning.

We recognize that requiring a clear assertion of the right to counsel might disadvantage some suspects who—because of fear, intimidation, lack of linguistic skills, or a variety of other reasons—will not clearly articulate their right to counsel although they actually want to have a lawyer present. But the primary protection afforded suspects subject to custodial interrogation is the *Miranda* warnings themselves. "[F]ull comprehension of the rights to remain silent and request an attorney [is] sufficient to dispel whatever coercion is inherent in the interrogation process." A suspect who knowingly and voluntarily waives his right to counsel after having that right explained to him has indicated his willingness to deal with the police unassisted. Although *Edwards* provides an additional protection—if a suspect subsequently requests an attorney, questioning must cease—it is one that must be affirmatively invoked by the suspect.

In considering how a suspect must invoke the right to counsel, we must consider the other side of the *Miranda* equation: the need for effective law enforcement. Although the courts ensure compliance with the *Miranda* requirements through the exclusionary rule, it is police officers who must actually decide whether or not they can question a suspect. The *Edwards* rule—questioning must cease if the suspect asks for a lawyer—provides a bright line that can be applied by officers in the real world of investigation and interrogation without unduly hampering the gathering of information. But if we were to require questioning to cease if a suspect makes a statement that might be a request for an attorney, this clarity and ease of application would be lost. Police officers would be forced to make difficult judgment calls about whether the suspect in fact wants a lawyer even though he has not said so, with the threat of suppression if they guess wrong. We therefore hold that, after a knowing and voluntary waiver of the *Miranda* rights, law enforcement officers may continue questioning until and unless the suspect clearly requests an attorney.

Of course, when a suspect makes an ambiguous or equivocal statement it will often be good police practice for the interviewing officers to clarify whether or not he actually wants an attorney. That was the procedure followed by the NIS agents in this case. Clarifying questions help protect the rights of the suspect by ensuring that he gets an attorney if he wants one, and will minimize the chance of a confession being suppressed due to subsequent judicial second-guessing as to the meaning of the suspect's statement regarding counsel. But we decline to adopt a rule requiring officers to ask clarifying questions. If the suspect's statement is not an unambiguous or unequivocal request for counsel, the officers have no obligation to stop questioning him.

To recapitulate: We held in *Miranda* that a suspect is entitled to the assistance of counsel during custodial interrogation even though the Constitution does not provide for such assistance. We held in *Edwards* that if the suspect invokes the right to counsel at any time, the police must immediately cease questioning him until an attorney is present. But we are unwilling to create a third layer of prophylaxis to prevent police questioning when the suspect might want a lawyer. Unless the suspect actually requests an attorney, questioning may continue.

The courts below found that petitioner's remark to the NIS agents—"Maybe I should talk to a lawyer"—was not a request for counsel, and we see no reason to disturb that conclusion. The NIS agents therefore were not required to stop questioning petitioner, though it was entirely proper for them to clarify whether petitioner in fact wanted a lawyer. . . .

Justice SOUTER, with whom Justice BLACKMUN, Justice STEVENS, and Justice GINSBURG join, concurring in the judgment.

In the midst of his questioning by naval investigators, petitioner said "Maybe I should talk to a lawyer." The investigators promptly stopped questioning Davis about the killing of Keith Shackleton and instead undertook to determine whether he meant to invoke his right to counsel. According to testimony accepted by the courts below, Davis answered the investigators' questions on that point by saying, "I'm not asking for a lawyer," and "No, I don't want to talk to a lawyer." Only then did the interrogation resume (stopping for good when petitioner said, "I think I want a lawyer before I say anything else").

I agree with the majority that the Constitution does not forbid law enforcement officers to pose questions (like those directed at Davis) aimed solely at clarifying whether a suspect's ambiguous reference to counsel was meant to assert his Fifth Amendment right. Accordingly I concur in the judgment affirming Davis's conviction, resting partly on evidence of statements given after agents ascertained that he did not wish to deal with them through counsel. I cannot, however, join in my colleagues' further conclusion that if the investigators here had been so inclined, they were at liberty to disregard Davis's reference to a lawyer entirely, in accordance with a general rule that interrogators have no legal obligation to discover what a custodial subject meant by an ambiguous statement that could reasonably be understood to express a desire to consult a lawyer.

Our own precedent, the reasonable judgments of the majority of the many courts already to have addressed the issue before us, and the advocacy of a considerable body of law enforcement officials are to the contrary. All argue against the Court's approach today, which draws a sharp line between interrogated suspects who "clearly" assert their right to counsel and those who say something that may, but may not, express a desire for counsel's presence, the former suspects being assured that questioning will not resume without counsel present, the latter being left to fend for themselves. The concerns of fairness and practicality that have long anchored our *Miranda* case law point to a different response: when law enforcement officials "reasonably do not know whether or not the suspect wants a lawyer," they should stop their interrogation and ask him to make his choice clear.

I

While the question we address today is an open one, its answer requires coherence with nearly three decades of case law addressing the relationship between police and criminal suspects in custodial interrogation. Throughout that period, two precepts have commanded broad assent: that the *Miranda* safeguards exist "to assure that the individual's right to choose between speech and silence remains unfettered throughout the interrogation process," and that the justification for *Miranda* rules, intended to operate in the real world, "must be consistent with ... practical realities." A rule barring government agents from further interrogation until they determine whether a suspect's ambiguous statement was meant as a request for counsel fulfills both ambitions. It assures that a suspect's choice whether or not to deal with police through counsel will be "scrupulously honored," and it faces both the real-world reasons why misunderstandings arise between suspect and interrogator and the real-world limitations on the capacity of police and trial courts to apply fine distinctions and intricate rules.

Tested against the same two principles, the approach the Court adopts does not fare so well. First, as the majority expressly acknowledges, criminal suspects who may (in *Miranda*'s words) be "thrust into an unfamiliar atmosphere and run through menacing police interrogation procedures," would seem an odd group to single out for the Court's demand of heightened linguistic care. A substantial percentage of them lack anything like a confident command of the English language and many more will be sufficiently intimidated by the interrogation process or overwhelmed by the uncertainty of their predicament that the ability to speak assertively will abandon them. Indeed, the awareness of just these realities has, in the past, dissuaded the Court from placing any burden of clarity upon individuals in custody, but has led it instead to require that requests for counsel be "give[n] a broad, rather than a narrow, interpretation" and that courts "indulge every reasonable presumption" that a suspect has not waived his right to counsel under *Miranda*. . . .

II

Although I am convinced that the Court has taken the wrong path, I am not persuaded by petitioner's contention, that even ambiguous statements require an end to all police questioning. I recognize that the approach petitioner urges on us can claim some support from our case law, most notably in the "indicates in any manner" language of *Miranda*, and I do not deny that the rule I endorse could be abused by "clarifying" questions that shade subtly into illicitly badgering a suspect who wants counsel. But petitioner's proposal is not entirely in harmony with all the major themes of *Miranda* case law, its virtues and demerits being the reverse images of those that mark the Court's rule. While it is plainly wrong, for example, to continue interrogation when the suspect wants it to stop (and so indicates), the strong bias in favor of individual choice may also be disserved by stopping questioning when a suspect wants it to continue (but where his statement might be understood otherwise). The costs to society of losing confessions would, moreover, be especially hard to bear where the suspect, if asked for his choice, would have chosen to continue. One need not sign the majority's opinion here to agree that resort to the rule petitioner argues for should be had only if experience shows that less drastic means of safeguarding suspects' constitutional rights are not up to the job.

Our cases are best respected by a rule that when a suspect under custodial interrogation makes an ambiguous statement that might reasonably be understood as expressing a wish that a lawyer be summoned (and questioning cease), interrogators' questions should be confined to verifying whether the individual meant to ask for a lawyer. . . .

NOTES & QUESTIONS ON AMBIGUOUS QUASI-INVOCATIONS

1. *The burden of ambiguity.* One way of understanding the *Davis* decision is to ask which party has the burden of clarifying an ambiguous *Edwards* statement. According to the majority, it is the suspect. If the suspect fails to make a clear request for counsel, police are free to continue their interrogation. Of course, the Court could have adopted the opposite rule: requiring that police have the burden to clarify ambiguous statements—a rule the majority explicitly refused to adopt. Between the suspect and the police, which party is in the best position to ensure that the right to counsel is protected? On the one hand, the police are repeat players who understand the important role that lawyers play during interrogations. On the other hand, the suspect has direct access to his preferences and is in the best position to articulate whether he or she wants a lawyer or not. Do you agree with the majority that it would needlessly hamper police interrogations if the police were required to stop an interrogation after hearing an ambiguous statement that might reflect a desire for counsel?

2. *Semantics and foreign languages.* Does the *Davis* rule fall equally on all suspects? Consider, for example, the following argument:

> The decision in *Davis* will have the greatest negative impact upon those suspects who are most in need of *Miranda* protections. The plurality and the concurring opinions both acknowledge that certain groups, including women and ethnic minorities, will feel the brunt of the decision to adopt the threshold-of-clarity approach. Due to cultural and sociolinguistic differences, these groups of suspects utilize ambiguous or equivocal language more often than other suspects, even in contexts in which they are trying to express a firm desire or imperative. Groups with a pronounced use of indirect or hedged speech patterns include, inter alia, women, African-Americans, and suspects who speak Arabic, Farsi, Yiddish, Japanese, Indonesian, and Greek. With regard to foreign cultures in the United States, this pattern of speech is often passed on to second, third, and even fourth generation members.

Samira Sadeghi, *Hung Up on Semantics: A Critique of* Davis v. United States, 23 Hastings Const. L.Q. 313, 330-31 (1995). Did the Supreme Court sufficiently appreciate this difficulty?

PROBLEM CASE

Typically, a suspect will invoke the right to counsel at the commencement of interrogation. But what happens if a suspect invokes his right to counsel *before* the police start to question him—as a preemptive strike to preserve the right to counsel? Although this is a rare occurrence, you could imagine a lawyer proactively informing the police that an individual is represented by counsel and is not willing to speak with the police. In theory, this would appear to be a valid invocation of the right to counsel.

But think again. Consider the case of Dennis Bland. The police suspect Bland of shooting and killing someone in Philadelphia. According to the police, Bland "fled" Philadelphia for Florida, where his mother lived. Authorities arrested Bland in Florida and placed him in detention there while awaiting extradition back to Pennsylvania.

While Bland was still in jail in Florida, a lawyer hired by the family drafted the following letter, which was signed by Bland and then faxed to the Philadelphia Police Department homicide unit and the Philadelphia District Attorney's Office:

> Please be advised that I . . . do not wish to speak without an attorney present. I wish to be represented by a lawyer. Until such time as I have an opportunity to fully discuss the details of my case with my lawyer . . . I state the following to you: I do not wish to be questioned or have any discussion with the police. I do not wish to speak with you without my attorney present. I will not waive or give you any of my rights under *Miranda v. Arizona*, nor will I give up any of my Pennsylvania or federal constitutional rights either orally or in writing without the presence of my lawyer.

Bland was subsequently interrogated without counsel in Philadelphia, confessed, and was convicted at trial. Was the invocation valid in this case? See *Commonwealth v. Bland*, 631 Pa. 644, 655, 115 A.3d 854, 861 (2015).

3. Waiver After Invocation

Edwards left many questions unresolved. Chief among them is what happens when a suspect invokes the right to counsel and then consults with the attorney. Can the police then interrogate the suspect again outside the presence of counsel in an attempt to secure a waiver of the right to counsel? Or is waiver only possible in the presence of counsel once the right has been invoked? Another way of putting the question is to ask whether the *Edwards* protection is temporally isolated—the right to consult with an attorney and to be free from interrogation during that limited time period—or whether the *Edwards* protection endures indefinitely.

Minnick v. Mississippi

Supreme Court of the United States
498 U.S. 146 (1990)

Justice KENNEDY delivered the opinion of the Court.

To protect the privilege against self-incrimination guaranteed by the Fifth Amendment, we have held that the police must terminate interrogation of an accused in custody if the accused requests the assistance of counsel. We reinforced the protections of *Miranda* in *Edwards v. Arizona*, 451 U.S. 477, 484-485 (1981), which held that once the accused requests counsel, officials may not reinitiate questioning "until counsel has been made available" to him. The issue in the case before us is whether *Edwards'* protection ceases once the suspect has consulted with an attorney.

Petitioner Robert Minnick and fellow prisoner James Dyess escaped from a county jail in Mississippi and, a day later, broke into a mobile home in search of weapons. In the course of the burglary they were interrupted by the arrival of the trailer's owner, Ellis Thomas, accompanied by Lamar Lafferty and Lafferty's infant son. Dyess and Minnick used the stolen weapons to kill Thomas and the senior Lafferty. Minnick's story is that Dyess murdered one victim and forced Minnick to shoot the other. Before the escapees could get away, two young women arrived at the mobile home. They were held at gunpoint, then bound hand and foot. Dyess and Minnick fled in Thomas' truck, abandoning the vehicle in New Orleans. The fugitives continued to Mexico, where they fought, and Minnick then proceeded alone to California. Minnick was arrested in Lemon Grove, California, on a Mississippi warrant, some four months after the murders.

The confession at issue here resulted from the last interrogation of Minnick while he was held in the San Diego jail, but we first recount the events which preceded it. Minnick was arrested on Friday, August 22, 1986. Petitioner testified that he was mistreated by local police during and after the arrest. The day following the arrest, Saturday, two Federal Bureau of Investigation (FBI) agents came to the jail to interview him. Petitioner testified that he refused to go to the interview, but was told he would "have to go down or else." The FBI report indicates that the agents read petitioner his *Miranda* warnings, and that he acknowledged he understood his rights. He refused to sign a rights waiver form, however, and said he would not answer "very many" questions. Minnick told the agents about the jailbreak and the flight, and described how Dyess threatened and beat him. Early in the interview, he sobbed "[i]t was my life or theirs," but otherwise he hesitated to tell what happened at the trailer. The agents reminded him he did not have to answer questions without a lawyer present. According to the report, "Minnick stated 'Come back Monday when I have a lawyer,' and stated that he would make a more complete statement then with his lawyer present." The FBI interview ended.

After the FBI interview, an appointed attorney met with petitioner. Petitioner spoke with the lawyer on two or three occasions, though it is not clear from the record whether all of these conferences were in person.

On Monday, August 25, Deputy Sheriff J.C. Denham of Clarke County, Mississippi, came to the San Diego jail to question Minnick. Minnick testified that his jailers again told him he would "have to talk" to Denham and that he "could not refuse." Denham advised petitioner of his rights, and petitioner again declined to sign a rights waiver form. Petitioner told

Denham about the escape and then proceeded to describe the events at the mobile home. According to petitioner, Dyess jumped out of the mobile home and shot the first of the two victims, once in the back with a shotgun and once in the head with a pistol. Dyess then handed the pistol to petitioner and ordered him to shoot the other victim, holding the shotgun on petitioner until he did so. Petitioner also said that when the two girls arrived, he talked Dyess out of raping or otherwise hurting them.

Minnick was tried for murder in Mississippi. He moved to suppress all statements given to the FBI or other police officers, including Denham. The trial court denied the motion with respect to petitioner's statements to Denham, but suppressed his other statements. Petitioner was convicted on two counts of capital murder and sentenced to death. . . .

In *Miranda v. Arizona,* we indicated that once an individual in custody invokes his right to counsel, interrogation "must cease until an attorney is present"; at that point, "the individual must have an opportunity to confer with the attorney and to have him present during any subsequent questioning." *Edwards* gave force to these admonitions, finding it "inconsistent with *Miranda* and its progeny for the authorities, at their instance, to reinterrogate an accused in custody if he has clearly asserted his right to counsel." We held that "when an accused has invoked his right to have counsel present during custodial interrogation, a valid waiver of that right cannot be established by showing only that he responded to further police-initiated custodial interrogation even if he has been advised of his rights." Further, an accused who requests an attorney, "having expressed his desire to deal with the police only through counsel, is not subject to further interrogation by the authorities until counsel has been made available to him, unless the accused himself initiates further communication, exchanges, or conversations with the police."

Edwards is "designed to prevent police from badgering a defendant into waiving his previously asserted *Miranda* rights." The rule ensures that any statement made in subsequent interrogation is not the result of coercive pressures. Edwards conserves judicial resources which would otherwise be expended in making difficult determinations of voluntariness, and implements the protections of *Miranda* in practical and straightforward terms. The merit of the *Edwards* decision lies in the clarity of its command and the certainty of its application. . . .

The Mississippi Supreme Court relied on our statement in *Edwards* that an accused who invokes his right to counsel "is not subject to further interrogation by the authorities until counsel has been made available to him. . . ." We do not interpret this language to mean, as the Mississippi court thought, that the protection of *Edwards* terminates once counsel has consulted with the suspect. In context, the requirement that counsel be "made available" to the accused refers to more than an opportunity to consult with an attorney outside the interrogation room.

In *Edwards,* we focused on *Miranda*'s instruction that when the accused invokes his right to counsel, "the interrogation must cease until an attorney is present," agreeing with Edwards' contention that he had not waived his right "to have counsel present during custodial interrogation." In the sentence preceding the language quoted by the Mississippi Supreme Court, we referred to the "right to have counsel present during custodial interrogation," and in the sentence following, we again quoted the phrase "interrogation must cease until an attorney is present" from *Miranda.* The full sentence relied on by the Mississippi Supreme Court, moreover, says: "We further hold that an accused, such as *Edwards,* having expressed his desire to deal with the police only through counsel, is not subject to further interrogation by the authorities until counsel has been made available to him, unless the accused himself initiates further communication, exchanges, or conversations with the police."

Our emphasis on counsel's presence at interrogation is not unique to *Edwards.* It derives from *Miranda,* where we said that in the cases before us "[t]he presence of counsel ... would be the adequate protective device necessary to make the process of police interrogation conform to the dictates of the [Fifth Amendment] privilege. His presence would insure that statements made in the government-established atmosphere are not the product of compulsion." Our cases following *Edwards* have interpreted the decision to mean that the authorities may not initiate questioning of the accused in counsel's absence. Writing for a plurality of the Court, for instance, then-Justice Rehnquist described the holding of *Edwards* to be "that subsequent incriminating statements made without [Edwards'] attorney present violated the rights secured to the defendant by the Fifth and Fourteenth Amendments to the United States Constitution." *Oregon v. Bradshaw,* 462 U.S. 1039, 1043 (1983). These descriptions of *Edwards*' holding are consistent with our statement that "[p]reserving the integrity of an accused's choice to communicate with police only through counsel is the essence of *Edwards* and its progeny." In our view, a fair reading of *Edwards* and subsequent cases demonstrates that we have interpreted the rule to bar police-initiated interrogation unless the accused has counsel with him at the time of questioning. Whatever the ambiguities of our earlier cases on this point, we now hold that when counsel is requested, interrogation must cease, and officials may not reinitiate interrogation without counsel present, whether or not the accused has consulted with his attorney.

We consider our ruling to be an appropriate and necessary application of the *Edwards* rule. A single consultation with an attorney does not remove the suspect from persistent attempts by officials to persuade him to waive his rights, or from the coercive pressures that accompany custody and that may increase as custody is prolonged. The case before us well illustrates the pressures, and abuses, that may be concomitants of custody. Petitioner testified that though he resisted, he was required to submit to both the FBI and the Denham interviews. In the latter instance, the compulsion to submit to interrogation followed petitioner's unequivocal request during the FBI interview that questioning cease until counsel was present. The case illustrates also that consultation is not always effective in instructing the suspect of his rights. One plausible interpretation of the record is that petitioner thought he could keep his admissions out of evidence by refusing to sign a formal waiver of rights. If the authorities had complied with Minnick's request to have counsel present during interrogation, the attorney could have corrected Minnick's misunderstanding, or indeed counseled him that he need not make a statement at all. We decline to remove protection from police-initiated questioning based on isolated consultations with counsel who is absent when the interrogation resumes.

The exception to *Edwards* here proposed is inconsistent with *Edwards*' purpose to protect the suspect's right to have counsel present at custodial interrogation. It is inconsistent as well with *Miranda*, where we specifically rejected respondent's theory that the opportunity to consult with one's attorney would substantially counteract the compulsion created by custodial interrogation. We noted in *Miranda* that "[e]ven preliminary advice given to the accused by his own attorney can be swiftly overcome by the secret interrogation process. Thus the need for counsel to protect the Fifth Amendment privilege comprehends not merely a right to consult with counsel prior to questioning, but also to have counsel present during any questioning if the defendant so desires."

The exception proposed, furthermore, would undermine the advantages flowing from *Edwards*' "clear and unequivocal" character. Respondent concedes that even after consultation with counsel, a second request for counsel should reinstate the *Edwards* protection. We are invited by this formulation to adopt a regime in which *Edwards*' protection could pass in and out of existence multiple times prior to arraignment, at which point the same protection might reattach by virtue of our Sixth Amendment jurisprudence. Vagaries of this sort spread confusion through the justice system and lead to a consequent loss of respect for the underlying constitutional principle.

In addition, adopting the rule proposed would leave far from certain the sort of consultation required to displace *Edwards*. Consultation is not a precise concept, for it may encompass variations from a telephone call to say that the attorney is en route, to a hurried interchange between the attorney and client in a detention facility corridor, to a lengthy in-person conference in which the attorney gives full and adequate advice respecting all matters that might be covered in further interrogations. And even with the necessary scope of consultation settled, the officials in charge of the case would have to confirm the occurrence and, possibly, the extent of consultation to determine whether further interrogation is permissible. The necessary inquiries could interfere with the attorney-client privilege.

Added to these difficulties in definition and application of the proposed rule is our concern over its consequence that the suspect whose counsel is prompt would lose the protection of *Edwards*, while the one whose counsel is dilatory would not. There is more than irony to this result. There is a strong possibility that it would distort the proper conception of the attorney's duty to the client and set us on a course at odds with what ought to be effective representation.

Both waiver of rights and admission of guilt are consistent with the affirmation of individual responsibility that is a principle of the criminal justice system. It does not detract from this principle, however, to insist that neither admissions nor waivers are effective unless there are both particular and systemic assurances that the coercive pressures of custody were not the inducing cause. The *Edwards* rule sets forth a specific standard to fulfill these purposes, and we have declined to confine it in other instances. It would detract from the efficacy of the rule to remove its protections based on consultation with counsel.

Edwards does not foreclose finding a waiver of Fifth Amendment protections after counsel has been requested, provided the accused has initiated the conversation or discussions with the authorities; but that is not the case before us. There can be no doubt that the interrogation in question was initiated by the police; it was a formal interview which petitioner was compelled to attend. Since petitioner made a specific request for counsel before the interview, the police-initiated interrogation was impermissible. Petitioner's statement to Denham was not admissible at trial. . . .

Justice SCALIA, with whom THE CHIEF JUSTICE joins, dissenting.

. . . In this case, of course, we have not been called upon to reconsider *Edwards*, but simply to determine whether its irrebuttable presumption should continue after a suspect has actually consulted with his attorney. Whatever justifications might support *Edwards* are even less convincing in this context.

Most of the Court's discussion of *Edwards*—which stresses repeatedly, in various formulations, the case's emphasis upon the "right to have counsel present during custodial interrogation," is beside the point. The existence and the importance of the *Miranda*-created right "to have counsel present" are unquestioned here. What is questioned is why a State should not be given the opportunity to prove that the right was voluntarily waived by a suspect who, after having been read his *Miranda* rights twice and having consulted with counsel at least twice, chose to speak to a police officer (and to admit his involvement in two murders) without counsel present.

Edwards did not assert the principle that no waiver of the *Miranda* right "to have counsel present" is possible. It simply adopted the presumption that no waiver is voluntary in certain circumstances, and the issue before us today is how broadly those circumstances are to be defined. They should not, in my view, extend beyond the circumstances present in *Edwards* itself—where the suspect in custody asked to consult an attorney and was interrogated before that attorney had ever been provided. In those circumstances, the *Edwards* rule rests upon an assumption similar to that of *Miranda* itself: that when a suspect in police custody is first questioned he is likely to be ignorant of his rights and to feel isolated in a hostile environment. This likelihood is thought to justify special protection against unknowing or coerced waiver of rights. After a suspect has seen his request for an attorney honored, however, and has actually spoken with that attorney, the probabilities change. The suspect then knows that he has an advocate on his side, and that the police will permit him to consult that advocate. He almost certainly also has a heightened awareness (above what the *Miranda* warning itself will provide) of his right to remain silent—since at the earliest opportunity "any lawyer worth his salt will tell the suspect in no uncertain terms to make no statement to the police under any circumstances."

Under these circumstances, an irrebuttable presumption that any police-prompted confession is the result of ignorance of rights, or of coercion, has no genuine basis in fact. After the first consultation, therefore, the *Edwards* exclusionary rule should cease to apply. . . .

One should not underestimate the extent to which the Court's expansion of *Edwards* constricts law enforcement. Today's ruling, that the invocation of a right to counsel permanently prevents a police-initiated waiver, makes it largely impossible for the police to urge a prisoner who has initially declined to confess to change his mind—or indeed, even to ask whether he has changed his mind. . . .

NOTES & QUESTIONS ON WAIVER AFTER INVOCATION

1. *A bright-line rule to preserve* Edwards. The outcome in *Minnick* creates a bright-line rule for the *Edwards* protection. Once the Fifth Amendment right to counsel is invoked, the police must cease all interrogation of the suspect unless counsel is present. The opposite rule would create some problems of application. If the police were entitled to commence interrogation again, the Court would have to articulate a particular standard for when interrogation is permissible again. Would the police have

to wait for a particular period of time? That's why the majority insisted that only a bright-line rule would preserve the spirit of the *Edwards* protection. Consequently, *Minnick* represents a decidedly expansive interpretation of *Edwards*. See Marcy Strauss, *Reinterrogation*, 22 Hastings Const. L.Q. 359, 372 (1995).

2. *Custody*. Recall that the rule from *Minnick* applies as long as the suspect is in custody. Once the suspect has been released from custody, the situation changes and the *Edwards* protection no longer applies in the same way. That's because *Edwards* is based on *Miranda*, and *Miranda* involves protection for custodial interrogations. The implications of this aspect of the doctrine are explored below in the following case.

4. Resumption of Interrogation

In the following case, the suspect, Michael Shatzer, invoked his right to counsel during a police interrogation. He was then released. Police subsequently re-interviewed him a second time—more than two years later. The question is whether his *Edwards* invocation of the right to counsel required the Court to treat the subsequent waiver of that right, obtained two years later, as invalid; or whether the break in police custody effectively ended his *Edwards* protection, thus liberating the police from the usual prohibition from seeking a waiver from a suspect without counsel present if the suspect has previously invoked the *Miranda* right to counsel.

The facts of *Shatzer* are a bit quirky. Shatzer's break in police custody involved him being sent back to prison, where he was incarcerated for another crime. In that sense, it is a bit odd to think of Shatzer being "released" by the police when, in fact, he was simply returning to incarceration—hardly a meaningful release in the lay sense of that term. However, as you read the case, try to strip away this factual oddity and focus on the conceptual legal issue: Does a break in custody terminate *Edwards* protection, or must police respect the prior attorney-client relationship even if the suspect has been released in between the first and second interviews? Do not forget that the *Edwards* framework involves a presumption of involuntariness that makes a statement "compelled" for purposes of the Fifth Amendment.

Maryland v. Shatzer

Supreme Court of the United States
559 U.S. 98 (2010)

Justice Scalia delivered the opinion of the Court.

We consider whether a break in custody ends the presumption of involuntariness established in *Edwards v. Arizona*.

I

In August 2003, a social worker assigned to the Child Advocacy Center in the Criminal Investigation Division of the Hagerstown Police Department referred to the department allegations that respondent Michael Shatzer, Sr., had sexually abused his 3-year-old son. At that time, Shatzer was incarcerated at the Maryland Correctional Institution–Hagerstown, serving a sentence for an unrelated child-sexual-abuse offense. Detective Shane Blankenship was assigned to the investigation and interviewed Shatzer at the correctional institution on August 7, 2003. Before asking any questions, Blankenship reviewed Shatzer's *Miranda* rights with him, and obtained a written waiver of those rights. When Blankenship explained that he was there to question Shatzer about sexually abusing his son, Shatzer expressed confusion–he had thought Blankenship was an attorney there to discuss the prior crime for which he was incarcerated. Blankenship clarified the purpose of his visit, and Shatzer declined to speak without an attorney. Accordingly, Blankenship ended the interview, and Shatzer was released back into the general prison population. Shortly thereafter, Blankenship closed the investigation.

Two years and six months later, the same social worker referred more specific allegations to the department about the same incident involving Shatzer. Detective Paul Hoover, from the same division, was assigned to the investigation. He and the social worker interviewed the victim, then eight years old, who described the incident in more detail. With this new information in hand, on March 2, 2006, they went to the Roxbury Correctional Institute, to which Shatzer had since been transferred, and interviewed Shatzer in a maintenance room outfitted with a desk and three chairs. Hoover explained that he wanted to ask Shatzer about the alleged incident involving Shatzer's son. Shatzer was surprised because he thought that the investigation had been closed, but Hoover explained they had opened a new file. Hoover then read Shatzer his *Miranda* rights and obtained a written waiver on a standard department form.

Hoover interrogated Shatzer about the incident for approximately 30 minutes. Shatzer denied ordering his son to perform fellatio on him, but admitted to masturbating in front of his son from a distance of less than three feet. Before the interview ended, Shatzer agreed to Hoover's request that he submit to a polygraph examination. At no point during the interrogation did Shatzer request to speak with an attorney or refer to his prior refusal to answer questions without one.

Five days later, on March 7, 2006, Hoover and another detective met with Shatzer at the correctional facility to administer the polygraph examination. After reading Shatzer his *Miranda* rights and obtaining a written waiver, the other detective administered the test and concluded that Shatzer had failed. When the detectives then questioned Shatzer, he became upset, started to cry, and incriminated himself by saying, "I didn't force him. I didn't force him." After making this inculpatory statement, Shatzer requested an attorney, and Hoover promptly ended the interrogation. . . .

II

The Fifth Amendment, which applies to the States by virtue of the Fourteenth Amendment, provides that "[n]o person ... shall be compelled in any criminal case to be a witness against himself." In *Miranda v. Arizona*, 384 U.S. 436 (1966), the Court adopted a set of prophylactic measures to protect a suspect's Fifth Amendment right from the "inherently compelling pressures" of custodial interrogation. The Court observed that "incommunicado interrogation" in an "unfamiliar," "police-dominated atmosphere" involves psychological pressures "which work to undermine the individual's will to resist and to compel him to speak where he would not otherwise do so freely." Consequently, it reasoned, "[u]nless adequate protective devices are employed to dispel the compulsion inherent in custodial surroundings, no statement obtained from the defendant can truly be the product of his free choice."

To counteract the coercive pressure, *Miranda* announced that police officers must warn a suspect prior to questioning that he has a right to remain silent, and a right to the presence of an attorney. After the warnings are given, if the suspect indicates that he wishes to remain silent, the interrogation must cease. Similarly, if the suspect states that he wants an attorney, the interrogation must cease until an attorney is present. Critically, however, a suspect can waive these rights. To establish a valid waiver, the State must show that the waiver was knowing, intelligent, and voluntary under the "high standar[d] of proof for the waiver of constitutional rights. . . ."

In *Edwards*, the Court determined that [this] traditional standard for waiver was not sufficient to protect a suspect's right to have counsel present at a subsequent interrogation if he had previously requested counsel; "additional safeguards" were necessary. The Court therefore superimposed a "second layer of prophylaxis." . . . The rationale of *Edwards* is that once a suspect indicates that "he is not capable of undergoing [custodial] questioning without advice of counsel," "any subsequent waiver that has come at the authorities' behest, and not at the suspect's own instigation, is itself the product of the 'inherently compelling pressures' and not the purely voluntary choice of the suspect." Under this rule, a voluntary *Miranda* waiver is sufficient at the time of an initial attempted interrogation to protect a suspect's right to have counsel present, but it is not sufficient at the time of subsequent attempts if the suspect initially requested the presence of counsel. The implicit assumption, of course, is that the subsequent requests for interrogation pose a significantly greater risk of coercion. That increased risk results not only from the police's persistence in trying to get the suspect to talk, but also from the continued pressure that begins when the individual is taken into custody as a suspect and sought to be interrogated—pressure likely to "increase as custody is prolonged." The *Edwards* presumption of involuntariness ensures that police will not take advantage of the mounting coercive pressures of "prolonged police custody," by repeatedly attempting to question a suspect who previously requested counsel until the suspect is "badgered into submission."

We have frequently emphasized that the *Edwards* rule is not a constitutional mandate, but judicially prescribed prophylaxis. Because *Edwards* is "our rule, not a constitutional command," "it is our obligation to justify its expansion." Lower courts have uniformly held that a break in custody ends the *Edwards* presumption, but we have previously addressed the issue only in dicta.

A judicially crafted rule is "justified only by reference to its prophylactic purpose." We begin with the benefits. *Edwards'* presumption of involuntariness has the incidental effect of "conserv[ing] judicial resources which would otherwise be expended in making difficult determinations of voluntariness." Its fundamental purpose, however, is to "[p]reserv[e] the integrity of an accused's choice to communicate with police only through counsel" by "prevent[ing] police from badgering a defendant into waiving his previously asserted *Miranda* rights." Thus, the benefits of the rule are measured by the number of coerced confessions it suppresses that otherwise would have been admitted.

It is easy to believe that a suspect may be coerced or badgered into abandoning his earlier refusal to be questioned without counsel in the paradigm *Edwards* case. That is a case in which the suspect has been arrested for a particular crime and is held in uninterrupted pretrial custody while that crime is being actively investigated. After the initial interrogation, and up to and including the second one, he remains cut off from his normal life and companions, "thrust into" and isolated in an "unfamiliar," "police-dominated atmosphere," where his captors "appear to control [his] fate." That was the situation confronted by the suspects in *Edwards, Roberson,* and *Minnick,* the three cases in which we have held the *Edwards* rule applicable. *Edwards* was arrested pursuant to a warrant and taken to a police station, where he was interrogated until he requested counsel. The officer ended the interrogation and took him to the county jail, but at 9:15 the next morning, two of the officer's colleagues reinterrogated Edwards at the jail. Roberson was arrested "at the scene of a just-completed burglary" and interrogated there until he requested a lawyer. *Roberson,* 486 U.S., at 678. A different officer interrogated him three days later while he "was still in custody pursuant to the arrest." Minnick was arrested by local police and taken to the San Diego jail, where two Federal Bureau of

Investigation agents interrogated him the next morning until he requested counsel. Minnick, 498 U.S., at 148-149. Two days later a Mississippi deputy sheriff reinterrogated him at the jail. None of these suspects regained a sense of control or normalcy after they were initially taken into custody for the crime under investigation.

When, unlike what happened in these three cases, a suspect has been released from his pretrial custody and has returned to his normal life for some time before the later attempted interrogation, there is little reason to think that his change of heart regarding interrogation without counsel has been coerced. He has no longer been isolated. He has likely been able to seek advice from an attorney, family members, and friends. And he knows from his earlier experience that he need only demand counsel to bring the interrogation to a halt; and that investigative custody does not last indefinitely. In these circumstances, it is farfetched to think that a police officer's asking the suspect whether he would like to waive his *Miranda* rights will any more "wear down the accused," than did the first such request at the original attempted interrogation—which is of course not deemed coercive. His change of heart is less likely attributable to "badgering" than it is to the fact that further deliberation in familiar surroundings has caused him to believe (rightly or wrongly) that cooperating with the investigation is in his interest. Uncritical extension of *Edwards* to this situation would not significantly increase the number of genuinely coerced confessions excluded. The "justification for a conclusive presumption disappears when application of the presumption will not reach the correct result most of the time."

At the same time that extending the *Edwards* rule yields diminished benefits, extending the rule also increases its costs: the in-fact voluntary confessions it excludes from trial, and the voluntary confessions it deters law enforcement officers from even trying to obtain. Voluntary confessions are not merely "a proper element in law enforcement," they are an "unmitigated good," "essential to society's compelling interest in finding, convicting, and punishing those who violate the law."

The only logical endpoint of *Edwards* disability is termination of *Miranda* custody and any of its lingering effects. Without that limitation—and barring some purely arbitrary time limit—every *Edwards* prohibition of custodial interrogation of a particular suspect would be eternal. The prohibition applies, of course, when the subsequent interrogation pertains to a different crime, when it is conducted by a different law enforcement authority, and even when the suspect has met with an attorney after the first interrogation. And it not only prevents questioning ex ante; it would render invalid, ex post, confessions invited and obtained from suspects who (unbeknownst to the interrogators) have acquired *Edwards* immunity previously in connection with any offense in any jurisdiction. In a country that harbors a large number of repeat offenders, this consequence is disastrous.

We conclude that such an extension of *Edwards* is not justified; we have opened its "protective umbrella" far enough. The protections offered by *Miranda,* which we have deemed sufficient to ensure that the police respect the suspect's desire to have an attorney present the first time police interrogate him, adequately ensure that result when a suspect who initially requested counsel is reinterrogated after a break in custody that is of sufficient duration to dissipate its coercive effects.

If Shatzer's return to the general prison population qualified as a break in custody, there is no doubt that it lasted long enough (two years) to meet that durational requirement. But what about a break that has lasted only one year? Or only one week? It is impractical to leave the answer to that question for clarification in future case-by-case adjudication; law enforcement officers need to know, with certainty and beforehand, when renewed interrogation is lawful. And while it is certainly unusual for this Court to set forth precise time limits governing police action, it is not unheard of. . . .

[This] is a case in which the requisite police action has not been prescribed by statute but has been established by opinion of this Court. We think it appropriate to specify a period of time to avoid the consequence that continuation of the *Edwards* presumption "will not reach the correct result most of the time." It seems to us that period is 14 days. That provides plenty of time for the suspect to get reacclimated to his normal life, to consult with friends and counsel, and to shake off any residual coercive effects of his prior custody.

The 14-day limitation meets Shatzer's concern that a break-in-custody rule lends itself to police abuse. He envisions that once a suspect invokes his *Miranda* right to counsel, the police will release the suspect briefly (to end the *Edwards* presumption) and then promptly bring him back into custody for reinterrogation. But once the suspect has been out of custody long enough (14 days) to eliminate its coercive effect, there will be nothing to gain by such gamesmanship—nothing, that is, except the entirely appropriate gain of being able to interrogate a suspect who has made a valid waiver of his *Miranda* rights.

Shatzer argues that ending the *Edwards* protections at a break in custody will undermine *Edwards*' purpose to conserve judicial resources. To be sure, we have said that "[t]he merit of the Edwards decision lies in the clarity of its command and the certainty of its application." But clarity and certainty are not goals in themselves. They are valuable only when they reasonably further the achievement of some substantive end—here, the exclusion of compelled confessions. Confessions obtained after a 2-week break in custody and a waiver of *Miranda* rights are most unlikely to be compelled, and hence are unreasonably excluded. In any case, a break-in-custody exception will dim only marginally, if at all, the bright-line nature of *Edwards*. In every case involving *Edwards*, the courts must determine whether the suspect was in custody when he requested counsel and when he later made the statements he seeks to suppress. Now, in cases where there is an alleged break in custody, they simply have to repeat the inquiry for the time between the initial invocation and reinterrogation. In most cases that determination will be easy. And when it is determined that the defendant pleading *Edwards* has been out of custody for two weeks before the contested interrogation, the court is spared the fact-intensive inquiry into whether he ever, anywhere, asserted his *Miranda* right to counsel. . . .

Justice THOMAS, concurring in part and concurring in the judgment.

. . . I do not join the Court's decision to extend the presumption of involuntariness established in *Edwards v. Arizona* for 14 days after custody ends.

It is not apparent to me that the presumption of involuntariness the Court recognized in *Edwards* is justifiable even in the custodial setting to which Edwards applies it. Accordingly, I would not extend the *Edwards* rule "beyond the circumstances present in *Edwards* itself." But even if one believes that the Court is obliged to apply *Edwards* to any case involving continuing custody, the Court's opinion today goes well beyond that. It extends the presumption of involuntariness *Edwards* applies in custodial settings to interrogations that occur after custody ends.

The Court concedes that this extension, like the *Edwards* presumption itself, is not constitutionally required. The Court nevertheless defends the extension as a judicially created prophylaxis against compelled confessions. Even if one accepts that such prophylaxis is both permissible generally and advisable for some period following a break in custody, the Court's 14-day rule fails to satisfy the criteria our precedents establish for the judicial creation of such a safeguard.

Our precedents insist that judicially created prophylactic rules like those in *Edwards* and *Miranda v. Arizona* maintain "the closest possible fit" between the rule and the Fifth Amendment interests they seek to protect. The Court's 14-day rule does not satisfy this test. The Court relates its 14-day rule to the Fifth Amendment simply by asserting that 14 days between release and recapture should provide "plenty of time for the suspect . . . to shake off any residual coercive effects of his prior custody."

This ipse dixit does not explain why extending the *Edwards* presumption for 14 days following a break in custody—as opposed to 0, 10, or 100 days—provides the "closest possible fit" with the Self-Incrimination Clause. Nor does it explain how the benefits of a prophylactic 14-day rule (either on its own terms or compared with other possible rules) "outweigh its costs" (which would include the loss of law enforcement information as well as the exclusion of confessions that are in fact voluntary).

To be sure, the Court's rule has the benefit of providing a bright line. But bright-line rules are not necessary to prevent Fifth Amendment violations, as the Court has made clear when refusing to adopt such rules in cases involving other *Miranda* rights. And an otherwise arbitrary rule is not justifiable merely because it gives clear instruction to law enforcement officers.

As the Court concedes, "clarity and certainty are not goals in themselves. They are valuable only when they reasonably further the achievement of some substantive end—here, the exclusion of compelled confessions" that the Fifth Amendment prohibits. The Court's arbitrary 14-day rule fails this test, even under the relatively permissive criteria set forth in our precedents. . . .

Justice STEVENS, concurring in the judgment.

While I agree that the presumption from *Edwards v. Arizona* is not "eternal" and does not mandate suppression of Shatzer's statement made after a 2 ½-year break in custody, I do not agree with the Court's newly announced rule: that *Edwards* always ceases to apply when there is a 14-day break in custody.

In conducting its "cost-benefit" analysis, the Court demeans *Edwards* as a "second layer" of "judicially prescribed prophylaxis." The source of the holdings in the long line of cases that includes both *Edwards* and *Miranda*, however, is the Fifth Amendment's protection against compelled self-incrimination applied to the "compulsion inherent in custodial" interrogation, and the "significan[ce]" of "the assertion of the right to counsel." The Court's analysis today is insufficiently sensitive to the concerns that motivated the *Edwards* line of cases.

The most troubling aspect of the Court's time-based rule is that it disregards the compulsion caused by a second (or third, or fourth) interrogation of an indigent suspect who was told that if he requests a lawyer, one will be provided for him. When police tell an indigent suspect that he has the right to an attorney, that he is not required to speak without an attorney present, and that an attorney will be provided to him at no cost before questioning, the police have made a significant promise. If they cease questioning and then reinterrogate the suspect 14 days later without providing him with a lawyer, the suspect is likely to feel that the police lied to him and that he really does not have any right to a lawyer. . . .

The Court never explains why its rule cannot depend on, in addition to a break in custody and passage of time, a concrete event or state of affairs, such as the police's having honored their commitment to provide counsel. Instead, the Court simply decides to create a time-based rule, and in so doing, disregards much of the analysis upon which *Edwards* and subsequent decisions were based. "[T]he assertion of the right to counsel" "[i]s a significant event." As the Court today acknowledges, the right to counsel, like the right to remain silent, is one that police may "coerc[e] or badge[r]" a suspect into abandoning. However, as discussed above, the Court ignores the effects not of badgering but of reinterrogating a suspect who took the police at their word that he need not answer questions without an attorney present. The Court, moreover, ignores that when a suspect asks for counsel, until his request is answered, there are still the same "inherently compelling" pressures of custodial interrogation on which the *Miranda* line of cases is based, and that the concern about compulsion is especially serious for a detainee who has requested a lawyer, an act that signals his "inability to cope with the pressures of custodial interrogation."

Instead of deferring to these well-settled understandings of the *Edwards* rule, the Court engages in its own speculation that a 14-day break in custody eliminates the compulsion that animated *Edwards*. But its opinion gives no strong basis for believing that this is the case. A 14-day break in custody does not eliminate the rationale for the initial *Edwards* rule: The detainee has been told that he may remain silent and speak only through a lawyer and that if he cannot afford an attorney, one will be provided for him. He has asked for a lawyer. He does not have one. He is in custody. And police are still questioning him. A 14-day break in custody does not change the fact that custodial interrogation is inherently compelling. It is unlikely to change the fact that a detainee "considers himself unable to deal with the pressures of custodial interrogation without legal assistance." And in some instances, a 14-day break in custody may make matters worse "[w]hen a suspect understands his (expressed) wishes to have been ignored" and thus "may well see further objection as futile and confession (true or not) as the only way to end his interrogation." . . .

Because, at the very least, we do not know whether Shatzer could obtain a lawyer, and thus would have felt that police had lied about providing one, I cannot join the Court's opinion. I concur in today's judgment, however, on another ground: Even if Shatzer could not consult a lawyer and the police never provided him one, the 2 1/2-year break in custody is a basis for treating the second interrogation as no more coercive than the first. Neither a break in custody nor the passage of time has an inherent, curative power. But certain things change over time. . . . In the case before us, however, the suspect was returned to the general prison population for two years. I am convinced that this period of time is sufficient. I therefore concur in the judgment.

NOTES & QUESTIONS ON RESUMPTION OF INTERROGATION

1. *The 14-day rule.* The outcome in *Shatzer* was supported by some, ridiculed by others, in part for being hopelessly arbitrary. Why 14 days? Why not 7 or 10 or 100? Do you think there was a solution to the problem of arbitrariness? One solution, of course, would be to hold that a break in custody—no

matter how long or short—always terminates the *Edwards* protection. Or, the Court might have held that a break in custody *never* terminates that *Edwards* protection. Why did the Supreme Court reject both of these extremes? As one scholar noted, "[t]he fourteen-day rule is arbitrary in that it invites police circumvention because police simply will wait two weeks after a suspect invokes the right to counsel before trying again to elicit incriminating statements." Erwin Chemerinsky, *The Roberts Court and Criminal Procedure at Age Five*, 43 Tex. Tech L. Rev. 13, 17 (2010). Do you agree that *Shatzer* gives police a temporal guideline for how to evade the protections of *Edwards*?

B. THE SIXTH AMENDMENT RIGHT TO COUNSEL

As noted above, the Fifth Amendment does not exhaust the right to counsel while subject to police interrogation. If a suspect becomes a defendant as the result of initiation of formal adversarial proceedings (indictment, information, formal charge, arraignment, preliminary hearing, or bail hearing), the Sixth Amendment right to counsel becomes applicable and continues to apply during subsequent police questioning, formal or informal, overt or covert. In many situations, the Fifth Amendment and Sixth Amendment rights will run in parallel, but in other situations one of the protections might evaporate while the other continues in force—depending on the doctrine. For example, if police use an undercover agent or informant to question the defendant, it will not implicate *Miranda*, but it will implicate the Sixth Amendment. It is therefore essential for scholars and practitioners alike to carefully distinguish between the Fifth and Sixth Amendment doctrines.

The following cases focus on: (1) the original derivation of the Sixth Amendment right to counsel; (2) whether the right is "offense specific" or continues to apply if police seek to interrogate the defendant in connection with a different crime; (3) whether police may approach a represented defendant to request a waiver, what happens if the defendant speaks with interrogators, and does this qualify as a "waiver" of the Sixth Amendment right; and (4) whether a conversation with a government informant constitutes a violation of the Sixth Amendment that requires suppression of the statement at trial.

1. The Derivation of the Right

The following case solidifies the application of the Sixth Amendment right to counsel to any police questioning, i.e., what the Court calls "deliberate elicitation" of a statement. So, in other words, the Sixth Amendment right applies not just in the interactions between the defendant, the prosecutor, and the judge during "all criminal prosecutions"—in the words of the Sixth Amendment—but that this right extends to encounters *outside* of the courtroom between the police and the defendant. As you read the following case, ask yourself why the Supreme Court considered it essential to recognize the application of the Sixth Amendment right to counsel in this context of undercover police questioning.

Massiah v. United States

Supreme Court of the United States
377 U.S. 201 (1964)

Mr. Justice Stewart delivered the opinion of the Court.

The petitioner was indicted for violating the federal narcotics laws. He retained a lawyer, pleaded not guilty, and was released on bail. While he was free on bail a federal agent succeeded by surreptitious means in listening to incriminating statements made by him. Evidence of these statements was introduced against the petitioner at his trial over his objection. He was convicted, and the Court of Appeals affirmed. We granted certiorari to consider whether, under the circumstances here presented, the prosecution's use at the trial of evidence of the petitioner's own incriminating statements deprived him of any right secured to him under the Federal Constitution.

The petitioner, a merchant seaman, was in 1958 a member of the crew of the S. S. Santa Maria. In April of that year federal customs officials in New York received information that he was going to transport a quantity of narcotics aboard that ship from South America to the United States. As a result of this and other information, the agents searched the Santa Maria upon its arrival in New York and found in the afterpeak of the vessel five packages containing about three and a half pounds of cocaine. They also learned of circumstances, not here relevant, tending to connect the petitioner with the cocaine. He was arrested, promptly arraigned, and subsequently indicted for possession of narcotics aboard a United States vessel. In July a superseding indictment was returned, charging the petitioner and a man named Colson with the same substantive offense, and in separate counts charging the petitioner, Colson, and others with having conspired to possess narcotics aboard a United States vessel, and to import, conceal, and facilitate the sale of narcotics. The petitioner, who had retained a lawyer, pleaded not guilty and was released on bail, along with Colson.

A few days later, and quite without the petitioner's knowledge, Colson decided to cooperate with the government agents in their continuing investigation of the narcotics activities in which the petitioner, Colson, and others had allegedly been engaged. Colson permitted an agent named Murphy to install a Schmidt radio transmitter under the front seat of Colson's automobile, by means of which Murphy, equipped with an appropriate receiving device, could overhear from some distance away conversations carried on in Colson's car.

On the evening of November 19, 1959, Colson and the petitioner held a lengthy conversation while sitting in Colson's automobile, parked on a New York street. By prearrangement with Colson, and totally unbeknown to the petitioner, the agent Murphy sat in a car parked out of sight down the street and listened over the radio to the entire conversation. The petitioner made several incriminating statements during the course of this conversation. At the petitioner's trial these incriminating statements were brought before the jury through Murphy's testimony, despite the insistent objection of defense counsel. The jury convicted the petitioner of several related narcotics offenses, and the convictions were affirmed by the Court of Appeals. . . .

In *Spano v. New York,* 360 U.S. 315, this Court reversed a state criminal conviction because a confession had been wrongly admitted into evidence against the defendant at his trial. In that case the defendant had already been indicted for first-degree murder at the time he confessed. The Court held that the defendant's conviction could not stand under the Fourteenth Amendment. While the Court's opinion relied upon the totality of the circumstances under which the confession had been obtained, four concurring Justices pointed out that the Constitution required reversal of the conviction upon the sole and specific ground that the confession had been deliberately elicited by the police after the defendant had been indicted, and therefore at a time when he was clearly entitled to a lawyer's help. It was pointed out that under our system of justice the most elemental concepts of due process of law contemplate that an indictment be followed by a trial, "in an orderly courtroom, presided over by a judge, open to the public, and protected by all the procedural safeguards of the law." It was said that a Constitution which guarantees a defendant the aid of counsel at such a trial could surely vouchsafe no less to an indicted defendant under interrogation by the police in a completely extrajudicial proceeding. Anything less, it was said, might deny a defendant "effective representation by counsel at the only stage when legal aid and advice would help him."

Ever since this Court's decision in the *Spano* case, the New York courts have unequivocally followed this constitutional rule. "Any secret interrogation of the defendant, from and after the finding of the indictment, without the protection afforded by the presence of counsel, contravenes the basic dictates of fairness in the conduct of criminal causes and the fundamental rights of persons charged with crime."

This view no more than reflects a constitutional principle established as long ago as *Powell v. Alabama*, 287 U.S. 45, where the Court noted that "during perhaps the most critical period of the proceedings . . . that is to say, from the time of their arraignment until the beginning of their trial, when consultation, thorough-going investigation and preparation (are) vitally important, the defendants . . . (are) as much entitled to such aid (of counsel) during that period as at the trial itself." And since the *Spano* decision the same basic constitutional principle has been broadly reaffirmed by this Court.

Here we deal not with a state court conviction, but with a federal case, where the specific guarantee of the Sixth Amendment directly applies. We hold that the petitioner was denied the basic protections of that guarantee when there was used against him at his trial evidence of his own incriminating words, which federal agents had deliberately elicited from him after he had been indicted and in the absence of his counsel. . . .

The Solicitor General, in his brief and oral argument, has strenuously contended that the federal law enforcement agents had the right, if not indeed the duty, to continue their investigation of the petitioner and his alleged criminal associates even though the petitioner had been indicted. He points out that the Government was continuing its investigation in order to uncover not only the source of narcotics found on the S. S. Santa Maria, but also their intended buyer. He says that the quantity of narcotics involved was such as to suggest that the petitioner was part of a large and well-organized ring, and indeed that the continuing investigation confirmed this suspicion, since it resulted in criminal charges against many defendants. Under these circumstances the Solicitor General concludes that the Government agents were completely "justified in making use of Colson's cooperation by having Colson continue his normal associations and by surveilling them."

We may accept and, at least for present purposes, completely approve all that this argument implies. . . . We do not question that in this case, as in many cases, it was entirely proper to continue an investigation of the suspected criminal activities of the defendant and his alleged confederates, even though the defendant had already been indicted. All that we hold is that the defendant's own incriminating statements, obtained by federal agents under the circumstances here disclosed, could not constitutionally be used by the prosecution as evidence against him at his trial.

Mr. Justice White, with whom Mr. Justice Clark and Mr. Justice Harlan join, dissenting.

. . . The importance of the matter should not be underestimated, for today's rule promises to have wide application well beyond the facts of this case. The reason given for the result here—the admissions were obtained in the absence of counsel—would seem equally pertinent to statements obtained at any time after the right to counsel attaches, whether there has been an indictment or not; to admissions made prior to arraignment, at least where the defendant has counsel or asks for it; to the fruits of admissions improperly obtained under the new rule; to criminal proceedings in state courts; and to defendants long since convicted upon evidence including such admissions. The new rule will immediately do service in a great many cases.

Whatever the content or scope of the rule may prove to be, I am unable to see how this case presents an unconstitutional interference with Massiah's right to counsel. Massiah was not prevented from consulting with counsel as often as he wished. No meetings with counsel were disturbed or spied upon. Preparation for trial was in no way obstructed. It is only a sterile syllogism—an unsound one, besides—to say that because Massiah had a right to counsel's aid before and during the trial, his out-of-court conversations and admissions must be excluded if obtained without counsel's consent or presence. The right to counsel has never meant as much before and its extension in this case requires some further explanation, so far unarticulated by the Court.

Since the new rule would exclude all admissions made to the police, no matter how voluntary and reliable, the requirement of counsel's presence or approval would seem to rest upon the probability that counsel would foreclose any admissions at all. This is nothing more than a thinly disguised constitutional policy of minimizing or entirely prohibiting the use in evidence of voluntary out-of-court admissions and confessions made by the accused. Carried as far as blind logic may compel some to go, the notion that statements from the mouth of the defendant should not be used in evidence would have a severe and unfortunate impact upon the great bulk of criminal cases. . . .

Applying the new exclusionary rule is peculiarly inappropriate in this case. At the time of the conversation in question, petitioner was not in custody but free on bail. He was not questioned in what anyone could call an atmosphere of official coercion. What he said was said to his partner in crime who had also been indicted. There was no suggestion or any possibility of coercion. What petitioner did not know was that Colson had decided to report the conversation to the police. Had there been no prior arrangements between Colson and the police, had Colson simply gone to the police after the conversation had occurred, his testimony relating Massiah's statements would be readily admissible at the trial, as would a recording which he might have made of the conversation. In such event, it would simply be said that Massiah risked talking to a friend who decided to disclose what he knew of Massiah's criminal activities. But, if, as occurred here, Colson had been cooperating with the police prior to his meeting with Massiah, both his evidence and the recorded conversation are somehow transformed into inadmissible evidence despite the fact that the hazard to Massiah remains precisely the same—the defection of a confederate in crime. . . .

NOTES & QUESTIONS ON MASSIAH

1. Massiah *and* Miranda. Recall that *Massiah* was decided two years before *Miranda* and therefore does not rely on that Fifth Amendment decision. The authority for *Massiah* is unambiguously the Sixth Amendment. While *Miranda* has been subject to a number of exceptions discussed above, the *Massiah* decision opened up an entirely new and conceptually distinct foundation for the right to counsel.

2. Massiah *in the state courts.* Professor Wayne Logan recently surveyed the application of *Massiah* in state courts and found that its protections were far from uniform. In fact, the government usually wins when a defendant brings a *Massiah* motion to suppress an interrogational statement that violates the Sixth Amendment:

> Analysis of forty-five years of caselaw suggests that, contrary to initial dire concern that *Massiah* would stifle police efforts to secure confessions, its actual impact has been limited. . . . Whether the outcome is perhaps attributable to *Massiah*'s purported amorphous constitutional rationale, or simply reflects the broader ongoing effort of conservative court majorities to limit Warren Court defense-oriented holdings, one cannot say for sure. There is no escaping, however, that based on the results reported on in this Article, *Massiah* has failed to live up to its promise as a protective shield for the criminally accused.

Wayne A. Logan, *False* Massiah*: The Sixth Amendment Revolution That Wasn't*, 50 Tex. Tech L. Rev. 153, 171 (2017). As you read the following subsections, ask yourself why *Massiah* has not had the impact that some lawyers initially hoped (or feared) that it would. Logan suggested the following explanation: "The data . . . underscores widespread strategic police use of a few formalistic requirements, such as securing information by means of what a court concludes is a non-government agent, lack of deliberate elicitation, and triggering prerequisites (critical stage and offense-specificity) to secure admissible confessions."

2. Interrogations for Different Offenses

In a law school or exam hypothetical, we are often lulled into a false sense of simplicity. Single defendants are charged with a single crime and go to trial for that one offense. In reality, defendants are often subject to multiple and overlapping investigations. In the following case, the defendant was protected by his Sixth Amendment right to counsel, thus requiring police to cease their questioning. However, police investigating another offense subsequently questioned the defendant. Does invoking the Sixth Amendment right to counsel in one criminal case stop the police from questioning the suspect in connection with a different criminal case? Or was he a "defendant" for one offense, but just a "suspect" for the other?

Texas v. Cobb

Supreme Court of the United States
532 U.S. 162 (2001)

Chief Justice REHNQUIST delivered the opinion of the Court.

The Texas Court of Criminal Appeals held that a criminal defendant's Sixth Amendment right to counsel attaches not only to the offense with which he is charged, but to other offenses "closely related factually" to the charged offense. We hold that our decision in *McNeil v. Wisconsin*, 501 U.S. 171 (1991), meant what it said, and that the Sixth Amendment right is "offense specific."

In December 1993, Lindsey Owings reported to the Walker County, Texas, Sheriff's Office that the home he shared with his wife, Margaret, and their 16-month-old daughter, Kori Rae, had been burglarized. He also informed police that his wife and daughter were missing. Respondent Raymond Levi Cobb lived across the street from the Owings. Acting on an anonymous tip that respondent was involved in the burglary, Walker County investigators questioned him about the events. He denied involvement. In July 1994, while under arrest for an unrelated offense, respondent was again questioned about the incident. Respondent then gave a written statement confessing to the burglary, but he denied knowledge relating to the disappearances. Respondent was subsequently indicted for the burglary, and Hal Ridley was appointed in August 1994 to represent respondent on that charge.

Shortly after Ridley's appointment, investigators asked and received his permission to question respondent about the disappearances. Respondent continued to deny involvement. Investigators repeated this process in September 1995, again with Ridley's permission and again with the same result.

In November 1995, respondent, free on bond in the burglary case, was living with his father in Odessa, Texas. At that time, respondent's father contacted the Walker County Sheriff's Office to report that respondent had confessed to him that he killed Margaret Owings in the course of the burglary. Walker County investigators directed respondent's father to the Odessa police station, where he gave a statement. Odessa police then faxed the statement to Walker County, where investigators secured a warrant for respondent's arrest and faxed it back to Odessa. Shortly thereafter, Odessa police took respondent into custody and administered warnings pursuant to *Miranda v. Arizona*, 384 U.S. 436 (1966). Respondent waived these rights.

After a short time, respondent confessed to murdering both Margaret and Kori Rae. . . . Respondent later led police to the location where he had buried the victims' bodies. Respondent was convicted of capital murder for murdering more than one person in the course of a single criminal transaction. He was sentenced to death. . . . [W]e granted certiorari to consider first whether the Sixth Amendment right to counsel extends to crimes that are "factually related" to those that have actually been charged. . . .

The Sixth Amendment provides that "[i]n all criminal prosecutions, the accused shall enjoy the right . . . to have the Assistance of Counsel for his defence." In *McNeil v. Wisconsin,* 501 U.S. 171 (1991), we explained when this right arises:

> The Sixth Amendment right [to counsel] . . . is offense specific. It cannot be invoked once for all future prosecutions, for it does not attach until a prosecution is commenced, that is, at or after the initiation of adversary judicial criminal proceedings—whether by way of formal charge, preliminary hearing, indictment, information, or arraignment.

Accordingly, we held that a defendant's statements regarding offenses for which he had not been charged were admissible notwithstanding the attachment of his Sixth Amendment right to counsel on other charged offenses.

Some state courts and Federal Courts of Appeals, however, have read into *McNeil*'s offense-specific definition an exception for crimes that are "factually related" to a charged offense. Several of these courts have interpreted *Brewer v. Williams,* 430 U.S. 387 (1977), and *Maine v. Moulton,* 474 U.S. 159 (1985)—both of which were decided well before *McNeil*—to support this view, which respondent now invites us to approve. We decline to do so.

Moulton is . . . unhelpful to respondent. That case involved two individuals indicted for a series of thefts, one of whom had secretly agreed to cooperate with the police investigation of his codefendant, Moulton. At the suggestion of police, the informant recorded several telephone calls and one face-to-face conversation he had with Moulton during which the two discussed their criminal exploits and possible alibis. In the course of those conversations, Moulton made various incriminating statements regarding both the thefts for which he had been charged and additional crimes. In a superseding indictment, Moulton was charged with the original crimes as well as burglary, arson, and three additional thefts. At trial, the State introduced portions of the recorded face-to-face conversation, and Moulton ultimately was convicted of three of the originally charged thefts plus one count of burglary. Moulton appealed his convictions to the Supreme Judicial Court of Maine, arguing that introduction of the recorded conversation violated his Sixth Amendment right to counsel. That court agreed . . . [and we] affirmed.

Respondent contends that, in affirming reversal of both the theft and burglary charges, the *Moulton* Court must have concluded that Moulton's Sixth Amendment right to counsel attached to the burglary charge. But the *Moulton* Court did not address the question now before us, and to the extent *Moulton* spoke to the matter at all, it expressly referred to the offense-specific nature of the Sixth Amendment right to counsel. . . .

Respondent predicts that the offense-specific rule will prove "disastrous" to suspects' constitutional rights and will "permit law enforcement officers almost complete and total license to conduct unwanted and uncounseled interrogations." Besides offering no evidence that such a parade of horribles has occurred in those jurisdictions that have not enlarged upon *McNeil*, he fails to appreciate the significance of two critical considerations. First, there can be no doubt that a suspect must be apprised of his rights against compulsory self-incrimination and to consult with an attorney before authorities may conduct custodial interrogation. In the present case, police scrupulously followed *Miranda*'s dictates when questioning respondent. Second, it is critical to recognize that the Constitution does not negate society's interest in the ability of police to talk to witnesses and suspects, even those who have been charged with other offenses.

Although it is clear that the Sixth Amendment right to counsel attaches only to charged offenses, we have recognized in other contexts that the definition of an "offense" is not necessarily limited to the four corners of a charging instrument. In *Blockburger v. United States*, 284 U.S. 299 (1932), we explained that "where the same act or transaction constitutes a violation of two distinct statutory provisions, the test to be applied to determine whether there are two offenses or only one, is whether each provision requires proof of a fact which the other does not." We have since applied the *Blockburger* test to delineate the scope of the Fifth Amendment's Double Jeopardy Clause, which prevents multiple or successive prosecutions for the "same offence." We see no constitutional difference between the meaning of the term "offense" in the contexts of double jeopardy and of the right to counsel. Accordingly, we hold that when the Sixth Amendment right to counsel attaches, it does encompass offenses that, even if not formally charged, would be considered the same offense under the *Blockburger* test. . . .

It remains only to apply these principles to the facts at hand. At the time he confessed to Odessa police, respondent had been indicted for burglary of the Owings residence, but he had not been charged in the murders of Margaret and Kori Rae. As defined by Texas law, burglary and capital murder are not the same offense under *Blockburger*. Accordingly, the Sixth Amendment right to counsel did not bar police from interrogating respondent regarding the murders, and respondent's confession was therefore admissible.

Justice BREYER, with whom Justice STEVENS, Justice SOUTER, and Justice GINSBURG join, dissenting.

. . . This case focuses [on] . . . the meaning of the words "offense specific." These words appear in this Court's Sixth Amendment case law, not in the Sixth Amendment's text. The definition of these words is not self-evident. Sometimes the term "offense" may refer to words that are written in a criminal statute; sometimes it may refer generally to a course of conduct in the world, aspects of which constitute the elements of one or more crimes; and sometimes it may refer, narrowly and technically, just to the conceptually severable aspects of the latter. This case requires us to determine whether an "offense"—for Sixth Amendment purposes—includes factually related aspects of a single course of conduct other than those few acts that make up the essential elements of the crime charged.

We should answer this question in light of the Sixth Amendment's basic objectives as set forth in this Court's case law. At the very least, we should answer it in a way that does not undermine those objectives. But the Court today decides that "offense" means the crime set forth within "the four corners of a charging instrument," along with other crimes that "would be considered the same offense" under the test established by *Blockburger v. United States*. In my view, this unnecessarily technical definition undermines Sixth Amendment protections while doing nothing to further effective law enforcement.

For one thing, the majority's rule, while leaving the Fifth Amendment's protections in place, threatens to diminish severely the additional protection that, under this Court's rulings, the Sixth Amendment provides when it grants the right to counsel to defendants who have been charged with a crime and insists that law enforcement officers thereafter communicate with them through that counsel. . . .

The majority's rule permits law enforcement officials to question those charged with a crime without first approaching counsel, through the simple device of asking questions about any other related crime not actually charged in the indictment. Thus, the police could ask the individual charged with robbery about, say, the assault of the cashier not yet charged, or about any other uncharged offense (unless under *Blockburger*'s definition it counts as the "same crime"), all without notifying counsel. Indeed, the majority's rule would permit law enforcement officials to question anyone charged with any crime in any one of the examples just given about his or her conduct on the single relevant occasion without notifying counsel unless the prosecutor has charged every possible crime arising out of that same brief course of conduct. What Sixth Amendment sense—what common sense—does such a rule make? What is left of the "communicate through counsel" rule? The majority's approach is inconsistent with any common understanding of the scope of counsel's representation. It will undermine the lawyer's role as "medium" between the defendant and the government. And it will, on a random basis, remove a significant portion of the protection that this Court has found inherent in the Sixth Amendment.

In fact, under the rule today announced by the majority, two of the seminal cases in our Sixth Amendment jurisprudence would have come out differently. In *Maine v. Moulton*, which the majority points out "expressly referred to the offense-specific nature of the Sixth Amendment right to counsel," we treated burglary and theft as the same offense for Sixth Amendment purposes. Despite the opinion's clear statement that "[i]ncriminating statements pertaining to other crimes, as to which the Sixth Amendment right has not yet attached, are, of course, admissible at a trial of those offenses," the Court affirmed the lower court's reversal of both burglary and theft charges even though, at the time that the incriminating statements at issue were made, Moulton had been charged only with theft by receiving. Under the majority's rule, in contrast, because theft by receiving and burglary each required proof of a fact that the other did not, only Moulton's theft convictions should have been overturned. . . .

At the same time, the majority's rule threatens the legal clarity necessary for effective law enforcement. That is because the majority, aware that the word "offense" ought to encompass something beyond "the four corners of the charging instrument," imports into Sixth Amendment law the definition of "offense" set forth in *Blockburger v. United States*, a case interpreting the Double Jeopardy Clause of the Fifth Amendment, which Clause uses the word "offence" but otherwise has no relevance here. Whatever Fifth Amendment virtues *Blockburger* may have, to import it into this Sixth Amendment context will work havoc.

In theory, the test says that two offenses are the "same offense" unless each requires proof of a fact that the other does not. That means that most of the different crimes mentioned above are not the "same offense." Under many States' laws, for example, the statute defining assault and the statute defining robbery each requires proof of a fact that the other does not. Hence the extension of the definition of "offense" that is accomplished by the use of the *Blockburger* test does nothing to address the substantial concerns about the circumvention of the Sixth Amendment right that are raised by the majority's rule.

But, more to the point, the simple-sounding *Blockburger* test has proved extraordinarily difficult to administer in practice. Judges, lawyers, and law professors often disagree about how to apply it. The test has emerged as a tool in an area of our jurisprudence that the Chief Justice has described as "a veritable Sargasso Sea which could not fail to challenge the most intrepid judicial navigator." Yet the Court now asks, not the lawyers and judges who ordinarily work with double jeopardy law, but police officers in the field, to navigate *Blockburger* when they question suspects. Some will apply the test successfully; some will not. Legal challenges are inevitable. The result, I believe, will resemble not so much the Sargasso Sea as the criminal law equivalent of Milton's "Serbonian Bog ... Where Armies whole have sunk."

There is, of course, an alternative. We can, and should, define "offense" in terms of the conduct that constitutes the crime that the offender committed on a particular occasion, including criminal acts that are "closely related to" or "inextricably intertwined with" the particular crime set forth in the charging instrument. This alternative is not perfect. The language used lacks the precision for which police officers may hope; and it requires lower courts to specify its meaning further as they apply it in individual cases. Yet virtually every lower court in the United States to consider the issue has defined "offense" in the Sixth Amendment context to encompass such closely related acts. These courts have found offenses "closely related" where they involved the same victim, set of acts, evidence, or motivation. They have found offenses unrelated where time, location, or factual circumstances significantly separated the one from the other. . . .

NOTES & QUESTIONS ON INTERROGATIONS FOR DIFFERENT OFFENSES

1. Massiah *and* Miranda. The *Cobb* decision holds that the Sixth Amendment right to counsel is offense-specific. So, the invocation of the right in connection with a criminal proceeding for one offense does not preclude the police from interrogating the suspect in an investigation into another offense (although remember that some other rule may apply to that questioning, such as *Miranda* or the due process voluntariness test). The definition of what constitutes a second "offense" is what became controversial. The Court's definition states that two offenses are separate if each requires proof of a fact that the other does not. Do you agree with this definition? As any student of the criminal law knows, one criminal transaction might involve several different offenses that, while considerably linked, nonetheless require different elements as part of their technical statutory definitions. In that situation, invocation of the right to counsel in one case would not preclude the police from interrogating the defendant with regard to a closely related—but technically "separate"—offense. Is this result too formalistic? As one commentator noted:

> This poverty of analysis is, sadly, par for the course in the *Massiah* line of cases and represents yet another missed opportunity to bring much needed clarity to the exclusion debate. In fact, with the narrowing of the *Massiah* right in *Cobb*, the need for a coherent understanding of the Sixth

> Amendment exclusionary rule becomes even more pressing. . . . Given the abundance of overlapping and related statutory offenses, a single criminal transaction can be characterized—and prosecuted—as a number of offenses, all just different enough from one another to satisfy the *Blockburger* test.

Michael J. Howe, *Tomorrow's* Massiah*: Towards a "Prosecution Specific" Understanding of the Sixth Amendment Right to Counsel*, 104 Colum. L. Rev. 134, 149-50 (2004).

STATE LAW REQUIREMENTS

Not all jurisdictions follow the federal rule that the Sixth Amendment right to counsel is offense-specific. For example, New York sticks to the rule that once the Sixth Amendment right to counsel attaches, police are forbidden, absent proof of waiver, from interrogating the defendant in relation to any crime or investigation, regardless of whether it is the same offense or not. See, e.g., *People v. Rogers*, 48 N.Y.2d 167, 173, 397 N.E.2d 709, 713 (1979) ("Our acknowledgment of an accused's right to the presence of counsel, even when the interrogation concerns unrelated matters, represents no great quantitative change in the protection we have extended to the individual as a shield against the awesome and sometimes coercive force of the State. An attorney is charged with protecting the rights of his client and it would be to ignore reality to deny the role of counsel when the particular episode of questioning does not concern the pending charge."). However, many states follow the federal rule from *Cobb*, which is far more police-friendly.

The diversity of rules across states can create a complicated conflict of laws when crimes in multiple jurisdictions—with multiple police agencies—are involved. For example, in *State v. Harvin*, 345 S.C. 190, 194 (2001), the defendant Larry Harvin was a suspect in a murder committed in Charleston, South Carolina. He left South Carolina for Rochester, New York. While living in New York, detectives in South Carolina were alerted by a witness that Harvin had allegedly confessed to the crime. He was interrogated first by Rochester police officers and then later by both Rochester and Charleston police officers together. At the time, the defendant was represented by counsel in connection with drug charges and petit larceny filed in a municipality near Rochester. The defendant provided a statement confessing that he was involved in the Charleston killing.

The defendant moved to suppress the statement that allegedly violated his Sixth Amendment right to counsel, since he already had counsel on the drug and petit larceny charges. Under New York law, the police were forbidden from interrogating him for any offense while he had counsel. However, under South Carolina law, which follows *Cobb*, police were entitled to interrogate him on the murder, which clearly involved a different offense. Which law governs?

In *Harvin*, the Supreme Court of South Carolina concluded that South Carolina law should control and that the evidence was properly admitted because "our State interest in deterring the conduct of out-of-state police officers, who should have known the law of their own state and acted in accordance therewith, seems minimal at best."

2. *Contrasting with* Miranda. Unlike the Sixth Amendment right to counsel, which is offense-specific, the *Miranda* rule is categorical and applies to any police interrogation. This rule was articulated most squarely in *Arizona v. Roberson*, 486 U.S. 675, 687 (1988). In *Roberson*, the officer who conducted the second interrogation was genuinely unaware that the suspect had invoked his right to counsel when speaking with the first officer. Nonetheless, this fact was irrelevant, the Court ruled, because "[i]n addition to the fact that *Edwards* focuses on the state of mind of the suspect and not of the police, custodial interrogation must be conducted pursuant to established procedures, and those procedures in turn must enable an officer who proposes to initiate an interrogation to determine whether the suspect has previously requested counsel."

3. Waiving the Sixth Amendment Right

This case asks whether police are permitted to approach a represented defendant to obtain a waiver of the Sixth Amendment right to counsel in the absence of counsel, or whether the same "unapproachability" *Edwards/Minnick* rule that applies to the *Miranda* right to counsel also applies to the Sixth Amendment. Furthermore, if the Sixth Amendment right to counsel can be waived, can it be waived by implication or must it be waived explicitly? What is the standard for a Sixth Amendment waiver?

Brewer v. Williams

Supreme Court of the United States
430 U.S. 387 (1977)

Mr. Justice Stewart delivered the opinion of the Court.

An Iowa trial jury found the respondent, Robert Williams, guilty of murder. The judgment of conviction was affirmed in the Iowa Supreme Court by a closely divided vote. In a subsequent habeas corpus proceeding a Federal District Court ruled that under the United States Constitution Williams is entitled to a new trial, and a divided Court of Appeals for the Eighth Circuit agreed. The question before us is whether the District Court and the Court of Appeals were wrong.

I

On the afternoon of December 24, 1968, a 10-year-old girl named Pamela Powers went with her family to the YMCA in Des Moines, Iowa, to watch a wrestling tournament in which her brother was participating. When she failed to return from a trip to the washroom, a search for her began. The search was unsuccessful.

Robert Williams, who had recently escaped from a mental hospital, was a resident of the YMCA. Soon after the girl's disappearance Williams was seen in the YMCA lobby carrying some clothing and a large bundle wrapped in a blanket. He obtained help from a 14-year-old boy in opening the street door of the YMCA and the door to his automobile parked outside. When Williams placed the bundle in the front seat of his car the boy "saw two legs in it and they were skinny and white." Before anyone could see what was in the bundle Williams drove away. His abandoned car was found the following day in Davenport, Iowa, roughly 160 miles east of Des Moines. A warrant was then issued in Des Moines for his arrest on a charge of abduction.

On the morning of December 26, a Des Moines lawyer named Henry McKnight went to the Des Moines police station and informed the officers present that he had just received a long-distance call from Williams, and that he had advised Williams to turn himself in to the Davenport police. Williams did surrender that morning to the police in Davenport, and they booked him on the charge specified in the arrest warrant and gave him the warnings required by *Miranda v. Arizona*. The Davenport police then telephoned their counterparts in Des Moines to inform them that Williams had surrendered. McKnight, the lawyer, was still at the Des Moines police headquarters, and Williams conversed with McKnight on the telephone. In the presence of the Des Moines chief of police and a police detective named Leaming, McKnight advised Williams that Des Moines police officers would be driving to Davenport to pick him up, that the officers would not interrogate him or mistreat him, and that Williams was not to talk to the officers about Pamela Powers until after consulting with McKnight upon his return to Des Moines. As a result of these conversations, it was agreed between McKnight and the Des Moines police officials that Detective Leaming and a fellow officer would drive to Davenport to pick up Williams, that they would bring him directly back to Des Moines, and that they would not question him during the trip.

In the meantime Williams was arraigned before a judge in Davenport on the outstanding arrest warrant. The judge advised him of his *Miranda* rights and committed him to jail. Before leaving the courtroom, Williams conferred with a lawyer named Kelly, who advised him not to make any statements until consulting with McKnight back in Des Moines.

Detective Leaming and his fellow officer arrived in Davenport about noon to pick up Williams and return him to Des Moines. Soon after their arrival they met with Williams and Kelly, who, they understood, was acting as Williams' lawyer. Detective Leaming repeated the *Miranda* warnings, and told Williams: "(W)e both know that you're being represented here by Mr. Kelly and you're being represented by Mr. McKnight in Des Moines, and . . . I want you to remember this because we'll be visiting between here and Des Moines."

Williams then conferred again with Kelly alone, and after this conference Kelly reiterated to Detective Leaming that Williams was not to be questioned about the disappearance of Pamela Powers until after he had consulted with McKnight back in Des Moines. When Leaming expressed some reservations, Kelly firmly stated that the agreement with McKnight was to be carried out that there was to be no interrogation of Williams during the automobile journey to Des Moines. Kelly was denied permission to ride in the police car back to Des Moines with Williams and the two officers.

The two detectives, with Williams in their charge, then set out on the 160-mile drive. At no time during the trip did Williams express a willingness to be interrogated in the absence of an attorney. Instead, he stated several times that "(w)hen I get to Des Moines and see Mr. McKnight, I am going to tell you the whole story." Detective Leaming knew that Williams was a former mental patient, and knew also that he was deeply religious.

The detective and his prisoner soon embarked on a wide-ranging conversation covering a variety of topics, including the subject of religion. Then, not long after leaving Davenport and reaching the interstate highway, Detective Leaming delivered what has been referred to in the briefs and oral arguments as the "Christian burial speech." Addressing Williams as "Reverend," the detective said:

> I want to give you something to think about while we're traveling down the road. . . . Number one, I want you to observe the weather conditions, it's raining, it's sleeting, it's freezing, driving is very treacherous, visibility is poor, it's going to be dark early this evening. They are predicting several inches of snow for tonight, and I feel that you yourself are the only person that knows where this little girl's body is, that you yourself have only been there once, and if you get a snow on top of it you yourself may be unable to find it. And, since we will be going right past the area on the way into Des Moines, I feel that we could stop and locate the body, that the parents of this little girl should be entitled to a Christian burial for the little girl who was snatched away from them on Christmas (E)ve and murdered. And I feel we should stop and locate it on the way in rather than waiting until morning and trying to come back out after a snow storm and possibly not being able to find it at all.

Williams asked Detective Leaming why he thought their route to Des Moines would be taking them past the girl's body, and Leaming responded that he knew the body was in the area of Mitchellville[,] a town they would be passing on the way to Des Moines. Leaming then stated: "I do not want you to answer me. I don't want to discuss it any further. Just think about it as we're riding down the road."

As the car approached Grinnell, a town approximately 100 miles west of Davenport, Williams asked whether the police had found the victim's shoes. When Detective Leaming replied that he was unsure, Williams directed the officers to a service station where he said he had left the shoes; a search for them proved unsuccessful. As they continued towards Des Moines, Williams asked whether the police had found the blanket, and directed the officers to a rest area where he said he had disposed of the blanket. Nothing was found. The car continued towards Des Moines, and as it approached Mitchellville, Williams said that he would show the officers where the body was. He then directed the police to the body of Pamela Powers. . . .

II

. . . There can be no doubt in the present case that judicial proceedings had been initiated against Williams before the start of the automobile ride from Davenport to Des Moines. A warrant had been issued for his arrest, he had been arraigned on that warrant before a judge in a Davenport courtroom, and he had been committed by the court to confinement in jail. The State does not contend otherwise.

There can be no serious doubt, either, that Detective Leaming deliberately and designedly set out to elicit information from Williams just as surely as and perhaps more effectively than if he had formally interrogated him. Detective Leaming was fully aware before departing for Des Moines that Williams was being represented in Davenport by Kelly and in Des Moines by McKnight. Yet he purposely sought during Williams' isolation from his lawyers to obtain as much incriminating information as possible. Indeed, Detective Leaming conceded as much when he testified at Williams' trial. . . . The state courts clearly proceeded upon the hypothesis that Detective Leaming's "Christian burial speech" had been tantamount to interrogation. Both courts recognized that Williams had been entitled to the assistance of counsel at the time he made the incriminating statements. Yet no such constitutional protection would have come into play if there had been no interrogation. . . .

III

The Iowa courts recognized that Williams had been denied the constitutional right to the assistance of counsel. They held, however, that he had waived that right during the course of the automobile trip from Davenport to Des Moines.

The District Court and the Court of Appeals were . . . correct in their understanding of the proper standard to be applied in determining the question of waiver as a matter of federal constitutional law—that it was incumbent upon the State to prove "an intentional relinquishment or abandonment of a known right or privilege." *Johnson v. Zerbst,* 304 U.S., at 464. That standard has been reiterated in many cases. This strict standard applies equally to an alleged waiver of the right to counsel whether at trial or at a critical stage of pretrial proceedings. . . .

We conclude, finally that the Court of Appeals was correct in holding that, judged by these standards, the record in this case falls far short of sustaining petitioner's burden. It is true that Williams had been informed of and appeared to understand his right to counsel. But waiver requires not merely comprehension but relinquishment, and Williams' consistent reliance upon the advice of counsel in dealing with the authorities refutes any suggestion that he waived that right. He consulted McKnight by long-distance telephone before turning himself in. He spoke with McKnight by telephone again shortly after being booked. After he was arraigned, Williams sought out and obtained legal advice from Kelly. Williams again consulted with Kelly after Detective Leaming and his fellow officer arrived in Davenport. Throughout, Williams was advised not to make any statements before seeing McKnight in Des Moines, and was assured that the police had agreed not to question him. His statements while in the car that he would tell the whole story after seeing McKnight in Des Moines were the clearest expressions by Williams himself that he desired the presence of an attorney before any interrogation took place. But even before making these statements, Williams had effectively asserted his right to counsel by having secured attorneys at both ends of the automobile trip, both of whom, acting as his agents, had made clear to the police that no interrogation was to occur during the journey. Williams knew of that agreement and, particularly in view of his consistent reliance on counsel, there is no basis for concluding that he disavowed it.

Despite Williams' express and implicit assertions of his right to counsel, Detective Leaming proceeded to elicit incriminating statements from Williams. Leaming did not preface this effort by telling Williams that he had a right to the presence of a lawyer, and made no effort at all to ascertain whether Williams wished to relinquish that right. The circumstances of record in this case thus provide no reasonable basis for finding that Williams waived his right to the assistance of counsel.

Is a waiver *presumed* to be involuntary if it takes place outside the presence of the defendant's appointed counsel? In *Michigan v. Jackson,* 475 U.S. 625 (1986), the Supreme Court essentially imported this *Edwards/Minnick*–style rule, which originated in the *Miranda* context, to Sixth Amendment waivers as well. So, in *Jackson,* the Court concluded that police could not initiate a conversation with a defendant, without counsel present, after he or she had asserted a Sixth Amendment right to counsel in connection with that offense;

any waiver of the right to counsel would be deemed invalid if it occurred outside the presence of counsel. Then, in *McNeil v. Wisconsin*, 501 U.S. 171 (1991), the Supreme Court clarified that an accused's invocation of his Sixth Amendment right to counsel during a judicial proceeding does not constitute an invocation of his *Miranda* right to counsel, which is separate, as long as the subsequent custodial interrogation was for a different offense than the one related to his Sixth Amendment invocation. The result of these decisions was that if a defendant invoked his Sixth Amendment right to counsel in one case, the police were not entitled to approach him, without counsel present, to discuss the same charges, but the police *were* entitled to approach the defendant to discuss unrelated charges involving some other crime.

But in the following case, *Montejo*, the Supreme Court reversed course and reconsidered the wisdom of the *Jackson* presumption.

Montejo v. Louisiana

Supreme Court of the United States
556 U.S. 778 (2009)

Justice SCALIA delivered the opinion of the Court.

We consider in this case the scope and continued viability of the rule announced by this Court in *Michigan v. Jackson*, 475 U.S. 625 (1986), forbidding police to initiate interrogation of a criminal defendant once he has requested counsel at an arraignment or similar proceeding.

I

Petitioner Jesse Montejo was arrested on September 6, 2002, in connection with the robbery and murder of Lewis Ferrari, who had been found dead in his own home one day earlier. Suspicion quickly focused on Jerry Moore, a disgruntled former employee of Ferrari's dry cleaning business. Police sought to question Montejo, who was a known associate of Moore.

Montejo waived his rights under *Miranda v. Arizona* and was interrogated at the sheriff's office by police detectives through the late afternoon and evening of September 6 and the early morning of September 7. During the interrogation, Montejo repeatedly changed his account of the crime, at first claiming that he had only driven Moore to the victim's home, and ultimately admitting that he had shot and killed Ferrari in the course of a botched burglary. These police interrogations were videotaped.

On September 10, Montejo was brought before a judge for what is known in Louisiana as a "72-hour hearing"—a preliminary hearing required under state law. Although the proceedings were not transcribed, the minute record indicates what transpired: "The defendant being charged with First Degree Murder, Court ordered N[o] Bond set in this matter. Further, Court ordered the Office of Indigent Defender be appointed to represent the defendant."

Later that same day, two police detectives visited Montejo back at the prison and requested that he accompany them on an excursion to locate the murder weapon (which Montejo had earlier indicated he had thrown into a lake). After some back-and-forth, the substance of which remains in dispute, Montejo was again read his *Miranda* rights and agreed to go along; during the excursion, he wrote an inculpatory letter of apology to the victim's widow. Only upon their return did Montejo finally meet his court-appointed attorney, who was quite upset that the detectives had interrogated his client in his absence.

At trial, the letter of apology was admitted over defense objection. The jury convicted Montejo of first-degree murder, and he was sentenced to death. . . .

II

Montejo and his amici raise a number of pragmatic objections to the Louisiana Supreme Court's interpretation of *Jackson*. We agree that the approach taken below would lead either to an unworkable standard, or to arbitrary and anomalous distinctions between defendants in different States. Neither would be acceptable.

Under the rule adopted by the Louisiana Supreme Court, a criminal defendant must request counsel, or otherwise "assert" his Sixth Amendment right at the preliminary hearing, before the *Jackson* protections are triggered. If he does so, the police may not initiate further interrogation in the absence of counsel. But if the court on its own appoints counsel, with the defendant taking no affirmative action to invoke his right to counsel, then police are free to initiate further interrogations provided that they first obtain an otherwise valid waiver by the defendant of his right to have counsel present.

This rule would apply well enough in States that require the indigent defendant formally to request counsel before any appointment is made, which usually occurs after the court has informed him that he will receive counsel if he asks for it. That is how the system works in Michigan, for example, whose scheme produced the factual background for this Court's decision in *Michigan v. Jackson*. Jackson, like all other represented indigent defendants in the State, had requested counsel in accordance with the applicable state law.

But many States follow other practices. In some two dozen, the appointment of counsel is automatic upon a finding of indigency, and in a number of others, appointment can be made either upon the defendant's request or sua sponte by the court. Nothing in our *Jackson* opinion indicates whether we were then aware that not all States require that a defendant affirmatively request counsel before one is appointed; and of course we had no occasion there to decide how the rule we announced would apply to these other States.

The Louisiana Supreme Court's answer to that unresolved question is troublesome. The central distinction it draws—between defendants who "assert" their right to counsel and those who do not—is exceedingly hazy when applied to States that appoint counsel absent request from the defendant. How to categorize a defendant who merely asks, prior to appointment, whether he will be appointed counsel? Or who inquires, after the fact, whether he has been? What treatment for one who thanks the court after the appointment is made? And if the court asks a defendant whether he would object to appointment, will a quick shake of his head count as an assertion of his right?

To the extent that the Louisiana Supreme Court's rule also permits a defendant to trigger *Jackson* through the "acceptance" of counsel, that notion is even more mysterious: How does one affirmatively accept counsel appointed by court order? An indigent defendant has no right to choose his counsel, so it is hard to imagine what his "acceptance" would look like, beyond the passive silence that Montejo exhibited.

In practice, judicial application of the Louisiana rule in States that do not require a defendant to make a request for counsel could take either of two paths. Courts might ask on a case-by-case basis whether a defendant has somehow invoked his right to counsel, looking to his conduct at the preliminary hearing—his statements and gestures—and the totality of the circumstances. Or, courts might simply determine as a categorical matter that defendants in these States—over half of those in the Union—simply have no opportunity to assert their right to counsel at the hearing and are therefore out of luck.

Neither approach is desirable. The former would be particularly impractical in light of the fact that, as amici describe, preliminary hearings are often rushed, and are frequently not recorded or transcribed. The sheer volume of indigent defendants would render the monitoring of each particular defendant's reaction to the appointment of counsel almost impossible. And sometimes the defendant is not even present. Police who did not attend the hearing would have no way to know whether they could approach a particular defendant; and for a court to adjudicate that question ex post would be a fact-intensive and burdensome task, even if monitoring were possible and transcription available. Because "clarity of . . . command" and "certainty of . . . application" are crucial in rules that govern law enforcement, this would be an unfortunate way to proceed.

The second possible course fares no better, for it would achieve clarity and certainty only at the expense of introducing arbitrary distinctions: Defendants in States that automatically appoint counsel would have no opportunity to invoke their rights and trigger *Jackson*, while those in other States, effectively instructed by the court to request counsel, would be lucky winners. That sort of hollow formalism is out of place in a doctrine that purports to serve as a practical safeguard for defendants' rights.

III

But if the Louisiana Supreme Court's application of *Jackson* is unsound as a practical matter, then Montejo's solution is untenable as a theoretical and doctrinal matter. Under his approach, once a defendant is represented by counsel, police may not initiate any further interrogation. Such a rule would be entirely untethered from the original rationale of *Jackson*.

It is worth emphasizing first what is not in dispute or at stake here. Under our precedents, once the adversary judicial process has been initiated, the Sixth Amendment guarantees a defendant the right to have counsel present at all "critical" stages of the criminal proceedings. Our precedents also place beyond doubt that the Sixth Amendment right to counsel may be waived by a defendant, so long as relinquishment of the right is voluntary, knowing, and intelligent. The defendant may waive the right whether or not he is already represented by counsel; the decision to waive need not itself be counseled. And when a defendant is read his *Miranda* rights (which include the right to have counsel present during interrogation) and agrees to waive those rights, that typically does the trick. . . .

The only question raised by this case, and the only one addressed by the *Jackson* rule, is whether courts must presume that such a waiver is invalid under certain circumstances. We created such a presumption in *Jackson* by analogy to a similar prophylactic rule established to protect the Fifth Amendment-based *Miranda* right to have counsel present at any custodial interrogation. *Edwards v. Arizona* decided that once "an accused has invoked his right to have counsel present during custodial interrogation . . . [he] is not subject to further interrogation by the authorities until counsel has been made available," unless he initiates the contact.

The *Edwards* rule is "designed to prevent police from badgering a defendant into waiving his previously asserted *Miranda* rights." It does this by presuming his postassertion statements to be involuntary, "even where the suspect executes a waiver and his statements would be considered voluntary under traditional standards." This prophylactic rule thus "protect[s] a suspect's voluntary choice not to speak outside his lawyer's presence."

Jackson represented a "wholesale importation of the *Edwards* rule into the Sixth Amendment." The *Jackson* Court decided that a request for counsel at an arraignment should be treated as an invocation of the Sixth Amendment right to counsel "at every critical stage of the prosecution," despite doubt that defendants "actually inten[d] their request for counsel to encompass representation during any further questioning," because doubts must be "resolved in favor of protecting the constitutional claim."

Citing *Edwards*, the Court held that any subsequent waiver would thus be "insufficient to justify police-initiated interrogation." In other words, we presume such waivers involuntary "based on the supposition that suspects who assert their right to counsel are unlikely to waive that right voluntarily" in subsequent interactions with police. . . .

With this understanding of what *Jackson* stands for and whence it came, it should be clear that Montejo's interpretation of that decision—that no represented defendant can ever be approached by the State and asked to consent to interrogation—is off the mark. When a court appoints counsel for an indigent defendant in the absence of any request on his part, there is no basis for a presumption that any subsequent waiver of the right to counsel will be involuntary. There is no "initial election" to exercise the right that must be preserved through a prophylactic rule against later waivers. No reason exists to assume that a defendant like Montejo, who has done nothing at all to express his intentions with respect to his Sixth Amendment rights, would not be perfectly amenable to speaking with the police without having counsel present. And no reason exists to prohibit the police from inquiring. *Edwards* and *Jackson* are meant to prevent police from badgering defendants into changing their minds about their rights, but a defendant who never asked for counsel has not yet made up his mind in the first instance. . . .

In practice, Montejo's rule would prevent police-initiated interrogation entirely once the Sixth Amendment right attaches, at least in those States that appoint counsel promptly without request from the defendant. As the dissent in *Jackson* pointed out, with no expressed disagreement from the majority, the opinion "most assuredly [did] not hold that the *Edwards* per se rule prohibiting all police-initiated interrogations applies from the moment the defendant's Sixth Amendment right to counsel attaches, with or without a request for counsel by the defendant." That would have constituted a "shockingly dramatic restructuring of the balance this Court has traditionally struck between the rights of the defendant and those of the larger society." . . .

IV

So on the one hand, requiring an initial "invocation" of the right to counsel in order to trigger the *Jackson* presumption is consistent with the theory of that decision, but would be unworkable in more than half the States of the Union. On the other hand, eliminating the invocation requirement would render the rule easy to apply but depart fundamentally from the *Jackson* rationale.

We do not think that stare decisis requires us to expand significantly the holding of a prior decision—fundamentally revising its theoretical basis in the process—in order to cure its practical deficiencies. To the contrary, the fact that a decision has proved "unworkable" is a traditional ground for overruling it. . . .

What does the *Jackson* rule actually achieve by way of preventing unconstitutional conduct? Recall that the purpose of the rule is to preclude the State from badgering defendants into waiving their previously asserted rights. The effect of this badgering might be to coerce a waiver, which would render the subsequent interrogation a violation of the Sixth Amendment. Even though involuntary waivers are invalid even apart from *Jackson*, mistakes are of course possible when courts conduct case-by-case voluntariness review. A bright-line rule like that adopted in *Jackson* ensures that no fruits of interrogations made possible by badgering-induced involuntary waivers are ever erroneously admitted at trial.

But without *Jackson*, how many would be? The answer is few if any. The principal reason is that the Court has already taken substantial other, overlapping measures toward the same end. Under *Miranda*'s prophylactic protection of the right against compelled self-incrimination, any suspect subject to custodial interrogation has the right to have a lawyer present if he so requests, and to be advised of that right. Under *Edwards*' prophylactic protection of the *Miranda* right, once such a defendant "has invoked his right to have counsel present," interrogation must stop. And under *Minnick*'s prophylactic protection of the *Edwards* right, no subsequent interrogation may take place until counsel is present, "whether or not the accused has consulted with his attorney."

These three layers of prophylaxis are sufficient. Under the *Miranda-Edwards-Minnick* line of cases (which is not in doubt), a defendant who does not want to speak to the police without counsel present need only say as much when he is first approached and given the *Miranda* warnings. At that point, not only must the immediate contact end, but "badgering" by later requests is prohibited. If that regime suffices to protect the integrity of "a suspect's voluntary choice not to speak outside his lawyer's presence" before his arraignment, it is hard to see why it would not also suffice to protect that same choice after arraignment, when Sixth Amendment rights have attached. And if so, then *Jackson* is simply superfluous. . . .

In sum, when the marginal benefits of the *Jackson* rule are weighed against its substantial costs to the truth-seeking process and the criminal justice system, we readily conclude that the rule does not "pay its way," *Michigan v. Jackson* should be and now is overruled. . . .

Justice Stevens, with whom Justice Souter and Justice Ginsburg join, and with whom Justice Breyer joins except for footnote 5, dissenting.

Today the Court properly concludes that the Louisiana Supreme Court's parsimonious reading of our decision in *Michigan v. Jackson* (1986), is indefensible. Yet the Court does not reverse. Rather, on its own initiative and without any evidence that the longstanding Sixth Amendment protections established in *Jackson* have caused any harm to the workings of the criminal justice system, the Court rejects *Jackson* outright on the ground that it is "untenable as a theoretical and doctrinal matter." That conclusion rests on a misinterpretation of *Jackson's* rationale and a gross undervaluation of the rule of stare decisis. The police interrogation in this case clearly violated petitioner's Sixth Amendment right to counsel.

I

. . . In *Jackson*, this Court considered whether the Sixth Amendment bars police from interrogating defendants who have requested the appointment of counsel at arraignment. Applying the presumption that such a request constitutes an invocation of the right to counsel "at every critical stage of the prosecution," we held that "a defendant who has been formally charged with a crime and who has requested appointment of counsel at his arraignment" cannot be subject to uncounseled interrogation unless he initiates "exchanges or conversations with the police."

II

. . . The majority's decision to overrule *Jackson* rests on its assumption that *Jackson*'s protective rule was intended to "prevent police from badgering defendants into changing their minds about their rights," just as the rule adopted in *Edwards v. Arizona* was designed to prevent police from coercing unindicted suspects into revoking their requests for counsel at interrogation. Operating on that limited understanding of the purpose behind *Jackson*'s protective rule, the Court concludes that *Jackson* provides no safeguard not already secured by this Court's Fifth Amendment jurisprudence.

The majority's analysis flagrantly misrepresents *Jackson*'s underlying rationale and the constitutional interests the decision sought to protect. While it is true that the rule adopted in *Jackson* was patterned after the rule in *Edwards*, the *Jackson* opinion does not even mention the antibadgering considerations that provide the basis for the Court's decision today. Instead, *Jackson* relied primarily on cases discussing the broad protections guaranteed by the Sixth Amendment right to counsel—not its Fifth Amendment counterpart. Jackson emphasized that the purpose of the Sixth Amendment is to "protec[t] the unaided layman at critical confrontations with his adversary," by giving him "the right to rely on counsel as a 'medium' between him[self] and the State." Underscoring that the commencement of criminal proceedings is a decisive event that transforms a suspect into an accused within the meaning of the Sixth Amendment, we concluded that arraigned defendants are entitled to "at least as much protection" during interrogation as the Fifth Amendment affords unindicted suspects. Thus, although the rules adopted in *Edwards* and *Jackson* are similar, *Jackson* did not rely on the reasoning of *Edwards* but remained firmly rooted in the unique protections afforded to the attorney-client relationship by the Sixth Amendment.

Once *Jackson* is placed in its proper Sixth Amendment context, the majority's justifications for overruling the decision crumble. . . . The Court exaggerates the considerations favoring reversal, however, and gives short shrift to the valid considerations favoring retention of the *Jackson* rule.

First, and most central to the Court's decision to overrule *Jackson*, is its assertion that *Jackson*'s "reasoning"—which the Court defines as "the weighing of the [protective] rule's benefits against its costs"—does not justify continued application of the rule it created. The balancing test the Court performs, however, depends entirely on its misunderstanding of *Jackson* as a rule designed to prevent police badgering, rather than a rule designed to safeguard a defendant's right to rely on the assistance of counsel.

Next, in order to reach the conclusion that the *Jackson* rule is unworkable, the Court reframes the relevant inquiry, asking not whether the *Jackson* rule as applied for the past quarter century has proved easily administrable, but instead whether the Louisiana Supreme Court's cramped interpretation of that rule is practically workable. The answer to that question, of course, is no. When framed more broadly, however, the evidence is overwhelming that *Jackson*'s simple, bright-line rule has done more to advance effective law enforcement than to undermine it. . . .

NOTES & QUESTIONS ON WAIVER

1. *Voluntary, knowing, and intelligent.* In *Montejo*, the Supreme Court returned to the basic rule that a waiver of the Sixth Amendment right to counsel is permissible if it is voluntary, knowing, and intelligent. This functional standard replaced the *Jackson* presumption that a waiver was "involuntary" if it took place after the invocation of counsel. Ironically, both the majority and the dissent agreed on a central insight: that a presumption of involuntariness should not depend on whether counsel was requested or assigned by the court during an initial court appearance. However, the majority and the dissent disagreed about the correct rule once this distinction was removed. For the majority, the presumption should be removed entirely; for the dissent, the presumption should apply regardless of whether the defendant requested or was assigned counsel. Who has the better of the argument?

2. *Turning back the clock.* Did *Montejo* simply turn the clock back to *Brewer*? Remember, in *Brewer* the Court indicated that a defendant was not immune from waiver requests, but only that the State was unable to prove valid waiver in that case. Or is the law post-*Montejo* distinguishable in some noticeable way?

4. Violations of the Sixth Amendment Right

What constitutes a violation of the Sixth Amendment right to counsel? According to the Supreme Court, the definition of a Sixth Amendment violation is a situation in which the police engage in conduct that is "deliberately eliciting" incriminating statements from the defendant while the defendant is represented by counsel. The following case requires a judicial application of the "deliberately eliciting" standard. Specifically, have the police violated the "deliberately eliciting" standard if they use a government informant to engage in a conversation with the defendant in the hope that the defendant might incriminate himself during the conversation? Does it matter whether the police speak with the defendant directly or use a government informant as an instrument to achieve the same result?

United States v. Henry

Supreme Court of the United States
447 U.S. 264 (1980)

Mr. Chief Justice BURGER delivered the opinion of the Court.

We granted certiorari to consider whether respondent's Sixth Amendment right to the assistance of counsel was violated by the admission at trial of incriminating statements made by respondent to his cellmate, an undisclosed Government informant, after indictment and while in custody.

I

The Janaf Branch of the United Virginia Bank/Seaboard National in Norfolk, Va., was robbed in August 1972. Witnesses saw two men wearing masks and carrying guns enter the bank while a third man waited in the car. No witnesses were able to identify respondent Henry as one of the participants. About an hour after the robbery, the getaway car was discovered. Inside was found a rent receipt signed by one "Allen R. Norris" and a lease, also signed by Norris, for a house in Norfolk. Two men, who were subsequently convicted of participating in the robbery, were arrested at the rented house. Discovered with them were the proceeds of the robbery and the guns and masks used by the gunman.

Government agents traced the rent receipt to Henry; on the basis of this information, Henry was arrested in Atlanta, Ga., in November 1972. Two weeks later he was indicted for armed robbery. He was held pending trial in the Norfolk city jail. Counsel was appointed on November 27.

On November 21, 1972, shortly after Henry was incarcerated, Government agents working on the Janaf robbery contacted one Nichols, an inmate at the Norfolk city jail, who for some time prior to this meeting had been engaged to provide confidential information to the Federal Bureau of Investigation as a paid informant. Nichols was then serving a sentence on local forgery charges. The record does not disclose whether the agent contacted Nichols specifically to acquire information about Henry or the Janaf robbery.

Nichols informed the agent that he was housed in the same cellblock with several federal prisoners awaiting trial, including Henry. The agent told him to be alert to any statements made by the federal prisoners, but not to initiate any conversation with or question Henry regarding the bank robbery. In early December, after Nichols had been released from jail, the agent again contacted Nichols, who reported that he and Henry had engaged in conversation and that Henry had told him about the robbery of the Janaf bank. Nichols was paid for furnishing the information.

When Henry was tried in March 1973, an agent of the Federal Bureau of Investigation testified concerning the events surrounding the discovery of the rental slip and the evidence uncovered at the rented house. Other witnesses also connected Henry to the rented house, including the rental agent who positively identified Henry as the "Allen R. Norris" who had rented the house and had taken the rental receipt described earlier. A neighbor testified that prior to the robbery she saw Henry at the rented house with John Luck, one of the two men who had by the time of Henry's trial been convicted for the robbery. In addition, palm prints found on the lease agreement matched those of Henry.

Nichols testified at trial that he had "an opportunity to have some conversations with Mr. Henry while he was in the jail," and that Henry told him that on several occasions he had gone to the Janaf Branch to see which employees opened the vault. Nichols also testified that Henry described to him the details of the robbery and stated that the only evidence connecting him to the robbery was the rental receipt. The jury was not informed that Nichols was a paid Government informant. On the basis of this testimony, Henry was convicted of bank robbery and sentenced to a term of imprisonment of 25 years.

On August 28, 1975, Henry moved to vacate his sentence. . . . At this stage, he stated that he had just learned that Nichols was a paid Government informant and alleged that he had been intentionally placed in the same cell with Nichols so that Nichols could secure information about the robbery. Thus, Henry contended that the introduction of Nichols' testimony violated his Sixth Amendment right to the assistance of counsel. The District Court denied the motion without a hearing. The Court of Appeals, however, reversed and remanded for an evidentiary inquiry into "whether the witness [Nichols] was acting as a government agent during his interviews with Henry." On remand, the District Court requested affidavits from the Government agents. An affidavit was submitted describing the agent's relationship with Nichols and relating the following conversation:

> I recall telling Nichols at this time to be alert to any statements made by these individuals [the federal prisoners] regarding the charges against them. I specifically recall telling Nichols that he was not to question Henry or these individuals about the charges against them, however, if they engaged him in conversation or talked in front of him, he was requested to pay attention to their statements. I recall telling Nichols not to initiate any conversations with Henry regarding the bank robbery charges against Henry, but that if Henry initiated the conversations with Nichols, I requested Nichols to pay attention to the information furnished by Henry.

The agent's affidavit also stated that he never requested anyone affiliated with the Norfolk city jail to place Nichols in the same cell with Henry. . . .

II

This Court has scrutinized postindictment confrontations between Government agents and the accused to determine whether they are "critical stages" of the prosecution at which the Sixth Amendment right to the assistance of counsel attaches. The present case involves incriminating statements made by the accused to an undisclosed and undercover Government informant while in custody and after indictment. The Government characterizes Henry's incriminating statements as voluntary and not the result of any affirmative conduct on the part of Government agents to elicit evidence. From this, the Government argues that Henry's rights were not violated, even assuming the Sixth Amendment applies to such surreptitious confrontations; in short, it is contended that the Government has not interfered with Henry's right to counsel.

This Court first applied the Sixth Amendment to postindictment communications between the accused and agents of the Government in *Massiah v. United States*. There, after the accused had been charged, he made incriminating statements to his codefendant, who was acting as an agent of the Government. In reversing the conviction, the Court held that the accused was denied "the basic protections of [the Sixth Amendment] when there was used against him at his trial evidence of his own incriminating words, which federal agents had deliberately elicited from him." The *Massiah* holding rests squarely on interference with his right to counsel.

The question here is whether under the facts of this case a Government agent "deliberately elicited" incriminating statements from Henry within the meaning of *Massiah.* Three factors are important. First, Nichols was acting under instructions as a paid informant for the Government; second, Nichols was ostensibly no more than a fellow inmate of Henry; and third, Henry was in custody and under indictment at the time he was engaged in conversation by Nichols.

The Court of Appeals viewed the record as showing that Nichols deliberately used his position to secure incriminating information from Henry when counsel was not present and held that conduct attributable to the Government. Nichols had been a paid Government informant for more than a year; moreover, the FBI agent was aware that Nichols had access to Henry and would be able to engage him in conversations without arousing Henry's suspicion. The arrangement between Nichols and the agent was on a contingent-fee basis; Nichols was to be paid only if he produced useful information. . . . Even if the agent's statement that he did not intend that Nichols would take affirmative steps to secure incriminating information is accepted, he must have known that such propinquity likely would lead to that result.

The Government argues that the federal agents instructed Nichols not to question Henry about the robbery. Yet according to his own testimony, Nichols was not a passive listener; rather, he had "some conversations with Mr. Henry" while he was in jail and Henry's incriminatory statements were "the product of this conversation.". . .

It is quite a different matter when the Government uses undercover agents to obtain incriminating statements from persons not in custody but suspected of criminal activity prior to the time charges are filed. In *Hoffa v. United States,* 385 U.S. 293, 302 (1966), for example this Court held that "no interest legitimately protected by the Fourth Amendment is involved" because "the Fourth Amendment [does not protect] a wrongdoer's misplaced belief that a person to whom he voluntarily confides his wrongdoing will not reveal it." Similarly, the Fifth Amendment has been held not to be implicated by the use of undercover Government agents before charges are filed because of the absence of the potential for compulsion. But the Fourth and Fifth Amendment claims made in those cases are not relevant to the inquiry under the Sixth Amendment here—whether the Government has interfered with the right to counsel of the accused by "deliberately eliciting" incriminating statements. . . .

It is undisputed that Henry was unaware of Nichols' role as a Government informant. The government argues that this Court should apply a less rigorous standard under the Sixth Amendment where the accused is prompted by an undisclosed undercover informant than where the accused is speaking in the hearing of persons he knows to be Government officers. That line of argument, however, seeks to infuse Fifth Amendment concerns against compelled self-incrimination into the Sixth Amendment protection of the right to the assistance of counsel. An accused speaking to a known Government agent is typically aware that his statements may be used against him. The adversary positions at that stage are well established; the parties are then "arms' length" adversaries.

When the accused is in the company of a fellow inmate who is acting by prearrangement as a Government agent, the same cannot be said. Conversation stimulated in such circumstances may elicit information that an accused would not intentionally reveal to persons known to be Government agents. Indeed, the *Massiah* Court noted that if the Sixth Amendment "is to have any efficacy it must apply to indirect and surreptitious interrogations as well as those conducted in the jailhouse." The Court pointedly observed that Massiah was more seriously imposed upon because he did not know that his codefendant was a Government agent.

Moreover, the concept of a knowing and voluntary waiver of Sixth Amendment rights does not apply in the context of communications with an undisclosed undercover informant acting for the Government. In that setting, Henry, being unaware that Nichols was a Government agent expressly commissioned to secure evidence, cannot be held to have waived his right to the assistance of counsel.

Finally Henry's incarceration at the time he was engaged in conversation by Nichols is also a relevant factor. As a ground for imposing the prophylactic requirements in *Miranda v. Arizona*, 384 U.S. 436, 467 (1966), this Court noted the powerful psychological inducements to reach for aid when a person is in confinement. While the concern in *Miranda* was limited to custodial police interrogation, the mere fact of custody imposes pressures on the accused; confinement may bring into play subtle influences that will make him particularly susceptible to the ploys of undercover Government agents. The Court of Appeals determined that on this record the incriminating conversations between Henry and Nichols were facilitated by Nichols' conduct and apparent status as a person sharing a common plight. That Nichols had managed to gain the confidence of Henry, as the Court of Appeals determined, is confirmed by Henry's request that Nichols assist him in his escape plans when Nichols was released from confinement.

. . . By intentionally creating a situation likely to induce Henry to make incriminating statements without the assistance of counsel, the Government violated Henry's Sixth Amendment right to counsel. This is not a case where, in Justice Cardozo's words, "the constable ... blundered"; rather, it is one where the "constable" planned an impermissible interference with the right to the assistance of counsel.

Mr. Justice REHNQUIST, dissenting.

The Court today concludes that the Government through the use of an informant "deliberately elicited" information from respondent after formal criminal proceedings had begun, and thus the statements made by respondent to the informant are inadmissible because counsel was not present. The exclusion of respondent's statements has no relationship whatsoever to the reliability of the evidence, and it rests on a prophylactic application of the Sixth Amendment right to counsel that in my view entirely ignores the doctrinal foundation of that right. The Court's ruling is based on *Massiah v. United States*, 377 U.S. 201 (1964), which held that a postindictment confrontation between the accused and his accomplice, who had turned State's evidence and was acting under the direction of the Government, was a "critical" stage of the criminal proceedings at which the Sixth Amendment right to counsel attached. While the decision today sets forth the factors that are "important" in determining whether there has been a *Massiah* violation, I think that *Massiah* constitutes such a substantial departure from the traditional concerns that underlie the Sixth Amendment guarantee that its language, if not its actual holding, should be re-examined.

The doctrinal underpinnings of *Massiah* have been largely left unexplained, and the result in this case, as in *Massiah*, is difficult to reconcile with the traditional notions of the role of an attorney. Here, as in *Massiah*, the accused was not prevented from consulting with his counsel as often as he wished. No meetings between the accused and his counsel were disturbed or spied upon. And preparation for trial was not obstructed.

Our decisions recognize that after formal proceedings have commenced an accused has a Sixth Amendment right to counsel at "critical stages" of the criminal proceedings. This principle derives from *Powell v. Alabama*, 287 U.S. 45 (1932), which held that a trial court's failure to appoint counsel until the trial began violated the Due Process Clause of the Fourteenth Amendment. *Powell* referred to the "critical period" as being "from the time of [the defendants'] arraignment until the beginning of their trial, when consultation, thorough-going investigation and preparation were vitally important." During that period, the defendants in *Powell* "did not have the aid of counsel in any real sense, although they were as much entitled to such aid during that period as at the trial itself." They thus were deprived of the opportunity to consult with an attorney, and to have him investigate their case and prepare a defense for trial. After observing that the duty to assign counsel "is not discharged by an assignment at such time or under such circumstances as to preclude the giving of effective aid in the preparation and trial of the case," this Court held that the defendants had been unconstitutionally denied effective assistance of counsel.

Powell was based on the rationale that an unaided layman, who has little or no familiarity with the law, requires assistance in the preparation and presentation of his case and in coping with procedural complexities in order to assure a fair trial. . . . More recently this Court has again observed that the concerns underlying the Sixth Amendment right to counsel are to provide aid to the layman in arguing the law and in coping with intricate legal procedure and to minimize the imbalance in the adversary system that otherwise resulted with the creation of the professional prosecuting official. Thus, in examining whether a stage of the proceedings is a "critical" one at which the accused is entitled to legal representation, it is important to recognize that the theoretical foundation of the Sixth Amendment right to counsel is based on the traditional role of an attorney as a legal expert and strategist.

"Deliberate elicitation" after formal proceedings have begun is thus not by itself determinative. *Ash* held that an accused has no right to be present at a photo display because there is no possibility that he "might be misled by his lack of familiarity with the law or overpowered by his professional adversary." If the event is not one that requires knowledge of legal procedure, involves a communication between the accused and his attorney concerning investigation of the case or the preparation of a defense, or otherwise interferes with the attorney-client relationship, there is in my view simply no constitutional prohibition against the use of incriminating information voluntarily obtained from an accused despite the fact that his counsel may not be present. In such circumstances, the accused at the least has been informed of his rights as required by *Miranda v. Arizona* and often will have received advice from his counsel not to disclose any information relating to his case.

Once the accused has been made aware of his rights, it is his responsibility to decide whether or not to exercise them. If he voluntarily relinquishes his rights by talking to authorities, or if he decides to disclose incriminating information to someone whom he mistakenly believes will not report it to the authorities, he is normally accountable for his actions and must bear any adverse consequences that result. Such information has not in any sense been obtained because the accused's will has been overborne, nor does it result from any "unfair advantage" that the State has over the accused: the accused is free to keep quiet and to consult with his attorney if he so chooses. In this sense, the decision today and the result in *Massiah* are fundamentally inconsistent with traditional notions of the role of the attorney that underlie the Sixth Amendment right to counsel. . . .

In cases such as this one and *Massiah*, the effect of the governmental action is to encourage an informant to reveal information to the authorities that the ordinary citizen most likely would reveal voluntarily. While it is true that the informants here and in *Massiah* were encouraged to "elicit" the information from the accused, I doubt that most people would find this type of elicitation reprehensible. It involves merely engaging the accused in conversation about his criminal activity and thereby encouraging him voluntarily to make incriminating remarks. There is absolutely no element of coercion, nor is there any interference whatsoever with the attorney-client relationship. Anything the accused might reveal to the informant should, as with revelations he might make to the ordinary citizen, be available for use at trial. This Court has never held that an accused is constitutionally protected from his inability to keep quiet, whether or not he has been encouraged by third-party citizens to voluntarily make incriminating remarks. I do not think the result should be different merely because the government has encouraged a third-party informant to report remarks obtained in this fashion. When an accused voluntarily chooses to make an incriminatory remark in these circumstances, he knowingly assumes the risk that his confidant may be untrustworthy. . . .

NOTES & QUESTIONS ON "DELIBERATELY INCITING"

1. *Third-party informants.* How much of the *Henry* decision relies on the assessment that the government informant was acting as an agent of the police? As Justice Rehnquist notes immediately above, the defendant's decision to speak voluntarily necessarily involves a risk that the "confidant may be untrustworthy." Is it correct to view the jailhouse informant in *Henry* as a mere "confidant," or does that label understate his role in the situation?

2. *Passive informants.* The holding in *Henry* is tied closely to the facts of the case and, in particular, the directions and instructions that the informant received from the police. In *Kuhlmann v. Wilson*, 477 U.S. 436, 440 (1986), the Supreme Court considered the case of a jailhouse informant who was told "to ask no questions of [respondent] about the crime but merely to listen as to what [respondent] might say in his presence." According to the Supreme Court, this passive informant was far different from the active informant in *Henry* that violated the "deliberately inciting" standard. Apparently, the mere act of listening was not enough to constitute an incitement to make an incriminating statement, because the informant "only listened" to respondent's "spontaneous" and "unsolicited" statements. Do you agree? Can mere presence ever be an invitation to divulge secrets?

HYPOTHETICAL

John is charged with murder and indicted by the local prosecutor. At arraignment, John asks for a public defender and receives one, who represents John for a bail application. John's application for bail is denied, given the severity of the charges, and he is returned to the local jail.

Initially, John is placed in a single cell. The next day, however, John receives a new cellmate. The cellmate has arranged with police that he will receive substantial concessions, including a transfer to a better prison, if he receives a confession from John. However, the police also tell the cellmate not to ask John any direct questions.

One morning, the cellmate receives a package, ostensibly from his family but in reality from the local authorities. The package includes a self-help book titled "Confession Is the Road to Redemption." When asked why he is reading the book, the cellmate tells John that he is reading it because he has decided that truthfulness is essential to his own salvation. However, the cellmate does not ask any direct questions of John—who responds without any prompting by confessing his involvement in the murder for which he was charged.

Does this interaction violate the Sixth Amendment? Was the government involved in deliberately inciting incriminating statements?

3. *Definitions of interrogation.* Recall the definition that the Supreme Court adopted for "interrogation" in the *Miranda* context, which the Court referred to as "express questioning or its functional equivalent." Specifically, the Court stated that *Miranda* is triggered whenever the suspect is subject "not only to express questioning, but also to any words or actions on the part of the police (other than those normally attendant to arrest and custody) that the police should know are reasonably likely to elicit an incriminating response from the suspect." *Rhode Island v. Innis*, 446 U.S. 291, 301 (1980). However, in *Massiah*, the Court developed a different definition for the Sixth Amendment context: words or conduct of the police that are "deliberately eliciting" incriminating statements from the defendant. In *Henry*, the defendant had a conversation with an undercover informant after he had invoked his Sixth Amendment right to counsel. Did this count as "deliberating eliciting"? Recall that under *Miranda*, speaking with an undercover agent does not count as an interrogation because the *lack of knowledge* that one is speaking with a potential government agent precludes any sense of coercion that might develop in the custodial environment. But in *Henry*, the Supreme Court refused to "infuse Fifth Amendment concerns against compelled self-incrimination into the Sixth Amendment protection of the right to the assistance of counsel." Does this divergent treatment under the two amendments make sense to you?

The differences between the *Miranda* right to counsel and the Sixth Amendment right to counsel are complex and, in some cases, interwoven. The following chart is a useful summary of the doctrinal differences between these two constitutional sources for the right to counsel.

	Miranda Right	Sixth Amendment Right
Trigger	Custody + interrogation	Suspect transformed into a defendant for the offense. State has initiated formal adversarial process + Deliberate Elicitation (questioning).
Offense-Specific	No. Both *Miranda* waiver and *Miranda* invocation apply to any offense, even if completely unrelated to the custody.	Yes, Sixth Amendment protects defendant only for offense he has been charged with. No impact on admissibility of statements elicited related to other offenses.
Undercover Cop/Jail Cell Snitch	*Miranda* does not apply if the suspect does not know the person is a cop; the "police questioning" does not produce inherent coercion necessitating *Miranda* neutralization (*Illinois v. Perkins*).	Sixth Amendment right is not triggered by coercion; therefore, it does not matter that defendant is unaware that he is being questioned by a government agent. Sixth Amendment right to counsel applies.
Poison Tree	No. See *Elstadt* and *Patane*.	Yes
Waiver	Waiver may express or implied (see *Butler* and *Thompkins*).	*Brewer v. Williams*: No implied waiver of fundamental trial right; must satisfy *Johnson v. Zerbst*.
Waiver Invalidation Rule	Yes Right to Silence: Police may not "badger" suspect to change his mind. Right to Counsel: Police may not re-initiate until 14 days after release from custody.	No Sixth Amendment does not produce an "unapproachable" defendant. Police always permitted to initiate contact and obtain waiver (normally a *Miranda* waiver will prove Sixth Amendment waiver).
Questioning	Express or functional equivalent	Express or functional equivalent
Impeachment	Yes. Statement in violation of *Miranda* may be used to impeach.	Yes. Statement in violation of Sixth Amendment may be used to impeach.

This chart was prepared by Professor Geoffrey Corn.

C. PRACTICE & POLICY

The materials in this chapter have focused on the constitutional rules regarding the right to counsel during police interrogations. Chief among these rules is a prohibition against communicating directly with a client, under certain circumstances, who has invoked his or her Sixth Amendment right to counsel. However, under certain circumstances, the rules of professional responsibility may be far more constraining on government prosecutors than the Sixth Amendment. Consequently, practicing criminal lawyers must be aware of both the constitutional and ethical constraints on communicating with suspects and defendants. All too often, young lawyers focus on the constitutional rules while assuming–erroneously–that the content of the norms of professional responsibility must, by logical necessity, track the exact contours of the Sixth Amendment. As the following materials demonstrate, the two normative regimes are not co-extensive.

The *Hammad* decision. In 1985, the Hammad Department Store in Brooklyn caught on fire, raising the suspicions of local fire investigators and federal agents investigating the fire. The investigation soon focused on Taiseer and Eid Hammad, the owners of the eponymous store. The two Hammad brothers were already under scrutiny for Medicaid fraud (involving orthopedic footwear) and the New York State Department of Social Services had already terminated their ability to participate in the Medicaid program. The authorities suspected that the fire was deliberately set to destroy voluminous records related to the illegal footwear scheme.

The Assistant United States Attorney (AUSA) assigned to work the case focused on a co-conspirator, Wallace Goldstein, who worked for a shoe supplier and was supplying fake invoices to the Hammad brothers as part of the Medicaid scheme. Goldstein confessed and agreed to work undercover to get the Hammad brothers to implicate themselves. Goldstein called the Hammads and claimed–falsely–that he had received a grand jury subpoena. During the conversation, the Hammads discussed how to respond to the fictitious subpoena and made incriminating statements about lying to the grand jury and concealing records. During a subsequent meeting in person, Goldstein showed the Hammads a fake subpoena that the AUSA had created and again had more discussions about how to respond to the situation. A grand jury then indicted the Hammads. Among other things, Eid Hammad was indicted for arson and Taiseer Hammad for obstruction of justice.

At this point, Taiseer Hammad made an innovative argument. He argued that the rules of professional responsibility prohibited the government, and in this case the AUSA, from speaking with him rather than through this attorney. Taiseer Hammad was represented by counsel in the Medicaid fraud matter. Although the AUSA did not speak with the Hammads directly, the AUSA did use a government informant, Wallace Goldstein, as an instrument of the government in order to conduct a de facto interrogation of the Hammads.

As for the rules of professional responsibility, consider Rule 4.2 of the Model Rules of Professional Conduct, which states:

> In representing a client, a lawyer shall not communicate about the subject of the representation with a person the lawyer knows to be represented by another lawyer in the matter, unless the lawyer has the consent of the other lawyer or is authorized to do so by law or a court order.

Other professional codes for lawyers include similar provisions.

The government responded that the Sixth Amendment right to counsel is "offense specific," as we learned in this chapter, so that the government is not restrained in the arson case by the existence of the attorney in the Medicaid matter. The government also argued that the Model Rules should not be read to apply in criminal cases at all, and if they were to apply in criminal cases, they should be interpreted as co-extensive with the Sixth Amendment, which is offense-specific.

The Second Circuit rejected the government argument and held that the Model Rules apply in criminal cases and represent a distinct normative constraint on government prosecutors:

> The Constitution defines only the "minimal historic safeguards" which defendants must receive rather than the outer bounds of those we may afford them. In other words, the Constitution prescribes a floor below which protections may not fall, rather than a ceiling beyond which they may not rise. The Model Code of Professional Responsibility, on the other hand, encompasses the attorney's duty "to maintain the highest standards of ethical conduct." The Code is designed to safeguard the integrity of the profession and preserve public confidence in our system of justice. It not only delineates an attorney's duties to the court, but defines his relationship with his client and adverse parties. Hence, the Code secures protections not contemplated by the Constitution.

United States v. Hammad, 858 F.2d 834, 839 (2d Cir. 1988).

The effect of this ruling was to clarify that the rules of professional responsibility go beyond the Constitution to help secure a general legal professional norm that goes well beyond the scope of the Sixth Amendment as interpreted by the Supreme Court. Although the Model Rules do not apply to police officers and other government employees, they do cover all prosecuting attorneys who are admitted to the bar.

Are government prosecutors covered by the Model Rules? The position of the federal government was that federal prosecutors in the Justice Department, such as AUSAs, were governed by Justice Department guidelines rather than local rules of professional responsibility, which in their details might diverge from jurisdiction to jurisdiction. However, Congress eventually passed legislation clarifying that federal prosecutors are attorneys governed by their local bar ethical rules of professional responsibility:

> (a) An attorney for the Government shall be subject to State laws and rules, and local Federal court rules, governing attorneys in each State where such attorney engages in that attorney's duties, to the same extent and in the same manner as other attorneys in that State.
> (b) The Attorney General shall make and amend rules of the Department of Justice to assure compliance with this section.
> (c) As used in this section, the term "attorney for the Government" includes any attorney described in . . . the Code of Federal Regulations and also includes any independent counsel, or employee of such a counsel, appointed under chapter 40.

28 U.S.C. § 530B.

Suppression. What is the appropriate remedy for a prosecutor who violates the rules of professional responsibility regarding communication with an opposing party represented by counsel? Is it simply reporting the attorney to the local bar disciplinary committee, or should the statement be suppressed from the trial? In *Hammad,* the Second Circuit concluded that a trial judge was entitled to, but not required to, order suppression in response to an ethical violation. While a Fifth or Sixth Amendment violation usually *requires* suppression as a matter of constitutional law, the appropriate remedy for an ethical violation might depend on the specific facts of the situation. The Second Circuit concluded that "[w]e have confidence that district courts will exercise their discretion cautiously and with clear cognizance that suppression imposes a barrier between the finder of fact and the discovery of truth." *Hammad,* 858 F.2d at 842. Consequently, an ethical violation regarding attorney communications can have far-reaching consequences beyond one attorney's individual career. The consequences could, in theory, doom a federal prosecution if the case is no longer viable without the suppressed evidence.

CHAPTER 9

IDENTIFICATIONS

INTRODUCTION

There is no moment more iconic in a criminal trial than when a witness, quite probably the victim him- or herself, takes the stand and when asked by the prosecuting attorney to identify the perpetrator, points to the defense table and says, simply, "him" or "her." At that point, the jury's decision about the defendant's fate represents, at least partly, an assessment of the witness's credibility and accuracy of observation and recollection. When the witness says that the defendant is the perpetrator, can this statement be trusted? If the answer to that question is yes, then a jury will likely convict.

The problem is that eyewitness identifications are not always reliable and accurate. Furthermore, once a person makes an identification, it is normally seared in his or her mind, and it is extremely rare that the individual will deviate from the certitude of such an identification when asked in the future to reaffirm it. This is troubling, as the volume of empirical data indicating the incidence of erroneous identifications is massive, all of which reveal that identifications are the product of human faculties and as such they are fallible. Consequently, it comes as no surprise that the moment when a witness identifies a suspect as a perpetrator is one of the most consequential moments in the criminal process, regardless of whether it occurs during a criminal trial; at a preliminary hearing; or before or after being formally charged by way of a physical lineup, or a photographic array, or an in-person "showup."

Both the Due Process Clauses of the Fifth and Fourteenth Amendments and the right to counsel provided by the Sixth Amendment play important, albeit limited roles in protecting defendants from the consequences of erroneous eyewitness identifications. As will be explored below, some out-of-court identifications represent a "critical stage" in the criminal confrontation between state and defendant that require the presence of counsel unless waived, a right provided by the Sixth Amendment right to counsel. Section A of this chapter explores the contours of the right to counsel during these out-of-court identification proceedings. The requirement of counsel is a recognition of the significance of the eyewitness identification; even if it occurs prior to trial, in a local police precinct, it may be the most important moment of the criminal case where the fate of the suspect is effectively sealed. Accordingly, counsel's presence as an observer may be the only feasible way to enable defense counsel to effectively confront the witness making the ID at trial.

But the right to counsel is not the only constitutional right designed to protect the interests of suspects and defendants with regard to identifications. The Supreme Court has declared that allowing the introduction of inherently unreliable identifications resulting from unnecessarily suggestive procedures arranged by the police violates due process. As Section B of this chapter will explore, "suggestive" means that the identification process was contaminated by forces that erroneously pushed the witness in one direction or the other.

Just because an identification process is declared suggestive does not mean that it must always be suppressed. As discussed in Section C below, suggestive identifications might still pass constitutional muster if the suggestive procedure was necessary under the circumstances, or if the eyewitness identification nonetheless demonstrates high *reliability*. For example, an identification might be deemed highly reliable based on the number of times that the witness encountered the perpetrator, in which contexts, and for how long. In other words, there is a profound difference between a fleeting encounter on a darkened street and repeated encounters indoors between two individuals over the course of many months who are negotiating a business transaction. While the first identification might be called into question if there is suggestiveness in a police lineup or if the police show the witness only one photo, it is unlikely that any police mistakes in the ID procedure would compromise the second identification, which might be declared reliable based on the totality of the circumstances. Of course, the vast majority of identifications fall somewhere in between these two extremes, and a trial judge must assess first the degree of suggestiveness, second whether there is a necessity justification, and ultimately the effect of the suggestiveness on the identification's reliability. Navigating this complex judicial assessment is the task of this chapter.

Finally, it is important to focus on where these two rules deviate and where they overlap. First, prior to the suspect being formally charged, the only relevant rule is the due process reliability test. Second, even after the suspect is formally charged, the Sixth Amendment applies only to identifications related to that charge, and only due process applies to uncharged offenses. Third, because the Sixth Amendment applies only to physical identifications, only due process applies to "non-corporeal" identification proceedings (like viewing photographs or video recordings) no matter when the proceeding occurs in the process. *If* a suspect is formally charged, and *if* police use a physical out-of-court procedure, and *if* it relates to that charge, and *if* defense counsel is not present (or has been waived), the Sixth Amendment is violated. But remember, even if police comply with the Sixth Amendment by having counsel present, a defendant may still assert a due process violation as the result of the physical lineup being unnecessarily suggestive, resulting in an unreliable ID.

These materials throw into sharp relief Herbert Packer's distinction–initially explored in Chapter 1 of this casebook–between the crime control and due process models of criminal justice. Under the crime control model, one might think that identifications should be evaluated generously with the goal of catching as many criminals as possible, even if the procedure sweeps up a few innocent individuals in the process. Under the due process model, however, one might think that identification procedures should produce inherently reliable identifications in order to ensure *fairness* to the targets of a criminal investigation. The following materials emphasize, at each turn, both of Packer's models.

A. RIGHT TO COUNSEL DURING IDENTIFICATIONS

As discussed in the prior chapter, the right to counsel applies not to just to the trial itself but also to other "critical stages" in the pretrial adversarial process, including post-indictment or post-arraignment interrogations. Out-of-court physical identification procedures qualify as one of those critical stages. Typically, the witness will make an identification, prior to trial, while working with the police or with prosecutors. At trial, a police officer might testify that the victim or witness identified the defendant during one of these encounters. Also, the witness may take the stand during the trial and pick out the defendant, sitting at the defense table, as the perpetrator, thus adding a second layer of identification to the situation. The prosecutor will then normally have the witness testify as to the prior out-of-court identification in order to bolster the credibility of the in-court identification.

Not all identifications are alike. Although there are many ways of structuring an identification, the following materials focus on three types of identifications that have drawn the scrutiny of the Supreme Court. The first is a "lineup" composed of the defendant and other individuals, who should be similar in appearance. The witness is then asked whether they recognize any of the individuals. The lineup usually takes place in a room that allows the witness to see the individuals in the lineup but not vice versa, thus preserving the privacy and safety of the witness and preventing witness intimidation. As will be explored below, the police might ask the individuals in the lineup to move in a particular way or even to speak a particular phrase if the witness heard the perpetrator say something and might be able to make an auditory identification of the perpetrator.

The second form of identification is a "showup," which is similar to a lineup except that the witness is only looking at a single individual, rather than a group of similar individuals. So, for example, say the police believe that the doorman of a building has committed a crime. The police could drive a witness in a police vehicle to the building and ask the witness to look out the car window at the person in front of the building. The witness might then respond that the doorman was the perpetrator of some crime that she witnessed, or she might respond that she doesn't recognize the doorman. A showup might also occur in a police precinct.

The third form of identification is a photographic, video, or audio identification. This replicates the multi-individual framework of the in-person lineup, except that neither the defendant nor the others are physically present—the witness simply looks at a group of photographs of individuals who are visually similar in the relevant way, and is asked by the police or prosecutors whether they recognize anyone depicted in the photographs. The photographs might be police mugshots from prior arrest bookings or they might be photographs taken in a different context.

Another way of distinguishing lineups is to focus on *when* they occur. Some identifications occur after the suspect has been formally charged, when the suspect has been transformed, formally speaking, into a defendant. Or, an identification—especially a photographic lineup or a showup—might occur prior to this point in time. As noted above, this *when* factor is critically important, because the Sixth Amendment protection applies only after the suspect becomes a defendant as the result of a formal charge (indictment, arraignment, bail hearing, preliminary hearing, information). The police do not need the cooperation of the suspect or any coercive authority to conduct a photographic lineup, nor do they need any judicial authority to drive a witness to a public place and ask the witness if they recognize any of the individuals there. On the other hand, a lineup requires the custody of the defendant, which is why a lineup frequently occurs after arrest and indictment.

As the following cases explore, the *temporal* location of the identification during the criminal process plays an important role in the Supreme Court's assessment of whether the suspect or defendant has a right to counsel during that identification. Generally speaking, the closer the identification is to the actual trial, the more likely it is that the Constitution requires access to counsel for the defendant, for various reasons. In general, as noted below, the Court asks whether the identification occurred during a "critical stage" of the proceedings and therefore necessitated the presence of counsel. The following materials explore these details and the intersection between the types of identifications and their temporal location during the criminal process.

1. Counsel for Physical Lineups After Initiation of Formal Charges

In the following case, the defendant was indicted for bank robbery. Subsequently, the defendant was placed in a lineup and told to recite the line "put the money in the bag," after which two bank employees identified the defendant as the robber. The question in the following case is whether this event constituted a "critical stage" that necessitated the presence of counsel pursuant to the Sixth Amendment. As you read the case, compare the significance of the lineup with other "critical stages" in the adversarial process when the Sixth Amendment right to counsel attaches.

United States v. Wade

Supreme Court of the United States
388 U.S. 218 (1967)

Mr. Justice BRENNAN delivered the opinion of the Court.

The question here is whether courtroom identifications of an accused at trial are to be excluded from evidence because the accused was exhibited to the witnesses before trial at a post-indictment lineup conducted for identification purposes without notice to and in the absence of the accused's appointed counsel.

The federally insured bank in Eustace, Texas, was robbed on September 21, 1964. A man with a small strip of tape on each side of his face entered the bank, pointed a pistol at the female cashier and the vice president, the only persons in the bank at the time, and forced them to fill a pillowcase with the bank's money. The man then drove away with an accomplice who had been waiting in a stolen car outside the bank. On March 23, 1965, an indictment was returned against respondent, Wade, and two others for conspiring to rob the bank, and against Wade and the accomplice for the robbery itself. Wade was arrested on April 2, and counsel was appointed to represent him on April 26. Fifteen days later an FBI agent, without notice to Wade's lawyer, arranged to have the two bank employees observe a lineup made up of Wade and five or six other prisoners and conducted in a courtroom of the local county courthouse. Each person in the line wore strips of tape such as allegedly worn by the robber and upon direction each said something like "put the money in the bag," the words allegedly uttered by the robber. Both bank employees identified Wade in the lineup as the bank robber.

At trial the two employees, when asked on direct examination if the robber was in the courtroom, pointed to Wade. The prior lineup identification was then elicited from both employees on cross-examination. . . .

II

. . . When the Bill of Rights was adopted, there were no organized police forces as we know them today. The accused confronted the prosecutor and the witnesses against him, and the evidence was marshalled, largely at the trial itself. In contrast, today's law enforcement machinery involves critical confrontations of the accused by the prosecution at pretrial proceedings where the results might well settle the accused's fate and reduce the trial itself to a mere formality. In recognition of these realities of modern criminal prosecution, our cases have construed the Sixth Amendment guarantee to apply to "critical" stages of the proceedings. The guarantee reads: "In all criminal prosecutions, the accused shall enjoy the right . . . to have the Assistance of Counsel for his defence." The plain wording of this guarantee thus encompasses counsel's assistance whenever necessary to assure a meaningful "defence."

As early as *Powell v. Alabama*, we recognized that the period from arraignment to trial was "perhaps the most critical period of the proceedings" during which the accused "requires the guiding hand of counsel" if the guarantee is not to prove an empty right. That principle has since been applied to require the assistance of counsel at the type of arraignment—for example, that provided by Alabama—where certain rights might be sacrificed or lost. . . .

[I]n addition to counsel's presence at trial, the accused is guaranteed that he need not stand alone against the State at any stage of the prosecution, formal or informal, in court or out, where counsel's absence might derogate from the accused's right to a fair trial. The security of that right is as much the aim of the right to counsel as it is of the other guarantees of the Sixth Amendment—the right of the accused to a speedy and public trial by an impartial jury, his right to be informed of the nature and cause of the accusation, and his right to be confronted with the witnesses against him and to have compulsory process for obtaining witnesses in his favor. The presence of counsel at such critical confrontations, as at the trial itself, operates to assure that the accused's interests will be protected consistently with our adversary theory of criminal prosecution.

In sum, the principle . . . requires that we scrutinize any pretrial confrontation of the accused to determine whether the presence of his counsel is necessary to preserve the defendant's basic right to a fair trial as affected by his right meaningfully to cross-examine the witnesses against him and to have effective assistance of counsel at the trial itself. It calls upon us to analyze whether potential substantial prejudice to defendant's rights inheres in the particular confrontation and the ability of counsel to help avoid that prejudice.

III

The Government characterizes the lineup as a mere preparatory step in the gathering of the prosecution's evidence, not different—for Sixth Amendment purposes—from various other preparatory steps, such as systematized or scientific analyzing of the accused's fingerprints, blood sample, clothing, hair, and the like. We think there are differences which preclude such stages being characterized as critical stages at which the accused has the right to the presence of his counsel. Knowledge of the techniques of science and technology is sufficiently available, and the variables in techniques few enough, that the accused has the opportunity for a meaningful confrontation of the Government's case at trial through the ordinary processes of cross-examination of the Government's expert witnesses and the presentation of the evidence of his own experts. The denial of a right to have his counsel present at such analyses does not therefore violate the Sixth Amendment; they are not critical stages since there is minimal risk that his counsel's absence at such stages might derogate from his right to a fair trial.

IV

But the confrontation compelled by the State between the accused and the victim or witnesses to a crime to elicit identification evidence is peculiarly riddled with innumerable dangers and variable factors which might seriously, even crucially, derogate from a fair trial. The vagaries of eyewitness identification are well-known; the annals of criminal law are rife with instances of mistaken identification. . . . A major factor contributing to the high incidence of miscarriage of justice from mistaken identification has been the degree of suggestion inherent in the manner in which the prosecution presents the suspect to witnesses for pretrial identification. . . . Suggestion can be created intentionally or unintentionally in many subtle ways. And the dangers for the suspect are particularly grave when the witness' opportunity for observation was insubstantial, and thus his susceptibility to suggestion the greatest.

Moreover, "(i)t is a matter of common experience that, once a witness has picked out the accused at the line-up, he is not likely to go back on his word later on, so that in practice the issue of identity may (in the absence of other relevant evidence) for all practical purposes be determined there and then, before the trial."

The pretrial confrontation for purpose of identification may take the form of a lineup. . . . It is obvious that risks of suggestion attend either form of confrontation and increase the dangers inhering in eyewitness identification. But as is the case with secret interrogations, there is serious difficulty in depicting what transpires at lineups and other forms of identification confrontations. . . . For the same reasons, the defense can seldom reconstruct the manner and mode of lineup identification for judge or jury at trial. Those participating in a lineup with the accused may often be police officers; in any event, the participants' names are rarely recorded or divulged at trial. The impediments to an objective observation are increased when the victim is the witness. Lineups are prevalent in rape and robbery prosecutions and present a particular hazard that a victim's understandable outrage may excite vengeful or spiteful motives. In any event, neither witnesses nor lineup participants are apt to be alert for conditions prejudicial to the suspect. And if they were, it would likely be of scant benefit to the suspect since neither witnesses nor lineup participants are likely to be schooled in the detection of suggestive influences. Improper influences may go undetected by a suspect, guilty or not, who experiences the emotional tension which we might expect in one being confronted with potential accusers. Even when he does observe abuse, if he has a criminal record he may be reluctant to take the stand and open up the admission of prior convictions. Moreover any protestations by the suspect of the fairness of the lineup made at trial are likely to be in vain; the jury's choice is between the accused's unsupported version and that of the police officers present. In short, the accused's inability effectively to reconstruct at trial any unfairness that occurred at the lineup may deprive him of his only opportunity meaningfully to attack the credibility of the witness' courtroom identification. . . .

[S]tate reports, in the course of describing prior identifications admitted as evidence of guilt, reveal numerous instances of suggestive procedures, for example, that all in the lineup but the suspect were known to the identifying witness, that the other participants in a lineup were grossly dissimilar in appearance to the suspect, that only the suspect was required to wear distinctive clothing which the culprit allegedly wore, that the witness is told by the police that they have caught the culprit after which the defendant is brought before the witness alone or is viewed in jail, that the suspect is pointed out before or during a lineup, and that the participants in the lineup are asked to try on an article of clothing which fits only the suspect.

The potential for improper influence is illustrated by the circumstances, insofar as they appear, surrounding the prior identifications in the three cases we decide today. In the present case, the testimony of the identifying witnesses elicited on cross-examination revealed that those witnesses were taken to the courthouse and seated in the courtroom to await assembly of the lineup. The courtroom faced on a hallway observable to the witnesses through an open door. The cashier testified that she saw Wade "standing in the hall" within sight of an FBI agent. Five or six other prisoners later appeared in the hall. The vice president testified that he saw a person in the hall in the custody of the agent who "resembled the person that we identified as the one that had entered the bank."

The lineup in *Gilbert* was conducted in an auditorium in which some 100 witnesses to several alleged state and federal robberies charged to Gilbert made wholesale identifications of Gilbert as the robber in each other's presence, a procedure said to be fraught with dangers of suggestion. And the vice of suggestion created by the identification in *Stovall* was the presentation to the witness of the suspect alone handcuffed to police officers. It is hard to imagine a situation more clearly conveying the suggestion to the witness that the one presented is believed guilty by the police.

The few cases that have surfaced therefore reveal the existence of a process attended with hazards of serious unfairness to the criminal accused and strongly suggest the plight of the more numerous defendants who are unable to ferret out suggestive influences in the secrecy of the confrontation. We do not assume that these risks are the result of police procedures intentionally designed to prejudice an accused. Rather we assume they derive from the dangers inherent in eyewitness identification and the suggestibility inherent in the context of the pretrial identification. . . .

Insofar as the accused's conviction may rest on a courtroom identification in fact the fruit of a suspect pretrial identification which the accused is helpless to subject to effective scrutiny at trial, the accused is deprived of that right of cross-examination which is an essential safeguard to his right to confront the witnesses against him. And even though cross-examination is a precious safeguard to a fair trial, it cannot be viewed as an absolute assurance of accuracy and reliability. Thus in the present context, where so many variables and pitfalls exist, the first line of defense must be the prevention of unfairness and the lessening of the hazards of eyewitness identification at the lineup itself. The trial which might determine the accused's fate may well not be that in the courtroom but that at the pretrial confrontation, with the State aligned against the accused, the witness the sole jury, and the accused unprotected against the overreaching, intentional or unintentional, and with little or no effective appeal from the judgment there rendered by the witness—"that's the man."

Since it appears that there is grave potential for prejudice, intentional or not, in the pretrial lineup, which may not be capable of reconstruction at trial, and since presence of counsel itself can often avert prejudice and assure a meaningful confrontation at trial, there can be little doubt that for Wade the postindictment lineup was a critical stage of the prosecution at which he was "as much entitled to such aid (of counsel) . . . as at the trial itself." *Powell v. Alabama*, 287 U.S. 45, 57. Thus both Wade and his counsel should have been notified of the impending lineup, and counsel's presence should have been a requisite to conduct of the lineup, absent an "intelligent waiver." No substantial countervailing policy considerations have been advanced against the requirement of the presence of counsel. Concern is expressed that the requirement will forestall prompt identifications and result in obstruction of the confrontations. As for the first, we note that in the two cases in which the right to counsel is today held to apply, counsel had already been appointed and no argument is made in either case that notice to counsel would have prejudicially delayed the confrontations. Moreover, we leave open the question whether the presence of substitute counsel might not suffice where notification and presence of the suspect's own counsel would result in prejudicial delay. And to refuse to recognize the right to counsel for fear that counsel will obstruct the course of justice is contrary to the basic assumptions upon which this Court has operated in Sixth Amendment cases. . . .

In our view counsel can hardly impede legitimate law enforcement; on the contrary, for the reasons expressed, law enforcement may be assisted by preventing the infiltration of taint in the prosecution's identification evidence. That result cannot help the guilty avoid conviction but can only help assure that the right man has been brought to justice. . . .

Mr. Justice WHITE, whom Mr. Justice HARLAN and Mr. Justice STEWART join, dissenting in part and concurring in part.

The Court has again propounded a broad constitutional rule barring the use of a wide spectrum of relevant and probative evidence, solely because a step in its ascertainment or discovery occurs outside the presence of defense counsel. This was the approach of the Court in *Miranda v. Arizona*. I objected then to what I thought was an uncritical and doctrinaire approach without satisfactory factual foundation. I have much the same view of the present ruling and therefore dissent from the judgment and from Parts II, IV, and V of the Court's opinion.

The Court's opinion is far-reaching. It proceeds first by creating a new per se rule of constitutional law: a criminal suspect cannot be subjected to a pretrial identification process in the absence of his counsel without violating the Sixth Amendment. If he is, the State may not buttress a later courtroom identification, of the witness by any reference to the previous identification. Furthermore, the courtroom identification is not admissible at all unless the State can establish by clear and convincing proof that the testimony is not the fruit of the earlier identification made in the absence of defendant's counsel—admittedly a heavy burden for the State and probably an impossible one. To all intents and purposes, courtroom identifications are barred if pretrial identifications have occurred without counsel being present.

The rule applies to any lineup, to any other techniques employed to produce an identification and a fortiori to a face-to-face encounter between the witness and the suspect alone, regardless of when the identification occurs, in time or place, and whether before or after indictment or information. It matters not how well the witness knows the suspect, whether the witness is the suspect's mother, brother, or long-time associate, and no matter how long or well the witness observed the perpetrator at the scene of the crime. The kidnap victim who has lived for days with his abductor is in the same category as the witness who has had only a fleeting glimpse of the criminal. Neither may identify the suspect without defendant's counsel being present. The same strictures apply regardless of the number of other witnesses who positively identify the defendant and regardless of the corroborative evidence showing that it was the defendant who had committed the crime.

The premise for the Court's rule is not the general unreliability of eyewitness identifications nor the difficulties inherent in observation, recall, and recognition. The Court assumes a narrower evil as the basis for its rule—improper police suggestion which contributes to erroneous identifications. The Court apparently believes that improper police procedures are so widespread that a broad prophylactic rule must be laid down, requiring the presence of counsel at all pretrial identifications, in order to detect recurring instances of police misconduct. I do not share this pervasive distrust of all official investigations. None of the materials the Court relies upon supports it. Certainly, I would bow to solid fact, but the Court quite obviously does not have before it any reliable, comprehensive survey of current police practices on which to base its new rule. Until it does, the Court should avoid excluding relevant evidence from state criminal trials.

The Court goes beyond assuming that a great majority of the country's police departments are following improper practices at pretrial identifications. To find the lineup a "critical" stage of the proceeding and to exclude identifications made in the absence of counsel, the Court must also assume that police "suggestion," if it occurs at all, leads to erroneous rather than accurate identifications and that reprehensible police conduct will have an unavoidable and largely undiscoverable impact on the trial. This in turn assumes that there is now no adequate source from which defense counsel can learn about the circumstances of the pretrial identification in order to place before the jury all of the considerations which should enter into an appraisal of courtroom identification evidence. But these are treacherous and unsupported assumptions resting as they do on the notion that the defendant will not be aware, that the police and the witnesses will forget or prevaricate, that defense counsel will be unable to bring out the truth and that neither jury, judge, nor appellate court is a sufficient safeguard against unacceptable police conduct occurring at a pretrial identification procedure. I am unable to share the Court's view of the willingness of the

> police and the ordinary citizen witness to dissemble, either with respect to the identification of the defendant or with respect to the circumstances surrounding a pretrial identification. . . .
>
> . . . [R]equiring counsel at pretrial identifications as an invariable rule trenches on other valid state interests. One of them is its concern with the prompt and efficient enforcement of its criminal laws. Identifications frequently take place after arrest but before an indictment is returned or an information is filed. The police may have arrested a suspect on probable cause but may still have the wrong man. Both the suspect and the State have every interest in a prompt identification at that stage, the suspect in order to secure his immediate release and the State because prompt and early identification enhances accurate identification and because it must know whether it is on the right investigative track. Unavoidably, however, the absolute rule requiring the presence of counsel will cause significant delay and it may very well result in no pretrial identification at all. . . .

NOTES & QUESTIONS ON POST-INDICTMENT LINEUPS

1. *Independent origin.* In *Gilbert v. California,* 388 U.S. 263 (1967), decided on the same day as *Wade*, the Supreme Court also held that a post-indictment lineup was unconstitutional because the defendant was not represented by counsel. The *Gilbert* Court first held that the out-of-court identification that violated the Sixth Amendment was per se inadmissible, no matter how reliable it may be. As to the in-court identification of the defendant, the Supreme Court held that an in-court identification should be excluded when it flowed from the unconstitutional police lineup. If prosecutors could establish that the in-court lineup had an "independent source," the in-court identification need not be excluded from evidence. The Court vacated Gilbert's conviction and remanded with instructions for the lower court to determine whether the in-court identification had an independent origin or whether it was inevitably tainted by the unconstitutional police lineup. For example, if the witness had adequate opportunity to reliably identify the defendant prior to the police lineup, the in-court identification could be based on that independent origin rather than on the tainted lineup.

2. *Lineups as compelled self-incrimination.* As noted above, lineups are not prohibited by the Fifth Amendment prohibition against compelled self-incrimination because a lineup is not "testimonial" in nature. Rather, the compelled nature of the lineup is more closely analogous to a bodily intrusion such as a blood test or DNA analysis, neither of which are testimonial in nature.

However, Wade *was* forced to speak during his lineup. Did the police forcing him to speak so that the witnesses could hear his voice constitute a form of compelled self-incrimination? The majority reasoned that it did not because Wade was forced to speak, not in order to communicate some information or idea, but rather to allow the witnesses to hear the sound of his voice as a means of identification. This fact made the speech "non-testimonial" and therefore not deserving of Fifth Amendment protection. The dissent in *Wade* disagreed, concluding that lineups violate the Fifth Amendment when suspects are forced to speak for the witness:

> In my view, however, the accused may not be compelled in a lineup to speak the words uttered by the person who committed the crime. I am confident that it could not be compelled in court. It cannot be compelled in a lineup. It is more than passive, mute assistance to the eyes of the victim or of witnesses. It is the kind of volitional act—the kind of forced cooperation by the accused—which is within the historical perimeter of the privilege against compelled self-incrimination.
>
> Our history and tradition teach and command that an accused may stand mute. The privilege means just that; not less than that. According to the Court, an accused may be jailed—indefinitely—until he is willing to say, for an identifying audience, whatever was said in the course of the commission of the crime. Presumably this would include, "Your money or your life"—or perhaps, words of assault in a rape case. This is intolerable under our constitutional system.

Having read this dissent, are you satisfied by the distinction between communicative speech and identificatory speech?

2. Counsel for Identifications Prior to Formal Charges

The following case involves an attempted extension of *Wade*. Unlike *Wade*, which involved a post-indictment identification, this case involves a pre-indictment identification. Also, unlike *Wade*, which involved a formal lineup, this case involves an informal "showup" of the suspect. A showup involves a situation where the witness sees a single individual—at the police station, at the crime scene, somewhere in public—and is asked by the police whether they recognize the person. While a lineup necessarily involves a plurality of individuals to select from, a showup typically involves a single individual. As you read the case, ask yourself whether the showup in this case constituted a "critical stage" of the proceedings for which the Sixth Amendment right to counsel should attach.

Kirby v. Illinois

Supreme Court of the United States
406 U.S. 682 (1972)

Mr. Justice STEWART announced the judgment of the Court and an opinion in which THE CHIEF JUSTICE, Mr. Justice BLACKMUN, and Mr. Justice REHNQUIST join.

In *United States v. Wade*, 388 U.S. 218, and *Gilbert v. California*, 388 U.S. 263, this Court held "that a post-indictment pretrial lineup at which the accused is exhibited to identifying witnesses is a critical stage of the criminal prosecution; that police conduct of such a lineup without notice to and in the absence of his counsel denies the accused his Sixth (and Fourteenth) Amendment right to counsel and calls in question the admissibility at trial of the in-court identifications of the accused by witnesses who attended the lineup." Those cases further held that no "in-court identifications" are admissible in evidence if their "source" is a lineup conducted in violation of this constitutional standard. "Only a per se exclusionary rule as to such testimony can be an effective sanction," the Court said, "to assure that law enforcement authorities will respect the accused's constitutional right to the presence of his counsel at the critical lineup." In the present case we are asked to extend the *Wade-Gilbert* per se exclusionary rule to identification testimony based upon a police station showup that took place before the defendant had been indicted or otherwise formally charged with any criminal offense.

On February 21, 1968, a man named Willie Shard reported to the Chicago police that the previous day two men had robbed him on a Chicago street of a wallet containing, among other things, traveler's checks and a Social Security card. On February 22, two police officers stopped the petitioner and a companion, Ralph Bean, on West Madison Street in Chicago. When asked for identification, the petitioner produced a wallet that contained three traveler's checks and a Social Security card, all bearing the name of Willie Shard. Papers with Shard's name on them were also found in Bean's possession. When asked to explain his possession of Shard's property, the petitioner first said that the traveler's checks were "play money," and then told the officers that he had won them in a crap game. The officers then arrested the petitioner and Bean and took them to a police station.

Only after arriving at the police station, and checking the records there, did the arresting officers learn of the Shard robbery. A police car was then dispatched to Shard's place of employment, where it picked up Shard and brought him to the police station. Immediately upon entering the room in the police station where the petitioner and Bean were seated at a table, Shard positively identified them as the men who had robbed him two days earlier. No lawyer was present in the room, and neither the petitioner nor

Bean had asked for legal assistance, or been advised of any right to the presence of counsel.

More than six weeks later, the petitioner and Bean were indicted for the robbery of Willie Shard. Upon arraignment, counsel was appointed to represent them, and they pleaded not guilty. A pretrial motion to suppress Shard's identification testimony was denied, and at the trial Shard testified as a witness for the prosecution. In his testimony he described his identification of the two men at the police station on February 22, and identified them again in the courtroom as the men who had robbed him on February 20. He was cross-examined at length regarding the circumstances of his identification of the two defendants. The jury found both defendants guilty, and the petitioner's conviction was affirmed on appeal. The Illinois appellate court held that the admission of Shard's testimony was not error, relying upon an earlier decision of the Illinois Supreme Court holding that the *Wade-Gilbert* per se exclusionary rule is not applicable to preindictment confrontations. . . .

I

We note at the outset that the constitutional privilege against compulsory self-incrimination is in no way implicated here. The Court emphatically rejected the claimed applicability of that constitutional guarantee in *Wade* itself. . . . It follows that the doctrine of *Miranda v. Arizona*, 384 U.S. 436, has no applicability whatever to the issue before us; for the *Miranda* decision was based exclusively upon the Fifth and Fourteenth Amendment privilege against compulsory self-incrimination, upon the theory that custodial interrogation is inherently coercive.

The *Wade-Gilbert* exclusionary rule, by contrast, stems from a quite different constitutional guarantee—the guarantee of the right to counsel contained in the Sixth and Fourteenth Amendments. Unless all semblance of principled constitutional adjudication is to be abandoned, therefore, it is to the decisions construing that guarantee that we must look in determining the present controversy.

In a line of constitutional cases in this Court stemming back to the Court's landmark opinion in *Powell v. Alabama*, 287 U.S. 45, it has been firmly established that a person's Sixth and Fourteenth Amendment right to counsel attaches only at or after the time that adversary judicial proceedings have been initiated against him.

This is not to say that a defendant in a criminal case has a constitutional right to counsel only at the trial itself. The *Powell* case makes clear that the right attaches at the time of arraignment, and the Court has recently held that it exists also at the time of a preliminary hearing. But the point is that, while members of the Court have differed as to existence of the right to counsel in the contexts of some of the above cases, all of those cases have involved points of time at or after the initiation of adversary judicial criminal proceedings–whether by way of formal charge, preliminary hearing, indictment, information, or arraignment. . . .

The initiation of judicial criminal proceedings is far from a mere formalism. It is the starting point of our whole system of adversary criminal justice. For it is only then that the government has committed itself to prosecute, and only then that the adverse positions of government and defendant have solidified. It is then that a defendant finds himself faced with the prosecutorial forces of organized society, and immersed in the intricacies of substantive and procedural criminal law. It is this point, therefore, that marks the commencement of the "criminal prosecutions" to which alone the explicit guarantees of the Sixth Amendment are applicable.

In this case we are asked to import into a routine police investigation an absolute constitutional guarantee historically and rationally applicable only after the onset of formal prosecutorial proceedings. We decline to do so. . . .

Mr. Justice BRENNAN, with whom Mr. Justice DOUGLAS and Mr. Justice MARSHALL join, dissenting.

After petitioner and Ralph Bean were arrested, police officers brought Willie Shard, the robbery victim, to a room in a police station where petitioner and Bean were seated at a table with two other police officers. Shard testified at trial that the officers who brought him to the room asked him if petitioner and Bean were the robbers and that he indicated they were. The prosecutor asked him, "And you positively identified them at the police station, is that correct?" Shard answered, "Yes." Consequently, the question in this case is whether, under *Gilbert v. California*, 388 U.S. 263 (1967), it was constitutional error to admit Shard's testimony that he identified petitioner at the pretrial station-house showup when that showup was conducted by the police without advising petitioner that he might have counsel present. *Gilbert* held, in the context of a post-indictment lineup, that "(o) nly a per se exclusionary rule as to such testimony can be an effective sanction to assure that law enforcement authorities will respect the accused's constitutional right to the presence of his counsel at the critical lineup." I would apply *Gilbert* and the principles of its companion case, *Wade*, 388 U.S. 218 (1967), and reverse. . . .

While it should go without saying, it appears necessary, in view of the plurality opinion today, to re-emphasize that *Wade* did not require the presence of counsel at pretrial confrontations for identification purposes simply on the basis of an abstract consideration of the words "criminal prosecutions" in the Sixth Amendment. Counsel is required at those confrontations because "the dangers inherent in eyewitness identification and the suggestibility inherent in the context of the pretrial identification" mean that protection must be afforded to the "most basic right (of) a criminal defendant—his right to a fair trial at which the witnesses against him might be meaningfully cross-examined." Indeed, the Court expressly stated that "legislative or other regulations, such as those of local police departments, which eliminate the risks of abuse and unintentional suggestion at lineup proceedings and the impediments to meaningful confrontation at trial may also remove the basis for regarding the stage as 'critical.'" Hence, "the initiation of adversary judicial criminal proceedings" is completely irrelevant to whether counsel is necessary at a pretrial confrontation for identification in order to safeguard the accused's constitutional rights to confrontation and the effective assistance of counsel at his trial.

In view of *Wade*, it is plain, and the plurality today does not attempt to dispute it, that there inheres in a confrontation for identification conducted after arrest the identical hazards to a fair trial that inhere in such a confrontation conducted "after the onset of formal prosecutional proceedings." The plurality apparently considers an arrest, which for present purposes we must assume to be based upon probable cause, to be nothing more than part of "a routine police investigation" and thus not "the starting point of our whole system of adversary criminal justice." An arrest, according to the plurality, does not face the accused "with the prosecutorial forces of organized society," nor immerse him "in the intricacies of substantive and procedural criminal law." Those consequences ensue, says the plurality, only with "(t)he initiation of judicial criminal proceedings," "(f)or it is only then that the government has committed itself to prosecute, and only then that the adverse positions of government and defendant have solidified." If these propositions do not amount to "mere formalism" it is difficult to know how to characterize them. An arrest evidences the belief of the police that the perpetrator of a crime has been caught. A post-arrest confrontation for identification is not "a mere preparatory step in the gathering of the prosecution's evidence." A primary, and frequently sole, purpose of the confrontation for identification at that stage is to accumulate proof to buttress the conclusion of the police that they have the offender in hand. The plurality offers no reason, and I can think of none, for concluding that a post-arrest confrontation for identification, unlike a post-charge confrontation, is not among those "critical confrontations of the accused by the prosecution at pretrial proceedings where the results might well settle the accused's fate and reduce the trial itself to a mere formality."

The highly suggestive form of confrontation employed in this case underscores the point. This showup was particularly fraught with the peril of mistaken identification. In the setting of a police station squad room where all present except petitioner and Bean were police officers, the danger was quite real that Shard's understandable resentment might lead him too readily to agree with the police that the pair under arrest, and the only persons exhibited to him, were indeed the robbers. The State had no case without Shard's identification testimony, and safeguards against that consequences were therefore of critical importance. Shard's testimony itself demonstrates the necessity for such safeguards. On direct examination, Shard identified petitioner and Bean not as the alleged robbers on trial in the courtroom, but as the pair he saw at the police station. . . .

Wade and *Gilbert*, of course, happened to involve post-indictment confrontations. Yet even a cursory perusal of the opinions in those cases reveals that nothing at all turned upon that particular circumstance. In short, it is fair to conclude that rather than "declin(ing) to depart from (the) rationale" of *Wade* and *Gilbert*, the plurality today, albeit purporting to be engaged in "principled constitutional adjudication," refuses even to recognize that "rationale." For my part, I do not agree that we "extend" *Wade* and *Gilbert* by holding that the principles of those cases apply to confrontations for identification conducted after arrest. Because Shard testified at trial about his identification of petitioner at the police station showup, the exclusionary rule of *Gilbert* requires reversal.

NOTES & QUESTIONS ON PRE-INDICTMENT SHOWUPS

1. *Pre-indictment versus post-indictment identifications.* The combination of *Wade* and *Kirby* make clear that the appropriate dividing line for the Sixth Amendment right to counsel is indictment. If the identification occurs after initiation of formal adversarial process (when the suspect becomes a defendant), the Sixth Amendment right to counsel applies, which means absence of counsel at a physical lineup renders that identification *per se* inadmissible (*Gilbert*), and an in-court identification of the defendant by the witness *presumptively* inadmissible unless the prosecution proves by clear and convincing evidence it is independent from the out-of-court identification (*Wade*). If, on the other hand, the identification occurs prior to formal adversarial process, as it did in *Kirby*, then the Sixth Amendment is not even applicable, and therefore the identification proceeding, even if physical, cannot qualify as a "critical stage" in the proceedings that requires the presence of counsel. Do you agree with the Supreme Court that the moment of indictment is this constitutionally significant?

3. Counsel for Non-Corporeal (Photographic) Identifications

The following case involves a post-indictment identification, so under the rule from *Wade* and *Gilbert*, the Sixth Amendment right to counsel has attached because the event takes place after the initiation of formal adversarial process.

In contrast, this case involves a *photographic* lineup, rather than an "in-person" corporeal lineup, thus distinguishing it from the facts of *Wade* and *Gilbert*. The question is therefore whether this type of identification is a critical stage in the adversarial process. As you read the case, ask yourself whether the rationale expressed in *Wade* and *Gilbert* applies with equal force in the case of photographic lineups. Or is there something distinctive or unique about the photographic lineup that is constitutionally significant?

United States v. Ash

Supreme Court of the United States
413 U.S. 300 (1973)

Mr. Justice BLACKMUN delivered the opinion of the Court.

In this case the Court is called upon to decide whether the Sixth Amendment grants an accused the right to have counsel present whenever the Government conducts a post-indictment photographic display, containing a picture of the accused, for the purpose of allowing a witness to attempt an identification of the offender. . . .

I

On the morning of August 26, 1965, a man with a stocking mask entered a bank in Washington, D.C., and began waving a pistol. He ordered an employee to hang up the telephone and instructed all others present not to move. Seconds later a second man, also wearing a stocking mask, entered the bank, scooped up money from tellers' drawers into a bag, and left. The gunman followed, and both men escaped through an alley. The robbery lasted three or four minutes.

A Government informer, Clarence McFarland, told authorities that he had discussed the robbery with Charles J. Ash, Jr., the respondent here. Acting on this information, an FBI agent, in February 1966, showed five black-and-white mug shots of Negro males of generally the same age, height, and weight, one of which was of Ash, to four witnesses. All four made uncertain identifications of Ash's picture. At this time Ash was not in custody and had not been charged. On April 1, 1966, an indictment was returned charging Ash and a codefendant, John L. Bailey, in five counts related to this bank robbery. . . .

Trial was finally set for May 1968, almost three years after the crime. In preparing for trial, the prosecutor decided to use a photographic display to determine whether the witnesses he planned to call would be able to make in-court identifications. Shortly before the trial, an FBI agent and the prosecutor showed five color photographs to the four witnesses who previously had tentatively identified the black-and-white photograph of Ash. Three of the witnesses selected the picture of Ash, but one was unable to make any selection. None of the witnesses selected the picture of Bailey which was in the group. This post-indictment identification provides the basis for respondent Ash's claim that he was denied the right to counsel at a "critical stage" of the prosecution. . . .

II

The Court of Appeals relied exclusively on that portion of the Sixth Amendment providing, "In all criminal prosecutions, the accused shall enjoy the right . . . to have the Assistance of Counsel for his defence." The right to counsel in Anglo-American law has a rich historical heritage, and this Court has regularly drawn on that history in construing the counsel guarantee of the Sixth Amendment. We re-examine that history in an effort to determine the relationship between the purposes of the Sixth Amendment guarantee and the risks of a photographic identification.

In *Powell v. Alabama,* 287 U.S. 45, 60-66 (1932), the Court discussed the English common-law rule that severely limited the right of a person accused of a felony to consult with counsel at trial. The Court examined colonial constitutions and statutes and noted that "in at least twelve of the thirteen colonies the rule of the English common law, in the respect now under consideration, had been definitely rejected and the right to counsel fully recognized in all criminal prosecutions, save that in one or two instances the right was limited to capital offenses or to the more serious crimes." The Sixth Amendment counsel guarantee, thus, was derived from colonial statutes and constitutional provisions designed to reject the English common-law rule.

Apparently several concerns contributed to this rejection at the very time when countless other aspects of the common law were being imported. One consideration was the inherent irrationality of the English limitation. Since the rule was limited to felony proceedings, the result, absurd and illogical, was that an accused misdemeanant could rely fully on counsel, but the accused felon, in theory at least, could consult counsel only on legal questions that the accused proposed to the court. English writers were appropriately critical of this inconsistency.

A concern of more lasting importance was the recognition and awareness that an unaided layman had little skill in arguing the law or in coping with an intricate procedural system. The function of counsel as a guide through complex legal technicalities long has been recognized by this Court. . . . The Court frequently has interpreted the Sixth Amendment to assure that the "guiding hand of counsel" is available to those in need of its assistance.

Another factor contributing to the colonial recognition of the accused's right to counsel was the adoption of the institution of the public prosecutor from the Continental inquisitorial system. . . . Thus, an additional motivation for the American rule was a desire to minimize imbalance in

As an alternative to a typical police lineup, a Dallas police officer shows a victim of a robbery a single headshot in an attempt to reduce the kinds of mistakes made by eyewitnesses trying to identify suspects. (LM Otero/AP/Shutterstock

the adversary system that otherwise resulted with the creation of a professional prosecuting official. . . .

This historical background suggests that the core purpose of the counsel guarantee was to assure "Assistance" at trial, when the accused was confronted with both the intricacies of the law and the advocacy of the public prosecutor. Later developments have led this Court to recognize that "Assistance" would be less than meaningful if it were limited to the formal trial itself.

This extension of the right to counsel to events before trial has resulted from changing patterns of criminal procedure and investigation that have tended to generate pretrial events that might appropriately be considered to be parts of the trial itself. At these newly emerging and significant events, the accused was confronted, just as at trial, by the procedural system, or by his expert adversary, or by both. . . .

The Court consistently has applied a historical interpretation of the guarantee, and has expanded the constitutional right to counsel only when new contexts appear presenting the same dangers that gave birth initially to the right itself. . . . The analogy between the unrepresented accused at the pretrial confrontation and the unrepresented defendant at trial, implicit in the cases mentioned above, was explicitly drawn in *Wade*. . . .

Throughout this expansion of the counsel guarantee to trial-like confrontations, the function of the lawyer has remained essentially the same as his function at trial. In all cases considered by the Court, counsel has continued to act as a spokesman for, or advisor to, the accused. The accused's right to the "Assistance of Counsel" has meant just that, namely, the right of the accused to have counsel acting as his assistant. . . .

The function of counsel in rendering "Assistance" continued at the lineup under consideration in *Wade* and its companion cases. Although the accused was not confronted there with legal questions, the lineup offered opportunities for prosecuting authorities to take advantage of the accused. Counsel was seen by the Court as being more sensitive to, and aware of, suggestive influences than the accused himself, and as better able to reconstruct the events at trial. Counsel present at lineup would be able to remove disabilities of the accused in precisely the same fashion that counsel compensated for the disabilities of the layman at trial. Thus, the Court mentioned that the accused's memory might be dimmed by "emotional tension," that the accused's credibility at trial would be diminished by his status as defendant, and that the accused might be unable to present his version effectively without giving up his privilege against compulsory self-incrimination. It was in order to compensate for these deficiencies that the Court found the need for the assistance of counsel.

This review of the history and expansion of the Sixth Amendment counsel guarantee demonstrates that the test utilized by the Court has called for examination of the event in order to determine whether the accused required aid in coping with legal problems or assistance in meeting his adversary. . . .

III

Although the Court of Appeals' majority recognized the argument that "a major purpose behind the right to counsel is to protect the defendant from errors that he himself might make if he appeared in court alone," the court concluded that "other forms of prejudice," mentioned and recognized in *Wade*, could also give rise to a right to counsel. These forms of prejudice were felt by the court to flow from the possibilities for mistaken identification inherent in the photographic display.

We conclude that the dangers of mistaken identification, mentioned in *Wade*, were removed from context by the Court of Appeals and were incorrectly utilized as a sufficient basis for requiring counsel. Although *Wade* did discuss possibilities for suggestion and the difficulty for reconstructing suggestivity, this discussion occurred only after the Court had concluded that the lineup constituted a trial-like confrontation, requiring the "Assistance of Counsel" to preserve the adversary process by compensating for advantages of the prosecuting authorities. . . .

The Court of Appeals considered its analysis complete after it decided that a photographic display lacks scientific precision and ease of accurate reconstruction at trial. That analysis, under *Wade*, however, merely carries one to the point where one must establish that the trial itself can provide no substitute for counsel if a pretrial confrontation is conducted in the absence of counsel. . . . We now undertake the threshold analysis that must be addressed.

IV

A substantial departure from the historical test would be necessary if the Sixth Amendment were interpreted to give Ash a right to counsel at the photographic identification in this case. Since the accused himself is not present at the time of the photographic display, and asserts no right to be present, no possibility arises that the accused might be misled by his lack of familiarity with the law or overpowered by his professional adversary. Similarly, the counsel guarantee would not be used to produce equality in a trial-like adversary confrontation. Rather, the guarantee was used by the Court of Appeals to produce confrontation at an event that previously was not analogous to an adversary trial.

Even if we were willing to view the counsel guarantee in broad terms as a generalized protection of the adversary process, we would be unwilling to go so far as to extend the right to a portion of the prosecutor's trial-preparation interviews with witnesses. Although photography is relatively new, the interviewing of witnesses before trial is a procedure that predates the Sixth Amendment. . . . The traditional counterbalance in the American adversary system for these interviews arises from the equal ability of defense counsel to seek and interview witnesses himself.

That adversary mechanism remains as effective for a photographic display as for other parts of pretrial interviews. No greater limitations are placed on defense counsel in constructing displays, seeking witnesses, and conducting photographic identifications than those applicable to the prosecution. Selection of the picture of a person other than the accused, or the inability of a witness to make any selection, will be useful to the defense in precisely the same manner that the selection of a picture of the defendant would be useful to the prosecution. In this very case, for example, the initial tender of the photographic display was by Bailey's counsel, who sought to demonstrate that the witness had failed to make a photographic identification. Although we do not suggest that equality of access to photographs removes all potential for abuse, it does remove any inequality in the adversary process itself and thereby fully satisfies the historical spirit of the Sixth Amendment's counsel guarantee. . . .

We are not persuaded that the risks inherent in the use of photographic displays are so pernicious that an extraordinary system of safeguards is required. We hold, then, that the Sixth Amendment does not grant the right to counsel at photographic displays conducted by the Government for the purpose of allowing a witness to attempt an identification of the offender. . . .

Mr. Justice BRENNAN, with whom Mr. Justice DOUGLAS and Mr. Justice MARSHALL join, dissenting.

The Court holds today that a pretrial display of photographs to the witnesses of a crime for the purpose of identifying the accused, unlike a lineup, does not constitute a "critical stage" of the prosecution at which the accused is constitutionally entitled to the presence of counsel. In my view, today's decision is wholly unsupportable in terms of such considerations as logic, consistency, and, indeed, fairness. As a result, I must reluctantly conclude that today's decision marks simply another step towards the complete evisceration of the fundamental constitutional principles established by this Court, only six years ago, in *United States v. Wade*, 388 U.S. 218 (1967); *Gilbert v. California*, 388 U.S. 263 (1967); and *Stovall v. Denno*, 388 U.S. 293 (1967). I dissent. . . .

III

As the Court of Appeals recognized, "the dangers of mistaken identification . . . set forth in *Wade* are applicable in large measure to photographic as well as corporeal identifications." To the extent that misidentification may be attributable to a witness' faulty memory or perception, or inadequate opportunity for detailed observation during the crime, the risks are obviously as great at a photographic display as at a lineup. . . .

Moreover, as in the lineup situation, the possibilities for impermissible suggestion in the context of a photographic display are manifold. Such suggestion, intentional or unintentional, may derive from three possible sources. First, the photographs themselves might tend to suggest which of the pictures is that of the suspect. For example, differences in age, pose, or other physical characteristics of the persons represented, and variations in the mounting, background, lighting, or markings of the photographs all might have the effect of singling out the accused.

Second, impermissible suggestion may inhere in the manner in which the photographs are displayed to the witness. The danger of misidentification is, of course, "increased if the police display to the witness . . . the pictures of several persons among which the photograph of a single such individual recurs or is in some way emphasized." And, if the photographs are arranged in an asymmetrical pattern, or if they are displayed in a time sequence that tends to emphasize a particular photograph, "any identification of the photograph which stands out from the rest is no more reliable than an identification of a single photograph, exhibited alone."

Third, gestures or comments of the prosecutor at the time of the display may lead an otherwise uncertain witness to select the "correct" photograph.

For example, the prosecutor might "indicate to the witness that (he has) other evidence that one of the persons pictured committed the crime," and might even point to a particular photograph and ask whether the person pictured "looks familiar." More subtly, the prosecutor's inflection, facial expressions, physical motions, and myriad other almost imperceptible means of communication might tend, intentionally or unintentionally, to compromise the witness' objectivity. . . .

Moreover, as with lineups, the defense can "seldom reconstruct" at trial the mode and manner of photographic identification. It is true, of course, that the photographs used at the pretrial display might be preserved for examination at trial. . . . Indeed, in reality, preservation of the photographs affords little protection to the unrepresented accused. For, although retention of the photographs may mitigate the dangers of misidentification due to the suggestiveness of the photographs themselves, it cannot in any sense reveal to defense counsel the more subtle, and therefore more dangerous, suggestiveness that might derive from the manner in which he photographs were displayed or any accompanying comments or gestures. . . .

Finally, and unlike the lineup situation, the accused himself is not even present at the photographic identification, thereby reducing the likelihood that irregularities in the procedures will ever come to light. . . .

Thus, the difficulties of reconstructing at trial an uncounseled photographic display are at least equal to, and possibly greater than, those involved in reconstructing an uncounseled lineup. And, as the Government argued in *Wade*, in terms of the need for counsel, "(t)here is no meaningful difference between a witness' pretrial identification from photographs and a similar identification made at a lineup." For in both situations, "the accused's inability effectively to reconstruct at trial any unfairness that occurred at the (pretrial identification) may deprive him of his only opportunity meaningfully to attack the credibility of the witness' courtroom identification." As a result, both photographic and corporeal identifications create grave dangers that an innocent defendant might be convicted simply because of his inability to expose a tainted identification. This being so, considerations of logic, consistency, and, indeed, fairness compel the conclusion that a pretrial photographic identification, like a pretrial corporeal identification, is a "critical stage of the prosecution at which (the accused is) as much entitled to such aid (of counsel) . . . as at the trial itself."

IV

Ironically, the Court does not seriously challenge the proposition that presence of counsel at a pretrial photographic display is essential to preserve the accused's right to a fair trial on the issue of identification. Rather, in what I can only characterize a triumph of form over substance, the Court seeks to justify its result by engrafting a wholly unprecedented—and wholly unsupportable–limitation on the Sixth Amendment right of "the accused . . . to have the Assistance of Counsel for his defence." Although apparently conceding that the right to counsel attaches, not only at the trial itself, but at all "critical stages" of the prosecution, the Court holds today that, in order to be deemed "critical," the particular "stage of the prosecution" under consideration must, at the very least, involve the physical "presence of the accused," at a "trial-like confrontation" with the Government, at which the accused requires the "guiding hand of counsel." According to the Court a pretrial photographic identification does not, of course, meet these criteria. . . .

The fundamental premise underlying all of this Court's decisions holding the right to counsel applicable at "critical" pretrial proceedings, is that a "stage" of the prosecution must be deemed "critical" for the purposes of the Sixth Amendment if it is one at which the presence of counsel is necessary "to protect the fairness of the trial itself." . . . Indeed, to exclude counsel from a pretrial proceeding at which his presence might be necessary to assure the fairness of the subsequent trial would, in practical effect, render the Sixth Amendment guarantee virtually meaningless, for it would "deny a defendant effective representation by counsel at the only stage when legal aid and advice would help him."

This established conception of the Sixth Amendment guarantee is, of course, in no sense dependent upon the physical "presence of the accused," at a "trial-like confrontation" with the Government, at which the accused requires the "guiding hand of counsel." On the contrary, in *Powell v. Alabama*, 287 U.S. 45 (1932), the seminal decision in this area, we explicitly held the right to counsel applicable at a stage of the pretrial proceedings involving none of the three criteria set forth by the Court today. In *Powell*, the defendants in a state felony prosecution were not appointed counsel until the very eve of trial. This Court held, in no uncertain terms, that such an appointment could not satisfy the demands of the Sixth Amendment. . . . In other words, *Powell* made clear that, in order to preserve the accused's right to a fair trial and to "effective and substantial" assistance of counsel at the trial, the Sixth Amendment guarantee necessarily encompasses a reasonable period of time before trial during which counsel might prepare the defense. Yet it can hardly be said that this preparatory period of research and investigation involves the physical "presence of the accused," at a "trial-like confrontation" with the Government, at which the accused requires the "guiding hand of counsel." . . .

There is something ironic about the Court's conclusion today that a pretrial lineup identification is a "critical stage" of the prosecution because counsel's presence can help to compensate for the accused's deficiencies as an observer, but that a pretrial photographic identification is not a "critical stage" of the prosecution because the accused is not able to observe at all. In my view, there simply is no meaningful difference, in terms of the need for attendance of counsel, between corporeal and photographic identifications. And applying established and well-reasoned Sixth Amendment principles, I can only conclude that a pretrial photographic display, like a pretrial lineup, is a "critical stage" of the prosecution at which the accused is constitutionally entitled to the presence of counsel.

NOTES & QUESTIONS ON PHOTOGRAPHIC LINEUPS

1. *The significance of presence.* The majority in *Ash* focused on the idea of presence. Unlike a lineup, which requires the physical presence of the defendant, a photographic lineup can be—and ought to be—conducted without the presence of the defendant. Since the defendant is not there, the photographic lineup is not a "trial-like confrontation" that requires defense counsel to protect the interests of the suspect. Do you agree with this assessment? This issue raises a major question about the role of the attorney in the criminal process. Is it to give advice to the client? Or is it to ensure counsel is armed with the information necessary to effectively confront the identifying witness at trial, as *Wade* suggests? Or should the attorney advocate for identification procedures that would best protect the client? The decision in *Ash* clearly rests on the assumption that the attorney's role is primarily centered around the giving of in-person advice. What sources might one consult in order to identify the true scope of a defense attorney's role during the criminal process?

B. DUE PROCESS AND UNNECESSARILY SUGGESTIVE IDENTIFICATIONS

In addition to the requirement of counsel during some identifications, the Supreme Court has stated that an identification that is unnecessarily "suggestive" that results in an inherently unreliable identification violates the protection of due process found in the Fifth Amendment and the Fourteenth Amendment. For example, if a witness tells the police that he was attacked by a short man who is five feet tall, and the police respond by organizing a lineup with one five-foot man and five other individuals who are each six feet ten inches in height, there is a strong likelihood that a court will look at the lineup and declare it unconstitutionally suggestive. Furthermore, if the police give the witness "hints" to indicate which individual in the lineup is the perpetrator or the defendant, the lineup is constitutionally suspect and is likely to be excluded. On the other hand, if the court concludes that the witness was able to make an accurate identification even without the suggestiveness, the testimony will be allowed.

The following two cases involve identifications that were attacked for being unconstitutionally suggestive. In the first case, ***Foster***, the Supreme Court concluded that the lineup was impermissibly suggestive, whereas in the second case, ***Simmons***, the Supreme Court concluded that the photographic lineup was appropriate under the circumstances. As you read the two cases, ask yourself why the second identification passed constitutional muster but not the first one. What role in the analysis is played by the likelihood that the identification procedure will lead to a risk of misidentification?

Foster v. California

Supreme Court of the United States
394 U.S. 440 (1969)

Mr. Justice FORTAS delivered the opinion of the Court.

Petitioner was charged by information with the armed robbery of a Western Union office. . . . The day after the robbery one of the robbers, Clay, surrendered to the police and implicated Foster and Grice. Allegedly, Foster and Clay had entered the office while Grice waited in a car. Foster and Grice were tried together. Grice was acquitted. Foster was convicted. . . .

Except for the robbers themselves, the only witness to the crime was Joseph David, the late-night manager of the Western Union office. After Foster had been arrested, David was called to the police station to view a lineup. There were three men in the lineup. One was petitioner. He is a tall man—close to six feet in height. The other two men were short—five feet, five or six inches. Petitioner wore a leather jacket which David said was similar to the one he had seen underneath the coveralls worn by the robber. After seeing this lineup, David could not positively identify petitioner as the robber. He "thought" he was the man, but he was not sure. David then asked to speak to petitioner, and petitioner was brought into an office and sat across from David at a table. Except for prosecuting officials there was no one else in the room. Even after this one-to-one confrontation David still was uncertain whether petitioner was one of the robbers: "truthfully—I was not sure," he testified at trial. A week or 10 days later, the police arranged for David to view a second lineup. There were five men in that lineup. Petitioner was the only person in the second lineup who had appeared in the first lineup. This time David was "convinced" petitioner was the man.

At trial, David testified to his identification of petitioner in the lineups, as summarized above. He also repeated his identification of petitioner in the courtroom. The only other evidence against petitioner which concerned the particular robbery with which he was charged was the testimony of the alleged accomplice Clay.

In *United States v. Wade* and *Gilbert v. California*, this Court held that because of the possibility of unfairness to the accused in the way a lineup is conducted, a lineup is a "critical stage" in the prosecution, at which the accused must be given the opportunity to be represented by counsel. That holding does not, however, apply to petitioner's case, for the lineups in which he appeared occurred before June 12, 1967. But in declaring the rule of *Wade* and *Gilbert* to be applicable only to lineups conducted after those cases were decided, we recognized that, judged by the "totality of the circumstances," the conduct of identification procedures may be "so unnecessarily suggestive and conducive to irreparable mistaken identification" as to be a denial of due process of law. *Stovall v. Denno*, 388 U.S. 293, 302 (1967).

Judged by that standard, this case presents a compelling example of unfair lineup procedures. In the first lineup arranged by the police, petitioner stood out from the other two men by the contrast of his height and by the fact that he was wearing a leather jacket similar to that worn by the robber. When this did not lead to positive identification, the police permitted a one-to-one confrontation between petitioner and the witness. This Court pointed out in *Stovall* that "(t)he practice of showing suspects singly to persons for the purpose of identification, and not as part of a lineup, has been widely condemned." Even after this the witness' identification of petitioner was tentative. So some days later another lineup was arranged. Petitioner was the only person in this lineup who had also participated in the first lineup. This finally produced a definite identification.

The suggestive elements in this identification procedure made it all but inevitable that David would identify petitioner whether or not he was in fact "the man." In effect, the police repeatedly said to the witness, "This is the man." This procedure so undermined the reliability of the eyewitness identification as to violate due process. . . .

Mr. Justice Black, dissenting.

The Court here directs the California courts to set aside petitioner Foster's conviction for armed robbery of the Western Union Telegraph Co. at Fresno, California. The night manager of the telegraph company testified before the court and jury that two men came into the office just after midnight, January 25, 1966, wrote a note telling him it was a holdup, put it under his face, and demanded money, flashed guns, took $531 and fled. The night manager identified Foster in the courtroom as one of the men, and he also related his identification of Foster in a lineup a week or so after the crime. The manager's evidence, which no witness disputed, was corroborated by the testimony of a man named Clay, who was Foster's accomplice in the robbery and who testified for the State. The testimony of these two eyewitnesses was also corroborated by proof that Foster and another person had committed a prior armed robbery of a Western Union office in another city six years before, when they appeared at the company's office, presented a note to an employee announcing their holdup, flashed a gun, and fled with company money. In this case Foster's attorney admitted conviction for the prior Western Union armed robbery. The circumstances of the two robberies appear to have been practically indistinguishable. Such evidence that a particular person committed a prior crime has been almost universally accepted as relevant and admissible to prove that the same person was responsible for a later crime of the same nature. A narration of these facts, falling from the lips of eyewitnesses, and not denied by other eyewitnesses, would be enough, I am convinced, to persuade nearly all lawyers and judges, unhesitatingly to say, "There was clearly enough evidence of guilt here for a jury to convict the defendant since, according to practice, and indeed constitutional command, the weight of evidence is for a jury, and not for judges." Nevertheless the Court in this case looks behind the evidence given by witnesses on the stand and decides that because of the circumstances under which one witness first identified the defendant as the criminal, the United States Constitution requires that the conviction be reversed. . . .

Far more fundamental, however, is my objection to the Court's basic holding that evidence can be ruled constitutionally inadmissible whenever it results from identification procedures that the Court considers to be "unnecessarily suggestive and conducive to irreparable mistaken identification." One of the proudest achievements of this country's Founders was that they had eternally guaranteed a trial by jury in criminal cases, at least until the Constitution they wrote had been amended in the manner they prescribed. . . .

That means that the jury must, if we keep faith with the Constitution, be allowed to hear eyewitnesses and decide for itself whether it can recognize the truth and whether they are telling the truth. It means that the jury must be allowed to decide for itself whether the darkness of the night, the weakness of a witness' eyesight, or any other factor impaired the witness' ability to make an accurate identification. To take that power away from the jury is to rob it of the responsibility to perform the precise functions the Founders most wanted it to perform. And certainly a Constitution written to preserve this indispensable, unerodible core of our system for trying criminal cases would not have included, hidden among its provisions, a slumbering sleeper granting the judges license to destroy trial by jury in whole or in part.

This brings me to the constitutional theory relied upon by the Court to justify its invading the constitutional right of jury trial. The Court here holds that: "(j)udged by the 'totality of the circumstances,' the conduct of identification procedures may be 'so unnecessarily suggestive and conducive to irreparable mistaken identification' as to be a denial of due process of law. . . . Judged by that standard, this case presents a compelling example of unfair lineup procedures."

I do not deny that the "totality of circumstances" can be considered to determine whether some specific constitutional prohibitions have been violated, such, for example, as the Fifth Amendment's command against compelling a witness to incriminate himself. Whether evidence has been compelled is, of course, a triable issue of fact. And the constitutional command not to compel a person to be a witness against himself, like other issues of fact, must be determined by a resolution of all facts and the "totality" of them offered in evidence. Consequently were the Court's legal formula posed for application in a coerced testimony case, I could agree to it. But it is not. Instead the Court looks to the "totality of circumstances" to show "unfair lineup procedures." This means "unfair" according to the Court's view of what is unfair. The Constitution, however, does not anywhere prohibit conduct deemed unfair by the courts. . . .

The Constitution sets up its own standards of unfairness in criminal trials in the Fourth, Fifth, and Sixth Amendments, among other provisions of the Constitution. Many of these provisions relate to evidence and its

PROBLEM CASE

Consider the following case. Ellis Lee reported to the Baltimore police that he had been victimized in the following crime: "[I w]as sitting on the bus stop, the 36 bus stop on Northern Parkway and Alameda, had my phone in my right hand, checking my phone, and in the corner of my ear, I hear 'Let me get your money.' I looked to my immediate right. There's a male looking at me with a gun aimed towards me. I told him I don't have anything. . . . There was no wallet on me. He said, 'Run, bitch.' So he has a gun, so I ran." Lee heard a gunshot and was hit in the back of the leg.

Lee described the assailant to the police in the following terms: "[a] black male, light skin, believed he had seen him before, a light [T]-shirt, tattoo on the right side of his neck, 5'8', regular sized, a short haircut. He held the bottom of his shirt up over his face, blue jeans, block letter tattoo on neck, had a letter M in it."

A police detective constructed a photographic lineup with mugshots culled from a police database. Each mugshot was of a man with a short haircut. None of the photos included a tattoo except one, which had a neck tattoo with the letter M on it. Lee identified that photo as probably being of the perpetrator, noting that his level of certainty was about 80 percent.

The police detective then constructed a second photographic lineup. All of the photos were of males with neck tattoos. Some of the tattoos had letters on them while others did not. One of the photographs in the second lineup pictured a man who was included in the first lineup—this was the only photograph that was common to both photo lineups. Lee then positively identified that photograph as being the perpetrator. That individual, Malik Small, was then arrested and eventually convicted.

Was the photo lineup impermissibly suggestive? If yes, why? If not, why not? If the photo lineup was defective in some way, how should the police have conducted it? For more on this case, see *Small v. State*, 235 Md. App. 648, 180 A.3d 163 (2018).

use in criminal cases. The Constitution provides that the accused shall have the right to compulsory process for obtaining witnesses in his favor. It ordains that evidence shall not be obtained by compulsion of the accused. It ordains that the accused shall have the right to confront the witnesses against him. In these ways the Constitution itself dictates what evidence is to be excluded because it was improperly obtained or because it is not sufficiently reliable. But the Constitution does not give this Court any general authority to require exclusion of all evidence that this Court considers improperly obtained or that this Court considers insufficiently reliable. . . .

Simmons v. United States

Supreme Court of the United States
390 U.S. 377 (1968)

Mr. Justice HARLAN delivered the opinion of the Court.

This case presents issues arising out of the petitioners' trial and conviction in the United States District Court for the Northern District of Illinois for the armed robbery of a federally insured savings and loan association.

The evidence at trial showed that at about 1:45 P.M. on February 27, 1964, two men entered a Chicago savings and loan association. One of them pointed a gun at a teller and ordered her to put money into a sack which the gunman supplied. The men remained in the bank about five minutes. After they left, a bank employee rushed to the street and saw one of the men sitting on the passenger side of a departing white 1960 Thunderbird automobile with a large scrape on the right door. Within an hour police located in the vicinity a car matching this description. They discovered that it belonged to a Mrs. Rey, sister-in-law of petitioner Simmons. She told the police that she had loaned the car for the afternoon to her brother, William Andrews.

At about 5:15 P.M. the same day, two FBI agents came to the house of Mrs. Mahon, Andrews' mother, about half a block from the place where the car was then parked. The agents had no warrant, and at trial it was disputed whether Mrs. Mahon gave them permission to search the house. They did search, and in the basement they found two suitcases, of which Mrs. Mahon disclaimed any knowledge. One suitcase contained, among other items, a gun holster, a sack similar to the one used in the robbery, and several coin cards and bill wrappers from the bank which had been robbed.

The following morning the FBI obtained from another of Andrews' sisters some snapshots of Andrews and of petitioner Simmons, who was said by the sister to have been with Andrews the previous afternoon. These snapshots were shown to the five bank employees who had witnessed the robbery. Each witness identified pictures of Simmons as representing one of the robbers. A week or two later, three of these employees identified photographs of petitioner Garrett as depicting the other robber, the other two witnesses stating that they did not have a clear view of the second robber.

The petitioners, together with William Andrews, subsequently were indicted and tried for the robbery, as indicated. Just prior to the trial, Garrett moved to suppress the Government's exhibit consisting of the suitcase containing the incriminating items. In order to establish his standing so to move, Garrett testified that, although he could not identify the suitcase with certainty, it was similar to one he had owned, and that he was the owner of clothing found inside the suitcase. The District Court denied the motion to suppress. Garrett's testimony at the "suppression" hearing was admitted against him at trial.

During the trial, all five bank employee witnesses identified Simmons as one of the robbers. Three of them identified Garrett as the second robber, the other two testifying that they did not get a good look at the second robber. . . . The jury found Simmons and Garrett, as well as Andrews, guilty as charged. . . .

I

The facts as to the identification claim are these. As has been noted previously, FBI agents on the day following the robbery obtained from Andrews' sister a number of snapshots of Andrews and Simmons. There seem to have been at least six of these pictures, consisting mostly of group photographs of Andrews, Simmons, and others. Later the same day, these were shown to the five bank employees who had witnessed the robbery at their place of work, the photographs being exhibited to each employee separately. Each of the five employees identified Simmons from the photographs. At later dates, some of these witnesses were again interviewed by the FBI and shown indeterminate numbers of pictures. Again, all identified Simmons. At trial, the Government did not introduce any of the photographs, but relied upon in-court identification by the five eyewitnesses, each of whom swore that Simmons was one of the robbers.

In support of his argument, Simmons looks to last Term's "lineup" decisions—*United States v. Wade* and *Gilbert v. California*—in which this Court first departed from the rule that the manner of an extra-judicial identification affects only the weight, not the admissibility, of identification testimony at trial. The rationale of those cases was that an accused is entitled to counsel at any "critical stage of the prosecution," and that a post-indictment lineup is such a "critical stage." Simmons, however, does not contend that he was entitled to counsel at the time the pictures were shown to the witnesses. Rather, he asserts simply that in the circumstances the identification procedure was so unduly prejudicial as fatally to taint his conviction. This is a claim which must be evaluated in light of the totality of surrounding circumstances. Viewed in that context, we find the claim untenable.

It must be recognized that improper employment of photographs by police may sometimes cause witnesses to err in identifying criminals. A witness may have obtained only a brief glimpse of a criminal, or may have seen him under poor conditions. Even if the police subsequently follow the most correct photographic identification procedures and show him the pictures of a number of individuals without indicating whom they suspect, there is some danger that the witness may make an incorrect identification. This danger will be increased if the police display to the witness only the picture of a single individual who generally resembles the person he saw, or if they show him the pictures of several persons among which the photograph of a single such individual recurs or is in some way emphasized. The chance of misidentification is also heightened if the police indicate to the witness that they have other evidence that one of the persons pictured committed the crime. Regardless of how the initial misidentification comes about, the witness thereafter is apt to retain in his memory the image of the photograph rather than of the person actually seen, reducing the trustworthiness of subsequent lineup or courtroom identification.

Despite the hazards of initial identification by photograph, this procedure has been used widely and effectively in criminal law enforcement, from the standpoint both of apprehending offenders and of sparing innocent suspects the ignominy of arrest by allowing eyewitnesses to exonerate them through scrutiny of photographs. The danger that use of the technique may result in convictions based on misidentification may be substantially lessened by a course of cross-examination at trial which exposes to the jury the method's potential for error. We are unwilling to prohibit its employment, either in the exercise of our supervisory power or, still less, as a matter of constitutional requirement. Instead, we hold that each case must be considered on its own facts, and that convictions based on eyewitness identification at trial following a pretrial identification by photograph will be set aside on that ground only if the photographic identification procedure was so impermissibly suggestive as to give rise to a very substantial likelihood of irreparable misidentification. This standard accords with our resolution of a similar issue in *Stovall v. Denno*, 388 U.S. 293, 301-302, and with decisions of other courts on the question of identification by photograph.

Applying the standard to this case, we conclude that petitioner Simmons' claim on this score must fail. In the first place, it is not suggested that it was unnecessary for the FBI to resort to photographic identification in this instance. A serious felony had been committed. The perpetrators were still at large. The inconclusive clues which law enforcement officials possessed led to Andrews and Simmons. It was essential for the FBI agents swiftly to determine whether they were on the right track, so that they could properly deploy their forces in Chicago and, if necessary, alert officials in other cities. The justification for this method of procedure was hardly less compelling than that which we found to justify the "one-man lineup" in *Stovall v. Denno*.

In the second place, there was in the circumstances of this case little chance that the procedure utilized led to misidentification of Simmons. The robbery took place in the afternoon in a well-lighted bank. The robbers wore no masks. Five bank employees had been able to see the robber later identified as Simmons for periods ranging up to five minutes. Those witnesses were shown the photographs only a day later, while their memories were still fresh. At least six photographs were displayed to each witness. Apparently, these consisted primarily of group photographs, with Simmons and Andrews each appearing several times in the series. Each witness was alone when he or she saw the photographs. There is no evidence to indicate that the witnesses were told anything about the progress of the investigation, or that the FBI agents in any other way suggested which persons in the pictures were under suspicion.

Under these conditions, all five eyewitnesses identified Simmons as one of the robbers. None identified Andrews, who apparently was as prominent in the photographs as Simmons. These initial identifications were confirmed by all five witnesses in subsequent viewings of photographs and at trial, where each witness identified Simmons in person. Notwithstanding cross-examination, none of the witnesses displayed any doubt about their respective identifications of Simmons. Taken together, these circumstances leave little room for doubt that the identification of Simmons was correct, even though the identification procedure employed may have in some respects fallen short of the ideal. We hold that in the factual surroundings of this case the identification procedure used was not such as to deny Simmons due process of law or to call for reversal under our supervisory authority. . . .

NOTES & QUESTIONS ON SUGGESTIVE IDENTIFICATIONS

1. *Risk of misidentification.* According to *Simmons*, an identification procedure violates due process if it creates a "very substantial likelihood of irreparable misidentification." 390 U.S. at 384. Why was there a risk of misidentification in *Foster* but not in *Simmons*? The standard for this analysis is the totality of the surrounding circumstances. In *Simmons*, the Court found it unlikely that the photographic lineup procedure would lead to a misidentification. Do you agree?

2. *Necessary identifications.* In *Simmons*, the Court rejects the defendant's argument that the photographic lineup was unnecessary under the circumstances. Instead, the Court concludes that the photographic lineup was *necessary*. But what relevance does necessity have in this context? In *Stovall v. Denno*, 388 U.S. 293, 302 (1967), the Court said that the relevant inquiry was whether the lineup "was so unnecessarily suggestive and conducive to irreparable mistaken identification" that the defendant was denied due process of law. The concept of being "unnecessarily suggestive" implies that a lineup that is necessarily suggestive—in the sense of being unavoidable—is not unconstitutional. As one scholar noted, "[n]o matter how necessary an identification procedure might have been, if the procedure was suggestive and the identification not reliable, its admission at trial would violate the 'fundamental fairness' guaranteed by the Due Process clause." Ofer Raban, *On Suggestive and Necessary Identification Procedures*, 37 Am. J. Crim. L. 53, 57 (2009). But perhaps a necessarily suggestive identification procedure is simply one where the police would be doing the best that they can. It would also be a recognition that no lineup is perfect. In practical terms, what this means for the advocate is that a successful argument attacking an identification procedure should articulate what the police or prosecutors should have done differently during the identification procedure. If the lawyer cannot articulate that alternate scenario, the argument will fail.

STATE LAW REQUIREMENTS

Several states have passed statutes imposing specific guidelines for eyewitness identifications in order to limit the possibility of suggestiveness. Instead of merely evaluating the legitimacy of identification procedures by a trial judge ex post, these statutes impose ex ante regulations in order to codify best practices. The statutes impose different requirements for in-person lineups, photographic lineups, and showups.

For example, North Carolina's Eyewitness Identification Reform Act includes the following requirements:

> (1) A lineup shall be conducted by an independent administrator or by an alternative method. . . .
> (2) Individuals or photos shall be presented to witnesses sequentially, with each individual or photo presented to the witness separately, in a previously determined order, and removed after it is viewed before the next individual or photo is presented.
> (3) Before a lineup, the eyewitness shall be instructed that:
> a. The perpetrator might or might not be presented in the lineup,
> b. The lineup administrator does not know the suspect's identity,
> c. The eyewitness should not feel compelled to make an identification,
> d. It is as important to exclude innocent persons as it is to identify the perpetrator, and
> e. The investigation will continue whether or not an identification is made.

The eyewitness shall acknowledge the receipt of the instructions in writing. If the eyewitness refuses to sign, the lineup administrator shall note the refusal of the eyewitness to sign the acknowledgement and shall also sign the acknowledgement.

(4) In a photo lineup, the photograph of the suspect shall be contemporary and, to the extent practicable, shall resemble the suspect's appearance at the time of the offense.

(5) The lineup shall be composed so that the fillers generally resemble the eyewitness's description of the perpetrator, while ensuring that the suspect does not unduly stand out from the fillers. In addition:

a. All fillers selected shall resemble, as much as practicable, the eyewitness's description of the perpetrator in significant features, including any unique or unusual features.

b. At least five fillers shall be included in a photo lineup, in addition to the suspect.

c. At least five fillers shall be included in a live lineup, in addition to the suspect.

d. If the eyewitness has previously viewed a photo lineup or live lineup in connection with the identification of another person suspected of involvement in the offense, the fillers in the lineup in which the current suspect participates shall be different from the fillers used in any prior lineups.

(6) If there are multiple eyewitnesses, the suspect shall be placed in a different position in the lineup or photo array for each eyewitness.

(7) In a lineup, no writings or information concerning any previous arrest, indictment, or conviction of the suspect shall be visible or made known to the eyewitness.

(8) In a live lineup, any identifying actions, such as speech, gestures, or other movements, shall be performed by all lineup participants.

(9) In a live lineup, all lineup participants must be out of view of the eyewitness prior to the lineup.

(10) Only one suspect shall be included in a lineup.

(11) Nothing shall be said to the eyewitness regarding the suspect's position in the lineup or regarding anything that might influence the eyewitness's identification.

(12) The lineup administrator shall seek and document a clear statement from the eyewitness, at the time of the identification and in the eyewitness's own words, as to the eyewitness's confidence level that the person identified in a given lineup is the perpetrator. The lineup administrator shall separate all witnesses in order to discourage witnesses from conferring with one another before or during the procedure. Each witness shall be given instructions regarding the identification procedures without other witnesses present.

(13) If the eyewitness identifies a person as the perpetrator, the eyewitness shall not be provided any information concerning the person before the lineup administrator obtains the eyewitness's confidence statement about the selection. There shall not be anyone present during the live lineup or photographic identification procedures who knows the suspect's identity, except the eyewitness and counsel as required by law.

N.C. Gen. Stat. Ann. § 15A-284.52. Illinois, Maryland, Ohio, West Virginia, and Wisconsin have similar statutes. See, e.g., Ohio Rev. Code § 2933.83; Md. Code § 3-506.1(c)(1). These statutory requirements add an additional layer of protection beyond the federal constitutional requirements.

Pay particular attention to Requirement (13). It requires that the officials conducting the lineup not know the identity of the suspect.

This statutory requirement of ignorance ensures that the lineup will be "double-blind" so that the police officers cannot unconsciously, by words or actions, taint the identification by virtue of their knowledge of the "correct" answer.

Would the identifications in *Foster* and *Simmons* satisfy the North Carolina statute? More generally, what is the purpose of the more robust requirements in these state statutes? Is it to ensure the *accuracy* of eyewitness identification based on empirically validated scientific research, or simply fairness to the defendant? How do police detectives and prosecutors view these requirements—as an impediment to a successful investigation or a set of best practices for modern police work?

C. RELIABILITY

Just because an identification procedure is unnecessarily suggestive does not automatically render it inadmissible at trial. Indeed, in a series of cases, the Supreme Court was quick to clarify that unnecessarily suggestive identifications do not violate due process if the identification carried "indicia of reliability" that outweighed the "corrupting effect" of the suggestive circumstances. In other words, the ultimate test of admissibility is reliability: If the identification is assessed by the court as reliable, the unnecessary suggestiveness will not result in due process–based exclusion. For example, there might be situations where the police fail to construct a photographic lineup in the appropriate way—thus making it unnecessarily suggestive—but the rest of the circumstances suggest that the identification is highly reliable. If the factors pointing toward reliability far outweigh the factors pointing *against* reliability (because of the corrupting influence of police suggestion), there is room for a trial judge to permit the identification to be admitted as evidence. Obviously, this balancing test is fraught with difficulty and falls to the trial judge to administer without much guidance.

The following materials focus on: (1) the basic idea of reliability as a pathway to admission, notwithstanding police suggestion; and (2) what happens when an identification is made unreliable through no deliberate fault of the police.

1. Reliability as a Pathway to Admission

In the following case, the witness is a rape victim who participated in a police showup. Although the Court conceded that the showup was inherently and unnecessarily suggestive, the identification was admissible because the Court found little risk of misidentification. Why? What specifically about the crime, and the victim's identification of the perpetrator during the attack, convinced the Court that the risk of misidentification was so low? As you read the case, look for any guidance the Court gives lower courts in how to determine whether an identification might be reliable notwithstanding the suggestiveness of the identification procedure.

Neil v. Biggers

Supreme Court of the United States
409 U.S. 188 (1972)

Mr. Justice POWELL delivered the opinion of the Court.

In 1965, after a jury trial in a Tennessee court, respondent was convicted of rape and was sentenced to 20 years' imprisonment. The State's evidence consisted in part of testimony concerning a station-house identification of respondent by the victim. . . .

II

We proceed, then, to consider respondent's due process claim. As the claim turns upon the facts, we must first review the relevant testimony at the jury trial and at the habeas corpus hearing regarding the rape and the identification. The victim testified at trial that on the evening of January 22, 1965, a youth with a butcher knife grabbed her in the doorway to her kitchen. . . . When the victim screamed, her 12-year-old daughter came out of her bedroom and also began to scream. The assailant directed the victim to "tell her (the daughter) to shut up, or I'll kill you both." She did so, and was then walked at knifepoint about two blocks along a railroad track, taken into a woods, and raped there. She testified that "the moon was shining brightly, full moon." After the rape, the assailant ran off, and she returned home, the whole incident having taken between 15 minutes and half an hour.

She then gave the police what the Federal District Court characterized as "only a very general description," describing him as "being fat and flabby with smooth skin, bushy hair and a youthful voice." Additionally, though not mentioned by the District Court, she testified at the habeas corpus hearing that she had described her assailant as being between 16 and 18 years old and between five feet ten inches and six feet, tall, as weighing between 180 and 200 pounds, and as having a dark brown complexion. This testimony was substantially corroborated by that of a police officer who was testifying from his notes.

On several occasions over the course of the next seven months, she viewed suspects in her home or at the police station, some in lineups and others in showups, and was shown between 30 and 40 photographs. She told the police that a man pictured in one of the photographs had features similar to those of her assailant, but identified none of the suspects. On August 17, the police called her to the station to view respondent, who was being detained on another charge. In an effort to construct a suitable lineup, the police checked the city jail and the city juvenile home. Finding no one at either place fitting respondent's unusual physical description, they conducted a showup instead.

The showup itself consisted of two detectives walking respondent past the victim. At the victim's request, the police directed respondent to say "shut up or I'll kill you." The testimony at trial was not altogether clear as to whether the victim first identified him and then asked that he repeat the words or made her identification after he had spoken. In any event, the victim testified that she had "no doubt" about her identification. . . .

We must decide whether, as the courts below held, this identification and the circumstances surrounding it failed to comport with due process requirements.

III

We have considered on four occasions the scope of due process protection against the admission of evidence deriving from suggestive identification procedures. In *Stovall v. Denno*, 388 U.S. 293 (1967), the Court held that the defendant could claim that "the confrontation conducted . . . was so unnecessarily suggestive and conductive to irreparable mistaken identification that he was denied due process of law." This we held, must be determined "on the totality of the circumstances." We went on to find that on the facts of the case then before us, due process was not violated, emphasizing that the critical condition of the injured witness justified a showup in her hospital room. At trial, the witness, whose view of the suspect at the time of the crime was brief, testified to the out-of-court identification, as did several police officers present in her hospital room, and also made an in-court identification. . . .

The only case to date in which this Court has found identification procedures to be violative of due process is *Foster v. California*, 394 U.S. 440, 442 (1969). There, the witness failed to identify Foster the first time he confronted him, despite a suggestive lineup. The police then arranged a showup, at which the witness could make only a tentative identification. Ultimately, at yet another confrontation, this time a lineup, the witness was able to muster a definite identification. We held all of the identifications inadmissible, observing that the identifications were "all but inevitable" under the circumstances.

In the most recent case of *Coleman v. Alabama*, 399 U.S. 1 (1970), we held admissible an in-court identification by a witness who had a fleeting but "real good look" at his assailant in the headlights of a passing car. The witness testified at a pretrial suppression hearing that he identified one of the petitioners among the participants in the lineup before the police placed the participants in a formal line. Mr. Justice Brennan for four members of the Court stated that this evidence could support a finding that the in-court identification was "entirely based upon observations at the time of the assault and not at all induced by the conduct of the lineup."

Some general guidelines emerge from these cases as to the relationship between suggestiveness and misidentification. It is, first of all, apparent that the primary evil to be avoided is "a very substantial likelihood of irreparable misidentification." While the phrase was coined as a standard for determining whether an in-court identification would be admissible in the wake of a suggestive out-of-court identification, with the deletion of "irreparable" it serves equally well as a standard for the admissibility of testimony concerning the out-of-court identification itself. It is the likelihood of misidentification which violates a defendant's right to due process, and it is this which was the basis of the exclusion of evidence in *Foster*. Suggestive confrontations are disapproved because they increase the likelihood of misidentification, and unnecessarily suggestive ones are condemned for the further reason that the increased chance of misidentification is gratuitous. But as *Stovall* makes clear, the admission of evidence of a showup without more does not violate due process.

What is less clear from our cases is whether, as intimated by the District Court, unnecessary suggestiveness alone requires the exclusion of evidence. While we are inclined to agree with the courts below that the police did not exhaust all possibilities in seeking persons physically comparable to respondent, we do not think that the evidence must therefore be excluded. The purpose of a strict rule barring evidence of unnecessarily suggestive confrontations would be to deter the police from using a less reliable procedure where a more reliable one may be available, and would not be based on the assumption that in every instance the admission of evidence of such a confrontation offends due process. . . .

We turn, then, to the central question, whether under the "totality of the circumstances" the identification was reliable even though the confrontation procedure was suggestive. As indicated by our cases, the factors to be considered in evaluating the likelihood of misidentification include the opportunity of the witness to view the criminal at the time of the crime, the witness' degree of attention, the accuracy of the witness' prior description of the criminal, the level of certainty demonstrated by the witness at the confrontation, and the length of time between the crime and the confrontation. Applying these factors, we disagree with the District Court's conclusion.

In part, as discussed above, we think the District Court focused unduly on the relative reliability of a lineup as opposed to a showup, the issue on which expert testimony was taken at the evidentiary hearing. It must be kept in mind also that the trial was conducted before *Stovall* and that therefore the incentive was lacking for the parties to make a record at trial of facts corroborating or undermining the identification. The testimony was addressed to the jury, and the jury apparently found the identification reliable. Some of the State's testimony at the federal evidentiary hearing may well have been self-serving in that it too neatly fit the case law, but it surely does nothing to undermine the state record, which itself fully corroborated the identification.

We find that the District Court's conclusions on the critical facts are unsupported by the record and clearly erroneous. The victim spent a considerable period of time with her assailant, up to half an hour. She was with him under adequate artificial light in her house and under a full moon outdoors, and at least twice, once in the house and later in the woods, faced him directly and intimately. She was no casual observer, but rather the victim of one of the most personally humiliating of all crimes. Her description to the police, which included the assailant's approximate age, height, weight, complexion, skin texture, build, and voice, might not have satisfied Proust but was more than ordinarily thorough. She had "no doubt" that respondent was the person who raped her. In the nature of the crime, there are rarely witnesses to a rape other than the victim, who often has a limited opportunity of observation. The victim here, a practical nurse by profession, had an unusual opportunity to observe and identify her assailant. She testified at the habeas corpus hearing that there was something about his face "I don't think I could ever forget."

There was, to be sure, a lapse of seven months between the rape and the confrontation. This would be a seriously negative factor in most cases. Here, though, the testimony is undisputed that the victim made no previous identification at any of the showups, lineups, or photographic showings. Her record for reliability was thus a good one, as she had previously resisted whatever suggestiveness inheres in a showup. Weighing all the factors, we find no substantial likelihood of misidentification. The evidence was properly allowed to go to the jury.

The following case expands upon, and applies, the factors for determining reliability that were first announced in *Biggers*: (1) the opportunity to view; (2) the degree of attention; (3) the accuracy of the description; (4) the witness's level of certainty; and (5) the time between the crime and the confrontation. Pay particular attention to how the Court applies these indicia of reliability to the facts of the case. Why specifically was the identification in this case considered reliable? Finally, pay attention to the role that the Supreme Court assigns to juries to weigh the credibility of identifications that have some questionable feature. Do juries have the "good sense and judgment" to assess the defects of an identification? And is it comforting to know that "evidence with some element of untrustworthiness is customary grist for the jury mill"?

Manson v. Brathwaite

Supreme Court of the United States
432 U.S. 98 (1972)

Mr. Justice Blackmun delivered the opinion of the Court.

This case presents the issue as to whether the Due Process Clause of the Fourteenth Amendment compels the exclusion, in a state criminal trial, apart from any consideration of reliability, of pretrial identification evidence obtained by a police procedure that was both suggestive and unnecessary. This Court's decisions in *Stovall v. Denno* and *Neil v. Biggers* are particularly implicated.

Jimmy D. Glover, a full-time trooper of the Connecticut State Police, in 1970 was assigned to the Narcotics Division in an undercover capacity. On May 5 of that year, about 7:45 P.M., and while there was still daylight, Glover and Henry Alton Brown, an informant, went to an apartment building at 201 Westland, in Hartford, for the purpose of purchasing narcotics from "Dickie Boy" Cicero, a known narcotics dealer. Cicero, it was thought, lived on the third floor of that apartment building. Glover and Brown entered the building, observed by back-up Officers D'Onofrio and Gaffey, and proceeded by stairs to the third floor. Glover knocked at the door of one of the two apartments served by the stairway. The area was illuminated by natural light from a window in the third floor hallway. The door was opened 12 to 18 inches in response to the knock. Glover observed a man standing at the door and, behind him, a woman. Brown identified himself. Glover then asked for "two things" of narcotics. The man at the door held out his hand, and Glover gave him two $10 bills. The door closed. Soon the man returned and handed Glover two glassine bags. While the door was open, Glover stood within two feet of the person from whom he made the purchase and observed his face. Five to seven minutes elapsed from the time the door first opened until it closed the second time.

Glover and Brown then left the building. This was about eight minutes after their arrival. Glover drove to headquarters where he described the seller to D'Onofrio and Gaffey. Glover at that time did not know the identity of the seller. He described him as being "a colored man, approximately five feet eleven inches tall, dark complexion, black hair, short Afro style, and having high cheekbones, and of heavy build. He was wearing at the time blue pants and a plaid shirt." D'Onofrio, suspecting from this description that respondent might be the seller, obtained a photograph of respondent from the Records Division of the Hartford Police Department. He left it at Glover's office. D'Onofrio was not acquainted with respondent personally but did know him by sight and had seen him "(s)everal times" prior to May 5. Glover, when alone, viewed the photograph for the first time upon his return to headquarters on May 7; he identified the person shown as the one from whom he had purchased the narcotics. . . .

Respondent was arrested on July 27 while visiting at the apartment of a Mrs. Ramsey on the third floor of 201 Westland. This was the apartment at which the narcotics sale had taken place on May 5.

Respondent was charged, in a two-count information, with possession and sale of heroin. At his trial in January 1971, the photograph from which Glover had identified respondent was received in evidence without objection on the part of the defense. Glover also testified that, although he had not seen respondent in the eight months that had elapsed since the sale, "there (was) no doubt whatsoever" in his mind that the person shown on the photograph was respondent. Glover also made a positive in-court identification without objection.

No explanation was offered by the prosecution for the failure to utilize a photographic array or to conduct a lineup. . . .

. . . *Biggers* well might be seen to provide an unambiguous answer to the question before us: The admission of testimony concerning a suggestive and unnecessary identification procedure does not violate due process so long as the identification possesses sufficient aspects of reliability. In one passage, however, the Court observed that the challenged procedure occurred pre-*Stovall* and that a strict rule would make little sense with regard to a confrontation that preceded the Court's first indication that a suggestive procedure might lead to the exclusion of evidence. One perhaps might argue that, by implication, the Court suggested that a different rule could apply post-*Stovall*. The question before us, then, is simply whether the *Biggers* analysis applies to post-*Stovall* confrontations as well to those pre-*Stovall*. . . .

Petitioner at the outset acknowledges that "the procedure in the instant case was suggestive (because only one photograph was used) and unnecessary" (because there was no emergency or exigent circumstance). The respondent . . . proposes a per se rule of exclusion that he claims is dictated by the demands of the Fourteenth Amendment's guarantee of due process. He rightly observes that this is the first case in which this Court has had occasion to rule upon strictly post-*Stovall* out-of-court identification evidence of the challenged kind.

Since the decision in *Biggers*, the Courts of Appeals appear to have developed at least two approaches to such evidence. The first, or per se approach, employed by the Second Circuit in the present case, focuses on the procedures employed and requires exclusion of the out-of-court identification evidence, without regard to reliability, whenever it has been obtained through unnecessarily suggested confrontation procedures. The justifications advanced are the elimination of evidence of uncertain reliability, deterrence of the police and prosecutors, and the stated "fair assurance against the awful risks of misidentification."

The second, or more lenient, approach is one that continues to rely on the totality of the circumstances. It permits the admission of the confrontation evidence if, despite the suggestive aspect, the out-of-court identification possesses certain features of reliability. Its adherents feel that the per se approach is not mandated by the Due Process Clause of the Fourteenth Amendment. This second approach, in contrast to the other, is ad hoc and serves to limit the societal costs imposed by a sanction that excludes relevant evidence from consideration and evaluation by the trier of fact. . . .

The respondent here stresses the same theme and the need for deterrence of improper identification practice, a factor he regards as pre-eminent. Photographic identification, it is said, continues to be needlessly employed. He notes that the legislative regulation "the Court had hoped *Wade* would engender," has not been forthcoming. He argues that a totality rule cannot be expected to have a significant deterrent impact; only a strict rule of exclusion will have direct and immediate impact on law enforcement agents. Identification evidence is so convincing to the jury that sweeping exclusionary rules are required. Fairness of the trial is threatened by suggestive confrontation evidence, and thus, it is said, an exclusionary rule has an established constitutional predicate.

There are, of course, several interests to be considered and taken into account. . . . Usually the witness must testify about an encounter with a total stranger under circumstances of emergency or emotional stress. The witness' recollection of the stranger can be distorted easily by the circumstances or by later actions of the police. Thus, *Wade* and its companion cases reflect the concern that the jury not hear eyewitness testimony unless that evidence has aspects of reliability. It must be observed that both approaches before us are responsive to this concern. The per se rule goes too far since its application automatically and peremptorily, and without consideration of alleviating factors, keeps evidence from the jury that is reliable and relevant.

The second factor is deterrence. Although the per se approach has the more significant deterrent effect, the totality approach also has an influence on police behavior. The police will guard against unnecessarily suggestive procedures under the totality rule, as well as the per se one, for fear that their actions will lead to the exclusion of identifications as unreliable.

The third factor is the effect on the administration of justice. Here the per se approach suffers serious drawbacks. Since it denies the trier reliable evidence, it may result, on occasion, in the guilty going free. Also, because of its rigidity, the per se approach may make error by the trial judge more likely than the totality approach. And in those cases in which the admission of identification evidence is error under the per se approach but not under the totality approach cases in which the identification is reliable despite an unnecessarily suggestive identification procedure reversal is a Draconian sanction. Certainly, inflexible rules of exclusion that may frustrate rather than promote justice have not been viewed recently by this Court with unlimited enthusiasm. . . .

The standard, after all, is that of fairness as required by the Due Process Clause of the Fourteenth Amendment. *Stovall*, with its reference to "the totality of the circumstances," and *Biggers*, with its continuing stress on the same totality, did not, singly or together, establish a strict exclusionary rule or new standard of due process. . . .

We therefore conclude that reliability is the linchpin in determining the admissibility of identification testimony for both pre- and post-*Stovall* confrontations. The factors to be considered are set out in *Biggers*. These include the opportunity of the witness to view the criminal at the time of the crime, the witness' degree of attention, the accuracy of his prior description of the criminal, the level of certainty demonstrated at the confrontation, and the time between the crime and the confrontation. Against these factors is to be weighed the corrupting effect of the suggestive identification itself.

We turn, then, to the facts of this case and apply the analysis:

1. *The opportunity to view.* Glover testified that for two to three minutes he stood at the apartment door, within two feet of the respondent. The door opened twice, and each time the man stood at the door. The moments passed, the conversation took place, and payment was made. Glover looked directly at his vendor. It was near sunset, to be sure, but the sun had not yet set, so it was not dark or even dusk or twilight. Natural light from outside entered the hallway through a window. There was natural light, as well, from inside the apartment.

2. *The degree of attention.* Glover was not a casual or passing observer, as is so often the case with eyewitness identification. Trooper Glover was a trained police officer on duty and specialized and dangerous duty when he called at the third floor of 201 Westland in Hartford on May 5, 1970. Glover himself was a Negro and unlikely to perceive only general features of "hundreds of Hartford black males," as the Court of Appeals stated. It is true that Glover's duty was that of ferreting out narcotics offenders and that he would be expected in his work to produce results. But it is also true that, as a specially trained, assigned, and experienced officer, he could be expected to pay scrupulous attention to detail, for he knew that subsequently he would have to find and arrest his vendor. In addition, he knew that his claimed observations would be subject later to close scrutiny and examination at any trial.

3. *The accuracy of the description.* Glover's description was given to D'Onofrio within minutes after the transaction. It included the vendor's

race, his height, his build, the color and style of his hair, and the high cheekbone facial feature. It also included clothing the vendor wore. No claim has been made that respondent did not possess the physical characteristics so described. D'Onofrio reacted positively at once. Two days later, when Glover was alone, he viewed the photograph D'Onofrio produced and identified its subject as the narcotics seller.

4. *The witness' level of certainty.* There is no dispute that the photograph in question was that of respondent. Glover, in response to a question whether the photograph was that of the person from whom he made the purchase, testified: "There is no question whatsoever." This positive assurance was repeated.

5. *The time between the crime and the confrontation.* Glover's description of his vendor was given to D'Onofrio within minutes of the crime. The photographic identification took place only two days later. We do not have here the passage of weeks or months between the crime and the viewing of the photograph.

These indicators of Glover's ability to make an accurate identification are hardly outweighed by the corrupting effect of the challenged identification itself. Although identifications arising from single-photograph displays may be viewed in general with suspicion, we find in the instant case little pressure on the witness to acquiesce in the suggestion that such a display entails. D'Onofrio had left the photograph at Glover's office and was not present when Glover first viewed it two days after the event. There thus was little urgency and Glover could view the photograph at his leisure. And since Glover examined the photograph alone, there was no coercive pressure to make an identification arising from the presence of another. The identification was made in circumstances allowing care and reflection. . . .

Surely, we cannot say that under all the circumstances of this case there is "a very substantial likelihood of irreparable misidentification." Short of that point, such evidence is for the jury to weigh. We are content to rely upon the good sense and judgment of American juries, for evidence with some element of untrustworthiness is customary grist for the jury mill. Juries are not so susceptible that they cannot measure intelligently the weight of identification testimony that has some questionable feature.

Of course, it would have been better had D'Onofrio presented Glover with a photographic array including "so far as practicable . . . a reasonable number of persons similar to any person then suspected whose likeness is included in the array." The use of that procedure would have enhanced the force of the identification at trial and would have avoided the risk that the evidence would be excluded as unreliable. But we are not disposed to view D'Onofrio's failure as one of constitutional dimension to be enforced by a rigorous and unbending exclusionary rule. The defect, if there be one, goes to weight and not to substance.

We conclude that the criteria laid down in *Biggers* are to be applied in determining the admissibility of evidence offered by the prosecution concerning a post-Stovall identification, and that those criteria are satisfactorily met and complied with here. . . .

Mr. Justice MARSHALL, with whom Mr. Justice BRENNAN joins, dissenting.

Today's decision can come as no surprise to those who have been watching the Court dismantle the protections against mistaken eyewitness testimony erected a decade ago in *United States v. Wade*, *Gilbert v. California*, and *Stovall v. Denno*. But it is still distressing to see the Court virtually ignore the teaching of experience embodied in those decisions and blindly uphold the conviction of a defendant who may well be innocent. . . .

II

Apparently, the Court does not consider *Biggers* controlling in this case. I entirely agree, since I believe that *Biggers* was wrongly decided. The Court, however, concludes that *Biggers* is distinguishable because it, like the identification decisions that preceded it, involved a pre-*Stovall* confrontation, and because a paragraph in *Biggers* itself seems to distinguish between pre- and post-*Stovall* confrontations. Accordingly, in determining the admissibility of the post-*Stovall* identification in this case, the Court considers two alternatives, a per se exclusionary rule and a totality-of-the circumstances approach. The Court weighs three factors in deciding that the totality approach, which is essentially the test used in *Biggers*, should be applied. In my view, the Court wrongly evaluates the impact of these factors.

First, the Court acknowledges that one of the factors, deterrence of police use of unnecessarily suggestive identification procedures, favors the per se rule. Indeed, it does so heavily, for such a rule would make it unquestionably clear to the police they must never use a suggestive procedure when a fairer alternative is available. I have no doubt that conduct would quickly conform to the rule.

Second, the Court gives passing consideration to the dangers of eyewitness identification recognized in the *Wade* trilogy. It concludes, however, that the grave risk of error does not justify adoption of the per se approach because that would too often result in exclusion of relevant evidence. In my view, this conclusion totally ignores the lessons of *Wade*. The dangers of mistaken identification are, as *Stovall* held, simply too great to permit unnecessarily suggestive identifications. Neither *Biggers* nor the Court's opinion today points to any contrary empirical evidence. Studies since *Wade* have only reinforced the validity of its assessment of the dangers of identification testimony. While the Court is "content to rely on the good sense and judgment of American juries," the impetus for *Stovall* and *Wade* was repeated miscarriages of justice resulting from juries' willingness to credit inaccurate eyewitness testimony.

Finally, the Court errs in its assessment of the relative impact of the two approaches on the administration of justice. The Court relies most heavily on this factor, finding that "reversal is a Draconian sanction" in cases where the identification is reliable despite an unnecessarily suggestive procedure used to obtain it. Relying on little more than a strong distaste for "inflexible rules of exclusion," the Court rejects the per se test. In so doing, the Court disregards two significant distinctions between the per se rule advocated in this case and the exclusionary remedies for certain other constitutional violations.

First, the per se rule here is not "inflexible." Where evidence is suppressed, for example, as the fruit of an unlawful search, it may well be forever lost to the prosecution. Identification evidence, however, can by its very nature be readily and effectively reproduced. The in-court identification, permitted under *Wade* and *Simmons* if it has a source independent of an uncounseled or suggestive procedure, is one example. Similarly, when a prosecuting attorney learns that there has been a suggestive confrontation, he can easily arrange another lineup conducted under scrupulously fair conditions. Since the same factors are evaluated in applying both the Court's totality test and the *Wade-Simmons* independent-source inquiry, any identification which is "reliable" under the Court's test will support admission of evidence concerning such a fairly conducted lineup. The evidence of an additional, properly conducted confrontation will be more persuasive to a jury, thereby increasing the chance of a justified conviction where a reliable identification was tainted by a suggestive confrontation. At the same time, however, the effect of an unnecessarily suggestive identification which has no value whatsoever in the law enforcement process will be completely eliminated.

Second, other exclusionary rules have been criticized for preventing jury consideration of relevant and usually reliable evidence in order to serve interest unrelated to guilt or innocence, such as discouraging illegal searches or denial of counsel. Suggestively obtained eyewitness testimony is excluded, in contrast, precisely because of its unreliability and concomitant irrelevance. Its exclusion both protects the integrity of the truth-seeking function of the trial and discourages police use of needlessly inaccurate and ineffective investigatory methods.

Indeed, impermissibly suggestive identifications are not merely worthless law enforcement tools. They pose a grave threat to society at large in a more direct way than most governmental disobedience of the law. For if the police and the public erroneously conclude, on the basis of an unnecessarily suggestive confrontation, that the right man has been caught and convicted, the real outlaw must still remain at large. Law enforcement has failed in its primary function and has left society unprotected from the depredations of an active criminal.

For these reasons, I conclude that adoption of the per se rule would enhance, rather than detract from, the effective administration of justice. In my view, the Court's totality test will allow seriously unreliable and misleading evidence to be put before juries. Equally important, it will allow dangerous criminals to remain on the streets while citizens assume that police action has given them protection. According to my calculus, all three of the factors upon which the Court relies point to acceptance of the per se approach. . . .

III

Despite my strong disagreement with the Court over the proper standards to be applied in this case, I am pleased that its application of the totality test does recognize the continuing vitality of *Stovall*. In assessing the reliability of the identification, the Court mandates weighing "the corrupting effect of the suggestive identification itself" against the "indicators of (a witness') ability to make an accurate identification." The Court holds, as *Neil v. Biggers* failed to, that a due process identification inquiry must take account of the suggestiveness of a confrontation and the likelihood that it led to misidentification, as recognized in *Stovall* and *Wade*. Thus, even if a witness did have an otherwise adequate opportunity to view a criminal, the later use of a highly suggestive identification procedure can render his testimony inadmissible. Indeed, it is my view that, assuming applicability of the totality test enunciated by the Court, the facts of the present case require that result. . . .

The use of a single picture (or the display of a single live suspect, for that matter) is a grave error, of course, because it dramatically suggests to the witness that the person shown must be the culprit. Why else would the police choose the person? And it is deeply ingrained in human nature to agree with the expressed opinions of others particularly others who should be more knowledgeable when making a difficult decision. In this case, moreover, the pressure was not limited to that inherent in the display of a single photograph. Glover, the identifying witness, was a state police officer on special assignment. He knew that D'Onofrio, an experienced Hartford narcotics detective, presumably familiar with local drug operations, believed respondent to be the seller. There was at work, then, both loyalty to another police officer and deference to a better-informed colleague. Finally, of course, there was Glover's knowledge that without an identification and arrest, government funds used to buy heroin had been wasted. . . .

I must conclude that this record presents compelling evidence that there was "a very substantial likelihood of misidentification" of respondent Brathwaite. The suggestive display of respondent's photograph to the witness Glover likely erased any independent memory that Glover had retained of the seller from his barely adequate opportunity to observe the criminal. . . .

NOTES & QUESTIONS ON INDICIA OF RELIABILITY

1. *The five factors.* In *Manson v. Brathwaite,* the Court offered five factors to guide the reliability analysis. The balancing process is clear. First, the trial judge is supposed to assess the degree of suggestiveness in the identification procedure. Part of that analysis is whether the suggestiveness was unnecessary. If the judge finds suggestiveness, he or she should then consider the overall reliability of the identification, using the five factors outlined in *Manson v. Brathwaite.* If those factors are sufficiently weighty so as to outweigh the risk of misidentification posed by the suggestiveness of the identification procedure, then the identification should be presented to the jury. The jury may consider any defects in the identification procedure but should not be barred from hearing the evidence. If, on the other hand, the five factors do not weigh the corrupting impact of the suggestiveness, then the identification should be suppressed and kept from the jury.

2. *Juries.* How much should trial judges trust juries to consider for themselves the corrupting influence of a defective identification? Empirical research shows that eyewitness identification is generally untrustworthy—even in situations where the identification procedure is not defective. (This issue will be explored in greater detail in the Practice & Policy section below.) Despite the inherent unreliability in eyewitness identifications, juries tend to exaggerate their significance and will be more encouraged to convict a defendant when there is eyewitness testimony identifying the defendant as the perpetrator. Does this fact suggest that the *Manson v. Brathwaite* factors should be tightened up so that fewer compromised identifications reach the jury? Or should judges simply take the empirical research into account when they *apply* the five *Manson v. Brathwaite* factors?

STATE LAW REQUIREMENTS

Not all states have followed the rule from *Brathwaite.* For example, Massachusetts maintains a per se exclusion rule for unnecessarily suggestive identifications, regardless of whether or not the identification is reliable under the totality of the circumstances. Although Due Process Clause of the Fourteenth Amendment does not mandate suppression of these identifications as a matter of the federal constitution, states are free to impose stricter requirements under state law, either constitutional or statutory.

Massachusetts courts have consistently rejected the reasoning in *Brathwaite* and have held that suppression is always required under article 12 of the Declaration of Rights of the Massachusetts Constitution when an identification was impermissibly suggestive:

> Our past resistance to the so-called reliability test reflects this court's concern that the dangers present whenever eyewitness evidence is introduced against an accused require the utmost protection against mistaken identifications. There is no question that the danger of mistaken identification by a victim or a witness poses a real threat to the truth-finding process of criminal trials. Indeed, mistaken identification is believed widely to be the primary cause of erroneous convictions. Compounding this problem is the tendency of juries to be unduly receptive to eyewitness evidence. . . .

Commonwealth v. Johnson, 420 Mass. 458, 465, 650 N.E.2d 1257, 1261 (1995). It should be noted that the majority of states that have considered the issue under state law have followed and incorporated the federal rule from *Brathwaite*.

New Jersey has adopted a unique approach. Under the New Jersey State Constitution, "when defendants can show some evidence of suggestiveness, all relevant system and estimator variables should be explored at pretrial hearings." *State v. Henderson,* 208 N.J. 208, 218, 27 A.3d 872, 878 (2011). This holding switched the New Jersey jurisprudence, which had been in line with *Brathwaite* in allowing reliability issues to be considered by a court only if the defendant had carried the burden to demonstrate suggestiveness.

Estimator variables are factors "beyond the control of the criminal justice system." According to the New Jersey Supreme Court, estimator variables "include factors related to the incident, the witness, or the perpetrator. Estimator variables are equally capable of affecting an eyewitness' ability to perceive and remember an event. Although the factors can be isolated and tested in lab experiments, they occur at random in the real world." *Id.* at 261, 27 A.3d at 904.

Under *Henderson,* trial judges are directed to always consider estimator variables and evaluate reliability, regardless of whether the defendant has established that the identification procedure was impermissibly suggestive:

> Remedying the problems with the current . . . test requires an approach that addresses its shortcomings: one that allows judges to consider all relevant factors that affect reliability in deciding whether an identification is admissible; that is not heavily weighted by factors that can be corrupted by suggestiveness; that promotes deterrence in a meaningful way; and that focuses on helping jurors both understand and evaluate the effects that various factors have on memory—because we recognize that most identifications will be admitted in evidence. Two principal changes to the current system are needed to accomplish that: first, the revised framework should allow all relevant system and estimator variables to be explored and weighed at pretrial hearings when there is some actual evidence of suggestiveness; and second, courts should develop and use enhanced jury charges to help jurors evaluate eyewitness identification evidence.

Id. at 288, 27 A.3d at 919. This departs significantly from the *Manson v. Brathwaite* sequence, which requires that courts make a finding that the procedure was impermissibly suggestive before moving to a second stage of the analysis focused on reliability.

2. Unreliable Identifications Without Police Misconduct

In the cases discussed above, the Court weighs reliability against suggestiveness in situations where the suggestiveness was the product of police misconduct. In most cases of police misconduct, the value of suppression is based on multiple goals: keeping unreliable evidence from the jury's consideration but also deterring police from misconduct during *future* identification procedures. In contrast, what rule should govern suggestive identifications that are the result not of police misconduct but simply of unfortunate circumstance? In other words, once one subtracts the value of deterrence, should suppression be ordered automatically or should a trial judge use a more flexible standard? In the following case, the Supreme Court answers this question.

Perry v. New Hampshire

Supreme Court of the United States
565 U.S. 228 (2012)

Justice GINSBURG delivered the opinion of the Court.

In our system of justice, fair trial for persons charged with criminal offenses is secured by the Sixth Amendment, which guarantees to defendants the right to counsel, compulsory process to obtain defense witnesses, and the opportunity to cross-examine witnesses for the prosecution. Those safeguards apart, admission of evidence in state trials is ordinarily governed by state law, and the reliability of relevant testimony typically falls within the province of the jury to determine. This Court has recognized, in addition, a due process check on the admission of eyewitness identification, applicable when the police have arranged suggestive circumstances leading the witness to identify a particular person as the perpetrator of a crime.

An identification infected by improper police influence, our case law holds, is not automatically excluded. Instead, the trial judge must screen the evidence for reliability pretrial. If there is "a very substantial likelihood of irreparable misidentification," *Simmons v. United States*, 390 U.S. 377, 384 (1968), the judge must disallow presentation of the evidence at trial. But if the indicia of reliability are strong enough to outweigh the corrupting effect of the police-arranged suggestive circumstances, the identification evidence ordinarily will be admitted, and the jury will ultimately determine its worth.

We have not extended pretrial screening for reliability to cases in which the suggestive circumstances were not arranged by law enforcement officers. Petitioner requests that we do so because of the grave risk that mistaken identification will yield a miscarriage of justice. Our decisions, however, turn on the presence of state action and aim to deter police from rigging identification procedures, for example, at a lineup, showup, or photograph array. When no improper law enforcement activity is involved, we hold, it suffices to test reliability through the rights and opportunities generally designed for that purpose, notably, the presence of counsel at postindictment lineups, vigorous cross-examination, protective rules of evidence, and jury instructions on both the fallibility of eyewitness identification and the requirement that guilt be proved beyond a reasonable doubt.

I

Around 3 A.M. on August 15, 2008, Joffre Ullon called the Nashua, New Hampshire, Police Department and reported that an African-American male was trying to break into cars parked in the lot of Ullon's apartment building. Officer Nicole Clay responded to the call. Upon arriving at the parking lot, Clay heard what "sounded like a metal bat hitting the ground." She then saw petitioner Barion Perry standing between two cars. Perry walked toward Clay, holding two car-stereo amplifiers in his hands. A metal bat lay on the ground behind him. Clay asked Perry where the amplifiers came from. "[I] found them on the ground," Perry responded.

Meanwhile, Ullon's wife, Nubia Blandon, woke her neighbor, Alex Clavijo, and told him she had just seen someone break into his car. Clavijo immediately went downstairs to the parking lot to inspect the car. He first observed that one of the rear windows had been shattered. On further inspection, he discovered that the speakers and amplifiers from his car stereo were missing, as were his bat and wrench. Clavijo then approached Clay and told her about Blandon's alert and his own subsequent observations.

By this time, another officer had arrived at the scene. Clay asked Perry to stay in the parking lot with that officer, while she and Clavijo went to talk to Blandon. Clay and Clavijo then entered the apartment building and took the stairs to the fourth floor, where Blandon's and Clavijo's apartments were located. They met Blandon in the hallway just outside the open door to her apartment.

Asked to describe what she had seen, Blandon stated that, around 2:30 A.M., she saw from her kitchen window a tall, African-American man roaming the parking lot and looking into cars. Eventually, the man circled Clavijo's car, opened the trunk, and removed a large box.

Clay asked Blandon for a more specific description of the man. Blandon pointed to her kitchen window and said the person she saw breaking into Clavijo's car was standing in the parking lot, next to the police officer. Perry's arrest followed this identification.

About a month later, the police showed Blandon a photographic array that included a picture of Perry and asked her to point out the man who had broken into Clavijo's car. Blandon was unable to identify Perry.

Perry was charged in New Hampshire state court with one count of theft by unauthorized taking and one count of criminal mischief. Before trial, he moved to suppress Blandon's identification on the ground that admitting it at trial would violate due process. Blandon witnessed what amounted to a one-person showup in the parking lot, Perry asserted, which all but guaranteed that she would identify him as the culprit. . . .

II

The Constitution, our decisions indicate, protects a defendant against a conviction based on evidence of questionable reliability, not by prohibiting introduction of the evidence, but by affording the defendant means to persuade the jury that the evidence should be discounted as unworthy of credit. Constitutional safeguards available to defendants to counter the State's evidence include the Sixth Amendment rights to counsel. . . . Apart from these guarantees, we have recognized, state and federal statutes and rules ordinarily govern the admissibility of evidence, and juries are assigned the task of determining the reliability of the evidence presented at trial. Only when evidence "is so extremely unfair that its admission violates fundamental conceptions of justice," have we imposed a constraint tied to the Due Process Clause. . . .

Perry concedes that, in contrast to every case in the *Stovall* line, law enforcement officials did not arrange the suggestive circumstances surrounding Blandon's identification. He contends, however, that it was mere happenstance that each of the *Stovall* cases involved improper police action. The rationale underlying our decisions, Perry asserts, supports a rule requiring trial judges to prescreen eyewitness evidence for reliability any time an identification is made under suggestive circumstances. We disagree.

Perry's argument depends, in large part, on the Court's statement in *Brathwaite* that "reliability is the linchpin in determining the admissibility of identification testimony." If reliability is the linchpin of admissibility under the Due Process Clause, Perry maintains, it should make no difference whether law enforcement was responsible for creating the suggestive circumstances that marred the identification.

Perry has removed our statement in *Brathwaite* from its mooring, and thereby attributes to the statement a meaning a fair reading of our opinion does not bear. As just explained, the *Brathwaite* Court's reference to reliability appears in a portion of the opinion concerning the appropriate remedy when the police use an unnecessarily suggestive identification procedure. The Court adopted a judicial screen for reliability as a course preferable to a per se rule requiring exclusion of identification evidence whenever law enforcement officers employ an improper procedure. The due process check for reliability, *Brathwaite* made plain, comes into play only after the defendant establishes improper police conduct. The very purpose of the check, the Court noted, was to avoid depriving the jury of identification evidence that is reliable, notwithstanding improper police conduct.

Perry's contention that improper police action was not essential to the reliability check *Brathwaite* required is echoed by the dissent. Both ignore a key premise of the *Brathwaite* decision: A primary aim of excluding identification evidence obtained under unnecessarily suggestive circumstances, the Court said, is to deter law enforcement use of improper lineups, showups, and photo arrays in the first place. Alerted to the prospect that identification evidence improperly obtained may be excluded, the Court reasoned, police officers will "guard against unnecessarily suggestive procedures." This deterrence rationale is inapposite in cases, like Perry's, in which the police engaged in no improper conduct. . . .

Perry's argument . . . would open the door to judicial preview, under the banner of due process, of most, if not all, eyewitness identifications. External suggestion is hardly the only factor that casts doubt on the trustworthiness of an eyewitness' testimony. . . . [M]any other factors bear on "the likelihood of misidentification"—for example, the passage of time between exposure to and identification of the defendant, whether the witness was under stress when he first encountered the suspect, how much time the witness had to observe the suspect, how far the witness was from the suspect, whether the suspect carried a weapon, and the race of the suspect and the witness. There is no reason why an identification made by an eyewitness with poor vision, for example, or one who harbors a grudge against the defendant, should be regarded as inherently more reliable, less of a "threat to the fairness of trial," than the identification Blandon made in this case. To embrace Perry's view would thus entail a vast enlargement of the reach of due process as a constraint on the admission of evidence.

Perry maintains that the Court can limit the due process check he proposes to identifications made under "suggestive circumstances." Even if we could rationally distinguish suggestiveness from other factors bearing on the reliability of eyewitness evidence, Perry's limitation would still involve trial courts, routinely, in preliminary examinations. Most eyewitness identifications involve some element of suggestion. Indeed, all in-court identifications do. Out-of-court identifications volunteered by witnesses are also likely to involve suggestive circumstances. For example, suppose a witness identifies the defendant to police officers after seeing a photograph of the defendant in the press captioned "theft suspect," or hearing a radio report implicating the defendant in the crime. Or suppose the witness knew that the defendant ran with the wrong crowd and saw him on the day and in the vicinity of the crime. Any of these circumstances might have "suggested" to the witness that the defendant was the person the witness observed committing the crime.

In urging a broadly applicable due process check on eyewitness identifications, Perry maintains that eyewitness identifications are a uniquely unreliable form of evidence. We do not doubt either the importance or the fallibility of eyewitness identifications. Indeed, in recognizing that defendants have a constitutional right to counsel at postindictment police lineups, we observed that "the annals of criminal law are rife with instances of mistaken identification."

We have concluded in other contexts, however, that the potential unreliability of a type of evidence does not alone render its introduction at the defendant's trial fundamentally unfair. We reach a similar conclusion here: The fallibility of eyewitness evidence does not, without the taint of improper state conduct, warrant a due process rule requiring a trial court to screen such evidence for reliability before allowing the jury to assess its creditworthiness.

Our unwillingness to enlarge the domain of due process as Perry and the dissent urge rests, in large part, on our recognition that the jury, not the judge, traditionally determines the reliability of evidence. We also take account of other safeguards built into our adversary system that caution juries against placing undue weight on eyewitness testimony of questionable reliability. These protections include the defendant's Sixth Amendment right to confront the eyewitness. Another is the defendant's right to the effective assistance of an attorney, who can expose the flaws in the eyewitness' testimony during cross-examination and focus the jury's attention on the fallibility of such testimony during opening and closing arguments. Eyewitness-specific jury instructions, which many federal and state courts have adopted, likewise warn the jury to take care in appraising identification evidence. The constitutional requirement that the government prove the defendant's guilt beyond a reasonable doubt also impedes convictions based on dubious identification evidence.

State and federal rules of evidence, moreover, permit trial judges to exclude relevant evidence if its probative value is substantially outweighed by its prejudicial impact or potential for misleading the jury. In appropriate cases, some States also permit defendants to present expert testimony on the hazards of eyewitness identification evidence.

Many of the safeguards just noted were at work at Perry's trial. . . . Given the safeguards generally applicable in criminal trials, protections availed of by the defense in Perry's case, we hold that the introduction of Blandon's eyewitness testimony, without a preliminary judicial assessment of its reliability, did not render Perry's trial fundamentally unfair. . . .

Justice Sotomayor, dissenting.

This Court has long recognized that eyewitness identifications' unique confluence of features—their unreliability, susceptibility to suggestion, powerful impact on the jury, and resistance to the ordinary tests of the adversarial process—can undermine the fairness of a trial. Our cases thus establish a clear rule: The admission at trial of out-of-court eyewitness identifications derived from impermissibly suggestive circumstances that pose a very substantial likelihood of misidentification violates due process. The Court today announces that that rule does not even "com[e] into play" unless the suggestive circumstances are improperly "police-arranged."

Our due process concern, however, arises not from the act of suggestion, but rather from the corrosive effects of suggestion on the reliability of the resulting identification. By rendering protection contingent on improper police arrangement of the suggestive circumstances, the Court effectively grafts a mens rea inquiry onto our rule. The Court's holding enshrines a murky distinction—between suggestive confrontations intentionally orchestrated by the police and, as here, those inadvertently caused by police actions—that will sow confusion. It ignores our precedents' acute sensitivity to the hazards of intentional and unintentional suggestion alike and unmoors our rule from the very interest it protects, inviting arbitrary results. And it recasts the driving force of our decisions as an interest in police deterrence, rather than reliability. Because I see no warrant for declining to assess the circumstances of this case under our ordinary approach, I respectfully dissent. . . .

Our precedents make no distinction between intentional and unintentional suggestion. To the contrary, they explicitly state that "[s]uggestion can be created intentionally or unintentionally in many subtle ways." Rather than equate suggestive conduct with misconduct, we specifically have disavowed the assumption that suggestive influences may only be "the result of police procedures intentionally designed to prejudice an accused." . . . The implication is that even police acting with the best of intentions can inadvertently signal "that's the man." . . .

More generally, our precedents focus not on the act of suggestion, but on suggestion's "corrupting effect" on reliability. Eyewitness evidence derived from suggestive circumstances, we have explained, is uniquely resistant to the ordinary tests of the adversary process. An eyewitness who has made an identification often becomes convinced of its accuracy. "Regardless of how the initial misidentification comes about, the witness thereafter is apt to retain in his memory the image of the photograph rather than of the person actually seen, reducing the trustworthiness of subsequent . . . courtroom identification." Suggestion bolsters that confidence.

At trial, an eyewitness' artificially inflated confidence in an identification's accuracy complicates the jury's task of assessing witness credibility and reliability. It also impairs the defendant's ability to attack the eyewitness' credibility. That in turn jeopardizes the defendant's basic right to subject his accuser to meaningful cross-examination. The end result of suggestion, whether intentional or unintentional, is to fortify testimony bearing directly on guilt that juries find extremely convincing and are hesitant to discredit. . . .

The majority today creates a novel and significant limitation on our longstanding rule: Eyewitness identifications so impermissibly suggestive that they pose a very substantial likelihood of an unreliable identification will be deemed inadmissible at trial only if the suggestive circumstances were "police-arranged." . . . I cannot agree.

The majority does not simply hold that an eyewitness identification must be the product of police action to trigger our ordinary two-step inquiry. Rather, the majority maintains that the suggestive circumstances giving rise to the identification must be "police-arranged," "police rigg[ed]," "police-designed," or "police-organized." Those terms connote a degree of intentional orchestration or manipulation. The majority categorically exempts all eyewitness identifications derived from suggestive circumstances that were not police-manipulated—however suggestive, and however unreliable—from our due process check. The majority thus appears to graft a mens rea requirement onto our existing rule.

As this case illustrates, police intent is now paramount. As the Court acknowledges, Perry alleges an "accidental showup." He was the only African-American at the scene of the crime standing next to a police officer. For the majority, the fact that the police did not intend that showup, even if they inadvertently caused it in the course of a police procedure, ends the inquiry. The police were questioning the eyewitness, Blandon, about the perpetrator's identity, and were intentionally detaining Perry in the parking lot—but had not intended for Blandon to identify the perpetrator from her window. Presumably, in the majority's view, had the police asked Blandon to move to the window to identify the perpetrator, that could have made all the difference.

I note, however, that the majority leaves what is required by its arrangement-focused inquiry less than clear. In parts, the opinion suggests that the police must arrange an identification "procedure," regardless of whether they "inten[d] the arranged procedure to be suggestive." Elsewhere, it indicates that the police must arrange the "suggestive circumstances" that lead the witness to identify the accused. Still elsewhere it refers to "improper" police conduct, connoting bad faith. Does police "arrangement" relate to the procedure, the suggestiveness, or both? If it relates to the procedure, do suggestive preprocedure encounters no longer raise the same concerns? If the police need not "inten[d] the arranged procedure to be suggestive," what makes the police action "improper"? And does that mean that good-faith, unintentional police suggestiveness in a police-arranged lineup can be "impermissibly suggestive"? . . .

The empirical evidence demonstrates that eyewitness misidentification is "the single greatest cause of wrongful convictions in this country." Researchers have found that a staggering 76% of the first 250 convictions overturned due to DNA evidence since 1989 involved eyewitness misidentification. Study after study demonstrates that eyewitness recollections are highly susceptible to distortion by postevent information or social cues; that jurors routinely overestimate the accuracy of eyewitness identifications; that jurors place the greatest weight on eyewitness confidence in assessing identifications even though confidence is a poor gauge of accuracy; and that suggestiveness can stem from sources beyond police-orchestrated procedures. The majority today nevertheless adopts an artificially narrow conception of the dangers of suggestive identifications at a time when our concerns should have deepened. . . .

NOTES & QUESTIONS ON SUGGESTIVENESS WITHOUT POLICE MISCONDUCT

1. *Police misconduct.* What is your assessment of the showup identification in *Perry*? Were the police at fault for creating the suggestive circumstances of the identification? The witness looked out her window and saw the police speaking with the man that she identified as the perpetrator of the robbery. Obviously, the showup was suggestive because the man was already talking with the police, suggesting that the police independently believed that the man was involved in the crime that they were investigating. Of course, this was a mere suggestion; it is possible that the police were simply speaking with another witness. But it is not unreasonable to conclude that the witness identification was tainted by the interaction she saw below her window; it is certainly possible, even likely, that the police were conducting the interview because Perry was a suspect. Could the police have done something differently to avoid this suggestiveness? Should they have prevented the witness from looking out the window until they could craft a more neutral showup?

2. *Deterrence.* Is there any deterrent rationale for excluding the identification in *Perry*? Is it possible that suppression might help eliminate cases of reckless or negligent lineups (which would still fall under the rubric of unintentional suggestiveness)? Do you agree with Justice Sotomayor that the majority's definition of "improper" police conduct remains elusive?

D. PRACTICE & POLICY

Although juries often consider an eyewitness identification as the "gold standard" of evidence that will move them to convict a defendant, empirical research has shown that eyewitness identifications are far less reliable than many had previously believed. The following materials focus on the reasons why eyewitness identifications are fallible and what, if anything, the criminal process can do to both limit the risk of misidentifications and appropriately calibrate expectations and assumptions about the value of eyewitness identifications. Most of these issues were explored in exhaustive detail in a pathbreaking

New Jersey case on the value of eyewitness identifications, *State v. Henderson*, 208 N.J. 208 (2011), which broke down the relevant problems into the following categories:

Blind administration. Police officers and prosecutors, even if they are well intentioned, might unintentionally render an identification procedure suggestive by subtly and unconsciously giving hints to the witness about the "correct" answer. The empirical literature on this effect is mixed, with some studies showing a significant risk of contamination and others showing only a modest effect. As one researcher noted, "[i]n consideration of the difficulty in observing an effect of experimenter knowledge and the variability of the effects obtained in earlier studies, we hypothesized that lineup procedures that increase choosing rates may increase the effects of administrator knowledge of the suspect's identity on identification accuracy. Lineup administrators who know the identity of a suspect may steer the witness to the suspect, either intentionally or unintentionally, but only under conditions that promote guessing among witnesses." Sarah M. Greathouse & Margaret Bull Kovera, *Instruction Bias and Lineup Presentation Moderate the Effects of Administrator Knowledge on Eyewitness Identification*, 33 Law & Hum. Behav. 70, 72 (2009). However, the costs of implementing a "double blind" system are very low, so there is little reason for police officers to use independent officers to conduct lineups, even if it only prevents misidentification in a small subset of cases.

Pre-identification instructions. Sometimes, the instructions prior to the lineup cause problems. For example, a witness might assume (reasonably) that the suspect is among the individuals present in the lineup or pictured in the photo lineup. With that assumption, the correct process from the witness's perspective is to select the individual in the lineup who looks *most* like the perpetrator. However, similarity is not the same thing as a positive identification. It might be the case that none of the individuals in the lineup is the perpetrator; in that scenario, selecting the closest match will yield a misidentification. As one researcher noted, "the effects of biased instructions were quite different for target-present (TP) lineups versus target-absent (TA) lineups. . . . [B]iased instructions produced a large, consistent decrease in the correct rejection rate for target-absent lineups, but inconsistent effects on correct identification rates in target-present lineups, which when averaged across studies showed an average effect size near zero." Steven E. Clark, *A Re-examination of the Effects of Biased Lineup Instructions in Eyewitness Identification*, 29 Law & Hum. Behav. 395 (2005). To remedy this problem, police officers should indicate to witnesses that the perpetrator may or may not be included in the lineup or showup.

Lineup construction. Lineups become suggestive when one of the options, whether in person or in a photograph, sticks out, on the basis of some noticeable characteristic that is present in that option but not in the others. A properly constructed lineup will therefore hold constant the various characteristics of the individuals presented, so that each of them has, for example, a tattoo, and the relevant color hair, and a similar height and build. For example, consider the following guidelines issued by the Attorney General of New Jersey: "Select fillers (nonsuspects) who generally fit the witness' description of the perpetrator. When there is a limited or inadequate description of the perpetrator provided by the witness, or when the description of the perpetrator differs significantly from the appearance of the suspect, fillers should resemble the suspect in significant features."

Preventing feedback loops. Feedback problems occur when the police or prosecutors indicate to the witness that they selected the "correct" individual from lineup. The result of this feedback is that witnesses then internalize this praise and increase their confidence in their own identification. For example, a witness who is 70 percent confident of their identification of a suspect may come to believe that they must be correct once they receive the police feedback. This, in turn, then impacts how the witness testifies before the jury at trial; an uncertain eyewitness identification is transformed into a certain one. Researchers refer to this as "confirmatory feedback." In the most extreme cases, the confirmatory feedback might even alter the actual memory of the witness, causing them to remember the event with the identified suspect as the perpetrator, even if the original memory of the incident was more vague and lacked precision. As one judge concluded, "[m]eta-analysis showed that across twenty studies of 2400 identifications, 'witnesses who received feedback "expressed significantly more . . . confidence in their decision compared with participants who received no feedback." "Witnesses who received feedback also tended to overstate the quality of their view of the events in question." Stuart Rabner, *Evaluating Eyewitness Identification Evidence in the 21st Century*, 87 N.Y.U. L. Rev. 1249, 1265-66 (2012); Amy Bradfield Douglass & Nancy Steblay, *Memory Distortion in Eyewitnesses: A Meta-Analysis of the Post-Identification Feedback Effect*, 20 Applied Cognitive Psychol. 859, 863 (2006).

Multiple viewings. One can distinguish between two types of multiple viewings. In the first, the witness fails to identify the suspect initially, but when the witness sees the suspect a second or third time, the witness reevaluates his or her lack of certainty and makes an identification. It should be obvious why these procedures might produce misidentifications.

However, the more subtle variation involves situations where the witness identifies the suspect the first time and then re-identifies the suspect again in subsequent identifications. Although this form of multiple identification would seem to be benign, the repeated identifications make the witness more certain about their identification and might alter their memory. Researchers refer to this as "mugshot commitment." Kenneth A. Deffenbacher et al., *Mugshot Exposure Effects: Retroactive Interference, Mugshot Commitment, Source Confusion, and Unconscious Transference*, 30 Law & Hum. Behav. 287, 299 (2006). The result is an increased risk of misidentifications.

Simultaneous or sequential lineups. The difference between the two forms of lineups is whether all options are presented at once or whether the options are presented one at a time. Although it sounds reasonable to present all options in a photographic lineup at the same time, the risk is that the witness will compare the features among the photos and select the one that is "closest." In contrast, if the photographs are presented sequentially, the witness is forced to compare each one to the mental picture of the perpetrator, thus producing a more reliable identification. However, research on this question is mixed and psychologists have not definitively established that sequential lineups are inherently more reliable. See Dawn McQuiston-Surrett et al., *Sequential vs. Simultaneous Lineups: A Review of Methods, Data, and Theory*, 12 Psychol. Pub. Pol'y & L. 137, 163 (2006) ("Although the concept of relative judgment is theoretically and intuitively appealing and of considerable interest here, we believe that the way this construct has been tested in much of the literature does not provide a strong basis for concluding that eyewitnesses preferentially use this strategy when choosing from [a simultaneous lineup] nor that they preferentially use an absolute judgment strategy when choosing from an [sequential lineup].").

Composite sketches. Visual composites produce their own set of accuracy problems. The problem, of course, is that it is impossible to ensure that the information is only unidirectional and does not flow back and contaminate the witness's memory. That's because the witness works collaboratively with an artist, through trial and error, to produce an image whose likeness matches the witness's memory. This process necessarily requires that the witness provide feedback to the artist about how close, or not close, the composite is to the witness's memory. In participating in this collaborative project, the composite image might end up contaminating the witness's memory. If the witness makes an in-court identification at a later stage, are they identifying the perpetrator who committed the crime or are they identifying an individual who strongly resembles the composite sketch?

Marvin Anderson smiles as he holds the unconditional pardon issued by Virginia Governor Mark Warner. Anderson spent 15 years in prison after he was identified by a rape victim in a lineup, despite the real perpetrator, Otis Lincoln, confessing to the attack in 1988. Anderson was exonerated in 2002 after DNA testing excluded him and implicated Lincoln. (Steve Helber/AP/Shutterstock)

The dangers inherent in showups. Showups are necessarily problematic because they are not organized with the clinical design of the photo or in-person lineup. When conducted in the police station, the witness is primed to assume that the individual is a perpetrator who the police already believe has committed the crime. As the Supreme Court of New Jersey noted: "By their nature, showups are suggestive and cannot be performed blind or double-blind. Nonetheless . . . 'the risk of misidentification is not heightened if a showup is conducted immediately after the witnessed event, ideally within two hours' because 'the benefits of a fresh memory seem to balance the risks of undue suggestion.'" *Henderson*, 208 N.J. at 259. Several states have imposed specific restrictions that limit when showup identifications will be admissible as evidence. See, e.g., *Commonwealth v. Martin*, 447 Mass. 274, 284, 850 N.E.2d 555, 563 (2006) (police must have "good reason" for conducting showup rather than some other form of identification); *People v. Duuvon*, 77 N.Y.2d 541, 544, 571 N.E.2d 654, 656 (1991) ("civilian showup identifications at police stations are inherently suggestive and should be suppressed as a matter of general principle unless exigency warrants otherwise"); *State v. Dubose*, 285 Wis. 2d 143, 148, 699 N.W.2d 582, 584-85 (2005) ("We hold that evidence obtained from such a showup will not be admissible unless, based on the totality of the circumstances, the showup was necessary. A showup will not be necessary, however, unless the police lacked probable cause to make an arrest or, as a result of other exigent circumstances, could not have conducted a lineup or photo array.").

Estimator variables. Finally, in addition to the problems associated with the design of the identification procedure, factors related to the witness may compromise the reliability of eyewitness identification. Some of these factors are inevitable and cannot be eliminated. For example, the witness is under an extreme amount of stress, both during the crime and during the identification, which might cloud the witness's ability to accurately recall the visual characteristics of the perpetrator. During a violent crime, the witness is most likely to focus on the weapon, rather than the face, of the perpetrator. Many crimes, even violent ones, occur quickly, rather than extending over a long time period, giving the witness insufficient time to record the details of the perpetrator's appearance. The crime might have occurred at night or in a dimly lit area, and the victim may have watched the events unfold from a significant distance. The perpetrator may have changed his physical appearance, making it difficult to assess and compare the current condition of the suspect with the prior characteristics recalled from the event in question. On top of all of this, the witness may suffer from explicit or implicit bias and might be more prone to identify an African-American suspect as the correct perpetrator. While some of these estimator variables can be remediated, some of them are merely hardwired into the nature of identifications. The police cannot change the lighting conditions that were in place during the commission of the crime. However, lawyers (and judges) can and should remain sensitive to the fact that identifications are plagued by human error. The procedural doctrine should evolve to filter out high-risk identifications as much as possible.

Cross-racial identifications. Substantial empirical research suggests that cross-racial eyewitness identifications are especially hazardous. In other words, a white eyewitness might be more likely to misidentify an African-American suspect than a white suspect. See Gary L. Wells & Elizabeth F. Loftus, *Eyewitness Testimony: Psychological Perspectives* (1984); John P. Rutledge, *They All Look Alike: The Inaccuracy of Cross-Racial Identifications*, 28 Am. J. Crim. L. 207, 228 (2001) (lamenting that the "wealth of social science data and abundance of case law has yet to inspire legal scholars to address the issue directly"). For example, in *Smith v. State*, the defendant's lawyer attempted to argue before the jury that a witness identification of his client might be compromised because it was a cross-racial identification. The identification was the key evidence in the trial. The trial court denied defense counsel's request for permission to discuss the subject during closing arguments and also rejected a request to discuss the issue in the judge's charge to the jury. On appeal, the Court of Appeals of Maryland reversed the conviction and concluded that although the scientific evidence on cross-racial identifications had not generated scientific consensus, the "the victim's identification of the defendants was anchored in her enhanced ability to identify faces" and under "these circumstances, defense counsel should have been allowed to argue the difficulties of cross-racial identification in closing argument." 388 Md. 468, 488-89, 880 A.2d 288, 300 (2005). In contrast, other courts have refused to allow the defense to introduce at trial scientific evidence regarding the problems of cross-racial identification. In *People v. Carrieri*, a New York court ruled against the introduction of the evidence because "procedural safeguards, to wit, cross-examination, summation, and a [jury] charge, combined with the life experiences of jurors, are sufficient tools for a jury to rationally decide if the accused has been accurately identified." 4 Misc. 3d 307, 308, 777 N.Y.S.2d 627, 628 (Sup. Ct. 2004). Which approach seems best to you?

PART IV

THE PRE-TRIAL PROCESS

CHAPTER 10

Prosecution and Discretion

INTRODUCTION

In some sense, the charging decision is the most consequential moment in all of criminal procedure. That is so because the charging decision is both reviewable and unreviewable *at the same time*. It is reviewable, of course, because the prosecutor's decision to charge must be confirmed by either a preliminary hearing or grand jury, followed by a full trial—i.e., the entire legal process associated with the criminal law. On the other hand, if the prosecutor declines to charge a suspect, the matter ends then and there, with no review by either judge or jury. In that sense, the decision to exercise prosecutorial discretion and decline to file charges is one that a single man or woman—or more properly the office of the local district attorney—is vested with complete discretion to make.

The prosecutorial discretion involved in the prosecutor's decision *not to charge* a defendant is entailed by the structural function of the public prosecutor. Private citizens who are victimized by a crime have no right to personally file criminal charges against a suspect and seek an indictment before a grand jury. Although a private citizen can file a civil lawsuit for private damages, criminal punishment will only be assessed after a criminal charge is filed by a public prosecutor who represents the community. Indeed, this is what makes the criminal law a branch of public law as opposed to private law.

Of course, the criminal law was not always entirely public. In England in the 1800s, for instance, surviving next of kin were permitted to file private prosecutions for murder—a procedural mechanism that is unknown in today's common law criminal justice system. In civil law jurisdictions, such as France, victims are still permitted to file criminal complaints on their own and ask a single court to resolve questions of criminal punishment and private remedies in a single proceeding. But common law jurisdictions such as the United States retain a strict separation between the resolution of private and public claims.

There are many reasons why a local prosecutor might refrain from commencing a criminal case against a suspect. The prosecutor might be unsure if the suspect is responsible for committing the crime or the prosecutor might assess that there is insufficient evidence to succeed at a trial. Or, in another vein, the prosecutor might take "mercy" on the suspect or might believe that a prosecution would not serve "the interests of justice" in the broadest sense. To take one example: If the case involves a child victim or a child witness, the prosecutor might conclude that the prosecution will do more harm to the innocent child than to the suspect. (Imagine a situation where the suspect is already incarcerated for another crime or is terminally ill and likely to die soon—both cases where additional criminal punishment is useless.) Or, there might be any number of illegitimate reasons why a prosecutor might decide to forgo criminal charges, such as the taking of a bribe or doing a favor for a personal friend or a politically well-connected individual. Or the prosecutor might have no reason at all. Then-Attorney General (and later Supreme Court Justice) Robert H. Jackson described prosecutorial discretion in the following terms during a 1940 speech to federal prosecutors:

> The prosecutor has more control over life, liberty, and reputation than any other person in America. His discretion is tremendous. He can have citizens investigated and, if he is that kind of person, he can have this done to the tune of public statements and veiled or unveiled intimations. Or the prosecutor may choose a more subtle course and simply have a citizen's friends interviewed. The prosecutor can order arrests, present cases to the grand jury in secret session, and on the basis of his one-sided presentation of the facts, can cause the citizen to be indicted and held for trial. He may dismiss the case before trial, in which case the defense never has a chance to be heard. Or he may go on with a public trial. If he obtains a conviction, the prosecutor can still make recommendations as to sentence, as to whether the prisoner should get probation or a suspended sentence, and after he is put away, as to whether he is a fit subject for parole. While the prosecutor at his best is one of the most beneficent forces in our society, when he acts from malice or other base motives, he is one of the worst.

Robert H. Jackson, *The Federal Prosecutor,* 31 Am. Inst. Crim. L. & Criminology 3 (1940-1941). The prosecutor's decision is so important because it is not reviewable by any court and the reasons for the decision are typically not disclosed. Since prosecutorial discretion falls within the discretion of the executive branch, the prosecutor usually owes no explanation to either the court or to the public regarding how that decision was made—at least as a matter of law. To the extent that a prosecutor's office feels compelled to defend its charging decisions to the public, that compulsion flows from politics. Prosecutors are either elected or appointed by politicians who themselves are elected, and political pressure may force prosecutors to explain their decisions in order to gain reelection.

The following materials explore the legal issues surrounding the exercise of charging discretion and commencement of the criminal adjudicatory process. Section A focuses on the pre-trial mechanisms that precede the trial: a preliminary hearing or a grand jury, depending on the jurisdiction and circumstance. Section B will focus on the exercise of prosecutorial discretion, particularly with regard to complaints about illegitimate forms of discretion: claims of selective prosecution ("why am I being charged when others were not?"), racially discriminatory charging, and vindictive prosecutions. Section C will focus on the difficult question of when to charge and try defendants together or separately—an issue that is especially complicated when a statement (such as a confession) is admissible against one defendant but not another. Finally, Section D, the Practice & Policy section, will explore deeper questions of prosecutorial discretion, including whether the law should require that prosecutors only charge defendants for the right reason (justice and probable cause versus discrimination and vindictiveness), rather than simply requiring that prosecutors meet a particular evidentiary burden regardless of their motivations.

A. PRE-TRIAL MECHANISMS

Typically, a prosecutor will have to provide some evidentiary justification for a charge before proceeding to trial. Depending on the jurisdiction and the severity of the charge, the prosecutor will either submit to a preliminary hearing or to a grand jury (sometimes to both). The two proceedings could not be more different. The preliminary hearing is an adversarial proceeding with the prosecution and the defense attorney presenting evidence before a judge, who rules on whether the prosecution has presented sufficient evidence to justify the charge and go forward to a full trial. On the other hand, the grand jury proceeding is directed by the prosecutor with neither a judge nor a defense attorney present—it is not a trial at all, but better understood as an investigation. After considering evidence from the prosecutor and any other evidence it requests, the grand jury either votes to return a "true bill of indictment" on one or more of the proposed charges or any other charge it determines is supported by the evidence, or returns a "no bill"—a refusal to indict on any charges. If the grand jury issues an indictment, it is "handed up" to a judge who will begin preparations for the holding of a trial, including any pre-trial motions (motions *in limine*) over evidentiary disputes.

1. Preliminary Hearing

In one sense, a preliminary hearing is a mini-trial, but the preliminary hearing should not be a replacement for a trial, i.e., a trial before the trial, which would be a waste of judicial resources. Rather, the preliminary hearing is best understood as an adversarial "screening" mechanism, designed to determine whether a particular evidentiary threshold has been met to justify moving forward with a charge or charges. Moreover, the standard of decision to be applied is far lower than the "beyond a reasonable doubt" standard used by the fact finder in a full criminal trial. The judge simply has to be convinced that the evidence gives him probable cause to believe that the defendant committed the crime and that a reasonable jury could convict the defendant. Expressed in the negative, if the judge believes that *no* reasonable jury could ever convict the defendant based on the paucity of evidence presented at the preliminary hearing, she should dismiss the charges. The determination is made for each charge, so it is entirely possible for the judge to dismiss one charge but schedule a trial for a second or third charge because there is sufficient evidence for one but not the other, or to reduce a charge presented by the prosecutor to a lesser included offense. In practical terms, the evidentiary bar at a preliminary hearing is low and it is rare for a case to be thrown out at the preliminary hearing stage.

Evaluated from the perspective of the adversarial process, the preliminary hearing is more advantageous to the defendant than a grand jury (in fact, in most cases the "target" of a grand jury investigation does not even qualify as a defendant until the true bill of indictment is issued). In the preliminary hearing, the defendant is present and capable of making arguments of both fact and law to the judge. In the latter, the "target" cannot make such arguments; indeed the target is not even present for the grand jury proceedings. In some states, such as California, the prosecution has the option of proceeding either through a grand jury indictment or through an "information" (a formal charge made under oath by a prosecutor) coupled with a preliminary hearing. In *Hawkins v. Superior Court*, 22 Cal. 3d 584, 586 P.2d 916 (1978), a defendant who was indicted by a grand jury filed a constitutional challenge claiming that he was denied the opportunity to contest the charges before a preliminary hearing and that this denial, which is afforded to other defendants, denied him equal protection. The California Supreme Court agreed and ruled that all defendants indicted by a grand jury in California were entitled to a post-indictment preliminary hearing if they so desired. This essentially created two tracks. Under track one, the defendant would be charged by "information" and brought before a preliminary hearing. Under track two, the defendant would be indicted by a grand jury and then also would be brought before a preliminary hearing if they asserted their right to a preliminary hearing. California voters eventually overruled *Hawkins* by amending the California State Constitution by including the following language: "If a felony is prosecuted by indictment, there shall be no postindictment preliminary hearing." Cal. Const. art. I, § 14.1. The result of the amendment was to again return to a pure grand-jury *or* preliminary hearing system.

2. Grand Juries

Although the grand jury is an important screening mechanism and an important procedural protection for defendants, the fact that only the prosecutor appears before the grand jury, presenting the state's evidence and the state's witnesses, means that most grand juries end with some kind of indictment being handed up to the judge. This fact has sparked the oft-repeated adage that a prosecutor can get a ham sandwich indicted. While certainly an exaggeration, the adage effectively communicates the reality that the grand jury proceeding deliberately sets the bar low for the prosecution, at least when compared to the proof beyond a reasonable doubt standard used at the criminal trial.

Since the grand jury is an ex parte (one-sided) proceeding, there are unique constitutional issues that are not raised by full, adversarial trials. For example, in the following case, the Supreme Court must decide whether an indictment should be sustained, and a defendant held for trial, when the sole evidence presented before the grand jury is evidence that would not be admissible at the trial itself. On the one hand, grand juries do not operate by regular rules of evidence since there is no judge to make evidentiary rulings (and no defense attorney to object to inadmissible evidence). On the other hand, a grand jury indictment based on entirely inadmissible evidence would seem to flout the probable cause standard insofar as it is based on what a reasonable jury would do based on evidence that it is entitled to consider. As you read the following case, ask yourself what the Supreme Court's ruling says about the proper role and function of the grand jury. Is it designed simply to protect the rights of the defendant or also to conserve precious judicial resources?

Costello v. United States

Supreme Court of the United States
350 U.S. 359 (1956)

Mr. Justice Black delivered the opinion of the Court.

We granted certiorari in this case to consider a single question: "May a defendant be required to stand trial and a conviction be sustained where only hearsay evidence was presented to the grand jury which indicted him?"

Petitioner, Frank Costello, was indicted for wilfully attempting to evade payment of income taxes due the United States for the years 1947, 1948 and 1949. The charge was that petitioner falsely and fraudulently reported less income than he and his wife actually received during the taxable years in question. Petitioner promptly filed a motion for inspection of the minutes of the grand jury and for a dismissal of the indictment. His motion was based on an affidavit stating that he was firmly convinced there could have been no legal or competent evidence before the grand jury which indicted him since he had reported all his income and paid all taxes due. The motion was denied. At the trial which followed the Government offered evidence designed to show increases is Costello's net worth in an attempt to prove that he had received more income during the years in question than he had reported. To establish its case the Government called and examined 144 witnesses and introduced 368 exhibits. All of the testimony and documents related to business transactions and expenditures by petitioner and his wife. The prosecution concluded its case by calling three government agents. Their investigations had produced the evidence used against petitioner at the trial. They were allowed to summarize the vast amount of evidence already heard and to introduce computations showing, if correct, that petitioner and his wife had received far greater income than they had reported. We have held such summarizations admissible in a "net worth" case like this.

Counsel for petitioner asked each government witness at the trial whether he had appeared before the grand jury which returned the indictment. This cross-examination developed the fact that the three investigating officers had been the only witnesses before the grand jury. After the Government concluded its case, petitioner again moved to dismiss the indictment on the ground that the only evidence before the grand jury was 'hearsay,' since the three officers had no firsthand knowledge of the transactions upon which their computations were based. Nevertheless the trial court again refused to dismiss the indictment, and petitioner was convicted. The Court of Appeals affirmed, holding that the indictment was valid even though the sole evidence before the grand jury was hearsay. Petitioner here urges: (1) that an indictment based solely on hearsay evidence violates that part of the Fifth Amendment providing that "No person shall be held to answer for a capital, or otherwise infamous crime, unless on a presentment or indictment of a Grand Jury . . ." and (2) that if the Fifth Amendment does not invalidate an indictment based solely on hearsay we should now lay down such a rule for the guidance of federal courts.

The Fifth Amendment provides that federal prosecutions for capital or otherwise infamous crimes must be instituted by presentments or indictments of grand juries. But neither the Fifth Amendment nor any other constitutional provision prescribes the kind of evidence upon which grand juries must act. The grand jury is an English institution, brought to this country by the early colonists and incorporated in the Constitution by the Founders. There is every reason to believe that our constitutional grand jury was intended to operate substantially like its English progenitor. The basic purpose of the English grand jury was to provide a fair method for instituting criminal proceedings against persons believed to have committed crimes. Grand jurors were selected from the body of the people and their work was not hampered by rigid procedural or evidential rules. In fact, grand jurors could act on their own knowledge and were free to make their presentments or indictments on such information as they deemed satisfactory. Despite its broad power to institute criminal proceedings the grand jury grew in popular favor with the years. It acquired an independence in England free from control by the Crown or judges. Its adoption in our Constitution as the sole method for preferring charges in serious criminal cases shows the high place it held as an instrument of justice. And in this country as in England of old the grand jury has convened as a body of laymen, free from technical rules, acting in secret, pledged to indict no one because of prejudice and to free no one because of special favor. As late as 1927 an English historian could say that English grand juries were still free to act on their own knowledge if they pleased to do so. And in 1852 Mr. Justice Nelson on circuit could say "No case has been cited, nor have we been able to find any, furnishing an authority for looking into and revising the judgment of the grand jury upon the evidence, for the purpose of determining whether or not the finding was founded upon sufficient proof. . . ."

In *Holt v. United States*, 218 U.S. 245, this Court had to decide whether an indictment should be quashed because supported in part by incompetent evidence. Aside from the incompetent evidence "there was very little evidence against the accused." The Court refused to hold that such an indictment should be quashed, pointing out that "The abuses of criminal practice would be enhanced if indictments could be upset on such a ground." The same thing is true where as here all the evidence before the grand jury was in the nature of "hearsay." If indictments were to be held open to challenge on the ground that there was inadequate or incompetent evidence before the grand jury, the resulting delay would be great indeed. The result of such a rule would be that before trial on the merits a defendant could always insist on a kind of preliminary trial to determine the competency and adequacy of the evidence before the grand jury. This is not required by the Fifth Amendment. An indictment returned by a legally constituted and unbiased grand jury, like an information drawn by the prosecutor, if valid on its face, is enough to call for trial of the charge on the merits. The Fifth Amendment requires nothing more.

Petitioner urges that this Court should exercise its power to supervise the administration of justice in federal courts and establish a rule permitting defendants to challenge indictments on the ground that they are not supported by adequate or competent evidence. No persuasive reasons are advanced for establishing such a rule. It would run counter to the whole history of the grand jury institution, in which laymen conduct their inquiries unfettered by technical rules. Neither justice nor the concept of a fair trial requires such a change. In a trial on the merits, defendants are entitled to a strict observance of all the rules designed to bring about a fair verdict. Defendants are not entitled, however, to a rule which would result in interminable delay but add nothing to the assurance of a fair trial.

In the next case, the Supreme Court must decide whether the government is under an obligation to provide exculpatory evidence—i.e., evidence that would tend to support an inference of the defendant's innocence—to the grand jury. At issue in this determination is nothing less than the proper role and function of the grand jury itself, and the extent to which the grand jury is subject to judicial supervision. Since the grand jury is not an adversarial process, does the prosecution therefore have an obligation to present exculpatory evidence to the grand jury since there is no defense attorney present to do so on behalf of the client? From an ethical standpoint, what is the prosecutor's obligation in the grand jury room: to indict the suspect or to find the truth wherever it might lead?

United States v. Williams

Supreme Court of the United States
504 U.S. 36 (1992)

Justice Scalia delivered the opinion of the Court.

The question presented in this case is whether a district court may dismiss an otherwise valid indictment because the Government failed to disclose to the grand jury "substantial exculpatory evidence" in its possession.

I

On May 4, 1988, respondent John H. Williams, Jr., a Tulsa, Oklahoma, investor, was indicted by a federal grand jury on seven counts of "knowingly mak[ing] [a] false statement or report . . . for the purpose of influencing . . . the action [of a federally insured financial institution]." According to the indictment, between September 1984 and November 1985 Williams supplied four Oklahoma banks with "materially false" statements that variously overstated the value of his current assets and interest income in order to influence the banks' actions on his loan requests. . . .

Shortly after arraignment, the District Court granted Williams' motion for disclosure of all exculpatory portions of the grand jury transcripts. Upon reviewing this material, Williams demanded that the District Court dismiss the indictment, alleging that the Government had failed to fulfill its obligation . . . to present "substantial exculpatory evidence" to the grand jury. His contention was that evidence which the Government had chosen not to present to the grand jury—in particular, Williams' general ledgers and tax returns, and Williams' testimony in his contemporaneous Chapter 11 bankruptcy proceeding—disclosed that, for tax purposes and otherwise, he had regularly accounted for the "notes receivable" (and the interest on them) in a manner consistent with the Balance Sheet and the Income Statement. This, he contended, belied an intent to mislead the banks, and thus directly negated an essential element of the charged offense. . . .

III

Respondent does not contend that the Fifth Amendment itself obliges the prosecutor to disclose substantial exculpatory evidence in his possession to the grand jury. Instead, building on our statement that the federal courts "may, within limits, formulate procedural rules not specifically required by the Constitution or the Congress," he argues that imposition of the . . . disclosure rule is supported by the courts' "supervisory power." We think not. [Our cases] deal strictly with the courts' power to control their own procedures. That power has been applied not only to improve the truth-finding process of the trial, but also to prevent parties from reaping benefit or incurring harm from violations of substantive or procedural rules (imposed by the Constitution or laws) governing matters apart from the trial itself. Thus . . . the supervisory power can be used to dismiss an indictment because of misconduct before the grand jury, at least where that misconduct amounts to a violation of one of those "few, clear rules which were carefully drafted and approved by this Court and by Congress to ensure the integrity of the grand jury's functions."

We did not hold . . . that the courts' supervisory power could be used, not merely as a means of enforcing or vindicating legally compelled standards of prosecutorial conduct before the grand jury, but as a means of prescribing those standards of prosecutorial conduct in the first instance—just as it may be used as a means of establishing standards of prosecutorial conduct before the courts themselves. It is this latter exercise that respondent demands. Because the grand jury is an institution separate from the courts, over whose functioning the courts do not preside, we think it clear that, as a general matter at least, no such "supervisory" judicial authority exists. . . .

"[R]ooted in long centuries of Anglo-American history," the grand jury is mentioned in the Bill of Rights, but not in the body of the Constitution. It has not been textually assigned, therefore, to any of the branches described in the first three Articles. It "is a constitutional fixture in its own right." In fact the whole theory of its function is that it belongs to no branch of the institutional Government, serving as a kind of buffer or referee between the Government and the people. Although the grand jury normally operates, of course, in the courthouse and under judicial auspices, its institutional relationship with the Judicial Branch has traditionally been, so to speak, at arm's length. Judges' direct involvement in the functioning of the grand jury has generally been confined to the constitutive one of calling the grand jurors together and administering their oaths of office.

The grand jury's functional independence from the Judicial Branch is evident both in the scope of its power to investigate criminal wrongdoing and in the manner in which that power is exercised. "Unlike [a] [c]ourt, whose jurisdiction is predicated upon a specific case or controversy, the grand jury can investigate merely on suspicion that the law is being violated, or even because it wants assurance that it is not." It need not identify the offender it suspects, or even "the precise nature of the offense" it is investigating. The grand jury requires no authorization from its constituting court to initiate an investigation, nor does the prosecutor require leave of court to seek a grand jury indictment. And in its day-to-day functioning, the grand jury generally operates without the interference of a presiding judge. It swears in its own witnesses and deliberates in total secrecy.

True, the grand jury cannot compel the appearance of witnesses and the production of evidence, and must appeal to the court when such compulsion is required. And the court will refuse to lend its assistance when the compulsion the grand jury seeks would override rights accorded by the Constitution, or even testimonial privileges recognized by the common law. Even in this setting, however, we have insisted that the grand jury remain "free to pursue its investigations unhindered by external influence or supervision so long as it does not trench upon the legitimate rights of any witness called before it." Recognizing this tradition of independence, we have said that the Fifth Amendment's "constitutional guarantee presupposes an investigative body acting independently of either prosecuting attorney or judge. . . ."

No doubt in view of the grand jury proceeding's status as other than a constituent element of a "criminal prosecutio[n]," we have said that certain constitutional protections afforded defendants in criminal proceedings have no application before that body. The Double Jeopardy Clause of the Fifth Amendment does not bar a grand jury from returning an indictment when a prior grand jury has refused to do so. We have twice suggested, though not held, that the Sixth Amendment right to counsel does not attach when an individual is summoned to appear before a grand jury, even if he is the subject of the investigation. And although "the grand jury may not force a witness to answer questions in violation of [the Fifth Amendment's] constitutional guarantee" against self-incrimination, our cases suggest that an indictment obtained through the use of evidence previously obtained in violation of the privilege against self-incrimination "is nevertheless valid."

Given the grand jury's operational separateness from its constituting court, it should come as no surprise that we have been reluctant to invoke the judicial supervisory power as a basis for prescribing modes of grand jury procedure. Over the years, we have received many requests to exercise supervision over the grand jury's evidence-taking process, but we have refused them all, including some more appealing than the one presented today. In *United States v. Calandra*, a grand jury witness faced questions that were allegedly based upon physical evidence the Government had obtained through a violation of the Fourth Amendment; we rejected the proposal that the exclusionary rule be extended to grand jury proceedings, because of "the potential injury to the historic role and functions of the grand jury." In *Costello v. United States*, we declined to enforce the hearsay rule in grand jury proceedings, since that "would run counter to the whole history of the grand jury institution, in which laymen conduct their inquiries unfettered by technical rules."

These authorities suggest that any power federal courts may have to fashion, on their own initiative, rules of grand jury procedure is a very limited one, not remotely comparable to the power they maintain over their own proceedings. It certainly would not permit judicial reshaping of the grand jury institution, substantially altering the traditional relationships between the prosecutor, the constituting court, and the grand jury itself. As we proceed to discuss, that would be the consequence of the proposed rule here.

Respondent argues that the . . . rule can be justified as a sort of Fifth Amendment "common law," a necessary means of assuring the constitutional right to the judgment "of an independent and informed grand jury." Respondent makes a generalized appeal to functional notions: Judicial supervision of the quantity and quality of the evidence relied upon by the grand jury plainly facilitates, he says, the grand jury's performance of its twin historical responsibilities, i.e., bringing to trial those who may be justly accused and shielding the innocent from unfounded accusation and prosecution. We do not agree. The rule would neither preserve nor enhance the traditional functioning of the institution that the Fifth Amendment demands. To the contrary, requiring the prosecutor to present exculpatory as well as inculpatory evidence would alter the grand jury's historical role, transforming it from an accusatory to an adjudicatory body.

It is axiomatic that the grand jury sits not to determine guilt or innocence, but to assess whether there is adequate basis for bringing a criminal charge. That has always been so; and to make the assessment it has always been thought sufficient to hear only the prosecutor's side. As Blackstone described the prevailing practice in 18th-century England, the grand jury was "only to hear evidence on behalf of the prosecution[,] for the finding of an indictment is only in the nature of an enquiry or accusation, which is afterwards to be tried and determined." So also in the United States. According to the description of an early American court, three years before the Fifth Amendment was ratified, it is the grand jury's function not "to enquire . . . upon what foundation [the charge may be] denied," or otherwise to try the suspect's defenses, but only to examine "upon what foundation [the charge] is made" by the prosecutor. As a consequence, neither in this country nor in England has the suspect under investigation by the grand jury ever been thought to have a right to testify or to have exculpatory evidence presented.

Imposing upon the prosecutor a legal obligation to present exculpatory evidence in his possession would be incompatible with this system. If a "balanced" assessment of the entire matter is the objective, surely the first thing to be done—rather than requiring the prosecutor to say what he knows in defense of the target of the investigation—is to entitle the target to tender his own defense. To require the former while denying (as we do) the latter would be quite absurd. It would also be quite pointless, since it would merely invite the target to circumnavigate the system by delivering his exculpatory evidence to the prosecutor, whereupon it would have to be passed on to the grand jury—unless the prosecutor is willing to take the chance that a court will not deem the evidence important enough to qualify for mandatory disclosure.

. . . [R]espondent argues that a rule requiring the prosecutor to disclose exculpatory evidence to the grand jury would, by removing from the docket unjustified prosecutions, save valuable judicial time. That depends, we suppose, upon what the ratio would turn out to be between unjustified prosecutions eliminated and grand jury indictments challenged—for the latter as well as the former consume "valuable judicial time." We need not pursue the matter; if there is an advantage to the proposal, Congress is free to prescribe it. For the reasons set forth above, however, we conclude that courts have no authority to prescribe such a duty pursuant to their inherent supervisory authority over their own proceedings. . . .

Justice STEVENS, with whom Justice BLACKMUN and Justice O'CONNOR join, and with whom Justice THOMAS joins as to Parts II and III, dissenting.

II

Like the Hydra slain by Hercules, prosecutorial misconduct has many heads. . . . The reported cases of this Court alone contain examples of the knowing use of perjured testimony, the suppression of evidence favorable to an accused person, and misstatements of the law in argument to the jury, to name just a few.

Nor has prosecutorial misconduct been limited to judicial proceedings: The reported cases indicate that it has sometimes infected grand jury proceedings as well. The cases contain examples of prosecutors presenting perjured testimony, questioning a witness outside the presence of the grand jury and then failing to inform the grand jury that the testimony was exculpatory, failing to inform the grand jury of its authority to subpoena witnesses, operating under a conflict of interest, misstating the law, and misstating the facts on cross-examination of a witness. . . .

The standard for judging the consequences of prosecutorial misconduct during grand jury proceedings is essentially the same as the standard applicable to trials. In *United States v. Mechanik*, 475 U.S. 66 (1986), we held that there was "no reason not to apply [the harmless error rule] to errors, defects, irregularities, or variances occurring before a grand jury just as we have applied it to such error occurring in the criminal trial itself." We repeated that holding in *Bank of Nova Scotia v. United States* when we rejected a defendant's argument that an indictment should be dismissed because of prosecutorial misconduct and irregularities in proceedings before the grand jury. Referring to the prosecutor's misconduct before the grand jury, we "concluded that our customary harmless-error inquiry is applicable where, as in the cases before us, a court is asked to dismiss an indictment prior to the conclusion of the trial." Moreover, in reviewing the instances of misconduct in that case, we applied precisely the same standard to the prosecutor's violations of Rule 6 of the Federal Rules of Criminal Procedure and to his violations of the general duty of fairness that applies to all judicial proceedings. . . .

In an opinion that I find difficult to comprehend, the Court today repudiates the assumptions underlying these cases and seems to suggest that the court has no authority to supervise the conduct of the prosecutor in grand jury proceedings so long as he follows the dictates of the Constitution, applicable statutes, and Rule 6 of the Federal Rules of Criminal Procedure. The Court purports to support this conclusion by invoking the doctrine of separation of powers and citing a string of cases in which we have declined to impose categorical restraints on the grand jury. Needless to say, the Court's reasoning is unpersuasive.

Although the grand jury has not been "textually assigned" to "any of the branches described in the first three Articles" of the Constitution, it is not an autonomous body completely beyond the reach of the other branches. Throughout its life, from the moment it is convened until it is discharged, the grand jury is subject to the control of the court. As Judge Learned Hand recognized over 60 years ago, "a grand jury is neither an officer nor an agent of the United States, but a part of the court." . . .

This Court has, of course, long recognized that the grand jury has wide latitude to investigate violations of federal law as it deems appropriate and need not obtain permission from either the court or the prosecutor. Correspondingly, we have acknowledged that "its operation generally is unrestrained by the technical procedural and evidentiary rules governing the conduct of criminal trials." But this is because Congress and the Court have generally thought it best not to impose procedural restraints on the grand jury; it is not because they lack all power to do so.

To the contrary, the Court has recognized that it has the authority to create and enforce limited rules applicable in grand jury proceedings. Thus, for example, the Court has said that the grand jury "may not itself violate a valid privilege, whether established by the Constitution, statutes, or the common law." And the Court may prevent a grand jury from violating such a privilege by quashing or modifying a subpoena or issuing a protective order forbidding questions in violation of the privilege. . . . Although the Court recognizes that it may invoke its supervisory authority to fashion and enforce privilege rules applicable in grand jury proceedings and suggests that it may also invoke its supervisory authority to fashion other limited rules of grand jury procedure, it concludes that it has no authority to prescribe "standards of prosecutorial conduct before the grand jury," because that would alter the grand jury's historic role as an independent, inquisitorial institution. I disagree.

We do not protect the integrity and independence of the grand jury by closing our eyes to the countless forms of prosecutorial misconduct that may occur inside the secrecy of the grand jury room. After all, the grand jury is not merely an investigatory body; it also serves as a "protector of citizens against arbitrary and oppressive governmental action." . . . It blinks reality to say that the grand jury can adequately perform this important historic role if it is intentionally misled by the prosecutor—on whose knowledge of the law and facts of the underlying criminal investigation the jurors will, of necessity, rely. . . .

III

What, then, is the proper disposition of this case? I agree with the Government that the prosecutor is not required to place all exculpatory evidence before the grand jury. A grand jury proceeding is an ex parte investigatory proceeding to determine whether there is probable cause to believe a violation of the criminal laws has occurred, not a trial. Requiring the prosecutor to ferret out and present all evidence that could be used at trial to create a reasonable doubt as to the defendant's guilt would be inconsistent with the purpose of the grand jury proceeding and would place significant burdens on the investigation. But that does not mean that the prosecutor may mislead the grand jury into believing that there is probable cause to indict by withholding clear evidence to the contrary. I thus agree with the Department of Justice that "when a prosecutor conducting a grand jury inquiry is personally aware of substantial evidence which directly negates the guilt of a subject of the investigation, the prosecutor must present or otherwise disclose such evidence to the grand jury before seeking an indictment against such a person." U.S. Dept. of Justice, United States Attorneys' Manual ¶ 9-11.233 (1988). . . .

NOTES & QUESTIONS ON GRAND JURIES

1. *Is the grand jury a judicial body?* The *Williams* case includes the startling assertion that the grand jury is not a judicial body at all. Rather, the Court considers it to be independent of all three branches of government—a "constitutional fixture in its own right." Do you agree that the grand jury is independent of all three branches of government? What is at stake in this debate? Under one view, the grand jury is a quasi-adjudicative body that requires the prosecutor to defend his decision to pursue charges before a citizen body. This view sees the grand jury as performing an essential function related to due process, i.e., a procedural hurdle that the prosecution must pass through in order to ensure that frivolous charges are not brought against innocent defendants—clearly a judicial function, and therefore subject to the direct oversight of the judicial branch. Under another view, the grand jury is purely an accusatory body that decides whom to charge with a crime. If the grand jury is accusatory, it should be viewed as providing assistance to the prosecutor to help decide which charges to pursue against which defendants. This view helps explain why no defense attorney or judge is present and why the technical rules of evidence are not observed during the grand jury proceeding. Which model is correct?

PROBLEM CASE

Consider the case of Officer Darren Wilson. In 2014, Officer Wilson shot and killed Michael Brown during a confrontation on the street. The shooting prompted public outrage and weeks of public demonstrations; many members of the local community believed that Wilson's use of deadly force was unjustified and called for the local authorities to initiate a criminal prosecution against him for murder.

The local district attorney, St. Louis County Prosecutor Robert P. McCulloch, came to the conclusion that Officer Wilson should not be prosecuted because he believed that the evidence suggested that Wilson reasonably believed that Brown was still a threat at the moment he was shot. In Missouri, district attorneys can either file charges against a defendant leading to a preliminary hearing or they can seek an indictment before a grand jury.

Ultimately, McCulloch decided to present the case to a grand jury and let it decide whether the case should go to trial or not. Ultimately, after hearing the evidence presented by McCulloch, the grand jury voted not to indict Wilson on any charges. The grand jury's decision was met with another round of public criticism. One member of the grand jury, who voted to indict, filed a "John Doe" lawsuit against McCulloch in federal court, seeking to be released from state rules that prohibit the release of grand jury information and also alleging that "the prosecutors presented evidence and explained the law differently in the Wilson matter than they had in the other matters presented to the grand jury," thus implying that the grand jury's decision was improperly influenced by the legal instructions and explanations offered by McCulloch. *Doe v. McCulloch*, 835 F.3d 785, 787 (8th Cir. 2016).

McCulloch defended his decision to go to the grand jury—rather than use a preliminary hearing—because the grand jury process allowed the "people" to decide whether Wilson should be prosecuted. Was there anything objectionable about McCulloch's recourse to the grand jury? Consider the view of Professor Ben Trachtenberg, who wrote:

Protesters in November 2014 gather across from City Hall in Los Angeles in support of the Ferguson riots and Michael Brown. (Chester Brown/Alamy)

> Ironically, it was McCulloch's apparent desire for "cover" that eventually helped to undermine public confidence in the grand jury's work. And it was his own failure to "stand up" and take responsibility for the decisions of his office—instead of hiding behind the anonymous lay persons on the grand jury—that deprived Missouri of what the people pay for when they hire a prosecutor. Like some other prosecutors before him in high-profile cases, McCulloch abdicated the usual role of the prosecutor, choosing instead to delegate his responsibilities to untrained citizens with inadequate guidance.

Ben Trachtenberg, *No, You "Stand Up": Why Prosecutors Should Stop Hiding Behind Grand Juries*, 80 Mo. L. Rev. 1099, 1100 (2015). Trachtenberg argued that using the grand jury in this type of situation created several risks: (1) it wastes time; (2) it sparks indictments contrary to the interests of justice; and (3) passing the buck to the grand jury allows the prosecutor to evade responsibility for his decisions.

However, some observers were more sympathetic to McCulloch's approach of allowing the grand jury to decide even though the prosecutor believed that criminal prosecution was inappropriate. Consider the following assessment:

> It is, of course, true that for Mr. McCulloch (or any other prosecutor) faced with the ticklish task of investigating a high-profile, potentially incendiary, case, there is a considerable advantage to be gleaned from having the final decision about whether or not to bring charges bear the imprimatur of a grand jury. The grand jury's verdict confers a democratic

stamp of approval on a choice that, if it issued from the prosecutor alone, is more easily attacked as biased or self-serving. And abstaining from a recommendation to the grand jury further reinforces the message of grand jury independence. This is a "political" advantage, if one wants to call it that. But being a public prosecutor is, unavoidably and quite properly, a political business. It is political in the personal sense inasmuch as elected prosecutors will inevitably keep at least one eye on the effects of their legal decisions on their electoral fortunes. But the prosecutor's job is also "political" in the larger sense that a criminal justice system in a democratic polity cannot function if the public sees it as merely a collection of rules enforced by the state's monopoly on official coercion. A democratic criminal justice system depends on its legitimacy. It must not only produce outcomes that are "correct" in some narrow legal sense, but must employ processes the public perceives to be fair.

Frank O. Bowman, III, *Vox Populi: Robert McCulloch, Ferguson and the Roles of Prosecutors and Grand Juries in High-Profile Cases,* 80 Mo. L. Rev. 1111, 1125 (2015). Which view do you think is correct? Is it appropriate for a prosecutor to bring a case to a grand jury even if the prosecutor believes that criminal charges are not warranted in the case? For another high-profile example, see the case of Joe Horn. See Brian Rogers, Ruth Rendon & Dale Lezon, *Joe Horn Cleared by Grand Jury in Pasadena Shootings: Panel Issues No-Bill After Two Weeks of Testimony,* Houston Chronicle, June 30, 2008.

B. PROSECUTORIAL DISCRETION

Prosecutors wield enormous power when they decide which suspects to pursue. As noted above, there is scrutiny for these charges in the form of either a grand jury indictment or a preliminary hearing. But for those suspects who are *not* charged through either device, there is no scrutiny. Or, at the very least, there is no *legal* scrutiny for these decisions. If the local prosecuting attorney works for an elected district attorney, the public might complain about non-prosecutions and vote the district attorney out of office during the next election cycle.

However, there are also ethical limits associated with the charging decision. For example, Rule 3.8(a) of the ABA Model Rules of Professional Conduct states: "The prosecutor in a criminal case shall: (a) refrain from prosecuting a charge that the prosecutor knows is not supported by probable cause. . . ." In contrast, Standard 3.9 of the ABA Standards for Criminal Justice states:

> A prosecutor should not institute, or cause to be instituted, or permit the continued pendency of criminal charges when the prosecutor knows that the charges are not supported by probable cause. A prosecutor should not institute, cause to be instituted, or permit the continued pendency of criminal charges in the absence of sufficient admissible evidence to support a conviction.

Although Standard 3.9 refers to probable cause in its first sentence, the second sentence imposes the additional requirement that the prosecutor not proceed unless there is "sufficient admissible evidence" to support the evidence, which is a higher standard. Most state ethics codes mirror Rule 3.8(a) from the Model Rules, i.e., they simply require that the prosecutor believe that the criminal charges are supported by probable cause. These rules impose an ethical overlay on a prosecutor bringing an unsupportable case to a grand jury or to a preliminary hearing. In addition to the legal consequence that the charges in such a case would be dismissed, either by the judge at the preliminary hearing or by the grand jury returning a "no bill," the prosecuting attorney could also face disciplinary charges before a state bar ethics committee for violating the "probable cause" professional ethics requirement for charging decisions.

The following materials focus on the legal issues that arise when prosecutors exercise their discretion in controversial ways. Subsection 1 focuses on complaints of selective prosecution, i.e., when a prosecutor charges a defendant even though many others who allegedly committed similar crimes were not prosecuted. Subsection 2 focuses on racially discriminatory charging practices and the legal standard for throwing out a charge motivated by racial discrimination. Finally, subsection 3 deals with complaints of vindictive prosecution, i.e., when a prosecutor's charging decision creates the perception that the charge is motivated by a desire to punish the defendant because the defendant chose to exercise a statutory or constitutional right. In each case, the question at stake is whether the allegedly unfair motivation for the charging decision is reason enough for a court to throw out the case even if there is sufficient evidence of guilt to proceed to a trial. In other words, does it matter *why* the prosecutor decided to file the case, or is the only relevant question whether there is sufficient evidence that the defendant committed the crime?

1. The Standard for Judging Claims of Selective Prosecution

Prosecutors make decisions about the allocation of scarce institutional resources all the time. Inevitably, this means that a prosecutor pursues charges against some individuals and not others, even if the prosecutor believes that he has probable cause to file charges against all of them. As Justice Jackson noted in 1940, "[o]ne of the greatest difficulties of the position of prosecutor is that he must pick his cases, because no prosecutor can ever investigate all of the cases in which he receives complaints. If the department of justice were to make even a pretense of reaching every probable violation of federal law, ten times its present staff would be inadequate." In most situations, this exercise of prosecutorial discretion is unobjectionable, almost banal. But occasionally cases of prosecutorial discretion can become so extreme that those who are prosecuted object that they are being treated unfairly—not because they fail to meet the probable cause standard but because there are others who were let free who meet the probable cause standard as well. Under what conditions might these cases of "selective prosecution" violate the Constitution and require a remedy?

Wayte v. United States

Supreme Court of the United States
470 U.S. 598 (1985)

Justice Powell delivered the opinion of the Court.

The question presented is whether a passive enforcement policy under which the Government prosecutes only those who report themselves as having violated the law, or who are reported by others, violates the First and Fifth Amendments.

I

On July 2, 1980 . . . the President issued Presidential Proclamation No. 4771. This Proclamation directed male citizens and certain male residents born during 1960 to register with the Selective Service System during the week of July 21, 1980. Petitioner fell within that class but did not register. Instead, he wrote several letters to Government officials, including the President, stating that he had not registered and did not intend to do so.

Petitioner's letters were added to a Selective Service file of young men who advised that they had failed to register or who were reported by others as having failed to register. For reasons we discuss infra, Selective Service adopted a policy of passive enforcement under which it would investigate and prosecute only the cases of nonregistration contained in this file. In furtherance of this policy, Selective Service sent a letter on June 17, 1981, to each reported violator who had not registered and for whom it had an address. The letter explained the duty to register, stated that Selective Service had information that the person was required to register but had not done so, requested that he either comply with the law by filling out an enclosed registration card or explain why he was not subject to registration, and warned that a violation could result in criminal prosecution and specified penalties. Petitioner received a copy of this letter but did not respond.

On July 20, 1981, Selective Service transmitted to the Department of Justice, for investigation and potential prosecution, the names of petitioner and 133 other young men identified under its passive enforcement system—all of whom had not registered in response to the Service's June letter. . . .

Petitioner moved to dismiss [his] indictment on the ground of selective prosecution. He contended that he and the other indicted nonregistrants were "vocal" opponents of the registration program who had been impermissibly targeted (out of an estimated 674,000 nonregistrants) for prosecution on the basis of their exercise of First Amendment rights.

III

In our criminal justice system, the Government retains "broad discretion" as to whom to prosecute. This broad discretion rests largely on the recognition that the decision to prosecute is particularly ill-suited to judicial review. Such factors as the strength of the case, the prosecution's general deterrence value, the Government's enforcement priorities, and the case's relationship to the Government's overall enforcement plan are not readily susceptible to the kind of analysis the courts are competent to undertake. Judicial supervision in this area, moreover, entails systemic costs of particular concern. Examining the basis of a prosecution delays the criminal proceeding, threatens to chill law enforcement by subjecting the prosecutor's motives and decisionmaking to outside inquiry, and may undermine prosecutorial effectiveness by revealing the Government's enforcement policy. All these are substantial concerns that make the courts properly hesitant to examine the decision whether to prosecute.

As we have noted in a slightly different context, however, although prosecutorial discretion is broad, it is not "unfettered." Selectivity in the enforcement of criminal laws is . . . subject to constitutional constraints." In particular, the decision to prosecute may not be "deliberately based upon an unjustifiable standard such as race, religion, or other arbitrary classification," including the exercise of protected statutory and constitutional rights.

It is appropriate to judge selective prosecution claims according to ordinary equal protection standards. Under our prior cases, these standards require petitioner to show both that the passive enforcement system had a discriminatory effect and that it was motivated by a discriminatory purpose. All petitioner has shown here is that those eventually prosecuted, along with many not prosecuted, reported themselves as having violated the law. He has not shown that the enforcement policy selected nonregistrants for prosecution on the basis of their speech. Indeed, he could not have done so given the way the "beg" policy was carried out. The Government did not prosecute those who reported themselves but later registered. Nor did it prosecute those who protested registration but did not report themselves or were not reported by others. In fact, the Government did not even investigate those who wrote letters to Selective Service criticizing registration unless their letters stated affirmatively that they had refused to comply with the law. The Government, on the other hand, did prosecute people who reported themselves or were reported by others but who did not publicly protest. These facts demonstrate that the Government treated all reported nonregistrants similarly. It did not subject vocal nonregistrants to any special burden. Indeed, those prosecuted in effect selected themselves for prosecution by refusing to register after being reported and warned by the Government.

Even if the passive policy had a discriminatory effect, petitioner has not shown that the Government intended such a result. The evidence he presented demonstrated only that the Government was aware that the passive enforcement policy would result in prosecution of vocal objectors and that they would probably make selective prosecution claims. As we have noted, however: "[D]iscriminatory purpose . . . implies more than . . . intent as awareness of consequences. It implies that the decisionmaker . . . selected or reaffirmed a particular course of action at least in part because of, not merely in spite of, its adverse effects upon an identifiable group." In the present case, petitioner has not shown that the Government prosecuted him *because of* his protest activities. Absent such a showing, his claim of selective prosecution fails. . . .

NOTES & QUESTIONS ON SELECTIVE PROSECUTION

1. *The equal protection argument.* Although the litigants in *Wayte* were ultimately unsuccessful, the Court's decision nonetheless lays out a roadmap for a successful claim of selective prosecution under equal protection. According to the Court, a successful equal protection argument would require that the defendant "show both that the passive enforcement system had a discriminatory effect and that it was motivated by a discriminatory purpose." Can you imagine situations of prosecutorial discretion that would run afoul of this standard? What would count as a discriminatory purpose? Also, what counts as a protected class in this context? Presumably, if prosecutors decided, pursuant to an office policy, to only prosecute the most "culpable" violators of a particular statute, this would not be problematic from the standpoint of equal protection standards. Indeed, simply prosecuting "the worst of the worst" would be garden-variety prosecutorial discretion that happens every day. What made the selective enforcement allegedly problematic in *Wayte* was that the selective prosecution went after the vocal objectors who had exercised their First Amendment rights. Can you imagine other examples of a protected class other than those exercising valid First Amendment rights?

2. *Elections for prosecutors.* U.S. Attorneys are appointed by the President of the United States, and their staff attorneys, called Assistant U.S. Attorneys (AUSAs), are appointed to their positions at the Justice Department. In contrast, local prosecutors are elected to their positions. Does the introduction of

direct democracy to the selection of prosecutors influence the exercise of prosecutorial discretion? Are elected prosecutors more likely to pursue harsher outcomes? At least some scholars argue that the answer to this question is yes, especially when compared with foreign legal systems without elected prosecutors and judges. See Michael Tonry, *Differences in National Sentencing Systems and the Differences They Make*, 45 Crime & Just. 1, 3 (2016) ("Substantial empirical evidence shows that prosecutorial and judicial decisions often become more severe when reelection campaigns loom.").

3. *Selective treatment in the immigration context.* As *Wayte* exemplifies, it is extraordinarily difficult for a defendant to succeed in a claim alleging selective prosecution. For example, a claim of selective prosecution is not available in the immigration context, i.e., arguing that the executive has impermissibly targeted an individual for removal from the country. As the Supreme Court stated in *Reno v. Am.-Arab Anti-Discrimination Comm.,* 525 U.S. 471, 491 (1999):

> The Executive should not have to disclose its "real" reasons for deeming nationals of a particular country a special threat—or indeed for simply wishing to antagonize a particular foreign country by focusing on that country's nationals—and even if it did disclose them a court would be ill equipped to determine their authenticity and utterly unable to assess their adequacy. Moreover, the consideration on the other side of the ledger in deportation cases—the interest of the target in avoiding "selective" treatment—is less compelling than in criminal prosecutions.

Is this deference to executive decision making in the immigration context advisable and appropriate? Moreover, do you agree with the Supreme Court that the danger of selective treatment in immigration is less "compelling" than in criminal prosecutions?

PROBLEM CASE

On April 7, 2018, Sarah Webb was driving down the street on her way to work. She was late and driving too fast. She was stopped by the police.

But this was no ordinary speeding ticket situation. The arresting officer noted that Webb had exceeded 80 miles per hour and that the road was wet. The officer threatened to upgrade the charge from mere speeding to "reckless driving"—a charge that could trigger an arrest. The officer returned to her squad car.

The police officer had a decision to make. She could either hand Webb a ticket for speeding and send her on her way—perhaps after giving her the customary admonition to slow down for the benefit of her own safety and the safety of her fellow motorists on the road. Or she could charge Webb with reckless driving and arrest her, with the expectation that the local prosecutor could argue that her conduct was sufficiently reckless under the circumstances to justify the charge. How to decide?

NYPD officer demonstrates how a body camera will be activated during a December 2014 news conference on the "Big Brother" pilot program of body cameras. (Shannon Stapleton/Reuters)

The officer's body camera captured the deliberations. As part of her discussion with her partner, the officer decided to pull out her smartphone and consult a so-called coin-flipping "app" that simulates the flipping of a coin. The "coin" in the app indicated that she should let Webb go with the ticket instead of arresting her. But after more consultation and discussion, the decision was reversed, and the police arrested Webb and took her to the police station.

As part of her case, Webb received access to the recording of the entire arrest, which included the coin-flip. She objected profusely, and the police chief was forced to explain how the flipping of a coin was a permissible form of police discretion. The officers were placed on administrative leave pending an investigation.

The incident raises a large question about the nature of discretion generally in the criminal justice system. Is there any legal or ethical prohibition on letting randomness factor into the decision? Is it essential that the state provide coherent *reasons* for its exercise of prosecutorial discretion? In other words, does an individual have the right to have their charging decision made based on a well-thought-out policy? For more discussion, see Jacey Fortin, *Before an Arrest, Officers Tossed a (Virtual) Coin*, N.Y. Times, July 14, 2018.

2. Charging Motivated by Racial Discrimination

There is something deeply unsettling about the prospect that a prosecutor might exercise his or her discretion in a racially discriminatory way. It is clear that the Constitution will not permit the state to allow racial discrimination to influence the charging decision. In the following case, the Supreme Court articulates and applies the exact standard that a defendant must satisfy in order to make out a claim of racially discriminatory charging: that the government did not prosecute "similarly situated suspects" of other races. As you read the case, make sure you remember the procedural posture of the case: a discovery dispute over whether the defendant is entitled to receive evidence from the prosecution regarding the charging decision.

United States v. Armstrong

Supreme Court of the United States
517 U.S. 456 (1996)

Chief Justice REHNQUIST delivered the opinion of the Court.

In this case, we consider the showing necessary for a defendant to be entitled to discovery on a claim that the prosecuting attorney singled him out for prosecution on the basis of his race. We conclude that respondents failed to satisfy the threshold showing: They failed to show that the Government declined to prosecute similarly situated suspects of other races.

In April 1992, respondents were indicted in the United States District Court for the Central District of California on charges of conspiring to possess with intent to distribute more than 50 grams of cocaine base (crack) and conspiring to distribute the same, and federal firearms offenses. . . . In response to the indictment, respondents filed a motion for discovery or for dismissal of the indictment, alleging that they were selected for federal prosecution because they are black. In support of their motion, they offered only an affidavit by a "Paralegal Specialist," employed by the Office of the Federal Public Defender representing one of the respondents. The only allegation in the affidavit was that, in every one of the 24 . . . cases closed by the office during 1991, the defendant was black. Accompanying the affidavit was a "study" listing the 24 defendants, their race, whether they were prosecuted for dealing cocaine as well as crack, and the status of each case. . . .

In *Wade v. United States*, 504 U.S. 181 (1992), we considered whether a federal court may review a Government decision not to file a motion to reduce a defendant's sentence for substantial assistance to the prosecution, to determine whether the Government based its decision on the defendant's race or religion. In holding that such a decision was reviewable, we assumed that discovery would be available if the defendant could make the appropriate threshold showing, although we concluded that the defendant in that case did not make such a showing. We proceed on a like assumption here.

A selective-prosecution claim is not a defense on the merits to the criminal charge itself, but an independent assertion that the prosecutor has brought the charge for reasons forbidden by the Constitution. Our cases delineating the necessary elements to prove a claim of selective prosecution have taken great pains to explain that the standard is a demanding one. These cases afford a "background presumption" that the showing necessary to obtain discovery should itself be a significant barrier to the litigation of insubstantial claims.

A selective-prosecution claim asks a court to exercise judicial power over a "special province" of the Executive. The Attorney General and United States Attorneys retain "broad discretion" to enforce the Nation's criminal laws. They have this latitude because they are designated by statute as the President's delegates to help him discharge his constitutional responsibility to "take Care that the Laws be faithfully executed." As a result, "[t]he presumption of regularity supports" their prosecutorial decisions and, "in the absence of clear evidence to the contrary, courts presume that they have properly discharged their official duties." In the ordinary case, "so long as the prosecutor has probable cause to believe that the accused committed an offense defined by statute, the decision whether or not to prosecute, and what charge to file or bring before a grand jury, generally rests entirely in his discretion."

Of course, a prosecutor's discretion is "subject to constitutional constraints." One of these constraints, imposed by the equal protection component of the Due Process Clause of the Fifth Amendment, is that the decision whether to prosecute may not be based on "an unjustifiable standard such as race, religion, or other arbitrary classification." A defendant may demonstrate that the administration of a criminal law is "directed so exclusively against a particular class of persons . . . with a mind so unequal and oppressive" that the system of prosecution amounts to "a practical denial" of equal protection of the law.

In order to dispel the presumption that a prosecutor has not violated equal protection, a criminal defendant must present "clear evidence to the contrary." We explained in *Wayte* why courts are "properly hesitant to examine the decision whether to prosecute." Judicial deference to the decisions of these executive officers rests in part on an assessment of the relative competence of prosecutors and courts. "Such factors as the strength of the case, the prosecution's general deterrence value, the Government's enforcement priorities, and the case's relationship to the Government's overall enforcement plan are not readily susceptible to the kind of analysis the courts are competent to undertake." It also stems from a concern not to unnecessarily impair the performance of a core executive constitutional function. "Examining the basis of a prosecution delays the criminal proceeding, threatens to chill law enforcement by subjecting the prosecutor's motives and decisionmaking to outside inquiry, and may undermine prosecutorial effectiveness by revealing the Government's enforcement policy."

The requirements for a selective-prosecution claim draw on "ordinary equal protection standards." The claimant must demonstrate that the federal prosecutorial policy "had a discriminatory effect and that it was motivated by a discriminatory purpose." To establish a discriminatory effect in a race case, the claimant must show that similarly situated individuals of a different race were not prosecuted. . . .

Having reviewed the requirements to prove a selective-prosecution claim, we turn to the showing necessary to obtain discovery in support of such a claim. If discovery is ordered, the Government must assemble from its own files documents which might corroborate or refute the defendant's claim. Discovery thus imposes many of the costs present when the Government must respond to a prima facie case of selective prosecution. It will divert prosecutors' resources and may disclose the Government's prosecutorial strategy. The justifications for a rigorous standard for the elements of a selective-prosecution claim thus require a correspondingly rigorous standard for discovery in aid of such a claim.

The parties, and the Courts of Appeals which have considered the requisite showing to establish entitlement to discovery, describe this showing with a variety of phrases, like "colorable basis," "substantial threshold showing," "substantial and concrete basis," or "reasonable likelihood." However, the many labels for this showing conceal the degree of consensus about the evidence necessary to meet it. The Courts of Appeals "require some evidence tending to show the existence of the essential elements of the defense," discriminatory effect and discriminatory intent.

In this case we consider what evidence constitutes "some evidence tending to show the existence" of the discriminatory effect element. The Court of Appeals held that a defendant may establish a colorable basis for discriminatory effect without evidence that the Government has failed to prosecute others who are similarly situated to the defendant. We think it was mistaken in this view. The vast majority of the Courts of Appeals require the defendant to produce some evidence that similarly situated defendants of other races could have been prosecuted, but were not, and this requirement is consistent with our equal protection case law. As the three-judge panel explained, "[s]elective prosecution implies that a selection has taken place."

The Court of Appeals reached its decision in part because it started "with the presumption that people of all races commit all types of crimes—not with the premise that any type of crime is the exclusive province of any particular racial or ethnic group." It cited no authority for this proposition, which seems contradicted by the most recent statistics of the United States Sentencing Commission. Those statistics show: More than 90% of the persons sentenced in 1994 for crack cocaine trafficking were black; 93.4% of convicted LSD dealers were white; and 91% of those convicted for pornography or prostitution were white. Presumptions at war with presumably reliable statistics have no proper place in the analysis of this issue.

The Court of Appeals also expressed concern about the "evidentiary obstacles defendants face." But all of its sister Circuits that have confronted the issue have required that defendants produce some evidence of differential treatment of similarly situated members of other races or protected classes. In the present case, if the claim of selective prosecution were well founded, it should not have been an insuperable task to prove that persons of other races were being treated differently than respondents. For instance, respondents could have investigated whether similarly situated persons of other races were prosecuted by the State of California and were known to federal law enforcement officers, but were not prosecuted in federal court. We think the required threshold—a credible showing of different treatment of similarly situated persons—adequately balances the Government's interest in vigorous prosecution and the defendant's interest in avoiding selective prosecution.

In the case before us, respondents' "study" did not constitute "some evidence tending to show the existence of the essential elements of" a selective-prosecution claim. The study failed to identify individuals who were not black and could have been prosecuted for the offenses for which respondents were charged, but were not so prosecuted. This omission was not remedied by respondents' evidence in opposition to the Government's motion for reconsideration. The newspaper article, which discussed the discriminatory effect of federal drug sentencing laws, was not relevant to an allegation of discrimination in decisions to prosecute. Respondents' affidavits, which recounted one attorney's conversation with a drug treatment center employee and the experience of another attorney defending drug prosecutions in state court, recounted hearsay and reported personal conclusions based on anecdotal evidence. The judgment of the Court of Appeals is therefore reversed. . . .

Justice STEVENS, dissenting.

Federal prosecutors are respected members of a respected profession. Despite an occasional misstep, the excellence of their work abundantly justifies the presumption that "they have properly discharged their official duties." Nevertheless, the possibility that political or racial animosity may infect a decision to institute criminal proceedings cannot be ignored. For that reason, it has long been settled that the prosecutor's broad discretion to determine when criminal charges should be filed is not completely unbridled. As the Court notes, however, the scope of judicial review of particular exercises of that discretion is not fully defined.

The United States Attorney for the Central District of California is a member and an officer of the bar of that District Court. As such, she has a duty to the judges of that Court to maintain the standards of the profession in the performance of her official functions. If a District Judge has reason to suspect that she, or a member of her staff, has singled out particular defendants for prosecution on the basis of their race, it is surely appropriate for the judge to determine whether there is a factual basis for such a concern. I agree with the Court that Rule 16 of the Federal Rules of Criminal Procedure is not the source of the District Court's power to make the necessary inquiry. I disagree, however, with its implicit assumption that a different, relatively rigid rule needs to be crafted to regulate the use of this seldom-exercised inherent judicial power.

The Court correctly concludes that in this case the facts presented to the District Court in support of respondents' claim that they had been singled out for prosecution because of their race were not sufficient to prove that defense. Moreover, I agree with the Court that their showing was not strong enough to give them a right to discovery, either under Rule 16 or under the District Court's inherent power to order discovery in appropriate circumstances. Like Chief Judge Wallace of the Court of Appeals, however, I am persuaded that the District Judge did not abuse her discretion when she concluded that the factual showing was sufficiently disturbing to require some response from the United States Attorney's Office. Perhaps the discovery order was broader than necessary, but I cannot agree with the Court's apparent conclusion that no inquiry was permissible.

The District Judge's order should be evaluated in light of three circumstances that underscore the need for judicial vigilance over certain types of drug prosecutions. First, the Anti-Drug Abuse Act of 1986 and subsequent legislation established a regime of extremely high penalties for the possession and distribution of so-called "crack" cocaine. Those provisions treat one gram of crack as the equivalent of 100 grams of powder cocaine. . . . These penalties result in sentences for crack offenders that average three to eight times longer than sentences for comparable powder offenders.

Second, the disparity between the treatment of crack cocaine and powder cocaine is matched by the disparity between the severity of the punishment imposed by federal law and that imposed by state law for the same conduct. For a variety of reasons, often including the absence of mandatory minimums, the existence of parole, and lower baseline penalties, terms of imprisonment for drug offenses tend to be substantially lower in state systems than in the federal system. The difference is especially marked in the case of crack offenses. . . . For example, if respondent Hampton is found guilty, his federal sentence might be as long as a mandatory life term. Had he been tried in state court, his sentence could have been as short as 12 years, less worktime credits of half that amount.

Finally, it is undisputed that the brunt of the elevated federal penalties falls heavily on blacks. While 65% of the persons who have used crack are white, in 1993 they represented only 4% of the federal offenders convicted of trafficking in crack. . . . Those figures represent a major threat to the integrity of federal sentencing reform, whose main purpose was the elimination of disparity (especially racial) in sentencing. . . .

The extraordinary severity of the imposed penalties and the troubling racial patterns of enforcement give rise to a special concern about the fairness of charging practices for crack offenses. Evidence tending to prove that black defendants charged with distribution of crack in the Central District of California are prosecuted in federal court, whereas members of other races charged with similar offenses are prosecuted in state court, warrants close scrutiny by the federal judges in that district. In my view, the District Judge, who has sat on both the federal and the state benches in Los Angeles, acted well within her discretion to call for the development of facts that would demonstrate what standards, if any, governed the choice of forum where similarly situated offenders are prosecuted. . . .

NOTES & QUESTIONS ON RACIALLY DISCRIMINATORY CHARGING

1. *How to prove discriminatory charging.* The Court's ruling in *Armstrong* would seem to create a difficult paradox for a victim of racially discriminatory charging to emerge from. In order to make out a claim of racial discrimination, the defendant will need access to discovery and the documents to prove the case. But in order to be entitled to discovery, *Armstrong* says that the defendant needs proof of racial discrimination. As one scholar wrote: "The statistical data you need to prove discrimination is always in the hands of the government, but *Armstrong* requires you to prove your claim of discrimination in order to get discovery of the evidence you need to prove your claim of discrimination! I regard *Armstrong* as one of the most perverse rulings of the very perverse Rehnquist court." Gerald F. Uelmen, *Selective Prosecution, Armed Career Criminal Act, Change of Venue*, Champion, March 2004, at 34. Do you agree with this assessment? Of course, one should pay careful attention to standards of decision. The evidentiary burden that the defendant has to satisfy in order to compel discovery is not as weighty as the burden that he has to satisfy in order to make out a final claim of discrimination on the merits. The discovery question merely requires "some" evidence while the merits decision requires a more demanding standard. So the Catch-22 situation that the defendant faces is perhaps no different from other areas of the law that require some factual showing before discovery is granted. For more discussion of this issue, see Richard H. McAdams, *Race and Selective Prosecution: Discovering the Pitfalls of* Armstrong, 73 Chi.-Kent L. Rev. 605, 623 (1998) ("for many crimes, *Armstrong* makes discovery impossible even where the defendant is a victim of selective prosecution").

2. *Discriminatory intent. Armstrong* deals with the standard required to prevail on a request for discovery. If the litigant succeeds in meeting the "similarly situated" requirement, the litigant will be entitled to discovery. At that point, the litigant will need to mine the materials produced in discovery in order to make out a showing of the prosecutor's discriminatory intent. How likely is it that the discovery process will yield evidence of discriminatory intent? Is it likely that the prosecutor would record his discriminatory intentions in the documentary record?

3. Vindictive Prosecution

What if the prosecutor's decision to charge creates a perception of vindictiveness, rather than that of a neutral application of an existing policy of prosecutorial discretion? For example, imagine a scenario where the defendant is charged and convicted of one crime, which he then successfully appeals. Imagine further that the appellate court's opinion overturning the conviction is highly critical of the prosecution's case and the prosecutor's conduct during the trial. In that situation, the prosecutor might feel embarrassed and might retaliate by bringing new, unrelated charges against the defendant that the prosecutor ordinarily would not prosecute. Assuming that the prosecutor can otherwise satisfy the demands of the probable cause standard for the second round of charges, would this be permissible? Or should the motivation itself—vindictiveness—taint the entire prosecution?

In the following case, the Supreme Court considers a real case of alleged vindictiveness—a prosecution taken in supposed retaliation for a defendant's assertion of his procedural rights. The defendant was convicted of a misdemeanor in a bench trial and then appealed the conviction, as was his right, to request a de novo jury trial on the same charges. This is a common procedural element for appealing misdemeanors; it does not violate double jeopardy because it is the defendant appealing the conviction rather than the prosecution appealing an acquittal. In the following case, however, the prosecution responded to the defendant's appeal by substituting the misdemeanor charge with a more serious felony charge. As you read the case, ask yourself whether the standards for unconstitutional vindictiveness should be the same for prosecutors as they are for judges.

Blackledge v. Perry

Supreme Court of the United States
417 U.S. 21 (1974)

Mr. Justice Stewart delivered the opinion of the Court.

While serving a term of imprisonment in a North Carolina penitentiary, the respondent Perry became involved in an altercation with another inmate. A warrant issued, charging Perry with the misdemeanor of assault with a deadly weapon. Under North Carolina law, the District Court Division of the General Court of Justice has exclusive jurisdiction for the trial of misdemeanors. Following a trial without a jury in the District Court of Northampton County, Perry was convicted of this misdemeanor and given a six-month sentence, to be served after completion of the prison term he was then serving.

Perry then filed a notice of appeal to the Northampton County Superior Court. Under North Carolina law, a person convicted in the District Court has a right to a trial de novo in the Superior Court. The right to trial de novo is absolute, there being no need for the appellant to allege error in the original proceeding. When an appeal is taken, the statutory scheme provides that the slate is wiped clean; the prior conviction is annulled, and the prosecution and the defense begin anew in the Superior Court.

After the filing of the notice of appeal, but prior to the respondent's appearance for trial de novo in the Superior Court, the prosecutor obtained an indictment from a grand jury, charging Perry with the felony of assault with a deadly weapon with intent to kill and inflict serious bodily injury. The indictment covered the same conduct for which Perry had been tried and convicted in the District Court. Perry entered a plea of guilty to the indictment in the Superior Court, and was sentenced to a term of five to seven years in the penitentiary, to be served concurrently with the identical prison sentence he was then serving.

A number of months later, the respondent filed an application for a writ of habeas corpus in the United States District Court for the Eastern District of North Carolina. He claimed that the indictment on the felony charge in the Superior Court constituted double jeopardy and also deprived him of due process of law. . . .

I

As in the District Court, Perry directs two independent constitutional attacks upon the conduct of the State in haling him into court on the felony charge after he took an appeal from the misdemeanor conviction. First, he contends that the felony indictment in the Superior Court placed him in double jeopardy, since he had already been convicted on the lesser included misdemeanor charge in the District Court. Second, he urges that the indictment on the felony charge constituted a penalty for his exercising his statutory right to appeal, and thus contravened the Due Process Clause of the Fourteenth Amendment. We find it necessary to reach only the latter claim.

Perry's due process arguments are derived substantially from *North Carolina v. Pearce*, 395 U.S. 711, and its progeny. In *Pearce*, the Court considered the constitutional problems presented when, following a successful appeal and reconviction, a criminal defendant was subjected to a greater punishment than that imposed at the first trial. While we concluded that such a harsher sentence was not absolutely precluded by either the Double Jeopardy or Due Process Clause, we emphasized that "imposition of a penalty upon the defendant for having successfully pursued a statutory right of appeal or collateral remedy would be . . . a violation of due process of law." Because "vindictiveness against a defendant for having successfully attacked his first conviction must play no part in the sentence he receives after a new trial," we held that an increased sentence could not be imposed upon retrial unless the sentencing judge placed certain specified findings on the record.

The lesson that emerges . . . is that the Due Process Clause is not offended by all possibilities of increased punishment upon retrial after appeal, but only by those that pose a realistic likelihood of "vindictiveness." Unlike the circumstances presented by those cases, however, in the situation here the central figure is not the judge or the jury, but the prosecutor. The question is whether the opportunities for vindictiveness in this situation are such as to impel the conclusion that due process of law requires a rule analogous to that of the *Pearce* case. We conclude that the answer must be in the affirmative.

A prosecutor clearly has a considerable stake in discouraging convicted misdemeanants from appealing and thus obtaining a trial de novo in the Superior Court, since such an appeal will clearly require increased expenditures of prosecutorial resources before the defendant's conviction becomes final, and may even result in a formerly convicted defendant's going free. And, if the prosecutor has the means readily at hand to discourage such appeals—by "upping the ante" through a felony indictment whenever a convicted misdemean[an]t pursues his statutory appellate remedy—the State can insure that only the most hardy defendants will brave the hazards of a de novo trial.

There is, of course, no evidence that the prosecutor in this case acted in bad faith or maliciously in seeking a felony indictment against Perry. The rationale of our judgment in the *Pearce* case, however, was not grounded upon the proposition that actual retaliatory motivation must inevitably exist. Rather, we emphasized that "since the fear of such vindictiveness may unconstitutionally deter a defendant's exercise of the right to appeal or collaterally attack his first conviction, due process also requires that a defendant be freed of apprehension of such a retaliatory motivation on the part of the sentencing judge." We think it clear that the same considerations apply here. A person convicted of an offense is entitled to pursue his statutory right to a trial de novo, without apprehension that the State will retaliate by substituting a more serious charge for the original one, thus subjecting him to a significantly increased potential period of incarceration.

Due process of law requires that such a potential for vindictiveness must not enter into North Carolina's two-tiered appellate process. We hold, therefore, that it was not constitutionally permissible for the State to respond to Perry's invocation of his statutory right to appeal by bringing a more serious charge against him prior to the trial de novo. . . .

Mr. Justice Rehnquist, dissenting.

I would find it more difficult than the Court apparently does in Part I of its opinion to conclude that the very bringing of more serious charges against respondent following his request for a trial de novo violated due process as defined in *North Carolina v. Pearce*. . . .

As the Court notes, in addition to his claim based on *Pearce*, respondent contends that his felony indictment in the Superior Court violated his rights under the Double Jeopardy Clause of the Fifth Amendment, made applicable to the States through the Fourteenth Amendment. Presumably because we have earlier held that "the jeopardy incident to" a trial does "not extent to an offense beyond (the trial court's) jurisdiction," the Court rests its decision instead on the Fourteenth Amendment due process doctrine of *Pearce*. In so doing, I think the Court too readily equates the role of the prosecutor, who is a natural adversary of the defendant and who, "often request(s) more than (he) can reasonably expect to get," with that of the sentencing judge in *Pearce*. . . .

The concurring opinion in *Pearce* took the position that the imposition of a penalty after retrial which exceeded the penalty imposed after the first trial violated the guarantee against double jeopardy. But the opinion of the Court . . . specifically rejected such an approach to the case. The Court went on to hold "that neither the double jeopardy provision nor the Equal Protection Clause imposes an absolute bar to a more severe sentence upon reconviction." The Court concluded by holding that due process "requires that vindictiveness against a defendant for having successfully attacked his first conviction must play no part in the sentence he receives after a new trial. And since the fear of such vindictiveness may unconstitutionally deter a defendant's exercise of the right to appeal or collaterally attack his first conviction, due process also requires that a defendant be freed of apprehension of such a retaliatory motivation on the part of the sentencing judge." To make certain that those requirements of due process were met, the Court laid down the rule that "whenever a judge imposes a more severe sentence upon a defendant after a new trial, the reasons for his doing so must affirmatively appear." Thus the avowed purpose of the remedy fashioned in *Pearce* was to prevent judicial vindictiveness from resulting in longer sentences after a retrial following successful appeal.

Since in theory if not in practice the second sentence in the *Pearce* situation might be expected to be the same as the first unless influenced

> by vindictiveness or by intervening conduct of the defendant, in theory at least the remedy mandated there reached no further than the identified wrong. The same cannot be said here. For while indictment on more serious charges after a successful appeal would present a problem closely analogous to that in *Pearce* in this respect, the bringing of more serious charges after a defendant's exercise of his absolute right to a trial de novo in North Carolina's two-tier system does not. The prosecutor here elected to proceed initially in the State District Court where felony charges could not be prosecuted, for reasons which may well have been unrelated to whether he believed respondent was guilty of and could be convicted of the felony with which he was later charged. Both prosecutor and defendant stand to benefit from an initial prosecution in the District Court, the prosecutor at least from its less burdensome procedures and the defendant from the opportunity for an initial acquittal and the limited penalties. With the countervailing reasons for proceeding only on the misdemeanor charge in the District Court no longer applicable once the defendant has invoked his statutory right to a trial de novo, a prosecutor need not be vindictive to seek to indict and convict a defendant of the more serious of the two crimes of which he believes him guilty. Thus even if one accepts the Court's equation of prosecutorial vindictiveness with judicial vindictiveness, here, unlike *Pearce*, the Court's remedy reaches far beyond the wrong it identifies. . . .

NOTES & QUESTIONS ON VINDICTIVE PROSECUTION

1. *Vindictive prosecution as a due process violation.* The Court in *Blackledge v. Perry* concluded that vindictive prosecutions violated due process, as opposed to equal protection. Do you agree that due process is a better framework than equal protection for considering the issue? What about the prosecution in Perry's case violated due process? More importantly, what general inferences can one make about the requirements of due process with regard to prosecutorial discretion? What is the underlying theory about the constitutional limits on prosecutorial discretion?

2. *The underlying theory.* What is the core theory underlying the doctrine of vindictive prosecution? Consider the following possibility:

> One reason a prosecutor might bring increased charges against a defendant who exercises a procedural right is to make future defendants think twice before exercising the same right. Indeed, a rational prosecutor might retaliate early in his or her career even if the marginal cost of doing so in an individual case exceeds the marginal benefit in that case, if only to establish

> a "tough" reputation. In any event, deterrence based on vocalized threats imperils constitutional rights the same way that deterrence based on patterns of past retaliation does. With a vocalized threat, a prosecutor may not even have to re-indict the defendant on the more severe charges; the defendant may self-chill. Thus, the prosecutor can save the effort of re-indicting the defendant and the attendant burdens that may accompany attempts to obtain a superseding indictment.

Tung Yin, *Coercion and Terrorism Prosecutions in the Shadow of Military Detention*, 2006 BYU L. Rev. 1255, 1314. Do you agree that the doctrine announced in *Blackledge v. Perry* is based on the need to encourage defendants to exercise their procedural rights? Or was the point merely to contain prosecutorial retaliation because it is per se impermissible and contrary to due process, irrespective of the larger consequences as a matter of policy?

3. *Prosecutorial vindictiveness versus judicial vindictiveness.* What is the difference between a judge's vindictiveness and a prosecutor's vindictiveness? Do you agree with Justice Rehnquist's complaint that the majority has conflated the two concepts? While the judge is clearly under a legal and an ethical obligation to approach a case with a sense of fairness and evenhandedness, does the same obligation run to the prosecutor? In what sense is the prosecutor obligated to treat potential defendants fairly? Does that obligation include a requirement to treat like cases alike? Does it include an obligation to avoid outcomes motivated by vindictiveness? Part of the answer to this question depends logically on our underlying conception of the public prosecutor. Is the prosecutor tasked with winning at all costs—balanced by a defense counsel seeking the opposite goal—or is the prosecutor tasked with a more nuanced goal?

4. *Due process limits on increasing sentences.* Imagine a situation where the defendant is convicted at trial and receives a sentence. The defendant successfully appeals the conviction and the appellate court orders a new trial. The second trial results in a conviction and the trial court is then in a position where it must resentence the defendant. The court then imposes a *higher* sentence than was originally imposed, even though the conviction is for the same charge. One could imagine this happening in either of two ways. Either the trial court is angered by the defendant's decision to appeal and angered by the appellate reversal, *or* the trial court simply has a change of heart, perhaps based on rehearing the evidence during the second trial. Does the increase in sentence in these hypothetical cases concern you? If so, why? In *North Carolina v. Pearce*, the Supreme Court concluded that an increased sentence, when motivated by vindictiveness, violated due process, but also recognized that there might be legitimate reasons for an increased sentence. To distinguish between these two possibilities, the Court noted:

> In order to assure the absence of such a [vindictive] motivation, we have concluded that whenever a judge imposes a more severe sentence upon a defendant after a new trial, the reasons for his doing so must affirmatively appear. Those reasons must be based upon objective information concerning identifiable conduct on the part of the defendant occurring after the time of the original sentencing proceeding. And the factual data upon which the increased sentence is based must be made part of the record, so that the constitutional legitimacy of the increased sentence may be fully reviewed on appeal.

North Carolina v. Pearce, 395 U.S. 711, 726 (1969). In *Alabama v. Smith*, 490 U.S. 794, 799 (1989), the Supreme Court clarified that there is no "presumption" of vindictiveness in these situations and that the "burden remains upon the defendant to prove actual vindictiveness."

C. CHARGING DEFENDANTS SEPARATELY OR TOGETHER

As a matter of law, prosecutors have the discretion to "join" for a common trial multiple defendants when the charges relate to the same criminal transaction. For example, Rule 8 of the Federal Rules of Criminal Procedure states that "[t]he indictment or information may charge two or more defendants if they are alleged to have participated in the same act or transaction, or in the same series of acts or transactions, constituting an offense or offenses. The defendants may be charged in one or more counts together or separately. All defendants need not be charged in each count." While a defendant may object to this joinder by filing a motion to sever, the defendant must demonstrate that the joint trial will result in unfair prejudice that cannot be offset by appropriate limiting instructions.

Even in situations where the defendants are indicted separately, the cases can be merged for the purpose of holding a combined trial. Rule 13 states that "[t]he court may order that separate cases be tried together as though brought in a single indictment or information if all offenses and all defendants could have been joined in a single indictment or information." However, if joinder results in unfair "prejudice" against either the defendant or the government, the court is permitted to "sever the defendants' trials, or provide any other relief that justice requires." See Rule 14.

As a matter of strategy, there are many reasons why a prosecutor might wish for the defendants to be tried together. For example, if the full nature of the criminality is best presented by both defendants appearing together, as in, for example, a conspiracy case, joinder might make it more likely that the jury will convict both defendants. On the other hand, there might be multiple reasons why joinder might be strategically inadvisable. Two defendants on trial together might blame each other, producing reasonable doubt and acquittals for both defendants if the jury believes that only one of them is guilty but cannot decide which one. Also, if the case against one defendant is built on the testimony of the other defendant, it might make more sense to indict the first defendant and negotiate a plea agreement, and then build a case against the second suspect.

In addition to these strategic issues, there are a number of situations where joint trials are *constitutionally* problematic. The following materials focus on the two most prominent situations: (1) inconsistent defenses among multiple defendants; and (2) limitations flowing from the demands of the Confrontation Clause.

1. Inconsistent Defenses

In the following case, the defendants, though tried together, implicated each other as responsible for the crime. The defendants claimed that their joint trial was impermissible because their defenses were mutually inconsistent. Why exactly is this impermissible? Do you agree with their assumption that juries confronted with inconsistent defenses will be more inclined to conclude that one or even both defendants are probably guilty? In other words, do mutually inconsistent defenses tend to produce more convictions? More importantly, is that reason enough to require the judge to sever the cases and try the defendants separately?

Zafiro v. United States

Supreme Court of the United States
506 U.S. 534 (1993)

Justice O'Connor delivered the opinion of the Court.

Rule 8(b) of the Federal Rules of Criminal Procedure provides that defendants may be charged together "if they are alleged to have participated in the same act or transaction or in the same series of acts or transactions constituting an offense or offenses." Rule 14 of the Rules, in turn, permits a district court to grant a severance of defendants if "it appears that a defendant or the government is prejudiced by a joinder." In this case, we consider whether Rule 14 requires severance as a matter of law when codefendants present "mutually antagonistic defenses."

I

Gloria Zafiro, Jose Martinez, Salvador Garcia, and Alfonso Soto were accused of distributing illegal drugs in the Chicago area, operating primarily out of Soto's bungalow in Chicago and Zafiro's apartment in Cicero, a nearby suburb. One day, Government agents observed Garcia and Soto place a large box in Soto's car and drive from Soto's bungalow to Zafiro's apartment. The agents followed the two as they carried the box up the stairs. When the agents identified themselves, Garcia and Soto dropped the box and ran into the apartment. The agents entered the apartment in pursuit and found the four petitioners in the living room. The dropped box contained 55 pounds of cocaine. After obtaining a search warrant for the apartment, agents found approximately 16 pounds of cocaine, 25 grams of heroin, and 4 pounds of marijuana inside a suitcase in a closet. Next to the suitcase was a sack containing $22,960 in cash. Police officers also discovered 7 pounds of cocaine in a car parked in Soto's garage.

The four petitioners were indicted and brought to trial together. At various points during the proceeding, Garcia and Soto moved for severance, arguing that their defenses were mutually antagonistic. Soto testified that he knew nothing about the drug conspiracy. He claimed that Garcia had asked him for a box, which he gave Garcia, and that he (Soto) did not know its contents until they were arrested. Garcia did not testify, but his lawyer argued that Garcia was innocent: The box belonged to Soto and Garcia was ignorant of its contents.

Zafiro and Martinez also repeatedly moved for severance on the ground that their defenses were mutually antagonistic. Zafiro testified that she was merely Martinez's girlfriend and knew nothing of the conspiracy. She claimed that Martinez stayed in her apartment occasionally, kept some clothes there, and gave her small amounts of money. Although she allowed Martinez to store a suitcase in her closet, she testified, she had no idea that the suitcase contained illegal drugs. Like Garcia, Martinez did not testify. But his lawyer argued that Martinez was only visiting his girlfriend and had no idea that she was involved in distributing drugs. The District Court denied the motions for severance. . . .

II

Rule 8(b) states that "[t]wo or more defendants may be charged in the same indictment or information if they are alleged to have participated in the same act or transaction or in the same series of acts or transactions constituting an offense or offenses." There is a preference in the federal system for joint trials of defendants who are indicted together. Joint trials "play a vital role in the criminal justice system." They promote efficiency and "serve the interests of justice by avoiding the scandal and inequity of inconsistent verdicts." For these reasons, we repeatedly have approved of joint trials. But Rule 14 recognizes that joinder, even when proper under Rule 8(b), may prejudice either a defendant or the Government. Thus, the Rule provides: "If it appears that a defendant or the government is prejudiced by a joinder of . . . defendants . . . for trial together, the court may order an election or separate trials of counts, grant a severance of defendants or provide whatever other relief justice requires."

In interpreting Rule 14, the Courts of Appeals frequently have expressed the view that "mutually antagonistic" or "irreconcilable" defenses may be so prejudicial in some circumstances as to mandate severance. Notwithstanding such assertions, the courts have reversed relatively few convictions for failure to grant a severance on grounds of mutually antagonistic or irreconcilable defenses. The low rate of reversal may reflect the inability of defendants to prove a risk of prejudice in most cases involving conflicting defenses.

Nevertheless, petitioners urge us to adopt a bright-line rule, mandating severance whenever codefendants have conflicting defenses. We decline to do so. Mutually antagonistic defenses are not prejudicial per se. Moreover, Rule 14 does not require severance even if prejudice is shown; rather, it leaves the tailoring of the relief to be granted, if any, to the district court's sound discretion.

We believe that, when defendants properly have been joined under Rule 8(b), a district court should grant a severance under Rule 14 only if there is a serious risk that a joint trial would compromise a specific trial right of one of the defendants, or prevent the jury from making a reliable judgment about guilt or innocence. Such a risk might occur when evidence that the jury should not consider against a defendant and that would not be admissible if a defendant were tried alone is admitted against a codefendant. For example, evidence of a codefendant's wrongdoing in some circumstances erroneously could lead a jury to conclude that a defendant was guilty. When many defendants are tried together in a complex case and they have markedly different degrees of culpability, this risk of prejudice is heightened. Evidence that is probative of a defendant's guilt but technically admissible only against a codefendant also might present a risk of prejudice. Conversely, a defendant might suffer prejudice if essential exculpatory evidence that would be available to a defendant tried alone were unavailable in a joint trial. The risk of prejudice will vary with the facts in each case, and district courts may find prejudice in situations not discussed here. When the risk of prejudice is high, a district court is more likely to determine that separate trials are necessary, but . . . less drastic measures, such as limiting instructions, often will suffice to cure any risk of prejudice.

Turning to the facts of this case, we note that petitioners do not articulate any specific instances of prejudice. Instead they contend that the very nature of their defenses, without more, prejudiced them. Their theory is that when two defendants both claim they are innocent and each accuses the other of the crime, a jury will conclude (1) that both defendants are lying and convict them both on that basis, or (2) that at least one of the two must be guilty without regard to whether the Government has proved its case beyond a reasonable doubt.

As to the first contention, it is well settled that defendants are not entitled to severance merely because they may have a better chance of acquittal in separate trials. Rules 8(b) and 14 are designed "to promote economy and efficiency and to avoid a multiplicity of trials, [so long as] these objectives can be achieved without substantial prejudice to the right of the defendants to a fair trial." While "[a]n important element of a fair trial is that a jury consider only relevant and competent evidence bearing on the issue of guilt or innocence," a fair trial does not include the right to exclude relevant and competent evidence. A defendant normally would not be entitled to exclude the testimony of a former codefendant if the district court did sever their trials, and we see no reason why relevant and competent testimony would be prejudicial merely because the witness is also a codefendant.

As to the second contention, the short answer is that petitioners' scenario simply did not occur here. The Government argued that all four petitioners were guilty and offered sufficient evidence as to all four petitioners; the jury in turn found all four petitioners guilty of various offenses. Moreover, even if there were some risk of prejudice, here it is of the type that can be cured with proper instructions, and "juries are presumed to follow their instructions." The District Court properly instructed the jury that the Government had "the burden of proving beyond a reasonable doubt" that each defendant committed the crimes with which he or she was charged. The court then instructed the jury that it must "give separate consideration to each individual defendant and to each separate charge against him. Each defendant is entitled to have his or her case determined from his or her own conduct and from the evidence [that] may be applicable to him or to her." In addition, the District Court admonished the jury that opening and closing arguments are not evidence and that it should draw no inferences from a defendant's exercise of the right to silence. These instructions sufficed to cure any possibility of prejudice.

Rule 14 leaves the determination of risk of prejudice and any remedy that may be necessary to the sound discretion of the district courts. Because petitioners have not shown that their joint trial subjected them to any legally cognizable prejudice, we conclude that the District Court did not abuse its discretion in denying petitioners' motions to sever.

NOTES & QUESTIONS ON INCONSISTENT DEFENSES

1. *What is the cure?* As the preceding case demonstrates, just because the defendant succeeds in demonstrating that there is a risk of prejudice, this

finding by itself is insufficient to establish that severance is required. Severance is called for only if the court is satisfied that no other remedy is adequate to mitigate the risk of prejudice. In many cases, the court can and will issue a particular instruction to the jury prior to deliberation. The task for the defendant seeking severance is to argue that the instruction itself is incapable of mitigating the risk of prejudice.

2. *Dual juries.* In some instances, a court can order the hybrid step of holding a single trial but impaneling two juries—one for each defendant. Although the procedure is a bit unorthodox, there is no procedural bar to it in the federal courts. See, e.g., *Lambright v. Stewart*, 191 F.3d 1181, 1186 (9th Cir. 1999) ("We are satisfied that the use of dual juries can actually palliate, rather than exacerbate, the risks of a joint trial . . . the use of dual juries can capture both the advantages of a joint trial and the protections of separate trials."). For evidence that is admissible against one defendant but not the other, the judge could excuse one jury from the courtroom while the other jury remains to hear the evidence. The result is a customizable trial that is both joint and severed at the same time. For more discussion, see Richard Vorosmarti, *Joinder and Severance*, 89 Geo. L.J. 1307, 1320 (2001).

2. Limitations Flowing from the Confrontation Clause

Imagine the following scenario: During an interrogation, a suspect confesses to the police that he committed a murder. During the investigation, the suspect also identifies his co-felon who co-perpetrated the murder with him. A grand jury indicts both of them for murder and the prosecutor seeks to try them together. Herein arises a constitutional puzzle of the highest order. The prosecutor intends to introduce into evidence at trial the first suspect's confession to the police *as evidence against the first defendant only*. But now the second defendant objects. He objects that the jury is incapable of considering his co-defendant's confession *as evidence against him*, and that unless his co-defendant actually testifies, he will never have an opportunity to confront the co-defendant as to the veracity of the aspects of his confession that implicate him. In short, the objecting co-defendant is asserting that while the confession is technically being offered only against the confession co-defendant, it is *functionally* being offered against both defendants. And, because this renders the confession testimonial evidence against him, he has a right to "confront"—through cross-examination—those who are giving testimony against him. But the first suspect will not normally be testifying at the trial because a defendant enjoys a right against self-incrimination and generally speaking the government cannot force a defendant to testify. The result is that the confession is admissible against the first defendant but not the second.

The following case, *Bruton*, is the Supreme Court's signature attempt to resolve the evidentiary paradoxes associated with joint trials and the Confrontation Clause. As you read the case, pay careful attention to the Supreme Court's legal framework for resolving the problem of "powerfully incriminating" statements.

Bruton v. United States

Supreme Court of the United States
391 U.S. 123 (1968)

Mr. Justice Brennan delivered the opinion of the Court.

This case presents the question . . . whether the conviction of a defendant at a joint trial should be set aside although the jury was instructed that a codefendant's confession inculpating the defendant had to be disregarded in determining his guilt or innocence.

A joint trial of petitioner and one Evans in the District Court for the Eastern District of Missouri resulted in the conviction of both by a jury on a federal charge of armed postal robbery. A postal inspector testified that Evans orally confessed to him that Evans and petitioner committed the armed robbery. The postal inspector obtained the oral confession, and another in which Evans admitted he had an accomplice whom he would not name, in the course of two interrogations of Evans at the city jail in St. Louis, Missouri, where Evans was held in custody on state criminal charges. Both petitioner and Evans appealed their convictions to the Court of Appeals for the Eighth Circuit. That court set aside Evans' conviction on the ground that his oral confessions to the postal inspector should not have been received in evidence against him. However, the court, relying upon *Delli Paoli*, affirmed petitioner' conviction because the trial judge instructed the jury that although Evans' confession was competent evidence against Evans it was inadmissible hearsay against petitioner and therefore had to be disregarded in determining petitioner's guilt or innocence. We granted certiorari to reconsider *Delli Paoli*.

. . . We have concluded . . . that *Delli Paoli* should be overruled. We hold that, because of the substantial risk that the jury, despite instructions to the contrary, looked to the incriminating extrajudicial statements in determining petitioner's guilt, admission of Evans' confession in this joint trial violated petitioner's right of cross-examination secured by the Confrontation Clause of the Sixth Amendment. We therefore overrule *Delli Paoli* and reverse.

The basic premise of *Delli Paoli* was that it is "reasonably possible for the jury to follow" sufficiently clear instructions to disregard the confessor's extrajudicial statement that his codefendant participated with him in committing the crime. If it were true that the jury disregarded the reference to the codefendant, no question would arise under the Confrontation Clause, because by hypothesis the case is treated as if the confessor made no statement inculpating the nonconfessor. But since *Delli Paoli* was decided this Court has effectively repudiated its basic premise. Before discussing this, we pause to observe that in *Pointer v. Texas*, 380 U.S. 400, we confirmed "that the right of cross-examination is included in the right of an accused in a criminal case to confront the witnesses against him" secured by the Sixth Amendment; "a major reason underlying the constitutional confrontation rule is to give a defendant charged with crime an opportunity to cross-examine the witnesses against him."

We applied *Pointer* in *Douglas v. Alabama*, 380 U.S. 415, in circumstances analogous to those in the present case. There two persons, Loyd and Douglas, accused of assault with intent to murder, were tried separately. Loyd was tried first and found guilty. At Douglas' trial the State called Loyd as a witness against him. An appeal was pending from Loyd's conviction and Loyd invoked the privilege against self-incrimination and refused to answer any questions. The prosecution was permitted to treat Loyd as a hostile witness. Under the guise of refreshing Loyd's recollection the prosecutor questioned Loyd by asking him to confirm or deny statements read by the prosecutor from a document purported to be Loyd's confession. These statements inculpated Douglas in the crime. We held that Douglas' inability to cross-examine Loyd denied Douglas "the right of cross-examination secured by the Confrontation Clause." We noted that "effective confrontation of Loyd was possible only if Loyd affirmed the statement as his. However, Loyd did not do so, but relied on his privilege to refuse to answer." The risk of prejudice in petitioner's case was even more serious than in *Douglas*. In *Douglas* we said, "Although the Solicitor's reading of Loyd's alleged statement, and Loyd's refusals to answer, were not technically testimony, the Solicitor's reading may well have been the equivalent in the jury's mind of testimony that Loyd in fact made the statement; and Loyd's reliance upon the privilege created a situation in which the jury might improperly infer both that the statement had been made and that it was true." Here Evans' oral confessions were in fact testified to, and were therefore actually in evidence. That testimony was legitimate evidence against Evans and to that extent was properly before the jury during its deliberations. Even greater, then, was the likelihood that the jury would believe Evans made the statements and that they were true—not just the self-incriminating portions but those implicating petitioner as well. Plainly, the introduction of Evans' confession added substantial, perhaps even critical, weight to the Government's case in a form not subject to cross-examination, since Evans did not take the stand. Petitioner thus was denied his constitutional right of confrontation.

Delli Paoli assumed that this encroachment on the right to confrontation could be avoided by the instruction to the jury to disregard the inadmissible hearsay evidence. But, as we have said, that assumption has since been effectively repudiated. True, the repudiation was not in the context of the admission of a confession inculpating a codefendant but in the context of a New York rule which submitted to the jury the question of the voluntariness of the confession itself. Nonetheless the message of *Jackson* for *Delli Paoli* was clear. We there held that a defendant is constitutionally entitled at least to have the trial judge first determine whether a confession was made voluntarily before submitting it to the jury for an assessment of its credibility. More specifically, we expressly rejected the proposition that a jury, when determining the confessor's guilt, could be relied on to ignore his confession of guilt should it find the confession involuntary. Significantly, we supported that conclusion in part by reliance upon the dissenting opinion of Mr. Justice Frankfurter for the four Justices who dissented in *Delli Paoli*.

That dissent challenged the basic premise of *Delli Paoli* that a properly instructed jury would ignore the confessor's inculpation of the nonconfessor in determining the latter's guilt. "The fact of the matter is that too often such admonition against misuse is intrinsically ineffective in that the effect of such a nonadmissible declaration cannot be wiped from the brains of the jurors. The admonition therefore becomes a futile collocation of words and fails of its purpose as a legal protection to defendants against whom such a declaration should not tell." The dissent went on to say . . . "The Government should not have the windfall of having the jury be influenced by evidence against a defendant which, as a matter of law, they should not consider but which they cannot put out of their minds." . . .

[O]ur action in 1966 in amending Rule 14 of the Federal Rules of Criminal Procedure also evidences our repudiation of *Delli Paoli*'s basic premise. Rule 14 authorizes a severance where it appears that a defendant might be prejudiced by a joint trial. The Rule was amended in 1966 to provide expressly that "(i)n ruling on a motion by a defendant for severance the court may order the attorney for the government to deliver to the court for inspection in camera any statements or confessions made by the defendants which the government intends to introduce in evidence at the trial." The Advisory Committee on Rules said in explanation of the amendment:

> A defendant may be prejudiced by the admission in evidence against a co-defendant of a statement or confession made by that co-defendant. This prejudice cannot be dispelled by cross-examination if the co-defendant does not take the stand. Limiting instructions to the jury may not in fact erase the prejudice. . . . The purpose of the amendment is to provide a procedure whereby the issue of possible prejudice can be resolved on the motion for severance.

Those who have defended reliance on the limiting instruction in this area have cited several reasons in support. Judge Learned Hand, a particularly severe critic of the proposition that juries could be counted on to disregard inadmissible hearsay, wrote the opinion for the Second Circuit which affirmed Delli Paoli's conviction. In Judge Hand's view the limiting instruction, although not really capable of preventing the jury from considering the prejudicial evidence, does as a matter of form provide a way around the exclusionary rules of evidence that is defensible because it "probably furthers, rather than impedes, the search for truth. . . ." Insofar as this implies the prosecution ought not to be denied the benefit of the confession to prove the confessor's guilt, however, it overlooks alternative ways of achieving that benefit without at the same time infringing the nonconfessor's right of confrontation. Where viable alternatives do exist, it is deceptive to rely on the pursuit of truth to defend a clearly harmful practice.

Finally, the reason advanced by the majority in *Delli Paoli* was to tie the result to maintenance of the jury system. "Unless we proceed on the basis that the jury will follow the court's instructions where those instructions are clear and the circumstances are such that the jury can reasonably be expected to follow them, the jury system makes little sense." . . . Nevertheless . . . there are some contexts in which the risk that the jury will not, or cannot, follow instructions is so great, and the consequences of failure so vital to the defendant, that the practical and human limitations of the jury system cannot be ignored. Such a context is presented here, where the powerfully incriminating extrajudicial statements of a codefendant, who stands accused side-by-side with the defendant, are deliberately spread before the jury in a joint trial. Not only are the incriminations devastating to the defendant but their credibility is inevitably suspect, a fact recognized when accomplices do take the stand and the jury is instructed to weigh their testimony carefully given the recognized motivation to shift blame onto others. The unreliability of such evidence is intolerably compounded when the alleged accomplice, as here, does not testify and cannot be tested by cross-examination. It was against such threats to a fair trial that the Confrontation Clause was directed.

In the following case, the Supreme Court considers options short of severance to solve the *Bruton* problem. In *Richardson*, the confession from the first defendant was introduced at trial but was redacted in order to remove the name of the second defendant from the document. Is this redaction strategy sufficient to resolve the Sixth Amendment Confrontation Clause problems identified by the Supreme Court in *Bruton*? Or is severance the only permissible remedy?

Richardson v. Marsh

Supreme Court of the United States
481 U.S. 200 (1987)

Justice SCALIA delivered the opinion of the Court.

In *Bruton v. United States*, 391 U.S. 123 (1968), we held that a defendant is deprived of his rights under the Confrontation Clause when his nontestifying codefendant's confession naming him as a participant in the crime is introduced at their joint trial, even if the jury is instructed to consider that confession only against the codefendant. Today we consider whether *Bruton* requires the same result when the codefendant's confession is redacted to omit any reference to the defendant, but the defendant is nonetheless linked to the confession by evidence properly admitted against him at trial.

I

Respondent Clarissa Marsh, Benjamin Williams, and Kareem Martin were charged with assaulting Cynthia Knighton and murdering her 4-year-old son, Koran, and her aunt, Ollie Scott. Respondent and Williams were tried jointly, over her objection. (Martin was a fugitive at the time of trial.) At the trial, Knighton testified as follows: On the evening of October 29, 1978, she and her son were at Scott's home when respondent and her boyfriend Martin visited. After a brief conversation in the living room, respondent announced that she had come to "pick up something" from Scott and rose from the couch. Martin then pulled out a gun, pointed it at Scott and the Knightons, and said that "someone had gotten killed and [Scott] knew something about it." Respondent immediately walked to the front door and peered out the peephole. The doorbell rang, respondent opened the door, and Williams walked in, carrying a gun. As Williams passed respondent, he asked, "Where's the money?" Martin forced Scott upstairs, and Williams went into the kitchen, leaving respondent alone with the Knightons. Knighton and her son attempted to flee, but respondent grabbed Knighton and held her until Williams returned. Williams ordered the Knightons to lie on the floor and then went upstairs to assist Martin. Respondent, again left alone with the Knightons, stood by the front door and occasionally peered out the peephole. A few minutes later, Martin, Williams, and Scott came down the stairs, and Martin handed a paper grocery bag to respondent. Martin and Williams then forced Scott and the Knightons into the basement, where Martin shot them. Only Cynthia Knighton survived.

In addition to Knighton's testimony, the State introduced (over respondent's objection) a confession given by Williams to the police shortly after his arrest. The confession was redacted to omit all reference to respondent—indeed, to omit all indication that anyone other than Martin and Williams participated in the crime. The confession largely corroborated Knighton's account of the activities of persons other than respondent in the house. In addition, the confession described a conversation Williams had with Martin as they drove to the Scott home, during which, according to Williams, Martin said that he would have to kill the victims after the robbery. At the time the confession was admitted, the jury was admonished not to use it in any way against respondent. Williams did not testify.

After the State rested, respondent took the stand. She testified that on October 29, 1978, she had lost money that Martin intended to use to buy drugs. Martin was upset, and suggested to respondent that she borrow money from Scott, with whom she had worked in the past. Martin and respondent picked up Williams and drove to Scott's house. During the drive, respondent, who was sitting in the backseat, "knew that [Martin and Williams] were talking" but could not hear the conversation because "the radio was on and the speaker was right in [her] ear." Martin and respondent were admitted into the home, and respondent had a short conversation with Scott, during which she asked for a loan. Martin then pulled a gun, and respondent walked to the door to see where the car was. When she saw Williams, she opened the door for him. Respondent testified that during the robbery she did not feel free to leave and was too scared to flee. She said that she did not know why she prevented the Knightons from escaping. She admitted taking the bag from Martin, but said that after Martin and Williams took the victims into the basement, she left the house without the bag. Respondent insisted that she had possessed no prior knowledge that Martin and Williams were armed, had heard no conversation about anyone's being harmed, and had not intended to rob or kill anyone.

During his closing argument, the prosecutor admonished the jury not to use Williams' confession against respondent. Later in his argument, however, he linked respondent to the portion of Williams' confession describing his conversation with Martin in the car. (Respondent's attorney did not object to this.) After closing arguments, the judge again instructed the jury that Williams' confession was not to be considered against respondent. The jury convicted respondent of two counts of felony murder in the perpetration of an armed robbery and one count of assault with intent to commit murder. . . .

II

The Confrontation Clause of the Sixth Amendment, extended against the States by the Fourteenth Amendment, guarantees the right of a criminal defendant "to be confronted with the witnesses against him." The right of confrontation includes the right to cross-examine witnesses. Therefore, where two defendants are tried jointly, the pretrial confession of one cannot be admitted against the other unless the confessing defendant takes the stand.

Ordinarily, a witness whose testimony is introduced at a joint trial is not considered to be a witness "against" a defendant if the jury is instructed to consider that testimony only against a codefendant. This accords with the almost invariable assumption of the law that jurors follow their instructions, which we have applied in many varying contexts. . . . In *Bruton*, however, we recognized a narrow exception to this principle: We held that a defendant is deprived of his Sixth Amendment right of confrontation when the facially incriminating confession of a nontestifying codefendant is introduced at their joint trial, even if the jury is instructed to consider the confession only against the codefendant. . . .

There is an important distinction between this case and *Bruton*, which causes it to fall outside the narrow exception we have created. In *Bruton*, the codefendant's confession "expressly implicat[ed]" the defendant as his accomplice. Thus, at the time that confession was introduced there was not the slightest doubt that it would prove "powerfully incriminating." By contrast, in this case the confession was not incriminating on its face, and became so only when linked with evidence introduced later at trial (the defendant's own testimony).

Where the necessity of such linkage is involved, it is a less valid generalization that the jury will not likely obey the instruction to disregard the evidence. Specific testimony that "the defendant helped me commit the crime" is more vivid than inferential incrimination, and hence more difficult to thrust out of mind. Moreover, with regard to such an explicit statement the only issue is, plain and simply, whether the jury can possibly be expected to forget it in assessing the defendant's guilt; whereas with regard to inferential incrimination the judge's instruction may well be successful in dissuading the jury from entering onto the path of inference in the first place, so that there is no incrimination to forget. In short, while it may not always be simple for the members of a jury to obey the instruction that they disregard an incriminating inference, there does not exist the overwhelming probability of their inability to do so that is the foundation of *Bruton*'s exception to the general rule.

Even more significantly, evidence requiring linkage differs from evidence incriminating on its face in the practical effects which application of the *Bruton* exception would produce. If limited to facially incriminating confessions, *Bruton* can be complied with by redaction—a possibility suggested in that opinion itself. If extended to confessions incriminating by connection, not only is that not possible, but it is not even possible to predict the admissibility of a confession in advance of trial. The "contextual implication" doctrine articulated by the Court of Appeals would presumably require the trial judge to assess at the end of each trial whether, in light of all of the evidence, a nontestifying codefendant's confession has been so "powerfully incriminating" that a new, separate trial is required for the defendant. This obviously lends itself to manipulation by the defense—and even without manipulation will result in numerous mistrials and appeals. It might be suggested that those consequences could be reduced by conducting a pretrial hearing at which prosecution and defense would reveal the evidence they plan to introduce, enabling the court to assess compliance with *Bruton* ex ante rather than ex post. If this approach is even feasible under the Federal Rules, it would be time consuming and obviously far from foolproof.

One might say, of course, that a certain way of assuring compliance would be to try defendants separately whenever an incriminating statement of one of them is sought to be used. That is not as facile or as just a remedy as might seem. Joint trials play a vital role in the criminal justice system, accounting for almost one-third of federal criminal trials in the past five years. Many joint trials—for example, those involving large conspiracies to import and distribute illegal drugs—involve a dozen or more codefendants. Confessions by one or more of the defendants are commonplace—and indeed the probability of confession increases with the number of participants, since each has reduced assurance that he will be protected by his own silence. It would impair both the efficiency and the fairness of the criminal justice system to require, in all these cases of joint crimes where incriminating statements exist, that prosecutors bring separate proceedings, presenting the same evidence again and again, requiring victims and witnesses to repeat the inconvenience (and sometimes trauma) of testifying, and randomly favoring the last-tried defendants who have the advantage of knowing the prosecution's case beforehand. Joint trials generally serve the interests of justice by avoiding inconsistent verdicts and enabling more accurate assessment of relative culpability—advantages which sometimes operate to the defendant's benefit. Even apart from these tactical considerations, joint trials generally serve the interests of justice by avoiding the scandal and inequity of inconsistent verdicts. The other way of assuring compliance with an expansive *Bruton* rule would be to forgo use of codefendant confessions. That price also is too high, since confessions "are more than merely desirable; they are essential to society's compelling interest in finding, convicting, and punishing those who violate the law."

The rule that juries are presumed to follow their instructions is a pragmatic one, rooted less in the absolute certitude that the presumption is true than in the belief that it represents a reasonable practical accommodation of the interests of the state and the defendant in the criminal justice process. On the precise facts of *Bruton*, involving a facially incriminating confession, we found that accommodation inadequate. As our discussion above shows, the calculus changes when confessions that do not name the defendant are at issue. While we continue to apply *Bruton* where we have found that its rationale validly applies, we decline to extend it further. We hold that the Confrontation Clause is not violated by the admission of a nontestifying codefendant's confession with a proper limiting instruction when, as here, the confession is redacted to eliminate not only the defendant's name, but any reference to his or her existence. . . .

Justice STEVENS, with whom Justice BRENNAN and Justice MARSHALL join, dissenting.

The rationale of our decision in *Bruton v. United States,* 391 U.S. 123, applies without exception to all inadmissible confessions that are "powerfully incriminating." Today, however, the Court draws a distinction of constitutional magnitude between those confessions that directly identify the defendant and those that rely for their inculpatory effect on the factual and legal relationships of their contents to other evidence before the jury. Even if the jury's indirect inference of the defendant's guilt based on an inadmissible confession is much more devastating to the defendant's case than its inference from a direct reference in the codefendant's confession, the Court requires the exclusion of only the latter statement. This illogical result demeans the values protected by the Confrontation Clause. Moreover, neither reason nor experience supports the Court's argument that a consistent application of the rationale of the *Bruton* case would impose unacceptable burdens on the administration of justice. . . .

Today the Court nevertheless draws a line between codefendant confessions that expressly name the defendant and those that do not. The Court relies on the presumption that in the latter category "it is a less valid generalization that the jury will not likely obey the instruction to disregard the evidence." I agree; but I do not read *Bruton* to require the exclusion of all codefendant confessions that do not mention the defendant. Some such confessions may not have any significant impact on the defendant's case. But others will. If we presume, as we must, that jurors give their full and vigorous attention to every witness and each item of evidence, the very acts of listening and seeing will sometimes lead them down "the path of inference." Indeed, the Court tacitly acknowledges this point; while the Court speculates that the judge's instruction may dissuade the jury from making inferences at all, it also concedes the probability of their occurrence, arguing that there is no overwhelming probability that jurors will be unable to "disregard an incriminating inference." *Bruton* has always required trial judges to answer the question whether a particular confession is or is not "powerfully incriminating" on a case-by-case basis; they should follow the same analysis whether or not the defendant is actually named by his or her codefendant.

Instructing the jury that it was to consider Benjamin Williams' confession only against him, and not against Clarissa Marsh, failed to guarantee the level of certainty required by the Confrontation Clause. The uncertainty arose because the prosecution's case made it clear at the time Williams' statement was introduced that the statement would prove "powerfully incriminating" of the respondent as well as of Williams himself. There can be absolutely no doubt that spreading Williams' carefully edited confession before the jury intolerably interfered with the jury's solemn duty to treat the statement as nothing more than meaningless sounds in its consideration of Marsh's guilt or innocence. . . .

The facts that joint trials conserve prosecutorial resources, diminish inconvenience to witnesses, and avoid delays in the administration of criminal justice have been well known for a long time. It is equally well known that joint trials create special risks of prejudice to one of the defendants, and that such risks often make it necessary to grant severances. The Government argues that the costs of requiring the prosecution to choose between severance and not offering the codefendant's confession at a joint trial outweigh the benefits to the defendant. On the scales of justice, however, considerations of fairness normally outweigh administrative concerns. . . .

PROBLEM CASE

Redaction is a permissible remedy to solve a *Bruton* problem, but what type of redaction is required? Consider the following case. In 1993, Stacey Williams was killed during a "severe beating." Anthony Bell confessed to the crime and also implicated Kevin Gray and Jacquin "Tank" Vanlandingham in the crime. Vanlandingham later died, but Gray and Bell were indicted for murder and tried together. Gray's motion for a separate trial was denied. When Bell's confession was read in court, here is how it was presented to the jury: "Question: Who was in the group that beat Stacey? Answer: Me, deleted, deleted, and a few other guys." Thus, Gray's name was redacted and replaced with blank spaces and the word "deleted"—thus signaling to the jury that Bell had implicated another person in the commission of the crime without explicitly naming Gray as that person. The jury was left to wonder, without explicitly knowing, whether the named individual was Gray, the co-defendant sitting next to Bell at the defense table. Does this situation require severance under the *Bruton* rule or is the use of the word "deleted" sufficient to solve the *Bruton* problem? Does the use of the word "deleted" call attention to the redaction in a way that makes the situation worse instead of better? On the other hand, would revising the grammar or syntax of the confession constitute an impermissible contamination/alteration of the evidence? See *Gray v. Maryland*, 523 U.S. 185 (1998).

NOTES & QUESTIONS ON BRUTON *PROBLEMS*

1. *The power of redaction.* Not all redactions are alike. Some of them are sufficiently leading that a jury might guess that the confessor implicated his or her co-defendant. How should this be solved? The Supreme Court did not provide a full answer to how statements should be redacted, a point hammered home by the dissent. The issue has been left to the lower appellate courts to apply. For example, courts have upheld the use of the phrase "another individual" as an acceptable redaction, *United States v. Logan*, 210 F.3d 820, 822 (8th Cir. 2000), and there are other grammatical solutions as well. *United States v. Barroso*, 108 F. Supp. 2d 338 (S.D.N.Y. 2000) (statement referred to conspiring with "more than one person").

2. *Gender-neutral pronouns.* Does the Constitution require gender-neutral pronouns in confessions so as not to give the jury information about the sex of the individual referred to in the statement? The argument in favor of gender-neutral pronouns is that they are more natural than symbols or the word "deletion"—so they do not call attention to the redaction in the minds of the jury. See Bryan M. Shay, *"So I Says to 'The Guy,' I Says . . .": The Constitutionality of Neutral Pronoun Redaction in Multidefendant Criminal Trials*, 48 Wm. & Mary L. Rev. 345, 396 (2006) ("allowing the admission of confessions redacted using neutral pronouns would be consistent with the *Bruton-Richardson-Gray* line of cases in light of the differences between neutral pronouns and symbols, as well as the tenuous inferential connection suggested by neutral pronoun redaction"). Would using neutral pronouns throughout a statement avoid the problems associated with using redaction symbols such as ellipses (. . .) or writing the word deletion?

EXAMPLES

Consider the following examples of redacted statements and decide whether they require severance or whether they are acceptable forms of redaction.

> So [we] went down to the store on 24th and Oxford and bought two Dutches and headed back to the house. That's when we seen the boy coming up 24th street. The other guy was like, let's get him. I was like, that boy is dirty. He ain't got no money. The other guy was like, I'm ready to fade him. I was like, okay. But he can't see my face because I got to come back here again. The other guy was going to put him on the ground and I was going to go into his pockets and take whatever he had. Next thing I knew, the other guy was on him. He got in front of him and pulled out his gun and then grabbed the boy trying

> to pull him in. The boy grabbed a hold of the other guy and then the other guy fired. I heard like four shots total. When the boy grabbed the other guy, the other guy pushed him off and fired the first shot. The boy went right down. . . .

Commonwealth v. Cannon, 610 Pa. 494, 22 A.3d 210, 214 (2011).

> The first time I heard about the idea of robbing the Brink's armored van was when a friend, whom I do not wish to name, spoke to me about it. He and I talked and my friend told me it would be easy to rob the armored car since there was an inside man. . . . The next time I met with my friend was on the day of the robbery.

United States v. Richards, 241 F.3d 335, 338 (3d Cir. 2001).

> Investigator Dominick West of the Sumter County Sheriff's Office then read the redacted versions of the four statements to the jury. He did not say Jackson's name, but instead said "another person" or "the other person" wherever Jackson's name appeared in the statements. Canty's redacted statements described how "another person" (1) asked Canty if he wanted to participate in robbing a pizza man; (2) told Canty to get Desmond to take them to Cherryvale Grocery; (3) used the pay phone to call Sambino's and order three large pizzas, requesting delivery to lot seven in O.C. Mobile Home Park; (4) bought a "Debbie snack cake donut sticks"; (5) returned to the mobile home park with Canty; (6) went behind the trailer on lot seven and waited for the pizza man to arrive; and (7) robbed and shot the pizza man, while Canty watched from his house.

State v. Jackson, 410 S.C. 584, 589-90, 765 S.E.2d 841, 844 (Ct. App. 2014). If a witness plays a surveillance video from the crime scene showing the defendant buying Debbie snack cakes, did the redaction-substitution ("another person") satisfy the *Gray v. Maryland* standard?

D. PRACTICE & POLICY

There are a number of deeper issues with prosecutorial discretion that deserve a deeper dive than the cases above have allowed. The first is the question of why the law should care about motives at all, in particular why the law should care about the reasons *why* a prosecutor decides to proceed with a case against a particular defendant. The second question builds on the first. Assuming that motives matter, how prevalent are racial stereotypes among prosecutors suffering from "implicit bias"—even if those prosecutors are otherwise progressive in their expressed attitudes about racial equality? The third question focuses on prosecutorial discretion in capital cases and whether a centralized system of review should constrain an individual prosecutor's discretion in order to improve consistency in capital charging decisions.

❧ **Why should motives matter?** One particular puzzle underneath much of the materials in this chapter is the question of why motives matter. If the prosecutor can prove to a jury's satisfaction, beyond a reasonable doubt, that an individual committed a particular crime, why should it matter why the prosecutor decided to pursue the charge against the individual? Under this view, all that matters is the guilt or innocence of the defendant, and perhaps the conduct of the trial itself—motives of the prosecutor in making the charging decision would be irrelevant. Indeed, one way of putting the point is to ask what right is violated when a *guilty* person is prosecuted for the *wrong* reason. Of course, there is something intuitively problematic about when an innocent person is prosecuted for the wrong reasons, because in that situation the wrong motives lead to a charging decision that is objectively unreasonable. But in the hypothetical case we are considering, the prosecutor decides to file charges that would be objectively reasonable if the prosecutor had the right motivation; the only problem is that in this situation, the prosecutor's motives are impure.

In asking this question, it is important to explain that motives might have *instrumental* and *intrinsic* value. Something has instrumental value when it can be a useful instrument for achieving some beneficial state of affairs. For example, a prosecutor motivated by justice is more likely to make appropriate charging decisions than a prosecutor motivated by discrimination or vengeance. For this reason, we should encourage prosecutors to have the right motives and discourage prosecutors to have the wrong motives. But this still leaves open the possibility that in some cases, the wrong motive might coincidentally produce the right decision. For example, a prosecutor motivated by racial discrimination might charge a defendant for the wrong reasons, but a prosecutor not motivated by racial discrimination might still have made the same decision. The answer to this question is that motives also have *intrinsic* value because we care about why state authorities act when they act on behalf of the community as public agents. But why? When state authorities act on behalf of the public, their motivations are not just an expression of *private* preference but also purport to express the preferences and desires of the public at large. For this reason, the public has a reason to complain about a public official who acts on their behalf with an impermissible motivation because the public objects to the imputation of that motive to the entire community. For more discussion of the inherent value of motives, see Steven Sverdlik, *Motive and Rightness* (2011).

❧ **Prosecutorial discretion, implicit bias, and race.** How easy is to spot racially discriminatory charging? In a situation where the prosecutor is outwardly bigoted, the discrimination might be easier to find. But most prosecutors are well-intentioned public servants who display no outward signs of bigotry. Is it nonetheless possible that inappropriate racial considerations taint their charging decisions, perhaps without them even knowing it? As one scholar has noted:

> There are many complex reasons for the unwarranted racial disparities that plague the American criminal justice system, but one of the most significant contributing factors is the exercise of prosecutorial discretion, especially at the charging and plea bargaining stages of the process. Few prosecutors consciously favor criminal defendants or victims based on race or class. Most prosecutors are motivated by a desire to enforce the law in ways that will produce justice for everyone in the communities they serve. However, all too often, prosecutors' well-intentioned charging and plea bargaining decisions result in dissimilar treatment of similarly situated victims and defendants, sometimes along race and class lines.

Angela J. Davis, *Racial Fairness in the Criminal Justice System: The Role of the Prosecutor*, 39 Colum. Hum. Rts. L. Rev. 202, 202-03 (2007). What accounts for the tension between "well-intentioned" charging and dissimilar treatment?

One possible answer is the existence of "implicit bias." According to psychologists, many members of the population display an implicit bias against particular ethnic groups or individuals that they associate with that group, even though they work hard to filter out those implicit biases in their actions. In other words, their initial assessments might reflect bias, but their cognition then works in overdrive to act in an unbiased manner. If the empirical conclusions of this literature are correct, many individuals have more bias than they are aware of, since the bias is "implicit" and they filter it out in their behavior. However, is it possible that some of this implicit bias still makes its way into the charging decisions of prosecutors? According to some researchers, the answer is clearly yes:

> Imagine a sixteen-year-old youth who steals a candy bar from a convenience store, the store clerk struggles to restrain the juvenile before he exits the store, and the juvenile punches the clerk in the face, rendering him unconscious. Did the juvenile strike the store clerk because it was the only way he could get free and avoid apprehension? Did the juvenile just panic? Or is the juvenile the type of person who will react violently at the drop of a dime? If the juvenile is black, the prosecutor assessing the facts of this case might be primed by the picture of the juvenile, the notation that he is black, or even the recognition of a stereotypically

> black name that triggers associations between the black juvenile and the concepts of aggression and hostility. The activation of these negative constructs can translate into a sense that the crime (or the offender) is more aggressive or violent than would be the case if the prosecutor assessed the facts of the case in a truly race-neutral manner. This implicitly biased evaluation process has been documented in juvenile probation officers and police officer participants. Sandra Graham and Brian Lowery, for example, found that when these participants were subliminally primed with words related to the category black, they judged an adolescent's behavior as more dispositional, of greater culpability, and more likely to lead to recidivism.

Robert J. Smith & Justin D. Levinson, *The Impact of Implicit Racial Bias on the Exercise of Prosecutorial Discretion*, 35 Seattle U. L. Rev. 795, 812 (2012). Does this evidence suggest that the law should impose a lower standard for throwing out claims of discriminatory charging, or is the existing standard correct? Recall that under *Armstrong*, a litigant must show that the prosecutor declined to charge "similarly situated" defendants. Once this showing is made, the litigant is entitled to discovery in order to demonstrate the racial motivation required under equal protection jurisprudence. However, if the racial discrimination was based on implicit bias, will the litigant be able to demonstrate the prosecutor's racial motivation?

Prosecutorial discretion and the death penalty. Is there too much discretion in the system? Is it problematic that individuals cannot predict in advance whether a particular crime would result in a capital charge from a prosecutor, let alone a capital conviction from a jury? The Supreme Court jurisprudence on capital sentencing has focused on the "guided discretion" of the jury, which is required to make a factual finding of aggravating circumstances in the case if it is going to make a capital sentencing recommendation. However, in addition to the discretion of the jury, the prosecutor's decision in deciding whether to *seek* the death penalty is even more clothed in secrecy. Some critics of capital punishment consider the process fundamentally arbitrary, with some prosecutors more likely to seek the death penalty and other prosecutors inclined against it except under truly extraordinary circumstances. The Supreme Court has focused all of its energy on constraining and guiding jury discretion but in the process has completely ignored prosecutorial discretion in capital cases. Each jurisdiction has its own regulations or policies regarding prosecutorial discretion in capital cases.

For example, U.S. Attorneys are required to follow a centralized process before charging a defendant with a capital offense, in order to promote consistency across the entire Department of Justice:

> Prior to seeking an indictment for an offense potentially punishable by death, the United States Attorney or Assistant Attorney General shall consult with the Capital Case Section. This consultation will help streamline the process of preparing submissions made pursuant to this Chapter, ensure that charging documents are crafted in accordance with applicable legal and policy requirements, and help ensure that applicable deadlines are met. In the event the Attorney General determines the death penalty will be sought in a particular case, the Capital Case Section can provide valuable litigation advice and support, as well as trial assistance.

U.S. Attorney Manual § 9-10.040. The purpose of the centralized process is to reduce arbitrariness:

> The review of cases under this Chapter culminates in a decision to seek, or not to seek, the death penalty against an individual defendant. Each such decision must be based upon the facts and law applicable to the case and be set within a framework of consistent and even-handed national application of Federal capital sentencing laws. Arbitrary or impermissible factors—such as a defendant's race, ethnicity, or religion—will not inform any stage of the decision-making process. The overriding goal of the review process is to allow proper individualized consideration of the appropriate factors relevant to each case.

U.S. Attorney Manual § 9-10.030. Should state jurisdictions impose a similar process in order remove capital decision making from local district attorneys?

CHAPTER 11

Pre-Trial and Non-Punitive Confinement

INTRODUCTION

When we think or talk of incarceration, the example that comes to mind is penal confinement: punishment after a conviction at trial according to the required burden of proof, i.e., proof beyond a reasonable doubt. In some ways, the paradigm of punitive incarceration is the default paradigm. It is clear that the Constitution envisions and permits post-conviction incarceration—the only issue is the correct procedures to be followed at trial and sentencing and the Eighth Amendment prohibition on cruel and unusual punishment. However, the Constitution also permits detention in situations other than post-trial punishment, though these examples are more controversial because they fall outside of the default paradigm. Examples of non-punitive confinement include: (a) pre-trial confinement; (b) involuntary commitment due to a dangerous mental illness; (c) post-punishment commitment for sexual offenders; (d) immigration detention; (e) material witness confinement; and (f) law of war detention.

Each of these examples of non-punitive confinement raises common constitutional questions. What standard governs committal? If the standard requires a finding of dangerousness, how dangerous must the detainee be? How long is confinement permitted to last? In cases where the confinement is long-lasting, does the detainee have the right to contest confinement through some regular process of judicial review after every few years? What role do doctors, experts, and other executive branch officials play in the determination? These and other questions have occupied courts as they have struggled to articulate a clear set of constitutional standards for these forms of non-punitive confinement.

What is clear is that non-punitive confinement is not based on a judicial determination of prior culpability—that is the role played by criminal punishment, which is inherently backward-looking. In contrast, non-punitive confinement is forward-looking. In other words, it is based on an assessment of future dangerousness or flight that the confinement is designed to prevent or incapacitate. For these reasons, the evidentiary standards for non-punitive confinement are entirely different than criminal punishment that follows a finding of guilt based on the elements of each criminal offence. Consequently, a "trial" for non-punitive confinement looks nothing like a criminal trial, because it is designed to help the court make an inherently predictive determination about the detainee's future behavior and its effect on the community. This raises important questions about the degree to which the judicial system, or the scientific evidence it relies on, can predict future dangerousness and the level of empirical certainty required for these determinations.

A. BAIL AND PRE-TRIAL DETENTION

When a defendant is arraigned, the judge will entertain an application for bail. The purpose of the bail is designed to ensure that the defendant appears for trial. The detainee either posts cash or applies for a bond from a bail bondsman, which involves posting a percentage of cash or assets in exchange for the bondsman's issuance of the bond. The court is entitled to impose other conditions as well, including but not limited to wearing an ankle monitor, house arrest, a curfew, no contact with certain acquaintances, travel restrictions, or a prohibition on possessing weapons.

If the defendant fails to appear for trial, the judge might issue a bench warrant and declare the bail forfeited. The bail bondsman would then seek to find and retrieve the defendant and haul him back to the jurisdiction, at which point the bondsman would receive his money back. Essentially, the bondsman would act as a bounty hunter.

In some situations where a court determines that bail will be ineffective in ensuring that the defendant appears for trial, the defendant might be denied bail entirely. For example, if the judge believes that the defendant is a flight risk and the crime is a serious one, the judge might deny bail entirely and order the defendant confined until trial. For example, federal law states that "[i]f, after a hearing . . . the judicial officer finds that no condition or combination of conditions will reasonably assure the appearance of the person as required and the safety of any other person and the community, such judicial officer shall order the detention of the person before trial." 18 U.S.C. § 3142. In the following case, the defendant challenges the constitutionality of this provision, arguing that it violates the Due Process Clause of the Fifth Amendment and the Eighth Amendment prohibition on excessive bail. As you read the case, pay particular attention to the majority's application of the Excessive Bail Clause to situations where bail is *denied*. Since the Eighth Amendment prohibits excessive bail, does this, by implication, provide an absolute right to bail?

United States v. Salerno

Supreme Court of the United States
481 U.S. 739 (1987)

Chief Justice REHNQUIST delivered the opinion of the Court.

The Bail Reform Act of 1984 (Act) allows a federal court to detain an arrestee pending trial if the Government demonstrates by clear and convincing evidence after an adversary hearing that no release conditions "will reasonably assure . . . the safety of any other person and the community." The United States Court of Appeals for the Second Circuit struck down this provision of the Act as facially unconstitutional, because, in that court's words, this type of pretrial detention violates "substantive due process." . . . We hold that, as against the facial attack mounted by these respondents, the Act fully comports with constitutional requirements. We therefore reverse.

I

Responding to "the alarming problem of crimes committed by persons on release," Congress formulated the Bail Reform Act of 1984, 18 U.S.C. § 3141, as the solution to a bail crisis in the federal courts. The Act represents the National Legislature's considered response to numerous perceived deficiencies in the federal bail process. By providing for sweeping changes in both the way federal courts consider bail applications and the circumstances under which bail is granted, Congress hoped to "give the courts adequate authority to make release decisions that give appropriate recognition to the danger a person may pose to others if released."

To this end, § 3141(a) of the Act requires a judicial officer to determine whether an arrestee shall be detained. Section 3142(e) provides that "[i]f, after a hearing pursuant to the provisions of subsection (f), the judicial officer finds that no condition or combination of conditions will reasonably assure the appearance of the person as required and the safety of any other person and the community, he shall order the detention of the person prior to trial." Section 3142(f) provides the arrestee with a number of procedural safeguards. He may request the presence of counsel at the detention hearing, he may testify and present witnesses in his behalf, as well as proffer evidence, and he may cross-examine other witnesses appearing at the hearing. If the judicial officer finds that no conditions of pretrial release can reasonably assure the safety of other persons and the community, he must state his findings of fact in writing and support his conclusion with "clear and convincing evidence."

The judicial officer is not given unbridled discretion in making the detention determination. Congress has specified the considerations relevant to that decision. These factors include the nature and seriousness of the charges, the substantiality of the Government's evidence against the arrestee, the arrestee's background and characteristics, and the nature and seriousness of the danger posed by the suspect's release. Should a judicial officer order detention, the detainee is entitled to expedited appellate review of the detention order. . . .

II

A facial challenge to a legislative Act is, of course, the most difficult challenge to mount successfully, since the challenger must establish that no set of circumstances exists under which the Act would be valid. The fact that the Bail Reform Act might operate unconstitutionally under some conceivable set of circumstances is insufficient to render it wholly invalid, since we have not recognized an "overbreadth" doctrine outside the limited context of the First Amendment. We think respondents have failed to shoulder their heavy burden to demonstrate that the Act is "facially" unconstitutional.

Respondents present two grounds for invalidating the Bail Reform Act's provisions permitting pretrial detention on the basis of future dangerousness. First . . . the Act exceeds the limitations placed upon the Federal Government by the Due Process Clause of the Fifth Amendment. Second . . . the Act contravenes the Eighth Amendment's proscription against excessive bail. We treat these contentions in turn.

The Due Process Clause of the Fifth Amendment provides that "No person shall . . . be deprived of life, liberty, or property, without due process of law. . . ." This Court has held that the Due Process Clause protects individuals against two types of government action. So-called "substantive due process" prevents the government from engaging in conduct that "shocks the conscience," or interferes with rights "implicit in the concept of ordered liberty." When government action depriving a person of life, liberty, or property survives substantive due process scrutiny, it must still be implemented in a fair manner. This requirement has traditionally been referred to as "procedural" due process.

Respondents first argue that the Act violates substantive due process because the pretrial detention it authorizes constitutes impermissible punishment before trial. The Government, however, has never argued that pretrial detention could be upheld if it were "punishment." The Court of Appeals assumed that pretrial detention under the Bail Reform Act is regulatory, not penal, and we agree that it is.

As an initial matter, the mere fact that a person is detained does not inexorably lead to the conclusion that the government has imposed punishment. To determine whether a restriction on liberty constitutes impermissible punishment or permissible regulation, we first look to legislative intent. Unless Congress expressly intended to impose punitive restrictions, the punitive/regulatory distinction turns on "whether an alternative purpose to which [the restriction] may rationally be connected is assignable for it, and whether it appears excessive in relation to the alternative purpose assigned [to it]."

We conclude that the detention imposed by the Act falls on the regulatory side of the dichotomy. The legislative history of the Bail Reform Act clearly indicates that Congress did not formulate the pretrial detention provisions as punishment for dangerous individuals. Congress instead perceived pretrial detention as a potential solution to a pressing societal problem. There is no doubt that preventing danger to the community is a legitimate regulatory goal.

Nor are the incidents of pretrial detention excessive in relation to the regulatory goal Congress sought to achieve. The Bail Reform Act carefully limits the circumstances under which detention may be sought to the most serious of crimes. The arrestee is entitled to a prompt detention hearing and the maximum length of pretrial detention is limited by the stringent time limitations of the Speedy Trial Act. Moreover, the conditions of confinement envisioned by the Act "appear to reflect the regulatory purposes relied upon by the" Government. . . . [T]he statute at issue here requires that detainees be housed in a "facility separate, to the extent practicable, from persons awaiting or serving sentences or being held in custody pending appeal." We conclude, therefore, that the pretrial detention contemplated by the Bail Reform Act is regulatory in nature, and does not constitute punishment before trial in violation of the Due Process Clause.

. . . Respondents characterize the Due Process Clause as erecting an impenetrable "wall" in this area that "no governmental interest—rational, important, compelling or otherwise—may surmount." We do not think the Clause lays down any such categorical imperative. We have repeatedly held that the Government's regulatory interest in community safety can, in appropriate circumstances, outweigh an individual's liberty interest. For example, in times of war or insurrection, when society's interest is at its peak, the Government may detain individuals whom the government believes to be dangerous. Even outside the exigencies of war, we have found that sufficiently compelling governmental interests can justify detention of dangerous persons. Thus, we have found no absolute constitutional barrier to detention of potentially dangerous resident aliens pending deportation proceedings. We have also held that the government may detain mentally unstable individuals who present a danger to the public and dangerous defendants who become incompetent to stand trial. We have approved of postarrest regulatory detention of juveniles when they present a continuing danger to the community. Even competent adults may face substantial liberty restrictions as a result of the operation of our criminal justice system. If the police suspect an individual of a crime, they may arrest and hold him until a neutral magistrate determines whether probable cause exists. Finally, respondents concede . . . that an arrestee may be incarcerated until trial if he presents a risk of flight or a danger to witnesses.

Respondents characterize all of these cases as exceptions to the "general rule" of substantive due process that the government may not detain a person prior to a judgment of guilt in a criminal trial. Such a "general rule" may freely be conceded, but we think that these cases show a sufficient number of exceptions to the rule that the congressional action challenged here can hardly be characterized as totally novel. Given the well-established authority of the government, in special circumstances, to restrain individuals' liberty prior to or even without criminal trial and conviction, we think that the present statute providing for pretrial detention on the basis of dangerousness must be evaluated in precisely the same manner that we evaluated the laws in the cases discussed above.

The government's interest in preventing crime by arrestees is both legitimate and compelling. In *Schall*, we recognized the strength of the State's interest in preventing juvenile crime. This general concern with crime prevention is no less compelling when the suspects are adults. Indeed, "[t]he harm suffered by the victim of a crime is not dependent upon the age of the perpetrator." *Schall v. Martin*, 467 U.S., at 264-265. The Bail Reform Act of 1984 responds to an even more particularized governmental interest than the interest we sustained in *Schall*. The statute we upheld in *Schall* permitted pretrial detention of any juvenile arrested on any charge after a showing that the individual might commit some undefined further crimes. The Bail Reform Act, in contrast, narrowly focuses on a particularly acute problem in which the Government interests are overwhelming. The Act operates only on individuals who have been arrested for a specific category of extremely serious offenses. Congress specifically found that these individuals are far more likely to be responsible for dangerous acts in the community after arrest. Nor is the Act by any means a scattershot attempt to incapacitate those who are merely suspected of these serious crimes. The Government must first of all demonstrate probable cause to believe that the charged crime has been committed by the arrestee, but that is not enough. In a full-blown adversary hearing, the Government must convince a neutral decisionmaker by clear and convincing evidence that no conditions of release can reasonably assure the safety of the community or any person. While the

Government's general interest in preventing crime is compelling, even this interest is heightened when the Government musters convincing proof that the arrestee, already indicted or held to answer for a serious crime, presents a demonstrable danger to the community. Under these narrow circumstances, society's interest in crime prevention is at its greatest.

On the other side of the scale, of course, is the individual's strong interest in liberty. We do not minimize the importance and fundamental nature of this right. But, as our cases hold, this right may, in circumstances where the government's interest is sufficiently weighty, be subordinated to the greater needs of society. We think that Congress' careful delineation of the circumstances under which detention will be permitted satisfies this standard. When the Government proves by clear and convincing evidence that an arrestee presents an identified and articulable threat to an individual or the community, we believe that, consistent with the Due Process Clause, a court may disable the arrestee from executing that threat. Under these circumstances, we cannot categorically state that pretrial detention "offends some principle of justice so rooted in the traditions and conscience of our people as to be ranked as fundamental."

Finally, we may dispose briefly of respondents' facial challenge to the procedures of the Bail Reform Act. To sustain them against such a challenge, we need only find them "adequate to authorize the pretrial detention of at least some [persons] charged with crimes," whether or not they might be insufficient in some particular circumstances. We think they pass that test. . . .

Under the Bail Reform Act, the procedures by which a judicial officer evaluates the likelihood of future dangerousness are specifically designed to further the accuracy of that determination. Detainees have a right to counsel at the detention hearing. They may testify in their own behalf, present information by proffer or otherwise, and cross-examine witnesses who appear at the hearing. The judicial officer charged with the responsibility of determining the appropriateness of detention is guided by statutorily enumerated factors, which include the nature and the circumstances of the charges, the weight of the evidence, the history and characteristics of the putative offender, and the danger to the community. The Government must prove its case by clear and convincing evidence. Finally, the judicial officer must include written findings of fact and a written statement of reasons for a decision to detain. The Act's review provisions provide for immediate appellate review of the detention decision. We think these extensive safeguards suffice to repel a facial challenge. . . .

Respondents also contend that the Bail Reform Act violates the Excessive Bail Clause of the Eighth Amendment. The Court of Appeals did not address this issue because it found that the Act violates the Due Process Clause. We think that the Act survives a challenge founded upon the Eighth Amendment.

The Eighth Amendment addresses pretrial release by providing merely that "[e]xcessive bail shall not be required." This Clause, of course, says nothing about whether bail shall be available at all. Respondents nevertheless contend that this Clause grants them a right to bail calculated solely upon considerations of flight. They rely on *Stack v. Boyle*, 342 U.S. 1, 5 (1951), in which the Court stated that "[b]ail set at a figure higher than an amount reasonably calculated [to ensure the defendant's presence at trial] is 'excessive' under the Eighth Amendment." In respondents' view, since the Bail Reform Act allows a court essentially to set bail at an infinite amount for reasons not related to the risk of flight, it violates the Excessive Bail Clause. Respondents concede that the right to bail they have discovered in the Eighth Amendment is not absolute. A court may, for example, refuse bail in capital cases. And, as the Court of Appeals noted and respondents admit, a court may refuse bail when the defendant presents a threat to the judicial process by intimidating witnesses. Respondents characterize these exceptions as consistent with what they claim to be the sole purpose of bail—to ensure the integrity of the judicial process.

While we agree that a primary function of bail is to safeguard the courts' role in adjudicating the guilt or innocence of defendants, we reject the proposition that the Eighth Amendment categorically prohibits the government from pursuing other admittedly compelling interests through regulation of pretrial release. The above- quoted dictum in *Stack v. Boyle* is far too slender a reed on which to rest this argument. The Court in *Stack* had no occasion to consider whether the Excessive Bail Clause requires courts to admit all defendants to bail, because the statute before the Court in that case in fact allowed the defendants to be bailed. Thus, the Court had to determine only whether bail, admittedly available in that case, was excessive if set at a sum greater than that necessary to ensure the arrestees' presence at trial. . . .

Nothing in the text of the Bail Clause limits permissible Government considerations solely to questions of flight. The only arguable substantive limitation of the Bail Clause is that the Government's proposed conditions of release or detention not be "excessive" in light of the perceived evil. Of course, to determine whether the Government's response is excessive, we must compare that response against the interest the Government seeks to protect by means of that response. Thus, when the Government has admitted that its only interest is in preventing flight, bail must be set by a court at a sum designed to ensure that goal, and no more. We believe that when Congress has mandated detention on the basis of a compelling interest other than prevention of flight, as it has here, the Eighth Amendment does not require release on bail. . . .

Justice MARSHALL, with whom Justice BRENNAN joins, dissenting.

This case brings before the Court for the first time a statute in which Congress declares that a person innocent of any crime may be jailed indefinitely, pending the trial of allegations which are legally presumed to be untrue, if the Government shows to the satisfaction of a judge that the accused is likely to commit crimes, unrelated to the pending charges, at any time in the future. Such statutes, consistent with the usages of tyranny and the excesses of what bitter experience teaches us to call the police state, have long been thought incompatible with the fundamental human rights protected by our Constitution. Today a majority of this Court holds otherwise. Its decision disregards basic principles of justice established centuries ago and enshrined beyond the reach of governmental interference in the Bill of Rights. . . .

. . . The majority concludes that the Act is a regulatory rather than a punitive measure. . . . The absurdity of this conclusion arises, of course, from the majority's cramped concept of substantive due process. The majority proceeds as though the only substantive right protected by the Due Process Clause is a right to be free from punishment before conviction. The majority's technique for infringing this right is simple: merely redefine any measure which is claimed to be punishment as "regulation," and, magically, the Constitution no longer prohibits its imposition. . . .

The logic of the majority's Eighth Amendment analysis is equally unsatisfactory. . . . Whether the magistrate sets bail at $1 million or refuses to set bail at all, the consequences are indistinguishable. It would be mere sophistry to suggest that the Eighth Amendment protects against the former decision, and not the latter. Indeed, such a result would lead to the conclusion that there was no need for Congress to pass a preventive detention measure of any kind; every federal magistrate and district judge could simply refuse, despite the absence of any evidence of risk of flight or danger to the community, to set bail. This would be entirely constitutional, since, according to the majority, the Eighth Amendment "says nothing about whether bail shall be available at all." . . .

The essence of this case may be found, ironically enough, in a provision of the Act to which the majority does not refer. Title 18 U.S.C. § 3142(j) provides that "[n]othing in this section shall be construed as modifying or limiting the presumption of innocence." But the very pith and purpose of this statute is an abhorrent limitation of the presumption of innocence. The majority's untenable conclusion that the present Act is constitutional arises from a specious denial of the role of the Bail Clause and the Due Process Clause in protecting the invaluable guarantee afforded by the presumption of innocence. . . .

NOTES & QUESTIONS ON BAIL AND PRE-TRIAL CONFINEMENT

1. *Denial of bail.* The majority argues that denying a detainee bail does not violate the Excessive Bail Clause because no bail is different from excessive bail. Do you agree with this argument? Or do you agree with the dissent's assessment that "[w]hether the magistrate sets bail at $1 million or refuses to set bail at all, the consequences are indistinguishable."

2. *An epidemic of pre-trial detention.* In the United States, bail is set for a vast number of crimes, leading to a massive population in pre-trial detention. For example, scholars have estimated that "local governments spent approximately $16.2 billion on pretrial detention of criminal defendants in 2010." See Robert A. Beattey Jr., Taiki Matsuura & Elizabeth L. Jeglic, *Judicial Bond-Setting Behavior: The Perceived Nature of the Crime May Matter More Than How Serious It Is*, 20 Psychol. Pub. Pol'y & L. 411, 412 (2014). The situation is different in some European countries, where many defendants are released without bail prior to criminal trial, though even some European states have been criticized for excessive use of pre-trial detention. See Sarah Nagy, *Use and Abuse of Pre-Trial Detention in Council of Europe States: A Path to Reform*, 13 Loy. U. Chi. Int'l L. Rev. 159, 173 (2015); Aya Fujimura-Fanselow & Elisabeth Wickeri, *"We Are Left to Rot": Arbitrary and Excessive Pretrial Detention in Bolivia*, 36 Fordham Int'l L.J. 812, 818 (2013). For more discussion on bail reform, see Section G, the Practice & Policy section, at the conclusion of this chapter.

STATE LAW REQUIREMENTS

In combination with a citizen referendum, New Jersey enacted the Criminal Justice Reform Act in 2017. The law created a presumption against monetary bail and in favor of non-monetary measures to ensure appearance at trial. The statute stated that trial courts should rely on

> pretrial release by non-monetary means to reasonably assure an eligible defendant's appearance in court when required, the protection of the safety of any other person or the community, that the eligible defendant will not obstruct or attempt to obstruct the criminal justice process, and that the eligible defendant will comply with all conditions of release, while authorizing the court, upon motion of a prosecutor, to order pretrial detention of the eligible defendant when it finds clear and convincing evidence that no condition or combination of conditions can reasonably assure the effectuation of these goals.

> Monetary bail may be set for an eligible defendant only when it is determined that no other conditions of release will reasonably assure the eligible defendant's appearance in court when required.

N.J. Stat. § 2A:162-15. The law was accompanied by the following amendment to the New Jersey State Constitution:

> All persons shall, before conviction, be eligible for pretrial release. Pretrial release may be denied to a person if the court finds that no amount of monetary bail, non-monetary conditions of pretrial release, or combination of monetary bail and non-monetary conditions would reasonably assure the person's appearance in court when required, or protect the safety of any other person or the community, or prevent the person from obstructing or attempting to obstruct the criminal justice process. It shall be lawful for the Legislature to establish by law procedures, terms, and conditions applicable to pretrial release and the denial thereof authorized under this provision.

N.J. Const. art. I, ¶11.

In practice, New Jersey courts now rarely use monetary bail. Proponents of the shift in the law argued that monetary bail was inherently unfair to poor and indigent defendants who could not afford to post monetary bail and had insufficient assets to secure a bond. In contrast, financially secure individuals were able to secure pre-trial freedom simply because they had the financial resources to do so.

The new system is designed to promote consistency across pre-trial determinations, based entirely on the likelihood that the defendant will appear for trial and the individual's level of dangerousness to the community. Under the new system, an algorithm computes the following scores: (1) Failure to Appear ("FTA"); (2) New Criminal Activity ("NCA"); and (3) New Violent Criminal Activity ("NVCA"). The scores are then aggregated to create a combined Public Safety Assessment ("PSA"), which determines whether pre-trial release will be granted.

Ironically, some defendants have objected to the new system. (Bail bond providers also objected to the law, which basically dried up their business overnight.) In one case, the defendant argued that he was constitutionally *entitled* to monetary bail. Brian Holland was arrested in April 2017 after a bar fight and charged with second-degree aggravated assault. Police alleged that Holland punched the victim in the face in the parking lot of the bar and continued to assault the victim as he lay on the ground. Holland was initially flagged for pre-trial detention because the algorithm suggested he was at risk for future violent behavior, although prosecutors eventually agreed to withdraw their motion for pre-trial detention if Holland accepted the conditions of home confinement and electronic monitoring.

The Third Circuit rejected Holland's constitutional challenge to the new system, concluding that the Excessive Bail Clause "does not dictate whether those assurances must be based on monetary or non-monetary conditions. Hence the Eighth Amendment does not require a New Jersey court to consider monetary bail with the same priority as non-monetary bail for a criminal defendant." *Holland v. Rosen*, No. 17-3104, 2018 WL 3340930, at *13 (3d Cir. July 9, 2018).

B. MENTAL ILLNESS

Every jurisdiction allows for the confinement of mentally ill individuals who are a danger to themselves or to others. Typically, confinement begins with a brief psychiatric hold after a family member or the police bring the individual to the hospital for a psychiatric evaluation. Or, a defense counsel may ask the court to order such an evaluation based on a concern that a client is not competent to stand trial. Then, a court hearing is scheduled to determine whether the individual is both ill and dangerous (such as acutely suicidal), at which point a judge might order the individual held in psychiatric confinement. The burden in these cases is often difficult to satisfy. The state is uninterested in holding all individuals with mental illness in the absence of indicia of dangerousness; if that were the policy, states would need to spend millions more on in-patient psychiatric care.

In the following case, the defendant was incarcerated in Louisiana following a different procedure from the one described immediately above. The defendant was put on trial and found not guilty by reason of insanity. Following psychiatric treatment, the defendant was declared free from mental disease but the doctors were unwilling to certify that he would not be a danger to the community—and on that basis a judge ordered his continued detention. The question for the Supreme Court was whether involuntary confinement for an individual who no longer met the criteria for mental illness was still permissible.

Foucha v. Louisiana

Supreme Court of the United States
504 U.S. 71 (1992)

Justice White delivered the opinion of the Court, except as to Part III.

When a defendant in a criminal case pending in Louisiana is found not guilty by reason of insanity, he is committed to a psychiatric hospital unless he proves that he is not dangerous. This is so whether or not he is then insane. After commitment, if the acquittee or the superintendent begins release proceedings, a review panel at the hospital makes a written report on the patient's mental condition and whether he can be released without danger to himself or others. If release is recommended, the court must hold a hearing to determine dangerousness; the acquittee has the burden of proving that he is not dangerous. If found to be dangerous, the acquittee may be returned to the mental institution whether or not he is then mentally ill. Petitioner contends that this scheme denies him due process and equal protection because it allows a person acquitted by reason of insanity to be committed to a mental institution until he is able to demonstrate that he is not dangerous to himself and others, even though he does not suffer from any mental illness.

I

Petitioner Terry Foucha was charged by Louisiana authorities with aggravated burglary and illegal discharge of a firearm. Two medical doctors were appointed to conduct a pretrial examination of Foucha. The doctors initially reported, and the trial court initially found, that Foucha lacked mental capacity to proceed, but four months later the trial court found Foucha competent to stand trial. The doctors reported that Foucha was unable to distinguish right from wrong and was insane at the time of the offense. On October 12, 1984, the trial court ruled that Foucha was not guilty by reason of insanity, finding that he "is unable to appreciate the usual, natural and probable consequences of his acts; that he is unable to distinguish right from wrong; that he is a menace to himself and others; and that he was insane at the time of the commission of the above crimes and that he is presently insane." He was committed to the East Feliciana Forensic Facility until such time as doctors recommend that he be released, and until further order of the court. In 1988, the superintendent of Feliciana recommended that Foucha be discharged or released. A three-member panel was convened at the institution to determine Foucha's current condition and whether he could be released or placed on probation without being a danger to others or himself. On March 21, 1988, the panel reported that there had been no evidence of mental illness since admission and recommended that Foucha be conditionally discharged. The trial judge appointed a two-member sanity commission made up of the same two doctors who had conducted the pretrial examination. Their written report stated that Foucha "is presently in remission from mental illness [but] [w]e cannot certify that he would not constitute a menace to himself or others if released." One of the doctors testified at a hearing that upon commitment Foucha probably suffered from a drug induced psychosis but that he had recovered from that temporary condition; that he evidenced no signs of psychosis or neurosis and was in "good shape" mentally; that he had, however, an antisocial personality, a condition that is not a mental disease and that is untreatable. The doctor also testified that Foucha had been involved in several altercations at Feliciana and that he, the doctor, would not "feel comfortable in certifying that [Foucha] would not be a danger to himself or to other people."

After it was stipulated that the other doctor, if he were present, would give essentially the same testimony, the court ruled that Foucha was dangerous to himself and others and ordered him returned to the mental institution. . . .

II

Addington v. Texas, 441 U.S. 418 (1979), held that to commit an individual to a mental institution in a civil proceeding, the State is required by the

Due Process Clause to prove by clear and convincing evidence the two statutory preconditions to commitment: that the person sought to be committed is mentally ill and that he requires hospitalization for his own welfare and protection of others. Proof beyond a reasonable doubt was not required, but proof by preponderance of the evidence fell short of satisfying due process.

When a person charged with having committed a crime is found not guilty by reason of insanity, however, a State may commit that person without satisfying the *Addington* burden with respect to mental illness and dangerousness. *Jones v. United States.* Such a verdict, we observed in *Jones*, "establishes two facts: (i) the defendant committed an act that constitutes a criminal offense, and (ii) he committed the act because of mental illness," 463 U.S., at 363, an illness that the defendant adequately proved in this context by a preponderance of the evidence. From these two facts, it could be properly inferred that at the time of the verdict, the defendant was still mentally ill and dangerous and hence could be committed.

We held, however, that "(t)he committed acquittee is entitled to release when he has recovered his sanity or is no longer dangerous"; i.e., the acquittee may be held as long as he is both mentally ill and dangerous, but no longer. We relied on *O'Connor v. Donaldson*, 422 U.S. 563 (1975), which held as a matter of due process that it was unconstitutional for a State to continue to confine a harmless, mentally ill person. Even if the initial commitment was permissible, "it could not constitutionally continue after that basis no longer existed." In the summary of our holdings in our opinion we stated that "the Constitution permits the Government, on the basis of the insanity judgment, to confine him to a mental institution until such time as he has regained his sanity or is no longer a danger to himself or society." In this case, Louisiana does not contend that Foucha was mentally ill at the time of the trial court's hearing. Thus, the basis for holding Foucha in a psychiatric facility as an insanity acquittee has disappeared, and the State is no longer entitled to hold him on that basis.

The State, however, seeks to perpetuate Foucha's confinement at Feliciana on the basis of his antisocial personality which, as evidenced by his conduct at the facility, the court found rendered him a danger to himself or others. There are at least three difficulties with this position. First, even if his continued confinement were constitutionally permissible, keeping Foucha against his will in a mental institution is improper absent a determination in civil commitment proceedings of current mental illness and dangerousness. . . . Due process requires that the nature of commitment bear some reasonable relation to the purpose for which the individual is committed. Here, according to the testimony given at the hearing in the trial court, Foucha is not suffering from a mental disease or illness. If he is to be held, he should not be held as a mentally ill person.

Second, if Foucha can no longer be held as an insanity acquittee in a mental hospital, he is entitled to constitutionally adequate procedures to establish the grounds for his confinement. ***Jackson v. Indiana*** indicates as much. There, a person under criminal charges was found incompetent to stand trial and was committed until he regained his sanity. It was later determined that nothing could be done to cure the detainee, who was a deaf mute. The state courts refused to order his release. We reversed, holding that the State was entitled to hold a person for being incompetent to stand trial only long enough to determine if he could be cured and become competent. If he was to be held longer, the State was required to afford the protections constitutionally required in a civil commitment proceeding. We noted . . . that a convicted criminal who allegedly was mentally ill was entitled to release at the end of his term unless the State committed him in a civil proceeding.

Third, "the Due Process Clause contains a substantive component that bars certain arbitrary, wrongful government actions 'regardless of the fairness of the procedures used to implement them.'" Freedom from bodily restraint has always been at the core of the liberty protected by the Due Process Clause from arbitrary governmental action. "It is clear that commitment for any purpose constitutes a significant deprivation of liberty that requires due process protection." We have always been careful not to "minimize the importance and fundamental nature" of the individual's right to liberty.

A State, pursuant to its police power, may of course imprison convicted criminals for the purposes of deterrence and retribution. But there are constitutional limitations on the conduct that a State may criminalize. Here, the State has no such punitive interest. As Foucha was not convicted, he may not be punished. Here, Louisiana has by reason of his acquittal exempted Foucha from criminal responsibility. . . .

The State may also confine a mentally ill person if it shows "by clear and convincing evidence that the individual is mentally ill and dangerous." Here, the State has not carried that burden; indeed, the State does not claim that Foucha is now mentally ill.

We have also held that in certain narrow circumstances persons who pose a danger to others or to the community may be subject to limited confinement. . . . [But under the Louisiana statute, unlike a pretrial bail hearing,] Foucha is not now entitled to an adversary hearing at which the State must prove by clear and convincing evidence that he is demonstrably dangerous to the community. Indeed, the State need prove nothing to justify continued detention, for the statute places the burden on the detainee to prove that he is not dangerous. At the hearing which ended with Foucha's recommittal, no doctor or any other person testified positively that in his opinion Foucha would be a danger to the community, let alone gave the basis for such an opinion. There was only a description of Foucha's behavior at Feliciana and his antisocial personality, along with a refusal to certify that he would not be dangerous. When directly asked whether Foucha would be dangerous, Dr. Ritter said only, "I don't think I would feel comfortable in certifying that he would not be a danger to himself or to other people." This, under the Louisiana statute, was enough to defeat Foucha's interest in physical liberty. It is not enough to defeat Foucha's liberty interest under the Constitution in being freed from indefinite confinement in a mental facility.

Furthermore, if Foucha committed criminal acts while at Feliciana, such as assault, the State does not explain why its interest would not be vindicated by the ordinary criminal processes involving charge and conviction, the use of enhanced sentences for recidivists, and other permissible ways of dealing with patterns of criminal conduct. These are the normal means of dealing with persistent criminal conduct. Had they been employed against Foucha when he assaulted other inmates, there is little doubt that if then sane he could have been convicted and incarcerated in the usual way.

It was emphasized in *United States v. Salerno* that the [pre-trial] detention we found constitutionally permissible was strictly limited in duration. Here, in contrast, the State asserts that because Foucha once committed a criminal act and now has an antisocial personality that sometimes leads to aggressive conduct, a disorder for which there is no effective treatment, he may be held indefinitely. This rationale would permit the State to hold indefinitely any other insanity acquittee not mentally ill who could be shown to have a personality disorder that may lead to criminal conduct. The same would be true of any convicted criminal, even though he has completed his prison term. It would also be only a step away from substituting confinements for dangerousness for our present system which, with only narrow exceptions and aside from permissible confinements for mental illness, incarcerates only those who are proved beyond reasonable doubt to have violated a criminal law. . . .

Justice KENNEDY, with whom THE CHIEF JUSTICE joins, dissenting.

As incarceration of persons is the most common and one of the most feared instruments of state oppression and state indifference, we ought to acknowledge at the outset that freedom from this restraint is essential to the basic definition of liberty in the Fifth and Fourteenth Amendments of the Constitution. I agree with the Court's reaffirmation of this first premise. But I submit with all respect that the majority errs in its failure to recognize that the conditions for incarceration imposed by the State in this case are in accord with legitimate and traditional state interests, vindicated after full and fair procedures. The error results from the majority's primary reliance on cases, such as *O'Connor v. Donaldson*, 422 U.S. 563 (1975), and *Addington v. Texas*, 441 U.S. 418 (1979), which define the due process limits for involuntary civil commitment. . . .

This is a criminal case. It began one day when petitioner, brandishing a .357 revolver, entered the home of a married couple, intending to steal. He chased them out of their home and fired on police officers who confronted him as he fled. Petitioner was apprehended and charged with aggravated burglary and the illegal use of a weapon. . . . There is no question that petitioner committed the criminal acts charged. Petitioner's response was to deny criminal responsibility based on his mental illness when he committed the acts. He contended his mental illness prevented him from distinguishing between right and wrong with regard to the conduct in question. . . .

The majority's failure to recognize the criminal character of these proceedings and its concomitant standards of proof leads it to conflate the standards for civil and criminal commitment in a manner not permitted by our precedents. *O'Connor v. Donaldson* and *Addington v. Texas* define the due process limits of involuntary civil commitment. Together they stand for the proposition that in civil proceedings the Due Process Clause requires the State to prove both insanity and dangerousness by clear and convincing evidence. Their precedential value in the civil context is beyond question. But it is an error to apply these precedents, as the majority does today, to criminal proceedings. . . .

The majority's opinion is troubling at a further level, because it fails to recognize or account for profound differences between clinical insanity and state-law definitions of criminal insanity. It is by now well established that insanity as defined by the criminal law has no direct analog in medicine or science. . . .

As provided by Louisiana law, and consistent with both federal criminal law and the law of a majority of the States, petitioner was found not guilty by reason of insanity under the traditional *M'Naghten* test. . . . Because the *M'Naghten* test for insanity turns on a finding of criminal irresponsibility at the time of the offense, it is quite wrong to place reliance on the fact, as the majority does, that Louisiana does not contend that petitioner is now insane. This circumstance should come as no surprise, since petitioner was competent at the time of his plea and indeed could not have entered a plea otherwise. Present sanity would have relevance if petitioner had been committed as a consequence of civil proceedings, in which dangerous conduct in the past was used to predict similar conduct in the future. It has no relevance here, however. Petitioner has not been confined based on predictions about future behavior but rather for past criminal conduct. Unlike civil commitment proceedings, which attempt to divine the future from the past, in a criminal trial whose outcome turns on *M'Naghten*, findings of past insanity and past criminal conduct possess intrinsic and ultimate significance. . . .

Because the majority conflates the standards for civil and criminal commitment, treating this criminal case as though it were civil, it upsets a careful balance relied upon by the States, not only in determining the conditions for continuing confinement, but also in defining the defenses permitted for

> mental incapacity at the time of the crime in question. In my view, having adopted a traditional and well-accepted test for determining criminal insanity . . . the State possesses the constitutional authority to incarcerate petitioner for the protection of society. . . .

NOTES & QUESTIONS ON MENTAL ILLNESS

1. *Preventive confinement.* The government argued that preventive detention was permissible in this case just as it was permissible in *Salerno*, which involved pre-trial detention. Do you agree that preventive detention in the pre-trial context provides an argument for preventive detention in other contexts? Although *Foucha* involved a criminal case, just as *Salerno* did, the two cases are at opposite ends of the temporal spectrum. One involved detention *prior* to the culpability determination of trial and the other involved detention *after* the culpability determination. Are there any significant differences suggested by this temporal difference?

2. *The mental illness diagnosis.* Ultimately, the government's detention of *Foucha* was ruled unconstitutional because the state failed to demonstrate that Foucha remained mentally ill. Do you agree that mental illness is a required element of the state's legal burden to justify preventive detention? If yes, how should mental illness be defined? Is it a legal category or a mental category? When mental "disease or defect" is considered in the context of an insanity plea in a criminal case, the concept is combined with a functional analysis of whether the disease prevented the defendant from appreciating the nature or wrongfulness of his action or caused the defendant to labor under an irresistible impulse (factors relevant for assessing the defendant's culpability or lack thereof). But in the context of a civil confinement proceeding, neither of these functional factors are relevant. As one scholar noted:

> *Foucha*'s rejection of hospitalization for an insanity acquittee who was diagnosed as having an antisocial personality disorder but no longer suffered from a treatable mental illness thus suggests an important clarification concerning the constitutional limits on state use of involuntary mental health interventions. At a minimum, such interventions will be limited to those who are mentally ill. Involuntary psychiatric hospitalization (and by extension psychiatric treatment) are not reasonable means of accomplishing even compelling governmental purposes when the individual in question is not mentally ill.

Bruce J. Winick, *Ambiguities in the Legal Meaning and Significance of Mental Illness*, 1 Psychol. Pub. Pol'y & L. 534, 550 (1995).

PROBLEM CASE

Loren Huss was charged in 1986 with the murder of his girlfriend, Marilyn Sheets, and found not guilty by reason of insanity. Huss was committed to a mental health facility pursuant to Iowa R. Civ. P. 2.22:

> If, upon hearing, the court finds that the defendant is not mentally ill and no longer dangerous to the defendant's self or to others, the court shall order the defendant released. If, however, the court finds that the defendant is mentally ill and dangerous to the defendant's self or to others, the court shall order the defendant committed to a state mental health institute or to the Iowa security and medical facility and retained in custody until the court finds that the defendant is no longer mentally ill and dangerous to the defendant's self or to others. The court shall give due consideration to the chief medical officer's findings and opinion along with any other relevant evidence that may be submitted.

As part of this process, a written evaluation by a staff psychologist concluded that Huss had "no signs or symptoms of mental illness . . . and is not seen as a danger to himself or others." Doctors testified that Huss suffered from bipolar affective disorder and had committed his crimes during manic phases of his disorder. As to his future dangerousness, another doctor testified:

> If we have an individual who has had a manic episode every spring for the last eight years, it becomes *relatively* easy. But in an individual such as Mr. Huss who experienced what sounded to be his first manic episode in 1986, it is totally impossible to predict if or when Mr. Huss might experience a future manic episode or episode of depression.

A third doctor testified that "in terms of his profile you'd have to say that he is certainly more of a danger to others than the average citizen because the best predictor of future behavior is past behavior."

The Iowa statute requires a finding that the inmate is both mentally ill and dangerous. This raises two questions. On the facts presented by the experts, should Huss be held in civil confinement? Also, is the Iowa statute constitutional or does it conflict with the Supreme Court's guidance in *Foucha v. Louisiana*? See *State v. Huss*, 666 N.W.2d 152, 155 (Iowa 2003).

C. SEXUAL OFFENDERS

Responding to perceived political pressure from constituents, several states have passed civil commitment statutes specifically directed to sexual predators. Although the statutes differ from state to state, many of the statutes allow for continued civil confinement after a defendant has been tried and convicted for a sexual offense and has completed his term of imprisonment. Instead of releasing the defendant, the state can apply for a civil commitment order based on a judicial determination that the defendant is a sexual predator who remains a danger to the community because there is a high risk of recidivism. The commitment is then periodically reviewed, which in theory could result in the offender's release, though in practice few are ever released and therefore remain committed indefinitely.

The following case involves a constitutional attack on Kansas's statute, the Sexually Violent Predator Act. The statute requires a finding that the detainee suffers from a "mental abnormality" but does not require that the detainee suffer from a "mental illness" in order to be confined. As you read the case, ask yourself whether the majority's decision to uphold the statute is consistent with the standard enunciated in *Foucha*, which required not just a finding of dangerousness but also a finding of mental illness as well.

Kansas v. Hendricks

Supreme Court of the United States
521 U.S. 346 (1997)

Justice THOMAS delivered the opinion of the Court.

In 1994, Kansas enacted the Sexually Violent Predator Act, which establishes procedures for the civil commitment of persons who, due to a "mental abnormality" or a "personality disorder," are likely to engage in "predatory acts of sexual violence." Kan. Stat. § 59-29a01. The State invoked the Act for the first time to commit Leroy Hendricks, an inmate who had a long history of sexually molesting children, and who was scheduled for release from prison shortly after the Act became law. Hendricks challenged his commitment on, inter alia, "substantive" due process, double jeopardy, and ex post facto grounds. The Kansas Supreme Court invalidated the Act, holding that its precommitment condition of a "mental abnormality" did not satisfy what the court perceived to be the "substantive" due process requirement that involuntary civil commitment must be predicated on a finding of "mental illness." . . . We granted certiorari . . . and now reverse the judgment below.

I

The Kansas Legislature enacted the Sexually Violent Predator Act (Act) in 1994 to grapple with the problem of managing repeat sexual offenders. Although Kansas already had a statute addressing the involuntary commitment of those defined as "mentally ill," the legislature determined that existing civil commitment procedures were inadequate to confront the risks presented by "sexually violent predators." . . .

As originally structured, the Act's civil commitment procedures pertained to: (1) a presently confined person who, like Hendricks, "has been convicted of a sexually violent offense" and is scheduled for release; (2) a person who has been "charged with a sexually violent offense" but has been found incompetent to stand trial; (3) a person who has been found "not guilty by reason of insanity of a sexually violent offense"; and (4) a person found "not guilty" of a sexually violent offense because of a mental disease or defect. . . .

In 1984, Hendricks was convicted of taking "indecent liberties" with two 13-year-old boys. After serving nearly 10 years of his sentence, he was slated for release to a halfway house. Shortly before his scheduled release, however, the State filed a petition in state court seeking Hendricks' civil confinement as a sexually violent predator. On August 19, 1994, Hendricks appeared before the court with counsel and moved to dismiss the petition on the grounds that the Act violated various federal constitutional provisions. Although the court reserved ruling on the Act's constitutionality, it concluded that there was probable cause to support a finding that Hendricks was a sexually violent predator, and therefore ordered that he be evaluated at the Larned State Security Hospital.

Hendricks subsequently requested a jury trial to determine whether he qualified as a sexually violent predator. During that trial, Hendricks' own testimony revealed a chilling history of repeated child sexual molestation and abuse, beginning in 1955 when he exposed his genitals to two young girls. . . . Hendricks admitted that he had repeatedly abused children whenever he was not confined. He explained that when he "get[s] stressed out," he "can't control the urge" to molest children. Although Hendricks recognized that his behavior harms children, and he hoped he would not sexually molest children again, he stated that the only sure way he could keep from sexually abusing children in the future was "to die." Hendricks readily agreed with the state physician's diagnosis that he suffers from pedophilia and that he is not cured of the condition; indeed, he told the physician that "treatment is bull——."

The jury unanimously found beyond a reasonable doubt that Hendricks was a sexually violent predator. The trial court subsequently determined, as a matter of state law, that pedophilia qualifies as a "mental abnormality" as defined by the Act, and thus ordered Hendricks committed to the Secretary's custody. . . .

II

Kansas argues that the Act's definition of "mental abnormality" satisfies "substantive" due process requirements. We agree. Although freedom from physical restraint "has always been at the core of the liberty protected by the Due Process Clause from arbitrary governmental action," that liberty interest is not absolute. The Court has recognized that an individual's constitutionally protected interest in avoiding physical restraint may be overridden even in the civil context. . . .

Accordingly, States have in certain narrow circumstances provided for the forcible civil detainment of people who are unable to control their behavior and who thereby pose a danger to the public health and safety. We have consistently upheld such involuntary commitment statutes provided the confinement takes place pursuant to proper procedures and evidentiary standards. It thus cannot be said that the involuntary civil confinement of a limited subclass of dangerous persons is contrary to our understanding of ordered liberty.

The challenged Act unambiguously requires a finding of dangerousness either to one's self or to others as a prerequisite to involuntary confinement. Commitment proceedings can be initiated only when a person "has been convicted of or charged with a sexually violent offense," and "suffers from a mental abnormality or personality disorder which makes the person likely to engage in the predatory acts of sexual violence." The statute thus requires proof of more than a mere predisposition to violence; rather, it requires evidence of past sexually violent behavior and a present mental condition that creates a likelihood of such conduct in the future if the person is not incapacitated. As we have recognized, "[p]revious instances of violent behavior are an important indicator of future violent tendencies."

A finding of dangerousness, standing alone, is ordinarily not a sufficient ground upon which to justify indefinite involuntary commitment. We have sustained civil commitment statutes when they have coupled proof of dangerousness with the proof of some additional factor, such as a "mental illness" or "mental abnormality." These added statutory requirements serve to limit involuntary civil confinement to those who suffer from a volitional impairment rendering them dangerous beyond their control. The Kansas Act is plainly of a kind with these other civil commitment statutes: It requires a finding of future dangerousness, and then links that finding to the existence of a "mental abnormality" or "personality disorder" that makes it difficult, if not impossible, for the person to control his dangerous behavior. The precommitment requirement of a "mental abnormality" or "personality disorder" is consistent with the requirements of these other statutes that we have upheld in that it narrows the class of persons eligible for confinement to those who are unable to control their dangerousness.

Hendricks nonetheless argues that our earlier cases dictate a finding of "mental illness" as a prerequisite for civil commitment. He then asserts that a "mental abnormality" is not equivalent to a "mental illness" because it is a term coined by the Kansas Legislature, rather than by the psychiatric community. Contrary to Hendricks' assertion, the term "mental illness" is devoid of any talismanic significance. Not only do "psychiatrists disagree widely and frequently on what constitutes mental illness," but the Court itself has used a variety of expressions to describe the mental condition of those properly subject to civil confinement. Indeed, we have never required state legislatures to adopt any particular nomenclature in drafting civil commitment statutes. Rather, we have traditionally left to legislators the task of defining terms of a medical nature that have legal significance. . . .

To the extent that the civil commitment statutes we have considered set forth criteria relating to an individual's inability to control his dangerousness, the Kansas Act sets forth comparable criteria and Hendricks' condition doubtless satisfies those criteria. The mental health professionals who evaluated Hendricks diagnosed him as suffering from pedophilia, a condition the psychiatric profession itself classifies as a serious mental disorder. Hendricks even conceded that, when he becomes "stressed out," he cannot "control the urge" to molest children. This admitted lack of volitional control, coupled with a prediction of future dangerousness, adequately distinguishes Hendricks from other dangerous persons who are perhaps more properly dealt with exclusively through criminal proceedings. Hendricks' diagnosis as a pedophile, which qualifies as a "mental abnormality" under the Act, thus plainly suffices for due process purposes.

We granted Hendricks' cross-petition to determine whether the Act violates the Constitution's double jeopardy prohibition or its ban on ex post facto lawmaking. The thrust of Hendricks' argument is that the Act establishes criminal proceedings; hence confinement under it necessarily constitutes punishment. He contends that where, as here, newly enacted "punishment" is predicated upon past conduct for which he has already been convicted and forced to serve a prison sentence, the Constitution's Double Jeopardy and Ex Post Facto Clauses are violated. We are unpersuaded by Hendricks' argument that Kansas has established criminal proceedings.

The categorization of a particular proceeding as civil or criminal "is first of all a question of statutory construction." We must initially ascertain whether the legislature meant the statute to establish "civil" proceedings. If so, we ordinarily defer to the legislature's stated intent. Here, Kansas' objective to create a civil proceeding is evidenced by its placement of the Act within the Kansas probate code, instead of the criminal code, as well as its description of the Act as creating a "civil commitment procedure." Nothing on the face of the statute suggests that the legislature sought to create anything other than a civil commitment scheme designed to protect the public from harm.

Although we recognize that a "civil label is not always dispositive," we will reject the legislature's manifest intent only where a party challenging the statute provides "the clearest proof" that "the statutory scheme [is] so punitive either in purpose or effect as to negate [the State's] intention" to deem it "civil." In those limited circumstances, we will consider the statute to have established criminal proceedings for constitutional purposes. Hendricks, however, has failed to satisfy this heavy burden.

As a threshold matter, commitment under the Act does not implicate either of the two primary objectives of criminal punishment: retribution or deterrence. The Act's purpose is not retributive because it does not affix culpability for prior criminal conduct. Instead, such conduct is used solely for evidentiary purposes, either to demonstrate that a "mental abnormality" exists or to support a finding of future dangerousness. We have previously concluded that an Illinois statute was nonpunitive even though it was triggered by the commission of a sexual assault, explaining that evidence of the prior criminal conduct was "received not to punish past misdeeds, but primarily to show the accused's mental condition and to predict future behavior." In addition, the Kansas Act does not make a criminal conviction a prerequisite for commitment—persons absolved of criminal responsibility may nonetheless be subject to confinement under the Act. An absence of the necessary criminal responsibility suggests that the State is not seeking retribution for a past misdeed. Thus, the fact that the Act may be "tied to criminal activity" is "insufficient to render the statut[e] punitive."

Moreover, unlike a criminal statute, no finding of scienter is required to commit an individual who is found to be a sexually violent predator; instead, the commitment determination is made based on a "mental abnormality" or "personality disorder" rather than on one's criminal intent. The existence of a scienter requirement is customarily an important element in distinguishing criminal from civil statutes. The absence of such a requirement here is evidence that confinement under the statute is not intended to be retributive.

Nor can it be said that the legislature intended the Act to function as a deterrent. Those persons committed under the Act are, by definition, suffering from a "mental abnormality" or a "personality disorder" that prevents them from exercising adequate control over their behavior. Such persons are therefore unlikely to be deterred by the threat of confinement. And the conditions surrounding that confinement do not suggest a punitive purpose on the State's part. The State has represented that an individual confined under the Act is not subject to the more restrictive conditions placed on state prisoners, but instead experiences essentially the same conditions as any involuntarily committed patient in the state mental institution. Because none of the parties argues that people institutionalized under the Kansas general civil commitment statute are subject to punitive conditions, even though they may be involuntarily confined, it is difficult to conclude that persons confined under this Act are being "punished."

Although the civil commitment scheme at issue here does involve an affirmative restraint, "the mere fact that a person is detained does not inexorably lead to the conclusion that the government has imposed punishment." The State may take measures to restrict the freedom of the dangerously mentally ill. This is a legitimate nonpunitive governmental objective and has been historically so regarded. The Court has, in fact, cited the confinement of "mentally unstable individuals who present a danger to the public" as one classic example of nonpunitive detention.

If detention for the purpose of protecting the community from harm necessarily constituted punishment, then all involuntary civil commitments would have to be considered punishment. But we have never so held.

Hendricks focuses on his confinement's potentially indefinite duration as evidence of the State's punitive intent. That focus, however, is misplaced. Far from any punitive objective, the confinement's duration is instead linked to the stated purposes of the commitment, namely, to hold the person until his mental abnormality no longer causes him to be a threat to others. If, at any time, the confined person is adjudged "safe to be at large," he is statutorily entitled to immediate release. . . .

Hendricks next contends that the State's use of procedural safeguards traditionally found in criminal trials makes the proceedings here criminal rather than civil. . . . The numerous procedural and evidentiary protections afforded here demonstrate that the Kansas Legislature has taken great care to confine only a narrow class of particularly dangerous individuals, and then only after meeting the strictest procedural standards. That Kansas chose to afford such procedural protections does not transform a civil commitment proceeding into a criminal prosecution.

Finally, Hendricks argues that the Act is necessarily punitive because it fails to offer any legitimate "treatment." Without such treatment, Hendricks asserts, confinement under the Act amounts to little more than disguised punishment. Hendricks' argument assumes that treatment for his condition is available, but that the State has failed (or refused) to provide it. . . . We have already observed that, under the appropriate circumstances and when accompanied by proper procedures, incapacitation may be a legitimate end of the civil law. . . . While we have upheld state civil commitment statutes that aim both to incapacitate and to treat, we have never held that the Constitution prevents a State from civilly detaining those for whom no treatment is available, but who nevertheless pose a danger to others. . . .

Justice Breyer, with whom Justice Stevens and Justice Souter join, and with whom Justice Ginsburg joins as to Parts II and III, dissenting.

I agree with the majority that the Kansas Sexually Violent Predator Act's definition of "mental abnormality" satisfies the "substantive" requirements of the Due Process Clause. Kansas, however, concedes that Hendricks' condition is treatable; yet the Act did not provide Hendricks (or others like him) with any treatment until after his release date from prison and only inadequate treatment thereafter. These, and certain other, special features of the Act convince me that it was not simply an effort to commit Hendricks civilly, but rather an effort to inflict further punishment upon him. The Ex Post Facto Clause therefore prohibits the Act's application to Hendricks, who committed his crimes prior to its enactment. . . .

II

Kansas' 1994 Act violates the Federal Constitution's prohibition of "any . . . ex post facto Law" if it "inflicts" upon Hendricks "a greater punishment" than did the law "annexed to" his "crime[s]" when he "committed" those crimes in 1984. The majority agrees that the Clause "forbids the application of any new punitive measure to a crime already consummated." But it finds the Act is not "punitive." With respect to that basic question, I disagree with the majority.

Certain resemblances between the Act's "civil commitment" and traditional criminal punishments are obvious. Like criminal imprisonment, the Act's civil commitment amounts to "secure" confinement and "incarceration against one's will." Moreover, the Act, like criminal punishment, imposes its confinement (or sanction) only upon an individual who has previously committed a criminal offense. And the Act imposes that confinement through the use of persons (county prosecutors), procedural guarantees (trial by jury, assistance of counsel, psychiatric evaluations), and standards ("beyond a reasonable doubt") traditionally associated with the criminal law.

These obvious resemblances by themselves, however, are not legally sufficient to transform what the Act calls "civil commitment" into a criminal punishment. Civil commitment of dangerous, mentally ill individuals by its very nature involves confinement and incapacitation. Yet "civil commitment," from a constitutional perspective, nonetheless remains civil. Nor does the fact that criminal behavior triggers the Act make the critical difference. The Act's insistence upon a prior crime, by screening out those whose past behavior does not concretely demonstrate the existence of a mental problem or potential future danger, may serve an important noncriminal evidentiary purpose. Neither is the presence of criminal law-type procedures determinative. Those procedures can serve an important purpose that in this context one might consider noncriminal, namely, helping to prevent judgmental mistakes that would wrongly deprive a person of important liberty.

If these obvious similarities cannot by themselves prove that Kansas' "civil commitment" statute is criminal, neither can the word "civil" written into the statute by itself prove the contrary. This Court has said that only the "clearest proof" could establish that a law the legislature called "civil" was, in reality, a "punitive" measure. But the Court has also reiterated that a "civil label is not always dispositive"; it has said that in close cases the label is "not of paramount importance" and it has looked behind a "civil" label fairly often.

In this circumstance, with important features of the Act pointing in opposite directions, I would place particular importance upon those features that would likely distinguish between a basically punitive and a basically nonpunitive purpose. . . . [W]hen a State believes that treatment does exist, and then couples that admission with a legislatively required delay of such treatment until a person is at the end of his jail term (so that further incapacitation is therefore necessary), such a legislative scheme begins to look punitive. . . .

III

To find that the confinement the Act imposes upon Hendricks is "punishment" is to find a violation of the Ex Post Facto Clause. Kansas does not deny that the 1994 Act changed the legal consequences that attached to Hendricks' earlier crimes, and in a way that significantly "disadvantage[d] the offender."

To find a violation of that Clause here, however, is not to hold that the Clause prevents Kansas, or other States, from enacting dangerous sexual offender statutes. A statute that operates prospectively, for example, does not offend the Ex Post Facto Clause. Neither does it offend the Ex Post Facto Clause for a State to sentence offenders to the fully authorized sentence, to seek consecutive, rather than concurrent, sentences, or to invoke recidivism statutes to lengthen imprisonment. Moreover, a statute that operates retroactively, like Kansas' statute, nonetheless does not offend the Clause if the confinement that it imposes is not punishment—if, that is to say, the legislature does not simply add a later criminal punishment to an earlier one. The statutory provisions before us do amount to punishment primarily because, as I have said, the legislature did not tailor the statute to fit the nonpunitive civil aim of treatment, which it concedes exists in Hendricks' case. . . .

PROBLEM CASE

In 2005, defendant pleaded guilty to two counts of second-degree burglary and was sentenced to prison. As the defendant neared his release date, the state filed a petition for sex offender civil management pursuant to New York's Sex Offender Management and Treatment Act. The state argued that although the burglary conviction was not a sexual offense, the defendant's motivation for committing the crime was sexual in nature because the defendant had broken into the residence looking for a child to molest. The state presented evidence that the defendant had a criminal history of prior convictions for offenses that had a sexual motivation, including crimes against children. The defendant was ordered detained after a civil commitment proceeding under the New York statute. The judge made the finding that the commitment was necessary by applying the standard of "clear and convincing evidence." See N.Y. Mental Hyg. Law § 10.07 (McKinney) ("The jury, or the court if a jury trial is waived, shall determine by clear and convincing evidence whether the respondent is a detained sex offender who suffers from a mental abnormality.").

The defendant argued that the "clear and convincing evidence" standard articulated in the statute violated his right to due process and that the U.S. Constitution required the application of the "beyond a reasonable doubt standard." In *In re Winship*, 397 U.S. 358 (1970), the Supreme Court concluded that the Constitution required the application of the "beyond a reasonable doubt" standard in all criminal cases. Does due process require the imposition of the same standard in proceedings held pursuant to the Sex Offender Management and Treatment Act? See *State v. Farnsworth*, 75 A.D.3d 14, 900 N.Y.S.2d 548 (2010).

NOTES & QUESTIONS ON SEXUAL PREDATORS

1. *Consistency with* Foucha. How is the decision in *Hendricks* consistent with *Foucha*? Recall that in *Foucha* the Court overturned a civil confinement based on dangerousness in the absence of a finding of a bona fide mental illness. Is *Hendricks* on all fours with *Foucha*? Unlike in *Foucha*, the Supreme Court in *Hendricks* rejected the notion that mental illness had any "talismanic significance" or was relevant in any way to the constitutional analysis. Does this suggest that *Foucha* is no longer good law? Should courts now uphold civil commitment statutes that do not require a finding of continued mental illness? Or is the rule from *Hendricks* that confinement for sexual predation is somehow constitutionally different?

2. *Minnesota's statute.* In 2015, a federal judge ruled that Minnesota's civil commitment system for sexual offenders was unconstitutional. The statistics for the program were unusually stark: 700 detainees were being subject to civil confinement and the judge ruled that even those detainees who failed to meet the statutory criteria were still being held—suggesting that the system was inherently punitive rather than preventive. But the Eighth Circuit reversed and upheld Minnesota's system, concluding:

> Reasonable relationship review is highly deferential to the legislature. No one can reasonably dispute that Minnesota has a real, legitimate interest in protecting its citizens from harm caused by sexually dangerous persons or persons who have a sexual psychopathic personality. . . . Any committed person can file a petition for reduction in custody. The petition is considered by a special review board consisting of experts in mental illness and at least one attorney. That panel conducts a hearing and issues a report

> with recommendations to a judicial appeal panel consisting of Minnesota district judges appointed to the judicial appeal panel by the Chief Justice of the Supreme Court. Through this process, the committed person "has the right to be represented by counsel" and the court "shall appoint a qualified attorney to represent the committed person if neither the committed person nor other provide counsel."

Karsjens v. Piper, 845 F.3d 394, 409-10 (8th Cir. 2017). Is the process outlined above sufficient to alleviate any concerns about due process? Would a stricter form of scrutiny (above reasonable relationship review) doom the statute?

3. *Ex post facto problems.* Several state legislatures have recently passed specific legislation authorizing civil confinement for sex offenders. Some courts have applied these statutes for offenders who were convicted before the enactment of the statutes. This raises the question of whether such an application violates the constitutional prohibition on ex post facto punishment. On the one hand, the temporal sequence suggests an obvious ex post facto problem. On the other hand, civil confinement statutes are forward-looking and non-punitive, thus suggesting that they should not be considered ex post facto *punishment* at all. The Supreme Court of New Jersey held that its Sex Offender Monitoring Act (SOMA) could not be applied retroactively because it was an element of post-conviction parole, and "[p]arole is a form of punishment under the Constitution." *Riley v. New Jersey State Parole Bd.*, 219 N.J. 270, 275, 98 A.3d 544, 547 (2014). However, other courts have upheld the retroactive application of civil confinement statutes that are not part of a parole monitoring system.

4. *Crane's lack of control requirement.* After *Hendricks*, the Supreme Court once again considered the Kansas Sexually Violent Predator Act in *Kansas v. Crane*, 534 U.S. 407 (2002). In *Crane*, the issue was whether Kansas could subject an individual to civil confinement without finding that the individual was incapable of controlling his behavior. In *Hendricks*, the Court assumed that it was considering the fate of individuals whose disorder makes it "difficult, if not impossible, for the [dangerous] person to control his dangerous behavior." The question is whether this statement implied a requirement of lack of control of behavior in order to render civil confinement constitutional. The Supreme Court answered this question in the affirmative, concluding that there "must be proof of serious difficulty in controlling behavior . . . sufficient to distinguish the dangerous sexual offender whose serious mental illness, abnormality, or disorder subjects him to civil commitment from the dangerous but typical recidivist convicted in an ordinary criminal case." *Crane*, 534 U.S. at 407.

STATE LAW REQUIREMENTS

Various state jurisdictions have considered the constitutionality of sexual predator confinement statutes under state constitutional law. These challenges have been equally unsuccessful as their counterparts under federal constitutional law. For example, New York State passed the following amendment to its state Mental Hygiene statute:

> Within sixty days after the court determines . . . that there is probable cause to believe that the respondent is a sex offender requiring civil management, the court shall conduct a jury trial to determine whether the respondent is a detained sex offender who suffers from a mental abnormality. The trial shall be held before the same court that conducted the probable cause hearing unless either the attorney general or counsel for the respondent has moved for a change of venue and the motion has been granted by the court.

N.Y. Mental Hyg. Law § 10.07. As in *Hendricks*, the statute requires a finding of a mental abnormality rather than a finding of mental illness.

In *State v. Myron P.*, 20 N.Y.3d 206, 981 N.E.2d 772 (2012), the New York State Court of Appeals heard a challenge from a confined sex offender. The petitioner, Myron P., argued that the state statute should be interpreted to require a preliminary determination that he suffered from a mental illness, and also that he was denied his right to a jury trial under federal and New York State constitutional law. (Article I, § 2 of the New York Constitution promises that "[t]rial by jury in all cases in which it has heretofore been guaranteed by constitutional provision shall remain inviolate forever.") In particular, Myron P. argued that the New York scheme was unconstitutional because his jury trial was only to determine whether or not he suffered from a mental abnormality. Once the jury concluded in the affirmative, then the judge alone determined that he was so dangerous as to require detention. According to the court, the scheme is consistent with historical practice because "in those historic civil commitment proceedings, once the jury made a finding of mental illness, the judge was statutorily mandated to confine the individual." 20 N.Y.3d at 213.

D. IMMIGRATION DETENTION

Like pre-trial detention and civil confinement for those who are mentally ill or sexual predators, immigration detention is also forward-looking. Pending a removal proceeding or an asylum hearing, which might be months away, the federal government is authorized by statute to detain aliens if an immigration judge determines that confinement is the only way to ensure the presence of the individual for those proceedings. The following case focuses on one particular type of immigration detention: the detention of an immigrant slated for removal from the country. By statute, these individuals should be removed, i.e., deported, within 90 days. But in some instances, removal does not occur within the window and a federal statute authorizes continued immigration detention beyond the 90-day period. The most likely reason for a delay in removal is an inability to find another country willing to accept the individual for repatriation. In that situation, faced with a possibly indefinite delay of removal, does the detainee have the right to a habeas hearing to contest his or her continued detention (or any other procedural protections)? And if yes, what standard would govern that judicial decision? Finally, is there some length of time during which it is reasonable to assume that the government might accomplish removal? Conversely (and stated in the negative), is there a time beyond which it is no longer reasonable to presume that the government will accomplish the removal?

Zadvydas v. Davis

Supreme Court of the United States
533 U.S. 678 (2001)

Justice BREYER delivered the opinion of the Court.

When an alien has been found to be unlawfully present in the United States and a final order of removal has been entered, the Government ordinarily secures the alien's removal during a subsequent 90-day statutory "removal period," during which time the alien normally is held in custody. A special statute authorizes further detention if the Government fails to remove the alien during those 90 days. It says:

> An alien ordered removed [1] who is inadmissible . . . [2] [or] removable [as a result of violations of status requirements or entry conditions, violations of criminal law, or reasons of security or foreign policy] or [3] who has been determined by the Attorney General to be a risk to the community or unlikely to comply with the order of removal, may be detained beyond the removal period and, if released, shall be subject to [certain] terms of supervision. . . .

8 U.S.C. § 1231(a)(6) (1994 ed., Supp. V).

In these cases, we must decide whether this post-removal-period statute authorizes the Attorney General to detain a removable alien indefinitely beyond the removal period or only for a period reasonably necessary to secure the alien's removal. We deal here with aliens who were admitted to the United States but subsequently ordered removed. Aliens who have not yet gained initial admission to this country would present a very different question. Based on our conclusion that indefinite detention of aliens in the former category would raise serious constitutional concerns, we construe the statute to contain an implicit "reasonable time" limitation, the application of which is subject to federal-court review.

I

The post-removal-period detention statute is one of a related set of statutes and regulations that govern detention during and after removal proceedings. While removal proceedings are in progress, most aliens may be released on bond or paroled. 8 U.S.C. §§ 1226(a)(2), (c). After entry of a final removal order and during the 90-day removal period, however, aliens must be held in custody. § 1231(a)(2). Subsequently, as the post-removal-period statute provides, the Government "may" continue to detain an alien who still remains here or release that alien under supervision. § 1231(a)(6).

Related Immigration and Naturalization Service (INS) regulations add that the INS District Director will initially review the alien's records to decide whether further detention or release under supervision is warranted after the 90-day removal period expires. 8 C.F.R. § 241.4(c)(1), (h), (k)(1)(i) (2001). If the decision is to detain, then an INS panel will review the matter further, at the expiration of a 3-month period or soon thereafter. And the panel will decide, on the basis of records and a possible personal interview, between still further detention or release under supervision. In making this decision, the panel will consider, for example, the alien's disciplinary record, criminal record, mental health reports, evidence of rehabilitation, history of flight, prior immigration history, and favorable factors such as family ties. To authorize release, the panel must find that the alien is not likely to be violent, to pose a threat to the community, to flee if released, or to violate the conditions of release. And the alien must demonstrate "to the satisfaction of the Attorney General" that he will pose no danger or risk of flight. If the panel decides against release, it must review the matter again within a year, and can review it earlier if conditions change. . . .

III

The post-removal-period detention statute applies to certain categories of aliens who have been ordered removed, namely, inadmissible aliens, criminal aliens, aliens who have violated their nonimmigrant status conditions, and aliens removable for certain national security or foreign relations reasons, as well as any alien "who has been determined by the Attorney General to be a risk to the community or unlikely to comply with the order of removal." 8 U.S.C. § 1231(a)(6). It says that an alien who falls into one of these categories "may be detained beyond the removal period and, if released, shall be subject to [certain] terms of supervision." The Government argues that the statute means what it literally says. It sets no "limit on the length of time beyond the removal period that an alien who falls within one of the Section 1231(a)(6) categories may be detained." Hence, "whether to continue to detain such an alien and, if so, in what circumstances and for how long" is up to the Attorney General, not up to the courts.

"[I]t is a cardinal principle" of statutory interpretation, however, that when an Act of Congress raises "a serious doubt" as to its constitutionality, "this Court will first ascertain whether a construction of the statute is fairly possible by which the question may be avoided." . . . [W]e read an implicit limitation into the statute before us. In our view, the statute, read in light of the Constitution's demands, limits an alien's post-removal-period detention to a period reasonably necessary to bring about that alien's removal from the United States. It does not permit indefinite detention.

A statute permitting indefinite detention of an alien would raise a serious constitutional problem. The Fifth Amendment's Due Process Clause forbids the Government to "depriv[e]" any "person . . . of . . . liberty . . . without due process of law." Freedom from imprisonment—from government custody, detention, or other forms of physical restraint—lies at the heart of the liberty that Clause protects. See *Foucha v. Louisiana,* 504 U.S. 71, 80 (1992). And this Court has said that government detention violates that Clause unless the detention is ordered in a criminal proceeding with adequate procedural protections, see *United States v. Salerno,* 481 U.S. 739, 746 (1987), or, in certain special and "narrow" nonpunitive "circumstances," *Foucha* at 80, where a special justification, such as harm-threatening mental illness, outweighs the "individual's constitutionally protected interest in avoiding physical restraint." *Kansas v. Hendricks,* 521 U.S. 346, 356 (1997).

The proceedings at issue here are civil, not criminal, and we assume that they are nonpunitive in purpose and effect. There is no sufficiently strong special justification here for indefinite civil detention—at least as administered under this statute. The statute, says the Government, has two regulatory goals: "ensuring the appearance of aliens at future immigration proceedings" and "[p]reventing danger to the community." But by definition the first justification—preventing flight—is weak or nonexistent where removal seems a remote possibility at best. As this Court said in *Jackson v. Indiana,* 406 U.S. 715 (1972), where detention's goal is no longer practically attainable, detention no longer "bear[s] [a] reasonable relation to the purpose for which the individual [was] committed."

The second justification—protecting the community—does not necessarily diminish in force over time. But we have upheld preventive detention based on dangerousness only when limited to specially dangerous individuals and subject to strong procedural protections. In cases in which preventive detention is of potentially indefinite duration, we have also demanded that the dangerousness rationale be accompanied by some other special circumstance, such as mental illness, that helps to create the danger.

The civil confinement here at issue is not limited, but potentially permanent. The provision authorizing detention does not apply narrowly to "a small segment of particularly dangerous individuals," *Hendricks* at 368, say, suspected terrorists, but broadly to aliens ordered removed for many and various reasons, including tourist visa violations. And, once the flight risk justification evaporates, the only special circumstance present is the alien's removable status itself, which bears no relation to a detainee's dangerousness.

Moreover, the sole procedural protections available to the alien are found in administrative proceedings, where the alien bears the burden of proving he is not dangerous, without (in the Government's view) significant later judicial review. This Court has suggested, however, that the Constitution may well preclude granting "an administrative body the unreviewable authority to make determinations implicating fundamental rights." The Constitution demands greater procedural protection even for property. The serious constitutional problem arising out of a statute that, in these circumstances, permits an indefinite, perhaps permanent, deprivation of human liberty without any such protection is obvious. . . .

IV

The Government seems to argue that, even under our interpretation of the statute, a federal habeas court would have to accept the Government's view about whether the implicit statutory limitation is satisfied in a particular case, conducting little or no independent review of the matter. In our view, that is not so. Whether a set of particular circumstances amounts to detention within, or beyond, a period reasonably necessary to secure removal is determinative of whether the detention is, or is not, pursuant to statutory authority. The basic federal habeas corpus statute grants the federal courts authority to answer that question. In doing so the courts carry out what this Court has described as the "historic purpose of the writ," namely, "to relieve detention by executive authorities without judicial trial."

In answering that basic question, the habeas court must ask whether the detention in question exceeds a period reasonably necessary to secure removal. It should measure reasonableness primarily in terms of the statute's basic purpose, namely, assuring the alien's presence at the moment of removal. Thus, if removal is not reasonably foreseeable, the court should hold continued detention unreasonable and no longer authorized by statute. In that case, of course, the alien's release may and should be conditioned on any of the various forms of supervised release that are appropriate in the circumstances, and the alien may no doubt be returned to custody upon a violation of those conditions. And if removal is reasonably foreseeable, the habeas court should consider the risk of the alien's committing further crimes as a factor potentially justifying confinement within that reasonable removal period.

We recognize, as the Government points out, that review must take appropriate account of the greater immigration-related expertise of the Executive Branch, of the serious administrative needs and concerns inherent in the necessarily extensive INS efforts to enforce this complex statute, and the Nation's need to "speak with one voice" in immigration matters. But we believe that courts can take appropriate account of such matters without abdicating their legal responsibility to review the lawfulness of an alien's continued detention.

Ordinary principles of judicial review in this area recognize primary Executive Branch responsibility. They counsel judges to give expert agencies decisionmaking leeway in matters that invoke their expertise. . . .

We realize that recognizing this necessary Executive leeway will often call for difficult judgments. In order to limit the occasions when courts will need to make them, we think it practically necessary to recognize some presumptively reasonable period of detention. . . . While an argument can be made for confining any presumption to 90 days, we doubt that when Congress shortened the removal period to 90 days in 1996 it believed that all reasonably foreseeable removals could be accomplished in that time. We do have reason to believe, however, that Congress previously doubted the constitutionality of detention for more than six months. Consequently, for the sake of uniform administration in the federal courts, we recognize that period. After this 6-month period, once the alien provides good reason to believe that there is no significant likelihood of removal in the reasonably foreseeable future, the Government must respond with evidence sufficient to rebut that showing. And for detention to remain reasonable, as the period of prior postremoval confinement grows, what counts as the "reasonably foreseeable future" conversely would have to shrink. This 6-month presumption, of course, does not mean that every alien not removed must be released after six months. To the contrary, an alien may be held in confinement until it has been determined that there is no significant likelihood of removal in the reasonably foreseeable future. . . .

Justice SCALIA, with whom Justice THOMAS joins, dissenting.

. . . A criminal alien under final order of removal who allegedly will not be accepted by any other country in the reasonably foreseeable future claims a constitutional right of supervised release into the United States. This claim can be repackaged as freedom from "physical restraint" or freedom from "indefinite detention," but it is at bottom a claimed right of release into this country by an individual who concededly has no legal right to be here. There is no such constitutional right.

Like a criminal alien under final order of removal, an inadmissible alien at the border has no right to be in the United States. In *Shaughnessy v. United States ex rel. Mezei*, 345 U.S. 206 (1953), we upheld potentially indefinite detention of such an inadmissible alien whom the Government was unable to return anywhere else. We said that "we [did] not think that respondent's continued exclusion deprives him of any statutory or constitutional right." While four Members of the Court thought that Mezei deserved greater procedural protections, no Justice asserted that Mezei had a substantive constitutional right to release into this country. And Justice Jackson's dissent,

> joined by Justice Frankfurter, affirmatively asserted the opposite, with no contradiction from the Court: "Due process does not invest any alien with a right to enter the United States, nor confer on those admitted the right to remain against the national will. Nothing in the Constitution requires admission or sufferance of aliens hostile to our scheme of government." Insofar as a claimed legal right to release into this country is concerned, an alien under final order of removal stands on an equal footing with an inadmissible alien at the threshold of entry: He has no such right. . . .

NOTES & QUESTIONS ON IMMIGRATION DETENTION

1. *The reasonably foreseeable future standard.* In *Zadvydas,* the Supreme Court concluded that immigration detainees who could not be removed within six months (because no country would take them) were entitled to a habeas hearing to determine whether their continued detention was "reasonably necessary." In other words, if the purpose of the detention is to facilitate removal, but removal is either impossible or indefinitely delayed, then the rationale for detention starts to evaporate. In the years immediately following the Court's decision, roughly 5,000 cases were reviewed, resulting in 3,000 releases, 1,700 continuing detentions, and 350 removals. Rachel Canty, *The New World of Immigration Custody Determinations After* Zadvydas v. Davis, 18 Geo. Immigr. L.J. 467, 468 (2004).

2. *Right to bail.* In *Demore v. Kim,* 538 U.S. 510 (2003), petitioners argued that prolonged immigration detention is only consistent with the Constitution if each detainee is given "an individualized bond hearing at which the Government proves by clear and convincing evidence that the class member's detention remains justified." The Supreme Court considered whether the immigration detention statute should be interpreted as containing an implicit six-month limit on detention as a way of avoiding a potential constitutional problem regarding indefinite detention without sufficient procedural protections. However, the majority considered detention pending removal as necessary for the proper functioning of immigration law and not one that required a bail hearing. The Eighth Amendment's Excessive Bail Clause only prohibits the imposition of "excessive bail"—literally—but does not address situations where individuals are denied bail entirely and remanded to custody.

E. MATERIAL WITNESS

The federal government is authorized by statute to hold a material witness even if the witness has committed no crime. The goal of the detention is purely forward-looking—to ensure the witness's availability for trial:

> If it appears from an affidavit filed by a party that the testimony of a person is material in a criminal proceeding, and if it is shown that it may become impracticable to secure the presence of the person by subpoena, a judicial officer may order the arrest of the person. . . . No material witness may be detained because of inability to comply with any condition of release if the testimony of such witness can adequately be secured by deposition, and if further detention is not necessary to prevent a failure of justice. Release of a material witness may be delayed for a reasonable period of time until the deposition of the witness can be taken pursuant to the Federal Rules of Criminal Procedure.

18 U.S.C. § 3144. According to 18 U.S.C. § 3145, the witness has the right to contest the issuance of the material witness order: "If a person is ordered detained by a magistrate judge, or by a person other than a judge of a court having original jurisdiction over the offense and other than a Federal appellate court, the person may file, with the court having original jurisdiction over the offense, a motion for revocation or amendment of the order. The motion shall be determined promptly."

Because material witness detention requires no finding of culpability, but simply a finding that it is required because a simple subpoena will be ineffective, it is potentially subject to great abuse. The government could detain as a material witness an individual who they suspect of a crime but for whom there is insufficient evidence to support a criminal conviction. The following case involves one such allegation of a pretextual use of the material witness statute. The litigant argues that he (and others) were detained by the federal government in the aftermath of 9/11 under the material witness statute even though the government had no intention of calling them as witnesses at trial. Do these allegations suggest that material witness detention is inherently flawed or does the litigation demonstrate precisely the opposite: appropriate judicial scrutiny of material witness detention?

Ashcroft v. al-Kidd

Supreme Court of the United States
563 U.S. 731 (2011)

Justice Scalia delivered the opinion of the Court.

We decide whether a former Attorney General enjoys immunity from suit for allegedly authorizing federal prosecutors to obtain valid material-witness warrants for detention of terrorism suspects whom they would otherwise lack probable cause to arrest.

I

The federal material-witness statute authorizes judges to "order the arrest of [a] person" whose testimony "is material in a criminal proceeding . . . if it is shown that it may become impracticable to secure the presence of the person by subpoena." 18 U.S.C. § 3144. Material witnesses enjoy the same constitutional right to pretrial release as other federal detainees, and federal law requires release if their testimony "can adequately be secured by deposition, and if further detention is not necessary to prevent a failure of justice."

U.S. Attorney General John Ashcroft holds a copy of the Strategic Plan for the Department of Justice at a 2004 hearing of the national commission investigating the 9/11 terrorist attacks. (Scott J. Ferrell/Congressional Quarterly/Alamy)

Because this case arises from a motion to dismiss, we accept as true the factual allegations in Abdullah al-Kidd's complaint. The complaint alleges that, in the aftermath of the September 11th terrorist attacks, then-Attorney General John Ashcroft authorized federal prosecutors and law enforcement officials to use the material-witness statute to detain individuals with suspected ties to terrorist organizations. It is alleged that federal officials had no intention of calling most of these individuals as witnesses, and that they were detained, at Ashcroft's direction, because federal officials suspected them of supporting terrorism but lacked sufficient evidence to charge them with a crime.

It is alleged that this pretextual detention policy led to the material-witness arrest of al-Kidd, a native-born United States citizen. FBI agents apprehended him in March 2003 as he checked in for a flight to Saudi Arabia. Two days earlier, federal officials had informed a Magistrate Judge that, if al-Kidd boarded his flight, they believed information "crucial" to the prosecution of Sami Omar al-Hussayen would be lost. Al-Kidd remained in federal custody for 16 days and on supervised release until al-Hussayen's trial concluded 14 months later. Prosecutors never called him as a witness.

II

Qualified immunity shields federal and state officials from money damages unless a plaintiff pleads facts showing (1) that the official violated a statutory or constitutional right, and (2) that the right was "clearly established" at the time of the challenged conduct. . . .

The Fourth Amendment protects "[t]he right of the people to be secure in their persons, houses, papers, and effects, against unreasonable searches and seizures." An arrest, of course, qualifies as a "seizure" of a "person" under this provision, and so must be reasonable under the circumstances. Al-Kidd does not assert that Government officials would have acted unreasonably if they had used a material-witness warrant to arrest him for the purpose of securing his testimony for trial. He contests, however (and the Court of Appeals here rejected), the reasonableness of using the warrant to detain him as a suspected criminal.

Fourth Amendment reasonableness "is predominantly an objective inquiry." We ask whether "the circumstances, viewed objectively, justify [the challenged] action." If so, that action was reasonable "whatever the subjective intent" motivating the relevant officials. This approach recognizes that the Fourth Amendment regulates conduct rather than thoughts, and it promotes evenhanded, uniform enforcement of the law.

Two "limited exception[s]" to this rule are our special-needs and administrative-search cases, where "actual motivations" do matter. A judicial warrant and probable cause are not needed where the search or seizure is justified by "special needs, beyond the normal need for law enforcement." . . . But those exceptions do not apply where the officer's purpose is not to attend to the special needs or to the investigation for which the administrative inspection is justified. The Government seeks to justify the present arrest on the basis of a properly issued judicial warrant—so that the special-needs and administrative-inspection cases cannot be the basis for a purpose inquiry here. . . .

A warrant issued by a neutral Magistrate Judge authorized al-Kidd's arrest. The affidavit accompanying the warrant application (as al-Kidd concedes) gave individualized reasons to believe that he was a material witness and that he would soon disappear. The existence of a judicial warrant based on individualized suspicion takes this case outside the domain of . . . our special-needs and administrative-search cases. . . .

A warrant based on individualized suspicion in fact grants more protection against the malevolent and the incompetent than existed in most of our cases eschewing inquiries into intent. . . . Because al-Kidd concedes that individualized suspicion supported the issuance of the material-witness arrest warrant; and does not assert that his arrest would have been unconstitutional absent the alleged pretextual use of the warrant; we find no Fourth Amendment violation. Efficient and evenhanded application of the law demands that we look to whether the arrest is objectively justified, rather than to the motive of the arresting officer. . . .

A Government official's conduct violates clearly established law when, at the time of the challenged conduct, "[t]he contours of [a] right [are] sufficiently clear" that every "reasonable official would have understood that what he is doing violates that right." . . . At the time of al-Kidd's arrest, not a single judicial opinion had held that pretext could render an objectively reasonable arrest pursuant to a material-witness warrant unconstitutional. A district-court opinion had suggested, in a footnoted dictum devoid of supporting citation, that using such a warrant for preventive detention of suspects "is an illegitimate use of the statute"—implying (we accept for the sake of argument) that the detention would therefore be unconstitutional. The Court of Appeals thought nothing could "have given John Ashcroft fair[er] warning" that his conduct violated the Fourth Amendment, because the footnoted dictum "call[ed] out Ashcroft by name"! We will indulge the assumption (though it does not seem to us realistic) that Justice Department lawyers bring to the Attorney General's personal attention all district judges' footnoted speculations that boldly "call him out by name." On that assumption, would it prove that for him (and for him only?) it became clearly established that pretextual use of the material-witness statute rendered the arrest unconstitutional? An extraordinary proposition. Even a district judge's ipse dixit of a holding is not "controlling authority" in any jurisdiction, much less in the entire United States; and his ipse dixit of a footnoted dictum falls far short of what is necessary absent controlling authority: a robust "consensus of cases of persuasive authority." . . .

We hold that an objectively reasonable arrest and detention of a material witness pursuant to a validly obtained warrant cannot be challenged as unconstitutional on the basis of allegations that the arresting authority had an improper motive. . . .

Justice GINSBURG, with whom Justice BREYER and Justice SOTOMAYOR join, concurring in the judgment.

. . . I agree with the Court that no "clearly established law" renders Ashcroft answerable in damages for the abuse of authority al-Kidd charged. But I join Justice Sotomayor in objecting to the Court's disposition of al-Kidd's Fourth Amendment claim on the merits. . . . In addressing al-Kidd's Fourth Amendment claim against Ashcroft, the Court assumes at the outset the existence of a validly obtained material witness warrant. That characterization is puzzling. Is a warrant "validly obtained" when the affidavit on which it is based fails to inform the issuing Magistrate Judge that "the Government has no intention of using [al-Kidd as a witness] at [another's] trial," and does not disclose that al-Kidd had cooperated with FBI agents each of the several times they had asked to interview him?

Casting further doubt on the assumption that the warrant was validly obtained, the Magistrate Judge was not told that al-Kidd's parents, wife, and children were all citizens and residents of the United States. In addition, the affidavit misrepresented that al-Kidd was about to take a one-way flight to Saudi Arabia, with a first-class ticket costing approximately $5,000; in fact, al-Kidd had a round-trip, coach-class ticket that cost $1,700. Given these omissions and misrepresentations, there is strong cause to question the Court's opening assumption—a valid material-witness warrant—and equally strong reason to conclude that a merits determination was neither necessary nor proper.

. . . [E]ven if the initial material witness classification had been proper, what even arguably legitimate basis could there be for the harsh custodial conditions to which al-Kidd was subjected: Ostensibly held only to secure his testimony, al-Kidd was confined in three different detention centers during his 16 days' incarceration, kept in high-security cells lit 24 hours a day, strip-searched and subjected to body-cavity inspections on more than one occasion, and handcuffed and shackled about his wrists, legs, and waist.. . . [H]is ordeal is a grim reminder of the need to install safeguards against disrespect for human dignity, constraints that will control officialdom even in perilous times. . . .

PROBLEM CASE

Consider the case of Nicole Schneyder, who was identified by local prosecutors as an indispensable witness in a murder case in Pennsylvania. Schneyder refused to testify after allegedly receiving a threat from the family of the defendant, Michael Overby. Schneyder was adamant that she would not testify and physically resisted her arrest by a police officer who was tasked with bringing her to court. Schneyder was not captured and did not appear at Overby's first trial, nor did she appear at the second trial. In lieu of her testimony, prosecutors introduced into evidence Schneyder's prior statements, and Overby was convicted. On appeal, Overby successfully argued that he was denied his right of confrontation and his conviction was overturned. Prosecutors began preparations for a third trial on February 2, 2005, this time with Schneyder's live testimony. Schneyder could not be served with a subpoena (because she could not be located). Instead, local prosecutors secured a material witness warrant.

Overby's trial was then pushed back more than three months, thus requiring Schneyder to stay in jail for 131 days while awaiting the commencement of the trial. Was the detention in this case for an unreasonable length of time? Was it longer than necessary given the facts of the case? If yes, does that make it constitutionally problematic? Was Schneyder's detention a continuing seizure in violation of the liberty interest protected by the Fourth Amendment? See *Schneyder v. Smith*, 653 F.3d 313, 315-16 (3d Cir. 2011).

NOTES & QUESTIONS ON MATERIAL WITNESSES

1. *The problem of pretext.* The *al-Kidd* case hits right at the weakness of the material witness statute: Since the detention is prospective in nature, the government need not demonstrate that the detainee has been called to testify in a past case but merely needs to make a showing that it plans to call the witness in a future case. However, there is little accountability if government prosecutors fail to follow through on their stated objective. Moreover, if the government never intended to call the witness at trial in the first place, there is little remedy—once the ruse comes to light, the detainee has already been subject to a deprivation of liberty. Is there any solution to this problem?

2. *Fourth Amendment concerns.* Although the Supreme Court has never articulated a constitutional concern with the material witness statute per se, lower courts have articulated a constitutional standard for material witness warrants. For example, in *Bacon,* the Ninth Circuit concluded: "Before a material witness arrest warrant may issue, the judicial officer must have probable cause to believe (1) 'that the testimony of a person is material' and (2) 'that it may become impracticable to secure his presence by subpoena.' These requirements are reasonable, and if they are met, an arrest warrant may issue." *Bacon v. United States,* 449 F.2d 933, 943 (9th Cir. 1971). Does this proposed "material witness probable cause" standard suffice to resolve any constitutional concerns about the deprivation of liberty of the witness, especially since the witness is not detained pursuant to any finding of guilt or culpability? Is there an alternative standard that would be preferable?

3. *Are material witness warrants "per se" unconstitutional?* Some scholars have argued that material witness warrants violate the Fourth Amendment because they allow detention in the absence of a criminal conviction. Consider the following argument:

> Section 3144 is facially unconstitutional because "no set of circumstances exists under which" it is legitimate to arrest someone who has not committed and is not committing a crime. The Supreme Court has long interpreted the Fourth Amendment as prohibiting arrests not supported by probable cause to believe the arrestee committed or imminently will commit a crime. Accordingly, the general rule is that seizures not based on probable cause to believe that the arrestee committed a crime are unreasonable under the Fourth Amendment. While there are some exceptions to that general rule, none of them justifies the detention of innocent witnesses in a criminal case prosecuted by civilian authorities.

Ricardo J. Bascuas, *The Unconstitutionality of "Hold Until Cleared": Reexamining Material Witness Detentions in the Wake of the September 11th Dragnet,* 58 Vand. L. Rev. 677, 732-33 (2005). Do you agree that the material witness statute is an impermissible exception to the probable cause standard? Does

Professor Bascuas's argument assume that the detention in question is punitive in nature? See also Donald Q. Cochran, *Material Witness Detention in a Post-9/11 World: Mission Creep or Fresh Start?*, 18 Geo. Mason L. Rev. 1, 17 (2010) (noting that courts use a probable cause standard for evaluating material witness warrants that is different from the probable cause standard "in the arrest context, which requires a belief that the suspect has committed or is committing a crime").

STATE LAW REQUIREMENTS

Many states have material witness statutes similar to the federal statute that was at issue in *al-Kidd*. For example, New York's provision states: "A material witness order may be issued upon the ground that there is reasonable cause to believe that a person whom the people or the defendant desire to call as a witness in a pending criminal action: (a) Possesses information material to the determination of such action; and (b) Will not be amenable or responsive to a subpoena at a time when his attendance will be sought." N.Y. Crim. Proc. Law §620.20. However, the statute also imposes particular constraints to ensure that the demand is legitimate as opposed to pretextual, including the requirement of a pending indictment or a grand jury proceeding or a felony complaint in a local criminal court.

Iowa's statute also requires the existence of an indictment:

> 1. When a law enforcement officer has probable cause to believe that a person is a necessary and material witness to a felony and that such person might be unavailable for service of a subpoena, the officer may arrest such person as a material witness with or without an arrest warrant.
>
> 2. At the time of the arrest, the law enforcement officer shall inform the person of: a. The officer's identity as a law enforcement officer. b. The reason for the arrest which is that the person is believed to be a material witness to an identified felony and that the person might be unavailable for service of a subpoena.

Iowa Code § 804.11. In *State v. Hernandez-Lopez*, 639 N.W.2d 226 (Iowa 2002), two witnesses arrested in connection with a fatal motor vehicle accident challenged the constitutionality of Iowa's material witness statute. The Iowa Supreme Court concluded that the statute complied with both substantive and procedural due process:

> We conclude the pre-trial detention imposed by the material witness statute does not constitute impermissible punishment without a trial. Our material witness statute does not possess a punitive purpose. The mere fact that an individual is subject to detention does not necessarily mean the government is imposing punishment. An individual deemed to be a material witness is subject to detention because the individual possesses critical knowledge of a felony and is unlikely to attend trial even if subpoenaed. The power to detain is utilized to secure a witness' attendance at trial, not to punish the witness.

Id. The court also noted that the statute was narrowly tailored to meet a compelling government interest in part because the statute allowed for alternatives to incarceration if those would be effective in securing the appearance of the witness at trial.

F. LAW OF WAR DETENTION

The laws of war are the rules of international law governing the conduct of warfare. Chief among these rules are regulations concerning the detention of captured enemy fighters, normally called combatants (although technically this term applies only to members of State armed forces). These rules, both treaty and customary, establish conditions of detention and the qualification for designating detainees as prisoners of war with the added protections resulting from this status. When soldiers successfully surrender to enemy forces, they are considered outside of combat and are no longer legitimate targets for killing. Instead, they are subject to capture and detention until the conclusion of hostilities. The rationale for detention during an armed conflict is to remove enemy fighters from the battlefield and prevent them from returning to the hostilities. For these reasons, law of war detention is inherently preventive in nature, i.e., designed to prevent soldiers from returning to the fight—and not punitive in nature.

The following case involves an American citizen captured overseas, allegedly fighting for the Taliban in Afghanistan during an armed conflict against U.S. forces. After the 9/11 terrorist attacks, U.S. armed forces launched a military invasion of Afghanistan. The goal of the intervention was to destroy al-Qaeda forces stationed there and to remove the Taliban government from power in Afghanistan. The rationale for this policy objective was that the Taliban government had given safe haven to al-Qaeda to operate a terrorist camp on its territory. During the military operation, Hamdi was captured by allied forces, transferred to U.S. forces, and placed in U.S. military detention. The Supreme Court was tasked with deciding whether the President had the authority to order Hamdi's military detention and whether this detention was consistent with the Due Process Clause. As you read the case, pay particular attention to the Court's invocation of the phrase "neutral decisionmaker" and what it might entail for other military detention cases.

Hamdi v. Rumsfeld

Supreme Court of the United States
542 U.S. 507 (2004)

Justice O'CONNOR announced the judgment of the Court and delivered an opinion, in which THE CHIEF JUSTICE, Justice KENNEDY, and Justice BREYER join.

Yaser Esam Hamdi during a prayer service performed by detainees in Camp X-Ray, Guantanamo Bay detention camp, April 2002. (Photographer's Mate 1st Class Shawn P. Eklund, United States Navy)

At this difficult time in our Nation's history, we are called upon to consider the legality of the Government's detention of a United States citizen on United States soil as an "enemy combatant" and to address the process that is constitutionally owed to one who seeks to challenge his classification as such. The United States Court of Appeals for the Fourth Circuit held that petitioner Yaser Hamdi's detention was legally authorized and that he was entitled to no further opportunity to challenge his enemy-combatant label. We now vacate and remand. We hold that although Congress authorized the detention of combatants in the narrow circumstances alleged here, due process demands that a citizen held in the United States as an enemy combatant be given a meaningful opportunity to contest the factual basis for that detention before a neutral decisionmaker.

I

On September 11, 2001, the al Qaeda terrorist network used hijacked commercial airliners to attack prominent targets in the United States. Approximately 3,000 people were killed in those attacks. One week later, in response to these "acts of treacherous violence," Congress passed a resolution authorizing the President to "use all necessary and appropriate force against those nations, organizations, or persons he determines planned, authorized, committed, or aided the terrorist attacks" or "harbored such organizations or persons, in order to prevent any future acts of international terrorism against the United States by such nations, organizations or persons." Authorization for Use of Military Force (AUMF), 115 Stat. 224. Soon thereafter, the President ordered United States Armed Forces to Afghanistan, with a mission to subdue al Qaeda and quell the Taliban regime that was known to support it.

This case arises out of the detention of a man whom the Government alleges took up arms with the Taliban during this conflict. His name is Yaser Esam Hamdi. Born in Louisiana in 1980, Hamdi moved with his family to Saudi Arabia as a child. By 2001, the parties agree, he resided in Afghanistan. At some point that year, he was seized by members of the Northern Alliance, a coalition of military groups opposed to the Taliban government, and eventually was turned over to the United States military. The Government asserts that it initially detained and interrogated Hamdi in Afghanistan before transferring him to the United States Naval Base in Guantanamo Bay in January 2002. In April 2002, upon learning that Hamdi is an American citizen, authorities transferred him to a naval brig in Norfolk, Virginia, where he remained until a recent transfer to a brig in Charleston, South Carolina. The Government contends that Hamdi is an "enemy combatant," and that this status justifies holding him in the United States indefinitely—without formal charges or proceedings—unless and until it makes the determination that access to counsel or further process is warranted. In June 2002, Hamdi's father, Esam Fouad Hamdi, filed the present petition for a writ of habeas corpus. . . .

II

The threshold question before us is whether the Executive has the authority to detain citizens who qualify as "enemy combatants." There is some debate as to the proper scope of this term, and the Government has never provided any court with the full criteria that it uses in classifying individuals as such. It has made clear, however, that, for purposes of this case, the "enemy combatant" that it is seeking to detain is an individual who, it alleges, was "part of or supporting forces hostile to the United States or coalition partners" in Afghanistan and who "engaged in an armed conflict against the United States" there. We therefore answer only the narrow question before us: whether the detention of citizens falling within that definition is authorized.

The Government maintains that no explicit congressional authorization is required, because the Executive possesses plenary authority to detain pursuant to Article II of the Constitution. We do not reach the question whether Article II provides such authority, however, because we agree with the Government's alternative position, that Congress has in fact authorized Hamdi's detention, through the AUMF. . . .

The AUMF authorizes the President to use "all necessary and appropriate force" against "nations, organizations, or persons" associated with the September 11, 2001, terrorist attacks. There can be no doubt that individuals who fought against the United States in Afghanistan as part of the Taliban, an organization known to have supported the al Qaeda terrorist network responsible for those attacks, are individuals Congress sought to target in passing the AUMF. We conclude that detention of individuals falling into the limited category we are considering, for the duration of the particular conflict in which they were captured, is so fundamental and accepted an incident to war as to be an exercise of the "necessary and appropriate force" Congress has authorized the President to use.

The capture and detention of lawful combatants and the capture, detention, and trial of unlawful combatants, by "universal agreement and practice," are "important incident[s] of war." The purpose of detention is to prevent captured individuals from returning to the field of battle and taking up arms once again.

There is no bar to this Nation's holding one of its own citizens as an enemy combatant. In *Quirin*, one of the detainees, Haupt, alleged that he was a naturalized United States citizen. 317 U.S., at 20. We held that "[c]itizens who associate themselves with the military arm of the enemy government, and with its aid, guidance and direction enter this country bent on hostile acts, are enemy belligerents within the meaning of . . . the law of war." While Haupt was tried for violations of the law of war, nothing in *Quirin* suggests that his citizenship would have precluded his mere detention for the duration of the relevant hostilities. Nor can we see any reason for drawing such a line here. A citizen, no less than an alien, can be "part of or supporting forces hostile to the United States or coalition partners" and "engaged in an armed conflict against the United States"; such a citizen, if released, would pose the same threat of returning to the front during the ongoing conflict.

In light of these principles, it is of no moment that the AUMF does not use specific language of detention. Because detention to prevent a combatant's return to the battlefield is a fundamental incident of waging war, in permitting the use of "necessary and appropriate force," Congress has clearly and unmistakably authorized detention in the narrow circumstances considered here.

Hamdi objects, nevertheless, that Congress has not authorized the indefinite detention to which he is now subject. The Government responds that "the detention of enemy combatants during World War II was just as 'indefinite' while that war was being fought." We take Hamdi's objection to be not to the lack of certainty regarding the date on which the conflict will end, but to the substantial prospect of perpetual detention. We recognize that the national security underpinnings of the "war on terror," although crucially important, are broad and malleable. As the Government concedes, "given its unconventional nature, the current conflict is unlikely to end with a formal cease-fire agreement." The prospect Hamdi raises is therefore not farfetched. If the Government does not consider this unconventional war won for two generations, and if it maintains during that time that Hamdi might, if released, rejoin forces fighting against the United States, then the position it has taken throughout the litigation of this case suggests that Hamdi's detention could last for the rest of his life.

It is a clearly established principle of the law of war that detention may last no longer than active hostilities. Hamdi contends that the AUMF does not authorize indefinite or perpetual detention. Certainly, we agree that indefinite detention for the purpose of interrogation is not authorized. Further, we understand Congress' grant of authority for the use of "necessary and appropriate force" to include the authority to detain for the duration of the relevant conflict, and our understanding is based on longstanding law-of-war principles. If the practical circumstances of a given conflict are entirely unlike those of the conflicts that informed the development of the law of war, that understanding may unravel. But that is not the situation we face as of this date. Active combat operations against Taliban fighters apparently are ongoing in Afghanistan. The United States may detain, for the duration of these hostilities, individuals legitimately determined to be Taliban combatants who "engaged in an armed conflict against the United States." If the record establishes that United States troops are still involved in active combat in Afghanistan, those detentions are part of the exercise of "necessary and appropriate force," and therefore are authorized by the AUMF. . . .

III

Even in cases in which the detention of enemy combatants is legally authorized, there remains the question of what process is constitutionally due to a citizen who disputes his enemy-combatant status. Hamdi argues that he is owed a meaningful and timely hearing and that "extra-judicial detention [that] begins and ends with the submission of an affidavit based on third-hand hearsay" does not comport with the Fifth and Fourteenth Amendments. The Government counters that any more process than was provided below would be both unworkable and "constitutionally intolerable." Our resolution of this dispute requires a careful examination both of the writ of habeas corpus, which Hamdi now seeks to employ as a mechanism of judicial review, and of the Due Process Clause, which informs the procedural contours of that mechanism in this instance.

Though they reach radically different conclusions on the process that ought to attend the present proceeding, the parties begin on common ground. All agree that, absent suspension, the writ of habeas corpus remains available to every individual detained within the United States. Only in the rarest of circumstances has Congress seen fit to suspend the writ. At all other times, it has remained a critical check on the Executive, ensuring that it does not detain individuals except in accordance with law. All agree suspension of the writ has not occurred here. Thus, it is undisputed that Hamdi was properly before an Article III court to challenge his detention under 28 U.S.C. § 2241. Further, all agree that § 2241 and its companion provisions provide at least a skeletal outline of the procedures to be afforded a petitioner in federal habeas review. Most notably, § 2243 provides that "the person detained may, under oath, deny any of the facts set forth in the return or allege any other material facts," and § 2246 allows the taking of evidence in habeas proceedings by deposition, affidavit, or interrogatories.

The simple outline of § 2241 makes clear both that Congress envisioned that habeas petitioners would have some opportunity to present and rebut facts and that courts in cases like this retain some ability to vary the ways in which they do so as mandated by due process. The Government recognizes the basic procedural protections required by the habeas statute, but asks us to hold that, given both the flexibility of the habeas mechanism and the circumstances presented in this case, the presentation of the Mobbs Declaration to the habeas court completed the required factual development. . . .

The ordinary mechanism that we use for balancing such serious competing interests, and for determining the procedures that are necessary to ensure that a citizen is not "deprived of life, liberty, or property, without due process of law," is the test that we articulated in *Mathews v. Eldridge*, 424 U.S. 319 (1976). *Mathews* dictates that the process due in any given instance is determined by weighing "the private interest that will be affected by the official action" against the Government's asserted interest, "including the function involved" and the burdens the Government would face in providing greater process. The *Mathews* calculus then contemplates a judicious balancing of these concerns, through an analysis of "the risk of an erroneous deprivation" of the private interest if the process were reduced and the "probable value, if any, of additional or substitute procedural safeguards." . . .

Striking the proper constitutional balance here is of great importance to the Nation during this period of ongoing combat. But it is equally vital that our calculus not give short shrift to the values that this country holds dear or to the privilege that is American citizenship. It is during our most challenging and uncertain moments that our Nation's commitment to due process is most severely tested; and it is in those times that we must preserve our commitment at home to the principles for which we fight abroad.

With due recognition of these competing concerns, we believe that neither the process proposed by the Government nor the process apparently envisioned by the District Court below strikes the proper constitutional balance when a United States citizen is detained in the United States as an enemy combatant. That is, "the risk of an erroneous deprivation" of a detainee's liberty interest is unacceptably high under the Government's proposed rule, while some of the "additional or substitute procedural safeguards" suggested by the District Court are unwarranted in light of their limited "probable value" and the burdens they may impose on the military in such cases.

We therefore hold that a citizen-detainee seeking to challenge his classification as an enemy combatant must receive notice of the factual basis for his classification, and a fair opportunity to rebut the Government's factual assertions before a neutral decisionmaker.

At the same time, the exigencies of the circumstances may demand that, aside from these core elements, enemy-combatant proceedings may be tailored to alleviate their uncommon potential to burden the Executive at a time of ongoing military conflict. Hearsay, for example, may need to be accepted as the most reliable available evidence from the Government in such a proceeding. Likewise, the Constitution would not be offended by a presumption in favor of the Government's evidence, so long as that presumption remained a rebuttable one and fair opportunity for rebuttal were provided. Thus, once the Government puts forth credible evidence that the habeas petitioner meets the enemy-combatant criteria, the onus could shift to the petitioner to rebut that evidence with more persuasive evidence that he falls outside the criteria. A burden-shifting scheme of this sort would meet the goal of ensuring that the errant tourist, embedded journalist, or local aid worker has a chance to prove military error while giving due regard to the Executive once it has put forth meaningful support for its conclusion that the detainee is in fact an enemy combatant. . . .

We think it unlikely that this basic process will have the dire impact on the central functions of warmaking that the Government forecasts. The parties agree that initial captures on the battlefield need not receive the process we have discussed here; that process is due only when the determination is made to continue to hold those who have been seized. The Government has made clear in its briefing that documentation regarding battlefield detainees already is kept in the ordinary course of military affairs. Any factfinding imposition created by requiring a knowledgeable affiant to summarize these records to an independent tribunal is a minimal one. . . .

Because we conclude that due process demands some system for a citizen-detainee to refute his classification, the proposed "some evidence" standard is inadequate. Any process in which the Executive's factual assertions go wholly unchallenged or are simply presumed correct without any opportunity for the alleged combatant to demonstrate otherwise falls constitutionally short. . . . Aside from unspecified "screening" processes, and military interrogations in which the Government suggests Hamdi could have contested his classification, Hamdi has received no process. An interrogation by one's captor, however effective an intelligence-gathering tool, hardly constitutes a constitutionally adequate factfinding before a neutral decisionmaker. That even purportedly fair adjudicators "are disqualified by their interest in the controversy to be decided is, of course, the general rule." Plainly, the "process" Hamdi has received is not that to which he is entitled under the Due Process Clause.

There remains the possibility that the standards we have articulated could be met by an appropriately authorized and properly constituted military tribunal. . . . In the absence of such process, however, a court that receives a petition for a writ of habeas corpus from an alleged enemy combatant must itself ensure that the minimum requirements of due process are achieved. . . . As we have discussed, a habeas court in a case such as this may accept affidavit evidence like that contained in the Mobbs Declaration, so long as it also permits the alleged combatant to present his own factual case to rebut the Government's return. . . . We have no reason to doubt that courts faced with these sensitive matters will pay proper heed both to the matters of national security that might arise in an individual case and to the constitutional limitations safeguarding essential liberties that remain vibrant even in times of security concerns. . . .

Justice SCALIA, with whom Justice STEVENS joins, dissenting.

. . . Where the Government accuses a citizen of waging war against it, our constitutional tradition has been to prosecute him in federal court for treason or some other crime. Where the exigencies of war prevent that, the Constitution's Suspension Clause allows Congress to relax the usual protections temporarily. Absent suspension, however, the Executive's assertion of military exigency has not been thought sufficient to permit detention without charge. No one contends that the congressional Authorization for Use of Military Force, on which the Government relies to justify its actions here, is an implementation of the Suspension Clause. Accordingly, I would reverse the judgment below. . . .

To be sure, certain types of permissible non criminal detention—that is, those not dependent upon the contention that the citizen had committed a criminal act—did not require the protections of criminal procedure. However, these fell into a limited number of well-recognized exceptions—civil commitment of the mentally ill, for example, and temporary detention in quarantine of the infectious. It is unthinkable that the Executive could render otherwise criminal grounds for detention noncriminal merely by disclaiming an intent to prosecute, or by asserting that it was incapacitating dangerous offenders rather than punishing wrongdoing. . . .

The relevant question, then, is whether there is a different, special procedure for imprisonment of a citizen accused of wrongdoing by aiding the enemy in wartime. Justice O'Connor, writing for a plurality of this Court, asserts that captured enemy combatants (other than those suspected of war crimes) have traditionally been detained until the cessation of hostilities and then released. That is probably an accurate description of wartime practice with respect to enemy aliens. The tradition with respect to American citizens, however, has been quite different. Citizens aiding the enemy have been treated as traitors subject to the criminal process. . . .

It follows from what I have said that Hamdi is entitled to a habeas decree requiring his release unless (1) criminal proceedings are promptly brought, or (2) Congress has suspended the writ of habeas corpus. A suspension of the writ could, of course, lay down conditions for continued detention, similar to those that today's opinion prescribes under the Due Process Clause. But there is a world of difference between the people's representatives' determining the need for that suspension (and prescribing the conditions for it), and this Court's doing so. . . .

NOTES & QUESTIONS ON LAW OF WAR DETENTION

1. *Neutral decision maker. Hamdi* stands for the proposition that due process requires that citizens captured on the battlefield have the right to contest their detention before a "neutral decisionmaker." However, the O'Connor opinion was careful not to equate "neutral decisionmaker" with a jury trial in an Article III federal court. In response to the *Hamdi* decision, the federal government created Combatant Status Review Tribunals (CSRTs), which are limited military tribunals (composed of three military officers), that allow captured detainees—not just U.S. citizens—the chance to contest their detention by arguing, for example, that they were not captured on the battlefield or were not acting as a belligerent. For more discussion, see Brandon L. Garrett, *Habeas Corpus and Due Process*, 98 Cornell L. Rev. 47, 79 (2012).

2. *The "some evidence" standard.* In *Hamdi,* the Court rejects the government's proposed "some evidence" standard for deciding whether continued

military detention is appropriate. Why did the Court reject this standard and which standard replaced it? For more discussion, see Stephen I. Vladeck, *The D.C. Circuit After* Boumediene, 41 Seton Hall L. Rev. 1451, 1470-71 (2011).

3. *Habeas at Guantanamo*. Although *Hamdi*'s due process analysis arose within the context of a petition from an American citizen, the Supreme Court later ruled that all detainees at Guantanamo had the right to file habeas petitions in federal court because the United States enjoyed "plenary and exclusive jurisdiction" over Guantanamo Bay, even if "ultimate sovereignty" rested with Cuba. *Rasul v. Bush*, 542 U.S. 466, 475 (2004). After *Rasul*, Congress passed the Military Commissions Act (MCA), which sharply curtailed the jurisdiction of federal courts to hear habeas petitions from military detainees at Guantanamo. In *Boumediene v. Bush*, 553 U.S. 723, 771 (2008), the Court declared the jurisdiction-stripping provisions unconstitutional because the "MCA does not purport to be a formal suspension of the writ; and the Government, in its submissions to us, has not argued that it is."

G. PRACTICE & POLICY

There are a number of issues with forward-looking detention that require a deeper level of analysis. Since each of the forms of detention described in this chapter are preventive in nature, they require making a prediction of future behavior—or the *risk* of future behavior—instead of assessing culpability for past behavior. Whether the court is making a prediction of the risk of flight (bail), risk of sexual violence (civil commitment for sexual predators), risk of failure to appear at trial (material witness), or risk of returning to the battlefield (law of war detention), each of these predictions could be made with reference to empirical data. In other words, the process of prediction could be made with the tools of actuarial science—broad generalizations and assumptions about the type of people and the type of situations that lead to future dangerousness. In the context of a criminal trial, which assesses past conduct, such social scientific data would be considered irrelevant to the question of the defendant's guilt or innocence. But if the preceding cases have demonstrated anything, it is that preventive detention is *not* criminal punishment and should not be constrained by the same constitutional standards. This then raises a deeper question: Should the law tolerate (or even encourage) the use of big data to make accurate predictions based on large data sets?

❧ **The rise of big data in bail determinations.** Although empirical data would be useful in any form of preventive detention, the area where it has been used most extensively is in bail determinations. Typically, in the past, judges assessed both dangerousness and risk of flight by considering the specifics of each case: the crime charged, the past criminal history of the defendant (if any), the defendant's familial and professional ties to the community, and the defendant's (financial) resources available for flight. Based on these factors the judge would then reach an all-things-considered (read unscientific) judgment about the likelihood that the defendant would commit another crime before trial or would flee the jurisdiction. This would then inform the judge's decision regarding the amount of bail, the conditions of pre-trial release (such as monitoring or home arrest), or the denial of bail entirely.

Now, all of these factors and more can be fed into a computer system that analyzes the patterns systematically. Versions of computer software are used at some level in 30 jurisdictions. Consequently, the advent of big data is not the future of predictive policing—it's the present. Consider the following description of one typical program, the Public Safety Assessment:

> The PSA looks to nine risk factors: age at current arrest, current violent offense, pending charges, prior misdemeanor conviction, prior felony conviction, prior violent conviction, prior failure to appear in past two years, prior failure to appear older than two years, and prior sentence to incarceration. Based on a combination of these factors, a person receives three prediction scores: a "failure to appear" score, a "new criminal activity" score, and a "new violent criminal activity" score. For example, with the "new criminal activity" score, a defendant could get two points for being younger than twenty-two and one point for having missed a court date during the last two years. Those numbers would be added up into a raw score that would determine the person's placement on a six-point scale from low to high risk.

Note, *Bail Reform and Risk Assessment: The Cautionary Tale of Federal Sentencing*, 131 Harv. L. Rev. 1125, 1131 (2018). It is easy to understand why jurisdictions would be drawn to the PSA. In addition to lowering the reliance on monetary bail, which is economically discriminatory, the PSA holds the promise of adding numerical precision—and objectivity—to a predictive determination that was previously vulnerable to subjective and even discriminatory factors. If the literature on "implicit bias" is correct, judges are not immune from social biases that make it more likely that they will assess an African-American defendant as dangerous. The promise of PSA is that it adds empirical rigor to an evaluation that is otherwise squishy at best, discriminatory at worse.

The criticism of predictive policing. But not everyone is enamored with the rise of empirical data in criminal procedure. Plenty of scholars and activists question whether assessments of dangerousness or recidivism should be made on the basis of statistical generalizations rather than individualized considerations. For example, consider the following criticisms of these software tools to predict future levels of dangerousness:

> I do not argue, nor could anybody, that group averages have nothing to do with individual behavior. But that does not always mean that the group average tells us much about what to expect for any given individual. The question is how much individual variation there is in a given population and how much of that variation the variables in the model explain. In the recidivism context (unlike, for instance, the Russian roulette context), the variables included in the instruments leave most of the variation unexplained.

Sonja B. Starr, *Evidence-Based Sentencing and the Scientific Rationalization of Discrimination*, 66 Stan. L. Rev. 803, 849 (2014). The question is whether the Constitution, and the Due Process Clause in particular, guarantees an individualized assessment that is walled off from statistical generalities. Is it the case that non-empirical analysis—the way it was done before PSA—has nothing to do with empirical generalities? In other words, is it the case that off-hand assessments by judges relied on assumptions and generalities as well, such as the idea that defendants without families are more likely to flee because they have fewer ties to the community, or that defendants with a history of violent offenses are more likely than others to commit additional crimes of violence? Is the idea of a purely individualized assessment a possibility or is it a fiction?

❧ **Democratic governance.** One problem with the use of big data in bail and other predictive policing is the criticism that the public has little access to the inner workings of the software and is therefore unable to critique any shortcomings or discriminatory patterns in its design. Since the computer software is often provided by a private vendor to the public entity, the user license sometimes prevents the release of the code to outside parties because the code is proprietary intellectual property. In other words, if the computer code was released publicly, a competitor might duplicate the software and release a competitor product, ultimately undermining the business model of the original vendor. In light of this business need for confidentiality, is secrecy appropriate? At least some critics say no:

> We have constitutional norms of public trial and we should have the same for mechanisms of policing. Thus, any underlying algorithm used in adjudication or policing should be publicly available, or—at the very least—available for and subject to inspection by independent authorities. If Amazon prefers not to share the code or ultimate algorithm it uses to better pitch products, so be it. But if a company prefers not to share the code or ultimate algorithm the State of Oklahoma uses in bail,

> diversion, sentencing, or parole decisions, society should have a ready answer: the state cannot do business with you. The societal cost in lack of trust is simply too high when our criminal justice system runs on knowable but nonetheless-kept-secret algorithms.

Stephen E. Henderson, *A Few Criminal Justice Big Data Rules*, 15 Ohio St. J. Crim. L. 527, 535 (2018). Do you agree with this assessment as a matter of democratic governance or is it unrealistic as a matter of contemporary business practice? In the quoted hypothetical above, could the State of Oklahoma find a vendor that would allow it to release its source code? One compromise might be to release the code to an independent evaluator who scrutinizes the code but does so pursuant to an order of confidentiality (a promise not to disclose the code to anyone else). For more discussion of the perils and promise of predictive policing, see Bernard E. Harcourt, *Against Prediction: Profiling, Policing, and Punishing in an Actuarial Age* (2008).

CHAPTER 12

DISCOVERY

INTRODUCTION

The criminal trial is not an investigatory tool designed to uncover evidence. Rather, the criminal trial is inherently performative and deliberative; it involves the testing and weighing of evidence gathered and introduced into evidence by the parties. The parties can only test the validity of the evidence by, for example, cross-examining a witness or submitting physical evidence for analysis to an expert of their choosing, if they have had prior access to the evidence in question. In other words, evidence must be disclosed in advance if the parties are going to use the trial as an opportunity to bring skeptical questions to bear on that evidence. This requires advance preparation.

Discovery obligations flow from two major sources of law: constitutional requirements of due process and statutes. The two sources of law are important to distinguish because they are so different. The constitutional obligation of discovery is fundamentally unilateral and imposes an obligation on the prosecution to disclose evidence to the defense to ensure a fair trial. In contrast, statutory discovery can be bilateral, in the sense that legislatures may impose an obligation on defense counsel to turn over particular kinds of evidence to the prosecution prior to trial or prior to the commencement of the defense case.

For example, Rule 16 of the Federal Rules of Criminal Procedure imposes obligations on federal prosecutors but also imposes a reciprocal obligation on the defense. However, the mechanism depends on whether the defendant has requested disclosure of the government's evidence. If they do, then they are required to turn over their own evidence that falls under particular categories outlined in Rule 16. This presents the defendant with a strategic decision to make: force the prosecution to show its hand in exchange for disclosing one's own hand or proceed to trial in the dark without either side having the benefit of discovery.

The following sections outline (a) the requirements of unilateral constitutional discovery; (b) the diverse schemes for bilateral statutory discovery in various jurisdictions; and (c) the duty to preserve evidence. The latter topic is logically prior to discovery, since one cannot disclose evidence that one never preserved. This is especially relevant with regard to evidence that might be exculpatory for the defendant but which the prosecution fails to safeguard appropriately.

A. CONSTITUTIONAL DISCOVERY

The Fifth and Fourteenth Amendments require due process of law, which entails that a fair trial must meet certain minimum standards before an individual can be deprived of liberty through the criminal process. Essential to a fair trial is that the prosecution team must turn over material evidence—including exculpatory evidence—in its possession to the defense, so that the defense has a fighting chance to put its best foot forward during the adversarial process.

There are different procedural postures through which discovery violations come to a court's attention. One possibility is that a defendant objects to the lack of disclosure by the prosecution team at the moment when the discovery is mandated, for example, on the eve of trial. If the judge agrees that the material must be disclosed, the violation can be remedied before the trial occurs. The other procedural posture involves a defendant who has been *convicted* who learns that evidence he believes he was entitled to was not disclosed as required. In that situation, a court will have to answer two questions. First, did the defendant receive all evidence that qualified as "favorable," meaning evidence that would tend to support a finding of not guilty at trial? If the defense specifically requested the evidence, then the prosecutor is on notice that the evidence is potentially favorable and should be disclosed. But if the defense communicated to the prosecution only a general request for evidence, or no request at all, then the prosecution could still be under a duty to disclose if the nature of the evidence made it obvious that it was favorable to the defense case.

If the defendant received all favorable evidence, there is no constitutional problem. On the other hand, if the defendant did *not* receive all favorable evidence, then the court will have to determine if the non-disclosed evidence was material, which means it would have created a reasonable probability of a different outcome in the trial. Thus, "favorable" is really the disclosure trigger: The State must disclose all favorable evidence. In contrast, "material" is the remedy trigger: The defendant is entitled to a new trial (or a new sentencing hearing) only if the favorable evidence was also material. Evidence cannot be material unless it was favorable, but just because it is favorable does not mean it was material.

So, when a defendant complains to a trial court that he has not been provided evidence required pursuant to the prosecution discovery obligation, the court can resolve this failure by ordering discovery. However, as will be seen in the cases that follow, when the defendant argues following conviction that fair process was corrupted because of a discovery failure, it is not enough to demonstrate that the prosecution failed to disclose evidence subject to the discovery obligation. In this sense, fairness is not defined by ensuring that a defendant received evidence subject to the disclosure obligation. Instead, the question will focus on whether the non-disclosed evidence would have created a reasonable probability of a different outcome, i.e., had the defendant received the evidence it would have created reasonable doubt in the minds of the jury. Thus, in a very real sense, fairness is not defined by ensuring the defendant received evidence he was entitled to, but whether the outcome of the trial, even conceding the prosecution's discovery failure, is one worthy of confidence.

The application of these principles leaves many unanswered questions regarding precisely what evidence needs to be turned over and what standards should be used to separate the crucial evidence that the Due Process Clause guarantees must be provided to the defense and peripheral pieces of evidence that the prosecution is entitled to keep close to its vest. The following materials focus on discovery as a due process requirement (the conceptual foundation for everything else to come), discovery of impeachment evidence (which will be used to attack the veracity of a witness), the standard for materiality, the cumulative effect of multiple discovery violations, and what happens when defense attorneys fail to object to the lack of discovery.

1. Discovery as a Due Process Requirement

In the following case, the Supreme Court outlines its conclusion that a failure to turn over material evidence to the defense violates the Constitution. As you read the case, ask yourself why a violation of this disclosure requirement should be categorized as a violation of due process. What does the protection of due process require in terms of ensuring a fair trial? Is advance notice of the prosecution's evidence that it will introduce at trial a fundamental feature of a fair trial? Recall that the defendant will always receive notice of the evidence when the prosecution introduces the evidence at trial. What *Brady* protects is the right to *advance* notice for purposes of adequate preparation.

Brady v. Maryland

Supreme Court of the United States
373 U.S. 83 (1963)

Opinion of the Court by Mr. Justice Douglas, announced by Mr. Justice Brennan.

Petitioner and a companion, Boblit, were found guilty of murder in the first degree and were sentenced to death, their convictions being affirmed by the Court of Appeals of Maryland. Their trials were separate, petitioner being tried first. At his trial Brady took the stand and admitted his participation in the crime, but he claimed that Boblit did the actual killing. And, in his summation to the jury, Brady's counsel conceded that Brady was guilty of murder in the first degree, asking only that the jury return that verdict "without capital punishment." Prior to the trial petitioner's counsel had requested the prosecution to allow him to examine Boblit's extrajudicial statements. Several of those statements were shown to him; but one dated July 9, 1958, in which Boblit admitted the actual homicide, was withheld by the prosecution and did not come to petitioner's notice until after he had been tried, convicted, and sentenced, and after his conviction had been affirmed. Petitioner moved the trial court for a new trial based on the newly discovered evidence that had been suppressed by the prosecution. . . .

We agree with the Court of Appeals that suppression of this confession was a violation of the Due Process Clause of the Fourteenth Amendment. . . . This ruling is an extension of *Mooney v. Holohan*, 294 U.S. 103, 112, where the Court ruled on what nondisclosure by a prosecutor violates due process:

> It is a requirement that cannot be deemed to be satisfied by mere notice and hearing if a state has contrived a conviction through the pretense of a trial which in truth is but used as a means of depriving a defendant of liberty through a deliberate deception of court and jury by the presentation of testimony known to be perjured. Such a contrivance by a state to procure the conviction and imprisonment of a defendant is as inconsistent with the rudimentary demands of justice as is the obtaining of a like result by intimidation.

In *Pyle v. Kansas*, 317 U.S. 213, 215-216, we phrased the rule in broader terms:

> Petitioner's papers are inexpertly drawn, but they do set forth allegations that his imprisonment resulted from perjured testimony, knowingly used by the State authorities to obtain his conviction, and from the deliberate suppression by those same authorities of evidence favorable to him. These allegations sufficiently charge a deprivation of rights guaranteed by the Federal Constitution, and, if proven, would entitle petitioner to release from his present custody.

The Third Circuit . . . construed that statement in *Pyle v. Kansas* to mean that the "suppression of evidence favorable" to the accused was itself sufficient to amount to a denial of due process. In *Napue v. Illinois*, 360 U.S. 264, 269, we extended the test formulated in *Mooney v. Holohan* when we said: "The same result obtains when the State, although not soliciting false evidence, allows it to go uncorrected when it appears."

We now hold that the suppression by the prosecution of evidence favorable to an accused upon request violates due process where the evidence is material either to guilt or to punishment, irrespective of the good faith or bad faith of the prosecution.

The principle of *Mooney v. Holohan* is not punishment of society for misdeeds of a prosecutor but avoidance of an unfair trial to the accused. Society wins not only when the guilty are convicted but when criminal trials are fair; our system of the administration of justice suffers when any accused is treated unfairly. An inscription on the walls of the Department of Justice states the proposition candidly for the federal domain: "The United States wins its point whenever justice is done its citizens in the courts." A prosecution that withholds evidence on demand of an accused which, if made available, would tend to exculpate him or reduce the penalty helps shape a trial that bears heavily on the defendant. That casts the prosecutor in the role of an architect of a proceeding that does not comport with standards of justice, even though, as in the present case, his action is not "the result of guile," to use the words of the Court of Appeals. . . .

NOTES & QUESTIONS ON BRADY *VIOLATIONS*

1. *The promise of* Brady. The scheme ratified in *Brady* involves voluntary disclosures, followed by coercive orders by the court when the defense believes that the prosecutor has not fulfilled its *Brady* obligations to disclose relevant

evidence. Having read the *Brady* case, it is worth asking whether the system has worked out as the *Brady* Court imagined it would. Do trial judges and appellate courts adequately force prosecutors to comply? Do defense attorneys have access to the required information to make timely objections? Assess this question again at the end of the chapter.

2. *The importance of remedies.* As discussed below, a key piece of the *Brady* system is the availability of a remedy—a new trial—for discovery violations that are discovered after trial. However, not all violations are eligible for this remedy; the evidence must be material to the outcome of the trial. Does this limitation on the availability of the new-trial remedy undermine the strength of the *Brady* regime? Does it conflict with the animating impulse behind *Brady* or does it remain faithful to it?

3. *Civil law alternatives to discovery.* The discovery system, and its constitutional obligation on the prosecution, is part of the deep structure of the Anglo-American common law legal system. The process is adversarial and party-driven, thus necessitating that prosecutors have an obligation to turn over to the defense material evidence that they collect. In contrast, some European legal systems appoint an "investigative judge" to oversee the investigation and keep custody of all evidence procured during the investigation. Instead of requiring the prosecution to send evidence to the defense, the investigative judge system is built around a comprehensive "dossier" of all evidence in the case. Both the state's attorney and the defendant's attorney are granted "access" to the dossier to prepare their arguments for trial. If the legal system includes "victim participation" in the trial (*partie civile* status), then the victim's lawyer will also have access to the dossier. Lawyers often debate which system is better. What's certainly clear is that the mechanics of the discovery regime are built into the very structure of the criminal justice system. For an argument that the defense should at least have "open file" access to all prosecution evidence, see Brian Gregory, Brady *Is the Problem: Wrongful Convictions and the Case for "Open File" Criminal Discovery*, 46 U.S.F. L. Rev. 819, 853 (2012).

2. Discovery of Impeachment Evidence

A major category of discovery violations involves a state's failure to provide the defense with evidence that could be used to impeach the credibility of one of the prosecution's witnesses. Although there are many categories of impeachment evidence, by far the most common is immunity agreements, i.e., agreements not to prosecute a witness in exchange for their testimony at trial against another target of the investigation. Witnesses who have received immunity from prosecution have an incentive to lie and therefore the defense is entitled to this information in order to impeach the witness at trial. But what happens if the state fails to turn over evidence of a promise not to prosecute? Furthermore, does it matter whether the failure to disclose the evidence is the result of bad faith or simple negligence?

Giglio v. United States

Supreme Court of the United States
405 U.S. 150 (1972)

Mr. Chief Justice BURGER delivered the opinion of the Court.

Petitioner was convicted of passing forged money orders and sentenced to five years' imprisonment. While appeal was pending in the Court of Appeals, defense counsel discovered new evidence indicating that the Government had failed to disclose an alleged promise made to its key witness that he would not be prosecuted if he testified for the Government. We granted certiorari to determine whether the evidence not disclosed was such as to require a new trial. . . .

The controversy in this case centers around the testimony of Robert Taliento, petitioner's alleged coconspirator in the offense and the only witness linking petitioner with the crime. The Government's evidence at trial showed that in June 1966 officials at the Manufacturers Hanover Trust Co. discovered that Taliento, as teller at the bank, had cashed several forged money orders. Upon questioning by FBI agents, he confessed supplying petitioner with one of the bank's customer signature cards used by Giglio to forge $2,300 in money orders; Taliento then processed these money orders through the regular channels of the bank. Taliento related this story to the grand jury and petitioner was indicted; thereafter, he was named as a coconspirator with petitioner but was not indicted.

Trial commenced two years after indictment. Taliento testified, identifying petitioner as the instigator of the scheme. Defense counsel vigorously cross-examined, seeking to discredit his testimony by revealing possible agreements or arrangements for prosecutorial leniency:

> **(Counsel.)** Did anybody tell you at any time that if you implicated somebody else in this case that you yourself would not be prosecuted?
> **(Taliento.)** Nobody told me I wouldn't be prosecuted.
> **Q.** They told you you might not be prosecuted?
> **A.** I believe I still could be prosecuted.
> . . .
> **Q.** Were you ever arrested in this case or charged with anything in connection with these money orders that you testified to?
> **A.** Not at that particular time.
> **Q.** To this date, have you been charged with any crime?
> **A.** Not that I know of, unless they are still going to prosecute.

In summation, the Government attorney stated, "(Taliento) received no promises that he would not be indicted."

The issue now before the Court arose on petitioner's motion for new trial based on newly discovered evidence. An affidavit filed by the Government as part of its opposition to a new trial confirms petitioner's claim that a promise was made to Taliento by one assistant, DiPaola, that if he testified before the grand jury and at trial he would not be prosecuted. DiPaola presented the Government's case to the grand jury but did not try the case in the District Court, and Golden, the assistant who took over the case for trial, filed an affidavit stating that DiPaola assured him before the trial that no promises of immunity had been made to Taliento. The United States Attorney, Hoey, filed an affidavit stating that he had personally consulted with Taliento and his attorney shortly before trial to emphasize that Taliento would definitely be prosecuted if he did not testify and that if he did testify he would be obliged to rely on the "good judgment and conscience of the Government" as to whether he would be prosecuted.

The District Court did not undertake to resolve the apparent conflict between the two Assistant United States Attorneys, DiPaola and Golden, but proceeded on the theory that even if a promise had been made by DiPaola it was not authorized and its disclosure to the jury would not have affected its verdict. We need not concern ourselves with the differing versions of the events as described by the two assistants in their affidavits. The heart of the matter is that one Assistant United States Attorney—the first one who dealt with Taliento—now states that he promised Taliento that he would not be prosecuted if he cooperated with the Government.

As long ago as *Mooney v. Holohan*, 294 U.S. 103, 112 (1935), this Court made clear that deliberate deception of a court and jurors by the presentation of known false evidence is incompatible with "rudimentary demands of justice." This was reaffirmed in *Pyle v. Kansas*, 317 U.S. 213 (1942). In *Napue v. Illinois*, 360 U.S. 264 (1959), we said, "(t)he same result obtains when the State, although not soliciting false evidence, allows it to go uncorrected when it appears." Thereafter *Brady v. Maryland* held that suppression of material evidence justifies a new trial "irrespective of the good faith or bad faith of the prosecution." When the "reliability of a given witness may well be determinative of guilt or innocence," nondisclosure of evidence affecting credibility falls within this general rule. We do not, however, automatically require a new trial whenever "a combing of the prosecutors' files after the trial has disclosed evidence possibly useful to the defense but not likely to have changed the verdict. . . ." A finding of materiality of the evidence is required under *Brady*. A new trial is required if "the false testimony could . . . . in any reasonable likelihood have affected the judgment of the jury. . . ."

In the circumstances shown by this record, neither DiPaola's authority nor his failure to inform his superiors or his associates is controlling. Moreover, whether the nondisclosure was a result of negligence or design, it is the responsibility of the prosecutor. The prosecutor's office is an entity and as such it is the spokesman for the Government. A promise made by one attorney must be attributed, for these purposes, to the Government. To the extent this places a burden on the large prosecution offices, procedures and regulations can be established to carry that burden and to insure communication of all relevant information on each case to every lawyer who deals with it.

Here the Government's case depended almost entirely on Taliento's testimony; without it there could have been no indictment and no evidence to carry the case to the jury. Taliento's credibility as a witness was therefore an important issue in the case, and evidence of any understanding or agreement as to a future prosecution would be relevant to his credibility and the jury was entitled to know of it. For these reasons, the due process requirements enunciated in *Napue* and the other cases cited earlier require a new trial, and the judgment of conviction is therefore reversed. . . .

In the following case, the state withheld from the defense the notes of a detective who had interviewed a key witness in a murder case. In fact, the witness testified at trial that the defendant was responsible for the murder. However, the witness told a different story to the detective in a pre-trial interview and implicated someone else. With access to these notes, defense counsel might have sought to impeach the witness's testimony at trial. Should the state have turned over the notes regarding the detective's conversation with the witness, and would it have made a difference to the outcome of the trial? In other words, was the evidence favorable and material?

Smith v. Cain

Supreme Court of the United States
565 U.S. 73 (2012)

Chief Justice Roberts delivered the opinion of the Court.

The State of Louisiana charged petitioner Juan Smith with killing five people during an armed robbery. At Smith's trial a single witness, Larry Boatner, linked Smith to the crime. Boatner testified that he was socializing at a friend's house when Smith and two other gunmen entered the home, demanded money and drugs, and shortly thereafter began shooting, resulting in the death of five of Boatner's friends. In court Boatner identified Smith as the first gunman to come through the door. He claimed that he had been face to face with Smith during the initial moments of the robbery. No other witnesses and no physical evidence implicated Smith in the crime.

The jury convicted Smith of five counts of first-degree murder. The Louisiana Court of Appeal affirmed Smith's conviction. The Louisiana Supreme Court denied review, as did this Court.

Smith then sought postconviction relief in the state courts. As part of his effort, Smith obtained files from the police investigation of his case, including those of the lead investigator, Detective John Ronquillo. Ronquillo's notes contain statements by Boatner that conflict with his testimony identifying Smith as a perpetrator. The notes from the night of the murder state that Boatner "could not . . . supply a description of the perpetrators other then [sic] they were black males." Ronquillo also made a handwritten account of a conversation he had with Boatner five days after the crime, in which Boatner said he "could not ID anyone because [he] couldn't see faces" and "would not know them if [he] saw them." And Ronquillo's typewritten report of that conversation states that Boatner told Ronquillo he "could not identify any of the perpetrators of the murder."

Smith requested that his conviction be vacated, arguing, inter alia, that the prosecution's failure to disclose Ronquillo's notes violated this Court's decision in *Brady v. Maryland*, 373 U.S. 83 (1963). The state trial court rejected Smith's *Brady* claim, and the Louisiana Court of Appeal and Louisiana Supreme Court denied review. We granted certiorari and now reverse.

Under *Brady*, the State violates a defendant's right to due process if it withholds evidence that is favorable to the defense and material to the defendant's guilt or punishment. The State does not dispute that Boatner's statements in Ronquillo's notes were favorable to Smith and that those statements were not disclosed to him. The sole question before us is thus whether Boatner's statements were material to the determination of Smith's guilt. We have explained that "evidence is 'material' within the meaning of *Brady* when there is a reasonable probability that, had the evidence been disclosed, the result of the proceeding would have been different." A reasonable probability does not mean that the defendant "would more likely than not have received a different verdict with the evidence," only that the likelihood of a different result is great enough to "undermine[] confidence in the outcome of the trial." *Kyles v. Whitley*, 514 U.S. 419, 434 (1995).

We have observed that evidence impeaching an eyewitness may not be material if the State's other evidence is strong enough to sustain confidence in the verdict. See *United States v. Agurs*, 427 U.S. 97, 112-113 (1976). That is not the case here. Boatner's testimony was the only evidence linking Smith to the crime. And Boatner's undisclosed statements directly contradict his testimony: Boatner told the jury that he had "[n]o doubt" that Smith was the gunman he stood "face to face" with on the night of the crime, but Ronquillo's notes show Boatner saying that he "could not ID anyone because [he] couldn't see faces" and "would not know them if [he] saw them." Boatner's undisclosed statements were plainly material.

The State and the dissent advance various reasons why the jury might have discounted Boatner's undisclosed statements. They stress, for example, that Boatner made other remarks on the night of the murder indicating that he could identify the first gunman to enter the house, but not the others. That merely leaves us to speculate about which of Boatner's contradictory declarations the jury would have believed. The State also contends that Boatner's statements made five days after the crime can be explained by fear of retaliation. Smith responds that the record contains no evidence of any such fear. Again, the State's argument offers a reason that the jury could have disbelieved Boatner's undisclosed statements, but gives us no confidence that it would have done so.

The police files that Smith obtained in state postconviction proceedings contain other evidence that Smith contends is both favorable to him and material to the verdict. Because we hold that Boatner's undisclosed statements alone suffice to undermine confidence in Smith's conviction, we have no need to consider his arguments that the other undisclosed evidence also requires reversal under *Brady*. . . .

NOTES & QUESTIONS ON IMPEACHMENT EVIDENCE

1. *The problem of implicit agreements.* What if the prosecution and a witness never formally agree that the witness will not be prosecuted, but there is an informal, non-binding understanding between them? The prosecutor might realize that a witness is less credible at trial if an immunity agreement is in place, so the prosecutor might prefer to vaguely suggest—without outright promising—that the witness will not be prosecuted. Then, in that situation, the prosecutor is not required to turn over evidence to the defense and the witness can truthfully declare at trial that they are testifying without a promise of immunity from the state. But if the prosecution has accomplished, with a wink and a nod, the same result as a formal immunity agreement, should it matter? Is this strategy an end-run around the *Brady-Giglio* disclosure regime? Some courts have held that *Giglio* requires disclosure even in the absence of a formal agreement with the prosecutor. Compare *Shabazz v. Artuz*, 336 F.3d 154, 157 (2d Cir. 2003) (favorable treatment to witness at sentencing insufficient to demonstrate the existence of an agreement that was required to be disclosed to second defendant) with *United States v. Shaffer*, 789 F.2d 682, 690 (9th Cir. 1986) ("While it is clear that an explicit agreement would have to be disclosed

. . . it is equally clear that facts which imply an agreement would also bear on [the witness's] credibility and would have to be disclosed."). For a discussion of this case law and an argument that prosecutors are required to disclose implicit agreements, see Peter A. Joy & Kevin C. McMunigal, *Implicit Plea Agreements and* Brady *Disclosure*, Crim. Just., Spring 2007, at 50, 52. Do you think that *Giglio* requires disclosure of all evidence that might impeach the witness's credibility, or just formal agreements?

2. Cain. Do you agree with the Supreme Court that the detective's notes could have been used to impeach the state's main witness at trial? Were the notes material to the outcome of the trial? Can you think of some reason why a state court would have refused to order a new trial?

3. *Impeachment evidence and plea bargaining*. Does the *Brady* disclosure regime apply to the plea bargaining process? One could certainly imagine that a defendant entering plea negotiations after indictment, but well before trial, would be interested in receiving full discovery. After all, if plea negotiations are designed to occur "in the shadow of the trial," in the famous phrase, it would be helpful for the defendant to understand the full scope of evidence in the possession of the state. In *United States v. Ruiz*, 536 U.S. 622 (2002), the defendant entered into "fast track" plea negotiations with prosecutors and agreed to plead guilty without the benefit of discovery. As it happens, the state was in possession of impeachment evidence regarding a potential witness; Ruiz argued that had she received this information, she might not have agreed to the plea deal. However, the Supreme Court concluded that plea negotiations are different from trials:

> [T]his Court has found that the Constitution, in respect to a defendant's awareness of relevant circumstances, does not require complete knowledge of the relevant circumstances, but permits a court to accept a guilty plea, with its accompanying waiver of various constitutional rights, despite various forms of misapprehension under which a defendant might labor. . . . It is difficult to distinguish, in terms of importance, (1) a defendant's ignorance of grounds for impeachment of potential witnesses at a possible future trial from (2) the varying forms of ignorance at issue in these cases.

Id. at 630. Do you agree with this decision? Does it place defendants in a disadvantageous position during plea bargaining? What is so special about a *trial* that entails that defendants are entitled to *Brady* disclosure of impeachment evidence in that context but not in others? On what basis are defendants expected to make decisions in plea negotiations without access to impeachment evidence? See also *People v. Gray*, 54 N.E.3d 841 (Ill. App. 2016).

PROBLEM CASE

Debra Milke was charged in Arizona with murder in connection with the death of her son, Christopher, who was only four years old at the time of his death. Milke was convicted in 1990 and sentenced to death. At the trial, the jury learned that young Christopher had wanted to go to the mall to see Santa Claus. Instead of taking him herself, Milke asked her roommate, James Styers, to take Christopher to the mall. On the way to the mall, Styers stopped and picked up one of his friends, Roger Scott. Instead of taking Christopher to the mall, the two men took Christopher to a deserted area and murdered him.

The police detective in charge of the case, Armando Saldate, suspected that Debra Milke was involved in the conspiracy as well. Saldate testified that after he informed Milke that Christopher had been killed, the two of them had a lengthy conversation. He said that during that conversation Milke had confessed to her involvement. However, Milke also testified at the trial and adamantly denied that she had confessed to Saldate. In the absence of other evidence, the jury apparently believed the police detective's story because the jury convicted Milke of murder.

Prosecutors failed to disclose to Milke information from Saldate's personnel file, including that he had engaged in sexual relations with a motorist on the job and later lied about it, that in previous cases he had lied under oath before grand juries or before a judge, and that he had been disciplined for lying. Did this information constitute impeachment evidence that the state was required to turn over to the defense under *Brady*?

3. What Is Material Evidence?

The *Brady* scheme includes its own enforcement mechanism. If the prosecution withholds material evidence and the defendant is convicted, then the defense is entitled to a new trial because the first trial under those conditions violated due process. The question is what qualifies as material evidence the withholding of which requires a new trial. Under *Brady*, materiality is defined as evidence that tends to affect the guilt or punishment of the defendant. In the following case, the Supreme Court applies that standard to the case of impeachment evidence that would impact the credibility of a witness at trial. At issue is what rule should be applied for the withholding of impeachment evidence—a per se rule that always requires a new trial or a more flexible standard that only requires a new trial if the withheld evidence affected the outcome of the jury's deliberations.

United States v. Bagley

Supreme Court of the United States
473 U.S. 667 (1985)

Justice Blackmun announced the judgment of the Court and delivered an opinion of the Court except as to Part III.

In *Brady v. Maryland* this Court held that "the suppression by the prosecution of evidence favorable to an accused upon request violates due process where the evidence is material either to guilt or punishment." The issue in the present case concerns the standard of materiality to be applied in determining whether a conviction should be reversed because the prosecutor failed to disclose requested evidence that could have been used to impeach Government witnesses.

I

In October 1977, respondent Hughes Anderson Bagley was indicted in the Western District of Washington on 15 charges of violating federal narcotics and firearms statutes. On November 18, 24 days before trial, respondent filed a discovery motion. The sixth paragraph of that motion requested: "The names and addresses of witnesses that the government intends to call at trial. Also the prior criminal records of witnesses, and any deals, promises or inducements made to witnesses in exchange for their testimony."

The Government's two principal witnesses at the trial were James F. O'Connor and Donald E. Mitchell. O'Connor and Mitchell were state law-enforcement officers employed by the Milwaukee Railroad as private security guards. Between April and June 1977, they assisted the federal Bureau of Alcohol, Tobacco and Firearms (ATF) in conducting an undercover investigation of respondent.

The Government's response to the discovery motion did not disclose that any "deals, promises or inducements" had been made to O'Connor or Mitchell. In apparent reply to a request in the motion's ninth paragraph for "[c]opies of all Jencks Act material," the Government produced a series of affidavits that O'Connor and Mitchell had signed between April 12 and May 4, 1977, while the undercover investigation was in progress. These affidavits recounted in detail the undercover dealings that O'Connor and Mitchell were having at the time with respondent. Each affidavit concluded with the statement, "I made this statement freely and voluntarily without any threats or rewards, or promises of reward having been made to me in return for it."

Respondent waived his right to a jury trial and was tried before the court in December 1977. At the trial, O'Connor and Mitchell testified about both the firearms and the narcotics charges. On December 23, the court found respondent guilty on the narcotics charges, but not guilty on the firearms charges.

In mid-1980, respondent filed requests for information pursuant to the Freedom of Information Act and to the Privacy Act of 1974, 5 U.S.C. §§ 552 and 552a. He received in response copies of ATF form contracts that O'Connor and Mitchell had signed on May 3, 1977. Each form was entitled "Contract for Purchase of Information and Payment of Lump Sum Therefor." The printed portion of the form stated that the vendor "will provide" information to ATF and that "upon receipt of such information by the Regional Director, Bureau of Alcohol, Tobacco and Firearms, or his representative, and upon the accomplishment of the objective sought to be obtained by the use of such information to the satisfaction of said Regional Director, the United States will pay to said vendor a sum commensurate with services and information rendered." Each form contained the following typewritten description of services:

> That he will provide information regarding T-I and other violations committed by Hughes A. Bagley, Jr.; that he will purchase evidence for ATF; that he will cut [sic] in an undercover capacity for ATF; that he will assist ATF in gathering of evidence and testify against the violator in federal court.

The figure "$300.00" was handwritten in each form on a line entitled "Sum to Be Paid to Vendor."

Because these contracts had not been disclosed to respondent in response to his pretrial discovery motion, respondent moved . . . to vacate his sentence. He alleged that the Government's failure to disclose the contracts, which he could have used to impeach O'Connor and Mitchell, violated his right to due process. . . .

II

The holding in *Brady v. Maryland* requires disclosure only of evidence that is both favorable to the accused and "material either to guilt or to punishment." . . . The evidence suppressed in *Brady* would have been admissible only on the issue of punishment and not on the issue of guilt, and therefore could have affected only Brady's sentence and not his conviction. Accordingly, the Court affirmed the lower court's restriction of Brady's new trial to the issue of punishment.

The *Brady* rule is based on the requirement of due process. Its purpose is not to displace the adversary system as the primary means by which truth is uncovered, but to ensure that a miscarriage of justice does not occur. Thus, the prosecutor is not required to deliver his entire file to defense counsel, but only to disclose evidence favorable to the accused that, if suppressed, would deprive the defendant of a fair trial. . . .

In *Brady* and *Agurs*, the prosecutor failed to disclose exculpatory evidence. In the present case, the prosecutor failed to disclose evidence that the defense might have used to impeach the Government's witnesses by showing bias or interest. Impeachment evidence, however, as well as exculpatory evidence, falls within the *Brady* rule. Such evidence is "evidence favorable to an accused," so that, if disclosed and used effectively, it may make the difference between conviction and acquittal.

The Court of Appeals treated impeachment evidence as constitutionally different from exculpatory evidence. According to that court, failure to disclose impeachment evidence is "even more egregious" than failure to disclose exculpatory evidence "because it threatens the defendant's right to confront adverse witnesses." Relying on *Davis v. Alaska*, 415 U.S. 308 (1974), the Court of Appeals held that the Government's failure to disclose requested impeachment evidence that the defense could use to conduct an effective cross-examination of important prosecution witnesses constitutes "constitutional error of the first magnitude" requiring automatic reversal.

This Court has rejected any such distinction between impeachment evidence and exculpatory evidence. In *Giglio v. United States*, the Government failed to disclose impeachment evidence similar to the evidence at issue in the present case, that is, a promise made to the key Government witness that he would not be prosecuted if he testified for the Government. This Court said:

> When the reliability of a given witness may well be determinative of guilt or innocence, nondisclosure of evidence affecting credibility falls within th[e] general rule [of *Brady*]. We do not, however, automatically require a new trial whenever a combing of the prosecutors' files after the trial has disclosed evidence possibly useful to the defense but not likely to have changed the verdict. . . . A finding of materiality of the evidence is required under *Brady*. . . . A new trial is required if the false testimony could . . . in any reasonable likelihood have affected the judgment of the jury. . . .

Thus, the Court of Appeals' holding is inconsistent with our precedents.

Moreover, the court's reliance on *Davis v. Alaska* for its "automatic reversal" rule is misplaced. In *Davis*, the defense sought to cross-examine a crucial prosecution witness concerning his probationary status as a juvenile delinquent. The defense intended by this cross-examination to show that the witness might have made a faulty identification of the defendant in order to shift suspicion away from himself or because he feared that his probationary status would be jeopardized if he did not satisfactorily assist the police and prosecutor in obtaining a conviction. Pursuant to a state rule of procedure and a state statute making juvenile adjudications inadmissible, the trial judge prohibited the defense from conducting the cross-examination. This Court reversed the defendant's conviction, ruling that the direct restriction on the scope of cross-examination denied the defendant "the right of effective cross-examination which would be constitutional error of the first magnitude and no amount of showing of want of prejudice would cure it."

The present case, in contrast, does not involve any direct restriction on the scope of cross-examination. The defense was free to cross-examine the witnesses on any relevant subject, including possible bias or interest resulting from inducements made by the Government. The constitutional error, if any, in this case was the Government's failure to assist the defense by disclosing information that might have been helpful in conducting the cross-examination. As discussed above, such suppression of evidence amounts to a constitutional violation only if it deprives the defendant of a fair trial. Consistent with "our overriding concern with the justice of the finding of guilt," a constitutional error occurs, and the conviction must be reversed, only if the evidence is material in the sense that its suppression undermines confidence in the outcome of the trial.

III

It remains to determine the standard of materiality applicable to the nondisclosed evidence at issue in this case. Our starting point is the framework for evaluating the materiality of *Brady* evidence established in *United States v. Agurs*. The Court in *Agurs* distinguished three situations involving the discovery, after trial, of information favorable to the accused that had been known to the prosecution but unknown to the defense. The first situation was the prosecutor's knowing use of perjured testimony or, equivalently, the prosecutor's knowing failure to disclose that testimony used to convict the defendant was false. The Court noted the well-established rule that "a conviction obtained by the knowing use of perjured testimony is fundamentally unfair, and must be set aside if there is any reasonable likelihood that the false testimony could have affected the judgment of the jury." Although this rule is stated in terms that treat the knowing use of perjured testimony as error subject to harmless-error review, it may as easily be stated as a materiality standard under which the fact that testimony is perjured is considered material unless failure to disclose it would be harmless beyond a reasonable doubt. The Court in *Agurs* justified this standard of materiality on the ground that the knowing use of perjured testimony involves prosecutorial misconduct and, more importantly, involves "a corruption of the truth-seeking function of the trial process."

At the other extreme is the situation in *Agurs* itself, where the defendant does not make a *Brady* request and the prosecutor fails to disclose certain evidence favorable to the accused. The Court rejected a harmless-error rule in that situation, because under that rule every nondisclosure is treated as error, thus imposing on the prosecutor a constitutional duty to deliver his entire file to defense counsel. At the same time, the Court rejected a standard that would require the defendant to demonstrate that the evidence if disclosed probably would have resulted in acquittal. The Court reasoned: "If the standard applied to the usual motion for a new trial based on newly discovered evidence were the same when the evidence was in the State's possession as when it was found in a neutral source, there would be no special significance to the prosecutor's obligation to serve the cause of justice." The standard of materiality applicable in the absence of a specific *Brady* request is therefore stricter than the harmless-error standard but more lenient to the defense than the newly-discovered-evidence standard.

The third situation identified by the Court in *Agurs* is where the defense makes a specific request and the prosecutor fails to disclose responsive evidence. The Court did not define the standard of materiality applicable in this situation, but suggested that the standard might be more lenient to the defense than in the situation in which the defense makes no request or only a general request. The Court also noted: "When the prosecutor receives a specific and relevant request, the failure to make any response is seldom, if ever, excusable."

The Court has relied on and reformulated the *Agurs* standard for the materiality of undisclosed evidence in two subsequent cases arising outside the *Brady* context. In neither case did the Court's discussion of the *Agurs* standard distinguish among the three situations described in *Agurs*. In *United States v. Valenzuela-Bernal*, 458 U.S. 858 (1982), the Court held that due process is violated when testimony is made unavailable to the defense by Government deportation of witnesses "only if there is a reasonable likelihood that the testimony could have affected the judgment of the trier of fact." And in *Strickland v. Washington*, 466 U.S. 668 (1984), the Court held that a new trial must be granted when evidence is not introduced because of the incompetence of counsel only if "there is a reasonable probability that, but for counsel's unprofessional errors, the result of the proceeding would have been different." The *Strickland* Court defined a "reasonable probability" as "a probability sufficient to undermine confidence in the outcome."

We find the *Strickland* formulation of the *Agurs* test for materiality sufficiently flexible to cover the "no request," "general request," and "specific request" cases of prosecutorial failure to disclose evidence favorable to the accused: The evidence is material only if there is a reasonable probability that, had the evidence been disclosed to the defense, the result of the proceeding would have been different. A "reasonable probability" is a probability sufficient to undermine confidence in the outcome. . . .

In the present case, we think that there is a significant likelihood that the prosecutor's response to respondent's discovery motion misleadingly induced defense counsel to believe that O'Connor and Mitchell could not be impeached on the basis of bias or interest arising from inducements offered by the Government. Defense counsel asked the prosecutor to disclose any inducements that had been made to witnesses, and the prosecutor failed to disclose that the possibility of a reward had been held out to O'Connor and Mitchell if the information they supplied led to "the accomplishment of the objective sought to be obtained . . . to the satisfaction of [the Government]." This possibility of a reward gave O'Connor and Mitchell a direct, personal stake in respondent's conviction. The fact that the stake was not guaranteed through a promise or binding contract, but was expressly contingent on the Government's satisfaction with the end result, served only to strengthen any incentive to testify falsely in order to secure a conviction. Moreover, the prosecutor disclosed affidavits that stated that O'Connor and Mitchell received no promises of reward in return for providing information in the affidavits implicating respondent in criminal activity. In fact, O'Connor and Mitchell signed the last of these affidavits the very day after they signed the ATF contracts. While the Government is technically correct that the blank contracts did not constitute a "promise of reward," the natural effect of these affidavits would be misleadingly to induce defense counsel to believe that O'Connor and Mitchell provided the information in the affidavits, and ultimately their testimony at trial recounting the same information, without any "inducements." . . .

NOTES & QUESTIONS ON MATERIALITY

1. *The reasonable probability standard.* The rule reaffirmed in *Bagley* is that a *Brady* violation only requires reversal and a new trial if there is a "reasonable probability" that the withheld evidence would have changed the outcome of the trial. In other words, if the appellate court determines that the jury would have voted to convict, even if its deliberations had included the withheld evidence, then reversal is not necessary. Do you agree that this standard is sufficient to vindicate any due process concerns arising from a *Brady* violation? How easy is it for an appellate court to make this counterfactual determination? Recall that the appellate court has no access to the jury's confidential deliberations and has no way of knowing how close the jury was to acquitting the defendant. Does this factor compromise the standard's workability?

2. *Specific versus general requests.* Should it matter whether the *Brady* violation arises from a general request, a specific request, or no request at all? In *Agurs*, the Supreme Court seemed to think that the situations were analytically and doctrinally distinct. But in *Bagley*, the Court threw out the distinction and decided that the "reasonable probability" standard was flexible enough to work for all three situations. Do you agree? As one scholar noted:

> *Bagley*'s effective equal treatment of specific and general/no requests runs counter to the intentions of at least five Justices (Blackmun, O'Connor, Stevens, Marshall, and Brennan), each of whom indicated that specific requests should receive favorable treatment. In addition, the equal treatment of specific and general/no requests represents a reversal of the *Brady-Agurs* materiality framework without any consideration by the Supreme Court of the notice and fairness rationales underlying that framework.

Paul G. Nofer, *Specific Requests and the Prosecutorial Duty to Disclose Evidence: The Impact of* United States v. Bagley, 1986 Duke L.J. 892, 913-14. It is important to remember that the distinction between specific and general/no requests is still relevant for the determination of whether a piece of evidence is favorable. If the defense specifically requests the evidence from the prosecution, then the prosecution is on notice about the significance of the evidence. If the defense provides no request, the prosecution can still be on notice that the evidence is favorable to the defendant's case, but only if the nature of the evidence itself makes it clear that it would tend to support the defendant's innocence.

PROBLEM CASE

A father was pushing his 16-month-old boy in a stroller when the unthinkable happened—a shot rang out and hit the boy in the head, killing him instantly. The police charged Daquan Wright with criminal possession of a weapon in the second degree. Another co-defendant was charged with murder. At trial, a witness testified that he saw Daquan Wright hand a gun to the triggerman, right before the triggerman fired at the little boy's father. (The prosecution's theory of the case was that the father was the intended target and that the boy was hit by mistake.)

Wright argued that the state violated its *Brady* obligation by failing to disclose to the defense that the witness had received $2,000 from the Crimestoppers Organization in exchange for coming forward. The state responded that the violation was immaterial because the state had already disclosed that the witnessed received $12,000 worth of government benefits, the witness was cross-examined about this fact, and there was not "a reasonable possibility that it would have changed the result of the proceedings." The defense countered that the $2,000 gave the witness a special reason to lie. Under these circumstances, was the evidence material? *People v. Wright*, 166 A.D.3d 1022, 88 N.Y.S.3d 457 (N.Y. App. Div. 2018).

4. Cumulative Effect of Discovery Violations

The following case considers the potentially paradoxical results that might flow from a *series* of discovery violations by the prosecution. Imagine that the prosecutor fails to turn over ten pieces of evidence to the defense—each one constituting a distinct *Brady* violation. If each piece of evidence, by itself, were insufficient to change the outcome of the trial, what remedy should the appellate court order? If each violation is viewed separately, and judged according to the standard of materiality, it would appear that no new trial is necessary. But that result seems deeply counterintuitive. As you read the following case, look for the Court's solution to this doctrinal quandary. What guidance does the Court give to trial judges faced with multiple *Brady* violations?

Kyles v. Whitley

Supreme Court of the United States
514 U.S. 419 (1995)

Justice SOUTER delivered the opinion of the Court.

After his first trial in 1984 ended in a hung jury, petitioner Curtis Lee Kyles was tried again, convicted of first-degree murder, and sentenced to death. On habeas review, we follow the established rule that the state's obligation under *Brady v. Maryland* to disclose evidence favorable to the defense, turns on the cumulative effect of all such evidence suppressed by the government, and we hold that the prosecutor remains responsible for gauging that effect regardless of any failure by the police to bring favorable evidence to the prosecutor's attention. Because the net effect of the evidence withheld by the State in this case raises a reasonable probability that its disclosure would have produced a different result, Kyles is entitled to a new trial. . . .

II

The record indicates that, at about 2:20 P.M. on Thursday, September 20, 1984, 60-year-old Dolores Dye left the Schwegmann Brothers' store (Schwegmann's) on Old Gentilly Road in New Orleans after doing some food shopping. As she put her grocery bags into the trunk of her red Ford LTD, a man accosted her and after a short struggle drew a revolver, fired into her left temple, and killed her. The gunman took Dye's keys and drove away in the LTD.

New Orleans police took statements from six eyewitnesses, who offered various descriptions of the gunman. They agreed that he was a black man, and four of them said that he had braided hair. The witnesses differed significantly, however, in their descriptions of height, age, weight, build, and hair length. Two reported seeing a man of 17 or 18, while another described the gunman as looking as old as 28. One witness described him as 5′4″ or 5′5″, medium build, 140-150 pounds; another described the man as slim and close to six feet. One witness said he had a mustache; none of the others spoke of any facial hair at all. One witness said the murderer had shoulder-length hair; another described the hair as "short."

Since the police believed the killer might have driven his own car to Schwegmann's and left it there when he drove off in Dye's LTD, they recorded the license numbers of the cars remaining in the parking lots around the store at 9:15 P.M. on the evening of the murder. Matching these numbers with registration records produced the names and addresses of the owners of the cars, with a notation of any owner's police record. Despite this list and the eyewitness descriptions, the police had no lead to the gunman until the Saturday evening after the shooting.

At 5:30 P.M., on September 22, a man identifying himself as James Joseph called the police and reported that on the day of the murder he had bought a red Thunderbird from a friend named Curtis, whom he later identified as petitioner, Curtis Kyles. He said that he had subsequently read about Dye's murder in the newspapers and feared that the car he purchased was the victim's. He agreed to meet with the police.

A few hours later, the informant met New Orleans Detective John Miller, who was wired with a hidden body microphone, through which the ensuing conversation was recorded. The informant now said his name was Joseph Banks and that he was called Beanie. His actual name was Joseph Wallace.

His story, as well as his name, had changed since his earlier call. In place of his original account of buying a Thunderbird from Kyles on Thursday, Beanie told Miller that he had not seen Kyles at all on Thursday and had bought a red LTD the previous day, Friday. Beanie led Miller to the parking lot of a nearby bar, where he had left the red LTD, later identified as Dye's. . . .

Beanie seemed eager to cast suspicion on Kyles, who allegedly made his living by "robbing people," and had tried to kill Beanie at some prior time. Beanie said that Kyles regularly carried two pistols, a .38 and a .32. . . . Beanie told the officers that after he bought the car, he and his "partner" (Burns) drove Kyles to Schwegmann's about 9 P.M. on Friday evening to pick up Kyles's car, described as an orange four-door Ford. When asked where Kyles's car had been parked, Beanie replied that it had been "[o]n the same side [of the lot] where the woman was killed at." . . .

At 10:40 A.M., Kyles was arrested as he left the apartment, which was then searched under a warrant. Behind the kitchen stove, the police found a .32-caliber revolver containing five live rounds and one spent cartridge. Ballistics tests later showed that this pistol was used to murder Dye. In a wardrobe in a hallway leading to the kitchen, the officers found a homemade shoulder holster that fit the murder weapon. In a bedroom dresser drawer, they discovered two boxes of ammunition, one containing several .32-caliber rounds of the same brand as those found in the pistol. Back in the kitchen, various cans of cat and dog food, some of them of the brands Dye typically purchased, were found in Schwegmann's sacks. No other groceries were identified as possibly being Dye's, and no potty was found. Later that afternoon at the police station, police opened the rubbish bags and found the victim's purse, identification, and other personal belongings wrapped in a Schwegmann's sack.

The gun, the LTD, the purse, and the cans of pet food were dusted for fingerprints. The gun had been wiped clean. Several prints were found on the purse and on the LTD, but none was identified as Kyles's. Dye's prints were not found on any of the cans of pet food. Kyles's prints were found, however, on a small piece of paper taken from the front passenger-side floorboard of the LTD. The crime laboratory recorded the paper as a Schwegmann's sales slip, but without noting what had been printed on it, which was obliterated in the chemical process of lifting the fingerprints. A second Schwegmann's receipt was found in the trunk of the LTD, but Kyles's prints were not found on it. Beanie's fingerprints were not compared to any of the fingerprints found.

The lead detective on the case, John Dillman, put together a photo lineup that included a photograph of Kyles (but not of Beanie) and showed the array to five of the six eyewitnesses who had given statements. Three of them picked the photograph of Kyles; the other two could not confidently identify Kyles as Dye's assailant.

Kyles was indicted for first-degree murder. Before trial, his counsel filed a lengthy motion for disclosure by the State of any exculpatory or impeachment evidence. The prosecution responded that there was "no exculpatory evidence of any nature," despite the government's knowledge of the following evidentiary items: (1) the six contemporaneous eyewitness statements taken by police following the murder; (2) records of Beanie's initial call to the police; (3) the tape recording of the Saturday conversation between Beanie and officers Eaton and Miller; (4) the typed and signed statement given by Beanie on Sunday morning; (5) the computer print-out of license numbers of cars parked at Schwegmann's on the night of the murder, which did not list the number of Kyles's car; (6) the internal police memorandum calling for the seizure of the rubbish after Beanie had suggested that the purse might be found there; and (7) evidence linking Beanie to other crimes at Schwegmann's and to the unrelated murder of one Patricia Leidenheimer, committed in January before the Dye murder. . . .

III

The prosecution's affirmative duty to disclose evidence favorable to a defendant can trace its origins to early 20th-century strictures against misrepresentation and is of course most prominently associated with this Court's decision in *Brady v. Maryland*. *Brady* held "that the suppression by the prosecution of evidence favorable to an accused upon request violates due process where the evidence is material either to guilt or to punishment, irrespective of the good faith or bad faith of the prosecution." In *United States v. Agurs*, 427 U.S. 97 (1976), however, it became clear that a defendant's failure to request favorable evidence did not leave the Government free of all obligation. There, the Court distinguished three situations in which a *Brady* claim might arise: first, where previously undisclosed evidence revealed that the prosecution introduced trial testimony that it knew or should have known was perjured; second, where the Government failed to accede to a defense request for disclosure of some specific kind of exculpatory evidence; and third, where the Government failed to volunteer exculpatory evidence never requested, or requested only in a general way. The Court found a duty on the part of the Government even in this last situation, though only when suppression of the evidence would be "of sufficient significance to result in the denial of the defendant's right to a fair trial."

In the third prominent case on the way to current *Brady* law, *United States v. Bagley*, 473 U.S. 667 (1985), the Court disavowed any difference between exculpatory and impeachment evidence for *Brady* purposes, and it abandoned the distinction between the second and third *Agurs* circumstances, i.e., the "specific-request" and "general- or no-request" situations. *Bagley* held that regardless of request, favorable evidence is material, and constitutional error results from its suppression by the government, "if there is a reasonable probability that, had the evidence been disclosed to the defense, the result of the proceeding would have been different."

Four aspects of materiality under *Bagley* bear emphasis. Although the constitutional duty is triggered by the potential impact of favorable but undisclosed evidence, a showing of materiality does not require demonstration by a preponderance that disclosure of the suppressed evidence would have resulted ultimately in the defendant's acquittal (whether based on the presence of reasonable doubt or acceptance of an explanation for the crime that does not inculpate the defendant). *Bagley*'s touchstone of materiality is a "reasonable probability" of a different result, and the adjective is important. The question is not whether the defendant would more likely than not have received a different verdict with the evidence, but whether in its absence he received a fair trial, understood as a trial resulting in a verdict worthy of confidence. A "reasonable probability" of a different result is accordingly shown when the government's evidentiary suppression "undermines confidence in the outcome of the trial."

The second aspect of *Bagley* materiality bearing emphasis here is that it is not a sufficiency of evidence test. A defendant need not demonstrate that after discounting the inculpatory evidence in light of the undisclosed evidence, there would not have been enough left to convict. The possibility of an acquittal on a criminal charge does not imply an insufficient evidentiary basis to convict. One does not show a *Brady* violation by demonstrating that some of the inculpatory evidence should have been excluded, but by showing that the favorable evidence could reasonably be taken to put the whole case in such a different light as to undermine confidence in the verdict.

Third, we note that . . . once a reviewing court applying *Bagley* has found constitutional error there is no need for further harmless-error review. Assuming, arguendo, that a harmless-error enquiry were to apply, a *Bagley* error could not be treated as harmless, since "a reasonable probability that, had the evidence been disclosed to the defense, the result of the proceeding would have been different," necessarily entails the conclusion that the suppression must have had "substantial and injurious effect or influence in determining the jury's verdict." This is amply confirmed by the development of the respective governing standards. . . .

The fourth and final aspect of *Bagley* materiality to be stressed here is its definition in terms of suppressed evidence considered collectively, not item by item. As Justice Blackmun emphasized in the portion of his opinion written for the Court, the Constitution is not violated every time the government fails or chooses not to disclose evidence that might prove helpful to the defense. We have never held that the Constitution demands an open file policy and the rule in *Bagley* requires less of the prosecution than the ABA Standards for Criminal Justice, which call generally for prosecutorial disclosures of any evidence tending to exculpate or mitigate.

While the definition of *Bagley* materiality in terms of the cumulative effect of suppression must accordingly be seen as leaving the government with a degree of discretion, it must also be understood as imposing a corresponding burden. On the one side, showing that the prosecution knew of an item of favorable evidence unknown to the defense does not amount to a *Brady* violation, without more. But the prosecution, which alone can know what is undisclosed, must be assigned the consequent responsibility to gauge the likely net effect of all such evidence and make disclosure when the point of "reasonable probability" is reached. This in turn means that the individual prosecutors has a duty to learn of any favorable evidence known to the others acting on the government's behalf in the case, including the police. But whether the prosecutor succeeds or fails in meeting this obligation (whether, that is, a failure to disclose is in good faith or bad faith, the prosecution's responsibility for failing to disclose known, favorable evidence rising to a material level of importance is inescapable).

[W]e were asked at oral argument to raise the threshold of materiality because the *Bagley* standard "makes it difficult . . . to know" from the "perspective [of the prosecutor at] trial . . . exactly what might become important later on." The State asks for "a certain amount of leeway in making a judgment call" as to the disclosure of any given piece of evidence.

Uncertainty about the degree of further "leeway" that might satisfy the State's request for a "certain amount" of it is the least of the reasons to deny the request. At bottom, what the State fails to recognize is that, with or without more leeway, the prosecution cannot be subject to any disclosure obligation without at some point having the responsibility to determine when it must act. . . . Unless, indeed, the adversary system of prosecution is to descend to a gladiatorial level unmitigated by any prosecutorial obligation for the sake of truth, the government simply cannot avoid responsibility for knowing when the suppression of evidence has come to portend such an effect on a trial's outcome as to destroy confidence in its result.

This means, naturally, that a prosecutor anxious about tacking too close to the wind will disclose a favorable piece of evidence. This is as it should be. Such disclosure will serve to justify trust in the prosecutor as "the representative . . . of a sovereignty . . . whose interest . . . in a criminal prosecution is not that it shall win a case, but that justice shall be done." And it will tend to preserve the criminal trial, as distinct from the prosecutor's private deliberations, as the chosen forum for ascertaining the truth about criminal accusations. The prudence of the careful prosecutor should not therefore be discouraged. . . .

IV

In this case, disclosure of the suppressed evidence to competent counsel would have made a different result reasonably probable. . . . [T]he question is not whether the State would have had a case to go to the jury if it had disclosed the favorable evidence, but whether we can be confident that the jury's verdict would have been the same. Confidence that it would have been cannot survive a recap of the suppressed evidence and its significance for the prosecution. The jury would have been entitled to find:

(a) that the investigation was limited by the police's uncritical readiness to accept the story and suggestions of an informant whose accounts were inconsistent to the point, for example, of including four different versions of the discovery of the victim's purse, and whose own behavior was enough to raise suspicions of guilt;
(b) that the lead police detective who testified was either less than wholly candid or less than fully informed;
(c) that the informant's behavior raised suspicions that he had planted both the murder weapon and the victim's purse in the places they were found;
(d) that one of the four eyewitnesses crucial to the State's case had given a description that did not match the defendant and better described the informant;
(e) that another eyewitness had been coached, since he had first stated that he had not seen the killer outside the getaway car, or the killing itself, whereas at trial he claimed to have seen the shooting, described the murder weapon exactly, and omitted portions of his initial description that would have been troublesome for the case;
(f) that there was no consistency to eyewitness descriptions of the killer's height, build, age, facial hair, or hair length.

Since all of these possible findings were precluded by the prosecution's failure to disclose the evidence that would have supported them, "fairness"

> cannot be stretched to the point of calling this a fair trial. Perhaps, confidence that the verdict would have been the same could survive the evidence impeaching even two eyewitnesses if the discoveries of gun and purse were above suspicion. Perhaps those suspicious circumstances would not defeat confidence in the verdict if the eyewitnesses had generally agreed on a description and were free of impeachment. But confidence that the verdict would have been unaffected cannot survive when suppressed evidence would have entitled a jury to find that the eyewitnesses were not consistent in describing the killer, that two out of the four eyewitnesses testifying were unreliable, that the most damning physical evidence was subject to suspicion, that the investigation that produced it was insufficiently probing, and that the principal police witness was insufficiently informed or candid. . . .

NOTES & QUESTIONS ON CUMULATIVE VIOLATIONS

1. *Cumulative constitutional violations. Kyles* represents one of the few areas where constitutional jurisprudence recognizes that cumulative violations require consolidated treatment. For an argument that cumulative constitutional violations should be recognized in many more areas, consider the following argument:

> As a result of the failure to properly apply cumulative harm, a truly unreliable verdict—one where the errors occur across different types of constitutional claims—may not be remedied. Cumulative harm should be more broadly remedied in criminal cases.

Kerry Abrams & Brandon L. Garrett, *Cumulative Constitutional Rights*, 97 B.U. L. Rev. 1309, 1322 (2017). Abrams and Garrett would even extend the methodology to situations where multiple constitutional provisions are violated—not simply the multiple but similar violations at issue in *Kyles*. Do you agree that the concept of cumulative constitutional violations can be extended in this way?

5. Failure to Object to Discovery Violations

Generally speaking, most objections are deemed waived—or procedurally defaulted—if they are not raised at trial or raised in prior appellate proceedings. So, for example, if the defendant failed to object to a discovery violation at trial, the defense may be prohibited from raising this objection during later stages of the case. These "procedural default" rules are usually codified in state procedural rules. However, if a convicted prisoner files a habeas corpus petition seeking review of their detention, the prisoner can overcome the procedural default rule if the prisoner can show both "cause" and "prejudice." The "cause" requirement simply means that the prisoner had cause, i.e., a necessary reason, for violating the state procedural rule. The "prejudice" requirement simply means that application of the state procedural rule caused real harm to the defendant. Although the procedural default rule is a substantial hurdle to post-conviction review, the cause-and-prejudice exception demonstrates that the hurdle is not insurmountable in all cases.

Procedural default, if universally applied without any exceptions, would produce a Catch-22 situation in the context of *Brady* discovery violations. If the prosecution fails to turn over material evidence to the defense, such as exculpatory or impeachment evidence, the defense might not be aware of the violation enough to object to the lack of disclosure. The situation is, in other words, an unknown unknown, rather than a known unknown. The following case concerns one of these situations. As you read the case, ask yourself whether there was sufficient cause for the defendant's failure to raise his constitutional claim earlier in the case and whether the application of the procedural rule prejudiced the defendant's case. Should the defendant be excused from responsibility for failing to abide by the state procedural rule?

Strickler v. Greene

Supreme Court of the United States
527 U.S. 263 (1999)

Justice STEVENS delivered the opinion of the Court.

The District Court for the Eastern District of Virginia granted petitioner's application for a writ of habeas corpus and vacated his capital murder conviction and death sentence on the grounds that the Commonwealth had failed to disclose important exculpatory evidence and that petitioner had not, in consequence, received a fair trial. The Court of Appeals for the Fourth Circuit reversed because petitioner had not raised his constitutional claim at his trial or in state collateral proceedings. In addition, the Fourth Circuit concluded that petitioner's claim was, "in any event, without merit." Finding the legal question presented by this case considerably more difficult than the Fourth Circuit, we granted certiorari to consider (1) whether the Commonwealth violated *Brady v. Maryland* and its progeny; (2) whether there was an acceptable "cause" for petitioner's failure to raise this claim in state court; and (3), if so, whether he suffered prejudice sufficient to excuse his procedural default.

I

In the early evening of January 5, 1990, Leanne Whitlock, an African-American sophomore at James Madison University, was abducted from a local shopping center and robbed and murdered. In separate trials, both petitioner and Ronald Henderson were convicted of all three offenses. Henderson was convicted of first-degree murder, a noncapital offense, whereas petitioner was convicted of capital murder and sentenced to death.

At both trials, a woman named Anne Stoltzfus testified in vivid detail about Whitlock's abduction. The exculpatory material that petitioner claims should have been disclosed before trial includes documents prepared by Stoltzfus, and notes of interviews with her, that impeach significant portions of her testimony. We begin, however, by noting that, even without the Stoltzfus testimony, the evidence in the record was sufficient to establish petitioner's guilt on the murder charge. Whether petitioner would have been convicted of capital murder and received the death sentence if she had not testified, or if she had been sufficiently impeached, is less clear. . . .

II

The first question that our order granting certiorari directed the parties to address is whether the Commonwealth violated the *Brady* rule. We begin our analysis by identifying the essential components of a *Brady* violation.

In *Brady*, this Court held "that the suppression by the prosecution of evidence favorable to an accused upon request violates due process where the evidence is material either to guilt or to punishment, irrespective of the good faith or bad faith of the prosecution." We have since held that the duty to disclose such evidence is applicable even though there has been no request by the accused and that the duty encompasses impeachment evidence as well as exculpatory evidence. Such evidence is material "if there is a reasonable probability that, had the evidence been disclosed to the defense, the result of the proceeding would have been different." Moreover, the rule encompasses evidence "known only to police investigators and not to the prosecutor." In order to comply with *Brady*, therefore, "the individual prosecutor has a duty to learn of any favorable evidence known to the others acting on the government's behalf in this case, including the police."

These cases, together with earlier cases condemning the knowing use of perjured testimony, illustrate the special role played by the American prosecutor in the search for truth in criminal trials. Within the federal system, for example, we have said that the United States Attorney is "the representative not of an ordinary party to a controversy, but of a sovereignty whose obligation to govern impartially is as compelling as its obligation to govern at all; and whose interest, therefore, in a criminal prosecution is not that it shall win a case, but that justice shall be done."

This special status explains both the basis for the prosecution's broad duty of disclosure and our conclusion that not every violation of that duty necessarily establishes that the outcome was unjust. Thus the term "*Brady* violation" is sometimes used to refer to any breach of the broad obligation to disclose exculpatory evidence—that is, to any suppression of so-called "*Brady* material"—although, strictly speaking, there is never a real "*Brady* violation" unless the nondisclosure was so serious that there is a reasonable probability that the suppressed evidence would have produced a different verdict. There are three components of a true *Brady* violation: The evidence at issue must be favorable to the accused, either because it is exculpatory, or because it is impeaching; that evidence must have been suppressed by the State, either willfully or inadvertently; and prejudice must have ensued.

Two of those components are unquestionably established by the record in this case. The contrast between (a) the terrifying incident that Stoltzfus confidently described in her testimony and (b) her initial perception of that event "as a trivial episode of college kids carrying on" that her daughter did not even notice, suffices to establish the impeaching character of the undisclosed documents. Moreover, with respect to at least five of those documents, there is no dispute about the fact that they were known to the Commonwealth but not disclosed to trial counsel. It is the third component—whether petitioner has established the prejudice necessary to satisfy the "materiality" inquiry—that is the most difficult element of the claimed Brady violation in this case.

Because petitioner acknowledges that his *Brady* claim is procedurally defaulted, we must first decide whether that default is excused by an adequate showing of cause and prejudice. In this case, cause and prejudice parallel two of the three components of the alleged *Brady* violation itself. The suppression of the Stoltzfus documents constitutes one of the causes for the failure to assert a *Brady* claim in the state courts, and unless those documents were "material" for *Brady* purposes, their suppression did not give rise to sufficient prejudice to overcome the procedural default.

III

Respondent expressly disavows any reliance on the fact that petitioner's *Brady* claim was not raised at trial. He states that the Commonwealth has consistently argued "that the claim is defaulted because it could have been raised on state habeas corpus through the exercise of due diligence, but was not." Despite this concession, it is appropriate to begin the analysis of the "cause" issue by explaining why petitioner's reasons for failing to raise his *Brady* claim at trial are acceptable under this Court's cases.

Three factors explain why trial counsel did not advance this claim: The documents were suppressed by the Commonwealth; the prosecutor maintained an open file policy; and trial counsel were not aware of the factual basis for the claim. The first and second factors—i.e., the nondisclosure and the open file policy—are both fairly characterized as conduct attributable to the Commonwealth that impeded trial counsel's access to the factual basis for making a *Brady* claim. . . . [I]t is just such factors that ordinarily establish the existence of cause for a procedural default.

If it was reasonable for trial counsel to rely on, not just the presumption that the prosecutor would fully perform his duty to disclose all exculpatory materials, but also the implicit representation that such materials would be included in the open files tendered to defense counsel for their examination, we think such reliance by counsel appointed to represent petitioner in state habeas proceedings was equally reasonable. Indeed, in *Murray* we expressly noted that "the standard for cause should not vary depending on the timing of a procedural default."

Respondent contends, however, that the prosecution's maintenance of an open file policy that did not include all it was purported to contain is irrelevant because the factual basis for the assertion of a *Brady* claim was available to state habeas counsel. He presses two factors to support this assertion. First, he argues that an examination of Stoltzfus' trial testimony, as well as a letter published in a local newspaper, made it clear that she had had several interviews with Detective Claytor. Second, the fact that the Federal District Court entered an order allowing discovery of the Harrisonburg police files indicates that diligent counsel could have obtained a similar order from the state court. We find neither factor persuasive.

Although it is true that petitioner's lawyers—both at trial and in post-trial proceedings—must have known that Stoltzfus had had multiple interviews with the police, it by no means follows that they would have known that records pertaining to those interviews, or that the notes that Stoltzfus sent to the detective, existed and had been suppressed. Indeed, if respondent is correct that Exhibits 2, 7, and 8 were in the prosecutor's "open file," it is especially unlikely that counsel would have suspected that additional impeaching evidence was being withheld. The prosecutor must have known about the newspaper articles and Stoltzfus' meetings with Claytor, yet he did not believe that his prosecution file was incomplete.

Furthermore, the fact that the District Court entered a broad discovery order even before federal habeas counsel had advanced a *Brady* claim does not demonstrate that a state court also would have done so. Indeed, as we understand Virginia law and respondent's position, petitioner would not have been entitled to such discovery in state habeas proceedings without a showing of good cause. Even pursuant to the broader discovery provisions afforded at trial, petitioner would not have had access to these materials under Virginia law, except as modified by *Brady*. Mere speculation that some exculpatory material may have been withheld is unlikely to establish good cause for a discovery request on collateral review. Nor, in our opinion, should such suspicion suffice to impose a duty on counsel to advance a claim for which they have no evidentiary support. Proper respect for state procedures counsels against a requirement that all possible claims be raised in

> state collateral proceedings, even when no known facts support them. The presumption . . . is inconsistent with the novel suggestion that conscientious defense counsel have a procedural obligation to assert constitutional error on the basis of mere suspicion that some prosecutorial misstep may have occurred. . . . In summary, petitioner has established cause for failing to raise a *Brady* claim prior to federal habeas. . . .
>
> IV
>
> . . . Petitioner has satisfied two of the three components of a constitutional violation under *Brady*: exculpatory evidence and nondisclosure of this evidence by the prosecution. Petitioner has also demonstrated cause for failing to raise this claim during trial or on state postconviction review. However, petitioner has not shown that there is a reasonable probability that his conviction or sentence would have been different had these materials been disclosed. He therefore cannot show materiality under *Brady*. . . .

NOTES & QUESTIONS ON FAILURE TO OBJECT

1. *The cause and prejudice standard.* When should courts conclude that a defendant has cause for his procedural default and has suffered prejudice? In *Strickler*, the defendant satisfied the "cause" prong of the standard but failed to demonstrate prejudice. However, other defendants have fared better. For example, in *Banks v. Dretke*, the defendant had cause for not raising his objection earlier and had suffered enough prejudice to warrant a new trial. Banks argued that the prosecutor failed to turn over evidence that a key witness named Farr was a police informant—evidence that Banks could have used to impeach the witness. The court applied the following standard for establishing cause:

> Banks's prosecutors represented at trial and in state postconviction proceedings that the State had held nothing back. Moreover, in state postconviction court, the State's pleading denied that Farr was an informant. It was not incumbent on Banks to prove these representations false; rather, Banks was entitled to treat the prosecutor's submissions as truthful. Accordingly, Banks has shown cause for failing to present evidence in state court capable of substantiating his Farr *Brady* claim.

Banks v. Dretke, 540 U.S. 668, 698 (2004). Unlike in *Strickler*, though, Banks also was prejudiced by the violation because "[a]t least as to the penalty phase, in sum, one can hardly be confident that Banks received a fair trial, given the jury's ignorance of Farr's true role in the investigation and trial of the case."

B. STATUTORY DISCOVERY

Unlike constitutional discovery, which is inherently unidirectional and requires the prosecutor to turn over evidence to the defense, statutory discovery can be bidirectional, or "reciprocal," meaning that both sides have an obligation to exchange relevant information. Another way of putting the point is that a prosecutor's duty to disclose information to the defense flows from multiple sources including the Constitution, statute, and ethical rules. In contrast, the defense's duty to disclose information is usually governed by state statutes. To further complicate matters, the extent of that statutory disclosure varies from jurisdiction to jurisdiction. For example, Arkansas state law includes two provisions codifying defense discovery obligations that are quite broad. The first states that

> the trial court may require that the prosecuting attorney be informed of and permitted to inspect and copy or photograph any reports or statements of experts, made in connection with the particular case, including results of physical or mental examinations and of scientific tests, experiments or comparisons.

Ark. R. Crim. P. 18.2. A second provision states that

> the prosecuting attorney shall, upon request, be informed as soon as practicable before trial of the nature of any defense which defense counsel intends to use at trial and the names and addresses of persons whom defense counsel intends to call as witnesses in support thereof.

Ark. R. Crim. P. 18.3. Taken together, these two provisions cover much of the defense case and function to put the prosecutor on equal terms with the defense. Think of the provisions this way: Constitutional discovery confers a benefit on the defense by imposing an obligation on the prosecutor. The statutory discovery quoted above confers a benefit on the prosecutor by imposing an obligation on the defense. The result is an information symmetry between the two sides of the trial.

Similarly, New York's bilateral discovery scheme allows the prosecution to request information in the defense's possession prior to trial:

> Except to the extent protected by court order, upon a demand to produce by the prosecutor, a defendant . . . shall disclose and make available for inspection, photographing, copying or testing, subject to constitutional limitations:
>
> (a) any written report or document, or portion thereof, concerning a physical or mental examination, or scientific test, experiment, or comparisons, made by or at the request or direction of, the defendant . . . and (b) any photograph, drawing, tape or other electronic recording which the defendant intends to introduce at trial.

N.Y. Crim. Proc. Law § 240.30. This mirrors the structure of Rule 16 of the Federal Rules of Criminal Procedure, which requires federal court defendants to turn over all evidence in their possession (and which they intend to introduce at trial during their case-in-chief) if the defendant requested and received discovery from the prosecution.

On the other hand, some states have more specific discovery obligations that require defendants to turn over discrete types of evidence, such as any material or witness statement designed to establish an alibi for the defendant. In the following case, the Supreme Court considers the constitutional validity of such requirements, in particular whether alibi-evidence discovery violates a defendant's Fifth Amendment right against self-incrimination. Much is at stake in this case, since if the disclosure of alibi evidence violates the Fifth Amendment, other categories of discovery from the defense to the prosecutor could be considered as compelled testimony as well.

Williams v. Florida

Supreme Court of the United States
399 U.S. 78 (1970)

Mr. Justice White delivered the opinion of the Court.

Prior to his trial for robbery in the State of Florida, petitioner filed a Motion for a Protective Order, seeking to be excused from the requirements of Rule 1.200 of the Florida Rules of Criminal Procedure. That rule requires a defendant, on written demand of the prosecuting attorney, to give notice in advance of trial if the defendant intends to claim an alibi, and to furnish the prosecuting attorney with information as to the place where he claims to have been and with the names and addresses of the alibi witnesses he intends to use. In his motion petitioner openly declared his intent to claim an alibi, but objected to the further disclosure requirements on the ground that the rule "compels the Defendant in a criminal case to be a witness against himself" in violation of his Fifth and Fourteenth Amendment rights. The motion was denied. . . .

I

Florida's notice-of-alibi rule is in essence a requirement that a defendant submit to a limited form of pretrial discovery by the State whenever he intends to rely at trial on the defense of alibi. In exchange for the defendant's disclosure of the witnesses he proposes to use to establish that defense, the State in turn is required to notify the defendant of any witnesses it proposes to offer in rebuttal to that defense. Both sides are under a continuing duty promptly to disclose the names and addresses of additional witnesses bearing on the alibi as they become available. The threatened sanction for failure to comply is the exclusion at trial of the defendant's alibi evidence—except for his own testimony—or, in the case of the State, the exclusion of the State's evidence offered in rebuttal of the alibi.

In this case, following the denial of his Motion for a Protective Order, petitioner complied with the alibi rule and gave the State the name and address of one Mary Scotty. Mrs. Scotty was summoned to the office of the State Attorney on the morning of the trial, where she gave pretrial testimony. At the trial itself, Mrs. Scotty, petitioner, and petitioner's wife all testified that the three of them had been in Mrs. Scotty's apartment during the time of the robbery. On two occasions during cross-examination of Mrs. Scotty, the prosecuting attorney confronted her with her earlier deposition in which she had given dates and times that in some respects did not correspond with the dates and times given at trial. Mrs. Scotty adhered to her trial story, insisting that she had been mistaken in her earlier testimony. The State also offered in rebuttal the testimony of one of the officers investigating the robbery who claimed that Mrs. Scotty had asked him for directions on the afternoon in question during the time when she claimed to have been in her apartment with petitioner and his wife.

We need not linger over the suggestion that the discovery permitted the State against petitioner in this case deprived him of "due process" or a "fair trial." Florida law provides for liberal discovery by the defendant against the State, and the notice-of-alibi rule is itself carefully hedged with reciprocal duties requiring state disclosure to the defendant. Given the ease with which an alibi can be fabricated, the State's interest in protecting itself against an eleventh-hour defense is both obvious and legitimate. Reflecting this interest, notice-of-alibi provisions, dating at least from 1927, are now in existence in a substantial number of States. The adversary system of trial is hardly an end in itself; it is not yet a poker game in which players enjoy an absolute right always to conceal their cards until played. We find ample room in that system, at least as far as "due process" is concerned, for the instant Florida rule, which is designed to enhance the search for truth in the criminal trial by insuring both the defendant and the State ample opportunity to investigate certain facts crucial to the determination of guilt or innocence.

Petitioner's major contention is that he was "compelled . . . to be a witness against himself" contrary to the commands of the Fifth and Fourteenth Amendments because the notice-of-alibi rule required him to give the State the name and address of Mrs. Scotty in advance of trial and thus to furnish the State with information useful in convicting him. No pretrial statement of petitioner was introduced at trial; but armed with Mrs. Scotty's name and address and the knowledge that she was to be petitioner's alibi witness, the State was able to take her deposition in advance of trial and to find rebuttal testimony. Also, requiring him to reveal the elements of his defense is claimed to have interfered with his right to wait until after the

State had presented its case to decide how to defend against it. We conclude, however, as has apparently every other court that has considered the issue, that the privilege against self-incrimination is not violated by a requirement that the defendant give notice of an alibi defense and disclose his alibi witnesses.

The defendant in a criminal trial is frequently forced to testify himself and to call other witnesses in an effort to reduce the risk of conviction. When he presents his witnesses, he must reveal their identity and submit them to cross-examination which in itself may prove incriminating or which may furnish the State with leads to incriminating rebuttal evidence. That the defendant faces such a dilemma demanding a choice between complete silence and presenting a defense has never been thought an invasion of the privilege against compelled self-incrimination. The pressures generated by the State's evidence may be severe but they do not vitiate the defendant's choice to present an alibi defense and witnesses to prove it, even though the attempted defense ends in catastrophe for the defendant. However "testimonial" or "incriminating" the alibi defense proves to be, it cannot be considered "compelled" within the meaning of the Fifth and Fourteenth Amendments.

Very similar constraints operate on the defendant when the State requires pretrial notice of alibi and the naming of alibi witnesses. Nothing in such a rule requires the defendant to rely on an alibi or prevents him from abandoning the defense; these matters are left to his unfettered choice. That choice must be made, but the pressures that bear on his pretrial decision are of the same nature as those that would induce him to call alibi witnesses at the trial: the force of historical fact beyond both his and the State's control and the strength of the State's case built on these facts. Response to that kind of pressure by offering evidence or testimony is not compelled self-incrimination transgressing the Fifth and Fourteenth Amendments.

In the case before us, the notice-of-alibi rule by itself in no way affected petitioner's crucial decision to call alibi witnesses or added to the legitimate pressures leading to that course of action. At most, the rule only compelled petitioner to accelerate the timing of his disclosure, forcing him to divulge at an earlier date information that the petitioner from the beginning planned to divulge at trial. Nothing in the Fifth Amendment privilege entitles a defendant as a matter of constitutional right to await the end of the State's case before announcing the nature of his defense, any more than it entitles him to await the jury's verdict on the State's case-in-chief before deciding whether or not to take the stand himself.

Petitioner concedes that absent the notice-of-alibi rule the Constitution would raise no bar to the court's granting the State a continuance at trial on the ground of surprise as soon as the alibi witness is called. Nor would there be self-incrimination problems if, during that continuance, the State was permitted to do precisely what it did here prior to trial: take the deposition of the witness and find rebuttal evidence. But if so utilizing a continuance is permissible under the Fifth and Fourteenth Amendments, then surely the same result may be accomplished through pretrial discovery, as it was here, avoiding the necessity of a disrupted trial. We decline to hold that the privilege against compulsory self-incrimination guarantees the defendant the right to surprise the State with an alibi defense. . . .

Mr. Justice Black, with whom Mr. Justice Douglas joins, concurring in part and dissenting in part.

The core of the majority's decision is an assumption that compelling a defendant to give notice of an alibi defense before a trial is no different from requiring a defendant, after the State has produced the evidence against him at trial, to plead alibi before the jury retires to consider the case. This assumption is clearly revealed by the statement that "the pressures that bear on (a defendant's) pre-trial decision are of the same nature as those that would induce him to call alibi witnesses at the trial: the force of historical fact beyond both his and the State's control and the strength of the State's case built on these facts." That statement is plainly and simply wrong as a matter of fact and law, and the Court's holding based on that statement is a complete misunderstanding of the protections provided for criminal defendants by the Fifth Amendment and other provisions of the Bill of Rights.

When a defendant is required to indicate whether he might plead alibi in advance of trial, he faces a vastly different decision from that faced by one who can wait until the State has presented the case against him before making up his mind. Before trial the defendant knows only what the State's case might be. Before trial there is no such thing as the "strength of the State's case"; there is only a range of possible cases. At that time there is no certainty as to what kind of case the State will ultimately be able to prove at trial. Therefore any appraisal of the desirability of pleading alibi will be beset with guesswork and gambling far greater than that accompanying the decision at the trial itself. Any lawyer who has actually tried a case knows that, regardless of the amount of pretrial preparation, a case looks far different when it is actually being tried than when it is only being thought about.

The Florida system, as interpreted by the majority, plays upon this inherent uncertainty in predicting the possible strength of the State's case in order effectively to coerce defendants into disclosing an alibi defense that may never be actually used. Under the Florida rule, a defendant who might plead alibi must, at least 10 days before the date of trial, tell the prosecuting attorney that he might claim an alibi or else the defendant faces the real threat that he may be completely barred from presenting witnesses in support of his alibi. According to the Court, however, if he gives the required notice and later changes his mind "(n)othing in such a rule requires (him) to rely on an alibi or prevents him from abandoning the defense; these matters are left to his unfettered choice." Thus in most situations defendants with any possible thought of pleading alibi are in effect compelled to disclose their intentions in order to preserve the possibility of later raising the defense at trial. Necessarily few defendants and their lawyers will be willing to risk the loss of that possibility by not disclosing the alibi. Clearly the pressures on defendants to plead an alibi created by this procedure are not only quite different from the pressures operating at the trial itself, but are in fact significantly greater. Contrary to the majority's assertion, the pretrial decision cannot be analyzed as simply a matter of "timing," influenced by the same factors operating at the trial itself.

The Court apparently also assumes that a defendant who has given the required notice can abandon his alibi without hurting himself. Such an assumption is implicit in and necessary for the majority's argument that the pretrial decision is no different from that at the trial itself. I, however, cannot so lightly assume that pretrial notice will have no adverse effects on a defendant who later decides to forgo such a defense. Necessarily the defendant will have given the prosecutor the names of persons who may have some knowledge about the defendant himself or his activities. Necessarily the prosecutor will have every incentive to question these persons fully, and in doing so he may discover new leads or evidence. Undoubtedly there will be situations in which the State will seek to use such information—information it would probably never have obtained but for the defendant's coerced cooperation.

It is unnecessary for me, however, to engage in any such intellectual gymnastics concerning the practical effects of the notice-of-alibi procedure, because the Fifth Amendment itself clearly provides that "(n)o person . . . shall be compelled in any criminal case to be a witness against himself." If words are to be given their plain and obvious meaning, that provision, in my opinion, states that a criminal defendant cannot be required to give evidence, testimony, or any other assistance to the State to aid it in convicting him of crime. The Florida notice-of-alibi rule in my opinion is a patent violation of that constitutional provision because it requires a defendant to disclose information to the State so that the State can use that information to destroy him. It seems to me at least slightly incredible to suggest that this procedure may have some beneficial effects for defendants. There is no need to encourage defendants to take actions they think will help them. The fear of conviction and the substantial cost or inconvenience resulting from criminal prosecutions are more than sufficient incentives to make defendants want to help themselves. If a defendant thinks that making

> disclosure of an alibi before trial is in his best interest, he will obviously do so. And the only time the State needs the compulsion provided by this procedure is when the defendant has decided that such disclosure is likely to hurt his case. . . .

AFTERMATH Florida eventually revised its discovery process. Under the current scheme, the defendant may elect to participate in the discovery process or not. If the defendant participates and receives discovery materials, the defendant is then required to turn over to the prosecutor "a written list of the names and addresses of all witnesses whom the defendant expects to call as witnesses at the trial or hearing," Fla. R. Crim. P. 3.220, as well as "reports or statements of experts, that the defendant intends to use as a witness at a trial or hearing, made in connection with the particular case, including results of physical or mental examinations and of scientific tests, experiments, or comparisons" and "any tangible papers or objects that the defendant intends to use in the hearing or trial." Fla. R. Crim. P. 3.220. This would include alibi witness information. However, if the defendant elects not to participate in discovery, there is no obligation for the defendant to provide information about alibi witnesses.

NOTES & QUESTIONS ON STATUTORY DISCOVERY

1. *Alibi evidence.* One method for enforcing alibi-evidence discovery provisions is to prevent the defense or its witnesses from testifying if the evidence was not properly disclosed in advance. Is this exclusion an impermissible constraint on a defendant's right to testify in their own defense? Consider the case of Luis Albert Alicea, who was charged with robbery and murder. Alicea claimed that he was at home and receiving phone calls at the time of the murder and therefore could not be held responsible. The trial court prevented Alicea from presenting the alibi at trial because he had failed to give timely notice to the prosecution pursuant to Wis. Stat. § 971.23. Alicea appealed, arguing that he had a constitutional right to testify that he was not the perpetrator. The Seventh Circuit agreed, concluding:

> In balancing the competing interests underlying Wisconsin's alibi-notice rule and the constitutional policies favoring petitioner's right to testify, we must closely examine the justification for the state interest. To be sure, Wisconsin has a legitimate interest in preventing the truly guilty from escaping justice by means of fabricated alibis. But we cannot see how that interest is promoted by precluding a defendant's testimony for failure to give notice.

Alicea v. Gagnon, 675 F.2d 913, 923-24 (7th Cir. 1982). Other courts have reached a similar result, though some of them on statutory grounds rather than constitutional grounds. See, e.g., *People v. Merritt*, 396 Mich. 67, 238 N.W.2d 31 (1976). For more discussion of his dilemma, see Lori Ann Irish, *Alibi Notice Rules: The Preclusion Sanction as Procedural Default*, 51 U. Chi. L. Rev. 254, 256 (1984).

STATUTORY REQUIREMENTS

State statutes often regulate the *timing* of pretrial discovery. For example, New York's criminal discovery statute gives the prosecution until the first day of trial to comply with its discovery obligations:

> 1. After the jury has been sworn and before the prosecutor's opening address, or in the case of a single judge trial after commencement and before submission of evidence, the prosecutor shall, subject to a protective order, make available to the defendant:
>
> (a) Any written or recorded statement, including any testimony before a grand jury and an examination videotaped . . . made by a person whom the prosecutor intends to call as a witness at trial, and which relates to the subject matter of the witness's testimony;
>
> (b) A record of judgment of conviction of a witness the people intend to call at trial if the record of conviction is known by the prosecutor to exist;
>
> (c) The existence of any pending criminal action against a witness the people intend to call at trial, if the pending criminal action is known by the prosecutor to exist.

N.Y. Crim. Proc. Law § 240.45. The timing of defense disclosure is similarly last minute. The same provision requires that the defense turn over relevant statements *after* the prosecution has finished its case-in-chief and just before the defense begins its case-in-chief. Louisiana, South Carolina, and Wyoming have similar discovery statutes, while other jurisdictions require earlier disclosure.

Many defense attorneys have complained bitterly about the lack of an earlier statutory discovery obligation. Lawyers sometimes refer to the New York statute as a "Blindfold Law" because it requires that the defense team prepare for trial without sufficient advance notice of the prosecution's case. Prosecutors like last-minute discovery because it reduces the risk that a prosecution witness will be harassed, intimidated, or tampered with. Even so, there is a pending bill in New York to change the discovery calendar, which includes the following provision: "The prosecution shall perform its Phase One discovery obligations under this section within fifteen calendar days after the defendant's arraignment. . . ." If you were a state legislator, would you support this bill?

C. THE DUTY TO PRESERVE EVIDENCE

The prosecution cannot disclose evidence that it does not have. This raises the possibility that the prosecution could frustrate the defense's access to exculpatory evidence by simply not keeping it. In the following case, the Supreme Court considers this exact scenario and asks whether the prosecution has a constitutional obligation to preserve evidence. The police failed to perform tests or refrigerate clothing so that it could be tested later. Defendant Larry Youngblood argued that these failures prevented him from receiving a fair trial. As you read the case, ask yourself what the police and prosecutors should have done differently.

Arizona v. Youngblood

Supreme Court of the United States
488 U.S. 51 (1988)

Chief Justice Rehnquist delivered the opinion of the Court.

Respondent Larry Youngblood was convicted by a Pima County, Arizona, jury of child molestation, sexual assault, and kidnaping. The Arizona Court of Appeals reversed his conviction on the ground that the State had failed to preserve semen samples from the victim's body and clothing. We granted certiorari to consider the extent to which the Due Process Clause of the Fourteenth Amendment requires the State to preserve evidentiary material that might be useful to a criminal defendant. . . .

Nine days after the attack, on November 7, 1983, the police asked the boy to pick out his assailant from a photographic lineup. The boy identified respondent as the assailant. Respondent was not located by the police until four weeks later; he was arrested on December 9, 1983.

On November 8, 1983, Edward Heller, a police criminologist, examined the sexual assault kit. He testified that he followed standard department procedure, which was to examine the slides and determine whether sexual contact had occurred. After he determined that such contact had occurred, the criminologist did not perform any other tests, although he placed the assault kit back in the refrigerator. He testified that tests to identify blood group substances were not routinely conducted during the initial examination of an assault kit and in only about half of all cases in any event. He did not test the clothing at this time.

Respondent was indicted on charges of child molestation, sexual assault, and kidnaping. The State moved to compel respondent to provide blood and saliva samples for comparison with the material gathered through the use of the sexual assault kit, but the trial court denied the motion on the ground that the State had not obtained a sufficiently large semen sample to make a valid comparison. The prosecutor then asked the State's criminologist to perform an ABO blood group test on the rectal swab sample in an attempt to ascertain the blood type of the boy's assailant. This test failed to detect any blood group substances in the sample.

In January 1985, the police criminologist examined the boy's clothing for the first time. He found one semen stain on the boy's underwear and another on the rear of his T-shirt. The criminologist tried to obtain blood group substances from both stains using the ABO technique, but was unsuccessful. He also performed a P-30 protein molecule test on the stains, which indicated that only a small quantity of semen was present on the clothing; it was inconclusive as to the assailant's identity. The Tucson Police Department had just begun using this test, which was then used in slightly more than half of the crime laboratories in the country.

Respondent's principal defense at trial was that the boy had erred in identifying him as the perpetrator of the crime. In this connection, both a criminologist for the State and an expert witness for respondent testified as to what might have been shown by tests performed on the samples shortly after they were gathered, or by later tests performed on the samples from the boy's clothing had the clothing been properly refrigerated. The court instructed the jury that if they found the State had destroyed or lost evidence, they might "infer that the true fact is against the State's interest."

The jury found respondent guilty as charged, but the Arizona Court of Appeals reversed the judgment of conviction. It stated that "when identity is an issue at trial and the police permit the destruction of evidence that could eliminate the defendant as the perpetrator, such loss is material to the defense and is a denial of due process." The Court of Appeals concluded on the basis of the expert testimony at trial that timely performance of tests with properly preserved semen samples could have produced results that might have completely exonerated respondent. The Court of Appeals reached this conclusion even though it did "not imply any bad faith on the part of the State." . . . We now reverse.

Decision of this case requires us to again consider "what might loosely be called the area of constitutionally guaranteed access to evidence." In *Brady v. Maryland* we held that "the suppression by the prosecution of evidence favorable to the accused upon request violates due process where the evidence is material either to guilt or to punishment, irrespective of the good faith or bad faith of the prosecution." In *United States v. Agurs* we held that the prosecution had a duty to disclose some evidence of this description even though no requests were made for it, but at the same time we rejected the notion that a "prosecutor has a constitutional duty routinely to deliver his entire file to defense counsel."

There is no question but that the State complied with *Brady* and *Agurs* here. The State disclosed relevant police reports to respondent, which contained information about the existence of the swab and the clothing, and the boy's examination at the hospital. The State provided respondent's expert with the laboratory reports and notes prepared by the police criminologist, and respondent's expert had access to the swab and to the clothing.

If respondent is to prevail on federal constitutional grounds, then, it must be because of some constitutional duty over and above that imposed by cases such as *Brady* and *Agurs.* Our most recent decision in this area of the law, *California v. Trombetta,* 467 U.S. 479 (1984), arose out of a drunk-driving prosecution in which the State had introduced test results indicating the concentration of alcohol in the blood of two motorists. The defendants sought to suppress the test results on the ground that the State had failed to preserve the breath samples used in the test. We rejected this argument for several reasons: first, "the officers here were acting in good faith and in accord with their normal practice"; second, in the light of the procedures actually used the chances that preserved samples would have exculpated the defendants were slim; and, third, even if the samples might have shown inaccuracy in the tests, the defendants had "alternative means of demonstrating their innocence." In the present case, the likelihood that the preserved materials would have enabled the defendant to exonerate himself appears to be greater than it was in *Trombetta,* but here, unlike in *Trombetta,* the State did not attempt to make any use of the materials in its own case in chief.

Our decisions in related areas have stressed the importance for constitutional purposes of good or bad faith on the part of the Government when the claim is based on loss of evidence attributable to the Government. In *United States v. Marion,* 404 U.S. 307 (1971), we said that "[n]o actual prejudice to the conduct of the defense is alleged or proved, and there is no showing that the Government intentionally delayed to gain some tactical advantage over appellees or to harass them." Similarly, in *United States v. Valenzuela-Bernal,* we considered whether the Government's deportation of two witnesses who were illegal aliens violated due process. We held that the prompt deportation of the witnesses was justified "upon the Executive's good-faith determination that they possess no evidence favorable to the defendant in a criminal prosecution."

The Due Process Clause of the Fourteenth Amendment, as interpreted in *Brady,* makes the good or bad faith of the State irrelevant when the State fails to disclose to the defendant material exculpatory evidence. But we think the Due Process Clause requires a different result when we deal with the failure of the State to preserve evidentiary material of which no more can be said than that it could have been subjected to tests, the results of which might have exonerated the defendant. Part of the reason for the difference in treatment is found in the observation made by the Court in *Trombetta* that "[w]henever potentially exculpatory evidence is permanently lost, courts face the treacherous task of divining the import of materials whose contents are unknown and, very often, disputed." Part of it stems from our unwillingness to read the "fundamental fairness" requirement of the Due Process Clause as imposing on the police an undifferentiated and absolute duty to retain and to preserve all material that might be of conceivable evidentiary significance in a particular prosecution. We think that requiring a defendant to show bad faith on the part of the police both limits the extent of the police's obligation to preserve evidence to reasonable bounds and confines it to that class of cases where the interests of justice most clearly require it, *i.e.*, those cases in which the police themselves by their conduct indicate that the evidence could form a basis for exonerating the defendant. We therefore hold that unless a criminal defendant can show bad faith on the part of the police, failure to preserve potentially useful evidence does not constitute a denial of due process of law.

In this case, the police collected the rectal swab and clothing on the night of the crime; respondent was not taken into custody until six weeks later. The failure of the police to refrigerate the clothing and to perform tests on the semen samples can at worst be described as negligent. None of this information was concealed from respondent at trial, and the evidence—such as it was—was made available to respondent's expert who declined to perform any tests on the samples. The Arizona Court of Appeals noted in its opinion—and we agree—that there was no suggestion of bad faith on the part of the police. It follows, therefore, from what we have said, that there was no violation of the Due Process Clause. . . .

Justice BLACKMUN, with whom Justice BRENNAN and Justice MARSHALL join, dissenting.

The Constitution requires that criminal defendants be provided with a fair trial, not merely a "good faith" try at a fair trial. Respondent here, by what may have been nothing more than police ineptitude, was denied the opportunity to present a full defense. That ineptitude, however, deprived respondent of his guaranteed right to due process of law. In reversing the judgment of the Arizona Court of Appeals, this Court, in my view, misreads the import of its prior cases and unduly restricts the protections of the Due Process Clause. An understanding of due process demonstrates that the evidence which was allowed to deteriorate was "constitutionally material," and that its absence significantly prejudiced respondent. Accordingly, I dissent.

I

The Court, with minimal reference to our past cases and with what seems to me to be less than complete analysis, announces that "unless a criminal defendant can show bad faith on the part of police, failure to preserve potentially useful evidence does not constitute a denial of due process of law." This conclusion is claimed to be justified because it limits the extent of police responsibility "to that class of cases where the interests of justice most clearly require it, i.e., those cases in which the police themselves by their conduct indicate that the evidence could form a basis for exonerating the defendant." The majority has identified clearly one type of violation, for police action affirmatively aimed at cheating the process undoubtedly violates the Constitution. But to suggest that this is the only way in which the Due Process Clause can be violated cannot be correct. Regardless of intent or lack thereof, police action that results in a defendant's receiving an unfair trial constitutes a deprivation of due process. . . .

Brady and *Agurs* could not be more clear in their holdings that a prosecutor's bad faith in interfering with a defendant's access to material evidence is *not* an essential part of a due process violation. Nor did *Trombetta* create such a requirement. *Trombetta*'s initial discussion focused on the due process requirement "that criminal defendants be afforded a meaningful opportunity to present a complete defense," and then noted that the delivery of exculpatory evidence to the defendant "protect[s] the innocent from erroneous conviction and ensur[es] the integrity of our criminal justice system." Although the language of *Trombetta* includes a quotation in which the words "in good faith" appear, those words, for two reasons, do not have the significance claimed for them by the majority. First, the words are the antecedent part of the fuller phrase "in good faith and in accord with their normal practice." That phrase has its source in *Killian v. United States,* 368 U.S. 231, 242 (1961), where the Court held that the practice of discarding investigators' notes, used to compile reports that were then received in evidence, did not violate due process. In both *Killian* and *Trombetta,* the importance of police compliance with *usual procedures* was manifest. Here, however, the same standard of conduct cannot be claimed. There has been no suggestion that it was the usual procedure to ignore the possible deterioration of important evidence, or generally to treat material evidence in a negligent or reckless manner. Nor can the failure to refrigerate the clothing be squared with the careful steps taken to preserve the sexual-assault kit. The negligent or reckless failure to preserve important evidence just cannot be "in accord with . . . normal practice."

Second, and more importantly, *Trombetta* demonstrates that the absence of bad faith does not end the analysis. The determination in *Trombetta* that the prosecution acted in good faith and according to normal practice merely prefaced the primary inquiry, which centers on the "constitutional materiality" of the evidence itself. There is nothing in *Trombetta* that intimates that good faith alone should be the measure. . . .

I also doubt that the "bad faith" standard creates the bright-line rule sought by the majority. Apart from the inherent difficulty a defendant would have in obtaining evidence to show a lack of good faith, the line between "good faith" and "bad faith" is anything but bright, and the majority's formulation may well create more questions than it answers. What constitutes bad faith for these purposes? Does a defendant have to show actual malice, or would recklessness, or the deliberate failure to establish standards for maintaining and preserving evidence, be sufficient? Does "good faith police work" require a certain minimum of diligence, or will a lazy officer, who does not walk the few extra steps to the evidence refrigerator, be considered to be acting in good faith? While the majority leaves these questions for another day, its quick embrace of a "bad faith" standard has not brightened the line; it only has moved the line so as to provide fewer protections for criminal defendants. . . .

Applying this standard to the facts of this case, I conclude that the Arizona Court of Appeals was correct in overturning respondent's conviction. The clothing worn by the victim contained samples of his assailant's semen. The appeals court found that these samples would probably be larger, less contaminated, and more likely to yield conclusive test results than would the samples collected by use of the assault kit. The clothing and the semen stains on the clothing therefore obviously were material. . . .

AFTERWORD Youngblood was eventually exonerated after a DNA test suggested that he was innocent. His original conviction was based on an eyewitness identification performed by the victim in the case, a ten-year-old boy. In 2000, his attorneys requested a DNA test of the clothing that was at issue in the above case. At the time the Supreme Court considered the case, the improper storage of the clothing meant that it could not be tested for DNA. However, as new and more sophisticated DNA testing became available, the clothing was tested; DNA results of the semen on the clothing excluded Youngblood as a suspect. In 2000, Youngblood was formally exonerated and released. Two years later, based on the DNA tests, another individual, Walter Cruise, was identified as the assailant and convicted.

NOTES & QUESTIONS ON PRESERVING EVIDENCE

1. *The bad faith standard.* The majority concluded that Youngblood would need to establish police bad faith in order to prevail. The failure to preserve evidence, absent bad faith, is not a basis for overturning a conviction as a denial of

due process. Consequently, incompetent or negligent police procedures would not be enough to establish a denial of due process of law. This raises the question: How can bad faith be demonstrated? As one scholar noted:

> Regardless of whether bad faith turns on knowledge or intent, the burden on the defendant is nearly impossible to bear. . . . Evidence of bad faith is likely to be within the peculiar control of the police, and an officer unprincipled enough to destroy evidence is unlikely to chronicle his actions. . . . Moreover, a number of jurisdictions have held that destroying evidence pursuant to routine procedure is not bad faith. Nor, under the facts of *Youngblood* itself, does mere negligence suffice to establish bad faith. Not surprisingly, perhaps, regardless of whether the test is based on knowledge or intent, in the two decades since *Youngblood* was decided, there are few reported cases in which a court has found bad faith.

Norman C. Bay, *Old Blood, Bad Blood, and Youngblood: Due Process, Lost Evidence, and the Limits of Bad Faith*, 86 Wash. U. L. Rev. 241, 291-93 (2008). Do you agree that the bad faith standard is almost impossible for litigants to satisfy? Was this the point of crafting the standard in the first place? The most obvious way to suggest bad faith is to demonstrate that the evidence was inevitably beneficial to the defense, since that would give the prosecution a motive to deliberately fail to preserve evidence. In contrast, if the evidence might be beneficial to either side of the case, it is much harder to establish an inference of bad faith, since in that case a self-interested prosecutor would have reason to want to preserve the evidence.

2. *Evidence relevant to the defense*. The state is not obligated to preserve every piece of evidence. Rather, the constitutional duty is limited to evidence that might be "expected to play a role" in the suspect's defense. In *California v. Trombetta*, 467 U.S. 479, 488-89 (1984), the Supreme Court concluded that the state must preserve evidence that "possess[es] an exculpatory value that was apparent before the evidence was destroyed, and [is] of such a nature that the defendant would be unable to obtain comparable evidence by other reasonably available means." In other words, the state commits no constitutional violation when it destroys evidence whose exculpatory character is only revealed at a later point in time. Can you imagine a situation where the exculpatory character of an evidence would only be apparent later? In *Trombetta*, the defendant argued that the state was under an obligation to preserve breath samples. The Supreme Court disagreed, concluding that the breath samples did not have an exculpatory quality that was apparent when the state disposed of them. Although the Court noted that it was technically possible to preserve breath samples, it is not a common police practice to do so.

STATUTORY REQUIREMENTS

In many jurisdictions, the defense can use depositions as a way of preserving testimonial evidence that will be unavailable at the time of trial. For example, consider the following statutory provision in North Carolina:

> In all criminal actions, hearings and investigations it shall be lawful for the defendant in any such action to make affidavit before the clerk of the superior court of the county in which said action is pending, that it is important for the defense that he have the testimony of any person, whose name must be given, and that such person is so infirm, or otherwise physically incapacitated, or nonresident of this State, that he cannot procure his attendance at the trial or hearing of said cause. Upon the filing of such affidavit, it shall be the duty of the clerk to appoint some responsible person to take the deposition of such witness, which deposition may be read in the trial of such criminal action under the same rules as now apply by law to depositions in civil actions: provided, that the district attorney or prosecuting attorney of the district, county or town in which such action is pending have 10 days' notice of the taking of such deposition, who may appear in person or by representative to conduct the cross-examination of such witness.

N.C. Gen. Stat. § 8-74. However, it is important to distinguish these depositions from traditional discovery depositions in civil litigation, which are designed to give the other party in the litigation access to testimonial evidence. Criminal depositions, however, are designed to preserve testimonial evidence that would otherwise be unavailable at the trial.

Notice that the constraint on the use of depositions is the right of confrontation protected by the Sixth Amendment and incorporated against the states by the Fourteenth Amendment. That right requires that testimonial evidence be subject to cross-examination and would generally prevent the prosecution's entry into evidence of a deposition transcript at trial if the defendant did not have the opportunity to cross-examine the witness.

For example, in *United States v. Dixon*, the defendant was convicted of transporting an illegal alien for profit. The government took a deposition from a witness and then subsequently *deported* that witness from the country. The deposition was introduced as evidence at trial without the benefit of cross-examination. The Ninth Circuit upheld the conviction because the government made a good faith effort to locate the witness for trial by sending letters to the witness's lawyer and offering money for travel expenses. More importantly, the defendant presumably had the opportunity to cross-examine the witness at the deposition, thus resolving any potential Confrontation Clause problem. 657 F. App'x 704, 705 (9th Cir. 2016).

PROBLEM CASE

Andrea Bloodworth was stopped by police during a traffic stop. During the traffic stop, police discovered a firearm. Since Bloodworth had a prior criminal record, he was charged with, and convicted of, possession of a firearm by a felon, in violation of 18 U.S.C. §§ 922(g)(1) et seq. The conviction resulted in a 204-month sentence. Bloodworth appealed and argued that the state had failed to preserve crucial evidence of the traffic stop, which was the key event in the case. Specifically, the state had produced an audio recording of the stop from an automatic recording system on the arresting officer. Prosecutors conceded that the audio recording had existed and was subsequently deleted. However, prosecutors contended that the recording was automatically deleted as part of the recording system's data retention protocol. The system keeps a certain number of recordings but due to storage recordings, older recordings are automatically deleted as new recordings are produced. Did the police department have a duty to preserve the evidence? Is the data retention policy constitutionally problematic? See *United States v. Bloodworth*, 412 F. App'x 639, 640 (4th Cir. 2011).

D. PRACTICE & POLICY

Discovery rules are meaningless if they are not followed by prosecutors (and defense attorneys too). The best way to ensure that discovery rules are followed is to develop a system of enforcement. Although defense attorneys complain repeatedly that discovery obligations are underenforced, an evaluation of that claim, and weighing potential remedies, requires an objective assessment of the current methods of enforcement. These include exclusion of the evidence, professional ethics, sanctions imposed by trial judges, and even criminal sanctions. This range of enforcement measures applies regardless of whether the discovery rule flows from *Brady* and its progeny or whether the discovery rule flows from statute.

❧ **Exclusion of evidence.** Violation of the prosecution's *Brady* obligations permits but does not require the court to exclude the evidence. However, the possibility of exclusion provides a built-in incentive for the prosecution to comply with its discovery obligations. Similarly, the possibility that the defense might be precluded from introducing alibi evidence provides a strong incentive for the defense to comply with its discovery obligations in this area. But suppression of evidence is not guaranteed after a discovery violation. For example, in *United States v. Golyansky*, the prosecution violated its discovery obligations by initially withholding information about the mental health history of a prosecution witness. The trial court judge responded by excluding the evidence from trial. On appeal, the Tenth Circuit noted that the proper sanction analysis should consider the following factors: "(1) the reasons the government delayed producing requested materials, including whether the government acted in bad faith; (2) the extent of prejudice to the defendant as a result of the delay; and (3) the feasibility of curing any prejudice with a continuance." 291 F.3d 1245, 1249 (10th Cir. 2002). The Tenth Circuit concluded that continuance of the trial was an adequate response to cure any potential prejudice to the defendant, because it would give the defense time to prepare its case, and therefore suppression of the evidence was unnecessary. For other examples where suppression was declared inappropriate as a remedy, see *People v. Lee*, 18 P.3d 192 (Colo. 2001) (noting that "in the absence of willful misconduct or a pattern of neglect demonstrating a need for modification of a party's discovery practices, the rationale for a deterrent sanction loses much of its force. . . . [T]he need to find the truth is the paramount interest at stake."); *People v. Daley*, 97 P.3d 295 (Colo. Ct. App. 2004) ("A trial court should avoid excluding evidence because 'the attendant windfall to the party against whom such evidence would have been offered defeats, rather than furthers, the objectives of discovery.'"). Consequently, there is a large class of discovery violations for which suppression is not a viable method of enforcement.

❧ **Ethical obligations.** In addition to statutory and constitutional requirements for discovery, the ABA Model Rules codify a prosecutor's ethical duty to turn over relevant evidence to the defense. For example, consider the following provision:

> The prosecutor in a criminal case shall . . . (d) make timely disclosure to the defense of all evidence or information known to the prosecutor that tends to negate the guilt of the accused or mitigates the offense, and, in connection with sentencing, disclose to the defense and to the tribunal all unprivileged mitigating information known to the prosecutor, except when the prosecutor is relieved of this responsibility by a protective order of the tribunal. . . .

Model Rule 3.8(d). Similarly, ABA Criminal Justice Standards for the Prosecution Function state:

> (a) After charges are filed if not before, the prosecutor should diligently seek to identify all information in the possession of the prosecution or its agents that tends to negate the guilt of the accused, mitigate the offense charged, impeach the government's witnesses or evidence, or reduce the likely punishment of the accused if convicted. . . .
> (c) Before trial of a criminal case, a prosecutor should make timely disclosure to the defense of information described in (a) above that is known to the prosecutor, regardless of whether the prosecutor believes it is likely to change the result of the proceeding, unless relieved of this responsibility by a court's protective order. A prosecutor should not intentionally attempt to obscure information disclosed pursuant to this standard by including it without identification within a larger volume of materials.

Standard 3-5.4.

Courts have generally upheld ethics sanctions against prosecutors. For example, in 2012, the Supreme Court of North Dakota considered a state disciplinary board's 60-day suspension of an assistant district attorney who withheld evidence in a criminal case. In the course of a fraud prosecution of a state employee regarding expense reimbursements, the prosecutor asked a state auditor to produce a memorandum. However, the prosecutor failed to turn over the memorandum to the defense. An appeals court refused to order a new trial because it concluded that the prosecutor had an open file policy and the defendant was unable to show that he was prejudiced by the discovery violation. Nonetheless, a state bar hearing committee found that the prosecution had violated North Dakota's Rules for Professional Conduct, which required disclosure, and imposed the 60-day suspension. The Supreme Court of North Dakota concluded that the ethics rules were stricter than both state and constitutional law, and that the prosecutor could be found to have acted unethically even if the defendant was not prejudiced by the violation. The court also concluded that the ethics rule "is not limited to a prosecutor's intentional failure to disclose exculpatory evidence, but also applies to a knowing or negligent failure to disclose." *In re Disciplinary Action Against Feland*, 2012 ND 174, ¶ 25, 820 N.W.2d 672, 681. Ultimately, given the limited nature of the violation, the Supreme Court overturned the suspension in favor of a formal "admonition" of the attorney. In short, state ethics proceedings can, in theory, punish discovery violations that do not meet the standard of "prejudice" needed to suppress evidence at trial.

❧ **Sanctions imposed by trial judges.** Prosecutors can get into serious trouble for violating their *Brady* obligations. In many cases, judges will hold prosecutors in contempt of court for violating disclosure obligations. New York has a court policy document that aims to encourage trial court judges to exercise this option. It states:

> Courts should adopt a form document to be issued by trial courts in criminal cases regarding certain disclosure obligations of the prosecuting authority and to provide recommended language for that document. . . . The order should provide that only willful and deliberate conduct will constitute a violation of the order or be eligible for personal sanctions against a prosecutor.

John W. McConnell, Request for Public Comment on Proposed Model Orders Regarding Disclosure Obligations of Prosecutors and Defense

Counsel in Criminal Matters, Appendix A: Summary of Recommendations Regarding Attorney Responsibility in Criminal Cases, April 6, 2017.

What sanctions might a trial judge impose when a prosecutor is held in contempt for violating a judge's discovery order? Consider the case of *Commonwealth v. Carney*, 458 Mass. 418, 419, 938 N.E.2d 866, 869 (2010). The trial judge in the case granted the defense's request for an order directing the prosecutors to grant a right of inspection to the key evidence seized in the case, namely a pistol, bullets, and a bag of marijuana. After finding that the prosecution and police failed to adhere to the requirements of the judge's order, the judge imposed punitive sanctions of $25,000 against the state. On appeal, the sanctions were reversed, not just because the appellate court concluded that there was no violation of the discovery order, but also because sanctions for discovery violations under the Massachusetts state discovery statute should be remedial rather than punitive. While it can often be difficult to distinguish between punitive and remedial sanctions, it is clear that the $25,000 fine was punitive rather than remedial. Remedial sanctions are inherently forward-looking and are designed to induce compliance. On the other hand, punitive sanctions are designed to punish individuals for past behavior, which is far less common with regard to discovery violations.

❧ **Criminal charges for discovery violations.** While it is certainly true that punitive sanctions for discovery violations are generally disfavored, there are notable exceptions. For example, California has passed a statute making severe disclosure violations a crime:

> A prosecuting attorney who intentionally and in bad faith alters, modifies, or withholds any physical matter, digital image, video recording, or relevant exculpatory material or information, knowing that it is relevant and material to the outcome of the case, with the specific intent that the physical matter, digital image, video recording, or relevant exculpatory material or information will be concealed or destroyed, or fraudulently represented as the original evidence upon a trial, proceeding, or inquiry, is guilty of a felony punishable by imprisonment . . . for 16 months, or two or three years.

Cal. Penal Code § 141. Should prosecutors face criminal charges for violating their *Brady* obligations? Or does the statute impose draconian consequences for violations that could be cured by one of the other enforcement mechanisms described above? For a discussion of this and similar statutes, see Jodi Nafzger, *Leveling Felony Charges at Prosecutors for Withholding Evidence*, 66 Drake L. Rev. 307, 313 (2018). Are there other solutions to the problem of enforcing discovery statutes? As one commentator noted regarding the general problem of enforcement:

> The increasing frustration of trial court judges with criminal discovery is the strongest evidence yet that criminal discovery must be reformed. When judges begin to complain, and more importantly, begin looking for alternative ways to achieve justice, it is time for rule makers to take notice.

Beth Brennan & Andrew King-Ries, *A Fall from Grace:* United States v. W.R. Grace *and the Need for Criminal Discovery Reform*, 20 Cornell J.L. & Pub. Pol'y 313, 359 (2010).

CHAPTER 13

NEGOTIATED JUSTICE

INTRODUCTION

A guilty plea can result from a negotiated plea bargain or simply a capitulation by the defendant and a full acceptance of responsibility (or resignation to an anticipated guilty verdict). It is often said that our current justice system would collapse without plea bargaining—the voluntary resolution of criminal cases through negotiation. While that is certainly true, it is important not to fall victim to the naturalistic fallacy—to assume, as it were, that how the system works today is how it should always work. Although a world with fewer plea bargains would be burdensome, the criminal justice system could certainly evolve to accommodate an increase in cases. Furthermore, even assuming that plea bargaining should continue, many questions remain about when plea bargains are appropriate, how they should be conducted, and when they should be enforced.

The constitutional requirements for pleading guilty flow from two distinct sources and it is important to keep them separate: the Fifth Amendment requirement of due process of law, which requires voluntariness and lack of coercion before the right to a jury trial is waived, and the Sixth Amendment requirement of counsel at critical stages of the process, which entails not just the assignment of counsel in a generic sense but also the *effective* assistance of counsel. If a defendant pleads guilty without the benefit of competent counsel advising him or her about the consequences of that decision, the Sixth Amendment (and by extension the Fourteenth Amendment) is violated.

Ideally, plea bargains would produce results that are factually correct. In other words, one goal of the criminal process is to ensure that only the guilty plead guilty while the innocent plead not guilty and are acquitted at trial. But there are other goals as well, including a fair process: Suspects and defendants should have access to the information and resources that are necessary to make an informed decision about pleading guilty. So, for example, defendants at trial should have access to at least some discovery information in order to make an informed decision and should have the benefit of effective assistance of counsel when evaluating a potential plea deal. Nonetheless, despite these and other procedural protections, it is undeniable that factually innocent defendants sometimes plead guilty.

The following sections focus on (a) the validity of plea bargains and the constitutional and statutory constraints placed on them; (b) the constitutional and statutory requirements for pleading guilty and waiving a jury trial; and (c) enforcing plea bargains, most notably when one party backs and out and reneges on the deal.

A. PLEA BARGAINS

The plea bargain represents an indelible part of the criminal justice system that is, nonetheless, somewhat difficult to integrate into the conceptual framework of criminal law and procedure. Typically, the paradigm for criminal justice is either a defendant who pleads guilty and, pursuant to an admission of guilt under oath during the plea is then found guilty by the court; or a defendant who is found guilty by the trier of fact (usually a jury or perhaps a judge if the defendant has voluntarily selected a bench trial) based on a determination that the prosecution has proven each material element of an offense beyond a reasonable doubt. It is important to note, however, that a plea of guilty is not the same as a finding of guilt. Ultimately, whether based on a guilty plea or as the result of a contested trial, there must be a finding of guilt that overcomes the presumption of innocence. Either way, the determination of guilt is made upon the hearing of the evidence. With a guilty plea, that evidence is typically the defendant's own admission under oath (although not always). With a plea of not guilty, in contrast, the evidence is presented at trial and then weighed by judicial or jury deliberation to determine if the prosecutor has demonstrated proof beyond a reasonable doubt as to each element of the offense.

Plea bargaining short-circuits the contested trial process. It is a form of negotiated justice that flows from a bilateral agreement rather than the bilateral contestation that typically comes to mind when one thinks of the adversarial process. The negotiated solution is a form of agreement that one might associate, more typically, with the field of contracts. The existence of a negotiated solution raises a host of difficult doctrinal and constitutional questions about the background requirements for these agreements. Must there be an equal playing field for the negotiated result to be legitimate? What if negotiations break down and the prosecutor decides to proceed to trial again? What if the statute only allows the maximum penalty if the defendant is convicted at trial, but removes that possibility if the defendant pleads guilty? Does such a scheme violate the constitutional requirements that a decision to plead guilty must be made voluntarily and without coercion?

STATUTORY REQUIREMENTS

Some of these questions are answered by state and federal statutes governing plea bargaining, but the floor is provided by the constitutional protections. The statutes can extend greater protections than those provided by the Constitution but obviously cannot abrogate them. To take a typical example, Rule 11 of the Federal Rules of Criminal Procedure lays out the requirements for a plea bargain:

> An attorney for the government and the defendant's attorney, or the defendant when proceeding pro se, may discuss and reach a plea agreement. The court must not participate in these discussions. If the defendant pleads guilty or nolo contendere to either a charged offense or a lesser or related offense, the plea agreement may specify that an attorney for the government will:
>
> (A) not bring, or will move to dismiss, other charges;
>
> (B) recommend, or agree not to oppose the defendant's request, that a particular sentence or sentencing range is appropriate or that a particular provision of the Sentencing Guidelines, or policy statement, or sentencing factor does or does not apply (such a recommendation or request does not bind the court); or
>
> (C) agree that a specific sentence or sentencing range is the appropriate disposition of the case, or that a particular provision of the Sentencing Guidelines, or policy statement, or sentencing factor does or does not apply (such a recommendation or request binds the court once the court accepts the plea agreement).

Rule 11 then lays out the process for what happens next if a plea agreement is reached:

> (2) Disclosing a Plea Agreement. The parties must disclose the plea agreement in open court when the plea is offered, unless the court for good cause allows the parties to disclose the plea agreement in camera.
>
> (3) Judicial Consideration of a Plea Agreement.
>
> (A) To the extent the plea agreement is of the type specified in Rule 11(c)(1)(A) or (C), the court may accept the agreement, reject it, or defer a decision until the court has reviewed the presentence report.
>
> (B) To the extent the plea agreement is of the type specified in Rule 11(c)(1)(B), the court must advise the defendant that the defendant has no right to withdraw the plea if the court does not follow the recommendation or request.

Also, even when the defense and prosecution enter into a plea agreement, that court retains some discretion to either accept or reject the plea bargain:

> (4) Accepting a Plea Agreement. If the court accepts the plea agreement, it must inform the defendant that to the extent the plea agreement is of the type

specified in Rule 11(c)(1)(A) or (C), the agreed disposition will be included in the judgment.

(5) Rejecting a Plea Agreement. If the court rejects a plea agreement containing provisions of the type specified in Rule 11(c)(1)(A) or (C), the court must do the following on the record and in open court (or, for good cause, in camera):

(A) inform the parties that the court rejects the plea agreement;

(B) advise the defendant personally that the court is not required to follow the plea agreement and give the defendant an opportunity to withdraw the plea; and

(C) advise the defendant personally that if the plea is not withdrawn, the court may dispose of the case less favorably toward the defendant than the plea agreement contemplated.

The following subsections discuss the constitutional considerations regarding the practice of plea bargaining, including constraints on capital plea bargains; whether plea bargaining is inherently coercive and therefore unconstitutional; and prosecutorial threats to pursue harsher charges if plea bargain negotiations fail. Although these materials focus on the practice of negotiated justice on the ground, they also implicate the deepest conceptual tension about negotiated justice: What room is there for negotiated solutions in a system built around the adversarial process?

1. Constraints on Capital Plea Bargains

The following case presents a particular constitutional riddle caused by the specific conditions that a federal statute outlined for the imposition of the death penalty in a federal kidnapping case. The statute stipulated that capital punishment could only be imposed by jury *verdict*; this suggested, by implication, that pleading guilty would automatically exempt the defendant from the possibility of the death penalty. This created an "incentive" for risk-averse defendants to plead guilty. Did this legislative scheme impermissibly coerce defendants into pleading guilty in order to avoid the possibility of the death penalty?

United States v. Jackson

Supreme Court of the United States
390 U.S. 570 (1968)

Mr. Justice STEWART delivered the opinion of the Court.

The Federal Kidnaping Act provides:

"Whoever knowingly transports in interstate . . . commerce, any person who has been unlawfully . . . kidnaped . . . and held for ransom . . . or otherwise . . . shall be punished (1) by death if the kidnaped person has not been liberated unharmed, and if the verdict of the jury shall so recommend, or (2) by imprisonment for any term of years or for life, if the death penalty is not imposed."

This statute thus creates an offense punishable by death "if the verdict of the jury shall so recommend." The statute sets forth no procedure for imposing the death penalty upon a defendant who waives the right to jury trial or upon one who pleads guilty.

On October 10, 1966, a federal grand jury in Connecticut returned an indictment charging in count one that three named defendants, the appellees in this case, had transported from Connecticut to New Jersey a person who had been kidnaped and held for ransom and who had been harmed when liberated. The District Court dismissed this count of the indictment, holding the Federal Kidnaping Act unconstitutional because it makes "the risk of death" the price for asserting the right to jury trial, and thereby "impairs . . . free exercise" of that constitutional right. The Government appealed directly to this Court, and we noted probable jurisdiction. We reverse.

We agree with the District Court that the death penalty provision of the Federal Kidnaping Act imposes an impermissible burden upon the exercise of a constitutional right, but we think that provision is severable from the remainder of the statute. There is no reason to invalidate the law in its entirety simply because its capital punishment clause violates the Constitution. The District Court therefore erred in dismissing the kidnaping count of the indictment. . . .

II

Under the Federal Kidnaping Act, therefore, the defendant who abandons the right to contest his guilt before a jury is assured that he cannot be executed; the defendant ingenuous enough to seek a jury acquittal stands forewarned that, if the jury finds him guilty and does not wish to spare his life, he will die. Our problem is to decide whether the Constitution permits the establishment of such a death penalty, applicable only to those defendants who assert the right to contest their guilt before a jury. The inevitable effect of any such provision, is of course, to discourage assertion of the Fifth Amendment right not to plead guilty and to deter exercise of the Sixth Amendment right to demand a jury trial. If the provision had no other purpose or effect than to chill the assertion of constitutional rights by penalizing those who choose to exercise them, then it would be patently unconstitutional. But, as the Government notes, limiting the death penalty to cases where the jury recommends its imposition does have another objective: It avoids the more drastic alternative of mandatory capital punishment in every case. In this sense, the selective death penalty procedure established by the Federal Kidnaping Act may be viewed as ameliorating the severity of the more extreme punishment that Congress might have wished to provide.

The Government suggests that, because the Act thus operates "to mitigate the severity of punishment," it is irrelevant that it "may have the incidental effect of inducing defendants not to contest in full measure." We cannot agree. Whatever might be said of Congress' objectives, they cannot be pursued by means that needlessly chill the exercise of basic constitutional rights. The question is not whether the chilling effect is "incidental" rather than intentional; the question is whether that effect is unnecessary and therefore excessive. In this case the answer to that question is clear. The Congress can of course mitigate the severity of capital punishment. The goal of limiting the death penalty to cases in which a jury recommends it is an entirely legitimate one. But that goal can be achieved without penalizing those defendants who plead not guilty and demand jury trial. In some States, for example, the choice between life imprisonment and capital punishment is left to a jury in every case—regardless of how the defendant's guilt has been determined. Given the availability of this and other alternatives, it is clear that the selective death penalty provision of the Federal Kidnaping Act cannot be justified by its ostensible purpose. Whatever the power of Congress to impose a death penalty for violation of the Federal Kidnaping Act, Congress cannot impose such a penalty in a manner that needlessly penalizes the assertion of a constitutional right.

It is no answer to urge, as does the Government, that federal trial judges may be relied upon to reject coerced pleas of guilty and involuntary waivers of jury trial. For the evil in the federal statute is not that it necessarily coerces guilty pleas and jury waivers but simply that it needlessly encourages them. A procedure need not be inherently coercive in order that it be held to impose an impermissible burden upon the assertion of a constitutional right. Thus the fact that the Federal Kidnaping Act tends to discourage defendants from insisting upon their innocence and demanding trial by jury hardly implies that every defendant who enters a guilty plea to a charge under the Act does so involuntarily. The power to reject coerced guilty pleas and involuntary jury waivers might alleviate, but it cannot totally eliminate, the constitutional infirmity in the capital punishment provision of the Federal Kidnaping Act.

The Government alternatively proposes that this Court, in the exercise of its supervisory powers, should simply instruct federal judges sitting in kidnaping cases to reject all attempts to waive jury trial and all efforts to plead guilty, however voluntary and well-informed such attempted waivers and pleas might be. In that way, we could assure that every defendant charged in a federal court with aggravated kidnaping would face a possible death penalty, and that no defendant tried under the federal statute would be induced to forgo a constitutional right. But of course the inevitable consequence of this "solution" would be to force all defendants to submit to trial, however clear their guilt and however strong their desire to acknowledge it in order to spare themselves and their families the spectacle and expense of protracted courtroom proceedings. It is true that a defendant has no constitutional right to insist that he be tried by a judge rather than a jury and it is also true "that a criminal defendant has (no) absolute right to have his guilty plea accepted by the court." But the fact that jury waivers and guilty pleas may occasionally be rejected hardly implies that all defendants may be required to submit to a full-dress jury trial as a matter of course. Quite apart from the cruel impact of such a requirement upon those defendants who would greatly prefer not to contest their guilt, it is clear—as even the Government recognizes—that the automatic rejection of all guilty pleas "would rob the criminal process of much of its flexibility." As one federal court has observed:

> The power of a court to accept a plea of guilty is traditional and fundamental. Its existence is necessary for the . . . practical . . . administration of the criminal law. Consequently, it should require an unambiguous expression on the part of the Congress to withhold this authority in specified cases.

If any such approach should be inaugurated in the administration of a federal criminal statute, we conclude that the impetus must come from Congress, not from this Court. The capital punishment provision of the Federal Kidnaping Act cannot be saved by judicial reconstruction. . . .

NOTES & QUESTIONS ON CAPITAL PLEA BARGAINS

1. *Factual innocence.* Why would factually innocent defendants plead guilty to a crime that they did not commit? This question is particularly vexing in the case of capital defendants who might plead guilty and accept a life sentence in order to avoid a death sentence. Professor John Blume and Rebecca Helm offer the following summary of the reasons why innocent defendants plead guilty:

> First, innocent persons charged with relatively minor offenses often plead guilty in order to get out of jail, to avoid the hassle of having criminal charges hanging over their heads, or to avoid being punished for exercising their right to trial. Second, defendants who were wrongfully convicted, but have

> their conviction vacated on direct appeal or in post-conviction review proceedings, plead guilty to receive a sentence of time served and obtain their immediate (or at least imminent) freedom. Third, some innocent defendants plead guilty due to the fear of a harsh alternative punishment, e.g., the death penalty.

John H. Blume & Rebecca K. Helm, *The Unexonerated: Factually Innocent Defendants Who Plead Guilty*, 100 Cornell L. Rev. 157, 173 (2014). With this information in hand, how would you revise plea bargaining procedures to reduce the risk of "false" guilty pleas? Although capital defendants often receive the greatest attention, consider those defendants who fall in the first category: those charged with minor offenses who have no jury trial right. Would expanding the offenses eligible for jury trial reduce this problem?

STATE LAW REQUIREMENTS

Some state death penalty statutes have confronted the same problem and generally speaking state courts have applied the result in *Jackson* to those statutes as well. For example, in 1995, the New York State legislature reintroduced capital punishment in the state. The statute barred the imposition of the death penalty after a guilty plea, effectively requiring a jury verdict in order for capital punishment to be applied. As the New York State Court of Appeals observed, the statute imposed the death penalty "only on those who assert innocence and proceed to trial." *Hynes v. Tomei*, 92 N.Y.2d 613, 620, 706 N.E.2d 1201, 1203 (1998).

Applying the rule from *Jackson*, the New York State Court of Appeals concluded that the state death penalty statute could not survive constitutional scrutiny. The N.Y. statute included the following provisions:

> A defendant may not enter a plea of guilty to the crime of murder in the first degree . . . provided, however, that a defendant may enter such a plea with both the permission of the court and the consent of the people when the agreed upon sentence is either life imprisonment without parole or a term of imprisonment . . . other than a sentence of life imprisonment without parole.

State prosecutors argued that the provision functioned to merely "codify permissible plea bargaining." They also argued that the statute also provided for bifurcated proceedings. The Court rejected both arguments, concluding that "bifurcation does not eliminate the statutory framework that allows the possibility of death only after a jury trial" and that "defendants under the New York statute who are awaiting trial and are offered a plea are still faced with the choice *Jackson* declared unconstitutional: exercise Fifth and Sixth Amendment rights and risk death, or abandon those rights and avoid the possibility of death." *Id.* at 626, 706 N.E.2d at 1207.

Do you agree that in order for a death penalty statute to be constitutional, it must preserve the option of imposing the death penalty on those defendants who plead guilty? Does it sound perverse to require that a statute *increase* the categories of individuals who face capital punishment?

2. Is Plea Bargaining Constitutional?

The *Jackson* holding pertains to capital punishment, but it articulates a particular vision of voluntariness and coercion that could, in theory, be extended to cover all cases of plea bargaining. In *Jackson*, the fact that the defendants were faced with the possibility of either pleading guilty and receiving a lesser punishment or pleading not guilty and risking the death penalty convinced the Supreme Court that the statute was unconstitutional. What then of all plea bargains? In any plea bargain, the defendant pleads guilty in exchange for consideration, which is usually a lesser sentence. If the defendant refuses to plead guilty and instead asserts his or her innocence at trial, the defendant runs the risk of a greater punishment, perhaps even a draconian one. Does this fact entail that *all* plea bargains are inherently coercive and involuntary? In the following case, the Supreme Court considers this exact question. What hangs in the balance is a practice—plea bargaining—that sits at the core of the criminal justice system.

Brady v. United States

Supreme Court of the United States
397 U.S. 742 (1970)

Mr. Justice WHITE delivered the opinion of the Court.

In 1959, petitioner was charged with kidnaping. . . . Since the indictment charged that the victim of the kidnaping was not liberated unharmed, petitioner faced a maximum penalty of death if the verdict of the jury should so recommend. Petitioner, represented by competent counsel throughout, first elected to plead not guilty. Apparently because the trial judge was unwilling to try the case without a jury, petitioner made no serious attempt to reduce the possibility of a death penalty by waiving a jury trial. Upon learning that his codefendant, who had confessed to the authorities, would plead guilty and be available to testify against him, petitioner changed his plea to guilty. His plea was accepted after the trial judge twice questioned him as to the voluntariness of his plea. Petitioner was sentenced to 50 years' imprisonment, later reduced to 30.

In 1967, petitioner sought relief . . . claiming that his plea of guilty was not voluntarily given because [the statute] operated to coerce his plea, because his counsel exerted impermissible pressure upon him, and because his plea was induced by representations with respect to reduction of sentence and clemency. . . .

I

In *United States v. Jackson* . . . the District Court . . . [held] the statute unconstitutional because it permitted imposition of the death sentence only upon a jury's recommendation and thereby made the risk of death the price of a jury trial. This Court held the statute valid, except for the death penalty provision; with respect to the latter, the Court agreed with the trial court "that the death penalty provision . . . imposes an impermissible burden upon the exercise of a constitutional right. . . ." The problem was to determine "whether the Constitution permits the establishment of such a death penalty, applicable only to those defendants who assert the right to contest their guilt before a jury." The inevitable effect of the provision was said to be to discourage assertion of the Fifth Amendment right not to plead guilty and to deter exercise of the Sixth Amendment right to demand a jury trial. Because the legitimate goal of limiting the death penalty to cases in which a jury recommends it could be achieved without penalizing those defendants who plead not guilty and elect a jury trial, the death penalty provision "needlessly penalize(d) the assertion of a constitutional right," and was therefore unconstitutional.

Since the "inevitable effect" of the death penalty provision . . . was said by the Court to be the needless encouragement of pleas of guilty and waivers of jury trial, Brady contends that *Jackson* requires the invalidation of every plea of guilty entered under that section, at least when the fear of death is shown to have been a factor in the plea. Petitioner, however, has read far too much into the *Jackson* opinion.

The Court made it clear in *Jackson* that it was not holding [the statute] inherently coercive of guilty pleas: "the fact that the Federal Kidnaping Act tends to discourage defendants from insisting upon their innocence and demanding trial by jury hardly implies that every defendant who enters a guilty plea to a charge under the Act does so involuntarily."

Moreover, the Court in *Jackson* rejected a suggestion that the death penalty provision . . . be saved by prohibiting in capital kidnaping cases all guilty pleas and jury waivers, "however clear (the defendants') guilt and however strong their desire to acknowledge it in order to spare themselves and their families the spectacle and expense of protracted courtroom proceedings." "(T)hat jury waivers and guilty pleas may occasionally be rejected" was no ground for automatically rejecting all guilty pleas under the statute, for such a rule "would rob the criminal process of much of its flexibility."

Plainly, it seems to us, *Jackson* ruled neither that all pleas of guilty encouraged by the fear of a possible death sentence are involuntary pleas nor that such encouraged pleas are invalid whether involuntary or not. *Jackson* prohibits the imposition of the death penalty . . . but that decision neither fashioned a new standard for judging the validity of guilty pleas nor mandated a new application of the test theretofore fashioned by courts and since reiterated that guilty pleas are valid if both "voluntary" and "intelligent."

That a guilty plea is a grave and solemn act to be accepted only with care and discernment has long been recognized. Central to the plea and the foundation for entering judgment against the defendant is the defendant's admission in open court that he committed the acts charged in the indictment. He thus stands as a witness against himself and he is shielded by the Fifth Amendment from being compelled to do so—hence the minimum requirement that his plea be the voluntary expression of his own choice. But the plea is more than an admission of past conduct; it is the defendant's consent that judgment of conviction may be entered without a trial—a waiver of his right to trial before a jury or a judge. Waivers of constitutional rights not only must be voluntary but must be knowing, intelligent acts done with sufficient awareness of the relevant circumstances and likely consequences. On neither score was Brady's plea of guilty invalid.

II

The trial judge in 1959 found the plea voluntary before accepting it; the District Court in 1968, after an evidentiary hearing, found that the plea was voluntarily made; the Court of Appeals specifically approved the finding of voluntariness. We see no reason on this record to disturb the judgment of those courts. Petitioner, advised by competent counsel, tendered his plea after his codefendant, who had already given a confession, determined to plead guilty and became available to testify against petitioner. It was this development that the District Court found to have triggered Brady's guilty plea.

The voluntariness of Brady's plea can be determined only by considering all of the relevant circumstances surrounding it. One of these circumstances was the possibility of a heavier sentence following a guilty verdict after a trial. It may be that Brady, faced with a strong case against him and recognizing that his chances for acquittal were slight, preferred to plead guilty and thus limit the penalty to life imprisonment rather than to elect a jury trial which could result in a death penalty. But even if we assume that Brady would not have pleaded guilty except for the death penalty provision of [the statute], this assumption merely identifies the penalty provision as a "but for" cause of his plea. That the statute caused the plea in this sense does not necessarily prove that the plea was coerced and invalid as an involuntary act.

The State to some degree encourages pleas of guilty at every important step in the criminal process. For some people, their breach of a State's law is alone sufficient reason for surrendering themselves and accepting punishment. For others, apprehension and charge, both threatening acts by the Government, jar them into admitting their guilt. In still other cases, the post-indictment accumulation of evidence may convince the defendant and his counsel that a trial is not worth the agony and expense to the defendant and his family. All these pleas of guilty are valid in spite of the State's responsibility for some of the factors motivating the pleas; the pleas are no more improperly compelled than is the decision by a defendant at the close of the State's evidence at trial that he must take the stand or face certain conviction.

Of course, the agents of the State may not produce a plea by actual or threatened physical harm or by mental coercion overbearing the will of the defendant. But nothing of the sort is claimed in this case; nor is there evidence that Brady was so gripped by fear of the death penalty or hope of leniency that he did not or could not, with the help of counsel, rationally weigh the advantages of going to trial against the advantages of pleading guilty. Brady's claim is of a different sort: that it violates the Fifth Amendment to influence or encourage a guilty plea by opportunity or promise of leniency and that a guilty plea is coerced and invalid if influenced by the fear of a possibly higher penalty for the crime charged if a conviction is obtained after the State is put to its proof.

Insofar as the voluntariness of his plea is concerned, there is little to differentiate Brady from (1) the defendant, in a jurisdiction where the judge and jury have the same range of sentencing power, who pleads guilty because his lawyer advises him that the judge will very probably be more lenient than the jury; (2) the defendant, in a jurisdiction where the judge alone has sentencing power, who is advised by counsel that the judge is normally more lenient with defendants who plead guilty than with those who go to trial; (3) the defendant who is permitted by prosecutor and judge to plead guilty to a lesser offense included in the offense charged; and (4) the defendant who pleads guilty to certain counts with the understanding that other charges will be dropped. In each of these situations, as in Brady's case, the defendant might never plead guilty absent the possibility or certainty that the plea will result in a lesser penalty than the sentence that could be imposed after a trial and a verdict of guilty. We decline to hold, however, that a guilty plea is compelled and invalid under the Fifth Amendment whenever motivated by the defendant's desire to accept the certainty or probability of a lesser penalty rather than face a wider range of possibilities extending from acquittal to conviction and a higher penalty authorized by law for the crime charged.

The issue we deal with is inherent in the criminal law and its administration because guilty pleas are not constitutionally forbidden, because the criminal law characteristically extends to judge or jury a range of choice in setting the sentence in individual cases, and because both the State and the defendant often find it advantageous to preclude the possibility of the maximum penalty authorized by law. For a defendant who sees slight possibility of acquittal, the advantages of pleading guilty and limiting the probable penalty are obvious—his exposure is reduced, the correctional processes can begin immediately, and the practical burdens of a trial are eliminated. For the State there are also advantages—the more promptly imposed punishment after an admission of guilt may more effectively attain the objectives of punishment; and with the avoidance of trial, scarce judicial and prosecutorial resources are conserved for those cases in which there is a substantial issue of the defendant's guilt or in which there is substantial doubt that the State can sustain its burden of proof. It is this mutuality of advantage that perhaps explains the fact that at present well over three-fourths of the criminal convictions in this country rest on pleas of guilty, a great many of them no doubt motivated at least in part by the hope or assurance of a lesser penalty than might be imposed if there were a guilty verdict after a trial to judge or jury.

Of course, that the prevalence of guilty pleas is explainable does not necessarily validate those pleas or the system which produces them. But we cannot hold that it is unconstitutional for the State to extend a benefit to a defendant who in turn extends a substantial benefit to the State and who demonstrates by his plea that he is ready and willing to admit his crime and to enter the correctional system in a frame of mind that affords hope for success in rehabilitation over a shorter period of time than might otherwise be necessary.

A contrary holding would require the States and Federal Government to forbid guilty pleas altogether, to provide a single invariable penalty for each crime defined by the statutes, or to place the sentencing function in a separate authority having no knowledge of the manner in which the conviction in each case was obtained. In any event, it would be necessary to forbid prosecutors and judges to accept guilty pleas to selected counts, to lesser included offenses, or to reduced charges. The Fifth Amendment does not reach so far. . . .

Under this standard, a plea of guilty is not invalid merely because entered to avoid the possibility of a death penalty. . . .

NOTES & QUESTIONS ON THE CONSTITUTIONALITY OF PLEA BARGAINING

1. *The balance of power.* Do defendants and prosecutors enjoy a level playing field such that their negotiations—and their resulting plea bargains—are fundamentally fair? Consider the following assessment:

> [T]o threaten defendants with harsher punishment if convicted at trial (the trial tax) is tantamount to a use of legal force that by no measure of reasoned consideration can be viewed as "consensual." Because the conditions on benefits in plea settings rely upon a distorted and . . . intellectually dishonest interpretation of consent by ignoring the power imbalances existing

> between defendants and prosecutors, and because of the force that is available to prosecutors to severely restrict or eliminate liberty, plea-bargaining amounts to an unconstitutional condition that violates the Bill of Rights.

Dr. Robert Schehr, *The Emperor's New Clothes: Intellectual Dishonesty and the Unconstitutionality of Plea-Bargaining*, 2 Tex. A&M L. Rev. 385, 429-30 (2015). Do you agree with the author's assertion that defendants have little power and therefore do not consent to plea bargains in any meaningful sense? Would a criminal justice system without plea bargains better protect the rights of defendants?

2. *The right to counsel.* As we saw in prior chapters, the right to counsel includes the right to effective assistance of counsel. That is important not just in trial situations but also during plea negotiations. The role of competent counsel is not just to represent the client at trial but to also advise the client of the best course of action. Sometimes that means accepting a plea deal and lowering one's criminal exposure. In other situations, it means risking a higher punishment by going to trial and seeking exoneration. While it is the defendant who must serve the prison sentence, it is the counsel who has the judgment and experience to assess the likelihood of prevailing at trial. Consequently, it is impossible to disentangle plea bargaining from the constitutional right to effective assistance of counsel.

3. Threats During Plea Bargaining

What if the prosecutor threatens the defendant with harsher treatment if the defendant fails to accept a plea agreement? Would this compromise the voluntariness of the agreement? In one sense, implicit threats abound in the plea bargaining context, in the sense that prosecutors might naturally pursue more serious punishment against a defendant who fails to accept a plea bargain. However, the following case introduces for our consideration a more specific type of threat. In *Bordenkircher,* the prosecutor threatened to indict the defendant on a more serious charge if the plea bargain was not accepted. Then, when the defendant failed to accept the terms of the plea bargain, the prosecutor carried out the threat. Should the Constitution permit such strong-arm tactics?

Bordenkircher v. Hayes

Supreme Court of the United States
434 U.S. 357 (1978)

Mr. Justice Stewart delivered the opinion of the Court.

The question in this case is whether the Due Process Clause of the Fourteenth Amendment is violated when a state prosecutor carries out a threat made during plea negotiations to reindict the accused on more serious charges if he does not plead guilty to the offense with which he was originally charged.

I

The respondent, Paul Lewis Hayes, was indicted by a Fayette County, Ky., grand jury on a charge of uttering a forged instrument in the amount of $88.30, an offense then punishable by a term of 2 to 10 years in prison. After arraignment, Hayes, his retained counsel, and the Commonwealth's Attorney met in the presence of the Clerk of the Court to discuss a possible plea agreement. During these conferences the prosecutor offered to recommend a sentence of five years in prison if Hayes would plead guilty to the indictment. He also said that if Hayes did not plead guilty and "save[d] the court the inconvenience and necessity of a trial," he would return to the grand jury to seek an indictment under the Kentucky Habitual Criminal Act, which would subject Hayes to a mandatory sentence of life imprisonment by reason of his two prior felony convictions. Hayes chose not to plead guilty, and the prosecutor did obtain an indictment charging him under the Habitual Criminal Act. It is not disputed that the recidivist charge was fully justified by the evidence, that the prosecutor was in possession of this evidence at the time of the original indictment, and that Hayes' refusal to plead guilty to the original charge was what led to his indictment under the habitual criminal statute. . . .

A jury found Hayes guilty on the principal charge of uttering a forged instrument and, in a separate proceeding, further found that he had twice before been convicted of felonies. As required by the habitual offender statute, he was sentenced to a life term in the penitentiary. . . .

II

It may be helpful to clarify at the outset the nature of the issue in this case. While the prosecutor did not actually obtain the recidivist indictment until after the plea conferences had ended, his intention to do so was clearly expressed at the outset of the plea negotiations. Hayes was thus fully informed of the true terms of the offer when he made his decision to plead not guilty. This is not a situation, therefore, where the prosecutor without notice brought an additional and more serious charge after plea negotiations relating only to the original indictment had ended with the defendant's insistence on pleading not guilty. As a practical matter, in short, this case would be no different if the grand jury had indicted Hayes as a recidivist from the outset, and the prosecutor had offered to drop that charge as part of the plea bargain.

The Court of Appeals nonetheless drew a distinction between "concessions relating to prosecution under an existing indictment," and threats to bring more severe charges not contained in the original indictment—a line it thought necessary in order to establish a prophylactic rule to guard against the evil of prosecutorial vindictiveness. Quite apart from this chronological distinction, however, the Court of Appeals found that the prosecutor had acted vindictively in the present case since he had conceded that the indictment was influenced by his desire to induce a guilty plea. The ultimate conclusion of the Court of Appeals thus seems to have been that a prosecutor acts vindictively and in violation of due process of law whenever his charging decision is influenced by what he hopes to gain in the course of plea bargaining negotiations.

III

We have recently had occasion to observe: "[W]hatever might be the situation in an ideal world, the fact is that the guilty plea and the often concomitant plea bargain are important components of this country's criminal justice system. Properly administered, they can benefit all concerned." The open acknowledgment of this previously clandestine practice has led this Court to recognize the importance of counsel during plea negotiations, the need for a public record indicating that a plea was knowingly and voluntarily made, and the requirement that a prosecutor's plea-bargaining promise must be kept. The decision of the Court of Appeals in the present case, however, did not deal with considerations such as these, but held that the substance of the plea offer itself violated the limitations imposed by the Due Process Clause of the Fourteenth Amendment. For the reasons that follow, we have concluded that the Court of Appeals was mistaken in so ruling.

IV

This Court held in *North Carolina v. Pearce*, 395 U.S. 711, 725, that the Due Process Clause of the Fourteenth Amendment "requires that vindictiveness against a defendant for having successfully attacked his first conviction must play no part in the sentence he receives after a new trial." The same principle was later applied to prohibit a prosecutor from reindicting a convicted misdemeanant on a felony charge after the defendant had invoked an appellate remedy, since in this situation there was also a "realistic likelihood of vindictiveness."

In those cases the Court was dealing with the State's unilateral imposition of a penalty upon a defendant who had chosen to exercise a legal right to attack his original conviction—a situation "very different from the give-and-take negotiation common in plea bargaining between the prosecution and defense, which arguably possess relatively equal bargaining power." The Court has emphasized that the due process violation . . . lay not in the possibility that a defendant might be deterred from the exercise of a legal right, but rather in the danger that the State might be retaliating against the accused for lawfully attacking his conviction. *Blackledge v. Perry*, 417 U.S., at 26-28.

To punish a person because he has done what the law plainly allows him to do is a due process violation of the most basic sort and for an agent of the State to pursue a course of action whose objective is to penalize a person's reliance on his legal rights is "patently unconstitutional." But in the "give-and-take" of plea bargaining, there is no such element of punishment or retaliation so long as the accused is free to accept or reject the prosecution's offer.

Plea bargaining flows from "the mutuality of advantage" to defendants and prosecutors, each with his own reasons for wanting to avoid trial. Defendants advised by competent counsel and protected by other procedural safeguards are presumptively capable of intelligent choice in response to prosecutorial persuasion, and unlikely to be driven to false self-condemnation. Indeed, acceptance of the basic legitimacy of plea bargaining necessarily implies rejection of any notion that a guilty plea is involuntary in a constitutional sense simply because it is the end result of the bargaining process. By hypothesis, the plea may have been induced by promises of a recommendation of a lenient sentence or a reduction of charges, and thus by fear of the possibility of a greater penalty upon conviction after a trial.

While confronting a defendant with the risk of more severe punishment clearly may have a "discouraging effect on the defendant's assertion of his trial rights, the imposition of these difficult choices [is] an inevitable"—and permissible—"attribute of any legitimate system which tolerates and encourages the negotiation of pleas." It follows that, by tolerating and encouraging the negotiation of pleas, this Court has necessarily accepted as constitutionally legitimate the simple reality that the prosecutor's interest at the bargaining table is to persuade the defendant to forgo his right to plead not guilty.

It is not disputed here that Hayes was properly chargeable under the recidivist statute, since he had in fact been convicted of two previous felonies. In our system, so long as the prosecutor has probable cause to believe that the accused committed an offense defined by statute, the decision whether or not to prosecute, and what charge to file or bring before a grand jury, generally rests entirely in his discretion. Within the limits set by the legislature's constitutionally valid definition of chargeable offenses, "the conscious exercise of some selectivity in enforcement is not in itself a federal constitutional violation" so long as "the selection was [not] deliberately based upon an unjustifiable standard such as race, religion, or other arbitrary classification." To hold that the prosecutor's desire to induce a guilty plea is an "unjustifiable standard," which, like race or religion, may play no part in his charging decision, would contradict the very premises that underlie the concept of plea bargaining itself. Moreover, a rigid constitutional rule that would prohibit a prosecutor from acting forthrightly in his dealings with the defense could only invite unhealthy subterfuge that would drive the practice of plea bargaining back into the shadows from which it has so recently emerged.

There is no doubt that the breadth of discretion that our country's legal system vests in prosecuting attorneys carries with it the potential for both individual and institutional abuse. And broad though that discretion may be, there are undoubtedly constitutional limits upon its exercise. We hold only that the course of conduct engaged in by the prosecutor in this case, which no more than openly presented the defendant with the unpleasant alternatives of forgoing trial or facing charges on which he was plainly subject to prosecution, did not violate the Due Process Clause of the Fourteenth Amendment.

Mr. Justice BLACKMUN, with whom Mr. Justice BRENNAN and Mr. Justice MARSHALL join, dissenting.

I feel that the Court, although purporting to rule narrowly . . . is departing from, or at least restricting, the principles established in *North Carolina v. Pearce* and in *Blackledge v. Perry*. If those decisions are sound and if those principles are salutary, as I must assume they are, they require, in my view, an affirmance, not a reversal, of the judgment of the Court of Appeals in the present case.

In *Pearce* . . . it was held that "vindictiveness against a defendant for having successfully attacked his first conviction must play no part in the sentence he receives after a new trial." Accordingly, if on the new trial, the sentence the defendant receives from the court is greater than that imposed after the first trial, it must be explained by reasons "based upon objective information concerning identifiable conduct on the part of the defendant occurring after the time of the original sentencing proceeding," other than his having pursued the appeal or collateral remedy. On the other hand, if the sentence is imposed by the jury and not by the court, if the jury is not aware of the original sentence, and if the second sentence is not otherwise shown to be a product of vindictiveness, *Pearce* has no application.

Then later, in *Perry*, the Court applied the same principle to prosecutorial conduct where there was a "realistic likelihood of vindictiveness." It held that the requirement of Fourteenth Amendment due process prevented a prosecutor's reindictment of a convicted misdemeanant on a felony charge after the defendant had exercised his right to appeal the misdemeanor conviction and thus to obtain a trial de novo. It noted the prosecution's "considerable stake" in discouraging the appeal.

The Court now says, however, that this concern with vindictiveness is of no import in the present case, despite the difference between five years in prison and a life sentence, because we are here concerned with plea bargaining where there is give-and-take negotiation, and where, it is said, "there is no such element of punishment or retaliation so long as the accused is free to accept or reject the prosecution's offer." Yet in this case vindictiveness is present to the same extent as it was thought to be in *Pearce* and in *Perry*; the prosecutor here admitted that the sole reason for the new indictment was to discourage the respondent from exercising his right to a trial. Even had such an admission not been made, when plea negotiations, conducted in the face of the less serious charge under the first indictment, fail, charging by a second indictment a more serious crime for the same conduct creates "a strong inference" of vindictiveness. . . . I therefore do not understand why, as in *Pearce*, due process does not require that the prosecution justify its action on some basis other than discouraging respondent from the exercise of his right to a trial. . . .

It might be argued that it really makes little difference how this case, now that it is here, is decided. The Court's holding gives plea bargaining full sway despite vindictiveness. A contrary result, however, merely would prompt the aggressive prosecutor to bring the greater charge initially in every case, and only thereafter to bargain. The consequences to the accused would still be adverse, for then he would bargain against a greater charge, face the likelihood of increased bail, and run the risk that the court would be less inclined to accept a bargained plea. Nonetheless, it is far preferable to hold the prosecution to the charge it was originally content to bring and to justify in the eyes of its public.

NOTES & QUESTIONS ON THREATS

1. *The coercive nature of plea bargain negotiations.* The Court in *Brady* viewed the prosecutor's threats as nothing more significant than the implicit threats already imbedded in plea negotiations. The fact that the prosecutor responded to the failed negotiations by pursuing more serious charges—which were ultimately upheld by the jury—is not an indication that the prosecutor did anything untoward. Indeed, the opposite result, which would have prevented the prosecutor from filing more serious charges, would seem to constrain the prosecutor if a deal is reached and also constrain the prosecutor if a deal is *not* reached—an odd result, to be sure. What is your assessment? Should the prosecutor be prevented from taking these actions if motivated by vindictiveness?

Why did the majority reject the application of *Pearce*, and its prohibition on vindictive prosecutions, to this case?

2. *Wired plea deals.* Is it permissible for the prosecution to tie the fate of two individuals together during plea bargaining? In other words, is it acceptable for the prosecution to promise not to prosecute a defendant's family members in exchange for the defendant's agreement to plead guilty? These are colloquially referred to as "wired" plea deals. To take an obvious example, imagine a situation where a suspect evades detection by police with the help of a family member. After the suspect is caught, the prosecutor threatens to charge the family member with harboring a fugitive or being an accessory after the fact, unless the defendant agrees to a plea agreement. Assuming that the prosecutor has an adequate basis for believing that the family member committed one of these crimes, is this global resolution of the charges acceptable? Or is it inherently coercive? Most courts that have considered the issue have upheld wired plea deals, though several have required that the prosecution inform the court of the existence of any wired deals so that the court can take this information into account when assessing whether the defendant's plea was coerced or voluntary. See, e.g., *United States v. Bennett*, 332 F.3d 1094, 1101 (7th Cir. 2003):

> We hold today that the government must advise the district court of any package deals or wired pleas during the Rule 11 plea colloquy of any defendant involved in the deal. The possibility of coercion resulting from plea agreements linking multiple defendants together, or defendants and third persons together, argues for the adoption of this rule. Therefore, the prosecution must comply with this rule or face the penalty of withdrawal of the accepted plea. Upon disclosure of a package deal, the district court should make a more detailed examination as to the voluntariness of each defendant's guilty plea pursuant to the package deal.

3. *Guilty pleas induced by improperly procured confessions.* As noted above, a guilty plea must be knowing and voluntary. Against that backdrop, consider the following situation, which could frequently arise. A defendant pleads guilty, pursuant to a plea agreement, but later files a habeas petition alleging that the guilty plea was induced by a coerced confession improperly obtained by a state agent, e.g., a police officer or a prosecutor. The convict argues that but for the coerced confession, the convict would not have accepted the plea agreement. In this circumstance, should a habeas court reverse the guilty plea? In *McMann v. Richardson*, 397 U.S. 759 (1970), the Supreme Court said no:

> A more credible explanation for a plea of guilty by a defendant who would go to trial except for his prior confession is his prediction that the law will

> permit his admissions to be used against him by the trier of fact. At least the probability of the State's being permitted to use the confession as evidence is sufficient to convince him that the State's case is too strong to contest and that a plea of guilty is the most advantageous course. Nothing in this train of events suggests that the defendant's plea, as distinguished from his confession, is an involuntary act. His later petition for collateral relief asserting that a coerced confession induced his plea is at most a claim that the admissibility of his confession was mistakenly assessed and that since he was erroneously advised, either under the then applicable law or under the law later announced, his plea was an unintelligent and voidable act. The Constitution, however, does not render pleas of guilty so vulnerable.

Id. at 769. Do you agree that a defendant who pleads guilty is making a rational decision based on a prediction about the admissibility of his confession? If the habeas court believes that the confession was coerced, is it appropriate to validate the defendant's decision to waive his rights and plead guilty?

B. CONDITIONS FOR PLEADING GUILTY

Instead of pleading guilty during a plea negotiation, a defendant might also plead guilty "free and clear," i.e., without any explicit agreement regarding treatment, such as a sentencing recommendation, in exchange for the guilty plea. There are a variety of reasons why a defendant might want to plead guilty. The defendant might *hope* for preferential treatment at sentencing, either from the prosecutor or from the judge, but not due to a formal agreement. Or the defendant might decide that contesting guilt is pointless, due to the substantial evidence in the prosecution's possession, and would prefer to focus on the sentencing phase of the trial. Or the defendant might feel genuinely guilty and believe that pleading guilty is an important element in a personal process of taking ownership of past misbehavior and the first step in the road to redemption. Either way, pleading guilty is not universally accepted by judges. First and foremost, the decision to plead guilty must be a knowing and voluntary one, and there are many situations when a defendant might plead guilty but then regret the decision. Regret, by itself, is not reason enough to contest a prior decision to plead guilty, but lack of access to the relevant information might be reason to overcome the prior decision. As you consider these materials, you might ask yourself why access to some types of information is considered by the law to be a necessary predicate for a knowing and voluntary decision.

STATUTORY REQUIREMENTS

Rule 11 of the Federal Rules of Criminal Procedure lays out the conditions for a guilty plea in the federal courts:

> Before the court accepts a plea of guilty or nolo contendere, the defendant may be placed under oath, and the court must address the defendant personally in open court. During this address, the court must inform the defendant of, and determine that the defendant understands, the following:
>
> (A) the government's right, in a prosecution for perjury or false statement, to use against the defendant any statement that the defendant gives under oath;
> (B) the right to plead not guilty, or having already so pleaded, to persist in that plea;
> (C) the right to a jury trial;
> (D) the right to be represented by counsel—and if necessary have the court appoint counsel—at trial and at every other stage of the proceeding;
> (E) the right at trial to confront and cross-examine adverse witnesses, to be protected from compelled self-incrimination, to testify and present evidence, and to compel the attendance of witnesses;
> (F) the defendant's waiver of these trial rights if the court accepts a plea of guilty or nolo contendere;
> (G) the nature of each charge to which the defendant is pleading;
> (H) any maximum possible penalty, including imprisonment, fine, and term of supervised release;
> (I) any mandatory minimum penalty;
> (J) any applicable forfeiture;
> (K) the court's authority to order restitution;
> (L) the court's obligation to impose a special assessment;
> (M) in determining a sentence, the court's obligation to calculate the applicable sentencing-guideline range and to consider that range, possible departures under the Sentencing Guidelines, and other sentencing factors . . .;
> (N) the terms of any plea-agreement provision waiving the right to appeal or to collaterally attack the sentence; and
> (O) that, if convicted, a defendant who is not a United States citizen may be removed from the United States, denied citizenship, and denied admission to the United States in the future.

However, not all states have specific statutory requirements covering the same ground. In those cases, the Constitution might step in to impose parallel requirements. In the following cases, the Supreme Court outlines the requirements of voluntariness. Over time, the Court has constructed a constitutional edifice that requires either the prosecutor or the court to inform the defendant about the consequences of his or her decision to plead guilty. But not every piece of information is required to be provided to the defendant as a matter of constitutional law. So, as you read the following materials, ask yourself why the Constitution requires an understanding of some consequences but not others.

1. Pleading Guilty While Maintaining Innocence

Normally, trial courts accept a guilty plea only after defendants declare, under oath, that they committed the crime to which they are pleading guilty. This is often accompanied by an "allocution," whereby defendants state, again under oath, the specifics of how they committed the crime. One goal of the allocution is to convince the trial court of the factual basis for the guilty plea. Some defendants, in some cases, refuse to follow this basic scheme, and insist on pleading guilty and maintaining their innocence at the same time. In some cases, the defendant might formalize this unique approach by pleading "nolo contendere," or no contest, to the charges. In other cases, such as the following case, the defendant might still plead not guilty while making a statement to the judge that they did not perpetrate the crime. Is the judge permitted to accept a guilty plea under these circumstances, or is a factual assertion of guilt constitutionally required?

North Carolina v. Alford

Supreme Court of the United States
400 U.S. 25 (1970)

Mr. Justice White delivered the opinion of the Court.

On December 2, 1963, Alford was indicted for first-degree murder, a capital offense under North Carolina law. The court appointed an attorney to represent him, and this attorney questioned all but one of the various witnesses who appellee said would substantiate his claim of innocence. The witnesses, however, did not support Alford's story but gave statements that strongly indicated his guilt. Faced with strong evidence of guilt and no substantial evidentiary support for the claim of innocence. Alford's attorney recommended that he plead guilty, but left the ultimate decision to Alford himself. The prosecutor agreed to accept a plea of guilty to a charge of second-degree murder, and on December 10, 1963, Alford pleaded guilty to the reduced charge.

Before the plea was finally accepted by the trial court, the court heard the sworn testimony of a police officer who summarized the State's case. Two other witnesses besides Alford were also heard. Although there was no eyewitness to the crime, the testimony indicated that shortly before the killing Alford took his gun from his house, stated his intention to kill the victim, and returned home with the declaration that he had carried out the killing. After the summary presentation of the State's case, Alford took the stand and testified that he had not committed the murder but that he was pleading guilty because he faced the threat of the death penalty if he did not do so. In response to the questions of his counsel, he acknowledged that his counsel had informed him of the difference between second- and first-degree murder and of his rights in case he chose to go to trial. The trial court then asked appellee if, in light of his denial of guilt, he still desired to plead guilty to second-degree murder and appellee answered, "Yes, sir. I plead guilty on—from the circumstances that he (Alford's attorney) told me." After eliciting information about Alford's prior criminal record, which was a long one, the trial court sentenced him to 30 years' imprisonment, the maximum penalty for second-degree murder.

Alford sought post-conviction relief in the state court. Among the claims raised was the claim that his plea of guilty was invalid because it was the product of fear and coercion. After a hearing, the state court in 1965 found that the plea was "willingly, knowingly, and understandingly" made on the advice of competent counsel and in the face of a strong prosecution case. Subsequently, Alford petitioned for a writ of habeas corpus, first in the United States District Court for the Middle District of North Carolina, and then in the Court of Appeals for the Fourth Circuit. . . .

As previously recounted after Alford's plea of guilty was offered and the State's case was placed before the judge, Alford denied that he had committed the murder but reaffirmed his desire to plead guilty to avoid a possible death sentence and to limit the penalty to the 30-year maximum provided for second-degree murder. Ordinarily, a judgment of conviction resting on a plea of guilty is justified by the defendant's admission that he committed the crime charged against him and his consent that judgment be entered without a trial of any kind. The plea usually subsumes both elements, and justifiably so, even though there is no separate, express admission by the defendant that he committed the particular acts claimed to constitute the crime charged in the indictment. Here Alford entered his plea but accompanied it with the statement that he had not shot the victim.

If Alford's statements were to be credited as sincere assertions of his innocence, there obviously existed a factual and legal dispute between him and the State. Without more, it might be argued that the conviction entered on his guilty plea was invalid, since his assertion of innocence negatived any admission of guilt, which, as we observed last Term in *Brady*, is normally "(c)entral to the plea and the foundation for entering judgment against the defendant. . . ." 397 U.S., at 748.

In addition to Alford's statement, however, the court had heard an account of the events on the night of the murder, including information from Alford's acquaintances that he had departed from his home with his gun stating his intention to kill and that he had later declared that he had carried out his intention. Nor had Alford wavered in his desire to have trial court determine his guilt without a jury trial. Although denying the charge against him, he nevertheless preferred the dispute between him and the State to be settled by the judge in the context of a guilty plea proceeding rather than by a formal trial. Thereupon, with the State's telling evidence and Alford's denial before it, the trial court proceeded to convict and sentence Alford for second-degree murder.

State and lower federal courts are divided upon whether a guilty plea can be accepted when it is accompanied by protestations of innocence and hence contains only a waiver of trial but no admission of guilt. Some courts, giving expression to the principle that "(o)ur law only authorizes a conviction where guilt is shown," require that trial judges reject such pleas. But others have concluded that they should not "force any defense on a defendant in a criminal case," particularly when advancement of the defense might "end in disaster. . . ." They have argued that, since "guilt, or the degree of guilt, is at times uncertain and elusive," "(a)n accused, though believing in or entertaining doubts respecting his innocence, might reasonably conclude a jury would be convinced of his guilt and that he would fare better in the sentence by pleading guilty. . . ." As one state court observed nearly a century ago, "(r)easons other than the fact that he is guilty may induce a defendant to so plead, . . . (and) (h)e must be permitted to judge for himself in this respect."

This Court has not confronted this precise issue, but prior decisions do yield relevant principles. In *Lynch v. Overholser*, 369 U.S. 705 (1962), Lynch, who had been charged in the Municipal Court of the District of Columbia with drawing and negotiating bad checks, a misdemeanor punishable by a maximum of one year in jail, sought to enter a plea of guilty, but the trial judge refused to accept the plea since a psychiatric report in the judge's possession indicated that Lynch had been suffering from "a manic depressive psychosis, at the time of the crime charged," and hence might have been not guilty by reason of insanity. Although at the subsequent trial Lynch did not rely on the insanity defense, he was found not guilty by reason of insanity and committed for an indeterminate period to a mental institution. On habeas corpus, the Court ordered his release, construing the congressional legislation seemingly authorizing the commitment as not reaching a case where the accused preferred a guilty plea to a plea of insanity. The Court expressly refused to rule that Lynch had an absolute right to have his guilty plea accepted, but implied that there would have been no constitutional error had his plea been accepted even though evidence before the judge indicated that there was a valid defense.

The issue in *Hudson v. United States*, 272 U.S. 451 (1926), was whether a federal court has power to impose a prison sentence after accepting a plea of nolo contendere, a plea by which a defendant does not expressly admit his guilt, but nonetheless waives his right to a trial and authorizes the court for purposes of the case to treat him as if he were guilty. The Court held that a trial court does have such power, and except for the cases which were rejected in *Hudson*, the federal courts have uniformly followed this rule, even in cases involving moral turpitude. Implicit in the nolo contendere cases is a recognition that the Constitution does not bar imposition of a prison sentence upon an accused who is unwilling expressly to admit his guilt but who, faced with grim alternatives, is willing to waive his trial and accept the sentence.

These cases would be directly in point if Alford had simply insisted on his plea but refused to admit the crime. The fact that his plea was denominated a plea of guilty rather than a plea of nolo contendere is of no constitutional significance with respect to the issue now before us, for the Constitution is concerned with the practical consequences, not the formal categorizations, of state law. Thus, while most pleas of guilty consist of both a waiver of trial and an express admission of guilt, the latter element is not a constitutional requisite to the imposition of criminal penalty. An individual accused of crime may voluntarily, knowingly, and understandingly consent to the imposition of a prison sentence even if he is unwilling or unable to admit his participation in the acts constituting the crime.

Nor can we perceive any material difference between a plea that refuses to admit commission of the criminal act and a plea containing a protestation of innocence when, as in the instant case, a defendant intelligently concludes that his interests require entry of a guilty plea and the record before the judge contains strong evidence of actual guilt. Here the State had a strong case of first-degree murder against Alford. Whether he realized or disbelieved his guilt, he insisted on his plea because in his view he had absolutely nothing to gain by a trial and much to gain by pleading. Because of the overwhelming evidence against him, a trial was precisely what neither Alford nor his attorney desired. Confronted with the choice between a trial for first-degree murder, on the one hand, and a plea of guilty to second-degree murder, on the other, Alford quite reasonably chose the latter and thereby limited the maximum penalty to a 30-year term. When his plea is viewed in light of the evidence against him, which substantially negated his claim of innocence and which further provided a means by which the judge could test whether the plea was being intelligently entered, its validity cannot be seriously questioned. In view of the strong factual basis for the plea demonstrated by the State and Alford's clearly expressed desire to enter it despite his professed belief in his innocence, we hold that the trial judge did not commit constitutional error in accepting it. . . .

NOTES & QUESTIONS ON ALFORD *PLEAS*

1. *The value of honesty.* Why would a defendant insist on making an *Alford* plea and why should the legal system accept its validity? One possible answer is the value of honesty or transparency. In some situations, a defendant might honestly feel innocent of the charges but might correctly anticipate that a jury

would disagree and convict him of the charges. A plea bargain would avoid the trial and produce a better result for the defendant, but the defendant prefers to maintain his innocence simply because the defendant honestly believes in his own innocence. If the defendant were "forced" to admit guilt as part of the guilty plea, then the defendant would be in the awkward dilemma of either "lying" to the court when he allocates to the offense or being forced to endure a trial that he does not want. *Alford* promotes transparency by allowing defendants to select strategic outcomes while remaining faithful to their moral compass.

2. *Collateral consequences.* Defendants will often prefer to take an *Alford* plea to avoid collateral consequences in other litigation. For example, Professor (now Judge) Stephanos Bibas has identified the following collateral consequences of a guilty plea that concern defendants: child-custody disputes, inability to secure post-conviction employment, and liability in civil litigation. Also, Bibas notes that a defendant who was intoxicated (or otherwise cognitively compromised) during the crime might not remember the event clearly, which might pose another barrier to pleading guilty. Despite these legitimate possibilities, Bibas also admits that these collateral consequences can sometimes be mere cover for feelings of shame and guilt that would be exacerbated by pleading guilty. See Stephanos Bibas, *Harmonizing Substantive-Criminal-Law Values and Criminal Procedure: The Case of* Alford *and Nolo Contendere Pleas*, 88 Cornell L. Rev. 1361, 1380 (2003). Does this suggest an argument against allowing *Alford* pleas, since it facilitates defendants' refusals to take responsibility for their actions?

STATE LAW REQUIREMENTS

The Supreme Court's *Alford* decision permits pleas of nolo contendere, or their functional equivalent, but does not require them. In other words, the U.S. Constitution is no bar to their use, but nothing in *Alford* requires a state to allow them. Some states refuse to accept the legitimacy of these pleas and require a guilty plea from defendants seeking to avoid a contested trial. See, e.g., *Ross v. State*, 456 N.E.2d 420, 423 (Ind. 1983) ("We hold, as a matter of law, that a judge may not accept a plea of guilty when the defendant both pleads guilty and maintains his innocence at the same time."). In Michigan, a judge who accepts a plea of nolo contendere must not "question the defendant about participation in the crime" and also "(a) state why a plea of nolo contendere is appropriate; and (b) hold a hearing, unless there has been one, that establishes support for a finding that the defendant is guilty of the offense charged or the offense to which the defendant is pleading." Mich. Code Crim. Proc. R. 6.302. The Michigan framework allows for nolo contendere pleas but is not capacious enough to encompass an *Alford* situation where the defendant affirmatively attests to innocence under oath. See also *Dep't of Law & Pub. Safety, Div. of Gaming Enforcement v. Gonzalez*, 273 N.J. Super. 239, 246, 641 A.2d 1060, 1063 (App. Div. 1994) ("To permit Gonzalez to assert such diametrically opposite positions, and to have the Commission reach conclusions at variance with the judicial record, hardly fosters public confidence in either the casino industry or the judicial system.").

2. Understanding the Elements of the Offense

In the following case, the defendant pleaded guilty without fully understanding the elements of the offense, in this case that conviction for second-degree "malice" murder required a finding of intent to kill. Apparently, the defendant was under the mistaken impression that he could plead guilty to the offense and still maintain that the crime was unintentional in nature. Does this misunderstanding compromise the voluntariness of the guilty plea? Should a guilty plea be limited to situations where the defendant understands the elements of the offense, such that the defendant has a full and rich picture of the crime for which he is pleading guilty?

Henderson v. Morgan

Supreme Court of the United States
426 U.S. 637 (1976)

Mr. Justice STEVENS delivered the opinion of the Court.

The question presented is whether a defendant may enter a voluntary plea of guilty to a charge of second-degree murder without being informed that intent to cause the death of his victim was an element of the offense. . . .

I

On April 6, 1965, respondent killed Mrs. Ada Francisco in her home. . . . Respondent was indicted for first-degree murder and arraigned on April 15, 1965. Two concededly competent attorneys were appointed to represent him. The indictment, which charged that he "willfully" stabbed his victim, was read in open court. His lawyers requested, and were granted, access to his written statement and to earlier psychiatric reports. A new psychiatric examination was requested and ordered.

Respondent was found competent to stand trial. Defense counsel held a series of conferences with the prosecutors, with the respondent, and with members of his family. The lawyers "thought manslaughter first would satisfy the needs of justice." They therefore endeavored to have the charge reduced to manslaughter, but the prosecution would agree to nothing less than second-degree murder and a minimum sentence of 25 years. The lawyers gave respondent advice about the different sentences which could be imposed for the different offenses, but, as the District Court found, did not explain the required element of intent.

On June 8, 1965, respondent appeared in court with his attorneys and entered a plea of guilty to murder in the second degree in full satisfaction of the first-degree murder charge made in the indictment. In direct colloquy with the trial judge respondent stated that his plea was based on the advice of his attorneys, that he understood he was accused of killing Mrs.

Francisco in Fulton County, that he was waiving his right to a jury trial, and that he would be sent to prison. There was no discussion of the elements of the offense of second-degree murder, no indication that the nature of the offense had ever been discussed with respondent, and no reference of any kind to the requirement of intent to cause the death of the victim.

At the sentencing hearing a week later his lawyers made a statement explaining his version of the offense, particularly noting that respondent "meant no harm to that lady" when he entered her room with the knife. The prosecutor disputed defense counsel's version of the matter, but did not discuss it in detail. After studying the probation officer's report, the trial judge pronounced sentence.

At the evidentiary hearing in the Federal District Court, respondent testified that he would not have pleaded guilty if he had known that an intent to cause the death of his victim was an element of the offense of second-degree murder. The District Judge did not indicate whether or not he credited this testimony.

II

Petitioner contends that the District Court applied an unrealistically rigid rule of law. Instead of testing the voluntariness of a plea by determining whether a ritualistic litany of the formal legal elements of an offense was read to the defendant, petitioner argues that the court should examine the totality of the circumstances and determine whether the substance of the charge, as opposed to its technical elements, was conveyed to the accused. We do not disagree with the thrust of petitioner's argument, but we are persuaded that even under the test which he espouses, this judgment finding respondent guilty of second-degree murder was defective.

We assume, as petitioner argues, that the prosecutor had overwhelming evidence of guilt available. We also accept petitioner's characterization of the competence of respondent's counsel and of the wisdom of their advice to plead guilty to a charge of second-degree murder. Nevertheless, such a plea cannot support a judgment of guilt unless it was voluntary in a constitutional sense. And clearly the plea could not be voluntary in the sense that it constituted an intelligent admission that he committed the offense unless the defendant received "real notice of the true nature of the charge against him, the first and most universally recognized requirement of due process."

The charge of second-degree murder was never formally made. Had it been made, it necessarily would have included a charge that respondent's assault was "committed with a design to effect the death of the person killed." That element of the offense might have been proved by the objective evidence even if respondent's actual state of mind was consistent with innocence or manslaughter. But even if such a design to effect death would almost inevitably have been inferred from evidence that respondent repeatedly stabbed Mrs. Francisco, it is nevertheless also true that a jury would not have been required to draw that inference. The jury would have been entitled to accept defense counsel's appraisal of the incident as involving only manslaughter in the first degree. Therefore, an admission by respondent that he killed Mrs. Francisco does not necessarily also admit that he was guilty of second-degree murder.

There is nothing in this record that can serve as a substitute for either a finding after trial, or a voluntary admission, that respondent had the requisite intent. Defense counsel did not purport to stipulate to that fact; they did not explain to him that his plea would be an admission of that fact; and he made no factual statement or admission necessarily implying that he had such intent. In these circumstances it is impossible to conclude that his plea to the unexplained charge of second-degree murder was voluntary.

Petitioner argues that affirmance of the Court of Appeals will invite countless collateral attacks on judgments entered on pleas of guilty, since frequently the record will not contain a complete enumeration of the elements of the offense to which an accused person pleads guilty. We think petitioner's fears are exaggerated.

Normally the record contains either an explanation of the charge by the trial judge, or at least a representation by defense counsel that the nature of the offense has been explained to the accused. Moreover, even without such an express representation, it may be appropriate to presume that in most cases defense counsel routinely explain the nature of the offense in sufficient detail to give the accused notice of what he is being asked to admit. This case is unique because the trial judge found as a fact that the element of intent was not explained to respondent. Moreover, respondent's unusually low mental capacity provides a reasonable explanation for counsel's oversight; it also forecloses the conclusion that the error was harmless beyond a reasonable doubt, for it lends at least a modicum of credibility to defense counsel's appraisal of the homicide as a manslaughter rather than a murder.

Since respondent did not receive adequate notice of the offense to which he pleaded guilty, his plea was involuntary and the judgment of conviction was entered without due process of law.

Mr. Justice REHNQUIST, with whom THE CHIEF JUSTICE joins, dissenting.

The Court's opinion affirms a judgment which directs the release on federal habeas of a state prisoner who, on advice of counsel, pleaded guilty in the New York State courts 11 years ago to a charge of second-degree murder. The Court declares its agreement with petitioner's contention that the test for reviewing the constitutional validity of a counseled plea of guilty should be "the totality of the circumstances." But the

Court's holding can be justified only if the Constitution requires that "a ritualistic litany of the formal legal elements of an offense (be) read to the defendant," a requirement which it purports to eschew. The Court accomplishes this result by imposing on state courts, as a constitutional requirement, a definition of "voluntariness" announced by this Court in *McCarthy v. United* States, 394 U.S. 459 (1969), in which the Court interpreted a provision of the Federal Rules of Criminal Procedure. Yet that case has been held to have only prospective application even as to the federal courts.

McCarthy extended the definition of voluntariness to include an "understanding of the essential elements of the crime charged, including the requirement of specific intent. . . ." But prior to *McCarthy* . . . the generally accepted standard for a valid guilty plea in federal courts was . . . a three-pronged test: The plea of guilty must be made voluntarily, it must be made after proper advice, and it must be made with full understanding of the consequences. There can be no doubt that respondent entered his plea "with full understanding of the consequences" because the District Court expressly so found. Nor can there be any serious doubt that respondent's plea was made "voluntarily" as that term is used in . . . the previous cases. . . .

There was no contention in the federal habeas court that respondent's guilty plea was not "voluntary" in the normal sense of that word. There was no hint of physical or psychological coercion, and respondent was represented by not one but two admittedly capable defense attorneys. While *McCarthy* expands the notion of "voluntariness" to include the concept that a defendant must have an "understanding of the essential elements of the crime charged, including the requirement of specific intent . . .," in order for a plea in the federal case to be valid under Fed. Rule Crim. Proc. 11, that decision was held prospective only. . . . Even had it not been, Rule 11 by its terms applies only to proceedings in federal courts. . . .

His attorneys were motivated by the eminently reasonable tactical judgment on their part that he should plead guilty to second-degree murder in order to avoid the possibility of conviction for first-degree murder with its more serious attendant penalties. Since the Court concedes both the competence of respondent's counsel and the wisdom of their advice, that should be the end of the matter. . . .

In adopting the rule it does, the Court opens the door to countless similarly situated prisoners to withdraw their guilty pleas many years after they were entered. Since it is unlikely that prosecutors will be able to reassemble witnesses and evidence at this late date to try these prisoners, the practical effect of the Court's ruling will be to release these prisoners who at one time freely admitted their guilt.

NOTES & QUESTIONS ON UNDERSTANDING THE ELEMENTS

1. *Why did he care?* Why was the defendant in *Henderson* so concerned about the intent element of second-degree malice murder? After all, the defendant clearly knew the name of the crime that he pleaded guilty to. What hinged on the intent element? Did it make him especially blameworthy from the perspective of community morals? Or did it offend his own internal moral compass? Or perhaps there were specific collateral legal consequences in other cases that he was concerned about?

2. *Which elements?* The Court in *Henderson v. Morgan* concluded that the defendant must understand the nature of the offense for his guilty plea to be considered voluntary. In that case, the defendant was unaware that the offense required an intentional killing, something that he wished to deny. *That* element is surely essential to a lay person's understanding of what they are pleading guilty to. But as any student of the criminal law knows, each criminal offense includes a lengthy list of material elements, some of which are contextual, or quite technical, and far less central than the "intentional" element that was at issue in *Henderson*. If the case goes to trial, the prosecutor is required to prove each material element beyond a reasonable doubt. Similarly, should a guilty plea require an understanding of *each* material element? For example, should ignorance about some background or contextual element of a complex offense entail that the guilty plea was involuntary? If not, is there a coherent way of distinguishing between core and peripheral material elements of an offense? In a short footnote in the *Henderson* opinion, the Court stated:

> There is no need in this case to decide whether notice of the true nature, or substance, of a charge always requires a description of every element of the offense; we assume it does not. Nevertheless, intent is such a critical element of the offense of second-degree murder that notice of that element is required.

How should courts address what counts as a "critical element"? Do you think that "critical element" is a workable standard?

PROBLEM CASE

Keith Patton pleaded guilty to attempted murder in Indiana in 1984. At the time of the crime, Patton was 17 years old and intoxicated. With his associate Leroy Johnson, Patton saw a parked car and used a sawed-off shotgun to fire once into the driver's-side window of the car. The bullet hit the passenger in the car and injured her. Patton then fired a second shot, which hit the driver of the car and killed him. Patton and Johnson then committed a sexual assault of the passenger. To resolve the case against him, Patton pleaded guilty to multiple charges, including murder of the driver, attempted murder of the passenger, and rape. At sentencing, Patton admitted that he killed the driver but insisted that he did so without the intent to kill. Patton was sentenced to death, but an appellate court overturned the sentence, concluding that the trial court should not have accepted the guilty plea to murder when Patton denied having the intent to kill the driver. A second trial resulted in another conviction and a total sentence of 222 years. In a subsequent appeal, Patton argued that the trial court erred in accepting his guilty plea for attempted murder of the passenger, because Patton was never told by the court that attempted murder required a finding that he acted with the specific intent to kill the victim—in this case, the passenger of the car. Is the specific intent requirement a "critical element" of the crime of attempted murder? If the judge failed to explain this requirement, should an appellate court vacate the guilty plea? See *Patton v. State*, 810 N.E.2d 690, 697 (Ind. 2004).

3. Understanding the Punishment

In addition to understanding the nature of the offense to which the defendant is pleading guilty, the defendant must also understand the practical consequences of the guilty plea—i.e., the punishment that the defendant will face. Although usually the maximum penalty for a particular crime is relatively straightforward, the complexities of modern sentencing can sometimes elude defense attorneys or even judges. In the following case, the defendant labored under a misperception regarding sentencing when he pleaded guilty to first-degree murder. Consequently, was the guilty plea involuntary?

Hill v. Lockhart

Supreme Court of the United States
474 U.S. 52 (1985)

Justice Rehnquist delivered the opinion of the Court.

Petitioner William Lloyd Hill pleaded guilty in the Arkansas trial court to charges of first-degree murder and theft of property. More than two years later he sought federal habeas relief on the ground that his court-appointed attorney had failed to advise him that, as a second offender, he was required to serve one-half of his sentence before becoming eligible for parole. . . . [W]e conclude that petitioner failed to allege the kind of prejudice from the allegedly incompetent advice of counsel that would have entitled him to a hearing.

Under Arkansas law, the murder charge to which petitioner pleaded guilty carried a potential sentence of 5 to 50 years or life in prison, along with a fine of up to $15,000. Petitioner's court-appointed attorney negotiated a plea agreement pursuant to which the State, in return for petitioner's plea of guilty to both the murder and theft charges, agreed to recommend that the trial judge impose concurrent prison sentences of 35 years for the murder and 10 years for the theft. Petitioner signed a written "plea statement" indicating that he understood the charges against him and the consequences of pleading guilty, that his plea had not been induced "by any force, threat, or promise" apart from the plea agreement itself, that he realized that the trial judge was not bound by the plea agreement and retained the sole "power of sentence," and that he had discussed the plea agreement with his attorney and was satisfied with his attorney's advice. The last two lines of the "plea statement," just above petitioner's signature, read: "I am aware of everything in this document. I fully understand what my rights are, and I voluntarily plead guilty because I am guilty as charged."

Petitioner appeared before the trial judge at the plea hearing, recounted the events that gave rise to the charges against him, affirmed that he had signed and understood the written "plea statement," reiterated that no "threats or promises" had been made to him other than the plea agreement itself, and entered a plea of guilty to both charges. The trial judge accepted the guilty plea and sentenced petitioner in accordance with the State's recommendations. The trial judge also granted petitioner credit for the time he had already served in prison, and told petitioner that "[y]ou will be required to serve at least one-third of your time before you are eligible for parole."

More than two years later petitioner filed a federal habeas corpus petition alleging, inter alia, that his guilty plea was involuntary by reason of ineffective assistance of counsel because his attorney had misinformed him as to his parole eligibility date. According to petitioner, his attorney had told him that if he pleaded guilty he would become eligible for parole after serving one-third of his prison sentence. In fact, because petitioner previously had been convicted of a felony in Florida, he was classified under Arkansas law as a "second offender" and was required to serve one-half of his sentence before becoming eligible for parole. . . .

The longstanding test for determining the validity of a guilty plea is "whether the plea represents a voluntary and intelligent choice among the alternative courses of action open to the defendant." Here petitioner does not contend that his plea was "involuntary" or "unintelligent" simply because the State through its officials failed to supply him with information about his parole eligibility date. We have never held that the United States Constitution requires the State to furnish a defendant with information about parole eligibility in order for the defendant's plea of guilty to be voluntary, and indeed such a constitutional requirement would be inconsistent with the current rules of procedure governing the entry of guilty pleas in the federal courts. Instead, petitioner relies entirely on the claim that his plea was "involuntary" as a result of ineffective assistance of counsel because his attorney supplied him with information about parole eligibility that was erroneous. Where, as here, a defendant is represented by counsel during the plea process and enters his plea upon the advice of counsel, the voluntariness of the plea depends on whether counsel's advice "was within the range of competence demanded of attorneys in criminal cases."

Our concern in *McMann v. Richardson* with the quality of counsel's performance in advising a defendant whether to plead guilty stemmed from the more general principle that all "defendants facing felony charges are entitled to the effective assistance of competent counsel." Two Terms ago, in *Strickland v. Washington*, we adopted a two-part standard for evaluating claims of ineffective assistance of counsel. There, citing *McMann*, we reiterated that "[w]hen a convicted defendant complains of the ineffectiveness of counsel's assistance, the defendant must show that counsel's representation fell below an objective standard of reasonableness." We also held, however, that "[t]he defendant must show that there is a reasonable probability that, but for counsel's unprofessional errors, the result of the proceeding would have been different." This additional "prejudice" requirement was based on our conclusion that "[a]n error by counsel, even if professionally unreasonable, does not warrant setting aside the judgment of a criminal proceeding if the error had no effect on the judgment."

Although our decision in *Strickland* dealt with a claim of ineffective assistance of counsel in a capital sentencing proceeding, and was premised in part on the similarity between such a proceeding and the usual criminal trial, the same two-part standard seems to us applicable to ineffective-assistance claims arising out of the plea process. . . .

In many guilty plea cases, the "prejudice" inquiry will closely resemble the inquiry engaged in by courts reviewing ineffective-assistance challenges to convictions obtained through a trial. For example, where the alleged error of counsel is a failure to investigate or discover potentially exculpatory evidence, the determination whether the error "prejudiced" the defendant by causing him to plead guilty rather than go to trial will depend on the likelihood that discovery of the evidence would have led counsel to change his recommendation as to the plea. This assessment, in turn, will depend in large part on a prediction whether the evidence likely would have changed the outcome of a trial. Similarly, where the alleged error of counsel is a failure to advise the defendant of a potential affirmative defense to the crime charged, the resolution of the "prejudice" inquiry will depend largely on whether the affirmative defense likely would have succeeded at trial. . . .

In the present case the claimed error of counsel is erroneous advice as to eligibility for parole under the sentence agreed to in the plea bargain. We find it unnecessary to determine whether there may be circumstances under which erroneous advice by counsel as to parole eligibility may be deemed constitutionally ineffective assistance of counsel, because in the present case we conclude that petitioner's allegations are insufficient to satisfy the *Strickland* requirement of "prejudice." Petitioner did not allege in his habeas petition that, had counsel correctly informed him about his parole eligibility date, he would have pleaded not guilty and insisted on going to trial. He alleged no special circumstances that might support the conclusion that he placed particular emphasis on his parole eligibility in deciding whether or not to plead guilty. Indeed, petitioner's mistaken belief that he would become eligible for parole after serving one-third of his sentence would seem to have affected not only his calculation of the time he likely would serve if sentenced pursuant to the proposed plea agreement, but also his calculation of the time he likely would serve if he went to trial and were convicted. . . .

NOTES & QUESTIONS ON UNDERSTANDING PUNISHMENT

1. *Mistakes about parole.* In *Hill*, both defense counsel and the judge gave the defendant erroneous information about his parole eligibility—falsely informing him that he would be eligible after serving a third of his sentence when the real time period was after half. How should other mistakes or confusions be evaluated? For example, in *Buchheit v. State*, 339 Ark. 481, 482-83, 6 S.W.3d 109, 110 (1999), the defendant was not told that he had to serve 70 percent of his sentence before he would become eligible for parole, arguably a similar situation to *Hill*. However, the Arkansas Supreme Court refused to disturb the guilty plea because the defendant was never told a different percentage but was instead simply told that parole eligibility would be decided by prison officials, information that could not have "induced Buchheit to forego a trial and plead guilty." Do you agree? Should defense counsel be under an affirmative obligation to inform all defendants about the exact parole eligibility rules in their case?

PROBLEM CASE

The defendant was charged with the Class B felony offense of drug trafficking in the second degree pursuant to Missouri Penal Code § 195.223. The defendant pleaded guilty, not in connection with a formal plea agreement with prosecutors, but rather with the understanding that he might receive a favorable sentencing recommendation from prosecutors "down the road" based on his future cooperation with federal authorities in a related investigation. At the plea hearing, the judge asked about the range of punishment associated with the Class B felony that the defendant was pleading guilty to. The prosecutor responded that the range was 5-10 years for a Class B felony and the defendant stipulated that he understood this sentencing range. The prosecutor's statement was an error because the statutory range for a Class B felony in Missouri is 5-15 years. The error was never corrected at the hearing. Eventually, the defendant received a prison sentence of 10 years, which was suspended, and probation. Consequently, the defendant was set free in accordance with the suspended sentence. After the defendant violated his probation, he was sent back to prison to serve the 10-year sentence. He filed a habeas petition arguing that his guilty plea was defective because he was not made aware of the true sentencing range for the offense to which he pleaded guilty; had he known that the statutory range was 5-15 years, he would not have pleaded guilty. What result in the case? Should the defendant have his guilty plea invalidated and should he be permitted to go to trial instead? *Cole v. State*, 850 S.W.2d 406, 407 (Mo. Ct. App. 1993).

4. Understanding the Collateral Consequences

What if the defendant is aware of the formal punishment associated with the offense but unaware of the collateral consequences that might flow from a guilty plea for that offense? Conviction can trigger many collateral consequences—some major and some minor. In the following case, the defendant said he was unaware of the immigration consequences—deportation—for pleading guilty. As you read the following case, ask yourself whether a defendant must be aware of all consequences, such as deportation, and whether failure to be so informed constitutes ineffective assistance of counsel. If the answer to that question is yes, should we extend that logic to other collateral consequences as well?

Padilla v. Kentucky

Supreme Court of the United States
559 U.S. 356 (2010)

Justice Stevens delivered the opinion of the Court.

Petitioner Jose Padilla, a native of Honduras, has been a lawful permanent resident of the United States for more than 40 years. Padilla served this Nation with honor as a member of the U.S. Armed Forces during the Vietnam War. He now faces deportation after pleading guilty to the transportation of a large amount of marijuana in his tractor-trailer in the Commonwealth of Kentucky.

In this postconviction proceeding, Padilla claims that his counsel not only failed to advise him of this consequence prior to his entering the plea, but also told him that he "did not have to worry about immigration status since he had been in the country so long." Padilla relied on his counsel's erroneous advice when he pleaded guilty to the drug charges that made his deportation virtually mandatory. He alleges that he would have insisted on going to trial if he had not received incorrect advice from his attorney. . . .

II

Before deciding whether to plead guilty, a defendant is entitled to "the effective assistance of competent counsel." The Supreme Court of Kentucky rejected Padilla's ineffectiveness claim on the ground that the advice he sought about the risk of deportation concerned only collateral matters, i.e., those matters not within the sentencing authority of the state trial court. In its view, "collateral consequences are outside the scope of representation required by the Sixth Amendment," and, therefore, the "failure of defense counsel to advise the defendant of possible deportation consequences is not cognizable as a claim for ineffective assistance of counsel." The Kentucky high court is far from alone in this view.

We, however, have never applied a distinction between direct and collateral consequences to define the scope of constitutionally "reasonable professional assistance" required under *Strickland*. Whether that distinction is appropriate is a question we need not consider in this case because of the unique nature of deportation.

We have long recognized that deportation is a particularly severe "penalty," but it is not, in a strict sense, a criminal sanction. Although removal proceedings are civil in nature, deportation is nevertheless intimately related to the criminal process. Our law has enmeshed criminal convictions and the penalty of deportation for nearly a century. And, importantly, recent changes in our immigration law have made removal nearly an automatic result for a broad class of noncitizen offenders. Thus, we find it "most difficult" to divorce the penalty from the conviction in the deportation context. Moreover, we are quite confident that noncitizen defendants facing a risk of deportation for a particular offense find it even more difficult.

Deportation as a consequence of a criminal conviction is, because of its close connection to the criminal process, uniquely difficult to classify as either a direct or a collateral consequence. The collateral versus direct distinction is thus ill suited to evaluating a *Strickland* claim concerning the specific risk of deportation. We conclude that advice regarding deportation is not categorically removed from the ambit of the Sixth Amendment right to counsel. *Strickland* applies to Padilla's claim.

III

Under *Strickland,* we first determine whether counsel's representation "fell below an objective standard of reasonableness." . . . "The proper measure of attorney performance remains simply reasonableness under prevailing professional norms." We long have recognized that "[p]revailing norms of practice as reflected in American Bar Association standards and the like . . . are guides to determining what is reasonable. . . ." Although they are "only guides" and not "inexorable commands," these standards may be valuable measures of the prevailing professional norms of effective representation, especially as these standards have been adapted to deal with the intersection of modern criminal prosecutions and immigration law.

The weight of prevailing professional norms supports the view that counsel must advise her client regarding the risk of deportation. We too have previously recognized that "[p]reserving the client's right to remain in the United States may be more important to the client than any potential jail sentence." Likewise, we have recognized that "preserving the possibility of" discretionary relief from deportation . . . "would have been one of the principal benefits sought by defendants deciding whether to accept a plea offer or instead to proceed to trial." We expected that counsel who were unaware of the discretionary relief measures would "follo[w] the advice of numerous practice guides" to advise themselves of the importance of this particular form of discretionary relief.

In the instant case, the terms of the relevant immigration statute are succinct, clear, and explicit in defining the removal consequence for Padilla's conviction. Padilla's counsel could have easily determined that his plea would make him eligible for deportation simply from reading the text of the statute, which addresses not some broad classification of crimes but specifically commands removal for all controlled substances convictions except for the most trivial of marijuana possession offenses. Instead, Padilla's counsel provided him false assurance that his conviction would not result in his removal from this country. This is not a hard case in which to find deficiency. . . .

NOTES & QUESTIONS ON COLLATERAL CONSEQUENCES

1. *The logical stopping point.* In dissent, both Justice Scalia and Justice Alito argued that there was no natural stopping point to the new collateral consequence rule articulated in *Padilla*—arguably any consequence that flowed from conviction could be potentially problematic for the defendant or constitute a severe penalty. For example, in *Taylor v. State*, 304 Ga. App. 878, 878, 698 S.E.2d 384, 385 (2010), the defendant pleaded guilty to child molestation, which triggered the state's sex offender registration statute. The plea deal included a sentence of one year of incarceration followed by nine years of probation. After pleading guilty, Taylor argued that he was never informed that he would also have to participate in mandatory treatment and counseling, including polygraph tests, while he was on probation. Applying *Padilla*, the Georgia Supreme Court concluded that "like deportation, registration as a sex offender is intimately related to the criminal process in that it is an

automatic result following certain criminal convictions." *Id.* at 883, 698 S.E.2d at 388. However, the court concluded that although defendant's counsel did not explain the program, it was outlined by the judge during the plea hearing, thus giving the defendant adequate notice. Do you agree that conditions of probation or other post-incarceration treatment programs should fall under the rule announced in *Padilla*? See also *People v. Fonville*, 291 Mich. App. 363, 392, 804 N.W.2d 878, 894-95 (2011) (holding that "applying the *Padilla* rationale to this case supports a holding that defense counsel must advise a defendant that registration as a sexual offender is a consequence of the defendant's guilty plea"). For a discussion of these two cases, see Joanna Rosenberg, *A Game Changer? The Impact of* Padilla v. Kentucky *on the Collateral Consequences Rule and Ineffective Assistance of Counsel Claims*, 82 Fordham L. Rev. 1407, 1444 (2013).

PROBLEM CASE

In July 2006, a police officer in Elizabethtown, Kentucky, suspected that Timothy Pridham had obtained pseudoephedrine, an ingredient in the manufacture of methamphetamine that is found in some medications. Pridham was a convicted methamphetamine manufacturer and was riding in a car with three other individuals. During the traffic stop, the police officer found 30 pseudoephedrine pills in the car. The police searched Pridham's residence and found other materials used in the manufacture of methamphetamine. A local grand jury indicted Pridham on several charges: manufacturing methamphetamine, complicity to commit unlawful distribution of a methamphetamine precursor, fourth-degree controlled substance endangerment to a child, and being a first-degree persistent felony offender.

The case was scheduled for trial. At the end of voir dire, but before the start of trial, Pridham agreed to plea deal. In exchange for a guilty plea, the state offered three concurrent sentences of 30 years, 5 years, and 5 years. Pridham accepted the deal and was sentenced to 30 years in prison. Later, Pridham filed a petition to reverse his guilty plea, contending that he was told by defense counsel that he would be eligible for parole after serving 20 percent of his 30-year sentence, or 6 years. However, because of the application of a separate "violent offender" statute to his case, Pridham was only eligible for parole after serving 20 years of his sentence. Since Pridham was 57 when he committed the crime, he would be eligible for parole on his 77th birthday. Pridham argued that he would not have accepted the plea if he understood how parole eligibility would work in his case. Under these circumstances, should an appeals court take steps to invalidate the guilty plea and permit Pridham to go to trial? See *Commonwealth v. Pridham*, 394 S.W.3d 867 (Ky. 2012).

5. Communicating Plea Offers to Clients

What if the prosecutor offers a plea deal but the defense attorney does not bother to relay the offer to his or her client before rejecting it? In that case, the defendant might claim that had he known about the offer, he might have accepted it. In the following case, the Supreme Court considers whether a rejected plea offer, not communicated to the client, might constitute ineffective assistance of client. In deciding that constitutional question under the Sixth Amendment, bear in mind that codified ethical standards are clear that plea offers should be communicated to the client. For example, the ABA Criminal Justice Standards for the Defense Function state that "[d]efense counsel should promptly communicate to the client every plea offer and all significant developments, motions, and court actions or rulings, and provide advice as outlined in this Standard." See Standard 4-5.1(c). Notice that the provision requires communication of "every" plea offer, rather than just plausible or highly beneficial plea offers. As you read the case, ask yourself whether the Sixth Amendment standard for effective assistance of counsel requires the same.

Missouri v. Frye

Supreme Court of the United States
566 U.S. 134 (2012)

Justice KENNEDY delivered the opinion of the Court.

The Sixth Amendment, applicable to the States by the terms of the Fourteenth Amendment, provides that the accused shall have the assistance of counsel in all criminal prosecutions. The right to counsel is the right to effective assistance of counsel. This case arises in the context of claimed ineffective assistance that led to the lapse of a prosecution offer of a plea bargain, a proposal that offered terms more lenient than the terms of the guilty plea entered later. The initial question is whether the constitutional right to counsel extends to the negotiation and consideration of plea offers that lapse or are rejected. If there is a right to effective assistance with respect to those offers, a further question is what a defendant must demonstrate in order to show that prejudice resulted from counsel's deficient performance. . . .

I

In August 2007, respondent Galin Frye was charged with driving with a revoked license. Frye had been convicted for that offense on three other occasions, so the State of Missouri charged him with a class D felony, which carries a maximum term of imprisonment of four years.

On November 15, the prosecutor sent a letter to Frye's counsel offering a choice of two plea bargains. The prosecutor first offered to recommend a 3-year sentence if there was a guilty plea to the felony charge, without a recommendation regarding probation but with a recommendation that Frye serve 10 days in jail as so-called "shock" time. The second offer was to reduce the charge to a misdemeanor and, if Frye pleaded guilty to it, to recommend a 90-day sentence. The misdemeanor charge of driving with a revoked license carries a maximum term of imprisonment of one year. The letter stated both offers would expire on December 28. Frye's attorney did not advise Frye that the offers had been made. The offers expired.

Frye's preliminary hearing was scheduled for January 4, 2008. On December 30, 2007, less than a week before the hearing, Frye was again arrested for driving with a revoked license. At the January 4 hearing, Frye waived his right to a preliminary hearing on the charge arising from the August 2007 arrest. He pleaded not guilty at a subsequent arraignment but then changed his plea to guilty. There was no underlying plea agreement. The state trial court accepted Frye's guilty plea. The prosecutor recommended a 3-year sentence, made no recommendation regarding probation, and requested 10 days shock time in jail. The trial judge sentenced Frye to three years in prison.

Frye filed for postconviction relief in state court. He alleged his counsel's failure to inform him of the prosecution's plea offer denied him the effective assistance of counsel. At an evidentiary hearing, Frye testified he would have entered a guilty plea to the misdemeanor had he known about the offer. . . .

II

It is well settled that the right to the effective assistance of counsel applies to certain steps before trial. The "Sixth Amendment guarantees a defendant the right to have counsel present at all 'critical' stages of the criminal proceedings." Critical stages include arraignments, postindictment interrogations, postindictment lineups, and the entry of a guilty plea. . . .

In the case now before the Court the State, as petitioner, points out that the legal question presented is different from that in *Hill* and *Padilla*. In those cases the claim was that the prisoner's plea of guilty was invalid because counsel had provided incorrect advice pertinent to the plea. In the instant case, by contrast, the guilty plea that was accepted, and the plea proceedings concerning it in court, were all based on accurate advice and information from counsel. The challenge is not to the advice pertaining to the plea that was accepted but rather to the course of legal representation that preceded it with respect to other potential pleas and plea offers.

To give further support to its contention that the instant case is in a category different from what the Court considered in *Hill* and *Padilla*, the State urges that there is no right to a plea offer or a plea bargain in any event. It claims Frye therefore was not deprived of any legal benefit to which he was entitled. Under this view, any wrongful or mistaken action of counsel with respect to earlier plea offers is beside the point.

The State is correct to point out that *Hill* and *Padilla* concerned whether there was ineffective assistance leading to acceptance of a plea offer, a process involving a formal court appearance with the defendant and all counsel present. Before a guilty plea is entered the defendant's understanding of the plea and its consequences can be established on the record. This affords the State substantial protection against later claims that the plea was the result of inadequate advice. At the plea entry proceedings the trial court and all counsel have the opportunity to establish on the record that the defendant understands the process that led to any offer, the advantages and disadvantages of accepting it, and the sentencing consequences or possibilities that will ensue once a conviction is entered based upon the plea. *Hill* and *Padilla* both illustrate that, nevertheless, there may be instances when claims of ineffective assistance can arise after the conviction is entered. Still, the State, and the trial court itself, have had a substantial opportunity to guard against this contingency by establishing at the plea entry proceeding that the defendant has been given proper advice or, if the advice received appears to have been inadequate, to remedy that deficiency before the plea is accepted and the conviction entered.

When a plea offer has lapsed or been rejected, however, no formal court proceedings are involved. This underscores that the plea-bargaining process is often in flux, with no clear standards or timelines and with no judicial supervision of the discussions between prosecution and defense. Indeed, discussions between client and defense counsel are privileged. So the prosecution has little or no notice if something may be amiss and perhaps no capacity to intervene in any event. And, as noted, the State insists there is no right to receive a plea offer. For all these reasons, the State contends, it is unfair to subject it to the consequences of defense counsel's inadequacies, especially when the opportunities for a full and fair trial, or, as here, for a later guilty plea albeit on less favorable terms, are preserved.

The State's contentions are neither illogical nor without some persuasive force, yet they do not suffice to overcome a simple reality. Ninety-seven percent of federal convictions and ninety-four percent of state convictions are the result of guilty pleas. The reality is that plea bargains have become so central to the administration of the criminal justice system that defense counsel have responsibilities in the plea bargain process, responsibilities that must be met to render the adequate assistance of counsel that the Sixth Amendment requires in the criminal process at critical stages. Because ours "is for the most part a system of pleas, not a system of trials," it is insufficient simply to point to the guarantee of a fair trial as a backstop that inoculates any errors in the pretrial process. "To a large extent . . . horse trading [between prosecutor and defense counsel] determines who goes to jail and for how long. That is what plea bargaining is. It is not some adjunct to the criminal justice system; it is the criminal justice system." In today's criminal justice system, therefore, the negotiation of a plea bargain, rather than the unfolding of a trial, is almost always the critical point for a defendant. . . .

This Court now holds that, as a general rule, defense counsel has the duty to communicate formal offers from the prosecution to accept a plea on terms and conditions that may be favorable to the accused. Any exceptions to that rule need not be explored here, for the offer was a formal one with a fixed expiration date. When defense counsel allowed the offer to expire without advising the defendant or allowing him to consider it, defense counsel did not render the effective assistance the Constitution requires.

Though the standard for counsel's performance is not determined solely by reference to codified standards of professional practice, these standards can be important guides. The American Bar Association recommends defense counsel "promptly communicate and explain to the defendant all plea offers made by the prosecuting attorney," and this standard has been adopted by numerous state and federal courts over the last 30 years. The standard for prompt communication and consultation is also set out in state bar professional standards for attorneys.

The prosecution and the trial courts may adopt some measures to help ensure against late, frivolous, or fabricated claims after a later, less advantageous plea offer has been accepted or after a trial leading to conviction with resulting harsh consequences. First, the fact of a formal offer means that its terms and its processing can be documented so that what took place in the negotiation process becomes more clear if some later inquiry turns on the conduct of earlier pretrial negotiations. Second, States may elect to follow rules that all offers must be in writing, again to ensure against later misunderstandings or fabricated charges. Third, formal offers can be made part of the record at any subsequent plea proceeding or before a trial on the merits, all to ensure that a defendant has been fully advised before those further proceedings commence. . . .

Here defense counsel did not communicate the formal offers to the defendant. As a result of that deficient performance, the offers lapsed. Under *Strickland*, the question then becomes what, if any, prejudice resulted from the breach of duty.

To show prejudice from ineffective assistance of counsel where a plea offer has lapsed or been rejected because of counsel's deficient performance, defendants must demonstrate a reasonable probability they would have accepted the earlier plea offer had they been afforded effective assistance of counsel. Defendants must also demonstrate a reasonable probability the plea would have been entered without the prosecution canceling it or the trial court refusing to accept it, if they had the authority to exercise that discretion under state law. To establish prejudice in this instance, it is necessary to show a reasonable probability that the end result of the criminal process would have been more favorable by reason of a plea to a lesser charge or a sentence of less prison time.

> ... In a case, such as this, where a defendant pleads guilty to less favorable terms and claims that ineffective assistance of counsel caused him to miss out on a more favorable earlier plea offer, *Strickland*'s inquiry into whether "the result of the proceeding would have been different," requires looking not at whether the defendant would have proceeded to trial absent ineffective assistance but whether he would have accepted the offer to plead pursuant to the terms earlier proposed. . . .

NOTES & QUESTIONS ON COMMUNICATING PLEA OFFERS

1. *Should plea offers be placed on the record?* One solution to the problem of uncommunicated plea offers is to place them on the record by, for example, filling out paperwork that the defense counsel is required to provide to the client. This would effectively take plea offers out of the shadows and reduce, if not eliminate, the possibility that plea offers will not be communicated to the client. Is this a good strategy? One scholar argues that the written plea offer should include the following elements:

> The overarching objective is to create a record that captures the elements of a lawyer's investigation and advice that defendants often challenge in ineffective assistance of counsel claims, while minimizing the time required to complete it. Therefore, the record should consist of at least three primary sections: expected trial outcome, terms of the plea bargain deal, and an evaluation of options. These are the key inputs into the defendant's decision to accept or reject a plea bargain deal—and those most needed to review a lawyer's advice after the fact.

Joel Mallord, *Putting Plea Bargaining on the Record*, 162 U. Pa. L. Rev. 683 (2014). Would this solve the problem? What if prosecutors communicated an unofficial, hypothetical plea offer of the following sort: "What would you say, hypothetically, if we were to offer manslaughter—is that something that your client would be interested in?" In other words, would it be difficult to enforce a written notice requirement?

2. *Would the plea deal be accepted?* In order to reverse a guilty plea, a habeas court must be satisfied that the end result of the case would have been different had defense counsel communicated the prosecution's offer to the client. As discussed above in the opinion, this requires answering the following counterfactual question: Would the client have accepted the plea deal? But in order to determine that the defendant suffered "prejudice," i.e., that the outcome would have been different, the convict must also demonstrate something

else: that the prosecution would have honored the deal after the client accepted it. What if the prosecution had changed its mind? Or more commonly, what if the judge had rejected the proposed plea agreement? In some jurisdictions, judges have the authority to review plea agreements and are under no obligation to accept the deal as negotiated by the parties. If the judge would have rejected the plea anyway, or if the prosecution would have withdrawn the plea, then the defendant suffered no prejudice by the defense counsel's failure to communicate the offer.

6. Rejecting a Favorable Plea Deal

The following case was decided by the Supreme Court on the same day as *Frye*. Instead of an uncommunicated plea deal, the case concerns a communicated plea deal that was subsequently rejected on advice of counsel. The defendant proceeded to trial and was convicted, thus leading to profound regret about the rejected plea offer. Had the defendant known that he would be convicted, he would have accepted the plea offer. Under what circumstances might a rejected plea offer constitute ineffective assistance of counsel under the Sixth Amendment? And is the defendant's regret—heightened by the benefit of hindsight—enough to ground a claim of ineffective assistance? As you read the case, ask yourself what standard the Court articulates to evaluate these ex post claims.

Lafler v. Cooper

Supreme Court of the United States
566 U.S. 156 (2012)

Justice KENNEDY delivered the opinion of the Court.

In this case, as in *Missouri v. Frye,* also decided today, a criminal defendant seeks a remedy when inadequate assistance of counsel caused nonacceptance of a plea offer and further proceedings led to a less favorable outcome. In *Frye*, defense counsel did not inform the defendant of the plea offer; and after the offer lapsed the defendant still pleaded guilty, but on more severe terms. Here, the favorable plea offer was reported to the client but, on advice of counsel, was rejected. In *Frye* there was a later guilty plea. Here, after the plea offer had been rejected, there was a full and fair trial before a jury. After a guilty verdict, the defendant received a sentence harsher than that offered in the rejected plea bargain. The instant case comes to the Court with the concession that counsel's advice with respect to the plea offer fell below the standard of adequate assistance of counsel guaranteed by the Sixth Amendment, applicable to the States through the Fourteenth Amendment.

I

On the evening of March 25, 2003, respondent pointed a gun toward Kali Mundy's head and fired. From the record, it is unclear why respondent did this, and at trial it was suggested that he might have acted either in self-defense or in defense of another person. In any event the shot missed and Mundy fled. Respondent followed in pursuit, firing repeatedly. Mundy was shot in her buttock, hip, and abdomen but survived the assault.

Respondent was charged under Michigan law with assault with intent to murder, possession of a firearm by a felon, possession of a firearm in the commission of a felony, misdemeanor possession of marijuana, and for being a habitual offender. On two occasions, the prosecution offered to dismiss two of the charges and to recommend a sentence of 51 to 85 months for the other two, in exchange for a guilty plea. In a communication with the court respondent admitted guilt and expressed a willingness to accept the offer. Respondent, however, later rejected the offer on both occasions, allegedly after his attorney convinced him that the prosecution would be unable to establish his intent to murder Mundy because she had been shot below the waist. On the first day of trial the prosecution offered a significantly less favorable plea deal, which respondent again rejected. After trial, respondent was convicted on all counts and received a mandatory minimum sentence of 185 to 360 months' imprisonment. . . .

II

Defendants have a Sixth Amendment right to counsel, a right that extends to the plea-bargaining process. . . . In *Hill,* the Court held "the two-part *Strickland v. Washington* test applies to challenges to guilty pleas based on ineffective assistance of counsel." The performance prong of *Strickland* requires a defendant to show "that counsel's representation fell below an objective standard of reasonableness." In this case all parties agree the performance of respondent's counsel was deficient when he advised respondent to reject the plea offer on the grounds he could not be convicted at trial. In light of this concession, it is unnecessary for this Court to explore the issue.

The question for this Court is how to apply *Strickland*'s prejudice test where ineffective assistance results in a rejection of the plea offer and the defendant is convicted at the ensuing trial.

To establish *Strickland* prejudice a defendant must "show that there is a reasonable probability that, but for counsel's unprofessional errors, the result of the proceeding would have been different." In the context of pleas a defendant must show the outcome of the plea process would have been different with competent advice. In *Hill,* when evaluating the petitioner's claim that ineffective assistance led to the improvident acceptance of a guilty plea, the Court required the petitioner to show "that there is a reasonable probability that, but for counsel's errors, [the defendant] would not have pleaded guilty and would have insisted on going to trial."

In contrast to *Hill,* here the ineffective advice led not to an offer's acceptance but to its rejection. Having to stand trial, not choosing to waive it, is the prejudice alleged. In these circumstances a defendant must show that but for the ineffective advice of counsel there is a reasonable probability that the plea offer would have been presented to the court (i.e., that the defendant would have accepted the plea and the prosecution would not have withdrawn it in light of intervening circumstances), that the court would have accepted its terms, and that the conviction or sentence, or both, under the offer's terms would have been less severe than under the judgment and sentence that in fact were imposed. Here, the Court of Appeals for the Sixth Circuit agreed with that test for *Strickland* prejudice in the context of a rejected plea bargain. This is consistent with the test adopted and applied by other appellate courts without demonstrated difficulties or systemic disruptions.

Petitioner and the Solicitor General propose a different, far more narrow, view of the Sixth Amendment. They contend there can be no finding of *Strickland* prejudice arising from plea bargaining if the defendant is later convicted at a fair trial. The three reasons petitioner and the Solicitor General offer for their approach are unpersuasive. . . .

In the instant case respondent went to trial rather than accept a plea deal, and it is conceded this was the result of ineffective assistance during the plea negotiation process. Respondent received a more severe sentence at trial, one 3½ times more severe than he likely would have received by pleading guilty. Far from curing the error, the trial caused the injury from the error. Even if the trial itself is free from constitutional flaw, the defendant who goes to trial instead of taking a more favorable plea may be prejudiced from either a conviction on more serious counts or the imposition of a more severe sentence. . . .

It is, of course, true that defendants have "no right to be offered a plea . . . nor a federal right that the judge accept it." In the circumstances here, that is beside the point. If no plea offer is made, or a plea deal is accepted by the defendant but rejected by the judge, the issue raised here simply does not arise. Much the same reasoning guides cases that find criminal defendants have a right to effective assistance of counsel in direct appeals even though the Constitution does not require States to provide a system of appellate review at all. As in those cases, "[w]hen a State opts to act in a field where its action has significant discretionary elements, it must nonetheless act in accord with the dictates of the Constitution."

Third, petitioner seeks to preserve the conviction obtained by the State by arguing that the purpose of the Sixth Amendment is to ensure "the reliability of [a] conviction following trial." This argument, too, fails to comprehend the full scope of the Sixth Amendment's protections. . . . The goal of a just result is not divorced from the reliability of a conviction, but here the question is not the fairness or reliability of the trial but the fairness and regularity of the processes that preceded it, which caused the defendant to lose benefits he would have received in the ordinary course but for counsel's ineffective assistance. . . .

In the end, petitioner's three arguments amount to one general contention: A fair trial wipes clean any deficient performance by defense counsel during plea bargaining. That position ignores the reality that criminal justice today is for the most part a system of pleas, not a system of trials. Ninety-seven percent of federal convictions and ninety-four percent of state convictions are the result of guilty pleas. As explained in *Frye*, the right to adequate assistance of counsel cannot be defined or enforced without taking account of the central role plea bargaining plays in securing convictions and determining sentences. . . .

III

Respondent has satisfied *Strickland*'s two-part test. Regarding performance, perhaps it could be accepted that it is unclear whether respondent's counsel believed respondent could not be convicted for assault with intent to murder as a matter of law because the shots hit Mundy below the waist, or whether he simply thought this would be a persuasive argument to make to the jury to show lack of specific intent. And, as the Court of Appeals for the Sixth Circuit suggested, an erroneous strategic prediction about the outcome of a trial is not necessarily deficient performance. Here, however, the fact of deficient performance has been conceded by all parties. The case comes to us on that assumption, so there is no need to address this question.

As to prejudice, respondent has shown that but for counsel's deficient performance there is a reasonable probability he and the trial court would have accepted the guilty plea. In addition, as a result of not accepting the plea and being convicted at trial, respondent received a minimum sentence 3½ times greater than he would have received under the plea. The standard for ineffective assistance under *Strickland* has thus been satisfied. . . .

Justice SCALIA, with whom Justice THOMAS joins, and with whom THE CHIEF JUSTICE joins as to all but Part IV, dissenting.

. . . [The] Court today opens a whole new field of constitutionalized criminal procedure: plea-bargaining law. The ordinary criminal process has become too long, too expensive, and unpredictable, in no small part as a consequence of an intricate federal Code of Criminal Procedure imposed on the States by this Court in pursuit of perfect justice. The Court now moves to bring perfection to the alternative in which prosecutors and defendants have sought relief. Today's opinions deal with only two aspects of counsel's plea-bargaining inadequacy, and leave other aspects (who knows what they might be?) to be worked out in further constitutional litigation that will burden the criminal process. And it would be foolish to think that "constitutional" rules governing *counsel*'s behavior will not be followed by rules governing the *prosecution*'s behavior in the plea-bargaining process that the Court today announces "*is* the criminal justice system." Is it constitutional, for example, for the prosecution to withdraw a plea offer that has already been accepted? Or to withdraw an offer before the defense has had adequate time to consider and accept it? Or to make no plea offer at all, even though its case is weak—thereby excluding the defendant from "the criminal justice system"?

Anthony Cooper received a full and fair trial, was found guilty of all charges by a unanimous jury, and was given the sentence that the law prescribed. The Court nonetheless concludes that Cooper is entitled to some sort of habeas corpus relief (perhaps) because his attorney's allegedly incompetent advice regarding a plea offer *caused* him to receive a full and fair trial. That conclusion is foreclosed by our precedents. Even if it were not foreclosed, the constitutional right to effective plea-bargainers that it establishes is at least a new rule of law, which does not undermine the Michigan Court of Appeals' decision and therefore cannot serve as the basis for habeas relief. . . .

In many—perhaps most—countries of the world, American-style plea bargaining is forbidden in cases as serious as this one, even for the purpose of obtaining testimony that enables conviction of a greater malefactor, much less for the purpose of sparing the expense of trial. In Europe, many countries adhere to what they aptly call the "legality principle" by requiring prosecutors to charge all prosecutable offenses, which is typically incompatible with the practice of charge-bargaining. Such a system reflects an admirable belief that the law is the law, and those who break it should pay the penalty provided.

In the United States, we have plea bargaining a-plenty, but until today it has been regarded as a necessary evil. It presents grave risks of prosecutorial overcharging that effectively compels an innocent defendant to avoid massive risk by pleading guilty to a lesser offense; and for guilty defendants it often—perhaps usually—results in a sentence well below what the law prescribes for the actual crime. But even so, we accept plea bargaining because many believe that without it our long and expensive process of criminal trial could not sustain the burden imposed on it, and our system of criminal justice would grind to a halt.

Today, however, the Supreme Court of the United States elevates plea bargaining from a necessary evil to a constitutional entitlement. It is no longer a somewhat embarrassing adjunct to our criminal justice system. . . . [E]ven though there is no doubt that the respondent here is guilty of the offense with which he was charged; even though he has received the exorbitant gold standard of American justice—a full-dress criminal trial with its innumerable constitutional and statutory limitations upon the evidence that the prosecution can bring forward, and (in Michigan as in most States) the requirement of a unanimous guilty verdict by impartial jurors; the Court says that his conviction is invalid because he was deprived of his *constitutional entitlement* to plea-bargain.

I am less saddened by the outcome of this case than I am by what it says about this Court's attitude toward criminal justice. The Court today embraces the sporting-chance theory of criminal law, in which the State functions like a conscientious casino-operator, giving each player a fair chance to beat the house, that is, to serve less time than the law says he deserves. And when a player is excluded from the tables, his *constitutional rights* have been violated. I do not subscribe to that theory. No one should, least of all the Justices of the Supreme Court. . . .

NOTES & QUESTIONS ON REJECTING FAVORABLE PLEA OFFERS

1. *The right to a jury trial.* Since he rejected the favorable plea deal that arguably he should have accepted, Lafler received a jury trial—a jury trial that all parties conceded was a fair trial. This fact alone makes the case an odd one because Lafler argued that forcing him to go through that fair trial was a constitutional violation because an effective attorney would have avoided the trial and recommended acceptance of the plea deal. Do you agree with the government's contention that there could be no constitutional violation given that the trial was fair? Put simply: What is the relationship between the constitutional right to a jury trial and the constitutional right to counsel? Is it possible that the right to counsel would entail that the defendant waive his right to a jury trial (by pleading guilty)? The majority says yes, exactly. In that vein, consider the following:

> The criminal justice system is not designed to prevent harsh consequences, but only unjust convictions. The result the defendant challenged was not due to a failure of the system but to its success; the sentence [he] received after jury trial was due simply to the exposure of the truth by the trial. Justice Kennedy admitted as much when he allowed that a sentencing judge did not need to disregard "information concerning the crime that was discovered after the plea offer was made." *Lafler*, therefore, found a violation of the

> Sixth Amendment despite the fact that the purpose of the right to counsel was fulfilled in this case.

George Dery & Anneli Soo, *Turning the Sixth Amendment Upon Itself: The Supreme Court in* Lafler v. Cooper *Diminished the Right to Jury Trial with the Right to Counsel*, 12 Conn. Pub. Int. L.J. 101, 116 (2012). Do you agree with this criticism? If the trial resulted in the "right" outcome, should it matter that the defendant missed out on an overly generous outcome?

PROBLEM CASE

A defendant is charged with ten counts of child sex abuse. The prosecutor proposed a plea deal. In exchange for pleading guilty, the defendant would serve ten years in prison. The prosecutor explained the rationale for the plea bargain:

> [T]he prosecutor from the first trial stated that she had made the ten-year plea offer because the victims were "going through a whole lot of things personally" at the time the offer was made and she was not sure about their ability to testify.

The defendant's counsel recommended that he reject the plea offer and proceed to trial. Following this advice, the defendant went to trial and was convicted, whereupon he was sentenced to eight *life* sentences, plus an additional sentence of 20 years. Facing the rest of his life in prison, the defendant filed an appeal arguing ineffective assistance of counsel, which was granted by the court. The prosecution then reoffered the original 10-year plea offer and the defendant accepted it, but the judge rejected the plea offer and told the defendant to accept a 25-year sentence or to go to trial. The defendant rejected the 25-year deal and filed a motion for the judge's recusal, arguing that the judge was prejudiced against him.

After the judge voluntarily recused himself from the case, a new judge was assigned in preparation for the second trial. Before the trial could start, the prosecution offered a 25-year plea deal, which the defendant accepted, thus eliminating the need for the second trial. At that point, the defendant appealed again, arguing that he was prejudiced by the original rejection of the 10-year plea bargain offer, which he did on the advice of counsel. Should an appeals court order the reinstatement of the original 10-year offer or should the appeals court let stand the 25-year sentence? See *Rodriguez v. State*, 470 S.W.3d 823, 829 (Tex. Crim. App. 2015).

C. ENFORCING PLEA BARGAINS

A plea bargain, like any agreement, isn't valuable unless it can be enforced. Some plea bargains are easier than others to enforce. Consider, for example, two different types of agreements. Imagine that the prosecutor agrees with a defendant that if he pleads guilty and testifies against a co-felon, he will receive a favorable sentencing recommendation from the prosecution. If the defendant then fails to testify, or fails to testify truthfully, the prosecutor could then give the court a recommendation for a harsher sentence than was first accommodated. The ease of the situation flows from the fact that the defendant's cooperation must take place prior to the prosecutor's reciprocating action, thus giving the defendant a built-in incentive to comply with the arrangement. Things are more complicated in the *reverse* situation: Imagine the same scenario but assume that the defendant cooperates and testifies against the co-felon, but the prosecutor refuses to honor the promise to make the light sentencing recommendation. At this point, the defendant has already performed under the agreement and so has no cards to play. If such an agreement is going to be vindicated, it will have to be through some form of judicial enforcement.

The following materials involve judicial interventions to enforce plea bargains. As you read the cases, compare the cases where defendants ask courts to enforce agreements against prosecutors and the cases where prosecutors are the ones responding to a breach by the defense. Are there pertinent differences? Do prosecutors have tools at their disposal that defense attorneys do not themselves enjoy?

1. Enforcing Agreements Against Prosecutors

In the following case, the prosecution refused to live up to its promise to make a favorable sentencing recommendation. Since the recommendation is, by definition, a *recommendation* (which the judge is free to accept or ignore), what remedy should be given to the defendant in the face of this breach? This raises a tricky problem, because simply forcing the prosecution to make the recommendation is unlikely to change the result in terms of the court's decision. On the other hand, ordering the trial court to impose the sentence contemplated in the negotiated recommendation would appear to unnecessarily compromise the discretion of the trial court to determine the appropriate sentence even in cases where there is a negotiated plea agreement. What to do? As you read the case, ask yourself whether the Court has adequately solved this quandary.

Santobello v. New York

Supreme Court of the United States
404 U.S. 257 (1971)

Mr. Chief Justice Burger delivered the opinion of the Court.

We granted certiorari in this case to determine whether the State's failure to keep a commitment concerning the sentence recommendation on a guilty plea required a new trial.

The facts are not in dispute. The State of New York indicted petitioner in 1969 on two felony [gambling] counts. Petitioner first entered a plea of not guilty to both counts. After negotiations, the Assistant District Attorney in charge of the case agreed to permit petitioner to plead guilty to a lesser-included offense, Possession of Gambling Records in the Second Degree, conviction of which would carry a maximum prison sentence of one year. The prosecutor agreed to make no recommendation as to the sentence.

On June 16, 1969, petitioner accordingly withdrew his plea of not guilty and entered a plea of guilty to the lesser charge. Petitioner represented to the sentencing judge that the plea was voluntary and that the facts of the case, as described by the Assistant District Attorney, were true. The court accepted the plea and set a date for sentencing. A series of delays followed, owing primarily to the absence of a pre-sentence report, so that by September 23, 1969, petitioner had still not been sentenced. By that date petitioner acquired new defense counsel.

Petitioner's new counsel moved immediately to withdraw the guilty plea. In an accompanying affidavit, petitioner alleged that he did not know at the time of his plea that crucial evidence against him had been obtained as a result of an illegal search. The accuracy of this affidavit is subject to challenge since petitioner had filed and withdrawn a motion to suppress, before pleading guilty. In addition to his motion to withdraw his guilty plea, petitioner renewed the motion to suppress and filed a motion to inspect the grand jury minutes.

These three motions in turn caused further delay until November 26, 1969, when the court denied all three and set January 9, 1970, as the date for sentencing. On January 9 petitioner appeared before a different judge, the judge who had presided over the case to this juncture having retired. Petitioner renewed his motions, and the court again rejected them. The court then turned to consideration of the sentence.

At this appearance, another prosecutor had replaced the prosecutor who had negotiated the plea. The new prosecutor recommended the maximum one-year sentence. In making this recommendation, he cited petitioner's criminal record and alleged links with organized crime. Defense counsel immediately objected on the ground that the State had promised petitioner before the plea was entered that there would be no sentence recommendation by the prosecution. He sought to adjourn the sentence hearing in order to have time to prepare proof of the first prosecutor's promise. The second prosecutor, apparently ignorant of his colleague's commitment, argued that there was nothing in the record to support petitioner's claim of a promise, but the

State, in subsequent proceedings, has not contested that such a promise was made. . . .

This record represents another example of an unfortunate lapse in orderly prosecutorial procedures, in part, no doubt, because of the enormous increase in the workload of the often understaffed prosecutor's offices. The heavy workload may well explain these episodes, but it does not excuse them. The disposition of criminal charges by agreement between the prosecutor and the accused, sometimes loosely called "plea bargaining," is an essential component of the administration of justice. Properly administered, it is to be encouraged. If every criminal charge were subjected to a full-scale trial, the States and the Federal Government would need to multiply by many times the number of judges and court facilities.

Disposition of charges after plea discussions is not only an essential part of the process but a highly desirable part for many reasons. It leads to prompt and largely final disposition of most criminal cases; it avoids much of the corrosive impact of enforced idleness during pre-trial confinement for those who are denied release pending trial; it protects the public from those accused persons who are prone to continue criminal conduct even while on pretrial release; and, by shortening the time between charge and disposition, it enhances whatever may be the rehabilitative prospects of the guilty when they are ultimately imprisoned.

However, all of these considerations presuppose fairness in securing agreement between an accused and a prosecutor. It is now clear, for example, that the accused pleading guilty must be counseled, absent a waiver. Fed. Rule Crim. Proc. 11, governing pleas in federal courts, now makes clear that the sentencing judge must develop, on the record, the factual basis for the plea, as, for example, by having the accused describe the conduct that gave rise to the charge. The plea must, of course, be voluntary and knowing and if it was induced by promises, the essence of those promises must in some way be made known. There is, of course, no absolute right to have a guilty plea accepted. A court may reject a plea in exercise of sound judicial discretion.

This phase of the process of criminal justice, and the adjudicative element inherent in accepting a plea of guilty, must be attended by safeguards to insure the defendant what is reasonably due in the circumstances. Those circumstances will vary, but a constant factor is that when a plea rests in any significant degree on a promise or agreement of the prosecutor, so that it can be said to be part of the inducement or consideration, such promise must be fulfilled.

On this record, petitioner "bargained" and negotiated for a particular plea in order to secure dismissal of more serious charges, but also on condition that no sentence recommendation would be made by the prosecutor. It is now conceded that the promise to abstain from a recommendation was made, and at this stage the prosecution is not in a good position to argue that its inadvertent breach of agreement is immaterial. The staff lawyers in a prosecutor's office have the burden of "letting the left hand know what the right hand is doing" or has done. That the breach of agreement was inadvertent does not lessen its impact.

We need not reach the question whether the sentencing judge would or would not have been influenced had he known all the details of the negotiations for the plea. He stated that the prosecutor's recommendation did not influence him and we have no reason to doubt that. Nevertheless, we conclude that the interests of justice and appropriate recognition of the duties of the prosecution in relation to promises made in the negotiation of pleas of guilty will be best served by remanding the case to the state courts for further consideration. The ultimate relief to which petitioner is entitled we leave to the discretion of the state court, which is in a better position to decide whether the circumstances of this case require only that there be specific performance of the agreement on the plea, in which case petitioner should be resentenced by a different judge, or whether, in the view of the state court, the circumstances require granting the relief sought by petitioner, i.e., the opportunity to withdraw his plea of guilty. We emphasize that this is in no sense to question the fairness of the sentencing judge; the fault here rests on the prosecutor, not on the sentencing judge. . . .

NOTES & QUESTIONS ON ENFORCING PLEA AGREEMENTS

1. *What is the remedy?* If the defense wants to enforce a plea agreement that the prosecutors have violated, should the appellate court enforce the agreement through specific performance and order the trial court to impose the negotiated sentence, or should the court merely order the trial court to conduct a new sentencing? State courts have taken a variety of perspectives on this issue. In his concurring opinion in *Santobello*, Justice Douglas offered the following assessment:

> Where the "plea bargain" is not kept by the prosecutor, the sentence must be vacated and the state court will decide in light of the circumstances of each case whether due process requires (a) that there be specific performance of the plea bargain or (b) that the defendant be given the option to

> go to trial on the original charges. One alternative may do justice in one case, and the other in a different case. In choosing a remedy, however, a court ought to accord a defendant's preference considerable, if not controlling, weight inasmuch as the fundamental rights flouted by a prosecutor's breach of a plea bargain are those of the defendant, not of the State.

Santobello v. New York, 404 U.S. 257, 267 (1971). This suggests that the appellate court should usually order the remedy that the defendant is requesting, i.e., either remand with an order to enforce the prior agreement or remand for a new sentencing hearing. For example, in *State v. Freeman*, 115 R.I. 523, 534-35, 351 A.2d 824, 829-30 (1976), the Rhode Island Supreme Court conceded that "there is no authority that due process requires the imposition of the remedy of specific performance where a plea bargain is breached by the state" but in this case specific performance was warranted because "the agreement was reached after extensive plea bargaining between the prosecutor and defendants, and the trial justice after extended questioning of defendants regarding the voluntariness of their pleas committed himself to a sentence of from 2 to 3 years. . . ."

2. Enforcing Agreements Against Defendants

When the defendant fails to live up to the obligations of a plea agreement, the prosecution has a trump card up its sleeve: It could, in theory, re-indict the defendant for a more serious crime than the one he pleaded guilty to. So, for example, if the defendant pleads guilty to manslaughter, agrees to testify, but then fails to follow through, the prosecution might respond by seeking a new indictment for first-degree murder. In the following case, the Supreme Court asks whether the Double Jeopardy Clause prohibits this move.

Ricketts v. Adamson

Supreme Court of the United States
483 U.S. 1 (1987)

Justice White delivered the opinion of the Court.

The question for decision is whether the Double Jeopardy Clause bars the prosecution of respondent for first-degree murder following his breach of a plea agreement under which he had pleaded guilty to a lesser offense, had been sentenced, and had begun serving a term of imprisonment. The Court of Appeals for the Ninth Circuit held that the prosecution of respondent violated double jeopardy principles and directed the issuance of a writ of habeas corpus. We reverse.

The damaged 1976 Datsun 710 in which reporter Don Bolles was fatally injured by a car bomb, on display at the Newseum, Washington, D.C. (Steve Terrell/Flickr)

In 1976, Donald Bolles, a reporter for the Arizona Republic, was fatally injured when a dynamite bomb exploded underneath his car. Respondent was arrested and charged with first-degree murder in connection with Bolles' death. Shortly after his trial had commenced, while jury selection was underway, respondent and the state prosecutor reached an agreement whereby respondent agreed to plead guilty to a charge of second-degree murder and to testify against two other individuals—Max Dunlap and James Robison—who were allegedly involved in Bolles' murder. Specifically, respondent agreed to "testify fully and completely in any Court, State or Federal, when requested by proper authorities against any and all parties involved in the murder of Don Bolles. . . ." The agreement provided that "[s]hould the defendant refuse to testify or should he at any time testify untruthfully . . . then this entire agreement is null and void and the original charge will be automatically reinstated." The parties agreed that respondent would receive a prison sentence of 48-49 years, with a total incarceration time of 20 years and 2 months. In January 1977, the state trial court accepted the plea agreement and the proposed sentence, but withheld imposition of the sentence. Thereafter, respondent testified as obligated under the agreement, and both Dunlap and Robison were convicted of the first-degree murder of Bolles. While their convictions and sentences were on appeal, the trial court, upon motion of the State, sentenced respondent. In February 1980, the Arizona Supreme Court reversed the convictions of Dunlap and Robison and remanded their cases for retrial. This event sparked the dispute now before us.

The State sought respondent's cooperation and testimony in preparation for the retrial of Dunlap and Robison. On April 3, 1980, however, respondent's counsel informed the prosecutor that respondent believed his obligation to provide testimony under the agreement had terminated when he was sentenced. Respondent would again testify against Dunlap and Robison only if certain conditions were met, including, among others, that the State release him from custody following the retrial. The State then informed respondent's attorney on April 9, 1980, that it deemed respondent to be in breach of the plea agreement. On April 18, 1980, the State called respondent to testify in pretrial proceedings. In response to questions, and upon advice of counsel, respondent invoked his Fifth Amendment privilege against self-incrimination. The trial judge, after respondent's counsel apprised him of the State's letter of April 9 indicating that the State considered respondent to be in breach of the plea agreement, refused to compel respondent to answer questions. . . .

On May 8, 1980, the State filed a new information charging respondent with first-degree murder. . . . [R]espondent offered to testify at the retrials, but the State declined his offer. . . . Respondent was then convicted of first-degree murder and sentenced to death. . . .

The State submits . . . that respondent's breach of the plea arrangement to which the parties had agreed removed the double jeopardy bar to prosecution of respondent on the first-degree murder charge. We agree with the State.

Under the terms of the plea agreement, both parties bargained for and received substantial benefits. The State obtained respondent's guilty plea and his promise to testify against "any and all parties involved in the murder of Don Bolles" and in certain specified other crimes. Respondent, a direct participant in a premeditated and brutal murder, received a specified prison sentence accompanied with a guarantee that he would serve actual incarceration time of 20 years and 2 months. He further obtained the State's promise that he would not be prosecuted for his involvement in certain other crimes.

The agreement specifies in two separate paragraphs the consequences that would flow from respondent's breach of his promises. Paragraph 5 provides that if respondent refused to testify, "this entire agreement is null and void and the original charge will be automatically reinstated." Similarly, Paragraph 15 of the agreement states that "[i]n the event this agreement becomes null and void, then the parties shall be returned to the positions they were in before this agreement." Respondent unquestionably understood the meaning of these provisions. At the plea hearing, the trial judge read the plea agreement to respondent, line by line, and pointedly asked respondent whether he understood the provisions in Paragraphs 5 and 15. Respondent replied "Yes, sir," to each question. On this score, we do not find it significant, as did the Court of Appeals, that "double jeopardy" was not specifically waived by name in the plea agreement. Nor are we persuaded by the court's assertion that "[a]greeing that charges may be reinstituted . . . is not equivalent to agreeing that if they are reinstituted a double jeopardy defense is waived." The terms of the agreement could not be clearer: in the event of respondent's breach occasioned by a refusal to testify, the parties would be returned to the status quo ante, in which case respondent would have no double jeopardy defense to waive. And, an agreement specifying that charges may be reinstated given certain circumstances is, at least under the provisions of this plea agreement, precisely equivalent to an agreement waiving a double jeopardy defense. . . .

We are also unimpressed by the Court of Appeals' holding that there was a good-faith dispute about whether respondent was bound to testify a second time and that until the extent of his obligation was decided, there could be no knowing and intelligent waiver of his double jeopardy defense. But respondent knew that if he breached the agreement he could be retried, and it is incredible to believe that he did not anticipate that the extent of his obligation would be decided by a court. Here he sought a construction of the agreement in the Arizona Supreme Court, and that court found that he had failed to live up to his promise. The result was that respondent was returned to the position he occupied prior to execution of the plea bargain: he stood charged with first-degree murder. Trial on that charge did not violate the Double Jeopardy Clause. . . .

Respondent cannot escape the Arizona Supreme Court's interpretation of his obligations under the agreement. The State did not force the breach; respondent chose, perhaps for strategic reasons or as a gamble, to advance an interpretation of the agreement that proved erroneous. And, there is no indication that respondent did not fully understand the potential seriousness of the position he adopted. In the April 3 letter, respondent's counsel advised the prosecutor that respondent "is fully aware of the fact that your office may feel that he has not completed his obligations under the plea agreement . . . and, further, that your office may attempt to withdraw the plea agreement from him, [and] that he may be prosecuted for the killing of Donald Bolles on a first degree murder charge." This statement of respondent's awareness of the operative terms of the plea agreement only underscores that which respondent's plea hearing made evident: respondent clearly appreciated and understood the consequences were he found to be in breach of the agreement. . . .

Finally, it is of no moment that following the Arizona Supreme Court's decision respondent offered to comply with the terms of the agreement. At this point, respondent's second-degree murder conviction had already been ordered vacated and the original charge reinstated. The parties did not agree that respondent would be relieved from the consequences of his refusal to testify if he were able to advance a colorable argument that a testimonial obligation was not owing. The parties could have struck a different bargain, but permitting the State to enforce the agreement the parties actually made does not violate the Double Jeopardy Clause. . . .

Justice Brennan, with whom Justice Marshall, Justice Blackmun, and Justice Stevens join, dissenting.

The critical question in this case is whether Adamson ever breached his plea agreement. Only by demonstrating that such a breach occurred can it plausibly be argued that Adamson waived his rights under the Double Jeopardy Clause. By simply assuming that such a breach occurred, the Court ignores the only important issue in this case. . . .

This Court has yet to address in any comprehensive way the rules of construction appropriate for disputes involving plea agreements. Nevertheless, it seems clear that the law of commercial contract may in some cases prove useful as an analogy or point of departure in construing a plea agreement, or in framing the terms of the debate. It is also clear, however, that commercial contract law can do no more than this, because plea agreements are constitutional contracts. The values that underlie commercial contract law, and that govern the relations between economic actors, are not coextensive with those that underlie the Due Process Clause, and that govern relations between criminal defendants and the State. Unlike some commercial contracts, plea agreements must be construed in light of the rights and obligations created by the Constitution.

The State argues and the Arizona Supreme Court seems to imply that a breach occurred when Adamson sent his letter of April 3, 1980, to the prosecutor in response to the State's demand for his testimony at the retrials of Dunlap and Robison. In this letter, Adamson stated that, under his interpretation of the agreement, he was no longer obligated to testify, and demanded additional consideration for any additional testimony.

Neither the State, the state courts, nor this Court has attempted to explain why this letter constituted a breach of the agreement. Of course, it could not plausibly be argued that merely sending such a letter constituted a breach by nonperformance, for nothing in the plea agreement states that Adamson shall not disagree with the State's interpretation of the plea agreement, or that Adamson shall not send the State a letter to that effect. But one might argue that, in the language of commercial contract law, the letter constituted a breach by anticipatory repudiation. Such a breach occurs when one party unequivocally informs the other that it no longer intends to honor their contract. . . .

In the conventional case of anticipatory repudiation, therefore, the announcement of an intention to default on the contract constitutes a breach. In his letter of April 3, however, Adamson did not announce such an intention. To the contrary, Adamson invoked the integrity of that agreement as a defense to what he perceived to be an unwarranted demand by the prosecutor that he testify at the retrials of Dunlap and Robison. And in insisting that he had no obligation to perform as the State demanded, Adamson advanced an objectively reasonable interpretation of his contract.

We have held in the commercial sphere that a letter of the sort that Adamson sent does not constitute anticipatory repudiation. In *New York Life Ins. Co. v. Viglas*, 297 U.S. 672 (1936), the Court addressed the question whether an insurance company's notification to a policyholder that it would henceforth refuse to continue paying disability benefits constituted a breach of the contract. The Court ultimately found that the company's subsequent action to stop payment constituted a breach of the agreement, noting that the insurance company's refusal was based on unfounded facts. But the Court held that the notification alone did not constitute a breach by repudiation. . . .

Adamson has done no more here to repudiate his plea agreement than did the New York Life Insurance Company in *Viglas*. . . . After his lawyers were informed, by telephone, of the State's view that his plea agreement obligated him to testify, he responded with a letter advancing his own reasonable interpretation of the agreement. Although the area of breach by repudiation, like other areas of commercial contract law, is not free from ambiguity, it seems plain that even under commercial contract principles Adamson did not breach his agreement. . . .

PROBLEM CASE

The defendant, Tracy Lynn Dyer, pleaded guilty to first-degree murder, assault, and conspiracy. In exchange for pleading guilty, Dyer agreed to a sentence of life for the murder and ten years each on the remaining two charges, which were to be served concurrently. As part of the plea bargain, Dyer was obligated to testify against his co-defendant at trial. Dyer signed a plea bargain that explicitly included a waiver of his right to a jury trial but no other explicit waivers. During the plea hearing, the judge asked the prosecution about its recourse in the event that the defendant breached the agreement; the prosecution responded that it could—or would—charge Dyer with perjury.

After sentencing, Dyer had a change of heart and declined to testify against his former co-defendant. The prosecution declared the plea agreement breached and moved to prosecute the defendant. Dyer was convicted at trial and sentenced to life without the possibility of parole for the murder, followed by ten-year sentences each on the second and third charges. The ten-year sentences were to be served ***consecutively*** with the life sentence, making this sentence harsher than the one he agreed to during the original plea agreement. Dyer objected, arguing that his trial violated the prohibition against double jeopardy, since jeopardy attached when he first pleaded guilty. How should an appeals court rule? Was the trial inconsistent with the Supreme Court's holding in *Ricketts v. Adamson*? See *Dyer v. State*, 34 P.3d 652 (Okla. Ct. Cr. App. 2001).

D. PRACTICE & POLICY

The materials in this chapter have delivered a front-row seat of the promise and perils of negotiated justice. While plea agreements accomplish many things—increased efficiency for courts and lawyers, lower risk for defendants—they come at great cost. In many ways, it is absurd that the vast majority of criminal defendants receive punishment without the benefit of a criminal trial. Just the possibility of a trial is enough to bring them to the bargaining table and ultimately waive their Fifth and Sixth Amendment rights. Consequently, many have lamented that plea bargaining has quietly taken over the entire justice system, delivering outcomes that are privately negotiated and shielded from the light of a public trial. As one legal scholar, now a judge, summarized it:

> Plea bargaining has semiprivatized public justice. That explains why the parties prefer it as a fast, cheap, discreet, consensual resolution that leaves prosecutors, defense lawyers, and judges all better off. That very semiprivate aspect also explains the many legitimate objections to plea bargaining: it commodifies justice, mutes its trumpet, excludes central and supporting actors, and bypasses the cathartic morality play of a jury trial.

Stephanos Bibas, *Incompetent Plea Bargaining and Extrajudicial Reforms*, 126 Harv. L. Rev. 150, 173-74 (2012). In response to these well-known anxieties over plea bargaining, scholars and lawyers have proposed a number of reforms that might, in theory, keep the benefits of plea bargaining while eliminating, or at the very least reducing, the costs to defendants who voluntarily waive their right to a jury trial. What follows is a survey of a handful of these reform proposals. Which ones do you find compelling? However, before proceeding to the proposals, a brief history lesson is in order:

❧ **The history of plea bargaining.** Plea bargaining was an innovation designed to cure a particular problem. According to legal historian George Fisher, plea bargaining emerged in the very early 1800s in Massachusetts in liquor prosecutions. An experimental prosecutor would charge defendants with multi-count indictments and later exercise his authority to drop certain charges (nolle prosequi) in exchange for a guilty plea on the remaining charges. George Fisher, *Plea Bargaining's Triumph: A History of Plea Bargaining in America* (2003). This practice drew the ire of local officials who complained that his lack of trials and lack of convictions were hurting revenue from fines. The authority to drop charges through nolle prosequi was eventually transferred to judges in order to prevent prosecutors from exercising their discretion in making plea deals. However, prosecutors eventually found other mechanisms to negotiate solutions by, for example, delaying cases, which functioned as a form of de facto probation, according to Fisher. Eventually, full blown plea bargaining became an accepted part of the system, and the underhanded mechanisms that prosecutors once employed to negotiate solutions were replaced with open negotiations and explicit agreements. Plea bargaining moved from the shadows to the light.

The standard argument for why judges were motivated to ratify plea deals is that caseloads increased dramatically and judges struggled to deal with the mountain of cases, thus preventing them from taking all cases to trial. However, Fisher's research suggests that the caseload increase wasn't criminal in nature—courts were facing an onslaught of *civil* cases that were burdening the courts, and courts responded by reducing their caseload in the only way they knew how: plea bargaining in criminal cases. While civil litigation can result in settlements, the timing of those negotiations is capricious and many of the reason why civil litigants settle today—the high cost of discovery and litigation generally—didn't apply back then. But criminal defendants might be quick to plead guilty in order to avoid the most serious charges against them.

What lessons might be learned from this history, particularly lessons that might be useful as one debates potential reforms to the plea bargaining process? Before considering specific reform proposals, it is help to remember that "bargaining is like a garden weed—malleable, organic, and exceedingly hard to eradicate. Even when its roots are chopped down, it manages to grow back elsewhere, wherever and whenever the most basic conditions for its survival are present." Jennifer L. Mnookin, *Uncertain Bargains: The Rise of Plea Bargaining in America*, 57 Stan. L. Rev. 1721, 1727 (2005) (also noting that "hardy and resilient though bargaining may be, its particular shape responds directly to the details of institutional arrangements"). Here are some possible reforms:

❧ **Change discovery rules.** One reason why defendants plead guilty is because they overestimate the strength of the prosecution's case. Although constitutional discovery requires that the prosecution turn over evidence to the defense prior to the commencement of trial, the timing of that discovery means that plea bargaining might occur before the defense has had the opportunity to fully evaluate the strength of the prosecution's case. So, one solution might be to impose greater statutory requirements for full discovery earlier in the process. Bibas notes that

> [t]hough there is no constitutional right to impeachment information in advance of trial, and likely no right to exculpatory material in advance of trial, prosecutors are free to provide this information earlier, and some do. Exculpatory information is particularly important to innocent defendants, who, as noted above, may be the least knowledgeable about the prosecution's case. One possible drawback of more discovery is that egocentrism skews interpretation of new information to reinforce self-serving beliefs.

Stephanos Bibas, *Plea Bargaining Outside the Shadow of Trial*, 117 Harv. L. Rev. 2463, 2531-32 (2004). Defendants would still plead guilty but they might hold out for a better deal than they would otherwise if they were kept in the dark about the full scope of the prosecution's evidence. The goal of the reform would be to make the information available for the negotiating process line up with the evidence that would be introduced at trial. Do you agree that liberalizing discovery rules in this way would have a substantial effect?

❧ **Devote more financial resources to public defenders.** Public defenders are often overworked and defendants might feel coerced into pleading guilty because they do not have confidence in their ability to secure an acquittal if they are represented by an underfunded and understaffed public defender's office. With more funding, the quality of the representation will be improved, in part by giving public defenders a lower caseload. In theory, defendants should factor their increased chances into their plea bargain decisions and therefore hold out for better deals. Prosecutors, also aware of the increased resources available to public defenders, will be forced to offer better deals or risk acquittals at jury trials. In this vein, one might think about the deficits in plea bargaining as simply a reflection of greater inequities in the criminal justice system. If there is an equality of arms between the prosecution and the defense, the results of a negotiated compromise will be just, but if there is fundamental inequality of arms between prosecution and the defense, their negotiations will be infected by that inequality. To solve the specific problem, one might need to solve the bigger problem.

❧ **Fixed discounts for pleading guilty.** Another possible solution is to take away some discretion from the actors to reached tailored outcomes. For example, one might construct a plea bargaining system that would require prosecutors and defendants to select from a range of outcomes that are defined by statute—if those options are not palatable to both parties, they would need to go to trial to vindicate their position. One version of this idea calls for plea-based ceilings:

> [P]lea-based ceilings would establish mandatory caps or ceilings on trial sentences. Pursuant to the ceiling, no defendant could receive a punishment after trial that exceeded the sentence he could have had as a result of a plea offer by more than a modest, predetermined amount. Ceilings would thus limit the sentencing differential and enforce a fixed discount by capping the punishment that could be imposed on the defendant who pleads not guilty.

Russell D. Covey, *Fixed Justice: Reforming Plea Bargaining with Plea-Based Ceilings*, 82 Tul. L. Rev. 1237, 1242 (2008). The idea of using a fixed discount for pleading guilty is controversial; it clearly creates uniformity across the system, but it also limits the ability of the parties to craft particular compromises uniquely tailored to the situation. However, assuming that the prosecution could still dismiss entire charges as part of the plea bargain, the fixed-discount system might work.

❧ **An increased role for judges.** Plea bargaining is a party-driven process. The prosecution and the defense negotiate a compromise that both sides are willing to accept rather than risk the uncertain outcome of a trial. The negotiated solution is then presented to the judge, who formally accepts the dismissal of any charges and also imposes a sentence—usually, though not always, in accordance with the terms of the plea agreement. Although in theory a judge could reject a plea bargain entirely and force a trial, this is very rare. Judges usually ratify the outcomes that the parties have negotiated privately. But if there was a judge controlling the entire process, a court hearing could be used to negotiate a compromise on the record. Consider the following proposal, which involves the judge actually setting two punishments: one if the defendant pleads guilty prior to trial and the other if the defendant is convicted at trial:

> At the conclusion of the conference, or after an appropriate interval, the judge would order two alternative dispositions of the defendant's case. The first would be imposed after conviction at trial, and would have been either selected from the dispositions submitted by counsel or formulated by the judge himself. It would include whatever charge reductions or dismissals the judge found appropriate and a sentence

> designation for each remaining charge. The second disposition would be imposed following a plea of guilty, and would be determined by reducing the total sentence designated for the post-trial disposition by a specific discount rate. This rate would be uniform for all defendants within a given jurisdiction and would embody the median plea concession necessary to induce an administratively acceptable volume of guilty pleas in that jurisdiction. The judge would be required to announce these alternative dispositions without recommendation or comment.

Note, *Restructuring the Plea Bargain*, 82 Yale L.J. 286, 301-02 (1972). Are there any downsides to this proposal? One possible defect is that the judge would need to impose a provisional sentence prior to the actual guilt phase of the trial and without the benefit of the evidence presented during that proceeding. This might strike some as putting the cart before the horse. However, one could separate this two-alternative-dispositions proposal from the more general point that judges could oversee the plea bargaining process rather than leaving it to the parties to hash out individually (and in private). The involvement of the judge might mitigate the risk that defense counsel might give erroneous or incompetent advice to the defendant.

❧ **A separate prosecutor just for negotiating plea bargains.** In most typical cases, the trial prosecutor will engage in negotiations with the defense counsel. The trial prosecutor not only knows the evidence but also can gauge his or her own willingness to bring the case to trial. If the prosecutor is hesitant because the evidence is weak, the prosecutor will be more likely to propose or accept a deal. The result of this process is that each prosecutor will handle his or her own negotiations, with different standards. What if each prosecutorial office appointed a single prosecutor in charge of negotiating all plea deals? Would this promote consistency? Consider the following assessment of the proposal:

> Implementation of these procedures would produce several improvements over the present system. By devoting himself exclusively to plea bargaining, the executive prosecutor should develop a rich background of experience useful in resolving the more difficult questions. He should prove a more efficient and objective plea negotiator because he will not be engaged in the trial of other cases and because possible conflict between office policies and his personal goals will be minimized. In addition, placing the authority for plea negotiation in fewer, more responsible hands would encourage uniform treatment of defendants. Finally, under the proposed procedure plea discussions would be initiated earlier, thus facilitating quick disposition of cases.

Welsh S. White, *A Proposal for Reform of the Plea Bargaining Process*, 119 U. Pa. L. Rev. 439, 454-55 (1971). This proposal would certainly increase consistency, although the flip side is that the plea bargaining prosecutor would have less familiarity with the facts and evidence of each case. Does that lack of familiarity strike you as a feature or a bug in the proposal?

PART V

CONDUCTING THE TRIAL

CHAPTER 14

Right to a Speedy Trial

INTRODUCTION

The right to a speedy trial is an essential component of the rule of law. As the saying goes, justice delayed is justice denied, not just for the victims and society more broadly, but for the accused as well. In the case of a defendant in pre-trial detention, this is literally true, insofar as the only way of getting out of jail is to win an acquittal at trial; any delay in the trial will delay even the possibility of obtaining freedom. But even in a case where a defendant is free on bail or free on their own recognizance, the delay of a trial, whether it occurs at the pre-charging or post-charging stage, delays the moment when a suspect or an accused can achieve formal exoneration. Until that time, a dark cloud of suspicion may hang over and follow the suspect.

For this and other reasons, the Framers saw fit to codify the right to a speedy trial in the Sixth Amendment, which reads:

> In all criminal prosecutions, the accused shall enjoy the right to a speedy and public trial, by an impartial jury of the state and district wherein the crime shall have been committed, which district shall have been previously ascertained by law, and to be informed of the nature and cause of the accusation. . . .

Because of the use of the word "accused," the Supreme Court has held that this Sixth Amendment protection applies only to post-charging delays, because prior to being charged, there is no "accused" at all, only a suspect. But that does not entail that a mere suspect has no rights to a speedy trial at all. As will be discussed below, courts have recognized that the principle of due process, protected in the Fifth and Fourteenth Amendments, encompasses a more general right to disposition of an allegation of criminal misconduct in a manner that is not unreasonably delayed with accordant prejudice—a right that sweeps more broadly than the Sixth Amendment protection.

The *application* of the right to a speedy trial is necessarily fact-dependent and must be made on a case-by-case basis. As the Supreme Court recognized long ago in *Beavers v. Haubert,* 198 U.S. 77, 87 (1905): "The right of a speedy trial is necessarily relative. It is consistent with delays and depends upon circumstances." Consequently, the actualization of the right is seen as where the rubber meets the road. How long is too long? Which reasons for delay will be considered as legitimate and which ones will be deemed unacceptable? While statutes may impose specific deadlines for the trial process, they include many exceptions. And as a matter of constitutional law, neither the Fifth nor the Sixth Amendment includes specific timelines to guide our decision making. There is no substitution for all-things-considered judgment about the nature of each case and whether a delay is unconstitutionally unjustified and excessive. Along the way, however, courts have established standards, which are outlined below, that help guide the analysis.

Section A of this chapter focuses on pre-charging delays governed by a Fifth Amendment analysis, while Section B focuses on post-charging delays governed by a Sixth Amendment standard. Then, Section C focuses on the federal Speedy Trial Act, which imposes additional statutory requirements in federal criminal trials, as well as analogous statutes in state jurisdictions. Finally, Section D, the Practice & Policy section at the end of the chapter, focuses on practical barriers to on-the-ground implementation of the speedy trial right, including expansive interpretations of statutory exceptions and a lack of judicial resources to conduct trials in an expeditious manner.

A. PRE-CHARGING DELAY

Recall that the Sixth Amendment does not protect the right to be free from a pre-charging delay in the commencement of trial. But it would be odd to suggest that the government could simply wait forever to charge a particular defendant. Moreover, one could imagine a situation where doing so would inure to the benefit of the prosecutor. For example, consider a case where the prosecution's case is based on forensic evidence that is unlikely to spoil with the passage in time. If, on the other hand, the defense case will be based on two alibi witnesses who will testify that the suspect could not have committed the crime, the prosecution would have an incentive to delay indicting the defendant until such time as the alibi witnesses died or otherwise became unavailable. The result would be a delay that does not harm the government's future case but utterly hamstrings the defendant's ability to present a defense. For this and other reasons, one might ask whether a delay of this kind, though not addressed by the Sixth Amendment, might nonetheless run afoul of a more general requirement of "fundamental fairness" protected by due process under the Fifth and Fourteenth Amendments.

In the following case, *United States v. Marion*, the Supreme Court considers whether to recognize a Fifth Amendment due process right to be free from an unreasonable pre-charging delay. As you read the case, ask yourself whether other procedural protections, such as statutes of limitations, are by themselves adequate to protect against unreasonable pre-charging delays.

United States v. Marion

Supreme Court of the United States
404 U.S. 307 (1971)

Mr. Justice WHITE delivered the opinion of the Court.

This appeal requires us to decide whether dismissal of a federal indictment was constitutionally required by reason of a period of three years between the occurrence of the alleged criminal acts and the filing of the indictment.

On April 21, 1970, the two appellees were indicted and charged in 19 counts with operating a business known as Allied Enterprises, Inc., which was engaged in the business of selling and installing home improvements such as intercom sets, fire control devices, and burglary detection systems. Allegedly, the business was fraudulently conducted and involved misrepresentations, alterations of documents, and deliberate nonperformance of contracts. The period covered by the indictment was March 15, 1965, to February 6, 1967; the earliest specific act alleged occurred on September 3, 1965, the latest on January 19, 1966.

On May 5, 1970, appellees filed a motion to dismiss the indictment "for failure to commence prosecution of the alleged offenses charged therein within such time as to afford (them their) rights to due process of law and to a speedy trial under the Fifth and Sixth Amendments to the Constitution of the United States." No evidence was submitted, but from the motion itself and the arguments of counsel at the hearing on the motion, it appears that Allied Enterprises had been subject to a Federal Trade Commission cease and desist order on February 6, 1967, and that a series of articles appeared in the Washington Post in October 1967, reporting the results of that newspaper's investigation of practices employed by home improvement firms such as Allied. The articles also contained purported statements of the then United States Attorney for the District of Columbia describing his office's investigation of these firms and predicting that indictments would soon be forthcoming. Although the statements attributed to the United States Attorney did not mention Allied specifically, that company was mentioned in the course of the newspaper stories. In the summer of 1968, at the request of the United States Attorney's office, Allied delivered certain of its records to that office, and in an interview there appellee Marion discussed his conduct as an officer of Allied Enterprises. The grand jury that indicted appellees was not impaneled until September 1969, appellees were not informed of the grand jury's concern with them until March 1970, and the indictment was finally handed down in April.

Appellees moved to dismiss because the indictment was returned "an unreasonably oppressive and unjustifiable time after the alleged offenses." They argued that the indictment required memory of many specific acts and conversations occurring several years before, and they contended that the delay was due to the negligence or indifference of the United States Attorney in investigating the case and presenting it to a grand jury. No specific prejudice was claimed or demonstrated. The District Court judge dismissed the indictment for "lack of speedy prosecution" at the conclusion of the hearing and remarked that since the Government must have become aware of the relevant facts in 1967, the defense of the case "is bound to have been seriously prejudiced by the delay of at least some three years in bringing the prosecution that should have been brought in 1967, or at the very latest early 1968." . . .

II

Appellees do not claim that the Sixth Amendment was violated by the two-month delay between the return of the indictment and its dismissal. Instead, they claim that their rights to a speedy trial were violated by the period of approximately three years between the end of the criminal scheme charged and the return of the indictment; it is argued that this delay is so substantial and inherently prejudicial that the Sixth Amendment required the dismissal of the indictment. In our view, however, the Sixth Amendment speedy trial provision has no application until the putative defendant in some way becomes an "accused," an event that occurred in this case only when the appellees were indicted on April 21, 1970.

The Sixth Amendment provides that "[i]n all criminal prosecutions, the accused shall enjoy the right to a speedy and public trial. . . ." On its face, the protection of the Amendment is activated only when a criminal prosecution has begun and extends only to those persons who have been "accused" in the course of that prosecution. These provisions would seem to afford no protection to those not yet accused, nor would they seem to require the Government to discover, investigate, and accuse any person within any particular period of time. The amendment would appear to guarantee to a criminal defendant that the Government will move with the dispatch that is appropriate to assure him an early and proper disposition of the charges against him. . . .

Our attention is called to nothing in the circumstances surrounding the adoption of the Amendment indicating that it does not mean what it appears to say, nor is there more than marginal support for the proposition that, at the time of the adoption of the Amendment, the prevailing rule was that prosecutions would not be permitted if there had been long delay in presenting a charge. The framers could hardly have selected less appropriate language if they had intended the speedy trial provision to protect against pre-accusation delay. No opinions of this Court intimate support for appellees' thesis, and the courts of appeals that have considered the question in constitutional terms have never reversed a conviction or dismissed an indictment solely on the basis of the Sixth Amendment's speedy trial provision where only pre-indictment delay was involved. . . .

No federal statute of general applicability has been enacted by Congress to enforce the speedy trial provision of the Sixth Amendment, but Federal Rule of Criminal Procedure 48(b), which has the force of law, authorizes dismissal of an indictment, information, or complaint "(i)f there is unnecessary delay in presenting the charge to a grand jury or in filing an information against a defendant who has been held to answer to the district court, or if there is unnecessary delay in bringing a defendant to trial. . . ." The rule clearly is limited to post-arrest situations.

Appellees' position is, therefore, at odds with longstanding legislative and judicial constructions of the speedy trial provisions in both national and state constitutions.

III

It is apparent also that very little support for appellees' position emerges from a consideration of the purposes of the Sixth Amendment's speedy trial provision, a guarantee that this Court has termed "an important safeguard to prevent undue and oppressive incarceration prior to trial, to minimize anxiety and concern accompanying public accusation and to limit the possibilities that long delay will impair the ability of an accused to defend himself." *United States v. Ewell*, 383 U.S. 116, 120 (1966). Inordinate delay between arrest, indictment, and trial may impair a defendant's ability to present an effective defense. But the major evils protected against by the speedy trial guarantee exist quite apart from actual or possible prejudice to an accused's defense. To legally arrest and detain, the Government must assert probable cause to believe the arrestee has committed a crime. Arrest is a public act that may seriously interfere with the defendant's liberty, whether he is free on bail or not, and that may disrupt his employment, drain his financial resources, curtail his associations, subject him to public obloquy, and create anxiety in him, his family and his friends. . . . So viewed, it is readily understandable that it is either a formal indictment or information or else the actual restraints imposed by arrest and holding to answer a criminal charge that engage the particular protections of the speedy trial provision of the Sixth Amendment.

Invocation of the speedy trial provision thus need not await indictment, information, or other formal charge. But we decline to extend that reach of the amendment to the period prior to arrest. Until this event occurs, a citizen suffers no restraints on his liberty and is not the subject of public accusation: his situation does not compare with that of a defendant who has been arrested and held to answer. Passage of time, whether before or after arrest, may impair memories, cause evidence to be lost, deprive the defendant of witnesses, and otherwise interfere with his ability to defend himself. But this possibility of prejudice at trial is not itself sufficient reason to wrench the Sixth Amendment from its proper context. Possible prejudice is inherent in any delay, however short; it may also weaken the Government's case.

The law has provided other mechanisms to guard against possible as distinguished from actual prejudice resulting from the passage of time between crime and arrest or charge. As we said in *United States v. Ewell*, 386 U.S., at 122, "the applicable statute of limitations . . . is . . . the primary guarantee against bringing overly stale criminal charges." . . . These statutes provide predictability by specifying a limit beyond which there is an irrebuttable presumption that a defendant's right to a fair trial would be prejudiced. . . . There is thus no need to press the Sixth Amendment into service to guard against the mere possibility that pre-accusation delays will prejudice the defense in a criminal case since statutes of limitation already perform that function. . . .

[T]he Government concedes that the Due Process Clause of the Fifth Amendment would require dismissal of the indictment if it were shown at trial that the pre-indictment delay in this case caused substantial prejudice to appellees' rights to a fair trial and that the delay was an intentional device to gain tactical advantage over the accused. However, we need not, and could not now, determine when and in what circumstances actual prejudice resulting from pre-accusation delays requires the dismissal of the prosecution. Actual prejudice to the defense of a criminal case may result from the shortest and most necessary delay; and no one suggests that every delay-caused detriment to a defendant's case should abort a criminal prosecution. To accommodate the sound administration of justice to the rights of the defendant to a fair trial will necessarily involve a delicate judgment based on the circumstances of each case. It would be unwise at this juncture to attempt to forecast our decision in such cases.

IV

In the case before us, neither appellee was arrested, charged, or otherwise subjected to formal restraint prior to indictment. It was this event, therefore, that transformed the appellees into "accused" defendants who are subject to the speedy trial protections of the Sixth Amendment.

The 38-month delay between the end of the scheme charged in the indictment and the date the defendants were indicted did not extend beyond the period of the applicable statute of limitations here. Appellees have not, of course, been able to claim undue delay pending trial, since the indictment was brought on April 21, 1970, and dismissed on June 8, 1970. Nor have appellees adequately demonstrated that the pre-indictment delay by the Government violated the Due Process Clause. No actual prejudice to the conduct of the defense is alleged or proved, and there is no showing that the Government intentionally delayed to gain some tactical advantage over appellees or to harass them. Appellees rely solely on the real possibility of prejudice inherent in any extended delay: that memories will dim, witnesses become inaccessible, and evidence be lost. In light of the applicable statute of limitations, however, these possibilities are not in themselves enough to demonstrate that appellees cannot receive a fair trial and to therefore justify the dismissal of the indictment. Events of the trial may demonstrate actual prejudice, but at the present time appellees' due process claims are speculative and premature.

PROBLEM CASE

Consider the following case. Ben Chester White was killed in 1966 in Homochitto National Forest in Mississippi; the murder appeared to have racial motivations. The next day, the chief suspect, James Jones, gave a statement to police implicating himself, Claude Fuller, and Ernest Avants in the murder.

Avants was indicted and scheduled to go on trial in state court in 1967. Before the trial, however, federal agents interviewed Avants in connection with another murder case, and during that interview Avants confessed to the White murder. The interview was recorded on videotape. It appears that state prosecutors were unaware of the videotaped statement with the federal agents, and Avants was acquitted of murder in his state trial.

In 1999, more than three decades later, a national news program was broadcast about the case, prompting renewed scrutiny, and federal lawyers reexamined it. The Justice Department launched a federal murder case with jurisdiction based on the fact that the killing occurred in a federal national forest. Because of the dual sovereign theory, the prohibition on double jeopardy did not prevent prosecution in federal court after a state court acquittal. The federal trial was held in 2003 and Avants was convicted and sentenced to life.

Avants appealed his conviction, arguing that the more than 30-year pre-indictment delay violated his Fifth Amendment right to due process, an argument that he also made prior to his trial. Do you agree that the delay violated his constitutional right to a speedy trial? See *United States v. Avants*, 367 F.3d 433, 442 (5th Cir. 2004).

Although the Supreme Court recognized a limited role for the Due Process Clause in the context of pre-charging delays, the Court's majority in *Marion* was uncomfortable ordering relief and instead remanded to the lower court to determine whether the defendant's due process rights were violated. In the following case, *Lovasco*, the Supreme Court asks what role prejudice plays in the due process analysis. If the defendant was prejudiced by the government's investigative delay, is this fact sufficient by itself to establish a due process violation?

United States v. Lovasco

Supreme Court of the United States
431 U.S. 783 (1977)

Mr. Justice MARSHALL delivered the opinion of the Court.

We granted certiorari in this case to consider the circumstances in which the Constitution requires that an indictment be dismissed because of delay between the commission of an offense and the initiation of prosecution.

I

On March 6, 1975, respondent was indicted for possessing eight firearms stolen from the United States mails, and for dealing in firearms without a license. The offenses were alleged to have occurred between July 25 and August 31, 1973, more than 18 months before the indictment was filed. Respondent moved to dismiss the indictment due to the delay.

The District Court conducted a hearing on respondent's motion at which the respondent sought to prove that the delay was unnecessary and that it had prejudiced his defense. In an effort to establish the former proposition, respondent presented a Postal Inspector's report on his investigation that was prepared one month after the crimes were committed, and a stipulation concerning the post-report progress of the probe. The report stated, in brief, that within the first month of the investigation respondent had admitted to Government agents that he had possessed and then sold five of the stolen guns, and that the agents had developed strong evidence linking respondent to the remaining three weapons. The report also stated, however, that the agents had been unable to confirm or refute respondent's claim that he had found the guns in his car when he returned to it after visiting his son, a mail handler, at work. The stipulation into which the Assistant United States Attorney entered indicated that little additional information concerning the crimes was uncovered in the 17 months following the preparation of the Inspector's report.

To establish prejudice to the defense, respondent testified that he had lost the testimony of two material witnesses due to the delay. The first witness, Tom Stewart, died more than a year after the alleged crimes occurred.

At the hearing respondent claimed that Stewart had been his source for two or three of the guns. The second witness, respondent's brother, died in April 1974, eight months after the crimes were completed. Respondent testified that his brother was present when respondent called Stewart to secure the guns, and witnessed all of respondent's sales. Respondent did not state how the witnesses would have aided the defense had they been willing to testify.

The Government made no systematic effort in the District Court to explain its long delay. The Assistant United States Attorney did expressly disagree, however, with defense counsel's suggestion that the investigation had ended after the Postal Inspector's report was prepared. The prosecutor also stated that it was the Government's theory that respondent's son, who had access to the mail at the railroad terminal from which the guns were "possibly stolen," was responsible for the thefts. Finally, the prosecutor elicited somewhat cryptic testimony from the Postal Inspector indicating that the case "as to these particular weapons involves other individuals"; that information had been presented to a grand jury "in regard to this case other than . . . (on) the day of the indictment itself"; and that he had spoken to the prosecutors about the case on four or five occasions.

Following the hearing, the District Court filed a brief opinion and order. The court found that by October 2, 1973, the date of the Postal Inspector's report, "the Government had all the information relating to defendant's alleged commission of the offenses charged against him," and that the 17-month delay before the case was presented to the grand jury "had not been explained or justified" and was "unnecessary and unreasonable." The court also found that "(a)s a result of the delay defendant has been prejudiced by reason of the death of Tom Stewart, a material witness on his behalf." Accordingly, the court dismissed the indictment. . . .

II

In *United States v. Marion*, 404 U.S. 307 (1971), this Court considered the significance, for constitutional purposes, of a lengthy preindictment delay. We held that as far as the Speedy Trial Clause of the Sixth Amendment is concerned, such delay is wholly irrelevant, since our analysis of the language, history, and purposes of the Clause persuaded us that only "a formal indictment or information or else the actual restraints imposed by arrest and holding to answer a criminal charge . . . engage the particular protections" of that provision. We went on to note that statutes of limitations, which provide predictable, legislatively enacted limits on prosecutorial delay, provide "the primary guarantee, against bringing overly stale criminal charges." But we did acknowledge that the "statute of limitations does not fully define (defendants') rights with respect to the events occurring prior to indictment" and that the Due Process Clause has a limited role to play in protecting against oppressive delay.

Respondent seems to argue that due process bars prosecution whenever a defendant suffers prejudice as a result of preindictment delay. To support that proposition respondent relies on the concluding sentence of the Court's opinion in *Marion* where, in remanding the case, we stated that "(e)vents of the trial may demonstrate actual prejudice, but at the present time appellees' due process claims are speculative and premature." But the quoted sentence establishes only that proof of actual prejudice makes a due process claim concrete and ripe for adjudication, not that it makes the claim automatically valid. . . . Thus *Marion* makes clear that proof of prejudice is generally a necessary but not sufficient element of a due process claim, and that the due process inquiry must consider the reasons for the delay as well as the prejudice to the accused.

The Court of Appeals found that the sole reason for the delay here was "a hope on the part of the Government that others might be discovered who may have participated in the theft. . . ." It concluded that this hope did not justify the delay, and therefore affirmed the dismissal of the indictment. But the Due Process Clause does not permit courts to abort criminal prosecutions simply because they disagree with a prosecutor's judgment as to when to seek an indictment. Judges are not free, in defining "due process," to impose on law enforcement officials our "personal and private notions" of fairness and to "disregard the limits that bind judges in their judicial function." Our task is more circumscribed. We are to determine only whether the action complained of here, compelling respondent to stand trial after the Government delayed indictment to investigate further violates those "fundamental conceptions of justice which lie at the base of our civil and political institutions," and which define "the community's sense of fair play and decency."

It requires no extended argument to establish that prosecutors do not deviate from "fundamental conceptions of justice" when they defer seeking indictments until they have probable cause to believe an accused is guilty; indeed it is unprofessional conduct for a prosecutor to recommend an indictment on less than probable cause. It should be equally obvious that prosecutors are under no duty to file charges as soon as probable cause exists but before they are satisfied they will be able to establish the suspect's guilt beyond a reasonable doubt. To impose such a duty "would have a deleterious effect both upon the rights of the accused and upon the ability of society to protect itself." From the perspective of potential defendants, requiring prosecutions to commence when probable cause is established is undesirable because it would increase the likelihood of unwarranted charges being filed, and would add to the time during which defendants stand accused but untried. . . .

It might be argued that once the Government has assembled sufficient evidence to prove guilt beyond a reasonable doubt, it should be constitutionally required to file charges promptly, even if its investigation of the entire criminal transaction is not complete. Adopting such a rule, however, would have many of the same consequences as adopting a rule requiring immediate prosecution upon probable cause.

First, compelling a prosecutor to file public charges as soon as the requisite proof has been developed against one participant on one charge would cause numerous problems in those cases in which a criminal transaction involves more than one person or more than one illegal act. In some instances, an immediate arrest or indictment would impair the prosecutor's ability to continue his investigation, thereby preventing society from bringing lawbreakers to justice. In other cases, the prosecutor would be able to obtain additional indictments despite an early prosecution, but the necessary result would be multiple trials involving a single set of facts. Such trials place needless burdens on defendants, law enforcement officials, and courts.

Second, insisting on immediate prosecution once sufficient evidence is developed to obtain a conviction would pressure prosecutors into resolving doubtful cases in favor of early and possibly unwarranted prosecutions. The determination of when the evidence available to the prosecution is sufficient to obtain a conviction is seldom clear-cut, and reasonable persons often will reach conflicting conclusions. . . . To avoid the risk that a subsequent indictment would be dismissed for preindictment delay, the prosecutor might feel constrained to file premature charges, with all the disadvantages that would entail.

Finally, requiring the Government to make charging decisions immediately upon assembling evidence sufficient to establish guilt would preclude the Government from giving full consideration to the desirability of not prosecuting in particular cases. The decision to file criminal charges, with the awesome consequences it entails, requires consideration of a wide range of factors in addition to the strength of the Government's case, in order to determine whether prosecution would be in the public interest. Prosecutors often need more information than proof of a suspect's guilt, therefore, before deciding whether to seek an indictment. . . .

We would be most reluctant to adopt a rule which would have these consequences absent a clear constitutional command to do so. We can find no such command in the Due Process Clause of the Fifth Amendment. In our view, investigative delay is fundamentally unlike delay undertaken by the Government solely "to gain tactical advantage over the accused," *United States v. Marion*, 404 U.S., at 324, precisely because investigative delay is not so one-sided. Rather than deviating from elementary standards of "fair play and decency," a prosecutor abides by them if he refuses to

> seek indictments until he is completely satisfied that he should prosecute and will be able promptly to establish guilt beyond a reasonable doubt. Penalizing prosecutors who defer action for these reasons would subordinate the goal of "orderly expedition" to that of "mere speed." This the Due Process Clause does not require. We therefore hold that to prosecute a defendant following investigative delay does not deprive him of due process, even if his defense might have been somewhat prejudiced by the lapse of time. . . .

NOTES & QUESTIONS ON PRE-CHARGING DELAYS

1. *The standard for judging pre-charging delays.* The Supreme Court in *Lovasco* failed to offer a complete standard for evaluating a pre-indictment delay. *Lovasco* simply concludes that the mere fact that the defendant was prejudiced by the delay is insufficient to establish a constitutional violation. Consequently, appellate courts have offered different standards to evaluate the question. Some Circuits require that the defendant show that (1) he or she suffered actual (or definite) prejudice resulting from the delay, and (2) the delay was purposefully designed to gain tactical advantage or to harass. See, e.g., *United States v. Colonna*, 360 F.3d 1169, 1177 (10th Cir. 2004). However, other Circuits require that the defendant demonstrate that they (1) suffered actual, non-speculative prejudice from the delay, at which point the court will conduct a balancing test to determine if (2) the delay, when balanced against the prosecution's reasons for it, offends fundamental conceptions of justice at the base of our civil and political institutions. See, e.g., *United States v. Doe*, 149 F.3d 945, 948 (9th Cir. 1998). Which test best gets to the heart of due process? For more discussion, see Michael J. Cleary, *Pre-Indictment Delay: Establishing a Fairer Approach Based on* United States v. Marion *and* United States v. Lovasco, 78 Temp. L. Rev. 1049 (2005).

PROBLEM CASE

Jack Humphrey was murdered in Evansville, Wyoming in 1977. The police focused their investigation on his wife, Rita Ann Humphrey, whose relationship with her husband had soured considerably. Rita Ann was interviewed by police detectives at the Natrona County Sheriff's Office. While there, in addition to speaking with the police, she also spoke with a relative, put her hands over her face, and stated: "God, what have I done?" Rita Ann was indicted for murder in 1980, but the government failed to meet its burden to establish probable cause at a preliminary hearing and the indictment was dismissed in August 1980.

In 1999, more than two decades after the murder, the Evansville Police Department reopened the case. Rita Ann alleged that the police department was pressured to reopen the case because Jack Humphrey's surviving sister had recently been elected mayor of Evansville. Rita Ann was re-indicted in 2004 and at a preliminary hearing later that year, this time the government succeeded in satisfying its burden to show probable cause. A trial date was scheduled for January 2005. In the intervening years, the transcript of the 1980 preliminary hearing had been destroyed and some of the investigators who worked on the original 1977 case had died.

Rita Ann sought dismissal, arguing that the 24-year delay in re-charging her violated her right to due process. Do you agree? Focus on her claim that the decision to reopen the case was spurred by the victim's sister recent election as the local mayor. What role does that fact play in the analysis? See *Humphrey v. State*, 2008 WY 67, ¶ 35, 185 P.3d 1236, 1247 (Wyo. 2008).

B. POST-CHARGING DELAY

Post-charging delays implicate the Sixth Amendment and its protection of the right to a speedy trial. This constitutional right only attaches once a suspect has been formally transformed into a "defendant" in the case by being arrested and bound over for trial. At that point a constitutional clock starts to run and unreasonable delays in the run-up to a trial might require dismissal of the charges.

Several important rules have emerged from the jurisprudence regarding post-charging delays. First, defense-requested delays, including requests to prepare motions or prepare for trial, are normally excluded from the calculation. Second, the constitutional clock does not run on a sealed indictment until it is unsealed, which has the effect of placing sealed indictments in limbo for purposes of post-charging delays. Third, if a charge is dismissed and later refiled, the gap between them is not included in the delay calculation.

In the following case, the Supreme Court outlines a four-pronged standard to determine whether the Sixth Amendment right to a speedy trial has been violated. Find the Court's articulation of the four factors and note its application to the present case. Note that the Court emphasizes that the factors will always require balancing and will necessarily involve a case-specific analysis. Perform that balancing and determine for yourself whether the delay in bringing Barker to trial violated the Sixth Amendment. Do you agree with the Supreme Court's conclusion?

Barker v. Wingo

Supreme Court of the United States
407 U.S. 514 (1972)

Mr. Justice Powell delivered the opinion of the Court.

Although a speedy trial is guaranteed the accused by the Sixth Amendment to the Constitution, this Court has dealt with that right on infrequent occasions. The Court's opinion in *Kloper v. North Carolina*, 386 U.S. 213 (1967), established that the right to a speedy trial is "fundamental" and is imposed by the Due Process Clause of the Fourteenth Amendment on the States. As Mr. Justice Brennan pointed out in his concurring opinion in *Dickey*, in none of these cases have we attempted to set out the criteria by which the speedy trial right is to be judged. This case compels us to make such an attempt.

I

On July 20, 1958, in Christian County, Kentucky, an elderly couple was beaten to death by intruders wielding an iron tire tool. Two suspects, Silas Manning and Willie Barker, the petitioner, were arrested shortly thereafter. The grand jury indicted them on September 15. Counsel was appointed on September 17, and Barker's trial was set for October 21. The Commonwealth had a stronger case against Manning, and it believed that Barker could not be convicted unless Manning testified against him. Manning was naturally unwilling to incriminate himself. Accordingly, on October 23, the day Silas Manning was brought to trial, the Commonwealth sought and obtained the first of what was to be a series of 16 continuances of Barker's trial. Barker made no objection. By first convicting Manning, the Commonwealth would remove possible problems of self-incrimination and would be able to assure his testimony against Barker.

The Commonwealth encountered more than a few difficulties in its prosecution of Manning. The first trial ended in a hung jury. A second trial resulted in a conviction, but the Kentucky Court of Appeals reversed because of the admission of evidence obtained by an illegal search. At his third trial, Manning was again convicted, and the Court of Appeals again reversed because the trial court had not granted a change of venue. A fourth trial resulted in a hung jury. Finally, after five trials, Manning was convicted, in March 1962, of murdering one victim, and after a sixth trial, in December 1962, he was convicted of murdering the other.

The Christian County Circuit Court holds three terms each year—in February, June, and September. Barker's initial trial was to take place in the September term of 1958. The first continuance postponed it until the February 1959 term. The second continuance was granted for one month only. Every term thereafter for as long as the Manning prosecutions were in process, the Commonwealth routinely moved to continue Barker's case to the next term. When the case was continued from the June 1959 term until the following September, Barker, having spent 10 months in jail, obtained his release by posting a $5,000 bond. He thereafter remained free in the community until his trial. Barker made no objection, through his counsel, to the first 11 continuances.

When on February 12, 1962, the Commonwealth moved for the twelfth time to continue the case until the following term, Barker's counsel filed a motion to dismiss the indictment. The motion to dismiss was denied two weeks later, and the Commonwealth's motion for a continuance was granted. The Commonwealth was granted further continuances in June 1962 and September 1962, to which Barker did not object.

In February 1963, the first term of court following Manning's final conviction, the Commonwealth moved to set Barker's trial for March 19. But on the day scheduled for trial, it again moved for a continuance until the June term. It gave as its reason the illness of the ex-sheriff who was the chief investigating officer in the case. To this continuance, Barker objected unsuccessfully.

The witness was still unable to testify in June, and the trial, which had been set for June 19, was continued again until the September term over Barker's objection. This time the court announced that the case would be dismissed for lack of prosecution if it were not tried during the next term. The final trial date was set for October 9, 1963. On that date, Barker again moved to dismiss the indictment, and this time specified that his right to a speedy trial had been violated. The motion was denied; the trial commenced with Manning as the chief prosecution witness; Barker was convicted and given a life sentence. . . .

III

Perhaps because the speedy trial right is so slippery, two rigid approaches are urged upon us as ways of eliminating some of the uncertainty which courts experience in protecting the right. The first suggestion is that we hold that the Constitution requires a criminal defendant to be offered a trial within a specified time period. The result of such a ruling would have the virtue of clarifying when the right is infringed and of simplifying courts' application of it. Recognizing this, some legislatures have enacted laws, and some courts have adopted procedural rules which more narrowly define the right. The United States Court of Appeals for the Second Circuit has promulgated rules for the district courts in that Circuit establishing that the government must be ready for trial within six months of the date of arrest, except in unusual circumstances, or the charge will be dismissed. This type of rule is also recommended by the American Bar Association.

But such a result would require this Court to engage in legislative or rulemaking activity, rather than in the adjudicative process to which we should confine our efforts. We do not establish procedural rules for the States, except when mandated by the Constitution. We find no constitutional basis for holding that the speedy trial right can be quantified into a specified number of days or months. The States, of course, are free to prescribe a reasonable period consistent with constitutional standards, but our approach must be less precise.

The second suggested alternative would restrict consideration of the right to those cases in which the accused has demanded a speedy trial. Most States have recognized what is loosely referred to as the "demand rule," although eight States reject it. It is not clear, however, precisely what is meant by that term. Although every federal court of appeals that has considered the question has endorsed some kind of demand rule, some have regarded the rule within the concept of waiver, whereas others have viewed it as a factor to be weighed in assessing whether there has been a deprivation of the speedy trial right. We shall refer to the former approach as the demand-waiver doctrine. The demand-waiver doctrine provides that a defendant waives any consideration of his right to speedy trial for any period prior to which he has not demanded a trial. Under this rigid approach, a prior demand is a necessary condition to the consideration of the speedy trial right. . . .

Such an approach, by presuming waiver of a fundamental right from inaction, is inconsistent with this Court's pronouncements on waiver of constitutional rights. The Court has defined waiver as "an intentional relinquishment or abandonment of a known right or privilege." Courts should "indulge every reasonable presumption against waiver," and they should "not presume acquiescence in the loss of fundamental rights." . . .

We reject, therefore, the rule that a defendant who fails to demand a speedy trial forever waives his right. This does not mean, however, that the defendant has no responsibility to assert his right. We think the better rule is that the defendant's assertion of or failure to assert his right to a speedy trial is one of the factors to be considered in an inquiry into the deprivation of the right. Such a formulation avoids the rigidities of the demand-waiver rule and the resulting possible unfairness in its application. It allows the trial court to exercise a judicial discretion based on the circumstances, including due consideration of any applicable formal procedural rule. It would permit, for example, a court to attach a different weight to a situation in which the defendant knowingly fails to object from a situation in which his attorney acquiesces in long delay without adequately informing his client, or from a situation in which no counsel is appointed. It would also allow a court to weigh the frequency and force of the objections as opposed to attaching significant weight to a purely pro forma objection. . . .

We, therefore, reject both of the inflexible approaches—the fixed-time period because it goes further than the Constitution requires; the demand-waiver rule because it is insensitive to a right which we have deemed fundamental. The approach we accept is a balancing test, in which the conduct of both the prosecution and the defendant are weighed.

IV

A balancing test necessarily compels courts to approach speedy trial cases on an ad hoc basis. We can do little more than identify some of the factors which courts should assess in determining whether a particular defendant has been deprived of his right. Though some might express them in different ways, we identify four such factors: Length of delay, the reason for the delay, the defendant's assertion of his right, and prejudice to the defendant.

The length of the delay is to some extent a triggering mechanism. Until there is some delay which is presumptively prejudicial, there is no necessity for inquiry into the other factors that go into the balance. Nevertheless, because of the imprecision of the right to speedy trial, the length of delay that will provoke such an inquiry is necessarily dependent upon the peculiar circumstances of the case. To take but one example, the delay that can be tolerated for an ordinary street crime is considerably less than for a serious, complex conspiracy charge.

Closely related to length of delay is the reason the government assigns to justify the delay. Here, too, different weights should be assigned to different reasons. A deliberate attempt to delay the trial in order to hamper the defense should be weighted heavily against the government. A more neutral reason such as negligence or overcrowded courts should be weighted less heavily but nevertheless should be considered since the ultimate responsibility for such circumstances must rest with the government rather than with the defendant. Finally, a valid reason, such as a missing witness, should serve to justify appropriate delay.

We have already discussed the third factor, the defendant's responsibility to assert his right. Whether and how a defendant asserts his right is closely related to the other factors we have mentioned. The strength of his efforts will be affected by the length of the delay, to some extent by the reason for the delay, and most particularly by the personal prejudice, which is not always readily identifiable, that he experiences. The more serious the deprivation, the more likely a defendant is to complain. The defendant's assertion of his speedy trial right, then, is entitled to strong evidentiary weight in determining whether the defendant is being deprived of the right. We emphasize that failure to assert the right will make it difficult for a defendant to prove that he was denied a speedy trial.

A fourth factor is prejudice to the defendant. Prejudice, of course, should be assessed in the light of the interests of defendants which the speedy trial right was designed to protect. This Court has identified three such interests: (i) to prevent oppressive pretrial incarceration; (ii) to minimize anxiety and concern of the accused; and (iii) to limit the possibility that the defense will be impaired. Of these, the most serious is the last, because the inability of a defendant adequately to prepare his case skews the fairness of the entire system. If witnesses die or disappear during a delay, the prejudice is obvious. There is also prejudice if defense witnesses are unable to recall accurately events of the distant past. Loss of memory, however, is not always reflected in the record because what has been forgotten can rarely be shown.

We have discussed previously the societal disadvantages of lengthy pretrial incarceration, but obviously the disadvantages for the accused who cannot obtain his release are even more serious. The time spent in jail awaiting trial has a detrimental impact on the individual. It often means loss of a job; it disrupts family life; and it enforces idleness. Most jails offer little or no recreational or rehabilitative programs. The time spent in jail is simply dead time. Moreover, if a defendant is locked up, he is hindered in his ability to gather evidence, contact witnesses, or otherwise prepare his defense. Imposing those consequences on anyone who has not yet been convicted is serious. It is especially unfortunate to impose them on those persons who are ultimately found to be innocent. Finally, even if an accused is not incarcerated prior to trial, he is still disadvantaged by restraints on his liberty and by living under a cloud of anxiety, suspicion, and often hostility.

We regard none of the four factors identified above as either a necessary or sufficient condition to the finding of a deprivation of the right of speedy trial. Rather, they are related factors and must be considered together with such other circumstances as may be relevant. In sum, these factors have no talismanic qualities; courts must still engage in a difficult and sensitive balancing process. But, because we are dealing with a fundamental right of the accused, this process must be carried out with full recognition that the accused's interest in a speedy trial is specifically affirmed in the Constitution.

V

The difficulty of the task of balancing these factors is illustrated by this case, which we consider to be close. It is clear that the length of delay between arrest and trial—well over five years—was extraordinary. Only seven months of that period can be attributed to a strong excuse, the illness of the ex-sheriff who was in charge of the investigation. Perhaps some delay would have been permissible under ordinary circumstances, so that Manning could be utilized as a witness in Barker's trial, but more than four years was too long a period, particularly since a good part of that period was attributable to the Commonwealth's failure or inability to try Manning under circumstances that comported with due process.

Two counterbalancing factors, however, outweigh these deficiencies. The first is that prejudice was minimal. Of course, Barker was prejudiced to some extent by living for over four years under a cloud of suspicion and anxiety. Moreover, although he was released on bond for most of the period, he did spend 10 months in jail before trial. But there is no claim that any of Barker's witnesses died or otherwise became unavailable owing to the delay. The trial transcript indicates only two very minor lapses of memory—one on the part of a prosecution witness—which were in no way significant to the outcome.

More important than the absence of serious prejudice, is the fact that Barker did not want a speedy trial. Counsel was appointed for Barker immediately after his indictment and represented him throughout the period. No question is raised as to the competency of such counsel. Despite the fact that counsel had notice of the motions for continuances, the record shows no action whatever taken between October 21, 1958, and February 12, 1962, that could be construed as the assertion of the speedy trial right. On the latter date, in response to another motion for continuance, Barker moved to dismiss the indictment. The record does not show on what ground this motion was based, although it is clear that no alternative motion was made for an immediate trial. Instead the record strongly suggests that while he hoped to take advantage of the delay in which he had acquiesced, and thereby obtain a dismissal of the charges, he definitely did not want to be tried. . . .

The probable reason for Barker's attitude was that he was gambling on Manning's acquittal. The evidence was not very strong against Manning, as the reversals and hung juries suggest, and Barker undoubtedly thought that if Manning were acquitted, he would never be tried. . . . That Barker was gambling on Manning's acquittal is also suggested by his failure, following the pro forma motion to dismiss filed in February 1962, to object to the Commonwealth's next two motions for continuances. Indeed, it was not until March 1963, after Manning's convictions were final, that Barker, having lost his gamble, began to object to further continuances. At that time, the Commonwealth's excuse was the illness of the ex-sheriff, which Barker has conceded justified the further delay.

We do not hold that there may never be a situation in which an indictment may be dismissed on speedy trial grounds where the defendant has failed to object to continuances. There may be a situation in which the defendant was represented by incompetent counsel, was severely prejudiced, or even cases in which the continuances were granted ex parte. But barring extraordinary circumstances, we would be reluctant indeed to rule that a defendant was denied this constitutional right on a record that strongly indicates, as does this one, that the defendant did not want a speedy trial. We hold, therefore, that Barker was not deprived of his due process right to a speedy trial. . . .

PROBLEM CASE

Consider the following case involving defendant James Ray Shell:

> Shell filed a false passport application in 1978 under the name Bonney. After a DEA investigation of his alleged involvement in a heroin conspiracy, he fled the United States and lived in Hong Kong for several years before he was deported to Guam. While abroad he used the alias Chris Weber. From 1980 to 1984, the government unsuccessfully attempted to locate him. In 1984, a grand jury indicted Shell on the 1978 passport charge. From 1984 to 1989, his file was misplaced and the government made no attempt to locate him. In 1989, a new search began for Shell, and the government located and arrested him in Guam in 1990. Shell moved to dismiss the indictment.

Apply each of the *Barker* factors to this case. Under the *Barker* standard, is Shell eligible for a dismissal with prejudice? Was Shell himself responsible for the delay because he was living abroad under a false name, or was the government responsible for the delay because of its negligence? See *United States v. Shell*, 974 F.2d 1035, 1035-36 (9th Cir. 1992).

Although Barker failed to prevail in his Sixth Amendment claim, the Court in other cases has been more sympathetic to speedy trial claims. Using the factors identified in *Barker*, evaluate the claims outlined below in *Doggett v. United States*. As you read the case, ask yourself why the Court was more sympathetic to Doggett's claim than Barker's. What role does prosecutorial negligence—something in between good faith diligence and bad faith delay—play in the analysis?

Doggett v. United States

Supreme Court of the United States
505 U.S. 647 (1992)

Justice SOUTER delivered the opinion of the Court.

In this case we consider whether the delay of 8½ years between petitioner's indictment and arrest violated his Sixth Amendment right to a speedy trial. We hold that it did.

I

On February 22, 1980, petitioner Marc Doggett was indicted for conspiring with several others to import and distribute cocaine. Douglas Driver, the Drug Enforcement Administration's (DEA's) principal agent investigating the conspiracy, told the United States Marshal's Service that the DEA would oversee the apprehension of Doggett and his confederates. On March 18, 1980, two police officers set out under Driver's orders to arrest Doggett at his parents' house in Raleigh, North Carolina, only to find that he was not there. His mother told the officers that he had left for Colombia four days earlier.

To catch Doggett on his return to the United States, Driver sent word of his outstanding arrest warrant to all United States Customs stations and to a number of law enforcement organizations. He also placed Doggett's name in the Treasury Enforcement Communication System (TECS), a computer network that helps Customs agents screen people entering the country, and in the National Crime Information Center computer system, which serves similar ends. The TECS entry expired that September, however, and Doggett's name vanished from the system.

In September 1981, Driver found out that Doggett was under arrest on drug charges in Panama and, thinking that a formal extradition request would be futile, simply asked Panama to "expel" Doggett to the United States. Although the Panamanian authorities promised to comply when their own proceedings had run their course, they freed Doggett the following July and let him go to Colombia, where he stayed with an aunt for several months. On September 25, 1982, he passed unhindered through Customs in New York City and settled down in Virginia. Since his return to the United States, he has married, earned a college degree, found a steady job as a computer operations manager, lived openly under his own name, and stayed within the law.

Doggett's travels abroad had not wholly escaped the Government's notice, however. In 1982, the American Embassy in Panama told the State Department of his departure to Colombia, but that information, for whatever reason, eluded the DEA, and Agent Driver assumed for several years that his quarry was still serving time in a Panamanian prison. Driver never asked DEA officials in Panama to check into Doggett's status, and only after his own fortuitous assignment to that country in 1985 did he discover Doggett's departure for Colombia. Driver then simply assumed Doggett had settled there, and he made no effort to find out for sure or to track Doggett down, either abroad or in the United States. Thus Doggett remained lost to the American criminal justice system until September 1988, when the Marshal's Service ran a simple credit check on several thousand people subject to outstanding arrest warrants and, within minutes, found out where Doggett lived and worked. On September 5, 1988, nearly 6 years after his return to the United States and 8½ years after his indictment, Doggett was arrested.

He naturally moved to dismiss the indictment, arguing that the Government's failure to prosecute him earlier violated his Sixth Amendment right to a speedy trial. The Federal Magistrate hearing his motion applied the criteria for assessing speedy trial claims set out in *Barker v. Wingo,* 407 U.S. 514 (1972): "[l]ength of delay, the reason for the delay, the defendant's assertion of his right, and prejudice to the defendant." The

Magistrate found that the delay between Doggett's indictment and arrest was long enough to be "presumptively prejudicial," that the delay "clearly [was] attributable to the negligence of the government," and that Doggett could not be faulted for any delay in asserting his right to a speedy trial, there being no evidence that he had known of the charges against him until his arrest. The Magistrate also found, however, that Doggett had made no affirmative showing that the delay had impaired his ability to mount a successful defense or had otherwise prejudiced him. In his recommendation to the District Court, the Magistrate contended that this failure to demonstrate particular prejudice sufficed to defeat Doggett's speedy trial claim. . . .

II

The Sixth Amendment guarantees that, "[i]n all criminal prosecutions, the accused shall enjoy the right to a speedy . . . trial. . . ." On its face, the Speedy Trial Clause is written with such breadth that, taken literally, it would forbid the government to delay the trial of an "accused" for any reason at all. Our cases, however, have qualified the literal sweep of the provision by specifically recognizing the relevance of four separate enquiries: whether delay before trial was uncommonly long, whether the government or the criminal defendant is more to blame for that delay, whether, in due course, the defendant asserted his right to a speedy trial, and whether he suffered prejudice as the delay's result.

The first of these is actually a double enquiry. Simply to trigger a speedy trial analysis, an accused must allege that the interval between accusation and trial has crossed the threshold dividing ordinary from "presumptively prejudicial" delay, since, by definition, he cannot complain that the government has denied him a "speedy" trial if it has, in fact, prosecuted his case with customary promptness. If the accused makes this showing, the court must then consider, as one factor among several, the extent to which the delay stretches beyond the bare minimum needed to trigger judicial examination of the claim. This latter enquiry is significant to the speedy trial analysis because, as we discuss below, the presumption that pretrial delay has prejudiced the accused intensifies over time. In this case, the extraordinary 8½ year lag between Doggett's indictment and arrest clearly suffices to trigger the speedy trial enquiry; its further significance within that enquiry will be dealt with later.

As for *Barker*'s second criterion, the Government claims to have sought Doggett with diligence. The findings of the courts below are to the contrary, however, and we review trial court determinations of negligence with considerable deference. The Government gives us nothing to gainsay the findings that have come up to us, and we see nothing fatal to them in the record. For six years, the Government's investigators made no serious effort to test their progressively more questionable assumption that Doggett was living abroad, and, had they done so, they could have found him within minutes. While the Government's lethargy may have reflected no more than Doggett's relative unimportance in the world of drug trafficking, it was still findable negligence, and the finding stands. . . .

III

The Government is left, then, with its principal contention: that Doggett fails to make out a successful speedy trial claim because he has not shown precisely how he was prejudiced by the delay between his indictment and trial.

We have observed in prior cases that unreasonable delay between formal accusation and trial threatens to produce more than one sort of harm, including "oppressive pretrial incarceration," "anxiety and concern of the accused," and "the possibility that the [accused's] defense will be impaired" by dimming memories and loss of exculpatory evidence. Of these forms of prejudice, "the most serious is the last, because the inability of a defendant adequately to prepare his case skews the fairness of the entire system." Doggett claims this kind of prejudice, and there is probably no other kind that he can claim, since he was subjected neither to pretrial detention nor, he has successfully contended, to awareness of unresolved charges against him.

The Government answers Doggett's claim by [claiming] . . . that the Speedy Trial Clause does not significantly protect a criminal defendant's interest in fair adjudication. In so arguing, the Government asks us, in effect, to read part of *Barker* right out of the law, and that we will not do. . . . [T]he Sixth Amendment right of the accused to a speedy trial has no application beyond the confines of a formal criminal prosecution. Once triggered by arrest, indictment, or other official accusation, however, the speedy trial enquiry must weigh the effect of delay on the accused's defense just as it has to weigh any other form of prejudice that *Barker* recognized.

As an alternative to limiting *Barker,* the Government claims Doggett has failed to make any affirmative showing that the delay weakened his ability to raise specific defenses, elicit specific testimony, or produce specific items of evidence. Though Doggett did indeed come up short in this respect, the Government's argument takes it only so far: consideration of prejudice is not limited to the specifically demonstrable, and, as it concedes, affirmative proof of particularized prejudice is not essential to every speedy trial claim. *Barker* explicitly recognized that impairment of one's defense is the most difficult form of speedy trial prejudice to prove because time's erosion of exculpatory evidence and testimony "can rarely be shown." And though time can tilt the case against either side, one cannot generally be sure which of them it has prejudiced more severely. Thus, we generally have to recognize that excessive delay presumptively compromises the reliability of a trial in ways that neither party can prove or, for that matter, identify. While such presumptive prejudice cannot alone carry a Sixth Amendment claim without regard to the other *Barker* criteria, it is part of the mix of relevant facts, and its importance increases with the length of delay.

This brings us to an enquiry into the role that presumptive prejudice should play in the disposition of Doggett's speedy trial claim. We begin with hypothetical and somewhat easier cases and work our way to this one.

Our speedy trial standards recognize that pretrial delay is often both inevitable and wholly justifiable. The government may need time to collect witnesses against the accused, oppose his pretrial motions, or, if he goes into hiding, track him down. We attach great weight to such considerations when balancing them against the costs of going forward with a trial whose probative accuracy the passage of time has begun by degrees to throw into question. Thus, in this case, if the Government had pursued Doggett with reasonable diligence from his indictment to his arrest, his speedy trial claim would fail. Indeed, that conclusion would generally follow as a matter of course however great the delay, so long as Doggett could not show specific prejudice to his defense.

The Government concedes, on the other hand, that Doggett would prevail if he could show that the Government had intentionally held back in its prosecution of him to gain some impermissible advantage at trial. That we cannot doubt. *Barker* stressed that official bad faith in causing delay will be weighed heavily against the government and a bad-faith delay the length of this negligent one would present an overwhelming case for dismissal.

Between diligent prosecution and bad-faith delay, official negligence in bringing an accused to trial occupies the middle ground. While not compelling relief in every case where bad-faith delay would make relief virtually automatic, neither is negligence automatically tolerable simply because the accused cannot demonstrate exactly how it has prejudiced him. It was on this point that the Court of Appeals erred, and on the facts before us, it was reversible error.

Barker made it clear that "different weights [are to be] assigned to different reasons" for delay. Although negligence is obviously to be weighed more lightly than a deliberate intent to harm the accused's defense, it still falls on the wrong side of the divide between acceptable and unacceptable reasons for delaying a criminal prosecution once it has begun. And such is the nature of the prejudice presumed that the weight we assign to official negligence compounds over time as the presumption of evidentiary prejudice grows. Thus, our toleration of such negligence varies inversely with its protractedness and its consequent threat to the fairness of the accused's trial. Condoning prolonged and unjustifiable delays in prosecution would both penalize many defendants for the state's fault and simply encourage the government to gamble with the interests of criminal suspects assigned a low prosecutorial priority. The Government, indeed, can hardly complain too loudly, for persistent neglect in concluding a criminal prosecution indicates an uncommonly feeble interest in bringing an accused to justice; the more weight the Government attaches to securing a conviction, the harder it will try to get it.

To be sure, to warrant granting relief, negligence unaccompanied by particularized trial prejudice must have lasted longer than negligence demonstrably causing such prejudice. But even so, the Government's egregious persistence in failing to prosecute Doggett is clearly sufficient. The lag between Doggett's indictment and arrest was 8½ years, and he would have faced trial 6 years earlier than he did but for the Government's inexcusable oversights. The portion of the delay attributable to the Government's negligence far exceeds the threshold needed to state a speedy trial claim; indeed, we have called shorter delays "extraordinary." When the Government's negligence thus causes delay six times as long as that generally sufficient to trigger judicial review and when the presumption of prejudice, albeit unspecified, is neither extenuated, as by the defendant's acquiescence, nor persuasively rebutted, the defendant is entitled to relief. . . .

Justice THOMAS, with whom THE CHIEF JUSTICE and Justice SCALIA join, dissenting.

Just as "bad facts make bad law," so too odd facts make odd law. Doggett's 8½-year odyssey from youthful drug dealing in the tobacco country of North Carolina, through stints in a Panamanian jail and in Colombia, to life as a computer operations manager, homeowner, and registered voter in suburban Virginia is extraordinary. But even more extraordinary is the Court's conclusion that the Government denied Doggett his Sixth Amendment right to a speedy trial despite the fact that he has suffered none of the harms that the right was designed to prevent. I respectfully dissent. . . .

Although being an "accused" is necessary to trigger the Clause's protection, it is not sufficient to do so. The touchstone of the speedy trial right, after all, is the substantial deprivation of liberty that typically accompanies an "accusation," *not* the accusation itself. That explains why a person who has been arrested but not indicted is entitled to the protection of the Clause, even though technically he has not been "accused" at all. And it explains why the lower courts consistently have held that, with respect to sealed (and hence secret) indictments, the protections of the Speedy Trial Clause are triggered *not* when the indictment is *filed,* but when it is *unsealed*. . . .

It remains to be considered, however, whether Doggett is entitled to relief under the Speedy Trial Clause because of the disruption of his life years after the criminal events at issue. In other words, does the Clause protect a right to repose, free from secret or unknown indictments? In my view, it does not, for much the same reasons set forth above.

The common law recognized no right of criminals to repose. . . . That is not to deny that our legal system has long recognized the value of repose, both to the individual and to society. But that recognition finds expression not in the sweeping commands of the Constitution, or in the common law, but in any number of specific statutes of limitations enacted by the federal and state legislatures. Such statutes not only protect a defendant from prejudice to his defense (as discussed above), but also balance his interest in repose against society's interest in the apprehension and punishment of criminals. In general, the graver the offense, the longer the limitations period; indeed, many serious offenses, such as murder, typically carry no limitations period at all. These statutes refute the notion that our society ever has recognized any general right of criminals to repose. . . .

There is no basis for concluding that the disruption of an accused's life years after the commission of his alleged crime is an evil independently protected by the Speedy Trial Clause. Such disruption occurs *regardless* of whether the individual is under indictment during the period of delay. Thus, had Doggett been indicted shortly before his 1988 arrest rather than shortly after his 1980 crime, his repose would have been equally shattered—but he would not have even a colorable speedy trial claim. To recognize a constitutional right to repose is to recognize a right to be tried speedily *after the offense*. That would, of course, convert the Speedy Trial Clause into a constitutional statute of limitations—a result with no basis in the text or history of the Clause or in our precedents. . . .

NOTES & QUESTIONS ON POST-CHARGING DELAYS

1. *Negligent violations of the Sixth Amendment. Barker* identified the four factors for analyzing a post-charging delay: (1) length of delay; (2) reason for delay; (3) defendant's assertion of speedy trial right; and (4) prejudice to defendant. *Doggett* stands for the proposition that even prosecutorial negligence can violate the Sixth Amendment right to a speedy trial under the *Barker* four-pronged standard. What this means, in practice, is that the government has a prosecutorial *duty* to prosecute defendants in a timely manner. The Constitution not only forbids intentional delays, but also forbids, in some situations, negligence in the discharge of that constitutional duty.

2. *How to catch a fugitive.* Which party is responsible for the fact that Doggett was not caught and put on trial earlier? Is it significant that the government finally located and apprehended Doggett after running a simple credit check—an investigative technique that it could have tried years earlier? Does this technique seem retrograde, and therefore obvious, or was it a clever investigative use of a tool designed for commercial financial transactions?

3. *Speedy sentencing.* What if the defendant faces a delay in sentencing? Does the Sixth Amendment right to a speedy trial encompass a right to a sentencing determination by a certain time frame? Recall that the Sixth Amendment does not apply to mere suspects—its protections are only triggered once a suspect is formally charged and is transformed into an accused. After conviction, the accused is now a convict and the trial itself (or at the very least the guilt phase of the trial) is concluded. In *Betterman v. Montana*, 136 S. Ct. 1609, 1617 (2016), the Supreme Court concluded that "at the third phase of the criminal-justice process, i.e., between conviction and sentencing, the Constitution's presumption-of-innocence-protective speedy trial right is not engaged." Does this entail that a convict could languish forever without being sentenced? Probably not, since the Supreme Court noted that statutes and rules of criminal procedure require prompt sentencing. Do statutory rules provide enough protection for convicts awaiting sentencing? Should the Sixth Amendment apply? Or, by analogy to pre-charging delays, might a more general Fifth Amendment right to due process apply to delays in sentencing?

4. *Remedies for speedy trial violations.* Assuming that a court finds that a post-charging delay was unconstitutional, what remedy is appropriate? In *Strunk v. United States*, 412 U.S. 434, 439 (1973), the defendant was subject to an unconstitutional delay. After reaching this conclusion, an appeals court rejected the defendant's request for a dismissal of the charges and instead remanded the case back to the trial court with instructions to reduce the sentence. On appeal, the Supreme Court concluded that dismissal, while an extreme remedy, is the only appropriate remedy when the government violates the Speedy Trial Clause and that a sentence reduction is insufficient as a remedy to the constitutional violation. *Strunk*'s holding only applies to constitutional violations; remedies for violations of statutory speedy trial requirements are not similarly constrained. For more discussion, see Anthony G. Amsterdam, *Speedy Criminal Trial: Rights and Remedies*, 27 Stan. L. Rev. 525, 538 (1975). If the only remedy to a Sixth Amendment violation is dismissal with prejudice, does this make judges reluctant to hold that a speedy trial violation has occurred?

STATUTORY REQUIREMENTS

In addition to the Speedy Trial Act, discussed in Section C below, federal judges have other statutory mechanisms to ensure speedy trials. For example, the Federal Rules of Criminal Procedure allow a trial judge to dismiss a case if the judge feels that the defendant has suffered an unreasonable delay:

> The court may dismiss an indictment, information, or complaint if unnecessary delay occurs in:
>
> (1) presenting a charge to a grand jury;
> (2) filing an information against a defendant; or
> (3) bringing a defendant to trial.

Fed. R. Crim. P. 48. The question is what counts as an "unnecessary" delay. In practice, district court judges have used this provision to issue dismissals in cases involving long delays. For example, in *United States v. Black*, 416 F. Supp. 59, 62 (M.D. Fla. 1976), a trial judge ruled that a delay of 44 months since the alleged offense and 33 months since the indictment was an unnecessary delay because the government had the information that it would need to locate the defendant but simply failed to act on it.

What is the exact relationship between the Sixth Amendment and Rule 48? One way of understanding the rule is that it is a specific codification that authorizes the remedy—dismissal—that trial courts can impose for violations of the Sixth Amendment. However, nothing in its text requires a finding of a constitutional violation. In theory, then, Rule 48 is more demanding than the Sixth Amendment because by its terms, Rule 48 could be applied in situations even where the court finds that no Sixth Amendment violation occurred, but dismissal is nevertheless warranted by virtue of the "unnecessary delay." See, e.g., *United States v. DeLuna*, 763 F.2d 897, 923 (8th Cir. 1985).

PROBLEM CASE

Consider the following case of prosecutorial negligence resulting in a post-charging delay.

In September 2005, the government charged Ferreira with conspiracy to distribute methamphetamine through a federal indictment. At the time of the indictment, Ferreira was already in custody in Georgia in connection with state criminal charges pending there. In October 2005, federal prosecutors filed a writ of habeas corpus ad prosequendum directing the authorities in Georgia to make Ferreira available for his initial federal appearance. The government filed a superseding indictment and therefore filed a second writ of habeas corpus ad prosequendum. During the interim, however, Ferreira had been transferred from one county in Georgia to another county, because there were multiple state cases against him in Georgia. Although the Federal Marshals Service was aware of this transfer and notified the Department of Justice, that notification was misplaced, leading to the second writ of habeas corpus ad prosequendum being sent to the wrong county in Georgia. In July 2008, a third writ of habeas corpus ad prosequendum was sent to the state prison in Georgia where Ferreira was incarcerated. By this time, Ferreira had already filed motions pro se requesting a speedy trial. Once counsel was appointed, counsel filed a motion to dismiss the indictment asserting that the three-year delay had violated Ferreira's right to a speedy trial.

If you were the judge, would you grant the motion to dismiss? Why or why not? See *United States v. Ferreira*, 665 F.3d 701, 706 (6th Cir. 2011).

C. THE SPEEDY TRIAL ACT

In 1974, Congress passed the Speedy Trial Act, 18 U.S.C. § 3161, and amended it in 1979. Congress designed the Act to establish minimum criteria for speedy trials. These statutory requirements are in addition to the constitutional requirements, but they only apply in federal prosecutions. State criminal proceedings are governed by analogous state statutes and by the federal constitutional requirements previously outlined in this chapter.

The Speedy Trial Act first outlines a general presumption that trials should be conducted as quickly as is reasonably possible: "In any case involving a defendant charged with an offense, the appropriate judicial officer, at the earliest practicable time, shall, after consultation with the counsel for the defendant and the attorney for the Government, set the case for trial on a day certain, or list it for trial on a weekly or other short-term trial calendar at a place within the judicial district, so as to assure a speedy trial." 18 U.S.C. § 3161. Then, the Act includes a specific set of deadlines for particular phases of the trial, including indictment or information 30 days after arrest; and a trial 70 days after indictment or first appearance, whichever is later.

Recognizing that the Speedy Trial Act might cause a problem by authorizing the government to bring defendants to trial too quickly, and prevent them from preparing an adequate defense, the Act was amended in 1979 to stipulate that unless the defendant waives this right in writing, the defendant gets at least 30 days to prepare for trial.

The temporal requirements for a speedy trial (30 days for indictment and 70 days for trial) are subject to long list of exceptions, including delays

- resulting from mental competency exam;
- resulting from trial for other charges;
- resulting from any interlocutory appeal;
- resulting from any pre-trial motion;
- resulting from any proceeding relating to the transfer of a case;
- resulting from transportation from another district, unless it takes more than ten days;
- resulting from consideration by the court of a proposed plea agreement;
- reasonably attributable to any period, not to exceed 30 days, during which any proceeding concerning the defendant is actually under advisement by the court.

The basic idea is that almost any pre-trial judicial proceeding or consideration might be a legitimate reason for a delay. In practice, then, federal trials need not occur within 70 days in complex cases or even in non-complex cases involving pre-trial motions—a description that could apply to almost any federal trial, since pre-trial motion practice is a routine aspect of federal criminal practice.

Another issue is whether a defendant can waive the protections of the Speedy Trial Act and if so, how a court should construe those waivers. For example, does the waiver have to be specific and based on a particular reason for the delay, or could a trial court get around the requirements of the Speedy Trial Act by procuring a permanent and complete waiver from the defendant? In the following case, the Supreme Court tackles this complex question.

Zedner v. United States

Supreme Court of the United States
547 U.S. 489 (2006)

Justice Alito delivered the opinion of the Court.

This case requires us to consider the application of the doctrines of waiver, judicial estoppel, and harmless error to a violation of the Speedy Trial Act. The Act generally requires a federal criminal trial to begin within 70 days after a defendant is charged or makes an initial appearance, but the Act contains a detailed scheme under which certain specified periods of delay are not counted. In this case, petitioner's trial did not begin within 70 days of indictment. Indeed, his trial did not commence until more than seven years after the filing of the indictment, but petitioner, at the suggestion of the trial judge, signed a blanket, prospective waiver of his rights under the Act. We address the following questions: whether this waiver was effective; whether petitioner is judicially estopped from challenging the validity of the waiver; and whether the trial judge's failure to make the findings required to exclude a period of delay under a particular provision of the Act was harmless error.

I

In March 1996, petitioner attempted to open accounts at seven financial institutions using counterfeit $10 million United States bonds. The quality of the counterfeiting was, to put it mildly, not expert. One bond purported to be issued by the "Ministry of Finance of U.S.A." Others contained misspelled words such as "Thunted States" and the "Onited States" (United States), "Dhtladelphla" (Philadelphia), "Cgicago" (Chicago), and "forevev" (forever). After petitioner presented these bonds, the Secret Service was contacted, and petitioner was arrested. Following arraignment on a criminal complaint, he was released on bond.

On April 4, 1996, a grand jury in the Eastern District of New York indicted petitioner. . . . On June 26, the District Court, citing the complexity of the case, granted what is termed an "ends-of-justice" continuance until September 6. On September 6, the District Court granted another continuance, this time until November 8.

At the November 8 status conference, petitioner requested, without opposition from the Government, a further adjournment to January 1997. Concerned about the difficulty of fitting petitioner's trial into its heavily scheduled calendar and the prospect that petitioner might "only waive [the Act] for so long as it is convenient for [him] to waive," the District Court instructed petitioner as follows. "I think if I'm going to give you that long an adjournment, I will have to take a waiver for all time." Petitioner's counsel responded that the defense would "waive for all time. That will not be a problem. That will not be an issue in this case."

The District Court then addressed petitioner directly and appears to have attempted to explain the operation of a provision of the Act, 18 U.S.C. § 3162(a)(2), under which a defendant whose trial does not begin on time is deemed to have waived the right to move for dismissal of the information or indictment if he or she does not file that motion prior to trial or entry of a guilty plea. The District Court reasoned: "[I]f you can waive [the Act] by inaction, i.e., not raising the motion to dismiss, you can waive affirmatively, knowledgeably, intelligently your right to do so, your right to a speedy trial and your right to make a motion to dismiss for the speedy trial." The court told petitioner that it was "prepared to start . . . trial right away," but that if a continuance was granted, petitioner might have to wait some time for trial because the court had a "fairly big cas[e] . . . which [wa]s set to take eight months for trial." "[I]f that [trial] starts before you start," the court warned, "you may have to wait until that is done."

The District Court then produced a preprinted form—apparently of its own devising—captioned "Waiver of Speedy Trial Rights." The court led petitioner and his counsel through the form, and both signed it. Among other things, the form stated: "I wish to waive my rights to a speedy trial . . . under the Speedy Trial Act of 1974 (18 U.S.C. § 3161 et seq.), under the Rules of this Circuit and under the Speedy Trial Plan adopted by this Court." The form also stated: "I have been advised and fully understand that . . . I also waive any and all rights to make a motion to dismiss the indictment . . . against me for failure of the Court to give me a speedy trial and that I waive all of such rights to a speedy trial and to make such a motion or motions for all time." After the form was signed, petitioner's counsel requested that a further status conference be scheduled for January 31, 1997, and the court agreed.

At the January 31 status conference, petitioner sought yet another continuance "to tap . . . the proper channels to authenticate [the] bonds." Petitioner and the Government emphasized that this request raised no issue under the Act because petitioner had "waived for all time," though the Government suggested that it "would like to try the case sometime in 1997." After a brief discussion between the court and petitioner's counsel about the need to investigate the authenticity of what seemed such obviously fake bonds, the court offered to set trial for May 5, 1997. The court admonished petitioner's counsel to "[g]et to work" and noted: "This [case] is a year old. That's enough for a criminal case." Nevertheless, apparently satisfied with petitioner's waiver "for all time," the District Court made no mention of the Act and did not make any findings to support exclusion of the 91 days between January 31 and petitioner's next court appearance on May 2, 1997.

The four years that followed saw a variety of proceedings in petitioner's case, but no trial. Counsel sought to be relieved because petitioner insisted that he argue that the bonds were genuine, and the court ultimately granted counsel's request to withdraw. At the court's suggestion, petitioner was examined by a psychiatrist, who determined that petitioner was competent to stand trial. Petitioner then asked to proceed pro se and sought to serve subpoenas on, among others, the President, the Chairman of the Federal Reserve Board, the Attorney General, the Secretary of State, the late Chinese leader Chiang Kai-shek, and "The Treasury Department of Treasury International Corporation." After a year of quashed subpoenas, the District Court set the case for trial, only to conclude on the morning of jury selection that it had to inquire once again into petitioner's competency. The court dismissed the jury panel, found petitioner incompetent, and committed him to the custody of the Attorney General for hospitalization and treatment. On interlocutory appeal, however, the Court of Appeals vacated that order and remanded for further hearings. In July and August 2000, the District Court held those hearings and received further briefing on the competency issue.

On March 7, 2001, while the competency issue remained under submission, petitioner moved to dismiss the indictment for failure to comply with the Act. The District Court denied the motion on the ground that petitioner had waived his Speedy Trial Act rights "for all time," mentioning in passing that the case was complex. In the same order, the court found petitioner incompetent. That latter determination was upheld on interlocutory appeal, and petitioner was committed for evaluation. After several months of hospitalization, petitioner was found to be delusional but competent to stand trial, and he was released.

Finally, on April 7, 2003, more than seven years after petitioner was indicted, his trial began. The jury found petitioner guilty on six counts of attempting to defraud a financial institution and the court sentenced him to 63 months of imprisonment. . . .

II

As noted above, the Speedy Trial Act generally requires a trial to begin within 70 days of the filing of an information or indictment or the defendant's initial appearance, 18 U.S.C. § 3161(c)(1), but the Act recognizes that criminal cases vary widely and that there are valid reasons for greater delay in particular cases. To provide the necessary flexibility, the Act includes a long and detailed list of periods of delay that are excluded in computing the time within which trial must start. For example, the Act excludes "delay resulting from other proceedings concerning the defendant," "delay resulting from the absence or unavailability of the defendant or an essential witness," "delay resulting from the fact that the defendant is mentally incompetent or physically unable to stand trial," and "[a] reasonable period of delay when the defendant is joined for trial with a codefendant as to whom the time for trial has not run and no motion for severance has been granted."

Much of the Act's flexibility is furnished by § 3161(h)(8), which governs ends-of-justice continuances. . . . This provision permits a district court to grant a continuance and to exclude the resulting delay if the court, after considering certain factors, makes on-the-record findings that the ends of justice served by granting the continuance outweigh the public's and defendant's interests in a speedy trial. This provision gives the district court discretion—within limits and subject to specific procedures—to accommodate limited delays for case-specific needs.

To promote compliance with its requirements, the Act contains enforcement and sanctions provisions. If a trial does not begin on time, the defendant may move, before the start of trial or the entry of a guilty plea, to dismiss the charges, and if a meritorious and timely motion to dismiss is filed, the district court must dismiss the charges, though it may choose whether to dismiss with or without prejudice. In making that choice, the court must take into account, among other things, "the seriousness of the offense; the facts and circumstances of the case which led to the dismissal; and the impact of a re-prosecution on the administration of [the Act] and on the administration of justice." § 3162(a)(2).

This scheme is designed to promote compliance with the Act without needlessly subverting important criminal prosecutions. The more severe sanction (dismissal with prejudice) is available for use where appropriate, and the knowledge that a violation could potentially result in the imposition of this sanction gives the prosecution a powerful incentive to be careful about compliance. The less severe sanction (dismissal without prejudice) lets the court avoid unduly impairing the enforcement of federal criminal laws—though even this sanction imposes some costs on the prosecution and the court, which further encourages compliance. When an indictment is dismissed without prejudice, the prosecutor may of course seek—and in the great majority of cases will be able to obtain—a new indictment, for even if "the period prescribed by the applicable statute of limitations has expired, a new indictment may be returned . . . within six calendar months of the date of the dismissal." § 3288.

With this background in mind, we turn to the questions presented by the unusual procedures followed in this case.

III

Petitioner contends, and the Government does not seriously dispute, that a defendant may not prospectively waive the application of the Act. We agree.

As our discussion above suggests, the Speedy Trial Act comprehensively regulates the time within which a trial must begin. Section 3161(h) specifies in detail numerous categories of delay that are not counted in applying the Act's deadlines. Conspicuously, § 3161(h) has no provision excluding periods of delay during which a defendant waives the application of the Act, and it is apparent from the terms of the Act that this omission was a considered one. Instead of simply allowing defendants to opt out of the Act, the Act demands that defense continuance requests fit within one of the specific exclusions set out in subsection (h). Subsection (h)(8), which permits ends-of-justice continuances, was plainly meant to cover many of these requests. Among the factors that a district court must consider in deciding whether to grant an ends-of-justice continuance are a defendant's need for "reasonable time to obtain counsel," "continuity of counsel," and "effective preparation" of counsel. § 3161(h)(8)(B)(iv). If a defendant could simply waive the application of the Act whenever he or she wanted more time, no defendant would ever need to put such considerations before the court under the rubric of an ends-of-justice exclusion.

The purposes of the Act also cut against exclusion on the grounds of mere consent or waiver. If the Act were designed solely to protect a defendant's right to a speedy trial, it would make sense to allow a defendant to waive the application of the Act. But the Act was designed with the public interest firmly in mind. That public interest cannot be served, the Act recognizes, if defendants may opt out of the Act entirely. . . .

It is significant that § 3162(a)(2) makes no mention of prospective waivers, and there is no reason to think that Congress wanted to treat prospective and retrospective waivers similarly. Allowing prospective waivers would seriously undermine the Act because there are many cases—like the case at hand—in which the prosecution, the defense, and the court would all be happy to opt out of the Act, to the detriment of the public interest. . . .

NOTES & QUESTIONS ON THE SPEEDY TRIAL ACT

1. *The correct remedy.* When faced with a violation of the Speedy Trial Act, trial courts have at least two potential remedies that could be granted to the defendant. The court could dismiss the indictment with prejudice or the court could dismiss the indictment without prejudice. In the former, the case is dead and cannot be refiled, but in the latter, a new indictment could be refiled. According to the Speedy Trial Act, 18 U.S.C. § 3162, in "determining whether to dismiss the case with or without prejudice, the court shall consider, among others, each of the following factors: the seriousness of the offense; the facts and circumstances of the case which led to the dismissal; and the impact of a reprosecution on the administration of this chapter and on the administration of justice." This discretionary scheme is in contrast with a violation of the Sixth Amendment right to a speedy trial. As noted above, the Supreme Court has interpreted *Barker* as standing for the proposition that a dismissal with prejudice, though an extreme action, is the "only remedy" for a violation of the Sixth Amendment right. *Strunk v. United States*, 412 U.S. 434, 439 (1973). See also *United States v. Moreno*, 789 F.3d 72, 78 (2d Cir. 2015).

2. *Not so speedy.* The goal of the Speedy Trial Act was to impose statutory requirements that would go beyond what the Sixth Amendment required. Not everyone agrees that the Speedy Trial Act, as applied, accomplished that goal. For example, consider the following assessment from one lawyer:

> STA violations occur with such regularity because there is no real incentive for anyone to follow the Act. Delay is a federal prosecutor's friend. The longer the delay, the greater the chance a prosecutor has to flip a co-defendant into a cooperating witness through a negotiated plea deal. Defense attorneys also desire and create delays. Trials take an enormous amount of preparation, so defense lawyers often will defer trials as long as possible out of convenience. For those defense lawyers who bill by the hour or are paid per CJA-appointment, there can be a direct correlation between delays and larger profits, and as a result, defense attorneys are sometimes incentivized to create delay. Defense attorneys may also act as proxies for defendants who wish to delay their trials as long as possible in order to avoid the consequences of a guilty verdict.

Shon Hopwood, *The Not So Speedy Trial Act*, 89 Wash. L. Rev. 709, 738-39 (2014). What is your reaction to this assessment? Does it suggest that we should not concern ourselves with trial delays because defense attorneys are often just as responsible for them? Or does it suggest the opposite: that we should be more concerned about trial delays because structural factors and incentives impose virtually insurmountable obstacles to reform, making the situation even worse than imagined?

STATE LAW REQUIREMENTS

Plenty of states have their own versions of the Speedy Trial Act that regulate the timing of state criminal processes. For example, consider New York State's provision:

> 1. Except as otherwise provided in subdivision three, a motion . . . must be granted where the people are not ready for trial within:
>
> > (a) six months of the commencement of a criminal action wherein a defendant is accused of one or more offenses, at least one of which is a felony;
> > (b) ninety days of the commencement of a criminal action wherein a defendant is accused of one or more offenses, at least one of which is a misdemeanor punishable by a sentence of imprisonment of more than three months and none of which is a felony;
> > (c) sixty days of the commencement of a criminal action wherein the defendant is accused of one or more offenses, at least one of which is a misdemeanor punishable by a sentence of imprisonment of not more than three months and none of which is a crime punishable by a sentence of imprisonment of more than three months;
> > (d) thirty days of the commencement of a criminal action wherein the defendant is accused of one or more offenses, at least one of which is a violation and none of which is a crime.

N.Y. Crim. Proc. Law § 30.30. However, like the federal statute, the New York provision includes several notable exceptions. A few serious crimes, such as murder, are excluded entirely from these deadlines. Also excluded are delays associated with competency proceedings, production demands, requests for a bill of particulars, pre-trial motions, interlocutory appeals, trials on other charges, and judicial consideration of motions related to these categories.

Other state statutes tie the length of the statutory deadlines to the defendant's decision to file an explicit "demand for a speedy trial." For example, Florida's statute sets the following deadlines if the defendant triggers the protections of the statute: The court must hold a "calendar call" hearing within 5 days after receiving the demand and hold the trial within 45 days of receiving the demand. In cases where the defendant fails to file a demand, the trial must still occur within 90 days of arrest for misdemeanors or within 175 days of arrest for felonies. Fla. R. Crim. P. 3.191.

PROBLEM CASE

Consider the following crime:

> On January 18, 1996, the victim, a 13-year-old male, was at home alone and answered a knock at the door. A person wearing a gray mask "pushed his way through the door with a knife," forced the victim to the victim's bedroom, made the victim lie down, and asked for his clothes. The perpetrator sat on the victim's chest and attempted to tie his hands with a telephone cord. The victim struggled with the perpetrator and "yanked the mask off his head," at which point the victim

recognized Thomas, his next door neighbor, who was 14 years old. Thomas fled from the victim's apartment. The victim reported the incident to his aunt, who called the police. Thomas was arrested the same day, taken to the police station, questioned, and released that night to his mother, Mrs. J., who signed a form upon Thomas's release into her custody.

In re Thomas J., 132 Md. App. 396, 400-01, 752 A.2d 699, 701 (2000). The state filed a delinquency petition on May 2, 1996, and summons were quickly issued for Thomas and his mother. However, the family moved to another house in Prince George County and neither Thomas nor his mother appeared at the hearing. The matter was rescheduled for June 21 with a request for a "sheriff service" against Thomas and his mother. The Deputy Sheriff returned the summons stating that he was unable to contact them and a summons sent by mail was returned by the Post Office as undeliverable because no forwarding address was provided. When Thomas failed to appear at the June 21 hearing, a "writ of body attachment" was issued. He was served with the writ three years later, on April 2, 1999, and appeared in court, at which point his attorney sought dismissal because he was denied a speedy trial.

Based on these facts, do you believe that Thomas was denied a speedy trial and the case should be dismissed?

D. PRACTICE & POLICY

The failure to implement the right to a speedy trial in concrete terms continues to haunt criminal courts across the country. The mere fact that the Sixth Amendment requires it is no guarantee that courts will transform this abstract right into a reality. Consider the case of Kalief Browder. Browder, a resident of New York City, was 16 years old when he was arrested in 2010 on a charge of stealing a backpack containing electronic items (which he denied). He was granted bail of $3,000 and sent to Riker's Island because neither he nor his family could afford the cash bail amount. So began Browder's incomprehensible encounter with the New York City criminal justice system. Browder stayed in jail for three years waiting for his trial to begin. After the delay, the charge was not dismissed due to a violation of his right to a speedy trial, but rather for the prosecution's failure to marshal sufficient evidence against him; a prosecution witness had left the contrary and could not testify. Browder's time in pre-trial confinement was extremely difficult; he spent two years in solitary confinement and alleged that he received regular beatings from corrections officers. After release, Browder struggle to readjust and committed suicide in 2015. (His mother, Venida Browder, died a year later of complications from a heart attack.) This is just one story among many others. Consequently, this section focuses briefly on two obstacles to holding speedy trials in all cases: the unavailability of witnesses and the lack of judicial resources. It concludes with a discussion of the relationship between the speedy trial right and the prohibition against excessive bail.

❧ Witness availability. Some judges will grant continuances, at the prosecutor's request, if the witness is not available. State statutes will often include special provisions that create an exception for these situations. For example, New York law grants an exception for a

> period of delay resulting from a continuance granted at the request of a district attorney if . . . the continuance is granted because of the unavailability of evidence material to the people's case, when the district attorney has exercised due diligence to obtain such evidence and there are reasonable grounds to believe that such evidence will become available in a reasonable period. . . .

N.Y. C.P.L.R. § 30.30. So, for example, if the prosecution is unable to locate a key prosecution witness and seeks a continuance of the trial date, a judge could grant this request and the witness unavailability would toll the speedy trial clock. In theory, the prosecution could continue to seek continuances if the witness remains unavailable. Does this exception threaten to swallow the rule that trials must be held within a certain time period?

Certainly, it is uncontroversial to suggest that a pre-charging delay resulting from failure to locate a key witness would not violate the right to a speedy trial, because in that instance the government would not be delaying the trial intentionally in order to achieve a strategic benefit. Assuming that the government was diligent in its search for the witness, there would be no negligence either. However, the situation with regard to post-charging delays is somewhat different. Surely, a court should not delay a trial indefinitely due to witness unavailability. Indeed, one of the reasons why Browder's trial was delayed so many times by the trial judge was the prosecution's persistent failure to locate a key witness. In his case, the doctrinal exception for witness unavailability really was a barrier to implementing the right to a speedy trial.

What solutions exist for this problem? One possibility is to include specific statutory limits for how long a case might be deferred based on witness or evidence unavailability. Or, in the alternative, the statute might limit the number of times a trial could be delayed absent an explicit waiver from the defense, regardless of the status of the evidence or witnesses. Can you think of other solutions to this problem? Would it be acceptable to remove the exception entirely and force prosecutors to proceed to trial even if they cannot locate a key witness? For more discussion, see Daniel Hamburg, *A Broken Clock: Fixing New York's Speedy Trial Statute*, 48 Colum. J.L. & Soc. Probs. 223, 246 (2015) (referring to the New York statutory scheme as having a "bizarre design").

❧ Lack of resources. A lack of judicial resources is another potential obstacle for achieving a speedy trial. If there are no judges, prosecutors, or courtrooms to hold trials, it will be impossible to give each defendant a speedy trial. Of course, prosecutors could solve this problem by simply dismissing cases, but they are usually loath to do so. Which side—the prosecution or the defense—should bear the burden of this lack of resources? Note that as a matter of constitutional law, a lack of resources may be counted against the government as part of the constitutional calculation, since the government itself decides how much resources to devote to criminal adjudication.

What if the governmental delay is the result of a paucity of judicial resources, such as an overcrowded court docket, a lack of prosecutors, or a lack of judges? Recall that in the Supreme Court's first speedy trial case, it noted that the right was "relative" and "depends upon circumstances." *Beavers v. Haubert*, 198 U.S. 77 (1905). On the other hand, the government itself has an obligation to properly fund the judicial system, such that chronic underfunding or understaffing is not a restriction flowing from the natural environment, but rather from specific choices made by the government. Consequently, "[u]nintentional delays caused by overcrowded court dockets or understaffed prosecutors are among the factors to be weighed less heavily than intentional delay, calculated to hamper the defense, in determining whether the Sixth Amendment has been violated. . . ." *Strunk v. United States*, 412 U.S. 434, 436 (1973). How far should this analysis be taken? Are there other examples of judicial resources that might impact the government's ability to offer speedy trials?

In 2016, the Bronx Defenders, along with two private law firms, filed a federal lawsuit against Janet DiFiore, the Chief Judge of New York State (and by extension Chief Judicial Officer of the Unified Court System), and New York Governor Andrew Cuomo, arguing that a lack of resources in the Bronx was causing a systematic denial of speedy trial rights: "Adjournment after adjournment, people wait for hours to see a judge only to be told to come back yet another day. The months often turn into years. People's lives are put on hold as their fate hangs in the balance. The process can feel interminable." See *Trowbridge et al. v. DiFiore*, Complaint, May 10, 2016. As an example, the class action lawsuit made the following allegations:

> For Sarah Bello, it took 1,166 days and 33 court dates—30 of which were scheduled trial dates—before the charges against her were adjourned in contemplation of dismissal. For Joseph Bermudez, it took 1,258 days and 38 court dates before he could get his day in court, have a trial, and be acquitted. At least 16 times, both sides were ready for trial, but there were no misdemeanor trial courtrooms ("Trial Parts") available. John Carridice waited 1,009 days and had 20 court dates before he finally got a trial and was acquitted. Though their cases were ultimately resolved in their favor, the damage inflicted by Court Delay—jobs and opportunities lost, lives disrupted, and relationships strained—had already been done.

Janet DiFiore, Westchester County district attorney, and United States Attorney for the Southern District of New York Michael Garcia announce an indictment against over 30 members of the Genovese crime family in February 2006. (Chip East/Reuters)

According to the complaint, these delays were not the result of prosecutorial bad faith, but simply a lack of resources allocated to the Bronx Criminal Court. The case settled on August 9, 2018 with the filing of a Stipulation and Order of Settlement that included a data-sharing agreement regarding court delays, a schedule for holding "stakeholder meetings" designed to discuss speedy trial problems, and the creation of a "trial request tracking" computer system to keep track of cases where the defendant has requested a speedy trial with the goal of ensuring that those cases are brought to trial in an expeditious manner. Do these reforms adequately respond to the problem? Are there other solutions to the problem of inadequate judicial resources?

Speedy trials and bail. Both the right to a speedy trial and the prohibition on excessive bail are concerned with the intrusion of liberty that is caused by pre-trial detention. If defendants are in pre-trial detention because they could not afford bail, or because a judge refused to grant bail, any trial delay is especially burdensome because it delays the moment when they might secure their freedom by winning a trial. Consequently, what makes trial delays so problematic is that they are combined with a system of bail that some critics consider unduly harsh and discriminatory against low-income families. In a hypothetical world without bail or pre-trial detention, trial delays would be far less worrisome, because incarceration during the delay would not be an option. Recall that Kalief Browder's painful odyssey in Riker's was so tragic because he could not afford cash bail, making the delays in his case especially difficult to endure. Indeed, many years ago, Richard Posner argued that trial delays were most burdensome to defendants in pre-trial custody, while trial delays were least burdensome, and even beneficial, to those free on bail. See Richard A. Posner, *Economic Analysis of Law* 563-64 (4th ed. 1992). For the latter group, a delay would give the defendant more time to develop a legal defense while the prosecution's evidence, especially eyewitness testimony, might become degraded. Finally, if the defendant is anticipating a conviction, a trial delay represents a delay in punishment, as well. One consequence of this distinction is that defendants denied bail, or unable to afford bail, are more likely to plead guilty than defendants who are free pending trial, potentially creating economic discrimination in the incentive structure for guilty pleas. See Crystal S. Yang, *Toward an Optimal Bail System*, 92 N.Y.U. L. Rev. 1399, 1488 (2017). For more discussion, see also Yair Listokin, *Crime and (with a Lag) Punishment: The Implications of Discounting for Equitable Sentencing*, 44 Am. Crim. L. Rev. 115 (2007).

CHAPTER 15

COUNSEL

INTRODUCTION

The right to legal representation at trial is one of the most fundamental rights that make up the core of the rule of law. At least with regard to criminal justice, the idea of the rule of law is that the executive branch does not have unilateral authority to imprison rule breakers. Instead, the executive authorities (police and prosecutors) must justify the imprisonment before the judiciary—a group of neutral decision makers tasked with determining whether an individual violated the criminal law and what criminal sentence is appropriate for that violation. Law enforcement authority is shared between the executive and judicial branches and necessarily so because concentrating that power within the same actor is inevitably totalitarian.

Our Founders understood that the trial is the primary mechanism for making decisions of criminal responsibility and punishment when an individual accused contests an accusation. It involves the presentation of evidence before the fact finder while a judge handles matters of law. The highly technical proceedings of the trial are virtually impossible to navigate without legal training, so fair trial rights are meaningless without counsel to exercise them as part of a coherent legal strategy. This chapter tells the story of the right to counsel and the role that it plays in creating fair trials. Section A focuses on the right to counsel in federal and state court; Section B focuses on the right to *effective* assistance of counsel (and when a reversal is required by virtue of ineffective assistance); and Section C focuses on the right to self-representation—an often-dangerous choice by defendants that courts are nonetheless duty-bound to respect as long as the defendant's decision is voluntary and intelligent, because, as will be seen, the Sixth Amendment right to counsel also encompasses the right to refuse counsel in most situations. Section D outlines the right to retain psychiatric experts. Finally, Section E, the Practice & Policy section, focuses on practical obstacles to fulfilling the right to counsel and whether that right should be extended beyond criminal trials to quasi-criminal proceedings (such as immigration hearings) and collateral habeas corpus proceedings.

A. THE RIGHT TO COUNSEL

The Sixth Amendment Counsel Clause is clear that defendants in federal criminal cases have a right to counsel:

> In all criminal prosecutions, the accused shall enjoy the right to a speedy and public trial, by an impartial jury of the State and district wherein the crime shall have been committed, which district shall have been previously ascertained by law, and to be informed of the nature and cause of the accusation; to be confronted with the witnesses against him; to have compulsory process for obtaining witnesses in his favor, and to have the Assistance of Counsel for his defence.

The right to counsel is therefore part of a suite of rights that are constitutive of the notion of a fair trial. Without counsel, few of the other rights matter. For example, the right to cross-examine witnesses is of little use without counsel—*competent* counsel—to ask the questions. So, the right to counsel is the instrument through which the other fair trial rights can be secured. Consequently, the materials in this section answer the key doctrinal questions related to the realization of the right to counsel in criminal practice: (1) the right to counsel in state prosecutions, (2) the right to counsel in prosecutions for petty offenses, and (3) the moment when the Sixth Amendment right to counsel attaches.

1. Proceedings in State Court

Does the right to counsel apply not just in federal court but also in state criminal proceedings? In some cases, the answer is clearly yes. For example, in *Powell v. Alabama*, 287 U.S. 45 (1932), the Supreme Court heard an appeal arising from the conviction of five African-American men for allegedly raping two white women in a freight train. When the train reached Scottsboro, the suspects were taken into custody by sheriff's deputies. According to the Court, the "proceedings, from beginning to end, took place in an atmosphere of tense, hostile, and excited public sentiment," and the governor was compelled to call out the Alabama National Guard to protect the defendants from members of the local community. What followed was a rushed trial that gave the defendants inadequate time to secure counsel or mount a defense:

> It is hardly necessary to say that the right to counsel being conceded, a defendant should be afforded a fair opportunity to secure counsel of his own choice. Not only was that not done here, but such designation of counsel as was attempted was either so indefinite or so close upon the trial as to amount to a denial of effective and substantial aid in that regard.

Id. at 53. At the time, in 1932, some states protected the right to counsel in all cases, others only in prosecutions for serious crimes, and others only in capital cases. *Powell* did not explicitly hold that the federal constitution required counsel in each and every case, only that in the case before it (indigent defendants facing the risk of capital punishment) the denial of counsel was so egregious as to make the resulting conviction unconstitutional:

> All that it is necessary now to decide, as we do decide, is that in a capital case, where the defendant is unable to employ counsel, and is incapable adequately of making his own defense because of ignorance, feeble-mindedness, illiteracy, or the like, it is the duty of the court, whether requested or not, to assign counsel for him as a necessary requisite of due process of law. . . .

Id. at 71. In other words, the *Powell* Court limited its decision to the egregious facts of the case and declined to establish a broad per se rule. In *Powell*, the capital defendants were indigent and unable to represent themselves on account of special circumstances, such as "ignorance, feeble-mindedness, [or] illiteracy."

Then, in *Betts v. Brady,* 316 U.S. 455, 473 (1942), the Supreme Court again considered whether the Fourteenth Amendment required the extension of this right to state prosecutions as a function of the Fifth Amendment protection of due process. The Court ultimately concluded that it did not:

> As we have said, the Fourteenth Amendment prohibits the conviction and incarceration of one whose trial is offensive to the common and fundamental ideas of fairness and right, and while want of counsel in a particular case may result in a conviction lacking in such fundamental fairness, we cannot say that the amendment embodies an inexorable command that no trial for any offense, or in any court, can be fairly conducted and justice accorded a defendant who is not represented by counsel.

According to the *Betts* Court, lack or denial of counsel *may,* under some circumstances, make a trial so unfair as to render it unconstitutional, though this finding would not be automatic. *Betts* explicitly held what was possibly left open by *Powell*, that in some circumstances a state court denial of counsel would not necessarily violate the federal constitution if that denial did not deprive of the trial of its fundamental fairness.

Justice Hugo Black dissented in *Betts* because he felt that *all* defendants in state court were entitled to counsel under the Sixth Amendment as incorporated by the Fourteenth Amendment. For decades, Black remained in the minority with this view. But with the prosecution of Mr. Clarence Earl Gideon in a Florida court for breaking and entering, the Supreme Court finally had the opportunity to reconsider its holding from *Betts* and its interpretation of *Powell*. The police investigated a theft and charged Gideon with breaking and entering. Some suggested that some teenagers—the main witnesses in the case who implicated Gideon—were probably the real culprits. Also, the prosecution presented an improbable theory of the case: The state alleged that Gideon carried away beer, wine, and 20 pounds of coins out of the building on his own. Denied counsel at public expense, Gideon was forced to represent himself at trial, and lost. But on appeal there was vindication, not just for Gideon but for Justice Black as well. The Supreme Court's opinion was authored by Black, this time writing for the majority. As you read the case, ask yourself whether there are reasons to move to a per se rule that requires the recognition of a right to counsel in all state court criminal cases.

Gideon v. Wainwright

Supreme Court of the United States
372 U.S. 335 (1963)

Mr. Justice Black delivered the opinion of the Court.

Petitioner was charged in a Florida state court with having broken and entered a poolroom with intent to commit a misdemeanor. This offense is a felony under Florida law. Appearing in court without funds and without a lawyer, petitioner asked the court to appoint counsel for him, whereupon the following colloquy took place:

The Court: Mr. Gideon, I am sorry, but I cannot appoint Counsel to represent you in this case. Under the laws of the State of Florida, the only time the Court can appoint Counsel to represent a Defendant is when that person is charged with a capital offense. I am sorry, but I will have to deny your request to appoint Counsel to defend you in this case.
The Defendant: The United States Supreme Court says I am entitled to be represented by Counsel.

Put to trial before a jury, Gideon conducted his defense about as well as could be expected from a layman. He made an opening statement to the jury, cross-examined the State's witnesses, presented witnesses in his own defense, declined to testify himself, and made a short argument "emphasizing his innocence to the charge contained in the Information filed in this case." The jury returned a verdict of guilty, and petitioner was sentenced to serve five years in the state prison. . . . Since 1942, when *Betts v. Brady*, 316 U.S. 455, was decided by a divided Court, the problem of a defendant's federal constitutional right to counsel in a state court has been a continuing source of controversy and litigation in both state and federal courts. . . .

I

The facts upon which Betts claimed that he had been unconstitutionally denied the right to have counsel appointed to assist him are strikingly like the facts upon which Gideon here bases his federal constitutional claim. Betts was indicted for robbery in a Maryland state court. On arraignment, he told the trial judge of his lack of funds to hire a lawyer and asked the court to appoint one for him. Betts was advised that it was not the practice in that county to appoint counsel for indigent defendants except in murder and rape cases. He then pleaded not guilty, had witnesses summoned, cross-examined the State's witnesses, examined his own, and chose not to testify himself. He was found guilty by the judge, sitting without a jury, and sentenced to eight years in prison. Like Gideon, Betts sought release by habeas corpus, alleging that he had been denied the right to assistance of counsel in violation of the Fourteenth Amendment. Betts was denied any relief, and on review this Court affirmed. It was held that a refusal to appoint counsel for an indigent defendant charged with a felony did not necessarily violate the Due Process Clause of the Fourteenth Amendment, which for reasons given the Court deemed to be the only applicable federal constitutional provision.

Treating due process as "a concept less rigid and more fluid than those envisaged in other specific and particular provisions of the Bill of Rights," the Court held that refusal to appoint counsel under the particular facts and circumstances in the *Betts* case was not so "offensive to the common and fundamental ideas of fairness" as to amount to a denial of due process. Since the facts and circumstances of the two cases are so nearly indistinguishable, we think the *Betts v. Brady* holding if left standing would require us to reject Gideon's claim that the Constitution guarantees him the assistance of counsel. Upon full reconsideration we conclude that *Betts v. Brady* should be overruled.

II

The Sixth Amendment provides, "In all criminal prosecutions, the accused shall enjoy the right . . . to have the Assistance of Counsel for his defence." We have construed this to mean that in federal courts counsel must be provided for defendants unable to employ counsel unless the right is competently and intelligently waived. Betts argued that this right is extended to indigent defendants in state courts by the Fourteenth Amendment. In response the Court stated that, while the Sixth Amendment laid down "no rule for the conduct of the states, the question recurs whether the constraint laid by the amendment upon the national courts expresses a rule so fundamental and essential to a fair trial, and so, to due process of law, that it is made obligatory upon the states by the Fourteenth Amendment." In order to decide whether the Sixth Amendment's guarantee of counsel is of this fundamental nature, the Court in *Betts* set out and considered "(r)elevant data on the subject . . . afforded by constitutional and statutory provisions subsisting in the colonies and the states prior to the inclusion of the Bill of Rights in the national Constitution, and in the constitutional, legislative, and judicial history of the states to the present date." On the basis of this historical data the Court concluded that "appointment of counsel is not a fundamental right, essential to a fair trial." It was for this reason the *Betts* Court refused to accept the contention that the Sixth Amendment's guarantee of counsel for indigent federal defendants was extended to or, in the words of that Court, "made obligatory upon the states by the Fourteenth Amendment." Plainly, had the Court concluded that appointment of counsel for an indigent criminal defendant was "a fundamental right, essential to a fair trial," it would have held that the Fourteenth Amendment requires appointment of counsel in a state court, just as the Sixth Amendment requires in a federal court.

We think the Court in *Betts* had ample precedent for acknowledging that those guarantees of the Bill of Rights which are fundamental safeguards of liberty immune from federal abridgment are equally protected against state invasion by the Due Process Clause of the Fourteenth Amendment. This same principle was recognized, explained, and applied in *Powell v. Alabama,* 287 U.S. 45 (1932), a case upholding the right of counsel, where the Court held that despite sweeping language to the contrary in *Hurtado v. California*, 110 U.S. 516 (1884), the Fourteenth Amendment "embraced" those "fundamental principles of liberty and justice which lie at the base of all our civil and political institutions," even though they had been "specifically dealt with in another part of the Federal Constitution." In many cases other than *Powell* and *Betts*, this Court has looked to the fundamental nature of original Bill of Rights guarantees to decide whether the Fourteenth Amendment makes them obligatory on the States. Explicitly recognized to be of this "fundamental nature" and therefore made immune from state invasion by the Fourteenth, or some part of it, are the First Amendment's freedoms of speech, press, religion, assembly, association, and petition for redress of grievances. . . .

We accept *Betts v. Brady*'s assumption, based as it was on our prior cases, that a provision of the Bill of Rights which is "fundamental and essential to a fair trial" is made obligatory upon the States by the Fourteenth Amendment. We think the Court in *Betts* was wrong, however, in concluding that the Sixth Amendment's guarantee of counsel is not one of these fundamental rights. Ten years before *Betts v. Brady,* this Court, after full consideration of all the historical data examined in *Betts,* had unequivocally declared that "the right to the aid of counsel is of this fundamental character." *Powell v. Alabama,* 287 U.S. 45, 68 (1932). While the Court at the close of its *Powell* opinion did by its language, as this Court frequently does, limit its holding to the particular facts and circumstances of that case, its conclusions about the fundamental nature of the right to counsel are unmistakable. Several years later, in 1936, the Court reemphasized what it had said about the fundamental nature of the right to counsel in this language: "We concluded that certain fundamental rights, safeguarded by the first eight amendments against federal action, were also safeguarded against state action by the due process of law clause of the Fourteenth Amendment, and among them the fundamental right of the accused to the aid of counsel in a criminal prosecution." *Grosjean v. American Press Co.,* 297 U.S. 233, 243-244 (1936). . . .

In light of these and many other prior decisions of this Court, it is not surprising that the *Betts* Court, when faced with the contention that "one charged with crime, who is unable to obtain counsel, must be furnished counsel by the state," conceded that "(e)xpressions in the opinions of this court lend color to the argument. . . ." The fact is that in deciding as it did—that "appointment of counsel is not a fundamental right, essential to a fair trial"—the Court in *Betts v. Brady* made an abrupt break with its own well-considered precedents. In returning to these old precedents, sounder we believe than the new, we but restore constitutional principles established to achieve a fair system of justice. Not only these precedents but also reason and reflection require us to recognize that in our adversary system of criminal justice, any person haled into court, who is too poor to hire a lawyer, cannot be assured a fair trial unless counsel is provided for him. This seems to us to be an obvious truth. Governments, both state and federal, quite properly spend vast sums of money to establish machinery to try defendants accused of crime. Lawyers to prosecute are everywhere deemed essential to protect the public's interest in an orderly society. Similarly, there are few defendants charged with crime, few indeed, who fail to hire the best lawyers they can get to prepare and present their defenses. That government hires lawyers to prosecute and defendants who have the money hire lawyers to defend are the strongest indications of the wide-spread belief that lawyers in criminal courts are necessities, not luxuries. The right of one charged with crime to counsel may not be deemed fundamental and essential to fair trials in some countries, but it is in ours. From the very beginning, our state and national constitutions and laws have laid great emphasis on procedural and substantive safeguards designed to assure fair trials before impartial tribunals in which every defendant stands equal before the law. This noble ideal cannot be realized if the poor man charged with crime has to face his accusers without a lawyer to assist him. A defendant's need for a lawyer is nowhere better stated than in the moving words of Mr. Justice Sutherland in *Powell v. Alabama,* 287 U.S., at 68-69:

> The right to be heard would be, in many cases, of little avail if it did not comprehend the right to be heard by counsel. Even the intelligent and educated layman has small and sometimes no skill in the science of law. If charged with crime, he is incapable, generally, of determining for himself whether the indictment is good or bad. He is unfamiliar with the rules of evidence. Left without the aid of counsel he may be put on trial without a proper charge, and convicted upon incompetent evidence, or evidence irrelevant to the issue or otherwise inadmissible. He lacks both the skill and knowledge adequately to prepare his defense, even though he have a perfect one. He requires the guiding hand of counsel at every step in the proceedings against him. Without it, though he be not guilty, he faces the danger of conviction because he does not know how to establish his innocence.

The Court in *Betts v. Brady* departed from the sound wisdom upon which the Court's holding in *Powell v. Alabama* rested. Florida, supported by two other States, has asked that *Betts v. Brady* be left intact. Twenty-two States, as friends of the Court, argue that *Betts* was "an anachronism when handed down" and that it should now be overruled. We agree. . . .

2. What Punishment Triggers the Right to Counsel?

Gideon and *Powell* both involved prosecutions for felonies. This raised the question of whether *Gideon*'s recognition of the right to counsel applied only in felony cases or whether a prosecution for some minor offenses might be exempted from *Gideon*'s requirements. In *Argersinger v. Hamlin,* 407 U.S. 25 (1972), the Supreme Court held that the federal right to counsel applied even in prosecutions for so-called petty offenses that are punishable by less than six months in jail. But *Argersinger* arguably left unresolved a key question. Is the trigger for the right to counsel whether the statute allows for incarceration as a punishment or is the issue whether the defendant in a particular case is sentenced to incarceration? In other words, is a state relieved from the obligation to provide counsel if the defendant is not sentenced to incarceration in that case?

Scott v. Illinois

Supreme Court of the United States
440 U.S. 367 (1979)

Mr. Justice Rehnquist delivered the opinion of the Court.

We granted certiorari in this case to resolve a conflict among state and lower federal courts regarding the proper application of our decision in *Argersinger v. Hamlin*, 407 U.S. 25 (1972). Petitioner Scott was convicted of theft and fined $50 after a bench trial in the Circuit Court of Cook County, Ill. His conviction was affirmed by the state intermediate appellate court and then by the Supreme Court of Illinois, over Scott's contention that the Sixth and Fourteenth Amendments to the United States Constitution required that Illinois provide trial counsel to him at its expense.

Petitioner Scott was convicted of shoplifting merchandise valued at less than $150. The applicable Illinois statute set the maximum penalty for such an offense at a $500 fine or one year in jail, or both. The petitioner argues that a line of this Court's cases culminating in *Argersinger v. Hamlin* requires state provision of counsel whenever imprisonment is an authorized penalty. The Supreme Court of Illinois rejected this contention, quoting the following language from *Argersinger*:

> We hold, therefore, that absent a knowing and intelligent waiver, no person may be imprisoned for any offense, whether classified as petty, misdemeanor, or felony, unless he was represented by counsel at his trial. . . .
>
> Under the rule we announce today, every judge will know when the trial of a misdemeanor starts that no imprisonment may be imposed, even though local law permits it, unless the accused is represented by counsel. He will have a measure of the seriousness and gravity of the offense and therefore know when to name a lawyer to represent the accused before the trial starts.

407 U.S., at 37, 40. The Supreme Court of Illinois went on to state that it was "not inclined to extend *Argersinger*" to the case where a defendant is charged with a statutory offense for which imprisonment upon conviction is authorized but not actually imposed upon the defendant. We agree with the Supreme Court of Illinois that the Federal Constitution does not require a state trial court to appoint counsel for a criminal defendant such as petitioner, and we therefore affirm its judgment.

In his petition for certiorari, petitioner referred to the issue in this case as "the question left open in *Argersinger v. Hamlin*." Whether this question was indeed "left open" in *Argersinger* depends upon whether one considers that opinion to be a point in a moving line or a holding that the States are required to go only so far in furnishing counsel to indigent defendants. The Supreme Court of Illinois, in quoting the above language from *Argersinger*, clearly viewed the latter as *Argersinger*'s holding. Additional support for this proposition may be derived from the concluding paragraph of the opinion in that case: "The run of misdemeanors will not be affected by today's ruling. But in those that end up in the actual deprivation of a person's liberty, the accused will receive the benefit of 'the guiding hand of counsel' so necessary where one's liberty is in jeopardy." 407 U.S., at 40.

Petitioner, on the other hand, refers to language in the Court's opinion, responding to the opinion of Mr. Justice Powell, which states that the Court "need not consider the requirements of the Sixth Amendment as regards the right to counsel where loss of liberty is not involved . . . for here petitioner was in fact sentenced to jail." *Id.*, at 37.

There is considerable doubt that the Sixth Amendment itself, as originally drafted by the Framers of the Bill of Rights, contemplated any guarantee other than the right of an accused in a criminal prosecution in a federal court to employ a lawyer to assist in his defense. In *Powell v. Alabama*, 287 U.S. 45 (1932), the Court held that Alabama was obligated to appoint counsel for the Scottsboro defendants, phrasing the inquiry as "whether the defendants were in substance denied the right of counsel, and if so, whether such denial infringes the due process clause of the Fourteenth Amendment." *Id.*, at 52. . . .

Betts v. Brady, 316 U.S. 455 (1942), held that not every indigent defendant accused in a state criminal prosecution was entitled to appointment of counsel. A determination had to be made in each individual case whether failure to appoint counsel was a denial of fundamental fairness. *Betts* was in turn overruled in *Gideon v. Wainwright*, 372 U.S. 335 (1963). In *Gideon*, *Betts* was described as holding "that a refusal to appoint counsel for an indigent defendant charged with a felony did not necessarily violate the Due Process Clause of the Fourteenth Amendment. . . ."

Several Terms later the Court held in *Duncan v. Louisiana*, 391 U.S. 145 (1968), that the right to jury trial in federal court guaranteed by the Sixth Amendment was applicable to the States by virtue of the Fourteenth Amendment. The Court held, however: "It is doubtless true that there is a category of petty crimes or offenses which is not subject to the Sixth Amendment jury trial provision and should not be subject to the Fourteenth Amendment jury trial requirement here applied to the States. Crimes carrying possible penalties up to six months do not require a jury trial if they otherwise qualify as petty offenses. . . ." In *Baldwin v. New York*, 399 U.S. 66, 69 (1970), the controlling opinion of Mr. Justice White concluded that "no offense can be deemed 'petty' for purposes of the right to trial by jury where imprisonment for more than six months is authorized."

In *Argersinger* the State of Florida urged that a similar dichotomy be employed in the right-to-counsel area: Any offense punishable by less than six months in jail should not require appointment of counsel for an indigent defendant. The *Argersinger* Court rejected this analogy, however, observing that "the right to trial by jury has a different genealogy and is brigaded with a system of trial to a judge alone." 407 U.S., at 29.

The number of separate opinions in *Gideon, Duncan, Baldwin,* and *Argersinger,* suggests that constitutional line drawing becomes more difficult as the reach of the Constitution is extended further, and as efforts are made to transpose lines from one area of Sixth Amendment jurisprudence to another. The process of incorporation creates special difficulties, for the state and federal contexts are often different and application of the same principle may have ramifications distinct in degree and kind. The range of human conduct regulated by state criminal laws is much broader than that of the federal criminal laws, particularly on the "petty" offense part of the spectrum. As a matter of constitutional adjudication, we are, therefore, less willing to extrapolate an already extended line when, although the general nature of the principle sought to be applied is clear, its precise limits and their ramifications become less so. We have now in our decided cases departed from the literal meaning of the Sixth Amendment. And we cannot fall back on the common law as it existed prior to the enactment of that Amendment, since it perversely gave less in the way of right to counsel to accused felons than to those accused of misdemeanors.

In *Argersinger* the Court rejected arguments that social cost or a lack of available lawyers militated against its holding, in some part because it thought these arguments were factually incorrect. But they were rejected in much larger part because of the Court's conclusion that incarceration was so severe a sanction that it should not be imposed as a result of a criminal trial unless an indigent defendant had been offered appointed counsel to assist in his defense, regardless of the cost to the States implicit in such a rule. The Court in its opinion repeatedly referred to trials "where an accused is deprived of his liberty" and to "a case that actually leads to imprisonment even for a brief period." The Chief Justice in his opinion concurring in the result also observed that "any deprivation of liberty is a serious matter."

Although the intentions of the *Argersinger* Court are not unmistakably clear from its opinion, we conclude today that *Argersinger* did indeed delimit the constitutional right to appointed counsel in state criminal proceedings. Even were the matter res nova, we believe that the central premise of *Argersinger*—that actual imprisonment is a penalty different in kind from fines or the mere threat of imprisonment—is eminently sound and warrants adoption of actual imprisonment as the line defining the constitutional right to appointment of counsel. *Argersinger* has proved reasonably workable, whereas any extension would create confusion and impose unpredictable, but necessarily substantial, costs on 50 quite diverse States. We therefore hold that the Sixth and Fourteenth Amendments to the United States Constitution require only that no indigent criminal defendant be sentenced to a term of imprisonment unless the State has afforded him the right to assistance of appointed counsel in his defense.

Mr. Justice BRENNAN, with whom Mr. Justice MARSHALL and Mr. Justice STEVENS join, dissenting.

. . . In my view petitioner could prevail in this case without extending the right to counsel beyond what was assumed to exist in *Argersinger*. Neither party in that case questioned the existence of the right to counsel in trials involving "non-petty" offenses punishable by more than six months in jail. The question the Court addressed was whether the right applied to some "petty" offenses to which the right to jury trial did not extend. The Court's reasoning in applying the right to counsel in the case before it—that the right to counsel is more fundamental to a fair proceeding than the right to jury trial and that the historical limitations on the jury trial right are irrelevant to the right to counsel—certainly cannot support a standard for the right to counsel that is more restrictive than the standard for granting a right to jury trial. As my Brother Powell commented in his opinion concurring in the result in *Argersinger*, 407 U.S., at 45-46: "It is clear that wherever the right-to-counsel line is to be drawn, it must be drawn so that an indigent has a right to appointed counsel in all cases in which there is a due process right to a jury trial." *Argersinger* thus established a "two dimensional" test for the right to counsel: the right attaches to any "non-petty" offense punishable by more than six months in jail and in addition to any offense where actual incarceration is likely regardless of the maximum authorized penalty.

The offense of "theft" with which Scott was charged is certainly not a "petty" one. It is punishable by a sentence of up to one year in jail. Unlike many traffic or other "regulatory" offenses, it carries the moral stigma associated with common-law crimes traditionally recognized as indicative of moral depravity. The State indicated at oral argument that the services of a professional prosecutor were considered essential to the prosecution of this offense. Likewise, nonindigent defendants charged with this offense would be well advised to hire the "best lawyers they can get." Scott's right to the assistance of appointed counsel is thus plainly mandated by the logic of the Court's prior cases, including *Argersinger* itself. . . .

NOTES & QUESTIONS ON CONFINEMENT

1. *Suspended sentences.* If *Scott* stands for the proposition that the state must provide counsel in any case that results in confinement as a punishment, there are still some unresolved questions. For example, what if the judge imposes

a sentence of incarceration but then "suspends" the sentence? In *Alabama v. Shelton*, 535 U.S. 654 (2002), the Supreme Court held that the right to counsel applies even cases that result in suspended sentences. If the defendant is released on probation during the suspended sentence, the convict's sentence can be reactivated by the court if the defendant violates the probation. In that case, suspended sentences can become *actual* terms of confinement, thus triggering the protections of *Argersinger* and *Scott*, and the "minimal procedures" of a parole revocation hearing are insufficient to mitigate the damage done by denying the right to counsel at the original trial. Consequently, the rule from *Shelton* is that the right to counsel applies in any case where the defendant is subject to punishment of confinement, whether actual or suspended.

3. What Is a Critical Stage of the Criminal Process?

Is there a difference between "attachment" of the right to counsel and the point at which a defendant is entitled to the assistance of counsel? The answer is yes. One way to understand this is that you do not get to claim the assistance of counsel before the right "attaches," but just because the right has "attached" does not mean counsel is constitutionally required to be present at every step of the process. This was explained initially in the right to counsel chapter, where we learned that once the right "attaches," counsel is required to be present only at "critical stages" of the adversarial process. This next case addresses the difference between "attachment" and the right to the presence of counsel to assist the accused. Given that there are a number of avenues through which a state can commence criminal proceedings—arrest, indictment, the filing of an information—when exactly must the defendant have access to counsel, at public expense if necessary? In the following case, the Supreme Court answers this question with regard to an initial appearance in Texas that was handled by the police but without the involvement of prosecutors.

Rothgery v. Gillespie County

Supreme Court of the United States
554 U.S. 191 (2008)

Justice Souter delivered the opinion of the Court.

This Court has held that the right to counsel guaranteed by the Sixth Amendment applies at the first appearance before a judicial officer at which a defendant is told of the formal accusation against him and restrictions are imposed on his liberty. The question here is whether attachment of the right also requires that a public prosecutor (as distinct from a police officer) be aware of that initial proceeding or involved in its conduct. We hold that it does not.

I

Although petitioner Walter Rothgery has never been convicted of a felony, a criminal background check disclosed an erroneous record that he had been, and on July 15, 2002, Texas police officers relied on this record to arrest him as a felon in possession of a firearm. The officers lacked a warrant, and so promptly brought Rothgery before a magistrate. Texas law has no formal label for this initial appearance before a magistrate, which is sometimes called the "article 15.17 hearing"; it combines the Fourth Amendment's required probable-cause determination with the setting of bail, and is the point at which the arrestee is formally apprised of the accusation against him.

Rothgery's article 15.17 hearing followed routine. The arresting officer submitted a sworn "Affidavit Of Probable Cause" that described the facts supporting the arrest and "charge[d] that . . . Rothgery . . . commit[ted] the offense of unlawful possession of a firearm by a felon—3rd degree felony [Tex. Penal Code Ann. § 46.04]," After reviewing the affidavit, the magistrate "determined that probable cause existed for the arrest." The magistrate informed Rothgery of the accusation, set his bail at $5,000, and committed him to jail, from which he was released after posting a surety bond. The bond, which the Gillespie County deputy sheriff signed, stated that "Rothgery stands charged by complaint duly filed . . . with the offense of a . . . felony, to wit: Unlawful Possession of a Firearm by a Felon." The release was conditioned on the defendant's personal appearance in trial court "for any and all subsequent proceedings that may be had relative to the said charge in the course of the criminal action based on said charge."

Rothgery had no money for a lawyer and made several oral and written requests for appointed counsel, which went unheeded. The following January, he was indicted by a Texas grand jury for unlawful possession of a firearm by a felon, resulting in rearrest the next day, and an order increasing bail to $15,000. When he could not post it, he was put in jail and remained there for three weeks.

On January 23, 2003, six months after the article 15.17 hearing, Rothgery was finally assigned a lawyer, who promptly obtained a bail reduction and assembled the paperwork confirming that Rothgery had never been convicted of a felony. Counsel relayed this information to the district attorney, who in turn filed a motion to dismiss the indictment, which was granted. . . .

II

The Sixth Amendment right of the "accused" to assistance of counsel in "all criminal prosecutions" is limited by its terms: "it does not attach until a prosecution is commenced." We have, for purposes of the right to counsel, pegged commencement to "the initiation of adversary judicial criminal proceedings—whether by way of formal charge, preliminary hearing, indictment, information, or arraignment." The rule is not "mere formalism," but a recognition of the point at which "the government has committed itself to prosecute," "the adverse positions of government and defendant have solidified," and the accused "finds himself faced with the prosecutorial forces of organized society, and immersed in the intricacies of substantive and procedural criminal law." The issue is whether Texas's article 15.17 hearing marks that point, with the consequent state obligation to appoint counsel within a reasonable time once a request for assistance is made.

When the Court of Appeals said no, because no prosecutor was aware of Rothgery's article 15.17 hearing or involved in it, the court effectively focused not on the start of adversarial judicial proceedings, but on the activities and knowledge of a particular state official who was presumably otherwise occupied. This was error.

As the Court of Appeals recognized, we have twice held that the right to counsel attaches at the initial appearance before a judicial officer. This first time before a court, also known as the "preliminary arraignment" or "arraignment on the complaint," is generally the hearing at which "the magistrate informs the defendant of the charge in the complaint, and of various rights in further proceedings," and "determine[s] the conditions for pretrial release." Texas's article 15.17 hearing is an initial appearance: Rothgery was taken before a magistrate, informed of the formal accusation against him, and sent to jail until he posted bail. . . .

. . . [T]he overwhelming consensus practice conforms to the rule that the first formal proceeding is the point of attachment. We are advised without contradiction that not only the Federal Government, including the District of Columbia, but 43 States take the first step toward appointing counsel "before, at, or just after initial appearance." And even in the remaining seven States (Alabama, Colorado, Kansas, Oklahoma, South Carolina, Texas, and Virginia) the practice is not free of ambiguity. In any event, to the extent these States have been denying appointed counsel on the heels of the first appearance, they are a distinct minority.

The only question is whether there may be some arguable justification for the minority practice. Neither the Court of Appeals in its opinion, nor the County in its briefing to us, has offered an acceptable one. . . .

The County . . . tries to downplay the significance of the initial appearance by saying that an attachment rule unqualified by prosecutorial involvement would lead to the conclusion "that the State has statutorily committed to prosecute every suspect arrested by the police," given that "state law requires [an article 15.17 hearing] for every arrestee." The answer, though, is that the State has done just that, subject to the option to change its official mind later. The State may rethink its commitment at any point: it

> may choose not to seek indictment in a felony case, say, or the prosecutor may enter nolle prosequi after the case gets to the jury room. But without a change of position, a defendant subject to accusation after initial appearance is headed for trial and needs to get a lawyer working, whether to attempt to avoid that trial or to be ready with a defense when the trial date arrives. . . .

NOTES & QUESTIONS ON THE RIGHT TO COUNSEL

1. *Attachment versus the right to have counsel present.* In *Rothgery*, the Supreme Court decided that the bail hearing is the moment when the Sixth Amendment right to counsel "attaches." However, attachment does not necessarily entail that counsel must be present for the bail hearing itself; the latter is only required if it constitutes a "critical stage." The attachment point merely establishes the dividing line when the Sixth Amendment counsel right attaches to the criminal process because the prosecution has begun in earnest. In that vein, consider the following paragraph from the Court's opinion:

> If, indeed, the County had simply taken the cases at face value, it would have avoided the mistake of merging the attachment question (whether formal judicial proceedings have begun) with the distinct "critical stage" question (whether counsel must be present at a postattachment proceeding unless the right to assistance is validly waived). Attachment occurs when the government has used the judicial machinery to signal a commitment to prosecute as spelled out in *Brewer* and *Jackson*. Once attachment occurs, the accused at least is entitled to the presence of appointed counsel during any "critical stage" of the postattachment proceedings; what makes a stage critical is what shows the need for counsel's presence. Thus, counsel must be appointed within a reasonable time after attachment to allow for adequate representation at any critical stage before trial, as well as at trial itself.

Rothgery v. Gillespie County, 554 U.S. 191, 211-12 (2008).

2. *Counsel of one's choosing.* Does the Sixth Amendment entail that defendants have the right to select counsel of their choosing? In *United States v. Gonzalez-Lopez*, 548 U.S. 140 (2006), the Supreme Court concluded that it does and reversed the conviction of a defendant whose choice of counsel had been rejected on account of the trial court's erroneous application of a state disciplinary rule. The doctrinal rubric for this conclusion was ineffective assistance of counsel pursuant to *Strickland v. Washington*, 466 U.S.

668 (1984). Under *Strickland,* a successful claim of ineffective assistance of counsel required a finding that the defendant was prejudiced by the defective counsel. In *Gonzalez-Lopez,* the Court concluded that *Strickland* prejudice is automatically presumed when the state violates the "respondent's Sixth Amendment right to paid counsel of his choosing." What is the ground for this decision? Why is counsel of one's choosing—if one can afford it—constitutionally protected? Is it based on the personal autonomy of the criminal defendant? Or some other rationale? See Janet Moore, *The Antidemocratic Sixth Amendment,* 91 Wash. L. Rev. 1705, 1747 (2016) ("*Gonzalez-Lopez* continued the development of the Sixth Amendment's root meaning into the right of the individual, autonomous consumer to purchase services in the marketplace").

3. *Appellate counsel.* The discussion above focused on the right to counsel during initial appearances at the beginning of the adjudicatory process. But does the Constitution guarantee a right to counsel for appeals? In *Douglas v. California,* 372 U.S. 353, 357 (1963), the Supreme Court concluded that indigent defendants have the right to counsel for a first appeal. The Court stated that "where the merits of the one and only appeal an indigent has as of right are decided without benefit of counsel, we think an unconstitutional line has been drawn between rich and poor." *Id.* at 357. In *Ross v. Moffitt,* 417 U.S. 600 (1974), the Supreme Court declined to extend the rule from *Douglas* to discretionary state appeals beyond the first "as of right" appeal. Of course, there is nothing in the federal constitution that prohibits a state from guaranteeing by statute a more expansive right to counsel.

4. *Accuracy or autonomy.* What is the conceptual foundation for the right to counsel in general? Is it a concern for accuracy, i.e., the idea that a trial conducted without the benefit of defense counsel is unlikely to produce an accurate result? This rationale would support a prejudice requirement; if the denial of the right to counsel failed to change the outcome of the trial, then it is hard to view the resulting verdict as inaccurate. On the other hand, the right to counsel might be justified by the concept of the autonomy, i.e., the idea that denial of the right to counsel infringes the autonomy of the defendant to present a legal strategy of their own choosing:

> A criminal defendant engages in communicative activity in the public forum of the courtroom largely through the attorney he chooses to advocate his positions. A crucial aspect of the participatory and autonomy values served by the right to counsel of choice is the selection and employment of the advocate who will assert the defendant's legal rights.

Bruce J. Winick, *Forfeiture of Attorneys' Fees Under RICO and CCE and the Right to Counsel of Choice: The Constitutional Dilemma and How to Avoid It,*

43 U. Miami L. Rev. 765, 803 (1989). Which rationale makes most sense to you? Is it possible that the Sixth Amendment right to counsel is based on both ideas? As the Supreme Court noted in *Flanagan v. United States*, 465 U.S. 259, 268 (1984), "the right reflects constitutional protection of the defendant's free choice independent of concern for the objective fairness of the proceeding."

STATUTORY REQUIREMENTS

Gideon v. Wainwright and *Argersinger v. Hamlin* require that states grant criminal defendants a right to counsel at trial, regardless of whether the prosecution is for a serious or petty offense. As noted above, the federal constitutional right to counsel attaches to trials and direct "as-of-right" appeals, but not to subsequent appeals or civil offenses. However, states are free to pass more generous statutes conferring the right to counsel on additional defendants.

For example, Washington's legislature passed a statute that provides for counsel at public expense when the defendant

> (3) Is under a sentence of death and requests counsel be appointed to file and prosecute a motion or petition for collateral attack. . . . Counsel may be provided at public expense to file or prosecute a second or subsequent collateral attack on the same judgment and sentence. . . .
> (4) Is not under a sentence of death and requests counsel to prosecute a collateral attack after the chief judge has determined that the issues raised by the petition are not frivolous, in accordance with the procedure contained in rules of appellate procedure 16.11. Counsel shall not be provided at public expense to file or prosecute a second or subsequent collateral attack on the same judgment and sentence;
> (5) Responds to a collateral attack filed by the state or responds to or prosecutes an appeal from a collateral attack that was filed by the state;
> (6) Prosecutes a motion or petition for review after the supreme court or court of appeals has accepted discretionary review of a decision of a court of limited jurisdiction; or
> (7) Prosecutes a motion or petition for review after the supreme court has accepted discretionary review of a court of appeals decision.

Wash. Stat. § 10.73.150. Similarly, Wisconsin will provide counsel to indigent defendants in the following categories:

> (a) Cases involving persons charged with a crime against life . . .
> (b) Cases involving persons charged with a felony not specified under par. (a).
> (c) Cases involving persons charged with a misdemeanor that is punishable by imprisonment but is not specified under par. (a).
> (e) Cases involving children who are entitled to counsel or are provided counsel at the discretion of the court . . .
> (g) Cases involving persons entitled to counsel under ch. 48.
> (h) Cases involving paternity determinations . . .

Wis. Stat. § 977.08. The list of cases subject to counsel at public expenses varies from jurisdiction to jurisdiction.

B. INEFFECTIVE ASSISTANCE OF COUNSEL

Denial of counsel can be literal or constructive. In the latter case, a defense counsel might be so ineffective or incompetent that the defendant is denied the right of legal representation. In other words, incompetent legal counsel is, in some sense, no legal counsel at all. This requires federal courts to scrutinize the conduct of attorneys to determine whether the defendant received effective assistance of counsel in a criminal case or whether the counsel's conduct was so defective and prejudicial as to be a violation of the Sixth Amendment. The following subsections first outline the articulation of a standard for evaluating ineffective assistance of counsel claims and then apply that standard to categories of cases where the effectiveness of counsel is called into question: (1) conflicts of interests, particularly between co-defendants; and (2) strategic decisions, in particular the decision to plead guilty in capital cases.

1. The *Strickland* Standard

In the following case, the Supreme Court outlines the controlling standard for evaluating a claim of ineffective assistance of counsel. Pay particular attention to how the Supreme Court defines and applies the concept of deficiency. Also, as you read the case, determine what level of prejudice the defendant must demonstrate in order to reverse a conviction. With what level of certainty must the defendant establish that the outcome of the trial would have been different with competent counsel representing the defendant? Must the defendant conclusively establish beyond a reasonable doubt that the conviction would not have occurred but for the ineffective counsel? Also, are there some ineffective assistance claims that do not require a finding of actual prejudice, or trigger a presumption of prejudice the state must rebut?

Strickland v. Washington

Supreme Court of the United States
466 U.S. 668 (1984)

Justice O'Connor delivered the opinion of the Court.

This case requires us to consider the proper standards for judging a criminal defendant's contention that the Constitution requires a conviction or death sentence to be set aside because counsel's assistance at the trial or sentencing was ineffective.

I

During a 10-day period in September 1976, respondent planned and committed three groups of crimes, which included three brutal stabbing murders, torture, kidnaping, severe assaults, attempted murders, attempted extortion, and theft. After his two accomplices were arrested, respondent surrendered to police and voluntarily gave a lengthy statement confessing to the third of the criminal episodes. The State of Florida indicted respondent for kidnaping and murder and appointed an experienced criminal lawyer to represent him.

Counsel actively pursued pretrial motions and discovery. He cut his efforts short, however, and he experienced a sense of hopelessness about the case, when he learned that, against his specific advice, respondent had also confessed to the first two murders. By the date set for trial, respondent was subject to indictment for three counts of first-degree murder and multiple counts of robbery, kidnaping for ransom, breaking and entering and assault, attempted murder, and conspiracy to commit robbery. Respondent waived his right to a jury trial, again acting against counsel's advice, and pleaded guilty to all charges, including the three capital murder charges.

In the plea colloquy, respondent told the trial judge that, although he had committed a string of burglaries, he had no significant prior criminal record and that at the time of his criminal spree he was under extreme stress caused by his inability to support his family. He also stated, however, that he accepted responsibility for the crimes. The trial judge told respondent that he had "a great deal of respect for people who are willing to step forward and admit their responsibility" but that he was making no statement at all about his likely sentencing decision.

Counsel advised respondent to invoke his right under Florida law to an advisory jury at his capital sentencing hearing. Respondent rejected the advice and waived the right. He chose instead to be sentenced by the trial judge without a jury recommendation.

In preparing for the sentencing hearing, counsel spoke with respondent about his background. He also spoke on the telephone with respondent's wife and mother, though he did not follow up on the one unsuccessful effort to meet with them. He did not otherwise seek out character witnesses for respondent. Nor did he request a psychiatric examination, since his conversations with his client gave no indication that respondent had psychological problems.

Counsel decided not to present and hence not to look further for evidence concerning respondent's character and emotional state. That decision reflected trial counsel's sense of hopelessness about overcoming the evidentiary effect of respondent's confessions to the gruesome crimes. It also reflected the judgment that it was advisable to rely on the plea colloquy for evidence about respondent's background and about his claim of emotional stress: the plea colloquy communicated sufficient information about these subjects, and by forgoing the opportunity to present new evidence on these subjects, counsel prevented the State from cross-examining respondent on his claim and from putting on psychiatric evidence of its own.

Counsel also excluded from the sentencing hearing other evidence he thought was potentially damaging. He successfully moved to exclude respondent's "rap sheet." Because he judged that a presentence report might prove more detrimental than helpful, as it would have included respondent's criminal history and thereby would have undermined the claim of no significant history of criminal activity, he did not request that one be prepared.

At the sentencing hearing, counsel's strategy was based primarily on the trial judge's remarks at the plea colloquy as well as on his reputation as a sentencing judge who thought it important for a convicted defendant to own up to his crime. Counsel argued that respondent's remorse and acceptance of responsibility justified sparing him from the death penalty. Counsel also argued that respondent had no history of criminal activity and that respondent committed the crimes under extreme mental or emotional disturbance, thus coming within the statutory list of mitigating circumstances. He further argued that respondent should be spared death because he had surrendered, confessed, and offered to testify against a codefendant and because respondent was fundamentally a good person who had briefly gone badly wrong in extremely stressful circumstances. The State put on evidence and witnesses largely for the purpose of describing the details of the crimes. Counsel did not cross-examine the medical experts who testified about the manner of death of respondent's victims. . . .

[After sentence of death], [r]espondent subsequently sought collateral relief in state court on numerous grounds, among them that counsel had rendered ineffective assistance at the sentencing proceeding. Respondent challenged counsel's assistance in six respects. He asserted that counsel was ineffective because he failed to move for a continuance to prepare for sentencing, to request a psychiatric report, to investigate and present character witnesses, to seek a presentence investigation report, to present meaningful arguments to the sentencing judge, and to investigate the medical examiner's reports or cross-examine the medical experts. In support of the claim, respondent submitted 14 affidavits from friends, neighbors, and relatives stating that they would have testified if asked to do so. He also submitted one psychiatric report and one psychological report stating that respondent, though not under the influence of extreme mental or emotional disturbance, was "chronically frustrated and depressed because of his economic dilemma" at the time of his crimes. . . .

II

In a long line of cases that includes *Powell v. Alabama*, 287 U.S. 45 (1932), *Johnson v. Zerbst*, 304 U.S. 458 (1938), and *Gideon v. Wainwright*,

372 U.S. 335 (1963), this Court has recognized that the Sixth Amendment right to counsel exists, and is needed, in order to protect the fundamental right to a fair trial. The Constitution guarantees a fair trial through the Due Process Clauses, but it defines the basic elements of a fair trial largely through the several provisions of the Sixth Amendment, including the Counsel Clause. . . . Thus, a fair trial is one in which evidence subject to adversarial testing is presented to an impartial tribunal for resolution of issues defined in advance of the proceeding. The right to counsel plays a crucial role in the adversarial system embodied in the Sixth Amendment, since access to counsel's skill and knowledge is necessary to accord defendants the "ample opportunity to meet the case of the prosecution" to which they are entitled.

Because of the vital importance of counsel's assistance, this Court has held that, with certain exceptions, a person accused of a federal or state crime has the right to have counsel appointed if retained counsel cannot be obtained. That a person who happens to be a lawyer is present at trial alongside the accused, however, is not enough to satisfy the constitutional command. The Sixth Amendment recognizes the right to the assistance of counsel because it envisions counsel's playing a role that is critical to the ability of the adversarial system to produce just results. An accused is entitled to be assisted by an attorney, whether retained or appointed, who plays the role necessary to ensure that the trial is fair.

For that reason, the Court has recognized that "the right to counsel is the right to the effective assistance of counsel." *McMann v. Richardson*, 397 U.S. 759, 771, n. 14 (1970). Government violates the right to effective assistance when it interferes in certain ways with the ability of counsel to make independent decisions about how to conduct the defense. Counsel, however, can also deprive a defendant of the right to effective assistance, simply by failing to render "adequate legal assistance," *Cuyler v. Sullivan*, 446 U.S., at 344.

The Court has not elaborated on the meaning of the constitutional requirement of effective assistance in the latter class of cases—that is, those presenting claims of "actual ineffectiveness." In giving meaning to the requirement, however, we must take its purpose—to ensure a fair trial—as the guide. The benchmark for judging any claim of ineffectiveness must be whether counsel's conduct so undermined the proper functioning of the adversarial process that the trial cannot be relied on as having produced a just result.

The same principle applies to a capital sentencing proceeding such as that provided by Florida law. We need not consider the role of counsel in an ordinary sentencing, which may involve informal proceedings and standardless discretion in the sentencer, and hence may require a different approach to the definition of constitutionally effective assistance. A capital sentencing proceeding like the one involved in this case, however, is sufficiently like a trial in its adversarial format and in the existence of standards for decision that counsel's role in the proceeding is comparable to counsel's role at trial—to ensure that the adversarial testing process works to produce a just result under the standards governing decision. For purposes of describing counsel's duties, therefore, Florida's capital sentencing proceeding need not be distinguished from an ordinary trial.

III

A convicted defendant's claim that counsel's assistance was so defective as to require reversal of a conviction or death sentence has two components. First, the defendant must show that counsel's performance was deficient. This requires showing that counsel made errors so serious that counsel was not functioning as the "counsel" guaranteed the defendant by the Sixth Amendment. Second, the defendant must show that the deficient performance prejudiced the defense. This requires showing that counsel's errors were so serious as to deprive the defendant of a fair trial, a trial whose result is reliable. Unless a defendant makes both showings, it cannot be said that the conviction or death sentence resulted from a breakdown in the adversary process that renders the result unreliable.

As all the Federal Courts of Appeals have now held, the proper standard for attorney performance is that of reasonably effective assistance. The Court indirectly recognized as much when it stated in *McMann v. Richardson*, 397 U.S., at 770, 771, that a guilty plea cannot be attacked as based on inadequate legal advice unless counsel was not "a reasonably competent attorney" and the advice was not "within the range of competence demanded of attorneys in criminal cases." When a convicted defendant complains of the ineffectiveness of counsel's assistance, the defendant must show that counsel's representation fell below an objective standard of reasonableness.

More specific guidelines are not appropriate. The Sixth Amendment refers simply to "counsel," not specifying particular requirements of effective assistance. It relies instead on the legal profession's maintenance of standards sufficient to justify the law's presumption that counsel will fulfill the role in the adversary process that the Amendment envisions. The proper measure of attorney performance remains simply reasonableness under prevailing professional norms.

Representation of a criminal defendant entails certain basic duties. Counsel's function is to assist the defendant, and hence counsel owes the client a duty of loyalty, a duty to avoid conflicts of interest. From counsel's function as assistant to the defendant derive the overarching duty to advocate the defendant's cause and the more particular duties to consult with the defendant on important decisions and to keep the defendant informed of important developments in the course of the prosecution. Counsel also has a duty to bring to bear such skill and knowledge as will render the trial a reliable adversarial testing process.

These basic duties neither exhaustively define the obligations of counsel nor form a checklist for judicial evaluation of attorney performance. In any case presenting an ineffectiveness claim, the performance inquiry must be whether counsel's assistance was reasonable considering all the circumstances. Prevailing norms of practice as reflected in American Bar Association standards and the like are guides to determining what is reasonable, but they are only guides. No particular set of detailed rules for counsel's conduct can satisfactorily take account of the variety of circumstances faced by defense counsel or the range of legitimate decisions regarding how best to represent a criminal defendant. Any such set of rules would interfere with the constitutionally protected independence of counsel and restrict the wide latitude counsel must have in making tactical decisions. Indeed, the existence of detailed guidelines for representation could distract counsel from the overriding mission of vigorous advocacy of the defendant's cause. Moreover, the purpose of the effective assistance guarantee of the Sixth Amendment is not to improve the quality of legal representation, although that is a goal of considerable importance to the legal system. The purpose is simply to ensure that criminal defendants receive a fair trial.

Judicial scrutiny of counsel's performance must be highly deferential. It is all too tempting for a defendant to second-guess counsel's assistance after conviction or adverse sentence, and it is all too easy for a court, examining counsel's defense after it has proved unsuccessful, to conclude that a particular act or omission of counsel was unreasonable. A fair assessment of attorney performance requires that every effort be made to eliminate the distorting effects of hindsight, to reconstruct the circumstances of counsel's challenged conduct, and to evaluate the conduct from counsel's perspective at the time. Because of the difficulties inherent in making the evaluation, a court must indulge a strong presumption that counsel's conduct falls within the wide range of reasonable professional assistance; that is, the defendant must overcome the presumption that, under the circumstances, the challenged action "might be considered sound trial strategy." There are countless ways to provide effective assistance in any given case. Even the best criminal defense attorneys would not defend a particular client in the same way.

The availability of intrusive post-trial inquiry into attorney performance or of detailed guidelines for its evaluation would encourage the proliferation of ineffectiveness challenges. Criminal trials resolved unfavorably to the defendant would increasingly come to be followed by a second trial, this one of counsel's unsuccessful defense. Counsel's performance and even willingness to serve could be adversely affected. Intensive scrutiny of counsel and rigid requirements for acceptable assistance could dampen the ardor and impair the independence of defense counsel, discourage the acceptance of assigned cases, and undermine the trust between attorney and client.

Thus, a court deciding an actual ineffectiveness claim must judge the reasonableness of counsel's challenged conduct on the facts of the particular case, viewed as of the time of counsel's conduct. A convicted defendant making a claim of ineffective assistance must identify the acts or omissions of counsel that are alleged not to have been the result of reasonable professional judgment. The court must then determine whether, in light of all the circumstances, the identified acts or omissions were outside the wide range of professionally competent assistance. In making that determination, the court should keep in mind that counsel's function, as elaborated in prevailing professional norms, is to make the adversarial testing process work in the particular case. At the same time, the court should recognize that counsel is strongly presumed to have rendered adequate assistance and made all significant decisions in the exercise of reasonable professional judgment.

These standards require no special amplification in order to define counsel's duty to investigate, the duty at issue in this case. As the Court of Appeals concluded, strategic choices made after thorough investigation of law and facts relevant to plausible options are virtually unchallengeable; and strategic choices made after less than complete investigation are reasonable precisely to the extent that reasonable professional judgments support the limitations on investigation. In other words, counsel has a duty to make reasonable investigations or to make a reasonable decision that makes particular investigations unnecessary. In any ineffectiveness case, a particular decision not to investigate must be directly assessed for reasonableness in all the circumstances, applying a heavy measure of deference to counsel's judgments.

The reasonableness of counsel's actions may be determined or substantially influenced by the defendant's own statements or actions. Counsel's actions are usually based, quite properly, on informed strategic choices made by the defendant and on information supplied by the defendant. In particular, what investigation decisions are reasonable depends critically on such information. For example, when the facts that support a certain potential line of defense are generally known to counsel because of what the defendant has said, the need for further investigation may be considerably diminished or eliminated altogether. And when a defendant has given counsel reason to believe that pursuing certain investigations would be fruitless or even harmful, counsel's failure to pursue those investigations may not later be challenged as unreasonable. In short, inquiry into counsel's conversations with the defendant may be critical to a proper assessment of counsel's investigation decisions, just as it may be critical to a proper assessment of counsel's other litigation decisions.

An error by counsel, even if professionally unreasonable, does not warrant setting aside the judgment of a criminal proceeding if the error had no effect on the judgment. The purpose of the Sixth Amendment guarantee of counsel is to ensure that a defendant has the assistance necessary to justify reliance on the outcome of the proceeding. Accordingly, any deficiencies in counsel's performance must be prejudicial to the defense in order to constitute ineffective assistance under the Constitution.

In certain Sixth Amendment contexts, prejudice is presumed. Actual or constructive denial of the assistance of counsel altogether is legally presumed to result in prejudice. So are various kinds of state interference with counsel's assistance. Prejudice in these circumstances is so likely that case-by-case inquiry into prejudice is not worth the cost. Moreover, such circumstances involve impairments of the Sixth Amendment right that are easy to identify and, for that reason and because the prosecution is directly responsible, easy for the government to prevent.

One type of actual ineffectiveness claim warrants a similar, though more limited, presumption of prejudice. In *Cuyler v. Sullivan*, 446 U.S., at 345-350, the Court held that prejudice is presumed when counsel is burdened by an actual conflict of interest. In those circumstances, counsel breaches the duty of loyalty, perhaps the most basic of counsel's duties. Moreover, it is difficult to measure the precise effect on the defense of representation corrupted by conflicting interests. Given the obligation of counsel to avoid conflicts of interest and the ability of trial courts to make early inquiry in certain situations likely to give rise to conflicts, it is reasonable for the criminal justice system to maintain a fairly rigid rule of presumed prejudice for conflicts of interest. Even so, the rule is not quite the per se rule of prejudice that exists for the Sixth Amendment claims mentioned above. Prejudice is presumed only if the defendant demonstrates that counsel "actively represented conflicting interests" and that "an actual conflict of interest adversely affected his lawyer's performance."

Conflict of interest claims aside, actual ineffectiveness claims alleging a deficiency in attorney performance are subject to a general requirement that the defendant affirmatively prove prejudice. The government is not responsible for, and hence not able to prevent, attorney errors that will result in reversal of a conviction or sentence. Attorney errors come in an infinite variety and are as likely to be utterly harmless in a particular case as they are to be prejudicial. They cannot be classified according to likelihood of causing prejudice. Nor can they be defined with sufficient precision to inform defense attorneys correctly just what conduct to avoid. Representation is an art, and an act or omission that is unprofessional in one case may be sound or even brilliant in another. Even if a defendant shows that particular errors of counsel were unreasonable, therefore, the defendant must show that they actually had an adverse effect on the defense.

It is not enough for the defendant to show that the errors had some conceivable effect on the outcome of the proceeding. Virtually every act or omission of counsel would meet that test and not every error that conceivably could have influenced the outcome undermines the reliability of the result of the proceeding. Respondent suggests requiring a showing that the errors "impaired the presentation of the defense." That standard, however, provides no workable principle. Since any error, if it is indeed an error, "impairs" the presentation of the defense, the proposed standard is inadequate because it provides no way of deciding what impairments are sufficiently serious to warrant setting aside the outcome of the proceeding.

On the other hand, we believe that a defendant need not show that counsel's deficient conduct more likely than not altered the outcome in the case. This outcome-determinative standard has several strengths. It defines the relevant inquiry in a way familiar to courts, though the inquiry, as is inevitable, is anything but precise. The standard also reflects the profound importance of finality in criminal proceedings. Moreover, it comports with the widely used standard for assessing motions for new trial based on newly discovered evidence. Nevertheless, the standard is not quite appropriate.

Even when the specified attorney error results in the omission of certain evidence, the newly discovered evidence standard is not an apt source from which to draw a prejudice standard for ineffectiveness claims. The high standard for newly discovered evidence claims presupposes that all the essential elements of a presumptively accurate and fair proceeding were present in the proceeding whose result is challenged. An ineffective assistance claim asserts the absence of one of the crucial assurances that the result of the proceeding is reliable, so finality concerns are somewhat weaker and the appropriate standard of prejudice should be somewhat lower. The result of a proceeding can be rendered unreliable, and hence the proceeding itself unfair, even if the errors of counsel cannot be shown by a preponderance of the evidence to have determined the outcome.

Accordingly, the appropriate test for prejudice finds its roots in the test for materiality of exculpatory information not disclosed to the defense by the prosecution and in the test for materiality of testimony made unavailable to the defense by Government deportation of a witness. The defendant must show that there is a reasonable probability that, but for counsel's unprofessional errors, the result of the proceeding would have been different. A reasonable probability is a probability sufficient to undermine confidence in the outcome.

In making the determination whether the specified errors resulted in the required prejudice, a court should presume, absent challenge to the judgment on grounds of evidentiary insufficiency, that the judge or jury acted according to law. An assessment of the likelihood of a result more favorable to the defendant must exclude the possibility of arbitrariness, whimsy, caprice, "nullification," and the like. A defendant has no entitlement to the luck of a lawless decisionmaker, even if a lawless decision cannot be reviewed. The assessment of prejudice should proceed on the assumption that the decisionmaker is reasonably, conscientiously, and impartially applying the standards that govern the decision. It should not depend on the idiosyncrasies of the particular decisionmaker, such as unusual propensities toward harshness or leniency. Although these factors may actually have entered into counsel's selection of strategies and, to that limited extent, may thus affect the performance inquiry, they are irrelevant to the prejudice inquiry. Thus, evidence about the actual process of decision, if not part of the record of the proceeding under review, and evidence about, for example, a particular judge's sentencing practices, should not be considered in the prejudice determination.

The governing legal standard plays a critical role in defining the question to be asked in assessing the prejudice from counsel's errors. When a defendant challenges a conviction, the question is whether there is a reasonable probability that, absent the errors, the factfinder would have had a reasonable doubt respecting guilt. When a defendant challenges a death sentence such as the one at issue in this case, the question is whether there is a reasonable probability that, absent the errors, the sentencer—including an appellate court, to the extent it independently reweighs the evidence—would have concluded that the balance of aggravating and mitigating circumstances did not warrant death. . . .

V

Having articulated general standards for judging ineffectiveness claims, we think it useful to apply those standards to the facts of this case in order to illustrate the meaning of the general principles. The record makes it possible to do so. There are no conflicts between the state and federal courts over findings of fact, and the principles we have articulated are sufficiently close to the principles applied both in the Florida courts and in the District Court that it is clear that the factfinding was not affected by erroneous legal principles.

Application of the governing principles is not difficult in this case. The facts as described above make clear that the conduct of respondent's counsel at and before respondent's sentencing proceeding cannot be found unreasonable. They also make clear that, even assuming the challenged conduct of counsel was unreasonable, respondent suffered insufficient prejudice to warrant setting aside his death sentence.

With respect to the performance component, the record shows that respondent's counsel made a strategic choice to argue for the extreme emotional distress mitigating circumstance and to rely as fully as possible on respondent's acceptance of responsibility for his crimes. Although counsel understandably felt hopeless about respondent's prospects, nothing in the record indicates, as one possible reading of the District Court's opinion suggests, that counsel's sense of hopelessness distorted his professional judgment. Counsel's strategy choice was well within the range of professionally reasonable judgments, and the decision not to seek more character or psychological evidence than was already in hand was likewise reasonable.

The trial judge's views on the importance of owning up to one's crimes were well known to counsel. The aggravating circumstances were utterly overwhelming. Trial counsel could reasonably surmise from his conversations with respondent that character and psychological evidence would be of little help. Respondent had already been able to mention at the plea colloquy the substance of what there was to know about his financial and emotional troubles. Restricting testimony on respondent's character to what had come in at the plea colloquy ensured that contrary character and psychological evidence and respondent's criminal history, which counsel had successfully moved to exclude, would not come in. On these facts, there can be little question, even without application of the presumption of adequate performance, that trial counsel's defense, though unsuccessful, was the result of reasonable professional judgment. . . .

With respect to the prejudice component, the lack of merit of respondent's claim is even more stark. The evidence that respondent says his trial counsel should have offered at the sentencing hearing would barely have altered the sentencing profile presented to the sentencing judge. As the state courts and District Court found, at most this evidence shows that numerous people who knew respondent thought he was generally a good person and that a psychiatrist and a psychologist believed he was under considerable emotional stress that did not rise to the level of extreme disturbance. Given the overwhelming aggravating factors, there is no reasonable probability that the omitted evidence would have changed the conclusion that the aggravating circumstances outweighed the mitigating circumstances and, hence, the sentence imposed. Indeed, admission of the evidence respondent now offers might even have been harmful to his case: his "rap sheet" would probably have been admitted into evidence, and the psychological reports would have directly contradicted respondent's claim that the mitigating circumstance of extreme emotional disturbance applied to his case. . . .

NOTES & QUESTIONS ON STRICKLAND

1. *Applying* Strickland. Do you agree with the application of the *Strickland* standard in this case? The Court concluded that the counsel "made a strategic

choice to argue for the extreme emotional distress mitigating circumstance and to rely as fully as possible on respondent's acceptance of responsibility for his crimes." The Court also concluded that the defendant suffered no prejudice either. Do you agree with these assessments?

2. *The burden of demonstrating prejudice.* Prior to *Strickland,* federal courts applied something akin to a harmless-error framework for analyzing ineffective assistance of counsel claims. Specifically, defendants had the burden of demonstrating that the counsel's performance was defective, at which point the burden shifted to the government to demonstrate that counsel's performance did not change the outcome of the trial—the same framework used in harmless-error cases. *Strickland* changed that structure by imposing on defendants the burden of not only showing that their counsel was defective but also that the ineffective assistance impacted the trial in some way ("reasonable probability" or "probability sufficient to undermine confidence in the outcome"). Does this allocation of the burden strike you as justified, or does it require the defendant to prove too much?

3. *Deficiency versus prejudice.* Imagine an alternate holding for *Strickland* in which the Court concluded that reversal was required in any case where the counsel's conduct was deficient—thus eliminating the prejudice requirement. Would this be a workable standard? Would it open up a floodgate of reversals and overwhelm the criminal justice system? How often do trial attorneys engage in deficient representation?

2. Conflicts of Interests

It is not uncommon for one defense attorney to represent multiple defendants at one time, some of whom might even be tried as co-defendants in the same trial. In most cases, this arrangement is not unusual and may even be essential for achieving a good outcome for the defendants. The strongest defense might be a *common* defense, a *united* defense. Or, as Justice Frankfurter noted in *Glasser v. United States,* 315 U.S. 60, 92 (1942), "[a] common defense often gives strength against a common attack." This strategy depends on the co-defendants having a common interest—something that might not be the case if one defendant's interests are best served by pleading guilty and testifying against the other co-defendants. In those situations, one lawyer would have difficulty faithfully representing the diverse interests of his clients.

In the following case, the Supreme Court asks whether a conflict of interest can render an otherwise competent counsel ineffective. Also, if a defendant succeeds in showing that the counsel was conflicted, what showing of prejudice is required? Must the defendant meet the "reasonable probability" standard for prejudice outlined in *Strickland* or some other standard?

Holloway v. Arkansas
Supreme Court of the United States
435 U.S. 475 (1978)

Mr. Chief Justice Burger delivered the opinion of the Court.

Petitioners, codefendants at trial, made timely motions for appointment of separate counsel, based on the representations of their appointed counsel that, because of confidential information received from the codefendants, he was confronted with the risk of representing conflicting interests and could not, therefore, provide effective assistance for each client. We granted certiorari to decide whether petitioners were deprived of the effective assistance of counsel by the denial of those motions.

I

Early in the morning of June 1, 1975, three men entered a Little Rock, Ark., restaurant and robbed and terrorized the five employees of the restaurant. During the course of the robbery, one of the two female employees was raped once; the other, twice. The ensuing police investigation led to the arrests of the petitioners.

On July 29, 1975, the three defendants were each charged with one count of robbery and two counts of rape. On August 5, the trial court appointed Harold Hall, a public defender, to represent all three defendants. Petitioners were then arraigned and pleaded not guilty. Two days later, their cases were set for a consolidated trial to commence September 4.

On August 13 Hall moved the court to appoint separate counsel for each petitioner because "the defendants ha[d] stated to him that there is a possibility of a conflict of interest in each of their cases . . . ." After conducting a hearing on this motion, and on petitioners' motions for a severance, the court declined to appoint separate counsel.

Before trial, the same judge who later presided at petitioners' trial conducted a *Jackson v. Denno* hearing to determine the admissibility of a confession purportedly made by petitioner Campbell to two police officers at the time of his arrest. The essence of the confession was that Campbell had entered the restaurant with his codefendants and had remained, armed with a rifle, one flight of stairs above the site of the robbery and rapes (apparently serving as a lookout), but had not taken part in the rapes. The trial judge ruled the confession admissible, but ordered deletion of the references to Campbell's codefendants. At trial one of the arresting officers testified to Campbell's confession.

On September 4, before the jury was empaneled, Hall renewed the motion for appointment of separate counsel "on the grounds that one or two of the defendants may testify and if they do, then I will not be able to cross-examine them because I have received confidential information from them." The court responded, "I don't know why you wouldn't," and again denied the motion.

The prosecution then proceeded to present its case. The manager of the restaurant identified petitioners Holloway and Campbell as two of the robbers. Another male employee identified Holloway and petitioner Welch. A third identified only Holloway. The victim of the single rape identified Holloway and Welch as two of the robbers but was unable to identify the man who raped her. The victim of the double rape identified Holloway as the first rapist. She was unable to identify the second rapist but identified Campbell as one of the robbers.

On the second day of trial, after the prosecution had rested its case, Hall advised the court that, against his recommendation, all three defendants had decided to testify. He then stated:

> Now, since I have been appointed, I had previously filed a motion asking the Court to appoint a separate attorney for each defendant because of a possible conflict of interest. This conflict will probably be now coming up since each one of them wants to testify.
>
> **The Court:** That's all right; let them testify. There is no conflict of interest. Every time I try more than one person in this court each one blames it on the other one.
> **Mr. Hall:** I have talked to each one of these defendants, and I have talked to them individually, not collectively.
> **The Court:** Now talk to them collectively.

The court then indicated satisfaction that each petitioner understood the nature and consequences of his right to testify on his own behalf, whereupon Hall observed:

> I am in a position now where I am more or less muzzled as to any cross-examination.
>
> **The Court:** You have no right to cross-examine your own witness.
> **Mr. Hall:** Or to examine them.
> **The Court:** You have a right to examine them, but have no right to cross-examine them. The prosecuting attorney does that.
> **Mr. Hall:** If one [defendant] takes the stand, somebody needs to protect the other two's interest while that one is testifying, and I can't do that since I have talked to each one individually.
> **The Court:** Well, you have talked to them, I assume, individually and collectively, too. They all say they want to testify. I think it's perfectly alright [sic] for them to testify if they want to, or not. It's their business.

> Each defendant said he wants to testify, and there will be no cross-examination of these witnesses, just a direct examination by you.
> **Mr. Hall:** Your Honor, I can't even put them on direct examination because if I ask them—
> **The Court:** (Interposing) You can just put them on the stand and tell the Court that you have advised them of their rights and they want to testify; then you tell the man to go ahead and relate what he wants to. That's all you need to do.

Holloway then took the stand on his own behalf, testifying that during the time described as the time of the robbery he was at his brother's home. His brother had previously given similar testimony. When Welch took the witness stand, the record shows Hall advised him, as he had Holloway, that "I cannot ask you any questions that might tend to incriminate any one of the three of you . . . . Now, the only thing I can say is tell these ladies and gentlemen of the jury what you know about this case . . . ." Welch responded that he did not "have any kind of speech ready for the jury or anything. I thought I was going to be questioned." When Welch denied, from the witness stand, that he was at the restaurant the night of the robbery, Holloway interrupted, asking:

> Your Honor, are we allowed to make an objection?
>
> **The Court:** No, sir. Your counsel will take care of any objections.
> **Mr. Hall:** Your Honor, that is what I am trying to say. I can't cross-examine them.
> **The Court:** You proceed like I tell you to, Mr. Hall. You have no right to cross-examine your own witnesses anyhow.

Welch proceeded with his unguided direct testimony, denying any involvement in the crime and stating that he was at his home at the time it occurred. Campbell gave similar testimony when he took the stand. He also denied making any confession to the arresting officers.

The jury rejected the versions of events presented by the three defendants and the alibi witness, and returned guilty verdicts on all counts. . . .

II

More than 35 years ago, in *Glasser v. United States,* 315 U.S. 60 (1942), this Court held that by requiring an attorney to represent two codefendants whose interests were in conflict the District Court had denied one of the defendants his Sixth Amendment right to the effective assistance of counsel. In that case the Government tried five codefendants in a joint trial for conspiracy to defraud the United States. Two of the defendants, Glasser and Kretske, were represented initially by separate counsel. On the second day of trial, however, Kretske became dissatisfied with his attorney and dismissed him. The District Judge thereupon asked Glasser's attorney, Stewart, if he would also represent Kretske. Stewart responded by noting a possible conflict of interests: His representation of both Glasser and Kretske might lead the jury to link the two men together. Glasser also made known that he objected to the proposal. The District Court nevertheless appointed Stewart, who continued as Glasser's retained counsel, to represent Kretske. Both men were convicted.

Glasser contended in this Court that Stewart's representation at trial was ineffective because of a conflict between the interests of his two clients. This Court held that "the 'Assistance of Counsel' guaranteed by the Sixth Amendment contemplates that such assistance be untrammeled and unimpaired by a court order requiring that one lawyer should simultaneously represent conflicting interests." The record disclosed that Stewart failed to cross-examine a Government witness whose testimony linked Glasser with the conspiracy and failed to object to the admission of arguably inadmissible evidence. This failure was viewed by the Court as a result of Stewart's desire to protect Kretske's interests, and was thus "indicative of Stewart's struggle to serve two masters . . . ." After identifying this conflict of interests, the Court declined to inquire whether the prejudice flowing from it was harmless and instead ordered Glasser's conviction reversed. Kretske's conviction, however, was affirmed.

One principle applicable here emerges from *Glasser* without ambiguity. Requiring or permitting a single attorney to represent codefendants, often referred to as joint representation, is not per se violative of constitutional guarantees of effective assistance of counsel. This principle recognizes that in some cases multiple defendants can appropriately be represented by one attorney; indeed, in some cases, certain advantages might accrue from joint representation. In Mr. Justice Frankfurter's view: "Joint representation is a means of insuring against reciprocal recrimination. A common defense often gives strength against a common attack."

Since *Glasser* was decided, however, the courts have taken divergent approaches to two issues commonly raised in challenges to joint representation where—unlike this case—trial counsel did nothing to advise the trial court of the actuality or possibility of a conflict between his several clients' interests. First, appellate courts have differed on how strong a showing of conflict must be made, or how certain the reviewing court must be that the asserted conflict existed, before it will conclude that the defendants were deprived of their right to the effective assistance of counsel. Second, courts have differed with respect to the scope and nature of the affirmative duty of the trial judge to assure that criminal defendants are not deprived of their right to the effective assistance of counsel by joint representation of conflicting interests.

We need not resolve these two issues in this case, however. Here trial counsel, by the pretrial motions of August 13 and September 4 and by his accompanying representations, made as an officer of the court, focused explicitly on the probable risk of a conflict of interests. The judge then failed either to appoint separate counsel or to take adequate steps to ascertain whether the risk was too remote to warrant separate counsel. We hold that the failure, in the face of the representations made by counsel weeks before trial and again before the jury was empaneled, deprived petitioners of the guarantee of "assistance of counsel." . . .

This reasoning has direct applicability in this case where the "possibility of [petitioners'] inconsistent interests" was "brought home to the court" by formal objections, motions, and defense counsel's representations. It is arguable, perhaps, that defense counsel might have presented the requests for appointment of separate counsel more vigorously and in greater detail. As to the former, however, the trial court's responses hardly encouraged pursuit of the separate-counsel claim; and as to presenting the basis for that claim in more detail, defense counsel was confronted with a risk of violating, by more disclosure, his duty of confidentiality to his clients.

Additionally, since the decision in *Glasser*, most courts have held that an attorney's request for the appointment of separate counsel, based on his representations as an officer of the court regarding a conflict of interests, should be granted. In so holding, the courts have acknowledged and given effect to several interrelated considerations. An "attorney representing two defendants in a criminal matter is in the best position professionally and ethically to determine when a conflict of interest exists or will probably develop in the course of a trial." Second, defense attorneys have the obligation, upon discovering a conflict of interests, to advise the court at once of the problem. Finally, attorneys are officers of the court, and "when they address the judge solemnly upon a matter before the court, their declarations are virtually made under oath." We find these considerations persuasive.

The State argues, however, that to credit Hall's representations to the trial court would be tantamount to transferring to defense counsel the authority of the trial judge to rule on the existence or risk of a conflict and to appoint separate counsel. In the State's view, the ultimate decision on those matters must remain with the trial judge; otherwise unscrupulous defense attorneys might abuse their "authority," presumably for purposes of delay or obstruction of the orderly conduct of the trial.

The State has an obvious interest in avoiding such abuses. But our holding does not undermine that interest. When an untimely motion for separate counsel is made for dilatory purposes, our holding does not impair the trial court's ability to deal with counsel who resort to such tactics. Nor does our holding preclude a trial court from exploring the adequacy of the basis of defense counsel's representations regarding a conflict of interests without improperly requiring disclosure of the confidential communications of the client. In this case the trial court simply failed to take adequate steps in response to the repeated motions, objections, and representations made to it, and no prospect of dilatory practices was present to justify that failure. . . .

III

The issue remains whether the error committed at petitioners' trial requires reversal of their convictions. . . .

[A] rule requiring a defendant to show that a conflict of interests—which he and his counsel tried to avoid by timely objections to the joint representation—prejudiced him in some specific fashion would not be susceptible of intelligent, evenhanded application. In the normal case where a harmless-error rule is applied, the error occurs at trial and its scope is readily identifiable. Accordingly, the reviewing court can undertake with some confidence its relatively narrow task of assessing the likelihood that the error materially affected the deliberations of the jury. But in a case of joint representation of conflicting interests the evil—it bears repeating—is in what the advocate finds himself compelled to refrain from doing, not only at trial but also as to possible pretrial plea negotiations and in the sentencing process. It may be possible in some cases to identify from the record the prejudice resulting from an attorney's failure to undertake certain trial tasks, but even with a record of the sentencing hearing available it would be difficult to judge intelligently the impact of a conflict on the attorney's representation of a client. And to assess the impact of a conflict of interests on the attorney's options, tactics, and decisions in plea negotiations would be virtually impossible. Thus, an inquiry into a claim of harmless error here would require, unlike most cases, unguided speculation. . . .

Mr. Justice Powell with whom Mr. Justice Blackmun and Mr. Justice Rehnquist join, dissenting.

While disavowing a per se rule of separate representation, the Court holds today that the trial judge's failure in this case "either to appoint separate counsel or take adequate steps to ascertain whether the risk was too remote to warrant separate counsel" worked a violation of the guarantee of "assistance of counsel" embodied in the Sixth and Fourteenth Amendments. The Court accepts defense counsel's representations of a possible conflict of interests among his clients and of his inability to conduct effective cross-examination as being adequate to trigger the trial court's duty of inquiry. The trial court should have held an appropriate hearing on defense counsel's motions for separate representation, but our task is to decide whether this omission assumes the proportion of a constitutional violation. . . .

It is useful to contrast today's decision with the Court's most relevant previous ruling, *Glasser v. United States*, 315 U.S. 60 (1942). In that case, the trial court ordered Glasser's retained lawyer, Stewart, to represent both Glasser and his codefendant, Kretske, even though Stewart had identified "inconsistency in the defense" that counseled against joint representation. This Court reversed Glasser's conviction because his lawyer had been required to undertake simultaneous representation of "conflicting interests." The *Glasser* decision did not rest only on the determination that "[t]he possibility of the inconsistent interests of Glasser and Kretske [had been] brought home to the court . . . ." Instead, the Court proceeded to find record support for Glasser's claim of "impairment" of his Sixth Amendment right to assistance of counsel. The evidence "indicative of Stewart's struggle to serve two masters [could not] seriously be doubted."

Today's decision goes well beyond the limits of *Glasser*. I agree that the representations made by defense counsel in this case, while not as informative as the affidavit of counsel Stewart in *Glasser*, were sufficient to bring into play the trial court's duty to inquire further into the possibility of "conflicting interests." I question, however, whether the Constitution is violated simply by the failure to conduct that inquiry, without any additional determination that the record reveals a case of joint representation in the face of "conflicting interests." The Court's approach in this case is not premised on an ultimate finding of conflict of interest or ineffective assistance of counsel. Rather, it presumes prejudice from the failure to conduct an inquiry, equating that failure with a violation of the Sixth Amendment guarantee. . . . I am not convinced of the need for a prophylactic gloss on the requirements of the Constitution in this area of criminal law. . . .

STATUTORY REQUIREMENTS

In federal criminal prosecutions, Federal Rule of Criminal Procedure 44 protects a defendant's right to counsel and places the onus on the court to inquire whether co-representation is going to infringe on that right:

> *Court's Responsibilities in Cases of Joint Representation.* The court must promptly inquire about the propriety of joint representation and must personally advise each defendant of the right to the effective assistance of counsel, including separate representation. Unless there is good cause to believe that no conflict of interest is likely to arise, the court must take appropriate measures to protect each defendant's right to counsel.

Fed. R. Crim. P. 44. Does this Rule go beyond what the Sixth Amendment requires? Consider the following passage from *Cuyler v. Sullivan*, 446 U.S. 335, 346-47 (1980):

> *Holloway* requires state trial courts to investigate timely objections to multiple representation. But nothing in our precedents suggests that the Sixth Amendment requires state courts themselves to initiate inquiries into the propriety of multiple representation in every case. Defense counsel have an ethical obligation to avoid conflicting representations and to advise the court promptly when a conflict of interest arises during the course of trial. Absent special circumstances, therefore, trial courts may assume either that multiple representation entails no conflict or that the lawyer and his clients knowingly accept such risk of conflict as may exist.

Consequently, although the Sixth Amendment imposes no duty to inquire on state trial courts, Federal Rule 44 arguably imposes a more demanding scheme for federal criminal trials.

NOTES & QUESTIONS ON CONFLICTS OF INTEREST

1. *Conflicts of interest and a per se prejudice rule.* The Supreme Court declared in *Holloway* that defendants need *not* demonstrate a "reasonable possibility" of prejudice in cases of conflicts of interests—the conflict itself allows the court to avoid the prejudice inquiry. In *Strickland*, the Supreme Court concluded that prejudice is legally presumed if counsel was actively representing conflicting interests and an actual conflict of interest adversely affected the lawyer's performance. While this requirement is not the same as demonstrating full-blown prejudice, it also is not the "per se rule of prejudice" that exists in situations where there was a complete denial of the Sixth Amendment right to counsel. What is the advantage of this middle-ground position?

2. *Actual versus potential conflict.* Before finding a conflict of interest that constitutes a Sixth Amendment violation, courts look for proof of an actual conflict rather than a potential or hypothetical conflict. The Supreme Court has defined an actual conflict as "an active representation of competing interests." *Burger v. Kemp*, 483 U.S. 776, 783 (1987). In other words, the mere fact that an attorney represents two individuals who may have competing interests in the *future* is insufficient to demonstrate a conflict of interest that will violate the Sixth Amendment; a *present* conflict is required. What was the active and present conflict of interest in *Holloway*?

3. *The need to object.* In *Cuyler v. Sullivan*, 446 U.S. 335 (1980), the Supreme Court considered a case that was remarkably similar to *Holloway*. The defendant demonstrated a conflict of interest, but the defendant had failed to object to that conflict of interest at trial, unlike in *Holloway*, where the defendant

had specifically objected to the assignment of counsel. Indeed, in Holloway, *both* co-defendants objected and filed motions seeking new counsel—and appointed counsel stipulated to the court that he was "confronted with the risk of representing conflicting interests" that threatened his ability to represent both defendants effectively. The Supreme Court in *Cuyler* concluded that the absence of a timely objection to the joint representation was significant and that Cuyler must then demonstrate that the conflict actually affected the adequacy of the representation that he received from his counsel. Is the Court's diverse treatment of these cases warranted? Why is timely objection at trial so important?

4. *The trial judge's duty to inquire.* In *Mickens v. Taylor*, 535 U.S. 162 (2002), the Supreme Court considered a case where the trial court failed to inquire into a potential conflict of interest that the court was either aware of or should have been aware of. The Supreme Court concluded that in that situation, the defendant must establish that the conflict of interest adversely affected counsel's performance. Is the holding in *Mickens* closer in spirit to *Cuyler* or to *Holloway*? The scheme outlined in *Holloway* clearly applies in situations where the defendant objects to the co-representation at trial and the trial court denies the request to appoint new counsel, but the Supreme Court has shown little interest in extending the *Holloway* scheme to other fact patterns involving conflicts of interest. Do you agree with this narrowing of *Holloway* or should the Court apply its requirements more broadly?

PROBLEM CASE

Evan Mounier was charged in federal court with conspiracy to possess, with the intent to distribute, five or more kilograms of cocaine. Mounier was represented in the federal case by attorney Matthew DePrim, who had earlier represented Mounier in a related criminal case in state court. In that earlier case, DePrim had also represented Mounier's co-defendant, who was named Miguel Antonio Montes. In the federal case, DePrim initially represented both of the defendants, although he eventually withdrew as Montes's counsel. Three months after that withdrawal, Mounier pleaded guilty.

On appeal, Mounier argued that he was deprived of effective assistance of counsel because DePrim had a conflict of interest. Mounier never objected to the conflict but he also never waived the conflict. Specifically, Mounier argued that *both* co-defendants were seeking to gain lower sentences from the prosecutor by agreeing to provide evidence against the other defendant. In the end, Mounier was unhappy because he received a longer sentence than his co-defendant Montes.

Is Mounier required to demonstrate that the conflict of interest had an adverse effect on his case? See *United States v. Mounier*, 307 F. App'x 379, 380 (11th Cir. 2009).

3. Strategic Decisions

From an ethics perspective, attorneys are not permitted to make strategic decisions on their own on behalf of the client. These strategic decisions include whether to plead guilty or not guilty, whether to testify, which forum to file a case in, etc. For these major, "strategic" decisions, the attorney is the *advisor* for the client who retains the position as the ultimate decider. After these macro-level decisions are made, however, come a whole set of more specific—but still important—decisions that must be made. One might call these "tactical" decisions to distinguish them from "strategic" decisions. Attorneys make tactical decisions on behalf of their clients all the time. In criminal trials, those tactical decisions might include whether to call a particular witness or not or to cross-examine a victim in an aggressive way. Each of these decisions implicate discretion about the best avenue to achieve a positive outcome for the client. In some situations, that positive outcome might be an acquittal, but in other situations, the most positive outcome that can be achieved is a conviction combined with an advantageous sentence.

In the case of a capital crime, the strategic decisions often loom large and cast a heavy shadow over the fate of the defendant. Attorneys of course are concerned about the guilt phase, but they also have one eye trained on the sentencing phase when the jury will decide whether the convicted defendant will receive death or a sentence of incarceration, often life in prison. While the particulars of the defense strategy are clearly tactical choices, the question of whether the defendant should concede guilt to the jury is a strategic one that is closely related to the decision to formally plead guilty or not guilty. Indeed, this strategic choice of informally "conceding guilt" is a difficult one to make. In an ideal situation, the attorney will vigorously contest guilt and then if they lose in the first phase, will argue against the death penalty during the sentencing phase. But as the cases below demonstrate, this aggressive strategy carries significant risk. If the defense attorney argues to the jury that the defendant is innocent, but the jury decides otherwise, the defense attorney's credibility (and by extension the defendant's credibility) with the jury will be harmed going into the sentencing phase. At that time, if the defense attorney argues for mercy, the jury might be inclined to dismiss the attorney's point of view as insincere. Consequently, if the defense attorney considers a conviction inevitable, the attorney may wish to concede guilt and instead reserve his credibility for a strong recommendation to the jury that the defendant does not deserve to die.

In *Florida v. Nixon*, 543 U.S. 175 (2004), the Supreme Court considered a defense counsel's decision to concede guilt after the defendant declined to participate in the construction of a trial strategy, leaving his defense counsel with no choice but to make strategic decisions on his behalf. But in the following case, *McCoy v. Louisiana*, the defendant actively objected to the strategy pursued by his defense counsel. In contrast to *Florida v. Nixon*, the defendant in *McCoy* was locked in an outright disagreement with his counsel over the strategy of conceding guilt. In the latter situation, should a court side with the learned judgment of the defense counsel or should the court side with the wishes of the defendant? On the one hand, the defense counsel has the professional experience to make the strategic calculation, but on the other hand it is the defendant's life that is at stake and perhaps the defendant's wishes deserve priority. As you read the following case, pay particular attention to the attitude of the defendant regarding this proposed strategy. Is this enough to distinguish the case from *Florida v. Nixon*?

McCoy v. Louisiana

Supreme Court of the United States
138 S. Ct. 1500 (2018)

Justice GINSBURG delivered the opinion of the Court.

In *Florida v. Nixon*, this Court considered whether the Constitution bars defense counsel from conceding a capital defendant's guilt at trial "when [the] defendant, informed by counsel, neither consents nor objects." In that case, defense counsel had several times explained to the defendant a proposed guilt-phase concession strategy, but the defendant was unresponsive. We held that when counsel confers with the defendant and the defendant remains silent, neither approving nor protesting counsel's proposed concession strategy, "[no] blanket rule demand[s] the defendant's explicit consent" to implementation of that strategy.

In the case now before us, in contrast to *Nixon*, the defendant vociferously insisted that he did not engage in the charged acts and adamantly objected to any admission of guilt. Yet the trial court permitted counsel, at the guilt phase of a capital trial, to tell the jury the defendant "committed three murders. . . . [H]e's guilty." We hold that a defendant has the right to insist that counsel refrain from admitting guilt, even when counsel's experienced-based view is that confessing guilt offers the defendant the best chance to avoid the death penalty. Guaranteeing a defendant the right "to have the *Assistance* of Counsel for *his* defence," the Sixth Amendment so demands. With individual liberty—and, in capital cases, life—at stake, it is the defendant's prerogative, not counsel's, to decide on the objective of his defense: to admit guilt in the hope of gaining mercy at the sentencing stage, or to maintain his innocence, leaving it to the State to prove his guilt beyond a reasonable doubt.

I

On May 5, 2008, Christine and Willie Young and Gregory Colston were shot and killed in the Youngs' home in Bossier City, Louisiana. The three victims were the mother, stepfather, and son of Robert McCoy's estranged wife, Yolanda. Several days later, police arrested McCoy in Idaho. Extradited to Louisiana, McCoy was appointed counsel from the public defender's office. A Bossier Parish grand jury indicted McCoy on three counts of first-degree murder, and the prosecutor gave notice of intent to seek the death penalty. McCoy pleaded not guilty. Throughout the proceedings, he insistently maintained he was out of State at the time of the killings and that corrupt police killed the victims when a drug deal went wrong. At defense counsel's request, a court-appointed sanity commission examined McCoy and found him competent to stand trial.

In December 2009 and January 2010, McCoy told the court his relationship with assigned counsel had broken down irretrievably. He sought and gained leave to represent himself until his parents engaged new counsel for him. In March 2010, Larry English, engaged by McCoy's parents, enrolled as McCoy's counsel. English eventually concluded that the evidence against McCoy was overwhelming and that, absent a concession at the guilt stage that McCoy was the killer, a death sentence would be impossible to avoid at the penalty phase. McCoy, English reported, was "furious" when told, two weeks before trial was scheduled to begin, that English would concede McCoy's commission of the triple murders. McCoy told English "not to make that concession," and English knew of McCoy's "complet[e] oppos[ition] to [English] telling the jury that [McCoy] was guilty of killing the three victims"; instead of any concession, McCoy pressed English to pursue acquittal.

At a July 26, 2011 hearing, McCoy sought to terminate English's representation and English asked to be relieved if McCoy secured other counsel. With trial set to start two days later, the court refused to relieve English and directed that he remain as counsel of record. "[Y]ou are the attorney," the court told English when he expressed disagreement with McCoy's wish to put on a defense case, and "you have to make the trial decision of what you're going to proceed with."

At the beginning of his opening statement at the guilt phase of the trial, English told the jury there was "no way reasonably possible" that they could hear the prosecution's evidence and reach "any other conclusion than Robert McCoy was the cause of these individuals' death." McCoy protested; out of earshot of the jury, McCoy told the court that English was "selling [him] out" by maintaining that McCoy "murdered [his] family." The trial court reiterated that English was "representing" McCoy and told McCoy that the court would not permit "any other outbursts." Continuing his opening statement, English told the jury the evidence is "unambiguous," "my client committed three murders." McCoy testified in his own defense, maintaining his innocence and pressing an alibi difficult to fathom. In his closing argument, English reiterated that McCoy was the killer. On that issue, English told the jury that he "took [the] burden off of [the prosecutor]." The jury then returned a unanimous verdict of guilty of first-degree murder on all three counts. At the penalty phase, English again conceded "Robert McCoy committed these crimes" but urged mercy in view of McCoy's "serious mental and emotional issues." The jury returned three death verdicts. . . .

II

The Sixth Amendment guarantees to each criminal defendant "the Assistance of Counsel for his defence." At common law, self-representation was the norm. As the laws of England and the American Colonies developed, providing for a right to counsel in criminal cases, self-representation remained common and the right to proceed without counsel was recognized. Even now, when most defendants choose to be represented by counsel, an accused may insist upon representing herself—however counterproductive that course may be. As this Court explained, "[t]he right to defend is personal," and a defendant's choice in exercising that right "must be honored out of 'that respect for the individual which is the lifeblood of the law.'"

The choice is not all or nothing: To gain assistance, a defendant need not surrender control entirely to counsel. For the Sixth Amendment, in "grant[ing] to the accused personally the right to make his defense," "speaks of the 'assistance' of counsel, and an assistant, however expert, is still an assistant." Trial management is the lawyer's province: Counsel provides his or her assistance by making decisions such as "what arguments to pursue, what evidentiary objections to raise, and what agreements to conclude regarding the admission of evidence." Some decisions, however, are reserved for the client—notably, whether to plead guilty, waive the right to a jury trial, testify in one's own behalf, and forgo an appeal.

Autonomy to decide that the objective of the defense is to assert innocence belongs in this latter category. Just as a defendant may steadfastly refuse to plead guilty in the face of overwhelming evidence against her, or reject the assistance of legal counsel despite the defendant's own inexperience and lack of professional qualifications, so may she insist on maintaining her innocence at the guilt phase of a capital trial. These are not strategic choices about how best to *achieve* a client's objectives; they are choices about what the client's objectives in fact *are*.

Counsel may reasonably assess a concession of guilt as best suited to avoiding the death penalty, as English did in this case. But the client may not share that objective. He may wish to avoid, above all else, the opprobrium that comes with admitting he killed family members. Or he may hold life in prison not worth living and prefer to risk death for any hope, however small, of exoneration. When a client expressly asserts that the objective of "*his* defence" is to maintain innocence of the charged criminal acts, his lawyer must abide by that objective and may not override it by conceding guilt.

Preserving for the defendant the ability to decide whether to maintain his innocence should not displace counsel's, or the court's, respective trial management roles. Counsel, in any case, must still develop a trial strategy and discuss it with her client, explaining why, in her view, conceding guilt would be the best option. In this case, the court had determined that McCoy was competent to stand trial, i.e., that McCoy had "sufficient present ability to consult with his lawyer with a reasonable degree of rational understanding." If, after consultations with English concerning the management of the defense, McCoy disagreed with English's proposal to concede McCoy committed three murders, it was not open to English to override McCoy's objection. English could not interfere with McCoy's telling the jury "I was not the murderer," although counsel could, if consistent with providing effective assistance, focus his own collaboration on urging that McCoy's mental state weighed against conviction.

Florida v. Nixon is not to the contrary. Nixon's attorney did not negate Nixon's autonomy by overriding Nixon's desired defense objective, for Nixon never asserted any such objective. Nixon "was generally unresponsive" during discussions of trial strategy, and "never verbally approved or protested" counsel's proposed approach. Nixon complained about the admission of his guilt only after trial. McCoy, in contrast, opposed English's assertion of his guilt at every opportunity, before and during trial, both in conference with his lawyer and in open court. If a client declines to participate in his defense, then an attorney may permissibly guide the defense pursuant to the strategy she believes to be in the defendant's best interest. Presented with express statements of the client's will to maintain innocence, however, counsel may not steer the ship the other way. . . .

III

Because a client's autonomy, not counsel's competence, is in issue, we do not apply our ineffective-assistance-of-counsel jurisprudence, *Strickland v. Washington,* or *United States v. Cronic,* to McCoy's claim. To gain redress for attorney error, a defendant ordinarily must show prejudice. Here, however, the violation of McCoy's protected autonomy right was complete when the court allowed counsel to usurp control of an issue within McCoy's sole prerogative.

Violation of a defendant's Sixth Amendment-secured autonomy ranks as error of the kind our decisions have called "structural"; when present, such an error is not subject to harmless-error review. Structural error "affect[s] the framework within which the trial proceeds," as distinguished from a lapse or flaw that is "simply an error in the trial process itself." An error may be ranked structural, we have explained, "if the right at issue is not designed to protect the defendant from erroneous conviction but instead protects some other interest," such as "the fundamental legal principle that a defendant must be allowed to make his own choices about the proper way to protect his own liberty." An error might also count as structural when its effects are too hard to measure, as is true of the right to counsel of choice, or where the error will inevitably signal fundamental unfairness, as we have said of a judge's failure to tell the jury that it may not convict unless it finds the defendant's guilt beyond a reasonable doubt.

Under at least the first two rationales, counsel's admission of a client's guilt over the client's express objection is error structural in kind. Such an admission blocks the defendant's right to make the fundamental choices about his own defense. And the effects of the admission would be immeasurable, because a jury would almost certainly be swayed by a lawyer's concession of his client's guilt. McCoy must therefore be accorded a new trial without any need first to show prejudice. . . .

NOTES & QUESTIONS ON STRATEGIC DECISIONS

1. *The autonomy rationale. McCoy* relied on an autonomy rationale for its holding that prohibited defense attorneys from conceding guilt over the objections of the client. According to the Court, to do so would be to rob defendants of their autonomy, i.e., a crucial determination about their fate. Why does the concept of autonomy dictate this result? Is it because defendants themselves have a better sense of what works for them? Or is it because defendants are the final arbiters of their values, which structure what they hope to achieve through the trial? For some defendants, the ultimate goal of the trial is to avoid incarceration, or to avoid the death penalty, or some other result that they find intolerable. For other defendants, the ultimate—and perhaps only—strategic objective that they care about is to achieve exoneration. A defendant might legitimately insist that this is the only outcome they care about; they may wish to pursue this objective even if it might result in a harsher sentence such as death. *McCoy* stands for the proposition that the defendant's articulation of that objective must be respected by defense counsel. Or, put another way, perhaps the point is that the defense counsel must evaluate the "best" strategic outcome relative to the defendant's stated objective—not the objective that the defense counsel would rather pursue.

2. *Freedom of speech.* Another constitutional ground for the result in *McCoy* might be freedom of expression. If counsel concedes guilt over the objection of the client, has the client been subject to a form of compelled speech?

Think of it this way: Since the lawyer is acting as an agent of the defendant, allowing counsel to concede guilt over the objection of the defendant is like putting words into the mouth of the defendant without the defendant's permission. In other contexts, this form of "compelled" speech would violate the First Amendment. Or are defense attorneys merely speaking for themselves? Is the defense attorney a government actor, a requirement for the First Amendment to apply?

3. *Bifurcation.* The strategic dilemma analyzed in *Florida v. Nixon* and *McCoy* is exacerbated by the fact that death penalty cases do not use bifurcated juries, though they employ bifurcated proceedings. Bifurcated proceedings involve one proceeding for the guilt phase and another proceeding for sentencing, but with the same jury for both. However, one could imagine a different regime where one jury handles the guilt phase of the trial. Then, if the defendant is found guilty, a *new* jury with different members is impaneled to hear the penalty phase of the trial to decide if the defendant should receive capital punishment or not. This would eliminate the problem that defense attorneys must decide whether to contest guilt or whether to preserve their credibility with the jury for sentencing. The attorney could, in theory, do both—contest guilt and then argue for mercy before a second, independent jury that did not hear the attorney's futile protestations that the client was innocent. Would you support this approach? Would it have any negative consequences? Would it require holding a second "mini-trial" during the sentencing phase?

C. THE RIGHT TO SELF-REPRESENTATION

There is an old saying: Only a fool has himself for a client. Nonetheless, many defendants may reject the opportunity to hire counsel, either at their own or at public expense, and prefer instead to represent themselves at trial. In what circumstances should this request be honored by a trial court? The issue raises multiple concerns. If the defendant is not competent to act as an attorney in the courtroom, would the trial court violate the right to effective counsel if the trial court grants the defendant's wishes to proceed pro se? On the other hand, if the trial court rejects the request, the autonomy of the defendant is compromised because the defendant made an affirmative decision in favor of self-representation. Should the trial court act paternalistically and impose competent counsel on the defendant or should the trial court defer to the defendant's strategic decision? More specifically, what standard should guide a trial court's discretion in this situation?

Faretta v. California

Supreme Court of the United States
422 U.S. 806 (1975)

Mr. Justice STEWART delivered the opinion of the Court.

The Sixth and Fourteenth Amendments of our Constitution guarantee that a person brought to trial in any state or federal court must be afforded the right to the assistance of counsel before he can be validly convicted and punished by imprisonment. This clear constitutional rule has emerged from a series of cases decided here over the last 50 years. The question before us now is whether a defendant in a state criminal trial has a constitutional right to proceed without counsel when he voluntarily and intelligently elects to do so. Stated another way, the question is whether a State may constitutionally hale a person into its criminal courts and there force a lawyer upon him, even when he insists that he wants to conduct his own defense. It is not an easy question, but we have concluded that a State may not constitutionally do so.

I

Anthony Faretta was charged with grand theft in an information filed in the Superior Court of Los Angeles County, Cal. At the arraignment, the Superior Court Judge assigned to preside at the trial appointed the public defender to represent Faretta. Well before the date of trial, however, Faretta requested that he be permitted to represent himself. Questioning by the judge revealed that Faretta had once represented himself in a criminal prosecution, that he had a high school education, and that he did not want to be represented by the public defender because he believed that that office was "very loaded down with . . . a heavy case load." The judge responded that he believed Faretta was "making a mistake" and emphasized that in further proceedings Faretta would receive no special favors. Nevertheless, after establishing that Faretta wanted to represent himself and did not want a lawyer, the judge, in a "preliminary ruling," accepted Faretta's waiver of the assistance of counsel. The judge indicated, however, that he might reverse this ruling if it later appeared that Faretta was unable adequately to represent himself.

Several weeks thereafter, but still prior to trial, the judge sua sponte held a hearing to inquire into Faretta's ability to conduct his own defense, and questioned him specifically about both the hearsay rule and the state law governing the challenge of potential jurors.

After consideration of Faretta's answers, and observation of his demeanor, the judge ruled that Faretta had not made an intelligent and knowing waiver of his right to the assistance of counsel, and also ruled that

Faretta had no constitutional right to conduct his own defense. The judge, accordingly, reversed his earlier ruling permitting self-representation and again appointed the public defender to represent Faretta. Faretta's subsequent request for leave to act as co-counsel was rejected, as were his efforts to make certain motions on his own behalf. Throughout the subsequent trial, the judge required that Faretta's defense be conducted only through the appointed lawyer from the public defender's office. At the conclusion of the trial, the jury found Faretta guilty as charged, and the judge sentenced him to prison. . . .

II

In the federal courts, the right of self-representation has been protected by statute since the beginnings of our Nation. Section 35 of the Judiciary Act of 1789, enacted by the First Congress and signed by President Washington one day before the Sixth Amendment was proposed, provided that "in all the courts of the United States, the parties may plead and manage their own causes personally or by the assistance of such counsel. . . ." The right is currently codified in 28 U.S.C. s 1654.

With few exceptions, each of the several States also accords a defendant the right to represent himself in any criminal case. The constitutions of 36 States explicitly confer that right. Moreover, many state courts have expressed the view that the right is also supported by the Constitution of the United States. . . .

This Court's past recognition of the right of self-representation, the federal-court authority holding the right to be of constitutional dimension, and the state constitutions pointing to the right's fundamental nature form a consensus not easily ignored. "(T)he mere fact that a path is a beaten one," Mr. Justice Jackson once observed, "is a persuasive reason for following it." We confront here a nearly universal conviction, on the part of our people as well as our courts, that forcing a lawyer upon an unwilling defendant is contrary to his basic right to defend himself if he truly wants to do so.

III

This consensus is soundly premised. The right of self-representation finds support in the structure of the Sixth Amendment, as well as in the English and colonial jurisprudence from which the Amendment emerged. . . .

The Sixth Amendment does not provide merely that a defense shall be made for the accused; it grants to the accused personally the right to make his defense. It is the accused, not counsel, who must be "informed of the nature and cause of the accusation," who must be "confronted with the witnesses against him," and who must be accorded "compulsory process for obtaining witnesses in his favor." Although not stated in the Amendment in so many words, the right to self-representation—to make one's own defense personally—is thus necessarily implied by the structure of the Amendment. The right to defend is given directly to the accused; for it is he who suffers the consequences if the defense fails.

The counsel provision supplements this design. It speaks of the "assistance" of counsel, and an assistant, however expert, is still an assistant. The language and spirit of the Sixth Amendment contemplate that counsel, like the other defense tools guaranteed by the Amendment, shall be an aid to a willing defendant—not an organ of the State interposed between an unwilling defendant and his right to defend himself personally. To thrust counsel upon the accused, against his considered wish, thus violates the logic of the Amendment. In such a case, counsel is not an assistant, but a master; and the right to make a defense is stripped of the personal character upon which the Amendment insists. It is true that when a defendant chooses to have a lawyer manage and present his case, law and tradition may allocate to the counsel the power to make binding decisions of trial strategy in many areas. This allocation can only be justified, however, by the defendant's consent, at the outset, to accept counsel as his representative. An unwanted counsel "represents" the defendant only through a tenuous and unacceptable legal fiction. Unless the accused has acquiesced in such representation, the defense presented is not the defense guaranteed him by the Constitution, for, in a very real sense, it is not his defense.

The Sixth Amendment, when naturally read, thus implies a right of self-representation. This reading is reinforced by the Amendment's roots in English legal history.

In the long history of British criminal jurisprudence, there was only one tribunal that ever adopted a practice of forcing counsel upon an unwilling defendant in a criminal proceeding. The tribunal was the Star Chamber. That curious institution, which flourished in the late 16th and early 17th centuries, was of mixed executive and judicial character, and characteristically departed from common-law traditions. For those reasons, and because it specialized in trying "political" defenses, the Star Chamber has for centuries symbolized disregard of basic individual rights. The Star Chamber not merely allowed but required defendants to have counsel. The defendant's answer to an indictment was not accepted unless it was signed by counsel. When counsel refused to sign the answer, for whatever reason, the defendant was considered to have confessed. . . . The Star Chamber was swept away in 1641 by the revolutionary fervor of the Long Parliament. The notion of obligatory counsel disappeared with it. . . .

In the American Colonies the insistence upon a right of self-representation was, if anything, more fervent than in England. The colonists brought with them an appreciation of the virtues of self-reliance and a traditional distrust of lawyers. . . . This is not to say that the Colonies were slow to recognize the value of counsel in criminal cases. Colonial judges soon departed from ancient English practice and allowed accused felons the aid of counsel for their defense. At the same time, however, the basic right of self-representation was never questioned. We have found no instance where a colonial court required a defendant in a criminal case to accept as his representative an unwanted lawyer. . . . In sum, there is no evidence that the colonists and the Framers ever doubted the right of self-representation. . . .

It is undeniable that in most criminal prosecutions defendants could better defend with counsel's guidance than by their own unskilled efforts. But where the defendant will not voluntarily accept representation by counsel, the potential advantage of a lawyer's training and experience can be realized, if at all, only imperfectly. To force a lawyer on a defendant can only lead him to believe that the law contrives against him. . . . It is the defendant, therefore, who must be free personally to decide whether in his particular case counsel is to his advantage. And although he may conduct his own defense ultimately to his own detriment, his choice must be honored out of "that respect for the individual which is the lifeblood of the law."

V

When an accused manages his own defense, he relinquishes, as a purely factual matter, many of the traditional benefits associated with the right to counsel. For this reason, in order to represent himself, the accused must "knowingly and intelligently" forgo those relinquished benefits. Although a defendant need not himself have the skill and experience of a lawyer in order competently and intelligently to choose self-representation, he should be made aware of the dangers and disadvantages of self-representation, so that the record will establish that "he knows what he is doing and his choice is made with eyes open."

Here, weeks before trial, Faretta clearly and unequivocally declared to the trial judge that he wanted to represent himself and did not want counsel. The record affirmatively shows that Faretta was literate, competent, and understanding, and that he was voluntarily exercising his informed free will. The trial judge had warned Faretta that he thought it was a mistake not to accept the assistance of counsel, and that Faretta would be required to follow all the "ground rules" of trial procedure. We need make no assessment of how well or poorly Faretta had mastered the intricacies of the hearsay rule and the California code provisions that govern challenges of potential jurors on voir dire. For his technical legal knowledge, as such, was not relevant to an assessment of his knowing exercise of the right to defend himself.

In forcing Faretta, under these circumstances, to accept against his will a state-appointed public defender, the California courts deprived him of his constitutional right to conduct his own defense. . . .

PROBLEM CASE

In 2009, Major Nidal Hasan opened fire at Fort Hood, ultimately killing 13 people and injuring many others. Hasan was motivated by a jihadist outlook after being radicalized during online conversations he had over the Internet. Hassan was charged with murder and put on trial before a military court martial under the Uniform Code of Military Justice (UCMJ), which governs the criminal trials of members of the armed forces. Hasan sought to defend himself, and the judge, Colonel Tara Osborn, agreed, but also appointed stand-by counsel for the trial. On the first day of the trial, the stand-by counsel grew concerned about Hasan's unorthodox "strategy." Hasan conceded that he was the shooter and also admitted that he was waging jihad against the United States. The defense team was concerned that Hasan was deliberately trying to induce both a guilty verdict and a death sentence. The stand-by counsel asked the judge for permission to take over the defense or to be removed from the case. That request was denied. The judge concluded that Hasan had a constitutional right to self-representation. During the prosecution case, Hasan elected not to cross-examine most of the prosecution witnesses. After the prosecution rested, Hasan declined to call any witnesses as part of his defense case and did not offer a closing argument. (Hasan had originally planned a "defense of others" strategy because he was allegedly acting to save the lives of members of the Taliban in Afghanistan, but the judge ruled that the proposed defense was inapplicable to the case.) Hasan was convicted and ultimately sentenced to death. Should the judge have rejected Hasan's original request to represent himself? Should the judge have granted the stand-by counsel's request to take over the defense case?

NOTES & QUESTIONS ON SELF-REPRESENTATION

1. *Determining intelligence.* The judge in *Faretta* questioned the defendant in the following way to determine whether to grant his motion to represent himself:

> **Court:** In the *Faretta* matter, I brought you back down here to do some reconsideration as to whether or not you should continue to represent yourself. How have you been getting along on your research?
> **Defendant:** Not bad, your Honor. Last night I put in the mail a 995 motion and it should be with the Clerk within the next day or two.
> **Court:** Have you been preparing yourself for the intricacies of the trial of the matter?
> **Defendant:** Well, your Honor, I was hoping that the case could possibly be disposed of on the 995. Mrs. Ayers informed me yesterday that it was the Court's policy to hear the pretrial motions at the time of trial. If possible, your

Honor, I would like a date set as soon as the Court deems adequate after they receive the motion, sometime before trial.
Court: Let's see how you have been doing on your research. How many exceptions are there to the hearsay rule?
Defendant: Well, the hearsay rule would, I guess, be called the best evidence rule, your Honor. And there are several exceptions in case law, but in actual statutory law, I don't feel there is none.
Court: What are the challenges to the jury for cause?
Defendant: Well, there is 12 peremptory challenges.
Court: And how many for cause?
Defendant: Well, as many as the Court deems valid.
Court: And what are they? What are the grounds for challenging a juror for cause?
Defendant: Well, numerous grounds to challenge a witness—I mean, a juror, your Honor, one being the juror is perhaps suffered, was a victim of the same type of offense, might be prejudiced toward the defendant. Any substantial ground that might make the juror prejudice(d) toward the defendant.
Court: Anything else?
Defendant: Well, a relative perhaps of the victim.
Court: Have you taken a look at that code section to see what it is?
Defendant: Challenge a juror?
Court: Yes.
Defendant: Yes, your Honor. I have done—
Court: What is the code section?
Defendant: On voir diring a jury, your Honor?
Court: Yes.
Defendant: I am not aware of the section right offhand.
Court: What code is it in?
Defendant: Well, the research I have done on challenging would be in Witkins Jurisprudence.
Court: Have you looked at any of the codes to see where these various things are taken up?
Defendant: No, your Honor, I haven't.
Court: Have you looked in any of the California Codes with reference to trial procedure?
Defendant: Yes, your Honor.
Court: What codes?
Defendant: I have done extensive research in the Penal Code, your Honor, and the Civil Code.
Court: If you have done extensive research into it, then tell me about it.
Defendant: On empaneling a jury, your Honor?
Court: Yes.
Defendant: Well, the District Attorney and the defendant, defense counsel, has both the right to 12 peremptory challenges of a jury. These 12 challenges

> are undisputable. Any reason that the defense or prosecution should feel that a juror would be inadequate to try the case or to rule on a case, they may then discharge that juror. But if there is a valid challenge due to grounds of prejudice or some other grounds, that these aren't considered in the 12 peremptory challenges. There are numerous and the defendant, the defense and the prosecution both have the right to make any inquiry to the jury as to their feelings toward the case.

422 U.S. at 811. What was the goal of the judge's colloquy with the defendant? The judge seemed particularly concerned with quizzing Faretta to determine if he had the requisite knowledge of specific legal provisions to conduct his defense competently. But is there any evidence in this dialogue that the judge assessed whether Faretta understood the *risk* of representing himself in terms of what was at stake in making this decision?

2. *Stand-by counsel.* In situations where a trial court grants a defendant's motion for self-representation, the trial judge might also assign "stand-by counsel" to work alongside the defendant. The purpose of assigning the stand-by counsel is at least two-fold. First, the stand-by counsel can advise the defendant regarding strategy and tactics and provide legal information that might be of assistance to the defendant in conducting the defense. Second, the stand-by counsel could be assigned to step in and conduct the defense directly if the defendant decides that he no longer wishes to represent himself or if it becomes clear during the case that the defendant is no longer able to do so. In the absence of stand-by counsel, the trial court would be in a difficult position without that option. If the defendant is no longer able to act as his own attorney, and with no stand-by counsel to step in, the trial court would need to declare a mistrial and conduct a new trial.

3. *Self-representation and ineffective assistance of counsel.* A defendant who represents himself might be giving himself poor representation. In fact, if a lawyer gave the defendant that quality of legal services, the defendant might successfully argue that he was provided ineffective assistance of counsel in violation of the Sixth Amendment. Based on this logic, can a defendant argue that their *own* self-representation was ineffective, thus triggering a Sixth Amendment violation? The answer is that a defendant who seeks to represent himself or herself necessarily waives any claim to ineffective assistance of counsel. In a footnote in the *Faretta* opinion, the Court stated:

> The right of self-representation is not a license to abuse the dignity of the courtroom. Neither is it a license not to comply with relevant rules of procedural and substantive law. Thus, whatever else may or may not be open to him on appeal, a defendant who elects to represent himself cannot

> thereafter complain that the quality of his own defense amounted to a denial of "effective assistance of counsel."

Id. at 834 n.46. What is the rationale for this rule?

PROBLEM CASE

The 1987 Unabomber sketch, drawn by forensic artist Jeanne Boylan.

Between 1978 and 1995, the American public was terrorized by periodic mail bombs sent from an anonymous individual. For years, the FBI and other federal investigators were unable to locate a suspect, though authorities released a sketch of an individual wearing a hooded sweatshirt based on information provided by an eyewitness. In 1995, still at large, the Unabomber sent a letter to major newspapers indicating his willingness to stop his terror campaign if the newspapers published a lengthy, meandering manifesto that he had written on the sources of modern decay. After discussing the request with the FBI, the Washington Post and the New York Times collaborated on a joint publication of the manifesto. Federal authorities encouraged the publication because they hoped that someone would read the manifesto and recognize the author based on its ideas or word patterns. The gambit worked, and David Kaczynski of Schenectady, New York, contacted authorities to say that he recognized the manifesto as the work of his estranged brother, Theodore (Ted). After a lengthy investigation, Ted Kaczynski was located and arrested in a remote cabin without electricity in a wooded area of Colorado. The Unabomber's reign of terror, which including 16 bombs, three murders, and several victims maimed—was finally over.

Kaczynski's trial was immediately contentious. Pursuant to *Faretta,* Kaczynski sought permission to represent himself—a request that was denied by the trial judge. Counsel was appointed for Kaczynski and counsel insisted on presenting evidence that Kaczynski suffered from schizophrenia, despite Kaczynski's wishes to the contrary, as part of the defense case. Kaczynski was fine with his lawyers presenting evidence that he suffered from some mental conditions and so consented to them filing motions to introduce evidence of his mental status, but he was adamant that his lawyers not argue that he was not guilty by reason of suffering from schizophrenia. In response to this difficulty, Kaczynski pleaded guilty in exchange for the prosecution's promise not to seek the death penalty at sentencing. On appeal, though, Kaczynski argued that the trial judge's denial of his *Faretta* request was an error. The trial

Ted Kaczynski's cabin in the woods of Lincoln, Montana, in April 1996. (Elaine Thompson/AP Images)

judge denied the request for self-representation because Kaczynski had disclaimed the "only defense that is likely to prevent his conviction and execution," because he had consented to his attorney's introduction of evidence of his mental state, and because the request for self-representation was tactically motivated to delay the trial process. Was the trial judge correct to deny the request for self-representation or did this violate the Sixth Amendment? See *United States v. Kaczynski,* 239 F.3d 1108, 1113 (9th Cir. 2001).

According to the Supreme Court in *Faretta*, the decision to proceed without counsel should not be second-guessed by the trial judge, as long as the defendant's decision is made "voluntarily and intelligently." Even if the trial judge firmly believes that the defendant is doing a disservice to the case by proceeding pro se, that decision must be respected as a matter of constitutional law. If there are two evils to be weighed—incompetent self-representation or forced counsel against the wishes of the defendant—the court should favor incompetent self-representation. In the following case, the Supreme Court considers a slightly different, though related, fact pattern: What if the state concludes that the defendant is mentally competent to stand trial but not competent enough to represent himself at trial?

Recall that the standard to determine competence to stand trial is whether the defendant understands the nature of the proceedings and is capable of *assisting* in the defense. In contrast, proceeding pro se requires that the defendant run the defense rather than merely assisting in it. Should the Supreme Court extend the rationale from *Faretta* and defer to the defendant's wishes, or should the Supreme Court allow some room for a state court to conclude that a defendant is not competent enough to represent himself?

Indiana v. Edwards

Supreme Court of the United States
554 U.S. 164 (2008)

Justice Breyer delivered the opinion of the Court.

This case focuses upon a criminal defendant whom a state court found mentally competent to stand trial if represented by counsel but not mentally competent to conduct that trial himself. We must decide whether in these circumstances the Constitution prohibits a State from insisting that the defendant proceed to trial with counsel, the State thereby denying the defendant the right to represent himself. We conclude that the Constitution does not forbid a State so to insist.

I

In July 1999, Ahmad Edwards, the respondent, tried to steal a pair of shoes from an Indiana department store. After he was discovered, he drew a gun, fired at a store security officer, and wounded a bystander. He was caught and then charged with attempted murder, battery with a deadly weapon, criminal recklessness, and theft. His mental condition subsequently became the subject of three competency proceedings and two self-representation requests, mostly before the same trial judge:

1. First Competency Hearing: August 2000. Five months after Edwards' arrest, his court-appointed counsel asked for a psychiatric evaluation. After hearing psychiatrist and neuropsychologist witnesses, the court found Edwards incompetent to stand trial and committed him to Logansport State Hospital for evaluation and treatment.

2. Second Competency Hearing: March 2002. Seven months after his commitment, doctors found that Edwards' condition had improved to the point where he could stand trial. Several months later, however, but still before trial, Edwards' counsel asked for another psychiatric evaluation. In March 2002, the judge held a competency hearing, considered additional psychiatric evidence, and (in April) found that Edwards, while "suffer[ing] from mental illness," was "competent to assist his attorneys in his defense and stand trial for the charged crimes."

3. Third Competency Hearing: April 2003. Seven months later but still before trial, Edwards' counsel sought yet another psychiatric evaluation of his client. And, in April 2003, the court held yet another competency hearing. Edwards' counsel presented further psychiatric and neuropsychological evidence showing that Edwards was suffering from serious thinking difficulties and delusions. A testifying psychiatrist reported that Edwards could understand the charges against him, but he was "unable to cooperate with his attorney in his defense because of his schizophrenic illness"; "[h]is delusions and his marked difficulties in thinking make it impossible for him to cooperate with his attorney." In November 2003, the court concluded that Edwards was not then competent to stand trial and ordered his recommitment to the state hospital.

4. First Self-Representation Request and First Trial: June 2005. About eight months after his commitment, the hospital reported that Edwards' condition had again improved to the point that he had again become competent to stand trial. And almost one year after that, Edwards' trial began. Just before trial, Edwards asked to represent himself. He also asked for a continuance, which, he said, he needed in order to proceed pro se. The court refused the continuance. Edwards then proceeded to trial represented by counsel. The jury convicted him of criminal recklessness and theft but failed to reach a verdict on the charges of attempted murder and battery.

5. Second Self-Representation Request and Second Trial: December 2005. The State decided to retry Edwards on the attempted murder and battery charges. Just before the retrial, Edwards again asked the court to permit him to represent himself. Referring to the lengthy record of psychiatric reports, the trial court noted that Edwards still suffered from schizophrenia and concluded that "[w]ith these findings, he's competent to stand trial but I'm not going to find he's competent to defend himself." The court denied Edwards' self-representation request. Edwards was represented by appointed counsel at his retrial. The jury convicted Edwards on both of the remaining counts. . . .

II

Our examination of this Court's precedents convinces us that those precedents frame the question presented, but they do not answer it. The two cases that set forth the Constitution's "mental competence" standard, *Dusky v. United States*, 362 U.S. 402, and *Drope v. Missouri*, 420 U.S. 162 (1975), specify that the Constitution does not permit trial of an individual who lacks "mental competency." *Dusky* defines the competency standard as including both (1) "whether" the defendant has "a rational as well as factual understanding of the proceedings against him" and (2) whether the defendant "has sufficient present ability to consult with his lawyer with a reasonable degree of rational understanding." *Drope* repeats that standard, stating that it "has long been accepted that a person whose mental condition is such that he lacks the capacity to understand the nature and object of the proceedings against him, to consult with counsel, and to assist in preparing his defense may not be subjected to a trial." Neither case considered the mental competency issue presented here, namely, the relation of the mental competence standard to the right of self-representation.

The Court's foundational "self-representation" case, *Faretta*, held that the Sixth and Fourteenth Amendments include a "constitutional right to proceed without counsel when" a criminal defendant "voluntarily and intelligently elects to do so." . . . *Faretta* does not answer the question before us both because it did not consider the problem of mental competency and because *Faretta* itself and later cases have made clear that the right of self-representation is not absolute. The question here concerns a mental-illness-related limitation on the scope of the self-representation right.

The sole case in which this Court considered mental competence and self-representation together, *Godinez*, presents a question closer to that at issue here. The case focused upon a borderline-competent criminal defendant who had asked a state trial court to permit him to represent himself and to change his pleas from not guilty to guilty. The state trial court had found that the defendant met *Dusky*'s mental competence standard, that he "knowingly and intelligently" waived his right to assistance of counsel, and that he "freely and voluntarily" chose to plead guilty. And the state trial court had consequently granted the defendant's self-representation and change-of-plea requests. A federal appeals court, however, had vacated the defendant's guilty pleas on the ground that the Constitution required the trial court to ask a further question, namely, whether the defendant was competent to waive his constitutional right to counsel. Competence to make that latter decision, the appeals court said, required the defendant to satisfy a higher mental competency standard than the standard set forth in *Dusky*. *Dusky*'s more general standard sought only to determine whether a defendant represented by counsel was competent to stand trial, not whether he was competent to waive his right to counsel.

This Court, reversing the Court of Appeals, "reject[ed] the notion that competence to plead guilty or to waive the right to counsel must be measured by a standard that is higher than (or even different from) the *Dusky* standard." The decision to plead guilty, we said, "is no more complicated than the sum total of decisions that a [represented] defendant may be called upon to make during the course of a trial." Hence "there is no reason to believe that the decision to waive counsel requires an appreciably higher level of mental functioning than the decision to waive other constitutional rights." And even assuming that self-representation might pose special trial-related difficulties, "the competence that is required of a defendant seeking to waive his right to counsel is the competence to waive the right, not the competence to represent himself." For this reason, we concluded, "the defendant's 'technical legal knowledge' is 'not relevant' to the determination."

We concede that *Godinez* bears certain similarities with the present case. Both involve mental competence and self-representation. Both involve a defendant who wants to represent himself. Both involve a mental condition that falls in a gray area between *Dusky*'s minimal constitutional requirement that measures a defendant's ability to stand trial and a somewhat higher standard that measures mental fitness for another legal purpose.

We nonetheless conclude that *Godinez* does not answer the question before us now. In part that is because the Court of Appeals' higher standard at issue in *Godinez* differs in a critical way from the higher standard at issue here. In *Godinez*, the higher standard sought to measure the defendant's ability to proceed on his own to enter a guilty plea; here the higher standard seeks to measure the defendant's ability to conduct trial proceedings. To put the matter more specifically, the *Godinez* defendant sought only to change his pleas to guilty, he did not seek to conduct trial proceedings, and his ability to conduct a defense at trial was expressly not at issue. Thus we emphasized in *Godinez* that we needed to consider only the defendant's "competence to waive the right." And we further emphasized that we need not consider the defendant's "technical legal knowledge" about how to proceed at trial. . . .

III

We now turn to the question presented. We assume that a criminal defendant has sufficient mental competence to stand trial and that the defendant insists on representing himself during that trial. We ask whether the Constitution permits a State to limit that defendant's self-representation right by insisting upon representation by counsel at trial—on the ground that the defendant lacks the mental capacity to conduct his trial defense unless represented.

Several considerations taken together lead us to conclude that the answer to this question is yes. First, the Court's precedent, while not answering the question, points slightly in the direction of our affirmative answer. *Godinez*, as we have just said, simply leaves the question open. But the Court's "mental competency" cases set forth a standard that focuses directly upon a defendant's "present ability to consult with his lawyer"; a "capacity . . . to consult with counsel," and an ability "to assist [counsel] in preparing his defense." These standards assume representation by counsel and emphasize the importance of counsel. They thus suggest (though do not hold) that an instance in which a defendant who would choose to forgo counsel at trial presents a very different set of circumstances, which in our view, calls for a different standard.

At the same time *Faretta*, the foundational self-representation case, rested its conclusion in part upon pre-existing state law set forth in cases all of which are consistent with, and at least two of which expressly adopt, a competency limitation on the self-representation right.

Second, the nature of the problem before us cautions against the use of a single mental competency standard for deciding both (1) whether a defendant who is represented by counsel can proceed to trial and (2) whether a defendant who goes to trial must be permitted to represent himself. Mental illness itself is not a unitary concept. It varies in degree. It can vary over time. It interferes with an individual's functioning at different times in different ways. The history of this case illustrates the complexity of the problem. In certain instances an individual may well be able to satisfy *Dusky*'s mental competence standard, for he will be able to work with counsel at trial, yet at the same time he may be unable to carry out the basic tasks needed to present his own defense without the help of counsel. . . .

Third, in our view, a right of self-representation at trial will not "affirm the dignity" of a defendant who lacks the mental capacity to conduct his defense without the assistance of counsel. To the contrary, given that defendant's uncertain mental state, the spectacle that could well result from his self-representation at trial is at least as likely to prove humiliating as ennobling. Moreover, insofar as a defendant's lack of capacity threatens an improper conviction or sentence, self-representation in that exceptional context undercuts the most basic of the Constitution's criminal law objectives, providing a fair trial. . . .

We consequently conclude that the Constitution permits judges to take realistic account of the particular defendant's mental capacities by asking whether a defendant who seeks to conduct his own defense at trial is mentally competent to do so. That is to say, the Constitution permits States to insist upon representation by counsel for those competent enough to stand trial under *Dusky* but who still suffer from severe mental illness to the point where they are not competent to conduct trial proceedings by themselves. . . .

Justice Scalia, with whom Justice Thomas joins, dissenting.

The Constitution guarantees a defendant who knowingly and voluntarily waives the right to counsel the right to proceed pro se at his trial. A mentally ill defendant who knowingly and voluntarily elects to proceed pro se instead of through counsel receives a fair trial that comports with the Fourteenth Amendment. The Court today concludes that a State may nonetheless strip a mentally ill defendant of the right to represent himself when that would be fairer. In my view the Constitution does not permit a State to substitute its own perception of fairness for the defendant's right to make his own case before the jury—a specific right long understood as essential to a fair trial. . . .

Until today, the right of self-representation has been accorded the same respect as other constitutional guarantees. The only circumstance in which we have permitted the State to deprive a defendant of this trial right is the one under which we have allowed the State to deny other such rights: when it is necessary to enable the trial to proceed in an orderly fashion. That overriding necessity, we have said, justifies forfeiture of even the Sixth Amendment right to be present at trial—if, after being threatened with removal, a defendant "insists on conducting himself in a manner so disorderly, disruptive, and disrespectful of the court that his trial cannot be carried on with him in the courtroom." A pro se defendant may not "abuse the dignity of the courtroom," nor may he fail to "comply with relevant rules of procedural and substantive law," and a court may "terminate" the self-representation of a defendant who "deliberately engages in serious and obstructionist misconduct." This ground for terminating self-representation is unavailable here, however, because Edwards was not even allowed to begin to represent himself, and because he was respectful and compliant and did not provide a basis to conclude a trial could not have gone forward had he been allowed to press his own claims. . . .

PROBLEM CASE

Consider the case of Colin Ferguson, who was arrested and put on trial for a 1993 shooting that occurred on a Long Island Rail Road train in Nassau County, New York. Ferguson used a pistol to murder six passengers on the train and wound 19 others. The massacre only stopped because three passengers on the train heroically subdued and disarmed Ferguson. In 1995, Ferguson went on trial in Nassau County for the massacre. Well-known defense attorneys William Kunstler and Ron Kuby announced that they were retained to represent Ferguson and prepared a defense based on temporary insanity, including the notion that Ferguson suffered from "black rage." Unfortunately, Ferguson refused to cooperate with that defense strategy and claimed that he had not perpetrated the shootings; he also refused to admit that he was insane, either permanently or temporarily. Kunstler and Kuby argued to the court that Ferguson was not competent to stand trial because of his bizarre statements and actions. The trial judge, based on a psychiatric assessment, concluded that Ferguson was competent to stand trial because he understood the nature of the proceedings and was capable of assisting in his defense.

Kunstler and Kuby insisted on proceeding with an insanity defense, leading to a direct conflict with Ferguson, who refused to admit that he perpetrated the shootings. The trial judge allowed Ferguson to fire Kunstler and Kuby and represent himself at trial instead.

The trial, with Ferguson at the helm, descended into chaos, with Ferguson cross-examining witnesses with nonsensical questions. Ferguson also made bizarre claims that someone else stole his gun and committed the shooting and that he was the victim of a racist conspiracy.

Should the trial court in this situation have allowed Ferguson to proceed pro se? Following

Indiana v. Edwards, should the trial court be permitted to find Ferguson competent to stand trial yet incompetent to represent himself? Should the trial judge in this circumstance force the defendant to be represented by Kunstler and Kuby against his wishes? See *People v. Ferguson*, 248 A.D.2d 725, 725, 670 N.Y.S.2d 327, 328 (1998).

D. RIGHT TO RETAIN EXPERTS

In the previous materials, we assumed that the hiring of effective counsel was the primary method of ensuring a competent defense. In some cases, though, the attorney is not the only professional required to bring an effective defense case to the courtroom. Where the defendant suffers from serious psychological issues, the defense case might require the hiring of a mental expert, such as a psychiatrist, to testify about the defendant's state of mind. To take just the most obvious example, if the defendant pleads not guilty by reason of insanity, the defendant may need to hire a psychiatrist to testify that the defendant suffered from a mental disease or defect that prevented the defendant from understanding the nature of their actions or appreciating the wrongfulness of the actions. Or, if the defendant wishes to argue that their responsibility is mitigated because the defendant acted under an extreme emotional disturbance, the retaining of a psychological expert will be crucial to the success of that defense strategy.

In the following case, the Supreme Court asks whether defendants have a constitutional right to retain experts at public expense. If the answer to that question is yes, the next question is under what circumstances this right might apply. What showing must a defendant make before an expert will be provided at public expense?

Ake v. Oklahoma

Supreme Court of the United States
470 U.S. 68 (1985)

Justice MARSHALL delivered the opinion of the Court.

The issue in this case is whether the Constitution requires that an indigent defendant have access to the psychiatric examination and assistance necessary to prepare an effective defense based on his mental condition, when his sanity at the time of the offense is seriously in question.

I

Late in 1979, Glen Burton Ake was arrested and charged with murdering a couple and wounding their two children. He was arraigned in the District Court for Canadian County. His behavior at arraignment, and in other prearraignment incidents at the jail, was so bizarre that the trial judge, sua sponte, ordered him to be examined by a psychiatrist "for the purpose of advising with the Court as to his impressions of whether the Defendant may need an extended period of mental observation." The examining psychiatrist reported: "At times [Ake] appears to be frankly delusional. . . . He claims to be the 'sword of vengeance' of the Lord and that he will sit at the left hand of God in heaven." He diagnosed Ake as a probable paranoid schizophrenic and recommended a prolonged psychiatric evaluation to determine whether Ake was competent to stand trial.

In March, Ake was committed to a state hospital to be examined with respect to his "present sanity," i.e., his competency to stand trial. On April 10, less than six months after the incidents for which Ake was indicted, the chief forensic psychiatrist at the state hospital informed the court that Ake was not competent to stand trial.. . . The court found Ake to be a "mentally ill person in need of care and treatment" and incompetent to stand trial, and ordered him committed to the state mental hospital.

Six weeks later, the chief forensic psychiatrist informed the court that Ake had become competent to stand trial. At the time, Ake was receiving 200 milligrams of Thorazine, an antipsychotic drug, three times daily, and the psychiatrist indicated that, if Ake continued to receive that dosage, his condition would remain stable. The State then resumed proceedings against Ake.

At a pretrial conference in June, Ake's attorney informed the court that his client would raise an insanity defense. To enable him to prepare and present such a defense adequately, the attorney stated, a psychiatrist would have to examine Ake with respect to his mental condition at the time of the offense. During Ake's 3-month stay at the state hospital, no inquiry had been made into his sanity at the time of the offense, and, as an indigent, Ake could not afford to pay for a psychiatrist. Counsel asked the court either to arrange to have a psychiatrist perform the examination, or to provide funds to allow the defense to arrange one. The trial judge rejected counsel's argument that the Federal Constitution requires that an indigent defendant receive the assistance of a psychiatrist when that assistance is necessary to the defense, and he denied the motion for a psychiatric evaluation at state expense. . . .

Ake was tried for two counts of murder in the first degree, a crime punishable by death in Oklahoma, and for two counts of shooting with intent to kill. At the guilt phase of trial, his sole defense was insanity. Although defense counsel called to the stand and questioned each of the psychiatrists who had examined Ake at the state hospital, none testified about his mental state at the time of the offense because none had examined him on that point. The prosecution, in turn, asked each of these psychiatrists whether he had performed or seen the results of any examination diagnosing Ake's mental state at the time of the offense, and each doctor replied that he had not. As a result, there was no expert testimony for either side on Ake's sanity at the time of the offense. The jurors were then instructed that Ake could be found not guilty by reason of insanity if he did not have the ability to distinguish right from wrong at the time of the alleged offense. They were further told that Ake was to be presumed sane at the time of the crime unless he presented evidence sufficient to raise a reasonable doubt about his sanity at that time. If he raised such a doubt in their minds, the jurors were informed, the burden of proof shifted to the State to prove sanity beyond a reasonable doubt. The jury rejected Ake's insanity defense and returned a verdict of guilty on all counts. . . .

III

This Court has long recognized that when a State brings its judicial power to bear on an indigent defendant in a criminal proceeding, it must take steps to assure that the defendant has a fair opportunity to present his defense. This elementary principle, grounded in significant part on the Fourteenth Amendment's due process guarantee of fundamental fairness, derives from the belief that justice cannot be equal where, simply as a result of his poverty, a defendant is denied the opportunity to participate meaningfully in a judicial proceeding in which his liberty is at stake. In recognition of this right, this Court held almost 30 years ago that once a State offers to criminal defendants the opportunity to appeal their cases, it must provide a trial transcript to an indigent defendant if the transcript is necessary to a decision on the merits of the appeal. Since then, this Court has held that an indigent defendant may not be required to pay a fee before filing a notice of appeal of his conviction, that an indigent defendant is entitled to the assistance of counsel at trial, and on his first direct appeal as of right, and that such assistance must be effective. . . .

Meaningful access to justice has been the consistent theme of these cases. We recognized long ago that mere access to the courthouse doors does not by itself assure a proper functioning of the adversary process, and that a criminal trial is fundamentally unfair if the State proceeds against an indigent defendant without making certain that he has access to the raw materials integral to the building of an effective defense. Thus, while the Court has not held that a State must purchase for the indigent defendant all the assistance that his wealthier counterpart might buy, it has often reaffirmed that fundamental fairness entitles indigent defendants to "an adequate opportunity to present their claims fairly within the adversary system." To implement this principle, we have focused on identifying the "basic tools of an adequate defense or appeal," and we have required that such tools be provided to those defendants who cannot afford to pay for them.

To say that these basic tools must be provided is, of course, merely to begin our inquiry. In this case we must decide whether, and under what conditions, the participation of a psychiatrist is important enough to preparation of a defense to require the State to provide an indigent defendant with access to competent psychiatric assistance in preparing the defense. Three factors are relevant to this determination. The first is the private interest that will be affected by the action of the State. The second is the governmental interest that will be affected if the safeguard is to be provided. The third is the probable value of the additional or substitute procedural safeguards that are sought, and the risk of an erroneous deprivation of the affected interest if those safeguards are not provided. We turn, then, to apply this standard to the issue before us.

The private interest in the accuracy of a criminal proceeding that places an individual's life or liberty at risk is almost uniquely compelling. Indeed, the host of safeguards fashioned by this Court over the years to diminish the risk of erroneous conviction stands as a testament to that concern. The interest of the individual in the outcome of the State's effort to overcome the presumption of innocence is obvious and weighs heavily in our analysis.

We consider, next, the interest of the State. Oklahoma asserts that to provide Ake with psychiatric assistance on the record before us would result in a staggering burden to the State. We are unpersuaded by this assertion. Many States, as well as the Federal Government, currently make psychiatric assistance available to indigent defendants, and they have not found the financial burden so great as to preclude this assistance. This is especially so when the obligation of the State is limited to provision of one competent psychiatrist, as it is in many States, and as we limit the right we recognize today. At the same time, it is difficult to identify any interest of the State, other than that in its economy, that weighs against recognition of this right. The State's interest in prevailing at trial—unlike that of a private litigant—is necessarily tempered by its interest in the fair and accurate adjudication of criminal cases. Thus, also unlike a private litigant, a State may not legitimately assert an interest in maintenance of a strategic advantage over the defense, if the result of that advantage is to cast a pall on the accuracy of the verdict obtained. We therefore conclude that the governmental interest in denying Ake the assistance of a psychiatrist is not substantial, in light of the compelling interest of both the State and the individual in accurate dispositions. . . .

Psychiatry is not . . . an exact science, and psychiatrists disagree widely and frequently on what constitutes mental illness, on the appropriate diagnosis to be attached to given behavior and symptoms, on cure and treatment, and on likelihood of future dangerousness. Perhaps because there often is no single, accurate psychiatric conclusion on legal insanity in a given case, juries remain the primary factfinders on this issue, and they

> must resolve differences in opinion within the psychiatric profession on the basis of the evidence offered by each party. . . .
>
> We therefore hold that when a defendant demonstrates to the trial judge that his sanity at the time of the offense is to be a significant factor at trial, the State must, at a minimum, assure the defendant access to a competent psychiatrist who will conduct an appropriate examination and assist in evaluation, preparation, and presentation of the defense. This is not to say, of course, that the indigent defendant has a constitutional right to choose a psychiatrist of his personal liking or to receive funds to hire his own. Our concern is that the indigent defendant have access to a competent psychiatrist for the purpose we have discussed, and as in the case of the provision of counsel we leave to the State the decision on how to implement this right. . . .

NOTES & QUESTIONS ON RIGHT TO RETAIN EXPERTS

1. *The significant factor standard.* The Court stated in *Ake* that a trial judge is required to appoint a psychiatric expert if the defendant shows that "sanity at the time of the offense is to be a significant factor at trial." Do you agree that this is the correct standard? Since the result of the trial is unknown, the standard cannot depend on an assessment of whether the defendant has a valid insanity defense. Even assuming that the standard does not require the trial court to make a determination on the merits, it does require that the court determine whether sanity will be a "significant factor." How is this inquiry to be made without the benefit of psychiatric testimony for the trial court to consider? Should the trial court simply make the assessment based on the defense's articulation of their trial strategy?

2. *Is* Ake *limited to capital cases? Ake* involved a capital case, thus leading to some uncertainty over whether the right it outlined applies in all criminal cases or just in capital cases where insanity is an issue. At least a few state courts have asserted that *Ake* is limited to capital cases. See *Marlow v. State*, 538 So. 2d 804, 807 (Ala. Crim. App. 1988) ("Furthermore, *Ake v. Oklahoma*, the authority upon which the appellant bases his argument does not apply in non-capital cases."). Can you think of any reason why the *Ake* rationale would apply only in the capital context?

3. *Ineffective assistance of counsel.* In some situations, a lawyer might not understand the state law governing the retention of, and reimbursement for, expert witnesses. That failure could constitute ineffective assistance of counsel. In *Hinton v. Alabama*, 571 U.S. 263 (2014), police investigated a rash of

robberies and murders of restaurant managers in Birmingham. In each case, the robber used a gun with .38 caliber bullets. After an eyewitness identification by the surviving victim of one of the robberies, the defendant Anthony Ray Hinton was charged with capital murder. Hinton's trial strategy was to question the validity of the eyewitness testimony and the forensic evidence, and therefore he needed to secure a defense expert. The defense applied for funding from the judge and the judge granted $1,000, which the judge believed was the statutory maximum allowed. In fact, the judge was wrong because the state statute had been recently amended and now provided funding for "any expenses reasonably incurred," rather than a specific dollar amount. The defense counsel did not challenge the judge's mistake. On appeal, Hinton argued that the defense counsel's failure to correct the judge constituted ineffective assistance of counsel, and the Supreme Court agreed: "The trial attorney's failure to request additional funding in order to replace an expert he knew to be inadequate because he mistakenly believed that he had received all he could get under Alabama law constituted deficient performance." *Hinton v. Alabama*, 571 U.S. 263, 274 (2014).

STATUTORY REQUIREMENTS

A defendant's right to hire experts, at public expense, is also protected by federal statutes that apply in all federal criminal prosecutions. In a sense, these provisions sweep broader than *Ake*, because they also apply to other experts outside of the psychiatric context. For example, federal law provides:

> Counsel for a person who is financially unable to obtain investigative, expert, or other services necessary for adequate representation may request them in an ex parte application. Upon finding, after appropriate inquiry in an ex parte proceeding, that the services are necessary and that the person is financially unable to obtain them, the court, or the United States magistrate judge if the services are required in connection with a matter over which he has jurisdiction, shall authorize counsel to obtain the services.

18 U.S.C. § 3006A. However, the statute also imposes a cap of $2,400 for services rendered by an expert "unless payment in excess of that limit is certified by the court."

Similar statutes exist in some states. For example, New York law requires that

> [u]pon a finding in an ex parte proceeding that investigative, expert or other services are necessary and that the defendant . . . is financially unable to obtain them, the court shall authorize counsel, whether or not assigned in accordance with a plan, to obtain the services on behalf of the defendant or such other person. The court upon a finding that timely procurement of necessary services could not await prior authorization may authorize the services nunc pro tunc. The court shall determine reasonable compensation for the services and direct payment to the person who rendered them or to the person entitled to reimbursement. Only in extraordinary circumstances may the court provide for compensation in excess of one thousand

> dollars per investigative, expert or other service provider.

N.Y. County Law § 722-c. Michigan's statute suggests that the defendant gets to select the psychiatrist:

> The defendant may, at his or her own expense, secure an independent psychiatric evaluation by a clinician of his or her choice on the issue of his or her insanity at the time the alleged offense was committed. If the defendant is indigent, the court may, upon showing of good cause, order that the county pay for an independent psychiatric evaluation.

Mich. Comp. Laws § 768.20a.

E. PRACTICE & POLICY

Most of this chapter has focused on the core legal doctrines recognizing the right to counsel in criminal cases. However, there are a number of practical obstacles that make it difficult to transform the promise of *Gideon* into a reality. Every day, poor individuals face difficult courtroom proceedings with insufficient legal resources, either because the right to counsel does not apply to that type of proceeding, or because the public defender offices are overworked and understaffed. This section focus on these obstacles.

The limits of *Gideon*. The *Gideon* right to counsel applies in more situations than the actual trial, but its reach is not universal. For example, the *Gideon* right also applies during direct criminal law appeals taken as a matter of right, according to *Johnson v. United States* and *Ellis v. United States*. As the Supreme Court noted in *Douglas v. California*, 372 U.S. 353, 357 (1963), "where the merits of the one and only appeal an indigent has as of right are decided without benefit of counsel, we think an unconstitutional line has been drawn between rich and poor." However, the principle does not extend to subsequent discretionary appeals, post-conviction habeas corpus petitions, or civil proceedings. The lack of a constitutional right for habeas proceedings is particularly problematic, since habeas litigation functions as a form of de facto appellate review. Is it excessively formalistic to provide counsel at public expense for a direct appeal but not provide counsel for a collateral attack via a writ of habeas corpus? Recall that habeas litigation is the process by which a defendant, convicted in state court, can receive federal court review of state court proceedings that may have violated federal constitutional requirements. Should these significant legal claims depend on the financial resources of the convict? Furthermore, taken to its logical extreme, the lack of a constitutional right to habeas counsel entails that there is no constitutional right to effective assistance of counsel either. So, while a trial counsel's conflict of interest would be unconstitutional, a habeas counsel's conflict of interest would not raise a constitutional issue.

❧ Resources for the right to counsel. Prior chapters discussed the possibility that a lack of judicial resources might violate the constitutional right to a speedy trial, because a lack of prosecutors and judges limits the number of trials that can be conducted in a particularly busy jurisdiction. Could a similar argument be made regarding the lack of resources for public defenders? In other words, public defenders are notoriously overworked and carry a high caseload. Although these defense counsel are usually diligent and competent, they can only devote so much time to each case, given the overall workload. To respond to this problem, public defenders are more likely to seek plea deals rather than take cases to trial. Does this state of affairs suggest that there are *structural* barriers to the Sixth Amendment right to counsel? Could an appeals court declare that an entire jurisdiction was violating the Sixth Amendment and order that jurisdiction to increase its spending on public defense? In 2017, the ACLU sued the Missouri State Public Defenders making exactly this argument. See *Church v. State of Missouri* (currently pending).

❧ A *Gideon* for immigration? Immigration removal proceedings are considered civil proceedings and therefore no right to counsel applies. As the Supreme Court noted in *I.N.S. v. Lopez-Mendoza*, 468 U.S. 1032, 1038 (1984), "[a] deportation proceeding is a purely civil action to determine eligibility to remain in this country, not to punish an unlawful entry, though entering or remaining unlawfully in this country is itself a crime." Given the stakes for the individual in a removal proceeding, should counsel be recognized as a constitutional right? Consider the following argument:

> As is often true for dichotomies, the differences between civil and criminal proceedings blur at the margins. There are civil cases where the stakes are extraordinarily high, so high that they arguably approximate the life and liberty interests implicated by a criminal prosecution. For example, a loss of public benefits or potential eviction from an apartment can have a devastating impact on the life of an indigent person. The assistance of a lawyer can make all the difference to the ultimate outcome of such high stakes civil proceedings.

Kevin R. Johnson, *An Immigration* Gideon *for Lawful Permanent Residents*, 122 Yale L.J. 2394, 2396 (2013). If the *Gideon* right to counsel was extended to immigration removal proceedings, either as a matter of federal constitutional law or as matter of federal *statute*, the federal government would have to expend significant resources to provide attorneys for the thousands of removal proceedings that are conducted every year.

❧ A *Gideon* for federal capital habeas? As it stands now, state prisoners are not entitled to habeas counsel at public expense as a matter of federal *constitutional* law. *Pennsylvania v. Finley*, 481 U.S. 551, 555 (1987) ("We have never held that prisoners have a constitutional right to counsel when mounting collateral attacks upon their convictions . . ."); *Murray v. Giarratano*, 492 U.S. 1, 10 (1989) ("We think that these cases require the conclusion that the rule of *Pennsylvania v. Finley* should apply no differently in capital cases than in noncapital cases."). A federal statute allows a judge to appoint counsel in federal habeas proceedings for *federal* inmates. 28 U.S.C. § 2255. One proposal would be to constitutionally guarantee public counsel for all state prisoners under a sentence of death when they file federal habeas petitions. Indeed, some states guarantee counsel for *state* post-conviction petitions because "in capital cases, state post-conviction efforts, though collateral, have become part of the death penalty appeal process at the state level." *Jackson v. State*, 732 So. 2d 187, 191 (Miss. 1999). These provisions create an inconsistent patchwork of statutory guarantees from state to state. Consider the following argument for an omnibus solution as matter of federal constitutional law:

> The final element of the right to counsel at all stages of a capital case is the uniqueness of the death penalty. The Supreme Court recognized this qualitive difference even in the early modern era of constitutional criminal procedure. *Powell v. Alabama* guaranteed lawyers for capital trials, while *Betts* left non-capital cases open to a sliding scale of necessity. The Court's modern death penalty jurisprudence stresses the need for "a greater degree of reliability when the death sentence is imposed." In restating the modern penalty, the Court has emphasized that it is "profoundly different from all other penalties."

Michael A. Mello, *Is There a Federal Constitutional Right to Counsel in Capital Post-Conviction Proceedings?*, 79 J. Crim. L. & Criminology 1065, 1099–100 (1989). See also Emily Garcia Uhrig, *A Case for a Constitutional Right to Counsel in Habeas Corpus*, 60 Hastings L.J. 541 (2009).

❧ Civil *Gideon*. As noted above, the *Gideon* holding applies only to criminal proceedings and there is no analogous Supreme Court precedent applying its reasoning to civil cases. In practice, this means that indigent plaintiffs might have a hard time filing a case against individuals who have harmed them in a business dispute, a tort case, a breach of contract case, or a landlord-tenant dispute. In theory, if the case might win the plaintiff a significant recovery, the plaintiff's attorney might agree to a representation on "contingency," meaning that the attorney will be paid a percentage, say 30 percent, of the damage recovery. However, the defendant will have no ability to hire an attorney on contingency because the defendant, by definition, will not recover damages. Also, some cases are pursued for equitable relief, such as an injunction, and will not generate a monetary recovery. In such cases, civil parties will need to either find financial resources, locate a non-governmental organization to represent them (such as a tenant's rights organization if the case involves a rental dispute), or represent themselves pro se. Is this state of affairs acceptable? Consider also civil lawsuits that a citizen might file against the government for violating the citizen's civil rights, such as a §1983 action for police brutality. *Gideon* is of no help to such a plaintiff, but in other countries, the government will pay for an indigent person's legal representation if they need to file a lawsuit against the government. Would such a scheme help make legal rights achievable for the indigent population or would it encourage the filing of meritless and frivolous cases? For more discussion, see Alan J. Stein, *The Indigent's "Right" to Counsel in Civil Cases*, 43 Fordham L. Rev. 989 (1975). The argument would not be that indigent litigants are permitted counsel in *all* civil cases, but simply that counsel should be provided at public expense in cases that have some *public* element, i.e., a governmental defendant, thus suggesting that the plaintiff or complainant suffered some wrong at the hands of a public official or public institution. Although some statutes allow for an award of attorneys' fees if the plaintiff is successful, that hardly solves the problem that an indigent defendant has inadequate financial resources to retain a lawyer in the first instance. An attorney might agree to take a case with the promise of recovering fees at the back-end of the litigation, though most attorneys would not agree to such an arrangement.

Not every legal sch olar is in favor of a civil *Gideon*. Consider the following dire assessment:

> If civil *Gideon* became a reality, it is extremely unlikely that civil lawyers would be better supported. Courts would likely not require limits on caseloads or increased expenditures on a guaranteed right to civil counsel. Nor would civil plaintiffs be guaranteed a competent lawyer with time to investigate, research, and try their cases. To the contrary, if the absolutely critical rights theoretically protected by *Gideon* can be so watered down, a civil *Gideon* would likely fare much worse. The

> government's long-term treatment (read: starvation) of civil legal aid societies also does not make civil *Gideon* look particularly promising.

Benjamin H. Barton, *Against Civil* Gideon *(and for Pro Se Court Reform)*, 62 Fla. L. Rev. 1227, 1231 (2010). In other words, since criminal *Gideon* is inadequate to protect the rights of criminal defendants, civil *Gideon* would simply import a broken system into the civil context.

CHAPTER 16

The Jury

INTRODUCTION

Before a trial can begin, the court must first empanel a jury (unless the defendant elects a bench trial in front of a judge or it is an offense for which a jury is not provided). For both the prosecution and defense, the assembly of the jury is crucial to a successful outcome, since the jury will act as the trier of fact. All the evidence in the world is not going to help a trial lawyer unless the lawyer can successfully package that evidence into a coherent narrative that will be considered compelling by the jury. To what degree that evidence is considered compelling will depend very much on the jury's composition. In other words, not all juries are created equal.

The following sections focus on the mechanics of assembling the jury and the constitutional and statutory rules that regulate that process. Section A focuses on the right to a jury trial as a fundamental right applicable to both the federal and state systems, with particular emphasis on which crimes are serious enough to trigger this constitutional protection. Section B focuses on the jury composition and deliberation, including the size of the jury, the requirement of unanimity, and the standard of proof to be applied by the jury in criminal cases. Section C focuses on the process for selecting jurors and the use of for-cause and peremptory challenges by prosecutors and defense attorneys—a process that allows trial lawyers to strategically exclude individuals from the jury, but which is nonetheless regulated by constitutional anti-discrimination norms. Finally, Section D, the Practice & Policy section, considers when a defense attorney might forgo a jury trial entirely in favor of a bench trial and what strategic decisions might impact this decision.

A. THE JURY TRIAL AS A FUNDAMENTAL RIGHT

While the Sixth Amendment provides a right to trial by jury, whether that right extends to the states, and whether the right applies in all cases, are two questions that necessitated Supreme Court interpretation. In the following case, the Supreme Court asks whether the jury trial is a fundamental right that is mandatory not just in federal cases but in all state cases as well. As you read the case, notice the distinction between "serious" and "petty" offenses and the role it plays in the argument. Is the Supreme Court able to offer a coherent definition of these categories?

Duncan v. Louisiana

Supreme Court of the United States
391 U.S. 145 (1968)

Mr. Justice WHITE delivered the opinion of the Court.

Appellant, Gary Duncan, was convicted of simple battery in the Twenty-fifth Judicial District Court of Louisiana. Under Louisiana law simple battery is a misdemeanor, punishable by a maximum of two years' imprisonment and a $300 fine. Appellant sought trial by jury, but because the Louisiana Constitution grants jury trials only in cases in which capital punishment or imprisonment at hard labor may be imposed, the trial judge denied the request. Appellant was convicted and sentenced to serve 60 days in the parish prison and pay a fine of $150. . . .

Appellant was 19 years of age when tried. While driving on Highway 23 in Plaquemines Parish on October 18, 1966, he saw two younger cousins engaged in a conversation by the side of the road with four white boys. Knowing his cousins, Negroes who had recently transferred to a formerly all-white high school, had reported the occurrence of racial incidents at the school, Duncan stopped the car, got out, and approached the six boys. At trial the white boys and a white onlooker testified, as did appellant and his cousins. The testimony was in dispute on many points, but the witnesses agreed that appellant and the white boys spoke to each other, that appellant encouraged his cousins to break off the encounter and enter his car, and that appellant was about to enter the car himself for the purpose of driving away with his cousins. The whites testified that just before getting in the car appellant slapped Herman Landry, one of the white boys, on the elbow. The Negroes testified that appellant had not slapped Landry, but had merely touched him. The trial judge concluded that the State had proved beyond a reasonable doubt that Duncan had committed simple battery, and found him guilty.

I

The Fourteenth Amendment denies the States the power to "deprive any person of life, liberty, or property, without due process of law." In resolving conflicting claims concerning the meaning of this spacious language, the Court has looked increasingly to the Bill of Rights for guidance; many of the rights guaranteed by the first eight Amendments to the Constitution have been held to be protected against state action by the Due Process Clause of the Fourteenth Amendment. . . . The test for determining whether a right extended by the Fifth and Sixth Amendments with respect to federal criminal proceedings is also protected against state action by the Fourteenth Amendment has been phrased in a variety of ways in the opinions of this Court. The question has been asked whether a right is among those "fundamental principles of liberty and justice which lie at the base of all our civil and political institutions," *Powell v. State of Alabama*, 287 U.S. 45, 67 (1932); whether it is "basic in our system of jurisprudence," *In re Oliver*, 333 U.S. 257, 273 (1948); and whether it is "a fundamental right, essential to a fair trial," *Gideon v. Wainwright*, 372 U.S. 335, 343-344 (1963). The claim before us is that the right to trial by jury guaranteed by the Sixth Amendment meets these tests. The position of Louisiana, on the other hand, is that the Constitution imposes upon the States no duty to give a jury trial in any criminal case, regardless of the seriousness of the crime or the size of the punishment which may be imposed. Because we believe that trial by jury in criminal cases is fundamental to the American scheme of justice, we hold that the Fourteenth Amendment guarantees a right of jury trial in all criminal cases which—were they to be tried in a federal court—would come within the Sixth Amendment's guarantee. Since we consider the appeal before us to be such a case, we hold that the Constitution was violated when appellant's demand for jury trial was refused. . . .

The history of trial by jury in criminal cases has been frequently told. It is sufficient for present purposes to say that by the time our Constitution was written, jury trial in criminal cases had been in existence in England for several centuries and carried impressive credentials traced by many to Magna Carta. Its preservation and proper operation as a protection against arbitrary rule were among the major objectives of the revolutionary settlement which was expressed in the Declaration and Bill of Rights of 1689. . . .

Jury trial came to America with English colonists, and received strong support from them. Royal interference with the jury trial was deeply resented. Among the resolutions adopted by the First Congress of the American Colonies (the Stamp Act Congress) on October 19, 1765—resolutions deemed by their authors to state "the most essential rights and liberties of the colonists"—was the declaration: "That trial by jury is the inherent and invaluable right of every British subject in these colonies." . . . The constitutions adopted by the original States guaranteed jury trial. Also, the constitution of every State entering the Union thereafter in one form or another protected the right to jury trial in criminal cases. Even such skeletal history is impressive support for considering the right to jury trial in criminal cases to be fundamental to our system of justice, an importance frequently recognized in the opinions of this Court. . . .

Jury trial continues to receive strong support. The laws of every State guarantee a right to jury trial in serious criminal cases; no State has dispensed with it; nor are there significant movements underway to do so. Indeed, the three most recent state constitutional revisions, in Maryland, Michigan, and New York, carefully preserved the right of the accused to have the judgment of a jury when tried for a serious crime.

We are aware of prior cases in this Court in which the prevailing opinion contains statements contrary to our holding today that the right to jury trial in serious criminal cases is a fundamental right and hence must be recognized by the States as part of their obligation to extend due process of law to all persons within their jurisdiction. None of these cases, however, dealt with a State which had purported to dispense entirely with a jury trial in serious criminal cases. . . .

The guarantees of jury trial in the Federal and State Constitutions reflect a profound judgment about the way in which law should be enforced and justice administered. A right to jury trial is granted to criminal defendants in order to prevent oppression by the Government. Those who wrote our constitutions knew from history and experience that it was necessary to protect against unfounded criminal charges brought to eliminate enemies and against judges too responsive to the voice of higher authority. The framers of the constitutions strove to create an independent judiciary but insisted upon further protection against arbitrary action. Providing an accused with the right to be tried by a jury of his peers gave him an inestimable safeguard against the corrupt or overzealous prosecutor and against the compliant, biased, or eccentric judge. If the defendant preferred the common-sense judgment of a jury to the more tutored but perhaps less sympathetic reaction of the single judge, he was to have it. Beyond this, the jury trial provisions in the Federal and State Constitutions reflect a fundamental decision about the exercise of official power—a reluctance to entrust plenary powers over the life and liberty of the citizen to one judge or to a group of judges. Fear of unchecked power, so typical of our State and Federal Governments in other respects, found expression in the criminal law in this insistence upon community participation in the determination of guilt or innocence. The deep commitment of the Nation to the right of jury trial in serious criminal cases as a defense against arbitrary law enforcement qualifies for protection under the Due Process Clause of the Fourteenth Amendment, and must therefore be respected by the States.

Of course jury trial has "its weaknesses and the potential for misuse." We are aware of the long debate, especially in this century, among those who write about the administration of justice, as to the wisdom of permitting untrained laymen to determine the facts in civil and criminal proceedings. Although the debate has been intense, with powerful voices on either side, most of the controversy has centered on the jury in civil cases. Indeed, some of the severest critics of civil juries acknowledge that the arguments for criminal juries are much stronger. In addition, at the heart of the dispute have been express or implicit assertions that juries are incapable of adequately understanding evidence or determining issues of fact, and that they are unpredictable, quixotic, and little better than a roll of dice. Yet, the most recent and exhaustive study of the jury in criminal cases concluded that juries do understand the evidence and come to sound conclusions in most of the cases presented to them and that when juries differ with the result at which the judge would have arrived, it is usually because they are serving some of the very purposes for which they were created and for which they are now employed.

The State of Louisiana urges that holding that the Fourteenth Amendment assures a right to jury trial will cast doubt on the integrity of every trial conducted without a jury. Plainly, this is not the import of our holding. Our conclusion is that in the American States, as in the federal judicial system, a general grant of jury trial for serious offenses is a fundamental right, essential for preventing miscarriages of justice and for assuring that fair trials are provided for all defendants. We would not assert, however, that every criminal trial—or any particular trial—held before a judge alone is unfair or that a defendant may never be as fairly treated by a judge as he would be by a jury. Thus we hold no constitutional doubts about the practices, common in both federal and state courts, of accepting waivers of jury trial and prosecuting petty crimes without extending a right to jury trial. However, the fact is that in most places more trials for serious crimes are to juries than to a court alone; a great many defendants prefer the judgment of a jury to that of a court. Even where defendants are satisfied with bench trials, the right to a jury trial very likely serves its intended purpose of making judicial or prosecutorial unfairness less likely. . . .

II

Louisiana's final contention is that even if it must grant jury trials in serious criminal cases, the conviction before us is valid and constitutional because here the petitioner was tried for simple battery and was sentenced to only 60 days in the parish prison. We are not persuaded. It is doubtless true that there is a category of petty crimes or offenses which is not subject to the Sixth Amendment jury trial provision and should not be subject to the Fourteenth Amendment jury trial requirement here applied to the States.

Crimes carrying possible penalties up to six months do not require a jury trial if they otherwise qualify as petty offenses. But the penalty authorized for a particular crime is of major relevance in determining whether it is serious or not and may in itself, if severe enough, subject the trial to the mandates of the Sixth Amendment. The penalty authorized by the law of the locality may be taken "as a gauge of its social and ethical judgments" of the crime in question. . . . In the case before us the Legislature of Louisiana has made simple battery a criminal offense punishable by imprisonment for up to two years and a fine. The question, then, is whether a crime carrying such a penalty is an offense which Louisiana may insist on trying without a jury.

We think not. So-called petty offenses were tried without juries both in England and in the Colonies and have always been held to be exempt from the otherwise comprehensive language of the Sixth Amendment's jury trial provisions. There is no substantial evidence that the Framers intended to depart from this established common-law practice. . . .

In determining whether the length of the authorized prison term or the seriousness of other punishment is enough in itself to require a jury trial, we are counseled . . . to refer to objective criteria, chiefly the existing laws and practices in the Nation. In the federal system, petty offenses are defined as those punishable by no more than six months in prison and a $500 fine. In 49 of the 50 States crimes subject to trial without a jury, which occasionally include simple battery, are punishable by no more than one year in jail. Moreover, in the late 18th century in America crimes triable without a jury were for the most part punishable by no more than a six-month prison term, although there appear to have been exceptions to this rule. We need not, however, settle in this case the exact location of the line between petty offenses and serious crimes. It is sufficient for our purposes to hold that a crime punishable by two years in prison is, based on past and contemporary standards in this country, a serious crime and not a petty offense. Consequently, appellant was entitled to a jury trial and it was error to deny it. . . .

NOTES & QUESTIONS ON THE RIGHT TO TRIAL BY JURY

1. *Petty versus serious offenses.* The *Duncan* holding is limited to its facts in the sense that the Court refused to decide "the exact location of the line between petty offenses and serious crimes." 391 U.S., at 161. Since Duncan was subject to punishment of two years, the Supreme Court concluded that he was certainly entitled to a jury trial because the offense qualified as "serious." But the Court refused to decide whether a crime subject to a lesser punishment, say 18 months, might also be entitled to a jury trial as a matter

of constitutional law. Are these dividing lines arbitrary? Is the difference between 12, 18, or 24 months in prison significant? Two years after *Duncan*, in *Baldwin v. New York*, 399 U.S. 66, 69 (1970), the Supreme Court clarified that the dividing line between a serious and petty offense, and thus whether the right to a jury trial attached, was not whether the offense was a misdemeanor or a felony but rather whether punishment of more than *six months* was authorized by the statute. Then, in *Lewis v. United States*, 518 U.S. 322, 323 (1996), the Supreme Court concluded that the Sixth Amendment jury trial right does not apply even if "the aggregate prison term authorized for the offenses" exceeds six months. For example, if the defendant is charged with multiple misdemeanors, each one carrying a maximum punishment of less than six months, but with an aggregate criminal exposure of *more* than six months, the Sixth Amendment does not require that the defendant receive a jury trial. Do you agree that the dividing line should be based on the maximum punishment *per* offense or should it be based instead on the aggregate total punishment authorized by the statute?

2. *The importance of punishment. Duncan, Baldwin,* and *Lewis* all focus on the length of the punishment to determine whether an offense is "serious" and therefore the right to a jury trial applies. Why is this the correct standard? Why the focus on punishment instead of public opprobrium or some other barometer of what counts as a "serious" offense? Or perhaps the proscribed punishment in the statute is itself a proxy—a reliable guide—to determine the level of seriousness that the legislature, and the community at large, attaches to that criminal conduct. Is there any other proxy that could be used to determine seriousness other than the maximum punishment listed in the statute?

3. *Exceptions to the jury trial right.* The right to a jury trial has some exceptions. For example, members of the military may be prosecuted before a military court under the Uniform Code of Military Justice, instead of a civilian court with a civilian jury. The Fifth Amendment includes an explicit exception for the military justice system, but by its terms only applies to the grand jury requirement: "No person shall be held to answer for a capital, or otherwise infamous crime, unless on a presentment or indictment of a Grand Jury, except in cases arising in the land or naval forces, or in the Militia, when in actual service in time of War or public danger. . . ." By extension, courts have also held that the constitutional right to a civilian petit jury does not apply to members of the armed forces. For more on the constitutional exceptions to criminal procedure in the military context, see Stephen I. Vladeck, *Military Courts and Article III*, 103 Geo. L.J. 933, 935-36 (2015) ("the Supreme Court has articulated different normative, historical, and textual rationales to justify three different classes of military adjudication: courts-martial, military commissions, and courts incident to military rule (for example, martial law or belligerent occupation)").

STATE LAW REQUIREMENTS

A few states protect the right to a jury trial even if the offense is punishable by less than six months in jail. For example, Arizona courts have held that the Arizona Constitution requires a jury trial even for misdemeanors punishable by less than six months in jail if the "statutory offense has a common law antecedent that guaranteed a right to trial by jury at the time of Arizona statehood." In *Bosworth v. Anagnost*, 234 Ariz. 453, 323 P.3d 736 (Ct. App. 2014), an appeals court considered the fate of a defendant charged with misdemeanor shoplifting. The court held that shoplifting was based on a common law crime for which defendants were entitled to a jury trial in Arizona at the time when the state constitution was adopted. They cited numerous examples from the 1600s and 1700s:

> Mary Jones, was tryed for stealing 10 Yards of Lute-string, value 30 s. out of the shop of William Wolfe, at the Royal-Exchange, on the 16th of April. . . . [T]he Jury found her Guilty of the Felony to the value of 9 s.
>
> Anne Jenkins, and Elizabeth Green, were both tried for Shop-lifting, in stealing 18 Yards of Muslin, value 52 s. the Goods of William Peat. They came to the Shop to cheapen some Goods, and one of them put the piece of Muslin under her Coats, which she was seen to do, by the Maid of the House, and being stopt, it so appear'd. . . . They both denied the Fact; yet were found guilty of Felony.
>
> James Reed alias Reeves, of St. Mary Whitechapel, was indicted for feloniously stealing 5 Hats, value 18 s. out of the shop of Edmund Juby in the Daytime, the 17th of Octob. last. The Prisoner was seen to come out of the shop with the Hats, by one passing by; who, suspecting him, stopp'd him, and carried him back to the Owner's house with the Hats. The Prisoner in his Defence, said he found the Hats, but that did not avail him. The Jury found him guilty of Shoplifting.

Based on these historical examples, the court concluded that shoplifting, regardless of the punishment, was afforded a jury trial at common law, and therefore this protection endured today under the Arizona State Constitution.

B. JURY COMPOSITION AND DELIBERATION

Popular conception of the role and function of the jury is very much dominated by portrayals of jury decision making in novels, TV, and film. For example, for many individuals, the famous movie *12 Angry Men* provided a template for understanding the working of the jury and established the following mental paradigm: 12 individuals deliberating confidentially in an attempt to achieve universal consensus on an outcome—either guilty or not guilty. In reality, though, there is far more variation regarding the specifics of jury compensation and deliberation than one would imagine. For example, while most juries are composed of 12 people, some state statutes allow for the use of smaller juries. Furthermore, while most state courts require that the jury reach a unanimous

A scene from *12 Angry Men* (1957), written and produced by Reginald Rose and starring Henry Fonda. (World History Archive/Alamy)

decision for the defendant to be convicted, this is not universally true, with some states allowing majority votes for conviction.

1. Size of the Jury

In federal courts, the defendant has the right to be tried by a jury of 12, according to the Federal Rules of Criminal Procedure. See Fed. R. Crim. P. 23 (requiring a jury size of 12 unless both parties stipulate in writing their agreement to a smaller jury). All state jurisdictions that have retained the death penalty require a 12-person jury for capital cases. For non-capital crimes, however, state courts often utilize juries with fewer than 12 members. If the Constitution's protection of the right to a jury trial under the Sixth and Fourteenth Amendments does not require a 12-person jury, the question is what the constitutionally required minimum should be. In the following case, the Supreme Court asks whether a conviction by a six-member jury is consistent with the requirements of a jury trial. As you read the case, focus on the reasons why the framers of the Constitution sought to protect the right to trial by jury and whether a six-person jury is large enough to function in a way that would preserve that right. What happens to deliberations when the size of the jury is expanded or contracted?

Williams v. Florida

Supreme Court of the United States
399 U.S. 78 (1970)

Mr. Justice White delivered the opinion of the Court.

Prior to his trial for robbery in the State of Florida, petitioner filed . . . a pretrial motion to impanel a 12-man jury instead of the six-man jury provided by Florida law in all but capital cases. That motion . . . was denied. Petitioner was convicted as charged and was sentenced to life imprisonment. . . .

II

In *Duncan v. Louisiana*, 391 U.S. 145 (1968), we held that the Fourteenth Amendment guarantees a right to trial by jury in all criminal cases that—were they to be tried in a federal court—would come within the Sixth Amendment's guarantee. Petitioner's trial for robbery on July 3, 1968, clearly falls within the scope of that holding. The question in this case then is whether the constitutional guarantee of a trial by "jury" necessarily requires trial by exactly 12 persons, rather than some lesser number—in this case six. We hold that the 12-man panel is not a necessary ingredient of "trial by jury," and that respondent's refusal to impanel more than the six members provided for by Florida law did not violate petitioner's Sixth Amendment rights as applied to the States through the Fourteenth.

We had occasion in *Duncan v. Louisiana*, to review briefly the oft-told history of the development of trial by jury in criminal cases. That history revealed a long tradition attaching great importance to the concept of relying on a body of one's peers to determine guilt or innocence as a safeguard against arbitrary law enforcement. That same history, however, affords little insight into the considerations that gradually led the size of that body to be generally fixed at 12. Some have suggested that the number 12 was fixed upon simply because that was the number of the presentment jury from the hundred, from which the petit jury developed. Other, less circular but more fanciful reasons for the number 12 have been given, "but they were all brought forward after the number was fixed," and rest on little more than mystical or superstitious insights into the significance of 12. Lord Coke's explanation that the "number of twelve is much respected in holy writ, as 12 apostles, 12 stones, 12 tribes, etc.," is typical. In short, while sometime in the 14th century the size of the jury at common law came to be fixed generally at 12, that particular feature of the jury system appears to have been a historical accident, unrelated to the great purposes which gave rise to the jury in the first place. The question before us is whether this accidental feature of the jury has been immutably codified into our Constitution.

This Court's earlier decisions have assumed an affirmative answer to this question. The leading case so construing the Sixth Amendment is *Thompson v. Utah*, 170 U.S. 343 (1898). There the defendant had been tried and convicted by a 12-man jury for a crime committed in the Territory of Utah. A new trial was granted, but by that time Utah had been admitted as a State. The defendant's new trial proceeded under Utah's Constitution, providing for a jury of only eight members. This Court reversed the resulting conviction, holding that Utah's constitutional provision was an ex post facto law as applied to the defendant. In reaching its conclusion, the Court announced that the Sixth Amendment was applicable to the defendant's trial when Utah was a Territory, and that the jury referred to in the Amendment was a jury "constituted, as it was at common law, of twelve persons, neither more nor less." Arguably unnecessary for the result, this announcement was supported simply by referring to the Magna Carta, and by quoting passages from treatises which noted—what has already been seen—that at common law the jury did indeed consist of 12. Noticeably absent was any discussion of the essential step in the argument: namely, that every feature of the jury as it existed at common law—whether incidental or essential to that institution—was necessarily included in the Constitution wherever that document referred to a "jury." Subsequent decisions have reaffirmed the announcement in *Thompson* often in dictum and usually by relying—where there was any discussion of the issue at all—solely on the fact that the common-law jury consisted of 12.

While "the intent of the Framers" is often an elusive quarry, the relevant constitutional history casts considerable doubt on the easy assumption in our past decisions that if a given feature existed in a jury at common law in 1789, then it was necessarily preserved in the Constitution. Provisions for jury trial were first placed in the Constitution in Article III's provision that "(t)he Trial of all Crimes . . . shall be by Jury; and such Trial shall be held in the State where the said Crimes shall have been committed." The "very scanty history (of this provision) in the records of the Constitutional Convention" sheds little light either way on the intended correlation between Article III's "jury" and the features of the jury at common law. Indeed, pending and after the adoption of the Constitution, fears were expressed that Article III's provision failed to preserve the common-law right to be tried by a "jury of the vicinage." That concern, as well as the concern to preserve the right to jury in civil as well as criminal cases, furnished part of the impetus for introducing amendments to the Constitution that ultimately resulted in the jury trial provisions of the Sixth and Seventh Amendments. As introduced by James Madison in the House, the Amendment relating to jury trial in criminal cases would have provided that: "The trial of all crimes

. . . shall be by an impartial jury of freeholders of the vicinage, with the requisite of unanimity for conviction, of the right of challenge, and other accustomed requisites. . . ."

The Amendment passed the House in substantially this form, but after more than a week of debate in the Senate it returned to the House considerably altered.. . . A conference committee was appointed.. . . The version that finally emerged from the Committee was the version that ultimately became the Sixth Amendment, ensuring an accused: "the right to a speedy and public trial, by an impartial jury of the State and district wherein the crime shall have been committed, which district shall have been previously ascertained by law. . . ." Gone were the provisions spelling out such common-law features of the jury as "unanimity," or "the accustomed requisites." . . .

Three significant features may be observed in this sketch of the background of the Constitution's jury trial provisions. First, even though the vicinage requirement was as much a feature of the common-law jury as was the 12-man requirement, the mere reference to "trial by jury" in Article III was not interpreted to include that feature. Indeed, as the subsequent debates over the Amendments indicate, disagreement arose over whether the feature should be included at all in its common-law sense, resulting in the compromise described above. Second, provisions that would have explicitly tied the "jury" concept to the "accustomed requisites" of the time were eliminated. Such action is concededly open to the explanation that the "accustomed requisites" were thought to be already included in the concept of a "jury." But that explanation is no more plausible than the contrary one: that the deletion had some substantive effect. Indeed, given the clear expectation that a substantive change would be effected by the inclusion or deletion of an explicit "vicinage" requirement, the latter explanation is, if anything, the more plausible. Finally, contemporary legislative and constitutional provisions indicate that where Congress wanted to leave no doubt that it was incorporating existing common-law features of the jury system, it knew how to use express language to that effect. . . .

We do not pretend to be able to divine precisely what the word "jury" imported to the Framers, the First Congress, or the States in 1789. It may well be that the usual expectation was that the jury would consist of 12, and that hence, the most likely conclusion to be drawn is simply that little thought was actually given to the specific question we face today. But there is absolutely no indication in "the intent of the Framers" of an explicit decision to equate the constitutional and common-law characteristics of the jury. Nothing in this history suggests, then, that we do violence to the letter of the Constitution by turning to other than purely historical considerations to determine which features of the jury system, as it existed at common law, were preserved in the Constitution. The relevant inquiry, as we see it, must be the function that the particular feature performs and its relation to the purposes of the jury trial. Measured by this standard, the 12-man requirement cannot be regarded as an indispensable component of the Sixth Amendment. . . .

The purpose of the jury trial . . . is to prevent oppression by the Government. . . Given this purpose, the essential feature of a jury obviously lies in the interposition between the accused and his accuser of the commonsense judgment of a group of laymen, and in the community participation and shared responsibility that results from that group's determination of guilt or innocence. The performance of this role is not a function of the particular number of the body that makes up the jury. To be sure, the number should probably be large enough to promote group deliberation, free from outside attempts at intimidation, and to provide a fair possibility for obtaining a representative cross-section of the community. But we find little reason to think that these goals are in any meaningful sense less likely to be achieved when the jury numbers six, than when it numbers 12—particularly if the requirement of unanimity is retained. And, certainly the reliability of the jury as a factfinder hardly seems likely to be a function of its size.

It might be suggested that the 12-man jury gives a defendant a greater advantage since he has more "chances" of finding a juror who will insist on acquittal and thus prevent conviction. But the advantage might just as easily belong to the State, which also needs only one juror out of twelve insisting on guilt to prevent acquittal. What few experiments have occurred—usually in the civil area—indicate that there is no discernible difference between the results reached by the two different-sized juries. In short, neither currently available evidence nor theory suggests that the 12-man jury is necessarily more advantageous to the defendant than a jury composed of fewer members.

Similarly, while in theory the number of viewpoints represented on a randomly selected jury ought to increase as the size of the jury increases, in practice the difference between the 12-man and the six-man jury in terms of the cross-section of the community represented seems likely to be negligible. Even the 12-man jury cannot insure representation of every distinct voice in the community, particularly given the use of the peremptory challenge. As long as arbitrary exclusions of a particular class from the jury rolls are forbidden, the concern that the cross-section will be significantly diminished if the jury is decreased in size from 12 to six seems an unrealistic one.

We conclude, in short, as we began: the fact that the jury at common law was composed of precisely 12 is a historical accident, unnecessary to effect the purposes of the jury system and wholly without significance "except to mystics." . . .

Having decided that a six-person jury is consistent with the right to trial by jury, the Supreme Court in the following case asks the next logical question: Does the Constitution permit conviction by a jury composed of *less* than six individuals? Since the Supreme Court blessed the reduction of jury size from 12 to six, could the same arguments justify a reduction even further? On the other hand, at some point the size of the jury becomes so vanishingly small that the essential deliberative function of the jury is compromised. When is that point reached?

Ballew v. Georgia

Supreme Court of the United States
35 U.S. 223 (1978)

Mr. Justice BLACKMUN announced the judgment of the Court and delivered an opinion in which Mr. Justice STEVENS joined.

This case presents the issue whether a state criminal trial to a jury of only five persons deprives the accused of the right to trial by jury guaranteed by him by the Sixth and Fourteenth Amendments. Our resolution of the issue requires an application of principles enunciated in *Williams v. Florida*, 399 U.S. 78 (1970), where the use of a six-person jury in a state criminal trial was upheld against similar constitutional attack.

I

In November 1973 petitioner Claude Davis Ballew was the manager of the Paris Adult Theatre at 320 Peachtree Street, Atlanta, Ga. On November 9 two investigators from the Fulton County Solicitor General's office viewed at the theater a motion picture film entitled "Behind the Green Door." After they had seen the film, they obtained a warrant for its seizure, returned to the theater, viewed the film once again, and seized it. Petitioner and a cashier were arrested. Investigators returned to the theater on November 26, viewed the film in its entirety, secured still another warrant, and on November 27 once again viewed the motion picture and seized a second copy of the film.

On September 14, 1974, petitioner was charged in a two-count misdemeanor accusation with "distributing obscene materials. . . ." Petitioner was brought to trial in the Criminal Court of Fulton County. After a jury of 5 persons had been selected and sworn, petitioner moved that the court impanel a jury of 12 persons. That court, however, tried its misdemeanor cases before juries of five persons. . . . The motion for a 12-person jury was overruled, and the trial went on to its conclusion before the 5-person jury that had been impaneled. At the conclusion of the trial, the jury deliberated for 38 minutes and returned a verdict of guilty on both counts of the accusation. . . .

III

When the Court in *Williams v. Florida* permitted the reduction in jury size—or, to put it another way, when it held that a jury of six was not unconstitutional—it expressly reserved ruling on the issue whether a number smaller than six passed constitutional scrutiny. The Court refused to speculate when this so called "slippery slope" would become too steep. We face now, however, the two-fold question whether a further reduction in the size of the state criminal trial jury does make the grade too dangerous, that is, whether it inhibits the functioning of the jury as an institution to a significant degree, and, if so, whether any state interest counterbalances and justifies the disruption so as to preserve its constitutionality.

Williams v. Florida and *Colgrove v. Battin*, 413 U.S. 149 (1973) (where the Court held that a jury of six members did not violate the Seventh Amendment right to a jury trial in a civil case), generated a quantity of scholarly work on jury size. These writings do not draw or identify a bright line below which the number of jurors would not be able to function as required by the standards enunciated in *Williams*. On the other hand, they raise significant questions about the wisdom and constitutionality of a reduction below six. We examine these concerns:

First, recent empirical data suggest that progressively smaller juries are less likely to foster effective group deliberation. At some point, this decline leads to inaccurate fact-finding and incorrect application of the common sense of the community to the facts. Generally, a positive correlation exists between group size and the quality of both group performance and group productivity. A variety of explanations have been offered for this conclusion. Several are particularly applicable in the jury setting. The smaller the group, the less likely are members to make critical contributions necessary for the solution of a given problem. Because most juries are not permitted to take notes, memory is important for accurate jury deliberations. As juries decrease in size, then, they are less likely to have members who remember each of the important pieces of evidence or argument. Furthermore, the smaller the group, the less likely it is to overcome the biases of its members to obtain an accurate result. When individual and group decisionmaking were compared, it was seen that groups performed better because prejudices of individuals were frequently counterbalanced, and objectivity resulted. Groups also exhibited increased motivation and self-criticism. All these advantages, except, perhaps, self-motivation, tend to diminish as the size of the group diminishes. Because juries frequently face complex problems laden with value choices, the benefits are important and should be retained. In particular, the counterbalancing of various biases is critical to the accurate application of the common sense of the community to the facts of any given case.

Second, the data now raise doubts about the accuracy of the results achieved by smaller and smaller panels. Statistical studies suggest that the risk of convicting an innocent person (Type I error) rises as the size of the jury diminishes. Because the risk of not convicting a guilty person (Type II error) increases with the size of the panel, an optimal jury size can be selected as a function of the interaction between the two risks. . . .

Another doubt about progressively smaller juries arises from the increasing inconsistency that results from the decreases. Saks argued that the "more a jury type fosters consistency, the greater will be the proportion of juries which select the correct (i.e., the same) verdict and the fewer 'errors' will be made." From his mock trials held before undergraduates and former jurors, he computed the percentage of "correct" decisions rendered by 12-person and 6-person panels. In the student experiment, 12-person groups reached correct verdicts 83% of the time; 6-person panels reached correct verdicts 69% of the time. . . .

Third, the data suggest that the verdicts of jury deliberation in criminal cases will vary as juries become smaller, and that the variance amounts to an imbalance to the detriment of one side, the defense. . . . Also, group theory suggests that a person in the minority will adhere to his position more frequently when he has at least one other person supporting his argument. In the jury setting the significance of this tendency is demonstrated by the following figures: If a minority viewpoint is shared by 10% of the community, 28.2% of 12-member juries may be expected to have no minority representation, but 53.1% of 6-member juries would have none. Thirty-four percent of 12-member panels could be expected to have two minority members, while only 11% of 6-member panels would have two. As the numbers diminish below six, even fewer panels would have one member with the minority viewpoint and still fewer would have two. The chance for hung juries would decline accordingly.

Fourth, what has just been said about the presence of minority viewpoint as juries decrease in size foretells problems not only for jury decisionmaking, but also for the representation of minority groups in the community. The Court repeatedly has held that meaningful community participation cannot be attained with the exclusion of minorities or other identifiable groups from jury service. . . . Although the Court in *Williams* concluded that the six-person jury did not fail to represent adequately a cross-section of the community, the opportunity for meaningful and appropriate representation does decrease with the size of the panels. Thus, if a minority group constitutes 10% of the community, 53.1% of randomly selected six-member juries could be expected to have no minority representative among their members, and 89% not to have two. Further reduction in size will erect additional barriers to representation. . . .

IV

While we adhere to, and reaffirm our holding in *Williams v. Florida*, these studies, most of which have been made since *Williams* was decided in 1970, lead us to conclude that the purpose and functioning of the jury in a criminal trial is seriously impaired, and to a constitutional degree, by a reduction in size to below six members. We readily admit that we do not pretend to discern a clear line between six members and five. But the assembled data raise substantial doubt about the reliability and appropriate representation of panels smaller than six. Because of the fundamental importance of the jury trial to the American system of criminal justice, any further reduction that promotes inaccurate and possibly biased decision-making, that causes untoward differences in verdicts, and that prevents juries from truly representing their communities, attains constitutional significance. . . .

[T]he retention by Georgia of the unanimity requirement does not solve the Sixth and Fourteenth Amendment problem. Our concern has to do with the ability of the smaller group to perform the functions mandated by the Amendments. That a five-person jury may return a unanimous decision does not speak to the questions whether the group engaged in meaningful deliberation, could remember all the important facts and arguments, and truly represented the sense of the entire community. . . .

NOTES & QUESTIONS ON JURY SIZE

1. *The deliberative function.* Why did the Supreme Court conclude that a jury of six is constitutional but a jury of five is not? Why is that number constitutionally significant? Is there strong empirical evidence that a jury of six is qualitatively better than a jury of five? Or is the line somewhat arbitrary?

2. *The hung jury paradox.* In accordance with these constitutional precedents, some states allow juries of less than 12 in felony cases, and many states allow juries of less than 12 in misdemeanor cases. One alleged rationale for using smaller juries is to decrease the number of mistrials; smaller juries should increase consensus because there are fewer individuals who could serve as holdouts and trigger a hung jury—which would result in the judge declaring a mistrial in the case. States have allowed lowered smaller juries on the theory that they will reach more verdicts and more of those verdicts will be convictions. However, scholars have noted that the predicted decrease in mistrials has not materialized. Why? Professors Luppi and Parisi note that paradoxically, smaller trials end up increasing the number of mistrials. The reason may have to do with the way initial assessments are first expressed as deliberations

begin. If each person around the table expresses an opinion in sequence, the first few answers end up influencing the assessment of the remaining jurors who hear, for example, that three or four individuals all agree on an outcome. This places pressure on the remaining two jurors to agree as well. Indeed, the remaining jurors might not just be hesitant to express discordant opinions, but in fact the unanimity of the first responses might actually influence the underlying remaining assessments. See Barbara Luppi & Francesco Parisi, *Jury Size and the Hung-Jury Paradox*, 42 J. Legal Stud. 399 (2013). Does this suggest that jurisdictions should reconsider their jury sizes and move back to a consistent jury size of 12 in all cases?

3. *Judicial constraints on retrials.* In cases where a hung jury results in a mistrial, the state is usually permitted to retry the defendant in a second trial. What result if a series of trials result in a series of hung juries? May the state simply continue to retry the defendant indefinitely as long as the jury does not return a verdict of acquittal? Some courts might step in and prohibit a retrial in the interests of justice. For example, in *United States v. Ingram*, 412 F. Supp. 384, 386 (D.D.C. 1976), a federal district court ordered the dismissal of a case against a defendant facing a third trial. In the first trial, the jury voted for acquittal 10-2, and in the second trial the jury voted 11-1 in favor of acquittal. The court refused to permit a third trial, concluding that "[t]o permit a retrial, after 21 of 24 jurors have already refused to convict, is to ignore the reasonable doubt standard." *Id.* at 386.

STATE LAW REQUIREMENTS

States impose different requirements for jury sizes depending on the type of case. For example, Arizona requires a 12-person jury for all cases that could result in a death sentence or incarceration of at least 30 years. All other criminal cases have juries with eight individuals. Ariz. Rev. Stat. § 21-102. However, the majority of states require juries of 12 in *felony* cases. Several states allow smaller jury sizes for misdemeanor cases. See Bureau of Justice Statistics, *State Court Organization, 2011* (November 2013).

2. Unanimity

Does the jury need to unanimously agree on a conviction or may it convict a defendant based on a majority or super-majority vote? For the defendant facing a substantial prison term if convicted, this is no mere theoretical distinction. If all that is required to avoid conviction is one vote of not guilty, the defense may channel its trial strategy toward finding that one vote. On the other hand, if the prosecution can convict the defendant even when multiple jurors vote for acquittal, the prognosis for the defendant at trial begins to look grim. In addition to other considerations, these facts will certainly alter the calculus that both sides use when they go into plea bargaining. Consequently, requiring unanimity will arguably result in more acquittals and also result in more favorable plea deals for defendants. Conversely, permitting non-unanimity will result in more convictions and also result in more favorable plea deals for prosecutors. In the following case, the Supreme Court asks whether unanimity is simply an accidental feature of our common law past or whether it is a constitutional requirement that states are prohibited from revising.

Apodaca v. Oregon

Supreme Court of the United States
406 U.S. 404 (1972)

Mr. Justice WHITE announced the judgment of the Court in an opinion in which THE CHIEF JUSTICE, Mr. Justice BLACKMUN, and Mr. Justice REHNQUIST joined.

Robert Apodaca, Henry Morgan Cooper, Jr., and James Arnold Madden were convicted respectively of assault with a deadly weapon, burglary in a dwelling, and grand larceny before separate Oregon juries, all of which returned less-than-unanimous verdicts. The vote in the cases of Apodaca and Madden was 11-1, while the vote in the case of Cooper was 10-2, the minimum requisite vote under Oregon law for sustaining a conviction. After their convictions had been affirmed by the Oregon Court of Appeals, and review had been denied by the Supreme Court of Oregon, all three sought review in this Court upon a claim that conviction of crime by a less-than-unanimous jury violates the right to trial by jury in criminal cases specified by the Sixth Amendment and made applicable to the States by the Fourteenth. . . .

In *Williams v. Florida*, 399 U.S. 78 (1970), we had occasion to consider a related issue: whether the Sixth Amendment's right to trial by jury requires that all juries consist of 12 men. After considering the history of the 12-man requirement and the functions it performs in contemporary society, we concluded that it was not of constitutional stature. We reach the same conclusion today with regard to the requirement of unanimity.

I

Like the requirement that juries consist of 12 men, the requirement of unanimity arose during the Middle Ages and had become an accepted feature of the common-law jury by the 18th century. But, as we observed in *Williams*, "the relevant constitutional history casts considerable doubt on the easy assumption . . . that if a given feature existed in a jury at common law in 1789, then it was necessarily preserved in the Constitution." . . .

II

Our inquiry must focus upon the function served by the jury in contemporary society. As we said in *Duncan*, the purpose of trial by jury is to prevent oppression by the Government by providing a "safeguard against the corrupt or overzealous prosecutor and against the complaint, biased, or eccentric judge." "Given this purpose, the essential feature of a jury obviously lies in the interposition between the accused and his accuser of the commonsense judgment of a group of laymen. . . ." A requirement of unanimity, however, does not materially contribute to the exercise of this commonsense judgment. As we said in *Williams*, a jury will come to such a judgment as long as it consists of a group of laymen representative of a cross section of the community who have the duty and the opportunity to deliberate, free from outside attempts at intimidation, on the question of a defendant's guilt. In terms of this function we perceive no difference between juries required to act unanimously and those permitted to convict or acquit by votes of 10 to two or 11 to one. Requiring unanimity would obviously produce hung juries in some situations where nonunanimous juries will convict or acquit. But in either case, the interest of the defendant in having the judgment of his peers interposed between himself and the officers of the State who prosecute and judge him is equally well served.

III

Petitioners nevertheless argue that unanimity serves other purposes constitutionally essential to the continued operation of the jury system. Their principal contention is that a Sixth Amendment "jury trial" made mandatory on the States by virtue of the Due Process Clause of the Fourteenth Amendment should be held to require a unanimous jury verdict in order to give substance to the reasonable-doubt standard otherwise mandated by the Due Process Clause. See *In re Winship*, 397 U.S. 358 (1970).

We are quite sure, however, that the Sixth Amendment itself has never been held to require proof beyond a reasonable doubt in criminal cases. The reasonable-doubt standard developed separately from both the jury trial and the unanimous verdict. As the Court noted in the *Winship* case, the rule requiring proof of crime beyond a reasonable doubt did not crystallize in this country until after the Constitution was adopted. And in that case, which held such a burden of proof to be constitutionally required, the Court purported to draw no support from the Sixth Amendment.

Petitioners' argument that the Sixth Amendment requires jury unanimity in order to give effect to the reasonable-doubt standard thus founders on the fact that the Sixth Amendment does not require proof beyond a reasonable doubt at all. The reasonable-doubt argument is rooted, in effect, in due process and has been rejected in *Johnson v. Louisiana*, 406 U.S. 356.

IV

Petitioners also cite quite accurately a long line of decisions of this Court upholding the principle that the Fourteenth Amendment requires jury panels to reflect a cross section of the community. They then contend that unanimity is a necessary precondition for effective application of the cross-section requirement, because a rule permitting less than unanimous verdicts will make it possible for convictions to occur without the acquiescence of minority elements within the community.

There are two flaws in this argument. One is petitioners' assumption that every distinct voice in the community has a right to be represented on every jury and a right to prevent conviction of a defendant in any case. All that the Constitution forbids, however, is systematic exclusion of identifiable segments of the community from jury panels and from the juries ultimately drawn from those panels; a defendant may not, for example, challenge the makeup of a jury merely because no members of his race are on the jury, but must prove that his race has been systematically excluded. No group, in short, has the right to block convictions; it has only the right to participate in the overall legal processes by which criminal guilt and innocence are determined.

We also cannot accept petitioners' second assumption—that minority groups, even when they are represented on a jury, will not adequately represent the viewpoint of those groups simply because they may be outvoted in the final result. They will be present during all deliberations, and their views will be heard. We cannot assume that the majority of the jury will refuse to weigh the evidence and reach a decision upon rational grounds, just as it must now do in order to obtain unanimous verdicts, or that a majority will deprive a man of his liberty on the basis of prejudice when a minority is presenting a reasonable argument in favor of acquittal. We simply find no proof for the notion that a majority will disregard its instructions and cast its votes for guilt or innocence based on prejudice rather than the evidence. . . .

NOTES & QUESTIONS ON UNANIMITY

1. *Sixth Amendment.* Why did the Court decide that the Sixth Amendment right to a jury trial does not require unanimous verdicts? Is the concept of unanimity logically entailed by the concept of a jury trial? Alternatively, is unanimity logically required by the notion of due process of law?

2. *Powell's concurrence.* The opinion excerpted above is a plurality opinion representing the views of four Justices. Justice Powell provided the fifth vote for the court's holding that Oregon's law did not violate due process. While he voted with the plurality, Powell's rationale was unique, insofar as he concluded that the Sixth Amendment required unanimity in federal cases but that

the Fourteenth Amendment did not incorporate this requirement against the states. It is sometimes stated that *Apodaca* held that the Sixth Amendment requires jury unanimity in federal cases. But that is an imprecise statement. It is more accurate to say that there were five votes for the proposition that the Sixth Amendment requires unanimity in federal cases, but the Court's four-vote plurality opinion rejected this point.

3. *Manner and means.* Although a jury is required to vote unanimously in favor of conviction, the jurors need not be unanimous about the underlying theory supporting the conviction. For example, a single indictment might charge the defendant with committing felony murder by virtue of multiple triggering felonies. If some jurors believe that the defendant should be convicted of felony murder based on an underlying sexual assault, while other jurors believe the defendant should be convicted of felony murder based on robbery, is this sufficient to qualify as unanimity? Courts have upheld this result as long as the jurors all agree on the resulting conviction, even if there is underlying disagreement about the mode of commission. As the Supreme Court has remarked:

> We have never suggested that in returning general verdicts in such cases the jurors should be required to agree upon a single means of commission, any more than the indictments were required to specify one alone. In these cases, as in litigation generally, "different jurors may be persuaded by different pieces of evidence, even when they agree upon the bottom line. Plainly there is no general requirement that the jury reach agreement on the preliminary factual issues which underlie the verdict."

Schad v. Arizona, 501 U.S. 624, 631-32 (1991), quoting *McKoy v. North Carolina,* 494 U.S. 433, 449 (1990) (Blackmun, J., concurring). See also *Kitchens v. State,* 823 S.W.2d 256, 258 (Tex. Crim. App. 1991); *Jacobsen v. State,* 325 S.W.3d 733, 736 (Tex. App. 2010). Another way of putting the point is that the government must prove every element beyond a reasonable doubt, but this does not entail that the jury must agree on every fact or every legal theory that the state asserts at trial. Do you agree that jury unanimity on the manner of commission is not required?

4. *Relationship to the standard of proof.* Does the requirement of unanimity help maintain a high standard of proof for conviction in criminal cases? Recall that the Supreme Court has concluded that the Sixth Amendment right to a jury trial does not require unanimity. But consider again the concept of due process embodied in the Fifth and Fourteenth Amendments. If due process entails that convictions require a jury finding of proof beyond a reasonable doubt, might jury unanimity help ensure that jurors are convinced to this degree of certainty? Or is the issue of jury unanimity simply a function of the number of jurors who are convinced and independent of their *level* of certainty?

STATE LAW REQUIREMENTS

Almost every state requires unanimous jury verdicts in criminal cases, and in some jurisdictions the requirement flows from state constitutional law. For example, Texas courts have concluded that jury unanimity is required in all state felony cases. See Tex. Const. art. V, § 13; *Jacobsen v. State*, 325 S.W.3d 733, 736 (Tex. App. 2010).

But the unanimity rule is not universal. Historically, the two outliers were Louisiana and Oregon—the latter jurisdiction being at issue in the *Apodaca* case. In 1898, Louisiana adopted a state constitution that permitted 9-3 jury verdicts in felony cases. In 2018, Louisiana voters repealed the provision and reinstated the requirement of unanimous jury verdicts. The original 1898 law was widely viewed by supporters of the change as racially motivated. Without slavery there was a labor shortage on plantations, with the main source of labor coming from convicts on work-release programs, most of whom were African-American inmates. The assumption behind the law was that non-unanimous jury verdicts would increase the number of convictions of African-Americans. As one state court judge wrote in an opinion holding that unanimity was constitutionally required:

> The convict-lease program was instituted in Louisiana to recreate free black labor, more or less. Convicts were leased out to white companies and landowners for a nominal fee and had no protections against abuse. In order to Redeem the South, free African-American labor was absolutely necessary. By creating a system where white supremacists could convict African-Americans with 25 percent of the jury dissenting, Louisiana could achieve its desired free labor pool. . . . [T]here was no possibility that the non-unanimous verdict scheme was race-neutral good governance . . . it was absolutely motivated by invidious racial discrimination.

Louisiana v. Melvin Cartez Maxie (11th Judicial District, Oct. 11, 2018). The decision relied heavily on the work of historian Thomas Aiello and his book *Jim Crow's Last Stand.* A few days later, Louisiana voters went to the polls and repealed the provision at issue, after an extensive grass-roots political campaign to revise the statute. In contrast, Oregon's non-unanimous jury verdict statute dates back to 1934, though scholars have also argued that it was motivated by racial animus. With the recent repeal of Louisiana's provision, the pressure on Oregon to repeal its provision will no doubt intensify. See R.J. Vogt, *Pressure Grows on Oregon to End Non-Unanimous Verdicts,* Law360.com, Nov. 18, 2018.

The leasing or sale of convicts to commercial enterprises to recreate slavery and its market of free black labor was common in several Southern states, not just Louisiana. See Douglas A. Blackmon, *Slavery by Another Name* (2008).

3. The Reasonable Doubt Standard

When the jury returns a verdict, what standard of proof is required for a conviction? More than any piece of evidence, often what determines the outcome of the trial is the standard of proof. In the following case, the Supreme Court must determine whether the popular "proof beyond a reasonable doubt" standard is constitutionally required or whether a state could, consistent with the Constitution, apply a lesser standard of "preponderance of the evidence" in its criminal trials. Doing so would presumably increase the number of convictions returned, but would it be consistent with the requirements of due process in the criminal justice system?

In re Winship

Supreme Court of the United States
397 U.S. 358 (1970)

Mr. Justice Brennan delivered the opinion of the Court.

Constitutional questions decided by this Court concerning the juvenile process have centered on the adjudicatory stage at "which a determination is made as to whether a juvenile is a 'delinquent' as a result of alleged misconduct on his part, with the consequence that he may be committed to a state institution." *In re Gault*, 387 U.S. 1, 13 (1967). *Gault* decided that, although the Fourteenth Amendment does not require that the hearing at this stage conform with all the requirements of a criminal trial or even of the usual administrative proceeding, the Due Process Clause does require application during the adjudicatory hearing of "the essentials of due process and fair treatment." This case presents the single, narrow question whether proof beyond a reasonable doubt is among the "essentials of due process and fair treatment" required during the adjudicatory stage when a juvenile is charged with an act which would constitute a crime if committed by an adult.

Section 712 of the New York Family Court Act defines a juvenile delinquent as "a person over seven and less than sixteen years of age who does any act which, if done by an adult, would constitute a crime." During a 1967 adjudicatory hearing, conducted pursuant to s 742 of the Act, a judge in New York Family Court found that appellant, then a 12-year-old boy, had entered a locker and stolen $112 from a woman's pocketbook. The petition which charged appellant with delinquency alleged that his act, "if done by an adult, would constitute the crime or crimes of Larceny." The judge acknowledged that the proof might not establish guilt beyond a reasonable doubt, but rejected appellant's contention that such proof was required by the Fourteenth Amendment. The judge relied instead on s 744(b) of the New York Family Court Act which provides that "(a)ny determination at the conclusion of (an adjudicatory) hearing that a (juvenile) did an act or acts must be based on a preponderance of the evidence." During a subsequent dispositional hearing, appellant was ordered placed in a training school for an initial period of 18 months, subject to annual extensions of his commitment until his 18th birthday—six years in appellant's case. . . .

I

The requirement that guilt of a criminal charge be established by proof beyond a reasonable doubt dates at least from our early years as a Nation. The "demand for a higher degree of persuasion in criminal cases was recurrently expressed from ancient times, (though) its crystallization into the formula 'beyond a reasonable doubt' seems to have occurred as late as 1798. It is now accepted in common law jurisdictions as the measure of persuasion by which the prosecution must convince the trier of all the essential elements of guilt." Although virtually unanimous adherence to the reasonable-doubt standard in common-law jurisdictions may not conclusively establish it as a requirement of due process, such adherence does "reflect a profound judgment about the way in which law should be enforced and justice administered." *Duncan v. Louisiana*, 391 U.S. 145, 155 (1968).

Expressions in many opinions of this Court indicate that it has long been assumed that proof of a criminal charge beyond a reasonable doubt is constitutionally required. Mr. Justice Frankfurter stated that "(i)t the duty of the Government to establish . . . guilt beyond a reasonable doubt. This notion—basic in our law and rightly one of the boasts of a free society—is a requirement and a safeguard of due process of law in the historic, procedural content of 'due process.'" *Leland v. Oregon*, 343 U.S., at 802-803 (dissenting opinion). In a similar vein, the Court said in *Brinegar v. United States*, 338 U.S., at 174, that "(g)uilt in a criminal case must be proved beyond a reasonable doubt and by evidence confined to that which long experience in the common-law tradition, to some extent embodied in the Constitution, has crystallized into rules of evidence consistent with that standard. These rules are historically grounded rights of our system, developed to safeguard men from dubious and unjust convictions, with resulting forfeitures of life, liberty and property." *Davis v. United States*, 160 U.S., at 488, stated that the requirement is implicit in "constitutions . . . (which) recognize the fundamental principles that are deemed essential for the protection of life and liberty." In *Davis* a murder conviction was reversed because the trial judge instructed the jury that it was their duty to convict when the evidence was equally balanced regarding the sanity of the accused. This Court said: "On the contrary, he is entitled to an acquittal of the specific crime charged, if upon all the evidence, there is reasonable doubt whether he was capable in law of committing crime. . . . No man should be deprived of his life under the forms of law unless the jurors who try him are able, upon their consciences, to say that the evidence before them . . . is sufficient to show beyond a reasonable doubt the existence of every fact necessary to constitute the crime charged."

The reasonable-doubt standard plays a vital role in the American scheme of criminal procedure. It is a prime instrument for reducing the risk of convictions resting on factual error. The standard provides concrete substance for the presumption of innocence—that bedrock "axiomatic and elementary" principle whose "enforcement lies at the foundation of the administration of our criminal law." As the dissenters in the New York Court of Appeals observed, and we agree, "a person accused of a crime . . . would be at a severe disadvantage, a disadvantage amounting to a lack of fundamental fairness, if he could be adjudged guilty and imprisoned for years on the strength of the same evidence as would suffice in a civil case."

The requirement of proof beyond a reasonable doubt has this vital role in our criminal procedure for cogent reasons. The accused during a criminal prosecution has at stake interest of immense importance, both because of the possibility that he may lose his liberty upon conviction and because of the certainty that he would be stigmatized by the conviction. Accordingly, a society that values the good name and freedom of every individual should not condemn a man for commission of a crime when there is reasonable doubt about his guilt. . . .

Moreover, use of the reasonable-doubt standard is indispensable to command the respect and confidence of the community in applications of the criminal law. It is critical that the moral force of the criminal law not be diluted by a standard of proof that leaves people in doubt whether innocent men are being condemned. It is also important in our free society that every individual going about his ordinary affairs have confidence that his government cannot adjudge him guilty of a criminal offense without convincing a proper factfinder of his guilt with utmost certainty.

Lest there remain any doubt about the constitutional stature of the reasonable-doubt standard, we explicitly hold that the Due Process Clause protects the accused against conviction except upon proof beyond a reasonable doubt of every fact necessary to constitute the crime with which he is charged. . . .

II

. . . Finally, we reject the Court of Appeals' suggestion that there is, in any event, only a "tenuous difference" between the reasonable-doubt and preponderance standards. The suggestion is singularly unpersuasive. In this very case, the trial judge's ability to distinguish between the two standards enabled him to make a finding of guilt that he conceded he might not have made under the standard of proof beyond a reasonable doubt. Indeed, the trial judge's action evidences the accuracy of the observation of commentators that "the preponderance test is susceptible to the misinterpretation that it calls on the trier of fact merely to perform an abstract weighing of the evidence in order to determine which side has produced the greater quantum, without regard to its effect in convincing his mind of the truth of the proposition asserted." . . .

NOTES & QUESTIONS ON REASONABLE DOUBT

1. *Defining reasonable doubt.* Although the Supreme Court in *Winship* declared that proof beyond a reasonable doubt is constitutionally required in criminal cases, the Supreme Court did not define the standard with more precise language. Inevitably, judges struggle with how to define the "reasonable doubt." For example, in *Cage v. Louisiana*, the Supreme Court considered the following jury instruction:

> If you entertain a reasonable doubt as to any fact or element necessary to constitute the defendant's guilt, it is your duty to give him the benefit of that doubt and return a verdict of not guilty. Even where the evidence demonstrates a probability of guilt, if it does not establish such guilt beyond a reasonable doubt, you must acquit the accused. This doubt, however, must be a reasonable one; that is one that is founded upon a real tangible substantial basis and not upon mere caprice and conjecture. It must be such doubt as would give rise to a grave uncertainty, raised in your mind by reasons of the unsatisfactory character of the evidence or lack thereof. A reasonable doubt is not a mere possible doubt. It is an actual substantial doubt. It is a doubt that a reasonable man can seriously entertain. What is required is not an absolute or mathematical certainty, but a moral certainty.

498 U.S. 39, 40 (1990). The Supreme Court concluded that the instruction altered, rather than explained, the reasonable doubt standard, particularly with regard to the language of a "grave uncertainty." On the other hand, courts have usually upheld jury instructions that use terms like "honest" or "conscientious" doubt. See, e.g., *State v. Cervantes*, 87 Wash. App. 440, 447, 942 P.2d 382, 385 (1997).

2. *Quantification of the standard.* Furthermore, when judges attempt to quantify reasonable doubt in numerical terms they are inevitably overturned on appeal. So, for a judge, the safest route to avoid a reversal on appeal is to either steadfastly refuse to define reasonable doubt or to resort to a restatement of sorts: Proof beyond a reasonable doubt is not proof that is beyond all doubt, nor does it require absolute certainly; it permits doubts that are reasonable. What counts as reasonable under the circumstances of the case is for the jury to decide. Any definition that is more explicit than that inevitably risks *changing* the standard rather than *defining* it. Indeed, "the better practice is to give no definition of reasonable doubt at all to the jury." *Paulson v. State*, 28 S.W.3d 570, 573 (Tex. Crim. App. 2000). Do you agree that reasonable doubt is beyond definition? For an argument against quantifying standards of decision, consider the following from Professor Clermont:

> [L]awmakers could begin to state the standards in numerical terms. That, however, would not be wise, at least in our prevailing legal system. First,

> quantification by itself imposes some costs in terms of accuracy and other values—arguably by such effects as inaccurate meshing with soft or unquantifiable variables and the dehumanization of the legal process—even though theorists often overstate those costs. Second, expressly translating a level of probability into something like a point estimate could be illusory, because probability in connection with standards of decision is a complex concept. Third, there is no convincing reason to expect that quantification would effectively invoke our imprecise internal scale of judgment, or otherwise accord with our ingrained way of thinking.

Kevin M. Clermont, *Procedure's Magical Number Three: Psychological Bases for Standards of Decision*, 72 Cornell L. Rev. 1115, 1147-48 (1987).

3. *Harmless error?* A flawed instruction to a jury regarding the belief beyond a reasonable doubt standard is a "structural" error that cannot be deemed harmless. In other words, if an appellate court concludes that a judge misinstructed the jury regarding proof beyond a reasonable doubt, a new trial must be ordered. There is no room for the judge to conclude that the jury would have convicted the defendant anyway even if properly instructed on reasonable doubt. See *Sullivan v. Louisiana*, 508 U.S. 275, 281 (1993).

4. *Crime control or due process.* Does one's attitude about the correct standard of proof track Herbert Packer's two models of criminal procedure? In Chapter 1, Packer argued that the criminal could be viewed through two lenses: a crime control model designed to protect the community or a due process model designed to protect the rights of defendants. If the criminal law is about crime control, we should make convictions easier to obtain, which suggests that we should water down the reasonable doubt requirement. On the other hand, the due process model suggests that we should zealously guard the reasonable doubt standard against these incursions. How should the law balance these competing desiderata? Is proof beyond a reasonable doubt the outcome of this balancing process? Does it strike the right balance?

5. *Proof beyond a reasonable doubt in campus adjudication.* What should be the standard of proof in campus proceedings to find a student responsible for sexual assault? During the Obama Administration, the Office of Civil Rights within the Department of Education released a "Dear Colleague" letter that advised colleges and universities that Title IX required that campus adjudication proceedings should determine responsibility based on the "preponderance of the evidence" standard. The reasoning was explicitly outcome-oriented; under the preponderance standard, the allegations by complainants would be more likely to be sustained, resulting in sanctions against respondents, up to and including expulsion from the school. Many colleges and universities responded to the Dear Colleague letter by lowering the standard of proof as suggested, though this prompted criticism that the standard was too lax and not in keeping

with prevailing standards of criminal justice articulated in *Winship*. Several respondents who were expelled from universities filed lawsuits arguing due process violations. Advocates of the preponderance standard responded that *Winship* and the reasonable doubt standard apply in criminal cases yielding criminal punishment and concluded that expulsion from a university should not be equated with state sponsored criminal punishment. In other words, the preponderance standard was appropriate for administrative hearings convened by educational institutions. In 2018, the Office of Civil Rights under Betsy DeVos released new proposed regulations suggesting that universities have the freedom to choose between a preponderance standard or a more demanding "clear and convincing proof" standard. Which standard is most appropriate for this context?

C. JURY SELECTION

Before a jury trial can begin, the trial judge must oversee the jury selection process. That process begins with the assembly of a jury venire—the pool of community members who have been called to courthouse to take part of the jury selection process. Typically, an office in the court oversees this process by sending out notices to individuals calling them to appear at the court on a particular day for potential jury service. Although practices differ, the names and addresses for this process might be culled from the records of the Department of Motor Vehicles or voting registration records. In *Strauder v. West Virginia*, 100 U.S. 303 (1879), the Supreme Court struck down a state statute that limited jury service to white men as a violation of the Fourteenth Amendment.

Once at the courthouse, members of the venire will participate in the jury selection process for individual trials. Venire members will be brought into the courtroom where the judge, prosecutor, defense attorney, and defendant will be present. The process will usually begin with an address by the judge to the members of the venire, who will usually be sitting in the jury box. At that point, both the prosecutor and the defense attorney will question the venire members about a wide range of topics. Questions might include past experiences they have had with the police or prosecutors, whether they or their family members have ever been victimized by criminal behavior, and their views on conduct that might be at issue in the trial (such as the taking of drugs). For example, if a potential jury member states that they do not believe that narcotics should be illegal and that the state has no business criminalizing consensual conduct, the prosecutor might want to know this.

After the questioning of the jury pool is complete, the prosecutor, defense attorney, and judge will usually confer privately to discuss which members of the jury pool should be included in the jury. The process begins with the judge asking about the first member of the jury pool. If neither side objects, that individual is seated on the jury. This continues until the court has assembled a full jury. Each side will have an unlimited number of challenges "for cause" and a certain number of "peremptory challenges." Challenges for cause involve jurors who have demonstrated, through the questioning process, that they will have difficulty applying the judge's instructions on the law or difficulty deliberating objectively. The hypothetical case above about the juror who does not believe in drug offenses might be one example where a judge might grant a prosecution request to dismiss the juror for cause. Similarly, if a potential juror is a former police officer who states that "police officers always tell the truth," the defense might ask that the trial judge dismiss that individual as well.

After the trial judge rules on these challenges for cause, the discussion will turn to peremptory challenges. Each side can exercise these challenges for strategic gain: to cull members from the jury pool that the lawyer believes, either from empirical research or just from a hunch, will be unsympathetic to the lawyer's presentation of the case. In other words, the defense will use peremptory challenges to get rid of potential jurors who are predicted to view the defendant harshly, while prosecutors will use peremptory challenges to get rid of potential jurors who are predicted to be sympathetic. Once the trial judge accepts the peremptory challenges, the remaining members are selected for the jury. If the number of selected jurors is too small to make up a full jury, the judge will ask the bailiff to bring in another group of potential jurors from the venire and seat them in the courtroom, at which point the process will begin again. The jury selection process might take a few minutes, or it might take an entire day, depending in part on how many are dismissed for cause.

Although prosecutors and defense attorneys who exercise a peremptory challenge are not required to articulate a "cause" for dismissing an individual from the jury, this is not to say that these challenges are beyond legal scrutiny. As the following materials make clear, the Fourteenth Amendment prohibits trial judges from accepting a peremptory challenge when the lawyer has deployed that peremptory challenge in a discriminatory way. The following subsections focus specifically on (1) prohibited racial discrimination; (2) prohibited gender discrimination; and (3) the question of whether age discrimination violates the Fourteenth Amendment.

STATUTORY REQUIREMENTS

Although some states leave it to case law to define what qualifies as a challenge for "cause," other states have codified criteria by statute. For example, Indiana lists the following among the appropriate reasons to dismiss a potential juror for cause in a criminal case. Cause is warranted if the individual

has formed or expressed an opinion about the outcome of the case, and is unable to set that opinion aside and render an impartial verdict based upon the law and the evidence;
was a member of a jury that previously considered the same dispute involving one or more of the same parties;
is related within the fifth degree to the parties, their attorneys, or any witness subpoenaed in the case;
has a personal interest in the result of the trial;
is biased or prejudiced for or against a party to the case;
is a person who has been subpoenaed in good faith as a witness in the case;
was a member of the grand jury that issued the indictment;
is a defendant in a pending criminal case;
in a case in which the death penalty is sought, is not qualified to serve in a death penalty case under law; or
has formed or expressed an opinion about the outcome of the case which appears to be founded upon a) a conversation with a witness to the transaction; b) reading or hearing witness testimony or a report of witness testimony.

Indiana Jury Rule 17. "Qualified to serve in a death penalty case" is a technical term that refers to someone who is willing to hand down a death sentence, i.e., not categorically opposed to the death penalty in all circumstances. Notice that while some of the categories are very specific and can be mechanically applied, the prohibition against being "biased" or "prejudiced" against a party is not otherwise defined by this statute and requires application of the facts at hand.

1. Racial Discrimination

In the following case, the Supreme Court considers the standard for reviewing a defendant's claim that the prosecutor impermissibly excluded African-Americans from the jury. As noted below, the Supreme Court concluded in *Swain v. Alabama*, 380 U.S. 202 (1965), that a defendant would need to present evidence of systematic discrimination by prosecutors in a number of cases to prevail on a Fourteenth Amendment challenge. In *Batson*, the Supreme Court reconsidered that position. As you read the case, look for the new standard that replaces the standard in *Swain*. In articulating that new standard, what does the Supreme Court view as the particular harm of racial discrimination in jury selection? Whose rights are violated—the defendant's or the excluded juror's?

Batson v. Kentucky

Supreme Court of the United States
476 U.S. 79 (1986)

Justice Powell delivered the opinion of the Court.

This case requires us to reexamine that portion of *Swain v. Alabama*, 380 U.S. 202 (1965), concerning the evidentiary burden placed on a criminal defendant who claims that he has been denied equal protection through the State's use of peremptory challenges to exclude members of his race from the petit jury.

I

Petitioner, a black man, was indicted in Kentucky on charges of second-degree burglary and receipt of stolen goods. On the first day of trial in Jefferson Circuit Court, the judge conducted voir dire examination of the venire, excused certain jurors for cause, and permitted the parties to exercise peremptory challenges. The prosecutor used his peremptory challenges to strike all four black persons on the venire, and a jury composed only of white persons was selected. Defense counsel moved to discharge the jury before it was sworn on the ground that the prosecutor's removal of the black veniremen violated petitioner's rights under the Sixth and Fourteenth Amendments to a jury drawn from a cross section of the community, and under the Fourteenth Amendment to equal protection of the laws. Counsel requested a hearing on his motion. Without expressly ruling on the request for a hearing, the trial judge observed that the parties were entitled to use their peremptory challenges to "strike anybody they want to." The judge then denied petitioner's motion, reasoning that the cross-section requirement applies only to selection of the venire and not to selection of the petit jury itself. The jury convicted petitioner on both counts. . . .

II

In *Swain v. Alabama*, this Court recognized that a "State's purposeful or deliberate denial to Negroes on account of race of participation as jurors in the administration of justice violates the Equal Protection Clause." 380 U.S., at 203-204. This principle has been "consistently and repeatedly" reaffirmed in numerous decisions of this Court both preceding and following *Swain*. We reaffirm the principle today.

More than a century ago, the Court decided that the State denies a black defendant equal protection of the laws when it puts him on trial before a jury from which members of his race have been purposefully excluded. *Strauder v. West Virginia*, 100 U.S. 303 (1880). That decision laid the foundation for the Court's unceasing efforts to eradicate racial discrimination in the procedures used to select the venire from which individual jurors are drawn. In *Strauder*, the Court explained that the central concern of the recently ratified Fourteenth Amendment was to put an end to governmental discrimination on account of race. Exclusion of black citizens from service as jurors constitutes a primary example of the evil the Fourteenth Amendment was designed to cure.

In holding that racial discrimination in jury selection offends the Equal Protection Clause, the Court in *Strauder* recognized, however, that a defendant has no right to a "petit jury composed in whole or in part of persons of his own race." "The number of our races and nationalities stands in the way of evolution of such a conception" of the demand of equal protection. But the defendant does have the right to be tried by a jury whose members are selected pursuant to nondiscriminatory criteria. The Equal Protection Clause guarantees the defendant that the State will not exclude members of his race from the jury venire on account of race or on the false assumption that members of his race as a group are not qualified to serve as jurors.

Purposeful racial discrimination in selection of the venire violates a defendant's right to equal protection because it denies him the protection that a trial by jury is intended to secure. "The very idea of a jury is a body . . . composed of the peers or equals of the person whose rights it is selected or summoned to determine; that is, of his neighbors, fellows, associates, persons having the same legal status in society as that which he holds." The petit jury has occupied a central position in our system of justice by safeguarding a person accused of crime against the arbitrary exercise of power by prosecutor or judge. Those on the venire must be "indifferently chosen," to secure the defendant's right under the Fourteenth Amendment to "protection of life and liberty against race or color prejudice."

Racial discrimination in selection of jurors harms not only the accused whose life or liberty they are summoned to try. Competence to serve as a juror ultimately depends on an assessment of individual qualifications and ability impartially to consider evidence presented at a trial. A person's race simply "is unrelated to his fitness as a juror." As long ago as *Strauder*, therefore, the Court recognized that by denying a person participation in jury service on account of his race, the State unconstitutionally discriminated against the excluded juror.

The harm from discriminatory jury selection extends beyond that inflicted on the defendant and the excluded juror to touch the entire community. Selection procedures that purposefully exclude black persons from juries undermine public confidence in the fairness of our system of justice. Discrimination within the judicial system is most pernicious because it is "a stimulant to that race prejudice which is an impediment to securing to [black citizens] that equal justice which the law aims to secure to all others."

In *Strauder*, the Court invalidated a state statute that provided that only white men could serve as jurors. We can be confident that no State now has such a law. The Constitution requires, however, that we look beyond the face of the statute defining juror qualifications and also consider challenged selection practices to afford "protection against action of the State through its administrative officers in effecting the prohibited discrimination." Thus, the Court has found a denial of equal protection where the procedures implementing a neutral statute operated to exclude persons from the venire on racial grounds, and has made clear that the Constitution prohibits all forms of purposeful racial discrimination in selection of jurors. While decisions of this Court have been concerned largely with discrimination during selection of the venire, the principles announced there also forbid discrimination on account of race in selection of the petit jury. Since the Fourteenth Amendment protects an accused throughout the proceedings bringing him to justice, the State may not draw up its jury lists pursuant to neutral procedures but then resort to discrimination at "other stages in the selection process."

Accordingly, the component of the jury selection process at issue here, the State's privilege to strike individual jurors through peremptory challenges, is subject to the commands of the Equal Protection Clause. Although a prosecutor ordinarily is entitled to exercise permitted peremptory challenges "for any reason at all, as long as that reason is related to his view concerning the outcome" of the case to be tried, the Equal Protection Clause forbids the prosecutor to challenge potential jurors solely on account of their race or on the assumption that black jurors as a group will be unable impartially to consider the State's case against a black defendant.

III

The principles announced in *Strauder* never have been questioned in any subsequent decision of this Court. Rather, the Court has been called upon repeatedly to review the application of those principles to particular facts. A recurring question in these cases, as in any case alleging a violation of the Equal Protection Clause, was whether the defendant had met his burden of proving purposeful discrimination on the part of the State. That question also was at the heart of the portion of *Swain v. Alabama* we reexamine today.

Swain required the Court to decide, among other issues, whether a black defendant was denied equal protection by the State's exercise of peremptory challenges to exclude members of his race from the petit jury. The record in *Swain* showed that the prosecutor had used the State's peremptory challenges to strike the six black persons included on the petit jury venire. While rejecting the defendant's claim for failure to prove purposeful discrimination, the Court nonetheless indicated that the Equal Protection Clause placed some limits on the State's exercise of peremptory challenges.

The Court sought to accommodate the prosecutor's historical privilege of peremptory challenge free of judicial control and the constitutional prohibition on exclusion of persons from jury service on account of race. While the Constitution does not confer a right to peremptory challenges, those challenges traditionally have been viewed as one means of assuring the selection of a qualified and unbiased jury. To preserve the peremptory nature of the prosecutor's challenge, the Court in *Swain* declined to scrutinize his actions in a particular case by relying on a presumption that he properly exercised the State's challenges.

The Court went on to observe, however, that a State may not exercise its challenges in contravention of the Equal Protection Clause. It was impermissible for a prosecutor to use his challenges to exclude blacks from the jury "for reasons wholly unrelated to the outcome of the particular case on trial" or to deny to blacks "the same right and opportunity to participate in the administration of justice enjoyed by the white population." Accordingly, a black defendant could make out a prima facie case of purposeful discrimination on proof that the peremptory challenge system was "being perverted" in that manner. For example, an inference of purposeful discrimination would be raised on evidence that a prosecutor, "in case after case, whatever the circumstances, whatever the crime and whoever the defendant or the victim may be, is responsible for the removal of Negroes who have been selected as qualified jurors by the jury commissioners and who have survived challenges for cause, with the result that no Negroes ever serve on petit juries." Evidence offered by the defendant in *Swain* did not meet that standard. While the defendant showed that prosecutors in the jurisdiction had exercised their strikes to exclude blacks from the jury, he offered no proof of the circumstances under which prosecutors were responsible for striking black jurors beyond the facts of his own case.

A number of lower courts following the teaching of *Swain* reasoned that proof of repeated striking of blacks over a number of cases was necessary to establish a violation of the Equal Protection Clause. Since this interpretation of *Swain* has placed on defendants a crippling burden of proof, prosecutors' peremptory challenges are now largely immune from constitutional scrutiny. For reasons that follow, we reject this evidentiary formulation as inconsistent with standards that have been developed since *Swain* for assessing a prima facie case under the Equal Protection Clause. . . .

The standards for assessing a prima facie case in the context of discriminatory selection of the venire have been fully articulated since *Swain*. These principles support our conclusion that a defendant may establish a prima facie case of purposeful discrimination in selection of the petit jury solely on evidence concerning the prosecutor's exercise of peremptory challenges at the defendant's trial. To establish such a case, the defendant first must show that he is a member of a cognizable racial group and that the prosecutor has exercised peremptory challenges to remove from the venire members of the defendant's race. Second, the defendant is entitled to rely on the fact, as to which there can be no dispute, that peremptory challenges constitute a jury selection practice that permits "those to discriminate who are of a mind to discriminate." Finally, the defendant must show that these facts and any other relevant circumstances raise an inference that the prosecutor used that practice to exclude the veniremen from the petit jury on account of their race. This combination of factors in the empaneling of the petit jury, as in the selection of the venire, raises the necessary inference of purposeful discrimination.

In deciding whether the defendant has made the requisite showing, the trial court should consider all relevant circumstances. For example, a "pattern" of strikes against black jurors included in the particular venire might give rise to an inference of discrimination. Similarly, the prosecutor's questions and statements during voir dire examination and in exercising his challenges may support or refute an inference of discriminatory purpose. These examples are merely illustrative. We have confidence that trial judges, experienced in supervising voir dire, will be able to decide if the circumstances concerning the prosecutor's use of peremptory challenges creates a prima facie case of discrimination against black jurors.

Once the defendant makes a prima facie showing, the burden shifts to the State to come forward with a neutral explanation for challenging black jurors. Though this requirement imposes a limitation in some cases on the full peremptory character of the historic challenge, we emphasize that the prosecutor's explanation need not rise to the level justifying exercise of a challenge for cause. But the prosecutor may not rebut the defendant's prima facie case of discrimination by stating merely that he challenged jurors of the defendant's race on the assumption—or his intuitive judgment—that they would be partial to the defendant because of their shared race. Just as the Equal Protection Clause forbids the States to exclude black persons from the venire on the assumption that blacks as a group are unqualified to serve as jurors, so it forbids the States to strike black veniremen on the assumption that they will be biased in a particular case simply because the defendant is black. The core guarantee of equal protection, ensuring citizens that their State will not discriminate on account of race, would be meaningless were we to approve the exclusion of jurors on the basis of such assumptions, which arise solely from the jurors' race. Nor may the prosecutor rebut the defendant's case merely by denying that he had a discriminatory motive or "affirm[ing] [his] good faith in making individual selections." If these general assertions were accepted as rebutting a defendant's prima facie case, the Equal Protection Clause "would be but a vain and illusory requirement." The prosecutor therefore must articulate a neutral explanation related to the particular case to be tried. The trial court then will have the duty to determine if the defendant has established purposeful discrimination.

IV

The State contends that our holding will eviscerate the fair trial values served by the peremptory challenge. Conceding that the Constitution does not guarantee a right to peremptory challenges and that *Swain* did state that their use ultimately is subject to the strictures of equal protection, the State argues that the privilege of unfettered exercise of the challenge is of vital importance to the criminal justice system.

While we recognize, of course, that the peremptory challenge occupies an important position in our trial procedures, we do not agree that our decision today will undermine the contribution the challenge generally makes to the administration of justice. The reality of practice, amply reflected in many state- and federal-court opinions, shows that the challenge may be, and unfortunately at times has been, used to discriminate against black jurors. By requiring trial courts to be sensitive to the racially discriminatory use of peremptory challenges, our decision enforces the mandate of equal protection and furthers the ends of justice. In view of the heterogeneous population of our Nation, public respect for our criminal justice system and the rule of law will be strengthened if we ensure that no citizen is disqualified from jury service because of his race. . . .

PROBLEM CASE

In 1997, Curtis Flowers went on trial for the 1996 killing of four individuals at a furniture store in Winona, Mississippi. Flowers was convicted and sentenced to death. The Mississippi Supreme Court overturned the conviction because the prosecutor presented prejudicial evidence to the jury. A second trial resulted in a conviction but was also overturned. A third jury, in 2004, convicted Flowers and sentenced him to death. But Flowers attacked the third conviction with a *Batson* challenge, noting that the prosecutor used the vast percentage of his peremptory challenges on African-Americans, with the result that the jury was composed of only two African-American jurors but ten white jurors. The third conviction was again overturned after an appeals court concluded that the prosecutor's race-neutral reasons were a mere pretext for racial discrimination; the court noted that "trial judges should not blindly accept any and every reason put forth by the State, especially where, as here, the State continues to exercise challenge after challenge only upon members of a particular race." *Flowers v. State*, 947 So. 2d 910, 937 (Miss. 2007).

Although the fourth and fifth trials ended in mistrials, attorneys for Flowers maintained that the prosecutor used peremptory challenges to systematically exclude African-Americans from the jury. In 2010, Flowers was convicted and sentenced to death in a sixth trial. Again, Flowers appealed, arguing that the prosecutor's use of peremptory challenges violated *Batson*. The Supreme Court of Mississippi upheld the conviction, concluding that there was insufficient evidence of racial discrimination in the jury selection in the sixth trial alone. *Flowers v. State*, 240 So. 3d 1082 (Miss. 2017).

The Supreme Court granted certiorari, 2018 WL 3159779 (U.S. Nov. 2, 2018), to determine whether a defendant may use evidence of racial discrimination from *prior* trials to establish a pattern of racial discrimination in the use of peremptory challenges or whether a successful *Batson* challenge must be based solely on evidence of racial discrimination from the most recent trial. Which view is correct? Should Flowers be entitled to establish racial discrimination by presenting evidence of the prosecutor's past use of peremptory challenges across all six cases? How would you rule on Flowers's *Batson* challenge?

NOTES & QUESTIONS ON RACIAL DISCRIMINATION

1. *Systematic versus case-specific discriminations. Swain* held that a defendant would need to demonstrate evidence of systematic discrimination—i.e., systematic exclusion of racial minorities as a matter of policy—in order to prevail on a Fourteenth Amendment challenge to the government's use of peremptory challenges. *Batson* changed that. Under *Batson,* the defendant is relieved of the burden of establishing a prima facie equal protection violation because the use of the peremptory challenge against a juror from a class that has historically suffered systematic exclusion from juries triggered a "presumptive" equal protection violation. That presumption then shifted the burden of persuasion to the prosecutor to provide a justification for the challenge that credibly rebutted the presumptive equal protection violation. The ultimate burden remained on the defendant to persuade the court that the proffered race-neutral basis was insufficient to justify the challenge. What were some of the reasons why the *Swain* framework was abandoned? What are some of the evidentiary obstacles to obtaining the widespread evidence required by *Swain*? In fact, the majority in *Batson* referred to the "crippling burden of proof" that made peremptory challenges "largely immune from constitutional scrutiny." Does this account for the low number of successful discrimination challenges prior to *Batson* and its new standard?

2. *Evaluating the prosecution's race-neutral reason.* Under *Batson,* if the defendant meets the initial burden, the burden shifts to the prosecutor to demonstrate a race-neutral reason for exercising the peremptory challenge. How should a trial judge evaluate the prosecutor's assertion of the race-neutral reason? In *Snyder v. Louisiana,* 552 U.S. 472 (2008), the Supreme Court considered the prosecution's challenge to an African-American male named Mr. Brooks. The proffered race-neutral reasons were (1) that Brooks looked nervous; and (2) that Brooks was a college senior who was scheduled, as part of his degree program, to complete a stint as a student teacher. The prosecution attempted to justify the challenge on that ground, but the Supreme Court noted that 50 venire members expressed concerns about fulfilling work or family obligations, thus suggesting that this was a mere pretext and not the real reason for Brooks's dismissal from the jury. In order to make this determination, the Court concluded that "all of the circumstances that bear upon the issue of racial animosity must be consulted." *Id.* at 478. Can you think of other "circumstances" that would be relevant in a *Batson* challenge?

3. *Standing to raise a* Batson *challenge.* In *Batson,* the defendant was a member of the same racial minority that was excluded from the jury. What if a defendant was a member of one racial group but the prosecution used peremptory challenges to exclude members of another racial group? Would

the defendant have standing to object, on Fourteenth Amendment groups, to this discrimination? In *Powers v. Ohio*, 499 U.S. 400 (1991), a white defendant was charged with aggravated murder. During jury selection, the prosecutor used nine peremptory challenges, six of which involved African-American members of the venire. The Supreme Court concluded that a prosecutor cannot

> exclude otherwise qualified and unbiased persons from the petit jury solely by reason of their race, a practice that forecloses a significant opportunity to participate in civic life. An individual juror does not have a right to sit on any particular petit jury, but he or she does possess the right not to be excluded from one on account of race.

Id. at 409. What does this statement imply about the underlying rationale for the prohibition on racial discrimination in jury selection? Is it the right of the defendant to be tried by a discrimination-free jury or is it the right of the citizen to be selected without racial discrimination for jury service?

4. *Extending* Batson *to the defense. Batson* and its progeny involve allegations that the prosecutor has used peremptory challenges to discriminate against potential jurors from a particular class. What if a *defense* counsel engages in a discriminatory peremptory challenge? May the prosecution appeal? The Equal Protection Clause requires state action; when the defense engages in the discrimination, where is the state action? In *Georgia v. McCollum*, 505 U.S. 42, 54 (1992), the Supreme Court concluded that there is state action in these cases: "In exercising a peremptory challenge, a criminal defendant is wielding the power to choose a quintessential governmental body—indeed, the institution of government on which our judicial system depends." In *Georgia v. McCollum*, the state objected to the peremptory challenge during jury selection; the trial judge denied the objection and the issue was appealed on an interlocutory basis. A state would not be able to appeal on this issue after the jury renders its verdict, as the defense would, because the state is not entitled to appeal a jury verdict of acquittal.

PROBLEM CASE

Timothy Foster was convicted of murder and sentenced to death. The murder occurred in 1986 and the trial shortly thereafter in 1987. In addition to direct appeals in state court, Foster filed a habeas petition challenging the jury selection under *Batson*. In 2002, while his habeas litigation was still pending, Foster filed a state open records request for all records related to his 1987 trial. Pursuant to that request, Foster received the following documents:

First, there was a jury venire list. The names of all African-American individuals on the venire list were highlighted in green and they also had the letter "B" next to their names. Second, there was a draft affidavit written for one of the prosecutors that explained the jury selection process in the following way: "If it comes down to having to pick one of the black jurors, [this one] might be okay. This is solely my opinion. . . . Upon picking of the jury after listening to all of the jurors we had to pick, if we had to pick a black juror I recommend that [this juror] be one of the jurors." Third, there were handwritten notes about three prospective black jurors who were referred to as B#1, B#2, and B#3. Fourth, there was a handwritten document titled "Church of Christ" with a notation that read: "NO. No Black Church."

Much of the case centered on the prosecutor's decision to use a peremptory challenge for Juror Garrett, who was African-America, as opposed to Juror Blackmon, who was white. Here was the prosecutor's explanation for his preferring Blackmon:

> [She] was 46 years old, married 13 years to her husband who works at GE, buying her own home and [was recommended by a third party to] this prosecutor. She was no longer employed at Northwest Georgia Regional Hospital and she attended Catholic church on an irregular basis. She did not hesitate when answering the questions concerning the death penalty, had good eye contact with the prosecutor and gave good answers on the insanity issue. She was perceived by the prosecutor as having a stable home environment, of the right age and no association with any disadvantaged youth organizations. . . . [T]he chances of [Blackmon] returning a death sentence were greater when all these factors were considered than Juror Garrett. Consequently, Juror Garrett was excused.

Should Foster prevail on his *Batson* challenge alleging unconstitutional discrimination in the jury selection process? Apply each step of the burden-shifting framework. See *Foster v. Chatman*, 136 S. Ct. 1737 (2016).

2. Gender Discrimination

In the following case, the Supreme Court considers whether to extend the *Batson* framework to gender discrimination in jury selection. In other words, if a prosecutor uses peremptory challenges to systematically exclude potential jurors of one gender, can the defendant challenge the jury selection as a violation of the Equal Protection Clause? As you read the following case, evaluate the similarities and dissimilarities between racial and gender discrimination. Are the similarities sufficient enough to bring gender discrimination within the *Batson* framework?

J.E.B. v. Alabama

Supreme Court of the United States
511 U.S. 127 (1994)

Justice BLACKMUN delivered the opinion of the Court.

In *Batson v. Kentucky*, this Court held that the Equal Protection Clause of the Fourteenth Amendment governs the exercise of peremptory challenges by a prosecutor in a criminal trial. The Court explained that although a defendant has "no right to a petit jury composed in whole or in part of persons of his own race," the "defendant does have the right to be tried by a jury whose members are selected pursuant to nondiscriminatory criteria." Since *Batson*, we have reaffirmed repeatedly our commitment to jury selection procedures that are fair and nondiscriminatory. We have recognized that whether the trial is criminal or civil, potential jurors, as well as litigants, have an equal protection right to jury selection procedures that are free from state-sponsored group stereotypes rooted in, and reflective of, historical prejudice.

Although premised on equal protection principles that apply equally to gender discrimination, all our recent cases defining the scope of *Batson* involved alleged racial discrimination in the exercise of peremptory challenges. Today we are faced with the question whether the Equal Protection Clause forbids intentional discrimination on the basis of gender, just as it prohibits discrimination on the basis of race. We hold that gender, like race, is an unconstitutional proxy for juror competence and impartiality.

I

On behalf of relator T.B., the mother of a minor child, respondent State of Alabama filed a complaint for paternity and child support against petitioner J.E.B. in the District Court of Jackson County, Alabama. On October 21, 1991, the matter was called for trial and jury selection began. The trial court assembled a panel of 36 potential jurors, 12 males and 24 females. After the court excused three jurors for cause, only 10 of the remaining 33 jurors were male. The State then used 9 of its 10 peremptory strikes to remove male jurors; petitioner used all but one of his strikes to remove female jurors. As a result, all the selected jurors were female.

Before the jury was empaneled, petitioner objected to the State's peremptory challenges on the ground that they were exercised against male jurors solely on the basis of gender, in violation of the Equal Protection Clause of the Fourteenth Amendment. Petitioner argued that the logic and reasoning of *Batson v. Kentucky*, which prohibits peremptory strikes solely on the basis of race, similarly forbids intentional discrimination on the basis of gender. The court rejected petitioner's claim and empaneled the all-female jury. The jury found petitioner to be the father of the child, and the court entered an order directing him to pay child support. . . .

II

Discrimination on the basis of gender in the exercise of peremptory challenges is a relatively recent phenomenon. Gender-based peremptory strikes were hardly practicable during most of our country's existence, since, until the 20th century, women were completely excluded from jury service. So well entrenched was this exclusion of women that in 1880 this Court, while finding that the exclusion of African-American men from juries violated the Fourteenth Amendment, expressed no doubt that a State "may confine the selection [of jurors] to males." *Strauder v. West Virginia*, 100 U.S., at 310.

Many States continued to exclude women from jury service well into the present century, despite the fact that women attained suffrage upon ratification of the Nineteenth Amendment in 1920. States that did permit women to serve on juries often erected other barriers, such as registration requirements and automatic exemptions, designed to deter women from exercising their right to jury service.

The prohibition of women on juries was derived from the English common law which, according to Blackstone, rightfully excluded women from juries under "the doctrine of propter defectum sexus, literally, the 'defect of sex.'" In this country, supporters of the exclusion of women from juries tended to couch their objections in terms of the ostensible need to protect women from the ugliness and depravity of trials. Women were thought to be too fragile and virginal to withstand the polluted courtroom atmosphere.

This Court in *Ballard v. United States*, 329 U.S. 187 (1946), first questioned the fundamental fairness of denying women the right to serve on juries. Relying on its supervisory powers over the federal courts, it held that women may not be excluded from the venire in federal trials in States where women were eligible for jury service under local law. . . . Fifteen years later, however, the Court still was unwilling to translate its appreciation for the value of women's contribution to civic life into an enforceable right to equal treatment under state laws governing jury service. In *Hoyt v. Florida*, 368 U.S., at 61, the Court found it reasonable, "[d]espite the enlightened emancipation of women," to exempt women from mandatory jury service by statute, allowing women to serve on juries only if they volunteered to serve. The Court justified the differential exemption policy on the ground that women, unlike men, occupied a unique position "as the center of home and family life."

In 1975, the Court finally repudiated the reasoning of *Hoyt* and struck down, under the Sixth Amendment, an affirmative registration statute nearly identical to the one at issue in *Hoyt*. See *Taylor v. Louisiana*, 419 U.S. 522 (1975). We explained: "Restricting jury service to only special groups or excluding identifiable segments playing major roles in the community cannot be squared with the constitutional concept of jury trial." The diverse and representative character of the jury must be maintained "partly as assurance of a diffused impartiality and partly because sharing in the administration of justice is a phase of civic responsibility."

III

Taylor relied on Sixth Amendment principles, but the opinion's approach is consistent with the heightened equal protection scrutiny afforded gender-based classifications. . . . Despite the heightened scrutiny afforded distinctions based on gender, respondent argues that gender discrimination in the selection of the petit jury should be permitted, though discrimination on the basis of race is not. Respondent suggests that "gender discrimination in this country . . . has never reached the level of discrimination" against African-Americans, and therefore gender discrimination, unlike racial discrimination, is tolerable in the courtroom.

While the prejudicial attitudes toward women in this country have not been identical to those held toward racial minorities, the similarities between the experiences of racial minorities and women, in some contexts, "overpower those differences." . . . Certainly, with respect to jury service, African-Americans and women share a history of total exclusion, a history which came to an end for women many years after the embarrassing chapter in our history came to an end for African-Americans.

We need not determine, however, whether women or racial minorities have suffered more at the hands of discriminatory state actors during the decades of our Nation's history. It is necessary only to acknowledge that "our Nation has had a long and unfortunate history of sex discrimination," a history which warrants the heightened scrutiny we afford all gender-based classifications today. Under our equal protection jurisprudence, gender-based classifications require "an exceedingly persuasive justification" in order to survive constitutional scrutiny. Thus, the only question is whether discrimination on the basis of gender in jury selection substantially furthers the State's legitimate interest in achieving a fair and impartial trial. In making this assessment, we do not weigh the value of peremptory challenges as an institution against our asserted commitment to eradicate invidious discrimination from the courtroom. Instead, we consider whether peremptory challenges based on gender stereotypes provide substantial aid to a litigant's effort to secure a fair and impartial jury.

Far from proffering an exceptionally persuasive justification for its gender-based peremptory challenges, respondent maintains that its decision to strike virtually all the males from the jury in this case "may reasonably have been based upon the perception, supported by history, that men otherwise totally qualified to serve upon a jury in any case might be more sympathetic and receptive to the arguments of a man alleged in a paternity action to be the father of an out-of-wedlock child, while women equally qualified to serve upon a jury might be more sympathetic and receptive to the arguments of the complaining witness who bore the child."

We shall not accept as a defense to gender-based peremptory challenges "the very stereotype the law condemns." Respondent's rationale, not unlike those regularly expressed for gender-based strikes, is reminiscent of the arguments advanced to justify the total exclusion of women from juries. Respondent offers virtually no support for the conclusion that gender alone is an accurate predictor of juror's attitudes; yet it urges this Court to condone the same stereotypes that justified the wholesale exclusion of women from juries and the ballot box. Respondent seems to assume that gross generalizations that would be deemed impermissible if made on the basis of race are somehow permissible when made on the basis of gender.

Discrimination in jury selection, whether based on race or on gender, causes harm to the litigants, the community, and the individual jurors who are wrongfully excluded from participation in the judicial process. The litigants are harmed by the risk that the prejudice that motivated the discriminatory selection of the jury will infect the entire proceedings. The community is harmed by the State's participation in the perpetuation of invidious group stereotypes and the inevitable loss of confidence in our judicial system that state-sanctioned discrimination in the courtroom engenders.

When state actors exercise peremptory challenges in reliance on gender stereotypes, they ratify and reinforce prejudicial views of the relative abilities of men and women. Because these stereotypes have wreaked injustice in so many other spheres of our country's public life, active discrimination by litigants on the basis of gender during jury selection "invites cynicism respecting the jury's neutrality and its obligation to adhere to the law." The potential for cynicism is particularly acute in cases where gender-related issues are prominent, such as cases involving rape, sexual harassment, or paternity. Discriminatory use of peremptory challenges may create the impression that the judicial system has acquiesced in suppressing full participation by one gender or that the "deck has been stacked" in favor of one side. . . .

NOTES & QUESTIONS ON GENDER DISCRIMINATION

1. *The nature of the harm.* Does *J.E.B.* rest on the harm to the excluded jurors, harm to the defendant, harm to the community at large, or some combination of these?

2. *The rationale for peremptory challenges.* Are peremptory challenges intertwined with some form of discrimination? The point of peremptory challenges is that the prosecutor does not have sufficient reason to seek an excusal for cause. By definition, then, the challenge is already problematic. Does *J.E.B.* portend the end of peremptory challenges? Consider the following opinion from an Alabama judge:

> In spite of the weak attempt by the majority in *J.E.B.* to assure that *J.E.B.* does not eliminate all peremptory challenges, I read *J.E.B.* as requiring a nongender, nonrace reason for striking any juror that is struck, and as requiring no prima facie showing of gender (sex) or racial discrimination before a

> disclosure of reason is required. Therefore, there is no more peremptory challenge. I believe that the peremptory challenge has served the litigants in this state (black, white, male, female, rich, poor, plaintiff, civil defendant, state, criminal defendant) well. I add this concurrence in the result to my too-frequent dissents in bemoaning the demise of an effective means of assuring that the litigants in the courts of Alabama are satisfied with the jurors to whom they entrust their lives, liberties, sacred honor, and property.

Ex parte Thomas, 659 So. 2d 3, 9 (Ala. 1994). Do you agree with the assessment that because of the need to articulate a non-racial and non-gender rationale for the challenge, there are effectively no more pure peremptory challenges? Do you agree that litigants should be "satisfied" with their jurors?

3. *The problem of mixed motives.* The entire *Batson* framework assumes that a prosecutor has only one motivation for excluding a juror—either an impermissible racial- or gender-based motivation or a permissible non-discriminatory reason. However, in real life, people usually have multiple motivations for their actions and there is no reason to think that the exercising of peremptory challenges is any different. Specifically, how does the *Batson* framework handle situations where a prosecutor has *two* motivations, one discriminatory and the other non-discriminatory? In that situation, should the non-discriminatory motive insulate the prosecution from a reversal? This seems like the wrong result, because "[a]s under Title VII, demonstration of even one discriminatory motive should suffice to establish a *Batson* violation." Russell D. Covey, *The Unbearable Lightness of* Batson*: Mixed Motives and Discrimination in Jury Selection*, 66 Md. L. Rev. 279, 346 (2007). In light of this problem, some Circuits have adopted explicit "mixed-motive" doctrines. For example, the Second Circuit has held that a defendant should prevail on a *Batson* challenge unless the prosecutor can establish that he would have exercised the challenge *solely* for race-neutral reasons:

> The cynical might suggest that prosecutors will take from our ruling a message of caution not to acknowledge that race was a factor in their use of peremptory challenges even in those instances when it was. We totally reject such a view. In the first place, we are unwilling to accept the premise of this argument that prosecutors will readily disregard the obligations of their office and violate the requirements of an oath by swearing false denials of racial motivation. Second, we have every confidence that trial judges can be relied upon to determine the true facts of the prosecutor's motive, just as they are relied upon to determine subjective mental states of parties and witnesses in all manner of cases.

Howard v. Senkowski, 986 F.2d 24, 31 (2d Cir. 1993). Do you agree with the proverbial cynic that adopting a mixed-motive doctrine will incentivize prosecutors to lie about their motivations?

STATUTORY REQUIREMENTS

The number of peremptory challenges that can be exercised in a particular case depends on whether the case is federal or state and what kind of crime the defendant is charged with. Also, the prosecutor and defendant might have a different umber of challenges. Consider the statute governing federal criminal prosecutions:

Each side is entitled to the number of peremptory challenges to prospective jurors specified below. The court may allow additional peremptory challenges to multiple defendants, and may allow the defendants to exercise those challenges separately or jointly.

> (1) Capital Case. Each side has 20 peremptory challenges when the government seeks the death penalty.
>
> (2) Other Felony Case. The government has 6 peremptory challenges and the defendant or defendants jointly have 10 peremptory challenges when the defendant is charged with a crime punishable by imprisonment of more than one year.
>
> (3) Misdemeanor Case. Each side has 3 peremptory challenges when the defendant is charged with a crime punishable by fine, imprisonment of one year or less, or both.

Fed. R. Crim. P. 24. In contrast, state statutes vary widely on the number of peremptory challenges. For example, in Texas, both the prosecution and the defendant in a capital case are permitted 15 peremptory challenges each; in non-capital cases, 10 peremptory challenges each; in misdemeanors, 5 each. See Tex. Code Crim. P. Rule 35.15.

PROBLEM CASE

The defendant, Jeffrey Ray Chatwin, pleaded not guilty to aggravated assault in connection with a domestic dispute. On the date set for trial, a jury venire was assembled and voir dire was conducted by the court and the parties. A jury was selected. The judge excused the jury from the room and the defense counsel objected that the prosecutor had used a peremptory challenge to strike the only person of a racial minority from the jury. The judge asked the prosecutor for an explanation for why the peremptory challenge was exercised against this particular individual. Under *Batson*, the prosecutor must offer a race-neutral reason for exercising the challenge. The prosecutor stated that he felt that

> this jury would be better able to deliberate the evidence that I anticipate[d] presenting to it if [the jury was] balanced between men and women. I therefore made efforts to take men off of the jury. That may not make a great deal of sense, but that was the game plan. [The venire person] was a man, I took him because he was a man. . . .

State v. Chatwin, 58 P.3d 867, 868 (Utah 2002). Defense counsel, upon hearing this explanation, then objected that the peremptory challenge was discriminatory on the basis of gender. The trial judge responded with the following statement:

> Well, I am not prepared to state that the challenge was inappropriate. It appears to me that there's been a justification for

exercising the challenge. . . . And moreover I'm not persuaded that in a case of this nature, specifically a spousal-abuse type of case, that selecting jurors, be they male or female which the Prosecutor or Defense for that matter decides might be more inclined to adhere to the Prosecution's theory of the case or the Defense's theory, for instance, that that was an inappropriate way or manner or justification for a challenge.

Id. at 869. Do you agree with the trial judge? Should an appellate court uphold or overturn the conviction?

3. Age Discrimination

Lawyers will attempt to remove other classes of jurors with peremptory challenges in order to achieve a strategic objective. For example, if a prosecutor believes that older jurors might be more lenient, the prosecutor might seek to exclude the older jurors and empanel a juror that is as young as possible. Lawyers for defendants in these cases have argued that age discrimination should be excluded as a permissible rationale for peremptory challenges, based on an analogous argument that led the Supreme Court to outlaw racial discrimination in *Batson* and gender discrimination in *J.E.B.* However, these efforts have mostly been unsuccessful, and the Supreme Court has never held that age discrimination in jury selection violates the Fourteenth Amendment. And most lower courts have rejected the argument as well. See, e.g., *Baxter v. United States*, 640 A.2d 714 (D.C. 1994); *Sanchez v. Roden*, 808 F.3d 85, 90 (1st Cir. 2015) (age is a race-neutral reason for exercising peremptory challenge and is consistent with *Batson*). Part of the underlying reason for the distinction is that under federal constitutional law, age discrimination is reviewed according to rational basis review, whereas racial and gender categorizations are reviewed under strict and intermediate scrutiny respectively.

STATE LAW REQUIREMENTS

State constitutional law provisions sometimes go further and prohibit additional forms of discrimination that have not yet been articulated by the Supreme Court as violating the federal constitution's Fourteenth Amendment. For example, several state courts have concluded that the prosecution cannot use peremptory challenges to systematically exclude jurors of a particular religious group. For example, in *Fields v. People*, 732 P.2d 1145, 1153 (Colo. 1987), the Supreme Court of Colorado concluded that excluding jurors of a particular religious group violated article 2, section 16 of the Colorado Constitution, in addition to the federal Sixth Amendment. Similarly, in *State v. Levinson*, 71 Haw. 492, 499, 795 P.2d 845, 849-50 (1990), the Supreme

Court of Hawaii concluded these peremptory challenges would violate the Equal Protection Clause of the Hawaii State Constitution:

> [W]hen a prima facie case of the use of peremptory challenges by the defense to discriminate against potential jurors because of their race, religion, sex or ancestry is established, it is incumbent upon the court to require a non-discriminatory explanation of the challenge, which satisfies it that the challenge is not based on a prohibited discriminatory basis, before excusing the juror.

PROBLEM CASE

In 2005, George Clinton Helmstetter and two other individuals were indicted by a federal grand jury on charges of passing, uttering, and possessing counterfeit notes with intent to defraud. Helmstetter was convicted but argued on appeal that his rights were violated by the prosecutor's use of peremptory challenges to keep young individuals off the jury, presumably on the theory that younger jurors would be more sympathetic to the defendant's plight, while older jurors would be more willing to condemn him. Helmstetter argued that age should be considered a protected class under *Batson* because Congress passed a statute, 28 U.S.C. § 1865, setting the minimum age of jury service at 18 years of age, and a prosecutor's deliberate strategy to exclude younger jurors undermines that legislative scheme. Specifically, discriminating against young jurors discriminates against a class of individuals whose right to serve on a jury has been specifically articulated by Congress. According to the defendant, "while discrimination against jurors on the basis of their youth does not carry with it the historical connotations of racial discrimination, the principle that individuals should be treated as individuals and not be discriminated against on the basis of an immutable characteristic . . . is . . . another form of stereotyping." Should an appeals court extend *Batson* to the category of age? See *United States v. Helmstetter*, 479 F.3d 750, 751-53 (10th Cir. 2007).

4. Erroneous Denial of Peremptory Challenge

The *Batson* framework imposes a special burden on trial courts. Whereas peremptory challenges were basically unreviewable before, now trial courts are directed by *Batson* to scrutinize the challenges and disallow them if they are motivated by racial or gender discrimination. In theory, the trial judge will make an accurate assessment and allow all proper peremptory challenges and disallow all improper challenges. In reality, though, trial judges will not always make the right call. A trial judge's error could go in either direction: The judge could erroneously uphold some discriminatory challenges or the judge might erroneously overrule some appropriate challenges. The question is what remedy might be offered in these cases. In the former case, the remedy is relatively simple: An appellate court should reverse the conviction because the jury composition was inappropriately influenced by racial discrimination. But what of the latter case? Suppose a defense attorney attempts to exercise a peremptory challenge but the judge disallows the challenge because the judge believes the challenge is racially discriminatory? Assume that the trial judge is mistaken, and the appeals court concludes that the defense attorney had a legitimate race-neutral reason for wanting to excuse the juror. If the defendant was ultimately convicted, can the defendant secure a new trial because the judge failed to allow the defendant to exercise their peremptory challenges? In the following case, the Supreme Court tackles this question.

Rivera v. Illinois

Supreme Court of the United States
556 U.S. 148 (2009)

Justice GINSBURG delivered the opinion of the Court.

This case concerns the consequences of a state trial court's erroneous denial of a defendant's peremptory challenge to the seating of a juror in a criminal case. If all seated jurors are qualified and unbiased, does the Due Process Clause of the Fourteenth Amendment nonetheless require automatic reversal of the defendant's conviction?

Following a jury trial in an Illinois state court, defendant-petitioner Michael Rivera was convicted of first-degree murder and sentenced to a prison term of 85 years. On appeal, Rivera challenged the trial court's rejection of his peremptory challenge to venire member Deloris Gomez. Gomez sat on Rivera's jury and indeed served as the jury's foreperson. It is conceded that there was no basis to challenge Gomez for cause. She met the requirements for jury service, and Rivera does not contend that she was in fact biased against him. The Supreme Court of Illinois held that the peremptory challenge should have been allowed, but further held that the error was harmless and therefore did not warrant reversal of Rivera's conviction. We affirm the judgment of the Illinois Supreme Court.

The right to exercise peremptory challenges in state court is determined by state law. This Court has "long recognized" that "peremptory challenges are not of federal constitutional dimension." States may withhold peremptory challenges "altogether without impairing the constitutional guarantee of an impartial jury and a fair trial." *Georgia v. McCollum,* 505 U.S. 42, 57 (1992). Just as state law controls the existence and exercise of peremptory challenges, so state law determines the consequences of an erroneous denial of such a challenge. Accordingly, we have no cause to disturb the Illinois Supreme Court's determination that, in the circumstances Rivera's case presents, the trial court's error did not warrant reversal of his conviction.

I

Rivera was charged with first-degree murder in the Circuit Court of Cook County, Illinois. The State alleged that Rivera, who is Hispanic, shot and killed Marcus Lee, a 16-year-old African-American, after mistaking Lee for a member of a rival gang.

During jury selection, Rivera's counsel questioned prospective juror Deloris Gomez, a business office supervisor at Cook County Hospital's outpatient orthopedic clinic. Gomez stated that she sometimes interacted with patients during the check-in process and acknowledged that Cook County Hospital treats many gunshot victims. She maintained, however, that her work experience would not affect her ability to be impartial. After questioning Gomez, Rivera's counsel sought to use a peremptory challenge to excuse her. At that point in the jury's selection, Rivera had already used three peremptory challenges. Two of the three were exercised against women; one of the two women thus eliminated was African-American. Illinois law affords each side seven peremptory challenges.

Rather than dismissing Gomez, the trial judge called counsel to chambers, where he expressed concern that the defense was discriminating against Gomez. [Under] *Batson v. Kentucky*, 476 U.S. 79 (1986), and later decisions building upon *Batson*, parties are constitutionally prohibited from exercising peremptory challenges to exclude jurors on the basis of race, ethnicity, or sex. Without specifying the type of discrimination he suspected or the reasons for his concern, the judge directed Rivera's counsel to state his reasons for excusing Gomez. Counsel responded, first, that Gomez saw victims of violent crime on a daily basis. Counsel next added that he was "pulled in two different ways" because Gomez had "some kind of Hispanic connection given her name." At that point, the judge interjected that Gomez "appears to be an African American"—the second "African American female" the defense had struck. Dissatisfied with counsel's proffered reasons, the judge denied the challenge to Gomez, but agreed to allow counsel to question Gomez further.

After asking Gomez additional questions about her work at the hospital, Rivera's counsel renewed his challenge. Counsel observed, outside the jury's presence, that most of the jurors already seated were women. Counsel said he hoped to "get some impact from possibly other men in the case." The court reaffirmed its earlier ruling, and Gomez was seated on the jury.

Rivera's case proceeded to trial. The jury, with Gomez as its foreperson, found Rivera guilty of first-degree murder. . . .

II

The Due Process Clause of the Fourteenth Amendment, Rivera maintains, requires reversal whenever a criminal defendant's peremptory challenge is erroneously denied. Rivera recalls the ancient lineage of the peremptory challenge and observes that the challenge has long been lauded as a means to guard against latent bias and to secure "the constitutional end of an impartial jury and a fair trial." When a trial court fails to dismiss a lawfully challenged juror, Rivera asserts, it commits structural error: The jury becomes an illegally constituted tribunal, and any verdict it renders is per se invalid. According to Rivera, this holds true even if the Constitution does not itself mandate peremptory challenges, because criminal defendants have a constitutionally protected liberty interest in their state-provided peremptory challenge rights.

The improper seating of a juror, Rivera insists, is not amenable to harmless-error analysis because it is impossible to ascertain how a properly constituted jury—here, one without juror Gomez—would have decided his case. Thus, he urges, whatever the constitutional status of peremptory challenges, automatic reversal must be the rule as a matter of federal law.

Rivera's arguments do not withstand scrutiny. If a defendant is tried before a qualified jury composed of individuals not challengeable for cause, the loss of a peremptory challenge due to a state court's good-faith error is not a matter of federal constitutional concern. Rather, it is a matter for the State to address under its own laws.

As Rivera acknowledges, this Court has consistently held that there is no freestanding constitutional right to peremptory challenges. We have characterized peremptory challenges as "a creature of statute" and have made clear that a State may decline to offer them at all. When States provide peremptory challenges (as all do in some form), they confer a benefit "beyond the minimum requirements of fair [jury] selection" and thus retain discretion to design and implement their own systems.

Because peremptory challenges are within the States' province to grant or withhold, the mistaken denial of a state-provided peremptory challenge does not, without more, violate the Federal Constitution. "[A] mere error of state law," we have noted, "is not a denial of due process." The Due Process Clause, our decisions instruct, safeguards not the meticulous observance of state procedural prescriptions, but "the fundamental elements of fairness in a criminal trial."

The trial judge's refusal to excuse juror Gomez did not deprive Rivera of his constitutional right to a fair trial before an impartial jury. Our decision in *Ross* is instructive. Ross, a criminal defendant in Oklahoma, used a peremptory challenge to rectify the trial court's erroneous denial of a for-cause challenge, leaving him with one fewer peremptory challenge to use at his discretion. The trial court's error, we acknowledged, "may have resulted in a jury panel different from that which would otherwise have decided [Ross's] case." But because no member of the jury as finally composed was removable for cause, we found no violation of Ross's Sixth

Amendment right to an impartial jury or his Fourteenth Amendment right to due process. . . .

Rivera insists that, even without a constitutional violation, the deprivation of a state-provided peremptory challenge requires reversal as a matter of federal law. We disagree. Rivera relies in part on *Swain*, 380 U.S. 202, which suggested that "[t]he denial or impairment of the right [to exercise peremptory challenges] is reversible error without a showing of prejudice." We disavowed this statement in *Martinez-Salazar*, observing, albeit in dicta, "that the oft-quoted language in *Swain* was not only unnecessary to the decision in that case . . . but was founded on a series of our early cases decided long before the adoption of harmless-error review." As our recent decisions make clear, we typically designate an error as "structural," therefore "requir[ing] automatic reversal," only when "the error necessarily render[s] a criminal trial fundamentally unfair or an unreliable vehicle for determining guilt or innocence." The mistaken denial of a state-provided peremptory challenge does not, at least in the circumstances we confront here, constitute an error of that character. . . .

NOTES & QUESTIONS ON ERRONEOUS DENIALS

1. *Is there a right to peremptory challenges?* The Supreme Court reiterated in *Rivera* that there is no general constitutional right to peremptory challenges. How can this statement be reconciled with *Batson*? The answer, it appears, is that peremptory statutes are guaranteed by statute and by state law, but not protected by the federal constitution. This creates a slightly odd situation. The state cannot deny the use of peremptory challenges in a discriminatory way, though it could remove a defendant's right to use all peremptory challenges completely, since this would be technically non-discriminatory. Does this result make sense to you? Why or why not? Is it part of the logic of discrimination?

D. PRACTICE & POLICY

Most of this chapter has focused on the rights associated with jury trials: i.e., the right to have a jury trial and what this means in terms of the jury's composition, including how large it is, how it conducts deliberations, and the exclusion of individuals from the jury through the system of peremptory and for-cause challenges. In some cases, though, a defendant may not want a jury trial and might want, instead, a "bench trial," which involves the judge sitting as both fact finder and trier of the law at the same time. The following materials focus on the strategic, doctrinal, and psychological justifications when a defendant voluntarily forgoes a jury trial.

Strategic argument for selecting a bench trial. Sometimes, defense lawyers will counsel a client that a jury trial will be dangerous. Especially in cases where the jury is likely to be inflamed by extraneous facts, the lawyer might conclude that the jury might convict the defendant for the "wrong reasons." In theory, of course, such extraneous information should be kept from the jury if its prejudicial value outweighs its probative value. In practice, what this means is that information with a high probative value will be presented to a jury even if it has some prejudicial effect. The jury might learn, for example, of a defendant's despicable conduct toward the victim and allow this fact to influence its determination of whether the defendant committed the crime. Assuming that the judge—a trained lawyer as opposed to a layperson—is immune to these biases, the defense counsel might recommend waiving a jury trial in order to receive a more neutral hearing.

The right to waive a jury trial. The next question is whether a defendant has a right to waive a jury trial. In most jurisdictions, the answer is emphatically yes; the jury trial right is an option afforded to the defendant but not one that the defendant must available himself of. However, as recently as 2014, defendants in North Carolina were not entitled to select a bench trial for serious offenses. This changed in 2014 when voters passed a new statute authorizing bench trials for all but capital offenses:

> A defendant accused of any criminal offense for which the State is not seeking a sentence of death in superior court may, knowingly and voluntarily, in writing or on the record in the court and with the consent of the trial judge, waive the right to trial by jury. When a defendant waives the right to trial by jury under this section, the jury is dispensed with as provided by law, and the whole matter of law and fact . . . shall be heard and judgment given by the court. If a motion for joinder of co-defendants is allowed, there shall be a jury trial unless all defendants waive the right to trial by jury, or the court, in its discretion, severs the case.

N.C. Gen. Stat. § 15A-1201. It is worth noting that the jury plays an important role in the criminal justice system and that role is not reducible to the protection of defendants' procedural rights. As a form of adjudication, the jury represents the community's access to the criminal justice system. The community's participation as a fact finder brings the judicial system one step away from the executive and judicial branches and closer to the people themselves. The new North Carolina statute embodies a determination that this community role is essential in the context of capital punishment and cannot be abrogated, even by voluntary election of the defendant. If the community, through the judicial system, is going to put someone to death for their misdeeds, then the community must be involved in that determination through the institution of the jury.

❧ **Cognitive biases among jurors.** Lawyers often assume that their strategic decision to opt for a bench trial is supported by empirical evidence from cognitive psychology. They assume, in other words, that judges will assess evidence objectively while jurors will not. The psychological literature indicates that even the most thoughtful individuals are prone to "cognitive biases," which one might describe as "mistakes" of rational inference or intuition that are hard to avoid in daily life. For example, one well-known cognitive bias is "confirmation bias," which is the tendency to focus on evidence that confirms one's hypothesis and to ignore or deemphasize evidence that undermines it. Lawyers often assume that jurors will succumb to cognitive biases while judges will be immune to them, with the result that a defendant might have a better shot with a judge. However, there are reasons to question this assumption. Are judges immune to cognitive biases simply because they have legal training or have experience running a courtroom? For example, Professor Rachlinski argues that the law should recognize that judges also are prone to cognitive bias:

> Courts are more likely to recognize the influence of cognitive biases in the types of cases that generally require trial by jury than in cases that typically require trial by judge. This distinction is consistent with an observation that cognitive psychologists have made between insider versus outsider perspectives on cognitive illusions. Psychologists argue that people can more easily identify cognitive biases when they treat a decision-making problem as one of a class of similar problems that many other people face than when they treat it as a unique problem that they face alone. As a consequence, cognitive biases are easier to spot in others than in oneself.
>
> As applied to the legal process, judges are more likely to adopt an outsider perspective to decision making by juries than by themselves or other judges. When judges both determine the procedural rules that govern fact-finding and decide the facts themselves they are inside the decision-making task. This insider perspective makes it difficult to identify cognitive illusions that might affect judgment. By contrast, a jury trial necessarily separates the fact-finding process from the process of adopting procedural rules to govern fact-finding. This creates an outsider perspective on the decision-making process thereby making it easier for courts to identify cognitive illusions.

Jeffrey J. Rachlinski, *Heuristics and Biases in the Courts: Ignorance or Adaptation?*, 79 Or. L. Rev. 61, 65-66 (2000). In other words, judges may easily identify the cognitive biases of the jury but fail to recognize their own cognitive biases. Does this finding change—or at least dampen—the empirical argument for strategically opting for a bench trial? How should a defense lawyer respond to this insight? One possibility, informed by empirical evidence, is to have the lawyer identify the particular cognitive bias that will be most relevant in the trial and then search for conclusions in the scholarly literature about whether judges, or juries, are more prone to that bias.

CHAPTER 17

Fair Trial Rights

INTRODUCTION

What is a fair trial and what principles underlie our Constitution's commitment to it? The Fifth and Sixth Amendments protect rights of due process, the right to a jury trial, the right to confront witnesses, the right to compulsory process, and the privilege against compelled self-incrimination. At the level of doctrine, each of these rights influences the unfolding of trial: what evidence may the defense produce, which witnesses can be called, what they can say on the stand, how the defense questions these witnesses on cross-examination, and which witnesses defense counsel may call to the stand during its defense case. In short, these rights constitute a cluster of rights that are constitutive of the concept of a fair trial.

Recalling Packer's two models of criminal justice, crime control and due process, this cluster of rights might be justified as instrumentally valuable because they help ensure the epistemic validity of criminal trials. The right to confront witnesses, for example, helps ensure that judges and juries will more likely than not return correct verdicts; the guilty will be convicted and the innocent will be acquitted. This vision makes fair trial rights subordinate to the value of truth-finding, which is the ultimate goal of the process. But Packer's due process model provides an alternative vision of the first trial: one committed to fairness wherein fairness has a value over and above its tendency to promote accuracy. What respect would we have for a criminal justice system that fails to give defendants a chance to confront witnesses against them, even if that system had a tendency to produce accurate results? Or how would we view a system of government that denies the privilege against self-incrimination and literally forces defendants to be witnesses against themselves? Probably as totalitarian rather than as a constitutional republic.

The following materials cycle through the following topics: (a) the danger of pre-trial publicity to a fair trial; (b) the public's and the defense's right to public access to the courtroom; (c) the defendant's right to "confront" adverse witnesses, which raises unique issues in an age of forensic science; (d) a defendant's privilege against compelled self-incrimination; and (e) the general right to present a defense and how it might constrain state rules of evidence in extreme cases. In some sense, the last right articulates most squarely the core of the fair trial rights: the right of defendants, when faced with the awesome power of state prosecution, to defend themselves before a neutral arbiter against the threat of coercive punishment. Each of the specific rights in this chapter advances this larger project of giving individuals a chance to vindicate their position in a court of law before punishment may be imposed.

A. PRE-TRIAL PUBLICITY

In theory, a jury should render its decision based on its consideration of the evidence presented at trial as applied to the law as explained by the judge; indeed, all jurors swear an oath or affirmation that they will do so. The confidential jury deliberations involve the jury's collective and considered application of law to fact. In reality, though, the jury process can be contaminated by outside information communicated to jury members. For example, members of the jury might have heard about the case prior to their being summoned for jury duty. Similarly, jury members might hear information about the case *during* the trial if the jurors listen to or read news reports about the trial. In both cases, it would be extremely hard for the jury to confine its deliberations to only the facts presented at trial according to the law as explained by the judge, wholly divorced from information received from outside sources.

At some point, a jury "contaminated" by pre-trial publicity may be so compromised that it is no longer able to function appropriately, thus jeopardizing the intended objective of the constitutional right to a jury trial flowing from both due process and the Sixth Amendment. The following subsections focus on (1) the foundational requirement of an "impartial" jury and what this means; (2) how to remediate pre-trial publicity that is so severe as to compromise the impartiality of a jury; and (3) the unique constitutional tensions raised when courts take the extraordinary step of ordering a change of venue for a trial.

1. The Impartial Jury Requirement

In the following case, the Supreme Court notes that due process requires that jury trials involve a "panel of impartial, indifferent jurors." At the same time, however, the Supreme Court is careful to concede that a jury that knows *nothing* of the alleged facts at issue in the trial is an unreasonable standard that would doom the possibility of finding any impartial jury in a highly publicized case of great public concern. Given that some prior knowledge of such a trial is consistent with due process, what standard does the Supreme Court articulate as the definition of what constitutes an "impartial" jury guaranteed by due process?

Irvin v. Dowd

Supreme Court of the United States
366 U.S. 717 (1961)

Mr. Justice Clark delivered the opinion of the Court.

This is a habeas corpus proceeding, brought to test the validity of petitioner's conviction of murder and sentence of death in the Circuit Court of Gibson County, Indiana. . . . During the course of the voir dire examination, which lasted some four weeks, petitioner filed two more motions for a change of venue and eight motions for continuances. All were denied. . . .

England, from whom the Western World has largely taken its concepts of individual liberty and of the dignity and worth of every man, has bequeathed to us safeguards for their preservation, the most priceless of which is that of trial by jury. This right has become as much American as it was once the most English. Although this Court has said that the Fourteenth Amendment does not demand the use of jury trials in a State's criminal procedure, every State has constitutionally provided trial by jury. In essence, the right to jury trial guarantees to the criminally accused a fair trial by a panel of impartial, "indifferent" jurors. The failure to accord an accused a fair hearing violates even the minimal standards of due process. . . .

It is not required, however, that the jurors be totally ignorant of the facts and issues involved. In these days of swift, widespread and diverse methods of communication, an important case can be expected to arouse the interest of the public in the vicinity, and scarcely any of those best qualified to serve as jurors will not have formed some impression or opinion as to the merits of the case. This is particularly true in criminal cases. To hold that the mere existence of any preconceived notion as to the guilt or innocence of an accused, without more, is sufficient to rebut the presumption of a prospective juror's impartiality would be to establish an impossible standard. It is sufficient if the juror can lay aside his impression or opinion and render a verdict based on the evidence presented in court.

. . . [T]he test is "whether the nature and strength of the opinion formed are such as in law necessarily . . . raise the presumption of partiality. The question thus presented is one of mixed law and fact. . . ." "The affirmative of the issue is upon the challenger. Unless he shows the actual existence of such an opinion in the mind of the juror as will raise the presumption of partiality, the juror need not necessarily be set aside. . . . If a positive and decided opinion had been formed, he would have been incompetent even though it had not been expressed." . . . .

The rule was established in *Reynolds* that "(t)he finding of the trial court upon that issue (the force of a prospective juror's opinion) ought not be set aside by a reviewing court, unless the error is manifest." In later cases this Court revisited *Reynolds*, citing it in each instance for the proposition that findings of impartiality should be set aside only where prejudice is "manifest." Indiana agrees that a trial by jurors having a fixed, preconceived opinion of the accused's guilt would be a denial of due process, but points out that the voir dire examination discloses that each juror qualified under the applicable Indiana statute. It is true that the presiding judge personally examined those members of the jury panel whom petitioner, having no more peremptory challenges, insisted should be excused for cause, and that each indicated that notwithstanding his opinion he could render an impartial verdict. But as Chief Justice Hughes observed in *United States v. Wood*, 299 U.S. 123, 145-146: "Impartiality is not a technical conception. It is a state of mind. For the ascertainment of this mental attitude of appropriate indifference, the Constitution lays down no particular tests and procedure is not chained to any ancient and artificial formula."

Here the build-up of prejudice is clear and convincing. An examination of the then current community pattern of thought as indicated by the popular news media is singularly revealing. For example, petitioner's first motion for a change of venue from Gibson County alleged that the awaited trial of petitioner had become the cause celebre of this small community—so much so that curbstone opinions, not only as to petitioner's guilt but even as to what punishment he should receive, were solicited and recorded on the public streets by a roving reporter, and later were broadcast over the local stations. A reading of the 46 exhibits which petitioner attached to his motion indicates that a barrage of newspaper headlines, articles, cartoons and pictures was unleashed against him during the six or seven months preceding his trial. The motion further alleged that the newspapers in which the stories appeared were delivered regularly to approximately 95% of the dwellings in Gibson County and that, in addition, the Evansville radio and TV stations, which likewise blanketed that county, also carried extensive newscasts covering the same incidents. These stories revealed the details of his background, including a reference to crimes committed when a juvenile, his convictions for arson almost 20 years previously, for burglary and by a court-martial on AWOL charges during the war. He was accused of being a parole violator. The headlines announced his police line-up identification, that he faced a lie detector test, had been placed at the scene of the crime and that the six murders were solved but petitioner refused to confess.

Finally, they announced his confession to the six murders and the fact of his indictment for four of them in Indiana. They reported petitioner's offer to plead guilty if promised a 99-year sentence, but also the determination, on the other hand, of the prosecutor to secure the death penalty, and that petitioner had confessed to 24 burglaries (the modus operandi of these robberies was compared to that of the murders and the similarity noted). One story dramatically relayed the promise of a sheriff to devote his life to securing petitioner's execution by the State of Kentucky, where petitioner is alleged to have committed one of the six murders, if Indiana failed to do so. Another characterized petitioner as remorseless and without conscience but also as having been found sane by a court-appointed panel of doctors. In many of the stories petitioner was described as the "confessed slayer of six," a parole violator and fraudulent-check artist. Petitioner's court-appointed counsel was quoted as having received "much criticism over being Irvin's counsel" and it was pointed out, by way of excusing the attorney, that he would be subject to disbarment should he refuse to represent Irvin. On the day before the trial the newspapers carried the story that Irvin had orally admitted the murder of Kerr (the victim in this case) as well as "the robbery-murder of Mrs. Mary Holland; the murder of Mrs. Wilhelmina Sailer in Posey County, and the slaughter of three members of the Duncan family in Henderson County, Ky."

It cannot be gainsaid that the force of this continued adverse publicity caused a sustained excitement and fostered a strong prejudice among the people of Gibson County. In fact, on the second day devoted to the selection of the jury, the newspapers reported that "strong feelings, often bitter and angry, rumbled to the surface," and that "the extent to which the multiple murders—three in one family—have aroused feelings throughout the area was emphasized Friday when 27 of the 35 prospective jurors questioned were excused for holding biased pretrial opinions. . . ." A few days later the feeling was described as "a pattern of deep and bitter prejudice against the former pipe-fitter." Spectator comments, as printed by the newspapers, were "my mind is made up"; "I think he is guilty"; and "he should be hanged."

Finally, and with remarkable understatement, the headlines reported that "impartial jurors are hard to find." The panel consisted of 430 persons. The court itself excused 268 of those on challenges for cause as having fixed opinions as to the guilt of petitioner; 103 were excused because of conscientious objection to the imposition of the death penalty; 20, the maximum allowed, were peremptorily challenged by petitioner and 10 by the State; 12 persons and two alternates were selected as jurors and the rest were excused on personal grounds, e.g., deafness, doctor's orders, etc. An examination of the 2,783-page voir dire record shows that 370 prospective jurors or almost 90% of those examined on the point (10 members of the panel were never asked whether or not they had any opinion) entertained some opinion as to guilt—ranging in intensity from mere suspicion to absolute certainty. A number admitted that, if they were in the accused's place in the dock and he in theirs on the jury with their opinions, they would not want him on a jury.

Here the "pattern of deep and bitter prejudice" shown to be present throughout the community was clearly reflected in the sum total of the voir dire examination of a majority of the jurors finally placed in the jury box. Eight out of the 12 thought petitioner was guilty. With such an opinion permeating their minds, it would be difficult to say that each could exclude this preconception of guilt from his deliberations. The influence that lurks in an opinion once formed is so persistent that it unconsciously fights detachment from the mental processes of the average man. Where one's life is at stake—and accounting for the frailties of human nature—we can only say that in the light of the circumstances here the finding of impartiality does not meet constitutional standards. Two-thirds of the jurors had an opinion that petitioner was guilty and were familiar with the material facts and circumstances involved, including the fact that other murders were attributed to him, some going so far as to say that it would take evidence to overcome their belief. One said that he "could not . . . give the defendant the benefit of the doubt that he is innocent." Another stated that he had a "somewhat" certain fixed opinion as to petitioner's guilt. No doubt each juror was sincere when he said that he would be fair and impartial to petitioner, but psychological impact requiring such a declaration before one's fellows is often its father. Where so many, so many times, admitted prejudice, such a statement of impartiality can be given little weight. As one of the jurors put it, "You can't forget what you hear and see." With his life at stake, it is not requiring too much that petitioner be tried in an atmosphere undisturbed by so huge a wave of public passion and by a jury other than one in which two-thirds of the members admit, before hearing any testimony, to possessing a belief in his guilt. . . .

NOTES & QUESTIONS ON THE IMPARTIAL JURY

1. *The burden.* According to the Supreme Court, which side bears the burden of proving or disproving the impartiality of the jury? Does the state have the burden to demonstrate that it has tried the defendant by an impartial jury, or does the defendant have the burden to demonstrate that his or her conviction resulted from a partial jury?

2. *The standard.* What standard does the Supreme Court articulate for figuring out whether a jury is impartial or not? What role does the "presumption"

play? Do the facts of pre-trial publicity in the opinion demonstrate that presumption of impartiality was negated?

3. *A duty to question jurors?* Does the constitutional requirement of an impartial jury obligate the trial court to question potential jurors during voir dire, regarding the particular *content* of any pre-trial publicity that they might have been exposed to prior to the trial? In other words, is a jury verdict of guilty inherently suspect if the trial judge failed to ask members of the voir dire about pre-trial publicity? In *Mu'Min v. Virginia,* 500 U.S. 415 (1991), the Supreme Court said no, reasoning that

> [a]cceptance of petitioner's claim would require that each potential juror be interrogated individually; even were the interrogation conducted in panels of four jurors, as the trial court did here, descriptions of one juror about pretrial publicity would obviously be communicated to the three other members of the panel being interrogated, with the prospect that more harm than good would be done by the interrogation. Petitioner says that the questioning can be accomplished by juror questionnaires submitted in advance at trial, but such written answers would not give counsel or the court any exposure to the demeanor of the juror in the course of answering the content questions. The trial court in this case expressed reservations about interrogating jurors individually because it might make the jurors feel that they themselves were on trial. While concern for the feelings and sensibilities of potential jurors cannot be allowed to defeat inquiry necessary to protect a constitutional right, we do not believe that "content" questions are constitutionally required.

Id. at 425. In *Mu'Min,* potential jurors had been asked whether they had heard anything about the case before the trial, and if they answered yes, whether they could still be impartial in the case. However, potential jurors were not asked to list in any meaningful detail the news reports that they had consumed about the case. Do you agree with the court that a more detailed colloquy is not constitutionally required?

2. Publicity and Change of Venue

When there is a risk that pre-trial publicity might compromise the impartiality of the jury, what options are available for resolving the problem? In *Irvin v. Dowd,* the Supreme Court faulted the trial judge for not ordering a change of venue to escape the substantial pre-trial publicity, but are there other less extreme options at the disposal of the trial court? For example, in *Sheppard v. Maxwell,* 384 U.S. 333, 355 (1966), the Supreme Court harshly criticized a trial judge for failing to take remedial action to eliminate the circus-like atmosphere caused by media publicity in a murder trial:

> While we cannot say that Sheppard was denied due process by the judge's refusal to take precautions against the influence of pretrial publicity alone, the court's later rulings must be considered against the setting in which the trial was held. . . . The fact is that bedlam reigned at the courthouse during the trial and newsmen took over practically the entire courtroom, hounding most of the participants in the trial, especially Sheppard. At a temporary table within a few feet of the jury box and counsel table sat some 20 reporters staring at Sheppard and taking notes. The erection of a press table for reporters inside the bar is unprecedented. The bar of the court is reserved for counsel, providing them a safe place in which to keep papers and exhibits, and to confer privately with client and co-counsel. It is designed to protect the witness and the jury from any distractions, intrusions or influences, and to permit bench discussions of the judge's rulings away from the hearing of the public and the jury. Having assigned almost all of the available seats in the courtroom to the news media the judge lost his ability to supervise that environment. The movement of the reporters in and out of the courtroom caused frequent confusion and disruption of the trial. And the record reveals constant commotion within the bar. Moreover, the judge gave the throng of newsmen gathered in the corridors of the courthouse absolute free rein. Participants in the trial, including the jury, were forced to run a gantlet of reporters and photographers each time they entered or left the courtroom. The total lack of consideration for the privacy of the jury was demonstrated by the assignment to a broadcasting station of space next to the jury room on the floor above the courtroom, as well as the fact that jurors were allowed to make telephone calls during their five-day deliberation.

In the most extreme situations, when all other avenues for protecting the jury from publicity are exhausted, trial courts resort to removing the trial to another locality that is free from the pre-trial publicity. For example, federal trial judges may transfer a case in the following circumstances:

> (a) For Prejudice. Upon the defendant's motion, the court must transfer the proceeding against that defendant to another district if the court is satisfied that so great a prejudice against the defendant exists in the transferring district that the defendant cannot obtain a fair and impartial trial there.
> (b) For Convenience. Upon the defendant's motion, the court may transfer the proceeding, or one or more counts, against that defendant to another district for the convenience of the parties, any victim, and the witnesses, and in the interest of justice.

Fed. R. Crim. P. 21. The common law has a tradition of hosting trials in the locality where the crime was committed, so the decision to change venue is not one that is taken lightly. In part, that is because the "community" itself stands in judgment of the accused through the operation of the local court and the community members sitting on the jury. This locality requirement is loosely codified in the Sixth Amendment, which requires that the trial be held in "the State and district wherein the crime shall have been committed," thus making clear, for example, that a crime in Florida cannot be prosecuted in New York. For this and other reasons, trial judges are hesitant about moving trials to another venue, preferring instead to manage the pre-trial publicity rather than giving up the case to a nearby court. As you read the following case, look for the standard that the Supreme Court articulates for when a change of venue is appropriate. In the following case, was the defendant denied a fair trial because the trial judge refused to move the trial?

Skilling v. United States

Supreme Court of the United States
561 U.S. 358 (2010)

Justice GINSBURG delivered the opinion of the Court.

In 2001, Enron Corporation, then the seventh highest-revenue-grossing company in America, crashed into bankruptcy. We consider . . . questions arising from the prosecution of Jeffrey Skilling, a longtime Enron executive, for crimes committed before the corporation's collapse. [D]id pretrial publicity and community prejudice prevent Skilling from obtaining a fair trial? . . .

I

Founded in 1985, Enron Corporation grew from its headquarters in Houston, Texas, into one of the world's leading energy companies. Skilling launched his career there in 1990 when Kenneth Lay, the company's founder, hired him to head an Enron subsidiary. Skilling steadily rose through the corporation's ranks, serving as president and chief operating officer, and then, beginning in February 2001, as chief executive officer. Six months later, on August 14, 2001, Skilling resigned from Enron.

Less than four months after Skilling's departure, Enron spiraled into bankruptcy. The company's stock, which had traded at $90 per share in August 2000, plummeted to pennies per share in late 2001. Attempting to comprehend what caused the corporation's collapse, the U.S. Department of Justice formed an Enron Task Force, comprising prosecutors and Federal Bureau of Investigation agents from around the Nation. The Government's investigation uncovered an elaborate conspiracy to prop up Enron's short-run stock prices by overstating the company's financial well-being. In the years following Enron's bankruptcy, the Government prosecuted dozens of Enron employees who participated in the scheme. In time, the Government worked its way up the corporation's chain of command: On July 7, 2004, a grand jury indicted Skilling, Lay, and Richard Causey, Enron's former chief accounting officer. . . .

In November 2004, Skilling moved to transfer the trial to another venue; he contended that hostility toward him in Houston, coupled with extensive pretrial publicity, had poisoned potential jurors. To support this assertion, Skilling, aided by media experts, submitted hundreds of news reports detailing Enron's downfall; he also presented affidavits from the experts he engaged portraying community attitudes in Houston in comparison to other potential venues. The U.S. District Court for the Southern District of Texas, in accord with rulings in two earlier instituted Enron-related prosecutions, denied the venue-transfer motion. . . .

In the months leading up to the trial, the District Court solicited from the parties questions the court might use to screen prospective jurors. Unable to agree on a questionnaire's format and content, Skilling and the Government submitted dueling documents. On venire members' sources of Enron-related news, for example, the Government proposed that they tick boxes from a checklist of generic labels such as "[t]elevision," "[n]ewspaper," and "[r]adio"; Skilling proposed more probing questions asking venire members to list the specific names of their media sources and to report on "what st[ood] out in [their] mind[s]" of "all the things [they] ha[d] seen, heard or read about Enron."

The District Court rejected the Government's sparer inquiries in favor of Skilling's submission. Skilling's questions "[we]re more helpful," the court said, "because [they] [we]re generally . . . open-ended and w[ould] allow the potential jurors to give us more meaningful information." The court converted Skilling's submission, with slight modifications, into a 77-question, 14-page document that asked prospective jurors about, inter alia, their sources of news and exposure to Enron-related publicity, beliefs concerning Enron and what caused its collapse, opinions regarding the defendants and their possible guilt or innocence, and relationships to the company and to anyone affected by its demise.

In November 2005, the District Court mailed the questionnaire to 400 prospective jurors and received responses from nearly all the addressees. The court granted hardship exemptions to approximately 90 individuals, and the parties, with the court's approval, further winnowed the pool by excusing another 119 for cause, hardship, or physical disability. The parties agreed to exclude, in particular, "each and every" prospective juror who said that a pre-existing opinion about Enron or the defendants would prevent her from impartially considering the evidence at trial.

. . . Skilling renewed his change-of-venue motion, arguing that the juror questionnaires revealed pervasive bias and that news accounts of Causey's guilty plea further tainted the jury pool. If Houston remained the trial venue, Skilling urged that "jurors need to be questioned individually by both the Court and counsel" concerning their opinions of Enron and "publicity issues."

The District Court again declined to move the trial. Skilling, the court concluded, still had not "establish[ed] that pretrial publicity and/or community prejudice raise[d] a presumption of inherent jury prejudice." The questionnaires and voir dire, the court observed, provided safeguards adequate to ensure an impartial jury.

Denying Skilling's request for attorney-led voir dire, the court said that in 17 years on the bench: "I've found . . . I get more forthcoming responses from potential jurors than the lawyers on either side. I don't know whether people are suspicious of lawyers—but I think if I ask a person a question, I will get a candid response much easier than if a lawyer asks the question."

But the court promised to give counsel an opportunity to ask followup questions and it agreed that venire members should be examined individually about pretrial publicity. The court also allotted the defendants jointly 14 peremptory challenges, 2 more than the standard number prescribed by Federal Rule of Criminal Procedure 24(b)(2) and (c)(4)(B).

Voir dire began on January 30, 2006. The District Court first emphasized to the venire the importance of impartiality and explained the presumption of innocence and the Government's burden of proof. The trial, the court next instructed, was not a forum "to seek vengeance against Enron's former officers," or to "provide remedies for" its victims. "The bottom line," the court stressed, "is that we want . . . jurors who . . . will faithfully, conscientiously and impartially serve if selected." In response to the court's query whether any prospective juror questioned her ability to adhere to these instructions, two individuals indicated that they could not be fair; they were therefore excused for cause.

After questioning the venire as a group, the District Court brought prospective jurors one by one to the bench for individual examination. Although the questions varied, the process generally tracked the following format: The court asked about exposure to Enron-related news and the content of any stories that stood out in the prospective juror's mind. Next, the court homed in on questionnaire answers that raised a red flag signaling possible bias. The court then permitted each side to pose followup questions. Finally, after the venire member stepped away, the court entertained and ruled on challenges for cause. In all, the court granted one of the Government's for-cause challenges and denied four; it granted three of the defendants' challenges and denied six. The parties agreed to excuse three additional jurors for cause and one for hardship.

By the end of the day, the court had qualified 38 prospective jurors, a number sufficient, allowing for peremptory challenges, to empanel 12 jurors and 4 alternates. Before the jury was sworn in, Skilling objected to the seating of six jurors. He did not contend that they were in fact biased; instead, he urged that he would have used peremptories to exclude them had he not exhausted his supply by striking several venire members after the court refused to excuse them for cause. The court overruled this objection.

After the jurors took their oath, the District Court told them they could not discuss the case with anyone or follow media accounts of the proceedings. "[E]ach of you," the court explained, "needs to be absolutely sure that your decisions concerning the facts will be based only on the evidence that you hear and read in this courtroom."

Following a four-month trial and nearly five days of deliberation, the jury found Skilling guilty of 19 counts, including the honest-services-fraud conspiracy charge, and not guilty of 9 insider-trading counts. The District Court sentenced Skilling to 292 months' imprisonment, 3 years' supervised release, and $45 million in restitution. . . .

II

Pointing to "the community passion aroused by Enron's collapse and the vitriolic media treatment" aimed at him, Skilling argues that his trial "never should have proceeded in Houston." And even if it had been possible to select impartial jurors in Houston, "[t]he truncated voir dire . . . did almost nothing to weed out prejudices," he contends, so "[f]ar from rebutting the presumption of prejudice, the record below affirmatively confirmed it." Skilling's fair-trial claim thus raises two distinct questions. First, did the District Court err by failing to move the trial to a different venue based on a presumption of prejudice? Second, did actual prejudice contaminate Skilling's jury?

The Sixth Amendment secures to criminal defendants the right to trial by an impartial jury. By constitutional design, that trial occurs "in the State where the . . . Crimes . . . have been committed." The Constitution's place-of-trial prescriptions, however, do not impede transfer of the proceeding to a different district at the defendant's request if extraordinary local prejudice will prevent a fair trial—a "basic requirement of due process."

"The theory of our [trial] system is that the conclusions to be reached in a case will be induced only by evidence and argument in open court, and not by any outside influence, whether of private talk or public print." When does the publicity attending conduct charged as criminal dim prospects that the trier can judge a case, as due process requires, impartially, unswayed by outside influence? Because most cases of consequence garner at least some pretrial publicity, courts have considered this question in diverse settings. We begin our discussion by addressing the presumption of prejudice from which the Fifth Circuit's analysis in Skilling's case proceeded. The foundation precedent is *Rideau v. Louisiana*, 373 U.S. 723 (1963).

Wilbert Rideau robbed a bank in a small Louisiana town, kidnaped three bank employees, and killed one of them. Police interrogated Rideau in jail without counsel present and obtained his confession. Without informing Rideau, no less seeking his consent, the police filmed the interrogation. On three separate occasions shortly before the trial, a local television station broadcast the film to audiences ranging from 24,000 to 53,000 individuals. Rideau moved for a change of venue, arguing that he could not receive a fair trial in the parish where the crime occurred, which had a population of approximately 150,000 people. The trial court denied the motion, and a jury eventually convicted Rideau. The Supreme Court of Louisiana upheld the conviction.

We reversed. "What the people [in the community] saw on their television sets," we observed, "was Rideau, in jail, flanked by the sheriff and two state troopers, admitting in detail the commission of the robbery, kidnapping, and murder." "[T]o the tens of thousands of people who saw and heard it," we explained, the interrogation "in a very real sense was Rideau's trial—at which he pleaded guilty." We therefore "d[id] not hesitate to hold, without pausing to examine a particularized transcript of the voir dire," that "[t]he kangaroo court proceedings" trailing the televised confession violated due process.

We followed *Rideau*'s lead in two later cases in which media coverage manifestly tainted a criminal prosecution. In *Estes v. Texas*, 381 U.S. 532, 538 (1965), extensive publicity before trial swelled into excessive exposure during preliminary court proceedings as reporters and television crews overran the courtroom and "bombard[ed] . . . the community with the sights and sounds of" the pretrial hearing. The media's overzealous reporting efforts, we observed, "led to considerable disruption" and denied the "judicial serenity and calm to which [Billie Sol Estes] was entitled."

Similarly, in *Sheppard v. Maxwell*, 384 U.S. 333 (1966), news reporters extensively covered the story of Sam Sheppard, who was accused of bludgeoning his pregnant wife to death. "[B]edlam reigned at the courthouse during the trial and newsmen took over practically the entire courtroom," thrusting jurors "into the role of celebrities." Pretrial media coverage, which we characterized as "months [of] virulent publicity about Sheppard and the murder," did not alone deny due process, we noted. But Sheppard's case involved more than heated reporting pretrial: We upset the murder conviction because a "carnival atmosphere" pervaded the trial.

In each of these cases, we overturned a "conviction obtained in a trial atmosphere that [was] utterly corrupted by press coverage"; our decisions, however, "cannot be made to stand for the proposition that juror exposure to . . . news accounts of the crime . . . alone presumptively deprives the defendant of due process." Prominence does not necessarily produce prejudice, and juror impartiality, we have reiterated, does not require ignorance. A presumption of prejudice, our decisions indicate, attends only the extreme case.

Relying on *Rideau, Estes,* and *Sheppard,* Skilling asserts that we need not pause to examine the screening questionnaires or the voir dire before declaring his jury's verdict void. We are not persuaded. Important differences separate Skilling's prosecution from those in which we have presumed juror prejudice.

First, we have emphasized in prior decisions the size and characteristics of the community in which the crime occurred. In Rideau, for example, we noted that the murder was committed in a parish of only 150,000 residents. Houston, in contrast, is the fourth most populous city in the Nation: At the time of Skilling's trial, more than 4.5 million individuals eligible for jury duty resided in the Houston area. Given this large, diverse pool of potential jurors, the suggestion that 12 impartial individuals could not be empaneled is hard to sustain.

Second, although news stories about Skilling were not kind, they contained no confession or other blatantly prejudicial information of the type readers or viewers could not reasonably be expected to shut from sight. Rideau's dramatically staged admission of guilt, for instance, was likely imprinted indelibly in the mind of anyone who watched it. Pretrial publicity about Skilling was less memorable and prejudicial. No evidence of the smoking-gun variety invited prejudgment of his culpability.

Third, unlike cases in which trial swiftly followed a widely reported crime, over four years elapsed between Enron's bankruptcy and Skilling's trial. Although reporters covered Enron-related news throughout this period, the decibel level of media attention diminished somewhat in the years following Enron's collapse.

Finally, and of prime significance, Skilling's jury acquitted him of nine insider-trading counts. Similarly, earlier instituted Enron-related prosecutions yielded no overwhelming victory for the Government. In *Rideau, Estes,* and *Sheppard,* in marked contrast, the jury's verdict did not undermine in any way the supposition of juror bias. It would be odd for an appellate court to presume prejudice in a case in which jurors' actions run counter to that presumption.

Skilling's trial, in short, shares little in common with those in which we approved a presumption of juror prejudice. . . . In this case, as just noted, news stories about Enron did not present the kind of vivid, unforgettable information we have recognized as particularly likely to produce prejudice, and Houston's size and diversity diluted the media's impact.

Nor did Enron's "sheer number of victims," trigger a presumption of prejudice. Although the widespread community impact necessitated careful identification and inspection of prospective jurors' connections to Enron, the extensive screening questionnaire and followup voir dire were well suited to that task. And hindsight shows the efficacy of these devices; jurors' links to Enron were either nonexistent or attenuated.. . . Persuaded that no presumption arose, we conclude that the District Court, in declining to order a venue change, did not exceed constitutional limitations. . . .

We next consider whether actual prejudice infected Skilling's jury. Voir dire, Skilling asserts, did not adequately detect and defuse juror bias. "[T]he record . . . affirmatively confirm[s]" prejudice, he maintains, because several seated jurors "prejudged his guilt." We disagree with Skilling's characterization of the voir dire and the jurors selected through it.

No hard-and-fast formula dictates the necessary depth or breadth of voir dire. Jury selection, we have repeatedly emphasized, is "particularly within the province of the trial judge."

When pretrial publicity is at issue, "primary reliance on the judgment of the trial court makes [especially] good sense" because the judge "sits in the locale where the publicity is said to have had its effect" and may base her evaluation on her "own perception of the depth and extent of news stories that might influence a juror." Appellate courts making after-the-fact assessments of the media's impact on jurors should be mindful that their judgments lack the on-the-spot comprehension of the situation possessed by trial judges.

Reviewing courts are properly resistant to second-guessing the trial judge's estimation of a juror's impartiality, for that judge's appraisal is ordinarily influenced by a host of factors impossible to capture fully in the record—among them, the prospective juror's inflection, sincerity, demeanor, candor, body language, and apprehension of duty. In contrast to the cold transcript received by the appellate court, the in-the-moment voir dire affords the trial court a more intimate and immediate basis for assessing a venire member's fitness for jury service. We consider the adequacy of jury selection in Skilling's case, therefore, attentive to the respect due to district-court determinations of juror impartiality and of the measures necessary to ensure that impartiality.

Skilling deems the voir dire insufficient because, he argues, jury selection lasted "just five hours," "[m]ost of the court's questions were conclusory[,] high-level, and failed adequately to probe jurors' true feelings," and the court "consistently took prospective jurors at their word once they claimed they could be fair, no matter what other indications of bias were present." Our review of the record, however, yields a different appraisal.

[T]he District Court initially screened venire members by eliciting their responses to a comprehensive questionnaire drafted in large part by Skilling. That survey helped to identify prospective jurors excusable for cause and served as a springboard for further questions put to remaining members of the array. Voir dire thus was, in the court's words, the "culmination of a lengthy process." . . .

> The District Court conducted voir dire, moreover, aware of the greater-than-normal need, due to pretrial publicity, to ensure against jury bias. At Skilling's urging, the court examined each prospective juror individually, thus preventing the spread of any prejudicial information to other venire members. To encourage candor, the court repeatedly admonished that there were "no right and wrong answers to th[e] questions." The court denied Skilling's request for attorney-led voir dire because, in its experience, potential jurors were "more forthcoming" when the court, rather than counsel, asked the question. The parties, however, were accorded an opportunity to ask followup questions of every prospective juror brought to the bench for colloquy. Skilling's counsel declined to ask anything of more than half of the venire members questioned individually, including eight eventually selected for the jury, because, he explained, "the Court and other counsel have covered" everything he wanted to know.
>
> Inspection of the questionnaires and voir dire of the individuals who actually served as jurors satisfies us that, notwithstanding the flaws Skilling lists, the selection process successfully secured jurors who were largely untouched by Enron's collapse. . . . The questionnaires confirmed that, whatever community prejudice existed in Houston generally, Skilling's jurors were not under its sway. . . .

NOTES & QUESTIONS ON CHANGE OF VENUE

1. *Houston.* Do you agree with Skilling that the environment in Houston was impermissibly toxic? List the various reasons why the community members in Houston were particularly angry about the Enron collapse. What did members of the community lose in that bankruptcy? Was it just an ordinary corporate event or did it have a greater salience for the residents of Houston? Finally, do you agree with the trial judge that community prejudice did not contaminate the jury?

2. *Social media.* In an era when all publicity, and press activity, was local, switching from one locality to another made sense as a solution for finding an impartial jury. But in today's world of social media and virtual networks, is it the case that physical locality (as opposed to virtual locality) determines the amount of pre-trial publicity in a case? Do Facebook, Twitter, and Instagram respect geographical or municipal boundaries? Does this fact make change of venue more or less appropriate as a solution in the future?

3. *Gag orders.* Courts may impose a gag order on the witnesses, police officers, and lawyers involved in the case. But what if a trial judge extended such an order to include journalists as well? In other words, in addition to

constraining what the ***lawyers*** say to the press, may a trial judge constrain what the ***journalists*** write, publish, or broadcast? Or would such an order constitute an unconstitutional "prior restraint" on the freedom of the press in violation of the First Amendment? In *Nebraska Press Ass'n v. Stuart,* the Supreme Court clarified that a trial judge imposing such an order would not only need to find that pre-trial publicity would foreclose the possibility of finding an impartial jury but also that no other remedy short of a gag order would achieve similar results:

> The record demonstrates, as the Nebraska courts held, that there was indeed a risk that pretrial news accounts, true or false, would have some adverse impact on the attitudes of those who might be called as jurors. But on the record now before us it is not clear that further publicity, unchecked, would so distort the views of potential jurors that 12 could not be found who would, under proper instructions, fulfill their sworn duty to render a just verdict exclusively on the evidence presented in open court. We cannot say on this record that alternatives to a prior restraint on petitioners would not have sufficiently mitigated the adverse effects of pretrial publicity so as to make prior restraint unnecessary. Nor can we conclude that the restraining order actually entered would serve its intended purpose. Reasonable minds can have few doubts about the gravity of the evil pretrial publicity can work, but the probability that it would do so here was not demonstrated with the degree of certainty our cases on prior restraint require.

Nebraska Press Ass'n v. Stuart, 427 U.S. 539, 568-69 (1976).

PROBLEM CASE

Consider the following two cases:

(1) Defendants Walter Lefight Church and Samuel Stephen Ealy were charged in connection with a triple homicide that occurred in 1999. The defendants were tried separately in 2002. Ealy went to trial first, was found guilty, but was spared the death penalty. Because the case involved a triple murder and carried a possible death sentence, there was substantial press coverage of the trial. Three months later, Church's trial was scheduled to begin. Church objected and filed a motion for a change of venue, arguing that the 45 articles that had been published in local newspapers about the case would make it impossible to find an impartial jury. To buttress his claim, Church filed affidavits from ten local residents, one of whom asserted:

> I am familiar with the allegations of capital murder against Walter "Pete" Church and Samuel S. Ealy. I am familiar with these allegations because of talk in the community among the citizens about the case, which is widespread, and the widespread publicity concerning the case from the newspapers circulated in the community, television news, and radio. I am also familiar with the sentiment in the community concerning this case and the victims involved. In my opinion, a fair trial, including the presumption of innocence would

> not be possible . . . due to, among other things, the nature of the charges, widespread publicity, and community feelings.

United States v. Church, 217 F. Supp. 2d 696, 699 (W.D. Va. 2002). Should the judge transfer the case to another venue?

(2) In 1961, someone robbed a bank in Lake Charles, Louisiana, kidnapped three employees from the bank, and killed one of them. Local police charged Wilbert Rideau with the crimes after he confessed during a police interrogation. The interrogation was conducted by the local sheriff's office and a video recording of the confession was publicly released and aired on a local television station three times. Calcasieu Parish (which includes Lake Charles) had a population of 150,00 and the viewership for the broadcasts of the confession was 24,000, 53,000, and 20,000, respectively. Under these circumstances, should the trial judge order a change of venue? See *Rideau v. Louisiana*, 373 U.S. 723 (1963).

STATE LAW REQUIREMENTS

State jurisdictions impose different standards to guide trial courts in exercising their discretion to change venue. For example, Florida courts articulate the following standard for when a change of venue is appropriate:

> The test for determining a change of venue is whether the general state of mind of the inhabitants of a community is so infected by knowledge of the incident and accompanying prejudice, bias, and preconceived opinions that jurors could not possibly put these matters out of their minds and try the case solely upon the evidence presented in the courtroom.

Serrano v. State, 64 So. 3d 93, 112 (Fla. 2011). In some jurisdictions, the standard for making a motion to change venue is codified by statute. For example, Texas law requires that

> [a] change of venue may be granted in any felony or misdemeanor case punishable by confinement on the written motion of the defendant, supported by his own affidavit and the affidavit of at least two credible persons, residents of the county where the prosecution is instituted, for either of the following causes, the truth and sufficiency of which the court shall determine:
>
> 1. That there exists in the county where the prosecution is commenced so great a prejudice against him that he cannot obtain a fair and impartial trial; and
> 2. That there is a dangerous combination against him instigated by influential persons, by reason of which he cannot expect a fair trial.

Tex. Crim. Proc. Code Ann. § 31.03. The Texas statute also provides that for "the convenience of parties and witnesses, and in the interest of justice," a judge may transfer the case to another district if both the prosecution and the defense consent to the transfer. Common to each of these state standards is the basic idea that the community prejudice is so severe that it impacts the defendant's ability to receive a fair jury trial.

B. OPEN PROCEEDINGS

Another solution for the problem of excessive publicity is to close the courtroom entirely to the press and the public. Although this will not solve the problem of *pre*-trial publicity, it will solve the problem of excessive publicity generated *during* the trial. In these cases, the object of protection is the jury. If members of the public or press do not have access to the trial, information from the trial will not be reported through news sources and then routed back to the jury during the proceedings, possibly contaminating the jury or its deliberations. Closing the courtroom is a drastic step, one that both compromises the public's access to an important branch of government under the First Amendment and also threatens to compromise the defendant's right to a jury trial under the Sixth Amendment. In cases where the defendant objects to the closing, the claim sounds under the Sixth Amendment; where a third party objects to the closing, the claim is usually pursued under the First Amendment.

In the following two cases, the Supreme Court explicitly considers open access to court proceedings under the Sixth Amendment. In other words, does the Sixth Amendment guarantee of trial by jury logically entail that proceedings must be open to the public? In the first case, *Gannett Co. v. DePasquale*, the defendant and the prosecutor both agreed that the court should be closed for pre-trial proceedings. In the second case, *Presley v. Georgia*, the defendant objected when the trial judge prevented members of the public from remaining in the courtroom during voir dire. As you read the cases, ask yourself whether this difference explains the divergent treatment these cases received from the Supreme Court.

Gannett Co. v. DePasquale

Supreme Court of the United States
443 U.S. 368 (1979)

Mr. Justice Stewart delivered the opinion of the Court.

The question presented in this case is whether members of the public have an independent constitutional right to insist upon access to a pretrial judicial proceeding, even though the accused, the prosecutor, and the trial judge all have agreed to the closure of that proceeding in order to assure a fair trial.

I

Wayne Clapp, aged 42 and residing at Henrietta, a Rochester, N. Y., suburb, disappeared in July 1976. He was last seen on July 16 when, with two male companions, he went out on his boat to fish in Seneca Lake, about 40 miles from Rochester. The two companions returned in the boat the same day and drove away in Clapp's pickup truck. Clapp was not with them. When he failed to return home by July 19, his family reported his absence to the police. An examination of the boat, laced with bulletholes, seemed to indicate that Clapp had met a violent death aboard it. Police then began an intensive search for the two men. They also began lake-dragging operations in an attempt to locate Clapp's body.

The petitioner, Gannett Co., Inc., publishes two Rochester newspapers, the morning Democrat & Chronicle and the evening Times-Union. . . .

III

This Court has long recognized that adverse publicity can endanger the ability of a defendant to receive a fair trial. To safeguard the due process rights of the accused, a trial judge has an affirmative constitutional duty to minimize the effects of prejudicial pretrial publicity. And because of the Constitution's pervasive concern for these due process rights, a trial judge may surely take protective measures even when they are not strictly and inescapably necessary.

Publicity concerning pretrial suppression hearings such as the one involved in the present case poses special risks of unfairness. The whole purpose of such hearings is to screen out unreliable or illegally obtained evidence and insure that this evidence does not become known to the jury. Publicity concerning the proceedings at a pretrial hearing, however, could influence public opinion against a defendant and inform potential jurors of inculpatory information wholly inadmissible at the actual trial.

The danger of publicity concerning pretrial suppression hearings is particularly acute, because it may be difficult to measure with any degree of certainty the effects of such publicity on the fairness of the trial. After the commencement of the trial itself, inadmissible prejudicial information about a defendant can be kept from a jury by a variety of means. When such information is publicized during a pretrial proceeding, however, it may never be altogether kept from potential jurors. Closure of pretrial proceedings is often one of the most effective methods that a trial judge can employ to attempt to insure that the fairness of a trial will not be jeopardized by the dissemination of such information throughout the community before the trial itself has even begun.

IV

The Sixth Amendment, applicable to the States through the Fourteenth, surrounds a criminal trial with guarantees such as the rights to notice, confrontation, and compulsory process that have as their overriding purpose the protection of the accused from prosecutorial and judicial abuses. Among the guarantees that the Amendment provides to a person charged with the commission of a criminal offense, and to him alone, is the "right to a speedy and public trial, by an impartial jury." The Constitution nowhere mentions any right of access to a criminal trial on the part of the public; its guarantee, like the others enumerated, is personal to the accused.

Our cases have uniformly recognized the public trial guarantee as one created for the benefit of the defendant. In *In re Oliver*, 333 U.S. 257, this Court held that the secrecy of a criminal contempt trial violated the accused's right to a public trial under the Fourteenth Amendment. The right to a public trial, the Court stated, "has always been recognized as a safeguard against any attempt to employ our courts as instruments of persecution. The knowledge that every criminal trial is subject to contemporaneous review in the forum of public opinion is an effective restraint on possible abuse of judicial power." . . .

Similarly, in *Estes v. Texas*, the Court held that a defendant was deprived of his right to due process of law under the Fourteenth Amendment by the televising and broadcasting of his trial. In rejecting the claim that the media representatives had a constitutional right to televise the trial, the Court stated that "[t]he purpose of the requirement of a public trial was to guarantee that the accused would be fairly dealt with and not unjustly condemned." 381 U.S., at 538-539. Thus, both the *Oliver* and *Estes* cases recognized that the constitutional guarantee of a public trial is for the benefit of the defendant. There is not the slightest suggestion in either case that there is any correlative right in members of the public to insist upon a public trial.

While the Sixth Amendment guarantees to a defendant in a criminal case the right to a public trial, it does not guarantee the right to compel a private trial. . . . But the issue here is not whether the defendant can compel a private trial. Rather, the issue is whether members of the public have an enforceable right to a public trial that can be asserted independently of the parties in the litigation.

There can be no blinking the fact that there is a strong societal interest in public trials. Openness in court proceedings may improve the quality of testimony, induce unknown witnesses to come forward with relevant testimony, cause all trial participants to perform their duties more conscientiously, and generally give the public an opportunity to observe the judicial system. But there is a strong societal interest in other constitutional guarantees extended to the accused as well. The public, for example, has a definite and concrete interest in seeing that justice is swiftly and fairly administered. Similarly, the public has an interest in having a criminal case heard by a jury, an interest distinct from the defendant's interest in being tried by a jury of his peers.

Recognition of an independent public interest in the enforcement of Sixth Amendment guarantees is a far cry, however, from the creation of a constitutional right on the part of the public. In an adversary system of criminal justice, the public interest in the administration of justice is protected by the participants in the litigation. Thus, because of the great public interest in jury trials as the preferred mode of fact-finding in criminal cases, a defendant cannot waive a jury trial without the consent of the prosecutor and judge. But if the defendant waives his right to a jury trial, and the prosecutor and the judge consent, it could hardly be seriously argued that a member of the public could demand a jury trial because of the societal interest in that mode of fact-finding. Similarly, while a defendant cannot convert his right to a speedy trial into a right to compel an indefinite postponement, a member of the general public surely has no right to prevent a continuance in order to vindicate the public interest in the efficient administration of justice. In short, our adversary system of criminal justice is premised upon the proposition that the public interest is fully protected by the participants in the litigation.

V

In arguing that members of the general public have a constitutional right to attend a criminal trial, despite the obvious lack of support for such a right in the structure or text of the Sixth Amendment, the petitioner and amici rely on the history of the public-trial guarantee. This history, however, ultimately demonstrates no more than the existence of a common-law rule of open civil and criminal proceedings.

Not many common-law rules have been elevated to the status of constitutional rights. The provisions of our Constitution do reflect an incorporation of certain few common-law rules and a rejection of others. The common-law right to a jury trial, for example, is explicitly embodied in the Sixth and Seventh Amendments. The common-law rule that looked upon jurors as interested parties who could give evidence against a defendant was explicitly rejected by the Sixth Amendment provision that a defendant is entitled to be tried by an "impartial jury." But the vast majority of common-law rules were neither made part of the Constitution nor explicitly rejected by it.

Our judicial duty in this case is to determine whether the common-law rule of open proceedings was incorporated, rejected, or left undisturbed by the Sixth Amendment. In pursuing this inquiry, it is important to distinguish between what the Constitution permits and what it requires. It has never been suggested that by phrasing the public-trial guarantee as a right of the accused, the Framers intended to reject the common-law rule of open proceedings. There is no question that the Sixth Amendment permits and even presumes open trials as a norm. But the issue here is whether the Constitution requires that a pretrial proceeding such as this one be opened to the public, even though the participants in the litigation agree that it should be closed to protect the defendants' right to a fair trial. . . .

Under English common law, the public had no right to attend pretrial proceedings. Closed pretrial proceedings have been a familiar part of the judicial landscape in this country as well. The original New York Field Code of Criminal Procedure published in 1850, for example, provided that pretrial hearings should be closed to the public "upon the request of a defendant." The explanatory report made clear that this provision was designed to protect defendants from prejudicial pretrial publicity. . . . Indeed, eight of the States that have retained all or part of the Field Code have kept the explicit provision relating to closed pretrial hearings. For these reasons, we hold that members of the public have no constitutional right under the Sixth and Fourteenth Amendments to attend criminal trials. . . .

Presley v. Georgia

Supreme Court of the United States
558 U.S. 209 (2010)

Per Curiam

After a jury trial in the Superior Court of DeKalb County, Georgia, petitioner Eric Presley was convicted of a cocaine trafficking offense. The conviction was affirmed by the Supreme Court of Georgia. Presley seeks certiorari, claiming his Sixth and Fourteenth Amendment right to a public trial was violated when the trial court excluded the public from the voir dire of prospective jurors. . . .

Before selecting a jury in Presley's trial, the trial court noticed a lone courtroom observer. The court explained that prospective jurors were about to enter and instructed the man that he was not allowed in the courtroom and had to leave that floor of the courthouse entirely. The court then questioned the man and learned he was Presley's uncle. . . . Presley's counsel objected to "the exclusion of the public from the courtroom," but the court explained, "[t]here just isn't space for them to sit in the audience." . . .

After Presley was convicted, he moved for a new trial based on the exclusion of the public from the juror voir dire. At a hearing on the motion, Presley presented evidence showing that 14 prospective jurors could have fit in the jury box and the remaining 28 could have fit entirely on one side of the courtroom, leaving adequate room for the public. The trial court denied the motion, commenting that it preferred to seat jurors throughout the entirety of the courtroom, and "it's up to the individual judge to decide . . . what's comfortable." The court continued: "It's totally up to my discretion whether or not I want family members in the courtroom to intermingle with the jurors and sit directly behind the jurors where they might overhear some inadvertent comment or conversation." . . .

This Court's rulings with respect to the public trial right rest upon two different provisions of the Bill of Rights. . . . The Sixth Amendment directs, in relevant part, that "[i]n all criminal prosecutions, the accused shall enjoy the right to a speedy and public trial. . . ."

An initial question is whether the right to a public trial in criminal cases extends to the jury selection phase of trial, and in particular the voir dire of prospective jurors. In the First Amendment context that question was answered in *Press-Enterprise I.* The Court there held that the voir dire of prospective jurors must be open to the public under the First Amendment. Later in the same Term as *Press-Enterprise I,* the Court considered a Sixth Amendment case concerning whether the public trial right extends to a pretrial hearing on a motion to suppress certain evidence. *Waller v. Georgia,* 467 U.S. 39 (1984). The *Waller* Court relied heavily upon *Press-Enterprise I* in finding that the Sixth Amendment right to a public trial extends beyond the actual proof at trial. It ruled that the pretrial suppression hearing must be open to the public because "there can be little doubt that the explicit Sixth Amendment right of the accused is no less protective of a public trial than the implicit First Amendment right of the press and public."

While *Press-Enterprise I* was heavily relied upon in *Waller,* the jury selection issue in the former case was resolved under the First, not the Sixth, Amendment. In the instant case, the question then arises whether it is so well settled that the Sixth Amendment right extends to jury voir dire that this Court may proceed by summary disposition.

The point is well settled under *Press-Enterprise I* and *Waller.* The extent to which the First and Sixth Amendment public trial rights are coextensive is an open question, and it is not necessary here to speculate whether or in what circumstances the reach or protections of one might be greater than the other. Still, there is no legitimate reason, at least in the context of juror selection proceedings, to give one who asserts a First Amendment privilege greater rights to insist on public proceedings than the accused has. . . . There could be no explanation for barring the accused from raising a constitutional right that is unmistakably for his or her benefit. That rationale suffices to resolve the instant matter. . . .

While the accused does have a right to insist that the voir dire of the jurors be public, there are exceptions to this general rule. "[T]he right to an open trial may give way in certain cases to other rights or interests, such as the defendant's right to a fair trial or the government's interest in inhibiting disclosure of sensitive information." *Waller,* 467 U.S., at 45. "Such circumstances will be rare, however, and the balance of interests must be struck with special care." *Waller* provided standards for courts to apply before excluding the public from any stage of a criminal trial: "[T]he party seeking to close the hearing must advance an overriding interest that is likely to be prejudiced, the closure must be no broader than necessary to protect that interest, the trial court must consider reasonable alternatives to closing the proceeding, and it must make findings adequate to support the closure."

In upholding exclusion of the public at juror voir dire in the instant case, the Supreme Court of Georgia concluded, despite our explicit statements to the contrary, that trial courts need not consider alternatives to closure absent an opposing party's proffer of some alternatives. While the Supreme Court of Georgia concluded this was an open question under this Court's precedents, the statement in *Waller* that "the trial court must consider reasonable alternatives to closing the proceeding" settles the point. . . .

The conclusion that trial courts are required to consider alternatives to closure even when they are not offered by the parties is clear not only from this Court's precedents but also from the premise that "[t]he process of juror selection is itself a matter of importance, not simply to the adversaries but to the criminal justice system." The public has a right to be present whether or not any party has asserted the right. In *Press-Enterprise I*, for instance, neither the defendant nor the prosecution requested an open courtroom during juror voir dire proceedings; in fact, both specifically argued in favor of keeping the transcript of the proceedings confidential. The Court, nonetheless, found it was error to close the courtroom.

Trial courts are obligated to take every reasonable measure to accommodate public attendance at criminal trials. Nothing in the record shows that the trial court could not have accommodated the public at Presley's trial. Without knowing the precise circumstances, some possibilities include reserving one or more rows for the public; dividing the jury venire panel to reduce courtroom congestion; or instructing prospective jurors not to engage or interact with audience members. . . .

There are no doubt circumstances where a judge could conclude that threats of improper communications with jurors or safety concerns are concrete enough to warrant closing voir dire. But in those cases, the particular interest, and threat to that interest, must "be articulated along with findings specific enough that a reviewing court can determine whether the closure order was properly entered."

We need not rule on this second claim of error, because even assuming, arguendo, that the trial court had an overriding interest in closing voir dire, it was still incumbent upon it to consider all reasonable alternatives to closure. It did not, and that is all this Court needs to decide. . . .

NOTES & QUESTIONS ON THE RIGHT TO OPEN PROCEEDINGS

1. *Specific findings.* If *Gannett Co. v. DePasquale* stands for the proposition that a closed courtroom is consistent with the Sixth Amendment, the more recent *Presley v. Georgia* is far more skeptical of the practice and stands for the proposition that a trial judge must explore all other alternatives before closing the courtroom. The court in *Presley v. Georgia* concluded that there might be security threats sufficient to justify a closed voir dire, but in that case, the justification must involve more than just vague or speculative concerns about security, but rather specific concerns articulated on the record that a reviewing court can scrutinize. Can you imagine a scenario where the security concerns would be specific enough to meet this standard? What type of evidence would a prosecutor need to present to the court to overcome the presumption of a public voir dire, especially over the defendant's objections?

2. *First Amendment right to open courts.* In addition to the Sixth Amendment, the First Amendment also imposes an open courts requirement, although in the case of the First Amendment the right inures to the benefit of the press and the public, not the defendant. In *Globe Newspaper Co. v. Superior Court*, 457 U.S. 596 (1982), a trial judge closed a courtroom pursuant to a Massachusetts statute that mandated closed trials for cases involving sexual offenses against minors. The case threw into sharp relief the tension between the state's desire to protect young victims and witnesses from testifying in open court and the public's interest, protected by the First Amendment, to directly observe (and to read contemporaneous news reports about) criminal cases of obvious public concern. The State of Massachusetts argued that the statute's infringement on public access was justified by the state's compelling interest in encouraging minors to report and testify about sexual abuse. According to the state, if minors envision that they will have to testify in open court, many will either refuse to testify in such cases or might even not report the abuse at all—a disastrous outcome from the perspective of public policy. The Supreme Court rejected this argument, concluding that it was not compelling enough to outweigh the First Amendment interest in public access. What result if the state statute were rewritten to *permit* rather than *require* judges to close the courtroom in cases of child witnesses or victims of sexual offenses? For example, such a statute could require that judges hear from both the defense and the prosecution and then make findings, on the record, about whether the case, and the likely testimony to be offered during it, is so sensitive that no other remedy short of court closure

will satisfy the public interest. Would such a revised statute pass constitutional muster?

C. THE RIGHT TO CONFRONTATION

The Sixth Amendment guarantees, along with "the right to a speedy and public trial, by an impartial jury," the right to be "confronted with the witnesses against him" and the right "to have compulsory process for obtaining witnesses in his favor." Taken together with the right to counsel, which is referred to immediately thereafter in the text of the Sixth Amendment, the right to confrontation is a constitutional directive regarding the process by which witnesses against the accused are subjected to adversarial testing. In other words, one might even consider it a specific directive laying out what is meant by the right to a trial. As an event, a trial is not merely a consideration of the defendant's guilt or innocence. That much could be accomplished by a judge or jury reviewing of a "dossier" of compiled evidence, including reports of forensic evidence and transcripts of testimony given under oath in the privacy of a magistrate's office. But the Sixth Amendment expresses a preference against such paper "trials" in favor of a far more performative event—a public contest of reasons between prosecution and defense, each side marshalling evidence that is presented by witnesses who are then cross-examined by opposing counsel in full view of the judge and jury. The Confrontation Clause is one embodiment of this performative ideal—a rejection of trial by paper, or trial by affidavit. The following two subsections focus on two aspects of this trial paradigm: the defendant's personal appearance at the trial and a face-to-face confrontation between the defendant and the witnesses who testify at trial. The final subsection focuses on the application of the Confrontation Clause when the prosecution seeks to introduce forensic evidence.

1. Presence at Trial

The basic building block of the right to confront witnesses starts from a general common law presumption that witnesses will present evidence in person at trial, rather than the civil law tradition of evidence by affidavit, which the framers explicitly rejected in drafting the Sixth Amendment. In addition to the presence of witnesses, the concept of confrontation also logically presupposes that the *defendant* will be present as well. After all, it is difficult for a defendant to confront adverse witnesses if the defendant is not even there. This suggests that removal of a defendant from the courtroom should never be taken lightly. On the other hand, a disruptive defendant can prevent a trial from functioning efficiently or at all, depending on the level of disruption. A defendant might speak when they are not supposed to, or yell, or even act violently. In *Illinois v. Allen,* 397 U.S. 337 (1970), the Supreme Court evaluated the decision of one trial judge to remove a disorderly defendant:

> It is not pleasant to hold that the respondent Allen was properly banished from the court for a part of his own trial. But our courts, palladiums of liberty as they are, cannot be treated disrespectfully with impunity. Nor can the accused be permitted by his disruptive conduct indefinitely to avoid being tried on the charges brought against him. It would degrade our country and our judicial system to permit our courts to be bullied, insulted, and humiliated and their orderly progress thwarted and obstructed by defendants brought before them charged with crimes. As guardians of the public welfare, our state and federal judicial systems strive to administer equal justice to the rich and the poor, the good and the bad, the native and foreign born of every race, nationality, and religion. Being manned by humans, the courts are not perfect and are bound to make some errors. But, if our courts are to remain what the Founders intended, the citadels of justice, their proceedings cannot and must not be infected with the sort of scurrilous, abusive language and conduct paraded before the Illinois trial judge in this case. . . . We do not hold that removing this defendant from his own trial was the only way the Illinois judge could have constitutionally solved the problem he had. We do hold, however, that there is nothing whatever in this record to show that the judge did not act completely within his discretion. Deplorable as it is to remove a man from his own trial, even for a short time, we hold that the judge did not commit legal error in doing what he did. . . .

In most criminal trials, the defendant wears civilian clothing and sits at a table beside defense counsel. But what if state authorities insist on using visible restraints, such as shackles, leg irons, or handcuffs, to restrain the defendant during the trial? If those restraints are visible to the jury, do they violate due process? In *Deck v. Missouri,* 544 U.S. 622 (2005), the Supreme Court concluded that shackling must be specially justified by the circumstances; otherwise, it will violate due process. Furthermore, a defendant shackled without the special justification need not make a showing of prejudice; the shackling is a per se due process violation: "We are mindful of the tragedy that can result if judges are not able to protect themselves and their courtrooms. But given their prejudicial effect, due process does not permit the use of visible restraints if the trial court has not taken account of the circumstances of the particular case." *Id.* at 632.

STATUTORY REQUIREMENTS

The Federal Rules of Criminal Procedure stipulate that a defendant in a federal criminal case must be present at initial appearance, arraignment, the plea, sentencing, and "every trial stage," including the jury impanelment and return of the verdict. See Fed. R. Crim. P. 43(a). Also, if the defendant is present at trial initially, but then fails to appear later, the Rules allow the trial to proceed on the theory that the defendant has waived his or her right to be present at trial. This would apply, for example, if a court has jurisdiction over the defendant by arresting and arraigning the defendant, but the defendant then flees the jurisdiction in the middle of the trial. Indeed, Rule 43 says that the waiver applies "when the defendant is voluntarily absent after the trial has begun, regardless of whether the court informed the defendant of an obligation to remain during trial." In that situation, the trial may continue even in the absence of the defendant. The defendant also is construed to have waived the right to be present at the trial "when the court warns the defendant that it will remove the defendant from the courtroom for disruptive behavior, but the defendant persists in conduct that justifies removal from the courtroom." Rule 43 does not otherwise define "disruptive behavior."

2. Personal Confrontations

Unlike some state constitutions that explicitly refer to face-to-face confrontations, the Sixth Amendment's Confrontation Clause does not explicitly say whether a defendant must have a personal, physical confrontation with the witness giving testimony against the defendant. So, to determine whether such personal confrontations are constitutionally required, one must look deeper into the Clause. The issue comes to a head in several situations. For example, *Maryland v. Craig* considers the use of a video-feed system to allow the victims of child abuse to testify remotely in a criminal trial. Another example is the introduction of a statement made out of court through another in-court witness pursuant to a hearsay exception (e.g., a police officer testifying about what someone at the scene of the crime told the officer she observed), where the defendant never has the opportunity to confront in court the declarant who made the damaging statement. In both of these examples, does the lack of a personal, face-to-face confrontation suggest that the procedure violates the Confrontation Clause?

Maryland v. Craig

Supreme Court of the United States
497 U.S. 836 (1990)

Justice O'CONNOR delivered the opinion of the Court.

This case requires us to decide whether the Confrontation Clause of the Sixth Amendment categorically prohibits a child witness in a child abuse case from testifying against a defendant at trial, outside the defendant's physical presence, by one-way closed circuit television.

I

In October 1986, a Howard County grand jury charged respondent, Sandra Ann Craig, with child abuse, first and second degree sexual offenses, perverted sexual practice, assault, and battery. The named victim in each count was a 6-year-old girl who, from August 1984 to June 1986, had attended a kindergarten and prekindergarten center owned and operated by Craig.

In March 1987, before the case went to trial, the State sought to invoke a Maryland statutory procedure that permits a judge to receive, by one-way closed circuit television, the testimony of a child witness who is alleged to be a victim of child abuse. To invoke the procedure, the trial judge must first "determin[e] that testimony by the child victim in the courtroom will result in the child suffering serious emotional distress such that the child cannot reasonably communicate." Md. Cts. & Jud. Proc. Code Ann. § 9-102(a)(1)(ii) (1989). Once the procedure is invoked, the child witness, prosecutor, and defense counsel withdraw to a separate room; the judge, jury, and defendant remain in the courtroom. The child witness is then examined and cross-examined in the separate room, while a video monitor records and displays the witness' testimony to those in the courtroom. During this time the witness cannot see the defendant. The defendant remains in electronic communication with defense counsel, and objections may be made and ruled on as if the witness were testifying in the courtroom.

In support of its motion invoking the one-way closed circuit television procedure, the State presented expert testimony that the named victim as well as a number of other children who were alleged to have been sexually abused by Craig, would suffer "serious emotional distress such that [they could not] reasonably communicate," § 9-102(a)(1)(ii), if required to testify in the courtroom. . . . Craig objected to the use of the procedure on Confrontation Clause grounds, but the trial court rejected that contention, concluding that although the statute "take[s] away the right of the defendant to be face to face with his or her accuser," the defendant retains the "essence of the right of confrontation," including the right to observe, cross-examine, and have the jury view the demeanor of the witness. The trial court further found that, "based upon the evidence presented . . . the testimony of each of these children in a courtroom will result in each child suffering serious emotional distress . . . such that each of these children cannot reasonably communicate." The trial court then found the named victim and three other children competent to testify and accordingly permitted them to testify against Craig via the one-way closed circuit television procedure. The jury convicted Craig on all counts. . . .

II

. . . The central concern of the Confrontation Clause is to ensure the reliability of the evidence against a criminal defendant by subjecting it to rigorous testing in the context of an adversary proceeding before the trier of fact. The word "confront," after all, also means a clashing of forces or ideas, thus carrying with it the notion of adversariness. As we noted in our earliest case interpreting the Clause:

> The primary object of the constitutional provision in question was to prevent depositions or ex parte affidavits, such as were sometimes admitted in civil cases, being used against the prisoner in lieu of a personal examination and cross-examination of the witness in which the accused has an opportunity, not only of testing the recollection and sifting the conscience of the witness, but of compelling him to stand face to face with the jury in order that they may look at him, and judge by his demeanor upon the stand and the manner in which he gives his testimony whether he is worthy of belief.

As this description indicates, the right guaranteed by the Confrontation Clause includes not only a "personal examination," but also "(1) insures that the witness will give his statements under oath—thus impressing him with the seriousness of the matter and guarding against the lie by the possibility of a penalty for perjury; (2) forces the witness to submit to cross-examination, the 'greatest legal engine ever invented for the discovery of truth'; [and] (3) permits the jury that is to decide the defendant's fate to observe the demeanor of the witness in making his statement, thus aiding the jury in assessing his credibility." *Green*, 99 U.S., at 158.

The combined effect of these elements of confrontation—physical presence, oath, cross-examination, and observation of demeanor by the trier of fact—serves the purposes of the Confrontation Clause by ensuring that evidence admitted against an accused is reliable and subject to the rigorous adversarial testing that is the norm of Anglo-American criminal proceedings.

We have recognized, for example, that face-to-face confrontation enhances the accuracy of factfinding by reducing the risk that a witness will wrongfully implicate an innocent person. We have also noted the strong symbolic purpose served by requiring adverse witnesses at trial to testify in the accused's presence.

Although face-to-face confrontation forms "the core of the values furthered by the Confrontation Clause," we have nevertheless recognized that it is not the sine qua non of the confrontation right. For this reason, we have never insisted on an actual face-to-face encounter at trial in every instance in which testimony is admitted against a defendant. Instead, we have repeatedly held that the Clause permits, where necessary, the admission of certain hearsay statements against a defendant despite the defendant's inability to confront the declarant at trial. In *Mattox*, for example, we held that the testimony of a Government witness at a former trial against the defendant, where the witness was fully cross-examined but had died after the first trial, was admissible in evidence against the defendant at his second trial. 156 U.S., at 240-244.

. . . We have accordingly stated that a literal reading of the Confrontation Clause would "abrogate virtually every hearsay exception, a result long rejected as unintended and too extreme." Thus, in certain narrow circumstances, "competing interests, if 'closely examined,' may warrant dispensing with confrontation at trial." We have recently held, for example, that hearsay statements of nontestifying co-conspirators may be admitted against a defendant despite the lack of any face-to-face encounter with the accused. Given our hearsay cases, the word "confronted," as used in the Confrontation Clause, cannot simply mean face-to-face confrontation, for the Clause would then, contrary to our cases, prohibit the admission of any accusatory hearsay statement made by an absent declarant—a declarant who is undoubtedly as much a "witness against" a defendant as one who actually testifies at trial.

In sum, our precedents establish that "the Confrontation Clause reflects a preference for face-to-face confrontation at trial," a preference that "must occasionally give way to considerations of public policy and the necessities of the case." . . . We have accordingly interpreted the Confrontation Clause in a manner sensitive to its purposes and sensitive to the necessities of trial and the adversary process. Thus, though we reaffirm the importance of face-to-face confrontation with witnesses appearing at trial, we cannot say that such confrontation is an indispensable element of the Sixth Amendment's guarantee of the right to confront one's accusers. Indeed, one commentator has noted that "[i]t is all but universally assumed that there are circumstances that excuse compliance with the right of confrontation."

This interpretation of the Confrontation Clause is consistent with our cases holding that other Sixth Amendment rights must also be interpreted in the context of the necessities of trial and the adversary process. We see no reason to treat the face-to-face component of the confrontation right any differently, and indeed we think it would be anomalous to do so.

That the face-to-face confrontation requirement is not absolute does not, of course, mean that it may easily be dispensed with. As we suggested in *Coy*, our precedents confirm that a defendant's right to confront accusatory witnesses may be satisfied absent a physical, face-to-face confrontation at trial only where denial of such confrontation is necessary to further an important public policy and only where the reliability of the testimony is otherwise assured.

III

Maryland's statutory procedure, when invoked, prevents a child witness from seeing the defendant as he or she testifies against the defendant at trial. We find it significant, however, that Maryland's procedure preserves all of the other elements of the confrontation right: The child witness must be competent to testify and must testify under oath; the defendant retains full opportunity for contemporaneous cross-examination; and the judge, jury, and defendant are able to view (albeit by video monitor) the demeanor (and body) of the witness as he or she testifies. Although we are mindful of the many subtle effects face-to-face confrontation may have on an adversary criminal proceeding, the presence of these other elements of confrontation—oath, cross-examination, and observation of the witness' demeanor—adequately ensures that the testimony is both reliable and subject to rigorous adversarial testing in a manner functionally equivalent to that accorded live, in-person testimony. These safeguards of reliability and adversariness render the use of such a procedure a far cry from the undisputed prohibition of the Confrontation Clause: trial by ex parte affidavit or inquisition. Rather, we think these elements of effective confrontation not only permit a defendant to "confound and undo the false accuser, or reveal the child coached by a malevolent adult," but may well aid a defendant in eliciting favorable testimony from the child witness. Indeed, to the extent the child witness' testimony may be said to be technically given out of court (though we do not so hold), these assurances of reliability and adversariness are far greater than those required for admission of hearsay testimony under the Confrontation Clause. We are therefore confident that use of the one-way closed circuit television procedure, where necessary to further an important state interest, does not impinge upon the truth-seeking or symbolic purposes of the Confrontation Clause. . . .

. . . [W]e will not second-guess the considered judgment of the Maryland Legislature regarding the importance of its interest in protecting child abuse victims from the emotional trauma of testifying. Accordingly, we hold that, if the State makes an adequate showing of necessity, the state interest in protecting child witnesses from the trauma of testifying in a child abuse case is sufficiently important to justify the use of a special procedure that permits a child witness in such cases to testify at trial against a defendant in the absence of face-to-face confrontation with the defendant.

The requisite finding of necessity must of course be a case-specific one: The trial court must hear evidence and determine whether use of the one-way closed circuit television procedure is necessary to protect the welfare of the particular child witness who seeks to testify. The trial court must also find that the child witness would be traumatized, not by the courtroom generally, but by the presence of the defendant. Denial of face-to-face confrontation is not needed to further the state interest in protecting the child witness from trauma unless it is the presence of the defendant that causes the trauma. In other words, if the state interest were merely the interest in protecting child witnesses from courtroom trauma generally, denial of face-to-face confrontation would be unnecessary because the child could be permitted to testify in less intimidating surroundings, albeit with the defendant present. Finally, the trial court must find that the emotional distress suffered by the child witness in the presence of the defendant is more than de minimis, i.e., more than "mere nervousness or excitement or some reluctance to testify." We need not decide the minimum showing of emotional trauma required for use of the special procedure, however, because the Maryland statute, which requires a determination that the child witness will suffer "serious emotional distress such that the child cannot reasonably communicate," § 9-102(a)(1)(ii), clearly suffices to meet constitutional standards. . . .

Justice SCALIA, with whom Justice BRENNAN, Justice MARSHALL, and Justice STEVENS join, dissenting.

Seldom has this Court failed so conspicuously to sustain a categorical guarantee of the Constitution against the tide of prevailing current opinion. The Sixth Amendment provides, with unmistakable clarity, that "[i]n all criminal prosecutions, the accused shall enjoy the right . . . to be confronted with the witnesses against him." The purpose of enshrining this protection in the Constitution was to assure that none of the many policy interests from time to time pursued by statutory law could overcome a defendant's right to face his or her accusers in court. . . .

Because of this subordination of explicit constitutional text to currently favored public policy, the following scene can be played out in an American courtroom for the first time in two centuries: A father whose young daughter has been given over to the exclusive custody of his estranged wife, or a mother whose young son has been taken into custody by the State's child welfare department, is sentenced to prison for sexual abuse on the basis of testimony by a child the parent has not seen or spoken to for many months; and the guilty verdict is rendered without giving the parent so much as the opportunity to sit in the presence of the child, and to ask, personally or through counsel, "it is really not true, is it, that I—your father (or mother) whom you see before you—did these terrible things?" Perhaps that is a procedure today's society desires; perhaps (though I doubt it) it is even a fair procedure; but it is assuredly not a procedure permitted by the Constitution. . . .

The Court makes the impossible plausible by recharacterizing the Confrontation Clause, so that confrontation (redesignated "face-to-face confrontation") becomes only one of many "elements of confrontation." The reasoning is as follows: The Confrontation Clause guarantees not only what it explicitly provides for—"face-to-face" confrontation—but also implied and collateral rights such as cross-examination, oath, and observation of demeanor (TRUE); the purpose of this entire cluster of rights is to ensure the reliability of evidence (TRUE); the Maryland procedure preserves the implied and collateral rights (TRUE), which adequately ensure the reliability of evidence (perhaps TRUE); therefore the Confrontation Clause is not violated by denying what it explicitly provides for—"face-to-face" confrontation (unquestionably FALSE). This reasoning abstracts from the right to its purposes, and then eliminates the right. It is wrong because the Confrontation Clause does not guarantee reliable evidence; it guarantees specific trial procedures that were thought to assure reliable evidence, undeniably among which was "face-to-face" confrontation. Whatever else it may mean in addition, the defendant's constitutional right "to be confronted with the witnesses against him" means, always and everywhere, at least what it explicitly says: the "right to meet face to face all those who appear and give evidence at trial." *Coy v. Iowa*, 487 U.S. 1012, 1016 (1988), *quoting California v. Green*, 399 U.S. 149, 175 (1970) (Harlan, J., concurring).

AFTERWORD Although Sandra Craig lost her appeal before the Supreme Court, she ultimately won her legal battle with state prosecutors. Her case centered around allegations that emerged from a daycare center that Craig ran with her husband, Jamal. A dozen of the children who attended the daycare center accused the husband and wife pair of sexual abuse. Some of the allegations reported by the children were particularly horrendous and included a report that one child had been buried in the backyard in a cage and other forms of ritualistic abuse. Defense attorneys for Craig contended that the accounts were the product of suggestive interrogations by psychologists who allegedly guided the patients toward similar accusations. The trial court ultimately rejected the defense arguments; Craig was convicted and sentenced to ten years in prison. On appeal, the conviction was reversed by a state appellate court that concluded that prosecutors had failed to turn over potentially exculpatory evidence, including statements from a victim that identified another individual as a perpetrator of the abuse. Despite winning at the Supreme Court on the Confrontation Clause issue, state prosecutors ultimately decided in 1991 not to retry Craig, concluding that a retrial would be too traumatic for the child witnesses.

NOTES & QUESTIONS ON THE CONFRONTATION CLAUSE

1. *Two-way video versus one-way video.* From the perspective of the Confrontation Clause, is there (and ought there be) a difference between one-way and two-way video testimony? A one-way link allows the court to hear the testimony of the remote witness, without providing any video feedback to the witness. In contrast, a two-way link allows the court to hear the testimony of the remote witness while also allowing the remote witness to see and hear what is happening in the courtroom. In *Craig*, the Supreme Court blessed the use of a one-way video link system. Most courts have applied the *Craig* framework to both one-way and two-way video links, while a few courts have concluded that two-way video links are less problematic and don't require the *Craig* showing of a necessity flowing from public policy. Do you agree that one-way and two-way video links are essentially the same for purposes of the Confrontation Clause or is the technology sufficiently different that the two systems should receive divergent constitutional treatment?

STATE LAW REQUIREMENTS

Although the Supreme Court blessed the use of a remote video feed for the testimony of the child witnesses in *Maryland v. Craig*, some state courts have rejected the use of video testimony under the Sixth Amendment and analogous state constitutional confrontation clauses. See, e.g., *State v. Deuter*, 839 S.W.2d 391, 395 (Tenn. 1992) ("The "face-to-face" language found in the Tennessee Constitution has been held to impose a higher right than that found in the federal constitution."). For example, in *State v. Thomas*, 376 P.3d 184 (N.M. 2016), the Supreme Court of New Mexico held that a trial judge erred in permitting two-way video testimony of a forensic scientist, concluding that "[n]othing in the record of this case demonstrates that the use of two-way video was necessary to further an important public policy as required by *Craig*." See also *State v. Rogerson*, 855 N.W.2d 495 (Iowa 2014) (trial judge erred in allowing two-way video testimony in the absence of evidence of necessity); *Harrell v. State*, 709 So. 2d 1364, 1368-69 (Fla. 1998). In most of these cases, the state courts have held that trial judges erred because the requisite finding of necessity in support of public policy, articulated in *Craig*, was not present. For example, the public policy rationale for allowing child abuse victims to testify remotely was well articulated in *Craig*, but in *Thomas*, *supra*, the trial judge in New Mexico failed to articulate a satisfying public policy rationale for allowing the forensics expert to testify remotely.

Other state courts have extended the ruling from *Craig* in other circumstances. For example, in *State v. Johnson*, 195 Ohio App. 3d 59, 958 N.E.2d 977, an Ohio court upheld the use of a two-way video system for the testimony of intimated witnesses. Similarly, in *Kramer v. State*, 277 P.3d 88, 91 (Wyo. 2012), the Wyoming Supreme Court upheld the use of video-conferencing testimony from patients confined to a state mental hospital.

3. Testimonial versus Non-testimonial Statements

Generally speaking, hearsay statements are not admissible at trial. One conceptual rationale for disallowing hearsay is that the defendant does not have the opportunity to confront, or cross-examine, the original declarant. However, there are many exceptions to the hearsay rule. Are these exceptions consistent with the Confrontation Clause? Should the prohibition on the hearsay rule be absolute? The Supreme Court concluded in *Ohio v. Roberts* that the introduction of hearsay evidence is consistent with the Confrontation Clause if the evidence bears "indicia of reliability," which it defined as falling within a "firmly rooted" exception to the hearsay rule or when the underlying declaration displayed "particularized guarantees of trustworthiness." *Ohio v. Roberts,* 448 U.S. 56, 66 (1980). In *Crawford v. Washington,* 541 U.S. 36 (2004), the Supreme Court reconsidered *Roberts,* concluding instead that out-of-court *testimonial* evidence can only be introduced into evidence if the witness is unavailable for trial and the defendant had prior opportunity to cross-examine the witness, regardless of the evidence's indicia of reliability. The *Crawford* rule is both narrower and wider than the older *Roberts* rule. It is narrower in the sense that it clarifies that the Confrontation Clause is only implicated when the out-of-court evidence is truly testimonial. But it is wider because it knocks out as unconstitutional testimonial hearsay evidence that bears indicia of reliability but that the defendant had no opportunity to cross-examine.

Crawford v. Washington

Supreme Court of the United States
541 U.S. 36 (2004)

Justice Scalia delivered the opinion of the Court.

Petitioner Michael Crawford stabbed a man who allegedly tried to rape his wife, Sylvia. At his trial, the State played for the jury Sylvia's tape-recorded statement to the police describing the stabbing, even though he had no opportunity for cross-examination. The Washington Supreme Court upheld petitioner's conviction after determining that Sylvia's statement was reliable. The question presented is whether this procedure complied with the Sixth Amendment's guarantee that, "[i]n all criminal prosecutions, the accused shall enjoy the right . . . to be confronted with the witnesses against him."

II

. . . As noted above, *Roberts* says that an unavailable witness's out-of-court statement may be admitted so long as it has adequate indicia of reliability—i.e., falls within a "firmly rooted hearsay exception" or bears "particularized guarantees of trustworthiness." 448 U.S., at 66. Petitioner argues that this test strays from the original meaning of the Confrontation Clause and urges us to reconsider it.

The Constitution's text does not alone resolve this case. One could plausibly read "witnesses against" a defendant to mean those who actually testify at trial, those whose statements are offered at trial, or something in-between. We must therefore turn to the historical background of the Clause to understand its meaning.

The right to confront one's accusers is a concept that dates back to Roman times. The founding generation's immediate source of the concept, however, was the common law. English common law has long differed from continental civil law in regard to the manner in which witnesses give testimony in criminal trials. The common-law tradition is one of live testimony in court subject to adversarial testing, while the civil law condones examination in private by judicial officers.

Nonetheless, England at times adopted elements of the civil-law practice. Justices of the peace or other officials examined suspects and witnesses before trial. These examinations were sometimes read in court in lieu of live testimony, a practice that "occasioned frequent demands by the prisoner to have his 'accusers,' i.e. the witnesses against him, brought before him face to face." In some cases, these demands were refused.

Pretrial examinations became routine under two statutes passed during the reign of Queen Mary in the 16th century. These Marian bail and committal statutes required justices of the peace to examine suspects and witnesses in felony cases and to certify the results to the court. It is doubtful that the original purpose of the examinations was to produce evidence admissible at trial. Whatever the original purpose, however, they came to be used as evidence in some cases, resulting in an adoption of continental procedure.

The most notorious instances of civil-law examination occurred in the great political trials of the 16th and 17th centuries. One such was the 1603 trial of Sir Walter Raleigh for treason. Lord Cobham, Raleigh's alleged accomplice, had implicated him in an examination before the Privy Council and in a letter. At Raleigh's trial, these were read to the jury. Raleigh argued that Cobham had lied to save himself: "Cobham is absolutely in the King's mercy; to excuse me cannot avail him; by accusing me he may hope for favour." Suspecting that Cobham would recant, Raleigh demanded that the judges call him to appear, arguing that "[t]he Proof of the Common Law is by witness and jury: let Cobham be here, let him speak it. Call my accuser before my face. . . ." The judges refused and, despite Raleigh's protestations that he was being tried "by the Spanish Inquisition," the jury convicted, and Raleigh was sentenced to death.

One of Raleigh's trial judges later lamented that "the justice of England has never been so degraded and injured as by the condemnation of Sir

Walter Raleigh." Through a series of statutory and judicial reforms, English law developed a right of confrontation that limited these abuses. For example, treason statutes required witnesses to confront the accused "face to face" at his arraignment. Courts, meanwhile, developed relatively strict rules of unavailability, admitting examinations only if the witness was demonstrably unable to testify in person. Several authorities also stated that a suspect's confession could be admitted only against himself, and not against others he implicated.

One recurring question was whether the admissibility of an unavailable witness's pretrial examination depended on whether the defendant had had an opportunity to cross-examine him. In 1696, the Court of King's Bench answered this question in the affirmative, in the widely reported misdemeanor libel case of *King v. Paine*, 5 Mod. 163, 87 Eng. Rep. 584. The court ruled that, even though a witness was dead, his examination was not admissible where "the defendant not being present when [it was] taken before the mayor . . . had lost the benefit of a cross-examination." The question was also debated at length during the infamous proceedings against Sir John Fenwick on a bill of attainder. Fenwick's counsel objected to admitting the examination of a witness who had been spirited away, on the ground that Fenwick had had no opportunity to cross-examine. The examination was nonetheless admitted on a closely divided vote after several of those present opined that the common-law rules of procedure did not apply to parliamentary attainder proceedings—one speaker even admitting that the evidence would normally be inadmissible. Fenwick was condemned, but the proceedings "must have burned into the general consciousness the vital importance of the rule securing the right of cross-examination." . . .

III

This history supports two inferences about the meaning of the Sixth Amendment.

First, the principal evil at which the Confrontation Clause was directed was the civil-law mode of criminal procedure, and particularly its use of ex parte examinations as evidence against the accused. It was these practices that the Crown deployed in notorious treason cases like Raleigh's; that the Marian statutes invited; that English law's assertion of a right to confrontation was meant to prohibit; and that the founding-era rhetoric decried. The Sixth Amendment must be interpreted with this focus in mind.

Accordingly, we once again reject the view that the Confrontation Clause applies of its own force only to in-court testimony, and that its application to out-of-court statements introduced at trial depends upon "the law of Evidence for the time being." Leaving the regulation of out-of-court statements to the law of evidence would render the Confrontation Clause powerless to prevent even the most flagrant inquisitorial practices. Raleigh was, after all, perfectly free to confront those who read Cobham's confession in court.

This focus also suggests that not all hearsay implicates the Sixth Amendment's core concerns. An off-hand, overheard remark might be unreliable evidence and thus a good candidate for exclusion under hearsay rules, but it bears little resemblance to the civil-law abuses the Confrontation Clause targeted. On the other hand, ex parte examinations might sometimes be admissible under modern hearsay rules, but the Framers certainly would not have condoned them.

The text of the Confrontation Clause reflects this focus. It applies to "witnesses" against the accused—in other words, those who "bear testimony." "Testimony," in turn, is typically "[a] solemn declaration or affirmation made for the purpose of establishing or proving some fact." An accuser who makes a formal statement to government officers bears testimony in a sense that a person who makes a casual remark to an acquaintance does not. The constitutional text, like the history underlying the common-law right of confrontation, thus reflects an especially acute concern with a specific type of out-of-court statement. . . .

Statements taken by police officers in the course of interrogations are also testimonial under even a narrow standard. Police interrogations bear a striking resemblance to examinations by justices of the peace in England. The statements are not sworn testimony, but the absence of oath was not dispositive. Cobham's examination was unsworn, yet Raleigh's trial has long been thought a paradigmatic confrontation violation. . . .

In sum, even if the Sixth Amendment is not solely concerned with testimonial hearsay, that is its primary object, and interrogations by law enforcement officers fall squarely within that class.

The historical record also supports a second proposition: that the Framers would not have allowed admission of testimonial statements of a witness who did not appear at trial unless he was unavailable to testify, and the defendant had had a prior opportunity for cross-examination. The text of the Sixth Amendment does not suggest any open-ended exceptions from the confrontation requirement to be developed by the courts. Rather, the "right . . . to be confronted with the witnesses against him," Amdt. 6, is most naturally read as a reference to the right of confrontation at common law, admitting only those exceptions established at the time of the founding. As the English authorities above reveal, the common law in 1791 conditioned admissibility of an absent witness's examination on unavailability and a prior opportunity to cross-examine. The Sixth Amendment therefore incorporates those limitations. The numerous early state decisions applying the same test confirm that these principles were received as part of the common law in this country. . . .

V

Although the results of our decisions have generally been faithful to the original meaning of the Confrontation Clause, the same cannot be said of our rationales. *Roberts* conditions the admissibility of all hearsay evidence on whether it falls under a "firmly rooted hearsay exception" or bears "particularized guarantees of trustworthiness." 448 U.S., at 66. This test departs from the historical principles identified above in two respects. First, it is too broad: It applies the same mode of analysis whether or not the hearsay consists of ex parte testimony. This often results in close constitutional scrutiny in cases that are far removed from the core concerns of the Clause. At the same time, however, the test is too narrow: It admits statements that do consist of ex parte testimony upon a mere finding of reliability. This malleable standard often fails to protect against paradigmatic confrontation violations. . . .

The unpardonable vice of the *Roberts* test, however, is not its unpredictability, but its demonstrated capacity to admit core testimonial statements that the Confrontation Clause plainly meant to exclude. . . .

Roberts' failings were on full display in the proceedings below. Sylvia Crawford made her statement while in police custody, herself a potential suspect in the case. Indeed, she had been told that whether she would be released "depend[ed] on how the investigation continues." In response to often leading questions from police detectives, she implicated her husband in Lee's stabbing and at least arguably undermined his self-defense claim. Despite all this, the trial court admitted her statement, listing several reasons why it was reliable. In its opinion reversing, the Court of Appeals listed several other reasons why the statement was not reliable. Finally, the State Supreme Court relied exclusively on the interlocking character of the statement and disregarded every other factor the lower courts had considered. The case is thus a self-contained demonstration of *Roberts*' unpredictable and inconsistent application.

Each of the courts also made assumptions that cross-examination might well have undermined. The trial court, for example, stated that Sylvia Crawford's statement was reliable because she was an eyewitness with direct knowledge of the events. But Sylvia at one point told the police that she had "shut [her] eyes and . . . didn't really watch" part of the fight, and that she was "in shock." The trial court also buttressed its reliability finding by claiming that Sylvia was "being questioned by law enforcement, and, thus, the [questioner] is . . . neutral to her and not someone who would be inclined to advance her interests and shade her version of the truth unfavorably toward the defendant." The Framers would be astounded to learn that ex parte testimony could be admitted against a criminal defendant because it was elicited by "neutral" government officers. But even if the court's assessment of the officer's motives was accurate, it says nothing about Sylvia's perception of her situation. Only cross-examination could reveal that. . . .

Where nontestimonial hearsay is at issue, it is wholly consistent with the Framers' design to afford the States flexibility in their development of hearsay law—as does *Roberts*, and as would an approach that exempted such statements from Confrontation Clause scrutiny altogether. Where testimonial evidence is at issue, however, the Sixth Amendment demands what the common law required: unavailability and a prior opportunity for cross-examination. . . . In this case, the State admitted Sylvia's testimonial statement against petitioner, despite the fact that he had no opportunity to cross-examine her. That alone is sufficient to make out a violation of the Sixth Amendment. . . .

NOTES & QUESTIONS ON TESTIMONIAL STATEMENTS

1. *Witness unavailability.* A witness may be unavailable to testify at trial. Normally, in the absence of sworn testimony at trial, a statement or affidavit from the witness would not be admissible as a substitute because to admit the statement into evidence would be to deprive the defendants of the right to confront the witnesses against them. But consider the following factual situation: A witness testifies at trial but for whatever reason, the defendant is subject to a second trial. (Perhaps the first trial ended in a hung jury or a guilty verdict was overturned on appeal.) If the witness is unavailable at the second trial, may the prosecutor introduce into evidence the sworn testimony from the first trial? Or would doing so violate the defendant's Sixth Amendment right to confront the witnesses against him? In *Mattox v. United States*, 156 U.S. 237 (1895), the witness died after the first trial, but the Court concluded that reading the witness's prior testimony was constitutional because the original testimony was under oath and the defendant had the opportunity to cross-examine the witness at the first trial: "To say that a criminal, after having once been convicted by the testimony of a certain witness, should go scot free simply because death has closed the mouth of that witness, would be carrying his constitutional protection to an unwarrantable extent." *Id.* at 243. The principle in *Mattox* only applies when prosecutors make a "good-faith effort" to obtain the witness's presence at trial. See *Barber v. Page*, 390 U.S. 719 (1968) (right to confrontation was violated when prior testimony was admitted from witness who was incarcerated and prosecutors failed to exhaust avenues to secure his presence at trial).

2. *Dying declarations. Crawford* discussed the long-standing common law exception for dying declarations. If a defendant makes a spontaneous utterance just prior to death, the testimony may be offered into evidence at trial, even though the defendant did not have the opportunity to cross-examine the witness. In a footnote in the *Crawford* opinion, Justice Scalia noted:

> The one deviation we have found involves dying declarations. The existence of that exception as a general rule of criminal hearsay law cannot be disputed. Although many dying declarations may not be testimonial, there is authority for admitting even those that clearly are. We need not decide in this case whether the Sixth Amendment incorporates an exception for testimonial dying declarations. If this exception must be accepted on historical grounds, it is sui generis.

541 U.S. at 56 n.6. Most courts that have considered the issue have ruled that dying declarations are an exception to the Confrontation Clause under the *Crawford* standard. See *People v. Clay*, 88 A.D.3d 14, 926 N.Y.S.2d 598 (2011); *Davis v. State*, 207 So. 3d 142 (Fla. 2016). Some states have statutes specifically allowing dying declarations. See, e.g., Colo. Rev. Stat. Ann. § 13-25-119. But a few courts have rejected the exception. See, e.g., *United States v. Mayhew*, 380 F. Supp. 2d 961, 965-66 (S.D. Ohio 2005).

3. *Forfeiture by wrongdoing.* In some situations, a court might allow prior testimony, or testimonial statements, to be read at trial if the judge determines that the witness's unavailability was caused by the defendant's conduct. But in that case, what explains the result (other than common sense)? Why does the Sixth Amendment right to confrontation no longer apply? One solution is to say that the defendant can forfeit the right by wrongdoing. This forfeiture-by-wrongdoing theory is a recognized exception to the Confrontation Clause. See *Reynolds v. United States*, 98 U.S. 145, 158 (1878) ("The Constitution gives the accused the right to a trial at which he should be confronted with the witnesses against him; but if a witness is absent by his own wrongful procurement, he cannot complain if competent evidence is admitted to supply the place of that which he has kept away. The Constitution does not guarantee an accused person against the legitimate consequences of his own wrongful acts."). However, the defendant's conduct must be *designed* to prevent the witness from testifying. In other words, the defendant's wrongful conduct must be engaged with the intent or purpose to prevent the witness from testifying. In *Giles v. California*, 554 U.S. 353 (2008), the Supreme Court refused to apply the exception to cases where the defendant's wrongful conduct was not performed with the purpose of preventing the witness from testifying, such as cases where the wrongful conduct had an independent criminal purpose.

4. *911 calls.* Courts have generally allowed into evidence recordings of 911 calls, even if the caller is not available to testify at the trial and undergo cross-examination. See, e.g., *People v. Brenn*, 152 Cal. App. 4th 166, 60 Cal. Rptr. 3d 830 (2007). Given that absence of cross-examination, one of the requirements under *Crawford*, the question is whether the evidence is "testimonial" or not. If the call is testimonial, the Confrontation Clause would bar its introduction into evidence. In *Davis v. Washington*, 547 U.S. 813 (2006), the Supreme Court concluded that 911 calls are usually, though not always, non-testimonial: "Moreover, any reasonable listener would recognize that McCottry (unlike Sylvia Crawford) was facing an ongoing emergency. Although one might call 911 to provide a narrative report of a crime absent any imminent danger, McCottry's call was plainly a call for help against bona fide physical threat." *Id.* at 827. However, consider *People v. Cortes*, 4 Misc. 3d 575, 583, 781 N.Y.S.2d 401, 407 (Sup. Ct. 2004), where a New York court declared a 911 call testimonial because "callers to 911 reporting crimes are likely to know the use to which the information will be put." In other words, if a 911 caller is primarily calling for a request for emergency services, the evidence is likely non-testimonial. On the other hand, if the individual is calling 911 to provide evidence to the authorities in the form of an anonymous tip, the call is likely testimonial.

5. *Statements to police.* If the statement in question is one that is made to the police, and then introduced at trial without the benefit of the original declarant's cross-examination, the question again is whether the statement was testimonial in nature. Under *Davis v. Washington, supra*, this question is answered by reference to the "primary purpose" of an interrogation. If the primary purpose is "to enable police assistance to meet an ongoing emergency," then the statement is likely non-testimonial. This requires a court to "objectively evaluate the circumstances in which the encounter occurs and the statements and actions of the parties." *Michigan v. Bryant*, 562 U.S. 344, 359 (2011). In *Bryant*, the police found the victim mortally wounded in a gas station parking lot, and the victim identified Bryant as the assailant. The Supreme Court found the statement non-testimonial, both because it was tendered to resolve an ongoing emergency and also because of the informality of the questioning. The inquiry into the "purpose" of the interrogation must remain an objective one rather than viewed from the subjective perspective of the declarant:

> During an ongoing emergency, a victim is most likely to want the threat to her and to other potential victims to end, but that does not necessarily mean that the victim wants or envisions prosecution of the assailant. A victim may want the attacker to be incapacitated temporarily or rehabilitated. Alternatively, a severely injured victim may have no purpose at all in answering questions posed; the answers may be simply reflexive. The victim's injuries could be so debilitating as to prevent her from thinking sufficiently clearly to understand whether her statements are for the purpose of

> addressing an ongoing emergency or for the purpose of future prosecution. Taking into account a victim's injuries does not transform this objective inquiry into a subjective one. The inquiry is still objective because it focuses on the understanding and purpose of a reasonable victim in the circumstances of the actual victim—circumstances that prominently include the victim's physical state.

Id. at 368-69.

4. Confronting Forensic Evidence

Increasingly, today's criminal convictions, at least in serious crimes, are built on sophisticated forensic evidence: DNA tests, blood-pattern analysis, fingerprint matches, and firearm forensics. Cases involving Internet activity involve sophisticated digital analysis of computer devices, while financial crimes almost always require a forensic accountant to review and explain the significance of complex financial records. In each of these cases, how does the defendant "confront" the scientific evidence that is being marshalled against them? State rules of criminal procedure and evidence allow the introduction of forensic evidence, usually in tandem with the testimony of the technician who performed the testing; this gives defense counsel the opportunity to cross-examine the technician.

In many cases, though, the conclusion of one technician will be built on the assumption that tests performed by other technicians or even other labs were done correctly. Can the second technician testify about the lab work that they received from the first lab? In *Williams v. Illinois*, 567 U.S. 50 (2012), the Supreme Court said yes. The case yielded no majority opinion; the following excerpt is from the four-vote plurality opinion authored by Justice Alito:

> Under settled evidence law, an expert may express an opinion that is based on facts that the expert assumes, but does not know, to be true. It is then up to the party who calls the expert to introduce other evidence establishing the facts assumed by the expert. While it was once the practice for an expert who based an opinion on assumed facts to testify in the form of an answer to a hypothetical question, modern practice does not demand this formality and, in appropriate cases, permits an expert to explain the facts on which his or her opinion is based without testifying to the truth of those facts. That is precisely what occurred in this case, and we should not lightly "swee[p] away an accepted rule governing the admission of scientific evidence." We now conclude that this form of expert testimony does not violate the Confrontation Clause because that provision has no application to out-of-court statements that are not offered to prove the truth of the matter asserted. When an expert testifies for the prosecution in a criminal case, the defendant has the opportunity to cross-examine the expert about any statements that are offered for

their truth. Out-of-court statements that are related by the expert solely for the purpose of explaining the assumptions on which that opinion rests are not offered for their truth and thus fall outside the scope of the Confrontation Clause. Applying this rule to the present case, we conclude that the expert's testimony did not violate the Sixth Amendment.

Given the lack of a majority opinion, *Williams v. Illinois* left some uncertainty in its wake. In the following case, the Supreme Court denied certiorari to review a state court determination that a trial judge was correct in allowing a lab analyst to report on the witness stand the results of a blood-alcohol lab test run by another technician who did not testify at trial. Although the majority of the Court voted not to review the case, Justice Gorsuch authored the following dissent, which argued that the Supreme Court had an obligation to clarify any uncertainty remaining after the fractured plurality opinion in *Williams*.

Stuart v. Alabama

Supreme Court of the United States
139 S.Ct. 36 (2018)

Justice Gorsuch, with whom Justice Sotomayor joins, dissenting from the denial of certiorari.

More and more, forensic evidence plays a decisive role in criminal trials today. But it is hardly "immune from the risk of manipulation." A forensic analyst "may feel pressure—or have an incentive—to alter the evidence in a manner favorable to the prosecution." Even the most well-meaning analyst may lack essential training, contaminate a sample, or err during the testing process. To guard against such mischief and mistake and the risk of false convictions they invite, our criminal justice system depends on adversarial testing and cross-examination. Because cross-examination may be "the greatest legal engine ever invented for the discovery of truth," the Constitution promises every person accused of a crime the right to confront his accusers.

That promise was broken here. To prove Vanessa Stuart was driving under the influence, the State of Alabama introduced in evidence the results of a blood-alcohol test conducted hours after her arrest. But the State refused to bring to the stand the analyst who performed the test. Instead, the State called a different analyst. Using the results of the test after her arrest and the rate at which alcohol is metabolized, this analyst sought to estimate for the jury Ms. Stuart's blood-alcohol level hours earlier when she was driving. Through these steps, the State effectively denied Ms. Stuart the chance to confront the witness who supplied a foundational piece of evidence in her conviction. The engine of cross-examination was left unengaged, and the Sixth Amendment was violated.

To be fair, the problem appears to be largely of our creation. This Court's most recent foray in this field, *Williams v. Illinois*, 567 U.S. 50 (2012), yielded no majority and its various opinions have sown confusion in courts across the country. This case supplies another example of that confusion. Though the opinion of the Alabama court is terse, the State defends it by arguing that, "[u]nder the rule of the *Williams* plurality," the prosecution was free to introduce the forensic report in this case without calling the analyst who prepared it. This is so, the State says, because it didn't offer the report for the truth of what it said about Ms. Stuart's blood-alcohol level at the time of the test, only to provide the State's testifying expert a basis for estimating Ms. Stuart's blood-alcohol level when she was driving.

But while *Williams* yielded no majority opinion, at least five Justices rejected this logic—and for good reason. After all, why would any prosecutor bother to offer in evidence the nontestifying analyst's report in this case except to prove the truth of its assertions about the level of alcohol in Ms. Stuart's blood at the time of the test? The whole point of the exercise was to establish—because of the report's truth—a basis for the jury to credit the testifying expert's estimation of Ms. Stuart's blood-alcohol level hours earlier. As the four dissenting Justices in *Williams* explained, "when a witness . . . repeats an out-of-court statement as the basis for a conclusion, . . . the statement's utility is then dependent on its truth." With this Justice Thomas fully agreed, observing that "[t]here is no meaningful distinction between disclosing an out-of-court statement so that the factfinder may evaluate the [testifying] expert's opinion and disclosing that statement for its truth."

Faced with this difficulty, the State offers an alternative defense of its judgment in this case. Even if it did offer the forensic report for the truth of its assertion about Ms. Stuart's blood-alcohol level at the time of her arrest, the State contends that the Sixth Amendment right to confrontation failed to attach because the report wasn't "testimonial."

But piecing together the fractured decision in *Williams* reveals this argument to be mistaken too—and this time in the view of eight Justices. The four-Justice *Williams* plurality took the view that a forensic report qualifies as testimonial only when it is "prepared for the primary purpose of accusing a targeted individual" who is "in custody [or] under suspicion." Meanwhile, four dissenting Justices took the broader view that even a report devised purely for investigatory purposes without a target in mind can qualify as testimonial when it is "made under circumstances which would lead an objective witness reasonably to believe that [it] would be available for use at a later trial." But however you slice it, a routine postarrest forensic report like the one here must qualify as testimonial. For even under the plurality's more demanding test, there's no question that Ms. Stuart was in custody when the government conducted its forensic test or that the report was prepared for the primary purpose of securing her conviction.

Respectfully, I believe we owe lower courts struggling to abide our holdings more clarity than we have afforded them in this area. *Williams* imposes on courts with crowded dockets the job of trying to distill holdings on two separate and important issues from four competing opinions. The errors here may be manifest, but they are understandable and they affect courts across the country in cases that regularly recur. I would grant review.

NOTES & QUESTIONS ON CONFRONTING FORENSIC EVIDENCE

1. *Testimonial evidence.* When is forensic evidence "testimonial" evidence that triggers the Confrontation Clause in the first place? In *Williams*, the four-vote plurality opinion noted that the Cellmark report was not created to be used as evidence against the defendant but was used as an investigative tool to *identify* and *catch* the rapist in that case. Do you agree that this distinction is convincing? Do police officers and their forensic experts distinguish their technical reports in this way? Is it not assumed that evidence used to identify an assailant will then be used to prosecute the assailant and that these two functions are inevitably intertwined? What is Justice Gorsuch's view on whether forensic reports are testimonial?

2. *Basis for expert testimony.* The *Williams* opinion suggested one novel reason for why a witness can refer to a prior forensic report without violating the Confrontation Clause: The witness may be referring to the report not to establish its truth but rather to use it as a *basis* for the witness's expert testimony. In other words, the witness needs to refer to the prior report or evidence in order to deliver his or her expert testimony. Does this distinction make sense to you and is it fundamentally different from offering the prior report for its truth value?

D. PRIVILEGE AGAINST SELF-INCRIMINATION

While a defendant can testify on his or her own behalf, the Fifth Amendment prohibits a defendant from being "compelled in any criminal case to be a witness against himself." So, for example, a defendant who wishes to remain silent cannot be called to the stand by the prosecutor. If the defendant elects to testify, the prosecution has the opportunity to cross-examine the defendant, but otherwise the defendant may remain silent throughout the entire trial. The following case asks a question that naturally arises when a defendant elects to remain silent. What inference, if any, may a prosecutor suggest that the jury draw from the defendant's decision to remain silent? May the prosecutor suggest to the jurors that they should draw a negative inference from that strategic decision not to testify? Of course, a juror has the raw power to draw any inference that she likes, since neither a trial judge nor an appellate court can look inside her head; nor are jurors generally required to make the reasons for their decisions publicly known. But in this case, the court asks a version of the question that can arise in many cases: What can the prosecutor say to the jury about the defendant's decision to invoke the privilege against self-incrimination?

Griffin v. California

Supreme Court of the United States
380 U.S. 609 (1965)

Mr. Justice DOUGLAS delivered the opinion of the Court.

Petitioner was convicted of murder in the first degree after a jury trial in a California court. He did not testify at the trial on the issue of guilt, though he did testify at the separate trial on the issue of penalty. The trial court instructed the jury on the issue of guilt, stating that a defendant has a constitutional right not to testify. But it told the jury:

> As to any evidence or facts against him which the defendant can reasonably be expected to deny or explain because of facts within his knowledge, if he does not testify or if, though he does testify, he fails to deny or explain such evidence, the jury may take that failure into consideration as tending to indicate the truth of such evidence and as indicating that among the inferences that may be reasonably drawn therefrom those unfavorable to the defendant are the more probable.

It added, however, that no such inference could be drawn as to evidence respecting which he had no knowledge. It stated that failure of a defendant to deny or explain the evidence of which he had knowledge does not create a presumption of guilt nor by itself warrant an inference of guilt nor relieve the prosecution of any of its burden of proof.

Petitioner had been seen with the deceased the evening of her death, the evidence placing him with her in the alley where her body was found. The prosecutor made much of the failure of petitioner to testify:

> The defendant certainly knows whether Essie Mae had this beat up appearance at the time he left her apartment and went down the alley with her.
>
> What kind of a man is it that would want to have sex with a woman that beat up is she was beat up at the time he left?

> He would know that. He would know how she got down the alley. He would know how the blood got on the bottom of the concrete steps. He would know how long he was with her in that box. He would know how her wig got off. He would know whether he beat her or mistreated her. He would know whether he walked away from that place cool as a cucumber when he saw Mr. Villasenor because he was conscious of his own guilt and wanted to get away from that damaged or injured woman.
>
> These things he has not seen fit to take the stand and deny or explain.
>
> And in the whole world, if anybody would know, this defendant would know.
>
> Essie Mae is dead, she can't tell you her side of the story. The defendant won't.

The death penalty was imposed. . . .

If this were a federal trial, reversible error would have been committed. . . . The question remains whether, statute or not, the comment rule, approved by California, violates the Fifth Amendment.

We think it does. It is in substance a rule of evidence that allows the State the privilege of tendering to the jury for its consideration the failure of the accused to testify. No formal offer of proof is made as in other situations; but the prosecutor's comment and the court's acquiescence are the equivalent of an offer of evidence and its acceptance.

. . . [C]omment on the refusal to testify is a remnant of the "inquisitorial system of criminal justice," which the Fifth Amendment outlaws. It is a penalty imposed by courts for exercising a constitutional privilege. It cuts down on the privilege by making its assertion costly. It is said, however, that the inference of guilt for failure to testify as to facts peculiarly within the accused's knowledge is in any event natural and irresistible, and that comment on the failure does not magnify that inference into a penalty for asserting a constitutional privilege. What the jury may infer, given no help from the court, is one thing. What it may infer when the court solemnizes the silence of the accused into evidence against him is quite another. . . .

Mr. Justice STEWART, with whom Mr. Justice WHITE joins, dissenting.

. . . It is not at all apparent to me, on any realistic view of the trial process, that a defendant will be at more of a disadvantage under the California practice than he would be in a court which permitted no comment at all on his failure to take the witness stand. How can it be said that the inferences drawn by a jury will be more detrimental to a defendant under the limiting and carefully controlling language of the instruction here involved than would result if the jury were left to roam at large with only its untutored instincts to guide it, to draw from the defendant's silence broad inferences of guilt? The instructions in this case expressly cautioned the jury that the defendant's failure to testify "does not create a presumption of guilt or by itself warrant an inference of guilt"; it was further admonished that such failure does not "relieve the prosecution of its burden of providing every essential element of the crime," and finally the trial judge warned that the prosecution's burden remained that of proof "beyond a reasonable doubt." Whether the same limitations would be observed by a jury without the benefit of protective instructions shielding the defendant is certainly open to real doubt.

Moreover, no one can say where the balance of advantage might lie as a result of the attorneys' discussion of the matter. No doubt the prosecution's argument will seek to encourage the drawing of inferences unfavorable to the defendant. However, the defendant's counsel equally has an opportunity to explain the various other reasons why a defendant may not wish to take the stand, and thus rebut the natural if uneducated assumption that it is because the defendant cannot truthfully deny the accusations made.

I think the California comment rule is not a coercive device which impairs the right against self-incrimination, but rather a means of articulating and bringing into the light of rational discussion a fact inescapably impressed on the jury's consciousness. The California procedure is not only designed to protect the defendant against unwarranted inferences which might be drawn by an uninformed jury; it is also an attempt by the State to recognize and articulate what it believes to be the natural probative force of certain facts. Surely no one would deny that the State has an important interest in throwing the light of rational discussion on that which transpires in the course of a trial, both to protect the defendant from the very real dangers of silence and to shape a legal process designed to ascertain the truth. . . .

NOTES & QUESTIONS ON SELF-INCRIMINATION

1. *The conceptual foundation.* If the defendant fails to testify at trial, why should the prosecutor be prevented from commenting on this fact? Given that the jury will no doubt draw some conclusions from the defendant's failure to testify, and the legal system's inability to police what inferences the jury might draw from the silence, how much difference does it make when the prosecutor mentions that silence to the jury?

2. *Cross-examination.* Why is a defendant who testifies not permitted to claim the privilege against self-incrimination during cross-examination? The answer is that the decision to testify constitutes a *waiver* of the privilege against self-incrimination. But the mere fact that the defendant has waived that privilege by testifying does not open the door completely at cross-examination. Cross-examination is limited to issues that the defendant has put in dispute by testifying to them during the initial testimony. As the Supreme Court has stated:

> [W]hen a witness voluntarily testifies, the privilege against self-incrimination is amply respected without need of accepting testimony freed from the antiseptic test of the adversary process. The witness himself, certainly if he is a party, determines the area of disclosure and therefore of inquiry. Such a witness has the choice, after weighing the advantage of the privilege against self-incrimination against the advantage of putting forward his version of the facts and his reliability as a witness, not to testify at all. He cannot reasonably claim that the Fifth Amendment gives him not only this choice but, if he elects to testify, an immunity from cross-examination on the matters he has himself put in dispute. It would make of the Fifth Amendment not only a humane safeguard against judicially coerced self-disclosure but a positive invitation to mutilate the truth a party offers to tell.

Brown v. United States, 356 U.S. 148, 155-56 (1958).

3. *Negative inferences at sentencing*. Although the jury should not draw a negative inference from the defendant's failure to testify during the trial, should the same rule apply to sentencing? In other words, can and should the judge or jury draw a negative inference from a defendant's failure to testify? As for guilt, the sentencing judge is already entitled to assume that the defendant is *guilty*, because the guilt phase of the trial is already over. However, a defendant who has been found guilty is still entitled to the privilege during sentencing, such that the sentencing judge should not draw an adverse inference—for example, as an aggravating factor—from the defendant's failure to testify at sentencing. See *Mitchell v. United States*, 526 U.S. 314, 324 (1999). One wrinkle is that a trial judge is permitted to inquire about the factual basis for a guilty plea, and if the judge is unsatisfied by the defendant's responses, the trial judge can and should reject the guilty plea. But the judge should not take the defendant's failure to say more during the sentencing hearing as evidence of more guilt deserving of a higher, rather than lower, sentence. As the Supreme Court has noted:

> The concerns which mandate the rule against negative inferences at a criminal trial apply with equal force at sentencing. Without question, the stakes are high: Here, the inference drawn by the District Court from petitioner's silence may have resulted in decades of added imprisonment. The Government often has a motive to demand a severe sentence, so the central purpose of the privilege—to protect a defendant from being the unwilling instrument of his or her own condemnation—remains of vital importance.

Mitchell v. United States, 526 U.S. 314, 329 (1999). How does this conclusion square with the assumption that sentencing judges are permitted to take into account at sentencing a defendant's failure to accept responsibility for his or her wrongful actions? Are these two principles compatible? Most federal appellate courts, though not all, have assumed that a judge should not *penalize* a convicted defendant for not accepting responsibility, but there is nothing wrong in denying the defendant a sentencing *reduction* (which is a benefit) authorized by the sentencing guidelines that is reserved for those who accept responsibility.

STATE LAW REQUIREMENTS

In *State v. Burgess,* a New Hampshire defendant was charged and convicted of attempted escape and sentenced to 10-30 years in prison, in addition to the sentences he was already serving. Burgess had used a shoelace to tinker with a leg brace that guards had placed on him for his court appearance. He used the shoelace to prevent the leg brace from locking properly and then bolted to the courtroom door, where he had to be subdued by guards. At sentencing, the judge made the following remarks:

> There isn't any real basis for mercy as asked for by defense counsel in this case. We have a defendant who has an extended record, has simply not accepted over the years in any constructive way his situation, made matters deliberately worse for himself time and time again. The tragedy involved here is entirely attributable to Mr. Burgess' actions. *He has not cooperated in terms of the Pre-Sentence report in terms of telling any—or talking to me as he's had opportunities to do about his situation.* The record is a fairly deplorable one and at the same time the kind of crimes we're talking about, the attempted escape and the implements of escape go to the very integrity and safety of the personnel that are involved with law enforcement and the judicial process and there needs to be a very stern message sent out that this is simply not going to be tolerated at all.

State v. Burgess, 156 N.H. 746, 750, 943 A.2d 727, 730 (2008). The appeals court found the adverse inference initially problematic under both the Sixth Amendment and the New Hampshire Constitution, which states: "No subject shall . . . be compelled to accuse or furnish evidence against himself." N.H. Const. Pt. 1, art. XV. The court concluded that because New Hampshire's sentencing scheme does not have an explicitly defined "benefit" for accepting responsibility codified in sentencing guidelines, the adverse inference at sentencing is basically a penalty. And levying that penalty on a defendant who refuses to speak at sentencing places them in a Hobson's Choice, though only if the defendant has maintained their innocence throughout the criminal process. Since Burgess *admitted* to the acts in question but simply denied that he had the requisite intent for the crime of escape, the New Hampshire court concluded that the defendant could have expressed remorse for his physical actions and therefore the judge's adverse inference from his refusal to do so did not violate the privilege against self-incrimination. However, other cases might come out differently if the defendant had steadfastly maintained complete innocence.

PROBLEM CASE

Consider the following case. The defendant, Thomas Moore, was prosecuted for a sexual assault. The victim was driving home after an evening class and was pulled over by a person that she believed to be a police officer. A man left the vehicle and approached the victim's car, shined a flashlight at her, and noted that she had been speeding, at which point he pretended to "arrest" the victim and then assaulted her in his car. At trial, Moore's attorneys presented an alibi defense, but Moore himself did not testify at the trial. The prosecutor said the following to the jury:

> [W]hen you look at the defendant's case and he chose to put on a case in this, he didn't choose to testify which is his right, and he certainly doesn't, isn't compelled to testify but he did choose to put on witnesses, that by examination of all the evidence, the more precise case which is [the State's] is not a matter of science but beyond a reasonable doubt.

Moore v. State, 669 N.E.2d 733, 735 (Ind. 1996). Moore's attorney requested a mistrial, which was denied, but the trial judge instructed the jury to ignore the prosecutor's statement. Did the comment violate the defendant's privilege against self-incrimination and should it result in a new trial?

E. RIGHT TO PRESENT A DEFENSE

After the prosecution rests its case-in-chief, the defense has an opportunity to present its case before the jury. There are many strategic options available depending on the situation at hand. Defense counsel might argue mistaken identity, or they might present an alibi witness. Or defense counsel might suggest that the defendant committed the act but not with the requisite mental state. Or the reverse. Or the defendant may need to offer evidence in support of an affirmative defense, such as the justification of self-defense, or that his conduct is legally excusable due to insanity or duress. The possible options are endless. However, the marshalling of particular pieces of evidence at trial, in service of that defense strategy, is governed by the law of evidence, which flows from state statutes. For various reasons of public policy, state legislators may have limited certain classes of evidence or dictated how they will be presented in court. To take just one example, many states have passed "rape shield laws" that severely restrict the ability of defense counsel to inquire about the sexual history of the victim in sexual assault cases, unless that evidence is material to the case.

In the following case, the defendant was charged with murdering a policeman but found that the statutory rules of evidence prevented his defense counsel from introducing any of the evidence required to present a compelling defense. While it is clear that state legislatures retain discretion to determine rules of evidence applicable in criminal trials in their jurisdiction, the question is whether that discretion is unlimited. If the rules of evidence are too restrictive, might they violate the defendant's right to due process? In other words, is the right to present a defense, free from unduly restrictive rules of evidence, implicit in the notion of due process? As you read the following case, look for the Court's specific articulation of the concept of the due process and ask yourself how it relates to the more specific right of the defendant to present a defense.

Chambers v. Mississippi

Supreme Court of the United States
410 U.S. 284 (1973)

Mr. Justice POWELL delivered the opinion of the Court.

Petitioner, Leon Chambers, was tried by a jury in a Mississippi trial court and convicted of murdering a policeman. The jury assessed punishment at life imprisonment. . . .

I

The events that led to petitioner's prosecution for murder occurred in the small town of Woodville in southern Mississippi. On Saturday evening, June 14, 1969, two Woodville policemen, James Forman and Aaron "Sonny" Liberty, entered a local bar and pool hall to execute a warrant for the arrest of a youth named C.C. Jackson. Jackson resisted and a hostile crowd of some 50 or 60 persons gathered. The officers' first attempt to handcuff Jackson was frustrated when 20 or 25 men in the crowd intervened and wrestled him free. Forman then radioed for assistance and Liberty removed his riot gun, a 12-gauge sawed-off shotgun, from the car. Three deputy sheriffs arrived shortly thereafter and the officers again attempted to make their arrest. Once more, the officers were attacked by the onlookers and during the commotion five or six pistol shots were fired. Forman was looking in a different direction when the shooting began, but immediately saw that Liberty had been shot several times in the back. Before Liberty died, he turned around and fired both barrels of his riot gun into an alley in the area from which the shots appeared to have come. The first shot was wild and high and scattered the crowd standing at the face of the alley. Liberty appeared, however, to take more deliberate aim before the second shot and hit one of the men in the crowd in the back of the head and neck as he ran down the alley. That man was Leon Chambers.

Officer Forman could not see from his vantage point who shot Liberty or whether Liberty's shots hit anyone. One of the deputy sheriffs testified at trial that he was standing several feet from Liberty and that he saw

Chambers shoot him. Another deputy sheriff stated that, although he could not see whether Chambers had a gun in his hand, he did see Chambers "break his arm down" shortly before the shots were fired. The officers who saw Chambers fall testified that they thought he was dead but they made no effort at that time either to examine him or to search for the murder weapon. Instead, they attended to Liberty, who was placed in the police car and taken to a hospital where he was declared dead on arrival. A subsequent autopsy showed that he had been hit with four bullets from a .22-caliber revolver.

Shortly after the shooting, three of Chambers' friends discovered that he was not yet dead. James Williams, Berkley Turner, and Gable McDonald loaded him into a car and transported him to the same hospital. Later that night, when the county sheriff discovered that Chambers was still alive, a guard was placed outside his room. Chambers was subsequently charged with Liberty's murder. He pleaded not guilty and has asserted his innocence throughout.

The story of Leon Chambers is intertwined with the story of another man, Gable McDonald. McDonald, a lifelong resident of Woodville, was in the crowd on the evening of Liberty's death. . . . [McDonald] gave a sworn confession that he shot Officer Liberty. . . . McDonald was turned over to the local police authorities and was placed in jail. One month later, at a preliminary hearing, McDonald repudiated his prior sworn confession. . . . The local justice of the peace accepted McDonald's repudiation and released him from custody. The local authorities undertook no further investigation of his possible involvement.

Chambers' case came on for trial in October of the next year. At trial, he endeavored to develop two grounds of defense. He first attempted to show that he did not shoot Liberty. . . . Petitioner's second defense was that Gable McDonald had shot Officer Liberty. He was only partially successful, however, in his efforts to bring before the jury the testimony supporting this defense. Sam Hardin, a lifelong friend of McDonald's, testified that he saw McDonald shoot Liberty. A second witness, one of Liberty's cousins, testified that he saw McDonald immediately after the shooting with a pistol in his hand. In addition to the testimony of these two witnesses, Chambers endeavored to show the jury that McDonald had repeatedly confessed to the crime. Chambers attempted to prove that McDonald had admitted responsibility for the murder on four separate occasions, once when he gave the sworn statement to Chambers' counsel and three other times prior to that occasion in private conversations with friends.

In large measure, he was thwarted in his attempt to present this portion of his defense by the strict application of certain Mississippi rules of evidence. Chambers asserts in this Court, as he did unsuccessfully in his motion for new trial and on appeal to the State Supreme Court, that the application of these evidentiary rules rendered his trial fundamentally unfair and deprived him of due process of law. It is necessary, therefore, to examine carefully the rulings made during the trial.

II

. . . At trial, after the State failed to put McDonald on the stand, Chambers called McDonald, laid a predicate for the introduction of his sworn out-of-court confession, had it admitted into evidence, and read it to the jury. The State, upon cross-examination, elicited from McDonald the fact that he had repudiated his prior confession. McDonald further testified, as he had at the preliminary hearing, that he did not shoot Liberty, and that he confessed to the crime only on the promise of Reverend Stokes that he would not go to jail and would share in a sizable tort recovery from the town. He also retold his own story of his actions on the evening of the shooting, including his visit to the cafe down the street, his absence from the scene during the critical period, and his subsequent trip to the hospital with Chambers.

At the conclusion of the State's cross-examination, Chambers renewed his motion to examine McDonald as an adverse witness. The trial court denied the motion. . . . Defeated in his attempt to challenge directly McDonald's renunciation of his prior confession, Chambers sought to introduce the testimony of the three witnesses to whom McDonald had admitted that he shot the officer. . . . The State objected to the admission of this testimony on the ground that it was hearsay. The trial court sustained the objection. . . .

In sum, then, this was Chambers' predicament. As a consequence of the combination of Mississippi's "party witness" or "voucher" rule and its hearsay rule, he was unable either to cross-examine McDonald or to present witnesses in his own behalf who would have discredited McDonald's repudiation and demonstrated his complicity. Chambers had, however, chipped away at the fringes of McDonald's story by introducing admissible testimony from other sources indicating that he had not been seen in the cafe where he said he was when the shooting started, that he had not been having beer with Turner, and that he possessed a .22 pistol at the time of the crime. But all that remained from McDonald's own testimony was a single written confession countered by an arguably acceptable renunciation. Chambers' defense was far less persuasive than it might have been had he been given an opportunity to subject McDonald's statements to cross-examination or had the other confessions been admitted.

III

The right of an accused in a criminal trial to due process is, in essence, the right to a fair opportunity to defend against the State's accusations. The rights to confront and cross-examine witnesses and to call witnesses in one's own behalf have long been recognized as essential to due process. . . .

Chambers was denied an opportunity to subject McDonald's damning repudiation and alibi to cross-examination. He was not allowed to test the witness' recollection, to probe into the details of his alibi, or to "sift" his conscience so that the jury might judge for itself whether McDonald's testimony was worthy of belief. The right of cross-examination is more than a desirable rule of trial procedure. It is implicit in the constitutional right of confrontation, and helps assure the "accuracy of the truth-determining process." It is, indeed, "an essential and fundamental requirement for the kind of fair trial which is this country's constitutional goal." Of course, the right to confront and to cross-examine is not absolute and may, in appropriate cases, bow to accommodate other legitimate interests in the criminal trial process. But its denial or significant diminution calls into question the ultimate "integrity of the fact-finding process" and requires that the competing interest be closely examined.

In this case, petitioner's request to cross-examine McDonald was denied on the basis of a Mississippi common-law rule that a party may not impeach his own witness. The rule rests on the presumption—without regard to the circumstances of the particular case—that a party who calls a witness "vouches for his credibility." . . . Whatever validity the "voucher" rule may have once enjoyed, and apart from whatever usefulness it retains today in the civil trial process, it bears little present relationship to the realities of the criminal process. . . . Moreover, as applied in this case, the "voucher" rule's impact was doubly harmful to Chambers' efforts to develop his defense. Not only was he precluded from cross-examining McDonald, but, as the State conceded at oral argument, he was also restricted in the scope of his direct examination by the rule's corollary requirement that the party calling the witness is bound by anything he might say. He was, therefore, effectively prevented from exploring the circumstances of McDonald's three prior oral confessions and from challenging the renunciation of the written confession. . . .

We need not decide, however, whether this error alone would occasion reversal since Chambers' claimed denial of due process rests on the ultimate impact of that error when viewed in conjunction with the trial court's refusal to permit him to call other witnesses. The trial court refused to allow him to introduce the testimony of Hardin, Turner, and Carter. Each would have testified to the statements purportedly made by McDonald, on three separate occasions shortly after the crime, naming himself as the murderer. The State Supreme Court approved the exclusion of this evidence on the ground that it was hearsay. . . .

Few rights are more fundamental than that of an accused to present witnesses in his own defense. In the exercise of this right, the accused, as is required of the State, must comply with established rules of procedure and evidence designed to assure both fairness and reliability in the ascertainment of guilt and innocence. Although perhaps no rule of evidence has been more respected or more frequently applied in jury trials than that applicable to the exclusion of hearsay, exceptions tailored to allow the introduction of evidence which in fact is likely to be trustworthy have long existed. The testimony rejected by the trial court here bore persuasive assurances of trustworthiness and thus was well within the basic rationale of the exception for declarations against interest. That testimony also was critical to Chambers' defense. In these circumstances, where constitutional rights directly affecting the ascertainment of guilt are implicated, the hearsay rule may not be applied mechanistically to defeat the ends of justice.

We conclude that the exclusion of this critical evidence, coupled with the State's refusal to permit Chambers to cross-examine McDonald, denied him a trial in accord with traditional and fundamental standards of due process. In reaching this judgment, we establish no new principles of constitutional law. Nor does our holding signal any diminution in the respect traditionally accorded to the States in the establishment and implementation of their own criminal trial rules and procedures. Rather, we hold quite simply that under the facts and circumstances of this case the rulings of the trial court deprived Chambers of a fair trial. . . .

NOTES & QUESTIONS ON PRESENTING A DEFENSE

1. *What is due process?* The Court says that due process is, in essence, the "right to a fair opportunity to defend against the State's accusations." Do you agree with this definition of due process? Does it imply that all rules of evidence are constitutionally suspect?

2. *State secrets.* What if the evidence that the defendant wishes to present in open court is classified or would otherwise damage national security? If the state objects to the presentation of the evidence on the ground that it would damage national security, might a defendant successfully argue that their

prosecution under the circumstances would violate the constitutional right to present a defense? The situation arguably puts the court in a difficult position, but are there ways to avoid the stark trade-offs? Consider the following list of possible solutions:

> As an alternative to excluding evidence that may reasonably persuade the jury of the defendant's innocence or placing the government in the disclose or dismiss dilemma, courts can bar the public from access to those portions of the trial touching upon sensitive national security secrets. Although this proposal implicates yet another competing constitutional claim, the right to an open trial, limited closure of the trial will not materially impair that right's underlying purposes.

Thomas G. Stacy, *The Constitution in Conflict: Espionage Prosecutions, the Right to Present a Defense, and the State Secrets Privilege*, 58 U. Colo. L. Rev. 177, 245 (1987). Do you agree that judges should close courtrooms to the public in order to allow defendants access to classified information? Even if defense attorneys have the relevant security clearances, what if the defendant *personally* does not have the appropriate security clearance to view the evidence that will be presented in closed court? Could the judge order that the trial proceed without the defendant present?

3. *Eliminating defenses.* What if the state simply *eliminates* a defense? *Chambers* stands for the possibility that a state may not use evidence rules to restrict a defendant's ability to present a defense to the point where it compromises the fundamental fairness of the trial. What if the defendant seeks to present a defense that is disallowed by statute? In *Montana v. Egelhoff*, 518 U.S. 37 (1996), a defendant argued on appeal that Montana had violated his due process rights when it eliminated the defense of voluntary intoxication by statute. The statute even disallowed the introduction of intoxication evidence that would negate the defendant's mens rea. The Supreme Court concluded that defense was only constitutionally protected if it was "fundamental":

> Although the rule allowing a jury to consider evidence of a defendant's voluntary intoxication where relevant to mens rea has gained considerable acceptance, it is of too recent vintage, and has not received sufficiently uniform and permanent allegiance, to qualify as fundamental, especially since it displaces a lengthy common-law tradition which remains supported by valid justifications today. . . .

The Court also distinguished *Chambers* as a case that involved *erroneous* evidentiary rulings whose cumulative effect was to rise to the level of a due process violation, rather than a single statutory rule that was consistent with common law precedents.

PROBLEM CASE

Defendant Adam Bradley was charged with attempted assault and harassment in a New York court. The charges stemmed from a fight in which the defendant allegedly threw a cup of hot tea at his wife and also slammed a door on her hand. At trial, the wife testified for the prosecution and stated that Bradley engaged in the acts intentionally. On cross-examination, the wife was asked whether she had ever told anyone that the incident with the door was an accident; she denied that she had characterized it as an accident to anyone.

Bradley took the stand in his own defense and argued that both incidents were "inadvertent" accidents. The defendant sought to call two witnesses to testify that the wife had allegedly described them as accidents, but the trial judge denied the request because the testimony was too "remote or speculative." Did the judge's decision deny the defendant his constitutional right to present a defense? *People v. Bradley*, 99 A.D.3d 934, 937, 952 N.Y.S.2d 260, 264 (2012).

F. PRACTICE & POLICY

In the age of electronic media, the lodestar for public access to the judicial system is live video coverage on television. The use of TV cameras in criminal trials was gradually introduced in the 1980s and has now become widespread. But its adoption is not universal, with each jurisdiction adopting different rules governing the cameras. In some jurisdictions, the presumption in favor of cameras is strong and the statutes govern how cameras should be positioned in the courtroom. In contrast, other courts disallow cameras entirely. This raises a host of policy questions for criminal justice: Does contemporaneous broadcasting of trials to a wide audience conflict with a defendant's right to a fair trial? Or conversely, does a court's *refusal* to allow cameras in the courtroom violate the right to a fair trial? Arguably, if the Sixth and First Amendments express a preference for an open courtroom, perhaps TV cameras are simply the logical culmination of that preference by opening the courtroom beyond its physical seating capacity. The following materials explore this and related policy questions.

State statutes and judicial rules. The State of Florida was an early pioneer in the use of TV cameras in state courtrooms. The state has a detailed judicial rule governing TV cameras, which includes the following guidance: at least one video camera and not more than one audio device and one still photography camera. If multiple news outlets want to cover the proceedings, it is the responsibility of the news organizations to create a "pool" to share the audio or video feed with each other. Camera operators should remain stationary and shall not move around to obtain different photographs. News organizations are permitted to install lighting at their own expense to improve the quality of the video or still photography. However, the "number of permitted cameras shall be within the sound discretion and authority of the presiding judge." Fla. St. J. Admin. R. 2.450. If the judge issues an order excluding the media from using cameras in the courtroom, that order is reviewable by an appellate court. See Fla. R. App. P. 9.100 ("The court shall immediately consider the petition to determine whether a stay of proceedings in the lower tribunal or the order under review is appropriate and, on its own motion or that of any party, the court may order a stay on such conditions as may be appropriate.").

TV cameras and the right to a fair trial. In some cases, a defendant might object to the lack of TV cameras during their trial. On the other hand, a defendant might object to the presence of TV cameras out of a concern that the unwanted public exposure will impair the completion of a fair trial—perhaps creating the very kind of media circus that undermined the *Sheppard* case, for example. In *Chandler v. Florida,* the defendants were police officers charged with burglarizing a Miami Beach restaurant. The defendants objected to the live TV coverage, which had been newly authorized by the state judicial rules, and the judge also denied a defense request to sequester the jury during the trial. The Supreme Court upheld the convictions, concluding that there was nothing inherently inconsistent about TV cameras and the right to a fair trial:

> An absolute constitutional ban on broadcast coverage of trials cannot be justified simply because there is a danger that, in some cases, prejudicial broadcast accounts of pretrial and trial events may impair the ability of jurors to decide the issue of guilt or innocence uninfluenced by extraneous matter. The risk of juror prejudice in some cases does not justify an absolute ban on news coverage of trials by the printed media; so also the risk of such prejudice does not warrant an absolute constitutional ban on all broadcast coverage.

Chandler v. Florida, 449 U.S. 560, 574-75 (1981). This resolves the constitutional question that states may, if they wish, permit the broadcasting of criminal trials *generally,* though it leaves open the possibility that in *specific* cases due process might require that the TV cameras be turned off. For example, in *Estes v. Texas,* 381 U.S. 532 (1965), the Supreme Court concluded that the presence of television cameras had deprived the defendant of a fair trial:

> Its presence is a form of mental—if not physical—harassment, resembling a police line-up or the third degree. The inevitable close-ups of his

> gestures and expressions during the ordeal of his trial might well transgress his personal sensibilities, his dignity, and his ability to concentrate on the proceedings before him—sometimes the difference between life and death—dispassionately, freely and without the distraction of wide public surveillance.

Id. at 549. The result of *Chandler* and *Estes* is that a state rule allowing the broadcast of criminal trials is constitutional but that an individual trial might violate due process if televised cameras impede the fairness of the trial or the ability of the defense to present its case. But this general assumption of constitutional permissiveness still leaves open the prudential question of whether states ought to allow the broadcasting of criminal trials.

❧ **The dignity argument.** One frequent policy argument made against televised trials is that the cameras compromise the "dignity" of the judicial proceedings. Indeed, notice the reference to dignity in the passage above quoted from *Estes*. Or consider the Second Circuit's worry that TV cameras would compromise "the required sense of solemnity, dignity and the search for truth." *Westmoreland v. Columbia Broad. Sys.*, 752 F.2d 16, 23 (2d Cir. 1984). It is not just the defendant's dignity that might be compromised; the dignity of the system itself might be undermined if the televised broadcasts turn the solemnity of the trial into a media circus. Is this process inevitable? Moreover, what assumption underlies the conclusion that increased media exposure—even raucous exposure—will compromise the dignity of the occasion? Is it that the public will not share the goals of the criminal process, i.e., to fairly judge whether a defendant has committed wrongdoing and deserves punishment? Or is the assumption that the criminal courts necessarily stand apart, as an autonomous system, from the public at large?

❧ **The distraction argument.** Another frequent argument is that TV cameras will prove a distraction to the proceedings. But the question is which participant will be distracted. In *Estes*, the Court argued that it was the juror: "But we know that distractions are not caused solely by the physical presence of the camera and its telltale red lights. It is the awareness of the fact of telecasting that is felt by the juror throughout the trial. We are all self-conscious and uneasy when being televised. Human nature being what it is, not only will a juror's eyes be fixed on the camera, but also his mind will be preoccupied with the telecasting rather than with the testimony." 381 U.S. at 546. The other possibility is that the defense lawyer might start playing to the public audience instead of faithfully fulfilling his client's interests. *Id.* at 566. This latter concern paints defense attorneys as vainglorious charlatans who are easily distracted from their ethical obligations. If this is the case, it would seem to prove too much and that public access generally, including regular reporting, might cause the defense attorney to seek publicity at the client's expense. Is this concern particular to the issue of TV cameras or rather a structural risk in the adversarial system? Consider the following argument rejecting the distraction concern:

> Trials subject to visual recordings may feel different to some participants, especially judges and attorneys who have been practicing for a number of years, but the novelty of being recorded would soon wear off. The cameras would surely be no more distracting than a stenographer who is seen as a normal and necessary element of court proceedings. After the initial transition period, cameras could fill the role of court reporters and even remove the distraction of having another person present in the courtroom.

Katherine Geldmacher, *Behind Closed Doors: Why the Federal Judiciary's Decision to Keep Cameras Out of District Courts Was a Mistake*, 30 Geo. J. Legal Ethics 753, 765 (2017).

❧ **Cameras in the federal courts.** In the federal court system, audio recordings of oral arguments are often released after the argument but are not broadcast contemporaneously. Some federal courts have experimented with video cameras in the courtroom as part of a pilot program—but not for criminal trials. The closest the pilot program came to criminal trials was civil trials related to criminal matters, such as civil rights lawsuits alleging unlawful searches and seizures by the police. As for appellate proceedings, the Supreme Court has never seriously entertained the idea of televising its oral arguments, despite considerable public interest in its jurisprudence. Although the Justices have offered varying reasons, Justice Alito explained that television coverage of the Court "would also in some ways change what now goes on. . . . Some lawyers arguing before the court in televised cases would use the occasion to address the television audience for political or other purposes." Sonja R. West, *The Monster in the Courtroom*, 2012 BYU L. Rev. 1953, 1973. Each of the other Justices who have spoken about the matter has expressed similar concerns, though it is unclear whether this concern is sufficiently grave to outweigh the increase in public access that broadcasting would enable. Chief Justice Roberts has often spoken of the respect that the public has for the federal judiciary, and the Supreme Court in particular, as an impartial and non-partisan guardian of the rule of law. Would TV cameras enhance or detract from public confidence in the federal judiciary as an institution?

❧ **Livestreaming on social media.** When state courts allow trials to be broadcast live on television, should they go the further step and allow (or should TV broadcasters support) livestreaming on social media sites such as Facebook or Twitter? On the one hand, the final destination (traditional cable TV or social media on the Internet) sounds rather arbitrary and in fact the two mediums are increasingly overlapping. However, social media viewing allows for dynamic feedback, through sharing, reposting, liking, and retweeting, while watching on TV is more passive and solitary. Does a future with criminal trials livestreamed on social media portend a *Black Mirror*–style dystopian justice system, or will it simply give regular people a view of the justice system that they ordinarily would be denied? After all, not every trial can be broadcast on TV because there simply are not enough hours in the day to do so, but it is certainly plausible to livestream every trial on social media on concurrent streams.

PART VI

AFTER THE TRIAL

CHAPTER 18

SENTENCING

INTRODUCTION

When punishment is imposed after conviction, the type and quantum of punishment is usually decided by reference to one or more theories of punishment. These theories provide a moral and legal rationale for punishment. They explain why, for example, the deprivation of liberty by coercive measures (being held in a prison) should not be considered a case of unlawful kidnapping. Something about the mechanism of punishment for past wrongdoing transforms what would otherwise constitute an illegal act into a lawful exercise of state power.

The traditional framework theories for punishment include retribution, expressivism, deterrence, rehabilitation, and incapacitation/protection of society. In practice, trial courts rarely rely on only one theory to justify their sentencing decisions. They are more likely to justify the sentence with regard to multiple theories and in some jurisdictions, statutes might explicitly direct the trial court to consider multiple theories. For example, the federal code, 18 U.S.C. § 3553, directs trial courts in all federal prosecutions to consider:

> (2) the need for the sentence imposed—
>
> (A) to reflect the seriousness of the offense, to promote respect for the law, and to provide just punishment for the offense;
>
> (B) to afford adequate deterrence to criminal conduct;
>
> (C) to protect the public from further crimes of the defendant; and
>
> (D) to provide the defendant with needed educational or vocational training, medical care, or other correctional treatment in the most effective manner[.]

Before proceeding further, it is important to analyze each of these theories. It is most useful to start with the second theory, deterrence. Deterrence works from the premise that the imposition of punishment will discourage future instances of law breaking, because the potential criminal will assess the risk of being punished and will incorporate that possibility into the decision whether to commit the crime in the first place. There are two flavors of deterrence. Specific deterrence focuses on the individual criminal, and the goal of the punishment is to deter that specific criminal from returning to a life of crime. General deterrence focuses on society in general, and the goal of punishment is to deter *others* from engaging in criminal behavior. For general deterrence, the punishment of the offender is a cautionary tale designed to influence the behavior of other members of the community. Both specific and general deterrence are inherently forward-looking.

The notion that a punishment should provide "just" punishment for the offense is usually associated with retributivism, which is often defined in contradistinction to deterrence. A retributive rationale focuses exclusively on giving the offender his or her just deserts; the goal is to ensure that the offender suffers in some way for the wrongdoing imposed on innocent victims. The conceptual foundation for retributivism is hotly debated and there are many plausible answers for why the offender "deserves" to be punished in this way. To take just one example, some retributivists will say that an offender has forfeited the right to liberty by virtue of his or her wrongdoing. But this is just one among many flavors of retributivism.

Expressivism is closely allied with retributivism—sometimes even viewed as a variant of retributivism. Expressivists believe that the institution of punishment is designed to "express" the community's disapproval of the wrongdoer's behavior. Although a token punishment might, in theory, communicate society's disapproval, most expressivists require that the punishment be proportional to the offender's wrongdoing. In practice, then, a substantial sentence adequately expresses the community's disapproval for a serious crime. On the ground, in its application, expressivist and retributive considerations may push a trial court in the same direction.

The last two theories, incapacitation and rehabilitation, are best considered together. Incapacitation focuses on the need to remove offenders from society to prevent them from engaging in future acts of criminality during their period of incarceration. Other forms of post-carceral control, such as parole, are similarly designed to supervise the offender in a way that gestures toward a form of incapacitation, i.e., preventing them from reoffending. Similarly, rehabilitation also aims to prevent reoccurrence of criminality, although this time by rehabilitating the offender into a productive member of society. Incarceration programs designed with a rehabilitative spirit will include educational and job training opportunities that will promote economic self-sufficiency and lessen the likelihood that the offender will fall back into criminal opportunities after release.

As noted above, trial courts usually focus on several—or all—of these theories when holding sentencing hearings. So, the major procedural question tackled in this chapter is who gets to decide what the sentence should be: the legislator, the judge, or the jury—or what combination of these is appropriate. The legislature enacts substantive statutes that proscribe the penalty for each offense. In some cases, the sentence might be mandatory and leave no discretion at all to the trial court. For example, a state statute might stipulate that an offender convicted of murder or some other serious offense should automatically receive a mandatory sentence of life in prison. In that situation, the trial court's imposition of the sentence becomes purely mechanical, and the defendant's only hope for mercy comes in the form of a pardon or clemency granted by the governor.

For all other offenses, the statute usually defines the minimum and maximum penalties for each offense. The trial court then has discretion to select the appropriate penalty between those two extremes, either through absolute discretion or guided discretion with factors outlined in sentencing guidelines. (Sometimes the sentencing guidelines originate from the legislature and in other jurisdictions the guidelines might be created by a sentencing commission composed of experts appointed by the government.) But the application of these sentencing guidelines could be handled by either the judge or the jury. This then raises the major constitutional question of this chapter: When sentencing guidelines are applied by a trial judge, does this process compromise the Sixth Amendment right to a jury trial? Or is the Sixth Amendment right limited to the guilt phase and silent about the relative role of judge and jury in sentencing? In the criminal process, the legislature, judge, and jury all have crucial roles, but the exact division of labor between them in the sentencing process has triggered some of the most intense constitutional litigation of the past 25 years.

The following sections explore that litigation in the following order: the Eighth Amendment prohibition on cruel and unusual punishment, which categorically limits punishment that is grossly disproportionate; constitutional limits on the application of the death penalty; and the proper role of the jury in sentencing decisions.

A. EIGHTH AMENDMENT CONSTRAINTS ON NON-CAPITAL SENTENCES

The Eighth Amendment provides that "[e]xcessive bail shall not be required, nor excessive fines imposed, nor cruel and unusual punishments inflicted." The text of the amendment gives no other guidance for what counts as cruel and unusual. The inquiry is complicated by the fact that penal practices have evolved considerably over the years. Forms of punishment that were once considered socially acceptable, such as corporal punishment, are now widely viewed as barbaric and not in keeping with a civilized form of government, at least according to a large percentage of the population. But what determines the content of the Eighth Amendment's prohibition: the social consensus at the time of the amendment or today's more "evolved" conception of humane punishment? Different theories of constitutional interpretation treat these questions differently. For originalists such as Justice Thomas or the late Justice Scalia, the question is tethered to the understanding of appropriate penal practices at the time of the adoption of the Bill of Rights. So, for example, Scalia was unwilling to consider capital punishment per se unconstitutional, since it was permitted at the nation's founding, nor did he see a significant role for the Eighth Amendment to play in non-capital sentencing, at least in terms of the imposition of life sentences. On the other hand, living constitutionalists believe that what counts as cruel and unusual punishment should be guided by evolving standards of decency. Under this hermeneutical approach, the meaning of the Eighth Amendment evolves over time as society continues to refine its moral and legal intuitions regarding acceptable practices of punishment. But if unmoored from a fixed historical period, how should the Supreme Court determine the content of these moral and legal intuitions?

In any event, setting aside this broader question of constitutional interpretation, one thing is certain: The Supreme Court's methodology in these cases is to consider what counts as cruel *and* what counts as unusual in modern penal practices. For example, in upholding a mandatory life term for a drug offense, the Supreme Court concluded that "[s]evere, mandatory penalties may be cruel, but they are not unusual in the constitutional sense, having been employed in various forms throughout our Nation's history." *Harmelin v. Michigan*, 501 U.S. 957, 994-95 (1991). To succeed in overturning a sentence, therefore, defendants must establish that their treatment was both cruel *and* unusual. Inevitably, this requires looking at the sentencing schemes of various state jurisdictions, and not just the statutory maximums. More contentiously, the Supreme Court also looks to the actual sentencing practices across state jurisdictions. So, for example, in determining what counts as a cruel and unusual punishment, it might be helpful not only to know what the maximum penalty is for theft in most jurisdictions, but also what thieves *actually* receive as punishment. If a maximum penalty is available but never handed down, this fact informs the inquiry of what counts as cruel and unusual.

More controversially, some Supreme Court Justices also make reference to sentencing practices in foreign jurisdictions. The impetus behind these references is to use foreign practices as a supporting benchmark to help determine whether a sentence is so out of step with international standards that it should be considered cruel and unusual. As you read the cases, keep both of these methodologies in the back of your mind. If, for example, a particular practice is relatively uncommon in American jurisdictions, or uncommon globally, should this lead us to conclude that the sentencing practice is indeed unusual? What tolerance does the Eighth Amendment have for punishment pluralism?

The following subsections focus on two particular areas of concern in the Eighth Amendment jurisprudence: disproportionate prison sentences and juvenile sentencing. The former focuses on so-called three-strikes statutes that permit judges to sentence recidivists to life in prison, even in the case of non-violent offenses, while the latter focuses on whether the Eighth Amendment allows a state to punish a juvenile offender to life in prison without the possibility of parole. The cases on the death penalty, though part of the Eighth Amendment jurisprudence, raise a number of distinct issues and are therefore covered in their own section of this chapter.

1. Proportionality and Prison Sentences

In determining whether a particular practice is cruel and unusual, the Supreme Court has scrutinized disproportionate punishment. The concept of proportionality requires reference to an application of the theories of punishment defined in the introduction above, including retribution, expressivism, deterrence, rehabilitation, and incapacitation. If the sentence is proportional (or alternatively, "not disproportionate") under at least one of the theories, then the Supreme Court is likely to uphold the sentence. At times, the Supreme Court has referred to the Eighth Amendment as embodying a "narrow" proportionality principle. This means that the Eighth Amendment does not require a strict or exact proportionality between crime or punishment; what it prohibits is simply a punishment that is so grossly disproportionate that it qualifies as both cruel and unusual.

Outside of the capital context, the Supreme Court has shown remarkably little interest in using the Eighth Amendment to scrutinize criminal sentences. Some penal *practices* have been struck down. For example, in *Hope v. Pelzer*, 536 U.S. 730 (2002), the Supreme Court concluded that the Eighth Amendment prohibited the handcuffing of an inmate to a hitching post for seven hours in hot weather with insufficient water and bathroom breaks. But as to the *length* of prison sentences, the Supreme Court has rarely, in the last 50 years, declared the length of a prison term disproportionately long. On the one hand, the Supreme Court declared 12 years of hard labor for falsifying records impermissibly excessive. *Weems v. United States*, 217 U.S. 349 (1910). On the other hand, though, the Supreme Court upheld a life sentence for a non-lethal drug crime in *Harmelin v. Michigan*, 501 U.S. 957 (1991). And in the following case, the Supreme Court considers California's "three strikes" statute for habitual offenders. As you read the case, ask yourself why defendants who have received lengthy sentences for non-violent offenses have had so little success with their Eighth Amendment challenges.

Ewing v. California

Supreme Court of the United States
538 U.S. 11 (2003)

Justice O'CONNOR announced the judgment of the Court and delivered an opinion, in which THE CHIEF JUSTICE and Justice KENNEDY join.

In this case, we decide whether the Eighth Amendment prohibits the State of California from sentencing a repeat felon to a prison term of 25 years to life under the State's "Three Strikes and You're Out" law.

I

California's three strikes law reflects a shift in the State's sentencing policies toward incapacitating and deterring repeat offenders who threaten the public safety. The law was designed "to ensure longer prison sentences and greater punishment for those who commit a felony and have been previously convicted of serious and/or violent felony offenses." On March 3, 1993, California Assemblymen Bill Jones and Jim Costa introduced Assembly Bill 971, the legislative version of what would later become the three strikes law. The Assembly Committee on Public Safety defeated the bill only weeks later. Public outrage over the defeat sparked a voter initiative to add Proposition 184, based loosely on the bill, to the ballot in the November 1994 general election.

On October 1, 1993, while Proposition 184 was circulating, 12-year-old Polly Klaas was kidnaped from her home in Petaluma, California. Her admitted killer, Richard Allen Davis, had a long criminal history that included two prior kidnaping convictions. Davis had served only half of his most recent sentence (16 years for kidnaping, assault, and burglary). Had Davis served his entire sentence, he would still have been in prison on the day that Polly Klaas was kidnaped. Polly Klaas' murder galvanized support for the three strikes initiative. . . .

California's current three strikes law consists of two virtually identical statutory schemes "designed to increase the prison terms of repeat felons." When a defendant is convicted of a felony, and he has previously been convicted of one or more prior felonies defined as "serious" or "violent" . . . sentencing is conducted pursuant to the three strikes law. Prior convictions must be alleged in the charging document, and the defendant has a right to a jury determination that the prosecution has proved the prior convictions beyond a reasonable doubt.

If the defendant has one prior "serious" or "violent" felony conviction, he must be sentenced to "twice the term otherwise provided as punishment for the current felony conviction." If the defendant has two or more prior "serious" or "violent" felony convictions, he must receive "an indeterminate term of life imprisonment." Defendants sentenced to life under the three strikes law become eligible for parole on a date calculated by reference to a "minimum term," which is the greater of (a) three times the term otherwise provided for the current conviction, (b) 25 years, or (c) the term determined by the court pursuant to § 1170 for the underlying conviction, including any enhancements.

Under California law, certain offenses may be classified as either felonies or misdemeanors. These crimes are known as "wobblers." Some crimes that would otherwise be misdemeanors become "wobblers" because of the defendant's prior record. For example, petty theft, a misdemeanor, becomes a "wobbler" when the defendant has previously served a prison term for committing specified theft-related crimes. Other crimes, such as grand theft, are "wobblers" regardless of the defendant's prior record. Both types of "wobblers" are triggering offenses under the three strikes law only when they are treated as felonies. Under California law, a "wobbler" is presumptively a felony and "remains a felony except when the discretion is actually exercised" to make the crime a misdemeanor.

In California, prosecutors may exercise their discretion to charge a "wobbler" as either a felony or a misdemeanor. Likewise, California trial courts have discretion to reduce a "wobbler" charged as a felony to a misdemeanor either before preliminary examination or at sentencing to avoid imposing a three strikes sentence. . . . California trial courts can also vacate allegations of prior "serious" or "violent" felony convictions, either on motion by the prosecution or sua sponte. . . . Thus, trial courts may avoid imposing a three strikes sentence in two ways: first, by reducing "wobblers" to misdemeanors (which do not qualify as triggering offenses), and second, by vacating allegations of prior "serious" or "violent" felony convictions.

On parole from a 9-year prison term, petitioner Gary Ewing walked into the pro shop of the El Segundo Golf Course in Los Angeles County on March 12, 2000. He walked out with three golf clubs, priced at $399 apiece, concealed in his pants leg. A shop employee, whose suspicions were aroused when he observed Ewing limp out of the pro shop, telephoned the police. The police apprehended Ewing in the parking lot.

Ewing is no stranger to the criminal justice system. In 1984, at the age of 22, he pleaded guilty to theft. The court sentenced him to six months in jail (suspended), three years' probation, and a $300 fine. In 1988, he was convicted of felony grand theft auto and sentenced to one year in jail and three years' probation. After Ewing completed probation, however, the sentencing court reduced the crime to a misdemeanor, permitted Ewing to withdraw his guilty plea, and dismissed the case. In 1990, he was convicted of petty theft with a prior and sentenced to 60 days in the county jail and three years' probation. In 1992, Ewing was convicted of battery and sentenced to 30 days in the county jail and two years' summary probation. One month later, he was convicted of theft and sentenced to 10 days in the county jail and 12 months' probation. In January 1993, Ewing was convicted of burglary and sentenced to 60 days in the county jail and one year's summary probation. In February 1993, he was convicted of possessing drug paraphernalia and sentenced to six months in the county jail and three years' probation. In July 1993, he was convicted of appropriating lost property and sentenced to 10 days in the county jail and two years' summary probation. In September 1993, he was convicted of unlawfully possessing a firearm and trespassing and sentenced to 30 days in the county jail and one year's probation.

In October and November 1993, Ewing committed three burglaries and one robbery at a Long Beach, California, apartment complex over a 5-week period. He awakened one of his victims, asleep on her living room sofa, as he tried to disconnect her video cassette recorder from the television in that room. When she screamed, Ewing ran out the front door. On another occasion, Ewing accosted a victim in the mailroom of the apartment complex. Ewing claimed to have a gun and ordered the victim to hand over his wallet. When the victim resisted, Ewing produced a knife and forced the victim back to the apartment itself. While Ewing rifled through the bedroom, the victim fled the apartment screaming for help. Ewing absconded with the victim's money and credit cards.

On December 9, 1993, Ewing was arrested on the premises of the apartment complex for trespassing and lying to a police officer. The knife used in the robbery and a glass cocaine pipe were later found in the back seat of the patrol car used to transport Ewing to the police station. A jury convicted Ewing of first-degree robbery and three counts of residential burglary. Sentenced to nine years and eight months in prison, Ewing was paroled in 1999.

Only 10 months later, Ewing stole the golf clubs at issue in this case. He was charged with, and ultimately convicted of, one count of felony grand theft of personal property in excess of $400. As required by the three strikes law, the prosecutor formally alleged, and the trial court later found, that Ewing had been convicted previously of four serious or violent felonies for the three burglaries and the robbery in the Long Beach apartment complex. . . . As a newly convicted felon with two or more "serious" or "violent" felony convictions in his past, Ewing was sentenced under the three strikes law to 25 years to life. . . .

II

The Eighth Amendment, which forbids cruel and unusual punishments, contains a "narrow proportionality principle" that "applies to noncapital sentences." *Harmelin v. Michigan*, 501 U.S. 957, 996-997 (1991) (Kennedy, J., concurring in part and concurring in judgment). We have most recently addressed the proportionality principle as applied to terms of years in a series of cases beginning with *Rummel v. Estelle*.

In *Rummel*, we held that it did not violate the Eighth Amendment for a State to sentence a three-time offender to life in prison with the possibility of parole. . . . Three years after *Rummel*, in *Solem v. Helm*, 463 U.S. 277 (1983), we held that the Eighth Amendment prohibited "a life sentence without possibility of parole for a seventh nonviolent felony." . . . We specifically stated that the Eighth Amendment's ban on cruel and unusual punishments "prohibits . . . sentences that are disproportionate to the crime committed," and that the "constitutional principle of proportionality has been recognized explicitly in this Court for almost a century." The *Solem* Court then explained that three factors may be relevant to a determination of whether a sentence is so disproportionate that it violates the Eighth Amendment: "(i) the gravity of the offense and the harshness of the penalty; (ii) the sentences imposed on other criminals in the same jurisdiction; and (iii) the sentences imposed for commission of the same crime in other jurisdictions." . . .

Our traditional deference to legislative policy choices finds a corollary in the principle that the Constitution "does not mandate adoption of any one penological theory." A sentence can have a variety of justifications, such as incapacitation, deterrence, retribution, or rehabilitation. Some or all of these justifications may play a role in a State's sentencing scheme. Selecting the sentencing rationales is generally a policy choice to be made by state legislatures, not federal courts.

When the California Legislature enacted the three strikes law, it made a judgment that protecting the public safety requires incapacitating criminals who have already been convicted of at least one serious or violent crime. Nothing in the Eighth Amendment prohibits California from making that choice. To the contrary, our cases establish that "States have a valid interest in deterring and segregating habitual criminals." Recidivism has long been recognized as a legitimate basis for increased punishment.

California's justification is no pretext. Recidivism is a serious public safety concern in California and throughout the Nation. According to a recent report, approximately 67 percent of former inmates released from state prisons were charged with at least one "serious" new crime within three years of their release. In particular, released property offenders like Ewing had higher recidivism rates than those released after committing violent, drug, or public-order offenses. Approximately 73 percent of the property offenders released in 1994 were arrested again within three years, compared to approximately 61 percent of the violent offenders, 62 percent of the public-order offenders, and 66 percent of the drug offenders. . . .

The State's interest in deterring crime also lends some support to the three strikes law. We have long viewed both incapacitation and deterrence as rationales for recidivism statutes: "[A] recidivist statute['s] . . . primary goals are to deter repeat offenders and, at some point in the life of one who repeatedly commits criminal offenses serious enough to be punished as felonies, to segregate that person from the rest of society for an extended period of time." Four years after the passage of California's three strikes law, the recidivism rate of parolees returned to prison for the commission of a new crime dropped by nearly 25 percent. . . .

To be sure, California's three strikes law has sparked controversy. Critics have doubted the law's wisdom, cost-efficiency, and effectiveness in reaching its goals. This criticism is appropriately directed at the legislature, which has primary responsibility for making the difficult policy choices that underlie any criminal sentencing scheme. We do not sit as a "superlegislature" to second-guess these policy choices. It is enough that the State of California has a reasonable basis for believing that dramatically enhanced sentences for habitual felons "advance[s] the goals of [its] criminal justice system in any substantial way."

III

Against this backdrop, we consider Ewing's claim that his three strikes sentence of 25 years to life is unconstitutionally disproportionate to his offense of "shoplifting three golf clubs." We first address the gravity of the offense compared to the harshness of the penalty. At the threshold, we note that Ewing incorrectly frames the issue. The gravity of his offense was not merely "shoplifting three golf clubs." Rather, Ewing was convicted of felony grand theft for stealing nearly $1,200 worth of merchandise after previously having been convicted of at least two "violent" or "serious" felonies. Even standing alone, Ewing's theft should not be taken lightly. His crime was certainly not "one of the most passive felonies a person could commit." To the contrary, the Supreme Court of California has noted the "seriousness" of grand theft in the context of proportionality review. . . .

In weighing the gravity of Ewing's offense, we must place on the scales not only his current felony, but also his long history of felony recidivism. Any other approach would fail to accord proper deference to the policy judgments that find expression in the legislature's choice of sanctions. In imposing a three strikes sentence, the State's interest is not merely punishing the offense of conviction, or the "triggering" offense: "[I]t is in addition the interest . . . in dealing in a harsher manner with those who by repeated criminal acts have shown that they are simply incapable of conforming to the norms of society as established by its criminal law." To give full effect to the State's choice of this legitimate penological goal, our proportionality review of Ewing's sentence must take that goal into account. Ewing's sentence is justified by the State's public-safety interest in incapacitating and deterring recidivist felons, and amply supported by his own long, serious criminal record. . . .

Justice SCALIA, concurring in the judgment.

In my opinion in *Harmelin v. Michigan*, 501 U.S. 957 (1991), I concluded that the Eighth Amendment's prohibition of "cruel and unusual punishments" was aimed at excluding only certain modes of punishment, and was not a "guarantee against disproportionate sentences." Out of respect for the principle of *stare decisis*, I might nonetheless accept the contrary holding of *Solem v. Helm*, 463 U.S. 277 (1983)—that the Eighth Amendment contains a narrow proportionality principle—if I felt I could intelligently apply it. This case demonstrates why I cannot.

Proportionality—the notion that the punishment should fit the crime—is inherently a concept tied to the penological goal of retribution. "[I]t becomes difficult even to speak intelligently of 'proportionality,' once deterrence and rehabilitation are given significant weight"—not to mention giving weight to the purpose of California's three strikes law: incapacitation. In the present case, the game is up once the plurality has acknowledged that "the Constitution does not mandate adoption of any one penological theory," and that a "sentence can have a variety of justifications, such as incapacitation, deterrence, retribution, or rehabilitation." That acknowledgment having been made, it no longer suffices merely to assess "the gravity of the offense compared to the harshness of the penalty"; that classic description of the proportionality principle (alone and in itself quite resistant to policy-free, legal analysis) now becomes merely the "first" step of the inquiry. Having completed that step (by a discussion which, in all fairness, does not convincingly establish that 25-years-to-life is a "proportionate" punishment for stealing three golf clubs), the plurality must then add an analysis to show that "Ewing's sentence is justified by the State's public-safety interest in incapacitating and deterring recidivist felons."

Which indeed it is—though why that has anything to do with the principle of proportionality is a mystery. Perhaps the plurality should revise its terminology, so that what it reads into the Eighth Amendment is not the unstated proposition that all punishment should be reasonably proportionate to the gravity of the offense, but rather the unstated proposition that all punishment should reasonably pursue the multiple purposes of the criminal law. That formulation would make it clearer than ever, of course, that the plurality is not applying law but evaluating policy.

Because I agree that petitioner's sentence does not violate the Eighth Amendment's prohibition against cruel and unusual punishments, I concur in the judgment.

Justice BREYER, with whom Justice STEVENS, Justice SOUTER, and Justice GINSBURG join, dissenting.

. . . [B]etween the end of World War II and 1994 (when California enacted the three strikes law), no one like Ewing could have served more than 10 years in prison. We know that for certain because the maximum sentence for Ewing's crime of conviction, grand theft, was for most of that period 10 years. From 1976 to 1994 (and currently, absent application of the three strikes penalty), a Ewing-type offender would have received a maximum sentence of four years. . . .

. . . California has reserved, and still reserves, Ewing-type prison time, i.e., at least 25 real years in prison, for criminals convicted of crimes far worse than was Ewing's. Statistics for the years 1945 to 1981, for example, indicate that typical (nonrecidivist) male first-degree murderers served between 10 and 15 real years in prison, with 90 percent of all such murderers serving less than 20 real years. Moreover, California, which has moved toward a real-time sentencing system (where the statutory punishment approximates the time served), still punishes far less harshly those who have engaged in far more serious conduct. It imposes, for example, upon nonrecidivists guilty of arson causing great bodily injury a maximum sentence of nine years in prison; it imposes upon those guilty of voluntary manslaughter a maximum sentence of 11 years. It reserves the sentence that it here imposes upon (former-burglar-now-golf-club-thief) Ewing for nonrecidivist, first-degree murderers. . . .

With three exceptions, we do not have before us information about actual time served by Ewing-type offenders in other States. We do know, however, that the law would make it legally impossible for a Ewing-type offender to serve more than 10 years in prison in 33 jurisdictions, as well as the federal courts, more than 15 years in 4 other States, and more than 20 years in 4 additional States. . . .

This is not the end of the matter. California sentenced Ewing pursuant to its "three strikes" law. That law represents a deliberate effort to provide stricter punishments for recidivists. And, it is important to consider whether special criminal justice concerns related to California's three strikes policy might justify including Ewing's theft within the class of triggering criminal conduct (thereby imposing a severe punishment), even if Ewing's sentence would otherwise seem disproportionately harsh. . . .

Neither do I see any other way in which inclusion of Ewing's conduct (as a "triggering crime") would further a significant criminal justice objective. One might argue that those who commit several property crimes should receive long terms of imprisonment in order to "incapacitate" them, i.e., to prevent them from committing further crimes in the future. But that is not the object of this particular three strikes statute. Rather, as the plurality says, California seeks "to reduce serious and violent crime." The statute's definitions of both kinds of crime include crimes against the person, crimes that create danger of physical harm, and drug crimes. They do not include even serious crimes against property, such as obtaining large amounts of money, say, through theft, embezzlement, or fraud. Given the omission of vast categories of property crimes—including grand theft (unarmed)—from the "strike" definition, one cannot argue, on property-crime-related incapacitation grounds, for inclusion of Ewing's crime among the triggers.

Nor do the remaining criminal law objectives seem relevant. No one argues for Ewing's inclusion within the ambit of the three strikes statute on grounds of "retribution." . . . [I]n terms of "deterrence," Ewing's 25-year term amounts to overkill. And "rehabilitation" is obviously beside the point. The upshot is that, in my view, the State cannot find in its three strikes law a special criminal justice need sufficient to rescue a sentence that other relevant considerations indicate is unconstitutional. . . .

NOTES & QUESTIONS ON PROPORTIONALITY

1. *Life imprisonment for parking.* The Court says that the Eighth Amendment's proportionality principle was not violated by California's three-strikes law but would be triggered by a state statute that allowed life imprisonment for a parking violation. What is the dividing line between these two extremes? Why is one of them grossly disproportionate but the other is constitutionally permissible?

2. *The carceral state.* For many critics of American criminal justice policy, the California statute, and the Supreme Court case that upheld it, are one piece of a much larger problem: the American obsession with incarceration as the only tool of law enforcement. In addition to the problem of serious prison terms for drug offenses, these critics complain that an unacceptably large percentage of the population is subject to incarceration. Moreover, the incarcerated population is disproportionately African-American when compared with the general population. As one scholar noted:

> Imprisonment is a method of criminal punishment employed the world over. But nowhere else has the possibility of consigning citizens to long-term state custody captured the political imagination to the extent it has in the United States. In American society, it is taken for granted that social exclusion enforced by the state is the appropriate response to the commission of antisocial acts. Yet judged from a policy perspective, it is not obvious why this should be. Precisely because social exclusion entails ongoing state control of the excluded, this penal strategy is extremely expensive, consuming resources that could otherwise be spent on more socially productive enterprises. It also takes a profound toll on children, families, and communities when individuals are removed from society as punishment. . . . And for all this, it is not even clear that punishing crime with social exclusion serves the aim of public safety, whether by rehabilitating offenders or deterring

> crime. Indeed, given the affirmatively harmful and arguably criminogenic conditions of many American prisons and jails, a strong case can be made that incarcerating convicted offenders as punishment is more likely to compromise public safety than to enhance it.

Sharon Dolovich, *Exclusion and Control in the Carceral State*, 16 Berkeley J. Crim. L. 259, 268-70 (2011). Do you agree with the author that the American obsession with incarceration is counterproductive?

3. *Harsh justice.* Not every nation follows the American carceral model. Many European nations deemphasize incarceration as a model for rehabilitation and when they do use incarceration, sentences are shorter and prison conditions are more favorable for prisoners. Professor James Q. Whitman argues in *Harsh Justice: Criminal Punishment and the Widening Divide Between America and Europe* (2005), that the American system of incarceration is built on the concept of degradation, while most European penal systems are much more likely to express mercy. Consequently, prisons in the United States have much harsher conditions than in Europe, and prisoners in the United States have to spend a much longer period in these harsher environments before being released. Based on what you read in the *Ewing* case, do you agree? Would you describe the Ewing's treatment as an exercise in degradation or would you describe it as his getting his "just deserts"?

STATUTORY REQUIREMENTS

The federal judicial system has its own version of California's statute. The federal Armed Career Criminal Act, 18 U.S.C. § 924(e), provides a substantial sentencing enhancement for federal offenders who have been previously convicted of at least three violent offenses or some drug offenses. Although the statute does not impose an automatic life sentence, it does mandate a 15-year prison sentence, even if the fourth offense would normally carry a much smaller penalty. In *Stokeling v. United States*, decided January 15, 2019, the Supreme Court concluded that all forms of robbery, even purse snatching and pickpocketing, qualify as violent felonies under the Armed Career Criminal Act because robbery inevitably involves the perpetrator's application of physical force over the resistance, however slight, of the victim. Justice Thomas noted:

> The force necessary to overcome a victim's physical resistance is inherently "violent." . . . This is true because robbery that must overpower a victim's will—even a feeble or weak-willed victim—necessarily involves a physical confrontation and struggle. The altercation need not cause pain or injury or even be prolonged; it is the physical contest between the criminal and the victim that is itself "capable of causing physical pain or injury."

Do you agree that the federal sentencing enhancement should apply in all of these cases?

2. Sentencing Juveniles to Life Without Parole

The harsh justice associated with the American system of incarceration will sometimes fall on juveniles who are tried as adults. In most jurisdictions, prosecutors retain substantial discretion to request permission to try a juvenile as an adult if they are charged with a serious offense. In such cases, the applicable penalty may be quite severe. In the following two cases, the Supreme Court considers the application of life sentences without the possibility for parole for juvenile offenders. (The issue in these cases is not the age of the defendant at trial but rather the age of the defendant when the crime was allegedly committed.) In both cases, the defendants were convicted of life without the possibility of parole, thus ensuring that the defendant would spend the rest of his life in prison. Whether this is consistent with the Eighth Amendment raises deep questions about the nature of punishment and the principle of proportionality. Is it based on retribution, deterrence, incapacitation, or rehabilitation? By definition, juvenile offenders sentenced to life in prison have no opportunity for meaningful rehabilitation, since they will not be returned to society.

The first case, *Graham v. Florida*, asks whether a juvenile may be sentenced to life without the possibility of parole for a non-homicide offense. The second case, *Miller v. Alabama*, asks whether a juvenile may receive this sentence for homicide—a question that was deliberately left open after the first case.

Graham v. Florida

Supreme Court of the United States
560 U.S. 48 (2010)

Justice KENNEDY delivered the opinion of the Court.

The issue before the Court is whether the Constitution permits a juvenile offender to be sentenced to life in prison without parole for a nonhomicide crime. The sentence was imposed by the State of Florida. Petitioner challenges the sentence under the Eighth Amendment's Cruel and Unusual Punishments Clause, made applicable to the States by the Due Process Clause of the Fourteenth Amendment.

I

Petitioner is Terrance Jamar Graham. He was born on January 6, 1987. Graham's parents were addicted to crack cocaine, and their drug use persisted in his early years. Graham was diagnosed with attention deficit hyperactivity disorder in elementary school. He began drinking alcohol and using tobacco at age 9 and smoked marijuana at age 13.

In July 2003, when Graham was age 16, he and three other school-age youths attempted to rob a barbeque restaurant in Jacksonville, Florida. One youth, who worked at the restaurant, left the back door unlocked just before closing time. Graham and another youth, wearing masks, entered through the unlocked door. Graham's masked accomplice twice struck the restaurant manager in the back of the head with a metal bar. When the manager started yelling at the assailant and Graham, the two youths ran out and escaped in a car driven by the third accomplice. The restaurant manager required stitches for his head injury. No money was taken.

Graham was arrested for the robbery attempt. Under Florida law, it is within a prosecutor's discretion whether to charge 16- and 17-year-olds as adults or juveniles for most felony crimes. Graham's prosecutor elected to charge Graham as an adult. The charges against Graham were armed burglary with assault or battery, a first-degree felony carrying a maximum penalty of life imprisonment without the possibility of parole and attempted armed robbery, a second-degree felony carrying a maximum penalty of 15 years' imprisonment.

On December 18, 2003, Graham pleaded guilty to both charges under a plea agreement. Graham wrote a letter to the trial court. After reciting "this is my first and last time getting in trouble," he continued, "I've decided to turn my life around." Graham said, "I made a promise to God and myself that if I get a second chance, I'm going to do whatever it takes to get to the [National Football League]."

The trial court accepted the plea agreement. The court withheld adjudication of guilt as to both charges and sentenced Graham to concurrent 3-year terms of probation. Graham was required to spend the first 12 months of his probation in the county jail, but he received credit for the time he had served awaiting trial, and was released on June 25, 2004.

Less than six months later, on the night of December 2, 2004, Graham again was arrested. The State's case was as follows: Earlier that evening, Graham participated in a home invasion robbery. His two accomplices were Meigo Bailey and Kirkland Lawrence, both 20-year-old men. According to the State, at 7 P.M. that night, Graham, Bailey, and Lawrence knocked on the door of the home where Carlos Rodriguez lived. Graham, followed by Bailey and Lawrence, forcibly entered the home and held a pistol to Rodriguez's chest. For the next 30 minutes, the three held Rodriguez and another man, a friend of Rodriguez, at gunpoint while they ransacked the home searching for money. Before leaving, Graham and his accomplices barricaded Rodriguez and his friend inside a closet.

The State further alleged that Graham, Bailey, and Lawrence, later the same evening, attempted a second robbery, during which Bailey was shot. Graham, who had borrowed his father's car, drove Bailey and Lawrence to the hospital and left them there. As Graham drove away, a police sergeant signaled him to stop. Graham continued at a high speed but crashed into a telephone pole. He tried to flee on foot but was apprehended. Three handguns were found in his car. . . .

On December 13, 2004, Graham's probation officer filed with the trial court an affidavit asserting that Graham had violated the conditions of his probation by possessing a firearm, committing crimes, and associating with persons engaged in criminal activity. The trial court held hearings on Graham's violations about a year later, in December 2005 and January 2006. The judge who presided was not the same judge who had accepted Graham's guilty plea to the earlier offenses. . . .

The trial court found Graham guilty of the earlier armed burglary and attempted armed robbery charges. It sentenced him to the maximum sentence authorized by law on each charge: life imprisonment for the armed burglary and 15 years for the attempted armed robbery. Because Florida has abolished its parole system, a life sentence gives a defendant no possibility of release unless he is granted executive clemency. . . .

III

The analysis begins with objective indicia of national consensus. "[T]he clearest and most reliable objective evidence of contemporary values is the legislation enacted by the country's legislatures." Six jurisdictions do not allow life without parole sentences for any juvenile offenders. Seven jurisdictions permit life without parole for juvenile offenders, but only for homicide crimes. Thirty-seven States as well as the District of Columbia permit sentences of life without parole for a juvenile nonhomicide offender in some circumstances. Federal law also allows for the possibility of life without parole for offenders as young as 13. Relying on this metric, the State and its amici argue that there is no national consensus against the sentencing practice at issue.

This argument is incomplete and unavailing. "There are measures of consensus other than legislation." Actual sentencing practices are an important part of the Court's inquiry into consensus. Here, an examination of actual sentencing practices in jurisdictions where the sentence in question is permitted by statute discloses a consensus against its use. Although these statutory schemes contain no explicit prohibition on sentences of life without parole for juvenile nonhomicide offenders, those sentences are most infrequent. According to a recent study, nationwide there are only 109 juvenile offenders serving sentences of life without parole for nonhomicide offenses. . . .

The evidence of consensus is not undermined by the fact that many jurisdictions do not prohibit life without parole for juvenile nonhomicide offenders. The Court confronted a similar situation in *Thompson*, where a plurality concluded that the death penalty for offenders younger than 16 was unconstitutional. A number of States then allowed the juvenile death penalty if one considered the statutory scheme. As is the case here, those States authorized the transfer of some juvenile offenders to adult court; and at that point there was no statutory differentiation between adults and juveniles with respect to authorized penalties. The plurality concluded that the transfer laws show "that the States consider 15-year-olds to be old enough to be tried in criminal court for serious crimes (or too old to be dealt with effectively in juvenile court), but tells us nothing about the judgment these States have made regarding the appropriate punishment for such youthful offenders." 487 U.S., at 826, n. 24. . . . The same reasoning obtains here. Many States have chosen to move away from juvenile court systems and to allow juveniles to be transferred to, or charged directly in, adult court under certain circumstances. Once in adult court, a juvenile offender may receive the same sentence as would be given to an adult offender, including a life without parole sentence. But the fact that transfer and direct charging laws make life without parole possible for some juvenile nonhomicide offenders does not justify a judgment that many States intended to subject such offenders to life without parole sentences. . . .

Community consensus, while "entitled to great weight," is not itself determinative of whether a punishment is cruel and unusual. In accordance with the constitutional design, "the task of interpreting the Eighth Amendment remains our responsibility." The judicial exercise of independent judgment requires consideration of the culpability of the offenders at issue in light of their crimes and characteristics, along with the severity of the punishment in question. In this inquiry the Court also considers whether the challenged sentencing practice serves legitimate penological goals.

Roper established that because juveniles have lessened culpability they are less deserving of the most severe punishments. As compared to adults, juveniles have a "lack of maturity and an underdeveloped sense of responsibility"; they "are more vulnerable or susceptible to negative influences and outside pressures, including peer pressure"; and their characters are "not as well formed." These salient characteristics mean that "[i]t is difficult even for expert psychologists to differentiate between the juvenile offender whose crime reflects unfortunate yet transient immaturity, and the rare juvenile offender whose crime reflects irreparable corruption." Accordingly, "juvenile offenders cannot with reliability be classified among the worst offenders." A juvenile is not absolved of responsibility for his actions, but his transgression "is not as morally reprehensible as that of an adult." No recent data provide reason to reconsider the Court's observations in *Roper* about the nature of juveniles. . . .

The Court has recognized that defendants who do not kill, intend to kill, or foresee that life will be taken are categorically less deserving of the most serious forms of punishment than are murderers. There is a line "between homicide and other serious violent offenses against the individual." Serious nonhomicide crimes "may be devastating in their harm . . . but in terms of moral depravity and of the injury to the person and to the public, . . . they cannot be compared to murder in their severity and irrevocability." This is because "[l]ife is over for the victim of the murderer," but for the victim of even a very serious nonhomicide crime, "life . . . is not over and normally is not beyond repair." Although an offense like robbery or rape is "a serious crime deserving serious punishment," those crimes differ from homicide crimes in a moral sense.

It follows that, when compared to an adult murderer, a juvenile offender who did not kill or intend to kill has a twice diminished moral culpability. The age of the offender and the nature of the crime each bear on the analysis. . . . Life without parole is an especially harsh punishment for a juvenile. Under this sentence a juvenile offender will on average serve more years and a greater percentage of his life in prison than an adult offender. A 16-year-old and a 75-year-old each sentenced to life without parole receive the same punishment in name only. This reality cannot be ignored.

The penological justifications for the sentencing practice are also relevant to the analysis. Criminal punishment can have different goals, and choosing among them is within a legislature's discretion. It does not follow, however, that the purposes and effects of penal sanctions are irrelevant to the determination of Eighth Amendment restrictions. A sentence lacking any legitimate penological justification is by its nature disproportionate to the offense. With respect to life without parole for juvenile nonhomicide offenders, none of the goals of penal sanctions that have been recognized as legitimate—retribution, deterrence, incapacitation, and rehabilitation—provides an adequate justification.

Retribution is a legitimate reason to punish, but it cannot support the sentence at issue here. Society is entitled to impose severe sanctions on a juvenile nonhomicide offender to express its condemnation of the crime and to seek restoration of the moral imbalance caused by the offense. But "[t]he heart of the retribution rationale is that a criminal sentence must be directly related to the personal culpability of the criminal offender." And as *Roper* observed, "[w]hether viewed as an attempt to express the community's moral outrage or as an attempt to right the balance for the wrong to the victim, the case for retribution is not as strong with a minor as with an adult." The case becomes even weaker with respect to a juvenile who did not commit homicide. Roper found that "[r]etribution is not proportional if the law's most severe penalty is imposed" on the juvenile murderer. The considerations underlying that holding support as well the conclusion that retribution does not justify imposing the second most severe penalty on the less culpable juvenile nonhomicide offender.

Deterrence does not suffice to justify the sentence either. Roper noted that "the same characteristics that render juveniles less culpable than adults suggest . . . that juveniles will be less susceptible to deterrence." Because juveniles' "lack of maturity and an underdeveloped sense of responsibility . . . often result in impetuous and ill-considered actions and decisions," they are less likely to take a possible punishment into consideration when making decisions. . . .

Incapacitation, a third legitimate reason for imprisonment, does not justify the life without parole sentence in question here. Recidivism is a serious risk to public safety, and so incapacitation is an important goal. But while incapacitation may be a legitimate penological goal sufficient to justify life without parole in other contexts, it is inadequate to justify that punishment for juveniles who did not commit homicide. To justify life without parole on the assumption that the juvenile offender forever will be a danger to society requires the sentencer to make a judgment that the juvenile is incorrigible. The characteristics of juveniles make that judgment questionable. . . .

Here one cannot dispute that this defendant posed an immediate risk, for he had committed, we can assume, serious crimes early in his term of supervised release and despite his own assurances of reform. Graham deserved to be separated from society for some time in order to prevent what the trial court described as an "escalating pattern of criminal conduct," but it does not follow that he would be a risk to society for the rest of his life. . . .

Finally there is rehabilitation, a penological goal that forms the basis of parole systems. The concept of rehabilitation is imprecise; and its utility and proper implementation are the subject of a substantial, dynamic field of inquiry and dialogue. It is for legislatures to determine what rehabilitative techniques are appropriate and effective. A sentence of life imprisonment without parole, however, cannot be justified by the goal of rehabilitation. The penalty forswears altogether the rehabilitative ideal. By denying the defendant the right to reenter the community, the State makes an irrevocable judgment about that person's value and place in society. This judgment is not appropriate in light of a juvenile nonhomicide offender's capacity for change and limited moral culpability. . . .

Terrance Graham's sentence guarantees he will die in prison without any meaningful opportunity to obtain release, no matter what he might do to demonstrate that the bad acts he committed as a teenager are not representative of his true character, even if he spends the next half century attempting to atone for his crimes and learn from his mistakes. The State has denied him any chance to later demonstrate that he is fit to rejoin society based solely on a nonhomicide crime that he committed while he was a child in the eyes of the law. This the Eighth Amendment does not permit. . . .

Miller v. Alabama

Supreme Court of the United States
567 U.S. 460 (2012)

Justice KAGAN delivered the opinion of the Court.

The two 14-year-old offenders in these cases were convicted of murder and sentenced to life imprisonment without the possibility of parole. In neither case did the sentencing authority have any discretion to impose a different punishment. State law mandated that each juvenile die in prison even if a judge or jury would have thought that his youth and its attendant characteristics, along with the nature of his crime, made a lesser sentence (for example, life with the possibility of parole) more appropriate. Such a scheme prevents those meting out punishment from considering a juvenile's "lessened culpability" and greater "capacity for change," and runs afoul of our cases' requirement of individualized sentencing for defendants facing the most serious penalties. We therefore hold that mandatory life without parole for those under the age of 18 at the time of their crimes violates the Eighth Amendment's prohibition on "cruel and unusual punishments."

I

In November 1999, petitioner Kuntrell Jackson, then 14 years old, and two other boys decided to rob a video store. En route to the store, Jackson learned that one of the boys, Derrick Shields, was carrying a sawed-off shotgun in his coat sleeve. Jackson decided to stay outside when the two other boys entered the store. Inside, Shields pointed the gun at the store clerk, Laurie Troup, and demanded that she "give up the money." Troup refused. A few moments later, Jackson went into the store to find Shields continuing to demand money. At trial, the parties disputed whether Jackson warned Troup that "[w]e ain't playin'," or instead told his friends, "I thought you all was playin'." When Troup threatened to call the police, Shields shot and killed her. The three boys fled empty-handed. . . .

Like Jackson, petitioner Evan Miller was 14 years old at the time of his crime. Miller had by then been in and out of foster care because his mother suffered from alcoholism and drug addiction and his stepfather abused him. Miller, too, regularly used drugs and alcohol; and he had attempted suicide four times, the first when he was six years old.

One night in 2003, Miller was at home with a friend, Colby Smith, when a neighbor, Cole Cannon, came to make a drug deal with Miller's mother. The two boys followed Cannon back to his trailer, where all three smoked marijuana and played drinking games. When Cannon passed out, Miller stole his wallet, splitting about $300 with Smith. Miller then tried to put the wallet back in Cannon's pocket, but Cannon awoke and grabbed Miller by the throat. Smith hit Cannon with a nearby baseball bat, and once released, Miller grabbed the bat and repeatedly struck Cannon with it. Miller placed a sheet over Cannon's head, told him "I am God, I've come to take your life," and delivered one more blow. The boys then retreated to Miller's trailer, but soon decided to return to Cannon's to cover up evidence of their crime. Once there, they lit two fires. Cannon eventually died from his injuries and smoke inhalation. . . .

II

Graham concluded . . . that life-without-parole sentences, like capital punishment, may violate the Eighth Amendment when imposed on children. To be sure, *Graham*'s flat ban on life without parole applied only to nonhomicide crimes, and the Court took care to distinguish those offenses from murder, based on both moral culpability and consequential harm. But none of what it said about children—about their distinctive (and transitory) mental traits and environmental vulnerabilities—is crime-specific. Those features are evident in the same way, and to the same degree, when (as in both cases here) a botched robbery turns into a killing. So *Graham*'s reasoning implicates any life-without-parole sentence imposed on a juvenile, even as its categorical bar relates only to nonhomicide offenses.

Most fundamentally, *Graham* insists that youth matters in determining the appropriateness of a lifetime of incarceration without the possibility of parole. In the circumstances there, juvenile status precluded a life-without-parole sentence, even though an adult could receive it for a similar crime. And in other contexts as well, the characteristics of youth, and the way they weaken rationales for punishment, can render a life-without-parole sentence disproportionate. "An offender's age," we made clear in *Graham*, "is relevant to the Eighth Amendment," and so "criminal procedure laws that fail to take defendants' youthfulness into account at all would be flawed." . . .

But the mandatory penalty schemes at issue here prevent the sentencer from taking account of these central considerations. By removing youth from the balance—by subjecting a juvenile to the same life-without-parole sentence applicable to an adult—these laws prohibit a sentencing authority from assessing whether the law's harshest term of imprisonment proportionately punishes a juvenile offender. That contravenes *Graham*'s (and also *Roper*'s) foundational principle: that imposition of a State's most severe penalties on juvenile offenders cannot proceed as though they were not children. . . .

. . . [M]andatory penalties, by their nature, preclude a sentencer from taking account of an offender's age and the wealth of characteristics and circumstances attendant to it. Under these schemes, every juvenile will receive the same sentence as every other—the 17-year-old and the 14-year-old, the shooter and the accomplice, the child from a stable household and the child from a chaotic and abusive one. And still worse, each juvenile (including these two 14-year-olds) will receive the same sentence as the vast majority of adults committing similar homicide offenses—but really, as *Graham* noted, a greater sentence than those adults will serve. In meting out the death penalty, the elision of all these differences would be strictly forbidden. And once again, *Graham* indicates that a similar rule should apply when a juvenile confronts a sentence of life (and death) in prison. . . .

We therefore hold that the Eighth Amendment forbids a sentencing scheme that mandates life in prison without possibility of parole for juvenile offenders. By making youth (and all that accompanies it) irrelevant to imposition of that harshest prison sentence, such a scheme poses too great a risk of disproportionate punishment. . . .

NOTES & QUESTIONS ON JUVENILE SENTENCING

1. *Mandatory LWOP.* What role in the constitutional analysis is played by the mandatory nature of the sentencing scheme in *Miller v. Alabama*? Recall that the Supreme Court explicitly couched its holding in terms related to the mandatory nature of the punishment, i.e., that Miller was subject to a *mandatory* sentence of life without the possibility of parole for murder. But what if a juvenile was sentenced to life without the possibility of parole for murder as part of a non-mandatory sentencing scheme? Is this consistent with the Eighth Amendment? Such a result would not offend *Graham*, since *Graham* involved the imposition of life without the possibility of parole for non-violent offenses.

2. *Why the need for a categorical remedy?* The Supreme Court could have concluded that the individual sentences in the *Graham* or *Miller* cases were disproportionately harsh and remanded for resentencing in those individual cases. But the Court went further and imposed a categorical remedy: prohibiting the imposition of life without the possibility of parole in similar cases. What factors support the imposition of a categorical, rather than individual, remedy in these cases?

3. *Juveniles are different.* Should the punishment of juveniles receive greater constitutional scrutiny for purposes of the Eighth Amendment? If yes, which characteristics about juveniles require this increased scrutiny as to the prohibition on cruel and unusual punishment? Compare the level of scrutiny—and by extension the level of deference to the legislature—in the juvenile cases with the level of scrutiny applied in *Ewing*, which involved an adult offender. Should Ewing have received this level of constitutional protection as well?

B. EIGHTH AMENDMENT CONSTRAINTS ON THE DEATH PENALTY

The Eighth Amendment had the greatest impact in the context of the death penalty. In *Furman v. Georgia,* 408 U.S. 238 (1972), the Supreme Court concluded that the death penalty violated the Eighth Amendment because it constituted cruel and unusual punishment. The 5-4 decision yielded no majority opinion but simply a collection of five separate opinions all concurring in the release. Just four years later, the Supreme Court reversed course and reinstated the death penalty in *Gregg v. Georgia,* 428 U.S. 153 (1976), holding that the death penalty was not a per se violation of the Eighth Amendment. In the decades since *Gregg,* the Supreme Court has reaffirmed its core holding while at the same time ruling that the death penalty is not permissible in certain contexts. The following materials focus on those prohibitions and the core constitutional arguments underlying them.

1. Mental Disability

In the following case, the Supreme Court considers whether the Eighth Amendment prohibits the imposition of the death penalty against an offender who suffers from a mental disability. This question opens up a third opportunity for the criminal justice system to consider the defendant's mental status, each with its own standard. The first starts with competence to stand trial, with the standard that the defendant must understand the proceedings and be capable of assisting in the defense. The second is the standard for an insanity plea, which includes some combination of cognitive or volitional tests, depending on the jurisdiction. The last is whether the defendant is so mentally disabled that the imposition of the death penalty is problematic. As you read the following case, ask yourself what the inquiry assumes about the nature of punishment. Why are especially culpable defendants put to death and what facts about mental disability pose an obstacle to that ultimate punishment?

Atkins v. Virginia

Supreme Court of the United States
536 U.S. 304 (2002)

STEVENS, J.

Those mentally retarded persons who meet the law's requirements for criminal responsibility should be tried and punished when they commit crimes. Because of their disabilities in areas of reasoning, judgment, and control of their impulses, however, they do not act with the level of moral culpability that characterizes the most serious adult criminal conduct.

Moreover, their impairments can jeopardize the reliability and fairness of capital proceedings against mentally retarded defendants. Presumably for these reasons, in the 13 years since we decided *Penry v. Lynaugh,* 492 U.S. 302 (1989), the American public, legislators, scholars, and judges have deliberated over the question whether the death penalty should ever be imposed on a mentally retarded criminal. The consensus reflected in those deliberations informs our answer to the question presented by this case: whether such executions are "cruel and unusual punishments" prohibited by the Eighth Amendment to the Federal Constitution.

I

Petitioner, Daryl Renard Atkins, was convicted of abduction, armed robbery, and capital murder, and sentenced to death. At approximately midnight on August 16, 1996, Atkins and William Jones, armed with a semiautomatic handgun, abducted Eric Nesbitt, robbed him of the money on his person, drove him to an automated teller machine in his pickup truck where cameras recorded their withdrawal of additional cash, then took him to an isolated location where he was shot eight times and killed. . . .

In the penalty phase, the defense relied on one witness, Dr. Evan Nelson, a forensic psychologist who had evaluated Atkins before trial and concluded that he was "mildly mentally retarded." His conclusion was based on interviews with people who knew Atkins, a review of school and court records, and the administration of a standard intelligence test which indicated that Atkins had a full scale IQ of 59.

The jury sentenced Atkins to death, but the Virginia Supreme Court ordered a second sentencing hearing because the trial court had used a misleading verdict form. At the resentencing, Dr. Nelson again testified. The State presented an expert rebuttal witness, Dr. Stanton Samenow, who expressed the opinion that Atkins was not mentally retarded, but rather was of "average intelligence, at least," and diagnosable as having antisocial personality disorder. The jury again sentenced Atkins to death. . . .

II

The Eighth Amendment succinctly prohibits "[e]xcessive" sanctions. It provides: "Excessive bail shall not be required, nor excessive fines imposed, nor cruel and unusual punishments inflicted.". . . A claim that punishment is excessive is judged not by the standards that prevailed in 1685 when Lord Jeffreys presided over the "Bloody Assizes" or when the Bill of Rights was adopted, but rather by those that currently prevail. As Chief Justice Warren explained in his opinion in *Trop v. Dulles,* 356 U.S. 86 (1958): "The basic concept underlying the Eighth Amendment is nothing less than the dignity of man. . . . The Amendment must draw its meaning from the evolving standards of decency that mark the progress of a maturing society."

Proportionality review under those evolving standards should be informed by "objective factors to the maximum possible extent." We have pinpointed that the "clearest and most reliable objective evidence of contemporary values is the legislation enacted by the country's legislatures." Relying in part on such legislative evidence, we have held that death is an impermissibly excessive punishment for the rape of an adult woman, *Coker v. Georgia,* 433 U.S. 584, 593-596 (1977) or for a defendant who neither took life, attempted to take life, nor intended to take life, *Enmund v. Florida,* 458 U.S. 782, 789-793 (1982). . . .

III

The parties have not called our attention to any state legislative consideration of the suitability of imposing the death penalty on mentally retarded offenders prior to 1986. In that year, the public reaction to the execution of a mentally retarded murderer in Georgia apparently led to the enactment of the first state statute prohibiting such executions. In 1988, when Congress enacted legislation reinstating the federal death penalty, it expressly provided that a "sentence of death shall not be carried out upon a person who is mentally retarded." In 1989, Maryland enacted a similar prohibition. It was in that year that we decided *Penry,* and concluded that those two state enactments, "even when added to the 14 States that have rejected capital punishment completely, do not provide sufficient evidence at present of a national consensus."

Much has changed since then. Responding to the national attention received by the Bowden execution and our decision in *Penry,* state legislatures across the country began to address the issue. In 1990, Kentucky and Tennessee enacted statutes similar to those in Georgia and Maryland, as did New Mexico in 1991, and Arkansas, Colorado, Washington, Indiana, and Kansas in 1993 and 1994. In 1995, when New York reinstated its death penalty, it emulated the Federal Government by expressly exempting the mentally retarded. Nebraska followed suit in 1998. There appear to have been no similar enactments during the next two years, but in 2000 and 2001 six more States—South Dakota, Arizona, Connecticut, Florida, Missouri, and North Carolina—joined the procession. The Texas Legislature unanimously adopted a similar bill, and bills have passed at least one house in other States, including Virginia and Nevada.

It is not so much the number of these States that is significant, but the consistency of the direction of change. Given the well-known fact that anticrime legislation is far more popular than legislation providing protections for persons guilty of violent crime, the large number of States prohibiting the execution of mentally retarded persons (and the complete absence of States passing legislation reinstating the power to conduct such executions) provides powerful evidence that today our society views mentally retarded offenders as categorically less culpable than the average criminal. The evidence carries even greater force when it is noted that the legislatures that have addressed the issue have voted overwhelmingly in favor of the prohibition. Moreover, even in those States that allow the execution of mentally retarded offenders, the practice is uncommon. Some States, for example New Hampshire and New Jersey, continue to authorize executions, but none have been carried out in decades. Thus there is little need to pursue legislation barring the execution of the mentally retarded in those States. And it appears that even among those States that regularly execute offenders and that have no prohibition with regard to the mentally retarded, only five have executed offenders possessing a known IQ less than 70 since we decided *Penry*. The practice, therefore, has become truly unusual, and it is fair to say that a national consensus has developed against it. . . .

IV

This consensus unquestionably reflects widespread judgment about the relative culpability of mentally retarded offenders, and the relationship between mental retardation and the penological purposes served by the death penalty. Additionally, it suggests that some characteristics of mental retardation undermine the strength of the procedural protections that our capital jurisprudence steadfastly guards.

As discussed above, clinical definitions of mental retardation require not only subaverage intellectual functioning, but also significant limitations in adaptive skills such as communication, self-care, and self-direction that became manifest before age 18. Mentally retarded persons frequently know the difference between right and wrong and are competent to stand trial. Because of their impairments, however, by definition they have diminished capacities to understand and process information, to communicate, to abstract from mistakes and learn from experience, to engage in logical reasoning, to control impulses, and to understand the reactions of others. There is no evidence that they are more likely to engage in criminal conduct than others, but there is abundant evidence that they often act on impulse rather than pursuant to a premeditated plan, and that in group settings they are followers rather than leaders. Their deficiencies do not warrant an exemption from criminal sanctions, but they do diminish their personal culpability.

In light of these deficiencies, our death penalty jurisprudence provides two reasons consistent with the legislative consensus that the mentally retarded should be categorically excluded from execution. First, there is a serious question as to whether either justification that we have recognized as a basis for the death penalty applies to mentally retarded offenders. *Gregg v. Georgia,* 428 U.S. 153, 183 (1976), identified "retribution and deterrence of capital crimes by prospective offenders" as the social purposes served by the death penalty. Unless the imposition of the death penalty on a mentally retarded person "measurably contributes to one or both of these goals, it 'is nothing more than the purposeless and needless imposition of pain and suffering,' and hence an unconstitutional punishment."

With respect to retribution—the interest in seeing that the offender gets his "just deserts"—the severity of the appropriate punishment necessarily depends on the culpability of the offender. Since *Gregg,* our jurisprudence has consistently confined the imposition of the death penalty to a narrow category of the most serious crimes. For example, in *Godfrey v. Georgia,* 446 U.S. 420 (1980), we set aside a death sentence because the petitioner's crimes did not reflect "a consciousness materially more 'depraved' than that of any person guilty of murder." If the culpability of the average murderer is insufficient to justify the most extreme sanction available to the State, the lesser culpability of the mentally retarded offender surely does not merit that form of retribution. Thus, pursuant to our narrowing jurisprudence, which seeks to ensure that only the most deserving of execution are put to death, an exclusion for the mentally retarded is appropriate.

With respect to deterrence—the interest in preventing capital crimes by prospective offenders—"it seems likely that 'capital punishment can serve as a deterrent only when murder is the result of premeditation and deliberation.'" Exempting the mentally retarded from that punishment will not affect the "cold calculus that precedes the decision" of other potential murderers. Indeed, that sort of calculus is at the opposite end of the spectrum from behavior of mentally retarded offenders. The theory of deterrence in capital sentencing is predicated upon the notion that the increased severity of the punishment will inhibit criminal actors from carrying out murderous conduct. Yet it is the same cognitive and behavioral impairments that make these defendants less morally culpable—for example, the diminished ability to understand and process information, to learn from experience, to engage in logical reasoning, or to control impulses—that also make it less likely that they can process the information of the possibility of execution as a penalty and, as a result, control their conduct based upon that information. Nor will exempting the mentally retarded from execution lessen the deterrent effect of the death penalty with respect to offenders who are not mentally retarded. Such individuals are unprotected by the exemption and will continue to face the threat of execution. Thus, executing the mentally retarded will not measurably further the goal of deterrence.

The reduced capacity of mentally retarded offenders provides a second justification for a categorical rule making such offenders ineligible for the death penalty. The risk "that the death penalty will be imposed in spite of factors which may call for a less severe penalty," is enhanced, not only by the possibility of false confessions, but also by the lesser ability

> of mentally retarded defendants to make a persuasive showing of mitigation in the face of prosecutorial evidence of one or more aggravating factors. Mentally retarded defendants may be less able to give meaningful assistance to their counsel and are typically poor witnesses, and their demeanor may create an unwarranted impression of lack of remorse for their crimes. . . .

NOTES & QUESTIONS ON MENTAL DISABILITY

1. *Applying* Atkins. *Atkins* stands for the proposition that some convicted murderers are so mentally disabled that they are ineligible for the death penalty. But how should a court assess whether a convict's mental disability is sufficiently grave to trigger the *Atkins* prohibition? The Supreme Court concluded that the definition of who counts as mentally disabled should be left to the states. Although there is some variety, states have used clinical standards from professional organizations to define mental or intellectual disability. Typically, the definitions focus on below-average intellectual functioning and limitations in adaptive behavior, with onset before the age of 18. The latter temporal constraint is designed to distinguish between a chronic mental disability and a mental illness, which might have emerged later in life. However, some states have departed from the clinical definitions and will define some defendants as death-eligible even with low IQ scores:

> The consequence is that some courts, failing to engage in the careful and thorough analysis called for by the various definitions of mental retardation, resort to stereotype. Stereotyping has long been a problem with regard to mental retardation. From early legal codes defining the criminal defense of "idiocy" for "a person who cannot account or number twenty pence," to the early twentieth-century view that "every imbecile . . . is a potential criminal," the "mentally retarded" have been regarded as a group both incompetent and dangerous. One would hope that a positive byproduct of the clinical shift from generalized assessment of adaptive behavior to a focus on the inability to perform particular core skills would have been acknowledgement that "[m]entally retarded people are individuals" and that "[a]ny attempt to describe them as a group risks false stereotyping and therefore demands the greatest caution." But despite scientific advances and evolving social perspective, stereotype still pervades adaptive behavior assessment in capital cases.

John H. Blume et al., *Of* Atkins *and Men: Deviations from Clinical Definitions of Mental Retardation in Death Penalty Cases,* 18 Cornell J.L. & Pub. Pol'y 689, 707-08 (2009). Should the Supreme Court step in and enforce a more rigorous and uniform federal standard for defining mental disability?

2. *The role of medical and clinical expertise.* The *Atkins* decision left open some ambiguity about the proper role of medical diagnoses in evaluating an *Atkins* claim. In *Moore v. Texas*, 137 S. Ct. 1039 (2017), the Supreme Court clarified that an *Atkins* claim should be based on the latest medical expertise rather than on "lay perceptions of intellectual disability," which are often based on lay stereotypes about which individuals should count as mentally disabled. A Texas appeals court had evaluated Moore's *Atkins* claim, and rejected it, based on the court's assumption that adaptive deficits must be "related" to intellectual-functioning deficits. The Supreme Court rejected this standard as inconsistent with the latest medical science regarding mental disability and the prevailing clinical consensus. Numerous mental health experts had testified at a state habeas proceeding that Moore was intellectually disabled.

3. *The role of IQ.* It is tempting to use an IQ test as a bright-line rule for determining whether a defendant is exempt from the death penalty under *Atkins*. The IQ test promises to bring quantitative rigor to a determination that can be frustratingly qualitative. The Supreme Court of Florida had announced a rule that a successful *Atkins* petition must demonstrate that the petitioner had an IQ of 70 or below. The bright-line rule was a judicial innovation motivated by a state statute that codified the following qualitative standard: "significantly subaverage general intellectual functioning existing concurrently with deficits in adaptive behavior and manifested during the period from conception to age 18." Fla. Stat. § 921.137(1) (2013). Petitioner Freddie Lee Hall had received an IQ score of 71 on one test, leading to the rejection of his *Atkins* petition. In *Hall v. Florida*, 572 U.S. 701 (2014), the Supreme Court ruled Florida's bright-line cutoff of 70 to be unconstitutional:

> Florida's rule disregards established medical practice in two interrelated ways. It takes an IQ score as final and conclusive evidence of a defendant's intellectual capacity, when experts in the field would consider other evidence. It also relies on a purportedly scientific measurement of the defendant's abilities, his IQ score, while refusing to recognize that the score is, on its own terms, imprecise.

Id. at 712. Although an IQ score may be relevant to the analysis, a bright-line cutoff that precludes a positive *Atkins* finding, regardless of other evidence, is unconstitutional.

4. *Competency for execution.* There are other situations besides a chronic mental disability recognized under *Atkins* that could make an individual incompetent to be executed. In *Panetti v. Quarterman*, 551 U.S. 930 (2007), the Supreme Court considered a condemned prisoner who suffered from delusions that made him believe that the state was using his criminal prosecution for murder as a sham event to prevent him from preaching. Specifically, an expert

testified that the "delusion has recast petitioner's execution as 'part of spiritual warfare . . . between the demons and the forces of the darkness and God and the angels and the forces of light.'" The Fifth Circuit concluded that the delusions were not relevant to his competency to be executed because the prisoner understood the link between his criminal prosecution and his punishment. On appeal, the Supreme Court rejected the Fifth Circuit's test, arguing that the defendant's delusions put him so far removed from reality that capital punishment served no proper purpose. According to the Court:

> [I]t might be said that capital punishment is imposed because it has the potential to make the offender recognize at last the gravity of his crime and to allow the community as a whole, including the surviving family and friends of the victim, to affirm its own judgment that the culpability of the prisoner is so serious that the ultimate penalty must be sought and imposed. The potential for a prisoner's recognition of the severity of the offense and the objective of community vindication are called in question, however, if the prisoner's mental state is so distorted by a mental illness that his awareness of the crime and punishment has little or no relation to the understanding of those concepts shared by the community as a whole.

Id. at 958-59. Applying this standard, should the state be allowed to execute Panetti?

PROBLEM CASE

Consider the case of Ricky Ray Rector. Rector was executed in 1992 for the killing of a police officer that occurred in Arkansas in 1981. Rector famously ordered a last meal that included a slice of pie, but declared that he wanted to save the pie for "later"—suggesting that he may not have totally understood his fate and the concept of a last meal. If this story is true, does it imply that Rector should not have been executed? For Rector, the *Atkins* decision came ten years too late. At the time of Rector's execution, there was no clear constitutional bar to executing a prisoner who suffers from a mental disability. (Rector's execution went poorly because the medical technicians failed to find a proper vein for the lethal injection, and he reportedly moaned extensively before finally succumbing.) Why is mental disability an obstacle to capital punishment? Does it depend on which theory of punishment justifies capital punishment?

2. Juvenile Death Penalty

A few years after the Supreme Court prohibited the imposition of the death penalty against the mentally disabled, the Supreme Court considered the use of capital punishment against juveniles. In a widely read opinion authored by Justice Kennedy, the Court looked at the infrequency of juvenile executions, both at home and abroad, in order to determine whether the practice was "unusual." As you read the following case, pay attention to the empirical evidence that Kennedy marshals to support his assessment of the culpability of juvenile offenders.

Roper v. Simmons

Supreme Court of the United States
543 U.S. 551 (2005)

KENNEDY, J.

This case requires us to address, for the second time in a decade and a half, whether it is permissible under the Eighth and Fourteenth Amendments to the Constitution of the United States to execute a juvenile offender who was older than 15 but younger than 18 when he committed a capital crime. . . .

I

At the age of 17, when he was still a junior in high school, Christopher Simmons, the respondent here, committed murder. About nine months later, after he had turned 18, he was tried and sentenced to death. There is little doubt that Simmons was the instigator of the crime. Before its commission Simmons said he wanted to murder someone. In chilling, callous terms he talked about his plan, discussing it for the most part with two friends, Charles Benjamin and John Tessmer, then aged 15 and 16 respectively. Simmons proposed to commit burglary and murder by breaking and entering, tying up a victim, and throwing the victim off a bridge. Simmons assured his friends they could "get away with it" because they were minors.

The three met at about 2 A.M. on the night of the murder, but Tessmer left before the other two set out. (The State later charged Tessmer with conspiracy, but dropped the charge in exchange for his testimony against Simmons.) Simmons and Benjamin entered the home of the victim, Shirley Crook, after reaching through an open window and unlocking the back door. Simmons turned on a hallway light. Awakened, Mrs. Crook called out, "Who's there?" In response Simmons entered Mrs. Crook's bedroom, where he recognized her from a previous car accident involving them both. Simmons later admitted this confirmed his resolve to murder her.

Using duct tape to cover her eyes and mouth and bind her hands, the two perpetrators put Mrs. Crook in her minivan and drove to a state park. They reinforced the bindings, covered her head with a towel, and walked her to a railroad trestle spanning the Meramec River. There they tied her hands and feet together with electrical wire, wrapped her whole face in duct tape and threw her from the bridge, drowning her in the waters below.

By the afternoon of September 9, Steven Crook had returned home from an overnight trip, found his bedroom in disarray, and reported his wife missing. On the same afternoon fishermen recovered the victim's body from the river. Simmons, meanwhile, was bragging about the killing, telling friends he had killed a woman "because the bitch seen my face.". . .

III

The evidence of national consensus against the death penalty for juveniles is similar, and in some respects parallel, to the evidence *Atkins* held sufficient to demonstrate a national consensus against the death penalty for the mentally retarded. When *Atkins* was decided, 30 States prohibited the death penalty for the mentally retarded. This number comprised 12 that had abandoned the death penalty altogether, and 18 that maintained it but excluded the mentally retarded from its reach. By a similar calculation in this case, 30 States prohibit the juvenile death penalty, comprising 12 that have rejected the death penalty altogether and 18 that maintain it but, by express provision or judicial interpretation, exclude juveniles from its reach. *Atkins* emphasized that even in the 20 States without formal prohibition, the practice of executing the mentally retarded was infrequent. . . .

As in *Atkins,* the objective indicia of consensus in this case—the rejection of the juvenile death penalty in the majority of States; the infrequency of its use even where it remains on the books; and the consistency in the trend toward abolition of the practice—provide sufficient evidence that today our society views juveniles, in the words *Atkins* used respecting the mentally retarded, as "categorically less culpable than the average criminal."

A majority of States have rejected the imposition of the death penalty on juvenile offenders under 18, and we now hold this is required by the Eighth Amendment.

Because the death penalty is the most severe punishment, the Eighth Amendment applies to it with special force. Capital punishment must be limited to those offenders who commit "a narrow category of the most serious crimes" and whose extreme culpability makes them "the most deserving of execution." This principle is implemented throughout the capital sentencing process. States must give narrow and precise definition to the aggravating factors that can result in a capital sentence. In any capital case a defendant has wide latitude to raise as a mitigating factor "any aspect of [his or her] character or record and any of the circumstances of the offense that the defendant proffers as a basis for a sentence less than death." There are a number of crimes that beyond question are severe in absolute terms, yet the death penalty may not be imposed for their commission. The death penalty may not be imposed on certain classes of offenders, such as juveniles under 16, the insane, and the mentally retarded, no matter how heinous the crime. These rules vindicate the underlying principle that the death penalty is reserved for a narrow category of crimes and offenders.

Three general differences between juveniles under 18 and adults demonstrate that juvenile offenders cannot with reliability be classified among the worst offenders. First, as any parent knows and as the scientific and sociological studies respondent and his *amici* cite tend to confirm, "[a] lack of maturity and an underdeveloped sense of responsibility are found in youth more often than in adults and are more understandable among the young. These qualities often result in impetuous and ill-considered actions and decisions." It has been noted that "adolescents are overrepresented statistically in virtually every category of reckless behavior." In recognition of the comparative immaturity and irresponsibility of juveniles, almost every State prohibits those under 18 years of age from voting, serving on juries, or marrying without parental consent.

The second area of difference is that juveniles are more vulnerable or susceptible to negative influences and outside pressures, including peer pressure. This is explained in part by the prevailing circumstance that juveniles have less control, or less experience with control, over their own environment.

The third broad difference is that the character of a juvenile is not as well formed as that of an adult. The personality traits of juveniles are more transitory, less fixed.

These differences render suspect any conclusion that a juvenile falls among the worst offenders. The susceptibility of juveniles to immature and irresponsible behavior means "their irresponsible conduct is not as morally reprehensible as that of an adult." Their own vulnerability and comparative lack of control over their immediate surroundings mean juveniles have a greater claim than adults to be forgiven for failing to escape negative influences in their whole environment. The reality that juveniles still struggle to define their identity means it is less supportable to conclude that even a heinous crime committed by a juvenile is evidence of irretrievably depraved character. From a moral standpoint it would be misguided to equate the failings of a minor with those of an adult, for a greater possibility exists that a minor's character deficiencies will be reformed. Indeed, "[t]he relevance of youth as a mitigating factor derives from the fact that the signature qualities of youth are transient; as individuals mature, the impetuousness and recklessness that may dominate in younger years can subside.". . .

Once the diminished culpability of juveniles is recognized, it is evident that the penological justifications for the death penalty apply to them with lesser force than to adults. We have held there are two distinct social purposes served by the death penalty: "'retribution and deterrence of capital crimes by prospective offenders.'" As for retribution, we remarked in *Atkins* that "[i]f the culpability of the average murderer is insufficient to justify the most extreme sanction available to the State, the lesser culpability of the mentally retarded offender surely does not merit that form of retribution." The same conclusions follow from the lesser culpability of the juvenile offender. Whether viewed as an attempt to express the community's moral outrage or as an attempt to right the balance for the wrong to the victim, the case for retribution is not as strong with a minor as with an adult. Retribution is not proportional if the law's most severe penalty is imposed on one whose culpability or blameworthiness is diminished, to a substantial degree, by reason of youth and immaturity.

As for deterrence, it is unclear whether the death penalty has a significant or even measurable deterrent effect on juveniles, as counsel for petitioner acknowledged at oral argument. In general we leave to legislatures the assessment of the efficacy of various criminal penalty schemes. Here, however, the absence of evidence of deterrent effect is of special concern because the same characteristics that render juveniles less culpable than adults suggest as well that juveniles will be less susceptible to deterrence. . . .

IV

Our determination that the death penalty is disproportionate punishment for offenders under 18 finds confirmation in the stark reality that the United States is the only country in the world that continues to give official sanction to the juvenile death penalty. This reality does not become controlling, for the task of interpreting the Eighth Amendment remains our responsibility. Yet at least from the time of the Court's decision in *Trop,* the Court has referred to the laws of other countries and to international authorities as instructive for its interpretation of the Eighth Amendment's prohibition of "cruel and unusual punishments."

As respondent and a number of *amici* emphasize, Article 37 of the United Nations Convention on the Rights of the Child, which every country in the world has ratified save for the United States and Somalia, contains an express prohibition on capital punishment for crimes committed by juveniles under 18. No ratifying country has entered a reservation to the provision prohibiting the execution of juvenile offenders. Parallel prohibitions are contained in other significant international covenants.

Respondent and his *amici* have submitted, and petitioner does not contest, that only seven countries other than the United States have executed juvenile offenders since 1990: Iran, Pakistan, Saudi Arabia, Yemen, Nigeria, the Democratic Republic of Congo, and China. Since then each of these countries has either abolished capital punishment for juveniles or made public disavowal of the practice. In sum, it is fair to say that the United States now stands alone in a world that has turned its face against the juvenile death penalty. . . .

It is proper that we acknowledge the overwhelming weight of international opinion against the juvenile death penalty, resting in large part on the

> understanding that the instability and emotional imbalance of young people may often be a factor in the crime. The opinion of the world community, while not controlling our outcome, does provide respected and significant confirmation for our own conclusions.
>
> Over time, from one generation to the next, the Constitution has come to earn the high respect and even, as Madison dared to hope, the veneration of the American people. The document sets forth, and rests upon, innovative principles original to the American experience, such as federalism; a proven balance in political mechanisms through separation of powers; specific guarantees for the accused in criminal cases; and broad provisions to secure individual freedom and preserve human dignity. These doctrines and guarantees are central to the American experience and remain essential to our present-day self-definition and national identity. Not the least of the reasons we honor the Constitution, then, is because we know it to be our own. It does not lessen our fidelity to the Constitution or our pride in its origins to acknowledge that the express affirmation of certain fundamental rights by other nations and peoples simply underscores the centrality of those same rights within our own heritage of freedom. . . .

NOTES & QUESTIONS ON JUVENILE DEATH PENALTY

1. *The international standard.* Should our interpretation of the Eighth Amendment and its prohibition on cruel and unusual punishment hinge on whether the international community considers this use of the death penalty acceptable? More than anything else in Kennedy's opinion, the reference to international jurisdictions drew the ire of Justice Scalia, who remarked in dissent:

> [T]he Court undertakes the majestic task of determining (and thereby prescribing) our Nation's current standards of decency. It is beyond comprehension why we should look, for that purpose, to a country that has developed, in the centuries since the Revolutionary War . . . a legal, political, and social culture quite different from our own. If we took the Court's directive seriously, we would also consider relaxing our double jeopardy prohibition. . . . We would also curtail our right to jury trial in criminal cases since, despite the jury system's deep roots in our shared common law, England now permits all but the most serious offenders to be tried by magistrates without a jury. The Court should either profess its willingness to reconsider all these matters in light of the views of foreigners, or else it should cease putting forth foreigners' views as part of the reasoned basis of its decisions. To

invoke alien law when it agrees with one's own thinking, and ignore it otherwise, is not reasoned decisionmaking, but sophistry.

Roper v. Simmons, 543 U.S. 551, 626-27 (2005). Do you agree with Scalia that there is something problematic about consulting the views of foreign jurisdictions? Or do you agree with Kennedy that international standards of decency confirm the Court's assessment that the juvenile death penalty is both cruel and unusual?

2. *The culpability of juveniles.* Do you agree with Kennedy that juveniles are not sufficiently mentally developed to be held fully responsible for their behavior? More importantly, why does this argument not compromise the state's authority to punish—even with incarceration—juveniles for lesser offenses? If it is really true that the minds and brains of juveniles are still being formed, what business does the state have punishing juveniles at all? The Court's jurisprudence regarding the limits of juvenile culpability is brought to its logical conclusion in *Graham v. Florida,* 560 U.S. 48 (2010), and *Miller v. Alabama,* 567 U.S. 460 (2012), which extend *Roper*'s analysis to the non-capital context.

3. Capital Punishment for Non-Killing Crimes

The Supreme Court has also limited the class of offenses that might be subject to capital punishment. In *Coker v. Georgia,* 433 U.S. 584 (1977), the Supreme Court concluded that a defendant could not be executed for conviction of rape and kidnapping. This led to some uncertainty as to whether the prohibition applied to all non-lethal offenses or whether some non-lethal offenses were nonetheless still subject to the death penalty. In another Kennedy opinion, reprinted here, the Supreme Court considered whether the rule from *Coker v. Georgia* should also apply to the rape of a child or whether that offense, with the added element of a young victim, was sufficiently brutal so as to make the death penalty constitutionally permissible.

Kennedy v. Louisiana

Supreme Court of the United States
554 U.S. 407 (2008)

KENNEDY, J.

II

The Eighth Amendment, applicable to the States through the Fourteenth Amendment, provides that "[e]xcessive bail shall not be required, nor excessive fines imposed, nor cruel and unusual punishments inflicted."

The Amendment proscribes "all excessive punishments, as well as cruel and unusual punishments that may or may not be excessive." The Court explained in *Atkins* and *Roper* that the Eighth Amendment's protection against excessive or cruel and unusual punishments flows from the basic "precept of justice that punishment for [a] crime should be graduated and proportioned to [the] offense." Whether this requirement has been fulfilled is determined not by the standards that prevailed when the Eighth Amendment was adopted in 1791 but by the norms that "currently prevail." The Amendment "draw[s] its meaning from the evolving standards of decency that mark the progress of a maturing society." This is because "[t]he standard of extreme cruelty is not merely descriptive, but necessarily embodies a moral judgment. The standard itself remains the same, but its applicability must change as the basic mores of society change."

Evolving standards of decency must embrace and express respect for the dignity of the person, and the punishment of criminals must conform to that rule. As we shall discuss, punishment is justified under one or more of three principal rationales: rehabilitation, deterrence, and retribution. It is the last of these, retribution, that most often can contradict the law's own ends. This is of particular concern when the Court interprets the meaning of the Eighth Amendment in capital cases. When the law punishes by death, it risks its own sudden descent into brutality, transgressing the constitutional commitment to decency and restraint.

For these reasons we have explained that capital punishment must "be limited to those offenders who commit 'a narrow category of the most serious crimes' and whose extreme culpability makes them 'the most deserving of execution.'" Though the death penalty is not invariably unconstitutional, the Court insists upon confining the instances in which the punishment can be imposed. . . .

Based both on consensus and our own independent judgment, our holding is that a death sentence for one who raped but did not kill a child, and who did not intend to assist another in killing the child, is unconstitutional under the Eighth and Fourteenth Amendments.

III

The existence of objective indicia of consensus against making a crime punishable by death was a relevant concern in *Roper, Atkins, Coker,* and *Enmund,* and we follow the approach of those cases here. The history of the death penalty for the crime of rape is an instructive beginning point.

In 1925, 18 States, the District of Columbia, and the Federal Government had statutes that authorized the death penalty for the rape of a child or an adult. Between 1930 and 1964, 455 people were executed for those crimes. To our knowledge the last individual executed for the rape of a child was Ronald Wolfe in 1964.

In 1972, *Furman* invalidated most of the state statutes authorizing the death penalty for the crime of rape; and in *Furman*'s aftermath only six States reenacted their capital rape provisions. Three States—Georgia, North Carolina, and Louisiana—did so with respect to all rape offenses. Three States—Florida, Mississippi, and Tennessee—did so with respect only to child rape. All six statutes were later invalidated under state or federal law.

Louisiana reintroduced the death penalty for rape of a child in 1995. Under the current statute, any anal, vaginal, or oral intercourse with a child under the age of 13 constitutes aggravated rape and is punishable by death. Mistake of age is not a defense, so the statute imposes strict liability in this regard. Five States have since followed Louisiana's lead: Georgia, Montana, Oklahoma, South Carolina, and Texas. Four of these States' statutes are more narrow than Louisiana's in that only offenders with a previous rape conviction are death eligible. Georgia's statute makes child rape a capital offense only when aggravating circumstances are present, including but not limited to a prior conviction.

By contrast, 44 States have not made child rape a capital offense. As for federal law, Congress in the Federal Death Penalty Act of 1994 expanded the number of federal crimes for which the death penalty is a permissible sentence, including certain nonhomicide offenses; but it did not do the same for child rape or abuse. Under 18 U.S.C. § 2245, an offender is death eligible only when the sexual abuse or exploitation results in the victim's death. . . .

The evidence of a national consensus with respect to the death penalty for child rapists, as with respect to juveniles, mentally retarded offenders, and vicarious felony murderers, shows divided opinion but, on balance, an opinion against it. Thirty-seven jurisdictions—36 States plus the Federal Government—have the death penalty. As mentioned above, only six of those jurisdictions authorize the death penalty for rape of a child. Though our review of national consensus is not confined to tallying the number of States with applicable death penalty legislation, it is of significance that, in 45 jurisdictions, petitioner could not be executed for child rape of any kind. . . .

IV

As we have said in other Eighth Amendment cases, objective evidence of contemporary values as it relates to punishment for child rape is entitled to great weight, but it does not end our inquiry. . . .

It must be acknowledged that there are moral grounds to question a rule barring capital punishment for a crime against an individual that did not result in death. These facts illustrate the point. Here the victim's fright, the sense of betrayal, and the nature of her injuries caused more prolonged physical and mental suffering than, say, a sudden killing by an unseen assassin. The attack was not just on her but on her childhood. For this reason, we should be most reluctant to rely upon the language of the plurality in *Coker,* which posited that, for the victim of rape, "life may not be nearly so happy as it was," but it is not beyond repair. Rape has a permanent psychological, emotional, and sometimes physical impact on the child. We cannot dismiss the years of long anguish that must be endured by the victim of child rape.

It does not follow, though, that capital punishment is a proportionate penalty for the crime. The constitutional prohibition against excessive or cruel and unusual punishments mandates that the State's power to punish "be exercised within the limits of civilized standards." Evolving standards of decency that mark the progress of a maturing society counsel us to be most hesitant before interpreting the Eighth Amendment to allow the extension of the death penalty, a hesitation that has special force where no life was taken in the commission of the crime. It is an established principle that decency, in its essence, presumes respect for the individual and thus moderation or restraint in the application of capital punishment.

To date the Court has sought to define and implement this principle, for the most part, in cases involving capital murder. One approach has been to insist upon general rules that ensure consistency in determining who receives a death sentence. At the same time the Court has insisted, to ensure restraint and moderation in use of capital punishment, on judging the "character and record of the individual offender and the circumstances of the particular offense as a constitutionally indispensable part of the process of inflicting the penalty of death." . . .

Our concern here is limited to crimes against individual persons. We do not address, for example, crimes defining and punishing treason, espionage, terrorism, and drug kingpin activity, which are offenses against the State. As it relates to crimes against individuals, though, the death penalty should not be expanded to instances where the victim's life was not taken. . . .

Consistent with evolving standards of decency and the teachings of our precedents we conclude that, in determining whether the death penalty is excessive, there is a distinction between intentional first-degree murder on the one hand and nonhomicide crimes against individual persons, even including child rape, on the other. The latter crimes may be devastating in their harm, as here, but "in terms of moral depravity and of the injury to the person and to the public," they cannot be compared to murder in their "severity and irrevocability." . . .

The goal of retribution, which reflects society's and the victim's interests in seeing that the offender is repaid for the hurt he caused, does not justify the harshness of the death penalty here. In measuring retribution, as well as other objectives of criminal law, it is appropriate to distinguish between a particularly depraved murder that merits death as a form of retribution and the crime of child rape.

There is an additional reason for our conclusion that imposing the death penalty for child rape would not further retributive purposes. In considering whether retribution is served, among other factors we have looked to whether capital punishment "has the potential . . . to allow the community as a whole, including the surviving family and friends of the victim, to affirm its own judgment that the culpability of the prisoner is so serious that the ultimate penalty must be sought and imposed." In considering the death penalty for nonhomicide offenses this inquiry necessarily also must include the question whether the death penalty balances the wrong to the victim.

It is not at all evident that the child rape victim's hurt is lessened when the law permits the death of the perpetrator. . . . Society's desire to inflict the death penalty for child rape by enlisting the child victim to assist it over the course of years in asking for capital punishment forces a moral choice on the child, who is not of mature age to make that choice. The way the death penalty here involves the child victim in its enforcement can compromise a decent legal system; and this is but a subset of fundamental difficulties capital punishment can cause in the administration and enforcement of laws proscribing child rape. . . .

In addition, by in effect making the punishment for child rape and murder equivalent, a State that punishes child rape by death may remove a strong incentive for the rapist not to kill the victim. Assuming the offender behaves in a rational way, as one must to justify the penalty on grounds of deterrence, the penalty in some respects gives less protection, not more, to the victim, who is often the sole witness to the crime. It might be argued that, even if the death penalty results in a marginal increase in the incentive to kill, this is counterbalanced by a marginally increased deterrent to commit the crime at all. Whatever balance the legislature strikes, however, uncertainty on the point makes the argument for the penalty less compelling than for homicide crimes. . . .

NOTES & QUESTIONS ON CAPITAL PUNISHMENT FOR RAPE

1. *Public offenses.* Kennedy's opinion included an exception for non-lethal offenses against the state, such as treason or espionage, which can still trigger the death penalty, regardless of whether a victim was killed or not. Can you think of a reason why these offenses should be treated differently under the Eighth Amendment?

2. *The remedy.* Does Kennedy's opinion support the conclusion that every offender convicted of a non-lethal offense is—by definition—less culpable than offenders convicted of murder? The Supreme Court might have simply created an obligation that trial juries make a finding that a perpetrator of a non-lethal offense is especially deserving of the death penalty for some particular reason. Instead, the Court simply prohibited the death penalty for the entire class of offenses. What justifies the imposition of this categorical, bright-line rule? The Court applied the same categorical remedy in *Atkins* and *Roper*, concluding that the risk of a constitutional violation was too severe to permit a case-by-case remedy.

3. *Countermajoritarianism after* Kennedy. Several states had legislatively imposed the death penalty for child rape. In *Kennedy*, the Supreme Court articulated a countermajoritarian constraint on that practice. Regardless of what the legislators decided as representatives of the majority of the polity, the Eighth Amendment prohibited the implementation of this legislative action. In that sense, the Court's Eighth Amendment jurisprudence, like much of its application of the Bill of Rights, is countermajoritarian because it vindicates constitutional limits on majoritarian legislative action. At the same time, however, the Court's methodology for determining the content of the Eighth Amendment requires consulting the penological practices of the majority of state jurisdictions in order to determine what counts as an "unusual" form of punishment. That methodology—formally speaking, consideration of "evolving standards of decency"—requires its own form of majoritarianism, but this time viewed across state jurisdictions instead of within them. In other words, while a majority of state voters in one jurisdiction might have approved the practice, the majority of jurisdictions across the United States have disapproved of the practice, and by implication, consider it inconsistent with evolving standards of decency. One might describe this methodology as majoritarian countermajoritarianism.

4. *The death penalty and felony murder.* Rape is not the only context in which the Supreme Court has prohibited capital punishment for some types of offenders and some types of offenses. For example, in *Enmund v. Florida*, 458 U.S. 782 (1982), the Supreme Court ruled that the death penalty was unconstitutionally disproportionate when applied to a defendant convicted of felony murder where the defendant participated in a robbery but did not share the intent to kill (because the killing was physically perpetrated by the defendant's co-felons). The Court concluded:

> [O]nly a small minority of jurisdictions—eight—allow the death penalty to be imposed solely because the defendant somehow participated in a robbery in the course of which a murder was committed. Even if the nine States are included where such a defendant could be executed for an unintended felony murder if sufficient aggravating circumstances are present to outweigh

> mitigating circumstances—which often include the defendant's minimal participation in the murder—only about a third of American jurisdictions would ever permit a defendant who somehow participated in a robbery where a murder occurred to be sentenced to die. Moreover, of the eight States which have enacted new death penalty statutes since 1978, none authorize capital punishment in such circumstances. While the current legislative judgment with respect to imposition of the death penalty where a defendant did not take life, attempt to take it, or intend to take life is neither "wholly unanimous among state legislatures," nor as compelling as the legislative judgments considered in *Coker*, it nevertheless weighs on the side of rejecting capital punishment for the crime at issue.

Id. at 792-93. In this vein, consider also the Problem Case below regarding the Tison brothers and their participation in a prison escape.

PROBLEM CASE

The Tison brothers planned, with the aid of other family members, an elaborate prison break for their father, who was incarcerated in an Arizona prison. At the time of the prison break, the father was serving a life sentence for having killed a prison guard during a prior escape attempt. The new escape plan involved the Tison brothers entering the prison with a large ice chest filled with firearms, which were then given to their father and his cellmate, another convicted murderer. Using the weapons, the brothers, their father, and the cellmate all escaped the prison grounds. After several days on the run, the car that they were traveling in suffered a flat tire. The group flagged down a passing car, whose occupants just happened to have the bad luck to be nearby. The occupants of the car included a husband and wife, their two-year-old son, and 15-year-old niece. One Tison brother showed the husband the flat tire, while the other Tison brother, Tison's father, and his cellmate were ready to ambush them. The Tison brothers walked back to the car and witnessed their father and his cellmate open fire on the family in a bloodbath—a decision that allegedly surprised them. The 15-year-old niece initially survived the shooting, ultimately crawling away and dying in the desert. The Tison brothers were convicted of murder and sentenced to death. Assuming that the Tison brothers were willing architects of the escape plan but did not intend for the family to get killed, is it proportional under the Eighth Amendment to execute the brothers? See *Tison v. Arizona*, 481 U.S. 137 (1987).

4. Racial Disparities

In the last 30 years, academic researchers have documented racial disparities in the imposition of the death penalty. For example, some researchers have focused not just on the race of the defendant but also on the race of the victim in a bid to demonstrate that the death penalty is racially discriminatory. In the following case, the Supreme Court must determine whether the death penalty is per se a violation of equal protection, given the disproportionate number of African-Americans who are sentenced to death. As you read the following case, look for the Court's discussion of the empirical evidence and the Court's assessment of it.

McCleskey v. Kemp

Supreme Court of the United States
481 U.S. 279 (1987)

POWELL, J.

This case presents the question whether a complex statistical study that indicates a risk that racial considerations enter into capital sentencing determinations proves that petitioner McCleskey's capital sentence is unconstitutional under the Eighth or Fourteenth Amendment.

I

. . . In support of his claim, McCleskey proffered a statistical study performed by Professors David C. Baldus, Charles Pulaski, and George Woodworth, and (the Baldus study) that purports to show a disparity in the imposition of the death sentence in Georgia based on the race of the murder victim and, to a lesser extent, the race of the defendant. The Baldus study is actually two sophisticated statistical studies that examine over 2,000 murder cases that occurred in Georgia during the 1970's. The raw numbers collected by Professor Baldus indicate that defendants charged with killing white persons received the death penalty in 11% of the cases, but defendants charged with killing blacks received the death penalty in only 1% of the cases. The raw numbers also indicate a reverse racial disparity according to the race of the defendant: 4% of the black defendants received the death penalty, as opposed to 7% of the white defendants.

Baldus also divided the cases according to the combination of the race of the defendant and the race of the victim. He found that the death penalty was assessed in 22% of the cases involving black defendants and white victims; 8% of the cases involving white defendants and white victims; 1% of the cases involving black defendants and black victims; and 3% of the cases involving white defendants and black victims. Similarly, Baldus found that prosecutors sought the death penalty in 70% of the cases involving black defendants and white victims; 32% of the cases involving white defendants and white victims; 15% of the cases involving black defendants and black victims; and 19% of the cases involving white defendants and black victims.

Baldus subjected his data to an extensive analysis, taking account of 230 variables that could have explained the disparities on nonracial grounds. One of his models concludes that, even after taking account of 39 nonracial variables, defendants charged with killing white victims were 4.3 times as likely to receive a death sentence as defendants charged with killing blacks. According to this model, black defendants were 1.1 times as likely to receive a death sentence as other defendants. Thus, the Baldus study indicates that black defendants, such as McCleskey, who kill white victims have the greatest likelihood of receiving the death penalty. . . .

II

McCleskey's first claim is that the Georgia capital punishment statute violates the Equal Protection Clause of the Fourteenth Amendment. He argues that race has infected the administration of Georgia's statute in two ways: persons who murder whites are more likely to be sentenced to death than persons who murder blacks, and black murderers are more likely to be sentenced to death than white murderers. As a black defendant who killed a white victim, McCleskey claims that the Baldus study demonstrates that he was discriminated against because of his race and because of the race of his victim. In its broadest form, McCleskey's claim of discrimination extends to every actor in the Georgia capital sentencing process, from the prosecutor who sought the death penalty and the jury that imposed the sentence, to the State itself that enacted the capital punishment statute and allows it to remain in effect despite its allegedly discriminatory application. We agree with the Court of Appeals, and every other court that has considered such a challenge, that this claim must fail.

Our analysis begins with the basic principle that a defendant who alleges an equal protection violation has the burden of proving "the existence of purposeful discrimination." A corollary to this principle is that a criminal defendant must prove that the purposeful discrimination "had a discriminatory effect" on him. Thus, to prevail under the Equal Protection Clause, McCleskey must prove that the decisionmakers in his case acted with discriminatory purpose. He offers no evidence specific to his own case that would support an inference that racial considerations played a part in his sentence. . . .

McCleskey also suggests that the Baldus study proves that the State as a whole has acted with a discriminatory purpose. He appears to argue that the State has violated the Equal Protection Clause by adopting the capital punishment statute and allowing it to remain in force despite its allegedly discriminatory application. . . . For this claim to prevail, McCleskey would have to prove that the Georgia Legislature enacted or maintained the death penalty statute because of an anticipated racially discriminatory effect. In *Gregg v. Georgia*, this Court found that the Georgia capital sentencing system could operate in a fair and neutral manner. There was no evidence then, and there is none now, that the Georgia Legislature enacted the capital punishment statute to further a racially discriminatory purpose.

Nor has McCleskey demonstrated that the legislature maintains the capital punishment statute because of the racially disproportionate impact suggested by the Baldus study. As legislatures necessarily have wide discretion in the choice of criminal laws and penalties, and as there were legitimate reasons for the Georgia Legislature to adopt and maintain capital punishment, we will not infer a discriminatory purpose on the part of the State of Georgia. Accordingly, we reject McCleskey's equal protection claims.

IV

. . . Although our decision in *Gregg* as to the facial validity of the Georgia capital punishment statute appears to foreclose McCleskey's disproportionality argument, he further contends that the Georgia capital punishment system is arbitrary and capricious in application, and therefore his sentence is excessive, because racial considerations may influence capital sentencing decisions in Georgia. We now address this claim.

To evaluate McCleskey's challenge, we must examine exactly what the Baldus study may show. Even Professor Baldus does not contend that his statistics prove that race enters into any capital sentencing decisions or that race was a factor in McCleskey's particular case. Statistics at most may show only a likelihood that a particular factor entered into some decisions. There is, of course, some risk of racial prejudice influencing a jury's decision in a criminal case. There are similar risks that other kinds of prejudice will influence other criminal trials. The question "is at what point that risk becomes constitutionally unacceptable." McCleskey asks us to accept the likelihood allegedly shown by the Baldus study as the constitutional measure of an unacceptable risk of racial prejudice influencing capital sentencing decisions. This we decline to do. . . .

At most, the Baldus study indicates a discrepancy that appears to correlate with race. Apparent disparities in sentencing are an inevitable part of our criminal justice system. The discrepancy indicated by the Baldus study is "a far cry from the major systemic defects identified in *Furman*." As this Court has recognized, any mode for determining guilt or punishment "has its weaknesses and the potential for misuse." Specifically, "there can be no perfect procedure for deciding in which cases governmental authority should be used to impose death." Despite these imperfections, our consistent rule has been that constitutional guarantees are met when "the mode [for determining guilt or punishment] itself has been surrounded with safeguards to make it as fair as possible." Where the discretion that is fundamental to our criminal process is involved, we decline to assume that what is unexplained is invidious. In light of the safeguards designed to minimize racial bias in the process, the fundamental value of jury trial in our criminal justice system, and the benefits that discretion provides to criminal defendants, we hold that the Baldus study does not demonstrate a constitutionally significant risk of racial bias affecting the Georgia capital sentencing process. . . .

V

Two additional concerns inform our decision in this case. First, McCleskey's claim, taken to its logical conclusion, throws into serious question the principles that underlie our entire criminal justice system. The Eighth Amendment is not limited in application to capital punishment, but applies to all penalties. Thus, if we accepted McCleskey's claim that racial bias has impermissibly tainted the capital sentencing decision, we could soon be faced with similar claims as to other types of penalty. Moreover, the claim that his sentence rests on the irrelevant factor of race easily could be extended to apply to claims based on unexplained discrepancies that correlate to membership in other minority groups, and even to gender. Similarly, since McCleskey's claim relates to the race of his victim, other claims could apply with equally logical force to statistical disparities that correlate with the race or sex of other actors in the criminal justice system, such as defense attorneys, or judges. Also, there is no logical reason that such a claim need be limited to racial or sexual bias. If arbitrary and capricious punishment is the touchstone under the Eighth Amendment, such a claim could—at least in theory—be based upon any arbitrary variable, such as the defendant's facial characteristics, or the physical attractiveness of the defendant or the victim, that some statistical study indicates may be influential in jury decisionmaking. As these examples illustrate, there is no limiting principle to the type of challenge brought by McCleskey. . . .

Second, McCleskey's arguments are best presented to the legislative bodies. It is not the responsibility—or indeed even the right—of this Court to determine the appropriate punishment for particular crimes. . . . Capital punishment is now the law in more than two-thirds of our States. It is the ultimate duty of courts to determine on a case-by-case basis whether these laws are applied consistently with the Constitution. Despite McCleskey's wide-ranging arguments that basically challenge the validity of capital punishment in our multiracial society, the only question before us is whether in his case, the law of Georgia was properly applied. We agree with the District Court and the Court of Appeals for the Eleventh Circuit that this was carefully and correctly done in this case.

NOTES & QUESTIONS ON RACIAL DISPARITIES

1. *The empirical evidence.* The Supreme Court concluded that the empirical evidence suggested only a *correlation* with race, rather than a causal conclusion. The causal conclusion would be that a defendant's race *causes* him or her to have a greater likelihood of being executed. The state of the empirical science is constantly changing, with new studies and new statistical analyses performed every year. If, in the future, the empirical science was to establish a causal connection to the Supreme Court's satisfaction, would this fact change the outcome? Would the Supreme Court then declare capital punishment a violation of the Equal Protection Clause?

2. *McCleskey's case.* The Supreme Court concluded that McCleskey himself did not receive a disproportionate punishment when he was sentenced to death. Does this methodology match, or conflict with, the methodology in the other death penalty cases above? In the other cases, the Supreme Court asked whether there was a significant risk that offenders in that class might receive a disproportionate punishment. Which is the correct methodology? Should the Court ask whether the individual defendant received a disproportionate punishment or whether that class of defendants is subject to the risk of disproportionate punishments?

3. *Discrimination.* The Supreme Court refused to recognize systemic racism in *McCleskey*. In contrast, the Supreme Court recognized the insidious impact of racism on the judicial system in *Batson v. Kentucky*, 476 U.S. 79 (1986), ultimately creating an entire procedural mechanism to prohibit racial discrimination in jury selection. What accounts for the different outcomes in *McCleskey* and *Batson*? What remedies were the petitioners asking for? Recall the role that evidence of systemic racism played in the *Batson* case.

5. Methods of Execution

The proper procedure for carrying out an execution has ignited no shortage of federal and state litigation. Although the death penalty was once carried out by electric chair or hanging, methods that are still on the books in some states, almost all modern executions are now carried out by lethal injection, which is widely viewed as more "humane" than its precursor methods. In recent years, death penalty opponents have attacked lethal injection as similarly inhumane because of the risk of botched executions. Indeed, there are many risks during the procedure. If the medical staff do not insert the IV correctly, the lethal injection procedure will definitely not work correctly because the full dose of the compounds will not enter the prisoner's vein. Also, the standard procedure, used for many years, was to deliver a three-drug sequence to first fully anesthetize/sedate the patient, paralyze him, and then kill him. When this sequence worked properly, the prisoner would not, in theory, feel any pain because the patient would not be conscious when he is killed. However, if the sedation fails to work properly, the lethal dose might cause pain to the offender.

In the following case, the Supreme Court considers whether Oklahoma's three-drug cocktail constitutes cruel and unusual punishment precisely because of an unacceptable risk that conscious offenders will suffer pain during the event. As you read the case, ask yourself what work the concept of "unacceptable risk" does in the analysis and also whether it is constitutionally required that executions be pain-free.

Glossip v. Gross

Supreme Court of the United States
135 S. Ct. 2726 (2015)

ALITO, J.

Prisoners sentenced to death in the State of Oklahoma filed an action in federal court . . . contending that the method of execution now used by the State violates the Eighth Amendment because it creates an unacceptable risk of severe pain. They argue that midazolam, the first drug employed in the State's current three-drug protocol, fails to render a person insensate to pain. After holding an evidentiary hearing, the District Court denied four prisoners' application for a preliminary injunction, finding that they had failed to prove that midazolam is ineffective. The Court of Appeals for the Tenth Circuit affirmed. . . .

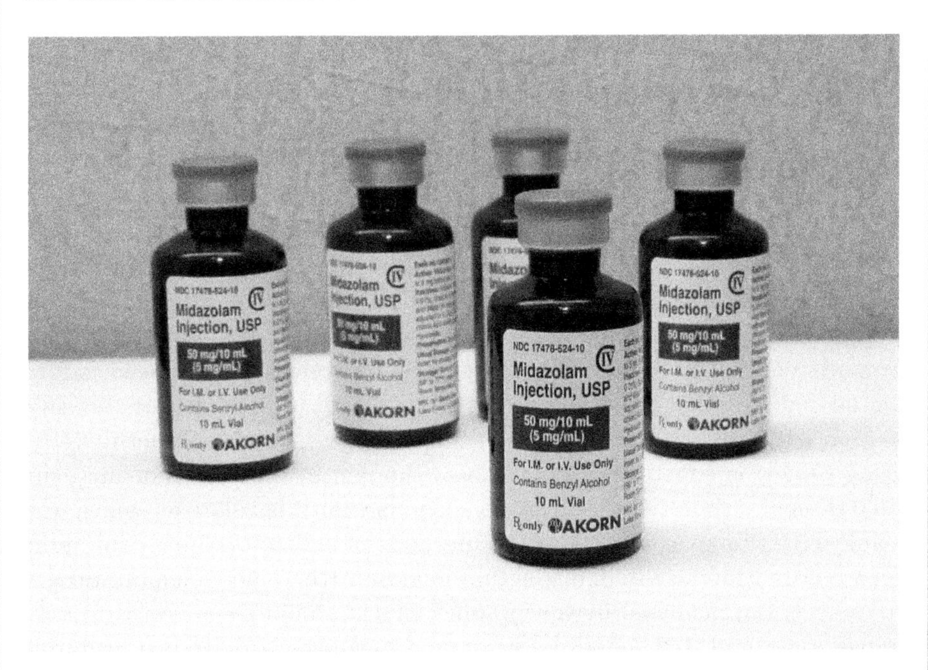

Bottles of the sedative midazolam at a hospital pharmacy in Oklahoma City. (Sue Ogrocki/AP Images)

For two independent reasons, we also affirm. First, the prisoners failed to identify a known and available alternative method of execution that entails a lesser risk of pain, a requirement of all Eighth Amendment method-of-execution claims. Second, the District Court did not commit clear error when it found that the prisoners failed to establish that Oklahoma's use of a massive dose of midazolam in its execution protocol entails a substantial risk of severe pain. . . .

IV

Our first ground for affirmance is based on petitioners' failure to satisfy their burden of establishing that any risk of harm was substantial when compared to a known and available alternative method of execution. In their amended complaint, petitioners proffered that the State could use sodium thiopental as part of a single-drug protocol. They have since suggested that it might also be constitutional for Oklahoma to use pentobarbital. But the District Court found that both sodium thiopental and pentobarbital are now unavailable to Oklahoma's Department of Corrections. The Court of Appeals affirmed that finding, and it is not clearly erroneous. On the contrary, the record shows that Oklahoma has been unable to procure those drugs despite a good-faith effort to do so.

Petitioners do not seriously contest this factual finding, and they have not identified any available drug or drugs that could be used in place of those that Oklahoma is now unable to obtain. Nor have they shown a risk of pain so great that other acceptable, available methods must be used. Instead, they argue that they need not identify a known and available method of execution that presents less risk. But this argument is inconsistent with the controlling opinion in *Baze*, 553 U.S., at 61, which imposed a requirement that the Court now follows. . . .

Readers can judge for themselves how much distance there is between the principal dissent's argument against requiring prisoners to identify an alternative and the view, now announced by Justices Breyer and Ginsburg, that the death penalty is categorically unconstitutional. The principal dissent goes out of its way to suggest that a State would violate the Eighth Amendment if it used one of the methods of execution employed before the advent of lethal injection. And the principal dissent makes this suggestion even though the Court held in *Wilkerson* that this method (the firing squad) is constitutional and even though, in the words of the principal dissent, "there is some reason to think that it is relatively quick and painless." Tellingly silent about the methods of execution most commonly used before States switched to lethal injection (the electric chair and gas chamber), the principal dissent implies that it would be unconstitutional to use a method that "could be seen as a devolution to a more primitive era." If States cannot return to any of the "more primitive" methods used in the past and if no drug that meets with the principal dissent's approval is available for use in carrying out a death sentence, the logical conclusion is clear. But we have time and again reaffirmed that capital punishment is not per se unconstitutional. We decline to effectively overrule these decisions.

V

We also affirm for a second reason: The District Court did not commit clear error when it found that midazolam is highly likely to render a person unable to feel pain during an execution. We emphasize four points at the outset of our analysis.

First, we review the District Court's factual findings under the deferential "clear error" standard. . . . Second, petitioners bear the burden of persuasion on this issue. . . . Third, numerous courts have concluded that the use of midazolam as the first drug in a three-drug protocol is likely to render an inmate insensate to pain that might result from administration of the paralytic agent and potassium chloride. . . . Fourth, challenges to lethal injection protocols test the boundaries of the authority and competency of federal courts. Although we must invalidate a lethal injection protocol if it violates the Eighth Amendment, federal courts should not "embroil [themselves] in ongoing scientific controversies beyond their expertise." Accordingly, an inmate challenging a protocol bears the burden to show, based on evidence presented to the court, that there is a substantial risk of severe pain.

Petitioners attack the District Court's findings of fact on two main grounds. First, they argue that even if midazolam is powerful enough to induce unconsciousness, it is too weak to maintain unconsciousness and insensitivity to pain once the second and third drugs are administered. Second, while conceding that the 500-milligram dose of midazolam is much higher than the normal therapeutic dose, they contend that this fact is irrelevant because midazolam has a "ceiling effect"—that is, at a certain point, an increase in the dose administered will not have any greater effect on the inmate. Neither argument succeeds.

The District Court found that midazolam is capable of placing a person "at a sufficient level of unconsciousness to resist the noxious stimuli which could occur from the application of the second and third drugs." This conclusion was not clearly erroneous. Respondents' expert, Dr. Evans, testified that the proper administration of a 500-milligram dose of midazolam would make it "a virtual certainty" that any individual would be "at a sufficient level of unconsciousness to resist the noxious stimuli which could occur from application of the 2nd and 3rd drugs" used in the Oklahoma protocol. And petitioners' experts acknowledged that they had no contrary scientific proof. . . .

Petitioners emphasize that midazolam is not recommended or approved for use as the sole anesthetic during painful surgery, but there are two reasons why this is not dispositive. First, as the District Court found, the 500-milligram dose at issue here "is many times higher than a normal therapeutic dose of midazolam." The effect of a small dose of midazolam has minimal probative value about the effect of a 500-milligram dose. Second, the fact that a low dose of midazolam is not the best drug for maintaining unconsciousness during surgery says little about whether a 500-milligram dose of midazolam is constitutionally adequate for purposes of conducting an execution. We recognized this point in *Baze*, where we concluded that although the medical standard of care might require the use of a blood pressure cuff and an electrocardiogram during surgeries, this does not mean those procedures are required for an execution to pass Eighth Amendment scrutiny.

Oklahoma has also adopted important safeguards to ensure that midazolam is properly administered. The District Court emphasized three requirements in particular: The execution team must secure both a primary and backup IV access site, it must confirm the viability of the IV sites, and it must continuously monitor the offender's level of consciousness. The District Court did not commit clear error in concluding that these safeguards help to minimize any risk that might occur in the event that midazolam does not operate as intended. . . .

[P]etitioners argue that there is no consensus among the States regarding midazolam's efficacy because only four States (Oklahoma, Arizona, Florida, and Ohio) have used midazolam as part of an execution. Petitioners rely on the plurality's statement in *Baze* that "it is difficult to regard a practice as 'objectively intolerable' when it is in fact widely tolerated," and the plurality's emphasis on the fact that 36 States had adopted lethal injection and 30 States used the particular three-drug protocol at issue in that case. But while the near-universal use of the particular protocol at issue in *Baze* supported our conclusion that this protocol did not violate the Eighth Amendment, we did not say that the converse was true, i.e., that other protocols or methods of execution are of doubtful constitutionality. That argument, if accepted, would hamper the adoption of new and potentially more humane methods of execution. . . .

Fourth, petitioners argue that difficulties with Oklahoma's execution of Lockett and Arizona's July 2014 execution of Joseph Wood establish that midazolam is sure or very likely to cause serious pain. We are not persuaded. Aside from the Lockett execution, 12 other executions have been conducted using the three-drug protocol at issue here, and those appear to have been conducted without any significant problems. Moreover, Lockett was administered only 100 milligrams of midazolam, and Oklahoma's investigation into that execution concluded that the difficulties were due primarily to the execution team's inability to obtain an IV access site. And the Wood execution did not involve the protocol at issue here. Wood did not receive a single dose of 500 milligrams of midazolam; instead, he received fifteen 50-milligram doses over the span of two hours. And Arizona used a different two-drug protocol that paired midazolam with hydromorphone, a drug that is not at issue in this case. When all of the circumstances are considered, the Lockett and Wood executions have little probative value for present purposes.

Finally, we find it appropriate to respond to the principal dissent's groundless suggestion that our decision is tantamount to allowing prisoners to be "drawn and quartered, slowly tortured to death, or actually burned at the stake." That is simply not true, and the principal dissent's resort to this outlandish rhetoric reveals the weakness of its legal arguments.

NOTES & QUESTIONS ON METHODS OF EXECUTION

1. *Known and available alternatives.* Why could the defendant not articulate a known and available alternative that would have a lower risk of pain? Also, do you agree that this requirement of the Eighth Amendment jurisprudence is appropriate? How can a petitioner prove that the state has alternatives to lethal injection, and is this too high of a burden to impose on petitioners? If there is no alternative that poses an acceptable level of risk, should the Supreme Court simply conclude that the death penalty is per se unconstitutional, regardless of which method is used?

2. *Examples of botched executions.* Do you agree with the majority's attempt to differentiate the examples of botched executions presented by the defendant? Does it matter that the dosing was different or that the medical staff failed to properly insert the IV?

3. *Severe pain.* The Court's standard requires a finding of a risk of severe pain from the execution. What is the significance of a risk of pain versus a risk of severe pain in this context? What is the dividing line between the two? If it were likely that an execution were to cause pain but not severe pain, would that be acceptable?

4. *Breyer versus Scalia.* In dueling dissenting and concurring opinions, Justices Breyer and Scalia wrote separately in *Glossip* to express their competing views about the constitutionality of the death penalty in general. Breyer argued that the death penalty suffers from three major constitutional deficits: unreliability, arbitrariness, and "unconscionably long delays that undermine the death penalty's penological purpose." Scalia responded that it is

convictions, not their associated punishment, that are "unreliable," and he also noted that "it is impossible to hold unconstitutional that which the Constitution explicitly contemplates" because the Fifth Amendment makes explicit reference to "capital" crimes. Which side has the better of the argument?

STATE LAW REQUIREMENTS

Some state courts have concluded that particular methods of execution are unconstitutional under state constitutional provisions. For example, Nebraska ruled in 2008 that the electric chair violated the cruel and unusual punishment clause of the Nebraska State Constitution. The defendant, Raymond Mata, was sentenced to death in a Nebraska trial court for premeditated murder. On appeal, the Nebraska Supreme Court considered whether electrocution violates the state constitution. The U.S. Supreme Court had never so held under the federal constitution, and typically the Nebraska courts interpret Nebraska's cruel and unusual punishment provision as coextensive with the federal constitutional provision. But in this case, the Nebraska Supreme Court decided to stake out its own state constitutional understanding of the provision:

> Our review of these early cases illustrates that the U.S. Supreme Court's case law on electrocution relies on unexamined factual assumptions about an electric current's physiological effects on a human. This obvious omission in the Court's jurisprudence results from three factors: (1) the Court's limited knowledge about an electrocution's effect on the human body, (2) the states' desire to find a more humane method of execution than hanging, and (3) the Court's view, when electrocution was first introduced, that the Eighth Amendment was not intended as a restraint on state legislatures' determinations of punishment. But that view has changed. The Supreme Court has specifically held that the Eighth Amendment is a restraint on legislative power to impose punishment. And it has held the 8th Amendment applies to the states through the 14th Amendment.

State v. Mata, 275 Neb. 1, 38, 745 N.W.2d 229, 260 (2008). In contrast, in November 2018, prison officials in Tennessee executed convicted killer Edmund Zagorski in the state's electric chair. (The previous execution using the electric chair in Tennessee was Daryl Horton in 2007.) Here was the local newspaper's account of the 2018 execution:

> The warden gave the signal to proceed. Zagorski lifted his right hand several times in what looked like attempts at a wave, before he clenched his hands into fists as the first charge of 1,750 volts of electricity was sent through his body for 20 seconds.
>
> Henry [his lawyer] said both pinkies appear to either be dislocated or broken due to the force with which he pulled against the straps. She also said there were signs that Zagorski was breathing during a short pause before the second jolt was administered for 15 seconds.
>
> The doctor overseeing the death appeared in view to check on Zagorski.
>
> Zagorski was dead. The blinds into the chamber closed.

Yihyun Jeong et al., *Tennessee Executes Edmund Zagorski by Electric Chair*, Nashville Tennessean, Nov. 2, 2018.

C. THE JURY'S ROLE IN SENTENCING

A criminal trial necessarily involves a collaboration between judge and jury. During the pre-trial and guilt phase, the division of labor is relatively clear: The judge is the law decider while the jury is the fact finder, applying the law to the facts. At trial's end, however, that division of labor becomes more complex and more fraught, especially as sentencing draws near. There is no question that judges may hand down sentences, following a jury determination of guilt, but the following cases all raise a particularly sticky point: In handing down that sentencing decision, can the judge "find facts" during that process or must the judge rely exclusively on the factual findings made by the jury during the guilt phase? This seemingly simple issue shows up in a vast array of cases, all of which implicate the Sixth Amendment right to a jury trial and by extension what it means for defendants to have their fates decided by a jury rather than by a judge.

1. Sentencing Enhancements

In the following case, New Jersey had passed a state statute imposing sentencing enhancements for crimes committed as a "hate crime." The statute did not create a new substantive offense, but simply created sentencing enhancements to existing offenses when the commission of the offense qualified as a hate crime. Under the statutory scheme, the determination of whether the offense was committed as a hate crime was decided by the judge at sentencing rather than by the jury during the guilt phase. Indeed, this was precisely by design. The goal of the statute was not to create a new class of offenses but merely to direct local judges to punish offenders more harshly in cases of hate crimes. But did bypassing the jury in this way cause a Sixth Amendment problem?

Apprendi v. New Jersey

Supreme Court of the United States
530 U.S. 466 (2000)

Justice STEVENS delivered the opinion of the Court.

A New Jersey statute classifies the possession of a firearm for an unlawful purpose as a "second-degree" offense. N.J. Stat. Ann. § 2C:39-4(a) (West 1995). Such an offense is punishable by imprisonment for "between five years and 10 years." A separate statute, described by that State's Supreme Court as a "hate crime" law, provides for an "extended term" of imprisonment if the trial judge finds, by a preponderance of the evidence, that "[t]he defendant in committing the crime acted with a purpose to intimidate an individual or group of individuals because of race, color, gender, handicap, religion, sexual orientation or ethnicity." The extended term authorized by the hate crime law for second-degree offenses is imprisonment for "between 10 and 20 years."

The question presented is whether the Due Process Clause of the Fourteenth Amendment requires that a factual determination authorizing an increase in the maximum prison sentence for an offense from 10 to 20 years be made by a jury on the basis of proof beyond a reasonable doubt.

I

At 2:04 A.M. on December 22, 1994, petitioner Charles C. Apprendi, Jr., fired several .22-caliber bullets into the home of an African-American family that had recently moved into a previously all-white neighborhood in Vineland, New Jersey. Apprendi was promptly arrested and, at 3:05 A.M., admitted that he was the shooter. After further questioning, at 6:04 A.M., he made a statement—which he later retracted—that even though he did not know the occupants of the house personally, "because they are black in color he does not want them in the neighborhood."

A New Jersey grand jury returned a 23-count indictment charging Apprendi with four first-degree, eight second-degree, six third-degree, and five fourth-degree offenses. The charges alleged shootings on four different dates, as well as the unlawful possession of various weapons. None of the counts referred to the hate crime statute, and none alleged that Apprendi acted with a racially biased purpose.

The parties entered into a plea agreement, pursuant to which Apprendi pleaded guilty to two counts of second-degree possession of a firearm for an unlawful purpose and one count of the third-degree offense of unlawful possession of an antipersonnel bomb; the prosecutor dismissed the other 20 counts. Under state law, a second-degree offense carries a penalty range of 5 to 10 years; a third-degree offense carries a penalty range of between 3 and 5 years. As part of the plea agreement, however, the State reserved the right to request the court to impose a higher "enhanced" sentence on count 18 (which was based on the December 22 shooting) on the ground that that offense was committed with a biased purpose, as described in § 2C:44-3(e). Apprendi, correspondingly, reserved the right to challenge the hate crime sentence enhancement on the ground that it violates the United States Constitution.

At the plea hearing, the trial judge heard sufficient evidence to establish Apprendi's guilt on counts 3, 18, and 22; the judge then confirmed that Apprendi understood the maximum sentences that could be imposed on those counts. Because the plea agreement provided that the sentence on the sole third-degree offense (count 22) would run concurrently with the other sentences, the potential sentences on the two second-degree counts were critical. If the judge found no basis for the biased purpose enhancement, the maximum consecutive sentences on those counts would amount to 20 years in aggregate; if, however, the judge enhanced the sentence on count 18, the maximum on that count alone would be 20 years and the maximum for the two counts in aggregate would be 30 years, with a 15-year period of parole ineligibility.

After the trial judge accepted the three guilty pleas, the prosecutor filed a formal motion for an extended term. The trial judge thereafter held an evidentiary hearing on the issue of Apprendi's "purpose" for the shooting on December 22. Apprendi adduced evidence from a psychologist and from seven character witnesses who testified that he did not have a reputation for racial bias. He also took the stand himself, explaining that the incident was an unintended consequence of overindulgence in alcohol, denying that he was in any way biased against African-Americans, and denying that his statement to the police had been accurately described. The judge, however, found the police officer's testimony credible, and concluded that the evidence supported a finding "that the crime was motivated by racial bias." Having found "by a preponderance of the evidence" that Apprendi's actions were taken "with a purpose to intimidate" as provided by the statute, the trial judge held that the hate crime enhancement applied. Rejecting Apprendi's constitutional challenge to the statute, the judge sentenced him to a 12-year term of imprisonment on count 18, and to shorter concurrent sentences on the other two counts. . . .

III

In his 1881 lecture on the criminal law, Oliver Wendell Holmes, Jr., observed: "The law threatens certain pains if you do certain things, intending thereby to give you a new motive for not doing them. If you persist in doing them, it has to inflict the pains in order that its threats may continue to be believed." New Jersey threatened Apprendi with certain pains if he unlawfully possessed a weapon and with additional pains if he selected his victims with a purpose to intimidate them because of their race. As a matter of simple justice, it seems obvious that the procedural safeguards designed to protect Apprendi from unwarranted pains should apply equally to the two acts that New Jersey has singled out for punishment. Merely using the label "sentence enhancement" to describe the latter surely does not provide a principled basis for treating them differently.

At stake in this case are constitutional protections of surpassing importance: the proscription of any deprivation of liberty without "due process of law" and the guarantee that "[i]n all criminal prosecutions, the accused shall enjoy the right to a speedy and public trial, by an impartial jury." Taken together, these rights indisputably entitle a criminal defendant to "a jury determination that [he] is guilty of every element of the crime with which he is charged, beyond a reasonable doubt."

[T]he historical foundation for our recognition of these principles extends down centuries into the common law. "[T]o guard against a spirit of oppression and tyranny on the part of rulers," and "as the great bulwark of [our] civil and political liberties," trial by jury has been understood to require that "the truth of every accusation, whether preferred in the shape of indictment, information, or appeal, should afterwards be confirmed by the unanimous suffrage of twelve of [the defendant's] equals and neighbours. . . ." Equally well founded is the companion right to have the jury verdict based on proof beyond a reasonable doubt. . . .

Any possible distinction between an "element" of a felony offense and a "sentencing factor" was unknown to the practice of criminal indictment, trial by jury, and judgment by court as it existed during the years surrounding our Nation's founding. As a general rule, criminal proceedings were submitted to a jury after being initiated by an indictment containing "all the facts and circumstances which constitute the offence, . . . stated with such certainty and precision, that the defendant . . . may be enabled to determine the species of offence they constitute, in order that he may prepare his defence accordingly . . . and that there may be no doubt as to the judgment which should be given, if the defendant be convicted." The defendant's ability to predict with certainty the judgment from the face of the felony indictment flowed from the invariable linkage of punishment with crime. . . .

Since *Winship*, we have made clear beyond peradventure that *Winship*'s due process and associated jury protections extend, to some degree, "to determinations that [go] not to a defendant's guilt or innocence, but simply to the length of his sentence." This was a primary lesson of *Mullaney v. Wilbur*, 421 U.S. 684 (1975), in which we invalidated a Maine statute that presumed that a defendant who acted with an intent to kill possessed the "malice aforethought" necessary to constitute the State's murder offense (and therefore, was subject to that crime's associated punishment of life imprisonment). The statute placed the burden on the defendant of proving, in rebutting the statutory presumption, that he acted with a lesser degree of culpability, such as in the heat of passion, to win a reduction in the offense from murder to manslaughter (and thus a reduction of the maximum punishment of 20 years).

The State had posited in *Mullaney* that requiring a defendant to prove heat-of-passion intent to overcome a presumption of murderous intent did not implicate *Winship* protections because, upon conviction of either offense, the defendant would lose his liberty and face societal stigma just the same. Rejecting this argument, we acknowledged that criminal law "is concerned not only with guilt or innocence in the abstract, but also with the degree of criminal culpability" assessed. Because the "consequences" of a guilty verdict for murder and for manslaughter differed substantially, we dismissed the possibility that a State could circumvent the protections of *Winship* merely by "redefin[ing] the elements that constitute different crimes, characterizing them as factors that bear solely on the extent of punishment." . . . .

V

The New Jersey statutory scheme that Apprendi asks us to invalidate allows a jury to convict a defendant of a second-degree offense based on its finding beyond a reasonable doubt that he unlawfully possessed a prohibited weapon; after a subsequent and separate proceeding, it then allows a judge to impose punishment identical to that New Jersey provides for crimes of the first degree, based upon the judge's finding, by a preponderance of the evidence, that the defendant's "purpose" for unlawfully possessing the weapon was "to intimidate" his victim on the basis of a particular characteristic the victim possessed. In light of the constitutional rule explained above, and all of the cases supporting it, this practice cannot stand.

. . . [New Jersey argues that the] required finding of biased purpose is not an "element" of a distinct hate crime offense, but rather the traditional "sentencing factor" of motive. . . . New Jersey's . . . point is nothing more than a disagreement with the rule we apply today. Beyond this, we do not see how the argument can succeed on its own terms. The state high court evinced substantial skepticism at the suggestion that the hate crime statute's "purpose to intimidate" was simply an inquiry into "motive." We share that skepticism. The text of the statute requires the factfinder to determine whether the defendant possessed, at the time he committed the subject act, a "purpose to intimidate" on account of, inter alia, race. By its very terms, this statute mandates an examination of the defendant's state of mind—a concept known well to the criminal law as the defendant's mens rea. It makes no difference in identifying the nature of this finding that Apprendi was also required, in order to receive the sentence he did for weapons possession, to have possessed the weapon with a "purpose to use [the weapon] unlawfully against the person or property of another." A second mens rea requirement hardly defeats the reality that the enhancement statute imposes of its own force an intent requirement necessary for the imposition of sentence. On the contrary, the fact that the language and structure of the "purpose to use" criminal offense is identical in relevant respects to the language and structure of the "purpose to intimidate" provision demonstrates to us that it is precisely a particular criminal mens rea that the hate crime enhancement statute seeks to target. The defendant's intent in committing a crime is perhaps as close as one might hope to come to a core criminal offense "element."

The foregoing notwithstanding, however, the New Jersey Supreme Court correctly recognized that it does not matter whether the required

> finding is characterized as one of intent or of motive, because "[l]abels do not afford an acceptable answer." That point applies as well to the constitutionally novel and elusive distinction between "elements" and "sentencing factors." *McMillan*, 477 U.S., at 86. Despite what appears to us the clear "elemental" nature of the factor here, the relevant inquiry is one not of form, but of effect—does the required finding expose the defendant to a greater punishment than that authorized by the jury's guilty verdict? . . .

NOTES & QUESTIONS ON SENTENCING ENHANCEMENTS

1. *Elements or enhancements. Apprendi* is based on demolishing the significance between elements of the offense and enhancements. An "element of an offense" is a material element, such as mens rea, actus reus, or attendant circumstance, that must be proven to the jury by the prosecutor according to the standard of proof beyond a reasonable doubt. Elements are either expressly stated in the statutory text of the offense description or are judicial elaborations of elements that are implicit in that definition. Either way, the state must demonstrate the elements of the offense to the satisfaction of the jury in order for a defendant to be convicted. Sentencing enhancements, by contrast, are factual findings that make the defendant eligible for a higher penalty or sentence. *Apprendi*'s significance was to declare that anything that increases a defendant's criminal exposure, including a mere sentencing enhancement, should be classified, for constitutional purposes, as an element.

2. *Function over form.* Does it matter whether a fact is labeled as an element of an offense or a sentencing factor? Traditionally, the former is determined by the jury, but the latter is determined by the judge. But according to the Supreme Court, what matters is the effect. Regardless of what it is called, if it increases the criminal exposure of the defendant, then it should be determined by the jury. Does this conclusion of function over form sweep more broadly than sentencing enhancements? Can you think of other situations where a judge's determination might increase the defendant's punishment?

3. *Reasonable doubt.* What role does *Winship* and the reasonable doubt requirement play in the Court's decision? How does the Court draw a line from the requirement that a jury must determine each element of the offense beyond a reasonable doubt to the conclusion that a judge is not entitled to make factual determinations underlying sentencing enhancements?

4. *Sentencing minima.* In *Alleyne v. United States*, 570 U.S. 99 (2013), the Supreme Court applied *Apprendi* to the context of factual findings that trigger mandatory minimum sentences. Because mandatory minimum sentences

increase the penalty for a crime, any fact that increases the mandatory minimum is an "element" that must be submitted to the jury. In *Alleyne*, the petitioner and an accomplice were accused of robbing a store manager who was driving to a local bank to deposit money from the day's business. The defendants pretended to have car trouble to get the manager to stop, at which point they pointed a gun at the manager and demanded the money. Alleyne was charged under a federal robbery statute that included different minimum sentences depending on whether the defendant carried a gun during the crime (five years) and whether that gun was "brandished" (seven years). The determination was made by the judge, rather than the jury. Applying *Apprendi*, the Supreme Court concluded that if the statutory trigger increases the mandatory minimum sentence faced by the defendant, it should be classified as an "element" of the offense and must be found by the jury pursuant to the Sixth Amendment.

2. Jury Determination of Capital Eligibility

The Supreme Court's Eighth Amendment jurisprudence requires that a jury exercise "guided discretion" in determining a defendant's eligibility for the death penalty. This means that a state must rationally narrow those eligible for the death penalty (so that only the most culpable are executed), and the sentence, in the decision whether capital punishment is warranted, must include consideration of individual circumstances of the defendant and the crime in question. The first requirement is a general and systemic one, while the second requirement is highly individualistic. These Eighth Amendment requirements flow from the need to balance between two opposite and intolerable extremes: a hypothetical system where defendants convicted of some crimes are automatically subject to the death penalty, thus giving the trial court no discretion whatsoever, or a hypothetical system where the trial court is given unlimited discretion, with no guidance, to determine whether the death penalty should be imposed. According to the Supreme Court in *Gregg v. Georgia*, 428 U.S. 153 (1976), a system with no discretion is problematic because it fails to ensure that only the most culpable defendants are executed, while a system with total discretion risks arbitrary decision making lacking in consistency and uniformity—and equally intolerable result. As the Court stated:

> [T]he concerns expressed in *Furman* that the penalty of death not be imposed in an arbitrary or capricious manner can be met by a carefully drafted statute that ensures that the sentencing authority is given adequate information and guidance. As a general proposition these concerns are best met by a system that provides for a bifurcated proceeding at which the sentencing authority is apprised of the information relevant to the imposition of sentence and provided with standards to guide its use of the information.

Id. at 195. In this context, "bifurcation" means that the jury first declares the defendant guilty or not guilty during the guilt phase of the trial. Then, only if the defendant is guilty will the court convene a sentencing hearing for both sides to argue to the jury that the defendant should receive the death penalty or, in the alternative, some lesser punishment such as life in prison. The bifurcation of the proceedings is essential to give the defendant maximum flexibility to both contest guilt while also pleading for mercy at sentencing. To understand the dilemma, consider a unified proceeding where the jury considers both guilt and punishment at the very same time. If defense counsel wishes to maintain their client's innocence, there is simply no way to seek mercy; the counsel's position is that their client did not commit the crime. Or, in the alternative, the counsel might ask for mercy and concede guilt to the jury, but this approach tags the request for mercy with a steep price indeed. Bifurcation takes the edge off this dilemma, because it allows the defendant to assert innocence (either directly through testimony on the stand or indirectly via counsel), while at the same time seeking mercy if the jury finds the defendant guilty. In *Gregg*, the Supreme Court concluded that bifurcation is constitutionally required in death penalty cases.

The use of "standards" required by *Gregg v. Georgia* usually boils down to aggravating and mitigating factors. In order to sentence the offender to death, the sentencer must find at least one aggravating factor and must also determine that the aggravating factors outweigh any mitigating factors. But notice the use of the phrase "sentencing authority" in the above quote from *Gregg*, which very carefully does not refer explicitly to the jury. In the following case, the Supreme Court inquires whether it is permissible for the judge to make the findings that are necessary to meet *Gregg*'s standard of guided discretion. If the findings are made by the judge rather than the jury, is this consistent with the vision of the Sixth Amendment articulated by *Apprendi*?

Ring v. Arizona

Supreme Court of the United States
536 U.S. 584 (2002)

Justice GINSBURG delivered the opinion of the Court.

This case concerns the Sixth Amendment right to a jury trial in capital prosecutions. In Arizona, following a jury adjudication of a defendant's guilt of first-degree murder, the trial judge, sitting alone, determines the presence or absence of the aggravating factors required by Arizona law for imposition of the death penalty.

In *Walton v. Arizona*, 497 U.S. 639 (1990), this Court held that Arizona's sentencing scheme was compatible with the Sixth Amendment because the additional facts found by the judge qualified as sentencing considerations, not as "element[s] of the offense of capital murder." Ten years later, however, we decided *Apprendi v. New Jersey*, 530 U.S. 466 (2000), which held that the Sixth Amendment does not permit a defendant to be "expose[d] . . . to a penalty exceeding the maximum he would receive if punished according to the facts reflected in the jury verdict alone." This prescription governs, *Apprendi* determined, even if the State characterizes the additional findings made by the judge as "sentencing factor[s]."

Apprendi's reasoning is irreconcilable with *Walton*'s holding in this regard, and today we overrule *Walton* in relevant part. Capital defendants, no less than noncapital defendants, we conclude, are entitled to a jury determination of any fact on which the legislature conditions an increase in their maximum punishment.

I

At the trial of petitioner Timothy Ring for murder, armed robbery, and related charges, the prosecutor presented evidence sufficient to permit the jury to find the facts here recounted. On November 28, 1994, a Wells Fargo armored van pulled up to the Dillard's department store at Arrowhead Mall in Glendale, Arizona. Courier Dave Moss left the van to pick up money inside the store. When he returned, the van, and its driver, John Magoch, were gone.

Later that day, Maricopa County Sheriff's Deputies found the van—its doors locked and its engine running—in the parking lot of a church in Sun City, Arizona. Inside the vehicle they found Magoch, dead from a single gunshot to the head. According to Wells Fargo records, more than $562,000 in cash and $271,000 in checks were missing from the van. . . .

The trial judge instructed the jury on alternative charges of premeditated murder and felony murder. The jury deadlocked on premeditated murder, with 6 of 12 jurors voting to acquit, but convicted Ring of felony murder occurring in the course of armed robbery. As later summed up by the Arizona Supreme Court, "the evidence admitted at trial failed to prove, beyond a reasonable doubt, that [Ring] was a major participant in the armed robbery or that he actually murdered Magoch." Although clear evidence connected Ring to the robbery's proceeds, nothing submitted at trial put him at the scene of the robbery. Furthermore, "[f]or all we know from the trial evidence," the Arizona court stated, "[Ring] did not participate in, plan, or even expect the killing. This lack of evidence no doubt explains why the jury found [Ring] guilty of felony, but not premeditated, murder."

Under Arizona law, Ring could not be sentenced to death, the statutory maximum penalty for first-degree murder, unless further findings were made. The State's first-degree murder statute prescribes that the offense "is punishable by death or life imprisonment as provided by § 13-703." The cross-referenced section, § 13-703, directs the judge who presided at trial to "conduct a separate sentencing hearing to determine the existence or nonexistence of [certain enumerated] circumstances . . . for the purpose of determining the sentence to be imposed." The statute further instructs: "The hearing shall be conducted before the court alone. The court alone shall make all factual determinations required by this section or the constitution of the United States or this state."

At the conclusion of the sentencing hearing, the judge is to determine the presence or absence of the enumerated "aggravating circumstances" and any "mitigating circumstances." The State's law authorizes the judge to sentence the defendant to death only if there is at least one aggravating circumstance and "there are no mitigating circumstances sufficiently substantial to call for leniency."

Between Ring's trial and sentencing hearing, Greenham pleaded guilty to second-degree murder and armed robbery. He stipulated to a 27½ year sentence and agreed to cooperate with the prosecution in the cases against Ring and Ferguson. Called by the prosecution at Ring's sentencing hearing, Greenham testified that he, Ring, and Ferguson had been planning the robbery for several weeks before it occurred. According to Greenham, Ring "had I guess taken the role as leader because he laid out all the tactics." On the day of the robbery, Greenham said, the three watched the armored van pull up to the mall. When Magoch opened the door to smoke a cigarette, Ring shot him with a rifle equipped with a homemade silencer. Greenham then pushed Magoch's body aside and drove the van away. At Ring's direction, Greenham drove to the church parking lot, where he and Ring transferred the money to Ring's truck. Later, Greenham recalled, as the three robbers were dividing up the money, Ring upbraided him and Ferguson for "forgetting to congratulate [Ring] on [his] shot."

On cross-examination, Greenham acknowledged having previously told Ring's counsel that Ring had nothing to do with the planning or execution of the robbery. Greenham explained that he had made that prior statement only because Ring had threatened his life. Greenham also acknowledged that he was now testifying against Ring as "pay back" for the threats and for Ring's interference in Greenham's relationship with Greenham's ex-wife.

On October 29, 1997, the trial judge entered his "Special Verdict" sentencing Ring to death. Because Ring was convicted of felony murder, not premeditated murder, the judge recognized that Ring was eligible for the death penalty only if he was Magoch's actual killer or if he was "a major participant in the armed robbery that led to the killing and exhibited a reckless disregard or indifference for human life." Citing Greenham's testimony at the sentencing hearing, the judge concluded that Ring "is the one who shot and killed Mr. Magoch." The judge also found that Ring was a major participant in the robbery and that armed robbery "is unquestionably a crime which carries with it a grave risk of death."

The judge then turned to the determination of aggravating and mitigating circumstances. He found two aggravating factors. First, the judge determined that Ring committed the offense in expectation of receiving something of "pecuniary value," as described in § 13-703; "[t]aking the cash from the armored car was the motive and reason for Mr. Magoch's murder and not just the result." Second, the judge found that the offense was committed "in an especially heinous, cruel or depraved manner." In support of this finding, he cited Ring's comment, as reported by Greenham at the sentencing hearing, expressing pride in his marksmanship. The judge found one nonstatutory mitigating factor: Ring's "minimal" criminal record. In his judgment, that mitigating circumstance did not "call for leniency"; he therefore sentenced Ring to death.

II

Based solely on the jury's verdict finding Ring guilty of first-degree felony murder, the maximum punishment he could have received was life imprisonment. This was so because, in Arizona, a "death sentence may not legally be imposed . . . unless at least one aggravating factor is found to exist beyond a reasonable doubt." The question presented is whether that aggravating factor may be found by the judge, as Arizona law specifies, or whether the Sixth Amendment's jury trial guarantee, made applicable to the States by the Fourteenth Amendment, requires that the aggravating factor determination be entrusted to the jury.

As earlier indicated, this is not the first time we have considered the constitutionality of Arizona's capital sentencing system. In *Walton v. Arizona*, 497 U.S. 639 (1990), we upheld Arizona's scheme against a charge that it violated the Sixth Amendment. The Court had previously denied a Sixth Amendment challenge to Florida's capital sentencing system, in which the jury recommends a sentence but makes no explicit findings on aggravating circumstances; we so ruled, *Walton* noted, on the ground that "the Sixth Amendment does not require that the specific findings authorizing the imposition of the sentence of death be made by the jury." *Walton* found unavailing the attempts by the defendant-petitioner in that case to distinguish Florida's capital sentencing system from Arizona's. In neither State, according to *Walton*, were the aggravating factors "elements of the offense"; in both States, they ranked as "sentencing considerations" guiding the choice between life and death. . . .

In an effort to reconcile its capital sentencing system with the Sixth Amendment as interpreted by *Apprendi*, Arizona first restates the *Apprendi* majority's portrayal of Arizona's system: Ring was convicted of first-degree murder, for which Arizona law specifies "death or life imprisonment" as the only sentencing options; Ring was therefore sentenced within the range of punishment authorized by the jury verdict. This argument overlooks *Apprendi*'s instruction that "the relevant inquiry is one not of form, but of effect." In effect, "the required finding [of an aggravated circumstance] expose[d] [Ring] to a greater punishment than that authorized by the jury's guilty verdict." The Arizona first-degree murder statute "authorizes a maximum penalty of death only in a formal sense," for it explicitly cross-references the statutory provision requiring the finding of an aggravating circumstance before imposition of the death penalty. If Arizona prevailed on its opening argument, *Apprendi* would be reduced to a "meaningless and formalistic" rule of statutory drafting.

Arizona also supports the distinction relied upon in *Walton* between elements of an offense and sentencing factors. As to elevation of the maximum punishment, however, *Apprendi* renders the argument untenable; *Apprendi* repeatedly instructs in that context that the characterization of a fact or circumstance as an "element" or a "sentencing factor" is not determinative of the question "who decides," judge or jury.

Even if facts increasing punishment beyond the maximum authorized by a guilty verdict standing alone ordinarily must be found by a jury, Arizona further urges, aggravating circumstances necessary to trigger a death sentence may nonetheless be reserved for judicial determination. As Arizona's counsel maintained at oral argument, there is no doubt that "[d]eath is different." States have constructed elaborate sentencing procedures in death cases, Arizona emphasizes, because of constraints we have said the Eighth Amendment places on capital sentencing.

Apart from the Eighth Amendment provenance of aggravating factors, Arizona presents "no specific reason for excepting capital defendants from the constitutional protections . . . extend[ed] to defendants generally, and none is readily apparent." The notion "that the Eighth Amendment's restriction on a state legislature's ability to define capital crimes should be compensated for by permitting States more leeway under the Fifth and Sixth Amendments in proving an aggravating fact necessary to a capital sentence . . . is without precedent in our constitutional jurisprudence."

In various settings, we have interpreted the Constitution to require the addition of an element or elements to the definition of a criminal offense in order to narrow its scope. If a legislature responded to one of these decisions by adding the element we held constitutionally required, surely the Sixth Amendment guarantee would apply to that element. We see no reason to differentiate capital crimes from all others in this regard.

Arizona suggests that judicial authority over the finding of aggravating factors "may . . . be a better way to guarantee against the arbitrary imposition of the death penalty." The Sixth Amendment jury trial right, however, does not turn on the relative rationality, fairness, or efficiency of potential factfinders. Entrusting to a judge the finding of facts necessary to support a death sentence might be "an admirably fair and efficient scheme of criminal justice designed for a society that is prepared to leave criminal justice to the State. . . . The founders of the American Republic were not prepared to leave it to the State, which is why the jury-trial guarantee was one of the least controversial provisions of the Bill of Rights. It has never been efficient; but it has always been free." *Apprendi*, 530 U.S., at 498, (Scalia, J., concurring).

In any event, the superiority of judicial factfinding in capital cases is far from evident. Unlike Arizona, the great majority of States responded to this Court's Eighth Amendment decisions requiring the presence of aggravating circumstances in capital cases by entrusting those determinations to the jury. . . . For the reasons stated, we hold that *Walton* and *Apprendi* are irreconcilable; our Sixth Amendment jurisprudence cannot be home to both. Accordingly, we overrule *Walton* to the extent that it allows a sentencing judge, sitting without a jury, to find an aggravating circumstance necessary for imposition of the death penalty. Because Arizona's enumerated aggravating factors operate as "the functional equivalent of an element of a greater offense," the Sixth Amendment requires that they be found by a jury.

NOTES & QUESTIONS ON THE JURY'S ROLE IN CAPITAL SENTENCING

1. *Judicial fact finding.* Would allowing a judge to make the factual findings for aggravating circumstances improve the consistency of capital decision making? In other words, is there any reason to believe that a jury is any better than a judge in meeting *Gregg*'s requirements?

2. *Aggravating factors as elements of the offense. Ring* is based on the premise that an aggravating factor finding that is necessary before the imposition of the death penalty is similar to an element of the offense—both must be found by the jury, according to the Sixth Amendment. In what ways are aggravating factors akin to elements of an offense?

3. *Recommendations versus findings. Ring* stands for the proposition that the jury must make the requisite findings that make the defendant eligible for the death penalty. But what if the jury makes a "recommendation" to the judge, who in turn makes the factual findings necessary and then makes the final decision? Florida had just such a scheme but it was deemed insufficient by the U.S. Supreme Court:

> . . . Florida argues that when Hurst's sentencing jury recommended a death sentence, it "necessarily included a finding of an aggravating circumstance." The State contends that this finding qualified Hurst for the death penalty under Florida law, thus satisfying *Ring*. "[T]he additional requirement that a judge also find an aggravator," Florida concludes, "only provides the defendant additional protection." The State fails to appreciate the central and singular role the judge plays under Florida law. As described above and by the Florida Supreme Court, the Florida sentencing statute does not make a defendant eligible for death until "*findings* by the court that such person shall be punished by death." Fla. Stat. § 775.082(1) (emphasis added). The trial court alone must find "the facts . . . [t]hat sufficient aggravating circumstances exist" and "[t]hat there are insufficient mitigating circumstances to

> outweigh the aggravating circumstances." § 921.141(3). The State cannot now treat the advisory recommendation by the jury as the necessary factual finding that *Ring* requires.

Hurst v. Florida, 136 S. Ct. 616, 622 (2016). Applying *Ring*, the jury must not only decide the existence of aggravating factors beyond a reasonable doubt but must also decide, again beyond a reasonable doubt, that the aggravating factors outweigh the mitigating factors. Do you agree with the Court's decision or is it excessively formalistic? What result if the statute were revised so that the trial court's decision was not described as "findings"?

4. *Death-eligible juries.* Prosecutors do not want jurors in capital cases who are unwilling to hand down a capital sentence in a capital prosecution. Specifically, prosecutors seek to avoid jurors who have a total objection to the death penalty, whether legal, moral, or religious. The question is whether prosecutors must use peremptory challenges to remove these potential jurors or whether an unwillingness to even consider the death penalty makes a person an inappropriate jury member—and therefore subject to a challenge "for cause." In *Witherspoon v. Illinois*, 391 U.S. 510 (1968), the Supreme Court upheld a state statute that allowed prosecutors unlimited challenges for jurors who "ha[ve] conscientious scruples against capital punishment." In *Wainwright v. Witt*, 469 U.S. 412, 424-25 (1985), the Supreme Court clarified that the correct standard "for determining when a prospective juror may be excluded for cause because of his or her views on capital punishment . . . is whether the juror's views would prevent or substantially impair the performance of his duties as a juror in accordance with his instructions and his oath." The decision overruled an earlier standard articulated in *Witherspoon*: that a juror's bias must be demonstrated with "unmistakable clarity."

The practice of excusing jurors in this context is now widespread, with judges allowing prosecutors to construct a "death eligible" jury—meaning a jury composed of members who have indicated a willingness to impose the death penalty in at least some cases. This process is often referred to, colloquially, as "Witherspooning" a jury. Do you agree that it is appropriate to limit a jury to individuals who have no objection to the death penalty? Or does it fundamentally stack the deck against the defense? If the defense cannot argue that the death penalty is immoral, their only recourse is to argue to the jury that this particular defendant deserves mercy. Does this voir dire process have some collateral benefits for the prosecution as well? For example, is a death-eligible jury more likely than a non–death-eligible jury to convict the defendant at the guilt phase? Pro-capital punishment individuals might be more sympathetic to the police and prosecutors and less sympathetic to defendants, especially when compared to death penalty opponents, who are more likely to be skeptical of state authorities.

STATE LAW REQUIREMENTS

States use different aggravating factors to determine whether an individual is culpable enough to face the death penalty. While it is constitutionally required for each state to have such criteria, to ensure that only the most culpable are executed, the exact aggravating factors are left to each state to consider and draft. For example, here are Florida's aggravating factors:

> (a) The capital felony was committed by a person previously convicted of a felony and under sentence of imprisonment or placed on community control or on felony probation.
> (b) The defendant was previously convicted of another capital felony or of a felony involving the use or threat of violence to the person.
> (c) The defendant knowingly created a great risk of death to many persons.
> (d) The capital felony was committed while the defendant was engaged, or was an accomplice, in the commission of, or an attempt to commit, or flight after committing or attempting to commit, any: robbery; sexual battery; aggravated child abuse; abuse of an elderly person or disabled adult resulting in great bodily harm, permanent disability, or permanent disfigurement; arson; burglary; kidnapping; aircraft piracy; or unlawful throwing, placing, or discharging of a destructive device or bomb.
> (e) The capital felony was committed for the purpose of avoiding or preventing a lawful arrest or effecting an escape from custody.
> (f) The capital felony was committed for pecuniary gain.
> (g) The capital felony was committed to disrupt or hinder the lawful exercise of any governmental function or the enforcement of laws.
> (h) The capital felony was especially heinous, atrocious, or cruel.
> (i) The capital felony was a homicide and was committed in a cold, calculated, and premeditated manner without any pretense of moral or legal justification.
> (j) The victim of the capital felony was a law enforcement officer engaged in the performance of his or her official duties.
> (k) The victim of the capital felony was an elected or appointed public official engaged in the performance of his or her official duties if the motive for the capital felony was related, in whole or in part, to the victim's official capacity.
> (l) The victim of the capital felony was a person less than 12 years of age.
> (m) The victim of the capital felony was particularly vulnerable due to advanced age or disability, or because the defendant stood in a position of familial or custodial authority over the victim.
> (n) The capital felony was committed by a criminal gang member. . . .
> (o) The capital felony was committed by a person designated as a sexual predator. . . .
> (p) The capital felony was committed by a person subject to an injunction. . . .

Fla. Stat. Ann. § 921.141. The statute then outlines a long list of mitigating factors to be weighed against any of the above factors that apply to the crime. In response to the Supreme Court's opinion in *Hurst v. Florida,* 136 S. Ct. 616 (2016), Florida altered its death penalty statute to require a unanimous jury *determination* that the case involves aggravating circumstances, proven beyond a reasonable doubt, that are sufficient to justify imposing a capital sentence on the defendant. At that point, the jury also then makes a sentencing recommendation to the judge, but the recommendation is only allowed if the jury first makes the required *finding* regarding aggravating circumstances.

3. Sentencing Guidelines

Several states have attempted to systematize sentencing practices by creating sentencing guidelines to give judges guidance on exercising their discretion in sentencing. Although sentencing guidelines vary from state to state, they typically are complex and technical documents that require the judge to assess a base score for the underlying offense and then a series of enhancements for aggravating factors. Also, the sentencing guidelines might call for sentence reductions based on certain mitigating factors. These are no mere "vague" categories but highly mathematical calculations designed to take the guesswork out of sentencing decisions and promote consistency across courtrooms and across judges. The idea that a criminal sentence should be affected by something as capricious as the judge that was assigned to one's case is precisely why rigorous sentencing guidelines were developed and codified in many jurisdictions.

In the following case, the defendant received an enhanced sentence for kidnapping because the judge found, in accordance with the Washington State Sentencing Guidelines, that the kidnapping was committed with deliberate cruelty. As you read the case, pay particular attention to the role that the *Apprendi* reasoning played in the case.

Blakely v. Washington

Supreme Court of the United States
542 U.S. 296 (2004)

Justice Scalia delivered the opinion of the Court.

Petitioner Ralph Howard Blakely, Jr., pleaded guilty to the kidnaping of his estranged wife. The facts admitted in his plea, standing alone, supported a maximum sentence of 53 months. Pursuant to state law, the court imposed an "exceptional" sentence of 90 months after making a judicial determination that he had acted with "deliberate cruelty." We consider whether this violated petitioner's Sixth Amendment right to trial by jury.

I

Petitioner married his wife Yolanda in 1973. He was evidently a difficult man to live with, having been diagnosed at various times with psychological and personality disorders including paranoid schizophrenia. His wife ultimately filed for divorce. In 1998, he abducted her from their orchard home in Grant County, Washington, binding her with duct tape and forcing her at knifepoint into a wooden box in the bed of his pickup truck. In the process, he implored her to dismiss the divorce suit and related trust proceedings.

When the couple's 13-year-old son Ralphy returned home from school, petitioner ordered him to follow in another car, threatening to harm Yolanda with a shotgun if he did not do so. Ralphy escaped and sought help when they stopped at a gas station, but petitioner continued on with Yolanda to a friend's house in Montana. He was finally arrested after the friend called the police.

The State charged petitioner with first-degree kidnaping. Upon reaching a plea agreement, however, it reduced the charge to second-degree kidnaping involving domestic violence and use of a firearm. Petitioner entered a guilty plea admitting the elements of second-degree kidnaping and the domestic-violence and firearm allegations, but no other relevant facts.

The case then proceeded to sentencing. In Washington, second-degree kidnaping is a class B felony. State law provides that "[n]o person convicted of a [class B] felony shall be punished by confinement . . . exceeding . . . a term of ten years." Other provisions of state law, however, further limit the range of sentences a judge may impose. Washington's Sentencing Reform Act specifies, for petitioner's offense of second-degree kidnaping with a firearm, a "standard range" of 49 to 53 months. A judge may impose a sentence above the standard range if he finds "substantial and compelling reasons justifying an exceptional sentence." The Act lists aggravating factors that justify such a departure, which it recites to be illustrative rather than exhaustive. Nevertheless, "[a] reason offered to justify an exceptional sentence can be considered only if it takes into account factors other than those which are used in computing the standard range sentence for the offense." When a judge imposes an exceptional sentence, he must set forth findings of fact and conclusions of law supporting it. A reviewing court will reverse the sentence if it finds that "under a clearly erroneous standard there is insufficient evidence in the record to support the reasons for imposing an exceptional sentence."

Pursuant to the plea agreement, the State recommended a sentence within the standard range of 49 to 53 months. After hearing Yolanda's description of the kidnaping, however, the judge rejected the State's recommendation and imposed an exceptional sentence of 90 months—37 months beyond the standard maximum. He justified the sentence on the ground that petitioner had acted with "deliberate cruelty," a statutorily enumerated ground for departure in domestic-violence cases.

Faced with an unexpected increase of more than three years in his sentence, petitioner objected. The judge accordingly conducted a 3-day bench hearing featuring testimony from petitioner, Yolanda, Ralphy, a police officer, and medical experts. After the hearing, he issued 32 findings of fact, concluding:

> The defendant's motivation to commit kidnapping was complex, contributed to by his mental condition and personality disorders, the pressures of the divorce litigation, the impending trust litigation trial and anger over his troubled interpersonal relationships with his spouse and

> children. While he misguidedly intended to forcefully reunite his family, his attempt to do so was subservient to his desire to terminate lawsuits and modify title ownerships to his benefit. The defendant's methods were more homogeneous than his motive. He used stealth and surprise, and took advantage of the victim's isolation. He immediately employed physical violence, restrained the victim with tape, and threatened her with injury and death to herself and others. He immediately coerced the victim into providing information by the threatening application of a knife. He violated a subsisting restraining order.

The judge adhered to his initial determination of deliberate cruelty. Petitioner appealed, arguing that this sentencing procedure deprived him of his federal constitutional right to have a jury determine beyond a reasonable doubt all facts legally essential to his sentence. . . .

II

This case requires us to apply the rule we expressed in *Apprendi v. New Jersey*, 530 U.S. 466, 490 (2000): "Other than the fact of a prior conviction, any fact that increases the penalty for a crime beyond the prescribed statutory maximum must be submitted to a jury, and proved beyond a reasonable doubt." This rule reflects two longstanding tenets of common-law criminal jurisprudence: that the "truth of every accusation" against a defendant "should afterwards be confirmed by the unanimous suffrage of twelve of his equals and neighbours," and that "an accusation which lacks any particular fact which the law makes essential to the punishment is . . . no accusation within the requirements of the common law, and it is no accusation in reason." . . .

In this case, petitioner was sentenced to more than three years above the 53-month statutory maximum of the standard range because he had acted with "deliberate cruelty." The facts supporting that finding were neither admitted by petitioner nor found by a jury. The State nevertheless contends that there was no *Apprendi* violation because the relevant "statutory maximum" is not 53 months, but the 10-year maximum for class B felonies. . . . It observes that no exceptional sentence may exceed that limit. Our precedents make clear, however, that the "statutory maximum" for *Apprendi* purposes is the maximum sentence a judge may impose solely on the basis of the facts reflected in the jury verdict or admitted by the defendant. In other words, the relevant "statutory maximum" is not the maximum sentence a judge may impose after finding additional facts, but the maximum he may impose without any additional findings. When a judge inflicts punishment that the jury's verdict alone does not allow, the jury has not found all the facts "which the law makes essential to the punishment," and the judge exceeds his proper authority.

The judge in this case could not have imposed the exceptional 90-month sentence solely on the basis of the facts admitted in the guilty plea. Those facts alone were insufficient because, as the Washington Supreme Court has explained, "[a] reason offered to justify an exceptional sentence can be considered only if it takes into account factors other than those which are used in computing the standard range sentence for the offense," which in this case included the elements of second-degree kidnaping and the use of a firearm. Had the judge imposed the 90-month sentence solely on the basis of the plea, he would have been reversed. The "maximum sentence" is no more 10 years here than it was 20 years in *Apprendi* (because that is what the judge could have imposed upon finding a hate crime) or death in *Ring* (because that is what the judge could have imposed upon finding an aggravator). . . .

III

Our commitment to *Apprendi* in this context reflects not just respect for longstanding precedent, but the need to give intelligible content to the right of jury trial. That right is no mere procedural formality, but a fundamental reservation of power in our constitutional structure. Just as suffrage ensures the people's ultimate control in the legislative and executive branches, jury trial is meant to ensure their control in the judiciary. *Apprendi* carries out this design by ensuring that the judge's authority to sentence derives wholly from the jury's verdict. Without that restriction, the jury would not exercise the control that the Framers intended. . . .

NOTES & QUESTIONS ON SENTENCING GUIDELINES

1. *Mandatory versus advisory guidelines.* What constitutional remedy was imposed in *Blakely*? Instead of making the guidelines disappear entirely (and preventing judges from making any reference to them), judges can still consult with the sentencing guidelines. Instead, just their mandatory nature was ruled unconstitutional in *Blakely*. Does the distinction between mandatory versus advisory guidelines carry constitutional significance? At the end of the day, if the guidelines help determine the fate of the defendant, does it matter whether the guidelines are merely advisory or mandatory? What if the number of judges utilizing the newly "advisory" guidelines is nearly universal? Does that change your assessment?

2. *The federal sentencing guidelines. Blakely* held state sentencing guidelines unconstitutional if they include sentencing enhancements determined by

the judge instead of the jury. In *United States v. Booker*, 543 U.S. 220 (2005), the Supreme Court evaluated the Federal Sentencing Guidelines. Predictably, the Federal Guidelines suffered the same fate as state guidelines on account of *Apprendi*. The Supreme Court noted:

> As the dissenting opinions in *Blakely* recognized, there is no distinction of constitutional significance between the Federal Sentencing Guidelines and the Washington procedures at issue in that case. This conclusion rests on the premise, common to both systems, that the relevant sentencing rules are mandatory and impose binding requirements on all sentencing judges.

Like the state guidelines at issue in *Blakely*, the Supreme Court concluded in *Booker* that judges could still consult the Federal Sentencing Guidelines but were no longer bound by them. In practice, this means that a judge can depart from the sentencing guidelines if the judge believes that the sentence contemplated by the guidelines would be too harsh.

3. *The Federal Sentencing Commission.* The federal sentencing guidelines were authored by the Federal Sentencing Commission, rather than by Congress. Why was this fact not sufficient to immunize them from constitutional attack? The Commission was composed of learned experts with deep knowledge of criminology and criminal justice, with a goal of producing a set of coherent standards to promote consistency across cases. The goal of the guidelines was to improve consistently while at the same time adding empirical and scientific rigor to the sentencing process. Should this have made a difference to the outcome of *United States v. Booker?*

4. *Sentencing diminution.* Imagine an alternate scheme not at issue in either *Blakely* or *Booker*. Say that Congress or a state legislature went through the penal code and increased the sentencing ranges for all crimes. Then, imagine that the sentencing guidelines were limited to sentencing diminutions based on mitigating circumstances. If the defendant failed to qualify for any sentencing diminution, then the defendant would receive the higher sentence called for in the statute. The mitigating factors would be found by the judge, rather than the jury. Unlike in *Blakely* and *Booker*, where the defendants faced higher sentences because of the judge's finding of certain aggravating factors, in this hypothetical situation the defendant would simply *fail* to qualify for mitigating circumstances. Would such a system satisfy the Sixth Amendment right to a jury trial?

D. THE ROLE OF VICTIMS

A key procedural element in many sentencing hearings is the reading of a victim impact statement before the judge renders a decision on the sentence.

This allows the victim to articulate how the crime has affected them as an individual, with concrete examples, and it also gives the victim an opportunity, in some situations, to say what punishment they believe would be appropriate (with the understanding that the victim's wishes do not control the sentencing decision). In a murder case, victim impact statements might be read by family and friends of the murder victim, who can attest to the hole in their lives left by the victim's absence. These statements are often the most gut-wrenching moments in the criminal process.

In *Booth v. Maryland*, 482 U.S. 496 (1987), the Supreme Court declared victim impact statements unconstitutional under the Eighth Amendment. But just a few years later, the Supreme Court reconsidered its decision. As you read the following case, identify the reasons for the Court's change of heart.

Payne v. Tennessee

Supreme Court of the United States
501 U.S. 808 (1991)

Chief Justice REHNQUIST delivered the opinion of the Court.

In this case we reconsider our holdings in *Booth v. Maryland*, 482 U.S. 496 (1987), and *South Carolina v. Gathers*, 490 U.S. 805 (1989), that the Eighth Amendment bars the admission of victim impact evidence during the penalty phase of a capital trial.

Petitioner, Pervis Tyrone Payne, was convicted by a jury on two counts of first-degree murder and one count of assault with intent to commit murder in the first degree. He was sentenced to death for each of the murders and to 30 years in prison for the assault.

The victims of Payne's offenses were 28-year-old Charisse Christopher, her 2-year-old daughter Lacie, and her 3-year-old son Nicholas. The three lived together in an apartment in Millington, Tennessee, across the hall from Payne's girlfriend, Bobbie Thomas. On Saturday, June 27, 1987, Payne visited Thomas' apartment several times in expectation of her return from her mother's house in Arkansas, but found no one at home. On one visit, he left his overnight bag, containing clothes and other items for his weekend stay, in the hallway outside Thomas' apartment. With the bag were three cans of malt liquor.

Payne passed the morning and early afternoon injecting cocaine and drinking beer. Later, he drove around the town with a friend in the friend's car, each of them taking turns reading a pornographic magazine. Sometime around 3 P.M., Payne returned to the apartment complex, entered the Christophers' apartment, and began making sexual advances towards Charisse. Charisse resisted and Payne became violent. A neighbor who resided in the apartment directly beneath the Christophers heard Charisse screaming, "'Get out, get out,'" as if she were telling the children to leave."

The noise briefly subsided and then began, "horribly loud." The neighbor called the police after she heard a "blood curdling scream" from the Christopher's apartment. . . .

During the sentencing phase of the trial . . . . [t]he State presented the testimony of Charisse's mother, Mary Zvolanek. When asked how Nicholas had been affected by the murders of his mother and sister, she responded: "He cries for his mom. He doesn't seem to understand why she doesn't come home. And he cries for his sister Lacie. He comes to me many times during the week and asks me, Grandmama, do you miss my Lacie. And I tell him yes. He says, I'm worried about my Lacie."

In arguing for the death penalty during closing argument, the prosecutor commented on the continuing effects of Nicholas' experience, stating: "But we do know that Nicholas was alive. And Nicholas was in the same room. Nicholas was still conscious. His eyes were open. He responded to the paramedics. He was able to follow their directions. He was able to hold his intestines in as he was carried to the ambulance. So he knew what happened to his mother and baby sister." . . . .

We granted certiorari to reconsider our holdings in *Booth* and *Gathers* that the Eighth Amendment prohibits a capital sentencing jury from considering "victim impact" evidence relating to the personal characteristics of the victim and the emotional impact of the crimes on the victim's family.

In *Booth* . . . [t]his Court held by a 5-to-4 vote that the Eighth Amendment prohibits a jury from considering a victim impact statement at the sentencing phase of a capital trial. The Court made clear that the admissibility of victim impact evidence was not to be determined on a case-by-case basis, but that such evidence was per se inadmissible in the sentencing phase of a capital case except to the extent that it "relate[d] directly to the circumstances of the crime." 482 U.S., at 507, n. 10. . . .

The *Booth* Court began its analysis with the observation that the capital defendant must be treated as a "uniquely individual human bein[g]," and therefore the Constitution requires the jury to make an individualized determination as to whether the defendant should be executed based on the "character of the individual and the circumstances of the crime." The Court concluded that while no prior decision of this Court had mandated that only the defendant's character and immediate characteristics of the crime may constitutionally be considered, other factors are irrelevant to the capital sentencing decision unless they have "some bearing on the defendant's 'personal responsibility and moral guilt." To the extent that victim impact evidence presents "factors about which the defendant was unaware, and that were irrelevant to the decision to kill," the Court concluded, it has nothing to do with the "blameworthiness of a particular defendant." . . .

Booth and *Gathers* were based on two premises: that evidence relating to a particular victim or to the harm that a capital defendant causes a victim's family do not in general reflect on the defendant's "blameworthiness," and that only evidence relating to "blameworthiness" is relevant to the capital sentencing decision. However, the assessment of harm caused by the defendant as a result of the crime charged has understandably been an important concern of the criminal law, both in determining the elements of the offense and in determining the appropriate punishment. Thus, two equally blameworthy criminal defendants may be guilty of different offenses solely because their acts cause differing amounts of harm. "If a bank robber aims his gun at a guard, pulls the trigger, and kills his target, he may be put to death. If the gun unexpectedly misfires, he may not. His moral guilt in both cases is identical, but his responsibility in the former is greater." The same is true with respect to two defendants, each of whom participates in a robbery, and each of whom acts with reckless disregard for human life; if the robbery in which the first defendant participated results in the death of a victim, he may be subjected to the death penalty, but if the robbery in which the second defendant participates does not result in the death of a victim, the death penalty may not be imposed. . . .

Whatever the prevailing sentencing philosophy, the sentencing authority has always been free to consider a wide range of relevant material. In the federal system, we observed that "a judge may appropriately conduct an inquiry broad in scope, largely unlimited either as to the kind of information he may consider, or the source from which it may come." . . .

The *Booth* Court reasoned that victim impact evidence must be excluded because it would be difficult, if not impossible, for the defendant to rebut such evidence without shifting the focus of the sentencing hearing away from the defendant, thus creating a "'mini-trial' on the victim's character." In many cases the evidence relating to the victim is already before the jury at least in part because of its relevance at the guilt phase of the trial. But even as to additional evidence admitted at the sentencing phase, the mere fact that for tactical reasons it might not be prudent for the defense to rebut victim impact evidence makes the case no different than others in which a party is faced with this sort of a dilemma. . . .

Payne echoes the concern voiced in *Booth*'s case that the admission of victim impact evidence permits a jury to find that defendants whose victims were assets to their community are more deserving of punishment than those whose victims are perceived to be less worthy. As a general matter, however, victim impact evidence is not offered to encourage comparative judgments of this kind—for instance, that the killer of a hardworking, devoted parent deserves the death penalty, but that the murderer of a reprobate does not. It is designed to show instead each victim's "uniqueness as an individual human being," whatever the jury might think the loss to the community resulting from his death might be. . . .

We are now of the view that a State may properly conclude that for the jury to assess meaningfully the defendant's moral culpability and blameworthiness, it should have before it at the sentencing phase evidence of the specific harm caused by the defendant. . . .

Justice MARSHALL, with whom Justice BLACKMUN joins, dissenting.

Power, not reason, is the new currency of this Court's decisionmaking. Four Terms ago, a five-Justice majority of this Court held that "victim impact" evidence of the type at issue in this case could not constitutionally be introduced during the penalty phase of a capital trial. *Booth v. Maryland,* 482 U.S. 496 (1987). By another 5-4 vote, a majority of this Court rebuffed an attack upon this ruling just two Terms ago. *South Carolina v. Gathers,* 490 U.S. 805 (1989). Nevertheless, having expressly invited respondent to renew the attack, today's majority overrules *Booth* and *Gathers* and credits the dissenting views expressed in those cases. Neither the law nor the facts supporting *Booth* and *Gathers* underwent any change in the last four years. Only the personnel of this Court did.

In dispatching *Booth* and *Gathers* to their graves, today's majority ominously suggests that an even more extensive upheaval of this Court's precedents may be in store. Renouncing this Court's historical commitment to a conception of "the judiciary as a source of impersonal and reasoned judgments," the majority declares itself free to discard any principle of constitutional liberty which was recognized or reaffirmed over the dissenting votes of four Justices and with which five or more Justices *now* disagree. The implications of this radical new exception to the doctrine of *stare decisis* are staggering. The majority today sends a clear signal that scores of established constitutional liberties are now ripe for reconsideration, thereby inviting the very type of open defiance of our precedents that the majority rewards in this case. Because I believe that this Court owes more to its constitutional precedents in general and to *Booth* and *Gathers* in particular, I dissent. . . .

NOTES & QUESTIONS ON VICTIM IMPACT STATEMENTS

1. *The content of the statement.* There were substantial differences between the victim impact statements in *Booth* and *Payne*. In *Booth*, the victim

impact statement included a family member of the deceased victim who articulated their conclusions about the defendant, the significant of his crime, and family members' opinion about an appropriate punishment. In *Payne*, though, the victim impact statement was different; the family members simply spoke about the significance of the victim's absence from their lives, without passing judgment on the defendant and expressing a view, pro or con, regarding the death penalty. In *Bosse v. Oklahoma*, 137 S. Ct. 1, 2 (2016), the Supreme Court concluded that *Payne* had not overruled *Booth*, and that the type of statements made in *Booth*—conclusions about the defendant—were still inappropriate at sentencing, at least at a capital sentencing hearing. *Payne*'s endorsement of victim impact statements appears limited to statements regarding the impact of the crime on the victim and the victim's family, friends, and colleagues. Do you agree that the content of the victim impact statement should determine its constitutionality?

2. *The value of a life.* An important objection to the use of victim impact statements is that the procedure inevitably prioritizes the lives of victims with a large and deep social network, while forgotten victims living on the margins of society (who are often victimized by crime) will be less likely to have their perpetrators punished severely, since they will have few family members or friends to speak of the void left by their absence. Did the majority in *Payne* do enough to counter this argument?

3. *The point of criminal punishment.* The issue addressed in *Payne* speaks to a fundamental question about the nature of criminal justice: What place do victims have in the basic structure of criminal procedure? Fundamentally, is trial and punishment designed to vindicate the interests of the victims or is it designed to protect the community at large? In the latter conception, the benefits to victims are collateral to the more basic goal of serving the public's interests. In the United States, the criminal process is controlled by a public prosecutor and defense counsel, with no formal role played by the victims or their legal representation. However, some foreign legal systems follow the French model, in which victims are formal parties to the legal proceedings (*partie civile*), including the right to make arguments to the court on all matters before it. With this comparative perspective in mind, re-evaluate the legitimacy of victim impact statements in American courts. Do they seem less significant and therefore less objectionable?

4. *The Crime Victims' Rights Act.* In 2004, Congress enacted the Crime Victims' Rights Act, 18 U.S.C. § 3771, which confers on victims in federal cases particular procedural protections during key stages of a criminal case. For example, the statute requires that federal prosecutions inform victims, in advance, of hearing dates, and also requires that prosecutors inform victims that a plea deal has been struck. Traditionally, prosecutors place great

weight on the opinions of the victims (or their families in murder cases) when deciding whether to agree to a proposed plea deal with a defendant, though formally the victims have no right to block a deal that they object to. After all, the prosecutor works for the public and represents the community at large; the prosecution, as a fiduciary of the public, may disagree with the victims regarding an appropriate dispensation of the case. The Crime Victims' Rights Act did not change that, though its notice requirement would give the victims an opportunity to appear before a district court and voice their objection before a judge decided whether to accept the terms of the plea deal. In theory, a judge could, after hearing these objections, refuse to ratify the terms of the deal by refusing to impose the sentence negotiated by the prosecution and the defense.

PROBLEM CASE

Between 2007-2008, state and federal prosecutors investigated billionaire Jeffrey Epstein after allegations surfaced that he had systematically paid underage girls to engage in sex acts with him at his Florida home. Epstein assembled a group of high-profile attorneys who negotiated an omnibus deal to resolve both his state and federal criminal exposure. The deal required Epstein to plead guilty to a state charge of soliciting prostitution and serve 18 months in jail, while at the same time he entered into a non-prosecution agreement with the federal government. (The federal non-prosecution agreement was negotiated with the approval of then-U.S. Attorney Alexander Acosta.) Victims in the case later filed a federal lawsuit alleging that the federal non-prosecution agreement, and Epstein's sentencing, violated the federal Crime Victims' Rights Act, since the victims were not informed about the deal. In February 2019, a federal district court considered whether the agreement violated the Crime Victims' Rights Act. The federal government argued that the Act's protections did not apply to non-prosecution agreements, but the court decided otherwise:

> The expansive context of the CVRA lends itself to only one interpretation; namely, that victims should be notified of significant events resulting in resolution of their case without a trial. Reading into the statute a negative implication that victims need not be informed of non-prosecution agreements, and only informed of the more common events of plea bargains or deferred prosecution agreements, would be inconsistent with the goal of the CVRA. In the context of plea agreements, the CVRA provides victims with rights prior to the acceptance of plea agreements. Furthermore, victims obtain rights under the CVRA even before prosecution. Based on this authority, the Court concludes that the CVRA must extend to conferral about non-prosecution agreements.

Doe 1 v. United States, No. 08-80736-CIV, 2019 WL 761702, at *15 (S.D. Fla. Feb. 21, 2019). Since the CVRA was violated, what remedy should the district court order? Can and should the district judge unwind the non-prosecution agreement?

E. PRACTICE & POLICY

The debate over methods of execution has plagued the moral and legal debate over capital punishment in America. For many years, abolitionists seeking to end capital punishment focused on a litigation strategy designed to get the Supreme Court to declare the entire practice unconstitutional as a violation of the Eighth Amendment. But with *Gregg v. Georgia* in 1976, the Supreme Court effectively closed that door, and leading death penalty opponents moved on to a new effort: litigating the methods and procedures used in executions themselves. The goal of this litigation strategy is itself contested. The anti–death penalty advocates argue that they seek to make the practice more humane, consistent with the Eighth Amendment's prohibition on cruel and unusual punishment, while death penalty supporters call foul and insist that the opponents are seeking to end capital punishment one method at a time. The following materials look at this controversy over methods of execution, which is very much ongoing.

❧ **Botched executions.** There have been several high-profile examples of botched executions. For example, on April 29, 2014, state officials executed Clayton D. Lockett in Oklahoma using lethal injection. The execution did not go as planned. The prison employees had problems inserting the IV in a vein in Lockett's arm and ended up placing the IV in Lockett's groin area. In retrospect it is unclear whether the even the groin placement worked correctly. After first receiving a sedative, a physician concluded that Lockett was sufficiently sedated that the rest of the execution process could proceed. After the second and third drugs were injected to paralyze Lockett and then stop his heart, however, it became clear that Lockett was not, in fact, fully sedated. *The New York Times* described what happened next:

> At that point, witnesses said, things began to go awry. Mr. Lockett's body twitched, his foot shook and he mumbled, witnesses said. At 6:37 P.M., he tried to rise and exhaled loudly. At that point, prison officials pulled a curtain in front of the witnesses and the doctor discovered a "vein failure" . . . .

Lockett subsequently died of a heart attack. One of his lawyers described the execution as torture. But despite these and other well-known press reports, the Supreme Court declined to intervene in lethal injection protocols in *Glossip*.

❧ **Which drugs to use.** Traditionally, the drug of choice for lethal injections was a three-drug sequence: sodium thiopental to sedate the prisoner, pancuronium bromide to induce paralysis, and potassium chloride to trigger heart failure. The goal of the sequence was to ensure that the condemned prisoner was fully unconscious before they suffered cardiac arrest, thus making the procedure, in theory at least, completely pain-free. Some states have abandoned the three-drug sequence, preferring instead to use a single, massive dose of a barbiturate, such as sodium pentobarbital. For example, the State of Ohio executed a prisoner, Johnnie Baston, in 2011, using the single-drug method. Recently, Nebraska decided to use a powerful opioid called fentanyl. Few states have adopted the one-drug method, though reasons vary. Some states might want to avoid the negative reaction to the one-drug method from lethal injection opponents, while others might have been wary of issues related to drug availability.

❧ **Drug companies refusing to provide drugs.** Some pharmaceutical companies have started to refuse to sell their compounds to prison systems for use in lethal injections, causing supply problems in these states. Pharmaceutical companies have multiple reasons to object. The first, and most basic, reason is an ethical or moral one: Pharmaceutical companies develop medicines to cure patients rather than to kill prisoners. Also, pharmaceutical corporations might object to being associated with lethal executions because the link could be the basis for a consumer boycott or just negative publicity. Whether motivated by ethics or economic self-interest, pharmaceutical companies receive little benefit from participating in executions. Finally, many pharmaceutical companies are headquartered in Europe where the death penalty is considered a violation of European human rights pursuant to Optional Protocol 13 of the European Convention on Human Rights. Even U.S.-based pharmaceutical companies dislike supplying the drugs, leaving states to resort to disguising their identity when attempting to purchase the drugs or to buying the drugs from after-market retailers. Some pharmaceutical companies have gone so far as to file lawsuits against states that attempt to use their drugs without permission. See, e.g., *Fresenius Kabi USA, LLC v. Nebraska*, 733 F. App'x 871, 872 (8th Cir. 2018) (review of German pharmaceutical company's request for temporary restraining order and preliminary injunction preventing Nebraska from using the corporation's drugs during an execution).

❧ **Doctors refusing to participate.** Besides the difficulty in securing the drugs, states also have difficulty securing the participation of physicians to oversee lethal injection. As noted above, the placement of the IV requires a trained nurse or doctor. Furthermore, the injection of the drugs in the three-drug sequence requires a physician who makes an assessment that the first drug has taken effect before the second and third drugs are administered, respectively. Many physicians refuse to participate because they consider lethal injections inconsistent with their professional obligation to heal (rather than to kill) their patients. Indeed, a central tenet of medical ethics is patient autonomy and in a lethal injection, the execution occurs against the express wishes of the prisoner. Some death penalty advocates complain that physicians are on the verge of effectively outlawing the death penalty by strategically wielding their power to refuse participation. But as the American Medical Association stated in a recent amicus brief to the Supreme Court:

> What people much prefer is a way to accomplish the deed while believing there is something humane about it. Society wants to delude itself into a belief that capital punishment no longer represents a weighted moral choice, but is now somehow scientific—nearly antiseptic. This delusion, however, cheapens life and makes its extinction easier. The medical profession, whose "essential quality" is an interest in humanity and which reveres human life, should have no part in this charade.

Brief of American Medical Association, Amicus Curiae, in Support of Neither Party, *Bucklew v. Precythe*, 2018 WL 3599463, at *12-13 (2018).

Some states have responded to the difficulty of finding trained physicians to participate in executions by promising absolute secrecy regarding their involvement in the execution. The hope, in other words, is to find physicians who believe that participation in executions is consistent with their ethical obligations but nonetheless do not want to face informal or formal professional sanctions. For example, Oklahoma has the following statute requiring secrecy in the death process: "The identity of all persons who participate in or administer the execution process and persons who supply the drugs, medical supplies or medical equipment for the execution shall be confidential and shall not be subject to discovery in any civil or criminal proceedings." Okla. Stat. Ann. tit. 22, § 1015. Although it is hard to determine whether the secrecy provisions are having a causal effect, a few physicians continue to participate—quietly—in executions. Indeed, consider the following assessment:

> [D]octors are not "prohibited" from participating in executions. As a legal matter, the ethical guidelines of the AMA and similar associations are not binding or enforceable. As a practical matter, they likewise do not impose a barrier to participation. No doctor has ever been disciplined for participating in an execution in this country, and every court that has considered the matter has concluded that state medical boards cannot impose discipline, particularly where, as in most states, the governing death penalty statute appears to contemplate some form of physician participation. Moreover, the ethical guidelines of other medical

> professionals (such as nurses and EMTs) are nearly identical to the AMA's guidelines, and these guidelines have not stopped those medical professionals from participating in executions. This suggests that the ethical guidelines themselves play little role in medical professionals' decisions about whether to participate in executions.

Ty Alper, *The Truth About Physician Participation in Lethal Injection Executions*, 88 N.C. L. Rev. 11, 26 (2009).

CHAPTER 19

Double Jeopardy

INTRODUCTION

The Fifth Amendment states that "nor shall any person be subject for the same offense to be twice put in jeopardy of life or limb." This provision constitutionalized the common law pleas of *autrefois acquit* and *autrefois convict*, meaning formerly acquitted or formerly convicted. Determining when the double jeopardy protection applies requires determining a series of threshold questions:

- When does jeopardy attach?
- If jeopardy did "attach," did the prior procedure result in a "bar" to reprosecution (in other words, was the defendant in prior jeopardy)?
- Was the prior offense "the same offense" for purposes of double jeopardy?
- Are the offenses being tried by the "same sovereign"?
- Does one of the recognized exceptions to double jeopardy apply?

Because of these complications, jurists have sometimes suggested that double jeopardy is not even a single doctrine but rather a cluster of related prohibitions that apply in the following contexts:

> The broad umbrella term we call "double jeopardy" today embraces (in its federal manifestation) four distinct species: 1) classic former jeopardy, arising out of the common law pleas at bar of autrefois convict and autrefois acquit; 2) simultaneous jeopardy, involving largely issues of merger and multiple punishment and lying on the at-times blurred boundary between constitutional law and statutory construction; 3) the problem of retrial following mistrial; and 4) collateral estoppel.

Fields v. State, 96 Md. App. 722, 725, 626 A.2d 1037, 1038-39 (1993).

Breaking down the categories outlined in this quote, one can see that the first category represents the most basic and uncomplicated form of double jeopardy. The second category shows up when the dividing line between offenses is unclear, so that a prosecutor might be accused of "double charging" or "double dipping" by treating a single offense as a series of separate offenses warranting separate charges and, ultimately, increased punishment. The third category deals with situations where the first trial ends in mistrial, thus leading to some uncertainty about (1) whether the jeopardy from the first trial has terminated, meaning that a retrial would constitute a second jeopardy; or (2) whether the jeopardy from the first trial never really ends, thus allowing a second trial as a continuation of the original jeopardy. As we will see below, courts have generally permitted retrial after mistrial in some cases but not in others, and the materials below will help identify the different triggering events for these rules: a hung jury, a defense request for a mistrial, or a trial judge's declaration of a mistrial following the prosecutor's conduct.

A. MECHANICS OF THE DOUBLE JEOPARDY RULE

At its most basic, the double jeopardy protection speaks to larger themes of finality and predictability that stand at the core of the rule of law and are also embodied by related doctrines in civil law, including res judicata. Statutes of limitations also perform a similar function. They are designed to give the individual the comfort of knowing that legal liability, whether civil liability or criminal "jeopardy," are not ongoing and eternal, but rather are finite and defined, and that there is a stopping point to the government's ability to lodge a criminal complaint and seek punishment. In the case of double jeopardy, that limitation is defined by the existence of a "first" jeopardy. This section will be devoted to defining and understanding the nature of that first jeopardy. Consequently, the two most important doctrinal elements of the double jeopardy rule are what constitute the "same offense" and when jeopardy first "attaches."

1. The Same Offense Requirement

In the following two cases, the Supreme Court deals with cases where the defendant alleges that they were prosecuted twice for the "same offense." The first case, *Blockburger,* established the test that has prevailed in the case law ever since. The second case, *Brown v. Ohio,* requires an application of the *Blockburger* test to a new set of facts.

Blockburger v. United States

Supreme Court of the United States
284 U.S. 299 (1932)

Mr. Justice SUTHERLAND delivered the opinion of the Court.

The petitioner was charged with violating provisions of the Harrison Narcotic Act. The indictment contained five counts. The jury returned a verdict against petitioner upon the second, third, and fifth counts only. Each of these counts charged a sale of morphine hydrochloride to the same purchaser. The second count charged a sale on a specified day of ten grains of the drug not in or from the original stamped package; the third count charged a sale on the following day of eight grains of the drug not in or from the original stamped package; the fifth count charged the latter sale also as having been made not in pursuance of a written order of the purchaser as required by the statute. The court sentenced petitioner to five years' imprisonment and a fine of $2,000 upon each count, the terms of imprisonment to run consecutively; and this judgment was affirmed on appeal.

The principal contentions here made by petitioner are as follows: (1) That, upon the facts, the two sales charged in the second and third counts as having been made to the same person constitute a single offense; and (2) that the sale charged in the third count as having been made not from the original stamped package, and the same sale charged in the fifth count as having been made not in pursuance of a written order of the purchaser, constitute but one offense, for which only a single penalty lawfully may be imposed.

One. The sales charged in the second and third counts, although made to the same person, were distinct and separate sales made at different times. It appears from the evidence that, shortly after delivery of the drug which was the subject of the first sale, the purchaser paid for an additional quantity, which was delivered the next day. But the first sale had been consummated, and the payment for the additional drug, however closely following, was the initiation of a separate and distinct sale completed by its delivery.

The contention on behalf of petitioner is that these two sales, having been made to the same purchaser and following each other, with no substantial interval of time between the delivery of the drug in the first transaction and the payment for the second quantity sold, constitute a single continuing offense. The contention is unsound. The distinction between the transactions here involved and an offense continuous in its character is well settled, as was pointed out by this court in the case of *In re Snow*, 120 U.S. 274. There it was held that the offense of cohabiting with more than one woman was a continuous offense, and was committed, in the sense of the statute, where there was a living or dwelling together as husband

and wife. The court said: "It is, inherently, a continuous offense, having duration; and not an offense consisting of an isolated act. . . . A distinction is laid down in adjudged cases and in text-writers between an offense continuous in its character, like the one at bar, and a case where the statute is aimed at an offense that can be committed uno ictu." 120 U.S., at 281, 286.

The Narcotic Act does not create the offense of engaging in the business of selling the forbidden drugs, but penalizes any sale made in the absence of either of the qualifying requirements set forth. Each of several successive sales constitutes a distinct offense, however closely they may follow each other. The distinction stated by Mr. Wharton is that, "when the impulse is single, but one indictment lies, no matter how long the action may continue. If successive impulses are separately given, even though all unite in swelling a common stream of action, separate indictments lie." *Wharton's Criminal Law* (11th Ed.) § 34. Or, as stated in note 3 to that section, "The test is whether the individual acts are prohibited, or the course of action which they constitute. If the former, then each act is punishable separately. . . . If the latter, there can be but one penalty."

In the present case, the first transaction, resulting in a sale, had come to an end. The next sale was not the result of the original impulse, but of a fresh one—that is to say, of a new bargain. The question is controlled, not by the *Snow* Case, but by such cases as that of *Ebeling v. Morgan*, 237 U.S. 625. There the accused was convicted under several counts of a willful tearing, etc., of mail bags with intent to rob. The court stated the question to be whether one who, in the same transaction, tears or cuts successively mail bags of the United States used in conveyance of the mails, with intent to rob or steal any such mail, is guilty of a single offense, or of additional offenses because of each successive cutting with the criminal intent charged." Answering this question, the court, after quoting the statute:

> These words plainly indicate that it was the intention of the lawmakers to protect each and every mail bag from felonious injury and mutilation. Whenever any one mail bag is thus torn, cut, or injured, the offense is complete. Although the transaction of cutting the mail bags was in a sense continuous, the complete statutory offense was committed every time a mail bag was cut in the manner described, with the intent charged. The offense as to each separate bag was complete when that bag was cut, irrespective of any attack upon, or mutilation of, any other bag.

Two. Section 1 of the Narcotic Act creates the offense of selling any of the forbidden drugs except in or from the original stamped package; and section 2 creates the offense of selling any of such drugs not in pursuance of a written order of the person to whom the drug is sold. Thus, upon the face of the statute, two distinct offenses are created. Here there was but one sale, and the question is whether, both sections being violated by the same act, the accused committed two offenses or only one.

The statute is not aimed at sales of the forbidden drugs qua sales, a matter entirely beyond the authority of Congress, but at sales of such drugs in violation of the requirements set forth in sections 1 and 2, enacted as aids to the enforcement of the stamp tax imposed by the act.

Each of the offenses created requires proof of a different element.

The applicable rule is that, where the same act or transaction constitutes a violation of two distinct statutory provisions, the test to be applied to determine whether there are two offenses or only one, is whether each provision requires proof of a fact which the other does not. . . . Applying the test, we must conclude that here, although both sections were violated by the one sale, two offenses were committed. . . .

Three. It is not necessary to discuss the additional assignments of error in respect of cross-examination, admission of testimony, statements made by the district attorney to the jury claimed to be prejudicial, and instructions of the court. These matters were properly disposed of by the court below. Nor is there merit in the contention that the language of the penal section of the Narcotic Act, "any person who violates or fails to comply with any of the requirements of this act," shall be punished, etc., is to be construed as imposing a single punishment for a violation of the distinct requirements of sections 1 and 2 when accomplished by one and the same sale. The plain meaning of the provision is that each offense is subject to the penalty prescribed; and, if that be too harsh, the remedy must be afforded by act of Congress, not by judicial legislation under the guise of construction. Under the circumstances, so far as disclosed, it is true that the imposition of the full penalty of fine and imprisonment upon each count seems unduly severe; but there may have been other facts and circumstances before the trial court properly influencing the extent of the punishment. In any event, the matter was one for that court, with whose judgment there is no warrant for interference on our part. Judgment affirmed.

While *Blockburger* required the Court to determine what constituted a single drug offense under the Narcotics Act, the following case requires an examination of lesser-included offenses. What counts as a lesser-included offense is sometimes difficult to determine, but there are some classic and relatively uncontroversial examples. For example, unlawful entry is a lesser-included offense of burglary, while theft is a lesser-included offense of robbery. In both cases, the greater offense will require an element that is missing from the lesser offense (such as the application of force that distinguishes robbery from theft). In the following case, the defendant was convicted of operating a vehicle without the owner's permission. Should this conviction bar the state from subsequently prosecuting the defendant for the greater offense of automobile theft?

Brown v. Ohio

Supreme Court of the United States
432 U.S. 161 (1977)

Mr. Justice POWELL delivered the opinion of the Court.

The question in this case is whether the Double Jeopardy Clause of the Fifth Amendment bars prosecution and punishment for the crime of stealing an automobile following prosecution and punishment for the lesser included offense of operating the same vehicle without the owner's consent.

I

On November 29, 1973, the petitioner, Nathaniel Brown, stole a 1965 Chevrolet from a parking lot in East Cleveland, Ohio. Nine days later, on December 8, 1973, Brown was caught driving the car in Wickliffe, Ohio. The Wickliffe police charged him with "joyriding" [—] taking or operating the car without the owner's consent in violation of Ohio Rev. Code Ann. 4549.04(D). . . . Brown pleaded guilty to this charge and was sentenced to 30 days in jail and a $100 fine.

Upon his release from jail on January 8, 1974, Brown was returned to East Cleveland to face further charges, and on February 5 he was indicted by the Cuyahoga County grand jury. The indictment was in two counts, the first charging the theft of the car "on or about the 29th day of November 1973," in violation of Ohio Rev. Code Ann. 4549.04(A), and the second charging joyriding on the same date in violation of s 4549.04(D). . . . Brown objected to both counts of the indictment on the basis of former jeopardy.

II

The Double Jeopardy Clause of the Fifth Amendment, applicable to the States through the Fourteenth, provides that no person shall "be subject for the same offence to be twice put in jeopardy of life or limb." It has long been understood that separate statutory crimes need not be identical either in constituent elements or in actual proof in order to be the same within the meaning of the constitutional prohibition. The principal question in this case is whether auto theft and joyriding, a greater and lesser included offense under Ohio law, constitute the "same offence" under the Double Jeopardy Clause.

Because it was designed originally to embody the protection of the common-law pleas of former jeopardy, the Fifth Amendment double jeopardy guarantee serves principally as a restraint on courts and prosecutors. The legislature remains free under the Double Jeopardy Clause to define crimes and fix punishments; but once the legislature has acted courts may not impose more than one punishment for the same offense and prosecutors ordinarily may not attempt to secure that punishment in more than one trial.

The Double Jeopardy Clause "protects against a second prosecution for the same offense after acquittal. It protects against a second prosecution for the same offense after conviction. And it protects against multiple punishments for the same offense." Where consecutive sentences are imposed at a single criminal trial, the role of the constitutional guarantee is limited to assuring that the court does not exceed its legislative authorization by imposing multiple punishments for the same offense. Where successive prosecutions are at stake, the guarantee serves "a constitutional policy of finality for the defendant's benefit." That policy protects the accused from attempts to relitigate the facts underlying a prior acquittal and from attempts to secure additional punishment after a prior conviction and sentence.

The established test for determining whether two offenses are sufficiently distinguishable to permit the imposition of cumulative punishment was stated in *Blockburger v. United States*, 284 U.S. 299, 304 (1932): "The applicable rule is that where the same act or transaction constitutes a violation of two distinct statutory provisions, the test to be applied to determine whether there are two offenses or only one, is whether each provision requires proof of an additional fact which the other does not. . . ." This test emphasizes the elements of the two crimes. "If each requires proof of a fact that the other does not, the *Blockburger* test is satisfied, notwithstanding a substantial overlap in the proof offered to establish the crimes. . . ." *Iannelli v. United States*, 420 U.S. 770, 785 n. 17 (1975).

If two offenses are the same under this test for purposes of barring consecutive sentences at a single trial, they necessarily will be the same for purposes of barring successive prosecutions. Where the judge is forbidden to impose cumulative punishment for two crimes at the end of a single proceeding, the prosecutor is forbidden to strive for the same result in successive proceedings. Unless "each statute requires proof of an additional fact which the other does not," the Double Jeopardy Clause prohibits successive prosecutions as well as cumulative punishment.

We are mindful that the Ohio courts "have the final authority to interpret . . . that State's legislation." Here the Ohio Court of Appeals has authoritatively defined the elements of the two Ohio crimes: Joyriding consists of taking or operating a vehicle without the owner's consent, and auto theft consists of joyriding with the intent permanently to deprive the owner of possession. Joyriding is the lesser included offense. The prosecutor who has established joyriding need only prove the requisite intent in order to establish auto theft; the prosecutor who has established auto theft necessarily has established joyriding as well.

Applying the *Blockburger* test, we agree with the Ohio Court of Appeals that joyriding and auto theft, as defined by the court, constitute "the same statutory offense" within the meaning of the Double Jeopardy Clause. For it is clearly not the case that "each (statute) requires proof of a fact which the other does not." As is invariably true of a greater and lesser included offense, the lesser offense joyriding requires no proof beyond that which is required for conviction of the greater auto theft. The greater offense is therefore by definition the "same" for purposes of double jeopardy as any lesser offense included in it.

This conclusion merely restates what has been this Court's understanding of the Double Jeopardy Clause at least since *In re Nielsen* was decided in 1889. In that case the Court endorsed the rule that "where . . . a person has been tried and convicted for a crime which has various incidents included in it, he cannot be a second time tried for one of those incidents without being twice put in jeopardy for the same offense." 131 U.S., at 188.

Although in this formulation the conviction of the greater precedes the conviction of the lesser, the opinion makes it clear that the sequence is immaterial. Thus, the Court treated the formulation as just one application of the rule that two offenses are the same unless each requires proof that the other does not. And as another application of the same rule, the Court cited with approval the decision of *State v. Cooper*, 13 N.J.L. 361 (1833), where the New Jersey Supreme Court held that a conviction for arson barred a subsequent felony-murder indictment based on the death of a man killed in the fire. Whatever the sequence may be, the Fifth Amendment forbids successive prosecution and cumulative punishment for a greater and lesser included offense.

III

After correctly holding that joyriding and auto theft are the same offense under the Double Jeopardy Clause, the Ohio Court of Appeals nevertheless concluded that Nathaniel Brown could be convicted of both crimes because the charges against him focused on different parts of his 9-day joyride. We hold a different view. The Double Jeopardy Clause is not such a fragile guarantee that prosecutors can avoid its limitations by the simple expedient of dividing a single crime into a series of temporal or spatial units. The applicable Ohio statutes, as written and as construed in this case, make the theft and operation of a single car a single offense. Although the Wickliffe and East Cleveland authorities may have had different perspectives on Brown's offense, it was still only one offense under Ohio law. Accordingly, the specification of different dates in the two charges on which Brown was convicted cannot alter the fact that he was placed twice in jeopardy for the same offense in violation of the Fifth and Fourteenth Amendments. Reversed.

NOTES & QUESTIONS ON THE SAME OFFENSE REQUIREMENT

1. *Joyriding.* Do you agree with the Court's assessment that joyriding and automobile theft are the same offense for purposes of the Fifth Amendment? Specifically, do you agree with the Court's application of the *Blockburger* test to lesser-included offenses? Following the logic of *Brown v. Smith,* the prosecution of any greater offense will be barred by double jeopardy if the state prosecutes the defendant for a lesser offense. Prosecutors need to be careful when making charging decisions, because the lesser-included rule from *Brown v. Smith* could reoccur in many situations.

2. *Separate offenses.* In some situations, two separate statutes might codify offenses that are strikingly similar. If the prosecutor charges the defendant under both statutes, should this violate double jeopardy? The only way to answer this question is to analyze both statutes and determine if the statutes are alternate codifications of the "same offense" or codifications of two distinct offenses. What standard should govern this inquiry? In *Garrett v. United States,* 471 U.S. 773 (1985), the Supreme Court clarified that

> [w]here the same conduct violates two statutory provisions, the first step in the double jeopardy analysis is to determine whether the legislature—in this case Congress—intended that each violation be a separate offense. If Congress intended that there be only one offense—that is, a defendant could be convicted under either statutory provision for a single act, but not under both—there would be no statutory authorization for a subsequent prosecution after conviction of one of the two provisions, and that would end the double jeopardy analysis.

Id. at 778. *Garrett* involved the Comprehensive Drug Abuse Prevention and Control Act of 1970, 21 U.S.C. § 848, which created the offense of a "continuing criminal enterprise" (CCE) when the defendant commits three predicate drug offenses. The question before the Court was whether Garrett could be convicted of both CCE *and* the predicate offenses at the same time. The Court concluded that there was no double jeopardy prohibition to multiple convictions, using congressional intent as its lodestar. Do you agree with this result?

3. *Civil and criminal offenses.* Government agencies, such as the IRS, the SEC, or the FCC, will sometimes levy "civil fines" against an individual who has violated agency rules. At the same time, the violator might also be subject to criminal action, which could result either in imprisonment or more fines, this time "criminal" fines. Does the imposition of both criminal and civil fines violate double jeopardy? In *Hudson v. United States*, 522 U.S. 93 (1997), the Supreme Court said no. The government imposed monetary penalties on the bankers for violations of federal banking regulations and subsequently indicted them on criminal charges related to the same underlying transactions. The Court noted:

> [W]e recognize that the imposition of both money penalties and debarment sanctions will deter others from emulating petitioners' conduct, a traditional goal of criminal punishment. But the mere presence of this purpose is insufficient to render a sanction criminal, as deterrence "may serve civil as well as criminal goals." For example, the sanctions at issue here, while intended to deter future wrongdoing, also serve to promote the stability of the banking industry. To hold that the mere presence of a deterrent purpose renders such sanctions "criminal" for double jeopardy purposes would severely undermine the Government's ability to engage in effective regulation of institutions such as banks.

Id. at 105. Do you agree with this assessment or should double jeopardy require that the government decide between criminal or civil enforcement?

4. *Understanding the difference between a mental element and crimes requiring proof of different facts.* The Court in *Brown* held that joyriding and grand theft of the same car were the same offense. But theft requires proof of intent to permanently deprive the victim of possession, a key mental element, whereas joyriding does not. The key to understanding this conclusion is that joyriding is "necessarily included" in a conviction for grand theft because the two offenses do not require proof of a distinct factual element; the only difference is that the "greater" offense requires proof of an *additional* mental element: intent to permanently deprive. Contrast this with *Blockburger*. In that case, the two offenses that arose out of the single sale of narcotics each required proof of a distinct factual element: no tax stamp for one offense, no prescription for the other. Accordingly, proving one did not automatically or "necessarily" prove the other.

PROBLEM CASE

Williams Charles Denton was charged in Texas with two counts each of aggravated robbery and aggravated assault after two complainants went to Denton's house and subsequently alleged that they were assaulted and robbed there. Denton was found guilty on all four counts and he was sentenced to concurrent sentences. The facts were as follows: Denton lived in a trailer and attached shed on his mother's property. The victims went to visit Denton to collect a debt related to a prior methamphetamine transaction. While there, the victims were strip searched and ordered to turn over their belongings to Denton and two co-felons. The victims were eventually allowed to leave but were told to leave their belongings behind.

Texas law defines aggravated assault thusly: "A person commits an offense if the person commits assault . . . . uses or exhibits a deadly weapon during the commission of the assault." The Texas definition of aggravated robbery states: "A person commits an offense if, in the course of committing theft . . . and with intent to obtain or maintain control of the property, he . . . intentionally or knowingly threatens or places another in fear of imminent bodily injury or death." Denton argued that he was impermissibly prosecuted and punished more than once for the same offense. Does double jeopardy prohibit this result? See *Ex parte Denton*, 399 S.W.3d 540 (Tex. Crim. App. 2013).

2. When Jeopardy Attaches

Double jeopardy only applies if the defendant is formally placed "in jeopardy." But when does that occur? In the following case, the Supreme Court considers a double jeopardy argument from a defendant who considered himself a contentious objector and was charged with draft evasion during the Vietnam War. The defendant made a successful motion to dismiss the indictment. Given that this motion came before the commencement of trial, could the government prosecute him again?

Serfass v. United States

Supreme Court of the United States
420 U.S. 377 (1975)

Mr. Chief Justice Burger delivered the opinion of the Court.

We granted certiorari to decide whether a Court of Appeals has jurisdiction of an appeal by the United States from a pretrial order dismissing an indictment based on a legal ruling made by the District Court after an examination of records and an affidavit setting forth evidence to be adduced at trial.

I

The material facts are not in dispute. Petitioner, whose military service had been deferred for two years while he was in the Peace Corps, was ordered to report for induction on January 18, 1971. On December 29, 1970, he requested the form for conscientious objectors, Selective Service Form 150, and after submitting the completed form to his local board, he requested an interview. Petitioner met with the local board on January 13, 1971, and thereafter he was informed by letter that it had considered his entire Selective Service file, had "unanimously agreed that there was no change over which (petitioner) had no control," and had therefore "decided not to re-open (petitioner's) file." He was also informed that he was "still under Orders to report for Induction on January 18, 1971 at 5:15 A.M." Petitioner appeared at the examining station and refused induction on January 18.

A grand jury returned an indictment charging petitioner with willfully failing to report for and submit to induction into the Armed Forces, in violation of 50 U.S.C. App. s 462(a). At petitioner's arraignment he pleaded not guilty and demanded a jury trial. The trial date was set for January 9, 1973. Prior to that time, petitioner filed a motion to dismiss the indictment on the ground that the local board did not state adequate reasons for its refusal to reopen his file. Attached to the motion was an affidavit of petitioner stating merely that he had applied for conscientious objector status and that the local board's letter was the only communication concerning his claim which he had received. At the same time, petitioner moved "to postpone the trial of the within matter which is now scheduled for January 9, 1973, for the reason that a Motion to Dismiss has been simultaneously filed and the expeditious administration of justice will be served best by considering the Motion prior to trial."

On January 5 the District Court granted petitioner's motion to continue the trial and set a date for oral argument on the motion to dismiss the indictment. Briefs were submitted, and after hearing oral argument, the District Court entered an order directing the parties to submit a copy of petitioner's Selective Service file. On July 16, 1973, it ordered that the indictment be dismissed. In its memorandum, the court noted that the material facts were derived from petitioner's affidavit, from his Selective Service file, and from the oral stipulation of counsel at the argument "that the information which Serfass submitted to the Board establishes a prima facie claim for conscientious objector status based upon late crystallization." The District Court held that dismissal of the indictment was appropriate. . . .

III

Although articulated in different ways by this Court, the purposes of, and the policies which animate, the Double Jeopardy Clause in this context are clear. "The constitutional prohibition against 'double jeopardy' was designed to protect an individual from being subjected to the hazards of trial and possible conviction more than once for an alleged offense. . . . The underlying idea, one that is deeply ingrained in at least the Anglo-American system of jurisprudence, is that the State with all its resources and power should not be allowed to make repeated attempts to convict an individual for an alleged offense, thereby subjecting him to embarrassment, expense and ordeal and compelling him to live in a continuing state of anxiety and insecurity, as well as enhancing the possibility that even though innocent he may be found guilty."

As an aid to the decision of cases in which the prohibition of the Double Jeopardy Clause has been invoked, the courts have found it useful to define a point in criminal proceedings at which the constitutional purposes and policies are implicated by resort to the concept of "attachment of jeopardy." In the case of a jury trial, jeopardy attaches when a jury is empaneled and sworn. In a nonjury trial, jeopardy attaches when the court begins to hear evidence. The Court has consistently adhered to the view that jeopardy does not attach, and the constitutional prohibition can have no application, until a defendant is "put to trial before the trier of facts, whether the trier be a jury or a judge."

Under our cases jeopardy had not yet attached when the District Court granted petitioner's motion to dismiss the indictment. Petitioner was not then, nor has he ever been, "put to trial before the trier of facts." The proceedings were initiated by his motion to dismiss the indictment. Petitioner had not waived his right to a jury trial, and, of course, a jury trial court not be waived by him without the consent of the Government and of the court. In such circumstances, the District Court was without power to make any determination regarding petitioner's guilt or innocence. Petitioner's defense was raised before trial precisely because "trial of the facts surrounding the commission of the alleged offense would be of no assistance in determining" its validity. His motion to postpone the trial was premised on the belief that "the expeditious administration of justice will be served best by considering the Motion (to dismiss the indictment) prior to trial." At no time during or following the hearing on petitioner's motion to dismiss the indictment did the District Court have jurisdiction to do more than grant or deny that motion, and neither before nor after the ruling did jeopardy attach.

IV

Petitioner acknowledges that "formal or technical jeopardy had not attached" at the time the District Court ruled on his motion to dismiss the indictment. However, he argues that because that ruling was based on "evidentiary facts outside of the indictment, which facts would constitute a defense on the merits at trial," it was the "functional equivalent of an acquittal on the merits" and "constructively jeopardy had attached."

The argument is grounded on two basic and interrelated premises. First, petitioner argues that the Court has admonished against the use of "technicalities" in interpreting the Double Jeopardy Clause, and he contends that the normal rule as to the attachment of jeopardy is merely a presumption which is rebuttable in cases where an analysis of the respective interests of the Government and the accused indicates that the policies of the Double Jeopardy Clause would be frustrated by further prosecution. Second, petitioner maintains that the disposition of his motion to dismiss the indictment was, in the circumstances of this case, the "functional equivalent of an acquittal on the merits," and he concludes that the policies of the Double Jeopardy Clause would in fact be frustrated by further prosecution. We disagree with both of petitioner's premises and with his conclusion.

It is true that we have disparaged "rigid, mechanical" rules in the interpretation of the Double Jeopardy Clause. However, we also observed . . . that "the conclusion that jeopardy has attached begins, rather than ends, the inquiry as to whether the Double Jeopardy Clause bars retrial." Implicit in the latter statement is the premise that the "constitutional policies underpinning the Fifth Amendment's guarantee" are not implicated before that point in the proceedings at which "jeopardy attaches." *United States v. Jorn*, 400 U.S., at 480. As we have noted above, the Court has consistently adhered to the view that jeopardy does not attach until a defendant is "put to trial before the trier of the facts, whether the trier be a jury or a judge." This is by no means a mere technicality, nor is it a "rigid, mechanical" rule. It is, of course, like most legal rules, an attempt to impart content to an abstraction.

When a criminal prosecution is terminated prior to trial, an accused is often spared much of the expense, delay, strain, and embarrassment which attend a trial. Although an accused may raise defenses or objections before trial which are "capable of determination without the trial of the general issue," Fed. Rule Crim. Proc. 12(b)(1), and although he must raise certain other defenses or objections before trial, Fed. Rule Crim. Proc. 12(b)(2), in neither case is he "subjected to the hazards of trial and possible conviction." Moreover, in neither case would an appeal by the United States "allow the prosecutor to seek to persuade a second trier of fact of the defendant's guilt after having failed with the first." Both the history of the Double Jeopardy Clause and its terms demonstrate that it does not come into play until a proceeding begins before a trier "having jurisdiction to try the question of the guilt or innocence of the accused." Without risk of a determination of guilt, jeopardy does not attach, and neither an appeal nor further prosecution constitutes double jeopardy.

Petitioner's second premise, that the disposition of his motion to dismiss the indictment was the "functional equivalent of an acquittal on the merits," and his conclusion that the policies of the Double Jeopardy Clause would be frustrated by further prosecution in his case need not, in light of the conclusion we reach above, long detain us. It is, of course, settled that "a verdict of acquittal . . . is a bar to a subsequent prosecution for the same offence." But the language of cases in which we have held that there can be no appeal from, or further prosecution after, an "acquittal" cannot be divorced from the procedural context in which the action so characterized was taken. The word itself has no talismanic quality for purposes of the Double Jeopardy Clause. In particular, it has no significance in this context unless jeopardy has once attached and an accused has been subjected to the risk of conviction.

NOTES & QUESTIONS ON WHEN JEOPARDY ATTACHES

1. *Bench trials.* In a jury trial, jeopardy attaches once the jury has been empaneled. But what about bench trials? The answer is that jeopardy attaches when the first witness is sworn, which is the functional equivalent of the empaneling of the jury—a moment of significance that suggests that the trial has begun in earnest and the defendant faces jeopardy, i.e., the possibility of conviction.

2. *Guilty pleas.* What if the defendant decides to forgo a trial and plead guilty instead? In that case, the jury is never empaneled, such that the rule from *Serfass* would seem to suggest that jeopardy has not attached when a defendant pleads guilty. Federal courts are split on the issue, with some ruling that jeopardy attaches the moment the defendant pleads guilty. The argument for this view is that the guilty plea is the functional equivalent of a guilty verdict, leaving nothing for the judge to do but accept the plea and move toward sentencing. See *United States v. McIntosh*, 580 F.3d 1222, 1229 (11th Cir. 2009). However, other Circuits have suggested the opposite, i.e., that jeopardy does not attach at that critical stage. See *United States v. Santiago Soto*, 825 F.2d 616, 620 (1st Cir. 1987) ("We hold that jeopardy did not attach when the district court accepted the guilty plea to the lesser included offense and then rejected the plea without having imposed sentence and entered judgment. Certainly in this case, in which the judge initially accepted the guilty plea but then rejected it within the same proceeding, defendant was not placed in jeopardy in any meaningful sense."); *State v. Thomas*, 296 Conn. 375, 397, 995 A.2d 65, 79 (2010).

STATE LAW REQUIREMENTS

Some states have tried to set the moment when jeopardy attaches by statute. For example, Kentucky passed a double jeopardy statute with the following language: "The former prosecution was improperly terminated after the first witness was sworn but before findings were rendered by a trier of fact." Ky. Rev. Stat. Ann. § 505.030. Why would Kentucky have adopted such a rule? The rule has the advantage of imposing the same triggering point for both bench and jury trials, thus harmonizing the standard and making it independent of whether the defendant elects a jury or bench trial. Similarly, Montana passed a statute declaring that jeopardy does not attach until the first witness is sworn in. However, in *Crist v. Bretz*, 437 U.S. 28, 37-38 (1978), the Supreme Court concluded that the Montana statute was unconstitutional, at least when applied in a jury trial:

> [T]he federal rule as to when jeopardy attaches in a jury trial is not only a settled part of federal constitutional law. It is a rule that both reflects and protects the defendant's interest in retaining a chosen jury. We cannot hold that this rule, so grounded, is only at the periphery of double jeopardy concerns. Those concerns—the finality of judgments, the minimization of harassing exposure to the harrowing experience of a criminal trial, and the valued right to continue with the chosen jury—have combined to produce the federal law that in a jury trial jeopardy attached when the jury is empaneled and sworn.

The Kentucky Supreme Court explicitly declared the similar Kentucky statute unconstitutional as well. See *Cardine v. Commonwealth*, 283 S.W.3d 641, 647 (Ky. 2009) ("Ultimately, the United States Supreme Court's interpretation of the federal constitution, as the supreme law of the land, trumps any competing interpretation by this Court and any inconsistent statute passed by this Commonwealth's General Assembly. Thus, to the extent that [the Kentucky statute] and the cases interpreting it guarantee anything less than the federal standard for attachment of double jeopardy, they are overruled."). Consequently, there is no state law variation regarding when jeopardy attaches.

PROBLEM CASE

Consider the case of Lt. Ehren Watada, a U.S. Army officer who refused to serve in Iraq. Watada was charged by the military with multiple offenses under the Uniform Code of Military Justice (UCMJ), including missing a troop movement and conduct unbecoming an officer. Watada argued that he should not be convicted because he believed that the war in Iraq was illegal and his participation would make him complicit in war crimes. Watada's defense counsel called multiple expert witnesses who questioned the legality of the war, including the U.N. Security Council's failure to pass a resolution authorizing the use of military force, as well as criticisms that the U.S. Congress only authorized the military action because of erroneous claims that Saddam Hussein possessed, or was actively developing and building, weapons of mass destruction. At trial, Watada's counsel attempted to assert a mistake of fact defense, arguing that his belief in the war effort's illegality negated the required intent for some of the charged offenses. Watada stipulated that he failed to report as ordered to his unit's deployment to Iraq because of his opinion about the war. The judge believed that the defense's stipulation was inconsistent with the defense's mistake of fact argument; consequently, the judge worried that the defendant did not understand the stipulation that he had just agreed to. The judge then rejected the stipulation and ordered a mistrial because the prosecution had no other evidence or witnesses ready to present at trial. When the military sought a second trial, Watada objected that a second trial would violate double jeopardy. The military's position was that a retrial was permitted because there was no verdict in the first case, nor was the mistrial the result of prosecutorial misconduct. A civilian district court issued a preliminary injunction while it considered the merits of the double jeopardy claim. Should a district judge in this situation stop the military from retrying the defendant? In particular, had jeopardy "attached" at the point in time when the prosecutor declared the mistrial? What is the correct standard for determining the moment of attachment? See *Watada v. Head,* No. C07-5549BHS, 2008 WL 4681577, at *18 (W.D. Wash. Oct. 21, 2008).

B. CONSEQUENCES OF THE DOUBLE JEOPARDY RULE

The major consequence of the application of the double jeopardy rule is to prevent the government from instituting a retrial of the defendant. In that sense, the rule is meant as a constraint on state authority in the criminal justice area. The underlying rationale was best explained by Justice Black:

> The underlying idea, one that is deeply ingrained in at least the Anglo-American system of jurisprudence, is that the State with all its resources and power should not be allowed to make repeated attempts to convict an individual for an alleged offense, thereby subjecting him to embarrassment, expense and ordeal and compelling him to live in a continuing state of anxiety and insecurity, as well as enhancing the possibility that even though innocent he may be found guilty.
>
> In accordance with this philosophy it has long been settled under the Fifth Amendment that a verdict of acquittal is final, ending a defendant's jeopardy, and even when "not followed by any judgment, is a bar to a subsequent prosecution for the same offence." Thus it is one of the elemental principles of our criminal law that the Government cannot secure a new trial by means of an appeal even though an acquittal may appear to be erroneous.

Green v. United States, 355 U.S. 184, 187-88 (1957). According to one legal historian, the prohibition on retrial has an ancient pedigree far older than the founding of the nation:

> An examination of early Greek and Roman law bears out Justice Black's assertion. Both legal systems contained some form of protection against double jeopardy. In 355 B.C., the Greek orator and pleader in law courts Demosthenes, in a speech against Leptines, stated that "the laws forbid the same man to be tried twice on the same issue, be it a civil action, a scrutiny, a contested claim, or anything else of the sort." Two years later, in a speech he wrote to be given by Diodorus against Timocrates, Demosthenes stated: "The legislator does not permit any question once decided by judgement of the court to be put a second time. . . ."

David S. Rudstein, *A Brief History of the Fifth Amendment Guarantee Against Double Jeopardy*, 14 Wm. & Mary Bill Rts. J. 193, 198 (2005).

The following subsections focus on the application of the retrial prohibition after acquittals, convictions, and appellate reversals of convictions. Each of these situations implicates the core rationale for the double jeopardy protection in unique ways. The case of a retrial after a full jury acquittal is straightforward—double jeopardy forbids it. But other cases require an understanding of what happens during the appellate process. For example, what happens when a reviewing court overturns a conviction? Should this event be viewed as the functional equivalent of a trial acquittal or is it somehow distinct?

1. Prohibition on Retrial Following Acquittal

Once jeopardy attaches and a defendant's trial results in an acquittal, the double jeopardy rule prohibits the state from prosecuting the defendant again for the same crime. This rule is relatively straightforward and intuitive. In the following case, though, the Supreme Court asks whether the same rule should be extended to situations where the defendant is convicted but that conviction is overturned on appeal for lack of sufficient evidence. In these cases, the appellate court determines, as a matter of law, that no reasonable fact finder could have found the defendant guilty beyond a reasonable doubt with the evidence that was presented at trial. In other words, the appellate court reverses the conviction because it concludes the prosecution failed not only to prove the case beyond a reasonable doubt, but to even satisfy its prima facie burden of production, meaning the trial court should have granted a motion to acquit the defendant and never allowed the prosecution to persuade the jury to convict (remember the simple axiom that before a prosecutor is permitted to persuade, she must first produce evidence that makes guilt at least a rational result). The defendant in the following case argues that an appellate reversal for inadequate evidence, by determining that no reasonable fact finder could have convicted the defendant, is the functional equivalent of a trial acquittal. Since the appellate court determines that the defendant *should* have been acquitted, should the state be constrained by the same double jeopardy rule that would apply if the defendant were actually acquitted at trial?

Burks v. United States

Supreme Court of the United States
437 U.S. 1 (1970)

Mr. Chief Justice BURGER delivered the opinion of the Court.

We granted certiorari to resolve the question of whether an accused may be subjected to a second trial when conviction in a prior trial was reversed by an appellate court solely for lack of sufficient evidence to sustain the jury's verdict.

I

Petitioner Burks was tried in the United States District Court for the crime of robbing a federally insured bank by use of a dangerous weapon, a violation of 18 U.S.C. § 2113(d). Burks' principal defense was insanity. To prove this claim petitioner produced three expert witnesses who testified, albeit with differing diagnoses of his mental condition, that he suffered from a mental illness at the time of the robbery, which rendered him substantially incapable of conforming his conduct to the requirements of the law. In rebuttal the Government offered the testimony of two experts, one of whom testified that although petitioner possessed a character disorder, he was not mentally ill. The other prosecution witness acknowledged a character disorder in petitioner, but gave a rather ambiguous answer to the question of whether Burks had been capable of conforming his conduct to the law. Lay witnesses also testified for the Government, expressing their opinion that petitioner appeared to be capable of normal functioning and was sane at the time of the alleged offense.

Before the case was submitted to the jury, the court denied a motion for a judgment of acquittal. The jury found Burks guilty as charged. Thereafter, he filed a timely motion for a new trial, maintaining, among other things, that "[t]he evidence was insufficient to support the verdict." The motion was denied by the District Court, which concluded that petitioner's challenge to the sufficiency of the evidence was "utterly without merit."

On appeal petitioner narrowed the issues by admitting the affirmative factual elements of the charge against him, leaving only his claim concerning criminal responsibility to be resolved. With respect to this point, the Court of Appeals agreed with petitioner's claim that the evidence was insufficient to support the verdict and reversed his conviction. . . . At this point, the Court of Appeals, rather than terminating the case against petitioner, remanded to the District Court "for a determination of whether a directed verdict of acquittal should be entered or a new trial ordered." Indicating that the District Court should choose the appropriate course "from a balancing of the equities," the court explicitly adopted the procedures utilized by the Fifth Circuit in *United States v. Bass*, 490 F.2d 846, 852-853 (1974), "as a guide" to be used on remand:

> [W]e reverse and remand the case to the district court where the defendant will be entitled to a directed verdict of acquittal unless the government presents sufficient additional evidence to carry its burden on the issue of defendant's sanity. As we noted earlier, the question of sufficiency of the evidence to make an issue for the jury on the defense of insanity is a question of law to be decided by the trial judge. . . . If the district court, sitting without the presence of the jury, is satisfied by the government's presentation, it may order a new trial. . . . Even if the government presents additional evidence, the district judge may refuse to order a new trial if he finds from the record that the prosecution had the opportunity fully to develop its case or in fact did so at the first trial.

The Court of Appeals assumed it had the power to order this "balancing" remedy by virtue of the fact that Burks had explicitly requested a new trial. . . .

II

. . . Petitioner's argument is straightforward. He contends that the Court of Appeals' holding was nothing more or less than a decision that the District Court had erred by not granting his motion for a judgment of acquittal. By implication, he argues, the appellate reversal was the operative equivalent of a district court's judgment of acquittal, entered either before or after verdict. Petitioner points out, however, that had the District Court found the evidence at the first trial inadequate, as the Court of Appeals said it should have done, a second trial would violate the Double Jeopardy Clause of the Fifth Amendment. Therefore, he maintains, it makes no difference that the determination of evidentiary insufficiency was made by a reviewing court since the double jeopardy considerations are the same, regardless of which court decides that a judgment of acquittal is in order.

The position advanced by petitioner has not been embraced by our prior holdings. Indeed, as the Court of Appeals here recognized, *Bryan v. United States*, would appear to be contrary. In *Bryan* the defendant was convicted in the District Court for evasion of federal income tax laws. Bryan had moved for a judgment of acquittal both at the close of the Government's case and when all of the evidence had been presented. After the verdict was returned he renewed these motions, but asked—in the alternative—for a new trial. These motions were all denied. The Court of Appeals reversed the conviction on the specific ground that the evidence was insufficient to sustain the verdict and remanded the case for a new trial. Certiorari was then granted to determine whether the Court of Appeals had properly ordered a new trial, or whether it should have entered a judgment of acquittal. In affirming the Court of Appeals, this Court decided, first, that the Court of Appeals had statutory authority, under 28 U.S.C. § 2106, to direct a new trial. But Bryan had also maintained that notwithstanding § 2106 a retrial was prohibited by the Double Jeopardy Clause, a contention which was dismissed in one paragraph: "Petitioner's contention that to require him to stand trial again would be to place him twice in jeopardy is not persuasive. He sought and obtained the reversal of his conviction assigning a number of alleged errors on appeal, including denial of his motion for judgment of acquittal. . . . [W]here the accused successfully seeks review of a conviction, there is no double jeopardy upon a new trial."

Five years after *Bryan* was decided, a similar claim of double jeopardy was presented to the Court in *Sapir v. United States*, 348 U.S. 373 (1955). Sapir had been convicted of conspiracy by a jury in the District Court. After the trial court denied a motion for acquittal, he obtained a reversal in the Court of Appeals, which held that the motion should have been granted since the evidence was insufficient to sustain a conviction. In a brief per curiam opinion, this Court, without explanation, reversed the Court of Appeals' decision to remand the petitioner's case for a new trial. . . .

Shortly after *Sapir*, in *Yates v. United States*, 354 U.S. 298 (1957), the Court adopted much the same reasoning. . . . In *Yates*, this Court—without citing *Sapir*—ordered acquittals for some defendants in the case, but new trials for others, when one of the main contentions of the petitioners concerned the insufficiency of the evidence. . . . The *Yates* decision thus paralleled [*Sapir*] in the sense that both would allow a new trial to correct evidentiary insufficiency if the defendant had requested such relief—even as an alternative to a motion for acquittal. But the language in *Yates* was also susceptible of a broader reading, namely, that appellate courts have full authority to order a new trial as a remedy for evidentiary insufficiency, even when the defendant has moved only for a judgment of acquittal.

Three years later in *Forman v. United States*, 361 U.S. 416 (1960), the Court again treated these questions. There a conviction was reversed by the Court of Appeals due to an improper instruction to the jury . . . as opposed to evidentiary insufficiency. Although the petitioner in *Forman* had moved for a new trial and judgment of acquittal, he argued that a new trial would not be appropriate relief since he had requested a judgment of acquittal with respect to the specific trial error on which this Court agreed with the Court of Appeals. Without distinguishing between a reversal due to trial error and reversal resulting solely from evidentiary insufficiency, this Court held that a new trial did not involve double jeopardy. . . .

The Court's holdings in this area, beginning with *Bryan*, can hardly be characterized as models of consistency and clarity. *Bryan* seemingly stood for the proposition that an appellate court could order whatever relief was "appropriate" or "equitable," regardless of what considerations prompted reversal. A somewhat different course was taken by the concurrence in

Sapir, where it was suggested that a reversal for evidentiary insufficiency would require a judgment of acquittal unless the defendant had requested a new trial. *Yates*, on the contrary, implied that new trials could be ordered to cure prior inadequacies of proof even when the defendant had not so moved. While not completely resolving these ambiguities, *Forman* suggested that a reviewing court could go beyond the relief requested by a defendant and order a new trial under some circumstances. In discussing *Sapir*, however, the *Forman* Court intimated that a different result might follow if the conviction was reversed for evidentiary insufficiency and the defendant had not requested a new trial.

After the *Bryan-Forman* line of decisions at least one proposition emerged: A defendant who requests a new trial as one avenue of relief may be required to stand trial again, even when his conviction was reversed due to failure of proof at the first trial. Given that petitioner here appealed from a denial of a motion for a new trial—although he had moved for acquittal during trial—our prior cases would seem to indicate that the Court of Appeals had power to remand on the terms it ordered. To reach a different result will require a departure from those holdings.

III

It is unquestionably true that the Court of Appeals' decision "represente[d] a resolution, correct or not, of some or all of the factual elements of the offense charged." By deciding that the Government had failed to come forward with sufficient proof of petitioner's capacity to be responsible for criminal acts, that court was clearly saying that Burks' criminal culpability had not been established. If the District Court had so held in the first instance, as the reviewing court said it should have done, a judgment of acquittal would have been entered and, of course, petitioner could not be retried for the same offense. Consequently, as Mr. Justice Douglas correctly perceived in *Sapir*, it should make no difference that the reviewing court, rather than the trial court, determined the evidence to be insufficient. The appellate decision unmistakably meant that the District Court had erred in failing to grant a judgment of acquittal. To hold otherwise would create a purely arbitrary distinction between those in petitioner's position and others who would enjoy the benefit of a correct decision by the District Court.

The Double Jeopardy Clause forbids a second trial for the purpose of affording the prosecution another opportunity to supply evidence which it failed to muster in the first proceeding. This is central to the objective of the prohibition against successive trials. The Clause does not allow "the State . . . to make repeated attempts to convict an individual for an alleged offense," since "[t]he constitutional prohibition against 'double jeopardy' was designed to protect an individual from being subjected to the hazards of trial and possible conviction more than once for an alleged offense."

> Nonetheless . . . our past holdings do not appear consistent with what we believe the Double Jeopardy Clause commands. A close reexamination of those precedents, however, persuades us that they have not properly construed the Clause, and accordingly should no longer be followed. . . .
>
> In our view it makes no difference that a defendant has sought a new trial as one of his remedies, or even as the sole remedy. It cannot be meaningfully said that a person "waives" his right to a judgment of acquittal by moving for a new trial. Moreover, as *Forman* has indicated, an appellate court is authorized by § 2106 to "go beyond the particular relief sought" in order to provide that relief which would be "just under the circumstances." Since we hold today that the Double Jeopardy Clause precludes a second trial once the reviewing court has found the evidence legally insufficient, the only "just" remedy available for that court is the direction of a judgment of acquittal. To the extent that our prior decisions suggest that by moving for a new trial, a defendant waives his right to a judgment of acquittal on the basis of evidentiary insufficiency, those cases are overruled. . . .

NOTES & QUESTIONS ON RETRIAL FOLLOWING ACQUITTAL

1. *Functional equivalent.* Do you agree that a reversal for lack of evidence is the functional equivalent of a trial acquittal for which jeopardy should attach?

2. *Legal error versus evidentiary insufficiency.* Why does an appellate reversal based on a finding of legal error at the trial not impose a jeopardy bar, but a reversal based on a finding of evidentiary insufficiency does? This can seem confusing. The key to understanding the difference is that the Double Jeopardy Clause is designed to prevent the government from taking multiple bites at the apple in its attempt to marshal enough evidence to support the defendant's conviction. A finding of legal error at the first trial does not trigger the same anxiety; the trial judge's legal error can hardly be attributed to the prosecutor. But in the case of evidentiary insufficiency, the deficiency can certainly be attributed to the prosecution. In the absence of sufficient evidence, the prosecution should not have gone to trial in the first place. Since the prosecutor did go to trial, the appellate reversal for evidentiary insufficiency bars retrial and prevents the prosecutor from getting a second bite at the prosecutorial apple.

3. *Equitable remedy.* Why did the Supreme Court reject the prior *Bryan* approach, which required a balancing of the equities to determine if retrial was appropriate after appellate reversal for lack of evidence?

PROBLEM CASE

Ernest Lee Brazzel was charged with attempted murder. At his trial, the jury convicted him of first-degree assault, as a lesser-included offense of attempted murder. The wrinkle in the case is that when the jury returned its verdict, it said nothing about the attempted murder charge. For example, the jury did not indicate that they were deadlocked or "hung" on that charge or that they were explicitly acquitting Brazzel of attempted murder. Instead, the jury simply said nothing. The government's position was that it was therefore entitled to try Brazzel again for attempted murder. Brazzel objected, arguing that the jury's silence should be construed as an implied acquittal, for which double jeopardy should attach. To try him again, Brazzel argued, would be to place him in jeopardy for the same offense twice. Do you agree with Brazzel or is the second prosecution allowed? See *Brazzel v. Washington*, 491 F.3d 976, 978 (9th Cir. 2007).

2. Prohibition on Retrial Following Conviction

Although less likely to occur in practice, double jeopardy also prohibits a retrial following a conviction. For example, if the prosecution is unsatisfied with the sentence imposed by the trial court, the state is not permitted to try the defendant a second time to secure a higher penalty, or a cumulative second penalty. Consider the following argument from *Ohio v. Johnson*, where the defendant pleaded guilty to involuntary manslaughter and grand theft. The defendant argued that after the guilty plea he could not subsequently be prosecuted for the more serious crimes of murder and aggravated robbery. The Supreme Court concluded that double jeopardy did not bar the second trial:

> Respondent urges, as an alternative basis for affirming the judgment of the Supreme Court of Ohio, that further prosecution of the counts which were dismissed would violate the double jeopardy prohibition against multiple prosecutions. He concedes that on the authority of our decision in *Brown v. Ohio*, the State is not prohibited by the Double Jeopardy Clause from charging respondent with greater and lesser included offenses and prosecuting those offenses in a single trial. But, he argues, his conviction and sentence on the charges of involuntary manslaughter and grand theft mean that further prosecution on the remaining offenses will implicate the double jeopardy protection against a second prosecution following conviction. The court below never had occasion to address this argument.
>
> The answer to this contention seems obvious to us. Respondent was indicted on four related charges growing out of a murder and robbery. The grand jury returned a single indictment, and all four charges were embraced within a single prosecution. Respondent's argument is apparently based on the assumption that trial proceedings, like amoebae, are capable of being infinitely subdivided, so that a determination of guilt and punishment on one

> count of a multicount indictment immediately raises a double jeopardy bar to continued prosecution on any remaining counts that are greater or lesser included offenses of the charge just concluded. We have never held that, and decline to hold it now.

Ohio v. Johnson, 467 U.S. 493, 500-01 (1984). Notice the basis for the Court's decision. Although the Court sided with the state, it was only because it viewed the more serious offenses as different from the offenses that the defendant pleaded guilty to. But implicitly the Court assumes that retrial for the same offense following conviction is prohibited by double jeopardy.

A distinct issue is raised when a defendant is convicted and then successfully appeals the conviction. It seems intuitively correct that if the appellate court reverses, for lack of evidence, a trial court's conviction, this should be treated as the functional equivalent of the trial court's acquittal. This was the issue addressed in the prior subsection. In contrast, if the appellate court reverses a trial court's conviction for trial error, a retrial is still permitted under the Double Jeopardy Clause. The argument here is that a reversal for trial error is not the functional equivalent of a reversal for lack of evidence. The appeals court is not determining that the trial court should have acquitted the defendant, but rather simply concluding that the trial court should have conducted the trial differently, with uncertain consequences for the result. In other words, it is conceptually coherent to conclude that the trial court made a reversible error but that the trial, conducted appropriately, would have still resulted in a conviction. For that reason, remand for a "do-over" trial is the appropriate remedy and not inconsistent with the Double Jeopardy Clause.

Does this pose particular problems of application? Consider the following observation:

> The Supreme Court's interpretation of the Double Jeopardy Clause in the area of appellate reversals of convictions thus has attached constitutional significance to the basis for the court's reversal: where a conviction is reversed for trial error, the Double Jeopardy Clause permits a retrial; where the reversal is based on insufficient evidence, the Double Jeopardy Clause bars retrial. This distinction is easy enough to apply when a convicted defendant raises a single claim, either of trial error or of insufficient evidence, on appeal. In the great many cases where a defendant asserts both claims as grounds for reversal, however, applying the distinction becomes more complicated.

Sarah O. Wang, *Insufficient Attention to Insufficient Evidence: Some Double Jeopardy Implications*, 79 Va. L. Rev. 1381, 1387 (1993). What if the appellate court determines that the trial court committed a reversible error *and* should have acquitted for lack of evidence? In that case, it seems clear that retrial should be barred. But what if the defendant appeals on both issues but the appellate court decides the reversible error question and refuses to reach the question of lack of evidence? Does the double jeopardy protection require the appellate court to consider and resolve the assertion that the trial court had insufficient evidence to support its verdict of conviction? Lower courts have grappled with this question, reaching a variety of different positions on the question. For more discussion of this issue, see, e.g., *United States v. Miller*, 952 F.2d 866 (5th Cir. 1992).

C. EXCEPTIONS TO DOUBLE JEOPARDY

Although the text of the Fifth Amendment says nothing about exceptions to the double jeopardy rule, courts have concluded that the rule should not be applied in all cases. These exceptions include hung jury mistrials and some other forms of mistrial, both of which allow the state to retry the defendant despite the fact that jeopardy attached when the jury was empaneled. In both cases, the operative question is whether the first jeopardy "terminated" when the mistrial was declared, such that a second trial would constitute a double jeopardy, or, in contrast, whether the first jeopardy was merely suspended when the mistrial was declared. Then, the second trial would simply be a continuation of the original jeopardy. In the following cases, these questions are more than mere definitional questions—they implicate deep questions of fundamental fairness underlying the Fifth Amendment's protections for individual defendants against excessive state power. The final exception involves dual sovereignty—the idea that a prosecution by one sovereign, such as the federal government, does not preclude a subsequent prosecution by a second sovereign, such as a state government.

1. Hung Jury Mistrials

The following case deals with a common occurrence. The jury is empaneled, and the trial is held, but not all the way to verdict because the jury fails to reach a consensus on an outcome. In these situations, the trial judge declares a mistrial due to a hung jury. The question is whether double jeopardy bars retrial in these circumstances. Another way of posing the question is whether a hung jury should be the functional equivalent of an acquittal, since a rule prohibiting a retrial on double jeopardy grounds would have the same practical effect as a jury returning a full acquittal, i.e., it would effectively end the state's prosecutorial efforts.

United States v. Sanford

Supreme Court of the United States
429 U.S. 14 (1976)

PER CURIAM.

Respondents were indicted for illegal game hunting in Yellowstone National Park. A jury trial in the United States District Court for the District of Montana resulted in a hung jury, and the District Court declared a mistrial. Four months later, while the Government was preparing to retry them, respondents moved to dismiss the indictment. The District Court, agreeing that the Government had consented to the activities which formed the basis of the indictment, dismissed it. The Government's appeal pursuant to the Criminal Appeals Act was dismissed by the Court of Appeals because that court thought retrial was barred by the Double Jeopardy Clause of the Fifth Amendment to the United States Constitution. The Government petitioned for certiorari, and we vacated the judgment of the Court of Appeals and remanded for further consideration. . . . On remand, the Court of Appeals . . . adhered to its prior determination. The Government now seeks certiorari from that ruling.

Buffalo herd in Yellowstone National Park. (Shadowmeld Photography/Wikimedia Commons)

The reasoning of the Court of Appeals is best summarized by this language from its opinion:

> Here appellees have undergone trial. There is no question but that jeopardy has attached. That being so, and since the proceedings in the district court have ended in appellees' favor and the consequences of a reversal in favor of the Government would be that appellees must be tried again, we conclude that they would, on retrial, be placed twice in jeopardy.

We agree with the Court of Appeals that jeopardy attached at the time of the empaneling of the jury for the first trial of respondents. But we do not agree with that court's conclusion that by reason of the sequence of events in the District Court the Government would be barred by the Double Jeopardy Clause from retrying respondents. The trial of respondents on the indictment terminated, not in their favor, but in a mistrial declared, sua sponte, by the District Court. Where the trial is terminated in this manner, the classical test for determining whether the defendants may be retried without violating the Double Jeopardy Clause is stated in Mr. Justice Story's opinion for this Court in *United States v. Perez*, 9 Wheat. 579, 580 (1824):

> We are of opinion, that the facts constitute no legal bar to a future trial. The prisoner has not been convicted or acquitted, and may again be put upon his defence. We think, that in all cases of this nature, the law has invested courts of justice with the authority to discharge a jury from giving any verdict, whenever, in their opinion, taking all the circumstances into consideration, there is a manifest necessity for the act, or the ends of public justice would otherwise be defeated.

The Government's right to retry the defendant, after a mistrial, in the face of his claim of double jeopardy is generally governed by the test laid down in *Perez*. The situation of a hung jury presented here is precisely the situation that was presented in *Perez* and therefore the Double Jeopardy Clause does not bar retrial of these respondents on the indictment which had been returned against them.

The District Court's dismissal of the indictment occurred several months after the first trial had ended in a mistrial, but before the retrial of respondents had begun. This case is, therefore, governed by *Serfass v. United States*, in which we held that a pretrial order of the District Court dismissing an indictment charging refusal to submit to induction into the Armed Forces was appealable. . . . The dismissal in this case, like that in *Serfass*, was prior to a trial that the Government had a right to prosecute and that the defendant was required to defend. Since in such cases a trial following the Government's successful appeal of a dismissal is not barred by double jeopardy, an appeal from the dismissal is authorized. . . .

NOTES & QUESTIONS ON HUNG JURY MISTRIALS

1. *Terminating jeopardy.* What explains why the government is entitled to retry a defendant after jeopardy attaches and the first trial ends in a hung jury mistrial? Think of it the following way: Although jeopardy attached when the first trial began, double jeopardy would only prohibit a second trial if the first jeopardy ended in some way. However, courts have sometimes suggested that in cases of a hung jury retrial, the original jeopardy is still ongoing—in part because a verdict was never reached. If the original jeopardy is ongoing despite the mistrial, then there is no "double" jeopardy at all, just one long "single" jeopardy that endures across two trials. Do you find this argument convincing? See *Richardson v. United States*, 468 U.S. 317, 325 (1984) ("the protection of the Double Jeopardy Clause by its terms applies only if there has been some event, such as an acquittal, which terminates the original jeopardy. Since jeopardy attached here when the jury was sworn, petitioner's argument necessarily assumes that the judicial declaration of a mistrial was an event which terminated jeopardy in his case and which allowed him to assert a valid claim of double jeopardy").

2. *Are all hung jury mistrials created equal?* The law treats every hung jury mistrial the same for purposes of the Double Jeopardy Clause. If the mistrial was the result of a hung jury, the government is entitled to retry the defendant again. This is a bright-line rule. Would it be possible to change the rule so that courts could inquire into the reason for the hung jury? Consider the following distinction:

> Most, perhaps almost all, hung juries result from evidence that is less than overwhelming but nonetheless sufficient to sustain a conviction on appeal. A small number, though, might be based on evidence that is insufficient to sustain a conviction on appeal. This number probably is small because the due process standard for legally sufficient evidence is a low one: whether any rational trier of fact could have found the essential elements of the crime beyond a reasonable doubt. Only egregiously defective cases meet this standard, and almost all of those cases will have produced an acquittal rather than a hung jury.

George C. Thomas III, *Solving the Double Jeopardy Mistrial Riddle*, 69 S. Cal. L. Rev. 1551, 1557 (1996). Under this proposed approach, a judge should bar retrial of the defendant if the hung jury results from evidence that was legally insufficient to sustain the conviction.

2. Other Mistrials

A hung jury is not the only situation that might trigger a judge to declare a mistrial. If a judge decides that the jury trial has become irretrievably tainted and that no instruction to the jury can cure the defect, the judge may have no alternative but to declare a mistrial. A variety of situations in the courtroom might trigger this situation. A lawyer might say something prejudicial or present evidence that the judge has declared inadmissible. Or a witness might blurt out something about the defendant that is not admissible. The general rule is that if the defendant asks for the mistrial, the mistrial request functions as an implicit waiver of double jeopardy, thus allowing the court to schedule a second trial after the mistrial is declared. But there are exceptions to this general rule. In the following case, the Supreme Court asks whether there should be an exception to the general rule when a defense counsel is baited into making the mistrial request. In that situation, has the defendant waived the protection of the double jeopardy rule, or should the baiting of the defense trigger an exception to the waiver rule?

United States v. Dinitz

Supreme Court of the United States
424 U.S. 600 (1976)

Mr. Justice STEWART delivered the opinion of the Court.

The question in this case is whether the Double Jeopardy Clause of the Fifth Amendment was violated by the retrial of the respondent after his original trial had ended in a mistrial granted at his request.

I

The respondent, Nathan Dinitz, was arrested on December 8, 1972, following the return of an indictment charging him with conspiracy to distribute LSD and with distribution of that controlled substance. On the day of his arrest, the respondent retained a lawyer named Jeffrey Meldon to represent him. Meldon appeared with the respondent at his arraignment, filed numerous pretrial motions on his behalf, and was completely responsible for the preparation of the case until shortly before trial. Some five days before the trial was scheduled to begin, the respondent retained another lawyer, Maurice Wagner, to conduct his defense. Wagner had not been admitted to practice before the United States District Court for the Northern District of Florida, but on the first day of the trial the court permitted him to appear pro hac vice. In addition to Meldon and Wagner, Fletcher Baldwin, a professor of law at the University of Florida, also appeared on the respondent's behalf.

The jury was selected and sworn on February 14, 1973, and opening statements by counsel began on the following afternoon. The prosecutor's opening statement briefly outlined the testimony that he expected an undercover agent named Steve Cox to give regarding his purchase of LSD from the respondent. Wagner then began his opening statement for the defense. After introducing himself and his co-counsel, Wagner turned to the case against the respondent:

> **Mr. Wagner:** After working on this case over a period of time it appeared to me that if we would have given nomenclature, if we would have named this case so there could be no question about identifying it in the future, I would have called it The Case[—]
> **Mr. Reed (AUSA):** Your Honor, we object to personal opinions.
> **The Court:** Objection sustained. The purpose of the opening statement is to summarize the facts the evidence will show, state the issues, not to give personal opinions. Proceed, Mr. Wagner.
> **Mr. Wagner:** Thank you, Your Honor. I call this the Case of the Incredible Witness.

The prosecutor again objected and the judge excused the jury. The judge then warned Wagner that he did not approve of his behavior and cautioned Wagner that he did not want to have to remind him again about the purpose of the opening statement.

Following this initial incident, the trial judge found it necessary twice again to remind Wagner of the purpose of the opening statement and to instruct him to relate "the facts that you expect the evidence to show, the admissible evidence." Later on in his statement, Wagner started to discuss an attempt to extort money from the respondent that had occurred shortly after his arrest. The prosecutor objected and the jury was again excused. Wagner informed the trial judge of some of the details of the extortion attempt and assured the court that he would connect it with the prospective Government witness Cox. But it soon became apparent that Wagner had no information linking Cox to the extortion attempt, and the trial judge then excluded Wagner from the trial and ordered him to leave the courthouse.

The judge then asked Meldon if he was prepared to proceed with the trial. Upon learning that Meldon had not discussed the case with the witnesses, the judge gave Meldon until 9 o'clock the following morning to prepare. Meldon informed the judge that the respondent was "in a quandary because he hired Mr. Wagner to argue the case and he feels he needs more time to obtain outside counsel to argue the case for him. The judge responded that "(y)ou are his counsel and have been" but stated that he would consider the matter "between now and 9:00 o'clock tomorrow morning."

The next morning, Meldon told the judge that the respondent wanted Wagner and not himself or Baldwin to try the case. The judge then set forth three alternative courses that might be followed (1) a stay or recess pending application to the Court of Appeals to review the propriety of expelling Wagner, (2) continuation of the trial with Meldon and Baldwin as counsel, or (3) a declaration of a mistrial which would permit the respondent to obtain other counsel. Following a short recess, Meldon moved for a mistrial, stating that, after "full consideration of the situation and an explanation of the alternatives before him, (the respondent) feels that he would move for a mistrial and that this would be in his best interest." The Government prosecutor did not oppose the motion. The judge thereupon declared a mistrial, expressing his belief that such a course would serve the interest of justice.

Before his second trial, the respondent moved to dismiss the indictment on the ground that a retrial would violate the Double Jeopardy Clause of the Constitution. This motion was denied. The respondent represented himself at the new trial, and he was convicted by the jury on both the conspiracy and distribution counts. A divided panel of the Court of Appeals for the Fifth Circuit reversed the conviction, holding that the retrial violated the respondent's constitutional right not to be twice put in jeopardy. The appellate court took the view that the trial judge's exclusion of Wagner and his questioning of Meldon had left the respondent no choice but to move for a mistrial. On that basis, the court concluded that the respondent's request for a mistrial should be ignored and the case should be treated as though the trial judge had declared a mistrial over the objection of the defendant. So viewing the case, the court held that the Double Jeopardy Clause barred the second trial of the respondent, because there had been no manifest necessity requiring the expulsion of Wagner. . . .

II

The Double Jeopardy Clause of the Fifth Amendment protects a defendant in a criminal proceeding against multiple punishments or repeated prosecutions for the same offense. Underlying this constitutional safeguard is the belief that "the State with all its resources and power should not be allowed to make repeated attempts to convict an individual for an alleged offense, thereby subjecting him to embarrassment, expense and ordeal and compelling him to live in a continuing state of anxiety and insecurity, as well as enhancing the possibility that even though innocent he may be found guilty." Where, as here, a mistrial has been declared, the defendant's "valued right to have his trial completed by a particular tribunal" is also implicated.

Since Mr. Justice Story's 1824 opinion for the Court in *United States v. Perez,* 9 Wheat. 579, this Court has held that the question whether under the Double Jeopardy Clause there can be a new trial after a mistrial has been declared without the defendant's request or consent depends on whether "there is a manifest necessity for the (mistrial), or the ends of public justice would otherwise be defeated." Different considerations obtain, however, when the mistrial has been declared at the defendant's request. The reasons for the distinction were discussed in the plurality opinion in the *Jorn* case:

> If that right to go to a particular tribunal is valued, it is because, independent of the threat of bad-faith conduct by judge or prosecutor, the defendant has a significant interest in the decision whether or not to take the case from the jury when circumstances occur which might be thought to warrant a declaration of mistrial. Thus, where circumstances develop not attributable to prosecutorial or judicial overreaching, a motion by the defendant for mistrial is ordinarily assumed to remove any barrier to reprosecution, even if the defendant's motion is necessitated by prosecutorial or judicial error. In the absence of such a motion, the *Perez* doctrine of manifest necessity stands as a command to trial judges not to foreclose the defendant's option until a scrupulous exercise of judicial discretion leads to the conclusion that the ends of public justice would not be served by a continuation of the proceedings.

The distinction between mistrials declared by the court sua sponte and mistrials granted at the defendant's request or with his consent is wholly consistent with the protections of the Double Jeopardy Clause. Even when judicial or prosecutorial error prejudices a defendant's prospects of securing an acquittal, he may nonetheless desire "to go to the first jury and, perhaps, end the dispute then and there with an acquittal." Our prior decisions recognize the defendant's right to pursue this course in the absence of circumstances of manifest necessity requiring a sua sponte judicial declaration of mistrial. But it is evident that when judicial or prosecutorial error seriously prejudices a defendant, he may have little interest in completing the trial and obtaining a verdict from the first jury. The defendant may reasonably conclude that a continuation of the tainted proceeding would result in a conviction followed by a lengthy appeal and, if a reversal is secured, by a second prosecution. In such circumstances, a defendant's mistrial request has objectives not unlike the interests served by the Double Jeopardy Clause the avoidance of the anxiety, expense, and delay occasioned by multiple prosecutions.

The Court of Appeals viewed the doctrine that permits a retrial following a mistrial sought by the defendant as resting on a waiver theory. The court concluded, therefore, that "something more substantial than a

Hobson's choice" is required before a defendant can "be said to have relinquished voluntarily his right to proceed before the first jury." The court thus held that no waiver could be imputed to the respondent because the trial judge's action in excluding Wagner left the respondent with "no choice but to move for or accept a mistrial." But traditional waiver concepts have little relevance where the defendant must determine whether or not to request or consent to a mistrial in response to judicial or prosecutorial error. In such circumstances, the defendant generally does face a "Hobson's choice" between giving up his first jury and continuing a trial tainted by prejudicial judicial or prosecutorial error. The important consideration, for purposes of the Double Jeopardy Clause, is that the defendant retain primary control over the course to be followed in the event of such error.

The Court of Appeals' determination that the manifest necessity standard should be applied to a mistrial motion when the defendant has "no choice" but to request a mistrial undermines rather than furthers the protections of the Double Jeopardy Clause. In the event of severely prejudicial error a defendant might well consider an immediate new trial a preferable alternative to the prospect of a probable conviction followed by an appeal, a reversal of the conviction, and a later retrial. Yet the Court of Appeals' decision, in effect, instructs trial judges to reject the most meritorious mistrial motion in the absence of manifest necessity and to require, instead, that the trial proceed to its conclusion despite a legitimate claim of seriously prejudicial error. For if a trial judge follows that course, the Double Jeopardy Clause will present no obstacle to a retrial if the conviction is set aside by the trial judge or reversed on appeal.

The Double Jeopardy Clause does protect a defendant against governmental actions intended to provoke mistrial requests and thereby to subject defendants to the substantial burdens imposed by multiple prosecutions. It bars retrials where "bad-faith conduct by judge or prosecutor," threatens the "(h)arassment of an accused by successive prosecutions or declaration of a mistrial so as to afford the prosecution a more favorable opportunity to convict" the defendant.

But here the trial judge's banishment of Wagner from the proceedings was not done in bad faith in order to goad the respondent into requesting a mistrial or to prejudice his prospects for an acquittal. As the Court of Appeals noted, Wagner "was guilty of improper conduct" during his opening statement which "may have justified disciplinary action." Even accepting the appellate court's conclusion that the trial judge overreacted in expelling Wagner from the courtroom, the court did not suggest, the respondent has not contended, and the record does not show that the judge's action was motivated by bad faith or undertaken to harass or prejudice the respondent.

Under these circumstances we hold that the Court of Appeals erred in finding that the retrial violated the respondent's constitutional right not to be twice put in jeopardy. Accordingly, the judgment before us is reversed, and the case is remanded to the Court of Appeals for further proceedings consistent with this opinion.

Oregon v. Kennedy

Supreme Court of the United States
456 U.S. 667 (1982)

Justice Rehnquist delivered the opinion of the Court.

The Oregon Court of Appeals decided that the Double Jeopardy Clause of the Fifth Amendment to the United States Constitution barred respondent's retrial after his first trial ended in a mistrial granted on his own motion. The Court of Appeals concluded that retrial was barred because the prosecutorial misconduct that occasioned the mistrial in the first instance amounted to "overreaching." Because that court took an overly expansive view of the application of the Double Jeopardy Clause following a mistrial resulting from the defendant's own motion, we reverse its judgment.

I

Respondent was charged with the theft of an oriental rug. During his first trial, the State called an expert witness on the subject of Middle Eastern rugs to testify as to the value and the identity of the rug in question. On cross-examination, respondent's attorney apparently attempted to establish bias on the part of the expert witness by asking him whether he had filed a criminal complaint against respondent. The witness eventually acknowledged this fact, but explained that no action had been taken on his complaint. On redirect examination, the prosecutor sought to elicit the reasons why the witness had filed a complaint against respondent, but the trial court sustained a series of objections to this line of inquiry. The following colloquy then ensued:

Prosecutor: Have you ever done business with the Kennedys?
Witness: No, I have not.
Prosecutor: Is that because he is a crook?

The trial court then granted respondent's motion for a mistrial.

When the State later sought to retry respondent, he moved to dismiss the charges because of double jeopardy. After a hearing at which the prosecutor testified, the trial court found as a fact that "it was not the intention of the prosecutor in this case to cause a mistrial." On the basis of this finding, the trial court held that double jeopardy principles did not bar retrial, and respondent was then tried and convicted.

Respondent then successfully appealed to the Oregon Court of Appeals, which sustained his double jeopardy claim. That court set out what it considered to be the governing principles in this kind of case: "The general rule is said to be that the double jeopardy clause does not bar reprosecution, . . . where circumstances develop not attributable to prosecutorial or judicial overreaching, . . . even if defendant's motion is necessitated by a prosecutorial error." However, retrial is barred where the error that prompted the mistrial is intended to provoke a mistrial or is "motivated by bad faith or undertaken to harass or prejudice" the defendant.

The Court of Appeals accepted the trial court's finding that it was not the intent of the prosecutor to cause a mistrial. Nevertheless, the court held that retrial was barred because the prosecutor's conduct in this case constituted what it viewed as "overreaching." Although the prosecutor intended to rehabilitate the witness, the Court of Appeals expressed the view that the question was in fact "a direct personal attack on the general character of the defendant." This personal attack left respondent with a "Hobson's choice—either to accept a necessarily prejudiced jury, or to move for a mistrial and face the process of being retried at a later time."

II

The Double Jeopardy Clause of the Fifth Amendment protects a criminal defendant from repeated prosecutions for the same offense. As a part of this protection against multiple prosecutions, the Double Jeopardy Clause affords a criminal defendant a "valued right to have his trial completed by a particular tribunal." The Double Jeopardy Clause, however, does not offer a guarantee to the defendant that the State will vindicate its societal interest in the enforcement of the criminal laws in one proceeding. If the law were otherwise, "the purpose of law to protect society from those guilty of crimes frequently would be frustrated by denying courts power to put the defendant to trial again."

Where the trial is terminated over the objection of the defendant, the classical test for lifting the double jeopardy bar to a second trial is the "manifest necessity" standard first enunciated in Justice Story's opinion for the Court in *United States v. Perez*, 9 Wheat. 579. *Perez* dealt with the most common form of "manifest necessity": a mistrial declared by the judge following the jury's declaration that it was unable to reach a verdict. While other situations have been recognized by our cases as meeting the "manifest necessity" standard, the hung jury remains the prototypical example. The "manifest necessity" standard provides sufficient protection to the defendant's interests in having his case finally decided by the jury first selected while at the same time maintaining "the public's interest in fair trials designed to end in just judgments."

But in the case of a mistrial declared at the behest of the defendant, quite different principles come into play. Here the defendant himself has elected to terminate the proceedings against him, and the "manifest necessity" standard has no place in the application of the Double Jeopardy Clause. Indeed, in *United States v. Tateo*, 377 U.S. 463, 467 (1964), the Court stated: "If Tateo had requested a mistrial on the basis of the judge's comments, there would be no doubt that if he had been successful, the Government would not have been barred from retrying him" (emphasis in original).

Our cases, however, have indicated that even where the defendant moves for a mistrial, there is a narrow exception to the rule that the Double Jeopardy Clause is no bar to retrial. The circumstances under which respondent's first trial was terminated require us to delineate the bounds of that exception more fully than we have in previous cases.

Since one of the principal threads making up the protection embodied in the Double Jeopardy Clause is the right of the defendant to have his trial completed before the first jury empaneled to try him, it may be wondered as a matter of original inquiry why the defendant's election to terminate the first trial by his own motion should not be deemed a renunciation of that right for all purposes. We have recognized, however, that there would be great difficulty in applying such a rule where the prosecutor's actions giving rise to the motion for mistrial were done "in order to goad the [defendant] into requesting a mistrial." In such a case, the defendant's valued right to complete his trial before the first jury would be a hollow shell if the inevitable motion for mistrial were held to prevent a later invocation of the bar of double jeopardy in all circumstances. But the precise phrasing of the circumstances which will allow a defendant to interpose the defense of double jeopardy to a second prosecution where the first has terminated on his own motion for a mistrial have been stated with less than crystal clarity in our cases which deal with this area of the law. In *United States v. Dinitz*, 424 U.S., at 611, we said: "The Double Jeopardy Clause does protect a defendant against governmental actions intended to provoke mistrial requests and thereby to subject defendants to the substantial burdens imposed by multiple prosecutions."

This language would seem to follow the rule of *United States v. Tateo* in limiting the exception to cases of governmental actions intended to provoke mistrial requests. But immediately following the quoted language we went on to say: "[The Double Jeopardy Clause] bars retrials where 'bad-faith conduct by judge or prosecutor,' threatens the '[h]arassment of an accused by successive prosecutions or declaration of a mistrial so as to afford the prosecution a more favorable opportunity to convict' the defendant."

The language just quoted would seem to broaden the test from one of intent to provoke a motion for a mistrial to a more generalized standard of "bad faith conduct" or "harassment" on the part of the judge or prosecutor. It was upon this language that the Oregon Court of Appeals apparently relied in concluding that the prosecutor's colloquy with the expert witness in this case amount to "overreaching."

The difficulty with the more general standards which would permit a broader exception than one merely based on intent is that they offer virtually no standards for their application. Every act on the part of a rational prosecutor during a trial is designed to "prejudice" the defendant by placing before the judge or jury evidence leading to a finding of his guilt. Given the complexity of the rules of evidence, it will be a rare trial of any complexity in which some proffered evidence by the prosecutor or by the defendant's attorney will not be found objectionable by the trial court. Most such objections are undoubtedly curable by simply refusing to allow the proffered evidence to be admitted, or in the case of a particular line of inquiry taken by counsel with a witness, by an admonition to desist from a particular line of inquiry.

More serious infractions on the part of the prosecutor may provoke a motion for mistrial on the part of the defendant, and may in the view of the trial court warrant the granting of such a motion. The "overreaching" standard applied by the court below and urged today by Justice Stevens, however, would add another classification of prosecutorial error, one requiring dismissal of the indictment, but without supplying any standard by which to assess that error.

By contrast, a standard that examines the intent of the prosecutor, though certainly not entirely free from practical difficulties, is a manageable standard to apply. It merely calls for the court to make a finding of fact. Inferring the existence or nonexistence of intent from objective facts and circumstances is a familiar process in our criminal justice system. When it is remembered that resolution of double jeopardy questions by state trial courts are reviewable not only within the state court system, but in the federal court system on habeas corpus as well, the desirability of an easily applied principle is apparent.

Prosecutorial conduct that might be viewed as harassment or overreaching, even if sufficient to justify a mistrial on defendant's motion, therefore, does not bar retrial absent intent on the part of the prosecutor to subvert the protections afforded by the Double Jeopardy Clause. A defendant's motion for a mistrial constitutes "a deliberate election on his part to forgo his valued right to have his guilt or innocence determined before the first trier of fact." Where prosecutorial error even of a degree sufficient to warrant a mistrial has occurred, "[t]he important consideration, for purposes of the Double Jeopardy Clause, is that the defendant retain primary control over the course to be followed in the event of such error." Only where the governmental conduct in question is intended to "goad" the defendant into moving for a mistrial may a defendant raise the bar of double jeopardy to a second trial after having succeeded in aborting the first on his own motion. . . .

NOTES & QUESTIONS ON OTHER MISTRIALS

1. *Goading. Oregon v. Kennedy* makes clear that the manifest necessity standard does not apply when the defendant has made the motion for a mistrial. (The manifest necessity standard applies in cases where the mistrial is declared over the objection of the defendant; in those cases, retrial is permitted if the mistrial was motivated by manifest necessity, usually a hung jury, but occasionally by other factors.) Instead, in cases where the defendant has requested the mistrial, retrial is ordinarily permitted unless the prosecution managed to "goad" the defendant into requesting the mistrial. Can you think of examples that would constitute impermissible goading?

2. *Prosecutorial avoidance.* The thread that runs through the Supreme Court's entire mistrial line of cases is that the Double Jeopardy Clause bars retrial following a mistrial when the record indicates that the mistrial was the result of a prosecutor seeking to avoid an inevitable acquittal. In that situation, the prosecution will not be allowed to use a mistrial—even when requested by defense in response to being baited—to avoid what appears to be an inevitable acquittal and regroup to improve its hand. So, if a witness fails to show up because she became ill that morning even though properly served with a subpoena, a state request for a mistrial will not erect a double jeopardy bar to retrial. But if the witness fails to show up because the prosecutor did not serve her, a state mistrial request will be viewed as opportunistic "acquittal avoidance" and will therefore trigger the protection of the Double Jeopardy Clause.

3. *Banishment.* The facts in *Dinitz* are striking. After the primary defense counsel was banished from the courtroom, the defense was given three options: (i) an interlocutory appeal regarding the judge's decision to exclude the primary counsel; (ii) continuing the case with the co-counsel; or (iii) mistrial. Do you agree with the Supreme Court that the judge's actions were neither taken in bad faith nor designed to goad the defense into requesting a mistrial? Because the Court concluded that there was no goading, the defense was stuck with the consequences of its acquiescence to the mistrial—a retrial.

PROBLEM CASE

The defendant, Gregory McDonald Williams, was charged with speeding, an open container violation, and driving under the influence. During closing arguments of the jury trial, the following events occurred:

> [T]he prosecutor incorrectly asserted that Williams "had some margaritas at 2:00[,]" which misstated the evidence that had been presented at trial. Williams did not interpose a timely objection when the misstatement was made. Rather, Williams's counsel did not discover the misstatement until after the jury had retired for deliberations, at which time he reviewed the videotape of Williams's traffic stop to determine what statements were made concerning Williams's alcohol consumption. When Williams's counsel raised the issue, the prosecutor acknowledged his mistake and moved for a mistrial. Williams's counsel initially opposed the mistrial motion, contending that a mistrial was not necessary and further stating that he knew that "the prosecution didn't make th[e] error to goad [the defense] into moving to mistrial[.]" The trial court denied the State's motion for a mistrial, but considered alternative curative actions.
>
> As a form of curative action, Williams's counsel proposed that the videotape evidence be replayed for the jury. The trial court, however, declined to replay the videotape in the absence of the jury's request. The trial court recessed the proceedings to allow counsel an opportunity to discuss other alternatives. When the proceedings resumed, Williams's counsel announced that he was joining in the State's motion for a mistrial, in light of the trial court's denial of his request to replay the videotape to the jury. In the absence of any further suggestions for resolving the issue, the trial court granted the joint motion for a mistrial.

See *Williams v. State*, 311 Ga. App. 783, 784-85, 717 S.E.2d 264, 265-66 (2011). Did the prosecution's behavior constitute impermissible "goading" of the defense into supporting the motion for a mistrial?

PROBLEM CASE

Consider the following case. James Fields was prosecuted along with a co-defendant in Baltimore County for armed robbery and related offenses. The trial was a contentious affair with open animosity between the judge and prosecutor breaking out in front of the jury. There were several angry exchanges, but the following exchange was the straw that broke the camel's back:

> **The Court:** [Ms. Prosecutor], get back up here, please.
>
> **The Court:** You are arrogant and obnoxious.
>
> **[The Prosecutor]:** That may very well be true, but I am also right, and that is what makes the difference.
>
> **The Court:** How do you know who is right, because I make the damn decision?

[THE PROSECUTOR]: You are making the decisions, and I am forced to abide by them, but that does not make them right.
THE COURT: Deal with them your own way. I do not deal with them the way you are dealing with them. Do you understand what I am talking about?
[THE PROSECUTOR]: No, sir, I do not understand that.
THE COURT: I am declaring a mistrial.
[THE PROSECUTOR]: No one is asking for a mistrial. You must make a finding of manifest [necessity].
THE COURT: I will do what I want to do! That is what you do not understand. Take a break.

Under these circumstances, does double jeopardy bar the prosecution from retrying the defendant? As discussed in this chapter, if the prosecutor goads the *defendant* into requesting a mistrial, there is an exception to the waiver rule and the double jeopardy rule still applies. But what happens if the prosecutor goads the *judge* into declaring a mistrial? Should the government be prohibited from retrying the defendant in these circumstances? See *Fields v. State*, 96 Md. App. 722 (1993).

3. Dual Sovereignty

Should the double jeopardy rule apply if the separate prosecutions are initiated by different sovereigns? The text of the Fifth Amendment says nothing about dual sovereigns, and the answer to this question requires a deep dive into the underlying purpose of the prohibition against subsequent prosecutions. From one perspective, if the prosecutions are initiated by different sovereigns, one might argue that the rule should not apply because the rule was designed to prevent the same sovereign power from having a second bite at the apple. On the other hand, from the perspective of the defendant, why should it matter whether the new prosecution is initiated by a separate, as opposed to the same, sovereign? Is the distinction between one or two sovereigns conceptually significant or is it a mere detail that should not fundamentally change the double jeopardy calculus?

Heath v. Alabama

Supreme Court of the United States
474 U.S. 82 (1985)

Justice O'CONNOR delivered the opinion of the Court.

The question before the Court is whether the Double Jeopardy Clause of the Fifth Amendment bars Alabama from trying petitioner for the capital offense of murder during a kidnaping after Georgia has convicted him of murder based on the same homicide. In particular, this case presents the issue of the applicability of the dual sovereignty doctrine to successive prosecutions by two States.

I

In August 1981, petitioner, Larry Gene Heath, hired Charles Owens and Gregory Lumpkin to kill his wife, Rebecca Heath, who was then nine months pregnant, for a sum of $2,000. On the morning of August 31, 1981, petitioner left the Heath residence in Russell County, Alabama, to meet with Owens and Lumpkin in Georgia, just over the Alabama border from the Heath home. Petitioner led them back to the Heath residence, gave them the keys to the Heaths' car and house, and left the premises in his girlfriend's truck. Owens and Lumpkin then kidnaped Rebecca Heath from her home. The Heath car, with Rebecca Heath's body inside, was later found on the side of a road in Troup County, Georgia. The cause of death was a gunshot wound in the head. The estimated time of death and the distance from the Heath residence to the spot where Rebecca Heath's body was found are consistent with the theory that the murder took place in Georgia, and respondent does not contend otherwise.

Georgia and Alabama authorities pursued dual investigations in which they cooperated to some extent. On September 4, 1981, petitioner was arrested by Georgia authorities. Petitioner waived his Miranda rights and gave a full confession admitting that he had arranged his wife's kidnaping and murder. In November 1981, the grand jury of Troup County, Georgia, indicted petitioner for the offense of "malice" murder. . . . Georgia then served petitioner with notice of its intention to seek the death penalty, citing as the aggravating circumstance the fact that the murder was "caused and directed" by petitioner. On February 10, 1982, petitioner pleaded guilty to the Georgia murder charge in exchange for a sentence of life imprisonment, which he understood could involve his serving as few as seven years in prison.

On May 5, 1982, the grand jury of Russell County, Alabama, returned an indictment against petitioner for the capital offense of murder during a kidnaping. Before trial on this indictment, petitioner entered pleas of autrefois convict and former jeopardy under the Alabama and United States Constitutions, arguing that his conviction and sentence in Georgia barred his prosecution in Alabama for the same conduct. Petitioner also entered a plea contesting the jurisdiction of the Alabama court on the ground that the crime had occurred in Georgia.

After a hearing, the trial court rejected petitioner's double jeopardy claims. It assumed, arguendo, that the two prosecutions could not have been brought in succession by one State but held that double jeopardy did not bar successive prosecutions by two different States for the same act. . . . On January 12, 1983, the Alabama jury convicted petitioner of murder during a kidnaping in the first degree. After a sentencing hearing, the jury recommended the death penalty. . . .

II

Successive prosecutions are barred by the Fifth Amendment only if the two offenses for which the defendant is prosecuted are the "same" for double jeopardy purposes. Respondent does not contravene petitioner's contention that the offenses of "murder during a kidnaping" and "malice murder," as construed by the courts of Alabama and Georgia respectively, may be considered greater and lesser offenses and, thus, the "same" offense under *Brown v. Ohio*, absent operation of the dual sovereignty principle. We therefore assume, arguendo, that, had these offenses arisen under the laws of one State and had petitioner been separately prosecuted for both offenses in that State, the second conviction would have been barred by the Double Jeopardy Clause.

The sole remaining question upon which we granted certiorari is whether the dual sovereignty doctrine permits successive prosecutions under the laws of different States which otherwise would be held to "subject [the defendant] for the same offence to be twice put in jeopardy." Although we have not previously so held, we believe the answer to this query is inescapable. The dual sovereignty doctrine, as originally articulated and consistently applied by this Court, compels the conclusion that successive prosecutions by two States for the same conduct are not barred by the Double Jeopardy Clause.

The dual sovereignty doctrine is founded on the common-law conception of crime as an offense against the sovereignty of the government. When a defendant in a single act violates the "peace and dignity" of two sovereigns by breaking the laws of each, he has committed two distinct "offences." As the Court explained in *Moore v. Illinois*, 14 How. 13, 19 (1852), "[a]n offence, in its legal signification, means the transgression of a law." Consequently, when the same act transgresses the laws of two sovereigns, "it cannot be truly averred that the offender has been twice punished for the same offence; but only that by one act he has committed two offences, for each of which he is justly punishable."

In applying the dual sovereignty doctrine, then, the crucial determination is whether the two entities that seek successively to prosecute a defendant for the same course of conduct can be termed separate sovereigns. This determination turns on whether the two entities draw their authority to punish the offender from distinct sources of power. Thus, the Court has uniformly held that the States are separate sovereigns with respect to the Federal Government because each State's power to prosecute is derived from its own "inherent sovereignty," not from the Federal Government. . . .

The States are no less sovereign with respect to each other than they are with respect to the Federal Government. Their powers to undertake criminal prosecutions derive from separate and independent sources of power and authority originally belonging to them before admission to the Union and preserved to them by the Tenth Amendment. The States are equal to each other "in power, dignity and authority, each competent to exert that residuum of sovereignty not delegated to the United States by the Constitution itself." Thus, "[e]ach has the power, inherent in any sovereign, independently to determine what shall be an offense against its authority and to punish such offenses, and in doing so each is exercising its own sovereignty, not that of the other."

The cases in which the Court has applied the dual sovereignty principle outside the realm of successive federal and state prosecutions illustrate the soundness of this analysis. *United States v. Wheeler,* 435 U.S. 313 (1978), is particularly instructive because there the Court expressly refused to find that only the State and Federal Governments could be considered distinct sovereigns with respect to each other for double jeopardy purposes, stating that "so restrictive a view of [the dual sovereignty] concept . . . would require disregard of the very words of the Double Jeopardy Clause." Instead, the *Wheeler* Court reiterated the principle that the sovereignty of two prosecuting entities for these purposes is determined by "the ultimate source of the power under which the respective prosecutions were undertaken." On the basis of this reasoning, the Court held that the Navajo Tribe, whose power to prosecute its members for tribal offenses is derived from the Tribe's "primeval sovereignty" rather than a delegation of federal authority, is an independent sovereign from the Federal Government for purposes of the dual sovereignty doctrine.

In those instances where the Court has found the dual sovereignty doctrine inapplicable, it has done so because the two prosecuting entities did not derive their powers to prosecute from independent sources of authority. Thus, the Court has held that successive prosecutions by federal and territorial courts are barred because such courts are "creations emanating from the same sovereignty." *Puerto Rico,* 302 U.S., at 264. Similarly, municipalities that derive their power to try a defendant from the same organic law that empowers the State to prosecute are not separate sovereigns with respect to the State. These cases confirm that it is the presence of independent sovereign authority to prosecute, not the relation between States and the Federal Government in our federalist system, that constitutes the basis for the dual sovereignty doctrine. . . .

III

Petitioner invites us to restrict the applicability of the dual sovereignty principle to cases in which two governmental entities, having concurrent jurisdiction and pursuing quite different interests, can demonstrate that allowing only one entity to exercise jurisdiction over the defendant will interfere with the unvindicated interests of the second entity and that multiple prosecutions therefore are necessary for the satisfaction of the legitimate interests of both entities. This balancing of interests approach, however, cannot be reconciled with the dual sovereignty principle. This Court has plainly and repeatedly stated that two identical offenses are not the "same offence" within the meaning of the Double Jeopardy Clause if they are prosecuted by different sovereigns. If the States are separate sovereigns, as they must be under the definition of sovereignty which the Court consistently has employed, the circumstances of the case are irrelevant.

Petitioner, then, is asking the Court to discard its sovereignty analysis and to substitute in its stead his difficult and uncertain balancing of interests approach. . . . The Court's express rationale for the dual sovereignty doctrine is not simply a fiction that can be disregarded in difficult cases. It finds weighty support in the historical understanding and political realities of the States' role in the federal system and in the words of the Double Jeopardy Clause itself, "nor shall any person be subject for the same offence to be twice put in jeopardy of life or limb."

It is axiomatic that "[i]n America, the powers of sovereignty are divided between the government of the Union, and those of the States. They are each sovereign, with respect to the objects committed to it, and neither sovereign with respect to the objects committed to the other." It is as well established that the States, "as political communities, [are] distinct and sovereign, and consequently foreign to each other." The Constitution leaves in the possession of each State "certain exclusive and very important portions of sovereign power." Foremost among the prerogatives of sovereignty is the power to create and enforce a criminal code. To deny a State its power to enforce its criminal laws because another State has won the race to the courthouse "would be a shocking and untoward deprivation of the historic right and obligation of the States to maintain peace and order within their confines."

Such a deprivation of a State's sovereign powers cannot be justified by the assertion that under "interest analysis" the State's legitimate penal interests will be satisfied through a prosecution conducted by another State. A State's interest in vindicating its sovereign authority through enforcement of its laws by definition can never be satisfied by another State's enforcement of its own laws. Just as the Federal Government has the right to decide that a state prosecution has not vindicated a violation of the "peace and dignity" of the Federal Government, a State must be entitled to decide that a prosecution by another State has not satisfied its legitimate sovereign interest. In recognition of this fact, the Court consistently has endorsed the principle that a single act constitutes an "offence" against each sovereign whose laws are violated by that act. The Court has always understood the words of the Double Jeopardy Clause to reflect this fundamental principle, and we see no reason why we should reconsider that understanding today. . . .

Justice MARSHALL, with whom Justice BRENNAN joins, dissenting.

Seizing upon the suggestion in past cases that every "independent" sovereign government may prosecute violations of its laws even when the defendant has already been tried for the same crime in another jurisdiction, the Court today gives short shrift to the policies underlying those precedents. The "dual sovereignty" doctrine, heretofore used to permit federal and state prosecutions for the same offense, was born of the need to accommodate complementary state and federal concerns within our system of concurrent territorial jurisdictions. It cannot justify successive prosecutions by different States. Moreover, even were the dual sovereignty doctrine to support successive state prosecutions as a general matter, it simply could not legitimate the collusion between Georgia and Alabama in this case to ensure that petitioner is executed for his crime. . . .

Had the Georgia authorities suddenly become dissatisfied with the life sentence petitioner received in their courts and reindicted petitioner in order to seek the death penalty once again, that indictment would without question be barred by the Double Jeopardy Clause of the Fifth Amendment, as applied to the States by the Fourteenth Amendment. Whether the second indictment repeated the charge of malice murder or instead charged murder in the course of a kidnaping, it would surely, under any reasonable constitutional standard, offend the bar to successive prosecutions for the same offense.

The only difference between this case and such a hypothetical volte-face by Georgia is that here Alabama, not Georgia, was offended by the notion that petitioner might not forfeit his life in punishment for his crime. The only reason the Court gives for permitting Alabama to go forward is that Georgia and Alabama are separate sovereigns. . . .

Because all but one of the cases upholding the dual sovereignty doctrine have involved the unique relationship between the Federal Government and the States, the question whether a similar rule should exempt successive prosecutions by two different States from the command of the Double Jeopardy Clause is one for which this Court's precedents provide all too little illumination. . . .

Where two States seek to prosecute the same defendant for the same crime in two separate proceedings, the justifications found in the federal-state context for an exemption from double jeopardy constraints simply do not hold. Although the two States may have opted for different policies within their assigned territorial jurisdictions, the sovereign concerns with whose vindication each State has been charged are identical. Thus, in contrast to the federal-state context, barring the second prosecution would still

> permit one government to act upon the broad range of sovereign concerns that have been reserved to the States by the Constitution. The compelling need in the federal-state context to subordinate double jeopardy concerns is thus considerably diminished in cases involving successive prosecutions by different States. Moreover, from the defendant's perspective, the burden of successive prosecutions cannot be justified as the quid pro quo of dual citizenship. . . .

NOTES & QUESTIONS ON DUAL SOVEREIGNTY

1. *Sham prosecutions.* Notwithstanding the dual sovereignty doctrine, there are some situations where a second prosecution would be barred. That would be situations where the second prosecution is performed in coordination with the prosecutors from the first trial. Although excluding this type of situation from the double jeopardy protection seems correct, the question is why. One argument is that the close coordination between the prosecutors makes the second prosecutors effectively state agents of the first state, thus eliminating the conceptual foundation (different sovereigns) upon which the dual sovereignty doctrine rests. For example, in *Bartkus v. Illinois*, 359 U.S. 121 (1959), federal prosecutors turned over to state prosecutors all evidence that they had gathered during their unsuccessful federal prosecutions. But the Supreme Court concluded that this fact was not enough to make the second state prosecution a "sham" federal prosecution: "It does not support the claim that the State of Illinois in bringing its prosecution was merely a tool of the federal authorities, who thereby avoided the prohibition of the Fifth Amendment against a retrial of a federal prosecution after an acquittal. It does not sustain a conclusion that the state prosecution was a sham and a cover for a federal prosecution, and thereby in essential fact another federal prosecution." *Id.* at 123-24.

2. *Gamble on dual sovereignty.* Will the Supreme Court reverse or limit the dual sovereignty doctrine? In 2019, the Supreme Court heard oral arguments in *Gamble v. United States*, an appeal from the Eleventh Circuit that will give the Court the chance to revisit *Heath v. Alabama* and the dual sovereignty doctrine. Gamble was prosecuted for gun possession under both Alabama criminal law and federal criminal law and received separate sentences in separate trials. Several Justices across conservative-liberal lines voted to grant certiorari to reconsider the application of the separate sovereigns doctrine in Gamble's case. At oral argument, those Justices were concerned about the potential unfairness of subjecting Gamble to multiple punishments, but the Justices were also aware of stare decisis and the long-standing history of the dual sovereignty doctrine.

3. *Vertical versus horizontal.* Should it make a difference whether the second prosecution involves a vertical relationship with the first prosecution (federal-state or state-federal) or whether the second prosecution is just horizontal to the first prosecution (state-state)? For example, if New York punishes a defendant for drug trafficking and Connecticut does the same, should double jeopardy bar this kind of double punishment? Recall that criminal jurisdiction usually attaches if part of the crime (at least one element) occurs in the state. It is therefore entirely plausible to imagine a criminal drug transaction that stretches among multiple state jurisdictions. What if the crime stretches among three or four states? Should the defendant be subject to multiple prosecutions and punishments in four separate states? Is there any limit to these horizontal prosecutions?

STATE LAW REQUIREMENTS

Some states have statutory double jeopardy protections that far exceed what the Fifth Amendment provides under federal constitutional law. For example, New York State's double jeopardy statute includes the following triggering condition:

> Except as otherwise provided in this section, a person "is prosecuted" for an offense . . . when he is charged therewith by an accusatory instrument filed in a court of this state or of any jurisdiction within the United States, and when the action either:
>
> (a) Terminates in a conviction upon a plea of guilty; or
>
> (b) Proceeds to the trial stage and a jury has been impaneled and sworn or, in the case of a trial by the court without a jury, a witness is sworn.

N.Y. Crim. Proc. Law § 40.30. Notice the reference to the person's prosecution in a court "of any jurisdiction." The practical impact of this language is a broad rejection of the dual sovereignty doctrine in New York courts. A person is deemed "prosecuted" and entitled to double jeopardy protection if they are charged for the same crime in another state court or in a federal court. Although a subsequent New York State prosecution would be consistent with the federal Double Jeopardy Clause under the dual sovereign doctrine, the state prosecution would be prohibited by the New York State double jeopardy statute.

The New York statute gained widespread notice in 2018 after the Justice Department prosecution of Paul Manafort, the former campaign manager of Donald Trump. Another section of the statute details exceptions to the double jeopardy rule, including when the offense is "prosecuted in such other jurisdiction and has there been terminated by a court order expressly founded upon insufficiency of evidence to establish some element of such offense. . . ." N.Y. Crim. Proc. Law § 40.20. Several lawyers noted that the provision does not list a presidential pardon as an exception. In other words, if a federal court were to dismiss charges against Manafort for lack of evidence, he could still be charged in a New York court, but if the federal prosecution ended because of a presidential pardon, a subsequent New York prosecution would be barred under the state statute. After this was noted, New York's Attorney General, Eric Schneiderman, urged New York legislators to revise the statute.

PROBLEM CASE

Terry Nichols was charged by Oklahoma for his involvement in the bombing of the Alfred P. Murrah Federal Building in Oklahoma City, a domestic terror attack committed by Timothy McVeigh. The bombing was carried out by detonating a truck packed with a massive bomb made from fertilizer and other ingredients. The bombing killed 168 people, including several children in a daycare center in the building. McVeigh was the principal perpetrator, but Terry Nichols was subsequently charged in federal court with conspiracy to use a weapon of mass destruction and involuntary manslaughter in the death of federal law enforcement agents who were killed in the bombing. In both the Nichols and McVeigh prosecutions, federal authorities went to trial first, and state prosecutors in Oklahoma offered to proceed second. McVeigh's federal trial resulted in a death sentence. (McVeigh suspended his effort to appeal his death sentence and was executed by the federal government in 2001.) Nichols was convicted at his federal trial but was spared the death penalty and received life in prison instead. But Terry Nichols then faced his state capital trial in Oklahoma. In 2004, Nichols was convicted of multiple counts of first-degree murder and a capital sentencing hearing was conducted, but the state jury deadlocked on the issue of the death penalty. Nichols was then sentenced to multiple life terms, one for each of the 161 victims of the bombing (including a fetal death), excluding the federal law enforcement officers. Nichols remains in federal custody serving his federal sentence. When the state charges against him were first announced, Oklahoma prosecutors insisted that the state charges were not motivated simply by a desire to seek an execution, but rather were a broader effort to seek justice in an Oklahoma court for the state's many victims. In reality, though, given the federal sentence, many observers interpreted the state trial as an attempt to get a capital sentence when federal prosecutors had failed in that effort. Is it appropriate for prosecutors, albeit from two different governments, to get two shots at convicting Nichols in a capital trial?

D. PRACTICE & POLICY

Although the dual sovereign or separate sovereign theory allows follow-on federal prosecutions after an initial state prosecution, federal prosecutors do not always have to exercise their prosecutorial discretion in favor of a second prosecution. Justice Department policy, codified in the Justice Manual (formerly known as the U.S. Attorney's Manual), outlines some of the policy considerations that federal prosecutors should consider before launching a federal prosecution. In some situations, the principles outlined in the policy will counsel in favor of forgoing prosecutions. Although not binding as a matter of federal statutory law, the Manual is considered binding on federal prosecutions as a matter of internal Justice Department regulations.

❧ **The three requirements.** In general, the Manual cautions against secondary federal prosecutions and only authorizes them when the following three conditions are met: (1) the case involves a "substantial federal interest"; (2) the state prosecution left the federal interest "demonstrably unvindicated"; and (3) prosecutors believe that the defendant's conduct constituted a federal crime and that they have enough admissible evidence to obtain a conviction. The Manual makes clear that if the criteria are not met, the Department should not proceed; however, the reverse does not apply. The satisfaction of the three criteria does not require the Department to initiate a federal prosecution and it may decline to do so on other grounds of prosecutorial discretion. Justice Manual § 9-2.031.

❧ Congressional intent. For some offenses, Congress has already made the decision for the Justice Department. In crafting some statutory offenses, Congress has expressed its intent to reject the dual sovereign doctrine; here the Justice Department is not permitted to commence a federal prosecution if state prosecutors had the first bite at the apple. Consider, for example, the federal crime of theft of an interstate shipment. After providing a lengthy definition of the types of theft and embezzlement of an interstate shipment, the statute notes that

> [a] judgment of conviction or acquittal on the merits under the laws of any State shall be a bar to any prosecution under this section for the same act or acts. Nothing contained in this section shall be construed as indicating an intent on the part of Congress to occupy the field in which provisions of this section operate to the exclusion of State laws on the same subject matter, nor shall any provision of this section be construed as invalidating any provision of State law unless such provision is inconsistent with any of the purposes of this section or any provision thereof.

18 U.S.C.A. § 659. Consequently, there is nothing that prevents Congress from constraining the executive branch from engaging in secondary prosecutions if that is what Congress so desires. Similarly, the general federal larceny and embezzlement statute states:

> Whoever steals, unlawfully abstracts, unlawfully and willfully converts to his own use or to the use of another, or embezzles any of the moneys, funds, securities, credits, property, or assets of any registered investment company shall be deemed guilty of a crime, and upon conviction thereof shall be subject to the penalties provided in . . . this title. A judgment of conviction or acquittal on the merits under the laws of any State shall be a bar to any prosecution under this section for the same act or acts.

15 U.S.C.A. § 80a-36. However, these crimes are exceptions to the general rule. Most federal offenses do not include any such directive from Congress, the Justice Department assumes that a federal prosecution is

permissible even if the same acts were charged in a state prosecution. As a policy matter, though, Congress could certainly use its authority over federal criminal law to walk back or sharply curtail the scope of the dual sovereign doctrine.

❧ Federal RICO. The federal RICO statute poses unique issues regarding double prosecutions. The statute was passed in 1970 and stands for "Racketeer Influenced and Corrupt Organizations." The criminal offense is highly unique in its construction and design. It allows federal prosecutors to charge individuals with participation in a corrupt organization or enterprise—initially organized crime. The enterprise is criminal if it engages in racketeering activity, which is defined according to a very long list of predicate criminal offenses that includes "murder, kidnapping, gambling, arson, robbery, bribery, extortion, dealing in obscene matter, or dealing in a controlled substance or listed chemical," 18 U.S.C.A. § 1961, but also many other predicate offenses as well. As one could imagine, then, a federal RICO prosecution may rightly cover at least some of the same ground as a prior state prosecution, given the extraordinary breadth of the RICO statute and the extraordinarily wide definition that it gives to racketeering activity. It should perhaps then come as no surprise that the Justice Manual allows RICO prosecutions to proceed even if they encompass some ground from a prior state prosecution:

> This policy does not apply, and thus prior approval is not required, where the prior prosecution involved only a minor part of the contemplated federal charges. For example, a federal conspiracy or RICO prosecution may allege overt acts or predicate offenses previously prosecuted as long as those acts or offenses do not represent substantially the whole of the contemplated federal charge, and, in a RICO prosecution, as long as there are a sufficient number of predicate offenses to sustain the RICO charge if the previously prosecuted offenses were excluded.

The question then is what constitutes the "whole of" the federal charge—a qualitative term that may allow prosecutors substantial room to maneuver.

RICO defendants have often argued that their federal prosecutions violate double jeopardy—and they usually lose. See, e.g., *United States v. Aleman*, 609 F.2d 298, 301 (7th Cir. 1979). Some scholars and defense attorneys worry that the current doctrine fails to adequately protect RICO defendants from double jeopardy problems:

> [F]ederal prosecutors . . . violate the spirit of the . . . policy by charging defendants with offenses for which they have already been prosecuted in state court. One . . . defendant, for instance, was convicted of a

> robbery in state court, served a prison term, and then was prosecuted under RICO based on a pattern of racketeering activity consisting of that robbery and two others. The basic purpose of RICO, and indeed the compelling interest of federal law enforcement behind RICO, is the eradication of organized crime. This purpose hardly is served by reprosecuting defendants who by no stretch of the imagination are organized crime members.

Linda Koenig Doris, *The Need for Greater Double Jeopardy and Due Process Safeguards in RICO Criminal and Civil Actions*, 70 Cal. L. Rev. 724, 733 (1982).

CHAPTER 20

APPEALS AND HABEAS CORPUS

INTRODUCTION

After a defendant is convicted and sentenced, the legal process is not complete; there remains a complex landscape of post-conviction legal review. One can describe that legal review process as tripartite: direct appellate review, state habeas relief, and federal habeas relief.

The first tier is "direct review" of the conviction and sentence in state appellate courts. Often this will include one appeal "as of right" to an intermediate appellate court, with further appeals to the state's highest court allowed on a certiorari basis, meaning that there is no guarantee that a state's highest court will agree to hear an appeal. The exact sequence and type of appeals before state appellate courts will vary between each state. Indeed, while every state has some direct appeal structure, the Supreme Court has never held that there is a federal constitutional right to a direct appeal.

The second tier is a state proceeding where the defendant files a petition for a writ of habeas corpus. In many states, the state habeas procedure is regulated by statute, but even in the absence of a statute, state courts can fall back on their common-law authority to issue a writ of habeas corpus. Habeas corpus is a Latin phrase that translates as "that you have the body" or some similar rendering, but a habeas corpus petition is really best understood as a show cause request: An inmate is demanding that the government show cause why her continued incarceration is consistent with law. Put differently, the procedure it refers to is one that forces the government to bring the prisoner's body to court and defend why that prisoner's continued detention is not illegal.

Strictly speaking, the writ of habeas corpus refers to the remedy that the court would issue if the court were to decide that continued detention would be illegal; counsel for the prisoner would make an application or a petition for a writ of habeas corpus. The court would then entertain the writ and then issue the writ if warranted, ordering the release of the individual.

The third tier is a federal proceeding, commenced in a federal district court, where the defendant files another petition for a writ of habeas corpus, alleging that his state criminal conviction or sentencing violated federal constitutional law. Taken together, the three tiers of post-conviction review are the three procedural mechanisms that a petitioner has to challenge their conviction. Both state and federal habeas petitions are referred to as "collateral" review proceedings to distinguish them from the review available in a direct review proceeding. (If the defendant was convicted in federal criminal court, rather than state court, the defendant would have only two tiers of review available: direct review in federal appellate courts and collateral review in a federal habeas corpus proceeding.) Federal habeas review is limited to claimed violations of "clearly established federal law," usually federal constitutional law, while state habeas proceedings can include allegations of violations of state law. State proceedings, either direct appellate review or state habeas review, must be exhausted before a petitioner files for federal habeas relief.

Whether the post-conviction review occurs in direct or collateral proceedings, the review is limited to questions of law, rather than findings of fact. In other words, higher courts are not permitted to engage in appellate proceedings that relitigate evidentiary questions, which would potentially transform appeals into a series of second and third "trials." This conceptual limitation is a distinct feature of the American judicial system that it inherited from the common law. In contrast, civil law countries in continental Europe often have a greater appetite for appellate proceedings that allow higher courts to engage in new fact finding and reassessments of the factual record below. In the United States, the higher court is deferential to the findings of facts made by the trial court and does not review them, since it is the trial court that heard from the witnesses, examined the evidence, and can properly balance their significance. There is one important exception to the general prohibition on reviewing matters of evidence: If an appellate court considers that no rational trier of fact could have convicted the defendant based on the admissible evidence at trial, the conviction could be overturned as a matter of law.

The writ of habeas corpus is often referred to as the Great Writ in recognition of its centrality to a divided form of government in the common law system. In addition to the criminal justice system, which requires a judicial determination (i.e., a trial) prior to the imposition of criminal punishment, non-punitive detention by the state also requires judicial review of its legality, thus explaining the need for the writ. As the following materials make clear, however, the writ is not confined to situations of non-punitive detention.

In fact, most habeas petitions involve "collateral" review of criminal convictions in state court. In that situation, the defendant has the opportunity to appeal the conviction on "direct review" to state appellate courts, including the supreme court or court of last resort of that state, at which point the defendant can then file a habeas petition in federal court to review the legality of the state proceedings.

Historically, the writ of habeas corpus was a "common law" writ, meaning the authority to issue the writ flowed just from the common law, the authority of judges in England to test the legality of executive detention. In England, the writ was codified by statute in 1679. In the United States, the writ is also codified by statute: "Writs of habeas corpus may be granted by the Supreme Court, any justice thereof, the district courts and any circuit judge within their respective jurisdictions. The order of a circuit judge shall be entered in the records of the district court of the district wherein the restraint complained of is had." 28 U.S.C.A. § 2241. Even in the absence of the federal statute, however, judges could rely on the common law writ to exercise their authority to release a prisoner.

The writ of habeas corpus is the only writ explicitly mentioned in the text of the Constitution, although interestingly the text does not "grant" a right to such a writ, but instead limits the government's ability to suspend the writ, suggesting our Founders understood the "privilege" of seeking such a writ as an inherent right. According to the Suspension Clause in Article I of the Constitution: "The privilege of the Writ of Habeas Corpus shall not be suspended, unless when in Cases of Rebellion or Invasion the public Safety may require it." The writ was suspended by President Lincoln in Maryland during the U.S. Civil War, an action that was declared illegal in *Ex parte Merryman*, 17 F. Cas. 144, 148 (C.C.D. Md. 1861), since the Constitution grants the suspension power to Congress rather than to the President. Since the writ represents a limit on executive power, it would be incongruous to conclude that the executive had the power to suspend the very legal mechanism that constrains it.

Habeas practice is often complex and technical. The following sections focus on the key elements of the habeas system, including the requirements for granting habeas relief. In particular, the materials focus on one particularly thorny obstacle for habeas petitioners: their inability to obtain relief if they have procedurally defaulted on their claims by failing to raise them in proceedings below in state court. Nonetheless, there are exceptions to procedural default, if the defendant can demonstrate either "cause and prejudice" or "actual innocence." These exceptions to procedural default, while difficult to satisfy, form an important part of the basic architecture of the habeas system.

The last sections of the chapter (and the casebook) focus on the territorial scope of the writ of habeas corpus, in particular whether it runs to territories over which the United States does not have formal, de jure, sovereignty, but over which it nonetheless exercises control. This question is of extreme importance during moments of armed conflict, when the armed forces of a state might exercise de facto control over territory that as a formal matter belongs to another sovereign state. Section F focuses on the suspension of the writ of habeas corpus and whether Congress can avoid the requirements of the Suspension Clause by simply providing an adequate substitute for the habeas process for some petitioners.

A. BUILDING BLOCKS OF POST-CONVICTION REVIEW

The mechanics of post-conviction review are complex. The rest of this chapter will explore the details of the tripartite structure described above, but before doing so, a few preliminary concepts must be introduced. The following subsections therefore focus on three essential concepts: evidentiary insufficiency, harmless error, and the concept of finality. What unites these concepts together is that they are basic concepts that structure the procedural framework for post-conviction review. The first question is when a habeas court may disturb a trial court's conviction due to insufficiency of evidence. As noted above, the dividing line between facts and law helps determine the scope of post-conviction review. Usually, assessing the facts is solely within the purview of the trial court and not subject to post-conviction review, but in some cases the insufficiency of evidence is so clear that it becomes transformed, almost by legal fiction, into a matter of law. In that case, a post-conviction court will have jurisdiction to overturn the conviction, though the question is what standard should govern a post-conviction court's assessment of the factual record.

The second question is whether a trial court's legal error, identified by a post-conviction court, requires the remedy of a new trial. Instead of adopting a bright-line rule that any legal error requires reversal of conviction, the Supreme Court has adopted the doctrine of harmless error, where some errors need not warrant the most extraordinary remedy of a new trial because the error did not impact the trial's result. One consequence of this rule is that it sets a very demanding standard for a petitioner to be victorious. It is not enough for the petitioner to establish that their trial violated a rule of federal constitutional law; the petitioner must also demonstrate that the error made a difference to the outcome. From the perspective of the defendant, the promise of post-conviction review is built around the possibility of obtaining a new trial. With the doctrine of harmless error, the petitioner may indeed achieve only a pyrrhic victory: a determination of a legal error without the sought after remedy.

Finally, the third question is when a state court judgment against a defendant is "final" for purposes of applying a new rule of constitutional law. This question shows up in the Supreme Court's retroactivity jurisprudence. But it speaks to a much broader issue, which is the concept of finality and the dividing line (and the associated significance) between direct appellate review and collateral review in the form of a petition for habeas corpus. The two forms of post-conviction review come with different legal standards and different legal consequences. To take just one example, new constitutional rulings may be applied retroactively to other cases that are still on direct appellate review but not to other habeas cases that have completed the direct review process. At issue in this debate is nothing less than the nature of the law that appellate courts and habeas courts apply in the cases before them.

1. Standard of Review for Insufficiency of Evidence

In re Winship, 397 U.S. 358 (1970), made clear that due process requires that the prosecution demonstrate each element of the crime beyond a reasonable doubt. Using this constitutional holding as its foundation, the following case asks how a federal habeas court should review an allegation that a state court criminal conviction did not satisfy the *Winship* standard. As you read the case, pay particular attention to the standard announced by the Supreme Court. How much deference does it require reviewing courts to give to the original trial court? How exactly is that level of deference codified in the standard?

Jackson v. Virginia

Supreme Court of the United States
443 U.S. 307 (1979)

Mr. Justice STEWART delivered the opinion of the Court.

The Constitution prohibits the criminal conviction of any person except upon proof of guilt beyond a reasonable doubt. *In re Winship,* 397 U.S. 358. The question in this case is what standard is to be applied in a federal habeas corpus proceeding when the claim is made that a person has been convicted in a state court upon insufficient evidence. . . .

III

This is the first of our cases to expressly consider the question whether the due process standard recognized in *Winship* constitutionally protects an accused against conviction except upon evidence that is sufficient fairly to support a conclusion that every element of the crime has been established beyond a reasonable doubt. . . .

It is axiomatic that a conviction upon a charge not made or upon a charge not tried constitutes a denial of due process. These standards no more than reflect a broader premise that has never been doubted in our constitutional system: that a person cannot incur the loss of liberty for an offense without notice and a meaningful opportunity to defend. A meaningful opportunity to defend, if not the right to a trial itself, presumes as well that a total want of evidence to support a charge will conclude the case in favor of the accused. Accordingly, we held in the *Thompson* case that a conviction based upon a record wholly devoid of any relevant evidence of a crucial element of the offense charged is constitutionally infirm. The "no evidence" doctrine of *Thompson v. Louisville* thus secures to an accused the most elemental of due process rights: freedom from a wholly arbitrary deprivation of liberty.

The Court in *Thompson* explicitly stated that the due process right at issue did not concern a question of evidentiary "sufficiency." The right established in *In re Winship*, however, clearly stands on a different footing. *Winship* involved an adjudication of juvenile delinquency made by a judge under a state statute providing that the prosecution must prove the conduct charged as delinquent—which in *Winship* would have been a criminal offense if engaged in by an adult—by a preponderance of the evidence. Applying that standard, the judge was satisfied that the juvenile was "guilty," but he noted that the result might well have been different under a standard of proof beyond a reasonable doubt. In short, the record in *Winship* was not totally devoid of evidence of guilt.

The constitutional problem addressed in *Winship* was thus distinct from the stark problem of arbitrariness presented in *Thompson v. Louisville*. In *Winship*, the Court held for the first time that the Due Process Clause of the Fourteenth Amendment protects a defendant in a criminal case against conviction "except upon proof beyond a reasonable doubt of every fact necessary to constitute the crime with which he is charged." In so holding, the Court emphasized that proof beyond a reasonable doubt has traditionally been regarded as the decisive difference between criminal culpability and civil liability. The standard of proof beyond a reasonable doubt, said the Court, "plays a vital role in the American scheme of criminal procedure," because it operates to give "concrete substance" to the presumption of innocence to ensure against unjust convictions, and to reduce the risk of factual error in a criminal proceeding. At the same time by impressing upon the factfinder the need to reach a subjective state of near certitude of the guilt of the accused, the standard symbolizes the significance that our society attaches to the criminal sanction and thus to liberty itself.

The constitutional standard recognized in the *Winship* case was expressly phrased as one that protects an accused against a conviction except on "proof beyond a reasonable doubt. . . ." In subsequent cases discussing the reasonable-doubt standard, we have never departed from this definition of the rule or from the *Winship* understanding of the central purposes it serves. In short, *Winship* presupposes as an essential of the due process guaranteed by the Fourteenth Amendment that no person shall be made to suffer the onus of a criminal conviction except upon sufficient proof—defined as evidence necessary to convince a trier of fact beyond a reasonable doubt of the existence of every element of the offense.

Although several of our cases have intimated that the factfinder's application of the reasonable-doubt standard to the evidence may present a federal question when a state conviction is challenged, the Federal Courts of Appeals have generally assumed that so long as the reasonable-doubt instruction has been given at trial, the no-evidence doctrine of *Thompson v. Louisville* remains the appropriate guide for a federal habeas corpus court to apply in assessing a state prisoner's challenge to his conviction as founded upon insufficient evidence. We cannot agree.

The *Winship* doctrine requires more than simply a trial ritual. A doctrine establishing so fundamental a substantive constitutional standard must also require that the factfinder will rationally apply that standard to the facts in evidence. A "reasonable doubt," at a minimum, is one based upon "reason." Yet a properly instructed jury may occasionally convict even when it can be said that no rational trier of fact could find guilt beyond a reasonable doubt, and the same may be said of a trial judge sitting as a jury. In a federal trial, such an occurrence has traditionally been deemed to require reversal of the conviction. Under *Winship,* which established proof beyond a reasonable doubt as an essential of Fourteenth Amendment due process, it follows that when such a conviction occurs in a state trial, it cannot constitutionally stand.

A federal court has a duty to assess the historic facts when it is called upon to apply a constitutional standard to a conviction obtained in a state court. For example, on direct review of a state-court conviction, where the claim is made that an involuntary confession was used against the defendant, this Court reviews the facts to determine whether the confession was wrongly admitted in evidence. The same duty obtains in federal habeas corpus proceedings.

After *Winship* the critical inquiry on review of the sufficiency of the evidence to support a criminal conviction must be not simply to determine whether the jury was properly instructed, but to determine whether the record evidence could reasonably support a finding of guilt beyond a reasonable doubt. But this inquiry does not require a court to "ask itself whether it believes that the evidence at the trial established guilt beyond a reasonable doubt." Instead, the relevant question is whether, after viewing the evidence in the light most favorable to the prosecution, any rational trier of fact could have found the essential elements of the crime beyond a reasonable doubt. This familiar standard gives full play to the responsibility of the trier of fact fairly to resolve conflicts in the testimony, to weigh the evidence, and to draw reasonable inferences from basic facts to ultimate facts. Once a defendant has been found guilty of the crime charged, the factfinder's role as weigher of the evidence is preserved through a legal conclusion that upon judicial review all of the evidence is to be considered in the light most favorable to the prosecution. The criterion thus impinges upon "jury" discretion only to the extent necessary to guarantee the fundamental protection of due process of law.

That the *Thompson* "no evidence" rule is simply inadequate to protect against misapplications of the constitutional standard of reasonable doubt is readily apparent. Any evidence that is relevant—that has any tendency to make the existence of an element of a crime slightly more probable than it would be without the evidence—could be deemed a "mere modicum." But it could not seriously be argued that such a "modicum" of evidence could by itself rationally support a conviction beyond a reasonable doubt. The *Thompson* doctrine simply fails to supply a workable or even a predictable standard for determining whether the due process command of *Winship* has been honored.

Under 28 U.S.C. § 2254, a federal court must entertain a claim by a state prisoner that he or she is being held in "custody in violation of the Constitution or laws or treaties of the United States." Under the *Winship* decision, it is clear that a state prisoner who alleges that the evidence in support of his state conviction cannot be fairly characterized as sufficient to have led a rational trier of fact to find guilt beyond a reasonable doubt has stated a federal constitutional claim. Thus, assuming that state remedies have been exhausted and that no independent and adequate state ground stands as a bar, it follows that such a claim is cognizable in a federal habeas corpus proceeding. The respondents have argued, nonetheless, that a challenge to the constitutional sufficiency of the evidence should not be entertained by a federal district court under 28 U.S.C. § 2254.

In addition to the argument that a *Winship* standard invites replication of state criminal trials in the guise of § 2254 proceedings—an argument that simply fails to recognize that courts can and regularly do gauge the sufficiency of the evidence without intruding into any legitimate domain of the trier of fact—the respondents have urged that any departure from the *Thompson* test in federal habeas corpus proceedings will expand the number of meritless claims brought to the federal courts, will duplicate the work of the state appellate courts, will disserve the societal interest in the finality of state criminal proceedings, and will increase friction between the federal and state judiciaries. . . . We disagree.

First, the burden that is likely to follow from acceptance of the *Winship* standard has, we think, been exaggerated. Federal-court challenges to the evidentiary support for state convictions have since *Thompson* been dealt with under § 2254. A more stringent standard will expand the contours of this type of claim, but will not create an entirely new class of cases cognizable on federal habeas corpus. Furthermore, most meritorious challenges to constitutional sufficiency of the evidence undoubtedly will be recognized in the state courts, and, if the state courts have fully considered the issue of sufficiency, the task of a federal habeas court should not be difficult. And this type of claim can almost always be judged on the written record without need for an evidentiary hearing in the federal court. . . .

The question whether a defendant has been convicted upon inadequate evidence is central to the basic question of guilt or innocence. The constitutional necessity of proof beyond a reasonable doubt is not confined to those defendants who are morally blameless. Under our system of criminal justice even a thief is entitled to complain that he has been unconstitutionally convicted and imprisoned as a burglar.

We hold that in a challenge to a state criminal conviction brought under 28 U.S.C. § 2254—if the settled procedural prerequisites for such a claim have otherwise been satisfied—the applicant is entitled to habeas corpus relief if it is found that upon the record evidence adduced at the trial no rational trier of fact could have found proof of guilt beyond a reasonable doubt. . . .

NOTES & QUESTIONS ON EVIDENTIARY INSUFFICIENCY

1. *Whose judgment?* The Court emphasized in *Jackson* that the reviewing court should not ask "whether it believes that the evidence at the trial established guilt beyond a reasonable doubt." Instead, the reviewing court is supposed to consider the question of guilt from the perspective of "rational trier of fact." Why is a reviewing court required to engage in this objective analysis? Why not engage in its own de novo assessment of the evidence? Recall that the reviewing court is not supposed to engage in its own fact finding and is instead limited to reviewing the factual record assembled by the state courts. Does this standard build in the required level of discretion to the trial court?

2. *Light most favorable to the prosecution.* The objective standard articulated in *Jackson* also requires the reviewing court to consider evidence "in the light most favorable to the prosecution" when it decides whether "any rational trier of fact could have found the essential elements of the crime beyond a reasonable doubt." Why should the reviewing court view the evidence in the light most favorable to the prosecution? Is it because the reviewing court should assume that if the trial court (whether a judge or jury) convicted the defendant, it probably weighed the conflicting evidence and judged that the weight of the evidence supported the prosecution rather than the defense case? Again, the standard appears designed to give deference to the trial court's primary role in assessing the evidence. With this deference in mind, what room is left for a reviewing court to engage in an independent and objective analysis of the prosecution's case?

2. Harmless Error Analysis

Not every constitutional error requires the extraordinary remedy of a reversal of a conviction ordered by a reviewing court. Some legal errors are truly significant because they altered the course of the defendant's trial; in the absence of the error, the defendant's case might have resulted in an acquittal, or at the very least, raised the chances of an acquittal significantly. On the other hand, many other errors, while certainly a violation of law, would not necessarily have changed the outcome of a trial; the defendant's conviction may have been inevitable even without the error. With this mind, the Supreme Court announced in *Chapman v. California*, 386 U.S. 18 (1967), that a habeas court need not grant a new trial if a constitutional error by the trial court was a "harmless error." However, not every constitutional violation is subject to the harmless error rule. Some rules are considered so fundamental that their violation will automatically trigger a retrial. In the following case, the Supreme Court asks whether the erroneous admission into evidence of an involuntary confession is subject to the harmless error rule or whether it should always vitiate the trial court's conviction of the defendant.

Arizona v. Fulminante

Supreme Court of the United States
499 U.S. 279 (1991)

Chief Justice Rehnquist . . . delivered the opinion of the Court with respect to Part II. . . .

II

Since this Court's landmark decision in *Chapman v. California*, 386 U.S. 18 (1967), in which we adopted the general rule that a constitutional error does not automatically require reversal of a conviction, the Court has applied harmless-error analysis to a wide range of errors and has recognized that most constitutional errors can be harmless.

The common thread connecting these cases is that each involved "trial error"—error which occurred during the presentation of the case to the jury, and which may therefore be quantitatively assessed in the context of other evidence presented in order to determine whether its admission was harmless beyond a reasonable doubt. In applying harmless-error analysis to these many different constitutional violations, the Court has been faithful to the belief that the harmless-error doctrine is essential to preserve the "principle that the central purpose of a criminal trial is to decide the factual question of the defendant's guilt or innocence, and promotes public respect for the criminal process by focusing on the underlying fairness of the trial rather than on the virtually inevitable presence of immaterial error."

In *Chapman v. California*, the Court stated:

> Although our prior cases have indicated that there are some constitutional rights so basic to a fair trial that their infraction can never be treated as harmless error, this statement in *Fahy* itself belies any belief that all trial errors which violate the Constitution automatically call for reversal. See, e.g., *Payne v. Arkansas*, 356 U.S. 560 (coerced confession); *Gideon v. Wainwright*, 372 U.S. 335 (right to counsel); *Tumey v. Ohio*, 273 U.S. 510 (impartial judge).

It is on the basis of this language in *Chapman* that Justice White in dissent concludes that the principle of stare decisis requires us to hold that an involuntary confession is not subject to harmless-error analysis. We believe that there are several reasons which lead to a contrary conclusion. In the first place, the quoted language from *Chapman* does not by its terms adopt any such rule in that case. The language that "[a]lthough our prior cases have indicated," coupled with the relegation of the cases themselves to a footnote, is more appropriately regarded as a historical reference to the holdings of these cases. This view is buttressed by an examination of the opinion in *Payne v. Arkansas*, 356 U.S. 560 (1958), which is the case referred to for the proposition that an involuntary confession may not be subject to harmless-error analysis. There the Court said:

> Respondent suggests that, apart from the confession, there was adequate evidence before the jury to sustain the verdict. But where, as here, an involuntary confession constitutes a part of the evidence before the jury and a general verdict is returned, no one can say what credit and weight the jury gave to the confession. And in these circumstances this Court has uniformly held that even though there may have been sufficient evidence, apart from the coerced confession, to support a judgment of conviction, the admission in evidence, over objection, of the coerced confession vitiates the judgment because it violates the Due Process Clause of the Fourteenth Amendment.

It is apparent that the State's argument which the Court rejected in *Payne* is not the harmless-error analysis later adopted in *Chapman*, but a much more lenient rule which would allow affirmance of a conviction if the evidence other than the involuntary confession was sufficient to sustain the verdict. This is confirmed by the dissent of Justice Clark in that case, which adopted the more lenient test. Such a test would, of course—unlike the harmless-error test—make the admission of an involuntary confession virtually risk-free for the State.

The admission of an involuntary confession—a classic "trial error"—is markedly different from the other two constitutional violations referred to in the *Chapman* footnote as not being subject to harmless-error analysis. One of those violations, involved in *Gideon v. Wainwright*, 372 U.S. 335 (1963), was the total deprivation of the right to counsel at trial. The other violation, involved in *Tumey v. Ohio*, 273 U.S. 510 (1927), was a judge who was not impartial. These are structural defects in the constitution of the trial mechanism, which defy analysis by "harmless-error" standards. The entire conduct of the trial from beginning to end is obviously affected by the absence of counsel for a criminal defendant, just as it is by the presence on the bench of a judge who is not impartial. Since our decision in *Chapman*, other cases have added to the category of constitutional errors which are not subject to harmless error the following: unlawful exclusion of members of the defendant's race from a grand jury, *Vasquez v. Hillery*, 474 U.S. 254 (1986); the right to self-representation at trial, *McKaskle v. Wiggins*, 465 U.S. 168, 177-178, n. 8 (1984); and the right to public trial, *Waller v. Georgia*, 467 U.S. 39, 49, n. 9 (1984). Each of these constitutional deprivations is a similar structural defect affecting the framework within which the trial proceeds, rather than simply an error in the trial process itself. "Without these basic protections, a criminal trial cannot reliably serve its function as a vehicle for determination of guilt or innocence, and no criminal punishment may be regarded as fundamentally fair."

It is evident from a comparison of the constitutional violations which we have held subject to harmless error, and those which we have held not, that involuntary statements or confessions belong in the former category. The admission of an involuntary confession is a "trial error," similar in both degree and kind to the erroneous admission of other types of evidence. The evidentiary impact of an involuntary confession, and its effect upon the composition of the record, is indistinguishable from that of a confession obtained in violation of the Sixth Amendment—of evidence seized in violation of the Fourth Amendment—or of a prosecutor's improper comment on a defendant's silence at trial in violation of the Fifth Amendment. When reviewing the erroneous admission of an involuntary confession, the appellate court, as it does with the admission of other forms of improperly admitted evidence, simply reviews the remainder of the evidence against the defendant to determine whether the admission of the confession was harmless beyond a reasonable doubt.

Nor can it be said that the admission of an involuntary confession is the type of error which "transcends the criminal process." This Court has applied harmless-error analysis to the violation of other constitutional rights similar in magnitude and importance and involving the same level of police misconduct. For instance, we have previously held that the admission of a defendant's statements obtained in violation of the Sixth Amendment is subject to harmless-error analysis. In *Milton v. Wainwright*, 407 U.S. 371 (1972), the Court held the admission of a confession obtained in violation of *Massiah v. United States*, 377 U.S. 201 (1964), to be harmless beyond a reasonable doubt. We have also held that the admission of an out-of-court statement by a nontestifying codefendant is subject to harmless-error analysis. The inconsistent treatment of statements elicited in violation of the Sixth and Fourteenth Amendments, respectively, can be supported neither by evidentiary or deterrence concerns nor by a belief that there is something more "fundamental" about involuntary confessions. This is especially true in a case such as this one where there are no allegations of physical violence on behalf of the police. A confession obtained in violation of the Sixth Amendment has the same evidentiary impact as does a confession obtained in violation of a defendant's due process rights. Government misconduct that results in violations of the Fourth and Sixth Amendments may be at least as reprehensible as conduct that results in an involuntary confession. For instance, the prisoner's confession to an inmate-informer at issue in *Milton*, which the Court characterized as implicating the Sixth Amendment right to counsel, is similar on its facts to the one we face today. Indeed, experience shows that law enforcement violations of these constitutional guarantees can involve conduct as egregious as police conduct used to elicit statements in violation of the Fourteenth Amendment. It is thus impossible to create a meaningful distinction between confessions elicited in violation of the Sixth Amendment and those in violation of the Fourteenth Amendment.

Of course an involuntary confession may have a more dramatic effect on the course of a trial than do other trial errors—in particular cases it may be devastating to a defendant—but this simply means that a reviewing court will conclude in such a case that its admission was not harmless error; it is not a reason for eschewing the harmless-error test entirely. The Supreme Court of Arizona, in its first opinion in the present case, concluded that the admission of Fulminante's confession was harmless error. That court concluded that a second and more explicit confession of the crime made by Fulminante after he was released from prison was not tainted by the first confession, and that the second confession, together with physical evidence from the wounds (the victim had been shot twice in the head with a large caliber weapon at close range and a ligature was found around her neck) and other evidence introduced at trial rendered the admission of the first confession harmless beyond a reasonable doubt. . . .

NOTES & QUESTIONS ON HARMLESS ERROR

1. *Shocking or common sense?* Do you find the Court's decision in *Fulminante* shocking? The Court concluded that a reviewing court could decide, in one breath, that the admission of an involuntary confession was unconstitutional,

but in the next breath declare the harm from that confession harmless and permit the conviction to stand. For some critics of the decision, this was an almost unconscionable result. For others, though, the decision was an exercise in common-sense constitutional rule making. In many cases, the error resulting from the admission of the involuntary confession will not be harmless; in which case the reviewing court will be entitled to order a new trial. In a handful of cases, where the error really is harmless, because of overwhelming evidence of guilt even without the confession, no retrial is required. In short, a retrial is permitted but not automatically required just because the confession was involuntary. Does this sound like a common-sense solution or a recipe for injustice? Does it offend our conception of justice to allow a conviction to stand when the trial included an involuntary confession? If yes, what is that conception of justice?

2. *The confession.* Fulminante's 11-year-old stepdaughter was murdered. While Fulminante was in a federal prison for an unrelated crime, the following incident occurred:

> There he became friends with another inmate, Anthony Sarivola, then serving a 60-day sentence for extortion. The two men came to spend several hours a day together. Sarivola, a former police officer, had been involved in loansharking for organized crime but then became a paid informant for the Federal Bureau of Investigation. While at Ray Brook, he masqueraded as an organized crime figure. After becoming friends with Fulminante, Sarivola heard a rumor that Fulminante was suspected of killing a child in Arizona. Sarivola then raised the subject with Fulminante in several conversations, but Fulminante repeatedly denied any involvement in Jeneane's death. During one conversation, he told Sarivola that Jeneane had been killed by bikers looking for drugs; on another occasion, he said he did not know what had happened. Sarivola passed this information on to an agent of the Federal Bureau of Investigation, who instructed Sarivola to find out more. Sarivola learned more one evening in October 1983, as he and Fulminante walked together around the prison track. Sarivola said that he knew Fulminante was "starting to get some tough treatment and whatnot" from other inmates because of the rumor. Sarivola offered to protect Fulminante from his fellow inmates, but told him, "'You have to tell me about it', you know. I mean, in other words, 'For me to give you any help.'" Fulminante then admitted to Sarivola that he had driven Jeneane to the desert on his motorcycle, where he choked her, sexually assaulted her, and made her beg for her life, before shooting her twice in the head.

Arizona v. Fulminante, 499 U.S. 279, 282-83 (1991). Fulminante argued that his confession was the product of illegal coercion, since Sarivola procured the confession by suggesting that Fulminante would only receive protection from the other inmates if he confessed. Do these facts alter your perception of the Supreme Court's ruling?

3. *Counterfactual inquiry*. When a habeas court asks whether a trial court's legal error was harmless, it necessarily engages in a counterfactual inquiry. The habeas court must imagine a hypothetical state of affairs that did not come to pass. In a world where the trial court had *not* made the legal error, would the jury have convicted the defendant anyway or would the jury have acquitted the defendant? That question is necessarily speculative, at least to some degree, because it requires an imaginative exercise. Does the harmless error analysis seem excessively or dangerously speculative? Or is it just the same as any legal analysis, like causation, that requires counterfactual analysis?

3. When Is a Case "Final"?

The following case is a key piece of the Supreme Court's jurisprudence on retroactivity. Specifically, it asks whether a new constitutional ruling should be applied retroactively to cases that are still on *direct* state or federal appellate review. For example, imagine a situation where the defendant is convicted and is in the midst of a direct appeal in state courts. Then, a new constitutional rule is announced by the Supreme Court in an unrelated case. Assuming that the state court that convicted the first defendant did not conduct its proceedings consistently with the new constitutional rule, should a new trial be ordered? This situation is, in fact, quite common. One could well imagine that the state trial court did not follow the constitutional rule, since it was announced after the trial occurred. In the following case, the Supreme Court supports the retroactive application of the federal rule because the state court conviction is not yet "final." What does finality mean in this context? When does a state court conviction become "final"?

Griffith v. Kentucky

Supreme Court of the United States
479 U.S. 314 (1987)

Justice BLACKMUN delivered the opinion of the Court.

These cases, one state and one federal, concern the retrospective application of *Batson v. Kentucky*, 476 U.S. 79 (1986). In *Batson*, this Court ruled that a defendant in a state criminal trial could establish a prima facie case of racial discrimination violative of the Fourteenth Amendment, based on the prosecution's use of peremptory challenges to strike members of the defendant's race from the jury venire, and that, once the defendant had made the prima facie showing, the burden shifted to the prosecution to come forward with a neutral explanation for those challenges. In the present cases we consider whether that ruling is applicable to litigation pending on direct state or federal review or not yet final when *Batson* was decided. We answer that question in the affirmative.

II

Twenty-one years ago, this Court adopted a three-pronged analysis for claims of retroactivity of new constitutional rules of criminal procedure. See *Linkletter v. Walker,* 381 U.S. 618 (1965). In *Linkletter,* the Court held that *Mapp v. Ohio,* 367 U.S. 643 (1961), which extended the Fourth Amendment exclusionary rule to the States, would not be applied retroactively to a state conviction that had become final before *Mapp* was decided. The Court explained that "the Constitution neither prohibits nor requires retrospective effect" of a new constitutional rule, and that a determination of retroactivity must depend on "weigh[ing] the merits and demerits in each case." The Court's decision not to apply *Mapp* retroactively was based on "the purpose of the *Mapp* rule; the reliance placed upon the [previous] doctrine; and the effect on the administration of justice of a retrospective application of *Mapp.*"

Shortly after the decision in *Linkletter,* the Court held that the three-pronged analysis applied both to convictions that were final and to convictions pending on direct review. See *Johnson v. New Jersey,* 384 U.S. 719 (1966); *Stovall v. Denno,* 388 U.S., at 300. In the latter case, the Court concluded that, for purposes of applying the three factors of the analysis, "no distinction is justified between convictions now final . . . and convictions at various stages of trial and direct review." Thus, a number of new rules of criminal procedure were held not to apply retroactively either to final cases or to cases pending on direct review.

In *United States v. Johnson,* 457 U.S. 537 (1982), however, the Court shifted course. In that case, we reviewed at some length the history of the Court's decisions in the area of retroactivity and concluded, in the words of Justice Harlan: "[R]etroactivity must be rethought." Specifically, we concluded that the retroactivity analysis for convictions that have become final must be different from the analysis for convictions that are not final at the time the new decision is issued. We observed that, in a number of separate opinions since *Linkletter,* various Members of the Court "have asserted that, at a minimum, all defendants whose cases were still pending on direct appeal at the time of the law-changing decision should be entitled to invoke the new rule." The rationale for distinguishing between cases that have become final and those that have not, and for applying new rules retroactively to cases in the latter category, was explained at length by Justice Harlan in *Desist v. United States,* 394 U.S., at 256, and in *Mackey v. United States,* 401 U.S. 667, 675 (1971) (opinion concurring in judgment). In *United States v. Johnson,* we embraced to a significant extent the comprehensive analysis presented by Justice Harlan in those opinions.

In Justice Harlan's view, and now in ours, failure to apply a newly declared constitutional rule to criminal cases pending on direct review violates basic norms of constitutional adjudication. First, it is a settled principle that this Court adjudicates only "cases" and "controversies." Unlike a legislature, we do not promulgate new rules of constitutional criminal procedure on a broad basis. Rather, the nature of judicial review requires that we adjudicate specific cases, and each case usually becomes the vehicle for announcement of a new rule. But after we have decided a new rule in the case selected, the integrity of judicial review requires that we apply that rule to all similar cases pending on direct review. . . .

As a practical matter, of course, we cannot hear each case pending on direct review and apply the new rule. But we fulfill our judicial responsibility by instructing the lower courts to apply the new rule retroactively to cases not yet final. Thus, it is the nature of judicial review that precludes us from "[s]imply fishing one case from the stream of appellate review, using it as a vehicle for pronouncing new constitutional standards, and then permitting a stream of similar cases subsequently to flow by unaffected by that new rule."

Second, selective application of new rules violates the principle of treating similarly situated defendants the same. As we pointed out in *United States v. Johnson*, the problem with not applying new rules to cases pending on direct review is "the actual inequity that results when the Court chooses which of many similarly situated defendants should be the chance beneficiary" of a new rule. Although the Court had tolerated this inequity for a time by not applying new rules retroactively to cases on direct review, we noted: "The time for toleration has come to an end."

In *United States v. Johnson*, our acceptance of Justice Harlan's views led to the holding that "subject to [certain exceptions], a decision of this Court construing the Fourth Amendment is to be applied retroactively to all convictions that were not yet final at the time the decision was rendered." The exceptions to which we referred related to three categories in which we concluded that existing precedent established threshold tests for the retroactivity analysis. In two of these categories, the new rule already was retroactively applied: (1) when a decision of this Court did nothing more than apply settled precedent to different factual situations, and (2) when the new ruling was that a trial court lacked authority to convict a criminal defendant in the first place.

The third category—where a new rule is a "clear break" with past precedent—is the one at issue in these cases. We described it in *United States v. Johnson*:

> [W]here the Court has expressly declared a rule of criminal procedure to be "a clear break with the past," it almost invariably has gone on to find such a newly minted principle nonretroactive. In this . . . type of case, the traits of the particular constitutional rule have been

> less critical than the Court's express threshold determination that the "new constitutional interpretatio[n] . . . so change[s] the law that prospectivity is arguably the proper course." Once the Court has found that the new rule was unanticipated, the second and third *Stovall* factors—reliance by law enforcement authorities on the old standards and effect on the administration of justice of a retroactive application of the new rule—have virtually compelled a finding of nonretroactivity.

Thus, we recognized what may be termed a "clear break exception." Under this exception, a new constitutional rule was not applied retroactively, even to cases on direct review, if the new rule explicitly overruled a past precedent of this Court, or disapproved a practice this Court had arguably sanctioned in prior cases, or overturned a longstanding practice that lower courts had uniformly approved. . . .

III

We . . . now reexamine the rationale for maintaining a "clear break" exception to the general proposition that new rules governing criminal procedure should be retroactive to cases pending on direct review. For the same reasons that persuaded us in *United States v. Johnson* to adopt different conclusions as to convictions on direct review from those that already had become final, we conclude that an engrafted exception based solely upon the particular characteristics of the new rule adopted by the Court is inappropriate.

First, the principle that this Court does not disregard current law, when it adjudicates a case pending before it on direct review, applies regardless of the specific characteristics of the particular new rule announced. The Court recognized in *United States v. Johnson* that the fact that a new rule is a clear break with the past is relevant primarily because it implicates the second and third *Stovall* factors of reliance by law enforcement officials and the burden on the administration of justice imposed by retroactive application. But even if these factors may be useful in deciding whether convictions that already have become final should receive the benefit of a new rule, the "clear break" exception, derived from the *Stovall* factors, reintroduces precisely the type of case-specific analysis that Justice Harlan rejected as inappropriate for cases pending on direct review.

Second, the use of a "clear break" exception creates the same problem of not treating similarly situated defendants the same. . . . The fact that the new rule may constitute a clear break with the past has no bearing on the "actual inequity that results" when only one of many similarly situated defendants receives the benefit of the new rule.

> We therefore hold that a new rule for the conduct of criminal prosecutions is to be applied retroactively to all cases, state or federal, pending on direct review or not yet final, with no exception for cases in which the new rule constitutes a "clear break" with the past. . . .

NOTES & QUESTIONS ON CASES ON DIRECT REVIEW

1. *The definition of finality.* Why does it matter whether a case is pending on direct review or not? One way of understanding the point is to consider the definition of "finality." Consider the following statement: "Finality attaches when this Court affirms a conviction on the merits on direct review or denies a petition for a writ of certiorari, or when the time for filing a certiorari petition expires." *Clay v. United States,* 537 U.S. 522, 527 (2003). Although there may be other definitions of finality in other contexts, finality in the post-conviction context only attaches when direct review is completed. If the defendant has filed a petition of certiorari, that moment of attachment is when the Supreme Court denies the cert petition. Or, if the defendant has elected not to pursue an appeal, finality would attach when the time period for filing the appeal has run its course. At that moment in time, the conviction becomes "final," after which a different retroactivity doctrine applies.

2. *Fairness.* What would post-conviction proceedings look like if constitutional rules were *not* applied retroactively to cases still on direct review? Would this raise a problem of fairness, i.e., some petitioners receiving the benefit of a new rule while others not? How should fairness be balanced with judicial efficiency? If new rules were *always* applied retroactively, even to cases that were already final on direct review, would this upend the legal system and overwhelm state courts with thousands of new trials? What if the convictions were years old and the witnesses no longer available? Consider the following assessment of the Supreme Court's jurisprudence in this area:

> The Court's doctrine has suffered from two shortcomings. First, it has failed to acknowledge the struggle animating traditional retroactivity doctrine: the effort to reconcile competing and often conflicting concerns about fairness and economic efficiency. Underlying these concerns are foundational assumptions about the process by which legal rules change.

Jill E. Fisch, *Retroactivity and Legal Change: An Equilibrium Approach,* 110 Harv. L. Rev. 1055, 1057 (1997). Did *Griffith* strike the right balance between fairness and efficiency?

B. LIMITS ON GRANTING HABEAS PETITIONS

Congress has the power to regulate the operation of the writ in federal courts. In 1996, responding to perceived public pressure regarding problems with the habeas system, Congress passed the Antiterrorism and Effective Death Penalty Act of 1996 (AEDPA), 110 Stat. 1214, 28 U.S.C. § 2254, which placed detailed constraints on the habeas process and explicitly excluded some claims as the basis for a successful habeas petition. The constraints imposed by the AEDPA largely now govern today's habeas practice and most of the cases in this chapter involve interpretations or applications of the AEDPA's requirements.

It is unclear whether the habeas reforms marshalled into law by the AEDPA were a response to clear criminological evidence of a broken habeas system, or whether the reforms were motivated by political pressure to appear tough on crime and criminals. For example, consider the following assessment from two legal scholars:

> The Republican Contract with America included a proposed Taking Back Our Streets Act that incorporated proposals concerning prisoner litigation. Arguing that "most petitions are totally lacking in merit," that "thousands upon thousands of frivolous petitions clog the federal district court dockets each year," and that "prisoners on death row [could] almost indefinitely delay their punishment," the Contract's authors sought to impose a one-year deadline for filing habeas corpus claims generally, and a more stringent six-month deadline for capital cases. They also wanted to "force[] federal courts to consider federal habeas petitions within a certain time frame." The justification for limiting prisoner lawsuits was confined to a single substantive sentence: "States are forced to spend millions of dollars defending prisoner lawsuits to improve prison conditions—many of which are frivolous." This treated institutional reform litigation as a version of frivolous litigation.

Mark Tushnet & Larry Yackle, *Symbolic Statutes and Real Laws: The Pathologies of the Antiterrorism and Effective Death Penalty Act and the Prison Litigation Reform Act*, 47 Duke L.J. 1, 20-21 (1997). While not everyone agrees about the significance of the political landscape leading up to the passage of the AEDPA, one thing is clear: The legislation, combined with analogous rules also articulated by judges in judicial decisions, have transformed habeas practice in many ways.

The following subsections outline the key constraints imposed by the AEDPA on habeas petitions. These limits include the requirement that the federal issue was properly preserved under state procedural rules, and the requirement that the state court engaged in an unreasonable application of clearly established federal law—a term of art that requires federal courts to determine not just whether the state court engaged in erroneous legal decision making but also whether its decision violated federal law that was already clearly established. So, a petition that asks a federal court to break new legal ground cannot, by definition, convince a federal court that the state court violated clearly established federal law. Also, the AEDPA requires that the habeas petition be filed according to a strict one-year clock, thus raising the question of whether a defendant's failure to meet that deadline can be excused, in some extreme circumstances, via the doctrine of "equitable tolling." The last habeas requirement prohibits a court from acting on successive habeas petitions, thus requiring that a successful habeas petition be the first one from the prisoner to raise the issue. As the cases below demonstrate, however, what counts as "successive" requires judicial interpretation and elaboration.

1. Procedural Default

A petition for a writ of habeas corpus is a civil attack on a final judgment, and for the vast majority of petitions, this arises out of a final state conviction where the petitioner is asking a federal court to rule that the state court's resolution of a federal constitutional right was flawed, and therefore the conviction violates federal constitutional law. The incorporation of most of the Bill of Rights through the Fourteenth Amendment makes such an argument viable in almost every state criminal case, because it is virtually impossible to conduct a state criminal trial without implicating a federal constitutional right. If the conduct of the trial is consistent with the federal right, there is no reason to grant a habeas petition, but if the conduct of the trial violated a federal right, there may be a basis for habeas relief. However, as the following case demonstrates, federal courts will almost never entertain such a petition unless the petitioner has preserved the federal issue in accordance with state procedural rules.

Teague v. Lane

Supreme Court of the United States
489 U.S. 288 (1989)

Justice O'Connor announced the judgment of the Court and delivered the opinion of the Court with respect to Parts I, II, and III. . . .

In *Taylor v. Louisiana*, 419 U.S. 522 (1975), this Court held that the Sixth Amendment required that the jury venire be drawn from a fair cross section of the community. The Court stated, however, that "in holding that petit juries must be drawn from a source fairly representative of the community we impose no requirement that petit juries actually chosen must mirror the community and reflect the various distinctive groups in the population. Defendants are not entitled to a jury of any particular composition." The principal question presented in this case is whether the Sixth Amendment's fair cross section requirement should now be extended to the petit jury. Because we adopt Justice Harlan's approach to retroactivity for cases on collateral review, we leave the resolution of that question for another day.

I

Petitioner, a black man, was convicted by an all-white Illinois jury of three counts of attempted murder, two counts of armed robbery, and one count of aggravated battery. During jury selection for petitioner's trial, the prosecutor used all 10 of his peremptory challenges to exclude blacks. Petitioner's counsel used one of his 10 peremptory challenges to exclude a black woman who was married to a police officer. After the prosecutor had struck six blacks, petitioner's counsel moved for a mistrial. The trial court denied the motion. When the prosecutor struck four more blacks, petitioner's counsel again moved for a mistrial, arguing that petitioner was "entitled to a jury of his peers." The prosecutor defended the challenges by stating that he was trying to achieve a balance of men and women on the jury. The trial court denied the motion, reasoning that the jury "appear[ed] to be a fair [one]."

On appeal, petitioner argued that the prosecutor's use of peremptory challenges denied him the right to be tried by a jury that was representative of the community. The Illinois Appellate Court rejected petitioner's fair cross section claim.

Petitioner then filed a petition for a writ of habeas corpus in the United States District Court for the Northern District of Illinois. Petitioner repeated his fair cross section claim. . . . He also argued, for the first time, that under *Swain* a prosecutor could be questioned about his use of peremptory challenges once he volunteered an explanation. The District Court, though sympathetic to petitioner's arguments, held that it was bound by *Swain* and Circuit precedent. . . .

II

Petitioner's first contention is that he should receive the benefit of our decision in *Batson* even though his conviction became final before *Batson* was decided. Before addressing petitioner's argument, we think it helpful to explain how *Batson* modified *Swain*. *Swain* held that a "State's purposeful or deliberate denial" to blacks of an opportunity to serve as jurors solely on account of race violates the Equal Protection Clause of the Fourteenth Amendment. 380 U.S., at 203-204. In order to establish a prima facie case of discrimination under *Swain*, a defendant had to demonstrate that the peremptory challenge system had been "perverted." A defendant could raise an inference of purposeful discrimination if he showed that the prosecutor in the county where the trial was held "in case after case, whatever the circumstances, whatever the crime and whoever the defendant or the victim may be," has been responsible for the removal of qualified blacks who had survived challenges for cause, with the result that no blacks ever served on petit juries.

In *Batson*, the Court overruled that portion of *Swain* setting forth the evidentiary showing necessary to make out a prima facie case of racial discrimination under the Equal Protection Clause. The Court held that a defendant can establish a prima facie case by showing that he is a "member of a cognizable racial group," that the prosecutor exercised "peremptory challenges to remove from the venire members of the defendant's race," and that those "facts and any other relevant circumstances raise an inference that the prosecutor used that practice to exclude the veniremen from the petit jury on account of their race." 476 U.S., at 96. Once the defendant makes out a prima facie case of discrimination, the burden shifts to the prosecutor "to come forward with a neutral explanation for challenging black jurors."

In *Allen v. Hardy*, the Court held that *Batson* constituted an "explicit and substantial break with prior precedent" because it overruled a portion of *Swain*. 478 U.S., at 258. Employing the retroactivity standard of *Linkletter v. Walker*, 381 U.S. 618 (1965), the Court concluded that the rule announced in *Batson* should not be applied retroactively on collateral review of convictions that became final before *Batson* was announced. The Court defined final to mean a case "where the judgment of conviction was rendered, the availability of appeal exhausted, and the time for petition for certiorari had elapsed before our decision in *Batson*. . . ."

Petitioner's conviction became final 2½ years prior to *Batson*, thus depriving petitioner of any benefit from the rule announced in that case. . . . We find that *Allen v. Hardy* is dispositive, and that petitioner cannot benefit from the rule announced in *Batson*.

III

Petitioner's second contention is that he has established a violation of the Equal Protection Clause under *Swain*. Recognizing that he has not shown any systematic exclusion of blacks from petit juries in case after case, petitioner contends that when the prosecutor volunteers an explanation for the use of his peremptory challenges, *Swain* does not preclude an examination of the stated reasons to determine the legitimacy of the prosecutor's motive.

Petitioner candidly admits that he did not raise the *Swain* claim at trial or on direct appeal. Because of this failure, petitioner has forfeited review of the claim in the Illinois courts. . . . The default prevents petitioner from raising the *Swain* claim in collateral proceedings under the Illinois Post-Conviction Act, unless fundamental fairness requires that the default be overlooked.

The fundamental fairness exception is a narrow one, and has been applied in limited circumstances. It is clear that collateral relief would be unavailable to petitioner. As a result, petitioner has exhausted his state remedies under 28 U.S.C. § 2254(b) with respect to the *Swain* claim

Under *Wainwright v. Sykes*, 433 U.S. 72, 87-91 (1977), petitioner is barred from raising the *Swain* claim in a federal habeas corpus proceeding unless he can show cause for the default and prejudice resulting therefrom. Petitioner does not attempt to show cause for his default. Instead, he argues that the claim is not barred because it was addressed by the Illinois Appellate Court. We cannot agree with petitioner's argument. The Illinois Appellate Court rejected petitioner's Sixth Amendment fair cross section claim without mentioning the Equal Protection Clause on which *Swain* was based or discussing whether *Swain* allows a prosecutor to be questioned about his use of peremptory challenges once he volunteers an explanation. Accordingly, we hold that petitioner's *Swain* claim is procedurally barred, and do not address its merits.

Our application of the procedural default rule here is consistent with *Harris v. Reed*, 489 U.S. 255, 263 (1989), which holds that a "procedural default does not bar consideration of a federal claim on either direct or habeas review unless the last state court rendering a judgment in the case 'clearly and expressly' states that its judgment rests on a state procedural bar." The rule announced in *Harris v. Reed* assumes that a state court has had the opportunity to address a claim that is later raised in a federal habeas proceeding. It is simply inapplicable in a case such as this one, where the claim was never presented to the state courts. . . .

2. Unreasonable Application of Clearly Established Federal Law

When has a state court engaged in an unreasonable application of clearly established federal law, as required by the AEDPA? The following case involves a constitutional violation that was outlined in prior chapters and is a common argument during collateral proceedings: ineffective assistance of counsel in violation of the Sixth Amendment and as articulated in *Strickland v. Washington*. The specific question at issue in this case is whether the state courts were correct in dismissing Williams's *Strickland* appeal or whether that dismissal was an unreasonable application of *Strickland*. The right to effective counsel is a key element of the criminal justice system, upon which the rest of the trial process depends. As you read the following case, ask yourself not just whether Williams's right to counsel was violated—from a de novo perspective—but also whether the Virginia courts acted unreasonably in dismissing the *Strickland* claim.

Williams v. Taylor

Supreme Court of the United States
529 U.S. 362 (2000)

Justice STEVENS announced the judgment of the Court and delivered the opinion of the Court with respect to Parts, I, III, and IV, and an opinion with respect to Parts II and V.

The questions presented are whether Terry Williams' constitutional right to the effective assistance of counsel as defined in *Strickland v. Washington*, 466 U.S. 668 (1984), was violated, and whether the judgment of the Virginia Supreme Court refusing to set aside his death sentence "was contrary to, or involved an unreasonable application of, clearly established Federal law, as determined by the Supreme Court of the United States," within the meaning of 28 U.S.C. § 2254(d)(1). We answer both questions affirmatively.

I

On November 3, 1985, Harris Stone was found dead in his residence on Henry Street in Danville, Virginia. Finding no indication of a struggle, local officials determined that the cause of death was blood alcohol poisoning, and the case was considered closed. Six months after Stone's death, Terry Williams, who was then incarcerated in the "I" unit of the city jail for an unrelated offense, wrote a letter to the police stating that he had killed "that man down on Henry Street" and also stating that he "did it" to that "lady down on West Green Street" and was "very sorry." The letter was unsigned, but it closed with a reference to "I cell." The police readily identified Williams as its author, and, on April 25, 1986, they obtained several statements from him. In one Williams admitted that, after Stone refused to lend him "a couple of dollars," he had killed Stone with a mattock and taken the money from his wallet. In September 1986, Williams was convicted of robbery and capital murder.

At Williams' sentencing hearing, the prosecution proved that Williams had been convicted of armed robbery in 1976 and burglary and grand larceny in 1982. The prosecution also introduced the written confessions that Williams had made in April. The prosecution described two auto thefts and two separate violent assaults on elderly victims perpetrated after the Stone murder. On December 4, 1985, Williams had started a fire outside one victim's residence before attacking and robbing him. On March 5, 1986, Williams had brutally assaulted an elderly woman on West Green Street—an incident he had mentioned in his letter to the police. That confession was particularly damaging because other evidence established that the woman was in a "vegetative state" and not expected to recover. Williams had also been convicted of arson for setting a fire in the jail while awaiting trial in this case. Two expert witnesses employed by the State testified that there was a "high probability" that Williams would pose a serious continuing threat to society.

The evidence offered by Williams' trial counsel at the sentencing hearing consisted of the testimony of Williams' mother, two neighbors, and a taped excerpt from a statement by a psychiatrist. One of the neighbors had not been previously interviewed by defense counsel, but was noticed by counsel in the audience during the proceedings and asked to testify on the spot. The three witnesses briefly described Williams as a "nice boy" and not a violent person. The recorded psychiatrist's testimony did little more than relate Williams' statement during an examination that in the course of one of his earlier robberies, he had removed the bullets from a gun so as not to injure anyone.

In his cross-examination of the prosecution witnesses, Williams' counsel repeatedly emphasized the fact that Williams had initiated the contact with the police that enabled them to solve the murder and to identify him as the perpetrator of the recent assaults, as well as the car thefts. In closing argument, Williams' counsel characterized Williams' confessional statements as "dumb," but asked the jury to give weight to the fact that he had "turned himself in, not on one crime but on four . . . that the [police otherwise] would not have solved." The weight of defense counsel's closing, however, was devoted to explaining that it was difficult to find a reason why the jury should spare Williams' life.

The jury found a probability of future dangerousness and unanimously fixed Williams' punishment at death. The trial judge concluded that such punishment was "proper" and "just" and imposed the death sentence. The Virginia Supreme Court affirmed the conviction and sentence. It rejected Williams' argument that when the trial judge imposed sentence, he failed to give mitigating weight to the fact that Williams had turned himself in. . . .

II

In 1867, Congress enacted a statute providing that federal courts "shall have power to grant writs of habeas corpus in all cases where any person may be restrained of his or her liberty in violation of the constitution, or of any treaty or law of the United States. . . ." 14 Stat. 385. Over the years, the federal habeas corpus statute has been repeatedly amended, but the scope of that jurisdictional grant remains the same. It is, of course, well settled that the fact that constitutional error occurred in the proceedings that led to a state-court conviction may not alone be sufficient reason for concluding that a prisoner is entitled to the remedy of habeas. On the other hand, errors that undermine confidence in the fundamental fairness of the state adjudication certainly justify the issuance of the federal writ. The deprivation of the right to the effective assistance of counsel recognized in *Strickland* is such an error.

The warden here contends that federal habeas corpus relief is prohibited by the amendment to 28 U.S.C. § 2254, enacted as a part of the Antiterrorism and Effective Death Penalty Act of 1996 (AEDPA). The relevant portion of that amendment provides:

> (d) An application for a writ of habeas corpus on behalf of a person in custody pursuant to the judgment of a State court shall not be granted with respect to any claim that was adjudicated on the merits in State court proceedings unless the adjudication of the claim—
>
> (1) resulted in a decision that was contrary to, or involved an unreasonable application of, clearly established Federal law, as determined by the Supreme Court of the United States. . . .

In this case, the Court of Appeals applied the construction of the amendment that it had adopted in its earlier opinion in *Green v. French*, 143 F.3d 865 (C.A.4 1998). It read the amendment as prohibiting federal courts from issuing the writ unless:

> (a) the state court decision is in "square conflict" with Supreme Court precedent that is controlling as to law and fact or (b) if no such controlling decision exists, "the state court's resolution of a question of pure law rests upon an objectively unreasonable derivation of legal principles from the relevant [S]upreme [C]ourt precedents, or if its decision rests upon an objectively unreasonable application of established principles to new facts[.]"

Accordingly, it held that a federal court may issue habeas relief only if "the state courts have decided the question by interpreting or applying the relevant precedent in a manner that reasonable jurists would all agree is unreasonable."

We are convinced that that interpretation of the amendment is incorrect. It would impose a test for determining when a legal rule is clearly established that simply cannot be squared with the real practice of decisional law. It would apply a standard for determining the "reasonableness" of state-court decisions that is not contained in the statute itself, and that Congress surely did not intend. And it would wrongly require the federal courts, including this Court, to defer to state judges' interpretations of federal law.

As the Fourth Circuit would have it, a state-court judgment is "unreasonable" in the face of federal law only if all reasonable jurists would agree that the state court was unreasonable. Thus, in this case, for example, even if the Virginia Supreme Court misread our opinion in *Lockhart*, we could not grant relief unless we believed that none of the judges who agreed with the state court's interpretation of that case was a "reasonable jurist." But the statute says nothing about "reasonable judges," presumably because all, or virtually all, such judges occasionally commit error; they make decisions that in retrospect may be characterized as "unreasonable." Indeed, it is most unlikely that Congress would deliberately impose such a requirement of unanimity on federal judges. As Congress is acutely aware, reasonable lawyers and lawgivers regularly disagree with one another. Congress surely did not intend that the views of one such judge who might think that relief is not warranted in a particular case should always have greater weight than the contrary, considered judgment of several other reasonable judges.

The inquiry mandated by the amendment relates to the way in which a federal habeas court exercises its duty to decide constitutional questions; the amendment does not alter the underlying grant of jurisdiction in § 2254(a). When federal judges exercise their federal-question jurisdiction under the "judicial Power" of Article III of the Constitution, it is "emphatically the province and duty" of those judges to "say what the law is." At the core of this power is the federal courts' independent responsibility—independent from its coequal branches in the Federal Government, and independent from the separate authority of the several States—to interpret federal law. A construction of AEDPA that would require the federal courts to cede this authority to the courts of the States would be inconsistent with the practice that federal judges have traditionally followed in discharging their duties under Article III of the Constitution. If Congress had intended to require such an important change in the exercise of our jurisdiction, we believe it would have spoken with much greater clarity than is found in the text of AEDPA.

This basic premise informs our interpretation of both parts of § 2254(d)(1): first, the requirement that the determinations of state courts be tested only against "clearly established Federal law, as determined by the Supreme Court of the United States," and second, the prohibition on the issuance of the writ unless the state court's decision is "contrary to, or involved an unreasonable application of," that clearly established law. We address each part in turn.

THE "CLEARLY ESTABLISHED LAW" REQUIREMENT

In *Teague v. Lane*, 489 U.S. 288 (1989), we held that the petitioner was not entitled to federal habeas relief because he was relying on a rule of federal law that had not been announced until after his state conviction became final. The antiretroactivity rule recognized in *Teague*, which prohibits reliance on "new rules," is the functional equivalent of a statutory provision commanding exclusive reliance on "clearly established law." Because there is no reason to believe that Congress intended to require federal courts to ask both whether a rule sought on habeas is "new" under *Teague*—which remains the law—and also whether it is "clearly established" under AEDPA, it seems safe to assume that Congress had congruent concepts in mind. It is perfectly clear that AEDPA codifies *Teague* to the extent that *Teague* requires federal habeas courts to deny relief that is contingent upon a rule of law not clearly established at the time the state conviction became final.

Teague's core principles are therefore relevant to our construction of this requirement. Justice Harlan recognized the "inevitable difficulties" that come with "attempting to determine whether a particular decision has really announced a new rule at all or whether it has simply applied a well-established constitutional principle to govern a case which is closely analogous to those which have been previously considered in the prior case law." But *Teague* established some guidance for making this determination, explaining that a federal habeas court operates within the bounds of comity and finality if it applies a rule "dictated by precedent existing at the time the defendant's conviction became final." A rule that "breaks new ground or imposes a new obligation on the States or the Federal Government," falls outside this universe of federal law.

To this, AEDPA has added, immediately following the "clearly established law" requirement, a clause limiting the area of relevant law to that "determined by the Supreme Court of the United States." 28 U.S.C. § 2254(d)(1). If this Court has not broken sufficient legal ground to establish an asked-for constitutional principle, the lower federal courts cannot themselves establish such a principle with clarity sufficient to satisfy the AEDPA bar. In this respect, we agree with the Seventh Circuit that this clause "extends the principle of *Teague* by limiting the source of doctrine on which a federal court may rely in addressing the application for a writ." . . . .

A rule that fails to satisfy the foregoing criteria is barred by *Teague* from application on collateral review, and, similarly, is not available as a basis for relief in a habeas case to which AEDPA applies. . . .

THE "CONTRARY TO, OR AN UNREASONABLE APPLICATION OF," REQUIREMENT

The message that Congress intended to convey by using the phrases "contrary to" and "unreasonable application of" is not entirely clear. The prevailing view in the Circuits is that the former phrase requires de novo review of "pure" questions of law and the latter requires some sort of "reasonability" review of so-called mixed questions of law and fact.

We are not persuaded that the phrases define two mutually exclusive categories of questions. Most constitutional questions that arise in habeas corpus proceedings—and therefore most "decisions" to be made—require the federal judge to apply a rule of law to a set of facts, some of which may be disputed and some undisputed. For example, an erroneous conclusion that particular circumstances established the voluntariness of a confession, or that there exists a conflict of interest when one attorney represents multiple defendants, may well be described either as "contrary to" or as an "unreasonable application of" the governing rule of law. In constitutional adjudication, as in the common law, rules of law often develop incrementally as earlier decisions are applied to new factual situations. But rules that depend upon such elaboration are hardly less lawlike than those that establish a bright-line test.

Indeed, our pre-AEDPA efforts to distinguish questions of fact, questions of law, and "mixed questions," and to create an appropriate standard of habeas review for each, generated some not insubstantial differences of opinion as to which issues of law fell into which category of question, and as to which standard of review applied to each. We thus think the Fourth Circuit was correct when it attributed the lack of clarity in the statute, in part, to the overlapping meanings of the phrases "contrary to" and "unreasonable application of."

The statutory text likewise does not obviously prescribe a specific, recognizable standard of review for dealing with either phrase. Significantly, it does not use any term, such as "de novo" or "plain error," that would easily identify a familiar standard of review. Rather, the text is fairly read simply as a command that a federal court not issue the habeas writ unless the state court was wrong as a matter of law or unreasonable in its application of law in a given case. The suggestion that a wrong state-court "decision"—a legal judgment rendered "after consideration of facts, and . . . law"—may no longer be redressed through habeas (because it is unreachable under the "unreasonable application" phrase) is based on a mistaken insistence that the § 2254(d)(1) phrases have not only independent, but mutually exclusive, meanings. Whether or not a federal court can issue the writ "under [the] 'unreasonable application' clause," the statute is clear that habeas may issue under § 2254(d)(1) if a state-court "decision" is "contrary to . . . clearly established Federal law." We thus anticipate that there will be a variety of cases, like this one, in which both phrases may be implicated. . . .

In sum, the statute directs federal courts to attend to every state-court judgment with utmost care, but it does not require them to defer to the opinion of every reasonable state-court judge on the content of federal law. If, after carefully weighing all the reasons for accepting a state court's judgment, a federal court is convinced that a prisoner's custody—or, as in this case, his sentence of death—violates the Constitution, that independent judgment should prevail. Otherwise the federal "law as determined by the Supreme Court of the United States" might be applied by the federal courts one way in Virginia and another way in California. In light of the well-recognized interest in ensuring that federal courts interpret federal law in a uniform way, we are convinced that Congress did not intend the statute to produce such a result.

III

In this case, Williams contends that he was denied his constitutionally guaranteed right to the effective assistance of counsel when his trial lawyers failed to investigate and to present substantial mitigating evidence to the sentencing jury. The threshold question under AEDPA is whether Williams seeks to apply a rule of law that was clearly established at the time his state-court conviction became final. That question is easily answered because the merits of his claim are squarely governed by our holding in *Strickland v. Washington*, 466 U.S. 668 (1984). . . .

It is past question that the rule set forth in *Strickland* qualifies as "clearly established Federal law, as determined by the Supreme Court of the United States." That the *Strickland* test "of necessity requires a case-by-case examination of the evidence," obviates neither the clarity of the rule nor the extent to which the rule must be seen as "established" by this Court. This Court's precedent "dictated" that the Virginia Supreme Court apply the *Strickland* test at the time that court entertained Williams' ineffective-assistance claim. And it can hardly be said that recognizing the right to effective counsel "breaks new ground or imposes a new obligation on the States." Williams is therefore entitled to relief if the Virginia Supreme Court's decision rejecting his ineffective-assistance claim was either "contrary to, or involved an unreasonable application of," that established law. It was both. . . .

NOTES & QUESTIONS ON CLEARLY ESTABLISHED FEDERAL LAW

1. *The* Strickland *standard.* Do you believe that Williams was denied his constitutional right to counsel? What facts in the record below were most important in convincing the habeas court that the Virginia Supreme Court's decision was contrary to established federal law? How much deference did the federal courts grant the state courts in making this determination?

2. *Determined by the Supreme Court.* The AEDPA requires more than that the state court acted contrary to clearly established federal law—that federal law must also be announced by the Supreme Court. Is this additional requirement too restrictive? How did it operate in Williams's case, especially the lower courts? In *Williams*, the ineffective assistance of counsel standard was articulated by the Supreme Court in *Strickland*. But what of other constitutional issues that have been mostly addressed by Circuit courts? What result in those cases under the AEDPA?

PROBLEM CASE

Three defendants were charged with the brutal rape, kidnapping, and robbery of a victim in 2001. Bunch, who was 16 at the time of the crime, was convicted of 10 counts, and sentenced by the trial court to 10 years for each count, the maximum, to be served consecutively, resulting in a combined sentence of 89 years in prison. Busch appealed, arguing that his sentence was cruel and unusual punishment, in violation of the Eighth Amendment. In his federal habeas petition, Bunch specifically cited Supreme Court precedent that disallows life sentences without the possibility of parole for non-homicide offenses (jurisprudence covered in the sentencing chapter of this casebook). See *Graham v. Florida*, 560 U.S. 48 (2010). *Graham* involved the imposition of a single sentence of life without the possibility of parole, while Bunch's case involved the functional equivalent of a life sentence due to the length of the prison terms and the fact that they were ordered served consecutively rather than concurrently. Did Bunch's sentencing violate clearly established federal law announced by the Supreme Court of the United States? See *Bunch v. Smith*, 685 F.3d 546 (6th Cir. 2012). For discussion of these issues, see also *Recent Case–Federal Habeas Review Under AEDPA*, 126 Harv. L. Rev. 860, 862 (2013).

3. Timeliness and Tolling

The AEDPA imposes a one-year limitations period. However, other limitation periods are often subject to the common law doctrine of equitable tolling to excuse delays through no fault of the petitioner. The question in this case is whether Congress intended, in passing the AEDPA, to allow or disallow equitable tolling. If the answer to that question is to permit equitable tolling, did Holland's situation warrant equitable tolling? As you read the following case, pay particular attention to the facts of Holland's situation that would explain why he could not comply with the one-year limitations period. Stepping back and viewing matters more globally, which policy factors support the recognition of equitable tolling in the habeas context? In answering that question, make reference both to the underlying goals of the writ of habeas corpus and to the congressional reforms embodied in the AEDPA.

Holland v. Florida

Supreme Court of the United States
560 U.S. 631 (2010)

Justice Breyer delivered the opinion of the Court.

We here decide that the timeliness provision in the federal habeas corpus statute is subject to equitable tolling. See Antiterrorism and Effective Death Penalty Act of 1996 (AEDPA), 28 U.S.C. § 2244(d). We also consider its application in this case. In the Court of Appeals' view, when a petitioner seeks to excuse a late filing on the basis of his attorney's unprofessional conduct, that conduct, even if it is "negligent" or "grossly negligent," cannot "rise to the level of egregious attorney misconduct" that would warrant equitable tolling unless the petitioner offers "proof of bad faith, dishonesty, divided loyalty, mental impairment or so forth." In our view, this standard is too rigid. We therefore reverse the judgment of the Court of Appeals and remand for further proceedings.

I

AEDPA states that "[a] 1-year period of limitation shall apply to an application for a writ of habeas corpus by a person in custody pursuant to the judgment of a State court." It also says that "[t]he time during which a properly filed application for State post-conviction . . . review" is "pending shall not be counted" against the 1-year period.

On January 19, 2006, Albert Holland filed a pro se habeas corpus petition in the Federal District Court for the Southern District of Florida. Both Holland (the petitioner) and the State of Florida (the respondent) agree that, unless equitably tolled, the statutory limitations period applicable to Holland's petition expired approximately five weeks before the petition was filed. Holland asked the District Court to toll the limitations period for equitable reasons. We shall set forth in some detail the record facts that underlie Holland's claim.

In 1997, Holland was convicted of first-degree murder and sentenced to death. The Florida Supreme Court affirmed that judgment. On October 1, 2001, this Court denied Holland's petition for certiorari. And on that date—the date that our denial of the petition ended further direct review of Holland's conviction—the 1-year AEDPA limitations clock began to run.

Thirty-seven days later, on November 7, 2001, Florida appointed attorney Bradley Collins to represent Holland in all state and federal postconviction proceedings. By September 19, 2002—316 days after his appointment and 12 days before the 1-year AEDPA limitations period expired—Collins, acting on Holland's behalf, filed a motion for postconviction relief in the state trial court. That filing automatically stopped the running of the AEDPA limitations period with, as we have said, 12 days left on the clock.

For the next three years, Holland's petition remained pending in the state courts. During that time, Holland wrote Collins letters asking him to make certain that all of his claims would be preserved for any subsequent federal habeas corpus review. Collins wrote back, stating, "I would like to reassure you that we are aware of state time-limitations and federal exhaustion requirements." He also said that he would "presen[t] . . . to the . . . federal courts" any of Holland's claims that the state courts denied. In a second letter Collins added, "should your Motion for Post-Conviction Relief be denied" by the state courts, "your state habeas corpus claims will then be ripe for presentation in a petition for writ of habeas corpus in federal court."

In mid-May 2003, the state trial court denied Holland relief, and Collins appealed that denial to the Florida Supreme Court. Almost two years later, in February 2005, the Florida Supreme Court heard oral argument in the case. But during that 2-year period, relations between Collins and Holland began to break down. Indeed, between April 2003 and January 2006, Collins communicated with Holland only three times—each time by letter.

Holland, unhappy with this lack of communication, twice wrote to the Florida Supreme Court, asking it to remove Collins from his case. In the second letter, filed on June 17, 2004, he said that he and Collins had experienced "a complete breakdown in communication." Holland informed the court that Collins had "not kept [him] updated on the status of [his] capital case" and that Holland had "not seen or spoken to" Collins "since April 2003." He wrote, "Mr. Collins has abandoned [me]" and said, "[I have] no idea what is going on with [my] capital case on appeal." He added that "Collins has never made any reasonable effort to establish any relationship of trust or confidence with [me]" and stated that he "does not trust" or have "any confidence in Mr. Collin's ability to represent [him]." Holland concluded by asking that Collins be "dismissed (removed) off his capital case" or that he be given a hearing in order to demonstrate Collins' deficiencies. The State responded that Holland could not file any pro se papers with the court while he was represented by counsel, including papers seeking new counsel. The Florida Supreme Court agreed and denied Holland's requests.

During this same period Holland wrote various letters to the Clerk of the Florida Supreme Court. In the last of these he wrote, "[I]f I had a competent, conflict-free, postconviction, appellate attorney representing me, I would not have to write you this letter. I'm not trying to get on your nerves. I just would like to know exactly what is happening with my case on appeal to the Supreme Court of Florida." During that same time period, Holland also filed a complaint against Collins with the Florida Bar Association, but the complaint was denied.

Collins argued Holland's appeal before the Florida Supreme Court on February 10, 2005. Shortly thereafter, Holland wrote to Collins emphasizing the importance of filing a timely petition for habeas corpus in federal court once the Florida Supreme Court issued its ruling. . . . Collins did not answer this letter. On June 15, 2005, Holland wrote again . . . [b]ut again, Collins did not reply.

Five months later, in November 2005, the Florida Supreme Court affirmed the lower court decision denying Holland relief. Three weeks after that, on December 1, 2005, the court issued its mandate, making its decision final. At that point, the AEDPA federal habeas clock again began to tick—with 12 days left on the 1-year meter. Twelve days later, on December 13, 2005, Holland's AEDPA time limit expired.

Four weeks after the AEDPA time limit expired, on January 9, 2006, Holland, still unaware of the Florida Supreme Court ruling issued in his case two months earlier, wrote Collins a third letter. . . . Collins did not answer.

Nine days later, on January 18, 2006, Holland, working in the prison library, learned for the first time that the Florida Supreme Court had issued a final determination in his case and that its mandate had issued—five weeks prior. He immediately wrote out his own pro se federal habeas petition and mailed it to the Federal District Court for the Southern District of Florida the next day. . . . The same day that he mailed that petition, Holland received a letter from Collins telling him that Collins intended to file a petition for certiorari in this Court from the State Supreme Court's most recent ruling. Holland answered immediately:

> Dear Mr. Bradley M. Collins:
>
> . . . Since recently, the Supreme Court of Florida has denied my [postconviction] and state writ of Habeas Corpus Petition. I am left to understand that you are planning to seek certiorari on these matters.
>
> It's my understanding that the AEDPA time limitations is not tolled during discretionary appellate reviews, such as certiorari applications resulting from denial of state post conviction proceedings.
>
> Therefore, I advise you not to file certiorari if doing so affects or jeopardizes my one year grace period as prescribed by the AEDPA.
>
> Thank you very much.

Holland was right about the law.

On January 26, 2006, Holland tried to call Collins from prison. But he called collect and Collins' office would not accept the call. Five days later, Collins wrote to Holland and told him for the very first time that, as Collins understood AEDPA law, the limitations period applicable to Holland's federal habeas application had in fact expired in 2000—before Collins had begun to represent Holland. . . .

Collins was wrong about the law. As we have said, Holland's 1-year limitations period did not begin to run until this Court denied Holland's petition for certiorari from the state courts' denial of relief on direct review, which occurred on October 1, 2001. And when Collins was appointed (on November 7, 2001) the AEDPA clock therefore had 328 days left to go. Holland immediately wrote back to Collins, pointing this out. . . . Collins did not answer this letter. Nor did he file a federal habeas petition as Holland requested. . . .

II

We have not decided whether AEDPA's statutory limitations period may be tolled for equitable reasons. Now, like all 11 Courts of Appeals that have considered the question, we hold that § 2244(d) is subject to equitable tolling in appropriate cases.

We base our conclusion on the following considerations. First, the AEDPA "statute of limitations defense . . . is not jurisdictional." It does not set forth "an inflexible rule requiring dismissal whenever" its "clock has run." We have previously made clear that a nonjurisdictional federal statute of limitations is normally subject to a "rebuttable presumption" in favor "of equitable tolling." In the case of AEDPA, the presumption's strength is reinforced by the fact that "equitable principles" have traditionally "governed" the substantive law of habeas corpus, for we will "not construe a statute to displace courts' traditional equitable authority absent the 'clearest command.'" . . . .

[W]e disagree with respondent that equitable tolling undermines AEDPA's basic purposes. We recognize that AEDPA seeks to eliminate delays in the federal habeas review process. But AEDPA seeks to do so without undermining basic habeas corpus principles and while seeking to harmonize the new statute with prior law, under which a petition's timeliness was always determined under equitable principles. When Congress codified new rules governing this previously judicially managed area of law, it did so without losing sight of the fact that the "writ of habeas corpus plays a vital role in protecting constitutional rights." It did not seek to end every possible delay at all costs. The importance of the Great Writ, the only writ explicitly protected by the Constitution, along with congressional efforts to harmonize the new statute with prior law, counsels hesitancy before interpreting AEDPA's statutory silence as indicating a congressional intent to close courthouse doors that a strong equitable claim would ordinarily keep open. . . .

III

We have previously made clear that a "petitioner" is "entitled to equitable tolling" only if he shows "(1) that he has been pursuing his rights diligently, and (2) that some extraordinary circumstance stood in his way" and prevented timely filing. In this case, the "extraordinary circumstances" at issue involve an attorney's failure to satisfy professional standards of care. The Court of Appeals held that, where that is so, even attorney conduct that is "grossly negligent" can never warrant tolling absent "bad faith, dishonesty, divided loyalty, mental impairment or so forth on the lawyer's part." But in our view, the Court of Appeals' standard is too rigid.

We have said that courts of equity "must be governed by rules and precedents no less than the courts of law." But we have also made clear that often the "exercise of a court's equity powers . . . must be made on a case-by-case basis." In emphasizing the need for "flexibility," for avoiding "mechanical rules," we have followed a tradition in which courts of equity have sought to "relieve hardships which, from time to time, arise from a hard and fast adherence" to more absolute legal rules, which, if strictly applied, threaten the "evils of archaic rigidity," The "flexibility" inherent in "equitable procedure" enables courts "to meet new situations [that] demand equitable intervention, and to accord all the relief necessary to correct . . . particular injustices." Taken together, these cases recognize that courts of equity can and do draw upon decisions made in other similar cases for guidance. Such courts exercise judgment in light of prior precedent, but with awareness of the fact that specific circumstances, often hard to predict in advance, could warrant special treatment in an appropriate case. . . .

In short, no pre-existing rule of law or precedent demands a rule like the one set forth by the Eleventh Circuit in this case. That rule is difficult to reconcile with more general equitable principles in that it fails to recognize that, at least sometimes, professional misconduct that fails to meet the Eleventh Circuit's standard could nonetheless amount to egregious behavior and create an extraordinary circumstance that warrants equitable tolling. And, given the long history of judicial application of equitable tolling, courts can easily find precedents that can guide their judgments. Several lower courts have specifically held that unprofessional attorney conduct may, in certain circumstances, prove "egregious" and can be "extraordinary" even though the conduct in question may not satisfy the Eleventh Circuit's rule. . . .

IV

The record facts that we have set forth in Part I of this opinion suggest that this case may well be an "extraordinary" instance in which petitioner's attorney's conduct constituted far more than "garden variety" or "excusable neglect." To be sure, Collins failed to file Holland's petition on time and appears to have been unaware of the date on which the limitations period expired—two facts that, alone, might suggest simple negligence. But, in these circumstances, the record facts we have elucidated suggest that the failure amounted to more: Here, Collins failed to file Holland's federal petition on time despite Holland's many letters that repeatedly emphasized the importance of his doing so. Collins apparently did not do the research necessary to find out the proper filing date, despite Holland's letters that went so far as to identify the applicable legal rules. Collins failed to inform Holland in a timely manner about the crucial fact that the Florida Supreme Court had decided his case, again despite Holland's many pleas for that information. And Collins failed to communicate with his client over a period of years, despite various pleas from Holland that Collins respond to his letters. . . .

NOTES & QUESTIONS ON TIMELINESS AND TOLLING

1. *Extraordinary events.* Was Collins's failure to file the habeas petition in this case extraordinary? Do you consider it extraordinary that Holland, the client, appeared to understand the structure and requirements of the AEDPA better than his attorney, Collins?

2. *Reasonable diligence.* What role does client diligence play in the case? Which facts support the conclusion that Holland was diligent in trying to comply with the limitations period? Is there any possible way that a habeas court could conclude that Holland did not demonstrate reasonable diligence in his desire to file a timely habeas petition?

3. *Other solutions.* Could a habeas court have concluded that Holland was constructively abandoned by his attorney—due to the long lapses in communication—and therefore the agency relationship between client and attorney was severed? If the agency relationship is broken, would that help or hurt Holland's argument?

PROBLEM CASE

In 1997, Rudin was charged with murder and using an unauthorized listening device in Nevada. Rudin was charged with killing her husband, Ron, whose body was located in Lake Mojave, Nevada. Rudin pleaded not guilty and secured the services of a private attorney. A few weeks before the trial, it became clear that her private attorney was incapable of handling the trial by himself, and the court appointed another attorney to assistant the private attorney. Court-appointed counsel soon learned that the private counsel had not reviewed thousands of pages of discovery documents that were turned over to the defense, nor had he interviewed key witnesses. While the trial did occur, the private attorney did a poor job, with a meandering opening statement. The court-appointed attorney described the performance as a "sham, a farce and a mockery." Rudin was convicted of murder and Nevada state appellate courts upheld the conviction. Rudin had separate, court-appointed attorneys for the appellate stage, but they withdrew once the Nevada Supreme Court upheld the conviction on direct review. Rudin petitioned for new counsel for the habeas petitions, and the court appointed attorney Dayvid Figler as "post-conviction" counsel. Rudin then personally filed a pro se petition, but instead of accepting the petition, the court turned over the petition to Figler. Figler never filed the papers, or drafted his own, and Rudin's second attempt to file another pro se petition was again rejected by the court because Rudin was represented by counsel. Rudin missed the statutory deadlines for filing state and federal habeas petitions. During this time, Rudin, who was incarcerated, had difficulty reaching Figler, though Figler did visit the prison a few times to meet with Rudin in person. On these facts, is Rudin eligible for equitable tolling? See *Rudin v. Myles,* 781 F.3d 1043 (9th Cir. 2015).

4. Exhaustion Requirement

The federal habeas statute directs federal district courts to reject a habeas petition if the petitioner has not already "exhausted" state remedies first. Consequently, the petitioner must complete the direct appellate process first, or pursue state habeas relief, if applicable, before filing for federal habeas relief. This truly makes the federal writ of habeas corpus a legal mechanism of last resort. A complex question of interpretation arises when the petitioner files a petition asserting *multiple* bases for habeas relief. What if some of the claims have been exhausted in state proceedings but other claims contained in the petition were not exhausted? Can a district court hear these "mixed" petitions or does the inclusion of the non-exhausted claims require the district court to dismiss the entire petition?

Rose v. Lundy

Supreme Court of the United States
455 U.S. 509 (1982)

Justice O'CONNOR delivered the opinion of the Court, except as to Part III-C.

In this case we consider whether the exhaustion rule in 28 U.S.C. §§ 2254(b), (c) requires a federal district court to dismiss a petition for a writ of habeas corpus containing any claims that have not been exhausted in the state courts. Because a rule requiring exhaustion of all claims furthers the purposes underlying the habeas statute, we hold that a district court must dismiss such "mixed petitions," leaving the prisoner with the choice of returning to state court to exhaust his claims or of amending or resubmitting the habeas petition to present only exhausted claims to the district court.

I

Following a jury trial, respondent Noah Lundy was convicted on charges of rape and crime against nature, and sentenced to the Tennessee State Penitentiary. After the Tennessee Court of Criminal Appeals affirmed the convictions and the Tennessee Supreme Court denied review, the respondent filed an unsuccessful petition for post-conviction relief in the Knox County Criminal Court.

The respondent subsequently filed a petition in Federal District Court for a writ of habeas corpus under 28 U.S.C. § 2254, alleging four grounds for relief: (1) that he had been denied the right to confrontation because the trial court limited the defense counsel's questioning of the victim; (2) that he had been denied the right to a fair trial because the prosecuting attorney stated that the respondent had a violent character; (3) that he had been denied the right to a fair trial because the prosecutor improperly remarked in his closing argument that the State's evidence was uncontradicted; and (4) that the trial judge improperly instructed the jury that every witness is presumed to swear the truth. After reviewing the state court records, however, the District Court concluded that it could not consider claims three and four "in the constitutional framework" because the respondent had not exhausted his state remedies for those grounds. The court nevertheless stated that "in assessing the atmosphere of the cause taken as a whole these items may be referred to collaterally."

Apparently in an effort to assess the "atmosphere" of the trial, the District Court reviewed the state trial transcript and identified 10 instances of prosecutorial misconduct, only five of which the respondent had raised before the state courts. In addition, although purportedly not ruling on the respondent's fourth ground for relief-that the state trial judge improperly charged that "every witness is presumed to swear the truth"—the court nonetheless held that the jury instruction, coupled with both the restriction of counsel's cross-examination of the victim and the prosecutor's "personal testimony" on the weight of the State's evidence, violated the respondent's right to a fair trial. . . . In short, the District Court considered several instances of prosecutorial misconduct never challenged in the state trial or appellate courts, or even raised in the respondent's habeas petition. . . .

II

The petitioner urges this Court to apply a "total exhaustion" rule requiring district courts to dismiss every habeas corpus petition that contains both exhausted and unexhausted claims. The petitioner argues at length that such a rule furthers the policy of comity underlying the exhaustion doctrine because it gives the state courts the first opportunity to correct federal constitutional errors and minimizes federal interference and disruption of state judicial proceedings. The petitioner also believes that uniform adherence to a total exhaustion rule reduces the amount of piecemeal habeas litigation.

Under the petitioner's approach, a district court would dismiss a petition containing both exhausted and unexhausted claims, giving the prisoner the choice of returning to state court to litigate his unexhausted claims, or of proceeding with only his exhausted claims in federal court. The petitioner believes that a prisoner would be reluctant to choose the latter route since a district court could, in appropriate circumstances under Habeas Corpus Rule 9(b), dismiss subsequent federal habeas petitions as an abuse of the writ. In other words, if the prisoner amended the petition to delete the unexhausted claims or immediately refiled in federal court a petition alleging only his exhausted claims, he could lose the opportunity to litigate his presently unexhausted claims in federal court. This argument is addressed in Part III-C of this opinion.

In order to evaluate the merits of the petitioner's arguments, we turn to the habeas statute, its legislative history, and the policies underlying the exhaustion doctrine.

III

A

The exhaustion doctrine existed long before its codification by Congress in 1948. In *Ex parte Royall*, 117 U.S. 241, 251 (1886), this Court wrote that as a matter of comity, federal courts should not consider a claim in a habeas corpus petition until after the state courts have had an opportunity to act. . . . Subsequent cases refined the principle that state remedies must be exhausted except in unusual circumstances. In *Ex parte Hawk*, 321 U.S. 114, 117 (1944), this Court reiterated that comity was the basis for the exhaustion doctrine: "it is a principle controlling all habeas corpus petitions to the federal courts, that those courts will interfere with the administration of justice in the state courts only in rare cases where exceptional circumstances of peculiar urgency are shown to exist." None of these cases, however, specifically applied the exhaustion doctrine to habeas petitions containing both exhausted and unexhausted claims.

In 1948, Congress codified the exhaustion doctrine in 28 U.S.C. § 2254, citing *Ex parte Hawk* as correctly stating the principle of exhaustion. Section 2254, however, does not directly address the problem of mixed petitions. To be sure, the provision states that a remedy is not exhausted if there exists a state procedure to raise "the question presented," but we believe this phrase to be too ambiguous to sustain the conclusion that Congress intended to either permit or prohibit review of mixed petitions. Because the legislative history of § 2254, as well as the pre-1948 cases, contains no reference to the problem of mixed petitions, in all likelihood Congress never thought of the problem. Consequently, we must analyze the policies underlying the statutory provision to determine its proper scope.

B

The exhaustion doctrine is principally designed to protect the state courts' role in the enforcement of federal law and prevent disruption of state judicial proceedings. Under our federal system, the federal and state "courts [are] equally bound to guard and protect rights secured by the Constitution." Because "it would be unseemly in our dual system of government for a federal district court to upset a state court conviction without an opportunity to the state courts to correct a constitutional violation," federal courts apply the doctrine of comity, which "teaches that one court should defer action on causes properly within its jurisdiction until the courts of another sovereignty with concurrent powers, and already cognizant of the litigation, have had an opportunity to pass upon the matter."

A rigorously enforced total exhaustion rule will encourage state prisoners to seek full relief first from the state courts, thus giving those courts the first opportunity to review all claims of constitutional error. As the number of prisoners who exhaust all of their federal claims increases, state courts may become increasingly familiar with and hospitable toward federal constitutional issues. Equally as important, federal claims that have been fully exhausted in state courts will more often be accompanied by a complete factual record to aid the federal courts in their review.

The facts of the present case underscore the need for a rule encouraging exhaustion of all federal claims. In his opinion, the District Court Judge wrote that "there is such mixture of violations that one cannot be separated from and considered independently of the others." Because the two unexhausted claims for relief were intertwined with the exhausted ones, the judge apparently considered all of the claims in ruling on the petition. Requiring dismissal of petitions containing both exhausted and unexhausted claims will relieve the district courts of the difficult if not impossible task of deciding when claims are related, and will reduce the temptation to consider unexhausted claims. . . .

Rather than increasing the burden on federal courts, strict enforcement of the exhaustion requirement will encourage habeas petitioners to exhaust all of their claims in state court and to present the federal court with a single habeas petition. To the extent that the exhaustion requirement reduces piecemeal litigation, both the courts and the prisoners should benefit, for as a result the district court will be more likely to review all of the prisoner's claims in a single proceeding, thus providing for a more focused and thorough review.

C

The prisoner's principal interest, of course, is in obtaining speedy federal relief on his claims. A total exhaustion rule will not impair that interest since he can always amend the petition to delete the unexhausted claims, rather than returning to state court to exhaust all of his claims. By invoking this procedure, however, the prisoner would risk forfeiting consideration of his unexhausted claims in federal court. Under 28 U.S.C. § 2254 Rule 9(b), a district court may dismiss subsequent petitions if it finds that "the failure of the petitioner to assert those [new] grounds in a prior petition constituted an abuse of the writ." . . . . Thus a prisoner who decides to proceed only with his exhausted claims and deliberately sets aside his unexhausted claims risks dismissal of subsequent federal petitions.

IV

In sum, because a total exhaustion rule promotes comity and does not unreasonably impair the prisoner's right to relief, we hold that a district court must dismiss habeas petitions containing both unexhausted and exhausted claims. . . .

NOTES & QUESTIONS ON EXHAUSTION

1. *Total exhaustion.* Under the Court's total exhaustion requirement, a petitioner must exhaust all of his or her habeas arguments in state court before filing a federal petition. Or, if the petitioner wishes to file the federal petition sooner rather than later, the petitioner may elect to only include the exhausted claims in the federal habeas petition. Does this force the petitioner into an unreasonable choice?

2. *Exhaustion and comity.* What is the conceptual basis for the exhaustion requirement? Courts have repeatedly referred to the exhaustion requirement as flowing from considerations of comity. What does the reference to comity mean in this context? What does it suggest about the relationship between federal and state jurisdictions?

3. *Total exhaustion and the AEDPA. Rose* was decided long before the AEDPA was passed. The total exhaustion requirement announced in *Rose* was maintained by the AEDPA, which added the one-year limitations period. This poses an obstacle for a petitioner who files for federal habeas review with a mixed petition. *Rose* directs the district court to reject such petitions, though by the time the unexhausted claims are then exhausted, the limitation period may have run, thus preventing federal review. This problem was recognized by the Supreme Court in *Rhines v. Weber*, 544 U.S. 269 (2005). Some district courts solved this problem by "staying" and holding in "abeyance" mixed petitions while petitioners exhaust the remaining claims in state court; this had the result of ensuring that the petition was still filed before the end of the limitation period. In *Rhines v. Weber*, the Supreme Court upheld the stay-and-abeyance procedure but concluded that it should be used sparingly:

> For these reasons, stay and abeyance should be available only in limited circumstances. Because granting a stay effectively excuses a petitioner's failure to present his claims first to the state courts, stay and abeyance is only appropriate when the district court determines there was good cause for the petitioner's failure to exhaust his claims first in state court. Moreover, even if a petitioner had good cause for that failure, the district court would abuse its discretion if it were to grant him a stay when his unexhausted claims are plainly meritless.

Id. at 277.

5. Successive Petitions

The AEDPA, 28 U.S.C. § 2244(b), prohibits a district court from granting a successive petition, in order to prevent federal courts from being flooded with repeat petitions simply rehashing old arguments. Specifically, the statute requires that

> (a) No circuit or district judge shall be required to entertain an application for a writ of habeas corpus to inquire into the detention of a person pursuant to a judgment of a court of the United States if it appears that the legality of such detention has been determined by a judge or court of the United States on a prior application for a writ of habeas corpus, except as provided in section 2255.
> (b)(1) A claim presented in a second or successive habeas corpus application under section 2254 that was presented in a prior application shall be dismissed.

28 U.S.C.A. § 2244. However, the statute *does* allow for the issuance of a writ of habeas corpus pursuant to a new claim raised for the first time in a successive petition, providing the following criteria are met:

> [T]he applicant shows that the claim relies on a new rule of constitutional law, made retroactive to cases on collateral review by the Supreme Court, that was previously unavailable; or
> (B)(i) the factual predicate for the claim could not have been discovered previously through the exercise of due diligence; and
>> (ii) the facts underlying the claim, if proven and viewed in light of the evidence as a whole, would be sufficient to establish by clear and convincing evidence that, but for constitutional error, no reasonable factfinder would have found nthe applicant guilty of the underlying offense.

28 U.S.C.A. § 2244. In the following case, the Supreme Court considers a unique fact pattern: A first habeas petition was granted, resulting in a second sentencing in state court. Then, the petitioner challenged the second sentence in a new habeas petition. For the purpose of the AEDPA, should this second habeas petition be considered "successive"?

Magwood v. Patterson

Supreme Court of the United States
561 U.S. 320 (2010)

Justice THOMAS delivered the opinion of the Court, except as to Part IV-B.

Petitioner Billy Joe Magwood was sentenced to death for murdering a sheriff. After the Alabama courts denied relief on direct appeal and in postconviction proceedings, Magwood filed an application for a writ of habeas corpus in Federal District Court, challenging both his conviction and his sentence. The District Court conditionally granted the writ as to the sentence, mandating that Magwood either be released or resentenced. The state trial court conducted a new sentencing hearing and again sentenced Magwood to death. Magwood filed an application for a writ of habeas corpus in federal court challenging this new sentence. The District Court once again conditionally granted the writ, finding constitutional defects in the new sentence. The Court of Appeals for the Eleventh Circuit reversed, holding in relevant part that Magwood's challenge to his new death sentence was an unreviewable "second or successive" challenge under 28 U.S.C. § 2244(b) because he could have mounted the same challenge to his original death sentence. We granted certiorari, and now reverse. Because Magwood's habeas application challenges a new judgment for the first time, it is not "second or successive" under § 2244(b).

I

After a conviction for a drug offense, Magwood served several years in the Coffee County Jail in Elba, Alabama, under the watch of Sheriff C.F. "Neil" Grantham. During his incarceration, Magwood, who had a long history of mental illness, became convinced that Grantham had imprisoned him without cause, and vowed to get even upon his release. Magwood followed through on his threat. On the morning of March 1, 1979, shortly after his release, he parked outside the jail and awaited the sheriff's arrival. When Grantham exited his car, Magwood shot him and fled the scene.

Magwood was indicted by a grand jury for the murder of an on-duty sheriff. . . . He was tried in 1981. The prosecution asked the jury to find Magwood guilty of aggravated murder as charged in the indictment, and sought the death penalty. Magwood pleaded not guilty by reason of insanity; however, the jury found him guilty of capital murder . . . and imposed the sentence of death. . . .

Eight days before his scheduled execution, Magwood filed an application for a writ of habeas corpus under 28 U.S.C. § 2254, and the District Court granted a stay of execution. After briefing by the parties, the District Court upheld Magwood's conviction but vacated his sentence and conditionally granted the writ based on the trial court's failure to find statutory mitigating circumstances relating to Magwood's mental state.

In response to the conditional writ, the state trial court held a new sentencing proceeding in September 1986. This time, the judge found that Magwood's mental state, as well as his age and lack of criminal history, qualified as statutory mitigating circumstances. As before, the court found that Magwood's capital felony under § 13-11-2(a)(5) included sufficient aggravation to render him death eligible. In his proposed findings, Magwood's attorney agreed that Magwood's offense rendered him death eligible, but argued that a death sentence would be inappropriate in light of the mitigating factors. The trial court imposed a penalty of death, stating on the record that the new "judgment and sentence [were] the result of a complete and new assessment of all of the evidence, arguments of counsel, and law." The Alabama courts affirmed and this Court denied certiorari. . . .

In April 1997, Magwood sought leave to file a second or successive application for a writ of habeas corpus challenging his 1981 judgment of conviction. The Court of Appeals denied his request. He simultaneously filed a petition for a writ of habeas corpus challenging his new death sentence, which the District Court conditionally granted. In that petition, Magwood again argued that his sentence was unconstitutional because he did not have fair warning at the time of his offense that his conduct would be sufficient to warrant a death sentence under Alabama law, and that his attorney rendered ineffective assistance during the resentencing proceeding. . . .

II

As amended by the Antiterrorism and Effective Death Penalty Act of 1996 (AEDPA), 28 U.S.C. § 2244(b) provides in relevant part:

> (1) A claim presented in a second or successive habeas corpus application under section 2254 that was presented in a prior application shall be dismissed.
> (2) A claim presented in a second or successive habeas corpus application under section 2254 that was not presented in a prior application shall be dismissed unless—
>> (A) the applicant shows that the claim relies on a new rule of constitutional law, made retroactive to cases on collateral review by the Supreme Court, that was previously unavailable; or
>> (B)(i) the factual predicate for the claim could not have been discovered previously through the exercise of due diligence; and
>>> (ii) the facts underlying the claim, if proven and viewed in light of the evidence as a whole, would be sufficient to establish by clear and convincing evidence that, but for constitutional error, no reasonable factfinder would have found the applicant guilty of the underlying offense.

This case turns on the meaning of the phrase "second or successive" in § 2244(b). More specifically, it turns on when a claim should be deemed to arise in a "second or successive habeas corpus application." If an application is "second or successive," the petitioner must obtain leave from the court of appeals before filing it with the district court. The district court must dismiss any claim presented in an authorized second or successive application unless the applicant shows that the claim satisfies certain statutory requirements. Thus, if Magwood's application was "second or successive," the District Court should have dismissed it in its entirety because he failed to obtain the requisite authorization from the Court of Appeals. If, however, Magwood's application was not second or successive, it was not subject to § 2244(b) at all, and his fair-warning claim was reviewable (absent procedural default).

The State contends that although § 2244(b), as amended by AEDPA, applies the phrase "second or successive" to "application[s]," it "is a claim-focused statute," and "[c]laims, not applications, are barred by § 2244(b)." According to the State, the phrase should be read to reflect a principle that "a prisoner is entitled to one, but only one, full and fair opportunity to wage a collateral attack." The State asserts that under this "one opportunity" rule, Magwood's fair-warning claim was successive because he had an opportunity to raise it in his first application, but did not do so.

Magwood, in contrast, reads § 2244(b) to apply only to a "second or successive" application challenging the same state-court judgment. According to Magwood, his 1986 resentencing led to a new judgment, and his first application challenging that new judgment cannot be "second or successive" such that § 2244(b) would apply. We agree.

We begin with the text. Although Congress did not define the phrase "second or successive," as used to modify "habeas corpus application under section 2254," it is well settled that the phrase does not simply "refe[r] to all § 2254 applications filed second or successively in time."

We have described the phrase "second or successive" as a "term of art." To determine its meaning, we look first to the statutory context. The limitations imposed by § 2244(b) apply only to a "habeas corpus application under section 2254," that is, an "application for a writ of habeas corpus on behalf of a person in custody pursuant to the judgment of a State court." The reference to a state-court judgment in § 2254(b) is significant because the term "application" cannot be defined in a vacuum. A § 2254 petitioner is applying for something: His petition "seeks invalidation (in whole or in part) of the judgment authorizing the prisoner's confinement." If his petition results in a district court's granting of the writ, "the State may seek a new judgment (through a new trial or a new sentencing proceeding)." Thus, both § 2254(b)'s text and the relief it provides indicate that the phrase "second or successive" must be interpreted with respect to the judgment challenged.

The State disagrees, contending that if the cross-reference to § 2254 is relevant, we should focus not on the statute's reference to a "judgment" but on its reference to "custody." The State explains that unlawful "custody" is the key "substance requirement" of § 2254, whereas being held pursuant to a state-court "judgment" is merely a "status requirement."

We find this argument unpersuasive. Section 2254 articulates the kind of confinement that may be challenged on the ground that the petitioner is being held "in violation of the Constitution or laws or treaties of the United States." The requirement of custody pursuant to a state-court judgment distinguishes § 2254 from other statutory provisions authorizing relief from constitutional violations—such as § 2255, which allows challenges to the judgments of federal courts, or Rev. Stat. § 1979, 42 U.S.C. § 1983, which allows federal-court suits against state and local officials. Custody is crucial for § 2254 purposes, but it is inextricable from the judgment that authorizes it. . . .

III

Appearing to recognize that Magwood has the stronger textual argument, the State argues that we should rule based on the statutory purpose. According to the State, a "one opportunity" rule is consistent with the statutory text, and better reflects AEDPA's purpose of preventing piecemeal litigation and gamesmanship.

We are not persuaded. AEDPA uses the phrase "second or successive" to modify "application." The State reads the phrase to modify "claims." We cannot replace the actual text with speculation as to Congress' intent. We have previously found Congress' use of the word "application" significant, and have refused to adopt an interpretation of § 2244(b) that would "elid[e] the difference between an application and a claim." Therefore, although we agree with the State that many of the rules under § 2244(b) focus on claims, that does not entitle us to rewrite the statute to make the phrase "second or successive" modify claims as well. . . .

In 2002, after exhausting his state sentencing appeal, the petitioner filed a § 2254 petition challenging only his 1998 sentence. The District Court denied relief on the merits and the Court of Appeals affirmed. We reversed, holding that the petition challenging the sentence should have been dismissed as an unauthorized "second or successive" application. We rejected the petitioner's argument "that his 1998 and 2002 petitions challenged different judgments. Although the petitioner had styled his first petition as a challenge to the 1994 conviction and his second petition as a challenge to the 1998 sentence, we concluded that both attacked the same "judgment" because the 1998 sentence was already in place when the petitioner filed his first application for federal habeas relief. In other words, the judgment he challenged in his 1998 application was "the same one challenged in the subsequent 2002 petition"; it "was the judgment pursuant to which [the petitioner] was being detained." We expressly recognized that the case might have been different had there been a "new judgment intervening between the two habeas petitions."

This is Magwood's first application challenging that intervening judgment. The errors he alleges are new. It is obvious to us—and the State does not dispute—that his claim of ineffective assistance at resentencing turns upon new errors. But, according to the State, his fair-warning claim does not, because the state court made the same mistake before. We disagree. An error made a second time is still a new error. . . .

NOTES & QUESTIONS ON SUCCESSIVE PETITIONS

1. *New errors.* Do you agree with the Court's assessment that an error, made for a second time, constitutes a new error? Are there some situations where one might conclude that there was simply one, continuous error?

2. *Successive petitions.* The exhaustion requirement is justified by reasons of comity and respect for the courts of another sovereign. What justifies the ban on successive petitions? Is it a reference to res judicata or is there another principle at play here?

PROBLEM CASE

Reconsider the case of *Panetti v. Quaterman*, excerpted in the sentencing chapter. The defendant, Scott Louis Panetti, was charged with capital murder in Texas. Panetti was sentenced to death, even though he suffered from mental illness. His stand-by counsel referred to his behavior during the trial as "bizarre . . . scary . . . trance-like. . . ," and Panetti may have stopped taking his anti-psychotic medications. Petitioner exhausted his state appeals and federal courts denied his habeas petition. The State of Texas then set a date for Panetti's execution. At that point, Panetti filed a new petition in state court arguing that he was incompetent to be executed due to his mental illness. In federal court, Panetti argued that the Texas courts violated federal law by failing to evaluate his competence for execution according to the appropriate federal constitutional standard, which was articulated in *Ford v. Wainwright*, 477 U.S. 399 (1986). Since this was the petitioner's second habeas petition, did a federal court have jurisdiction to entertain it? See *Panetti v. Quarterman*, 551 U.S. 930 (2007).

C. PROCEDURAL DEFAULT AND ITS EXCEPTIONS

The most likely reason that a petitioner will fail in his or her habeas petition is if the claims were procedurally defaulted in state court. Usually, legal issues are not properly preserved for appellate review unless they are reasserted at each stage of the litigation. So, for example, if the defendant fails to object to something at trial, or objects at trial but then fails to re-raise the issue on immediate appeal, a higher state appeals court might refuse to entertain the claim even if it is raised at a later point in time. The question is whether a federal court should uphold a state court's decision to refuse to entertain an otherwise valid constitutional claim because it was procedurally defaulted under the state's rules for procedural default. As one can imagine, this highly technical issue is often a bar to successful federal habeas review of a state court conviction. As the following subsections make clear, however, federal habeas jurisprudence recognizes two important exceptions to procedural default in some circumstances: "cause and prejudice" and "actual innocence."

1. The Cause-and-Prejudice Exception

In *Wainwright v. Sykes,* 433 U.S. 72 (1977), the Supreme Court considered whether federal habeas review is available to consider a potential *Miranda* violation when the petitioner failed to comply with Florida's state contemporaneous-objection rule. If habeas review is foreclosed by the application of the state rule, then it would appear to subordinate the federal requirements of *Miranda* to a procedural rule in the state courts. On the other hand, the federal habeas review is designed to review the legality of the state court proceedings, and the federal system has to give some credence to the legitimacy of the state procedural system. In other words, the state courts failed to vindicate the *Miranda* claim not because of the substance of the claim but rather because of a failure to satisfy some procedural requirements—and to completely ignore that fact would seem to make a mockery of the need for state procedures in the first instance. Consequently, the Supreme Court articulated a cause-and-prejudice exception to the procedural default rule. In so doing, the Court rejected an earlier rule that allowed a federal habeas court to consider any claim as long as there was no knowing and deliberate waiver by the defendant in state court. The cause-and-prejudice standard requires the petitioner to establish that there was cause for the failure to follow the state procedural rule—in short, a good reason—and that the defendant suffered actual prejudice from the alleged violation of federal law. The Court in *Wainwright v. Sykes* failed to define the full scope of the cause-and-prejudice exception standard but maintained that it would be sufficient to prevent miscarriages of justice.

In the following case, the Supreme Court further defined and applied the cause-and-prejudice standard as an exception to the procedural default rule. The facts of the case, recounted below, are shocking and a cautionary tale for a young associate in large firm practice. Two associates at a large firm agreed to defend a capital prisoner on a pro bono basis, but notified neither the prisoner nor the clerk of the court when they left the firm and dropped the case. As a result, the prisoner missed several important filing deadlines. As you read the case, ask yourself whether the situation that Cory Maples found himself in was sufficient to demonstrate the cause and prejudice necessary to negate a procedural default.

Maples v. Thomas

Supreme Court of the United States
565 U.S. 266 (2012)

Justice GINSBURG delivered the opinion of the Court.

Cory R. Maples is an Alabama capital prisoner sentenced to death in 1997 for the murder of two individuals. At trial, he was represented by two appointed lawyers, minimally paid and with scant experience in capital cases. Maples sought postconviction relief in state court, alleging ineffective assistance of counsel and several other trial infirmities. His petition, filed in August 2001, was written by two New York attorneys serving pro bono, both associated with the same New York-based large law firm. An Alabama attorney, designated as local counsel, moved the admission of the out-of-state counsel pro hac vice. As understood by New York counsel, local counsel would facilitate their appearance, but would undertake no substantive involvement in the case.

In the summer of 2002, while Maples' postconviction petition remained pending in the Alabama trial court, his New York attorneys left the law firm; their new employment disabled them from continuing to represent Maples. They did not inform Maples of their departure and consequent inability to serve as his counsel. Nor did they seek the Alabama trial court's leave to withdraw. Neither they nor anyone else moved for the substitution of counsel able to handle Maples' case. . . .

The sole question this Court has taken up for review is whether, on the extraordinary facts of Maples' case, there is "cause" to excuse the default. Maples maintains that there is, for the lawyers he believed to be vigilantly representing him had abandoned the case without leave of court, without informing Maples they could no longer represent him, and without securing any recorded substitution of counsel. We agree. Abandoned by counsel, Maples was left unrepresented at a critical time for his state postconviction petition, and he lacked a clue of any need to protect himself pro se. In these circumstances, no just system would lay the default at Maples' death-cell door. Satisfied that the requisite cause has been shown, we reverse the Eleventh Circuit's judgment.

I

. . . [I]n 1997, Alabama charged Maples with two counts of capital murder; the victims, Stacy Alan Terry and Barry Dewayne Robinson II, were Maples' friends who, on the night of the murders, had been out on the town with him. Maples pleaded not guilty, and his case proceeded to trial, where he was represented by two court-appointed Alabama attorneys. Only one of them had earlier served in a capital case. Neither counsel had previously tried the penalty phase of a capital case. Compensation for each lawyer was capped at $1,000 for time spent out-of-court preparing Maples' case, and at $40 per hour for in-court services.

Finding Maples guilty on both counts, the jury recommended that he be sentenced to death. The vote was 10 to 2, the minimum number Alabama requires for a death recommendation. Accepting the jury's recommendation, the trial court sentenced Maples to death. On direct appeal, the Alabama Court of Criminal Appeals and the Alabama Supreme Court affirmed the convictions and sentence. We denied certiorari.

Two out-of-state volunteers represented Maples in postconviction proceedings: Jaasi Munanka and Clara Ingen-Housz, both associates at the New York offices of the Sullivan & Cromwell law firm. At the time, Alabama required out-of-state attorneys to associate local counsel when seeking admission to practice pro hac vice before an Alabama court, regardless of the nature of the proceeding. The Alabama Rule further prescribed that the local attorney's name "appear on all notices, orders, pleadings, and other documents filed in the cause," and that local counsel "accept joint and several responsibility with the foreign attorney to the client, to opposing parties and counsel, and to the court or administrative agency in all matters [relating to the case]."

Munanka and Ingen-Housz associated Huntsville, Alabama attorney John Butler as local counsel. Notwithstanding his obligations under Alabama law, Butler informed Munanka and Ingen-Housz, "at the outset," that he would serve as local counsel only for the purpose of allowing the two New York attorneys to appear pro hac vice on behalf of Maples. Given his lack of "resources, available time [and] experience," Butler told the Sullivan & Cromwell lawyers, he could not "deal with substantive issues in the case." The Sullivan & Cromwell attorneys accepted Butler's conditions. This arrangement between out-of-state and local attorneys, it appears, was hardly atypical.

With the aid of his pro bono counsel, Maples filed a petition for postconviction relief under Alabama Rule of Criminal Procedure 32. Among other claims, Maples asserted that his court-appointed attorneys provided constitutionally ineffective assistance during both guilt and penalty phases of his capital trial. He alleged, in this regard, that his inexperienced and underfunded attorneys failed to develop and raise an obvious intoxication defense, did not object to several egregious instances of prosecutorial misconduct, and woefully underprepared for the penalty phase of his trial. The State responded by moving for summary dismissal of Maples' petition. On December 27, 2001, the trial court denied the State's motion.

Some seven months later, in the summer of 2002, both Munanka and Ingen-Housz left Sullivan & Cromwell. Munanka gained a clerkship with a federal judge; Ingen-Housz accepted a position with the European Commission in Belgium. Neither attorney told Maples of their departure from Sullivan & Cromwell or of their resulting inability to continue to represent him. In disregard of Alabama law, neither attorney sought the trial court's leave to withdraw. Compounding Munanka's and Ingen-Housz's inaction, no other Sullivan & Cromwell lawyer entered an appearance on Maples' behalf, moved to substitute counsel, or otherwise notified the court of any change in Maples' representation.

Another nine months passed. During this time period, no Sullivan & Cromwell attorneys assigned to Maples' case sought admission to the Alabama bar, entered appearances on Maples' behalf, or otherwise advised the Alabama court that Munanka and Ingen-Housz were no longer Maples' attorneys. Thus, Munanka and Ingen-Housz (along with Butler) remained Maples' listed, and only, "attorneys of record."

There things stood when, in May 2003, the trial court, without holding a hearing, entered an order denying Maples' Rule 32 petition. The clerk of the Alabama trial court mailed copies of the order to Maples' three attorneys of record. He sent Munanka's and Ingen-Housz's copies to Sullivan & Cromwell's New York address, which the pair had provided upon entering their appearances.

When those copies arrived at Sullivan & Cromwell, Munanka and Ingen-Housz had long since departed. The notices, however, were not forwarded to another Sullivan & Cromwell attorney. Instead, a mailroom employee sent the unopened envelopes back to the court. "Returned to Sender—Attempted, Unknown" was stamped on the envelope addressed to Munanka. A similar stamp appeared on the envelope addressed to Ingen-Housz, along with the handwritten notation "Return to Sender—Left Firm."

Upon receiving back the unopened envelopes he had mailed to Munanka and Ingen-Housz, the Alabama court clerk took no further action. In particular, the clerk did not contact Munanka or Ingen-Housz at the personal telephone numbers or home addresses they had provided in their pro hac vice applications. Nor did the clerk alert Sullivan & Cromwell or Butler. Butler received his copy of the order, but did not act on it. He assumed that Munanka and Ingen-Housz, who had been "cc'd" on the order, would take care of filing an appeal.

Meanwhile, the clock ticked on Maples' appeal. Under Alabama's Rules of Appellate Procedure, Maples had 42 days to file a notice of appeal from the trial court's May 22, 2003 order denying Maples' petition for postconviction relief. No appeal notice was filed, and the time allowed for filing expired on July 7, 2003.

A little over a month later, on August 13, 2003, Alabama Assistant Attorney General Jon Hayden, the attorney representing the State in Maples' collateral review proceedings, sent a letter directly to Maples. Hayden's letter informed Maples of the missed deadline for initiating an appeal within the State's system, and notified him that four weeks remained during which he could file a federal habeas petition. Hayden mailed the letter to Maples only, using his prison address. No copy was sent to Maples' attorneys of record, or to anyone else acting on Maples' behalf.

Upon receiving the State's letter, Maples immediately contacted his mother. She telephoned Sullivan & Cromwell to inquire about her son's case. Prompted by her call, Sullivan & Cromwell attorneys Marc De Leeuw, Felice Duffy, and Kathy Brewer submitted a motion, through Butler, asking the trial court to reissue its order denying Maples' Rule 32 petition, thereby restarting the 42-day appeal period.

The trial court denied the motion, noting that Munanka and Ingen-Housz had not withdrawn from the case and, consequently, were "still attorneys of record for the petitioner." Furthermore, the court added, attorneys De Leeuw, Duffy, and Brewer had not "yet been admitted to practice in Alabama" or "entered appearances as attorneys of record." "How," the court asked, "can a Circuit Clerk in Decatur, Alabama know what is going on in a law firm in New York, New York?" Declining to blame the clerk for the missed notice of appeal deadline, the court said it was "unwilling to enter into subterfuge in order to gloss over mistakes made by counsel for the petitioner."

Maples next petitioned the Alabama Court of Criminal Appeals for a writ of mandamus, granting him leave to file an out-of-time appeal. Rejecting Maples' plea, the Court of Criminal Appeals determined that, although the clerk had "assumed a duty to notify the parties of the resolution of Maples's Rule 32 petition," the clerk had satisfied that obligation by sending notices to the attorneys of record at the addresses those attorneys provided. Butler's receipt of the order, the court observed, sufficed to notify all attorneys "in light of their apparent co-counsel status." The Alabama Supreme Court summarily affirmed the Court of Criminal Appeals' judgment and this Court denied certiorari. Having exhausted his state postconviction remedies, Maples sought federal habeas corpus relief. . . .

II

As a rule, a state prisoner's habeas claims may not be entertained by a federal court "when (1) a state court [has] declined to address [those] claims because the prisoner had failed to meet a state procedural requirement, and (2) the state judgment rests on independent and adequate state procedural grounds." The bar to federal review may be lifted, however, if "the prisoner can demonstrate cause for the [procedural] default [in state court] and actual prejudice as a result of the alleged violation of federal law."

Given the single issue on which we granted review, we will assume, for purposes of this decision, that the Alabama Court of Criminal Appeals' refusal to consider Maples' ineffective-assistance claims rested on an independent and adequate state procedural ground: namely, Maples' failure to satisfy Alabama's Rule requiring a notice of appeal to be filed within 42 days from the trial court's final order. Accordingly, we confine our consideration to the question whether Maples has shown cause to excuse the missed notice of appeal deadline.

Cause for a procedural default exists where "something external to the petitioner, something that cannot fairly be attributed to him[,] . . . impeded [his] efforts to comply with the State's procedural rule." Negligence on the part of a prisoner's postconviction attorney does not qualify as "cause."

That is so, we reasoned in *Coleman*, because the attorney is the prisoner's agent, and under "well-settled principles of agency law," the principal bears the risk of negligent conduct on the part of his agent. Thus, when a petitioner's postconviction attorney misses a filing deadline, the petitioner is bound by the oversight and cannot rely on it to establish cause. We do not disturb that general rule.

A markedly different situation is presented, however, when an attorney abandons his client without notice, and thereby occasions the default. Having severed the principal-agent relationship, an attorney no longer acts, or fails to act, as the client's representative. His acts or omissions therefore "cannot fairly be attributed to [the client]." . . . We agree that, under agency principles, a client cannot be charged with the acts or omissions of an attorney who has abandoned him. Nor can a client be faulted for failing to act on his own behalf when he lacks reason to believe his attorneys of record, in fact, are not representing him. We therefore inquire whether Maples has shown that his attorneys of record abandoned him, thereby supplying the "extraordinary circumstances beyond his control," necessary to lift the state procedural bar to his federal petition.

From the time he filed his initial Rule 32 petition until well after time ran out for appealing the trial court's denial of that petition, Maples had only three attorneys of record: Munanka, Ingen-Housz, and Butler. Unknown to Maples, not one of these lawyers was in fact serving as his attorney during the 42 days permitted for an appeal from the trial court's order. . . .

Maples' only other attorney of record, local counsel Butler, also left him abandoned. Indeed, Butler did not even begin to represent Maples. Butler informed Munanka and Ingen-Housz that he would serve as local counsel only for the purpose of enabling the two out-of-state attorneys to appear pro hac vice. Lacking the necessary "resources, available time [and] experience," Butler told the two Sullivan & Cromwell lawyers, he would not "deal with substantive issues in the case." That the minimal participation he undertook was inconsistent with Alabama law, underscores the absurdity of holding Maples barred because Butler signed on as local counsel. . . .

Not only was Maples left without any functioning attorney of record, the very listing of Munanka, Ingen-Housz, and Butler as his representatives meant that he had no right personally to receive notice. He in fact received none or any other warning that he had better fend for himself. Had counsel of record or the State's attorney informed Maples of his plight before the time to appeal ran out, he could have filed a notice of appeal himself or enlisted the aid of new volunteer attorneys. Given no reason to suspect that he lacked counsel able and willing to represent him, Maples surely was blocked from complying with the State's procedural rule.

> "The cause and prejudice requirement," we have said, "shows due regard for States' finality and comity interests while ensuring that fundamental fairness [remains] the central concern of the writ of habeas corpus." In the unusual circumstances of this case, principles of agency law and fundamental fairness point to the same conclusion: There was indeed cause to excuse Maples' procedural default. Through no fault of his own, Maples lacked the assistance of any authorized attorney during the 42 days Alabama allows for noticing an appeal from a trial court's denial of postconviction relief. As just observed, he had no reason to suspect that, in reality, he had been reduced to pro se status. Maples was disarmed by extraordinary circumstances quite beyond his control. He has shown ample cause, we hold, to excuse the procedural default into which he was trapped when counsel of record abandoned him without a word of warning. . . .

NOTES & QUESTIONS ON CAUSE AND PREJUDICE

1. *Prejudice.* Because the court below had found that Maples did not demonstrate cause, that court never had occasion to consider whether Maples had demonstrated prejudice. After the Supreme Court concluded that Maples had, in fact, demonstrated cause, it remanded to the lower federal court for it to decide prejudice. Do you agree with this decision? Was there enough evidence in the record to allow the Supreme Court to rule on prejudice without requiring the further factual findings that could be made on remand?

2. *Abandonment.* Do you agree with the Court that Maples's attorneys abandoned him? What were the "extraordinary circumstances" beyond Maples's control? What is your assessment of the state's argument that Maples was represented by the firm, Sullivan & Cromwell, rather than the individual associates?

3. *Sua sponte.* What result if neither the state nor the prisoner raises the issue of state procedural default before the federal court? If there is no procedural default issue, then the silence is not surprising. But an odd situation results if there is a procedural default problem, but no one raises it. In *Trest v. Cain*, 522 U.S. 87, 89 (1997), the Supreme Court clarified that the federal habeas court is under no obligation to raise the procedural default sua sponte, since the procedural default is not a jurisdictional rule. Why? If the procedural default rule *were* jurisdictional, then the procedural default would deprive the federal court of jurisdiction, thus making it incumbent on the court to raise the issue and resolve it. Instead, procedural default goes to the merits as an application of the independent and adequate state ground doctrine.

PROBLEM CASE

Terry Harris was found guilty of murder in Illinois. According to the prosecution, Harris and the victim were co-workers and drove to a secluded forest preserve where the murder occurred. At trial, Harris testified in his own defense; in fact, he was the only defense witness. He conceded that he went to the forest with his co-worker to engage in consensual sex, and that the two of them got into an argument over a gun that Harris wanted to place in the glove compartment of the car. Harris said that he lost control and then strangled his co-worker to death. The jury then convicted Harris.

Harris was originally sentenced to death, but an appellate court overturned the sentence due to improper victim impact testimony at the sentencing hearing. On remand for a new sentencing hearing, Harris was sentenced to life in prison. Harris filed a state habeas petition, arguing among other things ineffective assistance of counsel. When it was denied, Harris filed a federal habeas petition, this time arguing, with the support of a neuropsychologist, that he suffered a mental disability and brain damage, that his IQ was 76, and that he was on the cusp of "mental retardation." Harris argued in the habeas petition that he received ineffective assistance of counsel because counsel failed to present evidence of his mental disability at the sentencing hearing. The district court denied the petition because the mental disability argument had not been raised below and was procedurally defaulted.

Did Harris's mental disability establish the "cause" that would excuse his default? See *Harris v. McAdory*, 334 F.3d 665, 669 (7th Cir. 2003).

2. Actual Innocence

Actual innocence can be relevant in one of two ways. Either it is a second exception to procedural default, in addition to "cause and prejudice," or it can also be a free-standing basis for a federal habeas petition. The following case discusses the standard for actual innocence, mostly in the first context. As you read the case, pay particular attention to the facts marshalled by the majority in support of its conclusion regarding actual innocence. Does the case give you confidence that actual innocence remains a viable doctrinal argument in habeas cases, or is this case the exception that proves the rule? Is it too easy or too hard for a prisoner to argue actual innocence?

House v. Bell

Supreme Court of the United States
547 U.S. 518 (2006)

Justice KENNEDY delivered the opinion of the Court.

Some 20 years ago in rural Tennessee, Carolyn Muncey was murdered. A jury convicted petitioner Paul Gregory House of the crime and sentenced him to death, but new revelations cast doubt on the jury's verdict. House, protesting his innocence, seeks access to federal court to pursue habeas corpus relief based on constitutional claims that are procedurally barred under state law. Out of respect for the finality of state-court judgments federal habeas courts, as a general rule, are closed to claims that state courts would consider defaulted. In certain exceptional cases involving a compelling claim of actual innocence, however, the state procedural default rule is not a bar to a federal habeas corpus petition. See *Schlup v. Delo,* 513 U.S. 298, 319-322 (1995). After careful review of the full record, we conclude that House has made the stringent showing required by this exception; and we hold that his federal habeas action may proceed. . . .

II

The State of Tennessee charged House with capital murder. At House's trial, the State presented testimony by Luttrell, Hensley, Adkins, Lora Muncey, Dr. Carabia, the sheriff, and other law enforcement officials. Through TBI Agents Presnell and Scott, the jury learned of House's false statements. Central to the State's case, however, was what the FBI testing showed—that semen consistent (or so it seemed) with House's was present on Mrs. Muncey's nightgown and panties, and that small bloodstains consistent with Mrs. Muncey's blood but not House's appeared on the jeans belonging to House.

Regarding the semen, FBI Special Agent Paul Bigbee, a serologist, testified that the source was a "secretor," meaning someone who "secrete[s] the ABO blood group substances in other body fluids, such as semen and saliva"—a characteristic shared by 80 percent of the population, including House. Agent Bigbee further testified that the source of semen on the gown was blood-type A, House's own blood type. As to the semen on the panties, Agent Bigbee found only the H blood-group substance, which A and B blood-type secretors secrete along with substances A and B, and which O-type secretors secrete exclusively. Agent Bigbee explained, however—using science an amicus here sharply disputes—that House's A antigens could have "degraded" into H. Agent Bigbee thus concluded that both semen deposits could have come from House, though he acknowledged that the H antigen could have come from Mrs. Muncey herself if she was a secretor—something he "was not able to determine"—and that, while Mr. Muncey was himself blood-type A (as was his wife), Agent Bigbee was again "not able to determine his secretor status." Agent Bigbee acknowledged on cross-examination that "a saliva sample" would have sufficed to determine whether Mr. Muncey was a secretor; the State did not provide such a sample, though it did provide samples of Mr. Muncey's blood.

As for the blood, Agent Bigbee explained that "spots of blood" appeared "on the left outside leg, the right bottom cuff, on the left thigh and in the right inside pocket and on the lower pocket on the outside." Agent Bigbee determined that the blood's source was type A (the type shared by

House, the victim, and Mr. Muncey). He also successfully tested for the enzyme phosphoglucomutase and the blood serum haptoglobin, both of which "are found in all humans" and carry "slight chemical differences" that vary genetically and "can be grouped to differentiate between two individuals if those types are different." Based on these chemical traces and on the A blood type, Agent Bigbee determined that only some 6.75 percent of the population carry similar blood, that the blood was "consistent" with Mrs. Muncey's (as determined by testing autopsy samples), and that it was "impossible" that the blood came from House.

A different FBI expert, Special Agent Chester Blythe, testified about fiber analysis performed on Mrs. Muncey's clothes and on House's pants. Although Agent Blythe found blue jean fibers on Mrs. Muncey's nightgown, brassiere, housecoat, and panties, and in fingernail scrapings taken from her body (scrapings that also contained trace, unidentifiable amounts of blood), he acknowledged that, as the prosecutor put it in questioning the witness, "blue jean material is common material," so "this doesn't mean that the fibers that were all over the victim's clothing were necessarily from [House's] pair of blue jeans." On House's pants, though cotton garments both transfer and retain fibers readily, Agent Blythe found neither hair nor fiber consistent with the victim's hair or clothing.

In the defense case House called Hankins, Clinton, and Turner, as well as House's mother, who testified that House had talked to her by telephone around 9:30 P.M. on the night of the murder and that he had not used her car that evening. House also called the victim's brother, Ricky Green, as a witness. Green testified that on July 2, roughly two weeks before the murder, Mrs. Muncey called him and "said her and Little Hube had been into it and she said she was wanting to leave Little Hube, she said she was wanting to get out—out of it, and she was scared." Green recalled that at Christmastime in 1982 he had seen Mr. Muncey strike Mrs. Muncey after returning home drunk.

As Turner informed the jury, House's shoes were found several months after the crime in a field near her home. Turner delivered them to authorities. Though the jury did not learn of this fact (and House's counsel claims he did not either), the State tested the shoes for blood and found none. House's shirt was not found.

The State's closing argument suggested that on the night of her murder, Mrs. Muncey "was deceived . . . . She had been told [her husband] had had an accident." The prosecutor emphasized the FBI's blood analysis, noting that "after running many, many, many tests," Agent Bigbee "was able to tell you that the blood on the defendant's blue jeans was not his own blood, could not be his own blood. He told you that the blood on the blue jeans was consistent with every characteristic in every respect of the deceased's, Carolyn Muncey's, and that ninety-three (93%) percent of the white population would not have that blood type. . . . He can't tell you one hundred (100%) percent for certain that it was her blood. But folks, he can sure give you a pretty good—a pretty good indication."

In the State's rebuttal, after defense counsel questioned House's motive "to go over and kill a woman that he barely knew[,] [w]ho was still dressed, still clad in her clothes," the prosecutor referred obliquely to the semen stains. While explaining that legally "it does not make any difference under God's heaven, what the motive was," the prosecutor told the jury, "you may have an idea why he did it":

> The evidence at the scene which seemed to suggest that he was subjecting this lady to some kind of indignity, why would you get a lady out of her house, late at night, in her night clothes, under the trick that her husband has had a wreck down by the creek? . . . Well, it is because either you don't want her to tell what indignities you have subjected her to, or she is unwilling and fights against you, against being subjected to those indignities. In other words, it is either to keep her from telling what you have done to her, or it is that you are trying to get her to do something that she nor any mother on that road would want to do with Mr. House, under those conditions, and you kill her because of her resistance. That is what the evidence at the scene suggests about motive.

In addition the government suggested the black rag Hensley said he saw in House's hands was in fact the missing blue tank top, retrieved by House from the crime scene. And the prosecution reiterated the importance of the blood. "[D]efense counsel," he said, "does not start out discussing the fact that his client had blood on his jeans on the night that Carolyn Muncey was killed . . . . He doesn't start with the fact that nothing that the defense has introduced in this case explains what blood is doing on his jeans, all over his jeans, that is scientifically, completely different from his blood." The jury found House guilty of murder in the first degree. . . .

III

The Tennessee Supreme Court affirmed House's conviction and sentence, describing the evidence against House as "circumstantial" but "quite strong." Two months later, in a state trial court, House filed a pro se petition for postconviction relief, arguing he received ineffective assistance of counsel at trial. The court-appointed counsel amended the petition to raise other issues, including a challenge to certain jury instructions. At a hearing before the same judge who conducted the trial, House's counsel offered no proof beyond the trial transcript. The trial court dismissed the petition, deeming House's trial counsel adequate and overruling House's other objections. On appeal House's attorney renewed only the jury-instructions argument. In an unpublished opinion the Tennessee Court of Criminal Appeals affirmed, and both the Tennessee Supreme Court and this Court denied review.

House filed a second postconviction petition in state court reasserting his ineffective-assistance claim and seeking investigative and/or expert assistance. After extensive litigation regarding whether House's claims were procedurally defaulted the Tennessee Supreme Court held that House's claims were barred under a state statute providing that claims not raised in prior postconviction proceedings are presumptively waived and that courts may not consider grounds for relief "which the court finds should be excluded because they have been waived or previously determined."

House next sought federal habeas relief, asserting numerous claims of ineffective assistance of counsel and prosecutorial misconduct. The United States District Court for the Eastern District of Tennessee, though deeming House's claims procedurally defaulted and granting summary judgment to the State on the majority of House's claims, held an evidentiary hearing to determine whether House fell within the "actual innocence" exception to procedural default that this Court recognized as to substantive offenses in *Schlup* and as to death sentences in *Sawyer v. Whitley*, 505 U.S. 333 (1992). Presenting evidence we describe in greater detail below, House attacked the semen and blood evidence used at his trial and presented other evidence, including a putative confession, suggesting that Mr. Muncey, not House, committed the murder. The District Court nevertheless denied relief, holding that House had neither demonstrated actual innocence of the murder under *Schlup* nor established that he was ineligible for the death penalty under *Sawyer*. . . .

IV

As a general rule, claims forfeited under state law may support federal habeas relief only if the prisoner demonstrates cause for the default and prejudice from the asserted error. The rule is based on the comity and respect that must be accorded to state-court judgments. The bar is not, however, unqualified. In an effort to "balance the societal interests in finality, comity, and conservation of scarce judicial resources with the individual interest in justice that arises in the extraordinary case," the Court has recognized a miscarriage-of-justice exception. "[I]n appropriate cases," the Court has said, "the principles of comity and finality that inform the concepts of cause and prejudice must yield to the imperative of correcting a fundamentally unjust incarceration."

In *Schlup*, the Court adopted a specific rule to implement this general principle. It held that prisoners asserting innocence as a gateway to defaulted claims must establish that, in light of new evidence, "it is more likely than not that no reasonable juror would have found petitioner guilty beyond a reasonable doubt." 513 U.S., at 327. This formulation, *Schlup* explains, "ensures that petitioner's case is truly 'extraordinary,' while still providing petitioner a meaningful avenue by which to avoid a manifest injustice." In the usual case the presumed guilt of a prisoner convicted in state court counsels against federal review of defaulted claims. Yet a petition supported by a convincing *Schlup* gateway showing "raise[s] sufficient doubt about [the petitioner's] guilt to undermine confidence in the result of the trial without the assurance that that trial was untainted by constitutional error"; hence, "a review of the merits of the constitutional claims" is justified.

For purposes of this case several features of the *Schlup* standard bear emphasis. First, although "[t]o be credible" a gateway claim requires "new reliable evidence—whether it be exculpatory scientific evidence, trustworthy eyewitness accounts, or critical physical evidence—that was not presented at trial," the habeas court's analysis is not limited to such evidence. There is no dispute in this case that House has presented some new reliable evidence; the State has conceded as much. In addition, because the District Court held an evidentiary hearing in this case, and because the State does not challenge the court's decision to do so, we have no occasion to elaborate on *Schlup*'s observation that when considering an actual-innocence claim in the context of a request for an evidentiary hearing, the District Court need not "test the new evidence by a standard appropriate for deciding a motion for summary judgment," but rather may "consider how the timing of the submission and the likely credibility of the affiants bear on the probable reliability of that evidence." Our review in this case addresses the merits of the *Schlup* inquiry, based on a fully developed record, and with respect to that inquiry *Schlup* makes plain that the habeas court must consider "all the evidence," old and new, incriminating and exculpatory, without regard to whether it would necessarily be admitted under "rules of admissibility that would govern at trial." Based on this total record, the court must make "a probabilistic determination about what reasonable, properly instructed jurors would do." The court's function is not to make an independent factual determination about what likely occurred, but rather to assess the likely impact of the evidence on reasonable jurors.

Second, it bears repeating that the *Schlup* standard is demanding and permits review only in the "extraordinary" case. At the same time, though, the *Schlup* standard does not require absolute certainty about the petitioner's guilt or innocence. A petitioner's burden at the gateway stage is to demonstrate that more likely than not, in light of the new evidence, no reasonable juror would find him guilty beyond a reasonable doubt—or, to remove the double negative, that more likely than not any reasonable juror would have reasonable doubt.

Finally, as the *Schlup* decision explains, the gateway actual-innocence standard is "by no means equivalent to the standard of *Jackson v. Virginia*, 443 U.S. 307 (1979)," which governs claims of insufficient evidence. When confronted with a challenge based on trial evidence, courts presume the jury resolved evidentiary disputes reasonably so long as sufficient evidence supports the verdict. Because a *Schlup* claim involves evidence the trial jury did not have before it, the inquiry requires the federal court to assess how reasonable jurors would react to the overall, newly supplemented record. If new evidence so requires, this may include consideration of "the credibility of the witnesses presented at trial." . . . .

[W]e turn to the evidence developed in House's federal habeas proceedings.

DNA Evidence

First, in direct contradiction of evidence presented at trial, DNA testing has established that the semen on Mrs. Muncey's nightgown and panties came from her husband, Mr. Muncey, not from House. The State, though conceding this point, insists this new evidence is immaterial. At the guilt phase at least, neither sexual contact nor motive were elements of the offense, so in the State's view the evidence, or lack of evidence, of sexual assault or sexual advance is of no consequence. We disagree. In fact we consider the new disclosure of central importance.

From beginning to end the case is about who committed the crime. When identity is in question, motive is key. The point, indeed, was not lost on the prosecution, for it introduced the evidence and relied on it in the final guilt-phase closing argument. Referring to "evidence at the scene," the prosecutor suggested that House committed, or attempted to commit, some "indignity" on Mrs. Muncey that neither she "nor any mother on that road would want to do with Mr. House." Particularly in a case like this where the proof was . . . circumstantial, we think a jury would have given this evidence great weight. Quite apart from providing proof of motive, it was the only forensic evidence at the scene that would link House to the murder.

Law and society, as they ought to do, demand accountability when a sexual offense has been committed, so not only did this evidence link House to the crime; it likely was a factor in persuading the jury not to let him go free. At sentencing, moreover, the jury came to the unanimous conclusion, beyond a reasonable doubt, that the murder was committed in the course of a rape or kidnaping. The alleged sexual motivation relates to both those determinations. This is particularly so given that, at the sentencing phase, the jury was advised that House had a previous conviction for sexual assault.

A jury informed that fluids on Mrs. Muncey's garments could have come from House might have found that House trekked the nearly two miles to the victim's home and lured her away in order to commit a sexual offense. By contrast a jury acting without the assumption that the semen could have come from House would have found it necessary to establish some different motive, or, if the same motive, an intent far more speculative. When the only direct evidence of sexual assault drops out of the case, so, too, does a central theme in the State's narrative linking House to the crime. In that light, furthermore, House's odd evening walk and his false statements to authorities, while still potentially incriminating, might appear less suspicious.

Bloodstains

The other relevant forensic evidence is the blood on House's pants, which appears in small, even minute, stains in scattered places. As the prosecutor told the jury, they were stains that, due to their small size, "you or I might not detect[,] [m]ight not see, but which the FBI lab was able to find on [House's] jeans." The stains appear inside the right pocket, outside that pocket, near the inside button, on the left thigh and outside leg, on the seat of the pants, and on the right bottom cuff, including inside the pants. Due to testing by the FBI, cuttings now appear on the pants in several places where stains evidently were found. (The cuttings were destroyed in the testing process, and defense experts were unable to replicate the tests.) At trial, the government argued "nothing that the defense has introduced in this case explains what blood is doing on his jeans, all over [House's] jeans, that is scientifically, completely different from his blood." House, though not disputing at this point that the blood is Mrs. Muncey's, now presents an alternative explanation that, if credited, would undermine the probative value of the blood evidence.

During House's habeas proceedings, Dr. Cleland Blake, an Assistant Chief Medical Examiner for the State of Tennessee and a consultant in forensic pathology to the TBI for 22 years, testified that the blood on House's pants was chemically too degraded, and too similar to blood collected during the autopsy, to have come from Mrs. Muncey's body on the night of the crime. The blood samples collected during the autopsy were placed in test tubes without preservative. Under such conditions, according to Dr. Blake, "you will have enzyme degradation. You will have different blood group degradation, blood marker degradation." The problem of decay, moreover, would have been compounded by the body's long exposure to the elements, sitting outside for the better part of a summer day. In contrast, if blood is preserved on cloth, "it will stay there for years"; indeed, Dr. Blake said he deliberately places blood drops on gauze during autopsies to preserve it for later testing. The blood on House's pants, judging by Agent Bigbee's tests, showed "similar deterioration, breakdown of certain of the named numbered enzymes" as in the autopsy samples. "[I]f the victim's blood had spilled on the jeans while the victim was alive and this blood had dried," Dr. Blake stated, "the deterioration would not have occurred," and "you would expect [the blood on the jeans] to be different than what was in the tube." Dr. Blake thus concluded the blood on the jeans came from the autopsy samples, not from Mrs. Muncey's live (or recently killed) body. . . .

In sum, considering "all the evidence," on this issue, we think the evidentiary disarray surrounding the blood, taken together with Dr. Blake's testimony and the limited rebuttal of it in the present record, would prevent reasonable jurors from placing significant reliance on the blood evidence. We now know, though the trial jury did not, that an Assistant Chief Medical Examiner believes the blood on House's jeans must have come from autopsy samples; that a vial and a quarter of autopsy blood is unaccounted for; that the blood was transported to the FBI together with the pants in conditions that could have caused vials to spill; that the blood did indeed spill at least once during its journey from Tennessee authorities through FBI hands to a defense expert; that the pants were stored in a plastic bag bearing both a large blood stain and a label with TBI Agent Scott's name; and that the styrofoam box containing the blood samples may well have been opened before it arrived at the FBI lab. Thus, whereas the bloodstains, emphasized by the prosecution, seemed strong evidence of House's guilt at trial, the record now raises substantial questions about the blood's origin.

A Different Suspect

Were House's challenge to the State's case limited to the questions he has raised about the blood and semen, the other evidence favoring the prosecution might well suffice to bar relief. There is, however, more; for in the post-trial proceedings House presented troubling evidence that Mr. Muncey, the victim's husband, himself could have been the murderer.

At trial, as has been noted, the jury heard that roughly two weeks before the murder Mrs. Muncey's brother received a frightened phone call from his sister indicating that she and Mr. Muncey had been fighting, that she was scared, and that she wanted to leave him. The jury also learned that the brother once saw Mr. Muncey "smac[k]" the victim. House now has produced evidence from multiple sources suggesting that Mr. Muncey regularly abused his wife. For example, one witness—Kathy Parker, a lifelong area resident who denied any animosity toward Mr. Muncey—recalled that Mrs. Muncey "was constantly with black eyes and busted mouth." In addition Hazel Miller, who is Kathy Parker's mother and a lifelong acquaintance of Mr. Muncey, testified at the habeas hearing that two or three months before the victim's death Mr. Muncey came to Miller's home and "tried to get my daughter [Parker] to go out with him." (Parker had dated Mr. Muncey at age 14.) According to Miller, Muncey said "[h]e was upset with his wife, that they had had an argument and he said he was going to get rid of that woman one way or the other."

Another witness—Mary Atkins, also an area native who "grew up" with Mr. Muncey and professed no hard feelings—claims she saw Mr. Muncey "backhan[d]" Mrs. Muncey on the very night of the murder. Atkins recalled that during a break in the recreation center dance, she saw Mr. Muncey and his wife arguing in the parking lot. Mr. Muncey "grabbed her and he just backhanded her." After that, Mrs. Muncey "left walking." There was also testimony from Atkins' mother, named Artie Lawson. A self-described "good friend" of Mr. Muncey, Lawson said Mr. Muncey visited her the morning after the murder, before the body was found. According to Lawson, Mr. Muncey asked her to tell anyone who inquired not only that she had been at the dance the evening before and had seen him, but also that he had breakfasted at her home at 6 o'clock that morning. Lawson had not in fact been at the dance, nor had Mr. Muncey been with her so early.

Of most importance is the testimony of Kathy Parker and her sister Penny Letner. They testified at the habeas hearing that, around the time of House's trial, Mr. Muncey had confessed to the crime. Parker recalled that she and "some family members and some friends [were] sitting around drinking" at Parker's trailer when Mr. Muncey "just walked in and sit down." Muncey, who had evidently been drinking heavily, began "rambling off . . . [t]alking about what happened to his wife and how it happened and he didn't mean to do it." According to Parker, Mr. Muncey "said they had been into [an] argument and he slapped her and she fell and hit her head and it killed her and he didn't mean for it to happen." Parker said she "freaked out and run him off." . . . .

Other testimony suggests Mr. Muncey had the opportunity to commit the crime. According to Dennis Wallace, a local law enforcement official who provided security at the dance on the night of the murder, Mr. Muncey left the dance "around 10:00, 10:30, 9:30 to 10:30." Although Mr. Muncey told law enforcement officials just after the murder that he left the dance only briefly and returned, Wallace could not recall seeing him back there again. . . .

The evidence pointing to Mr. Muncey is by no means conclusive. If considered in isolation, a reasonable jury might well disregard it. In combination, however, with the challenges to the blood evidence and the lack of motive with respect to House, the evidence pointing to Mr. Muncey likely would reinforce other doubts as to House's guilt. . . .

Conclusion

This is not a case of conclusive exoneration. . . . [A]lthough the issue is close, we conclude that this is the rare case where—had the jury heard all the conflicting testimony—it is more likely than not that no reasonable juror viewing the record as a whole would lack reasonable doubt. . . .

NOTES & QUESTIONS ON ACTUAL INNOCENCE

1. *Actual innocence versus not guilty.* When a jury returns a verdict of not guilty, the jury is not necessarily saying that it affirmatively believes that the defendant is innocent. Formally, a jury verdict of acquittal simply means that the jury concluded that the prosecution failed to satisfy its burden to demonstrate the guilt of the defendant beyond a reasonable doubt. The result of that failure may leave the jury in a state of agnosticism regarding the defendant's guilt, but that is enough to return a finding of not guilty. The actual innocence exception asks whether a reasonable juror would have reasonable doubt or not about the defendant's guilt. Even this standard is a far cry from the type of affirmative proof that a lay person would associate with the phrase "actual innocence."

2. *The two tracks for actual innocence.* In addition to his argument that actual innocence excused his procedural default, House also raised a "freestanding" actual innocence claim pursuant to *Herrera v. Collins*, 506 U.S. 390 (1993). Several Justices suggested in *Herrera* that in some cases an argument of actual innocence might be so compelling that the petitioner's execution might be unconstitutional under the Eighth Amendment and require the granting of habeas relief. Under this legal argument, the actual innocence claim is not raised merely within the context of procedural default but rather the merits of the habeas argument. In other words, a *Herrera*-style claim does not require an independent constitutional violation in the state court proceedings. Instead, the pending execution of the innocent man would itself be the constitutional violation. In *House v. Bell*, the Supreme Court articulated some uncertainty about the status of *Herrera*-style claims, but in any event concluded that House had not satisfied the high bar for them.

3. *Statute of limitations.* In addition to procedural default, should a claim of actual innocence also overcome a defect related to the habeas statute of limitations imposed by the AEDPA? In *McQuiggin v. Perkins*, 569 U.S. 383 (2013), the Supreme Court answered that question in the affirmative. As the Court noted:

> In other words, a credible showing of actual innocence may allow a prisoner to pursue his constitutional claims (here, ineffective assistance of counsel) on the merits notwithstanding the existence of a procedural bar to relief. "This rule, or fundamental miscarriage of justice exception, is grounded in the 'equitable discretion' of habeas courts to see that federal constitutional

> errors do not result in the incarceration of innocent persons." *Herrera*, 506 U.S., at 404.

McQuiggin, 569 U.S. at 392. According to the Court, there was a "miscarriage of justice" exception to the procedural requirements for habeas and that exception survived the passage of the AEDPA. Do you agree with this conclusion? Are there other powers that are implicit in the "equitable discretion" of habeas courts?

D. HABEAS COURT POWERS AND REMEDIES

What powers does a habeas court have? The following subsections focus on two important questions: Does a federal habeas court have the power to hold an evidentiary hearing or must it always remand back to the state court to hold such hearings and make factual findings? Second, are constitutional holdings to be given retroactive application in collateral proceedings? If yes, under what circumstances?

1. Holding Evidentiary Hearings

In the following case, the prisoner was a death row inmate who successfully argued that his assistance of counsel at sentencing was constitutionally defective because he failed to investigate, or present evidence of, mitigation that might have spared him the death penalty. The question is whether a habeas court, pursuant to the AEDPA, may hold an evidentiary hearing to gather facts pursuant to its inquiry. In this case, the evidentiary hearing involved expert testimony regarding the prisoner's mental state—evidence that the petitioner argues should have been unearthed and explored by his sentencing counsel.

Cullen v. Pinholster

Supreme Court of the United States
563 U.S. 170 (2011)

Justice Thomas delivered the opinion of the Court.

Scott Lynn Pinholster and two accomplices broke into a house in the middle of the night and brutally beat and stabbed to death two men who happened to interrupt the burglary. A jury convicted Pinholster of first-degree murder, and he was sentenced to death.

After the California Supreme Court twice unanimously denied Pinholster habeas relief, a Federal District Court held an evidentiary hearing and granted Pinholster habeas relief under 28 U.S.C. § 2254. The District Court concluded that Pinholster's trial counsel had been constitutionally ineffective at the penalty phase of trial. Sitting en banc, the Court of Appeals for the Ninth Circuit affirmed. Considering the new evidence adduced in the District Court hearing, the Court of Appeals held that the California Supreme Court's decision "was contrary to, or involved an unreasonable application of, clearly established Federal law." We granted certiorari and now reverse.

II

We first consider the scope of the record for a § 2254(d)(1) inquiry. The State argues that review is limited to the record that was before the state court that adjudicated the claim on the merits. Pinholster contends that evidence presented to the federal habeas court may also be considered. We agree with the State.

As amended by AEDPA, 28 U.S.C. § 2254 sets several limits on the power of a federal court to grant an application for a writ of habeas corpus on behalf of a state prisoner. Section 2254(a) permits a federal court to entertain only those applications alleging that a person is in state custody "in violation of the Constitution or laws or treaties of the United States." Sections 2254(b) and (c) provide that a federal court may not grant such applications unless, with certain exceptions, the applicant has exhausted state remedies.

If an application includes a claim that has been "adjudicated on the merits in State court proceedings," § 2254(d), an additional restriction applies. Under § 2254(d), that application "shall not be granted with respect to [such a] claim . . . unless the adjudication of the claim":

> (1) resulted in a decision that was contrary to, or involved an unreasonable application of, clearly established Federal law, as determined by the Supreme Court of the United States; or
> (2) resulted in a decision that was based on an unreasonable determination of the facts in light of the evidence presented in the State court proceeding.

This is a "difficult to meet," and "highly deferential standard for evaluating state-court rulings, which demands that state-court decisions be given the benefit of the doubt." The petitioner carries the burden of proof.

We now hold that review under § 2254(d)(1) is limited to the record that was before the state court that adjudicated the claim on the merits. Section 2254(d)(1) refers, in the past tense, to a state-court adjudication that "resulted in" a decision that was contrary to, or "involved" an unreasonable application of, established law. This backward-looking language requires an examination of the state-court decision at the time it was made. It follows that the record under review is limited to the record in existence at that same time i.e., the record before the state court.

This understanding of the text is compelled by "the broader context of the statute as a whole," which demonstrates Congress' intent to channel prisoners' claims first to the state courts. "The federal habeas scheme leaves primary responsibility with the state courts . . . ." Section 2254(b) requires that prisoners must ordinarily exhaust state remedies before filing for federal habeas relief. It would be contrary to that purpose to allow a petitioner to overcome an adverse state-court decision with new evidence introduced in a federal habeas court and reviewed by that court in the first instance effectively de novo.

Limiting § 2254(d)(1) review to the state-court record is consistent with our precedents interpreting that statutory provision. Our cases emphasize that review under § 2254(d)(1) focuses on what a state court knew and did. State-court decisions are measured against this Court's precedents as of "the time the state court renders its decision." To determine whether a particular decision is "contrary to" then-established law, a federal court must consider whether the decision "applies a rule that contradicts [such] law" and how the decision "confronts [the] set of facts" that were before the state court. If the state-court decision "identifies the correct governing legal principle" in existence at the time, a federal court must assess whether the decision "unreasonably applies that principle to the facts of the prisoner's case." It would be strange to ask federal courts to analyze whether a state court's adjudication resulted in a decision that unreasonably applied federal law to facts not before the state court. . . .

Pinholster's contention that our holding renders § 2254(e)(2) superfluous is incorrect. Section 2254(e)(2) imposes a limitation on the discretion of federal habeas courts to take new evidence in an evidentiary hearing. Like § 2254(d)(1), it carries out "AEDPA's goal of promoting comity, finality, and federalism by giving state courts the first opportunity to review [a] claim, and to correct any constitutional violation in the first instance."

Section 2254(e)(2) continues to have force where § 2254(d)(1) does not bar federal habeas relief. For example, not all federal habeas claims by state prisoners fall within the scope of § 2254(d), which applies only to claims "adjudicated on the merits in State court proceedings." At a minimum, therefore, § 2254(e)(2) still restricts the discretion of federal habeas courts to consider new evidence when deciding claims that were not adjudicated on the merits in state court.

Although state prisoners may sometimes submit new evidence in federal court, AEDPA's statutory scheme is designed to strongly discourage them from doing so. Provisions like §§ 2254(d)(1) and (e)(2) ensure that "[f]ederal courts sitting in habeas are not an alternative forum for trying facts and issues which a prisoner made insufficient effort to pursue in state proceedings."

Accordingly, we conclude that the Court of Appeals erred in considering the District Court evidence in its review under § 2254(d)(1). . . .

NOTES & QUESTIONS ON EVIDENTIARY HEARINGS

1. *Backward-looking versus forward-looking.* The Court concludes that the AEDPA asks the habeas court to review the record that the state court had before it, rather than engage in a forward looking analysis that would require the habeas court to engage in new fact finding. However, can you imagine situations where a habeas court might need to make factual findings in order to engage in the backward-looking analysis?

STATE LAW REQUIREMENTS

Although the AEDPA sharply limits the ability of a federal habeas court to hold an evidentiary hearing, state habeas proceedings are not similarly limited. State habeas proceedings are usually governed by state statutes, some of which explicitly grant state courts the authority to hold evidentiary hearings, even during collateral proceedings. For example, California law states:

> (b) A writ of habeas corpus may be prosecuted for, but not limited to, the following reasons:
>
> (1) False evidence that is substantially material or probative on the issue of guilt or punishment was introduced against a person at a hearing or trial relating to his or her incarceration.
>
> (2) False physical evidence, believed by a person to be factual, probative, or material on the issue of guilt, which was known by the person at the time of entering a plea of guilty, which was a material factor directly related to the plea of guilty by the person.
>
> (3)(A) New evidence exists that is credible, material, presented without substantial delay, and of such decisive force and value that it would have more likely than not changed the outcome at trial.
>
> (B) For purposes of this section, "new evidence" means evidence that has been discovered after trial, that could not have been discovered prior to trial by the exercise of due diligence, and is admissible and not merely cumulative, corroborative, collateral, or impeaching. . . .

Cal. Penal Code § 1473. California courts have interpreted this provision as implicitly allowing for evidentiary hearings as part of the habeas process, at least when the hearing is necessary to resolve factual disputes that the petition hinges on. *People v. Romero,* 8 Cal. 4th 728, 739, 883 P.2d 388, 392-93 (1994). The evidentiary hearing is, in some respects, both a mini-trial and not a mini-trial at the same time, because only some of the procedural mechanics of the criminal trial are implicated by the procedure. Some scholars have argued that similar discovery rules applicable to criminal trials should also apply in California habeas evidentiary hearings:

> A discovery statute would eliminate time consuming litigation concerning the availability and scope of discovery, thereby shortening the collateral proceeding. It would also promote uniformity in rulings and thereby render confidence in the outcome. Requiring that the proponent of a discovery motion show good cause prevents the use of habeas as an investigative tool and provides the referee a standard

with which to exercise his discretion. The statute should require: 1) a written motion that describes with specificity the items sought; 2) a statement that the item is not in the movants' possession and cannot be obtained otherwise; 3) a statement as to the materiality and relevance of the requested items to the issues; 4) and a brief statement, citation, or theory of admissibility.

Judge Joan Comparet-Cassani, *Evidentiary Hearings in California Capital Habeas Proceedings: What Are the Rules of Discovery?*, 39 Santa Clara L. Rev. 409, 446 (1999).

2. Retroactivity

A key question of habeas review is whether a given constitutional rule has been made retroactive and should be applied in collateral proceedings. In other words, if the constitutional ruling occurred after the trial, can it nonetheless be given retroactive effect in collateral proceedings? In the following case, the petitioner argued that his trial was compromised by a jury instruction that effectively diluted the requirement of proof beyond a reasonable doubt. As you read the case, ask yourself whether the vindication of the constitutional rule required retroactive effect. How does the procedural regime of the AEDPA figure into the analysis?

Tyler v. Cain

Supreme Court of the United States
533 U.S. 656 (2001)

Justice Thomas delivered the opinion of the Court.

Under *Cage v. Louisiana*, 498 U.S. 39 (1990), a jury instruction is unconstitutional if there is a reasonable likelihood that the jury understood the instruction to allow conviction without proof beyond a reasonable doubt. In this case, we must decide whether this rule was "made retroactive to cases on collateral review by the Supreme Court." We hold that it was not.

I

During a fight with his estranged girlfriend in March 1975, petitioner Melvin Tyler shot and killed their 20-day-old daughter. A jury found Tyler guilty of second-degree murder, and his conviction was affirmed on appeal. After sentencing, Tyler assiduously sought postconviction relief. By 1986, he had filed five state petitions, all of which were denied. He next filed a federal habeas petition, which was unsuccessful as well. After this Court's decision in *Cage*, Tyler continued his efforts. Because the jury instruction defining reasonable doubt at Tyler's trial was substantively identical to the instruction condemned in *Cage*, Tyler filed a sixth state postconviction petition, this time raising a *Cage* claim. The State District Court denied relief, and the Louisiana Supreme Court affirmed. . . .

In early 1997, Tyler returned to federal court. Seeking to pursue his *Cage* claim, Tyler moved the United States Court of Appeals for the Fifth Circuit for permission to file a second habeas corpus application, as required by the Antiterrorism and Effective Death Penalty Act of 1996 (AEDPA), 110 Stat. 1214. The Court of Appeals recognized that it could not grant the motion unless Tyler made "a prima facie showing" that his "claim relies on a new rule of constitutional law, made retroactive to cases on collateral review by the Supreme Court, that was previously unavailable." . . . The Courts of Appeals are divided on the question whether *Cage* was "made retroactive to cases on collateral review by the Supreme Court," as required by 28 U.S.C. § 2244(b)(2)(A). To resolve this conflict, we granted certiorari.

II

AEDPA greatly restricts the power of federal courts to award relief to state prisoners who file second or successive habeas corpus applications. If the prisoner asserts a claim that he has already presented in a previous federal habeas petition, the claim must be dismissed in all cases. § 2244(b)(1). And if the prisoner asserts a claim that was not presented in a previous petition, the claim must be dismissed unless it falls within one of two narrow exceptions. One of these exceptions is for claims predicated on newly discovered facts that call into question the accuracy of a guilty verdict. § 2244(b)(2)(B). The other is for certain claims relying on new rules of constitutional law. § 2244(b)(2)(A).

It is the latter exception that concerns us today. Specifically, § 2244(b)(2)(A) covers claims that "rel[y] on a new rule of constitutional law, made retroactive to cases on collateral review by the Supreme Court, that was previously unavailable." This provision establishes three prerequisites to obtaining relief in a second or successive petition: First, the rule on which the claim relies must be a "new rule" of constitutional law; second, the rule must have been "made retroactive to cases on collateral review by the Supreme Court"; and third, the claim must have been "previously unavailable." In this case, the parties ask us to interpret only the second requirement; respondent does not dispute that *Cage* created a "new rule" that was "previously unavailable." Based on the plain meaning of the text read as a whole, we conclude that "made" means "held" and, thus, the requirement is satisfied only if this Court has held that the new rule is retroactively applicable to cases on collateral review.

As commonly defined, "made" has several alternative meanings, none of which is entirely free from ambiguity. Out of context, it may thus be unclear which meaning should apply in § 2244(b)(2)(A), and how the term should be understood. We do not, however, construe the meaning of statutory terms in a vacuum. Rather, we interpret the words "in their context and with a view to their place in the overall statutory scheme." Quite significantly, under this provision, the Supreme Court is the only entity that can "ma[k]e" a new rule retroactive. The new rule becomes retroactive, not by the decisions of the lower court or by the combined action of the Supreme Court and the lower courts, but simply by the action of the Supreme Court.

The only way the Supreme Court can, by itself, "lay out and construct" a rule's retroactive effect, or "cause" that effect "to exist, occur, or appear," is through a holding. The Supreme Court does not "ma[k]e" a rule retroactive when it merely establishes principles of retroactivity and leaves the application of those principles to lower courts. In such an event, any legal conclusion that is derived from the principles is developed by the lower court (or perhaps by a combination of courts), not by the Supreme Court. We thus conclude that a new rule is not "made retroactive to cases on collateral review" unless the Supreme Court holds it to be retroactive.

To be sure, the statute uses the word "made," not "held." But we have already stated, in a decision interpreting another provision of AEDPA, that Congress need not use the word "held" to require as much. In *Williams v. Taylor*, 529 U.S. 362(2000), we concluded that the phrase "clearly established Federal law, as determined by the Supreme Court of the United States," "refers to the holdings, as opposed to the dicta, of this Court's decisions." The provision did not use the word "held," but the effect was the same. Congress, needless to say, is permitted to use synonyms in a statute. And just as "determined" and "held" are synonyms in the context of § 2254(d)(1), "made" and "held" are synonyms in the context of § 2244(b)(2)(A).

We further note that our interpretation is necessary for the proper implementation of the collateral review structure created by AEDPA. Under the statute, before a state prisoner may file a second or successive habeas application, he "shall move in the appropriate court of appeals for an order authorizing the district court to consider the application." The court of appeals must make a decision on the application within 30 days. In this limited time, the court of appeals must determine whether the application "makes a prima facie showing that [it] satisfies the [second habeas standard]." It is unlikely that a court of appeals could make such a determination in the allotted time if it had to do more than simply rely on Supreme Court holdings on retroactivity. The stringent time limit thus suggests that the courts of appeals do not have to engage in the difficult legal analysis that can be required to determine questions of retroactivity in the first instance.

Because "made" means "held" for purposes of § 2244(b)(2)(A), it is clear that the *Cage* rule has not been "made retroactive to cases on collateral review by the Supreme Court." *Cage* itself does not hold that it is retroactive. The only holding in *Cage* is that the particular jury instruction violated the Due Process Clause. . . .

Justice BREYER, with whom Justice STEVENS, Justice SOUTER, and Justice GINSBURG join, dissenting.

In *Cage v. Louisiana,* 498 U.S. 39 (1990), this Court held that a certain jury instruction violated the Constitution because it inaccurately defined "reasonable doubt," thereby permitting a jury to convict "based on a degree of proof below that required by the Due Process Clause." Here we must decide whether this Court has "made" *Cage* "retroactive to cases on collateral review." I believe that it has.

The Court made *Cage* retroactive in two cases taken together. Case One is *Teague v. Lane,* 489 U.S. 288 (1989). That case, as the majority says, held (among other things) that a new rule is applicable retroactively to cases on collateral review if (1) infringement of the new rule will "seriously diminish the likelihood of obtaining an accurate conviction," and (2) the new rule "alter[s] our understanding of the bedrock procedural elements that must be found to vitiate the fairness of a particular conviction."

Case Two is *Sullivan v. Louisiana,* 508 U.S. 275 (1993). This Court decided *Sullivan* after several lower courts had held that *Cage*'s rule did not fall within the *Teague* "watershed" exception I have just mentioned. The question in *Sullivan* was whether a violation of the *Cage* rule could ever count as harmless error. The Court answered that question in the negative. In so concluding, the Court reasoned that an instruction that violated *Cage* by misdescribing the concept of reasonable doubt "vitiates all the jury's findings," and deprives a criminal defendant of a "basic protection . . . without which a criminal trial cannot reliably serve its function." It renders the situation as if "there has been no jury verdict within the meaning of the Sixth Amendment."

To reason as the Court reasoned in *Sullivan* is to hold (in *Teague*'s language) (1) that infringement of the *Cage* rule "seriously diminish[es] the likelihood of obtaining an accurate conviction," and (2) that *Cage* "alter[s] our understanding of the bedrock procedural elements" that are essential to the fairness of a criminal trial. That is because an instruction that makes "all the jury's findings" untrustworthy must "diminish the likelihood of obtaining an accurate conviction." It is because a deprivation of a "basic protection" needed for a trial to "serve its function," is a deprivation of a "bedrock procedural elemen[t]." And it is because *Cage* significantly "alter[ed]" pre-existing law. That is what every Court of Appeals to have considered the matter has concluded. And I do not see how the majority can deny that this is so.

Consequently, *Sullivan,* in holding that a *Cage* violation can never be harmless because it leaves the defendant with no jury verdict known to the Sixth Amendment, also holds that *Cage* falls within *Teague*'s "watershed" exception. The matter is one of logic. If Case One holds that all men are mortal and Case Two holds that Socrates is a man, we do not need Case Three to hold that Socrates is mortal. It is also a matter of law. If Case One holds that a party's expectation measures damages for breach of contract and Case Two holds that Circumstances X, Y, and Z create a binding contract, we do not need Case Three to hold that in those same circumstances expectation damages are awarded for breach. Ordinarily, in law, to hold that a set of circumstances falls within a particular legal category is simultaneously to hold that, other things being equal, the normal legal characteristics of members of that category apply to those circumstances. . . .

I do not understand the basis for the Court's approach. I fear its consequences. For these reasons, with respect, I dissent.

NOTES & QUESTIONS ON RETROACTIVITY

1. *Watershed rules of criminal procedure.* The default rule is that constitutional holdings of criminal procedure are not given retroactive effect in collateral proceedings, except in limited circumstances. The exception at issue here is a "watershed" rule of criminal procedure. Do you consider the *Cage* holding a watershed rule of criminal procedure? If *Cage* does not qualify under that standard, which rules of criminal procedure would meet the test? Reflect back to *Gideon v. Wainwright*. Do you think that was a "watershed" rule? If not, the Court was bound to the law that applied at the time of Gideon's trial. But if it was a watershed rule, it was not just Gideon who deserved a remedy. Would every conviction that occurred without assistance of counsel, final on direct review but still subject to collateral review, require a new trial? Is the Court's desire to limit retroactivity motivated by concerns regarding efficiency and finality?

2. *The AEDPA standard.* The AEDPA allows the district court to apply a constitutional rule retroactively if the rule was decided by the Supreme Court and it held that the rule should be applied retroactively. Did the Supreme Court in *Sullivan* explicitly make *Cage* retroactive? According to the majority, the relevant standard regarding a new constitutional rule is whether "the Supreme Court holds it to be retroactive." Applying this standard, why did the majority conclude that Cage should not be applied retroactively? Did *Sullivan* hold, as the dissent suggests, that the *Cage* holding qualified as a "watershed" rule of criminal procedure? Should this count as an implied holding that *Cage* should be applied retroactively?

PROBLEM CASE

In 1998, a county corrections officer was screening outgoing mail from an inmate, Orlando Mora, which was addressed to his "common law wife." The letters directed her and others to sell drugs, collect debts, and engage in other activities that were part of a drug conspiracy. Search warrants were executed at several properties and police seized methamphetamine, materials related to the manufacture of methamphetamine, and a gun. Several people, include Mora, were indicted on drug conspiracy charges. In a federal habeas petition, Mora alleged that his sentencing violated *Apprendi* because the sentence relied on a determination of the quantity of the drugs in his case—a fact that was never found by the jury during his trial. *Apprendi* requires that all factors that increase a defendant's liability or punishment must be found by a jury beyond a reasonable doubt in accordance with the Sixth Amendment. *Apprendi* was decided in 2000 and triggered an entire line of Supreme Court cases regarding the Sixth Amendment, including *Booker*, *Blakely*, and *Ring*. Does *Apprendi* count as a "watershed" rule of criminal procedure that should be given retroactive effect in collateral proceedings? See *United States v. Mora*, 293 F.3d 1213, 1215 (10th Cir. 2002).

E. TERRITORIAL SCOPE OF THE WRIT

The vast majority of prisoners detained by the government are held within the territory of the United States. A few prisoners, though, are held by the government outside the United States. The fact that government agents often act extraterritorially—i.e., outside the country—raises a larger question of whether the protections of the U.S. Constitution, and federal statutes, apply wherever the government acts. This notion is often described with the shorthand question, Does the Constitution follow the flag? If answered in the negative, at least some constitutional protections stop at the nation's borders, opening up the possibility of unrestrained executive action on foreign territory.

In the context of the Great Writ, this larger question of extraterritoriality generates a very particular quandary: Once outside of the United States, how far does the writ of habeas corpus run? Much of this debate has taken on, and continues to take on, a decidedly historical turn, as both legal historians and constitutional scholars ask whether British courts had the power to issue writs of habeas corpus for prisoners detained in, say, Scotland or Ireland, or whether American courts had the power to issue the writ in incorporated territories such as Puerto Rice. But since 9/11, this historical inquiry has been supplemented with an urgent layer regarding the power of the executive in times of armed conflict, when the armed forces detain prisoners outside of the United States.

In the pathbreaking case of *Rasul v. Bush*, the petitioners argued that detainees housed at the U.S. military installation at Guantanamo Bay, Cuba, have the right to petition a federal district court for a writ of habeas corpus. As the Supreme Court debated the case, two questions floated to the surface. First, was the case governed by the Supreme Court's holding in *Johnson v. Eisentrager*, 339 U.S. 763 (1950), where the Court denied that federal courts had jurisdiction over German POWs held by the American military in a prison in post–World War II Germany? As you read *Rasul v. Bush*, ask yourself whether the federal government's control of Guantanamo Bay was analogous to its control over Germany in the years following the Second World War. Second, and relatedly, what is the most accurate description of the control and sovereignty that the federal government enjoyed, and continues to enjoy, over Guantanamo Bay? Is that level of control sufficient to conclude that the writ of habeas corpus issued by a federal district court "runs" to that location?

Rasul v. Bush

Supreme Court of the United States
542 U.S. 466 (2004)

Justice STEVENS delivered the opinion of the Court.

These two cases present the narrow but important question whether United States courts lack jurisdiction to consider challenges to the legality of the detention of foreign nationals captured abroad in connection with hostilities and incarcerated at the Guantanamo Bay Naval Base, Cuba.

Ruhal Ahmed and Shafiq Rasul, British citizens who were detained at the U.S. Guantanamo naval base as terror suspects. (Kim Kyung-Hoon/Reuters)

I

On September 11, 2001, agents of the al Qaeda terrorist network hijacked four commercial airliners and used them as missiles to attack American targets. While one of the four attacks was foiled by the heroism of the plane's passengers, the other three killed approximately 3,000 innocent civilians, destroyed hundreds of millions of dollars of property, and severely damaged the U.S. economy. In response to the attacks, Congress passed a joint resolution authorizing the President to use "all necessary and appropriate force against those nations, organizations, or persons he determines planned, authorized, committed, or aided the terrorist attacks . . . or harbored such organizations or persons." Authorization for Use of Military Force, Pub. L. 107-40, §§ 1-2, 115 Stat. 224. Acting pursuant to that authorization, the President sent U.S. Armed Forces into Afghanistan to wage a military campaign against al Qaeda and the Taliban regime that had supported it.

Petitioners in these cases are 2 Australian citizens and 12 Kuwaiti citizens who were captured abroad during hostilities between the United States and the Taliban. Since early 2002, the U.S. military has held them—along with, according to the Government's estimate, approximately 640 other non-Americans captured abroad—at the naval base at Guantanamo Bay. The United States occupies the base, which comprises 45 square miles of land and water along the southeast coast of Cuba, pursuant to a 1903 Lease Agreement executed with the newly independent Republic of Cuba in the aftermath of the Spanish-American War. Under the agreement, "the United States recognizes the continuance of the ultimate sovereignty of the Republic of Cuba over the [leased areas]," while "the Republic of Cuba consents that during the period of the occupation by the United States . . . the United States shall exercise complete jurisdiction and control over and within said areas." In 1934, the parties entered into a treaty providing that, absent an agreement to modify or abrogate the lease, the lease would remain in effect "[s]o long as the United States of America shall not abandon the . . . naval station of Guantanamo."

In 2002, petitioners, through relatives acting as their next friends, filed various actions in the U.S. District Court for the District of Columbia challenging the legality of their detention at the base. All alleged that none of the petitioners has ever been a combatant against the United States or has ever engaged in any terrorist acts. They also alleged that none has been charged with any wrongdoing, permitted to consult with counsel, or provided access to the courts or any other tribunal. . . .

II

Congress has granted federal district courts, "within their respective jurisdictions," the authority to hear applications for habeas corpus by any person who claims to be held "in custody in violation of the Constitution or laws or treaties of the United States." 28 U.S.C. §§ 2241(a), (c)(3). The statute traces its ancestry to the first grant of federal-court jurisdiction: Section 14 of the Judiciary Act of 1789 authorized federal courts to issue the writ of habeas corpus to prisoners who are "in custody, under or by colour of the authority of the United States, or are committed for trial before some court of the same." In 1867, Congress extended the protections of the writ to "all cases where any person may be restrained of his or her liberty in violation of the constitution, or of any treaty or law of the United States."

Habeas corpus is, however, "a writ antecedent to statute, . . . throwing its root deep into the genius of our common law." The writ appeared in English law several centuries ago, became "an integral part of our common-law heritage" by the time the Colonies achieved independence, and received explicit recognition in the Constitution, which forbids suspension of "[t]he Privilege of the Writ of Habeas Corpus . . . unless when in Cases of Rebellion or Invasion the public Safety may require it."

As it has evolved over the past two centuries, the habeas statute clearly has expanded habeas corpus "beyond the limits that obtained during the 17th and 18th centuries. But "[a]t its historical core, the writ of habeas corpus has served as a means of reviewing the legality of Executive detention, and it is in that context that its protections have been strongest." . . .

Consistent with the historic purpose of the writ, this Court has recognized the federal courts' power to review applications for habeas relief in a wide variety of cases involving executive detention, in wartime as well as in times of peace. The Court has, for example, entertained the habeas petitions of an American citizen who plotted an attack on military installations during the Civil War, *Ex parte Milligan*, 4 Wall. 2 (1866), and of admitted enemy aliens convicted of war crimes during a declared war and held in the United States, *Ex parte Quirin*, 317 U.S. 1 (1942), and its insular possessions, *In re Yamashita*, 327 U.S. 1 (1946).

The question now before us is whether the habeas statute confers a right to judicial review of the legality of executive detention of aliens in a territory over which the United States exercises plenary and exclusive jurisdiction, but not "ultimate sovereignty."

III

Respondents' primary submission is that the answer to the jurisdictional question is controlled by our decision in *Eisentrager*. In that case, we held that a Federal District Court lacked authority to issue a writ of habeas corpus to 21 German citizens who had been captured by U.S. forces in China, tried and convicted of war crimes by an American military commission headquartered in Nanking, and incarcerated in the Landsberg Prison in occupied Germany. . . . [T]his Court summarized the six critical facts in the case:

> We are here confronted with a decision whose basic premise is that these prisoners are entitled, as a constitutional right, to sue in some court of the United States for a writ of habeas corpus. To support that assumption we must hold that a prisoner of our military authorities is constitutionally entitled to the writ, even though he (a) is an enemy alien; (b) has never been or resided in the United States; (c) was captured outside of our territory and there held in military custody as a prisoner of war; (d) was tried and convicted by a Military Commission sitting outside the United States; (e) for offenses against laws of war committed outside the United States; (f) and is at all times imprisoned outside the United States.

On this set of facts, the Court concluded, "no right to the writ of habeas corpus appears."

Petitioners in these cases differ from the *Eisentrager* detainees in important respects: They are not nationals of countries at war with the United States, and they deny that they have engaged in or plotted acts of aggression against the United States; they have never been afforded access to any tribunal, much less charged with and convicted of wrongdoing; and for more than two years they have been imprisoned in territory over which the United States exercises exclusive jurisdiction and control. . . .

IV

. . . Application of the habeas statute to persons detained at the base is consistent with the historical reach of the writ of habeas corpus. At common law, courts exercised habeas jurisdiction over the claims of aliens detained within sovereign territory of the realm, as well as the claims of persons detained in the so-called "exempt jurisdictions," where ordinary writs did not run, and all other dominions under the sovereign's control. As Lord Mansfield wrote in 1759, even if a territory was "no part of the realm," there was "no doubt" as to the court's power to issue writs of habeas corpus if the territory was "under the subjection of the Crown." *King v. Cowle*, 2 Burr. 834, 854-855, 97 Eng. Rep. 587, 598-599 (K.B.). Later cases confirmed that the reach of the writ depended not on formal notions of territorial sovereignty, but rather on the practical question of "the exact extent and nature of the jurisdiction or dominion exercised in fact by the Crown."

In the end, the answer to the question presented is clear. Petitioners contend that they are being held in federal custody in violation of the laws of the United States. No party questions the District Court's jurisdiction over petitioners' custodians. Section 2241, by its terms, requires nothing more. We therefore hold that § 2241 confers on the District Court jurisdiction to hear petitioners' habeas corpus challenges to the legality of their detention at the Guantanamo Bay Naval Base. . . .

Justice SCALIA, with whom THE CHIEF JUSTICE and Justice THOMAS join, dissenting.

The Court today holds that the habeas statute, 28 U.S.C. § 2241, extends to aliens detained by the United States military overseas, outside the sovereign borders of the United States and beyond the territorial jurisdictions of all its courts. This is not only a novel holding; it contradicts a half-century-old precedent on which the military undoubtedly relied, *Johnson v. Eisentrager*, 339 U.S. 763 (1950). . . .

The reality is this: Today's opinion, and today's opinion alone, overrules *Eisentrager*; today's opinion, and today's opinion alone, extends the habeas statute, for the first time, to aliens held beyond the sovereign territory of the United States and beyond the territorial jurisdiction of its courts. No reasons are given for this result; no acknowledgment of its consequences made. . . . Normally, we consider the interests of those who have relied on our decisions. Today, the Court springs a trap on the Executive, subjecting Guantanamo Bay to the oversight of the federal courts even though it has never before been thought to be within their jurisdiction—and thus making it a foolish place to have housed alien wartime detainees. . . .

In abandoning the venerable statutory line drawn in *Eisentrager*, the Court boldly extends the scope of the habeas statute to the four corners of the earth. . . . The consequence of this holding, as applied to aliens outside the country, is breathtaking. It permits an alien captured in a foreign theater of active combat to bring a § 2241 petition against the Secretary of Defense. . . .

NOTES & QUESTIONS ON THE TERRITORIAL SCOPE OF HABEAS

1. *Reliance.* Evaluate Justice Scalia's argument that President Bush and the executive branch relied on prior precedents that the writ did not run to foreign territories and made crucial decisions accordingly, i.e., placing the detention camp in Guantanamo Bay. Assuming this reliance occurred, is it enough to dictate the outcome of the case?

2. *Black holes.* Some legal scholars complained that Guantanamo Bay operated as a legal black hole after 9/11. For example, here is Professor Fletcher's assessment:

> The current situation in Guantánamo Bay is best described as a black hole, namely a place where individuals are sent on military or executive order without any form of trial or hearing — not even a determination, as required by the Geneva Conventions—by a "competent tribunal" on whether they should be classified as prisoners of war. The nature of the black hole is that there is no way out, except through the good grace of the military. Those who fall in have no legal recourse, either under international law or under the writ of habeas corpus.

See George P. Fletcher, *Black Hole in Guantánamo Bay*, 2 J. Int'l Crim. Just. 121 (2004). If this is a correct statement of the state of affairs from 2000-2004, did *Rasul* effectively close that black hole? Is the existence of the writ of habeas corpus sufficient to return legal process to the detention facility or are other forms of legal process necessary to ensure legal accountability at the site? Or do you believe that the U.S. military should have relatively unfettered discretion to conduct detention operations there?

3. *Statutory or constitutional.* Was the decision in *Rasul* statutory or constitutional? Was the Court establishing a constitutional principle or interpreting the federal habeas statute and determining its reach?

F. SUSPENSION OF THE WRIT

The Constitution sets a defined limit on when Congress may suspend the writ of habeas corpus: "in cases of rebellion or invasion the public safety may require it." Although styled as a constraint, it acts as a shadow authorization as well because it entails that Congress has the power to suspend the operation of the writ. Consequently, the political branches have the power to detain individuals (the executive branch) and shield those detentions from judicial review (Congress). As noted in this chapter's introduction, President Lincoln attempted to suspend habeas corpus, though with that exception the writ has remained resilient throughout the nation's history.

The following case examines the particulars of Congress's power to suspend the writ. Following *Rasul*, which was decided on statutory grounds, Congress passed legislation to strip federal district courts of their jurisdiction to hear petitions for writs of habeas corpus and to provide an alternative substitute process. In *Boumediene,* the Supreme Court evaluates whether this substitute process is adequate; if it is, then Congress has not "suspended" the writ at all. But before the Court can engage in that analysis, it must first determine whether the Constitution's Suspension Clause even applies at Guantanamo Bay.

Boumediene v. Bush

Supreme Court of the United States
553 U.S. 723 (2008)

Justice KENNEDY delivered the opinion of the Court.

Petitioners are aliens designated as enemy combatants and detained at the United States Naval Station at Guantanamo Bay, Cuba. . . . Petitioners present a question not resolved by our earlier cases relating to the detention of aliens at Guantanamo: whether they have the constitutional privilege of habeas corpus, a privilege not to be withdrawn except in conformance with the Suspension Clause. We hold these petitioners do have the habeas corpus privilege. Congress has enacted a statute, the Detainee Treatment Act of 2005 (DTA), 119 Stat. 2739, that provides certain procedures for review of the detainees' status. We hold that those procedures are not an adequate and effective substitute for habeas corpus. Therefore § 7 of the Military Commissions Act of 2006 (MCA), 28 U.S.C. § 2241(e), operates as an unconstitutional suspension of the writ. . . .

IV

Drawing from its position that at common law the writ ran only to territories over which the Crown was sovereign, the Government says the Suspension Clause affords petitioners no rights because the United States does not claim sovereignty over the place of detention.

Guantanamo Bay is not formally part of the United States. And under the terms of the lease between the United States and Cuba, Cuba retains "ultimate sovereignty" over the territory while the United States exercises "complete jurisdiction and control." Under the terms of the 1934 Treaty, however, Cuba effectively has no rights as a sovereign until the parties agree to modification of the 1903 Lease Agreement or the United States abandons the base.

The United States contends, nevertheless, that Guantanamo is not within its sovereign control. This was the Government's position well before the events of September 11, 2001. And in other contexts the Court has held that questions of sovereignty are for the political branches to decide. Even if this were a treaty interpretation case that did not involve a political question, the President's construction of the lease agreement would be entitled to great respect.

We therefore do not question the Government's position that Cuba, not the United States, maintains sovereignty, in the legal and technical sense of the term, over Guantanamo Bay. But this does not end the analysis. Our cases do not hold it is improper for us to inquire into the objective degree of control the Nation asserts over foreign territory. As commentators have noted, "[s]overeignty" is a term used in many senses and is much abused." When we have stated that sovereignty is a political question, we have referred not to sovereignty in the general, colloquial sense, meaning the exercise of dominion or power, but sovereignty in the narrow, legal sense of the term, meaning a claim of right. Indeed, it is not altogether uncommon for a territory to be under the de jure sovereignty of one nation, while under the plenary control, or practical sovereignty, of another. This condition can occur when the territory is seized during war, as Guantanamo was during the Spanish-American War. Accordingly, for purposes of our analysis, we accept the Government's position that Cuba, and not the United States, retains de jure sovereignty over Guantanamo Bay. As we did in *Rasul,* however, we take notice of the obvious and uncontested fact that the United States, by virtue of its complete jurisdiction and control over the base, maintains de facto sovereignty over this territory. . . .

Fundamental questions regarding the Constitution's geographic scope first arose at the dawn of the 20th century when the Nation acquired noncontiguous Territories: Puerto Rico, Guam, and the Philippines—ceded to the United States by Spain at the conclusion of the Spanish-American War—and Hawaii—annexed by the United States in 1898. At this point Congress chose to discontinue its previous practice of extending constitutional rights to the territories by statute.

In a series of opinions later known as the Insular Cases, the Court addressed whether the Constitution, by its own force, applies in any territory that is not a State. The Court held that the Constitution has independent force in these territories, a force not contingent upon acts of legislative grace. Yet it took note of the difficulties inherent in that position.

Prior to their cession to the United States, the former Spanish colonies operated under a civil-law system, without experience in the various aspects of the Anglo-American legal tradition, for instance the use of grand and petit juries. At least with regard to the Philippines, a complete transformation of the prevailing legal culture would have been not only disruptive but also unnecessary, as the United States intended to grant independence to that Territory. The Court thus was reluctant to risk the uncertainty and instability that could result from a rule that displaced altogether the existing legal systems in these newly acquired Territories.

These considerations resulted in the doctrine of territorial incorporation, under which the Constitution applies in full in incorporated Territories surely destined for statehood but only in part in unincorporated Territories. As the Court later made clear, "the real issue in the Insular Cases was not whether the Constitution extended to the Philippines or Porto Rico when we went there, but which of its provisions were applicable by way of limitation upon the exercise of executive and legislative power in dealing with new conditions and requirements." *Balzac v. Porto Rico*, 258 U.S. 298, 312 (1922). It may well be that over time the ties between the United States and any of its unincorporated Territories strengthen in ways that are of constitutional significance. But, as early as *Balzac* in 1922, the Court took for granted that even in unincorporated Territories the Government of the United States was bound to provide to noncitizen inhabitants "guaranties of certain fundamental personal rights declared in the Constitution." Yet noting the inherent practical difficulties of enforcing all constitutional provisions "always and everywhere," the Court devised in the Insular Cases a doctrine that allowed it to use its power sparingly and where it would be most needed. This century-old doctrine informs our analysis in the present matter. . . .

The Government's formal sovereignty-based test raises troubling separation-of-powers concerns as well. The political history of Guantanamo illustrates the deficiencies of this approach. The United States has maintained complete and uninterrupted control of the bay for over 100 years. At the close of the Spanish-American War, Spain ceded control over the entire island of Cuba to the United States and specifically "relinquishe[d] all claim[s] of sovereignty . . . and title." From the date the treaty with Spain was signed until the Cuban Republic was established on May 20, 1902, the United States governed the territory "in trust" for the benefit of the Cuban people. And although it recognized, by entering into the 1903 Lease Agreement, that Cuba retained "ultimate sovereignty" over Guantanamo, the United States continued to maintain the same plenary control it had enjoyed since 1898. Yet the Government's view is that the Constitution had no effect there, at least as to noncitizens, because the United States disclaimed sovereignty in the formal sense of the term. The necessary implication of the argument is that by surrendering formal sovereignty over any unincorporated territory to a third party, while at the same time entering into a lease that grants total control over the territory back to the United States, it would be possible for the political branches to govern without legal constraint.

Our basic charter cannot be contracted away like this. The Constitution grants Congress and the President the power to acquire, dispose of, and govern territory, not the power to decide when and where its terms apply. Even when the United States acts outside its borders, its powers are not "absolute and unlimited" but are subject "to such restrictions as are expressed in the Constitution." Abstaining from questions involving formal sovereignty and territorial governance is one thing. To hold the political branches have the power to switch the Constitution on or off at will is quite another. The former position reflects this Court's recognition that certain matters requiring political judgments are best left to the political branches.

The latter would permit a striking anomaly in our tripartite system of government, leading to a regime in which Congress and the President, not this Court, say "what the law is." *Marbury v. Madison*, 1 Cranch 137, 177 (1803). . . .

We hold that Art. I, § 9, cl. 2, of the Constitution has full effect at Guantanamo Bay. If the privilege of habeas corpus is to be denied to the detainees now before us, Congress must act in accordance with the requirements of the Suspension Clause. This Court may not impose a de facto suspension by abstaining from these controversies. The MCA does not purport to be a formal suspension of the writ; and the Government, in its submissions to us, has not argued that it is. Petitioners, therefore, are entitled to the privilege of habeas corpus to challenge the legality of their detention.

V

In light of this holding the question becomes whether the statute stripping jurisdiction to issue the writ avoids the Suspension Clause mandate because Congress has provided adequate substitute procedures for habeas corpus. The Government submits there has been compliance with the Suspension Clause because the DTA review process in the Court of Appeals provides an adequate substitute. . . .

To determine the necessary scope of habeas corpus review, therefore, we must assess the CSRT process, the mechanism through which petitioners' designation as enemy combatants became final. Whether one characterizes the CSRT process as direct review of the Executive's battlefield determination that the detainee is an enemy combatant—as the parties have and as we do—or as the first step in the collateral review of a battlefield determination makes no difference in a proper analysis of whether the procedures Congress put in place are an adequate substitute for habeas corpus. What matters is the sum total of procedural protections afforded to the detainee at all stages, direct and collateral.

Petitioners identify what they see as myriad deficiencies in the CSRTs. The most relevant for our purposes are the constraints upon the detainee's ability to rebut the factual basis for the Government's assertion that he is an enemy combatant. As already noted at the CSRT stage the detainee has limited means to find or present evidence to challenge the Government's case against him. He does not have the assistance of counsel and may not be aware of the most critical allegations that the Government relied upon to order his detention. The detainee can confront witnesses that testify during the CSRT proceedings. But given that there are in effect no limits on the admission of hearsay evidence—the only requirement is that the tribunal deem the evidence "relevant and helpful"—the detainee's opportunity to question witnesses is likely to be more theoretical than real. . . .

> Although we make no judgment whether the CSRTs, as currently constituted, satisfy due process standards, we agree with petitioners that, even when all the parties involved in this process act with diligence and in good faith, there is considerable risk of error in the tribunal's findings of fact. . . . And given that the consequence of error may be detention of persons for the duration of hostilities that may last a generation or more, this is a risk too significant to ignore. . . .
>
> Although we do not hold that an adequate substitute must duplicate § 2241 in all respects, it suffices that the Government has not established that the detainees' access to the statutory review provisions at issue is an adequate substitute for the writ of habeas corpus. MCA § 7 thus effects an unconstitutional suspension of the writ. . . .

NOTES & QUESTIONS ON SUSPENSION

1. *Jurisdiction stripping.* Why did Congress decide to strip federal district courts of jurisdiction to hear habeas petitions? Was it motivated by a desire to streamline the process or was it motivated by a desire to decrease judicial scrutiny of executive detentions during the armed conflict with al-Qaeda?

2. *Collateral review in the absence of criminal trials.* What is the significance of the fact that the detainees at Guantanamo Bay filed habeas petitions but were not prosecuted in a criminal trial? Does this fact make "collateral" review in a habeas proceeding more or less imperative?

3. *De jure versus de facto sovereignty.* What is the significance of the fact that the United States has complete "control" over Guantanamo Bay and what role did it play in the majority's decision? Would it be correct to say that *Rasul* and *Boumediene* stand for the proposition that the writ should run to all territories where the United States has de facto sovereignty? If yes, is this holding correct? In answering this question, make reference to the underlying rationale for the writ of habeas corpus as a judicial check on the executive's power to engage in detentions. For more on de facto sovereignty, consider the following conclusion from Professor Colangelo:

> In the future, the Court may seize upon its practical sovereignty language in order to draw the lines for noncitizen habeas rights abroad as part of its functional approach. In that event, it will be anyone's guess what amount of control will qualify the United States as "practical sovereign" over a given territory. But as I've shown, that is not what the Court did in *Boumediene*. In *Boumediene*, the Court took notice of U.S. "de facto sovereignty" over Guantanamo, and used this concept not only to avoid the government's political question challenge but also to distinguish its arguments from common

> law history and precedent. As I've also shown, the concept of de facto sovereignty, in contrast to "practical sovereignty," comprises both control and jurisdiction.

Anthony J. Colangelo, *"De Facto Sovereignty":* Boumediene *and Beyond,* 77 Geo. Wash. L. Rev. 623, 669-70 (2009). Why did the Supreme Court conclude that the United States has both control *and* jurisdiction over Guantanamo Bay? What other territories would this standard apply to?

4. *The CSRT process.* The U.S. government created the Combatant Status Review Tribunals (CSRTs) after the Supreme Court decision in *Hamdi v. Rumsfeld,* which held that an American detainee captured on the battlefield had the right to contest his detention before a "neutral" decision maker. The CSRTs are rough-and-ready tribunals that bear little resemblance to the sophistication of an Article III court. The tribunals are headed by a panel of military officers who hear evidence from the government and the detainee, though the process is not constrained by the rules of evidence governing criminal trials. The purpose of a CSRT hearing is to determine whether the detainee is a combatant within the meaning of the Geneva Conventions and therefore subject to law-of-war detention. What did the Supreme Court conclude in *Boumediene* about these tribunals; do they constitute an adequate substitute for an Article III habeas hearing in a federal district court?

G. PRACTICE & POLICY

The debates over the application of the writ of habeas corpus at Guantanamo have taken place against a more general backdrop. Critics of President George W. Bush complained bitterly for years that the detention facility was a stain on the reputation of the United States and that its presence was a recruitment boon for Islamic extremists. On the other hand, other politicians were adamant that al-Qaeda detainees should remain at Guantanamo Bay indefinitely. To these politicians, the Supreme Court's decisions in *Rasul* and *Boumediene* were unwarranted judicial interventions in the executive branch's conduct of military operations. The following materials address the policy implications of the Supreme Court's habeas decisions in *Rasul* and *Boumediene*. In particular, was the "judicialization" of detention operations a good or bad thing? Did the Supreme Court's recognition and protection of the writ of habeas corpus at Guantanamo Bay bring meaningful judicial review to military detentions?

❧ The promise of *Rasul. Rasul* and *Boumediene* opened the door for habeas review of the legality of detention at Guantanamo Bay. It is safe to assume that the Supreme Court assumed that its decision would close the legal black hole that Professor Fletcher and others saw at Guantanamo Bay. But did that reality come to pass? See Muneer I. Ahmad, *Resisting Guantánamo: Rights at the Brink of Dehumanization*, 103 Nw. U. L. Rev. 1683, 1684-85 (2009) ("[C]ommentators greeted *Rasul* as a game-changing decision, and optimism spread among advocates and prisoners alike that the decision would bring law, and therefore justice, to the seemingly lawless zone of Guantánamo. *Rasul* seemed an important example of transformative legal practice—that is, a fundamental change in power arrangements, brought about through law—but the Executive managed to frustrate that decision for years."). As of 2018, a total of 780 detainees were housed at Guantanamo at one point in time (though not necessarily at the same time). About 500 detainees were released by President Bush, while 197 were released by the administration of President Obama. Over time, a total of 32 detainees were declared by federal courts to be detained illegally at the facility, while 21 detainees eventually lost their habeas challenges. Nine detainees died while housed at Guantanamo. See Human Rights First, *Guantánamo by the Numbers*, February 2018.

❧ Habeas in Afghanistan and Iraq. *Rasul* and *Boumediene* left open the question of whether the writ of habeas corpus would run to detention facilities operated by the United States in other foreign countries, such as Afghanistan or Iraq. If it did, it might fundamentally transform the legal practice of detention during armed conflict. But the *Rasul* and *Boumediene* majority decisions contained observations that make it unclear whether the Supreme Court would be willing to extend those decisions to detention facilities located in other countries. For example, the Supreme Court noted that habeas jurisdiction was denied in *Eisentrager*, when the military ran detention facilities in post–World War II Germany. In *Eisentrager*, although the U.S. military had complete control over the prison, and Germany remained in a state of occupation until 1955, the situation of the detainees was far different than those in Guantanamo Bay. The Germans were captured in China and had already been prosecuted and convicted before a U.S. military tribunal sitting in Nanking. This leaves some uncertainty about whether a military prison operated by the United States in, for example, Afghanistan, would be held to be analogous to Guantanamo or to the prison in *Eisentrager*.

In *Al Maqaleh v. Gates*, 604 F. Supp. 2d 205 (D.D.C. 2009), four detainees at Bagram Airfield in Afghanistan filed petitions for writs of habeas corpus in a D.C. district court. The district court found jurisdiction, concluding that the situation at Bagram was analogous to Boumediene's situation at Guantanamo Bay:

> Although the site of detention at Bagram is not identical to that at Guantanamo Bay, the "objective degree of control" asserted by the United States there is not appreciably different than at Guantanamo. Finally, it cannot be denied that the "practical obstacles" inherent in resolving a Bagram detainee's entitlement to habeas corpus are in some ways greater than those present for a Guantanamo detainee, because Bagram is located in an active theater of war. But those obstacles are not as great as respondents claim, and certainly are not insurmountable. And importantly, for these petitioners, such practical barriers are largely of the Executive's choosing—they were all apprehended elsewhere and then brought (i.e., rendered) to Bagram for detention now exceeding six years.

Id. at 209. On appeal, the D.C. Circuit reversed, concluding that

> [i]n Bagram, while the United States has options as to duration of the lease agreement, there is no indication of any intent to occupy the base with permanence, nor is there hostility on the part of the "host" country. Therefore, the notion that de facto sovereignty extends to Bagram is no more real than would have been the same claim with respect to Landsberg in the *Eisentrager* case. While it is certainly realistic to assert that the United States has de facto sovereignty over Guantanamo, the same simply is not true with respect to Bagram.

Al Maqaleh v. Gates, 605 F.3d 84, 97 (D.C. Cir. 2010). The Supreme Court has not addressed the question of Bagram Air Base and is not likely to do so in the near future. Although the abstract question is no doubt important for future armed conflict situations, the fate of American detention facilities in Afghanistan was largely mooted by the United States' decision to transfer detention operations to the government of Afghanistan. Since habeas only applies when the government has "custody" over an individual, detainees in the custody of the Afghanistan government arguably have no right to petition for a habeas writ in a U.S. district court.

❧ **Closing Guantanamo.** When Barack Obama became President in 2009, he suspended all transfers to Guantanamo and started the process of releasing detainees. Obama announced his intention to close Guantanamo Bay, end the CIA's detention authority, and prosecute remaining detainees in federal district court rather than military commissions. Of these three policy goals, only the second was fully achieved: The President, through an executive order, ended the CIA's authority to conduct ongoing detentions and interrogations. However, Obama's promise to end military commissions faltered when Congress passed legislation banning the use of federal funds to pay for the transfer of any detainee at Guantanamo Bay to the territory of the United States. This also prevented Obama from closing the detention facility and transferring the remaining detainees to a detention facility in the United States. Instead, Obama focused on transferring detainees out of Guantanamo Bay, a time-consuming and laborious process because it required negotiating with countries that were willing to accept them. Since 2009, no new prisoners have been brought to the detention facility and the population has slowly dwindled. As of 2018, there were 41 detainees housed there.

❧ **Continuing authorization?** The legal basis for the executive branch to hold al-Qaeda detainees at Guantanamo Bay flows from 2001 Authorization for the Use of Military Force (AUMF), passed by Congress in the immediate aftermath of 9/11. The authorization states the following:

> That the President is authorized to use all necessary and appropriate force against those nations, organizations, or persons he determines planned, authorized, committed, or aided the terrorist attacks that occurred on September 11, 2001, or harbored such organizations or persons, in order to prevent any future acts of international terrorism against the United States by such nations, organizations or persons.

Courts have consistently held that the broad AUMF language of "necessary and appropriate force" includes the power to capture and detain individuals covered by the AUMF. In 2018, 11 of the remaining detainees at Guantanamo Bay filed a combined habeas petition arguing that their continued detention was unlawful because the 2001 AUMF passed by Congress was no longer applicable, given the defeat of most of the core al-Qaeda organization in Pakistan and Afghanistan: "Petitioners are ostensibly being held in connection with an ever-expanding 'war' against terrorism involving new actors bearing no actual connection to Al Qaeda or 9/11, which appears to have neither geographic, durational nor organizational constraints." See *Al Bihani et al. v. Trump*, Case 1:09-cv-00745-RCL.

Table of Cases

Principal cases are indicated by italics.

C

INDEX

B

C

G

H

N

O

P